Published by Chambers and Partners Publishing
(a division of Orbach & Chambers Ltd)
Saville House, 23 Long Lane, London EC1A 9HL
Tel: (020) 7606 1300 Fax: (020) 7600 3191
email: info@ChambersandPartners.co.uk
www.ChambersandPartners.com

Our thanks to the many students, trainees, pupils,
solicitors, barristers and graduate recruitment personnel
who assisted us in our research. Also to Chambers and
Partners recruitment team for their knowledge and
assistance and to the researchers of Chambers UK
2004-2005 from which all firm rankings are drawn.

Publisher: Michael Chambers
Managing Editor: Fiona Boxall
Editor: Anna Williams
Writers: Anna Saunders, Hannah Langworth, Michael
Lovatt, Sam Wallace, Craig Giles
Editorial assistants: Tom Stevens, Michelle Madsen
Database: Andrew Taylor
A-Z Co-ordinator: Jill Tugwell
Production: Jasper John, Paul Cummings
Business Development Manager: Brad D. Sirott
Business Development Team: Neil Murphy, Richard
Ramsay, Jane Walker
Proofreaders: Sarah Weise, John Bradley, Sarah Reardon,
Sarah Margetts, Jennifer Munka

Printed by: Polestar Wheatons Limited

CONTENTS

first steps

solicitors

the true picture

do all law firm recruitment brochures look the same to you? the true picture is the antidote. it is the product of six months spent interviewing hundreds of trainees and newly qualified solicitors at 140 firms in england and wales. we asked them to tell us about their training contracts in their own words...and they did!

solicitors a-z

the phone numbers, addresses and e-mails you need to make your applications. plus loads of really useful facts and figures on the top law firms. all in simple easy to follow a-z format

barristers

chambers reports

impeneterable, incomprehensible and in another world...it's too easy to stereotype the bar. we banged on the doors of 44 chambers to have a nose around and quiz the inhabitants

bar a-z
details of some of the leading pupillages

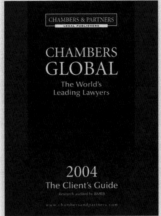

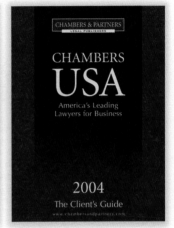

Chambers and Partners publishes a suite of legal guides that you should find helpful in your search for a training contract or pupillage.

- **Chambers UK** is the product of over 10,500 interviews with solicitors, barristers and their clients. It identifies the leading firms, sets and players across the full sweep of legal practice in the UK.

- **Chambers Global** sets out the results of our research into legal jurisdictions worldwide from Australia to Zambia. If you are considering a training contract with an international law firm, it's a must-read book.

- **Chambers USA** provides a more detailed analysis of the performance of the best firms across all US states.

These guides are available for reference in your university careers service or law library and can all be read online:

www.chambersandpartners.com.

first steps

so you want to be a lawyer...

If you want to train as a lawyer, you'll have to decide whether you want to be a barrister or a solicitor. This section should straighten out the basic differences in your mind, and we've also detailed a number of other career opportunities.

barrister

With the exception of drag queen, there aren't many careers in which donning a ridiculous wig is considered de rigueur. The Bar is one of those few (though perhaps not for much longer as wigs maybe on the endangered list). Before you invest in your wig – which is likely to be among the most expensive accessories you will ever buy – be sure that this is the profession for you.

Barristers are first and foremost professional advocates who stand up and argue real cases for real clients. It's not just about abstract legal argument. Ask any barrister, and they will tell you that academic strength is vital, but they also tell you that you need to be able to think about things practically and innovatively – what does my client want, and how can I utilise the law to help them to get it? To make the brilliant ideas in their heads work, barristers also need to be persuasive on their feet. That doesn't necessarily mean delivering an Oscar-winning performance in court, but it does mean being able to present a clear and logical argument, and being able to defend it in the face of opposition.

Barristers are also valued for their expert knowledge of the litigation process and the likelihood of certain outcomes given a set of circumstances. As such, they will also find themselves instructed to give written opinions. For some practitioners, particularly at the Chancery Bar, this kind of work is the staple diet.

It's this specialist ability in advocacy, and in giving detailed legal advice on the merits or demerits of a case, that differentiates barristers from their solicitor colleagues. Of course, if they wanted to, solicitors could do this all for themselves, and since 1991 following government efforts to eliminate restrictive practices in the legal profession, solicitor-advocates have been able to appear in even the highest courts. Increasingly, particularly where more straightforward litigation is concerned, that is exactly what they are doing, but the market for barristers is still very much intact. The reality is that most solicitors prefer to send their more time-consuming and difficult advocacy to the Bar.

The other quality that makes the Bar unique is its independence: barristers are self-employed. It's one of the fundamental tenets of professional ethics that a barrister should be able to fight for his or her client and fulfil an overriding duty to the court without fear of sanction from an employer. Though they group together in sets of chambers, each barrister is responsible for developing their own career and will stand or fall on their reputation. There is no salary at the end of the month, only the fees earned for each case taken. Theoretically, you can take as much time off as you want, but in practice you'll have to work hard to keep a roof over your head and pay the bills. And there won't be any holiday pay!

For all its insecurities, the Bar offers a dynamic, fast-moving and challenging career with the potential for some quite substantial earnings if you succeed. If you want to know more, the final section of this book will guide you through the recruitment process and some of the Bar's unique traditions, and our Chambers Reports will give you an insight into life as a young barrister in some of the best chambers in both London and the regions. If you're worried about how to pay for the vocational training you'll need in order to qualify, the Funding section on page 43 sets out the basics.

solicitor

Most budding lawyers qualify as solicitors rather than barristers. Over 5,000 trainees start contracts each year, while the number of pupillages available is about one tenth of this figure. The job of a solicitor places far greater emphasis on ongoing file or case management and many solicitors find they have little or nothing to do with the courts. Clients can include everyone from the battered wife to the biggest blue-chip companies.

The career path of a solicitor is regarded as being smoother and more certain. It starts with a two-year training contract, and unless you plan to take a year out for travel or other experience, for those seeking to train in a commercial firm (as opposed to a high street practice) the decision-making process should start in the second year of a three-year law degree or the final year of a non-law degree. These firms generally offer training contracts two years in advance: leave it too late and your preferred firms will no longer be recruiting for the year you want to start. Your choice of training contract is crucial, as it will determine your finances, your geography and your experiences.

After your degree, law school awaits. Law graduates need spend only one year on the Legal Practice Course (LPC). Those with a non-law degree must also complete the one-year CPE/PgDL before being eligible for the LPC. We discuss both cases later in this section. Larger commercial firms often offer scholarships to cover course fees and some maintenance for the LPC and, if necessary, the CPE/PgDL. A handful of big City firms require students to attend specific law schools that offer quite specialised City-oriented courses. Smaller firms in general/'high street' practice rather than commercial practice tend not to offer law school sponsorship and recruit closer to the start date of the training contract. For students headed for this type of firm, the CPE and LPC years can be an uncertain and expensive time.

Selecting the right firm for you is a crucial decision because the client base, work and reputation of the firm you train at will determine the experience you gain and your future marketability as a lawyer. In addition to finding out about the size and location of a firm and the work it handles, you should research the firm's reputation and learn about its culture. At Chambers and Partners, we've made it our business to know who does what, how well they do it and what it might be like working at a particular firm. In the Practice Areas section of this book, you'll find the core results of the research carried out for our parent publication *Chambers UK.* Our league tables show which firms command greatest respect from clients and other professionals in different areas of practice. An enormous amount of additional information is available in *Chambers UK,* including details of law firms' top clients and deals. Copies of the book should be available in your university careers office or law department library, or you can read the whole thing online at **www.chambersandpartners.com**. If you want to throw your research net even wider, you can find out about a firm's international work and reputation in *Chambers Global* and *Chambers USA.*

In the **True Picture** we've profiled 140 of the leading firms in England and Wales. This section of the book should help you understand what kind of firm might suit you and the kind of work you can expect to receive when you get there. Law firms come in all shapes and sizes. Do your research, do a bit of navel-gazing and work out what's best for you.

magic circle: Slaughter and May, Clifford Chance, Freshfields, Allen & Overy and Linklaters. These are seen by many as the elite firms and are high paying, hardworking and very corporate and finance-oriented. The prestige that attaches to a magic circle training is undeniable and, to that end, there are many students who'd consider going nowhere else. Whether this is because of the advice they are given by course directors, careers advisors, friends already at these firms or plain herd mentality, the fact is these firms do have the pick of the best and brightest students and offer a superb training. Their size and big-money deals will not appeal to all students and it's important that those who'd fare better in a different or smaller environment feel able to make an alternative choice.

london – large commercial: The top ten City of London firms account for around 1,000 training contracts between them, representing around 20% of all training contracts registered with the solicitors governing body – the Law Society. There's not a huge difference between the magic circle and firms such as Lovells, Herbert Smith and others of their ilk. In the largest commercial firms, work is almost entirely focused around business law, although a tiny number retain specialists in private client practice. Working hours are often long, but the money is very good. Expect to work on high-profile matters (though you won't always have particularly challenging duties). Expect to be pushed and, at times, be prepared to give 110%. If you are working against a deadline on a deal then you will be expected to stay until it is finished. This can mean working through the night and coming in at weekends from time to time.

To get into one of the top City firms you will need a consistently excellent academic record from A-levels through to your first and second-year exam results or final degree. Unfortunately you'll need to go right to the back of a very long queue if you failed to gain at least a 2:1. Recruitment personnel in City firms are also keen to ensure that prospective trainees possess commercial awareness. In other words, understanding what businesses want, how they work and what lawyers can do to help them. You need to show that you have an interest in law, an interest in business and an interest in the firm you are going to. If you can't...there's something wrong with your decision.

regionals: The City of London may be the beating heart of big, blue-chip international business, but there's more to life than an EC postcode. Out in the regions, firms such as Dickinson Dees, Burges Salmon and Wragge & Co – to name but a few – offer top-notch clients and some international work. Some regional firms might as well be top London firms,

which just happen to be based in the regions; others focus on regional clients and smaller work.

Regional firms can be every bit as difficult to get into as their City rivals. In some cases you are statistically more likely to get into a magic circle firm, as the ratio of vacancies to applications can be much better at the bigger practices. If the magic circle has refused you, don't assume you'll walk into a top regional firm...they are unimpressed by sloppy seconds applications. If you are applying to join a firm in Bristol, for example, and have studied and lived in London all your life, be prepared to be asked why you want to move to the area. The last thing firms want is to spend a fortune on training only for newly qualified lawyers to swan off to jobs in the City. Recruitment personnel at the top regional practices are looking for exactly the same abilities and experience as the top City firms.

Salaries are lower outside London, in some cases significantly so, but the cost of living is much more reasonable than in the capital. You will also benefit from less frenetic hours than in City-based practices and regional firms have a reputation for being a bit friendlier, a bit calmer and a bit more human than those in the City. As you will see in the **True Picture**, however, it is all about finding a firm that suits you.

nationals: National firms have offices in a number of UK cities. Eversheds has ten offices in England and Wales; DLA has eight in England and Scotland. Hammonds and Pinsents each have four in London, Birmingham, Leeds and Manchester, while Addleshaw Goddard skips the Birmingham option and Irwin Mitchell works in Sheffield rather than Manchester. Some nationals avoid these major cities: Shoosmiths operates in smaller cities and towns from the south coast up to Nottingham. Each of these firms has a different approach to recruitment and whether or not trainees move around the country, so make sure you know the policy adopted by your chosen firm.

niche: Particularly in London, there are a variety of niche firms to choose from. Construction, entertainment, IP, insurance litigation, family...the list goes on. If you are absolutely certain that you want to specialise in a particular practice area (especially if you have already worked in the relevant industry), a niche firm is a sound choice. Be aware that many firms described as niche practices actually offer other types of work. Be aware also that some niche firms do try to woo students by talking at great length about their other areas of practice.

general practice/'high street': Practices range from substantial, long-established firms in large town centres to sole practitioners working above shops in the suburbs. These firms act for legally aided clients, individuals funding themselves and local businesses. Staple work includes matrimonial, landlord and tenant, personal injury, employment, family, wills and probate, and crime. It's increasingly likely that firms have an additional specialism in small-ticket commercial work for local businesses. Be prepared to earn considerably less than your peers in commercial practice. Commonly, you'll receive at or around the minimum salary permitted by the Law Society (£14,200pa for the provinces and £15,900pa for inner London) of if you're lucky the recommended salary (£14,870 and £16,680 respectively). The hours can be unsociable if you find yourself working in crime, but in this kind of firm you will get to handle clients and real work from a very early stage. You'll grow up fast and you'll also see how the law actually affects individuals and the community in which you practice. Unlike commercial firms, most do not recruit two years in advance and most do not sponsor students through the LPC. Larger firms may take on four or five trainees a year, while the smallest will recruit on an ad hoc basis.

law centres

From its roots in North Kensington in 1970, the network of UK law centres has grown to around 54 today, each set up as either a registered charity or a not-for-profit company and run by its own local management committee. Advice is given to the public for free and funding comes from local government grants (approx 60%) or the Legal Services Commission by way of 'Legal Help' certificated payments. The kinds of legal problems handled by a law centre may vary from one to another, but they can all be described as social welfare law specialists. Employment, discrimination, housing, immigration and public law (eg education and community care) form the main diet. Crime is not handled.

Law centres see themselves as more than just providers of legal advice to the public; they tend to take on cases that have a wider social impact. A client who has a dispute with their window cleaner or a consumer problem is less likely to be taken on than someone who is affected by, say, a decision of a local authority on how rent arrears are dealt with. The number of cases brought by social landlords for rent arrears has increased to around 30,000 a year and law centres regard this as a trend that adversely affects a sufficiently large number of people such that their time will be well spent on tackling individual problems while also trying to bring about policy change.

Law Centres employ qualified solicitors and barristers. Most work is carried out by these lawyers with only around 10% of the typical centre's hours being clocked up by volunteers assisting at evening drop-in sessions. The majority of law centre lawyers will have originally come from private practice, although some will have earned their stripes in a law centre. Traditionally, those lawyers who have qualified while working at a law centre have done so by combining part-time study with work. This is the route most commonly followed by experienced advice workers.

From 2003 the Legal Services Commission is funding some 20 or so training contracts in 14 law centres up and down the country. These will mirror the typical training contract in private practice with trainees spending periods of time with different lawyers in the law centre learning about their specialist areas of work. Before you go rushing down to the postbox with your CV, take note: an Equal Ops Policy means that candidates will only be considered if they respond to an advertisement. Look for these in *The Guardian* (Wednesdays), local newspapers, a bi-monthly publication called *Legal Action* (your university law library should have it), and on the Law Centres Federation website **www.law centres.org.uk**. Salaries for qualified lawyers are around £24-30,000 (or more in London). At the junior level this compares favourably with high street practice, but the gap widens the more senior you get. Law centres operate along different lines to private practices: less hierarchy, more of an equal say for staff at all levels – some even operate as collectives with all staff drawing the same salary. Terms and conditions at work emulate those in local government and, as such, pension and holiday provisions, etc, are good, while flexible and part-time working is common.

Most law centres employ 10-15 lawyers and, if you're attracted to working with colleagues who share your ideals and social conscience, you may want to investigate a career in the sector. See our section on **Pro Bono Opportiunities** for info on the chances of volunteering while still studying.

working in-house with a company

A number of large companies and banks offer training contracts/pupillages. For information on in-house legal teams registered to take trainees check the Law Society's website and for pupillages, refer to the Bar Council. *Chambers UK* lists contact details for the legal teams of FTSE 100 companies.

government legal service

About 30 trainee solicitors and pupil barristers are recruited each year by the Government Legal Service to work within different government departments and offices. Customs & Excise; the Inland Revenue; the DTI; the Department for Work & Pensions/Department of Health; the Treasury Solicitor's Department; the Home Office; the Department for Environment, Food and Rural Affairs; the Office of the Deputy Prime Minister and the Department for Transport have all welcomed new recruits over the past few years. The GLS recruits centrally in London (though occasionally some regional offices may have vacancies, advertising them in national and local newspapers), and to discover what sort of person it is looking to attract, we spoke to James Murphy of the recruitment team.

The first thing he told us was how varied the work can be. At one end of the scale there are full-time litigators, and at the other people drafting new legislation or advising ministers. To satisfy such diverse needs, the GLS wants candidates with "*good legal minds...people who can get to the root of a problem very quickly.*" James also stressed the importance of working to deadlines and as part of the team. To find out if applicants have what it takes, the GLS holds one-day assessments, involving a written problem (a general legal topic so as not to disadvantage CPE candidates), a group exercise and a board interview.

We'd recommend anyone applying to the GLS to have a long think about the role government lawyers take, particularly how "*law and politics interact*" and the impact that they can have on life and society in the UK. Whether this is by bringing about the prosecution of drugs smugglers or human traffickers, or drafting new sexual offences or employment legislation. If you feel you need to gain a greater awareness, you can simply start by reading a good broadsheet newspaper regularly – they always cover topics of note, such as the evolution of the Lord Chancellor's Department into the Department for Constitutional Affairs, and plans for a new Supreme Court.

Successful applicants are asked to nominate the department in which they would like to work, though it is worth noting that some, like the Home Office, are often over-subscribed. While most training positions are based in a single department, it is sometimes possible to be seconded to another. Legal teams vary in size from a single lawyer in the smaller bodies to 300 or so in larger departments and agencies, in particular the Treasury Solicitor's Department and the Department for Constitutional Affairs.

Within departments, trainee solicitors do 'seats' just like their peers in private practice. Most pupil barristers will follow the traditional 'two sixes' system found at the independent Bar, whereby six months are spent in barristers chambers and the other six within the GLS. Some departments have adopted the newer 'four four four' system, starting pupils in the department then sending them out to barristers chambers before bringing them back to the department again.

According to Mark James-Dawson, a solicitor with the Health and Safety Executive, the main attractions of the GLS are the variety of work on offer, the high level of responsibility and the opportunity to have a hand in shaping legislation and government policy. *"You get to do interesting, high-profile work from an early stage,"* he told us. *"From the start, you can be working on a case that is being defended by a partner in a big City firm."* Lawyers are also positively encouraged to move between departments, meaning *"the potential for career development is greater than in private practice."* This is coupled with the traditional benefits of working in the public sector – a clear career structure and relative security at a time where a number of major firms are making people redundant; pension provisions and flexible hours to suit those with children.

On the downside, we've heard that lawyers sometimes get frustrated by budgetary constraints and bureaucracy, and at senior level, the astronomical sums enjoyed by their partners in top City firms simply aren't there. However, we sense that other compensations come in the form of job satisfaction and kinder hours. The current salary rates for newly qualified lawyers in London are within the range of £27,000 to £38,000, depending upon department. The first stage in securing training with the GLS is to contact its recruitment team, rather than the departments themselves. Sponsorship for the LPC or BVC is available and there is a vacation scheme offering two or three-week insights into life as a government lawyer. This year, having had the opportunity to interview a number of its trainees, we have included the GLS in our **True Picture** and **Chambers Reports** features.

local government

There are hundreds of local authority legal departments in the UK, some of which offer training contracts. There's no centralised list of vacancies and no single recruitment office, so you must contact each legal department separately and keep an eye open for advertisements in the legal and national press.

Your clients will all be officers within different departments of the local authority, and it is because the business of LAs is so varied that a training contract with one entails such a breadth of work. Contracts usually conform to the seat system that prevails in private practice and you're quite likely to undertake property, planning and environmental law; litigation and prosecution work; consumer protection, housing, education and childcare; employment, personal injury, administrative and commercial/contracts. Excellent news for aspiring advocates – LA trainees have rights of audience in civil and criminal courts and tribunals that outstrip their peers in private practice.

For many, the real appeal is working for a public sector organisation that's concerned with the local environment and community. For others it's the excellent working conditions and benefits; part-time working, flexi-time and job sharing are not uncommon. Most local government lawyers remain in the public sector, but the job is portable across the UK, and lawyers can also transfer to the GLS or CPS or even go into private practice. Some local authorities operate their legal departments along commercial principles and all must adhere to the principle of 'Best Value'.

Law School sponsorship is rare, but there are opportunities for both vacation work experience and/or paralegalling. For further information on a career in local government try **www.lgcareers.com**.

the crown prosecution service

If you have a passion for criminal law, and the idea of billable hours and contract drafting leaves you cold, the CPS may appeal. The service employs about 2,500 lawyers in England and Wales to handle cases involving well over a million defendants each year.

prosecutors review and prosecute criminal cases following investigation by the police and advise the police on matters of criminal and evidence law. Prosecutors are stationed in one of two units. Criminal Justice Units were established within police stations to combat the problem of failed prosecutions. Lawyers here advise police on the appropriate charge for the crime. They spend one day in the office preparing cases and the next in the magistrates' court, dealing with administrative matters relating to each case. Lawyers in the Trial Unit deal with Crown Court cases, including murder, rape and robbery. Because Crown Court matters are more serious, prosecutors often act as instructing counsel, although they can become higher court advocates and conduct prosecutions themselves. While it may lack the grit and glamour of *Law and Order* the work of the CPS is exciting and varied.

Prosecutors can expect to deal with 30 or 40 cases each day, and although they don't have the same intense client contact as defence lawyers, CPS prosecutors interact with everyone from magistrates, clerks, solicitors, probation officers and police to civilian and expert witnesses, and even serving prisoners. They also liaise with victim support and racial equality agencies. Where a prosecution is abandoned, the prosecutor must inform the victims why. It's easy to see why one prosecutor told us: *"You must be flexible and prepared for anything."* You must also be fairly *"bulletproof"* as the service sometimes gets bad press for failed prosecutions; at times, you'll not be the most popular person at the party, although you're guaranteed to have some pretty entertaining anecdotes!

More recently, the CPS has brought in new initiatives such as 'Narrowing the Justice Gap' (reducing the time between arrest and trial) and 'CPS Direct', which ensures that prosecutors are on call 24 hours a day to attend police stations and charge suspects in complicated cases. Each year the service recruits trainees and pupils on a starting salary of £17,888. A qualified prosecutor's salary ranges from £25,648-£45,388 nationally and £26,954-£51,082 in London.

caseworkers assist prosecutors by researching cases and making recommendations on information required and charges to be brought; liaising with counsel, witnesses, police and court staff; and providing support to witnesses and victims. They also attend court to assist counsel on a regular basis. London caseworkers will usually be able to do a three-month stint at the Old Bailey. Impressive organisational skills and an ability to relate to people are essential.

Jim Federick graduated with a non-law degree in 1998 and got a job in finance at the CPS, later becoming a caseworker. The CPS allowed him study leave for two years, during which he completed his CPE and the LPC and then returned to complete his training contract. When we spoke to him he was working in a Criminal Justice Unit in Brighton. Melanie Walfall began her legal career in private practice, completing her training with a criminal defence firm before moving to the CPS. She was also working in a Criminal Justice Unit when we caught up with her. Each of them were proud to be a part of an institution that is dedicated to *"serving the public."* As Jim told us, you can sleep soundly at night knowing that *"you are doing good work and making the world a safer place."*

The CPS is a supportive employer, providing ongoing training and educational opportunities to its staff as well as decent benefits and flexitime. However, it shares the same burden of bureaucracy and budget constraints as any other part of the civil service, and in a recent survey, staff raised these issues and also the volume of cases they were expected to handle.

Individual area offices run vacation placements and work experience, but apply early as demand is high, especially in London. The website **www.cps.gov.uk** is a useful starting point and for information about forthcoming vacancies, vacation placements or work experience, contact one of the local CPS Service Centres:

Eastern: 0172 779 8700; London: 020 7802 3800; North East: 0191 262 4200; South East: 0148 346 8200; Wales: 0292 080 3910; East Midlands: 0115 852 3300; West Midlands: 0121 262 1300; North West: 0151 239 6400; South West: 0139 228 8000; Yorkshire & Humberside: 0192 420 5315

the court service

The Court Service is an executive agency of the Department for Constitutional Affairs and is responsible for the daily business of the court system. It employs about 10,000 people (although Gordon Brown recently announced that this figure would be cut) and fulfils the administrative functions of each of the UK's various courts. As well as providing ushers and dealing with timetabling, it is also engaged in modernising the physical appearance of courts.

Because it is an administrative agency, there are few opportunities for lawyers, but the service does recruit Judicial Assistants at various times throughout the year. JA appointments are temporary, and each lasts for a three-month term. Appointments are sometimes renewed, but only for a maximum of 12 months. JAs undertake legal tasks for the Lord Justices in the Civil Division of the Court of Appeal at the Royal Courts of Justice, including legal research, advice and providing assistance in drafting judgments. Applicants for JA positions must be qualified lawyers who have completed pupillage or traineeship. They also need word-processing skills, be able to demonstrate intellectual ability (by way of a 2:1 degree) and have the ability to work under pressure as part of a team. JA appointments pay around £100 per day and the positions are advertised in *The Times* weekly law supplement and the *Law Society's*

Gazette as well as on the Court Service website **www.courtservice.gov.uk**.

Those looking for a longer term career might consider the roles of administrative officer, bailiff, and county and crown court ushers or clerks. The 91 crown courts and 233 county courts are presided over by members of the judiciary, so court clerks do not have a legal advisory role and do not need legal qualifications. You can register your interest in the Court Service by contacting your local area office. Find details via the Court Service website.

Magistrates' clerks are slightly different in that they do give legal advice to lay magistrates and managers of the court. Approximately 430 magistrates' courts operate in England and Wales, and between them they handle the majority of the country's criminal proceedings. In a busy port city like Hull, for instance, as well as the usual TV licence and traffic offences, the clerks will see drug trafficking cases and other serious crimes. A rural court is likely to be quieter and crimes of violence will be less common, while clerks in busy metropolitan centres will experience the greatest variety of cases.

A magistrates' court clerk needs to be able to think on their feet and deal confidently with people. Those we spoke to said that the vast majority of defendants treat them with respect and only occasionally must they exercise the power to order individuals into custody for contempt of court. The magistrates need to know they can rely on the clerks for sound advice on issues like self-defence, identification of suspects, and inferences from the silence of defendants after arrest.

A shift in recruitment policy has seen the traditional route (by which those without degrees could train while studying for the Diploma in Magisterial Law) overtaken by the recruitment of LPC and BVC graduates as trainee court clerks. As the individual progresses through a structured training programme, the number and complexity of their court duties will increase until ultimately they are advising lay magistrates on points of law and procedure.

Most courts operate nine or ten sessions a week and most clerks will be in court for the majority of these. The remaining time will be spent exercising powers delegated to them by the magistrates, such as issuing summonses. For more information about careers with the magistrates' courts and how to apply for positions refer to **www.ccmcc.co.uk**.

the law commission

Many laws are the product of political expediency and are drawn up at the will of the government of the day. However, the government is not always best placed to see where reforms could best be made. The Law Commission was set up by Parliament to keep the laws of England and Wales under review and propose reform where necessary. In order to formulate proposals to modernise, improve or simplify the law, the Commission undertakes research and wide-ranging consultation exercises with experts and those who may be affected. Its recommendations are then put forward for consideration by Parliament. The Commission employs about 15 research assistants to help with this task.

At any one time, it will be engaged in about 20 projects of law reform, and as a researcher you could be dealing with both common law and statutes going back many centuries. In a varied role, you could be analysing different areas of law, identifying defects in the current system, examining foreign law models to see how they deal with similar problems, helping to draft consultation papers or preparing a report of recommendations for the Lord Chancellor (or whatever he may be called at the time). The commission also works on the consolidation of statutes and the repeal of obsolete statutory provisions. Recent papers were published on such diverse subjects as a partial defence to murder, the termination of tenancies and partnership law.

If you are a law graduate looking for a centre stage experience, and have a keen interest in the workings of the law, this could be an ideal position for you. Thus far, more than two-thirds of the Commission's recommendations have been implemented by the government, so you will also get the satisfaction of seeing your work put into practice. For more details on the role of the Commission and information on a career in this field, check out **www.lawcom.gov.uk**.

legal services commission

This is the government body that replaced the Legal Aid Board in 2000. Operating from London and 12 regional offices, it manages the distribution of public funds for both civil legal services and criminal defence services. The Commission is split into four separate functions, each offering differing employment opportunities:

the operations division is the largest and handles civil cases. Caseworkers deal with the merits of applications for legal funding and means test applicants, as well as assessing and authorising claims for payment for legal services. Salaries start at £12,000 and there are also roles for administrators.

the criminal defence service performs an audit role, dealing with authorised providers of criminal legal advice. There are no financial or other limits as to who is entitled to claim free legal advice, so it is merely the lawyer's financial claims and the quality of their services that are scrutinised.

the contracting section audits claims for 'Legal Help' – the funding used for preliminary and basic advice on how individuals might be represented.

the planning and partnership section employs consultants and executives in order to better understand how the Commission should spend funds and place its resources.

Jobs at the Commission are advertised in local and/or national newspapers and you should consult its website **www.legalservices.gov.uk**. A few work experience placements crop up, usually in the operations group and usually lasting for about six weeks.

becoming a legal executive

If you haven't found a training contract or you are moving sideways into the law, the Institute of Legal Executives (ILEX) course may be right for you. Those who complete the course become legal executives – qualified lawyers who are sometimes known as the 'third branch' of the legal profession. There are over 22,000 legal executives and trainee legal executives across the country. No prior legal training is required to enrol on the course, and hence it is suitable for school leavers, graduates or those already engaged in a career and looking to branch out. It can be taken on a part-time basis, giving trainees an opportunity to combine study with practical experience.

Trainees initially study for a Professional Diploma in Law, which takes about two years part time. The course includes an introduction to both key concepts of law and legal practice and procedures. Trainees then progress to the Professional Higher Diploma in Law, which provides an opportunity to specialise in a particular area of practice, usually guided by the job the trainee is doing at the time. On completion of this, trainees become members of ILEX. However, it is necessary to gain five years' qualifying experience in a legal background, and be over 25 years of age, before becoming a fully qualified ILEX fellow.

Law graduates are exempt from the academic part of the course, and can take examinations solely in legal practice, enabling the qualification to be gained in a little over 12 months. For those without a law degree, the professional qualification will usually take three or four years to complete while in full-time employment. There is no set time to complete the examinations, so trainees can work at their own pace. ILEX graduates end up in employment across the full spectrum of legal services from private practice, to government departments, to the in-house legal departments at major corporations.

Some ILEX fellows eventually become fully qualified solicitors. As they have already been examined in some of the core subjects required by the CPE Board, and the others can be taken as single subjects over another one or two years of part-time study, most fellows can seek exemption from the CPE and move straight on to the Legal Practice Course. ILEX fellows may also be exempted from the two-year training contract.

Although ILEX can provide a useful route to qualification as a solicitor, it is by no means the quickest. Yet, positions for trainee legal executives may be available when formal training contracts are not and, crucially, students can earn whilst studying. A full list of colleges offering the course (including distance learning) is available at **www.ilex.org.uk**.

paralegal work

If you have time to fill before starting your training contract, paralegal work can provide a useful introduction to legal practice. Firms regard time spent paralegalling favourably as it demonstrates commitment to the profession and enables you to gain valuable experience and commercial or sector insight. Some firms, though not all, offer traineeships to the most impressive of their own paralegals, but you should always keep in mind that the job is a valuable position in its own right. Guard against giving the impression that you will leave as soon as something better crops up.

The paralegal market is highly competitive, so those with no legal qualifications or practical experience may find it difficult to secure a position. Indeed, some top City firms require all applicants to have completed the LPC. When starting out, it may be necessary to work a number of short-term contracts until one firm decides it wants you on a long-term basis.

Working as a paralegal can be a career in its own right, and experienced paralegals who develop specialist skills can make a very decent living from their work. For information on current vacancies, check the legal press or register with a recruitment agency. You should also find out if your law school's careers office has contacts and regularly check the websites of any firms in your area. Some firms may even select paralegals from people who write to them on spec.

how will i fare in the recruitment game?

It's rarely 'who you know' and mostly 'who you are' that secures you a job these days. Clearly there are some things you can't change about yourself – your age, roots, ethnicity, gender, a disability. There are other things you shouldn't have to change – your sexual orientation, personality, values. Having said that, you can't approach the world of work without making a few nips and tucks to your identity and addressing the content of your CV to see if it can be improved upon.

a matter of degrees

So you've not got a law degree. So what? From the top sets at the Bar to the little known solicitors firms on the high street, non-law graduates fare just as well as their LLB peers in the recruitment game. In the few cases where employers prefer law grads they will specify this, so unless you hear differently, conversion route applicants should proceed with confidence. Many recruiters tell us just how highly they regard staff with language skills and scientific and technical degrees, particularly where their clients' businesses will benefit.

Whether they admit it or not, many firms and chambers subscribe to the idea that there's a pecking order of universities. Every two years we conduct a survey into law firms' preferences and you'll find our 2004 results on our website.

Your degree result is perhaps the single thing on your CV that has most impact. Net a First and you'll impress all and sundry (at least on paper); walk away with a 2:1 and your path to employment will be made smoother; end up with a 2:2 and you're going to have to perform some fancy footwork. In some cases the effect of a poor degree result can be softened by a letter from your tutor stipulating the reason why you underachieved. Alas, it's rarely relevant that you just missed a 2:1 by a percentage point

or two; however, if you were a star student who suffered a serious accident or illness as finals loomed, confirmation of this (perhaps also by way of a doctor's letter) should assist.

Having spoken to a number of trainees and a couple of pupil barristers who left university with 2:2s, we would never discourage anyone from applying for a training position; nonetheless, these people all had other impressive qualities and/or CV-enhancing experiences. If you find yourself at the back of the queue in the job market, think hard about what you can do to overcome that 2:2 – a year or more in a relevant job, a further degree, a commitment to voluntary work perhaps.

Possibly unaware that they could be applying for training contracts and vacation schemes in their second year, many new students are lulled into a false sense of security concerning their academic performance in the first year. If the only marks you have to show recruiters are amazing thirds, you'll struggle to make headway. As boring as it may sound, work for good results throughout your time at university. At the very least, doing so will maximise your chances of a great final result.

student daze

But don't become a dullard! Your first year away from home (or for some, full-time employment) is a time to explore new-found freedom and practically unlimited opportunities. Almost every uni will have a wide range of societies, meeting groups and sports clubs. At the vast majority, if your leisure pursuit of choice is not on offer, they'll give you the cash to set it up, provided you can rustle up a handful of like-minded individuals and it's not illegal. Pursuing your interests will give an extra dimension to both your university experience and, crucially, your CV.

Sometimes the flood of info from university bodies such as the students' union and careers service can be so heavy you feel like you are drowning in e-mails, flyers and posters telling you of this job vacancy, that Amnesty meeting, or the other CV workshop. Resist the temptation to let it all wash over you. Relevant work experience is vital to almost every successful job application, so keep your eyes open for suitable positions, and use them to test your own ideas of what you would like to do. Many universities run law-specific careers seminars in association with firms of solicitors or sets of chambers. As Clare Harris, head of graduate recruitment at City law firm Lovells advises: *"Be savvy, go along and find out as much as you can by talking to trainee solicitors and recruiters."*

Do remember that only a minority of law firms and chambers throw drinks parties or sponsor libraries – the legal profession is not limited to the folk who've actually bought you a drink! Build up a decent understanding of the structure of the profession before deciding what kind of lawyer you want to be and which firm you want to work for. Just because your friends seem to know what they want doesn't mean their choices are right for you. Similarly, your tutors and family can only help you so far. Research, research and research some more until you are confident of your preferences. Take it from the horse's mouth. As Clare says, *"demonstrating your understanding of what the work will entail and being able to explain honestly and realistically why you want to do it will be one of the most important things to get across to recruiters."*

If you want to become a commercial lawyer, you'll need this thing they call commercial awareness. We're not suggesting you become a Sir John Harvey-Jones, rather that you should gain a sense of what's going on in the commercial world. Stock market down, a boom in China, insurgence in Iraq – do you see how they're all connected to rising oil prices? If you have zero interest in all this stuff, what makes you think commercial law will interest you? Why not read the *FT* now and again, or find an internet site that will give you headline bulletins in bite-sized chunks. Keep up to date in a way that suits you, just don't be oblivious to the events going on around you at national and international level.

ahh...those tuareg camp fires

It's official! Travel does broaden the mind. Recruiters know this too, so don't feel that you need to play down the time you've spent exploring the world. If you've itchy feet and if you haven't already been out there for a look-see, what's stopping you?

you're not from round here are you?

London attracts young professionals from all over the world, so you can skip this bit if you're a Brit intending to work in the capital. If you hold an EU passport or have a pre-existing right to live and work in the UK and you are following the appropriate path to qualification, you can probably also proceed with optimism. Applicants who tick none of these boxes will probably find doors are easier to push open if they apply to firms with business interests in the country or region from which they come. This is because law firms have to show sound reasons why an overseas applicant is worth employing over someone who needs no work permit. Generally, the people we encountered who were neither EU nationals nor had a permanent right to live and work in the UK were training in the largest City firms or with specialist shipping practices. Additionally, a number of barristers chambers will take pupils who intend to return to practice in their home jurisdiction. In all cases, excellent written and spoken English is essential and you will need a convincing reason why you have chosen to commence your career in Ol' Blighty.

Regional firms and sets are often most comfortable recruiting those with a local connection, be this through family or education. Quite simply, they want to know that whoever they take on will be committed to a long-term career with them;

they are wary of having their brightest and best skipping off to London as soon as they qualify. The picture across the UK is a variable one: some firms clearly state their preferences for local lads and lasses; others tell us that most of their applicants do have links with the region, but that they are happy to consider anyone. Over the years we've found Irish trainees in Staffordshire, Londoners in Exeter and Scots in Birmingham, but we've also found that law firms in certain cities tend to pick people with strong ties – ever-popular Bristol is the most obvious example.

grey matter

Older applicants often worry needlessly that they are at a disadvantage. Far from it! So long as you have something to show for your extra years, you may find it easier to impress recruiters. You already know how to work, your people/client-handling skills are doubtlessly better developed, and you may even have relevant industry-specific experience. We've chatted with successful barristers and solicitors who've done everything from secretarial work, pub management and film production to police work and PR. Certain past-life work experiences – healthcare, the armed forces, accountancy and engineering – make candidates particularly interesting.

But when is old too old? If you're still in your 20s, get over yourself – you're still a baby! If you're in your 30s, ask what it is you can offer a law firm. And if you're older still? Never say never. We have run into a small number of 40-something trainees. Given that each year after qualification a certain percentage of the UK's lawyers move firms or even drop out of the profession for good, we don't buy the argument that employers want 30 years of service out of each of their new recruits. More relevant is the adage concerning old dogs and new tricks, so if your coat is greying, consider carefully how you'd cope with being asked to revert to puppyhood.

breaking down barriers

Despite the legal profession being more diverse than ever before, for students with mental or physical disabilities, the route to a training contract or pupillage can be a difficult one. In a recent survey conducted by the Group for Solicitors with Disabilities (GSD) 500 randomly chosen law firms were asked to provide information on the provisions they made for disabled applicants in their training contract recruitment practices. At the time of writing, a disappointing 1% of those firms had responded. In the experience of the GSD, many students with disabilities have great difficulty in securing work placements and training contracts. The good news is that there are sources of advice and assistance available for students with disabilities seeking to enter the legal profession. The GSD has been actively involved in approaching law firms to set up designated work placement schemes for disabled students, and is in the process of writing its own guide to disability-friendly firms. The group also provides a forum in which disabled students and practitioners can meet in order to share experiences and provide one another with guidance and support. For would-be barristers, the Equal Opportunities (Disability) Committee of the Bar Council also provides students with advice and assistance.

single white male

An apt description for the legal profession 30 years ago maybe. In the course of our research, around 150 firms provided us with lists identifying their trainees. In most firms the girls outnumber the boys. The names reflect a healthy spread of ethnic backgrounds and in more than 1,000 interviews with trainees and pupil barristers in 2004 we heard just one complaint of racial discrimination. It is worth mentioning, however, that female and non-white trainees still have too few senior-level role models and there are always a small number of law firm sex or race discrimination claims going through the employment tribunals. Indeed, the

Law Society itself was the subject of a discrimination claim by its own vice president (though the latest decision found in favour of the society). For the record, we know scores of gay and lesbian lawyers for whom sexual orientation is entirely a non-career matter.

In the USA, diversity has been a hot topic for longer than it has in the UK, and as with other things that have travelled east across the Altlantic (including higher salaries and a greater commitment to pro bono work) the Brits are now paying more attention to it.

help!

Did someone mention pro bono? In case you've been on the moon for the last year and haven't noticed the flurry of interest in the topic, pro bono means working for free for the good of others. The benefits for those who receive pro bono assistance – and for those who give it – are so great that we've devoted a whole section (overleaf) to how students can get involved.

balancing act

What with studying hard, reading the *FT*, helping out at the local CAB, canoeing and playing hockey (you could try combining them), debating, acting as student law society president, acting on stage and attending all the careers events that crop up throughout the year, you'll hardly have time for a pint, let alone the ten that students supposedly put away in between lectures. Your mum and dad may tell you university is supposed to be a fun, carefree time, but frankly back in their day the job market was less competitive and no one built up a small mortgage in debt before the age of 21...well, only if they had a really wild time. Besides, what do the olds know? They were too busy listening to Backman Turner Overdrive and having sit-down protests.

Of course you must have fun, and you absolutely must develop your interests and friendships because these, in many cases, last far longer and can be more rewarding than any career. Ultimately, it all comes down to finding the right balance.

pro bono opportunities

Even if your idea of a dream come true is handling mergers and acquisitions in a top-flight City firm, it's time to dig deep into the corners of your soul and find your inner altruist. Recruiters, both barristers and solicitors, are always looking for candidates with practical experience of working in a legal environment. As Kara Irwin, Director of the BPP Pro Bono Centre puts it: *"Lawyers always see this as the most interesting thing on a candidate's CV. As well as being something tangible that students can contribute to the community, it gives them the opportunity to really develop important legal skills."* Volunteering can often be the best way to gain such skills, and there are plenty of available options for students who are willing to give up some of their spare time.

Every little bit counts, whether it's a half day a week helping out at your local CAB or six months overseas working as an intern on death row appeals, as long as you can offer some kind of long-term commitment. If you're just doing something to add a notch to your CV bedpost, it's going to look pretty obvious. We've spoken to some of the law schools and pro bono organisations to find out about the sort of things on offer. We've also put together a non-exhaustive list of other organisations involved in pro bono to get you started in your quest to save the world.

make the most of your law school

Most post-graduate law schools, and increasingly many university law departments, now have some kind of pro bono initiative in place. At some colleges, pro bono is not just an option; it's a compulsory element of the course. At the Student Law Office of Northumbria University, which has achieved Legal Services Commission Quality Marks for its housing and employment advice, all LPC and BVC students advise real clients, from the initial interview and advice stage through to advocacy before tribunals

and the small claims court.

As well as running legal advice clinics, many law schools are finding new and innovative ways of offering their students pro bono experience by engaging in outreach work in the local community. Take the Streetlaw Plus programme at the York branch of the College of Law. Here, students are actively helping local residents in Doncaster to address their concerns about dilapidated housing and planning through regular letter-writing surgeries.

Pro bono is not necessarily just about providing advice to individuals; it can involve carrying out research for pressure groups and international organisations. At BPP's Pro Bono Centre students have set up an intellectual property group, and recently helped to conduct research in association with a leading IP firm giving advice to the International Chamber of Commerce. Its human rights unit was involved in providing research support to the International Bar Association's Human Rights Institute in a recent review of the Somali legal system.

For undergraduates, it can often be more difficult to find a centrally organised pro bono initiative within their university. If this is the case where you are studying, that doesn't stop you using your initiative to seek out experience of your own. If you're young and inexperienced, don't worry; providing administrative support to an over-worked legal charity still looks great on your CV, and may well lead into other things later on.

the free representation unit (fru)

Becoming a ratified member of the FRU is a really good idea if you're thinking of going to the Bar, but it's an equally good idea if you are intending to be a solicitor specialising in any area of law involving contentious work (think crime, employment, family and commercial litigation) because chances are you'll be doing at least some of the advocacy yourself.

FRU representatives offer free advice and representation to clients who are not eligible for legal aid, appearing on their behalf before employment and social security tribunals. There is also a limited amount of work in criminal injuries compensation appeals and some immigration matters. Law students can train to become a social security representative in the final year of an LLB, or alternatively non-law graduates can do this in their CPE year. The employment option is only open to LPC and BVC students, and it should also be noted that FRU only operates in and around London, though several of the regional BVC and LPC providers have advice clinics that allow students to gain experience of tribunal advocacy.

To qualify, you'll need to attend an induction day and satisfactorily complete a legal opinion exercise. Once that's done, you'll be able to sign out a case of your own after discussing it with one of the caseworkers. Cases are graded to match differing levels of experience, but otherwise reps have free rein to choose whatever they want; a luxury that lawyers won't get in their early years of practice! Once a case is yours, you must see it through from beginning to end. A pupil barrister with a series of employment tribunal wins behind her told us: *"As a rep you'll get experience in using a whole bundle of practical legal skills. You'll conference with your client, conduct legal research, draft submissions, negotiate with your opponent, and if the case doesn't settle, you'll make oral submissions to the tribunal and get to examine and cross-examine witnesses."* From time to time, seasoned FRU reps have been known to take cases to the Employment Appeal Tribunal or the Social Security Commissioners and it's not unheard of for their names to appear in the reported decision.

If we haven't sold it to you already, it might also be pointed out that a very high number of the pupils and junior barristers that we interviewed for our **Chambers Reports** had worked for FRU or another similar organisation at some time in their training. It could well be the thing that saves your application from the shredder.

some other ideas to get you started

Below is a sample of the many pro bono opportunities on offer for students. For more information on other schemes, it's worth doing some research of your own.

the student pro bono group: This runs in conjunction with the Solicitors Pro Bono Group and is a good source of advice and information. Students can join the group for free by registering on its website at **www.students.probonogroup.org.uk**

aire (advice on individual rights in europe): AIRE provides information and advice throughout Europe on international human rights law, including the rights of individuals under the provisions of European Community law. It also offers direct legal advice and assistance on a case-by-case basis to legal practitioners or advisers. Internships are available for students who have a good working knowledge of international human rights law and EU law. Students must be able to commit a minimum of one day per week. A second European language is an advantage. Contact: Gabi Schlick on 020 7831 4276 or gschlick@airecentre.org.

amicus: Amicus is a charity providing assistance to US attorneys working on death-row cases. It gives training and arranges internships in the USA for UK post-graduate students. As internships are unpaid (though a limited number of scholarships do exist), interested applicants should have a plan for funding the placement. Contact: Sophie Garner sophiegarner @amicus-alj.org.

the bar pro bono unit: Established in 1996 by Attorney-General Lord Goldsmith QC, the unit matches individuals in need of legal representation with barristers in private practice willing to undertake work on a pro bono basis. Opportunities are available for students to provide administrative support to the unit on a part-time basis. This could mean anything from envelope stuffing to allocating cases to members of the panel. Contact: **www.barprobono.org.uk**

citizens advice bureaux: We spoke to the Citizens Advice service, which has over 22,000 volunteers in over 2,000 bureaux. Those with real commitment and enough time can train with the CAB on its Adviser Training Programme, which is a widely recognised qualification that may subsequently enable the period of your law firm training contract to be reduced by up to six months. Not all volunteers have the time or the inclination to train as advisers, and if admin, IT or reception work is enough for you, why not request one of these roles, or perhaps even help out with publicity and media activities? Debt, benefits, housing, employment, consumer issues, family matters and immigration are the most commonly raised problems, some six million of which are handled each year. Contact: **www.citizensadvice.org.uk/join-us**

independent custody visiting: A good idea for anyone interested in a criminal practice. Independent custody visiting began in the wake of the Scarman Report following the Brixton riots of 1981. Independent custody visitors (ICVs) work in pairs, conducting regular unannounced checks on police stations in their area to monitor the welfare of the detainees. Anyone over the age of 18 can apply to become an ICV. Applications are made to the local police authority. To download an application form, visit the Independent Custody Visiting Association website **www.icva.org.uk**

law centres: Law centres provide a free and independent professional legal service to people who live or work in their catchment areas, typically covering areas where legal aid is not available such as employment and immigration. Working at a law centre is very much a career in itself (see page 11); however, many centres accept student volunteers to provide administrative support and assistance with casework. The website **www.lawcentres.org.uk** provides links to individual law centres across the UK.

liberty: Liberty is a well-established human rights organisation providing advice and representation to groups and individuals in relation to domestic law cases involving the Human Rights Act. Liberty has opportunities for a small number of students to provide general office assistance and help with casework. Students should be able to commit at least one day a week. Apply by sending a CV and cover letter to the organisation. **www.liberty-human-rights.org.uk**

victim support: The Victim Support Witness Service operates in every crown court across England and Wales, providing guidance and support to witnesses, victims and their families before, during and after court proceedings. Volunteers need to be able to commit at least two hours per week. For details of the nearest local office, visit **www.victimsupport.org.uk**

Remember: these are just a few of the organisations you can become involved with. And it's worth pointing out that we've focused here on law-related matters.

cpe/pgdl/gdl: law for non-lawyers

To explain: the Law Society determines the training required to qualify as a solicitor in England and Wales. The training process has an academic stage and a vocational one. The vocational bit is the LPC but first, the academic element must be satisfied by completing one of the following: a qualifying law degree, the Common Professional Examination (CPE), or the Institute of Legal Executives' ILEX exams (see page 17). Likewise, the Bar Council requires aspiring barristers who lack a qualifying law degree to pass the CPE.

The CPE appears in a variety of different guises and goes by different names, but don't worry – there is no real difference between the Postgraduate Diploma in Law (PgDL), the Graduate Diploma in Law (GDL) and the CPE. As far as the Law Society and the Bar Council are concerned, all are equally valid. For simplicity, we use the term CPE throughout this book.

admission requirements

The standard requirement for admission to the CPE is a degree from a university in the UK or the Republic of Ireland. Some other non-standard qualifications are recognised, such as certain overseas degrees and degree equivalent or professional qualifications. Additionally, non-graduate mature persons who have gained considerable experience and shown exceptional ability in academic, professional, business or administrative fields may be considered. Check out the table of CPE providers on our website for more particular admission requirements: some institutions (especially in the regions) will look closely at your reason for studying in the area, while others are so heavily subscribed they tend to only consider applicants who name them as their first choice.

the course

This is no cakewalk. Full-time CPE courses last for a minimum of 36 weeks, during which you'll be expected to undertake 45 hours of lectures, tutorials, private study and research per week. With such a rigorous timetable, you can kiss goodbye to weekday hangovers and lazy afternoons of *Countdown* and *Fifteen-to-One*.

Whether done as a two-year part-time course, or one-year full time, the course covers seven "foundations of legal knowledge":
- **Contract**
- **Tort**
- **Criminal**
- **Equity and trusts**
- **EU law**
- **Property**
- **Public law**

Assessment is usually by way of written exams – these will mostly be traditional three-hour papers – and many institutions also require you to submit coursework assignments and/or a dissertation. Typically, the teaching is a combination of lectures and classroom-based activities. Some institutions require you to write several academic essays per term, while at law schools that favour a more practical approach, you'll have to prepare topics for moots or draft solutions to problem questions.

There is no gentle introduction to the CPE. This is a fast-track course, and it is essential that you remain on top of the workload, as well as the law. While really bright students may find reams of photocopied material a little elementary, no one passes without putting in the hours. Commendations and distinctions are up for grabs, and at certain firms, these may earn you a cheeky little bonus on top of any sponsorship you've been given. But remember:

if you are being sponsored, your firm won't be impressed if you just scrape through.

Good organisation, a consistent approach and commitment go a long way on the CPE, and with these it is possible to do very well without being in the library 24/7. Many people manage to squeeze in part-time jobs to keep the wolf from the door.

If you worked hard at university and got a good degree, you're perfectly capable of succeeding on the CPE. Essentially, it's a case of applying the skills you already have to industrial quantities of new material. If you do this in bite-sized chunks as you go along, the whole process is relatively palatable. However, if you are in two minds about the course, you may want to think hard before committing to it. People do the CPE for a variety of reasons, but if you are just looking for something to keep you out of trouble for a year after uni, there are considerably cheaper, easier and less demanding ways of going about it.

institutions

No two CPE courses are the same, so do your research. Contact institutions to request a prospectus and speak to former students to find out what course suits you best. At some institutions you will be taught by practising solicitors, while elsewhere, professors offer a more academic slant; the course may be characterised by the need to memorise great swathes of photocopied material, or it can be an exciting challenge for the intellectually astute.

Quite apart from the teaching style, you may also want to consider that different institutions attract a different type of student. For example, at providers that offer City-oriented LPC programmes you'll find a higher proportion of cut-and-thrust corporate types, while at somewhere like City Uni a more academic course attracts those looking to go to the Bar.

At most institutions you will find City slickers rubbing shoulders with champions of human rights. The course draws people of all ages and from a variety of backgrounds. Of course, there will be plenty of new and recent graduates, but there will also be those who have left other careers to train as lawyers, people who have already worked in law firms in a non-qualified capacity and people from overseas who are tailoring their qualifications to the English system. For every person who arrives at law school with training contract in hand, finances sorted, career done and dusted, and halfway to partnership already, there will be plenty of others whose CVs are still a Joycean stream of consciousness. Whichever category you fall into, the course can be tough and tiring, so you must be clear that you are doing it for your own benefit (rather than Mum and Dad's). The best advice we can give is to throw yourself into it wholeheartedly.

applications

Those wishing to study the CPE full time must apply through the Central Applications Board. To ensure the best chance of securing a place at your college of choice, apply early in the calendar year and in the first round of applications. It is possible to apply for a place in the second round in the late spring but popular, oversubscribed schools are unlikely to still have places. If you are hoping to do your LPC at a very popular school it is really worthwhile trying to get a CPE place there because most schools guarantee LPC places to those of their students who are successful at the CPE.

The course is now offered at 34 different universities and colleges in England and Wales. Check our website for a full list of course providers, fees and other details.

the legal practice course

The LPC is the year-long course undertaken by prospective solicitors after either a qualifying law degree or the CPE. The course is designed to equip them with the skills needed for practice rather than as a further period of scholarship. The first part of the year is spent on the compulsory elements of the course: knowledge areas include litigation, conveyancing and business law, and legal skills such as interviewing, advocacy, drafting and IT. After taking exams on these compulsory sections, the remaining months are devoted to three elective subjects. The range of options varies from one course provider to another. For a full list of who offers what, refer to the Chambers Student website **www.chambersandpartners.com**.

Currently, those students with training contracts from eight City firms – Allen & Overy, Clifford Chance, Freshfields, Herbert Smith, Linklaters, Lovells, Norton Rose, and Slaughter and May – must study an LPC course that is oriented to City practice at BPP in London, Nottingham Law School or the Oxford Institute of Legal Practice. They have no choice over elective subjects, being required to choose the private acquisitions, debt finance and equity finance options. Places are also available to students who will train with other firms, but the course content makes it appropriate only for those headed for City practice. This scenario will all change from September 2006, when new arrangements for the eight firms come into effect. Three firms – Linklaters, Allen & Overy and Clifford Chance – will each offer a tailor-made course in conjunction with the College of Law in London. The other five firms will all continue to send their future trainees to BPP in London.

Note that there are other institutions offering City electives, so not studying at BPP, Oxford or Nottingham is no bar to gaining a City-compatible LPC.

Each of these three providers also offers non-City electives.

What of the new firm-specific LPC courses to be run by the College of Law? In essence, these will be merely a refinement of the current City LPC, which in itself represented a leap forward when introduced for the eight so-called 'consortium firms'.

Linklaters' trainee development partner Simon Firth outlined some of the changes proposed for the 2006/7 academic year and beyond. There will be additional premises for the COL Store Street branch, tutors recruited specifically to teach the Linklaters course, firm-specific documentation, greater participation from Linklaters lawyers, and even some training in the firm's offices. "*We want to break down the boundary between the classroom and practice,*" he explained, adding: "*We're not going to be micromanaging it and controlling every aspect though.*" Just as you can't imagine people who train as doctors never seeing real patients, Simon thinks legal training shouldn't be divorced from real practice.

Plenty has been written about the pros and cons of such tailored courses, and whether they are elitist. Linklaters, however, is quite clear that the move to a tailored course will benefit both the firm and its trainees. Simon told us: "*They should find it more relevant and motivational. The Linklaters context of the course means that they will recognise the firm's documents and procedures and how we organise ourselves.*" Aware that some students might worry about their fitness for practice elsewhere if they didn't stay at Linklaters on qualification, Simon was keen to stress that the new course was no more specialised than the current City LPC. We're inclined to agree that such concerns are unfounded...unless, of course, someone intends to give up the City entirely and practice in crime or wills and probate!

LAW SOCIETY ASSESSMENT GRADES	
Anglia Polytechnic University	Good
Bournemouth University	Good
BPP Law School	Excellent
Bristol Institute of Legal Practice at UWE	Excellent
Cardiff Law School	Excellent
College of Law at Birmingham	Very Good
College of Law at Chester	Very Good
College of Law at Guildford	Very Good
College of Law at London	Very Good
College of Law at York	Very Good
De Montfort University	Good
Inns of Court School of Law	Excellent
Leeds Metropolitan University	Good
Liverpool John Moores University (p/t)	Good
London Metropolitan University	Satisfactory
Manchester Metropolitan University	Good
Nottingham Law School	Excellent
Oxford Institute of Legal Practice	Very Good
Staffordshire University	Excellent
Thames Valley University	Good
University of Central England	Satisfactory
University of Central Lancashire	Very Good
University of Exeter	Good
University of Glamorgan	Good
University of Hertfordshire (p/t)	Good
University of Huddersfield	Good
University of Northumbria	Good
University of Sheffield	Very Good
University of Westminster	Very Good
University of Wolverhampton	Good

These grades were accurate at the time of going to press in September 2004.

How do you choose a law school?

Applications are administered centrally by the LPC Applications Board. Before filling in the LawCabs application form, get hold of as much information as possible – digest the content of **www.lawcabs.ac.uk**, request law school prospectuses, chat to representatives visiting your university and current students, if possible. When choosing a school, there are plenty of considerations:

career issues: A future employer may well have a preferred list of schools. At the very least, it should be able to give you advice about your choice of provider, based on the experiences of its current trainees. If the firm is paying your fees, it's probably only polite to ask. If you don't yet have a training contract, think about the quality of careers advice on offer at each institution. Have they got a good record of getting students placements and training contracts with the kind of firms you want to work for? In the summer of 2004 we surveyed law firms in England and Wales to establish their preferred LPC providers. The results are on our website.

electives: Find out which institutions offer the electives best suited to the type of practice you want to move into. Some may have restrictions on elective combinations or run electives only when there is sufficient demand. For a full rundown on who offers what, see the Chambers Student website.

assessment grades and pass rates: Pass rates are published on the Law Society's website each autumn, but be aware that direct comparisons are impossible as each institution examines and marks independently of the others. The Law Society visits and inspects each institution and then publishes an Ofsted-style report on its website along with an assessment grade. The grades are set out opposite.

teaching methods: Most institutions timetable around 14 hours of classes per week. In some places you might be able to catch up on sleep in the back row of a lecture theatre; at others you'll be swanning around mock offices during sessions designed to replicate a morning in a firm. Exam and assessment methods also vary. Some institutions offer significantly more coursework, and as for exams, some are entirely open-book, while others only allow statute books and practitioner texts into the exam room. A larger provider may not be right for you, if you want to be more than a number to your tutors. Then again, relative anonymity may suit you.

tactics: Some of the most popular institutions require you to put them as first choice on the Law-Cabs application form before they will even consider you. We have included this type of information on the LPC Providers table on our website. Check also whether your university or CPE provider or your law firm has an agreement with an LPC provider.

money and fees: Fees vary and so do the institutions' policies on the inclusion of the cost of textbooks, Law Society membership, etc. Even if you have sponsorship from a law firm, living expenses still need to be taken into account and London, especially, can be a nasty shock if you haven't lived there before. The latest available information about the fees for each course is on our website.

location: For many students, tight finances restrict their choice of school. Living at home will save you a packet...if you can stand it! If you're lucky enough to be able to strike out on your own, it's worth considering what you like and don't like about your university or CPE provider, and whether you want to prolong your undergraduate experience or escape it. And remember, certain LPC providers are dominated by graduates of local universities. While some providers are part of a university law faculty, elsewhere elaborate floral arrangements and acres of plate glass may make you feel like you're studying in the offices of a City firm.

social mix and social life: It's worth thinking about whether you'd prefer to be somewhere with students following a similar career path or whether you want to mix it up with a wider cross-section of people. Size also matters: it can be harder to bond with your cohorts where you're one of several hundred. Studenty cities such as Nottingham and Bristol are always a lot of fun; however, students in the Big Smoke warn us that everyone turns into pumpkins after classes end.

In the following pages we've drawn out some of the differences between the 11 LPC providers that currently boast an Excellent or Very Good rating from the Law Society. The reports have been written with assistance from current and former students of each provider.

lpc providers – the inside story

bpp law school, london

number of places: 756 full-time, 144 part-time

BPP Law School is part of a worldwide professional education network. It was one of three law schools that pioneered the City LPC and from 2006 will be the sole LPC provider for future Slaughter and May, Freshfields, Lovells, Norton Rose and Herbert Smith trainees. Most students have training contracts when they start the course and *"magic circle trainees* [and others of that ilk] *dominate."* The law school has grown exponentially since opening in London and is now offering the course at its new Leeds branch and opens in Manchester in September 2005. This report is based on feedback from London students.

Most of the tutors are *"ex-City lawyers, not academic lecturers."* On a vocational course, that's no bad thing, and students say they were *"incredibly charismatic and on top of their game."* Although the course can feel a bit *"learn and regurgitate,"* the pace is brisk and the schedule is *"heavy,"* starting with the massive stack of books you'll find in your locker on the first day. Approximately 15 hours of classes per week are weighted towards two-hour sessions for groups of around 18. Teaching incorporates ferocious exploitation of PowerPoint and smartboards. Plenty of prep is needed. You'll be subjected to *"constant* [closed book] *examining all the time,"* culminating in the compulsory assessments in April, including a four-hour business law whopper.

The elective part of the course is *"less hectic."* Most students opt for 'City' and commercial electives, though plenty of other options are on offer if demand is sufficiently high. These courses are taught with the same military efficiency that you'll find across BPP and *"as you may only have three or four in your group you'll really benefit."* Minority options may mean early morning, evening and lunchtime classes and the loss of your weekly day off (sorry, 'individual study day'), as you're fitted in around the majority.

There's been a tendency for the building to become uncomfortably cramped at peak hours, but the transfer of CPE students to new premises near Waterloo in September 2004 should have eased this problem for the LPC and BVC students remaining in the *"very corporate looking"* Red Lion Street premises.

BPP's City orientation means the student mix, particularly on the full-time course, is not exactly diverse – Old Etonians and willowy girls are two a penny. Expect half of your class to spend their holidays in Dubai and Kenya, and the other half to be dashing off to see uni mates in Bristol or Cambridge every weekend. As most people know plenty of their fellow students from either university or the CPE course, or have located the people who will be joining the same firm as them, *"people don't invest much time in making other new friends."* Some students found the subterranean social areas *"a bit depressing."* Perhaps explaining the popularity of two nearby bars, The Square Pig and Sway. BPP has traditionally preferred not to become involved in students' lives outside their courses; however, the law school is establishing a counselling service and recently hired a massively enthusiastic pro bono co-ordinator, so we expect things to develop on both fronts.

bristol institute of legal practice at uwe

number of places: up to 340 full-time, up to 120 part-time

The West Country law school was the first to be given an Excellent grading by the Law Society in 1995 and has retained this seal of approval ever since. Part of its success must be down to the above-average staff-to-student ratio: students found that tutors were *"very available"* and *"made an effort to get to know you."* And friendly chats aren't all they can do. All the alumni we spoke to concluded that the LPC here is *"excellent and very well structured;" "an intensive course that was programmed well."* The calibre of teaching staff was judged to be *"high with exceptions"* and tutors were often willing to provide extra support – *"they really looked out for the individual."* The workload will be as heavy here as anywhere else, but the teaching pattern is slightly different. You'll spend most of your time in three-and-a-half-hour group sessions (which get the gold medal in a competitive field for duration) and lectures are only an occasional treat. A number of the students we spoke to had welcomed this format for the delivery of the course. The institute also wins the prize for the most electives on offer – 15 by our count, which reflects the diverse destinations of the students who come here. If you still want more, an LLM can be taken as a top-up qualification.

The institute's only real downside is its location on the UWE campus. We shudder at the slip in our 2003 edition, which turned the word 'lane' into 'track', so implying that the university took on the proportions of a barnyard. For the record, the road to UWE is fully tarmacked and sufficiently wide for traffic in both directions. But...*"if you live in the city centre it's a difficult drive or bus to UWE. And if you live near the uni you can have a difficult time getting a taxi back at night."* Although the campus has faced accusations that it has *"no character,"* once you're there *"the facilities are good."* LPC students have access to *"our own separate law library and the main uni library, and each tutor room has PCs."* The year can be an excellent one socially and most students choose to live in Bristol's vibrant student enclaves – Redlands, Cotham and Clifton or around Gloucester Road. Bristol is a superb city by any measure and, frankly, if the entire *Student Guide* team could move there, we would.

cardiff law school
number of places: 160 full-time

Having long borne a much coveted Excellent rating from the Law Society, it's rare that we hear any criticism about the quality of the LPC on offer in the buzzing Welsh capital. The course here is as much of a slog as anywhere else: *"The LPC is like going back to school – you have to go to classes and do your homework, otherwise you look at bit stupid."* But former students were full of praise for this *"really well-structured and well-presented course."* For many, what makes Cardiff outstanding is the quality of the staff/student relationship: *"The teaching standards are high and the law school staff are so supportive;" "they quickly catch on to what individuals need."* Class sizes are average (16-18 people), but because the overall intake is small, *"teachers are available and know you."*

The school aims to cater for a diverse range of students and the spread of electives should have something for everyone. It looks as if Cardiff will be going one step further and offering a new public services pathway LPC for those interested in legal aid practice. Alumni head for a wide range of firms across the country, and we don't just mean Wales. While two-thirds of students arrive for the LPC without a training contract, strong links with Welsh firms mean they are all guaranteed a work placement.

As part of Cardiff university, the law school offers a wealth of services. There are *"top-rate facilities,"* the library is *"well stocked"* (though we hear there's a tendency for cross-desk gossip), there are *"plenty of PCs"* and *"a great student union."* While in the gym or the student refectory, you'll note that *"the Cardiff LPC is a honey pot for those from Welsh universities."* Cardiff is described as a *"fun," "friendly,"* but *"small and compact"* city. You can sample the nightlife of the newly redeveloped Tiger Bay, and who knows, as you stumble out of a bar you may even bump into Charlotte Church. Prefer nights in? No problem. *"After classes together every day, we became close and there were lots of parties. People knew each other very well."* For the sporty, South Wales is fast becoming Britain's answer to Bondi. One student told us: *"Loads of my friends go down to the Gower Peninsula all the time."* This being Wales, another student insisted we give rugby a mention.

college of law
number of places: 3,628 full-time, 532 part-time

The College of Law is the oldest and largest LPC provider and, with five branches, it is accessible from pretty much every corner of England and Wales. After weathering the rejection of its City LPC tender, the biggest blow in COL history, it has bounced back by winning a contract to provide bespoke LPCs for Allen & Overy, Clifford Chance and Linklaters trainees from September 2006. Determined to retain the diversity of its student intake, from September 2005 the college will also offer a Public Services Pathway LPC designed for students with an interest in legal aid work. What's more, with 13 choices in total, COL offers students one of the longest elective menus.

Students at all branches follow a standard LPC course and are taught with the same materials and in the same way. Occupying around 14 hours a week, teaching is delivered by way of a mixture of lectures and small-group sessions. You can choose whether to attend classes in the morning or the afternoon, something which students at some other institutions envied. *"From a work perspective doing mornings is better and from a social perspective afternoons are better."* We'd venture to suggest that the nature of the LPC course means that you'll be doing a pretty solid day either way as *"there's a constant workload"* and *"always exams or coursework coming up."* One past student told us: *"It felt like you had a steam roller behind you."*

As at other institutions, some people felt their success on the course was due to the fact that it is *"not too demanding in terms of academic depth."* Others, however, were quick to praise teachers who had *"been in practice for a long time"* and who were *"good at getting what they needed out of you."* A few people also said the course materials were of real use to them in practice. Another possible benefit of the course here is that all exams are 'open-book', so *"you just need to know where everything is."* Given that several rainforests are felled each week to provide LPC students with paperwork, that's easier said than done.

The careers support available at COL is superb. Those without a training contract will be given plenty of advice and help with applications. One past student had found a pre-course session particularly helpful. *"They helped people who were having trouble getting interviews. It was really useful – you brought along a CV and an application you had done and they made suggestions."* In London, a 'commercial awareness forum' was set up by students a few years ago to host speakers and run networking events. Across the country the prestigious and highly successful Streetlaw project continues to prosper as part of a comprehensive commitment to pro bono initiatives.

store street, london
number of places: 1,248 full-time, 192 part-time

Store Street is the country's largest law school and here you'll find students embarking on all kinds of legal careers. On balance, most students felt that their needs were catered for, saying: *"The teaching was by and large good and did the job."* However, some felt that the buildings *"could do with brushing up"* and the large numbers on the LPC, BVC and CPE meant *"there are not enough facilities for the number of students."* We understand that the introduction of bespoke courses in 2006 will result in extra premises being brought into play.

Located just off Tottenham Court Road, Store Street enjoys the advantages of close proximity to the West End, but as with the other London law schools, bonding between fellow students can be patchy. Some thought *"the social scene was really good,"* whereas others felt that *"Store Street is a nice place to be, if you just want to keep yourself to yourself and get on with things."* Mostly, *"everyone plays with their own friends."*

guildford
number of places: 720 full-time, 100 part-time

Students love the Guildford branch's picturesque setting in a country manor house, saying: *"You can study on the grass"* and *"If I didn't want to work, I could go for a wander in the grounds."* For the more active, there are squash courts and sports facilities at the college. All that fresh air and healthy living predispose former students to think back fondly to their LPC year, with one confessing *"I even went back there recently!"* Guildford may not boast the pace or varied pleasures of London, but students didn't feel that their social life had been put out to pasture – *"everyone was always getting together and doing things."* Accommodation can be pricey, but look on the bright side: you're unlikely to have a gangland killing on your doorstep.

The course itself seems to progress smoothly: *"There were no problems with the teaching; the tutors were good and always there to give you extra help if you needed it."*

chester
number of places: 600 full-time, 80 part-time

In historic Chester, the COL is located in a former seminary, which is *"quite nice, if a bit like a school."* Although we didn't sense much religious zeal for the LPC, we did hear that many of the tutors here are *"excellent"* and *"prepared to hold your hand when you need it."* Chester attracts students who are originally from the North West, those heading for the big Manchester and Liverpool firms and also *"lots of Irish people,"* particularly from Queen's Uni in Belfast.

Depending on who you speak to, Chester is *"gorgeous," "picturesque"* and *"a nice place to have a year out – no hustle and bustle."* Others tired of it quickly: *"It's full of tourists, students and pensioners – and none of them like each other very much!"* Anyone more naturally suited to bright lights and big cities is likely to find this tiny city *"small and stifling."* As the college is located some distance from the centre of town, you'll need to chat up someone with a car if you don't have your own wheels. Consequently many people choose to live in the law student enclave in Boughton and walk to classes along the canal towpath.

"Everyone knows each other" on campus, and even off campus you won't go very far without recognising someone. *"There are only two places to go out on the town and so you get to see the same faces."* Remembering the nightlife with a mixture of fondness and embarrassment, one past student told us: *"There was this one night club called Rosie's that was horrible...but good fun. We all went every Thursday."*

york
number of places: 532 full-time, 80 part-time

Former students told us they'd had a straight-up LPC: *"York is very professionally run"* and *"the tutors know what they're talking about."* The arrival of the former head of the ICSL LPC seems to be keeping things sharp. The charms of the college's location also help: not only do students benefit from *"fantastically comfy seats"* (essential for academic success in the *Student Guide's* experience), but York racecourse is on the doorstep. Students *"remember creeping out to watch the horse races in the 15-minute break or catching the last one and having a beer."*

Speaking of York's attributes, one source said: *"The college is small enough so that you don't disappear, but it's in a reasonably sized town."* The beautiful old city was the real star for many, and if you're the sort who likes ghost walks and ancient pubs, you'll be in your element. When you do get fed up of the place, *"it's handy for social events in Leeds"* and *"pretty much four hours away from anywhere else in the UK."* (We knew what they meant!) Most students are staunchly pro-Yorkshire, and this branch has been seen as the place to come for anyone headed for the big firms in Leeds. It now has competition from the new BPP branch in Leeds, and we look forward to seeing how each fares in the popularity stakes in the next couple of years.

birmingham
number of places: 528 full-time, 80 part-time

The Birmingham branch is only a few years old, but students told us the course was *"well structured and well organised"* and that *"generally the quality of the teaching was excellent."* The facilities are *"pretty good,"* but with a doubling of student numbers since the branch opened, crowding can be an issue at busy times, particularly when it comes to PCs.

Outside working life, students got a buzz out of living in a city that finally feels *"up and coming."* *"In the last two to three years we've got Selfridges and the new Bullring shopping centre, which is a huge landmark."* The college is located in the Jewellery District, which is *"OK-ish"* and not too far from the city centre with its canalside bars and developments such as Brindleyplace. Much of student life revolves around Selly Oak and Edgbaston, near to Birmingham University.

inns of court school of law
number of places: 176 full-time

ICSL has traditionally been a BVC provider and, as you'd expect with such a well-established law school, the five-year-old ICSL LPC is going from strength to strength. When it upgraded the law school from Very Good to Excellent last year, practically the only slap on the wrist from the Law Society was a reprimand for not having enough whiteboards. Hardly crime of the century. Here the small intake is well taught (*"they really make sure people understand the course"*) by solid tutors. Perhaps because of the size of the intake and the relative newness of the course, there are slightly fewer electives on offer, but students should find something to suit their career path. The delivery of the course is slightly different from the norm: teaching always comes in 90-minute chunks and, in addition to small group sessions and lectures, there will also be workshops and, unusually, 15% of the course is taught to groups of eight or fewer students. The recently reno-vated lecture hall is *"great because it has interactive screens for every two or three people in a lecture."* Underneath is a common room with plenty of space and a few internet connections.

ICSL is also unique in that barrister types vastly outnumber future solicitors. LPC students have their own facilities, and we heard *"there's not much mixing unless you knew them from uni or school."* Nonetheless, ICSL's location in beautiful Gray's Inn will bring you into frequent contact with all things barristerial, and the close proximity of the Royal Courts of Justice and Chancery Lane are ideal for keeping you motivated through the more turgid elements of the course. If it all gets too much, the lawns of Gray's Inn and Lincoln's Inn Fields are a hop and a skip away. If you want to venture further afield, the school's recent incorporation into City University's Faculty of Law means there are sports facilities, a student union, counselling and accommodation services in nearby Islington.

nottingham law school
number of places: 650 full-time, 70 part-time

Part of Nottingham Trent University, this law school has long had an excellent reputation for providing a top-class LPC and a cracking social life. With such renown among students, competition for places has long been fierce, especially as NLS has up to now reserved a large number of places for students with training contracts at eight City law firms. This will change when these firms put their future trainees through school in London, and that can only be a good thing for students heading to other firms. Effectively, you've a better chance of getting a place than ever before. Unlike some law schools, Nottingham is not in favour of tailored courses for particular types of firm; rather the opposite. It plans to adapt and broaden its LPC now that many of its ties to the largest City firms have been loosened.

Students spoke approvingly of the *"young lecturers who knew what they were doing,"* the *"helpful tutors"* and the *"up-to-date, practical and well-organised course."* You'll have to do your bit, too, as the course is *"rigorous"* and *"tough,"* if only in *"intensity rather than difficulty."* There's no timetabled day off and you'll be in school from nine to five, mostly in classes of around 15 students. So no dozing at the back! The calibre of student is high: *"Everyone was sharp and there were a couple of stars."* Constant closed-book exams mean *"the whole course feels like jumping through a series of hoops like a performing seal,"* as it builds up to the compulsory subject assessments in April. After this, *"the pressure on the elective course is not half as much."*

One of Nottingham's major selling points is its *"real campus feel."* Students love the facilities, with one telling us: *"It was great to be able to go to the gym three times a week."* Facilities include a great accommodation office; however, one source who'd been placed in a flat share told us: *"I was stuck in a nasty area in the middle of the red light district. We had a gangland shooting nearby."* Others were luckier: *"I didn't know anyone when I arrived but was put in a house with six LPC students on a terrace full of LPC students."* Time and time again we hear that *"socially it's such a great place."* Nottingham never fails to please on this score: *"I seem to remember there were 300 pubs in a square mile."*

oxford institute of legal practice
number of places: 353 full-time

Oxilp is also being dropped as an LPC provider of choice by the consortium of eight City firms that sent it many of their recruits. Nevertheless, this institution retains a Very Good rating from the Law Society and continues to be popular, particularly with Oxford University alumni. Now free of the stranglehold on places by the consortium firms, and with a few years of experience behind it, Oxilp will be able to develop an independent persona.

Some of the former students we spoke to had attended the institute during its well-documented troubles, when a number of people had finished the year with disappointing results. All that to one side,

we heard plenty that bodes well for the future. Here's a sample. *"The quality of teaching was very good." "They had some absolutely brilliant tutors." "The course was very practical"* and *"a good background"* for a training contract. Up till now, most students have arrived on the course with training contracts already in the bag, and it will be interesting to see if this changes when the consortium firms no longer hog places.

The working week will contain the standard mixture of 90-minute small-group sessions and lectures, totalling around 14 hours. The range of electives is not as wide as at some other providers, but there is something to suit those headed for both City practice and smaller firms. As we've found elsewhere, the course here is *"demanding on hours,"* and the content can tend towards *"tedious form-filling and research tasks"* at times. Examinations are closed-book.

Located near Oxford's railway station and slightly separate from university territory, Oxilp is within easy walking distance of the city centre. There's a library on site, and students also have access to the university's world-class law libraries, which enjoy stupendous opening hours thanks to the generosity of several City firms eager to woo some of the country's brightest legal talent. When you're not studying, this student paradise offers plenty for those who want to prolong their undergraduate days. And there are plenty doing precisely that – Oxilp has thus far been dominated by Oxford graduates. If you are new to the city, an active social scene centred around a few bars and clubs is easy to infiltrate.

sheffield university
number of places: 216 full and part-time

This well-regarded law school is a part of Sheffield University: a definite plus for some people. Students benefit from the university's wide-ranging facilities (sports, library, accommodation and counselling services and the students' union) and enjoy feeling part of an academic community. Said one: *"I didn't want to be somewhere everyone was living and breathing the LPC."* Although growing steadily, year on year, the intake is relatively small compared with some LPC providers, and consequently some bemoaned the fact that *"you're not likely to meet a lot of other trainees going to your firm."* On the plus side *"you get a lot of individual attention and help,"* and each study group is assigned a personal tutor.

Some 80% of the teaching is imparted to groups of 16 or 18 via one-hour lectures and three-hour workshops and the quality of teaching is praised. Timetabling is sensible and predictable and all lectures take place on Mondays. Expect a heavy emphasis on the use of primary resources, such as practitioner texts as opposed to course manuals, in teaching sessions. And if you're worried about having forgotten much of the black letter law you learned at uni, you'll appreciate the contract law revision session in the two-week foundation course at the start of the LPC. Other core areas are recapped at appropriate times throughout the course. Eschewing the specialisation found elsewhere, Sheffield continues to teach a generalist course and offers a good spread of electives, including the relatively rare advanced criminal litigation.

Sheffield has developed excellent links with local firms – an LPC 'steering committee' gets practitioners involved in the running of the course – and committed careers service staff are particularly useful for the 70% of students who start the course without a training contract. They can be called upon for advice up to three years after completing the LPC. Sheffield is a proud city with a lot going for it, and the Derbyshire Dales are just minutes away for weekend walking and mountain biking.

university of central lancashire, preston
number of places: 60 full-time, 48 part-time

LPC students at this Preston-based law school are integrated closely with the university: many come here after graduating from its LLB and *"lots of tutors teach on the degree course as well, so people stay as they know them."* As we found at other providers with smaller student numbers, the personal touch enhances student enjoyment of what can be a tough year. *"It was because of the teachers that I didn't mind it as much,"* confided one source. LPC students have access to all university facilities (accommodation, the 'Bridge' part-time employment fixer-upper service, sports, counselling etc) and the law faculty, which is housed in *"one of the oldest buildings at the university"* and includes a very decent library that is also used by local law firms.

Uclan has recently experienced a technology push and so PC numbers are now up to scratch, with LPC students getting their own computer suite. As most students start the course without a training contract, the *"good, active"* careers service is prominent and runs a number of events. *"They have a work experience course and they try to place everyone in a firm in the North West for a week."*

The course is taught in three-hour workshops for groups of 20, combined with lectures for the entire intake. One student commented on the workshops: *"There's lots of interaction and I made plenty of new friends."* Elective subjects include a course pertaining to the elderly client, immigration and welfare law, employment and residential tenancies, as well as some commercial options.

Though a lot of the Uclan graduates treat the LPC year as *"an extra year of uni,"* we're assured that newcomers are able to fit in easily. Preston arrivistes can avail themselves of university accommodation, while those whose families live in East Lancashire tend to save their pennies by putting up with the olds for a further year. Preston was inaugerated as England's 50th city in 2001 to mark the Queen's Golden Jubilee. Rich in history, it is the capital of Lancashire and boasts some pleasing architecture and the National Football Museum. The lovely Lake District is within yomping distance and Blackpool beckons for cheesy nights out and donkey-on-the-beach days.

university of staffordshire
number of places: 150 full-time

The University of Staffordshire is going great guns; upgraded this year from Very Good to Excellent, it's obviously doing something right. Perhaps it's the commitment to keeping class sizes down to 16 or fewer people. Or perhaps it's the forward-thinking teaching methods: this institution not only has mock courtrooms (found in many law schools), but also simulates the solicitors' office to get students accustomed to working life. We reckon if they can sort out some dodgy modern art, tea and coffee by the bucketload and, of course, doors swinging off their hinges in a bid to be 'open' they'll be spot on. Students praise the law school's premises for their usability, and they are just a five-minute walk from Stoke-on-Trent railway station. Our sources tell us the teaching standard was mostly *"excellent"* and *"lectures give you a good starting point for the work for you to do in the workshops."*

Most students tend to have grown up or studied at universities in the Midlands and only a few arrive on the course with training contracts in hand. The careers service and individual mentors all help with CVs and applications, so as the months go on more people find employment. Many go to local general practice or smaller commercial firms. The mentor system in school is supplemented by external mentoring by lawyers in local law firms, who are often great at finding word-of-mouth opportunities.

As an LPC student, *"you don't feel so much a part of the wider university,"* though sports, student union and accommodation services are all available. Usually students make friendships within their small groups, but these do not overshadow their lives away from uni. Those more inclined to prolong their time as a student rather than plunge headfirst into the realm of fee earning, will be pleased to hear successful LPC students can take the university's LLM as a top-up qualification.

university of westminster
number of places: 120 full-time, 60 part-time

Westminster is an excellent choice for anyone looking for an alternative in London to the pile-'em-high, sell-the-course-very-expensive approach of some of its larger rivals. Self-funding students take note: this course is cheaper than BPP or the College of Law by a round-the-world ticket, two nights in Waikiki and a couple of pina coladas. Money issues aside, Westminster's real selling point is the small size of its intake; classes are guaranteed to be no more than 16 for the compulsories and *"everyone knows everyone by first name, including the tutors."* Teaching standards are good – the Law Society praised the knowledgeable and enthusiastic staff, who students say *"help you a lot."*

The course is delivered by way of one-hour lectures followed by two-hour classes. There's a good number of electives on offer, including some more unusual choices such as international commercial arbitration (sadly not including a trip to Hawaii), media and entertainment and e-commerce. An interesting mix of students includes a significant number who have come to the law after a past life in something other than academia. Few students arrive with their future plans sewn up, yet in spite of this *"there is no negative culture, even though there are not that many people with training contracts."* The explanation is simple: the majority of students are interested in smaller commercial firms and high-street practices, where recruitment well in advance is uncommon. At Westminster, you'll be well placed to find a training contract as the law school nurtures relationships with West End firms, and the electives are all taught by practitioners. Certain firms sponsor electives, offering cash prizes or work experience to the best performers.

LPC students can avail themselves of the university's wider facilities and the school of law has an excellent location just behind Oxford Circus. With shops, bars and the peerless clubs of Piccadilly close at hand, you'll have to be careful not to say goodbye to those aloha savings you made on course fees!

the bar vocational course

The compulsory academic stage of a barrister's training, this course is available at eight law schools. Applications are made through an online system, found at **www.bvconline.co.uk**. The closing date for first-round applications is in the January of the year you intend to commence the course, though a clearing system operates from March through to July. You can apply to as many institutions as you like, but only the first three will consider you in the first round.

Leave academia behind you – the focus of the BVC is on practical vocational skills and essential knowledge. As well as studying compulsory, fact-intensive knowledge subjects (including criminal and civil litigation, evidence, remedies and professional conduct), you'll develop a grounding in the basics of legal drafting and opinion writing and get up on your feet and develop your advocacy skills in front of tutors and fellow students. Client conferencing and negotiation are also part of the drill. Towards the end of the course, students choose two elective subjects in the areas of practice of most interest to them.

The assessment process will vary from one provider to another. Knowledge subjects like criminal and civil procedure are usually assessed by a written exam, often a multiple choice test (though don't assume that these will be an easy ride). You can expect a mixture of seen and unseen assessments for the other skills, with advocacy and conferencing usually involving the use of professional (or sometimes pretty amateur) actors. Expect the unexpected. As one student told us: "*During my conference assessment, the actor playing my client burst into tears when I told her there was a remote chance that she might go to prison.*"

what students think

Each year we speak to a great many students who've undertaken the BVC and we're sad to report that most have little to say about it that's positive. Many feel the course is overly long, or as one described it: "*A summer school strung out into a full-time course.*" Certainly, the Bar Council is awake to this kind of feedback, and is in the process of reviewing the structure and duration of the BVC. That's not to say that the BVC year will be a walk in the park – we have spoken to students with Firsts at degree level who found the transition from academia a difficult one. Picking up the niceties of legal drafting and opinion writing, for example, can be a real challenge. What concerned us most was the view held by many practising barristers that the BVC institutions are accepting students "*without a hope of getting tenancy.*"

Several people gave us examples of students who'd struggled to pass the BVC. These included students who had difficulties with spoken English, those who had "*really struggled to respond effectively to judicial intervention in the advocacy exercises,*" and students with weaker academic track records who "*would tend to miss some of the critical legal issues in the assessments.*" This kind of feedback gains a real resonance when you look at the shortfall between those starting out on the BVC and those gaining employment at the Bar. We've reproduced the statistics for you in our Bar section, and the point cannot be overstated: before you think about committing time and money to the BVC, understand just how competitive the hunt for pupillage and tenancy is.

The next section gives an overview of what's on offer at the various BVC providers. Though the core subject areas will be common to all of them, there are differences in course structures, electives and fees. Certainly, the myth that doing the BVC in London is in any way better has long been dispelled, and if you are looking for pupillage on the circuits, then doing the BVC at a regional provider can be a distinct advantage. Read brochures, and if possible attend open days, to get a feel for the different providers.

bpp law school, london

number of places: 216 full-time, 46 part-time

Located in the heart of legal London, this is one of the larger BVC providers. Step through the doors and you can't help but be reminded that you've left university far behind you – a shrine to glass and steel, BPP plc has a distinctly corporate feel to it. Indeed, an air of professionalism is very much at the heart of BPP's philosophy, and it refers to its students as clients. Don't even think of turning up for an advocacy class in your 501s; suits are the order of the day. As course director Richard Holt told us: "*We're trying to provide a rigorous training for our students that will prepare them for practice.*"

Expect the usual compulsory knowledge subjects and practical skills, along with a variety of options that include family, international trade and public law. The school also has a new pro bono centre that guarantees all committed students work experience in a variety of projects ranging from legal advice clinics to research for human rights charities.

BPP also trains prospective solicitors, many of them headed for big City law firms. While they have their own dedicated communal area, lockers and classrooms, BVC students share the wider facilities with hordes of LPC and CPE students. These facilities are extensive and include a large subsidised canteen and a library with super-long opening hours seven days a week and plenty of PCs. Advocacy classes are taken in groups of six, and the school's six mock court rooms are fully kitted out with video, PowerPoint, smartboards and actors. The majority of teaching is done in small groups of 12, which generally has a long-lasting impact on friendships post Bar school.

Most of those we spoke to were positive about the course, saying that lectures and classes are "*planned to the last detail*" and that the quality of the teaching is "*excellent*." At just under £11,500, so they should be! The part-time course runs over two years with weekend classes once a month.

bristol institute of legal practice at uwe

number or places: 72 full-time

You could do a lot worse than spend a year of your life in Bristol. There are plenty of ways to entertain yourself in this culture-rich city, and it also has a thriving local Bar, being home to many of the best sets on the Western Circuit. If you're aiming for a pupillage in the South West, it seems madness not to get on the course and start taking advantage of the strong links the school has with local practitioners and judges on the Western Circuit. Many of these people play an active and continuing role in designing the course structure and teaching it.

The student body is not overly large and this makes it easier for staff to build good relationships with the students. Our sources tell us this is exactly what happens. Students are divided into groups of 12 and allocated base rooms equipped with state-of-the-art IT and courtroom-style furniture. Much of the teaching and learning is carried out in these base rooms, but there are also larger groups for the knowledge-based subjects. Among the usual range of available electives, students can study options in alternative dispute resolution, clinical negligence the law of international trade, and the Free Legal Representation Service.

One of the highlights of the course is a compulsory two weeks of work experience; one week is spent marshalling with a High Court, circuit or district judge, and the other sees students in a working legal environment, eg chambers, the CPS or a Citizens Advice Bureau. For all you Bad Girls fans out there, prison visiting is also available.

The only downside to choosing this course is the dreary UWE campus on the edge of Bristol. Our sources recommend living side by side with the LPC gang in one of the city's vibrant student areas for maximum fun and only trekking out to school when necessary.

cardiff law school

number of places: 60 full-time

With the lowest course fees around and the smallest intake of students, Cardiff is, to quote course co-ordinator Andrew Jerram: *"the ASDA of BVC providers."* Benefiting from a high ratio of staff to students (around one member of staff for every ten students), the teaching corps is able to offer an open-door policy to students. Advocacy, conferencing and negotiation skills are all taught in small groups of six, while other knowledge and skills-based subjects are taught in groups of 12. Students also benefit from two weeks of work experience, which includes a week spent in a local chambers and a week's marshalling with a circuit judge or district judge.

In the third term of the course electives are available in advanced criminal practice, company law, employment law, family law, international trade, pupillage advocacy and, new this year, alternative dispute resolution.

A significant number – anything up to a third in some years – of the students intend to practise overseas and this makes for a diverse student body. This is interesting because, by contrast, LPC students at Cardiff tell us it's a seriously Welsh experience. For those looking for pupillage in the UK, the school has fostered close links with sets on the Wales and Chester Circuit, where many students have obtained pupillage in the past, though a number have also found pupillage in other parts of the country. Bear in mind that the Cardiff BVC is one of the most oversubscribed and so you'll have to make a convincing application. As for what the admissions tutors are looking for, Andrew says: *"We only take people who put us first. We're looking for evidence of a commitment to the profession – students should have undertaken mini-pupillage and should indicate why they have chosen to become a barrister rather than a solicitor."*

A city well known for its culture and vibrant nightlife, Cardiff has recently been voted one of the best places to work and study.

the college of law, store street, london

number of places: 120 full-time

The College of Law is smaller and just about cheaper than its two London rivals, and students say that there are real benefits to being in a smaller school. Most obvious is *"a close and supportive working relationship"* between students and staff. The general satisfaction of BVC students here is a testament to what the COL can achieve when it runs a course for a smaller number of students. The feedback from past BVC students is always positive, unlike the mixed reviews we hear from the 650-strong full-time LPC cohort with whom they share Store Street.

The majority of teaching is delivered to small groups of six and you'll find that full preparation is essential throughout the course. Skills teaching focuses on the use of recurring case studies, using the same set of facts to develop a variety of oral and written skills. There are plenty of opportunities for extra advocacy experience, including a pro bono elective in the third term in which students can represent clients before the London Residential Property Tribunals. Pro bono is something the COL has been committed to for some time and its programme is both comprehensive and a draw for students on not only the BVC, but the LPC and CPE too.

Students take part in an externally judged mock trial as part of the course, and so-called 'practitioner evenings' provide further regular opportunities to participate in advocacy exercises in front of practising members of the Bar. There is also an annual internal mooting competition. Students tell us that the range of events on offer *"provides a great chance to do some of that all-important networking."* The range of elective subjects offered is comprehensive.

Store Street is a packed and busy environment, but its library is extensive. The location off Tottenham Court Road is ideal should you need to buy a sofa or a laptop, but it's further from the Inns than the other two London BVC providers.

the inns of court school of law, city university, london

number of places: 575 full-time, 75 part-time

ICSL is the biggest of them all and Grand Dame of BVC providers; indeed it used to be the only institution teaching the course. Just off Gray's Inn Square, ICSL has a distinctly barristerial air about it, a beautiful setting, excellent library access and an interactive lecture theatre. A response to previous feedback concerning the diseconomies of scale, the student body is now in four cohorts, each with its own course director. Students are taught in a combination of large-group lectures of around 100 students and small-group classes of 12. Advocacy is taught in still smaller groups of six. In addition to the usual selection of compulsory courses and electives, there are weekly practitioner classes delivered by practising barristers and judges. There is also the possibility of doing work for the Free Representation Unit as an elective. As you might expect, the range of electives is extensive.

Students' verdicts are mixed. All confirm that there are *"too many people without a shot of tenancy"* and that *"a lot of the students were struggling."* Some express concern that course assessment criteria do not correspond well with what will be expected of a pupil in real-life practice. Others say that although *"some tutors are really well respected,"* there is *"a degree of despondency among some of the teaching staff"* and the quality of the teaching can be variable. For the record, particular praise is reserved for the *"well-prepared and well-delivered"* advocacy classes. As one student told us: *"you will be made to stand up and perform on video from day one. It's great for building up confidence."*

ICSL has the most experience in teaching the course, and its well-respected manuals are used by a number of other providers. As one of the pricier providers on the BVC market, you'll need to start pawning your valuables now, but you will get a shed-load of books as part of the deal. For many students this is *"the default choice,"* but perhaps they should ask whether bigger really does mean better.

manchester metropolitan university

number of places: 120 full-time

With its space-age new building and swanky lecture theatres complete with interactive whiteboards, Manchester Met certainly looks the part. Classes here are predominantly taught in small groups, and students are assigned to a 'syndicate group' of 12 students and expected to perform regularly in front of their colleagues from the word go. Former students say that this close working relationship gives you *"a good, realistic idea of your strengths and weaknesses."* As well as the compulsory subjects, there are plenty of options to choose from, including Chancery practice, sale of goods and credit, child law, judicial review of administrative action and personal injury litigation.

Students say that the staff here are a *"friendly and approachable"* bunch. Anyone looking for pupillage will also be glad to know that Manchester Met has forged strong links with chambers on the Northern Circuit. As course director Alan Gibb explains: *"practising barristers from the circuit regularly deliver master classes at the school. It provides an excellent opportunity for students to impress."* The school also offers all students the opportunity of undertaking mini-pupillage with a local chambers, and will soon be setting up a pro bono advice clinic. According to Alan, 30% of UK students obtained pupillage in the year 2002/3, a majority of them on the Northern Circuit.

With course fees currently at £7,750 for a year, Manchester remains in the BVC bargain basement. If you're considering applying, the admissions tutors are looking for *"good, clear and articulate reasons why students want to join the course."* Those without a commitment to studying in Manchester should think twice before putting fingers to keyboard as the school receives at least 300 applications every year from students selecting Manchester as their first choice. Students picking Manchester as their number three are unlikely to even get a look in.

university of northumbria at newcastle

number of places: 80 full-time + up to 40 on exempting LLB

As the home of Byker Grove, trendy late-night bars and Newcastle United FC, there is no doubting the credentials of this northern city. But what about the course? Northumbria has been at the forefront of developments in legal education – as well as offering a full-time BVC course, the School of Law is also pioneering a four-year LLB exempting degree, which incorporates all necessary elements of either the LPC or the BVC in the last two years of study. In their final year, students on the programme spend on average 50% of their time undertaking pro bono casework in the highly respected Student Law Office. This is the largest and longest established student legal advice centre in the UK, and its impact on the course cannot be underestimated. As students told us: *"The major selling point of Northumbria is that you get hands-on experience of real cases. You even get to do some of the advocacy, which you will dread at first, but in retrospect it's fantastic experience."* If you want to get a bit of practice in first, try out the school's own courtroom, which was transported from a real court in Morpeth a few years ago.

The BVC course is taught to small groups, each with its own skills practice room. Amongst the usual range of options are judicial review and alternative dispute resolution. The school maintains good links with local practitioners on the Northern Circuit, and barristers and judges regularly pop their heads around the door to give guest lectures or to judge moots. There are also visits from police and forensic experts and an established court visits programme.

Very popular, especially with students from the North West, your application is going to have to be impressive to stand a chance. Make sure you can demonstrate an interest in and some experience of advocacy, mooting or debating.

nottingham law school

number of places: 90-100 full-time

Nottingham Law school has done remarkably well in building itself a name as a centre of excellence for academic and professional legal training. So popular is its BVC course, Nottingham will now only take on students who have *"a fighting chance of getting pupillage."* A good academic track record and evidence of a really firm commitment to the profession are must-haves if you are thinking of applying. The admissions strategy seems to be paying off, because on average at least 50% of the school's BVC graduates go straight into pupillage in any given year. Regular buses are laid on to take students to London to dine at their Inns.

The teaching style here is designed to prepare students for practice by focusing on seven fact-intensive briefs, which are used to teach a variety of the core legal skills and simulate the progress of a real case from its commencement through to a full trial. Teaching is delivered to small groups of 12, with advocacy training taken by smaller groups of six students and held in the old Guildhall Courtroom with its Victorian wood panelling.

Elective subjects are available in advanced civil, advanced criminal, commercial, employment, family, landlord and tenant and immigration. Students receive their own copy of Archbold's Criminal Practice and the civil procedure text The White Book. As well as being a vital tool for any practitioner, they also make an effective doorstop.

With fairly competitive course fees and reasonable accommodation costs, Nottingham is a smart choice money-wise as well as quality-wise. What's more, the city has one of the largest student populations in the country (many of them law students), so there is always plenty going on. It's also home to some of the best chambers on the Midlands Circuit.

funding

With so much in the press about tuition fees and student debt, you could be forgiven for thinking you'll never be back in the black again. We say: don't take fashion tips from politicians – red is not the colour to be seen in and, with a little effort and creative thinking, you could soon be better off than you think.

grants

You've already established that the Student Loans Company is no longer your new best friend, so where next? There is a super-slim chance that you'll qualify for a local education authority grant, but alas, there isn't anything out there for you if you're plain, old, bog-ordinary skint. If your circumstances are at all unusual, however, pay close attention to the qualification criteria: whether you are a mature student, single parent or independent student might make a difference. Discretionary awards are means-tested, which means marathon form filling, and your chances are improved if you apply early. Look at **www.dfes.gov.uk/studentsupport** for more info.

hardship funds, access funds and charities

Your LEA or law school may be able to point you in the direction of local charities or trusts that could be good for an award. Some schools operate a hardship fund, so find out whether you qualify. And scrutinise college notice boards: amongst the flatshare ads and posters inviting you to take up obscure martial arts, there may be leaflets about scholarships and prizes.

bank loans

Already got a huge overdraft? No problem! You could still qualify for a deal from a high street bank. Perhaps believing the rich lawyer stereotype, many go out of their way to provide loans to impoverished law students. Interest rates are low and the repayment terms usually favourable, but sniff around to see what different banks are offering. And ask your law school if it has an arrangement with a specific bank to give its students an enhanced package. Many high street banks have graduate loan schemes tailored to the needs of the legal profession, and include pupillage as a formal part of the training when it comes to repayment.

Scott Jago, manager of Legal Student Services at NatWest's Legal Centre, advises students to arrange any required loan as soon as they have been accepted onto the course, rather than waiting until the fees are due. "*Law students need to plan their expenditure carefully,*" he told us. Scott also recommends that students prepare and stick to a budget, drawing down against their loan on a monthly basis. "*If you want a manageable student debt when you start work then monthly budgeting during your studies is essential.*"

career development loans

Barclays Bank, the Co-operative Bank and the Royal Bank of Scotland provide these on behalf of the DfES. See **www.lifelonglearning.co.uk/cdl**. In essence, if you don't have a government grant or employer sponsorship, you can borrow up to £8,000 to fund up to two years' study, with the DfES paying the interest while you study and for a month after you finish.

benefits, benefactors, begging...

Living at home while you study may not sound that appealing, especially if you made a bid for freedom when you started your degree. But, sometimes, needs must...and home-cooked meals after long days in the library are not to be sniffed at. If you are in a position whereby your family can – and will – help keep your head above water, they will be expecting results and you probably owe it to them to work hard. Ditto for those holding training contracts or pupillages that come with law school funding. No matter how much (or how little) you have been given, at the very least your firm or chambers will want to see a good record on exam marks and attendance.

There has been talk of a loophole in the law that almost begs students to declare bankruptcy and evade student debt. We do not recommend this. Why not consider other creative ways to ease the debt burden:

- You won't be able to claim social security benefits while at college, but a student card will get you cheap travel, discount haircuts and, if nothing else, student cinema tickets that will make you a highly desirable, cheap date.
- Books are pricey so don't go on a spending spree before term starts. College libraries have the core texts, and we guarantee you'll find former students wanting to recoup some of the cash they've spent, so check noticeboards for second-hand tomes.
- You'd be amazed at how few people go in for the big-money competitions open to students. A number of law schools, chambers and solicitors firms run them. A quick Google search will throw up plenty of other competitions, both in and outside the law, so stop whingeing about how much debt you've got and throw your hat into the ring.
- Market research focus groups pay decent money for an hour or two of your time, and if you get really desperate, how about being a human guinea pig – medical establishments will pay for the privilege of giving you the 'flu, or a few electric shocks.

part-time work

Officially, full-time courses are exactly that – full-time. This is true, even for courses that leave you with a large chunk of the day, or whole days free. Most law schools accept that students may need to work a few hours a week or during holidays, but think long and hard about your ability to earn while you study. Lack of time or energy can lead to failed exams, so if you need to earn stacks just to keep afloat, a part-time course might be more realistic.

solicitors

law firm sponsorship: You may be lucky enough to secure a training contract with a firm that stumps up the cash for CPE and/or LPC fees; if you're really lucky, it may even give you a modest maintenance grant. Our Salaries Table on pages 74-82 details the funding on offer from leading firms. However, very many students start their course without the guarantee of a training contract offer, and for them it's a gamble as to whether they will get any funding – or even a training contract. Sadly, there's no easy way around the problem of having to commit to course fees before knowing if it will all be worth it in the end. Nonetheless, in response to the government's decision to make undergraduates pay top-up fees, the Young Solicitors Group is piling on the pressure to have student loans extended to those who are studying to be Legal Aid solicitors and therefore won't be in receipt of sponsorship.

the law society: The society has its own bursary scheme. Application forms are available from February to April, but be quick; the closing date is 30 April in the year your course starts. There are also various trust funds advertised on the Society's website.

barristers

Pupils and students studying the CPE or BVC can apply for a range of scholarships from the four Inns of Court. Many Bar students base their choice of Inn on the likelihood of their getting their hands on some of the £3 million plus that is paid out each year by the Inns. Some are merit-based, while others consider financial hardship, so you need to do a bit of research. See our section on the **Inns of Court**.

Since 2003 all pupillages must be backed by a minimum chambers award of £10,000. Some sets pay far in excess of this sum – the highest is presently £40,500 from commercial set 3 Verulam Buidings – and many allow students to draw on these awards while studying the BVC. The majority of students, however, still have to depend on bank loans and/or parental support.

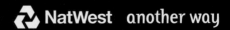

The Law Society
113 Chancery Lane,
London WC2A 1PL
Tel: 020 7242 1222
E-mail: info.services@lawsociety.org.uk
www.lawsoc.org.uk

Legal Education and Training Department
Tel: 0870 606 2555
E-mail: legaled@lawsociety.org.uk
www.training.lawsociety.org.uk

Trainee Solicitors Group
The Law Society
113 Chancery Lane,
London WC2A 1PL
Helpline: 08000 856 131
E-mail: info@tsg.org
www.tsg.org.uk

The Bar Council
289-293 High Holborn
London WC1V 7HZ
020 7242 0082
www.barcouncil.org.uk
For all other departments including the Education and
Training Department and the Equality and Diversity
Committee contact the main switchboard.

Gray's Inn, Education Department
8 South Square. Gray's Inn,
London WC1R 5ET
Tel: 020 7458 7800
www.graysinn.org.uk

Inner Temple, Education & Training Department
Treasury Office, Inner Temple,
London EC4Y 7HL
Tel: 020 7797 8250
www.innertemple.org.uk

Lincoln's Inn, Students' Department
Treasury Office, Lincoln's Inn,
London WC2A 3TL
Tel: 020 7405 0138
www.lincolnsinn.org.uk

Middle Temple, Students' Department
Treasury Office, Middle Temple,
London EC4Y 9AT
Tel: 0207 427 4800
www.middletemple.org.uk

The Institute of Legal Executives
Kempston Manor, Kempston,
Bedfordshire MK42 7AB
Tel: 01234 841000
E-mail: info@ilex.org.uk
www.ilex.org.uk

Government Legal Service
Recruitment Team GLS Secretariat,
Queen Anne's Chambers, 28 Broadway,
London SW1H 9JS
Tel: 020 7210 3574/3304/3386
E-mail: recruit@gls.gsi.gov.uk
www.gls.gov.uk

Crown Prosecution Service
50 Ludgate Hill,
London EC4M 7EX
Tel: 020 7796 8053
www.cps.gov.uk

The Law Commission
Conquest House, 37-38 John Street,
Theobalds Road,
London WC1N 2BQ
Tel: 020 7453 1220
E-mail: secretary@lawcommission.gsi.gov.uk
www.lawcom.gov.uk

Citizens Advice Bureaux
Head Office, Myddelton House,
115-123 Pentonville Road,
London N1 9LZ
Tel: 020 7833 2181
Volunteer Hotline: 08451 264264
www.citizensadvice.org.uk

Legal Services Commission
Head office, 85 Gray's Inn Road,
London WC1X 8TX
Tel: 020 7759 0000
www.legalservices.gov.uk

Chartered Institute of Patent Agents
95 Chancery Lane,
London WC2A IDT
Tel: 020 7405 9450
E-mail: mail@cipa.org.uk
www.cipa.org.uk

Institute of Trade Mark Attorneys
Canterbury House, 2-6 Sydenham Road, Croydon,
Surrey CR0 9XE
Tel: 020 8686 2052
www.itma.org.uk

CONTACTS

**Institute of Chartered Secretaries
and Administrators:**
16 Park Crescent,
London W1B 1AH
Tel: 020 7580 4741
www.icsa.org.uk

The Law Centres Federation
Duchess House,
18-19 Warren Street,
London W1T 5LR
Tel: 020 7387 8570
E-mail: info@lawcentres.org.uk
www.lawcentres.org.uk

Free Representation Unit
6th Floor 289-293 High Holborn
London WC1V 7HZ
Tel: 0207 611 9555
Email: admin@freerepresentationunit.org.uk
www.freerepresentationunit.org.uk

The Bar Lesbian & Gay Group
Email: info@blagg.org
(BLAGG) www.blagg.org
Lesbian & Gay Lawyers Association
www.lagla.org.uk

The Society of Asian Lawyers
c/o Aamir Khan Richards Butler
Beaufort House 15 St Botolph Street
London EC3A 7EE
Tel: 020 7772 5994
www.societyofasianlawyers.com

The Society of Black Lawyers
9 Winchester House 11 Cranmer Road
Kennington Road Park
London SW9 6EJ
Tel: 020 7735 652

The Association of Muslim Lawyers
PO Box 148 High Wycombe
Bucks HP13 5WJ
Email: aml@aml.org.uk
www.aml.org.uk

The Association of Women Barristers
Jane Hoyal 1 Pump Court Temple
London EC4Y 7AB
Email: Janehoyal@aol.com
www.womenbarristers.co.uk

Group for Solicitors with Disabilities
c/o Judith McDermott
The Law Society, 113 Chancery Lane
London WC2A 1PL
Tel: 020 7320 5793
Email: secretary@gsdnet.org.uk
www.gsdnet.org.uk

LPC Central Applications Board
P.O. Box No. 84, Guildford,
Surrey GU3 1YX
Tel: 01483 301282
www.lawcabs.ac.uk

CPE Central Applications Board
P.O. Box No. 84, Guildford,
Surrey GU3 1YX
Tel: 01483 451080
www.lawcabs.ac.uk O)

Online Pupillage Application System
Technical Assistance Helpline: 01491 828918
E-mail: pupillages@gtios.com
http://olpas.gti.co.uk

Career Development Loans
Freepost, Warrington WA4 6FB
Tel: (freephone) 0800 585505
www.lifelonglearning.co.uk/cdl

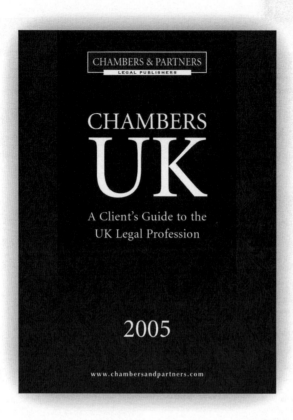

universities and law schools a-z

BPP Professional Education

Leeds - London - Manchester
Tel: (0845) 678 6868
Email: law@bpp.com
Website: www.bpp.com

contact
For further information or for the dates and times of open days, please call the school's national enquire line on: 0845 678 6868, email: law@bpp.com or visit the website: www.bpp.com

college profile

BPP is the leading provider of professional legal education in the country with over 3,500 full, part time and distance learning law students. It has three Law Schools, two in London (Holborn and Waterloo) and one in Leeds. A fourth school is due to open in Manchester in September 2005 (subject to validation). All courses are taught by highly trained and experienced academics and practitioners using hi-tech facilities. As a specialist Law School, BPP has a first rate, careers service dedicated to helping you achieve your career aspirations. All courses are provided in full and part time modes.

graduate diploma in law

The GDL is essentially a conversion course preparing graduates in any non-law subject to progress onto the Legal Practice and Bar Vocational Courses. The school's GDL is stimulating, topical and is assessed by way of examination and coursework. Graduates from the BPP GDL are guaranteed a place on the full or part time LPC at BPP and can apply for the school's BVC. The school's one week Law Summer School is ideal for those who are unsure whether a career in law is for them.

legal practice course

BPP's LPC has been prepared in conjunction with many of the UK's leading city and international Law firms. Since 2001 BPP has been one of only three institutions in the country to provide trainee solicitors to eight of the country's top law firms and from 2006 BPP will be the exclusive national provider to five of these firms. The Law Society has awarded BPP's LPC an Excellent rating - making BPP one of the few institutions in the country to achieve this accolade.

bar vocational course

As well as developing a sound understanding of the knowledge areas of law, the school's BVC concentrates on developing the essential barristerial skills of drafting, advocacy, negotiation and conference. These skills are practised in tutorial groups as small as six students and take place in one of the Law School's mock courtrooms. For added realism, you will practice advocacy and negotiation not only with your fellow students on the course, but also with practising barristers and professional actors.

Cardiff Law School

Cardiff Law School, Cardiff University, PO Box 294, Cardiff CF10 3UX
Tel: (029) 2087 4941/6660 Fax: (029) 2087 4984
Email: JonesBL@Cardiff.ac.uk
Website: www.cardiff.ac.uk/claws/cpls

contact
LPC: Mr Byron Jones
Tel: (029) 2087 4941

BVC: Mr Andrew Jerram
Tel: (029) 2087 4964

Other postgraduate law
courses:
The Postgraduate Secretary
Tel: (029) 2087 6102

university profile

Cardiff Law School is long established, well-resourced and enjoys an international reputation for its teaching and research. In the most recent assessment of research quality conducted by the Higher Education Funding Council, Cardiff achieved a grade 5 rating, placing it in the top law schools in the country. Cardiff offers opportunities for students to pursue postgraduate study by research leading to the degrees of M.Phil and Ph.D. In addition, taught Masters degrees in the areas of canon, commercial, European legal studies, marine affairs and medical law are offered in full and part-time mode.

legal practice course and bar vocational course

Within the Law School, the Centre for Professional Legal Studies is validated to offer both the Legal Practice Course and the Bar Vocational Course. Students are taught by experienced solicitors and barristers who have been specifically recruited for this purpose. Placements with solicitors' firms or sets of Chambers are available to students pursuing the vocational courses, while students studying the Bar Vocational Course additionally enjoy a one week placement with a Circuit or District Judge. Cardiff's Legal Practice Course has consistently been rated 'Excellent' by the Law Society; one of the few providers of this course to hold the top ranking.

facilities

Recent developments within the Law School include extensive IT provision together with dedicated accommodation for the vocational courses which house a practitioner library, courtroom facilities, and fixed and movable audio visual equipment for recording inter-active practitioner skills activities. In addition, the main law library contains one of the largest collections of primary and secondary material within the UK. The Law School is housed in its own building at the heart of the campus, itself located in one of the finest civic centres in Britain and only a short walk from the main shopping area. The University has its own postgraduate centre, together with a full range of sporting and social facilities.

University of Central England in Birmingham

School of Law, Franchise Street, Perry Barr, Birmingham B42 2SU
Tel: (0121) 331 6600/6614 Fax: (0121) 331 6622

college profile

UCE School of Law has been a major centre for legal education and training in the city for over 30 years. UCE is committed to providing a service that meets your needs – whether academic, professional or personal. It can be seen in the distinctly informal staff-student relationships, in the extensive support provision and learning facilities that you would expect to find in a large university such as UCE, including a legal practice resource centre, IT workrooms and mock courtroom, and of course in the quality and relevance of its courses.

postgraduate diploma in legal practice/lpc (full or part-time)

UCE's LPC maintains a generalist approach, reflecting the fact that the majority of students progress to general practice in small and medium sized firms. However, UCE is also committed to making sure that this is not at the cost of those students who aim for commercial practice – UCE offers distinctive electives for this sector including mergers and acquisitions, commercial property and commercial law. UCE aims to develop the problem-solving skills, commercial awareness and self-sufficiency that a trainee solicitor needs. Small class sizes and accessible staff ensure that individual study needs are met and that you receive the support you need to maximize personal development.

graduate diploma in law/gdl (full or part-time)

The GDL course is designed for non-law graduates wishing to enter the profession as solicitors or barristers. The purpose of the GDL is to provide legal training, which although primarily academic in nature, also reflects the demands that legal practice will place on that academic knowledge. UCE's teaching emphasises participation and student-centred learning. A variety of teaching methods are employed in order to develop the legal skills which form the basis of a successful career in law. An 'open door' policy and a commitment to individual personal development ensures you receive the support needed to maximize your potential.

pgcert/pgdip/llm corporate and business law

Explores relevant and topical legal issues relating to the corporate and business world.

pgcert/pgdip/ma immigration & refugee policy, law & practice

Examines the implications of current law and practice in the UK.

pgdip/llm international human rights

USA Pathway: Explores the conflict between the US Death Penalty and international standards. Students may undertake a semester's internship in the USA.

European Pathway: Studies the increasing importance of Human Rights in the UK and European law, including international environmental law and conflict, and refugees.

pgdip/ma criminal justice policy & practice

Studies how criminal justice policy is formulated and how criminological theory relates to practice.

contact
Apply to:
Full-time GDL and LPC courses
Central Appllctions Board
Part-time GDL and LPC courses
Direct to university
Other courses
Direct to university

contact names
GDL   Keith Gompertz
LPC   Martyn Packer

Other postgraduate courses
Karen D'Arcy

Email: lhss@uce.ac.uk
Website: www.lhss.uce.ac.uk
Website: www.uce.ac.uk

UCE Birmingham

A-Z UNIVERSITIES AND LAW SCHOOLS

City University, London - Institute of Law

City University, Institute of Law, Northampton Square, London EC1V 0HB
Tel: Dept of Law: (020) 7040 8301   ICSL: (020) 7404 5787
Fax: Dept of Law: (020) 7040 8578   ICSL: (020) 7831 4188
Email: Dept of Law: cpe@city.ac.uk   ICSL: ICSLcourses@city.ac.uk
Website: www.city.ac.uk/law

college profile

Law has been taught at City since 1977. In 2001 the Inns of Court School of Law (ICSL) joined the established Department of Law (also known as City Law School) to form a new Institute of Law. This formalised a long-standing relationship, and made City the first university in London to offer courses for students and practitioners in both branches of the profession at all stages of legal education. In addition to postgraduate legal training for both solicitors and barristers ICSL offers a well-established CPD programme which includes the PSC for trainee solicitors and Higher Rights training. Its successful Pro Bono project gives vocational course students the opportunity to work with live clients at the School's Advice Clinic or to work with a voluntary partner.

courses

cpe/graduate diploma in law (full or part time) Designed to enable non-law graduates to complete the first stage of professional training, this CPE course is one of the largest and most respected CPE courses in the UK, with a long-standing reputation with the Bar and a strong and growing reputation amongst City law firms.

graduate entry llb (two years full time) A well-established broader conversion course providing an opportunity to develop special interests.

llm programme (full or part time) A modular programme in International Law, with opportunities to specialise in human rights or environmental law, and a unique LLM in Criminal Litigation (icsl).

bar vocational course (ICSL - full or part-time) A forward looking IT based course focusing on the needs of the modern bar, particularly advocacy.

legal practice course (ICSL - full or part-time) Rated Excellent by the Law Society.

contact
Full course brochures are available from the Department of Law or ICSL as appropriate

department of law
Tel: (020) 7040 8301
Fax (020) 7040 8578
Email: cpe@city.ac.uk

icsl
Tel: (020) 7404 5787
Fax: (020) 7831 4188
Email: ICSLcourses@city.ac.uk

City University
London

Inns of Court
School of Law

The College of Law

Braboeuf Manor, Portsmouth Road, Guildford GU3 1HA
Freephone: (0800) 328 0153 Fax: (01483) 460460
Email: admissions@lawcol.co.uk
Website: www.college-of-law.co.uk

contact

Freephone:
(0800) 328 0153
If calling from overseas:
+44 (0) 1483 460382
Email:
admissions@lawcol.co.uk
Website:
www.college-of-law.co.uk

college profile

The College of Law is the largest legal training provider in Europe, with centres in Birmingham, Chester, Guildford, London and York. Training more than 5300 students each year, the College's size means that it has the depth of resources and flexibility to offer legal education, training and experience tailored to an individual's needs. Its Careers Service is the biggest and best-resourced, law-focused careers service in the UK, providing students with practical, relevant and up-to-date advice and support to maximise their chances of securing a training contract or pupillage. The College offers the following courses:

graduate diploma in law (GDL) full-time/part-time/distance learning

The College's GDL is purpose-built to introduce students not only to the law, but to the law in practice. As every student's academic profile is different, the College's GDL is dedicated to ensuring that students receive precisely the training and support their personal academic development requires. Large group sessions explore the wider issues surrounding topics, while small group sessions allow students to receive and learn from feedback to develop critical skills, practise legal research skills, sharpen problem-solving skills and polish presentation skills.

legal practice course (LPC) full-time/part-time/weekend learning

The College's LPC has been redesigned to ensure that a student's personal learning needs are at the heart of the course. Over 70% of the College's LPC is based around student-centred, small group workshops with a practical focus, involving realistic transactions and cases. Students receive individual feedback from the tutor as they progress, and knowledge and skills are further developed through independent reading and legal research, analysing and drafting legal documents and preparing written or oral advice for clients.

bar vocational course (BVC) full-time, London centre only

The College's BVC offers a practice-focused course structured around case-work at the Bar. In each area, as in real life, students follow work from instruction through to appeal, and every stage in-between. The course is litigation-based, with a heavy emphasis on developing and honing skills. Students appear in mock trials before real judges, with many other opportunities for advocacy through competitions and pro bono work.

The College runs open days at all its centres in the Autumn and Spring.
Visit the College's website at www.college-of-law.co.uk for details and to book a place.

The College of Law
of England and Wales

Manchester Metropolitan University

School of Law, All Saints West, Lower Ormond Street, Manchester M15 6HB
Tel: (0161) 247 3050   Fax: (0161) 247 6309
Email: law@mmu.ac.uk

contact
CPE/GDL: Harriet Roche

CPC: Shuma Chwdhury

BVC: Lucy Holland

college profile

The School of Law is one of the largest providers of legal education in the UK, and enjoys an excellent reputation for the quality and range of its courses. It is one of only six providers that offer the full range of law courses LLB, GDipL, LPC and BVC. The School's courses are well designed and taught, combining rigorous academic standards with practical application. In September 2003, the School moved into a brand new, state of the art building, in the heart of Manchester.

bar vocational course (full-time)

This course provides the vocational stage of training for intending practising barristers. However, skills learnt on the course such as advocacy and drafting are transferable to other professions. The BVC is skills based and interactive with particular emphasis on advocacy which is taught in groups of six. The course adopts a syndicate (mini-chambers) approach. Students are allocated to a particular group which has its own base room which contains extensive practitioner legal resources both in hard copy and online form. Each room has the latest in IT and AV equipment. There is also a BVC court room and a separate BVC resource room. Excellent student support is provided including careers advice and an additional professional programme that is designed to bridge the gap between student and professional life. A particular feature of the course is the close links it enjoys with the Northern Circuit whose members are involved in Advocacy Master Classes, the teaching of professional conduct and in a student mentoring scheme.

legal practice course
(full-time or part-time: part-time = attendance on Thursdays over two years)

The legal practice course provides the vocational stage of training for those wishing to qualify as a solicitor. Offering a full range of private client and commercial electives, the school aims to cater to students who are looking to practice in specialised areas (eg entertainment law or advanced criminal litigation) as well as students who wish to develop a broad subject base. A mentor scheme operates to put students in touch with local practitioners. Consistently recommended for its state of the art resources, student support and careers guidance and staffed by approachable and knowledgeable teaching staff, the LPC at Manchester Metropolitan University will provide a sound foundation for your legal career.

graduate diploma in law/cpe
(full-time or part-time or distance learning)

An increasing number of graduates enter the legal profession this way, with employers attracted by the applicant's maturity and transferable skills. The course places emphasis on the acquisition of legal research and other relevant legal skills. On completion students normally join the School's LPC or BVC Course. This means that if the full-time mode is followed a non-law graduate can become professionally qualified in two years. There is a guaranteed place for CPE students on the school's LPC course.

the
MANCHESTER
METROPOLITAN
UNIVERSITY

Northumbria University

School of Law, Northumbria University, Sutherland Building,
Newcastle-upon-Tyne NE1 8ST
Tel: (0191) 227 4494
Fax: (0191) 227 4557
Website: http://law.northumbria.ac.uk

contact
School of Law Admissions
Office
Tel: (0191) 227 4494
Fax: (0191) 227 4557
Email:
la.information@
northumbria.ac.uk

LPC/BVC/CPE:
Dawn Haynes

LLM: Elaine Conroy

college profile
Situated in the heart of Newcastle City Centre, Northumbria University Law School is known throughout the country for its distinctive and innovative programmes and the commitment of the staff to legal teaching and research is reflected in the rating of 'Excellent' received by the School from the Higher Education Funding Council for England. The School of Law has its own Legal Skills Centre with a large practitioner library, three mock courtrooms with video facilities and a Student Law Office.

lpc (full-time or part-time)
The Legal Practice Course at Northumbria has been rated by the Law Society as 'Very Good' in the most recent visit. Students study three compulsory areas of general legal practice (civil and criminal litigation, property law and practice and business law and practice) and three electives from an extensive range. The electives now cover the full range of commercial and private client practice and students many chose a 'High Street' or 'Commercial' focus. The Student Law Office is now an elective on the LPC where students work on real cases. The school offers 150 full time places, and 80 part time.

bvc (full-time)
Northumbria University is one of only five institutions outside of London to offer the Bar Vocational Course (BVC). Lectures which focus on key areas of practice are given regularly by senior practitioners and the programme is delivered from modern purpose built accommodation. The Student Law Office is now an optional module on the BVC where students are able to work with clients on live cases. The school offers 80 full time places.

cpe (full-time or distance learning)
The CPE is the conversion course for those students who have a non-law degree and would like to enter into the legal profession. It is offered on a one year full-time basis or two years distance-learning and covers the seven core subjects stipulated by the professional bodies as being the foundations of legal knowledge. Students are also required to choose an eighth optional subject from a wide range available.

other postgraduate programmes
LLM in Advanced Commercial Property Law, LLM in Advanced Legal Practice, LLM in Claims and Risk Management in Health Care, LLM in Commercial Law, LLM in EU Law, LLM in International Commercial Law, LLM in International Trade Law. LLM in Medical Law, LLM in Mental Health Law, LLM in Mental Health Law, Policy and Practice.

Nottingham Law School

Nottingham Law School, Belgrave Centre, Nottingham NG1 5LP
Tel: (0115) 848 6871 Fax: (0115) 848 6878
Email: linda.green2@ntu.ac.uk
Website: www.nls.ntu.ac.uk

contact
Nottingham Law School
Belgrave Centre
Nottingham NG1 5LP
Tel: (0115) 848 6871
Fax: (0115) 848 6878
Email:linda.green2@ntu.ac.uk
Website:www.nls.ntu.ac.uk

bar vocational course

Nottingham Law School has designed its BVC to develop to a high standard a range of core practical skills, and to equip students to succeed in the fast-changing environment of practice at the Bar. Particular emphasis is placed on the skill of advocacy. Advocacy sessions are conducted in groups of six and the School uses the Guildhall courtrooms for most sessions. The BVC is taught entirely by qualified barristers, and utilises the same integrated and interactive teaching methods as all of the School's other professional courses. Essentially, students learn by doing and Nottingham Law School provides an environment in which students are encouraged to realise, through practice and feedback, their full potential.

legal practice course

The LPC is offered by full-time and part-time block study. This course has been designed to be challenging and stimulating for students and responsive to the needs of firms, varying from large commercial to smaller high street practices, and it still carries the endorsement of a large cross section of firms from major corporate through to high street.

Nottingham Law School's LPC features: integration of the transactions and skills, so that each advances the other, whilst ensuring the transferability of skills between different subject areas. Carefully structured interactive group work which develops an ability to handle skills and legal transactions effectively, and in an integrated way. A rigorous assessment process that nevertheless avoids 'assessment overload', to maintain a teaching and learning emphasis to the course. A professionally qualified team, retaining substantial links with practice. An excellent rating from The Law Society's Assessment Panel in every year of its operation.

the graduate diploma in law (full-time)

The Nottingham Law School GDL is a one year conversion course designed for any non-law graduate who intends to become a solicitor or barrister in the UK. The intensive course effectively covers the seven core subjects of an undergraduate law degree in one go. It is the stepping stone to the LPC or the BVC, and a legal career thereafter. It is a graduate Diploma (Dip Law) in its own right and operates on a similar basis to the LPC (see above), though inevitably it has a more academic basis.

University of Wolverhampton

School of Legal Studies, Molineux Street, Wolverhampton WV1 1SB
Tel: (01902) 321000 Fax: (01902) 321570

contact

Ms Loraine Houlton
Head of Corporate &
Professional Division
Tel: (01902) 321999
Fax: (01902) 321567

college profile

Based in Wolverhampton and offers courses for students intending to follow a variety of careers within the legal profession. The law school has been offering these courses for over 20 years. Its LPC programme has had consistently good ratings. The lecturers are drawn from experienced solicitors, barristers, academics and individuals from business and industry. There are excellent IT facilities, a well-stocked library, bookshop and a sports centre. The School also offers an LLM in International Corporate and Financial Law, which draws together a number of legal issues with an international dimension such as the regulation of financial services and financial crime. It also deals with matters such as international banking law, international corporate finance and international corporate. The School also offers an MA in Practice Management a course developed in connection with the management section of the Law Society. It is taught on a flexible, part-time, block-delivery basis and is designed to provide an outlet to complex managerial and organisational issues facing practice managers.

legal practice course (full/part-time)

The vocational training course for those intending to practise as solicitors, the University's LPC offers a sound basis for a professional career. The core subjects of Business, Litigation and Conveyancing are taught, together with a range of commercial and private client options. Professional skills courses, practical workshops and seminars are all part of the training. Additional benefits include close links with local practitioners, mentoring, CV distribution and group social activities. The Legal Practice Course is housed in modern purpose-built dedicated accommodation which includes a court room, LPC Resources room and solicitors offices. The course is taught by experienced professionally-qualified staff with close links with the local profession. It has active personal tutor support, in-house and guest practitioners, a Practitioner Liaison Committee and a careers tutor.

common professional examination (full/part-time)

The academic stage of training for non-law graduates wishing to become solicitors or barristers. A full programme of lectures and tutorials is offered on this demanding course. Students are taught by experienced practitioners. Places on the LPC are guaranteed for successful students. New flexible studying choices are under discussion. Teaching methods on the CPE are varied and include lectures, group-led discussion and debate, workshops, oral presentations and independent research. The course includes an intensive induction programme involving use of library, methodology and an introduction to IT. The course as a whole is designed to provide the essential skills necessary for a successful career in law.

UNIVERSITY OF
WOLVERHAMPTON

solicitors

SOLICITORS TIMETABLE

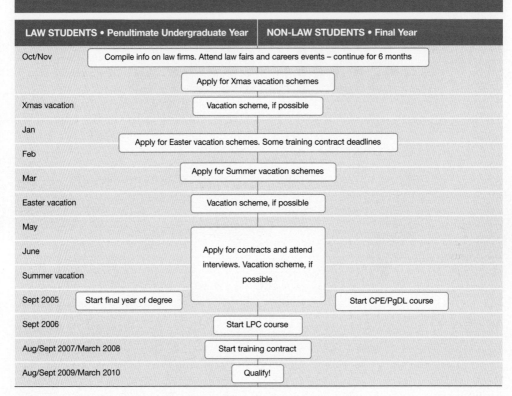

LAW STUDENTS • Penultimate Undergraduate Year	NON-LAW STUDENTS • Final Year
Oct/Nov	Compile info on law firms. Attend law fairs and careers events – continue for 6 months
	Apply for Xmas vacation schemes
Xmas vacation	Vacation scheme, if possible
Jan	Apply for Easter vacation schemes. Some training contract deadlines
Feb	
Mar	Apply for Summer vacation schemes
Easter vacation	Vacation scheme, if possible
May	Apply for contracts and attend interviews. Vacation scheme, if possible
June	
Summer vacation	
Sept 2005	Start final year of degree / Start CPE/PgDL course
Sept 2006	Start LPC course
Aug/Sept 2007/March 2008	Start training contract
Aug/Sept 2009/March 2010	Qualify!

Notes

1   *It is important to check application closing dates for each firm as these will vary.*

2   *Some firms will only accept applications for vacation schemes from penultimate year students whether law or non-law. See A-Z pages for further information.*

3   *Some firms require very early applications from non-law graduates. See A-Z pages for further information.*

4   *The timetable refers primarily to those firms that recruit two years in advance. Smaller firms often recruit just one year in advance or for immediate vacancies.*

vacation schemes

Vacation schemes provide a valuable insight into life as a solicitor and can be an important first step to gaining a training contract. If you spend your time wisely, you can discover a lot about a firm's character. Of course you might also discover that you don't want to be a solicitor after all, in which case you're going to save yourself a good deal of time and money.

According to Tom Purton, recruitment partner at Travers Smith: "*Vacation schemes are important for both students and the firm. In essence they greatly reduce the risk of recruitment going wrong on both sides.*" Some firms place great weight on their schemes, viewing them as integral to the recruitment process. Don't overestimate their importance though – having a couple of placements under your belt doesn't miraculously transform you into a better candidate. As Tom says: "*If a person has done a vacation scheme it demonstrates their commitment to obtaining a training contract, but is only one of the factors that we consider when making an offer.*"

Although some firms offer more vac scheme places than training contracts, they are still hard to get because of the huge number of applicants, and it's a sad fact that spaces are often filled by students doing multiple schemes. The key to success is to take the application process seriously – the firms certainly do. It's also worth taking your time to research the firms you want to apply to, and if you do want to go on more than one scheme, consider applying to different styles of firm to see where you feel most at home.

So you've got a place! Well done, but don't raise your expectations too high concerning the work you'll be doing. Firms will not expect you to spot a hole in their precedent documents or wow their biggest client. What they are looking for are keen, attentive, polite and punctual students, who "*grab every opportunity that is presented to them.*" If there is a cricket match after work, ask if you can go along (who knows, they might need you to play). If you are put on the firm's intranet, resist the temptation to e-mail your mates and do not indulge in sending around funnies, even if other members of staff do. In a less formal scheme, if you are introduced to people in the department and you have spare capacity, there's nothing to stop you making an offer of help, but if you have a minder, always check with them first as there may be a full programme of events and jobs to keep you busy. Get to know the trainees and ask them questions about what they like about the firm. This will be useful for you and will show them that you're interested.

Always take a written note when someone asks you to do a job. If necessary, recap what they've asked of you and clarify whether they envisaged a timescale or if they have a deadline. Keep a notebook with you and list the tasks you have been given, by whom, and when they need to be done by. If someone then asks you to do something else, you'll have a better idea of your capacity and priorities. Finally, if there's anyone who seems important and with whom you've had dealings, do remember to say goodbye and thank them for any help they've given you.

The experience is as much about your personality as your work, so make sure you speak to as many people as possible. Tom advises: "*Enjoy yourself, but also take it seriously. Although firms are looking for characters rather than drones, there is a balance to be struck.*" Blinded by a hectic schedule of social events and copious quantities of alcohol, students have been known to return to the office drunk, fall asleep in the library or even give up and go shopping for the day. And although the trainees might be a lot of fun, they're probably keeping an eye on you, and will report back if you criticise the partners or fail to suppress your raging hormones on the big night out. There's always one.

If you don't get on a scheme, it's not the end of the world. Most firms state that they will consider candidates for training contracts, even if they didn't get on their vac scheme. Firms also run open days, which can be almost as useful for getting a feel for the firm and speaking to trainees. Remember, too, that other work experience will set you out from the crowd just as effectively – helping a high street solicitor, a summer job in an office environment or voluntary work with a charity.

VACATION SCHEMES

FIRM NAME	NUMBER OF PLACES	DURATION	REMUN-ERATION	DEADLINE
Addleshaw Goddard	75	2 weeks	Not known	11 February 2005
Allen & Overy	75	3 weeks	£250 p.w.	31 January 2005
Arnold & Porter (UK)	Yes	Not known	Not known	4 February 2005
Ashurst	Easter (graduates & final year non-law); Summer (penult year law)	Easter: 2 weeks Summer: 3 weeks	£250 p.w.	31 January 2005
Baker & McKenzie	London: 30 International: 3-5*	3 weeks/*6-12 weeks in Lon/o'seas office	£250 p.w.	31 January 2005
Barlow Lyde & Gilbert	Yes, plus open days and drop in days	Not known	Not known	31 January 2005
Beachcroft Wansbroughs	16	Not known	Not known	1 May 2005
Berwin Leighton Paisner	50	2 weeks	Not known	28 February 2005
Bevan Brittan	60	Not known	Not known	31 March 2005
Bird & Bird	14	3 weeks	£220 p.w.	29 January 2005
Boodle Hatfield	10	2 weeks	Not known	1 January 2005
Bristows	Yes	Christmas/Easter: 1 week summer: 2 weeks	£200 p.w.	Xmas: 26 November 2004; Easter/summer: 28 Feb 2005
Burges Salmon	40	2 weeks	£200 p.w.	31 January 2005
Capsticks	Yes	2 weeks	Not known	28th February 2005
Clifford Chance	Christmas, Easter and summer (some overseas)	2-4 weeks	£270 p.w.	Christmas: 19 Nov 2004 Easter/Summer: 31 Jan 2005
Clyde & Co	15	2 weeks	Not known	31 January 2005
CMS Cameron McKenna	55	2 weeks	£225 p.w.	Not known
Coffin Mew & Clover	Open week in July	Not known	Not known	Not known
Covington & Burling	16	Not known	Not known	28 February 2005
Davenport Lyons	12	2 weeks	£175 p.w.	January 2005
Dechert	up to 16, plus 20-30 assessment days in both March and July	2 weeks	Min. £225 p.w.	Vac scheme: 28 February 2005
Denton Wilde Sapte	yes, plus open days	Not known	Not known	(OD: 26 November 2004) 11 February 2005

VACATION SCHEMES

FIRM NAME	NUMBER OF PLACES	DURATION	REMUN-ERATION	DEADLINE
Dickinson Dees	36	1 week	£125 p.w.	28 February 2005
DLA	200	2 weeks	£210 p.w (Lon) £170 p.w (Ors)	28 February 2005
DMH	Yes	1 week	Unpaid	31 January 2005
Eversheds	180	2 weeks summer, 1 week Easter	Regional variations	31 January 2005
Farrer & Co	30: Easter and summer	2 weeks	£230 p.w.	31 January 2005
Field Fisher Waterhouse	Yes	Not known	Not known	31 January 2005
Foot Anstey Sargent	Yes	Not known	Not known	31 March 2005
Freshfields Bruckhaus Deringer	100	2 weeks	£500 total	31 January 2005 (apply asap after 1 December 2004)
Gateley Wareing	12	2 weeks	Not known	11 February 2005
Government Legal Service	70	2-3 weeks	£200-250pw	31 March 2005
Halliwells	45	2 weeks	£133 p.w.	31 March 2005
Hammonds	64	2 weeks	£230 p.w. (Lon) £180 p.w. (Ors)	31 January 2005
Herbert Smith	115 (Christmas: non-law; Easter/summer: law and non-law) some o/seas	Not known	Not known	Xmas: 12 November 2004 Easter/summer: 31 Jan 2005
Hewitsons	Yes	1 week	Not known	Not known
Hill Dickinson	Yes	1 week	Not known	30th April 2005
Holman Fenwick & Willan	16	2 weeks	£250 p.w.	1 January to 14 February 2005
Howes Percival	Yes	Not known	Not known	Not known
Hugh James	Yes	Not known	Not known	Not known
Ince & Co	18	2 weeks	£250 p.w.	14 February 2005
Irwin Mitchell	50	1 week	£75 p.w.	31 January 2005
Jones Day	20 at Christmas: non-law 16 at Easter: non-law 40 in summer: law	2 weeks	£275 p.w.	Christmas: 31 Oct 2004 Easter/summer: 14 February 2005
Lawrence Graham	32 in Easter & summer	2 weeks	£220 p.w.	31 January 2005
Laytons	6	1 week	Not known	31 March 2005

VACATION SCHEMES

FIRM NAME	NUMBER OF PLACES	DURATION	REMUN-ERATION	DEADLINE
Lester Aldridge	8	2 weeks	£75 p.w.	31 March 2005
Lewis Silkin	12	Not known	Not known	Not known
Linklaters	30 in Christmas (non-law), 60 in summer (law), some o/seas	Not known	£275 p.w.	Not known
Lovells	90 Christmas, Easter and summer	Not known	Not known	Xmas: 12 Nov 2004 Easter/summer: 11 February 2005
Macfarlanes	36	2 weeks	£250 p.w.	28 February 2005
Manches	24	1 week	Under review	31 January 2005
Masons	Approx 12 in London	2 weeks	Not known	18 February 2005
Mayer, Brown, Rowe & Maw	25 Easter and summer	2 weeks	Not known	Not known
McCormicks	Yes	Not known	Not known	25 February 2005
Mills & Reeve	Yes	2 weeks	Not known	1 March 2005
Mishcon de Reya	12	2 weeks	£200 p.w.	15 March 2005
Morgan Cole	6 open days	n/a	n/a	31 March 2005
Nabarro Nathanson	60	3 weeks	Not known	28 February 2005
Norton Rose	15 in Christmas 45 in summer	Christmas: 2 weeks summer: 3 weeks	£250 p.w.	31 October 2004 31 January 2005
Olswang	Yes	2 weeks	£250 p.w.	31 January 2005
Orchard	Yes	Not known	Not known	Not known
Osborne Clarke	20-25 Easter and summer	1 week	£175-200 p.w.	31 January 2005
Pannone & Partners	50 Easter and summer	1 week	None	Easter: 28 January 2005 summer: 29 April 2005
Penningtons	open day places + vac scheme	Not known	Not known	31 March 2005
Pinsents	90	2 weeks	Not known	31 January 2005
Reed Smith	12	3 weeks (Lon) 2 weeks (Mids)	£600 (Lon) £300 (Mids)	31 January 2005
Reynolds Porter Chamberlain	18	2 weeks	£250 p.w.	28 February 2005

VACATION SCHEMES

FIRM NAME	NUMBER OF PLACES	DURATION	REMUN-ERATION	DEADLINE
Richards Butler	30 in London plus overseas placements	2 weeks	£200 p.w.	6 February 2005
Shadbolt & Co	6	2 weeks	£170 p.w.	28 February 2005
Shoosmiths	30	2 weeks	£200 p.w.	28 February 2005
Simmons & Simmons	Not known	Not known	£250 p.w.	31 January 2005
SJ Berwin	60	2 weeks	£225 p.w.	31 January 2005
Slaughter and May	60 (penult. year of degree)	2 weeks	£250 p.w.	28 January 2005
Speechly Bircham	12	3 weeks	£250 p.w.	14 February 2005
Steeles (law)	Yes	Not known	Not known	Not known
Stephenson Harwood	16	2 weeks	£250 p.w.	18 February 2005
Taylor Walton	8	Up to 3 weeks	£150 p.w.	30 March 2005
Taylor Wessing	20	2 weeks	£225 p.w.	mid February 2005
Teacher Stern Selby	Approx 10	Not known	Not known	Not known
Thomas Eggar	yes	1 week	Travel Expenses	31 March 2005
TLT Solicitors	12	1 week	Not known	31 March 2005
Travers Smith	45 summer + Christmas & Easter places	2 weeks	£250	31 January 2005
Trowers & Hamlins	25-30 plus open days	2 weeks	£225 p.w.	1 March 2005
Walker Morris	45	1 week	£165 p.w.	28 February 2005
Ward Hadaway	Yes	1 week	Not known	30 April 2005
Watson, Farley & Williams	30	2 weeks	£200 p.w.	25 February 2005
Wedlake Bell	6	3 weeks	£150 pw	28 February 2005
Weil, Gotshal & Manges	12	Not known	Not known	14 February 2005
White & Case	40-50	2 weeks	£300 p.w.	31 January 2005
Withers	6 in Easter and 24 in summer + Milan opportunities	2 weeks	Not known	31 January 2005
Wragge & Co	Easter and summer	Not known	Not known	31 January 2005

applications and selection

The race to find a training contract attracts an increasingly crowded field of candidates and, consequently, law firms can be ever more selective about who they invite to join their stable. The following guide to the applications procedure has been compiled by a panel of expert tipsters.

studying the form

Your first step is to find out which firms you want to apply to, and why. Consider which practice areas you might find interesting and work out who does them well. The **Solicitors Practice Areas** section summarises some of the main types of work and includes ranking tables showing the best firms. For more information on these runners and riders, or to learn about more specialist areas, consult our parent publication *Chambers UK*, which is available online or in your university or law school careers office. You should also consult law firms' own websites and any promotional material they produce. Because each firm is different in size, practice orientation and culture, you'll probably find reading the *True Picture* section of this guide helpful in deciding which ones appeal. Once you've made your choices (we cannot tell you how many to make), consider how your skills, qualifications and interests are relevant to these firms.

Remember, most commercial firms recruit two years in advance of the start of the training contract. Miss the starting gun and you'll probably have to wait another year to join the race. If they want to go straight from their LPC to their training contract with no time out, law students should apply before or during the summer vacation between the second and third years of their degree, and non-law degree candidates before starting their CPE. However, be aware that a few of the big City firms have early application deadlines – some even earlier than the spring of the year in which the CPE course starts.

Smaller firms recruit one year in advance or even closer to the start of the contract; some will test ride applicants by offering paralegal work to see how they perform, only then allowing the prospect of a training contract to be discussed.

As a rule, it's far better to make fewer, targeted applications and to tailor them to individual firms than to send off hundreds of one-size-fits-all covering letters and CVs. Recruiters can always spot blanket applications, and rather than hedging your bets, this tactic could turn you into a non-runner. Our student website **www.chambersandpartners.com** contains a detailed CV and application forms workshop, but here are a few basic tips:

- Don't put anything in your CV unless you can expand on it at interview. Your professed passion for sailing will ring hollow if you can't tell your aft from your anchor.
- Avoid chronological gaps in your experience. If you've taken time off, put it down and be prepared to explain why.
- Your CV gives you an opportunity to make your achievements shine, so keep it to two or three pages max and make the most of your strengths by effective use of headings or bold text.
- Don't make your application gimmicky - photos, bizarre fonts and lurid colours should be avoided. One recruiter recalled the time when one bright spark sent a piece of fruit with their application, accompanied by a note instructing them not to be a lemon and to pick her for a training contract. Of course, it didn't work.

Unless stated otherwise, CVs should be accompanied by a covering letter. This gives you a chance to expand on why you want to work for that particular firm and maybe what you usefully learned from that expedition to Borneo. The letter should convey why you and the firm are a good fit, and give the reader a more personal insight into your qualities. Keep it to one page in length. Recruiters won't be impressed by waffle or padding, and certainly don't want to read a treatise on how amazing their firm is. Finally, make sure that someone checks it over for you – one of the major reasons for rejecting applicants is that they haven't managed to spell the name of the firm correctly, or even their own in some cases.

If the firm doesn't ask for a CV, it will require you to complete a dreaded application form. These forms can take a surprising amount of time to fill in, so get started early. Most firms adhere to strict deadlines, and we've heard stories about candidates sending off electronic applications at two minutes past midnight and being told that they cannot be accepted. If the form is to be handwritten, take a photocopy and practise writing on that first. A form covered in Tippex and three different colours of ink will get attention for all the wrong reasons. Also, make sure you don't leave gaps: if you are struggling to complete a box, write slightly bigger to make sure there are no glaring empty spaces. Plan what you want to say in each section and make sure the form covers your whole range of skills and attributes. Read each question carefully to work out what the firm is really asking. Unless you do there's a danger you'll only give half an answer. Again, unless asked not to, you can include a short covering letter to highlight the best aspects of your application, include experiences you couldn't fit in and confirm your dedication to the cause. Finally, make sure you keep a copy of the form to read over should you be invited for interview.

getting ahead of the field

Almost all firms now demand a uniformly high level of academic achievement – a minimum 2:1 degree and, increasingly, excellent A-levels. As always, some thoroughbred applicants will gallop away with a host of offers, but for the rest, a little attention to what firms are looking for could save a trip to the knacker's yard. According to Sally Carthy from DLA: "*Academics are only a starting point. You have to be able to market yourself better than your contemporaries. Applicants should be able to demonstrate a broad range of interests, show commitment to the profession, and have done their research on the firm.*" Look at what else you can do to demonstrate your teamwork and problem-solving skills, as well as your business acumen. If you can get work experience or a vacation scheme place this will really help you understand the reality of practice. And if you can't, try and speak to lawyers at every opportunity. Ask family and friends if they know someone you can chat to, or perhaps there is someone at university or law school who can give you advice or contacts.

When it comes to interviews, anyone can get nervous or flustered, but effective preparation should boost your confidence and give your performance added credibility. As Sally Carthy says: "*Interviews are an oral examination. If you don't prepare for an examination, you prepare to fail.*" First things first, it always pays to be up to date with news and current affairs by reading both mainstream quality newspapers and the legal press. For the latter, try Tuesday's law supplement in *The Times* as well as *The Lawyer* or *Legal Week* and *The Law Society Gazette*. These mags are all online. According to Sally, it's not so much about the opinions you form on various topics, but "*how you stand by your convictions and put forward a reasoned response.*"

Make sure you have studied the firm's own literature just prior to interview. If you know which partner will be interviewing you, find out as much as you can about him or her from the firm's website, or they may even be profiled in *Chambers UK*.

Think about how you would answer the most obvious questions. Amazing as it may seem, we are regularly told that candidates seem incapable of explaining why they want to be a lawyer.

Some firms use reasoning tests, and although it's not possible to prepare for these as such, your careers service may well have something similar so that you can get an idea of what sort of questions might be posed. And don't forget to ask around; friends of friends may have attended the same firm's assessment day just a week before, and may be willing to pass on a few tips.

race day

When the big day comes, aim to turn up an hour early and find a café somewhere nearby to sit down and have a cup of tea. Then you can have a last look through a copy of the application you sent and any crib notes you've made. If you're rushing to make it on time, you won't be thinking clearly. Worse still, you might get sweaty. If you are travelling a long way, make sure that you take the firm's number with you in case you are delayed. Both partners and HR people are very busy and will not appreciate being kept waiting, especially without warning. Whilst waiting in reception for your interview, make sure that you are polite to everyone you meet. Recruiters will quickly find out if you've been rude or arrogant to receptionists or secretaries.

If more than one person interviews you, try to speak to everyone on the panel. Listen carefully and think clearly before answering questions. Sally Brewis from Dickinson Dees has a word of advice: "*Don't try to dodge a question as experienced interviewers will always come back to it. Hardly surprisingly; lawyers are quite good at doing that.*" Keep an eye on your body language, don't fidget and maintain eye contact as far as possible without scaring anyone. V. important: prepare a couple of sensible questions for the end of the interview, but make sure you couldn't easily have found the answers on the firm's website.

falling at the first fence

Do try to dress appropriately. Jeans and trainers, however smart, won't convey the right impression, nor will anything too racy or alternative. Whether you see yourself as a suit person or not, you should probably wear one (or something equally formal if you're female).

Even strong candidates can ruin their chances by trying too hard to impress. Sally Carthy advises people to "*remember that the legal profession is a conservative one, and so your style should be in keeping with that.*" It's probably best to avoid making too many wise cracks because even the most amiable partners won't appreciate you horsing around.

reaching the winner's enclosure

It's now relatively rare to be offered a training contract after one simple interview. These days, many firms employ a variety of psychometric tests, group exercises and case studies to weed out the also-rans. Non-law students can take comfort from the fact that these exercises and tests are designed to be completed by those without prior legal training. When embarking on a group exercise, remember that the aim is to determine how well you work in a team rather than how quickly you start jockeying for position. Listening to others in the group does not simply mean being quiet when they're talking: pick up on what they have said and make your own comments on their suggestions. According to Sally Brewis: "*Firms are not necessarily looking for the person who shouts the loudest, but the one who is making the most sense. It's good to show that you can organise people, but make sure that you're not leading them down the wrong path.*" If there is a social event at lunchtime or at the end of the day, remember that you are still being watched. Even the friendly trainee who adopts you as you hide by the buffet table may comment on your performance once you've gone home.

Keep in mind that you have been invited to meet recruiters because they are genuinely interested in you. As Sally Brewis says: "*Interviewers usually want to give you the best opportunity to shine, not trip you up.*" Finally, don't forget that an interview or assessment day is a two-way thing. Make sure you take the opportunity to find out more about the place – for example, what the atmosphere is like, which departments are popular to train in, and what kind of client contact trainees have. If it helps give you some much-needed confidence, just remind yourself that you're on a fact-finding mission as you walk through the door.

APPLICATIONS AND SELECTION

FIRM NAME	METHOD OF APPLICATION	SELECTION PROCESS	DEGREE CLASS	NUMBER OF CONTRACTS	NUMBER OF APPLICATIONS
Addleshaw Goddard	See website	Interview, assessment centre	2:1	50	2,000
Allen & Overy	Online	Interview	2:1	120	3,000
Arnold & Porter (UK)	Application form	Interview	2:1	2	Not known
asb law	See website	2 interviews, psychometric test + written exercise	2:1	10	500
Ashurst	Online	1 interview with assistant & another with 2 partners	2:1	45-50	2,500
B P Collins	Handwritten letter & CV	Screening interview & selection day	Not known	Not known	Not known
Baker & McKenzie	Online	Oral presentation, interview with 2 partners & meet a trainee	2:1	30	2,000
Barlow Lyde & Gilbert	Application form & covering letter	Interview day	Not known	16-18	2,000
Beachcroft Wansbroughs	Application form	Assessment centre & panel interview	2:1 preferred	28	Not known
Berwin Leighton Paisner	Online	Assessment day & partner interview	2:1	35	2,000
Bevan Brittan	Application form	Not known	Not known	Not known	Not known
Bird & Bird	Online	Assessment morning	2:1	14	1,500
Boodle Hatfield	Online	interviews with training principal, a partner and HR director plus verbal reasoning test	2.1	4	Not known
Boyes Turner	Letter & CV/online	2 interviews & 1 week work placement	2:1	4	Not known
Brabners Chaffe Street	Application form	Interview & assessment day	2:1/post-grad	7	Not known
Brachers	Online application form	Interview day with partners	2:1	6	400
Bristows	Application form	2 interviews	2.1 preferred	Up to 10	3,500
Browne Jacobson	Online	Assessment centre	2:1	8	1,500
Burges Salmon	Application form	Not known	2:1	20-25	1,500
Cadwalader, Wickersham & Taft	CV & covering letter	2 interviews	Not Known	4-6	Not Known
Capsticks	Application form	Summer placement then interview with Training Principal & partners	2:1 or above	4-5	300
Charles Russell	Online	Assessment day	2:1	12-14	Approx 2,000

APPLICATIONS AND SELECTION

FIRM NAME	METHOD OF APPLICATION	SELECTION PROCESS	DEGREE CLASS	NUMBER OF CONTRACTS	NUMBER OF APPLICATIONS
Cleary Gottlieb Steen & Hamilton	Cover letter & CV	Usually 2 interviews	2:1	4	1,000
Clifford Chance	Online application	Assessment day: interview + group exercise & verbal reasoning test	2:1	120	2,000
Clyde & Co	Online	Assessment session+interview with 2 partners	2:1	20	1,400+
CMS Cameron McKenna	Online application form	Initial interview + verbal reasoning test followed by assessment centre	2:1	80	1,500
Coffin Mew & Clover	CV & covering letter	Interview	2:1 (usually)	4-5	400+
Coudert Brothers	Letter & CV	2 interviews with partners	2:1	4	Not known
Covington & Burling	Application form & covering letter	2 interviews	2:1	4	Not known
Cripps Harries Hall	Application form on website	1 interview with managing partner & head of HR	2.1	8	Up to 750
Davenport Lyons	CV & covering letter	Interviews	2:1	5	2,000
Dechert	Application form	Communication exercises & interviews	2:1	up to 12	Approx 1,500
Denton Wilde Sapte	Application form	First interview; selection test; second interview + case study	2:1	35	2,000
Devonshires	Online	Not known	2:1 and higher	5	500
Dickinson Dees	Online application	Interview + test, exercise & personality questionnaire	2:1	up to 15	750
DLA	Application form	1st interview, 2nd interview & assessment afternoon	2:1	85+	2,500
DMH	Application form	1st interview & assessments; work experience & 2nd interview	2:1	6-7	400
Dorsey & Whitney	Letter & CV	Not known	2:1	4	Not known
DWF	Application form	Two-stage interview/selection process	2:1	8	Approx 1,000
Eversheds	Online	Selection day: group & individual exercises, presentations & interview	2:1	86	4,000
Farrer & Co	Application form & covering letter	Interviews with GR partner and partners	2:1	8-10	1,500
Field Fisher Waterhouse	Online	Interview	2:1	12	1,200
Finers Stephens Innocent	CV & covering letter	2 interviews with the training partners	2:1	5	800
Fisher Meredith	Application Form	Psychometric assessments and competitive interviews	Not known	Not known	Not known

APPLICATIONS AND SELECTION

FIRM NAME	METHOD OF APPLICATION	SELECTION PROCESS	DEGREE CLASS	NUMBER OF CONTRACTS	NUMBER OF APPLICATIONS
Foot Anstey Sargent	Letter & CV or online form	Assessment day	2:1 preferred	8	Not known
Forbes	Handwritten letter & CV	Interview with partners	2:1	4	350+
Ford & Warren	Letter & CV	Interviews & exercise	2:1	6	700
Forsters	Application form	1st interview with HR manager & GR partner; 2nd with 2 partners	Not known	Not known	Not known
Freeth Cartwright	Online Application form	Interview & selection day	Not known	Not known	Not known
Freshfields Bruckhaus Deringer	Application form	2 Interviews & written test	2:1	100	c.2,500
Government Legal Service	Online	Assessment day: group exercises, written questions & interview	2:2	30	1,200+
Gateley Wareing	See website	Not known	2:1	Not known	Not known
Halliwells	Application form	Group exercise, presentation & interview	2:1	13	1,000
Hammonds	Online	Assessment & interview	2:1	40	1,500
Harbottle & Lewis	CV & letter	Interview	2:1	4	800
Henmans	Application form on website	Interview with HR manager & partners	Not known	3	450
Herbert Smith	Online application form	Case study & interview	2:1	up to 100	2,027
Hewitsons	Application form	Interview	2:1	8	1,400
Hill Dickenson	CV & letter Online	Assessment day	not known	not known	not known
Hodge Jones & Allen	Online application form	Interview with 2 partners	2:1	3-4	400
Holman Fenwick & Willan	Online application form	2 interviews with partners & written exercise	2:1	8	1,000
Howes Percival	Online application form	Assess. centre & 2nd interview with training principal & partner	2:1	6	300
Hugh James	Application form	Interview & presentation	2:2	10	350
Ince & Co	Letter & CV	Interview with HR; interview with 2 partners & written test	2:1	8-10	1,500
Irwin Mitchell	Application form & covering letter	Assessment centre and interview; second interview	Not known	15	1,000
Jones Day	CV & letter online	2 interviews with partners	2:1	20	1,500
Kendall Freeman	Online application	Interview with 2 partners	2:1	8	Not known
Keoghs	CV & covering letter	Two-stage interview	2:1	4	800

APPLICATIONS AND SELECTION

FIRM NAME	METHOD OF APPLICATION	SELECTION PROCESS	DEGREE CLASS	NUMBER OF CONTRACTS	NUMBER OF APPLICATIONS
Lawrence Graham	Application form	Interview	2:1	18	1,000
Laytons	Application form	2 interviews	1 or 2:1	8	2,000
LeBoeuf, Lamb, Greene & MacRae	CV & covering letter	2 interviews	2:1	5	1,300
Lester Aldridge	Letter, CV & application form	Interview by a panel of partners	2:1	10	300
Lewis Silkin	Application form	Assessment day: interview with 2 partners & analytical exercise	2:1	7	1,000
Linklaters	Application form	2 interviews & commercial case study	2:1	130	4,000
Lovells	Online application form	Assessment day: critical thinking test, group exercise, interview	2:1	90	2,000
Lupton Fawcett	Application form & handwritten letter	Interviews & assessment days	2:1 preferred	2-3	300
Mace & Jones	Online	Interview with partners	2:1	varies	1,500
Macfarlanes	Online application	Assessment day	2:1	25	1,500
Manches	Application form	Interview with HR; interview with 2 partners	2:1	10	860
Martineau Johnson	Online application form	Half-day assessment centre	2:1	10-12	500
Masons	Online	Assessment day & an interview	2:1	15-18	1,600
Mayer, Brown, Rowe & Maw	Online application form	Selection workshop: interview, business analysis exercise & group exercise	2:1	25-30	720
McCormicks	Application form	Assessment day & interview with 2 partners	2:1	4	350
McDermott, Will & Emery	CV & covering letter	Not known	Not known	Not known	Not known
McGrigors	Application form	Assessment day	2:1	12-15	Not known
Mills & Reeve	Application form	One-day assessment centre	2:1	15-20	Approx 600
Mishcon de Reya	Application form	Not known	2:1	6-8	800+
Morgan Cole	Online	Assessment centre & interview	2.1 preferred	Not known	Not known
Nabarro Nathanson	Online	Interview & assessment day	2:1	25	1,500
Nicholson Graham & Jones	Online	Interview & assessment	2:1	10	1,500
Norton Rose	Online application form	Interview & group exercise	2:1	60-70	3,500+

APPLICATIONS AND SELECTION

FIRM NAME	METHOD OF APPLICATION	SELECTION PROCESS	DEGREE CLASS	NUMBER OF CONTRACTS	NUMBER OF APPLICATIONS
Olswang	Online	Business case scenario, interview, psychometric test + written exercises	2:1	Up to 20	2,500
Orchard	Application form	2 interviews	2:1	4-6	350
Osborne Clarke	Online	Assessment day: interviews, group exercises etc; 2nd interview + presentation	2:1 preferred	20-25	1,000-1,500
Pannone & Partners	Application form & CV	1st interview; 2nd interview comprises tour of firm & lunch	2:1	10	900
Payne Hicks Beach	Letter & CV	Interview	2:1	3	1,000
Penningtons	Online	Not known	2:1	12	1,000
Pinsents	Online application form	Assessment centre including interview	2:1	35	2,000
Prettys	Letter & CV	Not known	2:1 preferred	5	Not known
Pritchard Englefield	Application form	Interview	Generally 2:1	3	300-400
Reed Smith	Online	Assessment day: 2 interviews, aptitude test & presentation	2:1	6	700
Reynolds Porter Chamberlain	Online	Assessment day	2.1	15	900
Richards Butler	Online	Selection exercise & interview	2:1	20	2,000
Salans	Handwritten letter & CV	Interviews & workshop	2:1	3-4	500+
Shadbolt & Co	Application form	Interview, written assessment & group exercise	usually 2:1	4	100
Shearman & Sterling	Application form	Interviews	2:1	10	Not known
Shoosmiths	Application form	Full-day selection centre	2:1	11	1,000
Sidley Austin Brown & Wood	Covering letter & application form	Interview(s)	2:1	6-8	500
Simmons & Simmons	Online	Assessment day: interview + written & document exercises	2:1	50	2,500
SJ Berwin	Online application form	2 interviews	2:1	30	2,000
Slaughter and May	Covering letter & CV or online	Interview	2:1	85	2,500+
Speechly Bircham	Application form	Interview	2:1	5	1,000
Steeles (Law)	Online or CV & covering letter	Interview/assessment day	2:1	6	300-400
Stephenson Harwood	Online	Assessment centre	2:1	12	Not known

APPLICATIONS AND SELECTION

FIRM NAME	METHOD OF APPLICATION	SELECTION PROCESS	DEGREE CLASS	NUMBER OF CONTRACTS	NUMBER OF APPLICATIONS
Stevens & Bolton	Letter & application form	2 interviews	2:1	3	450
Tarlo Lyons	Application form	2 interviews	2:1	3	200
Taylor Walton	CV & covering letter	First & second interviews	2:1 or above	Not known	Not known
Taylor Wessing	Online	2 interviews, 1 with a partner	2:1	20	1,150
Teacher Stern Selby	Letter & application form	2 interviews	2:1 (not absolute)	3-6	1,000
Thomas Eggar	Letter & CV	Assessment centre & interview	2:1	Not known	Not known
Thomson Snell & Passmore	Letter & application form	Assessment Interview	2:1	4	Approx 500
TLT Solicitors	Application form	Assessment centre	2:1 preferred	8	500+
Travers Smith	CV and covering letter	Interviews (2 stage process)	2:1	up to 25	2,000
Trowers & Hamlins	Letter, application form & CV	Interview(s), essay & practical test	2:1+	12-15	1,600
Walker Morris	Application form	Telephone & face-to-face interviews	2:1	15	Approx 800
Ward Hadaway	Application form & letter	Interview	2:1	8	400+
Watson, Farley & Williams	Online	Assessment centre & interview	2:1 min	10	1,000
Wedlake Bell	CV & covering letter	Interviews	2:1	6	Not known
Weightmans	Online	Not known	Not known	Not known	Not known
Weil, Gotshal & Manges	Online	Not known	2:1	12	Not known
White & Case	Online	Interview	2:1	20-25	1,500
Wiggin and Co	CV & covering letter	selection exercise & interview	2:1	3	500
Withers	Application form	2 interviews	2:1	14	1,000
Wollastons	CV & application form	3-stage Interview	2:1	2	500
Wragge & Co	Online or application form	Telephone discussion & assessment day	2:1	25	1,000

offer and acceptance

After the hard work of securing a training contract, you'll need to know what to do when you actually land one. Law students will already know all about offer and acceptance; if you haven't yet been introduced to the timeless delights of Carlill v The Carbolic Smokeball Company, what better time to learn!

By accepting a training contract offer you enter into a legally binding contract with the law firm, so accept the right offer. Appreciating the minefield into which inexperienced students step, the Society has recently issued a revised set of good practice guidelines by which law firms should manage the recruitment process. The guidelines are detailed and we advise anyone who is unsure about their position to read them. They are on the Law Society's website, **www.lawsociety.org.uk**. To give you a feel for things, we've summarised them here.

If you're still an undergraduate, training contract interviews can only be scheduled for 1 September onwards in your final undergraduate year. If you've impressed the firm while on a vacation scheme or after work experience, the firm must wait until this date before interviewing you or offering a contract. At interview, you will be told if there is a further stage to the process. You should also be told within two weeks of reaching the end of the process whether or not you have been successful. An offer should be made in writing. However, we've found that many recruiters now seem to be making initial offers to students by phone. You need not accept a verbal offer; be polite and confirm with them that they will send the formal offer in writing for you to consider.

No deadline for acceptance of an offer should expire earlier than four weeks from the date of the offer. This new guideline is less helpful to students than the one it replaces. Under the old guidelines no offer should have expired before 1st November in a law undergrad's final year, or a non-law grad's CPE year, so allowing them to attend other interviews before accepting an offer made by a firm earlier in the year. If you need more time to consider an offer, firms are supposed to consider your request 'sympathetically' provided you have a good reason. No definition of 'good reason' is given in the guidelines.

If a firm is going to pay your law school fees, it should set out the terms and conditions of the arrangement in the training contract offer letter. The firm's willingness to provide financial assistance should not affect the time limit for accepting the contract.

We get calls from students who want to hang on to an offer from one firm while they pursue applications with others. In the initial wave of relief, it's too easy to forget that the balance of power has shifted in your favour. Too many trainees just take the first offer they receive because the firm has a decent enough reputation and is prepared to fund law school. Our advice always used to be that so long as you understand and respect the rules concerning offers, you could sit on an offer while your remaining applications ran their course. The change in the guidelines makes this more difficult, so guard against allowing a deadline to elapse while you attend subsequent interviews. If your top choice firm offers you a job, and you're confident it's the one for you, then go for it.

Students are supposed to respond promptly to a firm that's made an offer, either by accepting or rejecting it. If you feel you need more time, you will have to enter into diplomatic discussions with the law firm, telling them how much longer you need. Make sure you get written confirmation of any extension to the deadline. You can hold only two offers at a time. Accept your preferred offer in writing and confirm to everyone else that you are withdrawing your application. This is only fair to recruiters, who are really busy at this time of year, and other applicants who may suffer if you are still hogging the shortlist.

SALARIES AND BENEFITS

FIRM NAME	1ST YEAR SALARY	2ND YEAR SALARY	SPONSORSHIP/ AWARDS	OTHER BENEFITS	QUALIFICATION SALARY
Addleshaw Goddard	£20,000 (Manch/Leeds) £28,000 (London)	£22,000 (Manch/Leeds) £30,000 (London)	CPE & LPC: fees + £4,500 maintenance	Corporate gym m'ship, STL, subsd restaurant, pension, pte healthcare	£33,000 (Manch/Leeds) £48,000 (London)
Allen & Overy	£29,000	£33,000	CPE & LPC: fees + £5,000 p.a. maintenance (£4,500 outside London, Oxford & Guildford)	Pte healthcare scheme, PMI, STL, subsd restaurant, gym m'ship, 6 weeks unpaid leave on qual	£50,000
Arnold & Porter (UK)	Minimum £30,000	Not known	CPE & LPC: sponsorship	PHI, STL, life ass	£55,000
asb law	£17,500	Not known	Interest-free loan	Not known	Not known
Ashurst	£28,000-29,000	£31,000-32,000	CPE & LPC: fees + £5,000 p.a. maintenance (£4,500 outside London & Guildford), £500 LPC distinction award, language tuition bursaries	PHI, pension, life ass, STL, gym m'ship	£48,000
Baker & McKenzie	£29,000 + £3,000 'golden hello'	£32,000	CPE & LPC: fees + £5,000 p.a. maintenance + laptop or £2,000 for LPC	PHI, life ins, PMI, pension, subsd gym m'ship, STL, subsd restaurant	£50,000
Barlow Lyde & Gilbert	£28,000	£30,000	CPE & LPC: fees + maintenance	Not known	£47,000
Beachcroft Wansbroughs	£28,000 (London) £20,000 (regions)	£30,000 (London) £22,500 (regions)	CPE & LPC fees + £3,500 bursary	Flexible scheme (buy & sell benefits, inc. holiday, pension, pte healthcare)	Not known
Berwin Leighton Paisner	£28,000	£32,000	CPE & LPC: fees + £4,500 p.a. maintenance	Flexible package inc. PHI, PMI, subsd conveyancing, subsd gym m'ship	£50,000
Bevan Brittan	Not known	Not known	CPE & LPC: yes	Not known	Not known
Bird & Bird	£26,000	£28,000	CPE & LPC: fees + £3,500 p.a. maintenance	BUPA, STL, subsd sports club m'ship, life cover, PHI, pension	£46,000
Boodle Hatfield	£27,500	£29,500	CPE & LPC: fees + maintenance	Pte healthcare, life ass, STL, pension, PHI, conveyancing grant	£44,000
Boyes Turner	£18,000	£19,200	LPC: £4,000 interest-free loan	Pension, life ass	Not known
BP Collins	£18,000	£19,000	50% LPC costs refund when TC starts	Not known	Not known
Brabners Chaffe Street	£19,000	Not known	LPC: yes	Not known	Not known

Notes: PHI = Permanent Health Insurance; STL = Season Travel Ticket Loan; PMI = Private Medical Insurance

SALARIES AND BENEFITS

FIRM NAME	1ST YEAR SALARY	2ND YEAR SALARY	SPONSORSHIP/ AWARDS	OTHER BENEFITS	QUALIFICATION SALARY
Brachers	£16,975	£18,565	LPC/CPE: £6,000 discretionary award	Not known	£30,000
Bristows	£26,000	£28,000	CPE & LPC: fees + £5,000 p.a. maintenance	Pension, life ass & health ins	£43,000
Browne Jacobson	£19,000	Not known	CPE & LPC: fees + maintenance	Not known	Regional variations
Burges Salmon	£21,000	£22,000	CPE & LPC: fees + maintenance £4,500 p.a.	Bonus, pension, pmi, mobile phone, laptop, gym m'ship, social club, xmas gift	£34,500
Cadwalader, Wickersham & Taft	£30,000	£33,600	CPE & LPC: fees + £4,500 p.a maintenance	STL, pte dental & health, life ass	£65,000
Capsticks	Not known	Not known	CPE & LPC: scholarship contributions	Bonus, pension, PHI, death in service, STL	£41,000
Charles Russell	£27,000	£29,500	London & Guildford: CPE & LPC fees + £4,500 p.a. maintenance Chelt: one off LPC grant	BUPA, PHI, life ass, pension, STL	£44,000
Cleary Gottlieb Steen & Hamilton	£33,000	£39,000	LPC: fees + £5,000 maintenance	Pension, PHI, health club	£74,000
Clifford Chance	£29,000	£33,000	CPE & LPC: fees + £5,000 p.a. maintenance (Lon/Guild/Oxf), £4,500 p.a. (elsewhere), prizes for first class degree & LPC distinction	Interest-free loan, PMI, subsd restaurant, fitness centre, life ass, occupational health service, PHI	£50,000
Clyde & Co	£27,000	£30,000	CPE & LPC: fees + maintenance	Subsd sports club, STL, staff restaurant	£46,000
CMS Cameron McKenna	£28,000	£32,000	CPE & LPC: fees + £5,000 p.a. maintenance (Lon/Guild/Oxf), £4,500 (elsewhere)	Not known	£49,000
Coffin Mew & Clover	Competitive	Competitive	CPE & LPC: discussed with candidates	Not known	£27,750
Coudert Brothers	£28,000	£32,000	CPE & LPC: fees + £4,000 p.a. maintenance (discretionary)	Pension, pmi, subsd gym m'ship, STL, pte med & dental care	Not known
Covington & Burling	£30,000	£33,000	CPE & LPC: fees + £5,000 p.a. maintenance	Pension, PHI, pmi, life ass, STL	Not known
Cripps Harries Hall	£17,000	£19,500	LPC fees: 50% interest-free loan, 50% bursary	Not known	£30,000

Notes: PHI = Permanent Health Insurance; STL = Season Travel Ticket Loan; PMI = Private Medical Insurance

SALARIES AND BENEFITS

FIRM NAME	1ST YEAR SALARY	2ND YEAR SALARY	SPONSORSHIP/ AWARDS	OTHER BENEFITS	QUALIFICATION SALARY
Davenport Lyons	Not known	Not known	Not normally	STL, client intro bonus, contrib to gym m'ship, discretionary bonus	Not known
Dechert	£28,000	£32,000	LPC: fees + £4,500 p.a. maintenance	PHI, life ass, subsd gym m'ship, STL	£48,000
Denton Wilde Sapte	£28,000	£31,000	CPE & LPC: fees + £4,500 p.a. maintenance (£5,000 in London)	Flexible benefit scheme	£48,000
Devonshires	£24,500	£25,500	Under review	STL, healthcare scheme, subsd health-club m'ship	Competitive
Dickinson Dees	£18,000	£19,500	CPE & LPC: fees + £4,000 interest-free loan	Not known	£30,000
DLA	£28,000 (London) £20,000 (regions) £16,000 (Scotland)	£31,000 (London) £22,000 (regions) £18,000 (Scotland)	CPE & LPC: fees + maintenance	Not known	£48,000 (London) £33,000 (Birmingham) £32,500 (other English) £30,000 (Scotland)
DMH	£17,500	£20,250	Not known	Not known	£30,000
Dorsey & Whitney	£28,500	£31,500	Not known	Pension, health ins, life ass	£52,000
DWF	£18,000	Not known	LPC: fees	Life ass, pension	Not known
Eversheds	£28,000 (London)	£31,000 (London)	CPE & LPC: fees + maintenance	Regional variations	£48,000 (London)
Farrer & Co	£26,000	£28,500	CPE & LPC: fees + £4,500 p.a. maintenance	Health & life ins, subsd gym m'ship, STL	£43,000
Field Fisher Waterhouse	£27,000	£30,000	CPE & LPC: fees + £4,500 maintenance	STL, BUPA, life ass, pension, subsd gym m'ship, gp service	£46,000
Finers Stephens Innocent	Highly competitive	Highly competitive	LPC & CPE: fees	Pension, PMI, life ins, long-term disability ins, STL	Highly competitive

Notes: PHI = Permanent Health Insurance; STL = Season Travel Ticket Loan; PMI = Private Medical Insurance

SALARIES AND BENEFITS

FIRM NAME	1ST YEAR SALARY	2ND YEAR SALARY	SPONSORSHIP/ AWARDS	OTHER BENEFITS	QUALIFICATION SALARY
Foot Anstey Sargent	£16,750	£19,000	LPC: £8,000	Contributory pension	£28,500
Forbes	At least Law Soc min	£17,200	Not known	Not known	Highly competitive
Forsters	£25,000	£27,000	None	STL, PHI, life ins, subsd gym m'ship	£42,500
Freeth Cartwright	£17,000	Not known	Not known	Not known	Not known
Freshfields Bruckhaus Deringer	£29,000	£33,000	CPE & LPC: fees + £5,000 p.a. maintenance (Lon/Oxf), £4,500 p.a. (elswhere)	Life ass, PHI, pension, interest-free loan, STL, PMI, subsd staff restaurant, gym	£50,000
Gateley Wareing	£20,000	£22,000	LPC: fees + £4,000 maintenance CPE: fees	Not known	£32,000
Government Legal Service	£18,500 - £22,000	£20,200 - £25,000	LPC fees + £5–7,000 CPE: possibly	Pension, subsd canteen	£27,000– £38,000
Halliwells	£21,500	£22,500	CPE & LPC: fees + £4,500 p.a. maintenance	Pension, subsd gym m'ship	£32,000
Hammonds	£20,500	£23,000	CPE & LPC fees paid & maintenance grant of £4,500 p.a.	Subsd accom (rotational trainees), flexible benefits scheme	£46,000 (London) £33,000- 34,000 (other)
Harbottle & Lewis	£25,000	£26,000	LPC: fees + interest-free loan	Lunch, STL	£43,000
Henmans	£17,000	£18,650	Not known	Not known	£29,000
Herbert Smith	£28,500	£32,000	CPE & LPC: fees + £5,000 p.a. maintenance	Profit share, PHI, PMI, STL, life ass, gym, group personal accident ins, matched contrib. pension	£50,000
Hewitsons	£17,500	£18,500	None	Not known	£31,500
Hill Dickinson	£18,000	£19,500	LPC: fees (further funding under review)	Not known	Not known
Hodge Jones & Allen	£20,000	Not known	Not known	Pension, life ass, disability ins	£25,750
Holman Fenwick & Willan	£28,000	£30,000	CPE & LPC: fees + £5,000 p.a. maintenance	PMI, PHI, accident ins, subsd gym m'ship, STL	£46,000
Howes Percival	£19,300	£20,800	CPE & LPC: funding + maintenance grant	Pension, PHI	Not known

Notes: PHI = Permanent Health Insurance; STL = Season Travel Ticket Loan; PMI = Private Medical Insurance

SALARIES AND BENEFITS

FIRM NAME	1ST YEAR SALARY	2ND YEAR SALARY	SPONSORSHIP/ AWARDS	OTHER BENEFITS	QUALIFICATION SALARY
Hugh James	Competitive	Competitive	Not known	Contribution to stakeholder pension	Not known
Ince & Co	£27,000	£30,000	LPC: fees + £4,750 grant (London), £4,000 (elsewhere), CPE: discretionary	STL, PMI, PHI, contributory pension	£47,000
Irwin Mitchell	£18,000 (outside London)	£20,000 (outside London)	CPE & LPC: fees + £3,000 maintenance	Not known	Not known
Jones Day	£33,000	£37,000	CPE & LPC: fees + £5,000 p.a. maintenance	PMI, STL, subsd sports club m'ship, group life cover	£55,000
Kendall Freeman	£28,500	£32,000	CPE & LPC: fees + maintenance of £5,000 (London) or £4,500 (elsewhere)	Not known	£49,000
Keoghs	Under review	Under review	Not known	Not known	£27,500
Lawrence Graham	£28,000	£32,000	CPE & LPC: fees + £4,000 p.a. maintenance	STL, on-site gym	£46,000
Laytons	Market rate	Market rate	CPE & LPC: funding considered	Not known	Market rate
LeBoeuf, Lamb, Greene & MacRae	£33,000	£37,000	CPE & LPC: fees + £4,500 maintenance	Health, life & disability insurance contribs, STL	£65,000
Lester Aldridge	£16,500-17,000	£17,500-18,000	LPC: yes	Life ass, pension	£29,000
Lewis Silkin	£28,000	£30,000	LPC: fees	Life ass, critical illness cover, PMI, STL, pension, subsd gym m'ship	£43,000
Linklaters	£29,100	Not known	CPE & LPC: fees + £4,500-£5,000 p.a. maintenance.	Bonus schemes, health & w'wide travel ins, life ass, pension, STL, subsd gym m'ship	£51,000 +
Lovells	£28,000	£32,000	CPE & LPC: fees + £5,000 p.a. maintenance (Lon/Guild/Oxf), £4,500 p.a.(elsewhere), £500 bonus & £1,000 salary advance on joining, £500 prize for first class degree	PPP med ins, life ass, PHI, STL, in-house gym, staff restaurant, in-house dentist, doctor & physio, local retail discounts	£50,000

Notes: PHI = Permanent Health Insurance; STL = Season Travel Ticket Loan; PMI = Private Medical Insurance

SALARIES AND BENEFITS

FIRM NAME	1ST YEAR SALARY	2ND YEAR SALARY	SPONSORSHIP/ AWARDS	OTHER BENEFITS	QUALIFICATION SALARY
Lupton Fawcett	Competitive	Competitive	LPC: interest-free loan	PMI, STL	Competitive
Mace & Jones	£16,000	£16,500	Not known	Not known	Negotiable
Macfarlanes	£28,000	£32,000	CPE & LPC: fees + £5,000 p.a. maintenance (Lon/Guild/Oxf), £4,500 (elsewhere), prizes for LPC distinction or commendation	Comprehensive package	£50,000
Manches	£26,500 (London)	£30,000 (London)	CPE & LPC: fees + £4,000 p.a. maintenance	STL, BUPA, PHI, PMI, pension	£43,000 (London)
Martineau Johnson	£20,000	£21,500	Not known	Not known	£34,000
Masons	£25,000 (London) (varies between offices)	£27,000 (London) (varies between offices)	CPE & LPC: fees + maintenance	Life ass, PMI (all offices) Subsd restaurant & STL (London)	£44,500 (London)
Mayer, Brown, Rowe & Maw	£28,000	Not known	CPE & LPC: + £4,500 p.a. maintenance (£5,000 for Lon/Guild)	STL, subsd sports club m'ship, PMI	£50,000
McCormicks	Highly competitive	Highly competitive	Not known	Not known	Highly competitive
McDermott, Will & Emery	£30,000	Not known	CPE & LPC: fees + maintenance	PMI, life ass, PHI, STL, subisdised gym m'ship, employee assistance programme	Not known
McGrigors	£28,000	£32,000	CPE & LPC: fees + £4,500 p.a. maintenance	Life ass, pension, lunch allowance	£48,000
Mills & Reeve	£20,000	£21,000	LPC: fees + maintenance CPE: fees	Life ass, contrib pension, bonus, subsd gym, BUPA discount	Not known
Mishcon de Reya	£27,000	£29,000	CPE & LPC: fees + bursary	PMI, subsd gym m'ship, STL, PHI, life ass, pension	Not known
Morgan Cole	Competitive	Competitive	CPE & LPC: fees + maintenance	Not known	Not known

Notes: PHI = Permanent Health Insurance; STL = Season Travel Ticket Loan; PMI = Private Medical Insurance

SALARIES AND BENEFITS

FIRM NAME	1ST YEAR SALARY	2ND YEAR SALARY	SPONSORSHIP/ AWARDS	OTHER BENEFITS	QUALIFICATION SALARY
Nabarro Nathanson	£28,000 (Lond/Reading) £20,000 (Sheffield)	£32,000 (Lond/Reading) £22,000 (Sheffield)	CPE & LPC: fees + £5,000 p.a. maintenance (Lon/Guild), £4,500 (elsewhere)	PMI, pension, STL, subsd restaurant, subsd corporate gym m'ship	£48,000 (London) £32,000 (Sheffield)
Nicholson Graham & Jones	£28,000	£31,000	CPE & LPC: fees + £4,500 p.a. maintenance	Life ass, STL, subsd gym m'ship, BUPA	£46,000
Norton Rose	£28,500	£32,000	CPE & LPC: fees + £5,000 p.a. maintenance, £1,000 travel scholarship	£800 loan on arrival, life ass, pte health ins, STL, subsd gym m'ship	Not known
Olswang	£28,000	£32,000	CPE & LPC: fees + £4,500 maintenance, (London) or £4,000 (o/s London)	Pension, PMI, life cover, dental scheme, STL, subsd gym m'ship, PHI	£48,000
Osborne Clarke	£26,500 (London/TV) £20,500 (Bristol)	Not known	CPE & LPC: fees + £3,000 p.a. maintenance	Pension contributions, PMI, STL, PHI, life ass	£47,000 (London) £43,000 (TV) £34,000 (Bristol)
Pannone & Partners	£20,000	£22,000	LPC: fees	Not known	£32,000
Payne Hicks Beach	£26,000	£28,500	CPE & LPC: fees	STL, life ass, PHI, pension	Not known
Penningtons	£26,500 (London)	£28,500 (London)	LPC: fees + £4,000 maintenance	Subsd sports & social club, life ass, PMI, STL, crit ill cover	Not known
Pinsents	£28,000 (London)	£32,000 (London)	CPE & LPC: fees + maintenance (CPE: £3,000, LPC: £5,000)	Not known	Approx £48,000
Pritchard Englefield	£21,750	£22,250	LPC: fees	Some subsd training, luncheon vouchers	Approx £40,000
Reed Smith	£27,000 (London) £19,500 (Coventry)	£31,000 (London) £22,000 (Coventry)	CPE: fees + £2,500; LPC: fees + £5,000	BUPA, STL, life ass, PHI, pension contributions	£48,000
Reynolds Porter Chamberlain	£28,000	£30,000	CPE & LPC: fees + £4,500 p.a. maintenance	Bonus, PMI, income protection, STL, subsd gym m'ship	£47,000
Richards Butler	£28,000	£31,000	CPE & LPC: fees + £5,000 p.a. maintenance	Bonus, life ins, BUPA, STL, subsd staff restaurant, conveyancing allowance	£48,000 + bonus
Salans	£26,500	£28,500	LPC: fees	PMI, pension, STL, crit ill cover	Variable

Notes: PHI = Permanent Health Insurance; STL = Season Travel Ticket Loan; PMI = Private Medical Insurance

SALARIES AND BENEFITS

FIRM NAME	1ST YEAR SALARY	2ND YEAR SALARY	SPONSORSHIP/ AWARDS	OTHER BENEFITS	QUALIFICATION SALARY
Shadbolt & Co	£24,000	£28,000	LPC: 50% fee refund when TC starts	PMI, PHI, life ass, paid study leave, STL, bonus, prof m'ships + subs	£42,000
Shearman & Sterling	£35,000	£37,500	CPE & LPC: fees + £5,000 maintenance	Not known	£55,000
Shoosmiths	Competitive	Competitive	LPC: £12,500	Life ass, pension, staff discounts, Xmas bonus	Market rate
Sidley Austin Brown & Wood	£28,500	£32,000	CPE & LPC: fees + maintenance	PMI, disability cover, life ass, contrib to gym m'ship, STL	Not known
SJ Berwin	£28,000	£32,000	CPE & LPC: fees + £4,500 p.a. maintenance (£5,000 in London)	Corporate sports m'ship, free lunch, PMI	£50,000
Simmons & Simmons	£28,000	£32,000	CPE & LPC: fees + £5,000 p.a. maintenance (Lon/Guild/Oxf), £4,500 (elsewhere)	STL, fitness loan, trav ins, accident ins, death in service, PMI, staff restaurant	£48,000
Slaughter and May	£29,000	£32,500	CPE & LPC: fees + maintenance	BUPA, STL, pension, subsd health club m'ship, 24-hour accident cover	£50,000
Speechly Bircham	£26,000-27,000	£28,000-29,000	CPE & LPC: fees + maintenance	STL, PMI, life ass	£45,000
Stephenson Harwood	£26,000	£29,000	CPE & LPC: fees + maintenance	Subsd health club m'ship, PMI, BUPA, STL	£46,000
Stevens & Bolton	£21,500	£23,500	CPE & LPC: fees + £4,000 p.a. maintenance	PMI, life ass, pension, STL, PHI	£38,000
Tarlo Lyons	£27,000 (on average)	£29,000 (on average)	LPC: fees	Bonus, PMI, pension plan, gym m'ship	£42,000
Taylor Walton	Not known	Not known	LPC: full sponsorship	Not known	Not known
Taylor Wessing	£28,000	£31,000	CPE & LPC: fees + £4,500 p.a. maintenance	PMI, PHI, STL, subsd staff restaurant, pension	£48,000
Teacher Stern Selby	£25,000	Not known	LPC: occasional funding	Not known	£36,000
Thomas Eggar	Market rate	Market rate	LPC: 50% grant, 50% loan	Travel allowance	Not known
Thomson Snell & Passmore	£17,250	£18,750	LPC: grant & interest free loan	Not known	Not known

Notes: PHI = Permanent Health Insurance; STL = Season Travel Ticket Loan; PMI = Private Medical Insurance

SALARIES AND BENEFITS

FIRM NAME	1ST YEAR SALARY	2ND YEAR SALARY	SPONSORSHIP/ AWARDS	OTHER BENEFITS	QUALIFICATION SALARY
TLT Solicitors	Not known	Not known	LPC: fees + maintenance	Pension, subsd sports & health club m'ship, life ass	Market rate
Travers Smith	£28,000	£32,000	LPC & CPE: fees + 5,000 p.a. maintenance (£4,500 o/side Lon)	PMI, permanent sickness cover, life ass, STL, subsd bistro, subsd sports club m'ship	£50,000
Trowers & Hamlins	£26,000	£27,500	CPE & LPC: fees + £4,250–£4,500 p.a. maintenance	STL, PMI, employee assistance programme, bonus, death in service	£43,500
Walker Morris	£20,000	£22,000	CPE & LPC: fees + £4,500 maintenance	Not known	£33,000
Ward Hadaway	£17,500	£18,500	LPC: fees + £2,000 int-free loan	Death in service insurance, pension	£31,000
Watson, Farley & Williams	£28,500	£32,500	CPE & LPC: fees + £4,500 p.a. maintenance (£4,000 o/side London)	Life ass, PHI, BUPA, STL, pension, subsd gym m'ship	£50,000
Wedlake Bell	Not known	Not known	LPC & CPE: fees + £2,500 p.a. maintenance (if no LEA grant)	Pension, STL, subsd gym m'ship. On qual: life ass, PMI, PHI	Not known
Weil, Gotshal & Manges	£35,000	Not known	Not known	Not known	Not known
White & Case	£33,000-34,500	£36,000-37,500	CPE & LPC: fees + £5,500 p.a. maintenance, prize for LPC commendation or distinction	BUPA, gym m'ship contrib, life ins, pension, PHI, STL, bonuses	£60,000
Wiggin and Co	£26,500	£31,500	CPE & LPC: fees + £3,500 p.a. maintenance	Life ass, pte health cover, pension scheme, PHI	£41,600
Withers	£27,000	£30,000	CPE & LPC: fees + £4,500 p.a. maintenance, prize for CPE/LPC distinction or commendation	STL, PMI, life ass, Xmas bonus, subsd cafe	£45,000
Wollastons	£20,000	£21,000	LPC: fees	Not known	Not known
Wragge & Co	£21,000 (Birmingham) £28,000 (London)	£24,000 (Birmingham) £31,000 (London)	CPE & LPC: fees + £4,500 p.a. maintenance, prizes for LPC distinction	£1,000 int-free loan, pension, life ass, PHI, travel schemes, PMI, sports & social club, indep fin advice, subsd gym m'ship, Xmas gift	£34,000 (Birmingham) £48,000 (London)

Notes: PHI = Permanent Health Insurance; STL = Season Travel Ticket Loan; PMI = Private Medical Insurance

solicitors

specialist practice areas

banking & finance

Banking and finance covers a multitude of specialist areas, but in essence it is the management and documentation of the movement of money. From straightforward bank loans, through property finance, project finance, capital markets, securitisations and structured loans to leveraged finance involving complex cross-border structures, there's a mass of terminology and concepts that will, at this stage, leave you dazed and confused. But in time, and after exposure to different styles of transaction, you'll soon know your equity from your elbow.

type of work

Some deals follow a well-worn path, never veering from standard-form documentation; others require a great deal more brainpower and break new ground. Here, at the pointy end of finance, lawyers actually assist with the structuring of the deal, as well as ensuring compliance with relevant laws. The job is intellectually challenging, but commercial awareness is just as important. As Richard Kendall, a partner at Ashurst, told us: "*You need an understanding of where the client wants to get to and an understanding of the legal risks involved in getting there.*" This may involve taking security in several jurisdictions and the movement of money across borders, through different currencies and financial products.

Most of the day you'll be at your desk, working on documentation or managing deals; the rest of the time is spent in meetings with clients or other lawyers, either familiarising yourself with the commercial context of the deal, getting involved in the cut and thrust of negotiating its terms, or bringing it to completion. During negotiations, the lawyer must understand when he can compromise and when he must hold out on a point – he will be guided by the client and by a good understanding of market standards.

The type and location of the firm you join will determine your experiences. City firms act for international banks whereas regional firms' work is of a more domestic nature, usually for UK banks and building societies, or the companies they lend to. If you want to be a hotshot in international finance then it's the City for you, and if you want international travel, you're likely to be able to find a job that caters to your wanderlust – though you'll rarely have time to explore the places you visit.

skills needed

...an interest in the City...initiative and quick thinking...comfortable with complex documentation...attention to detail...teamworking...good communicator...stamina...

Richard likes the fact that clients are "*smart, dynamic and demanding.*" It's a challenge working with them and it requires "*intellectual rigour.*" He also enjoys building up longer-term relationships with investment bank clients.

The volume and complexity of the work requires a diligent, organised approach. As for having to be a genius with numbers, Richard told us: "*You'll get the odd have-a-go finance lawyer who'll try and check the formula, but it's best to let the experts do the checking.*" With some types of finance the hours have peaks and troughs; when a deal is building up you might work every weekend for three or four weeks with some all-nighters, but you can see the deals coming and plan for them. With other types, the diet is more regular, and a junior solicitor in a top firm might work 12-hour days with only occasional all-nighters. It's important to pick the right group or department to suit your preferred work pattern, but in all areas you'll have to work hard and you'll need physical stamina.

career options

In City firms there's a greater chance that you'll become specialised early on in your career. This may or may not appeal to you, and if it doesn't then a smaller or regional firm may be a better choice. Secondments to international banks are available from City firms – even for trainees – and, as Richard pointed out, are *an excellent opportunity to view things from a client's perspective.*" Subsequent moves in-house are common, especially for capital markets work or compliance roles to ensure that banks work within financial services regulations. Finally, banking law can be an ideal platform for a career in the financial markets; however, if you already know you want to be a banker, don't waste time training as a lawyer.

LEADING FIRMS FROM CHAMBERS UK 2004-2005

INVESTMENT GRADE/SYNDICATED LENDING
■ LONDON

1. Allen & Overy
   Clifford Chance
2. Linklaters
3. Slaughter and May
   White & Case
4. Ashurst
   Denton Wilde Sapte
   Freshfields Bruckhaus Deringer
   Norton Rose
5. Cleary Gottlieb Steen & Hamilton
   CMS Cameron McKenna
   Herbert Smith
   Lovells

ACQUISITION FINANCE
■ LONDON

1. Allen & Overy
   Clifford Chance
2. Ashurst
   Linklaters
3. Freshfields Bruckhaus Deringer
   Lovells
   Shearman & Sterling
4. Macfarlanes
   White & Case
5. Denton Wilde Sapte
   Herbert Smith
   Latham & Watkins
   Simpson Thacher & Bartlett
   Slaughter and May
   Travers Smith

BANKING & FINANCE: MID-MARKET DEALS
■ LONDON

1. Ashurst
   CMS Cameron McKenna
   DLA
   Lovells
2. Addleshaw Goddard
   Baker & McKenzie
   Berwin Leighton Paisner
   Eversheds
   Macfarlanes
   Simmons & Simmons
   Travers Smith
3. Pinsents
   SJ Berwin
4. Barlow Lyde & Gilbert
   Bird & Bird
   Cleary Gottlieb Steen & Hamilton
   Dechert
   Dickson Minto WS
   Jones Day
   Lawrence Graham
   Osborne Clarke

BANKING & FINANCE
THAMES VALLEY

[1] **Osborne Clarke** Reading
[2] **Pitmans** Reading
[3] **Clarks** Reading
EMW Law Milton Keynes
Howes Percival Milton Keynes
Matthew Arnold & Baldwin Watford
Morgan Cole Oxford
Olswang Thames Valley Reading
Shoosmiths Reading

BANKING & FINANCE
■ SOUTH

[1] **Blake Lapthorn Linnell** Southampton
Bond Pearce Southampton
[2] **asb law** Crawley
Paris Smith & Randall Southampton

BANKING & FINANCE
■ EAST ANGLIA

[1] **Eversheds** Cambridge
Mills & Reeve Norwich
[2] **Taylor Vinters** Cambridge

BANKING & FINANCE
■ SOUTH WEST

[1] **Burges Salmon** Bristol
Osborne Clarke Bristol
[2] **Bond Pearce** Bristol
[3] **Bevan Brittan** Bristol
Rickerbys Cheltenham
[4] **Clarke Willmott** Bristol
Foot Anstey Sargent Plymouth
TLT Bristol

BANKING & FINANCE
■ MIDLANDS

[1] **Eversheds** Birmingham
Pinsents Birmingham
[2] **Wragge & Co** Birmingham
[3] **DLA** Birmingham
Gateley Wareing Birmingham
Hammonds Birmingham
Martineau Johnson Birmingham
[4] **Browne Jacobson** Nottingham
Cobbetts Birmingham
Freeth Cartwright Birmingham

BANKING & FINANCE
■ WALES

[1] **Eversheds** Cardiff
Morgan Cole Cardiff
[2] **Edwards Geldard** Cardiff

BANKING & FINANCE
YORKSHIRE

[1] **Addleshaw Goddard** Leeds
DLA Leeds
Eversheds Leeds
[2] **Hammonds** Leeds
Pinsents Leeds
Walker Morris Leeds

BANKING & FINANCE
■ NORTH WEST

[1] **Addleshaw Goddard** Manchester
DLA Manchester
Eversheds Manchester
[2] **Halliwells** Manchester
Hammonds Manchester
[3] **Cobbetts** Manchester
Pinsents Manchester
[4] **Brabners Chaffe Street** Liverpool
DWF Manchester
Kuit Steinart Levy Manchester

BANKING & FINANCE
■ NORTH EAST

[1] **Dickinson Dees** Newcastle upon Tyne
Eversheds Newcastle upon Tyne
[2] **Robert Muckle** Newcastle upon Tyne
Ward Hadaway Newcastle upon Tyne

competition

The basic aim of both the UK and EU regulatory authorities is to ensure that markets function effectively on the basis of fair and open competition. According to Herbert Smith partner James Quinney, the Competition Act 1998 revolutionised UK domestic competition law. *"Before it came into effect, domestic law was toothless and many companies could safely ignore it. Under the new regime, regulatory bodies have extensive investigation powers – such as carrying out dawn raids – and can impose hefty fines. Now all parts of British business have had to sit up and take notice."* Recently there have been huge fines for a cartel that kept the price of vitamins artificially high, companies alleged to be involved in the price-fixing of replica football shirts, and Argos/Littlewoods, which the OFT found to have fixed the prices of Hasbro toys and games.

type of work

The work can be divided into three main areas: negotiating clearance from the appropriate authorities for acquisitions, mergers and joint ventures; advising on the structuring of commercial or co-operation agreements to ensure they withstand a competition challenge; and dealing with investigations by the regulators into the way a client conducts business (eg, alleged exploitation of customers or cartels). Most lawyers engage in work across all three areas, and typically a mixture of both contentious and non-contentious matters. There are also opportunities to work in more specialised areas such as cross-border trade or anti-dumping (preventing companies exporting a product at a lower price than it normally charges in its home market).

EU and UK competition rules are substantially similar, but the UK bodies concentrate on those rules that have their greatest effect domestically, while the EU authorities deal with matters where the rules affect more than one member state. However, unlike the EU position, individuals can be sent to prison for 5 years for certain breaches of the UK competition regime. In the UK, the main competition institutions are the Office of Fair Trade (OFT), the Competition Commission and the Competition Appeal Tribunal; on matters also affecting other EU countries, it is the European Commission. Additionally, there are industry-specific regulatory bodies, such as Ofcom for the media and telecoms industry. The recently introduced EU Modernisation Programme will allow national bodies to apply EU provisions, a development that may shift the focus from the Commission towards the national regulators.

As a trainee you will conduct plenty of research, perhaps into a particular market or how the authorities have approached a certain type of agreement in the past. It is unlikely that you'll get much independence and even junior lawyers usually work under the close supervision of a partner. As James says: *"It can be a difficult area of the law to dip into. You need a degree of practical day-to-day experience to provide good competition advice, but there are lots of interesting points to latch onto."*

skills needed

... clear, analytical mind...good judgement and confidence...articulate, both orally and on paper... mediation and lobbying skills...attention to detail...numeracy...decisiveness...

As competition law is so diverse, lawyers constantly need to keep on their toes. Says James: *"You need an ability to think laterally. Competition is a broad discipline involving a mix of interesting law, economics and politics. You have to be prepared to learn, and be engaged in more serious academic thought than there would be in a standard corporate law job, where the emphasis is more on doing the deal."*

Competition lawyers also need a high level of

business acumen. As James says: *"You need to have a close relationship with your client, because you have to understand their business. And clients really appreciate it if you can speak their language."* Indeed, one of the attractions of the job is that you get to find out about a range of different industries.

Students who want to learn more about competition law could think about enrolling on a course or possibly studying for a master's degree. James also recommends reading either *The Economics of EC Competition Law* by Simon Bishop and Mike Walker or periodicals such as *EU Competition Law Review* or *Competition Law Journal*. It is also desirable to have a good understanding of economics. As a great deal of business is done in Brussels, fluency in another language can also be useful.

career options

This is a highly competitive area and there will never be as many opportunities available as qualifying trainees wanting jobs. However, it would appear that the government sees the development of competition law as a priority in order to promote UK and EU productivity, so the increase in regulation – and legal work – is set to continue. Moreover, there might be a need for specialist competition advocates to conduct the more important cases before the High Court or Competition Appeal Tribunal. In international law firms, the potential to travel or to be posted abroad is also increasing as more governments across the world are adopting competition and merger laws. As for the regulatory authorities, OFT, for example, has doubled its number of investigators in recent years, so the potential for in-house roles is increasing.

LEADING FIRMS FROM CHAMBERS UK 2004-2005

COMPETITION/ANTI-TRUST
■ LONDON

[1] **Freshfields Bruckhaus Deringer**	**Herbert Smith**
Linklaters	**Slaughter and May**
[2] **Ashurst**	**Lovells**
SJ Berwin	
[3] **Allen & Overy**	**Baker & McKenzie**
Clifford Chance	**Simmons & Simmons**
[4] **Addleshaw Goddard**	**Bristows**
CMS Cameron McKenna	**Denton Wilde Sapte**
Eversheds	**Macfarlanes**
Richards Butler	
[5] **DLA**	**Mayer, Brown, Rowe & Maw**
McDermott Will & Emery	**Norton Rose**
Shearman & Sterling	

COMPETITION/ANTI-TRUST
■ THE SOUTH/SOUTH WEST

[1] **Burges Salmon** Bristol
[2] **Bond Pearce** Plymouth
Osborne Clarke Bristol
TLT Bristol

COMPETITION/ANTI-TRUST
■ MIDLANDS

[1] **Pinsents** Birmingham
[2] **Wragge & Co** Birmingham
[3] **Eversheds** Birmingham
Martineau Johnson Birmingham
Shoosmiths Nottingham

COMPETITION/ANTI-TRUST
■ THE NORTH

[1] **Addleshaw Goddard** Manchester
Eversheds Leeds
[2] **Dickinson Dees** Newcastle upon Tyne

COMPETITION/ANTI-TRUST
■ WALES

[1] **Eversheds** Cardiff
Morgan Cole Cardiff

construction & projects

While some lawyers are happy to deal with intangibles like share offerings and Eurobonds, construction lawyers prefer to spend their time working on the things that actually exist in the real world, be they skyscrapers, shopping centres or sewerage treatment plants. One person for whom the real world holds greater appeal is Bob Maynard, a partner at Berwin Leighton Paisner. "*Sewerage systems may not sound that glamorous, but bad sanitation is the world's biggest killer*," Bob told us. "*And you can see what a difference something like, say, a bridge can make to people's lives – whether they are driving cattle or a Cadillac across it.*" We can indeed...

type of work

Our subject lawyers assist their clients at both the 'procurement end' of construction and engineering projects – ie developing the contractual arrangements that allow things to be built – and the dispute end – picking up the pieces when things go wrong. It is because these arrangements involve so many different parties and continue for a far longer period of time than your average contractual relationship that there is so much scope for difficulties. No wonder, then, that construction features so prominently in contract and tort case law.

Perhaps as a consequence of the amount of time and money spent on resolving disputes, over the last decade the industry has set about adopting a new philosophy, whereby parties work in partnership with each other rather than expecting to have to sue each other at some stage. Furthermore, instead of mammoth, drawn-out court battles, adjudication of disputes has become the industry norm and all contracts now contain mandatory provisions detailing how any dispute will be resolved.

Normally people have a natural bias for contentious or non-contentious work, so if you want to concentrate on one rather than the other, be aware that some firms like their construction lawyers to handle both aspects. *Chambers UK* outlines the nature of the leading construction practices across the country.

skills needed

...attention to detail... excellent drafting... good judgement... down-to-earth attitude... comfortable with technical information... industry background a major boon... stamina... imagination... team worker... good interpersonal skills...

Those who take the non-contentious path will, according to Bob, be faced with "*the challenge of getting the contractual arrangements right*," something which requires a clear understanding of how construction projects work and the interrelationships between parties. You will draft documents that need to account for all the potential problems in a complex, and reasonably long-term, arrangement between a number of parties.

On the contentious side, "*you need particularly good analytical skills as there is always a lot of information to sift through.*" You need to have an affinity with case law and be prepared to keep up to date with the reports as well as industry trends and thinking. Since the Technology and Construction Court introduced its Pre-action Protocol, many more disputes have been resolved through mediation and this, in turn, means more time spent negotiating.

Perhaps more so than in other areas you should expect to spend more of your time with non-lawyers and non-City people. "*I like the clients,*" Bob said; "*they are down-to-earth, unstuffy people. They are people who build things.*" You could be dealing with technical individuals, such as geotechnical and structural engineers, or creative types – architects and designers – or even the owners of small construction companies who have been on and off building sites since their first day as an apprentice brickie. As a lawyer, you'll probably never be regarded as 'one of them', but relationship building is frequently as important as legal knowledge for winning and keeping clients.

career options

Nearly all international construction and engineering projects are governed (to varying degrees) by English or New York law, which means that experience in this field is internationally marketable. Those who make a name for themselves in top-end arbitration may get the chance to take on work in places like Hong Kong and Singapore.

Back on home turf, and for those looking to get out of private practice, many companies in the construction industry have lawyers working in-house, be this as a general corporate counsel or as a litigator.

Construction law isn't a subject that bewitches many students – certainly not like environment or competition law – but it can become rather appealing once they've sampled it in practice. Anyone coming from a science or engineering academic background, or those who've had some direct experience of the construction industry, tend to see the potential of the area more readily, and these people are certainly very attractive to the profession.

LEADING FIRMS FROM CHAMBERS UK 2004-2005

PROJECTS
■ **LONDON**

1. **Allen & Overy**
   Clifford Chance
   Linklaters
   Shearman & Sterling
2. **Freshfields Bruckhaus Deringer**
   Milbank, Tweed, Hadley & McCloy
   Norton Rose
   White & Case
3. **Denton Wilde Sapte**
   Herbert Smith
   Trowers & Hamlins
4. **Baker & McKenzie**
   CMS Cameron McKenna
   Dewey Ballantine
5. **Cadwalader, Wickersham & Taft**
   Chadbourne & Parke
   Latham & Watkins
   LeBoeuf, Lamb, Greene & MacRae
   Vinson & Elkins

CONSTRUCTION
■ **THE SOUTH**

1. **Shadbolt & Co** Reigate
2. **Blake Lapthorn Linnell** Southampton
   Cripps Harries Hall Tunbridge Wells
   Lester Aldridge Bournemouth
3. **Charles Russell** Guildford
   DMH Brighton
   Thomas Eggar Reigate

CONSTRUCTION
■ **THAMES VALLEY**

1. **Blake Lapthorn Linnell** Oxford
   Clarks Reading
   Morgan Cole Reading
2. **Boyes Turner** Reading
   Henmans Oxford

CONSTRUCTION
■ **EAST ANGLIA**

1. **Mills & Reeve** Cambridge
2. **Eversheds** Cambridge
3. **Greenwoods Solicitors** Peterborough
   Hewitsons Cambridge

CONSTRUCTION
■ **SOUTH WEST**

1. **Bevan Brittan** Bristol
   Masons Bristol
   Osborne Clarke Bristol
2. **Ashfords** Exeter
   Beachcroft Wansbroughs Bristol
   Burges Salmon Bristol
3. **Bond Pearce** Plymouth
   Clarke Willmott Bristol
   Veale Wasbrough Bristol
   Withy King Bath

CONSTRUCTION
■ **WALES**

1. **Eversheds** Cardiff
2. **Hugh James** Cardiff
   Morgan Cole Cardiff

CONSTRUCTION: MAINLY SUPPLIER LED
■ LONDON

1. **Masons**
2. **CMS Cameron McKenna**
   Fenwick Elliott
   Mayer, Brown, Rowe & Maw
   Shadbolt & Co
3. **Beale and Company**
   Berrymans Lace Mawer
   Kennedys
   Winward Fearon
4. **Barlow Lyde & Gilbert**
   Corbett & Co Teddington
   Davies Arnold Cooper
   Glovers
   Kingsley Napley
   Lane & Partners
   Reynolds Porter Chamberlain

CONSTRUCTION
■ MIDLANDS

1. **Wragge & Co** Birmingham
2. **Gateley Wareing** Birmingham
   Hammonds Birmingham
3. **Eversheds** Birmingham
   Freeth Cartwright Nottingham
   Pinsents Birmingham
4. **Beachcroft Wansbroughs** B'ham
   Cobbetts Birmingham
   DLA Birmingham
   Martineau Johnson Birmingham
5. **Edwards Geldard** Derby
   Nelsons Derby
   Putsman.wlc Birmingham
   Wright Hassall Leamington Spa

CONSTRUCTION
■ NORTH WEST

1. **Hammonds** Manchester
   Masons Manchester
2. **Addleshaw Goddard** Manchester
   Halliwells Manchester
   Mace & Jones Manchester
3. **DLA** Liverpool
   Eversheds Manchester
   Hill Dickinson Liverpool
4. **Beachcroft Wansbroughs** Manchester
   Cobbetts Manchester
   DWF Manchester

CONSTRUCTION
■ YORKSHIRE

1. **Addleshaw Goddard** Leeds
   Hammonds Leeds
2. **Masons** Leeds
3. **DLA** Leeds
   Eversheds Leeds
   Pinsents Leeds
4. **Denison Till** York
   Hawkswell Kilvington P'ship Leeds
   Walker Morris Leeds

CONSTRUCTION
■ NORTH EAST

1. **Dickinson Dees** Newcastle upon Tyne
   Watson Burton Newcastle upon Tyne
2. **Eversheds** Newcastle upon Tyne
3. **Hay & Kilner** Newcastle upon Tyne
   Ward Hadaway Newcastle upon Tyne

CONSTRUCTION: MAINLY PURCHASER LED
■ NATIONAL

1. **Allen & Overy**
   Berwin Leighton Paisner
   Clifford Chance
   Herbert Smith
   Linklaters
2. **Ashurst**
   Freshfields Bruckhaus Deringer
   Lovells
   Macfarlanes
   Norton Rose
   Trowers & Hamlins
3. **Addleshaw Goddard**
   Baker & McKenzie
   Campbell Hooper
   Denton Wilde Sapte
   Eversheds
   Hammonds
   Lewis Silkin
   Nabarro Nathanson
   Nicholson Graham & Jones
   Simmons & Simmons
   Taylor Wessing
4. **Clyde & Co**
   Field Fisher Waterhouse
   Fladgate Fielder
   Lawrence Graham
   SJ Berwin
   Slaughter and May
   Wedlake Bell

corporate law

It's the beating heart of most commercial firms, but in corporate departments top salaries and big deals accompany long hours. Large City firms act for companies listed on stock exchanges, while smaller City and regional firms tend to advise leading regional private companies and a handful of the FTSE 250. There are other differences, most notably extended hours and reduced chances for junior lawyers to take on significant responsibility in the largest City firms.

type of work

You'll have heard many of the terms: mergers and acquisitions (M&A); corporate restructurings; going public; rights issues; venture capital; MBOs. Soon enough this foreign lexicon will become familiar – at base, it all relates to the buying, selling and financing of businesses. And because all deals are interlinked with finance we have the umbrella term 'corporate finance'.

Here's an example. A company wants to buy a smaller competitor's business and needs to get the money together to do so. It might restructure its own business, disposing of certain assets it no longer requires. If it is a privately owned company (not listed on a stock exchange), it could raise money by becoming listed and offering shares to the public and institutional investors. If it is already a publicly listed company, it could offer new shares for sale. Alternatively it could raise money via debt; eg loans from the market (bonds) or from banks.

Or how about a company that hasn't been performing as well as it could. Let's say its management team believe they could do a better job if they owned the company. Bring on the private equity lawyer, a breed of corporate lawyer that helps his client to complete a management buyout (MBO). Most of the time the management team doesn't actually have enough money to do the deal, hence the involvement of a private equity company – an investor looking to

back the business for a healthy return and usually an influence in decision making.

The key phases to any type of deal are: negotiating and drafting the agreements; arranging financing; and carrying out 'due diligence', which is an investigation exercise to verify the accuracy of information passed from the purchase target to the buyer, or from the company raising money to the funder. We spoke to one of the City's top corporate lawyers, Charles Martin of Macfarlanes. He told us that transaction management was increasingly being influenced by US practices, particularly the due diligence phase, which he likened to "carpet-bombing – everything is looked at now and documentation is longer." To put this in context, Charles believes that after Enron, the dot.com crash and scandals involving City analysts, the role of the legal advisor in business transactions and corporate affairs has never been more important.

skills needed

...good all-rounder...stamina...can handle demanding, intelligent clients...commercially savvy...decisive and confident...tact and clear communication...eye for detail...organised...

The role is mainly transactional, but you may also be the first port of call for the client. And what of the idea that corporate lawyers are deal doers who know little 'pure' law? Actually, you need to be conversant in a variety of disciplines, and know when to refer matters to a specialist in, say, merger control, employment or tax.

Contrast the transactional lawyer's job with that of a litigator. The litigator is instructed only when a client has a problem, which he then has to resolve by relying on technical legal issues and procedures. Those who gain greater satisfaction from enabling a venture to reach fruition might find the idea of a life spent resolving disputes about as appealing as a career in an aspirin-packing factory.

Team spirit is essential and it will get you through a deal. Working three 20-hour days in a row may be rare, but it does happen. *"The hours are very lump*y," Charles admitted, *"but there's no point in fighting it; you just have to enjoy the peaks and troughs."* The long hours arise through client demand, and their expectations have risen as instant communication via mobile phones, e-mail and now BlackBerry has exploded. But being surrounded by busy, intelligent, high-achieving people is half of the appeal, Charles explained.

A robust and confident manner is typical in this field. Softies take note: stamina and good health are a must because you simply can't duck off home or pull a sicky whenever you need to; you have to keep pushing yourself because the deals wait for no one.

career options

As the new millennium fireworks fizzled, corporate departments became unnervingly quiet. The oomph had gone from the market. Jobs were lost. It was a reminder that the fortunes of corporate lawyers are tied to the general economy. There's a sense that things are picking up now but, even so, keep your fingers crossed for a boom when you qualify in 2009. Many trainee lawyers head for the City, assuming that there is nothing of worth in the regions. While regional firms do usually work on lower-value matters, the best ones are winning a number of important instructions, some with a cross-border element. If you do want international work in the regions or a smaller London firm then judge a practice by its overseas offices, associations and client base. *Chambers UK* should give you a few pointers.

A sound grounding in corporate finance makes an excellent springboard for working in industry. Lawyers move in-house to major companies, tempted by decent hours and salaries. Some go to banks, usually as in-house lawyers, occasionally as corporate finance execs or analysts. Company secretarial positions suit lawyers with a taste for internal management and compliance issues.

If you have a hunch that you want to be a corporate lawyer, why not try Charles' foolproof home-testing method: *"Read the City pages in your newspaper. It's not going to do it for you in the first two weeks, but if after six to nine months you are still basically not interested, then this job is not for you."* Simple.

LEADING FIRMS FROM CHAMBERS UK 2004-2005

CORPORATE FINANCE: LARGER DEALS/ LARGER RESOURCES
1 **Freshfields Bruckhaus Deringer**
  Linklaters
  Slaughter and May
2 **Allen & Overy**
  Clifford Chance
  Herbert Smith

CORPORATE FINANCE: LARGER DEALS/ MEDIUM RESOURCES
■ LONDON
1 **Ashurst**
2 **Lovells**
  Macfarlanes
3 **Norton Rose**
  Simmons & Simmons
4 **CMS Cameron McKenna**
  Shearman & Sterling
  Weil, Gotshal & Manges
5 **Skadden, Arps, Slate, Meagher**

CORPORATE FINANCE
■ EAST ANGLIA
1 **Eversheds** Norwich
  Mills & Reeve Norwich
2 **Hewitsons** Cambridge
  Taylor Vinters Cambridge
3 **Birketts** Ipswich
  Prettys Ipswich
4 **Greene & Greene** Bury St Edmunds
  Greenwoods Solicitors Peterborough
  Howes Percival Norwich
  Taylor Wessing Cambridge

CORPORATE FINANCE: MID-MARKET DEALS/ LARGER RESOURCES
■ LONDON

[1] Baker & McKenzie
Jones Day
Mayer, Brown, Rowe & Maw
Travers Smith
White & Case
[2] Addleshaw Goddard
Berwin Leighton Paisner
Denton Wilde Sapte
Lawrence Graham
[3] DLA
Eversheds
Field Fisher Waterhouse
McDermott Will & Emery
Nicholson Graham & Jones
SJ Berwin
[4] Charles Russell
Lewis Silkin
Nabarro Nathanson
Olswang
Taylor Wessing
[5] Dechert
Hammonds
Stephenson Harwood

CORPORATE FINANCE SOUTH WEST:
■ DEVON & CORNWALL

[1] Ashfords Exeter
Bond Pearce Exeter, Plymouth
[2] Foot Anstey Sargent Plymouth
Michelmores Exeter

CORPORATE FINANCE: MID-MARKET DEALS/ MEDIUM RESOURCES
■ LONDON

[1] Faegre Benson Hobson Audley
Memery Crystal
Reed Smith
[2] Bird & Bird
Osborne Clarke
Richards Butler
[3] Barlow Lyde & Gilbert
Clyde & Co
Fox Williams
Harbottle & Lewis
Marriott Harrison
Reynolds Porter Chamberlain
[4] Beachcroft Wansbroughs
Finers Stephens Innocent
Howard Kennedy
Pinsents
Watson, Farley & Williams

CORPORATE FINANCE
■ THE SOUTH: KENT & SUSSEX

[1] asb law Crawley
Cripps Harries Hall Tunbridge Wells
Davies Lavery Maidstone
Rawlison Butler Crawley
Thomas Eggar Worthing
Thomson Snell Tunbridge Wells
[2] Brachers Maidstone
Clarkson Wright & Jakes Orpington
DMH Crawley
[3] Mundays Cobham

CORPORATE FINANCE SOUTH WEST:
■ BRISTOL & SURROUND

[1] Burges Salmon Bristol
Osborne Clarke Bristol
[2] TLT Solicitors Bristol
[3] Bond Pearce Bristol
BPE Solicitors Cheltenham
Charles Russell Cheltenham
Clark Holt Swindon
[4] Bevan Brittan Bristol
Clarke Willmott Bristol
Rickerbys Cheltenham
Veale Wasbrough Lawyers Bristol
[5] Laytons Bristol
Lyons Davidson Bristol
Thring Townsend Bath, Swindon
Withy King Bath, Swindon

CORPORATE FINANCE
■ THAMES VALLEY

[1] Osborne Clarke Reading
[2] Manches Oxford
Nabarro Nathanson Reading
Pitmans Reading
Shoosmiths Reading
[3] Boyes Turner Reading
Clarks Reading
Howes Percival Milton Keynes
Kimbells Milton Keynes
Wilmer Cutler Pickering Oxford
[4] Darbys Oxford
EMW Law Milton Keynes
Field Seymour Parkes Reading
Moorcrofts Marlow

CORPORATE FINANCE
■ NORTH WEST

1. **Addleshaw Goddard** Manchester
   DLA Manchester
   Eversheds Manchester
2. **Halliwells** Manchester
   Hammonds Manchester
3. **Brabners Chaffe Street** Manchester
   Cobbetts Manchester
   Kuit Steinart Levy Manchester
   Pannone & Partners Manchester
   Pinsents Manchester
4. **Beachcroft Wansbroughs** Manchstr
   DWF Manchester
   Nexus Solicitors Manchester
5. **Wacks Caller** Manchester

CORPORATE FINANCE
■ THE SOUTH: SURREY, HAMPSHIRE & DORSET

1. **Blake Lapthorn Linnell** Fareham
   Bond Pearce Southampton
   Stevens & Bolton Guildford
2. **Clyde & Co** Guildford
   Lester Aldridge Southampton
   Paris Smith & Randall Southampton
   Penningtons Basingstoke, Godalming
   Shadbolt & Co Reigate
   Shoosmiths Fareham
3. **Coffin Mew & Clover** Southampton
   Lamport Bassitt Southampton
   Moore & Blatch Southampton

CORPORATE FINANCE
■ NORTH EAST

1. **Dickinson Dees** Stockton on Tees
2. **Eversheds** Newcastle upon Tyne
   Ward Hadaway Newcastle upon Tyne
3. **Robert Muckle** Newcastle upon Tyne
4. **Hay & Kilner** Newcastle upon Tyne
   Watson Burton Newcastle upon Tyne

CORPORATE FINANCE
■ YORKSHIRE

1. **Addleshaw Goddard** Leeds
   DLA Leeds
2. **Eversheds** Leeds
   Walker Morris Leeds
3. **Gordons** Bradford
   Hammonds Leeds
   Pinsents Leeds
4. **Andrew M Jackson** Hull
   Cobbetts Leeds
   Irwin Mitchell Leeds
   Lupton Fawcett Leeds
5. **Denison Till** York
   Gosschalks Hull
   Keeble Hawson Sheffield
   Lee & Priestley Leeds
   McCormicks Leeds
   Rollits Hull
   Schofield Sweeney Bradford
   Wake Smith Sheffield
6. **HLW** Sheffield

CORPORATE FINANCE
■ WALES

1. **Edwards Geldard** Cardiff
   Eversheds Cardiff
2. **M and A Solicitors** Cardiff
   Morgan Cole Cardiff
3. **Berry Smith** Cardiff
   Capital Law Cardiff Bay
   Dolmans Cardiff

CORPORATE FINANCE
■ EAST MIDLANDS

1. **Browne Jacobson** Nottingham
   Eversheds Nottingham
2. **Freeth Cartwright** Nottingham
   Gateley Wareing Nottingham
   Shoosmiths Nottingham
3. **Edwards Geldard** Derby
   Hewitsons Northampton
   Howes Percival Northampton

CORPORATE FINANCE
■ WEST MIDLANDS

1. **Wragge & Co** Birmingham
2. **Eversheds** Birmingham
   Pinsents Birmingham
3. **DLA** Birmingham
   Gateley Wareing Birmingham
   Hammonds Birmingham
4. **Cobbetts** Birmingham
   Heatons Birmingham
   Martineau Johnson Birmingham

crime

Criminal solicitors act for defendants in cases brought before the criminal courts. Lesser offences are usually dealt with exclusively by solicitors in the magistrates' courts, while for more serious charges in the Crown Courts, most defendants still prefer a barrister to conduct the advocacy.

type of work

general crime: For most lawyers, 'everyday crime' is their staple. Jae Carwardine at London firm Russell-Cooke, says: "*Diversity is the appeal of the job – you really don't know what each day is going to present you with.*" A hectic schedule of visits to police stations, prisons and magistrates' courts, plenty of face-to-face client meetings and advocacy means this is definitely not a desk job. The work is date-driven and cases have a fast turnover; lawyers who are accredited to work as Duty Solicitors in the magistrates' courts are certainly likely to see the fruits of their labour quickly.

Criminal law has evolved rapidly over the past decade, evidenced by a succession of Crime Bills. With changes in mode of trial issues, the handling of youth work, sexual offences, a new Proceeds of Crime Act and of course the Human Rights Act, Jae says it is essential that you keep up to date on changes. She also notes that "*the abolition of means testing is diminishing private work greatly – the number of people eligible for legal aid has significantly increased.*"

criminal fraud: Jae explained the difference between this and everyday crime: "*It involves mountains of paperwork and analysis of figures – you need to understand business operations.*" Fraud specialists usually have a much smaller caseload, but cases can run for years. A limited number of firms undertake this work.

skills needed...

...an eye for detail...sharp and resolute on your feet...excellent people skills...empathy...good organisational and IT skills...100% commitment...

Trainees used to be thrown in at the deep end, but the Law Society's accreditation process now means that, until accredited, they cannot attend police station interviews by themselves, nor make magistrates' court appearances. Once accredited, they will start with simple hearings to build confidence. Jae says: "*You have to be confident because it is nerve-racking – no one ever forgets their first bail application!*"

In court or at the station, the ability to think on one's feet, analyse matters quickly and deal with last-minute evidence or unexpected changes is key. And when handling casework, you will be looking for the things others have missed, so a questioning mind is essential, especially when faced with forensic or medical evidence, or a number of expert witnesses.

Criminal clients can be challenging: they may come from deprived backgrounds or have drink, drug and/or psychiatric problems, so "*accomplished people skills*" are essential. The need to maintain a professional stance is also vital, but Jae notes: "*You build very strong relationships with clients; you get to know the whole family, and receive Christmas cards. People never forget you because you are their lifeline.*"

There's a certain camaraderie amongst criminal solicitors as they're always meeting in police stations and courts, and they have a 'common enemy', so to speak, in the CPS. However, Jae warns: "*You do have to be quite thick-skinned; be prepared to be humiliated in public, and take it.*" This is not law for the fainthearted; "*If you are desperately shy, it probably won't work for you.*"

Criminal lawyers need to be able to deal with stress. Jae advised: "*This is a job for someone who really enjoys hard work and is committed. There is huge job satisfaction, but without great remuneration."* If a fat-cat salary is your biggest priority, reconsider now before it's too late...

career options

In 2001, the Legal Services Commission introduced a franchise system limiting the number of firms that handle publicly funded criminal defence. Changes in 2004 are expected to limit that number still further. To find the best criminal firms, look at our parent publication, *Chambers UK*, or alternatively ask a Citizens Advice Bureau or your local Law Society to recommend crime specialists. Training contracts at firms handling specialist or high-profile work are rare, but general crime firms will have more openings. Some lawyers actively promote the idea of trying paralegal work or outdoor clerking before applying for a training contract. Various government bodies such as the Serious Fraud Office or Customs provide a more prosecution-based approach, while work in the voluntary sector is a practical way to gain a realistic view of people and real life. Refer to page 14 for info on the CPS.

LEADING FIRMS FROM CHAMBERS UK 2004-2005

CRIME
■ LONDON

[1] **Bindman & Partners**
Edward Fail Bradshaw & Waterson
Taylor Nichol

[2] **BCL Burton Copeland**
Edwards Duthie
Hodge Jones & Allen
Saunders & Co
TV Edwards

[3] **Andrew Keenan & Co**
Hallinan, Blackburn, Gittings & Nott
Iliffes Booth Bennett (IBB) Uxbridge
McCormacks
Simons Muirhead & Burton
Victor Lissack, Roscoe & Coleman

[4] **Alistair Meldrum & Co** Enfield
Birds Solicitors
Galbraith Branley & Co
Moss & Co
Peters & Peters
Russell-Cooke
Whitelock & Storr

Birnberg Peirce & Partners
Kingsley Napley
Tuckers

Corker Binning Solicitors
Henry Milner & Co
Powell Spencer & Partners
TNT Solicitors (Thaki Novy Taube)

Fisher Meredith
Hickman & Rose
Kaim Todner
Russell Jones & Walker
Stokoe Partnership

Bark & Co
Claude Hornby & Cox
Joy Merriam & Co
Murray & Co
Reynolds Dawson
Venters Solicitors

FRAUD: CRIMINAL
■ LONDON

[1] **BCL Burton Copeland**
Kingsley Napley
Peters & Peters

[2] **Corker Binning Solicitors**
Irwin Mitchell

[3] **Byrne & Partners**
Russell Jones & Walker
Simons Muirhead & Burton

[4] **Claude Hornby & Cox**
Garstangs
Tarlo Lyons
Victor Lissack, Roscoe & Coleman

FRAUD: CRIMINAL
■ THE SOUTH/SOUTH WEST

[1] **Blake Lapthorn Linnell**
Hodkinsons Solicitors Locks Heath

[2] **Bobbetts Mackan** Bristol

CRIME
■ THE SOUTH

[1] **Blake Lapthorn Linnell** Fareham
Clarke Kiernan Tunbridge Wells
Coffin Mew & Clover Fareham
Knights Tunbridge Wells

CRIME
■ SOUTH WEST

1 **Bobbetts Mackan** Bristol
   Douglas & Partners Bristol
   Kelcey & Hall Bristol
   Sansbury Campbell Bristol
2 **Nunn Rickard Advocates** Exeter
   Russell Jones & Walker Bristol
   St James Solicitors Exeter
   Stone King Bath
   Walker Lahive Plymouth
3 **Aidan Woods & Co** Bristol
   Allen & Partners Bristol
   Bay Advocates Torquay
   Stones Exeter
   WBW Solicitors Newton Abbot

CRIME
■ MIDLANDS

1 **Cartwright King** Nottingham
   Fletchers Nottingham
   The Johnson Partnership Nottingham
2 **Glaisyers** Birmingham
   Kieran Clarke Solicitors Chesterfield
   Nelsons Nottingham
3 **Banner Jones Middleton** Chesterfield
   Barrie Ward & Julian Griffiths Nottingham
   Elliot Mather Chesterfield
   Jonas Roy Bloom Birmingham
   Lanyon Bowdler Telford
   Purcell Parker Birmingham
   Richard Nelson Solicitors Nottingham
   The Smith Partnership Derby
   Tyndallwoods Birmingham
   Varley Hadley Siddall Nottingham
   Woodford-Robinson Northampton

FRAUD: CRIMINAL
■ MIDLANDS

1 **Cartwright King** Nottingham
   Richard Nelson Solicitors Nottingham
2 **Glaisyers** Birmingham
   Nelsons Nottingham

CRIME
■ EAST ANGLIA

1 **Belmores** Norwich
   Hatch Brenner Norwich
   TMK Solicitors Southend-on-Sea
2 **David Charnley & Co** Romford
   Hunt & Coombs Peterborough
   Lucas & Wyllys Great Yarmouth
   Norton Peskett Lowestoft
   TNT Solicitors Harlow
3 **Cole Bentley & Co** Great Yarmouth
   Copleys Huntingdon
   Fosters Norwich
   Gepp & Sons Chelmsford
   Greenwoods Solicitors Peterborough
   Hegarty & Co Solicitors Peterborough

FRAUD: CRIMINAL
■ THE NORTH

1 **Cooper Kenyon Burrows** Manchester
2 **Pannone & Partners** Manchester
3 **Betesh Fox & Co** Manchester
   David Hanman Associates Manchester
   DLA Manchester
   Irwin Mitchell Sheffield
4 **Burton Copeland** Manchester
   Hill Dickinson Manchester
   Russell Jones & Walker Manchester

CRIME
■ NORTH EAST

1 **David Gray Solicitors** Newcastle
   Irwin Mitchell Sheffield
   McCormicks Leeds
   Sugaré & Co Leeds
2 **Grahame Stowe, Bateson** Leeds
   Henry Hyams Leeds
   Howells Cardiff
   Lester Morrill Leeds
   Levi & Co Leeds
   The Max Gold Partnership Hull
   Williamsons Solicitors Hull

CRIME
■ NORTH WEST

1 **Brian Koffman & Co** Manchester
   Burton Copeland Liverpool
   Draycott Browne Manchester
   JMW Solicitors Manchester
   Tuckers Manchester
2 **Betesh Fox & Co** Manchester
   Cunninghams Manchester
   Farleys Blackburn
   Forbes Blackburn
   Maidments Manchester
   Olliers Manchester
3 **Cobleys** Salford
   Kristina Harrison Solicitors Salford
   Pearson Fielding Partnership Liverpool
   RM Broudie & Co Liverpool
   Rowlands Manchester
   Russell & Russell Bolton

CRIME
■ WALES

1 **Gamlins** Rhyl
   Huttons Cardiff
   Martyn Prowel Solicitors Cardiff
2 **Clarke & Hartland** Cardiff
   Colin Jones Barry
   Douglas-Jones Mercer Swansea
   Goldstones Swansea
   Harding Evans Newport
   Howe & Spender Port Talbot
   Hugh James Blackwood
   Robertsons Cardiff
   Savery Pennington Cardiff
   Spiro Grech & Harding Roberts Cardiff
   Wilson Devonald Swansea

FRAUD: CRIMINAL
■ WALES

1 **Martyn Prowel Solicitors** Cardiff
   Roy Morgan & Co Cardiff

employment law

It's a current hot favourite with trainees, but is employment law the tamagotchi craze of the profession or is it destined to endure as one of the most engaging areas of legal practice? If the rapidity with which the body of law is changing and expanding means anything, then it is likely that employment lawyers will have plenty of work to keep them busy and interested for a long time to come.

type of work

Employment lawyers are intimately involved in the relationships between employers and employees. For employers they offer precautionary advice, negotiate senior level staff exits, and limit the damage when things go wrong and disgruntled ex-employees bring claims for, say, unfair dismissal or discrimination. For employees they can be pillars of strength, helping to secure sometimes life-changing tribunal decisions or assisting in contract negotiations. Some lawyers have particularly close ties with trade unions, or act for employers dealing with broader labour issues.

When picking a firm, decide whether you have a strong preference for acting for employees (applicants) or employers (respondents), or perhaps unions. Similarly, do you want your work to be primarily contentious or non-contentious? Certain firms work along partisan lines; others like Mike Burd's firm Lewis Silkin believe that the best employment lawyers become well rounded through exposure to all aspects of practice. Mike puts much of the appeal of the job down to "*shifting gears between hugely differing roles*." Additionally, "*every case is a drama with its own cast of characters – it's like going to the theatre every time*." But, a word of warning: some (although not all) of the very big commercial firms offer a heavy diet of 'corporate support' work to their employment lawyers, effec-tively rendering them mere ancillaries to the gun-slinging deal doers of the corporate department.

skills needed

...being a 'people' person...emotional intelligence tempered by commerciality...communication and negotiation skills...a talent for advocacy...practicality... quick assimilation of changes in strategy and advice...detailed knowledge of relevant law...

Flexibility and rapid response are vital. Mike explained that on the contentious side problems flare up unpredictably and need to be resolved quickly. "*It's a rare day when my plans are not blown out of the water. I might be drafting complex bonus provisions for an executive and end up on the phone to the chief exec of a company who has just been sacked and wants to see me urgently*." Of course you have to be good with people, but it's more than that: "*You have to be sanguine about the foibles of human beings...which can be endless!*" You also need to know when to be tough, particularly in negotiations with other lawyers. As for advocacy, this is where bared teeth and hardball tactics will work against you: employment tribunals are less formal and less legalistic in their language and procedure than normal court hearings.

career options

After a hard-core trainee seat in corporate, where one's role is essentially that of a remora fish, employment can be a reminder of what you thought the law was all about when still an idealistic student. It's usually easier to relate to the case scenario – by then you'll have been an employee yourself – and lawyers in this field are amongst the most pleasant in the profession. Factor in the never-a-dull-day aspect to the job and it's no wonder NQs are queuing around the block for the few jobs that crop up. Unless you can cast a spell over the head of department, you'd be well advised to steal a march on peers by ensuring that your training is fulsome, and perhaps supplemented by voluntary work at a CAB, law centre or FRU. With these organisations there's even a chance you might get some tribunal experience. If your employment seat combines pensions and employment law, and the emphasis is on the P and not the E, then this extra-curricular activity could make all the difference.

In the dozen or so years since employment law has become a specialist practice area, the number of practitioners has mushroomed, both in private prac-tice and in-house at larger companies – eg Warner Bros, M&S and Shell, for example. And if the law doesn't do it for you, you could sidestep into HR. If it's just fee earning that you've had enough of, a know-how position could see you collating and explaining the avalanche of new legislation and regulations to your colleagues in a law firm, a task Mike likens to *"playing 30 games of chess, blindfold, every day!"*

Chambers UK will give you information about the nature of the work and the clients of the best employ-ment law practices across the country.

LEADING FIRMS FROM CHAMBERS UK 2004-2005

EMPLOYMENT
■ THE SOUTH

1 **Blake Lapthorn Linnell** Fareham
DMH Crawley
2 **asb law** Crawley
Bond Pearce Southampton
Charles Russell Guildford
Clyde & Co Guildford
Cripps Harries Hall Tunbridge Wells
Paris Smith & Randall Southampton
Stevens & Bolton Guildford
3 **Brachers** Maidstone
Clarkson Wright & Jakes Orpington
Coffin Mew & Clover Southampton
Lamport Bassitt Southampton
Lester Aldridge Southampton
Moore & Blatch Southampton
Mundays Cobham
Pattinson & Brewer Chatham
Rawlison Butler Crawley
Sherrards Haywards Heath
Thomas Eggar Chichester
Thomson Snell Tunbridge Wells

EMPLOYMENT
■ THAMES VALLEY

1 **Clarks** Reading
2 **Olswang** Reading
Osborne Clarke Reading
3 **Henmans** Oxford
Manches Oxford
Morgan Cole Reading
Pitmans Reading
4 **Pictons** St Albans
Shoosmiths Reading

EMPLOYMENT
■ SOUTH WEST

1 **Ashfords** Exeter
Bevan Brittan Bristol
Burges Salmon Bristol
Osborne Clarke Bristol
2 **Bond Pearce** Plymouth
Veale Wasbrough Bristol
3 **Burroughs Day** Bristol
Clarke Willmott Taunton
TLT Bristol
4 **Lyons Davidson** Bristol
Rickerbys Cheltenham
Thompsons Bristol
Withy King Bath
5 **Beachcroft Wansbroughs** Bristol
Bevans Bristol
BPE Solicitors Cheltenham
Charles Russell Cheltenham
Michelmores Exeter
Pattinson & Brewer Bristol
Stephens & Scown Exeter
Thring Townsend Bath
Wolferstans Plymouth

EMPLOYMENT:
MAINLY RESPONDENT
■ LONDON

[1] Allen & Overy	Simmons & Simmons
[2] Baker & McKenzie	Herbert Smith
Lewis Silkin	Lovells
Mayer, Brown, Rowe & Maw	McDermott Will & Emery
[3] Beachcroft Wansbroughs	Charles Russell
Clifford Chance	CMS Cameron McKenna
Dechert	Eversheds
Fox Williams	Hammonds
Linklaters	Olswang
[4] Addleshaw Goddard	Denton Wilde Sapte
Farrer & Co	Freshfields Bruckhaus Deringer
Macfarlanes	Nabarro Nathanson
Travers Smith	
[5] Ashurst	Barlow Lyde & Gilbert
Berwin Leighton Paisner	Bird & Bird
Masons	Osborne Clarke
Salans	SJ Berwin
Slaughter and May	Taylor Wessing
[6] Archon	Doyle Clayton
Lawrence Graham	Mishcon de Reya
Norton Rose	Pinsents
Speechly Bircham	Stephenson Harwood
Withers	

EMPLOYMENT:
MAINLY APPLICANT
■ LONDON

[1] Russell Jones & Walker
[2] Pattinson & Brewer
Thompsons
[3] Bindman & Partners
Irwin Mitchell
Rowley Ashworth

EMPLOYMENT
■ MIDLANDS

[1] **Eversheds** Nottingham
Wragge & Co Birmingham
[2] **Hammonds** Birmingham
Martineau Johnson Birmingham
Pinsents Birmingham
[3] **Bevan Brittan** Bristol
Browne Jacobson Nottingham
Cobbetts Birmingham
DLA Birmingham
Gateley Wareing Birmingham
[4] **Freeth Cartwright** Nottingham
Higgs & Sons Brierley Hill
Shakespeares Birmingham
Shoosmiths Birmingham

EMPLOYMENT
■ EAST ANGLIA

[1] **Eversheds** Cambridge
Mills & Reeve Cambridge
[2] **Greenwoods Solicitors** Peterborough
Hewitsons Cambridge
Taylor Vinters Cambridge
[3] **Hegarty & Co Solicitors** Peterborough
Steeles Norwich
[4] **Ashton Graham** Ipswich
Prettys Ipswich
Wollastons Chelmsford

EMPLOYMENT
■ WALES

[1] **Eversheds** Cardiff
[2] **Edwards Geldard** Cardiff
Morgan Cole Cardiff
[3] **Hugh James** Cardiff
Russell Jones & Walker Cardiff
[4] **Capital Law** Cardiff Bay
Dolmans Cardiff
Harding Evans Newport

EMPLOYMENT
■ NORTH WEST

1. **Addleshaw Goddard** Manchester
   Eversheds Manchester
   Hammonds Manchester
2. **Cobbetts** Manchester
   DLA Manchester
   DWF Manchester
   Mace & Jones Manchester
3. **Brabners Chaffe Street** Manchester
   Halliwells Manchester
   Pannone & Partners Manchester
   Thompsons Manchester
4. **Berg & Co** Manchester
   Burnetts Carlisle
   Hill Dickinson Liverpool
   Keoghs Bolton
   Weightmans Liverpool
   Whittles Manchester

EMPLOYMENT
■ NORTH EAST

1. **Dickinson Dees** Newcastle upon Tyne
   Eversheds Newcastle upon Tyne
2. **Crutes** Newcastle upon Tyne
   Jacksons Stockton on Tees
   Robert Muckle Newcastle upon Tyne
   Samuel Phillips & Co Newcastle upon Tyne
   Short Richardson & Forth Newcastle
   Thompsons Newcastle upon Tyne
   Ward Hadaway Newcastle upon Tyne
   Watson Burton Newcastle upon Tyne
3. **Archers** Stockton on Tees
   Hay & Kilner Newcastle upon Tyne

EMPLOYMENT
■ YORKSHIRE

1. **Pinsents** Leeds
2. **Addleshaw Goddard** Leeds
   DLA Leeds
   Eversheds Leeds
3. **Cobbetts** Leeds
   Ford & Warren Leeds
   Hammonds Leeds
   Walker Morris Leeds
4. **Irwin Mitchell** Sheffield
   Lupton Fawcett Leeds
   Rollits Hull
   Wake Smith Sheffield

environmental law

Typically acting for corporate clients seeking damage limitation, pre-emptive advice and defence from prosecution, few environmental lawyers fit the whale-saving stereotype.

type of work

Head of environmental law at City practice Simmons & Simmons, Kathy Mylrea says: "*The beauty of environmental law is that it is extremely varied.*" Overlapping with property law, criminal matters and European legislation, the work breaks down into three broad areas:

- transactional, project and property support;
- compliance and regulatory advice; and
- litigation, including criminal and civil disputes, judicial reviews and statutory appeals.

With such diversity, it is unsurprising that a single day can see a solicitor handle matters as assorted as health and safety prosecutions, corporate transactions and environmental permit applications. We heard that "*job satisfaction is generally high because environmental law is relevant – it is there every day when you have a drink of water or put the rubbish out.*" The work isn't as desk-bound as many areas of law and, while "*visiting a rubbish tip is not everybody's idea of a great day out,*" if you prefer a real breeze to aircon, and river beds to sleeping pods, welcome to the great outdoors. That said, the whole sector is constantly evolving and, back at the office, there is plenty of paperwork: trainees and junior solicitors find that there are always new areas to be researched, legislation to be untangled, and manuals to be updated.

skills needed

...deal with intellectual problems commercially... be an all-rounder...understand corporate structures...awareness of environmental issues...basic grasp of science...research, interpretation and presentation skills...

Kathy says that above all "*you need strong basic legal skills*" – simply because environmental law is so broad, overlapping with so many other areas. A genuine interest in a specialist area such as renewable energy, conservation or water pollution is also vital, because "*no one gets on in environmental law unless they are really interested in i*t." Bags of research and complex legislation means academic skills are crucial, but Kathy warns: "*You can't be too purist – environment law is largely about looking for solutions,*" so sound judgement, pragmatism and commercial nous are all equally important. Expect lots of client contact, often over many years. Indeed, the ability to establish strong relationships is crucial, and as environmental risks are inherently difficult to quantify, you must develop a good gut instinct about matters and learn to think laterally to find appropriate solutions.

career options

Environmental law is increasingly integrated into other areas: legal developments in related fields such as the Utility Bill and the review of EC chemicals legislation all generate activity, yet environmental lawyers are quite a rare breed. You won't find a team of 20 or 30 lawyers, even in the largest practice, and this means that it is a competitive area to break into as an NQ. Kathy explained that environmental lawyers often have another string to their bow "*in case the need for legal advice in the area shrinks in the long term, or there is a reduction of environment work in the shorter term.*"

Genuine interest, commitment and a willingness to be flexible are essential to private practice, but there are other options. Kathy says: "*Private practice doesn't have a monopoly,*" and while it shouldn't be dismissed, she notes that "*if your objective is to change environment law, you should consider the other routes too."* In a local authority legal department you'll handle regulatory work, planning issues, waste management and air pollution prosecutions, and have a role in advising the authority on its own liability. In-house positions are rarer, except in large organisations such as Greenpeace, Friends of the Earth and the RSPB.

The Department for Environment, Food and Rural Affairs employs over 80 lawyers, including trainees on GLS-funded schemes. Work here includes litigation, drafting of subordinate legislation, advisory work and contract drafting.

The Environment Agency has lawyers in Bristol and eight regional offices, and is responsible for protecting and enhancing the environment through regulation of those corporate activities that have the greatest potential to pollute. The scope of work is vast, extending from waste management to flood defence, contaminated land to environmental impact assessment. Further, the agency is the prosecution body for environmental crimes, so there is plenty of prosecution work as well as enforcement activity and close involvement with government lawyers on the drafting and implementation of legislation.

LEADING FIRMS FROM CHAMBERS UK 2004-2005

ENVIRONMENT
■ NORTH WEST

[1] **Eversheds** Manchester

[2] **Addleshaw Goddard** Manchester

Cobbetts Manchester

Hammonds Manchester

McCool Patterson Hemsi Manchester

WDL Solicitors Chester

ENVIRONMENT
■ WALES

[1] **Edwards Geldard** Cardiff

[2] **Eversheds** Cardiff

Hugh James Cardiff

Morgan Cole Cardiff

ENVIRONMENT
■ NORTH EAST/YORKSHIRE

[1] **Eversheds** Leeds

[2] **DLA** Sheffield

Nabarro Nathanson Sheffield

[3] **Addleshaw Goddard** Leeds

Denison Till York

Dickinson Dees Newcastle upon Tyne

Hammonds Leeds

Pinsents Leeds

ENVIRONMENT
■ LONDON

[1] **Allen & Overy**
Freshfields Bruckhaus Deringer

[2] **Ashurst**
Barlow Lyde & Gilbert
Berwin Leighton Paisner
Clifford Chance
CMS Cameron McKenna
Leigh Day & Co
Linklaters
Simmons & Simmons

[3] **Baker & McKenzie**
Denton Wilde Sapte
Hammonds
Herbert Smith
Jones Day
Lovells
Mayer, Brown, Rowe & Maw
SJ Berwin
Slaughter and May

[4] **Lawrence Graham**
Macfarlanes
Nabarro Nathanson
Nicholson Graham & Jones
Trowers & Hamlins

[5] **Addleshaw Goddard**
Bircham Dyson Bell
Norton Rose
Stephenson Harwood

ENVIRONMENT
■ THE SOUTH

[1] **Bond Pearce** Southampton

[2] **Blake Lapthorn Linnell** Southampton
DMH Brighton

[3] **Brachers** Maidstone
Stevens & Bolton Guildford

ENVIRONMENT
■ THAMES VALLEY

[1] **Clarks** Reading

ENVIRONMENT
■ SOUTH WEST

[1] **Burges Salmon** Bristol

[2] **Bond Pearce** Plymouth
Clarke Willmott Bristol
Osborne Clarke Bristol

[3] **Bevan Brittan** Bristol
Veale Wasbrough Lawyers Bristol

ENVIRONMENT
■ EAST ANGLIA

[1] **Mills & Reeve** Cambridge
Richard Buxton Cambridge

[2] **Eversheds** Norwich
Hewitsons Cambridge

ENVIRONMENT
■ MIDLANDS

[1] **Wragge & Co** Birmingham

[2] **Browne Jacobson** Nottingham
Eversheds Nottingham
Hammonds Birmingham
Pinsents Birmingham

family law

Family lawyers handle divorce, disputes between cohabitants, inheritance disputes between family members, prenuptial and cohabitation agreements, and all matters relating to children. They will also deal with issues arising from registration of same-sex relationships, after the Civil Partnership Bill becomes law as is expected during 2004.

type of work

Your experience as a family lawyer will depend on whether you opt for general practice on the high street or one of the specialist practices that deal more with higher-value divorces and complex child or international matters. The former may be less glamorous, but, in general practice, you'll be thrown in at the deep end. So which route is best? James Pirrie at Family Law in Partnership points out that in general practice, you are more likely to have your own caseload from the start, which will increase your client skills. If you start in a specialist practice, you're more likely to be consigned to *"back-room duties – drafting documents and form-filling as part of a team."*

Whichever route you take, the ambit of your work will be wider than you'd expect as family law cases may involve inheritance and wills issues, conveyancing knowledge, judicial review (especially in connection with public funding, formerly legal aid) welfare benefits and the CSA, corporate law, tax, trusts and pensions – and that's before we start taking into account foreign jurisdictions. According to James, *"a good family lawyer's career profile should look more like Ayers Rock than Nelson's Column!"*

Clients will be husbands, wives, cohabitants, local authorities, children's guardians and, occasionally, children in their own right. You will also regularly encounter social workers, psychologists, probation officers and medical professionals, accountants, financial and pensions advisors, family lawyers from foreign jurisdictions and a wide variety of other experts. It is helpful to have some experience of people, relationships and the ways of the world in order to handle what can sometimes be distressing case scenarios. No two clients are ever the same, and neither are their stories; however, one thing that remains a constant is the need to keep the interests of any children paramount.

The first meeting with a client is crucial. At this stage you must *"try to understand what they want to achieve, help them understand the process options (and crucially, which of them are affordable), explain how the court might approach the issue, and do the sums to see what is sensible."* Subsequent tasks include drafting petitions, putting together skeleton arguments for court, and negotiating settlements. As a junior, you'll prepare bundles of case documentation and attend court to take notes. The more experienced you become, the greater the advocacy opportunities.

James thinks it is fairly easy to become immersed in the work and to take on responsibility. He reassures us that *"there isn't the same burnout in family law as in City work."* Family law is not a static area of practice – the Human Rights Act has opened up new possibilities; how children are dealt with has moved under the spotlight with the activities of men's groups such as Fathers For Justice, and acquiring psychological insights and negotiation skills is a never ending process

skills needed

...good listener...life experience...professional distance...interest in human relationships...commercial acumen...enjoy advocacy...carrying your clients' confidence

Empathy and sensitivity are invaluable traits, but James stresses: *"It is not important to have been through the wringer yourself. You can be very good contextually,* or technically brilliant." One of the first things you'll learn is that "it is no good to just act like a sponge, absorbing all your client's emotions." Instead, "you need to have a clear focus and strong communication skills because you are the conduit for your client's realities and concerns."

While family law may sound soft around the edges, at the negotiating table when your client's home, children or livelihood are at stake, "you need to be tough, and able to look someone in the eye and not blink for as long as it takes."

career options

Most family lawyers opt for private practice, in a range from the tough litigator, through the seasoned negotiator, to mediation and the new kid on the block – collaborative family law. This is a new model where the lawyers act for their clients in round-table negotiations but contract out of subsequently litigating the case. Others may pursue in-house positions with local authorities instead of private practice.

LEADING FIRMS FROM CHAMBERS UK 2004-2005

FAMILY/MATRIMONIAL
■ THE SOUTH

[1] **Lester Aldridge** Bournemouth
[2] **Blake Lapthorn Linnell** Fareham
Brachers Maidstone
Paris Smith & Randall Southampton
Thomson Snell Tunbridge Wells
[3] **Charles Russell** Guildford
Coffin Mew & Clover Portsmouth
Cripps Harries Hall Tunbridge Wells
Ellis Jones Bournemouth
Max Barford & Co Tunbridge Wells
Watson Nevill Solicitors Maidstone
Williams Thompson Christchurch

FAMILY/MATRIMONIAL
■ THAMES VALLEY

[1] **Blandy & Blandy** Reading
Manches Oxford
[2] **Boodle Hatfield** Oxford
Darbys Oxford
Henmans Oxford
[3] **Horsey Lightly Fynn** Newbury
Iliffes Booth Bennett (IBB) Uxbridge
Morgan Cole Reading

FAMILY/MATRIMONIAL
■ NORTH WEST

[1] **Pannone & Partners** Manchester
[2] **Addleshaw Goddard** Manchester
Cobbetts Manchester
Cuff Roberts Liverpool
Green & Co Manchester
Mace & Jones Knutsford, Liverpool
[3] **Brabners Chaffe Street** Liverpool
JMW Solicitors Altrincham
Laytons Manchester
Morecrofts Liverpool
Stephensons Leigh

FAMILY/MATRIMONIAL
■ NORTH EAST

[1] **Dickinson Dees** Newcastle upon Tyne
[2] **Hay & Kilner** Newcastle upon Tyne
Mincoffs Newcastle upon Tyne
Samuel Phillips Newcastle upon Tyne
Sintons Newcastle upon Tyne
Ward Hadaway Newcastle upon Tyne
Watson Burton Newcastle upon Tyne

FAMILY/MATRIMONIAL
■ WALES

[1] **Hugh James** Cardiff
Larby Williams Cardiff
Nicol Denvir & Purnell Cardiff
Wendy Hopkins & Co Cardiff
[2] **Avery Naylor** Swansea
Harding Evans Newport
Howells Cardiff
Leo Abse & Cohen Cardiff
Martyn Prowel Solicitors Cardiff
Robertsons Cardiff

FAMILY/MATRIMONIAL
■ LONDON

[1] **Manches**

Withers

[2] **Alexiou Fisher Philipps**

Charles Russell

Hughes Fowler Carruthers

Levison Meltzer Pigott

Miles Preston & Co

Payne Hicks Beach

Sears Tooth

[3] **Bindman & Partners**

Clintons

Collyer-Bristow

Dawson Cornwell

Farrer & Co

Goodman Ray

Gordon Dadds

Kingsley Napley

Mishcon de Reya

Reynolds Porter Chamberlain

[4] **Anthony Gold**

CKFT

Family Law In Partnership

Harcus Sinclair

International Family Law Chambers

[5] **Dawsons**

Fisher Meredith

Forsters

Hodge Jones & Allen

Margaret Bennett

Osbornes

Russell-Cooke

FAMILY/MATRIMONIAL
■ EAST ANGLIA

[1] **Mills & Reeve** Norwich

[2] **Buckles** Peterborough

Hunt & Coombs Peterborough

Silver Fitzgerald Cambridge

[3] **Cozens-Hardy & Jewson** Norwich

Gotelee & Goldsmith Ipswich

Hansells Norwich

Hatch Brenner Norwich

Leonard Gray Chelmsford

Marchant-Daisley Cambridge

Prettys Ipswich

Rudlings & Wakelam Thetford

Taylor Vinters Cambridge

FAMILY/MATRIMONIAL
■ SOUTH WEST

[1] **Burges Salmon** Bristol

Clarke Willmott Bristol

Foot Anstey Sargent Plymouth

Stephens & Scown Exeter

TLT Bristol

Tozers Exeter

Wolferstans Plymouth

[2] **Hartnell Chanot & Partners** Exeter

Ian Downing Plymouth

Stone King Bath

Stones Exeter

[3] **Bevan Brittan** Bristol

brains St Austell

Ford Simey Exeter

Gill Akaster Plymouth

Hooper & Wollen Torquay

Rickerbys Cheltenham

Veale Wasbrough Bristol

WBW Solicitors Newton Abbot

Withy King Bath

FAMILY/MATRIMONIAL
■ MIDLANDS

[1] **Blair Allison & Co** Birmingham

Challinors Lyon Clark West Bromwich

Rupert Bear Murray Davies Nottingham

[2] **Anthony Collins Solicitors** Birmingham

Nelsons Nottingham

Tyndallwoods Birmingham

[3] **Divorce & Family Law** Birmingham

Freeth Cartwright Birmingham

Hadens Walsall

Lanyon Bowdler Shrewsbury

Osborne & Co Birmingham

Turnbull Garrard Shrewsbury

Wace Morgan Shrewsbury

Young & Lee Birmingham

FAMILY/MATRIMONIAL
■ YORKSHIRE

[1] **Addleshaw Goddard** Leeds

[2] **Andrew M Jackson** Hull

Gordons Bradford

Grahame Stowe, Bateson Leeds

Irwin Mitchell Leeds

Jones Myers Gordon Leeds

Zermansky & Partners Leeds

[3] **Armitage Sykes Tullie** Huddersfield

Lupton Fawcett Leeds

Walker Morris Leeds

intellectual property

Intellectual property law is commonly divided into hard IP (patents) and soft IP (trade marks, design rights, copyright, passing off, anti-counterfeiting and confidential information). Unless a firm is very specialist, it will deal with both types of work.

type of work

Patents protect new, industrially applicable inventions, providing the proprietor with a monopoly to work the invention for a certain period. A trade mark provides a limited monopoly to use that mark on certain goods or services; and a registered design gives the owner an exclusive right to use the design. IP can be contentious or non-contentious and patent litigation, in particular, can be very complex, often with high stakes. The IP lawyer's role ranges from simple advice on the results of trade mark searches to trade mark opposition work, advice on a worldwide trade mark filing strategy and drafting sponsorship, endorsement and merchandising contracts.

James Love, Head of IP at Pinsents, explained what this means on a day-to-day basis: "*A large proportion of time is spent letter-writing, as disputes often don't go beyond a letter to the other side.*" And the rest of the time? "*Reading the patents once a case has taken off means wading through lots of material, seeking the smoking guns that are going to help your case.*" It isn't all paper-based: James described the typical IP lawyer's office as "*littered with the kind of products you find on supermarket shelves.*"

And rather like UN weapons inspectors, patent lawyers get out and about – perhaps, visiting factories to learn about production processes. The work is increasingly international (not least because of the internet) and is set to become more so as the European Community gets up to speed on trans-EC rights.

IP lawyers might be stuck into trade mark infringement proceedings, or they could just as eas-ily be called upon to work as a part of a multidisciplinary team on a large corporate transaction. Trainees and NQs usually have a decent number of smaller, discrete matters to work on, but there are times when they might feel like an insignificant cog in a vast machine when a high-value dispute takes off.

Clients include manufacturers and suppliers of hi-tech, engineering, pharmaceutical and agrochemical products, leading brand owners, universities, scientific institutions and media organisations. Lawyers must be able to handle a diverse range of individuals from the "*sophisticated, dynamic and pushy director of a big company to the mad inventor type who is pernickety and convinced his invention will make him millions.*"

skills needed

patent law ...a basic understanding of science (min. A-levels; ideally a degree)...aptitude for technical matters...well-organised...precise drafting...
general ip ...curiosity for all things creative, artistic and technological...handle quirky/artistic types...interest in the internet...up with consumer trends...

James stressed the importance of attention to detail, precision and accuracy: "*You need to be able to think in a very accurate, concentrated way – words are very important, and you have to analyse them in meticulous detail.*" Good drafting skills are absolutely critical, particularly in patent work, but beyond this, and especially in general IP matters, you'll need to have a good sense of commercial strategy and branding issues, and be innovative in the way you think.

Many lawyers have a science background. While this is going to be a huge bonus, James was quick to counsel young hopefuls against putting themselves through science A-Levels to bolster their CV. Some large firms do send NQs on a course in Bristol run by the Intellectual Property Lawyers Association, but James assured us that students would do better to *"hone their legal skills than become an armchair scientist."* Equally, while a science background may help you keep up when people start discussing the intricacies of electrode potential, *"if you are too much of a techy, you may leave the judge swamped; however, if you have had to go through the mental gymnastics yourself it can be helpful when it comes to explaining it all to someone else."*

career options

The Thames Valley has a concentration of IT companies and Cambridge's 'Silicon Fen' has grown on the back of the hi-tech and biotech companies that have spun out of the university. *Chambers UK* identifies the leading IP practices and gives details of their particular specialisms and clients.

Manufacturing, pharmaceutical and research companies employ patent specialists and there are in-house legal teams at all the large pharmaceutical companies, for example Procter & Gamble, Reckitt Benckiser and Unilever. Non-patent lawyers find their way into the media world: all major publishers and television companies have in-house IP lawyers. Many broadcasting companies now employ lawyers in positions such as head of business and legal affairs. Additionally, there is a visible drift of lawyers into firms of trade mark agents and patent attorneys where a good living is to be made. Equally, there is a drift in the other direction too.

LEADING FIRMS FROM CHAMBERS UK 2004-2005

INTELLECTUAL PROPERTY: PATENT LITIGATION
■ LONDON

[1] **Bird & Bird**
Bristows
Taylor Wessing
[2] **Herbert Smith**
Linklaters
Simmons & Simmons
[3] **Lovells**
Wragge & Co
[4] **Baker & McKenzie**
Clifford Chance
Freshfields Bruckhaus Deringer
Olswang
Roiter Zucker

INTELLECTUAL PROPERTY
■ MIDLANDS

[1] **Wragge & Co** Birmingham
[2] **Pinsents** Birmingham
[3] **Browne Jacobson** Nottingham
Eversheds Nottingham
Martineau Johnson Birmingham

INTELLECTUAL PROPERTY
■ EAST ANGLIA

[1] **Eversheds** Cambridge
Mills & Reeve Norwich
[2] **Greenwoods Solicitors** Peterborough
Taylor Vinters Cambridge
Taylor Wessing Cambridge

INTELLECTUAL PROPERTY
■ NORTH EAST

[1] **Addleshaw Goddard** Leeds
[2] **DLA** Leeds
Pinsents Leeds
Walker Morris Leeds
[3] **Dickinson Dees** Newcastle upon Tyne
Eversheds Leeds
Hammonds Leeds
Irwin Mitchell Leeds
Lupton Fawcett Leeds

INTELLECTUAL PROPERTY
■ WALES

[1] **Edwards Geldard** Cardiff
[2] **Eversheds** Cardiff

INTELLECTUAL PROPERTY: GENERAL
■ LONDON

1 Bird & Bird
Bristows
Taylor Wessing

2 Herbert Smith
Linklaters
Lovells
Simmons & Simmons
Willoughby & Partners

3 Ashurst
Baker & McKenzie
Denton Wilde Sapte
Field Fisher Waterhouse
Wragge & Co

4 Allen & Overy
Clifford Chance
Freshfields Bruckhaus Deringer
Olswang
Slaughter and May

5 Addleshaw Goddard
Briffa
DLA
Finers Stephens Innocent
Hammonds
Howrey Simon Arnold & White
Jones Day
Lewis Silkin
Mayer, Brown, Rowe & Maw
Redd
Richards Butler
Roiter Zucker
SJ Berwin
White & Case
Withers

INTELLECTUAL PROPERTY
■ THE SOUTH

1 Blake Lapthorn Linnell London
2 DMH Brighton
3 Bond Pearce Southampton
Lester Aldridge Bournemouth
Shadbolt & Co Reigate

INTELLECTUAL PROPERTY
■ NORTH WEST

1 Addleshaw Goddard Manchester
Halliwells Manchester
2 DLA Manchester
Eversheds Manchester
Hill Dickinson Liverpool
3 Berg & Co Manchester
Cobbetts Manchester
Hammonds Manchester
4 Kuit Steinart Levy Manchester
Pannone & Partners Manchester
Taylors Blackburn

INTELLECTUAL PROPERTY
■ SOUTH WEST

1 Bevan Brittan Bristol
Osborne Clarke Bristol
2 Beachcroft Wansbroughs Bristol
Bond Pearce Bristol
Burges Salmon Bristol
3 Humphreys & Co Solicitors Bristol

INTELLECTUAL PROPERTY
■ THAMES VALLEY

1 Willoughby & Partners Oxford
2 Nabarro Nathanson Reading
Olswang Thames Valley Reading
Shoosmiths Milton Keynes
3 Manches Oxford
Morgan Cole Reading
Osborne Clarke Reading
Marcus J O'Leary wokingham

litigation/dispute resolution

You probably think litigators live for protracted courtroom battles and entertain the idea of an early case settlement in much the same way as a mortician would view his latest masterpiece sitting up and asking for the Sunday papers. You'd be wrong. It's a grim fact of commercial reality that clients rarely wish to emerge from the courtroom to pose triumphantly on the steps for photographers. On the contrary, clients generally hope to reach a commercial settlement as quickly, cheaply and unobtrusively as possible. Result? Most cases never reach trial.

Unless they can be settled by correspondence, disputes are often concluded in one of three ways. The first is through litigation itself – the issue and pursuit of court proceedings, which can be expensive and time-consuming. For this reason, contracts often provide for disputes between the parties to be referred to the second method: binding arbitration. Arbitration is usually conducted by an expert in the subject matter if it is particularly specialised and, unlike court proceedings, arbitration is confidential. The third method is alternative dispute resolution (ADR). Although it can take various forms, the most common form of ADR is mediation. This involves structured negotiations between the parties, which are overseen and directed by an independent mediator. The parties retain the right to litigate if they find it impossible to reach an agreement.

type of work

Put simply, litigation is a process. Once a case has been commenced, it follows a predetermined course laid down by the rules of court: statement of case; disclosure of documents; witness statements; various procedural applications; and in a small number of cases, trial. Managing this process is the litigator's primary role, and this requires not only a mastery of the rules, but also a keen appreciation of tactics and attention to detail. The Civil Procedure Rules (CPR) introduced in 1999 were intended to speed up the exchange of information between the parties and cut the number of cases reaching the courts. Simon Willis, a partner at Barlow Lyde & Gilbert, believes that the CPR have made a difference: "*Parties are generally more inclined to be reasonable in their approach to litigation, and there is more emphasis on resolving disputes without resorting to trial. The reforms have got rid of some of the worst excesses under the old rules – there is less litigation by numbers.*"

Commercial litigation covers a multitude of business disputes, ranging from a skirmish over a tenancy agreement to full-scale combat over the terms of a multimillion-dollar contract. Some litigators specialise, for example in insurance, construction, media or shipping cases – for more information, look at the other relevant practice area sections in this guide. Specialisation usually has more to do with acquiring market knowledge than learning different skills or procedures; many litigators will tell you that it's better to start off as a generalist, so you can develop the requisite core skills and make yourself more marketable.

As a trainee, your workload will depend entirely on the type of firm you go to. Magic circle firms are unlikely to give eager young recruits free rein on the latest international banking dispute, but they will get an opportunity to observe experienced lawyers at work on headline-grabbing cases, even if their own role is far from glamorous. By contrast, in firms that handle much smaller matters, trainees are given the opportunity to deal with all aspects of a case, from drafting correspondence and conducting meetings with clients and counsel to trotting along to court to make small procedural applications.

While we're on the subject of court appearances, let's examine the role of the solicitor advocate following the extension of High Court rights of audience to solicitors. Some see this as natural evolution of the legal market, a visible erosion of the artificial barriers between solicitors and barristers. Yet, while many firms do offer advocacy training to their solicitors, it is not always as high up on the list of priorities as you might think. As Simon explains: "*Although it is growing, it is a gradual process. The business case is not there for bringing all advocacy in house. While firms are placing less reliance on counsel generally, the Bar still has an important role to play.*" When it comes to the crunch and there's a compelling need for someone to display an encyclopaedic knowledge of complex procedural rules, or demonstrate a mesmerising talent for cross-examination, clients and solicitors still feel more comfortable turning to the Bar.

Despite there not being a flood of solicitors seeking rights of audience in the higher courts, many firms are aiming to keep more advocacy in-house and draft more of their own pleadings. Students can certainly ask a firm to outline its policy on this issue: Will becoming a solicitor advocate be possible at all, purely optional, actively encouraged or mandatory? Students should also bear in mind that specialist litigation firms and those handling smaller cases may provide greater scope for advocacy than large City firms.

skills needed

...drive...commercial awareness...tactical thinking ...enjoy formulating and articulating arguments...a need to win...assimilate information quickly...think laterally...good negotiator...thick-skinned but sensitive to clients' needs...

This is, in essence, an adversarial area of practice, which will suit those who relish a good old battle of wits. As Simon says: "*It's a good choice if you enjoy an intellectual challenge and want to get close to the law – if you can see yourself exercising your judgement, taking a view, and then having the confidence to stand by it.*" This is still a relevant insight even if the current trend for ADR continues. "*A mediation requires many of the same skills as the litigation process: you still have to understand and present your case and identify the weaknesses in your opponent's. Equally, litigation is not always daggers drawn, and good litigators will be looking for opportunities to negotiate and compromise – whether or not a formal mediation is in progress.*"

According to Simon, some of the most important skills for a litigator are "*the ability to assimilate complex facts, to identify the important issues in a dispute, and to explain those issues, and your view, in a way your clients can understand.*" You need to be able to speak and write both concisely and precisely, especially when a high degree of legal analysis is involved. As you will not always be the sole lawyer working on a case it is also important to be able to work effectively as part of a team and earn the trust of those around you.

Litigators also need an ability to understand the commercial pressures facing clients at what can be a particularly taxing time. Simon explains: "*You have to look beyond the legal issues in a case and take account of your client's commercial position and objectives.*" On the other hand it does not pay to get too carried away. "*You not only have to manage the case, but also your client's expectations in terms of their realistic position, and what would be the likely cost of pursuing or defending an action.*"

career options

The Law Society requires all trainee solicitors to undertake contentious work, and in almost all cases you tend to discover fairly quickly whether you are suited to litigation. If you want to get a feel for advocacy prior to applying for training contracts, we'd recommend you join your local mooting or debating society.

Once qualified, litigation skills are less transferable than the other professional and business skills that you will have developed. As such, it may not be as easy to take up an in-house role as it would be for transactional lawyers. Better make sure private practice suits you...

LEADING FIRMS FROM CHAMBERS UK 2004-2005

LITIGATION: GENERAL COMMERCIAL (LARGER TEAMS)
■ LONDON

1 Herbert Smith

2 Clifford Chance

Freshfields Bruckhaus Deringer

Lovells

3 Allen & Overy

Linklaters

Slaughter and May

4 Ashurst

Barlow Lyde & Gilbert

Norton Rose

Richards Butler

Simmons & Simmons

5 Baker & McKenzie

Clyde & Co

CMS Cameron McKenna

Denton Wilde Sapte

SJ Berwin

LITIGATION: GENERAL COMMERCIAL
■ THE SOUTH: SURREY, HAMPSHIRE & DORSET

1 Blake Lapthorn Linnell Fareham

Bond Pearce Southampton

Clyde & Co Guildford

2 Lester Aldridge Southampton

Paris Smith & Randall Southampton

Stevens & Bolton Guildford

3 asb law Crawley

Charles Russell Guildford

Thomas Eggar Reigate

4 Barlows Guildford

Clarke Willmott Southampton

Moore & Blatch Southampton

Shadbolt & Co Reigate

Shoosmiths Fareham

LITIGATION: GENERAL COMMERCIAL (MEDIUM TEAMS)
■ LONDON

1 Eversheds

Jones Day

Macfarlanes

Mayer, Brown, Rowe & Maw

Stephenson Harwood

2 Berwin Leighton Paisner

Dechert

Ince & Co

Masons

Nabarro Nathanson

Reynolds Porter Chamberlain

Taylor Wessing

3 Addleshaw Goddard

Hammonds

Kendall Freeman

Morgan, Lewis & Bockius

Nicholson Graham & Jones

Pinsents

White & Case

4 Charles Russell

DLA

Howrey Simon Arnold & White

Lawrence Graham

Lewis Silkin

Memery Crystal

Mishcon de Reya

Olswang

Shook, Hardy & Bacon

Travers Smith

Watson, Farley & Williams

LITIGATION: GENERAL COMMERCIAL
■ THAMES VALLEY

1 Clarks Reading

Manches Oxford

2 Boyes Turner Reading

Morgan Cole Reading

Nabarro Nathanson Reading

Pitmans Reading

3 B P Collins Gerrards Cross

Henmans Oxford

Matthew Arnold & Baldwin Watford

Olswang Thames Valley Reading

Shoosmiths Reading

4 Iliffes Booth Bennett (IBB) Uxbridge

LITIGATION: GENERAL COMMERCIAL
■ MIDLANDS

1 Pinsents Birmingham

Wragge & Co Birmingham

2 Eversheds Birmingham

Hammonds Birmingham

3 Cobbetts Birmingham

DLA Birmingham

Gateley Wareing Birmingham

4 Browne Jacobson Nottingham

Freeth Cartwright Nottingham

Martineau Johnson Birmingham

Shoosmiths Northampton

5 Challinors Lyon Clark West Bromwich

George Green Cradley Heath

Kent Jones & Done Stoke-on-Trent

Moran & Co Tamworth

Shakespeares Birmingham

LITIGATION: GENERAL COMMERCIAL
■ SOUTH WEST

[1] **Burges Salmon** Bristol

Osborne Clarke Bristol

[2] **Ashfords** Exeter

Beachcroft Wansbroughs Bristol

Bevan Brittan Bristol

Bond Pearce Exeter

Foot Anstey Sargent Exeter, Plymouth

TLT Bristol

Veale Wasbrough Bristol

[3] **Bevans** Bristol

BPE Solicitors Cheltenham

Charles Russell Cheltenham

Clarke Willmott Taunton

Laytons Bristol

Michelmores Exeter

Rickerbys Cheltenham

LITIGATION: GENERAL COMMERCIAL
■ THE SOUTH: KENT & SUSSEX

[1] **Cripps Harries Hall** Tunbridge Wells

DMH Brighton

Thomas Eggar Worthing

[2] **Brachers** Maidstone

Thomson Snell Tunbridge Wells

LITIGATION: GENERAL COMMERCIAL
■ WALES

[1] **Edwards Geldard** Cardiff

Eversheds Cardiff

Hugh James Cardiff

[2] **Capital Law** Cardiff Bay

Morgan Cole Cardiff

LITIGATION: GENERAL COMMERCIAL
■ NORTH WEST

[1] **Addleshaw Goddard** Manchester

DLA Manchester

Eversheds Manchester

[2] **Cobbetts** Manchester

Halliwells Manchester

Hammonds Manchester

Hill Dickinson Liverpool

[3] **Brabners Chaffe Street** Liverpool

DWF Manchester

Kuit Steinart Levy Manchester

Pannone & Partners Manchester

Wacks Caller Manchester

[4] **Beachcroft Wansbroughs** Manchester

Berg & Co Manchester

Cuff Roberts Liverpool

Kershaw Abbott Manchester

Mace & Jones Manchester

Rowe Cohen Manchester

LITIGATION: GENERAL COMMERCIAL
■ EAST ANGLIA

[1] **Mills & Reeve** Cambridge

[2] **Birketts** Ipswich

Eversheds Cambridge

Hewitsons Cambridge

Taylor Vinters Cambridge

[3] **Howes Percival** Norwich

Prettys Ipswich

[4] **Greenwoods Solicitors** Peterborough

Steeles Norwich

LITIGATION: GENERAL COMMERCIAL
■ YORKSHIRE

[1] **DLA** Leeds

Eversheds Leeds

Pinsents Leeds

[2] **Addleshaw Goddard** Leeds

Hammonds Leeds

[3] **Irwin Mitchell** Sheffield

Walker Morris Leeds

[4] **Cobbetts** Leeds

Gordons Bradford

Keeble Hawson Leeds

Lupton Fawcett Leeds

Nabarro Nathanson Sheffield

[5] **Andrew M Jackson** Hull

Beachcroft Wansbroughs Leeds

Ford & Warren Leeds

Rollits Hull

LITIGATION: GENERAL COMMERCIAL
■ NORTH EAST

[1] **Ward Hadaway** Newcastle upon Tyne

[2] **Dickinson Dees** Newcastle upon Tyne

Eversheds Newcastle upon Tyne

[3] **Hay & Kilner** Newcastle upon Tyne

Robert Muckle Newcastle upon Tyne

[4] **Crutes** Newcastle upon Tyne

Watson Burton Newcastle upon Tyne

media & entertainment

advertising and marketing

Advertising and marketing law is split into pure and general work. Pure advertising law focuses on the client's products or advertisements, ensuring the content is legal and appropriate. General work encompasses commercial contracts with suppliers, clients and the media, plus corporate transactions, litigation and employment issues.

type of work: Copy clearance lawyers advise clients on issues such as comparative advertising, unauthorised references to living individuals and parodies of films or TV shows. A solid grasp of defamation and intellectual property law is essential. Legislation such as the Lotteries and Amusements Act and the Consumer Protection Act feature, and copy clearance work is further governed by regulatory codes such as those of the Advertising Standards Authority (ASA) and Ofcom. The lawyer must help the client to say exactly what he or she wants to say without falling foul of these regulations.

Sometimes you will be defending the client against allegations that their work has infringed the rights of third parties or advising on whether an ad should be pulled. At other times you will go on the offensive, helping clients to bring complaints about competitors' advertising, for example if a competitor is 'knocking copy' (making disparaging references to your client's products) or making claims that your client wouldn't be allowed to make.

As clients are often already committed to a course of action before they speak to you, the answer to a query is rarely a straightforward 'no'. Instead, advice is often about damage limitation or risk management and it's up to the lawyer to identify the risks and, if not eliminate them, manage them as best they can. Rather than a slow wade through turgid legal documents, advertising law is fast-moving and refreshing, with immediate results. Clients are similarly creative and lively, and always looking for fast, practical advice.

reputation management

Reputation management work oozes sex appeal, celebrity and intrigue. Until recently, libel cases were the order of the day; now the planetary alignment of the Human Rights Act (particularly Article 8, the right to privacy, and Article 10, the right to freedom of expression) and the nation's unhealthy obsession with celeb gossip and pics has opened up a whole new galaxy of claims. Naomi Campbell, Sara Cox, and Catherine and Michael are the vanguard and their lawyers are also fast becoming 'names' in their own right.

type of work: We spoke with Caroline Kean of media boutique Wiggin & Co about a life in libel and reputation management. She told us there were fundamental differences between acting for defendants (newspapers, other publishers and broadcasters) and claimants (commonly celebrities and politicians). *"Defendants instruct you as a part of their business. They have commercial nous, and a budget, and they don't usually have hysterics."* By contrast, the individual claimants probably feel they are going through the worst episode of their life and will need a good deal of handholding. Claimant lawyers need a heck of a lot of patience and the ability to get clients to really open up and expose their weaknesses.

When libel claims are made or threatened, the burden of proof switches to the defendant and, as such, their lawyers have to think and act strategically to prove that there has been no libel. At times, Caroline says: *"You get to be an investigative journalist,"* and she's even been to meetings wired-up. Less dramatic, maybe, but no less important to the client, are the non-contentious elements of the job including pre-publication or pre-broadcast advice to authors, editors and TV companies.

Caroline believes those destined to build a career in this field need *"an affinity with publishing matters"* and must be up to date with the news and gossip in the media world. In short, listen to the radio, watch TV, and read newspapers and magazines. *"One of my first jobs in the morning is to read The Mirror's celebrity and sports pages,"* Caroline chuckled. But she reminded us that *"you are first and foremost a lawyer – and not a failed luvvie."* In a similar vein, while it won't hurt to have edited your student newspaper or to have had some media experience, recruiters are aware that some applicants would indeed be better suited to journalism than the law. Ultimately, issues like freedom of speech and the right to privacy must matter to you as legal concepts and, to best serve your clients' interests, you'll need to build an armoury of legal tools. If you have your heart set on this kind of work, try reading a monthly magazine called *Media Lawyer*.

Jobs exist in-house at larger publishing and broadcasting concerns and it is relatively common for lawyers to hop over the fence from private practice…and back again. Even in private practice, regular office hours don't really apply. *"Near to a copy deadline your phone is going all the time, and you're likely to get calls late on a Friday or on a Sunday. If the client needs you, you have to be there."* The upside, Caroline reports, is that the job is *"the most enormous fun."* Sounds like great work, if you can get it!

entertainment

At parties, when asked what they do, many lawyers kill conversations. Not entertainment specialists.

type of work: Lawyers handle film and broadcasting, music, theatre and publishing work. We spoke to The Simkins Partnership's Robin Hilton and Julian Bentley, who explained that, while these areas of the entertainment industry each have different demands, with all of them *"you need to know how to give commercial advice in a legal context."* Essentially, all clients need contract, employment and litigation advice, and intellectual property is also very relevant.

When it comes to film and TV work, Robin says: *"Like any industrial process, you have to research and develop the product, make it and market it."* Legal advice is required at each stage, particularly those involving contractual arrangements (including banking and secured lending) and the law of copyright. *"You have to hold the producer's hand and take them through it; engaging artists, dealing with the director, putting together a patchwork of finance and then going through production."* A film lawyer may have to manage the contractual relationships with tax funds, banks and studios and several producers as well as giving clearance and classification advice.

Television lawyers only tend to be drafted in when issues or problems arise relating to the content of a programme, defamation claims, engaging talent or negotiating deal terms and contracts. Robin described film and TV work as *"reasonably office-bound"* and warned that *"people who think being a TV lawyer is a form of the entertainment business will be in for a shock. First and foremost, you're a lawyer not a show-biz person."* In fact, *"clients look to you to apply the rigour they often don't apply"* and expect an awareness of compliance, defamation, privacy, confidence and finance law. Robin added: *"You do need a passion for the industry itself, but that comes second to understanding the commercial framework – you can't just say 'I love watching telly' or 'I'm a film buff'."*

Music law divides evenly between work for major companies, the independent sector and talent, including record producers, songwriters and artists. Contract, copyright and competition law are key. Litigation can arise when there is a dispute over contract terms or ownership of rights in a composition, or if there is a split in a band or with management. Even when there are no musical differences, clients need help in negotiating contracts and so Julian warns that potential music lawyers *"need to be aware that it is document intensive – you have to be able to write well."* Julian also stressed that *"you really have to be ensconced in the business – live it and breathe it."*

Just a handful of London lawyers work for theatre and opera companies, producers, theatrical agents and actors, negotiating contracts and arranging funding. Publishing law is also a pocket-sized area of practice, as much of the contractual, licensing, copyright and libel advice for newspapers and publishers is carried out in-house.

skills needed

...people skills...patience...prepared to immerse yourself in the industry...a thorough knowledge of contract and copyright law...creativity in problem solving...commercial aptitude...methodical nature...being inquisitive...

career options

For all the industry's apparently laid-back approach, competition for legal positions is ferocious, and that applies to training contracts too. There are two basic routes in: train at a niche entertainment firm or at a large City firm with a specialism in entertainment. In either case, a demonstrable commitment to the field and an understanding of industry trends and new technology will really help. Try and get some relevant work experience, read the trade press and the media pages of the general press and watch lots of TV. Julian said: *"A lot of people in the music industry who aren't frontline musicians probably once were, and that includes lawyers...to say we're all failed musicians is not quite right, but music was top of our list of hobbies!"* Turning your hand to a bit of DJing, music journalism or booking bands at university will go down well as *"it demonstrates you might know people and can work the industry."*

Lawyers can quite easily transfer between private practice and jobs with media and entertainment organisations. The hours and regularity of in-house jobs appeal to some, as does the perception that you are closer to the production process. There are fewer in-house positions available in the music sector; in television they are plentiful, with all the big names such as BBC, Warners, Channel 5, Clear Channel and Endemol employing their own lawyers.

LEADING FIRMS FROM CHAMBERS UK 2004-2005

PUBLISHING
■ LONDON

1 **Denton Wilde Sapte**
2 **Finers Stephens Innocent**
  Taylor Wessing
3 **Harbottle & Lewis**
  Lovells
  Olswang
4 **Davenport Lyons**
  Farrer & Co
  Reynolds Porter Chamberlain
  The Simkins Partnership

FILM FINANCE
■ LONDON

1 **Richards Butler**
  SJ Berwin
2 **Davenport Lyons**
  Denton Wilde Sapte
3 **Addleshaw Goddard**
  Howard Kennedy
  Olswang
  The Simkins Partnership

THEATRE
■ LONDON

1 **Clintons**
2 **The Simkins Partnership**
3 **Bates, Wells & Braithwaite**
  Harbottle & Lewis
  Harrison Curtis
4 **Campbell Hooper**
  Tarlo Lyons

ADVERTISING & MARKETING
■ LONDON

[1] Lewis Silkin
Osborne Clarke
[2] Hammonds
Macfarlanes
The Simkins Partnership
[3] Addleshaw Goddard
Lawrence Graham
Mayer, Brown, Rowe & Maw
Olswang
Taylor Wessing
Wragge & Co
[4] Baker & McKenzie
CMS Cameron McKenna
Field Fisher Waterhouse
Harbottle & Lewis
Harrison Curtis
Kaye Scholer
Lovells

MUSIC
■ LONDON

[1] Russells
[2] Clintons
Lee & Thompson
[3] Sheridans
The Simkins Partnership
[4] Addleshaw Goddard
Bray & Krais
Davenport Lyons
[5] Eversheds
Hamlins
Harbottle & Lewis
Mishcon de Reya
[6] Collyer-Bristow
Engel Monjack
Forbes Anderson
Harrison Curtis
Marriott Harrison
Spraggon Stennett Brabyn

DEFAMATION/REPUTATION MANAGEMENT
■ LONDON

[1] Carter-Ruck
Davenport Lyons
David Price Solicitors & Advocates
Farrer & Co
Olswang
Schillings
[2] Addleshaw Goddard
Reynolds Porter Chamberlain
[3] Charles Russell
Simons Muirhead & Burton
Wiggin & Co
[4] Bindman & Partners
Clifford Chance
Goodman Derrick
Lovells
Russell Jones & Walker
[5] Dechert
Finers Stephens Innocent
Harbottle & Lewis
Lee & Thompson
Lewis Silkin
Mishcon de Reya
Richards Butler
[6] DLA
Eversheds
M Law
Taylor Wessing
Teacher Stern Selby
The Simkins Partnership

COMPUTER GAMES
■ LONDON

[1] Harbottle & Lewis
Osborne Clarke
[2] Bird & Bird
Bristows
Lovells
Olswang

FILM & TV PRODUCTION
■ LONDON

[1] Olswang
[2] Davenport Lyons
Harbottle & Lewis
Lee & Thompson
[3] Denton Wilde Sapte
Richards Butler
SJ Berwin
The Simkins Partnership
[4] Addleshaw Goddard
Howard Kennedy
[5] Bates, Wells & Braithwaite
Charles Russell
Harrison Curtis
Osborne Clarke
Simons Muirhead & Burton

BROADCASTING
■ LONDON

[1] Denton Wilde Sapte
Olswang
[2] Goodman Derrick
Wiggin & Co
[3] Davenport Lyons
Field Fisher Waterhouse
Herbert Smith
Lovells
Richards Butler
[4] Bird & Bird
Clifford Chance
Harbottle & Lewis
SJ Berwin
Taylor Wessing
The Simkins Partnership
Travers Smith

MEDIA & ENTERTAINMENT
■ NATIONWIDE

[1] Manches Oxford
McCormicks Leeds
MLM Cardiff
Morgan Cole Cardiff
Wiggin & Co Cheltenham

personal injury and clinical negligence

From simple pavement trippers to those suffering from industrial diseases, members of the public call upon personal injury lawyers to help them bring claims. In the majority of cases, it will be an insurance company that is liable to pay compensation and, accordingly, they too instruct PI lawyers. Some lawyers act for both claimant and defendant clients, but most concentrate on one or the other.

Clinical negligence claims are made where individuals have suffered injury or illness as a result of medical treatment that has gone wrong. Examples include orthopaedic surgery, cerebral palsy caused by birth trauma, incorrect dental treatment and delay in diagnosis by GPs. In all cases, the defendant will be a medical professional or body, usually the NHS, but sometimes the Medical Defence Union or insurance companies. As with PI, lawyers tend to act for either claimants or defendants.

type of work

We spoke to Rod Findlay, a partner specialising in clinical negligence at Newcastle firm Samuel Phillips & Co, who told us just how much work had to be done before a claim could be issued. After hearing the client's story, the lawyer spends several months obtaining and considering the medical records to see if they support what the client is saying and can provide the basis for a good claim. *"Some cases are really simple and some are a right old mess! You can have a huge volume of records, several different specialists and different hospitals. One client of mine had 14 sets of records."* Only after the initial review period is complete will the lawyer know whether there's a good chance of success for the claimant and be in a position to issue proceedings. At this stage he can also begin to prepare the case for a possible trial, although this may be a couple of years down the line. The basic procedural steps of litigation include taking witness statements,

instructing experts to prepare reports, disclosure of documentary evidence and, inevitably, negotiations with the other party. As with any type of litigation, most cases never reach trial and are settled.

Legal aid is still available for clinical negligence work – although practitioners do worry for how much longer – and the government is promoting schemes whereby legal work and costs are minimised. For example, its Chief Medical Officer has suggested that all claims below £30,000 and brain-damaged baby cases should be concluded by reference to a single expert's report. The PI scene has already undergone huge changes since the loss of legal aid, the rise and demise of various claims companies, and the predominance of 'no win, no fee' agreements.

skills needed

...a good bedside manner...sympathetic but detached...patience...tact...organised and methodical...logical thinker...good negotiator...interest in medical matters...

This kind of work, particularly clinical negligence, is especially suited to those with experience in the healthcare sector or who have studied medicine, although most young lawyers have no such background. *"The first thing I did when I qualified was buy a medical dictionary,"* Rod said, adding that clin neg can be a difficult area for those starting out and that good guidance is essential. *"It's because you're not just dealing with an injury, you're criticising another professional. You're just out of law school and you just about know about your own profession. But as you progress, you see cases crop up again and again, and you are better able to make experienced-based judgement calls."*

A trap for young players is *"listening to the story without picking up on the legal issues."* No matter how tragic or awful the client's experience, you have to remember to stick to your role – you are neither a medical advisor nor a best friend. Some of the facts in these cases can be quite gruesome, so this is not a job for the squeamish, or indeed for those overly sensitive to human misery. Defendant lawyers also have to accept that their role is to minimise their client's liability to the claimant, and this requires faith in the fairness and integrity of the legal process.

The job as a whole is very paper based, although there is the odd court hearing or home visit to a client. Be prepared to knuckle down to a lot of perusing and summarising of medical reports.

career options

Most lawyers stay in private practice for their whole careers, but don't assume that defendant lawyers never switch to working for claimants, and vice versa. Rod doubts there are differences in the type of person working on either side, although he suggests that those interested in PI and clinical negligence should pick their firm carefully. Some have specialisms (asbestos-related diseases, head and spine injuries, dental malpractice) and their lawyers become niche players; at others, lawyers remain generalists. On the defendant side, the NHS Litigation Authority has a near monopoly when it comes to issuing instructions, and every three years it reviews its panel of law firms. The review in January 2004 should have fixed the market until 2007. Interested students can choose PI and medical law options at university and law school, and the superkeen may find a publication called *Healthcare Risk Report* edifying.

LEADING FIRMS FROM CHAMBERS UK 2004-2005

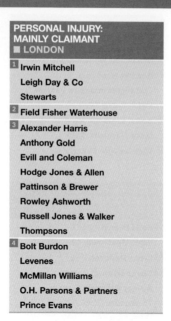

PERSONAL INJURY: MAINLY DEFENDANT
■ LONDON

[1] Barlow Lyde & Gilbert
Beachcroft Wansbroughs
[2] Berrymans Lace Mawer
[3] Greenwoods
Kennedys
Plexus Law
Vizards Wyeth
[4] Badhams Law Croydon
Davies Arnold Cooper
Davies Lavery
Reynolds Porter Chamberlain
Watmores

PERSONAL INJURY: MAINLY CLAIMANT
■ LONDON

[1] Irwin Mitchell
Leigh Day & Co
Stewarts
[2] Field Fisher Waterhouse
[3] Alexander Harris
Anthony Gold
Evill and Coleman
Hodge Jones & Allen
Pattinson & Brewer
Rowley Ashworth
Russell Jones & Walker
Thompsons
[4] Bolt Burdon
Levenes
McMillan Williams
O.H. Parsons & Partners
Prince Evans

PERSONAL INJURY: MAINLY DEFENDANT
■ THE SOUTH

1 **Beachcroft Wansbroughs** Winchester
Berrymans Lace Mawer Southampton
Clarke Willmott Southampton
Davies Lavery Maidstone
Vizards Wyeth Dartford
2 **Bond Pearce** Southampton
3 **Capital Law** Southampton
Lamport Bassitt Southampton

PERSONAL INJURY: MAINLY CLAIMANT
■ THE SOUTH

1 **Lamport Bassitt** Southampton
2 **Blake Lapthorn Linnell** Southampton
George Ide, Phillips Chichester
Moore & Blatch Southampton
Shoosmiths Basingstoke
Thomson Snell Tunbridge Wells
3 **Coffin Mew & Clover** Southampton
Colemans-ctts Kingston-upon-Thames
DMH Crawley

PERSONAL INJURY: MAINLY DEFENDANT
■ EAST ANGLIA

1 **Eversheds** Ipswich
2 **Edwards Duthie** Ilford
Kennedys Brentwood
Mills & Reeve Norwich
Prettys Ipswich

PERSONAL INJURY: MAINLY CLAIMANT
■ EAST ANGLIA

1 **Kester Cunningham John** Thetford
Taylor Vinters Cambridge
2 **Edwards Duthie** Ilford
Morgan Jones & Pett Great Yarmouth

PERSONAL INJURY: MAINLY DEFENDANT
■ THAMES VALLEY

1 **Henmans** Oxford
Morgan Cole Reading
Pitmans Reading
Thring Townsend Swindon

PERSONAL INJURY: MAINLY CLAIMANT
■ THAMES VALLEY

1 **Boyes Turner** Reading
Osborne Morris & Morgan
Thring Townsend Swindon
2 **Blake Lapthorn Linnell** Oxford
Fennemores Milton Keynes
Harris & Cartwright Slough
3 **Field Seymour Parkes** Reading
Henmans Oxford

PERSONAL INJURY: MAINLY DEFENDANT
■ SOUTH WEST

1 **Beachcroft Wansbroughs** Bristol
2 **Bond Pearce** Bristol
Cartwrights Insurance Partners Bristol
Veitch Penny Exeter
3 **Bevan Brittan** Bristol
Lyons Davidson Bristol
4 **Wansbroughs** Devizes

PERSONAL INJURY: MAINLY CLAIMANT
■ SOUTH WEST

1 **Bond Pearce** Plymouth
Veale Wasbrough Lawyers Bristol
2 **Lyons Davidson** Bristol
3 **Clarke Willmott** Bristol
Rowley Ashworth Exeter
Thompsons Bristol
Withy King Bath

PERSONAL INJURY: MAINLY CLAIMANT
■ MIDLANDS

1 **Irwin Mitchell** Birmingham
2 **Alexander Harris** Solihull
Barratt, Goff & Tomlinson Nottingham
Freeth Cartwright Nottingham
Rowley Ashworth Birmingham
Russell Jones & Walker Birmingham
Thompsons Birmingham
3 **Flint, Bishop & Barnett** Derby
Higgs & Sons Stourbridge

PERSONAL INJURY: MAINLY DEFENDANT
■ MIDLANDS

1 **Beachcroft Wansbroughs** Birmingham
Browne Jacobson Nottingham
Buller Jeffries Birmingham
Weightmans Birmingham
2 **Berrymans Lace Mawer** Birmingham
Davies Lavery Birmingham
DLA Birmingham
Everatt & Company Evesham
Keoghs Coventry

PERSONAL INJURY: MAINLY DEFENDANT
■ WALES

1 **Hugh James** Cardiff
Morgan Cole Cardiff
2 **Capital Law** Cardiff Bay
Dolmans Cardiff
Eversheds Cardiff
3 **Douglas-Jones Mercer** Swansea

PERSONAL INJURY: MAINLY CLAIMANT
■ WALES

1 **Hugh James** Cardiff
  Leo Abse & Cohen Cardiff
2 **John Collins & Partners** Swansea
  Thompsons Cardiff
3 **Edwards Geldard** Cardiff
  Loosemores Cardiff
  MLM Cardiff
  Russell Jones & Walker Cardiff

PERSONAL INJURY: MAINLY DEFENDANT
■ NORTH EAST

1 **Berrymans Lace Mawer** Stockton on Tees
  Eversheds Newcastle upon Tyne
2 **Crutes Law Firm** Newcastle upon Tyne
  Dickinson Dees Newcastle upon Tyne
  Hay & Kilner Newcastle upon Tyne
  Sintons Newcastle upon Tyne

PERSONAL INJURY: MAINLY CLAIMANT
■ NORTH EAST

1 **Thompsons** Newcastle upon Tyne
2 **Browell Smith & Co** Newcastle
  Hay & Kilner Newcastle
  Marrons Newcastle
  Sintons Newcastle
3 **Beecham Peacock** Newcastle
  Gorman Hamilton Newcastle
  Russell Jones & Walker Newcastle

PERSONAL INJURY: MAINLY DEFENDANT
■ NORTH WEST

1 **James Chapman & Co** Manchester
2 **Berrymans Lace Mawer** Liverpool
  Keoghs Bolton
  Weightmans Liverpool
3 **Beachcroft Wansbroughs** Manchester
  Halliwells Manchester
  Hill Dickinson Liverpool
4 **Ricksons** Manchester

PERSONAL INJURY: MAINLY CLAIMANT
■ NORTH WEST

1 **Pannone & Partners** Manchester
2 **John Pickering & Partners** Oldham
  McCool Patterson Manchester
  Thompsons Liverpool
3 **Colemans-ctts** Manchester
  Donns Solicitors Manchester
  Hugh Potter & Company Manchester
  Linder Myers Manchester
  Russell Jones & Walker Manchester

PERSONAL INJURY: MAINLY DEFENDANT
■ YORKSHIRE

1 **Beachcroft Wansbroughs** Leeds
  Berrymans Lace Mawer Leeds
  DLA Sheffield
  Nabarro Nathanson Sheffield
2 **Ford & Warren** Leeds
  Irwin Mitchell Sheffield
  Keeble Hawson Leeds
  Langleys York
  Praxis Partners Leeds

PERSONAL INJURY: MAINLY CLAIMANT
■ YORKSHIRE

1 **Irwin Mitchell** Leeds
2 **Russell Jones & Walker** Sheffield
  Stewarts Leeds
3 **Bridge McFarland Solicitors** Grimsby
  Keeble Hawson Sheffield
  Morrish & Co Leeds
  Pattinson & Brewer York
  Rowley Ashworth Leeds

CLINICAL NEGLIGENCE: MAINLY DEFENDANT
■ LONDON

[1] **Capsticks**

Hempsons

[2] **Bevan Brittan**

Kennedys

RadcliffesLeBrasseur

Weightmans

[3] **Barlow Lyde & Gilbert**

Berrymans Lace Mawer

Reynolds Porter Chamberlain

Trowers & Hamlins

CLINICAL NEGLIGENCE: MAINLY CLAIMANT
■ LONDON

[1] **Leigh Day & Co**

[2] **Irwin Mitchell**

Parlett Kent

[3] **Charles Russell**

Field Fisher Waterhouse

Kingsley Napley

[4] **Alexander Harris**

Anthony Gold

Bindman & Partners

Evill and Coleman

Stewarts

CLINICAL NEGLIGENCE: MAINLY DEFENDANT
■ THE SOUTH

[1] **Beachcroft Wansbroughs** Winchester

Brachers Maidstone

CLINICAL NEGLIGENCE: MAINLY CLAIMANT
■ THE SOUTH

[1] **Blake Lapthorn Linnell** Fareham

Penningtons Godalming

Thomson Snell Tunbridge Wells

[2] **George Ide, Phillips** Chichester

Moore & Blatch Southampton

Wynne Baxter Brighton

CLINICAL NEGLIGENCE: MAINLY DEFENDANT
■ EAST ANGLIA

[1] **Kennedys** Newmarket

[2] **Mills & Reeve** Norwich

CLINICAL NEGLIGENCE: MAINLY CLAIMANT
■ EAST ANGLIA

[1] **Kester Cunningham John** Thetford

[2] **Attwater & Liell** Harlow

Gadsby Wicks Chelmsford

Morgan Jones & Pett Great Yarmouth

Scrivenger Seabrook St Neots

CLINICAL NEGLIGENCE: MAINLY DEFENDANT
■ SOUTH WEST

[1] **Bevan Brittan** Bristol

[2] **Beachcroft Wansbroughs** Bristol

CLINICAL NEGLIGENCE: MAINLY CLAIMANT
■ SOUTH WEST

[1] **Barcan Woodward** Bristol

Parlett Kent Exeter

[2] **Clarke Willmott** Bristol

John Hodge & Co Weston-super-Mare

Preston Goldburn Falmouth

Withy King Bath

Wolferstans Plymouth

[3] **Bond Pearce** Bristol

Foot Anstey Sargent Exeter

Over Taylor Biggs Exeter

Russell Jones & Walker Bristol

CLINICAL NEGLIGENCE: MAINLY CLAIMANT
■ THAMES VALLEY

[1] **Boyes Turner** Reading

Osborne Morris Leighton Buzzard

[2] **Harris Cartwright** Slough

CLINICAL NEGLIGENCE: MAINLY DEFENDANT
■ MIDLANDS

[1] **Browne Jacobson** Birmingham

[2] **Bevan Brittan** Birmingham

[3] **Weightmans** Leicester

CLINICAL NEGLIGENCE: MAINLY CLAIMANT
■ MIDLANDS

[1] **Anthony Collins** Birmingham

Challinors Lyon Clark Birmingham

Freeth Cartwright Nottingham

Irwin Mitchell Birmingham

[2] **Alexander Harris** Solihull

Brindley Twist Tafft Coventry

CLINICAL NEGLIGENCE: MAINLY DEFENDANT
■ NORTH EAST

1 **Eversheds** Newcastle upon Tyne

2 **Ward Hadaway** Newcastle upon Tyne

CLINICAL NEGLIGENCE: MAINLY CLAIMANT
■ NORTH EAST

1 **Peter Maughan & Co** Gateshead

Samuel Phillips & Co Newcastle

2 **Ben Hoare Bell** Sunderland

Hay & Kilner Newcastle upon Tyne

CLINICAL NEGLIGENCE: MAINLY DEFENDANT
■ NORTH WEST

1 **Hempsons** Manchester

Hill Dickinson Liverpool

CLINICAL NEGLIGENCE: MAINLY CLAIMANT
■ NORTH WEST

1 **Alexander Harris** Altrincham

Pannone & Partners Manchester

2 **JMW Solicitors** Manchester

3 **Edwards Abrams Doherty** Liverpool

Linder Myers Manchester

McCool Patterson Hemsi Manchester

4 **Donns Solicitors** Manchester

Maxwell Gillott Lancaster

CLINICAL NEGLIGENCE: MAINLY DEFENDANT
■ WALES

1 **RadcliffesLeBrasseur** Cardiff

CLINICAL NEGLIGENCE: MAINLY CLAIMANT
■ WALES

1 **Hugh James** Cardiff

Huttons Cardiff

2 **Harding Evans** Newport

3 **Edwards Geldard** Cardiff

John Collins & Partners Swansea

CLINICAL NEGLIGENCE: MAINLY DEFENDANT
■ YORKSHIRE

1 **Hempsons** Harrogate

2 **Eversheds** Leeds

CLINICAL NEGLIGENCE: MAINLY CLAIMANT
■ YORKSHIRE

1 **Irwin Mitchell** Sheffield

2 **Lester Morrill** Leeds

3 **Heptonstalls** Goole

private client

Private client lawyers give advice on wealth management to individuals, families and trusts. Some additionally handle matrimonial matters or provide small-scale commercial advice; others focus on specialist tax and trusts or wills and probate. A few work in related areas such as heritage property and charities.

type of work

Trust law can be a bit turgid, but those who are best suited to private client practice tend to develop a real interest in it. Trusts are a means of holding assets and avoiding tax, allowing family members or other beneficiaries to access funds without the donor losing all control. Often trusts are held in an offshore jurisdiction, in which case these lawyers must ensure their client understands any foreign law implications. Increasingly, lawyers advise overseas clients wanting to invest in the UK, and banks whose overseas clients have UK interests.

In an average private client department, will drafting and probate forms a significant part of the work and can provide young lawyers with a hands-on role from day one. While your friends in the corporate department might be paginating and bundling rooms full of documents, you will be drafting wills or even organising house clearances.

Specialist charities lawyers work for national charities and local private charitable trusts on matters such as charity registrations and reorganisations, Charity Commission investigations or the development of trading subsidiaries. Such organisations also require mainstream commercial advice.

skills needed

...common sense...lateral thinking...communication and 'people' skills...pragmatism.. objectivity... organised mind...natural curiosity...eye for detail...a desire to help people...a good bedside manner...

If other people's personal affairs make you sit up and listen you'll be in your element. Private client solicitors necessarily become party to very personal information, so impartiality is essential. Chris Belcher at Farrer & Co points out: "*You have to be able to step back and maintain a professional, objective point of view.*" Fear not, the client list is unlikely to be exclusively made up of little old ladies; some clients will be famous, perhaps even super rich. Yet, the job is never going to be as spicy as a position in the offices of *Heat* or *Hello!* and you must always bear in mind that the highly confidential nature of your work means you won't be able to name-drop with your mates in the pub.

Private client practice may lack the fast and furious pace of corporate work, but it does make other demands: the work can be technical and you have to be interested in the academic side. For example, with all that tax and accounts work, it helps to be numerate, though fortunately "*you don't have to be Einstein!*"

Chris is very clear that "*there is no typical lawyer, as there is no typical client.*" Despite the green-welly image of specialist private client practices, more and more of their clients have made their money through property, business or even a lottery win, so a public school education and country retreat are not essential. Clients instruct lawyers for their technical legal knowledge not their pedigree, and they are even more inclined to instruct those who can combine know-how with practical skills and a personable approach.

career options

After a lull in the 1990s the field is experiencing a period of growth. Along with more wealth and more clients, the passing of three new Trustee Acts has seen the sector evolving. General social trends and greater life expectancy are also having an impact.

In-house opportunities are rare so most lawyers remain in private practice. While few City firms offer private client services, there are a number of small and medium-sized London firms with an established reputation, and plenty of excellent practices nationwide. Moves between high street firms and those servicing wealthy individuals are rare, so try and get a training contract with the right type of firm for you.

There is less scope for charity lawyers in terms of specialist law firms, but working at one will enable you to make good client contacts, which could lead to a move into the charities sector itself. For an overview of the leading private client and charities law practices refer to *Chambers UK*.

LEADING FIRMS FROM CHAMBERS UK 2004-2005

TRUSTS & PERSONAL TAX
■ THE SOUTH

[1] **Cripps Harries Hall** Tunbridge Wells
Thomas Eggar Chichester
[2] **Paris Smith & Randall** Southampton
Penningtons Godalming
Stevens & Bolton Guildford
Thomson Snell Tunbridge Wells
[3] **Adams & Remers** Lewes
Blake Lapthorn Linnell Fareham
Brachers Maidstone
Buss Murton Tunbridge Wells
Charles Russell Guildford
DMH Brighton
Godwins Winchester
Lester Aldridge Bournemouth
Moore & Blatch Lymington
Mundays Cobham
Rawlison Butler Crawley
White & Bowker Winchester
[4] **asb law** Horsham
Barlows Guildford
Griffith Smith Brighton
Whitehead Monckton Maidstone

TRUSTS & PERSONAL TAX
■ SOUTH WEST

[1] **Burges Salmon** Bristol
Wilsons Salisbury
[2] **Charles Russell** Cheltenham
Osborne Clarke Bristol
Wiggin & Co Cheltenham
[3] **Bond Pearce** Plymouth
Foot Anstey Sargent Plymouth
[4] **Clarke Willmott** Bristol
Coodes St Austell
Hooper & Wollen Torquay
Michelmores Exeter
[5] **Rickerbys** Cheltenham
TLT Bristol
Veale Wasbrough Bristol

TRUSTS & PERSONAL TAX
■ EAST ANGLIA

[1] **Mills & Reeve** Norwich
[2] **Hewitsons** Cambridge
Taylor Vinters Cambridge
Willcox & Lewis Norwich
[3] **Birketts** Ipswich
Greene & Greene Bury St Edmunds
Howes Percival Norwich
[4] **Ashton Graham** Ipswich
Barker Gotelee Ipswich
Cozens-Hardy & Jewson Norwich
Hansells Norwich
Hood Vores & Allwood Dereham
Prettys Ipswich
Roythorne & Co Spalding
Wollastons Chelmsford

TRUSTS & PERSONAL TAX
■ LONDON

1. **Macfarlanes**
   Withers
2. **Allen & Overy**
   Baker & McKenzie
   Boodle Hatfield
   Charles Russell
   Currey & Co
   Lawrence Graham
3. **Bircham Dyson Bell**
   Farrer & Co
   Forsters
   Hunters
   Payne Hicks Beach
   Speechly Bircham
   Taylor Wessing
4. **Berwin Leighton Paisner**
   Herbert Smith
   Linklaters
   Nicholson Graham & Jones
5. **Collyer-Bristow**
   Davenport Lyons
   Dawsons
   Finers Stephens Innocent
   Harbottle & Lewis
   Harcus Sinclair
   Howard Kennedy
   Lee & Pembertons
   May, May & Merrimans
   RadcliffesLeBrasseur
   Rooks Rider
   Simmons & Simmons
   Smyth Barkham
   Trowers & Hamlins
   Wedlake Bell

TRUSTS & PERSONAL TAX: CONTENTIOUS
■ LONDON

1. **Allen & Overy**
   Boodle Hatfield
   Herbert Smith
   Withers
2. **Baker & McKenzie**
   Charles Russell
   Clifford Chance
   Lawrence Graham
   Macfarlanes
3. **Berwin Leighton Paisner**
   Harcus Sinclair
   Laytons
   Norton Rose
   Speechly Bircham

TRUSTS & PERSONAL TAX
■ MIDLANDS

1. **Martineau Johnson** Birmingham
2. **Browne Jacobson** Nottingham
   Hewitsons Northampton
   Higgs & Sons Brierley Hill
   Lodders Stratford-upon-Avon
3. **Cobbetts** Birmingham
   Wragge & Co Birmingham
4. **Edwards Geldard** Derby
   Freeth Cartwright Nottingham
   Gateley Wareing Birmingham
   Hallmarks Worcester
   Mills & Reeve Birmingham
   Pinsents Birmingham
   Shakespeares Birmingham

TRUSTS & PERSONAL TAX
■ WALES

1. **Edwards Geldard** Cardiff
   Hugh James Cardiff
2. **Margraves** Llandrindod Wells

TRUSTS & PERSONAL TAX
■ NORTH EAST

1. **Dickinson Dees** Newcastle upon Tyne
   Wrigleys Leeds
2. **Addleshaw Goddard** Leeds
   Gordons Leeds
   Irwin Mitchell Sheffield
3. **Andrew M Jackson** Hull
   Grays York
   Lupton Fawcett Leeds
   Rollits Hull
   Ward Hadaway Newcastle upon Tyne

TRUSTS & PERSONAL TAX
■ NORTH WEST

1. **Halliwells** Manchester
2. **Addleshaw Goddard** Manchester
   Birch Cullimore Chester
   Brabners Chaffe Street Liverpool
   Cobbetts Manchester
   Cuff Roberts Liverpool
   Pannone & Partners Manchester

TRUSTS & PERSONAL TAX
■ THAMES VALLEY

1. **B P Collins** Gerrards Cross
   Boodle Hatfield Oxford
   Boyes Turner Reading
   Henmans Oxford
2. **Blandy & Blandy** Reading
   Iliffes Booth Bennett (IBB) Uxbridge
   Matthew Arnold & Baldwin Watford
3. **Penningtons** Newbury
   Pictons Hemel Hempstead
   Stanley Tee Bishops Stortford

CHARITIES
■ LONDON

1. **Bates, Wells & Braithwaite**
   Farrer & Co
2. **Nabarro Nathanson**
   Stone King
   Withers
3. **Allen & Overy**
   Berwin Leighton Paisner
   Bircham Dyson Bell
   Charles Russell
   Russell-Cooke
4. **Campbell Hooper**
   Claricoat Phillips
   Hempsons
   Herbert Smith
   RadcliffesLeBrasseur
   Speechly Bircham
   Trowers & Hamlins
5. **CMS Cameron McKenna**
   Gordon Dadds
   Harbottle & Lewis
   Howard Kennedy
   Lawrence Graham
   Macfarlanes
   Winckworth Sherwood

CHARITIES
■ THAMES VALLEY

1. **Blake Lapthorn Linnell** Oxford
   BrookStreet Des Roches Witney
   Winckworth Sherwood Oxford
2. **Henmans** Oxford
   Iliffes Booth Bennett (IBB) Ingatestone
   Manches Oxford
   Morgan Cole Oxford

CHARITIES
■ THE SOUTH

1. **Blake Lapthorn Linnell** Portsmouth
2. **Cripps Harries Hall** Tunbridge Wells
   Griffith Smith Brighton
   Thomson Snell & Passmore
   Tunbridge Wells
3. **Lester Aldridge** Bournemouth
   Thomas Eggar Chichester
4. **DMH** Brighton

CHARITIES
■ THE SOUTH WEST

1. **Stone King** Bath
2. **Burges Salmon** Bristol
   Osborne Clarke Bristol
   Wilsons Salisbury
3. **Bond Pearce** Plymouth
   Rickerbys Cheltenham
   Tozers Exeter
4. **Foot Anstey Sargent** Exeter
   Thring Townsend Bath
   Veale Wasbrough Lawyers Bristol

CHARITIES
■ MIDLANDS

1. **Anthony Collins Solicitors** Birmingham
   Martineau Johnson Birmingham
2. **Cobbetts** Birmingham
   Wragge & Co Birmingham
3. **Band Hatton** Coventry
   Pinsents Birmingham
   Shakespeares Birmingham

CHARITIES
■ WALES

1. **Edwards Geldard** Cardiff

CHARITIES
■ NORTH WEST

1. **Brabners Chaffe Street** Liverpool
   Halliwells Manchester
   Oswald Goodier & Co Preston
   Pannone & Partners Manchester
2. **Addleshaw Goddard** Manchester
   Birch Cullimore Chester
   Kuit Steinart Levy Manchester

CHARITIES
■ NORTH EAST

1. **Rollits** York
   Wrigleys Leeds
2. **Addleshaw Goddard** Leeds
   Dickinson Dees Newcastle upon Tyne
   McCormicks Leeds
3. **Grays** York
   Irwin Mitchell Sheffield
   Robert Muckle Newcastle upon Tyne
   Ward Hadaway Newcastle upon Tyne

CHARITIES
■ EAST ANGLIA

1. **Mills & Reeve** Norwich
   Taylor Vinters Cambridge
2. **Greenwoods Solicitors** Peterborough
   Hewitsons Cambridge
3. **Hegarty & Co Solicitors** Peterborough

property/real estate

It's a conundrum: the UK population watches property development shows on TV 24/7, yet few law students aspire to be property lawyers. Admittedly land law lectures at uni or law school usually baffle and bore in equal measure, but it's worth digging a little deeper because the reality of practice is very different.

type of work

We spoke to Mike Bothamley, head of Beachcroft Wansbroughs' property practice, and asked him to tell us what gets property lawyers out of bed in the mornings. *"The deals – I love deals!"* he explained, adding that buildings and the built environment *"and what they can do for peoples' quality of life"* were also important to him. Factor in the ongoing relationships with clients and various other professionals and you begin to see that daily life in practice is no snooze in the lecture theatre.

Mike, who concentrates on large-scale developments, talked about the life cycle of deals. They start with site assembly (buying all the required land) and planning permissions, progress through the funding and construction stages, and culminate in the sale or letting of completed buildings. The clients you act for will determine the sort of work you do. Developers tend to be more entrepreneurial and risk-taking than, for example, financiers who operate within narrower parameters and require more i-dotting and t-crossing from their lawyers. You might want to bear this in mind when choosing a firm. Many of the lawyers we speak to find the development side of the job the most interesting; others specialise in particular types of property: retail premises, agricultural land or offices, for example.

Whatever specialisation you end up in, the law and, more importantly, the market both keep evolving. Recently, for instance, the government has introduced the concept of commonhold land ownership, and there's a growing trend for 'outsourcing', whereby companies divest themselves of real estate ownership and management functions so they can concentrate on their core business. Mike also explained that the pensions crisis has led to greater interest in development and investment. He's right – you can see this at either end of the scale: the bloke down the road who's just taken out a buy-to-let mortgage and the fact that there's hardly a city centre in the UK that's not already been, or is currently being, redeveloped. Apparently, *"lowest common denominator development is a thing of the past,"* and there's a greater emphasis on the impact the built environment has on the business and residential communities that use it, in particular upon good design and sustainable development.

skills needed

cool-headed and unflappable...collaborative nature...lead others or work alone...analytical mind...grasp commercial and practical realities...see big picture while delving into detail...good drafter and negotiator...

One of the most satisfying aspects of the job is the co-operative process between all the parties to a deal – clients, opposite numbers, builders, surveyors, banks, planners, etc. Basically, *"everybody is after the same result;"* so if writing nasty letters and threatening court action leaves you cold, this could be your field. Yet you can't be a pushover; your client will expect you to negotiate favourable terms for them and you'll need to be firm. Happily, as you progress, industry knowledge becomes second nature, and it becomes easier to understand the commercial logic of a transaction, so that – as Mike puts it – *"you only expend powder and shot on the points that really matter."*

Property lawyers are jugglers. Usually they have several transactions on the go at any one time and, to stay on top of things, they need to be organised, proactive and fully aware of the consequences of each move in a transaction. But no matter how exciting things are for experienced lawyers, they all had to earn their stripes by doing their fair share of drafting and negotiating bog-standard leases and contracts. There are times when this can be tedious, but there are now more standardised documents in use, a development which makes life easier.

career options

There are several allied career options for lawyers – planning, environmental, local authority, banks and funders, contractors, surveyors, property companies – and ex-property lawyers often make good developers themselves. There's also been a rise in the number of openings for professional support lawyers – ideal for those with less interest in doing deals than in the documentation or the legal principles holding them together.

LEADING FIRMS FROM CHAMBERS UK 2004-2005

REAL ESTATE: MEDIUM DEALS
■ LONDON

1 DLA	Forsters
Wragge & Co	
2 Addleshaw Goddard	Eversheds
Field Fisher Waterhouse	Maxwell Batley
Richards Butler	Taylor Wessing
Travers Smith Braithwaite	
3 Boodle Hatfield	Fladgate Fielder
Nicholson Graham & Jones	Osborne Clarke
Simmons & Simmons	Speechly Bircham
4 Davies Arnold Cooper	Finers Stephens Innocent
Howard Kennedy	Manches
Mishcon de Reya	Trowers & Hamlins
5 Hammonds	Harbottle & Lewis
Julian Holy	Lewis Silkin
Park Nelson	Penningtons
Solomon Taylor & Shaw	Stepien Lake Gilbert & Paling
Tite & Lewis	

REAL ESTATE: LARGER DEALS
■ LONDON

1 Berwin Leighton Paisner
Clifford Chance
Linklaters
2 Herbert Smith
Lovells
3 Ashurst
Freshfields Bruckhaus Deringer
Nabarro Nathanson
SJ Berwin
4 Allen & Overy
CMS Cameron McKenna
Lawrence Graham
Macfarlanes
Slaughter and May
5 Dechert
Denton Wilde Sapte
Jones Day
Mayer, Brown, Rowe & Maw
Norton Rose
Olswang
Paul, Hastings, Janofsky & Walker

SPECIALIST PRACTICE AREAS PROPERTY/REAL ESTATE

REAL ESTATE
■ THE SOUTH

[1] **Blake Lapthorn Linnell** Fareham
Cripps Harries Hall Tunbridge Wells
[2] **Bond Pearce** Southampton
Paris Smith & Randall Southampton
[3] **Clyde & Co** Guildford
DMH Crawley
Lester Aldridge Bournemouth
Stevens & Bolton Guildford
Thomas Eggar Chichester
[4] **Coffin Mew & Clover** Southampton
GCL Solicitors Guildford
Rawlison Butler Crawley
Shoosmiths Fareham
Thomson Snell Tunbridge Wells
[5] **asb law** Crawley
Brachers Maidstone
Mundays Cobham
Penningtons Basingstoke
Steele Raymond Bournemouth
[6] **Davies Lavery** Maidstone
Lamport Bassitt Southampton
Laytons Guildford
Moore & Blatch Southampton

REAL ESTATE
■ SOUTH WEST

[1] **Burges Salmon** Bristol
[2] **Ashfords** Exeter
Beachcroft Wansbroughs Bristol
Bevan Brittan Bristol
Bond Pearce Plymouth
[3] **BPE Solicitors** Cheltenham
Charles Russell Cheltenham
Clarke Willmott Bristol
Davitt Jones Bould Taunton
Michelmores Exeter
Osborne Clarke Bristol
Rickerbys Cheltenham
TLT Solicitors Bristol
Veale Wasbrough Lawyers Bristol
[4] **Clark Holt** Swindon
Davies and Partners Gloucester
Foot Anstey Sargent Plymouth
Stephens & Scown Exeter
Thring Townsend Swindon
Withy King Bath

REAL ESTATE
■ EAST ANGLIA

[1] **Hewitsons** Cambridge
Mills & Reeve Cambridge
[2] **Birketts** Ipswich
Eversheds Cambridge
Taylor Vinters Cambridge
[3] **Ashton Graham** Bury St Edmunds
Greene & Greene Bury St Edmunds
Greenwoods Solicitors Peterborough
Kester Cunningham John Cambridge
Prettys Ipswich

REAL ESTATE
■ THAMES VALLEY

[1] **Pitmans** Reading
[2] **Boyes Turner** Reading
BrookStreet Des Roches Witney
Clarks Reading
Denton Wilde Sapte Milton keynes
Iliffes Booth Bennett (IBB) Uxbridge
[3] **Blake Lapthorn Linnell** Oxford
Harold Benjamin Harrow
Manches Oxford
Matthew Arnold & Baldwin Watford
Nabarro Nathanson Reading
[4] **Blandy & Blandy** Oxford
BPC Business Lawyers Gerrards Cross
Fennemores Milton Keynes
Field Seymour Parkes Reading
Morgan Cole Reading
Pictons Luton
Stanley Tee Bishops Stortsord

REAL ESTATE
■ WALES

[1] **Edwards Geldard** Cardiff
Eversheds Cardiff
[2] **Berry Smith** Cardiff
Capital Law Cardiff
[3] **Morgan LaRoche** Swansea
[4] **Hugh James** Cardiff
Morgan Cole Cardiff
Robertsons Cardiff

132

REAL ESTATE
WEST MIDLANDS

1. **Eversheds** Birmingham
   Wragge & Co Birmingham
2. **Pinsents** Birmingham
3. **Cobbetts** Birmingham
   DLA Birmingham
   Hammonds Birmingham
   Shoosmiths Northampton
4. **Knight & Sons** Newcastle
   Martineau Johnson Birmingham
   Wright Hassall Leamington Spa

REAL ESTATE
EAST MIDLANDS

1. **Browne Jacobson** Nottingham
   Eversheds Nottingham
   Freeth Cartwright Nottingham
2. **Edwards Geldard** Derby
   Harvey Ingram Owston Leicester
   Shoosmiths Nottingham

REAL ESTATE
NORTH WEST

1. **Addleshaw Goddard** Manchester
   Cobbetts Manchester
   DLA Liverpool
   Eversheds Manchester
2. **Beachcroft Wansbroughs** Manchstr
   Hammonds Manchester
3. **DWF** Liverpool
   Halliwells Manchester
   Mace & Jones Manchester
4. **Brabners Chaffe Street** Liverpool
   Cuff Roberts Liverpool
   Field Cunningham & Co Manchester
   JMW Solicitors Manchester
   Land Law Solicitors Altrincham
   Masons Manchester
   Pannone & Partners Manchester

REAL ESTATE
NORTH EAST

1. **Dickinson Dees** Newcastle upon Tyne
2. **Eversheds** Newcastle upon Tyne
3. **Robert Muckle** Newcastle upon Tyne
4. **Ward Hadaway** Newcastle upon Tyne
   Watson Burton Newcastle upon Tyne

REAL ESTATE
YORKSHIRE

1. **Addleshaw Goddard** Leeds
   Walker Morris Leeds
2. **DLA** Leeds
   Pinsents Leeds
3. **Cobbetts** Leeds
   Eversheds Leeds
   Hammonds Leeds
   Nabarro Nathanson Sheffield
4. **Andrew M Jackson** Hull
5. **Irwin Mitchell** Sheffield
   Keeble Hawson Leeds
   Shulmans Leeds
6. **Denison Till** York
   Gosschalks Hull
   Rollits Hull
   Wake Smith Sheffield

public interest

Are you the kind of person who won't shrug their shoulders and allow an injustice to continue unchallenged simply because it is lawful? This field is incredibly popular with students, yet academic argument and the rigours of practice are worlds apart...

civil liberties and human rights

Human rights issues crop up in both civil and criminal cases. On the civil side examples include claims of rights to education and community care under the Mental Health Act, or cases of discrimination at work, where people are unfairly passed over for promotion, miss out on benefits or equal pay. The right to family life is enshrined in the HRA and family lawyers have to consider human rights in relation to child access and residency. In housing cases, the issue might be a gay or lesbian partner's right to succeed to a tenancy previously held by their deceased partner.

Danny Simpson, head of the criminal and civil liberties department at Howells in Sheffield, explained how *"a lot of human rights issues relate to people's interactions with the state"* and judicial review is a key tool by which the decisions of public bodies can be challenged. A *"tidal wave of legislation"* spanning terrorism and antisocial behaviour intersects with the Public Order Acts and the Human Rights Act to throw up a multitude of issues in relation to asylum seeker's rights, treatment of people in police custody and local authorities' obligations towards people who are mentally ill, all of which have been the subject of recent cases.

Danny's caseload contains miscarriages of justice and files relating to public order convictions arising out of demonstrations and confrontations with the police. He also handles a wide range of police complaints and prisoners' issues. In July 2004, the House of Lords made a ruling on whether the fingerprints of a detainee in police custody could be retained even if no charges were laid against them. And consider for a moment the fact that the Home Secretary decides whether or not prisoners serving life sentences may be released. The European Court of Human Rights says it is wrong that a politician should make a decision based on whether or not a person has been sufficiently punished or the likelihood that their imprisonment has acted as a deterrent to others. The only valid criterion for a politician, says the court, is whether or not the person is a continuing danger.

skills needed

...passion...determination...demonstrated commitment...creativity...initiative... communicate well with Joe Public and with the court...love of advocacy...

Danny is clear that *"there is no point in doing this work for the money – you will be considerably worse paid than in other areas."* Instead, *"you do it because you have a desire or a vocation to improve another's situation."* As you'll have extensive contact with people who are mentally ill or *"don't appreciate the full extent of their legal predicament,"* empathy and sympathy are required in equal measure. Strong analytical skills are also vital because it's your job to *"identify the legal issues you can do something about, and those economic or political situations that, as a lawyer, you can't help with."* Organisational skills will serve you well, and you will need patience to battle against bureaucracy and red tape. Importantly, you must be able to manage a client's expectations; it will not help them if your idealism clouds a situation.

career options

The number of people who tell us they are looking for training contracts in this field outstrips the number of contracts available by some margin. However, as the work is largely legally aided (or done for free if no funding is available) the firms that specialise cannot offer trainees attractive salaries and certainly don't sponsor them through law school. "*In one respect there is a bottomless pit of work; in another it is difficult for practices to do the work at all without going bust.*"

"*Firms distinguish between those applicants who say they are interested and those who really are interested,*" so carrying out voluntary work for a law centre or specialist voluntary organisation such as the Howard League for Penal Reform or the Children's Legal Centre, or joining a relevant organisation such as Liberty or Justice, will improve your chances. The *Legal Action Group Bulletin* is an accessible publication covering the area and you'll find it enormously helpful in gaining a better understanding of the issues that concern lawyers in this field. It also goes without saying that regularly reading good quality newspapers is important, if only to keep track of Mr Blunkett's new measures.

Law centres and the voluntary sector pick up from where private practice leaves off, and it is not uncommon for dedicated lawyers to move between the two arenas during their careers. For more information on life inside law centres, see page 11.

immigration law

The subject of immigration is close to the hearts of many, not least among them the Home Secretary and readers of the *Daily Mail*. For better or worse, politics and public opinion are inexorably linked to the practice of immigration law. There are two strands of practice: business and personal, the latter being the one that motivates most students to enter the field, as it addresses one of the most fundamental issues in a person's life – the question of whether they will be permitted to live and work or study in the country they choose. For some clients, this will determine whether they can be together with their spouse/partner and family. For others, who have fled from persecution in their countries of origin, removal could mean torture or death.

2004 has seen a further reduction in the number of firms undertaking legal aid immigration work,

following a new set of cuts to legal aid funding. Publicly funded work has always been the preserve of the most committed of practitioners, and so it is sad to see a number of excellent firms now bowing out because the work is becoming uneconomic. Twinned with financial cut backs is the continuing raft of restrictive legislative activity in the linked areas of immigration and asylum, such as the recently overturned policy to refuse accommodation and assistance to destitute asylum seekers. Those entering practice must be more committed than ever.

On the business side, things are looking rosier. Immigration lawyer Jonathan Kingham explained: "*Until recently, there was a vilification of economic migrants, now the government has a new approach – managed migration. It is trying to cut down on asylum seekers and those seeking leave to remain on other human rights grounds, and instead ensure that those who come to the UK are coming to work and bringing skills.*" Business immigration work includes advice and assistance on work permits for employers and employees, and related schemes for Highly Skilled Migrants and investors. Jonathan believes that dealing with corporate clients and businessmen requires a particular set of skills, in particular managing client expectations: "*You have to be able to see their commercial concerns. At worst, a businessman might need to travel abroad for a high level meeting, yet the Home Office wants their passport.*" By contrast, "*for an asylum client, nothing is more important than getting leave to remain in the UK*".

skills needed

...sensitivity...compassion and commitment...able to deal with emotional clients...tenacity...willing to question the authorities...language skills...an understanding of the broader commercial context...

Unless you're organised, you'll find the job impossible. "*It's the nature of the game – everything has a deadline and you've got to meet them,*" says Jonathan. Furthermore, publicly funded work is accompanied by a mountain of unremunerated form filling and red tape, which you just can't ignore. You'll need to be familiar with several different sources of law – UK law and Home Office policy, European law, human rights legislation – and you'll need to know which will be most advantageous to your client. If advocacy is important to you, the good news is there's plenty of opportunity to develop this skill. Certainly it means an enormous amount to the client to have the same person take their case from start to finish. If you do end up working with asylum seekers, there's a delicate balance to be struck. *"You will hear some horrific stories and you'll have to be tough enough to elicit the right information, while also being sensitive towards the client."*

career options

Of those who have quit private practice recently, some went into the administrative side, becoming immigration adjudicators; others headed for the voluntary sector. Generally speaking immigration lawyers are motivated by higher ideals than money; in fact, working in the voluntary sector can be more satisfying as there are less funding constraints than in private practice. There are branches of the Refugee Legal Centre and the Immigration Advisory Service across the country and these organisations, and others like them, will doubtless continue to be very busy and offer employment opportunities.

As a student it is important to test your commitment to the field and to keep up to date by becoming a student member of the Immigration Law Practitioners Association. Consider joining organisations like the Joint Council for the Welfare of Immigrants, Amnesty or the Medical Foundation (which helps torture victims). Wherever possible, take immigration law subjects at law school or uni.

LEADING FIRMS FROM CHAMBERS UK 2004-2005

HUMAN RIGHTS
LONDON

1. **Bhatt Murphy**
   Bindman & Partners
2. **Birnberg Peirce & Partners**
   Christian Khan
   Hickman & Rose
   Leigh Day & Co
3. **Scott-Moncrieff, Harbour & Sinclair**
   Simons Muirhead & Burton
4. **Deighton Guedalla**
   Palmer Wade
   Taylor Nichol

HUMAN RIGHTS: COMMERCIAL
■ **LONDON**

1. **Clifford Chance**
   Freshfields Bruckhaus Deringer
   Herbert Smith

HUMAN RIGHTS
■ **MIDLANDS**

1. **Public Interest Lawyers** Birmingham
   Public Law Solicitors Birmingham
2. **Tyndallwoods** Birmingham

HUMAN RIGHTS
■ **THE NORTH**

1. **Harrison Bundey** Leeds
   Howells Sheffield
   Irwin Mitchell Sheffield
2. **A S Law** Liverpool
3. **Ben Hoare Bell** Sunderland
   Robert Lizar Manchester

IMMIGRATION: PERSONAL
■ LONDON

1 Bindman & Partners

Birnberg Peirce & Partners

Wesley Gryk

2 Deighton Guedalla

Glazer Delmar

Luqmani Thompson

Wilson & Co

3 Bartram & Co Hounslow

Bates, Wells & Braithwaite

DJ Webb & Co

Elder Rahimi

Powell & Co

IMMIGRATION
■ THAMES VALLEY

1 Darbys Oxford

Turpin Miller & Higgins Oxford

IMMIGRATION: BUSINESS
■ LONDON

1 CMS Cameron McKenna

Kingsley Napley

2 Bates, Wells & Braithwaite

Laura Devine Solicitors

Magrath & Co

Reed Smith

3 Baker & McKenzie

Mishcon de Reya

Penningtons

Sturtivant & Co

4 DJ Webb & Co

Fox Williams

Gherson & Co

Harbottle & Lewis

Lovells

Taylor Wessing

IMMIGRATION
■ EAST ANGLIA

1 Gross & Co Bury St Edmunds

Wollastons Chelmsford

IMMIGRATION
■ MIDLANDS

1 The Rights Partnership Birmingham

Tyndallwoods Birmingham

IMMIGRATION
■ THE NORTH

1 David Gray Newcastle upon Tyne

Harrison Bundey Leeds

2 A S Law Liverpool

Howells Sheffield

3 Henry Hyams Leeds

Jackson & Canter Liverpool

shipping

p&i club: Protection and Indemnity Club – a marine insurance club run mutually by and for shipowners.
charter party: a commercial instrument; essentially a contract for the hire of the whole or a part of a ship.
bill of lading: a receipt given by the master of the ship for goods loaded, a contract of carriage between the owners of the ships and the owners of the goods and a negotiable certificate of title to the goods themselves.
salvage: reward payable by owners of recovered ships; goods saved at sea by 'salvors'.

Do you dream of being a master and commander like Russell Crowe, or cavorting with pirates in the Caribbean? Careers in shipping law are diverse, unpredictable and truly international. For a land-locked nine-to-five desk job, look elsewhere.

type of work

Shipping law concerns the carriage of goods or people by sea. Contentious work is divided into wet ('Admiralty') work and dry ('marine') work. Wet work is broadly tortious, and concerns disputes arising from accidents or misadventure at sea (collision, salvage, total loss or modern-day piracy). It often attracts former naval officers or ex-mariners. In this area, lawyers need to act fast: delays cost money, and clients expect quick analysis and sensible answers. Dry work, on the other hand, concerns disputes related to contracts made on dry land, such as charter parties, bills of lading, and sale of goods contracts.

Non-contentious work primarily concerns ship finance and ship building contracts, sale and purchase agreements, employment contracts for crew members, affreightment contracts, and the registration and re-flagging of ships. Further niche areas include yachting or fishing, which usually involve regulatory matters. Be under no illusion – ship finance is nowhere near as exciting as casualty work,

nor does it offer the same opportunities for travel.

Dry shipping specialist Tony Rooth of Watson, Farley & Williams divides his time between court and arbitration appearances, conferences with counsel, client meetings, and giving internal advice and taking witness statements – a caseload that is nothing if not diverse. While shipping law does not have a work-all-night culture, there is often an element of unpredictability about it. Wet lawyers, especially, may have to jet off to Panama or Piraeus at short notice to take a witness statement or deal with a casualty. Tony tells us it's a case of "*have passport, will travel.*" And when you consider that you'll often be dealing with people or problems located in a different time zone, it becomes clear why shipping law doesn't suit the routine junkie. "*In a worst-case scenario, you'll have a client in the East, and a ship in the West.*"

In spite of headline-hitting cases – such as the Herald of Free Enterprise or Exxon Valdez disasters, "*shipping may not be as sexy or remunerative as some other areas of the law.*" Yet all is not lost; globalisation and industry consolidation mean that the area is far from static, and one can't really envisage world trade grinding to a halt. Trainees and NQs must expect to get chucked in at the deep end fairly early on. Research, client meetings, taking witness statements and drafting basic documents all mean "*lots of devilling, lots of exposure and certainly no photocopying.*" Devilling, by the way, means doing work for someone more senior (and busier) than you.

skills needed

...always up to speed on legal developments/industry trends...firm grip on contract, tort and court procedure...available to travel at short notice...good communicator...team spirit and self motivation...

Dry lawyers need to develop a good knowledge of conflicts, contract and tort. Wet lawyers need to be bold, as they will face adversity and the unexpected. All shipping lawyers will be interacting with people from different cultures and countries and at different ends of the social scale; many of them will have been schooled in the university of life and, as Tony notes, are strong characters who can sometimes be *"suspicious or difficult to handle."* From shipowners, operators, traders and charterers through to P&I clubs and hull underwriters – it's a really mixed bag, so people skills and good communication are crucial.

In wet work, naval or marine experience is common, but this is not to say you can't build a career without it. Most shipping lawyers start out with little industry knowledge, but soon acquire it. As Tony explained: *"It does help if you know your port from your starboard, especially when dealing with navigation matters."*

career options

The majority of UK-based jobs are to be found in London, with the remainder in larger port cities. In international firms, assistants can choose to work abroad, something that is generally considered to be a good career move. If, following qualification, you decide shipping is not for you, as a contentious shipping lawyer you'll have gained a solid grounding in commercial litigation. If you've taken the non-contentious route, you should be able to shift relatively seamlessly into general finance or corporate work. And if private practice disappoints, then P&I clubs, shipowners, operators and marine insurers all have openings for lawyers, but the financial rewards will be less than in private practice, as will the legal component of the position. Failing all else, there's always piracy...

LEADING FIRMS FROM CHAMBERS UK 2004-2005

SHIPPING
■ **LONDON**

[1] **Ince & Co**	
[2] **Clyde & Co**	**Holman Fenwick & Willan**
[3] **Bentleys, Stokes & Lowless**	**Hill Taylor Dickinson**
Richards Butler	
[4] **Barlow Lyde & Gilbert**	**Jackson Parton**
More Fisher Brown	**Shaw and Croft**
Waltons & Morse	**Winter Scott**
[5] **Clifford Chance**	**Curtis Davis Garrard**
Lawrence Graham	**Middleton Potts**
Stephenson Harwood	**Thomas Cooper & Stibbard**
Waterson Hicks	
[6] **Davies Arnold Cooper**	**Fishers**
Hill Dickinson	**Mays Brown, Solicitors**
Norton Rose	**Watson, Farley & Williams**

SHIPPING
■ **THE REGIONS**

[1] **Eversheds** Newcastle	
[2] **Andrew M Jackson** Hull	
Henderson Boyd Edinburgh	
Mills & Co Newcastle	
Rayfield Mills Newcastle	
[3] **Davies, Johnson & Co** Plymouth	
DLA Manchester	
Hill Dickinson Liverpool	
Lester Aldridge Southampton	
Mackinnons Aberdeen	
[4] **Bond Pearce** Plymouth	
Dale & Co Felixstowe	
Foot Anstey Sargent Plymouth	
John Weston & Co Felixstowe	
Maclay Murray & Spens Glasgow	
Prettys Ipswich	

sports law

Rather than being a discipline in its own right, sports law is an industry focus. Consequently, many of the firms that offer this kind of service do so by drawing upon the services of lawyers from other practice groups, and only a few have a team of dedicated sports lawyers. Broadly speaking, sports law encompasses:

- regulatory advice to teams and ruling bodies;
- advice on media, advertising and sponsorship;
- general corporate and commercial advice.

type of work

Like it or not, sport is a business. What this means for the sports lawyer is that advice must always be given in a commercial context. As Stephen Hornsby of The Simkins Partnership notes: "*Ultimately the most important things are the contracts. It is better to be a good contract lawyer than a good sports lawyer.*" On top of this, the lawyer needs to develop an understanding of intellectual property, sponsorship and broadcasting issues. On occasion, they may also need to tackle crime, personal injury and employment matters and, of late, some have been at the forefront of developments in the law regarding image rights and privacy.

Consider the juxtaposition of commercial considerations with sports regulations and domestic and EU law. The Bosman case, which concerned player transfer fees, is a prime example of where industry-specific and EU laws can collide. EU employment law prevailed, resulting in a tremendous knock-on effect in the football industry. The same can be said about the current attempt by the Inland Revenue to abolish football's 'super creditor' rule. That rule requires a club in administration to pay other clubs and its own players before creditors, on pain of expulsion from the league. If the challenge succeeds, clubs will tighten up on the amount of money and players they are willing to lend to each other, per-

haps leading to reductions in players' wages and a restricted transfer market. However, as Stephen notes: "*Sport, and especially football, will shortly be run as any other business. As the legal immunities begin to collapse, and the false liquidity in the market comes to an end, this will result in greater legal involvement.*"

Both the globalisation and commercialisation of sport has brought new issues that the legal framework must encompass. Intrusive press coverage has resulted in concerns over the accuracy of reports and potential claims for defamation or breach of privacy. The interests of broadcasters and sponsors often compete with those of the players and spectators – should players have to undertake rounds of press interviews after completing a match, rather than going home to their families? Should teams have to play late at night to maximise TV viewing figures? Does the ubiquitous sponsor's logo projected across the pitch detract from the enjoyment of the paying spectator? These are all conflicting interests that sports lawyers must face when negotiating the next round of broadcasting rights.

skills needed

...strong on contract law...commercial nous...interpersonal skills...entrepreneurial approach...innovation...passion for the subject...ability to see the other side of the argument...

It's important that you have a genuine interest in the industry. You've don't need to have read every edition of *The Racing Post* since the age of nine or be able to recite the names of past winners of the FA Cup, but if you want to work for a particular client, you ought to know a bit about the sport's relevant governing body and its professional organisation.

In this industry, perhaps more so than any other, you've got to be able to impress clients with your personality and passion. As well as executing the technical aspects of the job, you must be prepared to run what may in fact be closer to a consultancy service to help your client to manage his image. As Stephen says: *"The idea is to be a trusted advisor. If you have an idea, you pick up the phone and tell them about it, and give them a plan how to action it. It's not about just waiting for the phone to ring."* If emotions are running high, you must stay cool and rational and consider the merits of an alternative game plan. *"You must always understand that the opposition have a valid point of view themselves, and it is usually well thought out and sincerely held."* It's at this point that a sports lawyer needs that extra bit of imagination to make sure the ball stays in play.

career options

Lawyers move into this area by both accident and design. Some leading practitioners specialised in a field that affects sport, say IP or competition law, and then realised that their efforts had earned them a reputation on the sports field. Others had actively sought employment as a junior lawyer in one of the dedicated sports law practices. Stephen believes that opportunities in private practice will grow, especially if more lawyers take on work that was previously the preserve of agents.

Some lawyers find they are more satisfied working in-house at one of the governing bodies such as the RFU, MCC or FA. There are also roles within media organisations, say negotiating broadcasting rights on behalf of terrestrial or satellite broadcasters.

LEADING FIRMS FROM CHAMBERS UK 2004-2005

SPORT: REGULATORY
■ LONDON

1. **Denton Wilde Sapte**
2. **Farrer & Co**
   Hammonds
3. **Charles Russell**
   Max Bitel Greene
4. **Freshfields Bruckhaus Deringer**
   Simmons & Simmons
   Teacher Stern Selby
   The Simkins Partnership

SPORT: COMMERCIAL/MEDIA
■ LONDON

1. **Denton Wilde Sapte**
2. **Hammonds**
3. **Bird & Bird**
   Couchman Harrington Associates
   Olswang
4. **Addleshaw Goddard**
   Freshfields Bruckhaus Deringer
   Harbottle & Lewis
   Herbert Smith
   Nicholson Graham & Jones
   The Simkins Partnership
5. **Clintons**
   Collyer-Bristow
   Farrer & Co
   Field Fisher Waterhouse
   Fladgate Fielder
   Macfarlanes
   SJ Berwin
   Wiggin & Co

SPORT
■ WALES

1. **Hugh James** Cardiff

SPORT
■ SOUTH WEST

1. **Clarke Willmott** Bristol
2. **Osborne Clarke** Bristol

SPORT
■ THE NORTH

1. **James Chapman & Co** Manchester
2. **Addleshaw Goddard** Manchester
   McCormicks Leeds
3. **Cramers Solicitors** Leeds
   George Davies Solicitors Manchester
   Hill Dickinson Liverpool
   Walker Morris Leeds

tax

The tax lawyer's primary role is to advise on the most tax-efficient means of structuring and running a business. If you thought tax was all dusty books and dull conversation, think again!

type of work

The work comes in three main varieties: tax planning; transactional advice; and litigation. Nigel Popplewell, head of corporate tax at Burges Salmon in Bristol, told us: "*Some tax lawyers are happiest with planning, others like the rough and tumble of negotiation, and there are some who like the crack of court work and investigations – and a good fight with the Revenue.*" Sounds like there's something for everyone.

Tax law evolves with incredible speed, so you need to have your finger on the pulse when it comes to judicial decisions and new legislation. The simple fact is that there's a lot of tax law and you must make a commitment to learning it. Although qualifying into tax can "*be a bit like starting all over again,*" Nigel stressed that a junior lawyer can get up to speed on the technical aspects of the work relatively quickly: "*After 18 months you can do a huge amount. You may not be able to make judgement calls, but you can stand your ground and deal with the tax authorities.*" Taking the Chartered Tax Advisor exams will help, but a few more years of investment in your career may be required before your instincts become fully tuned and you have the requisite experience to handle any situation solo.

Much of a tax lawyer's work comes from other departments in the firm – perhaps a question from the property department on how VAT applies to a land purchase and construction project, or maybe assistance required by corporate colleagues in structuring a joint venture or a company reorganisation. The role is a blend of advisory work on large projects and ad hoc queries that require immediate answers. Tax lawyers are key to corporate deals, but generally they do not take a seat alongside their M&A counterparts on the all-night, deal-closing roller coaster. Nigel pointed out that "*no one wants to argue about tax at 2am,*" and so the tax points tend to be covered early on in a deal. Moreover, "*as soon as someone says 'tax', people say 'over to you', which gives you more control over your hours and environment.*"

skills needed

...excellent academics...analytical mind...willing to challenge and test...technical excellence...good on interpretation of black letter law...clear communication...commerciality...

While there is always room for the tax lawyer with an academic leaning and "*there is an element of truth in the anorak stereotype,*" if you have the hermit-like tendencies of a Howard Hughes and would hate being wheeled out in front of clients, you may have a problem. An essential element of your job will be to distil difficult principles into palatable, client-friendly language. In this sense, your job is just like that of any other corporate lawyer except your subject matter can be much more impenetrable and convoluted. In short, knowing the rules isn't enough: "*If you haven't got the communication skills, you won't be terribly good.*"

career options

Nigel observed that "*it can be difficult to get people involved in tax,*" but a career in this field should ensure you are well treated. "*Tax lawyers are highly thought of, and firms guard their employees very jealously.*" Despite these specialists being hugely in demand, tax lawyers tend not to move around much, and firms must ensure they "*grow their own.*" Moves to the Bar are not unheard of; indeed, some of the most respected tax barristers first achieved success as tax solicitors.

Outside private practice, you can work in-house in the tax department of a large corporation or financial institution, or you can work for the government in the Inland Revenue or Customs & Excise. Occasionally solicitors move to accountancy firms in a tax consultancy role. Overall, the skills and knowledge gained in private practice are transferable at all levels of qualification. We heartily agree with Nigel's parting shot: "*You are probably amongst the most employable lawyers in the world.*"

LEADING FIRMS FROM CHAMBERS UK 2004-2005

TAX
■ **LONDON**

[1] **Freshfields Bruckhaus Deringer**
  Linklaters
  Slaughter and May
[2] **Allen & Overy**
  Clifford Chance
[3] **Ashurst**
  Herbert Smith
  Macfarlanes
[4] **Berwin Leighton Paisner**
  Denton Wilde Sapte
  Lovells
  Norton Rose
  Simmons & Simmons
  SJ Berwin
  Travers Smith
[5] **CMS Cameron McKenna**
  Nabarro Nathanson
  Olswang
  Shearman & Sterling
  Watson, Farley & Williams
[6] **Addleshaw Goddard**
  Clyde & Co
  Field Fisher Waterhouse
  Jones Day
  McDermott Will & Emery
  Weil, Gotshal & Manges

TAX
■ **THE SOUTH / SOUTH WEST**

[1] **Burges Salmon** Bristol
  Osborne Clarke Bristol
[2] **Blake Lapthorn Linnell** Fareham
  TLT Solicitors Bristol

TAX
■ **MIDLANDS**

[1] **Pinsents** Birmingham
  Wragge & Co Birmingham
[2] **DLA** Birmingham
  Eversheds Nottingham
  Hammonds Birmingham
[3] **Mills & Reeve** Cambridge

TAX
■ **THE NORTH**

[1] **Addleshaw Goddard** Leeds
  Pinsents Leeds
[2] **Eversheds** Leeds
  Hammonds Leeds
[3] **Dickinson Dees** Newcastle upon Tyne
  Walker Morris Leeds

tmt

Lawyers who specialise in Technology, Media & Telecoms must keep up to date with both changes in the law and developments in this ever-changing sector. And thanks to the concept of 'convergence', they are increasingly advising clients from a number of media. It's no longer sufficient to be, say, a broadcasting specialist or an internet specialist – as these two technologies fuse, lawyers need to be familiar with both strands.

type of work

The average TMT lawyer spends much of his time advising on commercial transactions and drafting the requisite agreements. However, according to Mark O'Conor, an IT partner at Bird & Bird: "*You need to differentiate yourself from a standard commercial lawyer so that you can add value.*" To achieve this you need to be familiar with the latest industry know-how and understand how the most recent set of regulations is going to impact your client's business. You will be frequently applying your legal knowledge to new commercial situations: Does your client need a disclaimer on its website? Is a contract made online legally enforceable? Does your client's marketing e-mail count as unsolicited spam? How can you ascertain whether someone is abusing your client's software licence by allowing too many users of their product? What are the consequences of the change of the media regulator from Oftel to Ofcom? If these issues press your buttons, read on...

Large commercial companies commonly have their own in-house lawyers. Mark explained: "*You have to be able to deal with a real mix of people – some want you to stay in the back room, whereas others may want you to write the hymn sheet for them.*" The prevalence of in-house legal teams is good news for junior solicitors and trainees keen on a secondment. Whether or not clients have their own advisors, "*part of your job is to keep one eye on the latest cases and trade journals and to keep your clients informed. It is always good practice to send out a quick e-mail or bulletin; even if they don't read it, it lets them know that you're still on their case.*"

skills needed

...grounding in corporate and contractual law...understanding regulations and their application to real situations... comfortable with technical jargon...innovative...knowledge of competition and copyright matters...

It's not necessary to know absolutely everything about computers and technology. As Mark says: "*What you need is a real interest in the industry. You don't have to know what goes on when you take the cover off every gadget, but you should have an idea of the jargon. When you're presented with a schedule of things in a contract, you have to know what they're talking about. It always helps if you know your LAN from your WAN.*" Mark recommends reading *Wired* ("*a men's lifestyle magazine with computers in it*") or more serious publications such as *Computer Weekly* or *New Scientist*.

More generally, you'll need to be in possession of a full set of commercial skills. One minute you could be working on a plan to charge for online music; the next you'll be called away because an ISP has a domain name issue. For much of your work there may be no direct precedent, so it will be necessary to demonstrate innovative thinking and logical analysis. Yet, you'll still need to be prepared to spend time in the library researching black letter law.

career options

Although the market is competitive, there is still room for a few more junior lawyers. "*The work can be quite collegiate or team-based. I would expect trainees to be doing the raw research and attending meetings and negotiation sessions with the client. They may have to be the person making the notes, but why not let them also prepare the first draft of the contract?"* And more good news – British TMT lawyers are well respected elsewhere: *"IT law in the UK is at the forefront, so US companies won't hesitate to fly you over there. If you get big Silicon Valley companies or large users as clients, you can expect to travel anywhere."*

It's reasonably easy to join the in-house legal team of a telecoms or IT company. Or, because the tools of a TMT lawyer's trade are honed in general commercial law, (albeit with a technology slant), any large organisation with a serious IT component would be happy to log you on.

LEADING FIRMS FROM CHAMBERS UK 2004-2005

INFORMATION TECHNOLOGY
■ LONDON

[1] **Allen & Overy**
  Baker & McKenzie
  Bird & Bird
[2] **Clifford Chance**
  Denton Wilde Sapte
  Field Fisher Waterhouse
  Kemp Little
  Linklaters
  Lovells
  Masons
[3] **Barlow Lyde & Gilbert**
  DLA
  Freshfields Bruckhaus Deringer
  Herbert Smith
  Mayer, Brown, Rowe & Maw
  Olswang
  Osborne Clarke
  Shaw Pittman
  Simmons & Simmons
  Slaughter and May
  Taylor Wessing
[4] **Berwin Leighton Paisner**
  Bristows
  Eversheds
  Harbottle & Lewis
  Latham & Watkins
  Nicholson Graham & Jones
  Norton Rose

TELECOMMUNICATIONS
■ LONDON AND THE REGIONS

[1] **Allen & Overy**
  Bird & Bird
  Clifford Chance
  Linklaters
[2] **Baker & McKenzie**
  Olswang
[3] **Field Fisher Waterhouse**
  Freshfields Bruckhaus Deringer
  Herbert Smith
  Mayer, Brown, Rowe & Maw
  Taylor Wessing
[4] **Ashurst**
  Charles Russell
  Denton Wilde Sapte
  Norton Rose
  Simmons & Simmons
  Wilmer Cutler Pickering Hale & Dorr
[5] **Addleshaw Goddard**
  DLA
  Eversheds
  Kemp Little
  Lawrence Graham
  Lovells
  Nicholson Graham & Jones
  Osborne Clarke
  Slaughter and May
  White & Case
  Wragge & Co

INFORMATION TECHNOLOGY
■ THE SOUTH

[1] **Bond Pearce** Southampton
  DMH Brighton
[2] **Blake Lapthorn Linnell** Southampton
  Clyde & Co Guildford
  Shadbolt & Co Reigate

INFORMATION TECHNOLOGY
■ SOUTH WEST

[1] **Beachcroft Wansbroughs** Bristol
  Osborne Clarke Bristol
[2] **Bevan Brittan** Bristol
  Burges Salmon Bristol
[3] **Foot Anstey Sargent** Plymouth

INFORMATION TECHNOLOGY
■ THAMES VALLEY

[1] **Nabarro Nathanson** Reading
  Marcus J O'Leary Wokingham
[2] **Boyes Turner** Reading
  Clark Holt Swindon
  Manches Oxford
  Osborne Clarke Reading
[3] **Moorcrofts** Marlow
  Olswang Thames Valley Reading
  Willoughby & Partners Oxford

INFORMATION TECHNOLOGY
■ MIDLANDS & EAST ANGLIA

1. **Wragge & Co** Birmingham
2. **Eversheds** Nottingham
3. **Mills & Reeve** Birmingham
   Pinsents Birmingham
   Technology Law Alliance Birmingham
   V-Lex Ltd Worksop

INFORMATION TECHNOLOGY
■ WALES

1. **Edwards Geldard** Cardiff
   Eversheds Cardiff
2. **Hugh James** Cardiff
   Morgan Cole Cardiff

INFORMATION TECHNOLOGY
■ THE NORTH

1. **Addleshaw Goddard** Leeds
2. **Eversheds** Leeds
   Pinsents Leeds
3. **Halliwells** Manchester
   Irwin Mitchell Leeds
   Masons Manchester

international opportunities

The idea of the international law firm is far from new: UK law firms have ventured overseas since the 19th century. What has changed in recent times is the number of firms with offices overseas and the desire on the part of the largest firms to plant flags all over the globe. The Brits weren't the first in the game but they've certainly made up for lost time, and the largest firm worldwide is now our very own Clifford Chance. It still has some way to go though to catch up with Baker & McKenzie for the prize for most offices in most countries.

There are so many UK and US firms with overseas networks that students are spoiled for choice. Keeping track of which firms are opening or closing offices in different countries is almost a full-time occupation, but wherever possible we have mentioned the main changes of the past year in our True Picture reports. What we can never predict though is exactly who is going to merge with who. The last five years have been characterised by not only European mergers and alliances but transatlantic tie-ups. Recently we've seen the creation of Mayer, Brown, Rowe & Maw; Jones Day hoovering up Gouldens and next on the cards is the merger between Nicholson Graham & Jones in London with ten-office US firm Kirkpatrick & Lockhart. DLA is also in advanced negotiations with US firm Piper Rudnick. Save for one or two notable exceptions, the US law firms already in London have expanded their British operations.

If you are determined to spend part of your training contract overseas then you need to do a bit of research into the overseas activities of the firms that most interest you. A good place to start might be *Chambers Global,* which you can read online at www.chambersandpartners.com/chambersglobal or your university's careers library or law department may have its own copy.

let's get out of here!

Although time abroad gives you experience of working in another jurisdiction, you'll not normally practise foreign law. An overseas seat is without doubt a very rewarding and challenging experience. It will usually be taken in an office that is smaller than your firm's home office in the UK, and you should find that you are working on tasks offering greater responsibility. The trick to securing the most popular overseas seats is to wage an effective campaign of self-promotion and to get the prerequisite experience in the UK office before you go. The key to getting a particular seat may be as simple as having the right second language, but remember that language skills may also act as a handcuff. Quite simply, if the firm has a Moscow office and you are the only Russian-speaking trainee you won't be going to New York - the purpose of sending you abroad is so you can work for the best interests of the firm, not have a fab holiday!

It may be hard work. It may be an eye opener. It may even be lonely, if you're in a less popular location; nevertheless, the overwhelming feeling is that time abroad is very worthwhile. Each year we chat to trainees who are either there or have recently come back from time abroad. Here are their postcards...

amsterdam

Legend has it that Amsterdam was founded by two fishermen and a seasick dog after the dog jumped ship to deposit the contents of its stomach. If you think Amsterdam is only good for stag weekends, red light districts, clogs, and of course, Holland's most famous plant exports - marijuana and tulips - then think again. This city is one of the world's most liveable and loveable. Cars and buses give way to scores of bicycles, and some 100 kms of romantic tree-lined canals weave between distinctive 17th century town houses. Amsterdam offers the exuberance and cultural vibrancy of a big city, with the manageability of a small town. And although the city is known for its liberal, and often experimental, attitudes to drugs and prostitution, it also has a reputation for tolerance and safety.

work: Several firms offer trainee seats in Amsterdam and CMS Cameron McKenna, for example, also posts them to an allied firm in Utrecht. Being in a smaller office, you can expect much more responsibility so don't be surprised if you find yourself regularly meeting with clients or running a due diligence exercise by yourself. If you speak Dutch, you might even get some court time. However, the Dutch are famously laid back, and have a *"fantastic approach to the work/life balance - you need a very good reason to work past 6pm."* Partners are often more approachable than in the UK...and don't be shocked by their more relaxed attitudes. Smoking tobacco in offices and at your desk is not as uncommon as in the UK. If you're easily offended, this is probably not the place for you - the Dutch can also be blunt to the point of apparent rudeness. As one trainee put it: *"If you're doing something badly, they'll just say 'That's appalling!'"*

rest and play: Like the seasick dog, trainees in Amsterdam might find the social activities available at times a little dizzying. But fear not, should the bars, restaurants and clubs become overwhelming, a sobering visit to one of the city's many galleries and museums, housing Van Gogh, Rembrandt and Vermeer, will perk you up. Forget the horrors of the Central Line, trainees are offered firm bicycles upon their arrival. Apartments are surprisingly spacious and centrally located in *"trendy"* canal districts, like Nieuwmarkt or Keizersgracht. Most trainees can cycle canal-side to work in around five minutes. As one remarked: *"It has given me an extra two hours a day!"* Another said: *"There's something really great*

about being able to open your window and look out onto a canal." Flexible licensing hours allow trainees to go home after work, eat and then walk to the bars or brown cafes. *"There's no mad dash to the pub at 6pm."* Just remember, if you hope to return to a club, you should tip the bouncers on leaving - they never forget a face. Like everything, eating out is cheaper than in London and you'll have a ready-made set of friends to dine with as the city is home to a dozen or more UK trainees. In summer, the locals take to the streets and myriad pavement cafes, and descend naked on Vondelpark. At weekends you can cycle to the pretty Monacon Dam, about 15 kms to the north, to eat pancakes and drink beer before wobbling your way back. If ever your bike gets stolen you can buy a replacement for as little as €10. There's no shortage of boat-owners at the major UK firms, so you could find yourself baking on the deck of a barge in summer. In winter, when the canals freeze over, it's all about ice skating and sipping on hot chocolate.

best things: Safety, biking to work, brown cafés.
worst things: Constant hangovers, stag parties, Dutch directness.

brussels

Home of bureaucracy and Tintin, Brussels plays host to the headquarters of many EU institutions. Nearly 160 embassies are based there, in addition to 120 IGOs and 1,400 NGOs. Political powerhouse it may be, but it is probably fair to say that you can cram most of Brussels' attractions into a weekend. So what about spending a whole six months out there? Though competition for seats is *"not exactly fierce"* as most trainees prefer warmer, more romantic climes, one fan of the city said: *"Brussels gets a slating, but I thought it was cool. All those cobbley streets and bars and cafes - it was quite quirky."* It's also worth pointing out that this could be one of the most cosmopolitan places on the planet: *"I don't think there were any Belgian people in Brussels!"*

work: If you have a particular interest in EU or competition law, Brussels is the place for you. Several trainees opted for the city because they spoke French and wanted to improve it, but language skills are not considered to be a particular advantage, especially since many firms will provide tuition. *"Competition law can be quite intense at times,"* but all-nighters and Saturdays in the office are *"very rare."* In addition to EU law, *"there is also a lot of quality trade work coming through the city."* A DLA trainee said her work was characterised by *"big deals, lots of research and lots of responsibility."* Much of her day was spent monitoring public affairs and reviewing EU publications and websites. Don't underestimate the volume of research-based tasks that will come your way. *"You won't get much client contact but there are a lot more conferences and seminars to attend."* Litigation also rears its head, not only in the court of first instance but also the European Court of Justice.

rest and play: Most of the law firms have apartments for trainees located close to the office. Many of the 50-odd UK trainees live in an enclave in the Schumann area near to the Commission buildings and tend to flock together on arrival for tours and events laid on by the firms. The climate may be English but there's *"a much better quality of life and much better food."* After working your way through an almost endless selection of local beers, you'll never again settle for a pint of XXXX. Brussels is only two and a half hours from London, so persuading friends and family to visit won't prove difficult. Said one trainee: *"I haven't had a weekend on my own since I got here."* Brussels is a manageable city with a pleasant pace of life, though one trainee found it *"a bit too catholic - all the shops shut on Sundays, so everyone goes to the cinema."* Of course, its most famous symbol is the Mannekin Pis, a small statue of a boy relieving himself into a fountain, but if the excitement wears off after a couple of visits, you could always follow the lead of the trainees who hired a car and made a pilgrimage to Ostende, Belgian refuge of the late great Marvin Gaye.

best things: Restaurants, European lifestyle, internationalism.

worst things: Cobblestones in high heels, poodles.

frankfurt

Frankfurt is the European capital of Capital, and is clean, cosmopolitan and friendly. If you want an unforgettable time in a radically different environment then politely decline, but Frankfurt is a good place to live as a professional. *"It's definitely a working person's city,"* said one trainee; *"it's much livelier during the week."* The city is famous for its enormous airport (incorporating a nightclub and an adult cinema) and its business conventions, which include a major book fair. Even though most business is done in English, being able to speak German is of real advantage in terms of building up a rapport with clients and locals and making the most of your time there. The consensus was that the ski season is the best time of year to be in Frankfurt, but in the summer you can enjoy the riverbanks, lovely parks and open-air pools. Think Tooting Lido, but clean and green and pleasant.

work: There are a dozen or more UK trainees in Frankfurt at any one time, invariably working in banking and capital markets. A lot of work is done in English and pertains to English or New York law, but *"you can't be afraid of German law."* Trainees say the work, hours, atmosphere and manners in the office are essentially the same as found back in London. There's always a danger of being roped into mundane translation work, but if you know what to expect of a finance seat in the UK, there should be few surprises in Frankfurt.

rest and play: Trainees apartments are of an excellent standard and located within walking distance of the office, which always makes for a more pleasant start to the day. It also means *"you can go shopping after work and afford a taxi home."* Ladies: Frankfurt has its own equivalent of Bond Street as well as recognisable favourites such as H&M; unfortunately they're all closed on Sundays, *"even the supermarkets."* All the UK trainees are clustered in the same part of town so you've a readymade social circle. *"The city benefits from having a lot of professionals who want to spend money so there are lots of bars and restaurants and clubs."* The best thing is that you never have to stand up or queue to buy a drink and, we're told, the waiters have excellent memories. If you fancy a more authentic German experience, simply cross to the south of the river and pop into a cafe for schnitzel and apple wine. Frankfurt's location in the heart of Germany means it's easy to hop on a train to pretty much anywhere else in the country at weekends.

best things: Standard of living, structure, ease of travel.
worst things: No shopping on Sundays.

hong kong

An island of capitalism within a communist state, despite having returned to the tight embrace of China in 1997, Hong Kong is still *"beyond fabulous,"* according to trainees. From the moment you arrive at Chek Lap Kok Airport the island city will tire, amaze and entertain you in equal measure. Hong Kong exists for people to make money and shop, and its inspiration is more Ronald McDonald than Chairman Mao. The crowds, noise and smog could send your blood pressure soaring, so take a leaf out of the locals' book and take a free T'ai Chi class in the park or visit the region's Buddhist temples and remote islands. It must work, as HK residents enjoy very high life expectancy. September to March is mild; otherwise it gets exceedingly hot and sweaty.

work: One trainee had been drawn to the *"new business culture and travel opportunities in the region."* And there's plenty of both, even with a dip in the Asian economy. With the bonded zone of Guangzhou so close, the city's law firms have found plenty to occupy themselves on trade agreements. Mostly trainees deal with general commercial work, but corporate transactions do crop up and there is also some litigation and IP. You must be ready to master a whole new set of traditions and etiquette before you can deal effectively with clients and colleagues. One trainee reported on the long hours local lawyers put in: *"They have an obsession with working and that was very very hard for me to adjust to. Usually I did 9.30am until 7pm, but the locals stayed later."* One Herbert Smith trainee told us that anyone wanting to put a bit back into the community could get involved in various projects including beach clean-ups, catching stray cats on Lantau Island (really!) and spending time at the JFK Centre for severely disabled people.

rest and play: Typically trainees' apartments are on The Levels, a residential hill where your relative altitude reflects your wealth. *"At the top is The Peak where the temperature is always a couple of degrees cooler so that became the popular place to live. Plus it has fantastic views."* Most trainees live halfway up with the expats, where there's a pleasant village feel. The nicest flats are the *"palatial"* A&O ones. Apparently the firm moved trainees from their old digs when they became rat-infested! Partying on the island is easy; *"my Hong Kong seat was one of the most intense periods of fun I've ever had,"* said one trainee. Full of clubs, Wanchai is the old sailors' hangout, just ten minutes from the CBD and *"never feels threatening."* Clubs stay open until 4am and sometimes 8am; many supply free drinks for girls on Wednesdays. Less crazy is Lan Kwai Fong, with its concentration of expat bars. The Chinese tend not to drink as often; indeed, one source thought *"the opportunities to meet local people socially are limited,"* so make sure you make friends in the office. You can easily get to mainland China for a round of golf, black market shopping or to visit trainees in Shanghai and taste the *"swinging Shanghai scene"* at a New Year's ball. One trainee managed to do so much travelling that he likened his time in HK to *"the life of an international playboy."* You may laugh...we heard his stories!

best things: nightlife, junk trips around the harbour, proximity to China.
worst things: pollution, humidity, blowing your budget.

madrid

Having come through a bloody civil war and spent decades languishing under Franco, Spain has played a hard game of catch-up with its neighbours, but now, according to one trainee we spoke to, "*Spain is really starting to move on the international scene...it's an exciting time to be out here.*" Madrid is everything a capital city should be: vibrant, affordable and fun. "*For young, single people it is ideal.*" You would be wise to avoid a summer seat, however, since Madrid can become scorching hot and the savvy locals all flee to the coast.

work: Being a trainee solicitor is not the best way to soak up the easy going 'mañana' ethos for which the locals are famous. Madrid is a regional commercial centre like Paris or Frankfurt, and you can expect to be handling the same kind of commercial and corporate work, with plenty of private M&A and corporate housekeeping etc. Good Spanish is essential, since you will mostly be handling Spanish law. "*You end up working just as hard as in London, but people are less likely to come up to you and tell you that something's urgent.*" Even if your office is dressed down on Friday, the working environment will be "*smart and conservative.*" For trainees there will be a fair amount of translation and checking, but when there's chargeable work, it always takes priority. A two or three-hour siesta in the middle of the day can jar with Protestant sensibilities and, when the work is flooding in, the long lunch break means you can be in the office until 10 or 11pm. People guard their weekends quite jealously though.

rest and play: Trainees' apartments are smart and central and within easy walking distance of work.

Madrid is a real cultural oasis in the otherwise barren central plains of Spain. Bar culture dominates and the city boasts three of the best art collections in Europe: the Prado, the Reina Sofia and the Thyssen. Queues for the latest movies stretch twice around the block, but tickets cost a quarter of what you would pay in London's West End. Madrid is an ideal base for trips to the surrounding towns and countryside. The locals are open and friendly, making it easy to immerse yourself in Spanish life. Whether you want to go to a bullfight, hang out in cafés or watch some proper football, Madrid has it all, including half our top football players!

best things: Food, weather, footie.
worst things: Long days, having to go out so late.

the middle east

The big business centres of the Middle East attract trainees with the guarantee of fine weather, high-profile work and exotic glitz. Oil has turned Abu Dhabi from a small fishing village into one of the richest cities in the world in just 40 years, and skyscrapers and palm trees now dominate the landscape. Trainees find the city is incredibly Westernised and that culture shock minimal. If Abu Dhabi isn't to your liking, beautiful Muscat, the capital of Oman, offers a more authentic taste of life in the Gulf. March to September is the best time to go, although you'll be air-conditioned all year round. Temperatures of up to 50°C make the summer months the quietest (and cheapest), but you won't get as many public holidays.

work: In the Gulf "*they have a different way of doing business,*" but they still tend to do it in English. Commercial advice features highly and there is an emphasis on projects and finance work, much of it oil related, of course. One trainee from Trowers & Hamlins tells us that work is "*split between dealing with UAE Government departments and multinational con-*

sortiums that want to set up business in the UAE." You can expect plenty of client contact, and you may get PR and marketing experiences that you'd never have back in London. The typical working day runs from 8am-1pm and then 4pm-7pm, with your lunch break best spent swimming, waterskiing or taking a nap. The week runs from Saturday to Wednesday, with some trainees required to work Thursday mornings. Because there are only three days in common with foreign offices the pressure can build up. "*When someone phones up and asks for something to be done by the end of the week, it often means it has to be done there and then.*"

rest and play: Luxurious apartments with sea views are par for the course, as are membership of swanky hotel health clubs, cars and free petrol. If it's culture you're after, think twice about Abu Dhabi since "*there isn't much.*" Trainees agree that there's an "*excellent quality of life*" however, and with the Maldives, Oman and Petra all within striking distance, adventures will never be far from mind. The ex-pat community and office colleagues make up a big part of a trainee's social life, with Abu Dhabi's 'Brit Club' all important. The scene in Muscat is much smaller and socialising takes place in the city's half dozen hotels. By the end of your six months the waiters will know exactly what you are going to drink and where you are going to sit. If you tire of looking at them, pop over to the Souk for a spot of souvenir shopping - that hookah pipe will look fab in your living room back in Clapham. The smaller pool of Brit lawyers in Muscat means you're more likely to build a wider group of friends including teachers, engineers and oil workers, with whom you can rent a 4x4 and take off to explore the wadis and dunes.

best things: Experiencing a new lifestyle, quality work, desert adventures.
worst things: Heat, isolation, the unfamiliar working week.

milan/rome

Famous for its comedy politics, appalling TV and a diet that no doubt has Dr Atkins turning in his grave, Italy is an exciting prospect for trainees. Its business and fashion capital, Milan, is home to the country's stock exchange and most of its major banks and corporates. "Although "*not the most beautiful city in the world,*" it is wealthy, glamorous and fast paced. Nestled in the plains of the Po Valley, it's a short journey into the Alps or to the beautiful lakes region. The Eternal City, Rome, meanwhile, remains Italy's traditional regulatory centre. It lacks the relentless commercial pace of Milan, but none of its style, and is "*the most stunning city in the world,*" according to one besotted trainee. Milan's winters can be cool, with temperatures falling below zero. In the summer, both cities become hot and muggy, and Rome can be stifling. Sensibly, the locals flee to the coast, and you'd be well advised to do the same whenever you can.

work: Competition for Italian seats is tough and language skills are essential. Expect either corporate, capital markets or banking work. When the office is busy you could be drafting advices and prospectuses on top of the usual pre-transaction due diligence. When the office is quiet, you'll be unlikely to avoid translation jobs. "*It is a working city and you become acutely aware of that,*" one trainee cautioned of Milan, adding: "*People work until they feel their bosses are going home.*" Expect more finance and securitisation work in Rome, but as with most foreign offices, "*it was the equivalent of doing three seats in terms of variety.*" Forget Starbucks, you'll be quaffing real coffee here, and you'll need it, since working hours are much the same as London, and sometimes longer. While this will be no Roman Holiday, you will enjoy long lunches, regular coffee breaks and a generally relaxed office environment. Trainees noted a more deferential attitude towards partners, who tend to be older and highly academically qualified. "*There's a real focus on the partners being everything, and to be fair,* *it's mostly true."* Despite this, trainees spoke of a *"warm"* atmosphere in the office. *"If you make an effort to speak Italian, you'll be rewarded."* As one put it, *"it's almost like a family."* Not to be confused, of course, with The Family.

rest and play: Italians are famously welcoming, and as one trainee told us, *"I loved being alone in Rome; I wasn't going to Irish bars and talking English the entire time."* Apartments are usually centrally located (the Clifford Chance pad overlooks the Roman Forum), but wherever you can, always route your journey to work past something spectacular. One source described his journey to work on a Vespa, whizzing past the Colosseum. Whether it's sipping an £8 espresso in Piazza Navona, getting lost in cobbled streets, or admiring the views from atop St Peter's Basilica, there'll be something about Rome that'll have you tossing a coin in the Trevi Fountain. In Milan, *"everywhere is a fashion show, so when you come here you have to smarten up your act or barmen won't serve you!"* When you're not bankrupting yourself at Prada, you can enjoy one of Italy's *"most civilised traditions"* – the mid-evening aperetivo, which is drinks plus everything from tapas to sushi. Miraculously, you can just turn up at football games in the afternoon and get tickets to see the city's famous clubs – AC Milan or Inter Milan.

best things: Real coffee, shopping, football.
worst things: Queuing for the Sistine Chapel, bankruptcy, bum-pinching.

MOSCOW

With its fascinating history, stunning architecture and a metro system with more chandeliers than your average palace, much like a Dostoevsky novel Moscow is rounded off with an appealing edge of madness. When asked to characterise the Russian capital, one trainee said: *"It's best to describe what it isn't. It's not west, it's not Soviet and it's not Asian. I suppose it's on the way to being Western."* If you keep up

with the news, you'll already have gathered that there's a fair amount of crime and punishment going on, and of late Russia has faced a series of horrific acts of terrorism. We've no indication that any of this has impeded on the availability of trainee seats however. Visit Moscow in winter for the full effect of plenty of *"fresh, crisp snow"* and the thermometer plummeting to minus 30°C - a perfect excuse to buy one of those furry hats and pretend you're Anna Karenina...or Omar Sharif.

work: *"It's all oil related below the surface,"* announced one past visitor to Moscow. Several firms offer energy work in addition to a regular diet of banking and corporate. Trainees tell us the office life is *"more regimented than in London,"* but that *"you can expect to do things that are well beyond trainee level."* Indeed, it's easy to feel that you've accepted an important mission when you agree to a posting here, particularly if you find yourself *"fast tracked through customs and immigration."* Though English is spoken in the office, even pidgin Russian will be useful, if only for getting around in the city and making sense of the mind-boggling Cyrillic alphabet.

rest and play: Most firms in Moscow provide their trainees with good-sized apartments within the Zone 1 Garden Ring, although some provide an allowance for suitable accommodation. White & Case trainees get to live *"right by Pushkin Square in Tverskaya* [the main shopping drag] *with the old Czar's shop opposite."* Apparently, *"you can buy anything in Moscow, even the blue lights that exempt you from observing traffic lights."* One source said he went shopping only twice in six months because *"unless you have silly money for designer stuff, it is simply not the place for it."* It's perfectly possible to find ex-pat friends, even Irish bars, if you can't match the locals and their love of vodka. The usual tourist attractions – Lenin's Mausoleum and Red Square – are impressive, although the view of St Basil's Cathedral is somewhat marred by an endless procession of women in white wedding dresses waiting to have their photo taken. You can escape as far as St Petersburg on an overnight train and there's a circuit of picturesque towns around the city known as the Golden Ring.

best things: Surreal social life, anarchy.
worst things: Corruption, dire supermarkets, traffic.

new york

New York, and more particularly Manhattan, life is 24/7. Of course, you'll already know that if you watched SATC. What you'll also know is that NY is a sassy, smoke-free, carb-free, cab-honking, cosmopolitan-drinking, style-conscious, your-name's-not-on-the-list kinda of town. At least, it is if you're doing it right. Despite overseas allowances and cheap taxis, even trainees coming from London find the city extremely expensive, if only because everyone needs tipping. Don't accept a posting unless you're prepared to spend big and make the most of everything the city has to offer. The best time to visit is in the fall, when the New York is *"absolutely beautiful"* and you don't have to put up with intense heat or cold.

work: New York law is reasonably similar to UK law and trainees are also likely to come in contact with work similar in nature to London experiences. That said similarities can be deceptive, and there can be times where you feel like an Englishman in New York: *"I did a lot bankruptcy work which functions in a very different way to the English system of insolvency."* Overall though, the variations are mainly on a theme and those you notice will offer *"interesting contrasts"* rather than initiation into a foreign system. Banking and capital markets are high on the agenda, and a lot of work from Latin America comes through the city. New York offices can feel more formal than their counterparts in the UK; yet in spite of this, US firms often have better developed diversity and pro bono programmes. During a busy period, you might be in the office until the wee hours, racking up those bill-able hours, but generally 9am to 8pm are more typical. One massive difference that will mark you out as a legal alien to most US lawyers is the simple fact that you're a trainee. *"It's not a concept that the US system understands, so you're often treated as an associate in terms of the work you're given.* On top of this responsibility-boost, any trainee working at a US firm in London will doubtless get an awful lot out of experience closer to the homeland: *"I'd done international work before, but I worked on a huge refinancing deal across 15 different jurisdictions and got a real sense of the firm's clout."*

rest and play: Trainees get apartments with fantastic views on the Upper East and Upper West sides. You'll need a head for heights and a taste for marble atria guarded by the ubiquitous and all-seeing concierge. Beyond the daily cost of living, the main expense is weekend travel, be this for skiing upstate in the winter or trips to the Hamptons in the summer. Culturally, New York is in a league of its own and between them the Whitney, the Met, the Guggenheim and the Moma contain some of the most important art of the last century. By the same token, with big brash musicals on Broadway and a decent, if not always ground-breaking selection of work off-Broadway, off-off-Broadway and off-off-off Broadway, neither would you want to miss a trip to theatre. But it's not all satisfaction for the mind: when it comes to satisfying the stomach and scratching that party-itch New York has a bewildering array of opportunities. Sustained by a potent mix of cwaffee and cocktails, you could keep going for the entire six months without sleep, though you're likely to be exhausted long before the possibilities. With so many other international trainees in town, you'll find many willing colleagues in social endeavour, but we're reliably informed that the best friend any sociable trainee could hope for comes in the slim, burgundy form of the *Zagat Guide*, which includes over 2,000 eateries and bars, polled from over 18,000 New Yorkers. And if you've got any time to spare, walks in an autumnal Central Park or a skinny latte at your local bookstore/coffee house are clichés to tick off in your Eye Spy NY.

best things: Convenience, the buzz, discovering your limits.
worst things: Tipping, working hours.

paris

"If your life is rubbish, at least you are in a beautiful place!" So said one trainee of the city of romance, style, art and haughty grandeur. Whether you feel more at home in the cafés of the Left Bank or on the leather sofas at the National Bank, there is everything a young bourgeois or bohemian could wish for, from haute couture to basement jazz clubs. May is the perfect time to invite friends across as it's not too hot and there are no tourists around. There's no need to be one of les miserables if there's no 'special friend' with whom you can stroll, hand in hand, along the Champs Elisee, *"it's a great place to be single; you can fall in love with Paris."*

work: Seats in Paris range from broad-based finance options through asset finance, capital markets, corporate and even international arbitration as the ICA is based in the city. Trainees have to manage themselves far more in Paris than in London, and find they are given considerably more responsibility than they are used to as *"the concept of supervisor isn't really there."* One trainee told us: *"I grew up in the Paris office."* It's imperative that you speak French; you'll want to blend in with the locals rather than the tourists, and in the office much of your work can involve translating documents from English into French or vice versa. There's a notional 9.00am-5.30pm work schedule with an hour or two for a proper sit-down lunch. *"They're a bit keen on their food,"* said one trainee, while another admitted to leaving Paris *"double the size"* she'd been when she arrived. Most lawyers usually leave the office by six or seven in the evening.

rest and play: Whether it's a 30th-floor apartment in the 15th arrondissement in the south west of the city or a pad in Le Marais, right in the thick of things, you'll probably end up walking to work to soak up the atmosphere. A readymade, e-mail-based social scene awaits all new arrivals and we hear you have to make an effort not to fall into the ex-pat scene. Bars and restaurants stay open until late, even on school nights. *"You can be eating at midnight and then still go on somewhere else as nothing closes."* Your tastes may become distinctly French, even in the space of six months - *"everyone drinks champagne!"* Weekend travel options are endless. Depending on the time of year, you can be on the slopes or the sands within a few hours thanks to the high speed TGV.

best things: Food, springtime, romance.
worst things: French TV, no bacon sarnies, arrogance.

piraeus/athens

Greece is a delight for hellenophiles, historians and hedonists alike. Having impressed even the most doubtful of Thomases when it hosted the 2004 Olympic Games, Athens now benefits from improved infrastructure and huge civic pride. Of course, national pride had already been boosted when Greece beat Portugal in the final of Euro 2004. While temperatures in the capital can reach 40° C in summer, this is compensated for by post-work swims at the beach. If Athens is the cradle of civilisation, Piraeus is its hospital waiting room. The guidebooks would have us believe it's the sort of place you end up in if you're waiting for a ferry to take you somewhere better...or in this case if you're a trainee in a UK law firm. Piraeus is a port city, and although this means ships and less than inspiring architecture, there's also an abundance of sunshine, seafood and sailors. Athens is only nine kms and a three-quid taxi fare away, and the blinding white sands of the Greek islands are at your feet. Whether it's weekend island hopping, the sleep-when-you're-dead nightlife, or the spectacular ruins of the Acropolis, a trainee seat in Piraeus or Athens is sure to be no Greek tragedy.

work: If your interest lies in shipping, then a seat in Piraeus is perfect. Most trainees work on ship finance with the occasional piece of litigation floating into the seat. The law that governs their work is largely English, and transactions and negotiations are also handled mainly in English, although knowledge of Greek is a definite advantage. Work in Athens tends to revolve more around corporate finance, with Greek law playing a greater role. At Norton Rose, solicitors speak to each other and to clients in Greek, so if it's all Greek to you, best stay in London. You can expect to be drafting your own loan agreements, attending closing and signing meetings solo, and have plenty of contact with often colourful shipping clients. Working hours are more or less the same as in the UK; so although the day starts later, you'll also work later. Thanks be to Zeus that bars stay open for post-toil retsina and post-deal plate smashing.

rest and play: Norton Rose's Piraeus trainees live in an *"amazing"* fourth floor apartment overlooking the Marina Zea, a ten-minute walk from the office. The deal is much the same at Stephenson Harwood and Watson, Farley & Williams, both of which offer two-bedroom flats just minutes from work. (Add an extra 15 minutes for each street you have to cross.) Most of the trainees we spoke to already had contacts in Greece, but for those who don't, there is a trainee welcoming committee ready and willing to introduce you to everything from hip hop clubs to bouzouki nights and hair-raising spins around go-kart tracks before breakfasting in a taverna. All on a school night too! Some trainees wax lyrical about Greece's epicurean delights, while others decry the ubiquitous *"grease and cheese pie."* Either way, a seat in Greece is a baklava-sweet deal. Earning a London salary, living rent-free in a relatively inexpensive and vibrant city with easy access to the Greek islands every weekend leaves the Central Line and the occasional weekend in Stow-on-the-Wold flailing in its wake.

best things: Fresh seafood, bouzouki nights, watching ferries from your office window.
worst things: Stifling summer heat, traffic.

prague

Like sleeping beauty, Prague has awoken from her 40 years of hibernation under Soviet rule and reappeared as a magical fairyland of spires, towers, cobbled streets and endless churches. Only Prague could have described her emergence from communism as the Velvet Revolution, and indeed, the city brims with elegance and romance. Situated on the Vltava River, the entire city is a UNESCO world heritage site dominated by a castle. Weekends hold trips to the western spa towns, while the Sumava Mountains of south Bohemia offer superb hiking. Prague has reclaimed her cultural, artistic and musical life, and from the eclectic mixture of artistic and architectural styles – gothic to art deco, cubist to high renaissance – to the clink and chatter of Czechs enjoying a post-work drink, Prague will enchant even the most cynical trainee. As one put it: *"I've been here six months now and every time I leave the office and walk into the main square, I think 'Wow, this is fantastic!'"*

work: A dab of corporate here, a dash of finance there, spots of litigation and privatisation, the occasional joint venture and a splash of IP - it's a diverse experience. Interaction with the local authorities provided some trainees with a lesson in post-communist bureaucracy, with one remarking how interesting it had been working in such a highly regulated economy. The work is international in nature, which is doubtless why UK firm's offices are English speaking. You'll be surrounded by the Czech Republic's brightest and best, those who were first in their class at law school, so it's not surprising that our sources noted a deferential attitude towards partners, who are often *"truly exceptional"* lawyers. Nevertheless, the office atmosphere is relaxed and quintessentially Czech; *"everyone makes an effort to go out for a proper lunch every day."* White & Case maintains an intimate festive tradition of meeting at the Christmas market in the old town square for a quick drink before returning to the office.

rest and play: Trainees' apartments are all within minutes of the office in the centre of Prague. Visiting mothers: don't be alarmed by the austere communist entrance to the digs; *"While it's all dour soviet misery outside, it's Ikea-tastic on the inside!"* Prague boasts a large expat community, and with half a dozen UK trainees in the city each six months it's all too easy to slip into. You can still eat and drink in Prague cheaply, and although fairly *"stodgy"* and *"not to everyone's tastes,"* the traditional Czech menu of meat, potatoes and dumplings will certainly keep you warm in the winter, if not supermodel svelte. In any case, you can walk off those extra pounds, since the city is safe and best experienced on foot. Drinking is the most popular pastime: *"You tend to take over a whole cocktail bar, there's no closing time and staff don't go home until you've finished."* When you're not listening to the strains of Dvorak wafting out of the apartment downstairs, you hear live jazz, opera, rock and dance music for a fraction of London prices. You certainly won't be short of visitors, since *"you suddenly grow all these friends who want to stay on weekends!"*

best things: The Christmas market, reading Kundera in an old town square café.
worst things: Aloof customer service, Czech bureaucracy, leaving.

singapore

The Singapore of the 21st century, with its three million inhabitants is a far cry from the tiny fishing village Stamford Raffles found in 1819. With its polyglot society, full employment, 90% home ownership and general all-round efficiency, Singapore is seen by many as a model city state. The opium dens and rickshaws of its colonial past have been swept aside to make way for a brave, new civic utopia where the streets are safe and clean, everything is air conditioned, and an automated taxi system means you'll never wait more than four minutes for a cab or pay much more than a pound. *"Precision"* is what it's all about, and the city runs like a Swiss timepiece. Singapore is known as 'The Fine City' as much for its rigorously enforced penalties (jaywalking, failing to flush the toilet or importing packs of chewing gum that are surplus to personal use) as for its splendour. Singapore is non-seasonal, but the humidity makes you feel like you're walking out into soup as you leave Changi Airport. Many people take a spare shirt to work and peel off the moist one upon arriving in the office.

work: Singapore is much more developed than its ASEAN counterparts, yet its legal profession has experienced both a recession and SARS of late. Some international firms have abandoned their joint venture agreements with local law firms or left the jurisdiction entirely, but a number remain heavily engaged in the market, perhaps even using the city as a hub for work in the wider region. Trainees are mostly involved in litigation, project and asset finance, corporate and debt restructuring work, with shipping and aviation law on offer in some firms. Don't be deceived by the *"efficient and relaxed atmosphere,"* as in times of plenty, you'll be rushed off your feet. One trainee told us: *"I would work from 9am 'til 6pm or 7pm but if I was there 'til 8pm I would be locking the door and turning the lights off."* A word of caution from one trainee: *"The air con is so cold we were sitting at our desk with coats on!"*

rest and play: Norton Rose trainees share an apartment with its own pool, just behind Orchard Road, which is the Singaporean equivalent of

Oxford Street. In fact all the trainees we spoke to reported having immaculate, centrally located accommodation and one even had *"a maid who did the ironing."* If you're addicted to designer labels, whoop for joy because shopping is the national pastime. Home cooking is nonsensical as you can eat out after work very cheaply while exploring different districts, such as China Town and Little India. For those who can't resist (or are hosting Ma and Pa for a week or two), there's always the Raffles Hotel and their world famous gin slings. At the moment, the trainees favourite is Equinox on the 72nd floor of the Stamford hotel, but there are any number of bars to choose from and on Wednesdays ladies drink for free. There's a well-established social scene amongst ex-pats and UK trainees, who all arrive within the same three-week window, and group weekends away are frequent. You can take a bus to Malaysia in an hour, fly to Oz for the weekend or even hire a private Indonesian island for 25 of your brand new best friends.

best things: Travel opportunities, cultural difference, food.
worst things: Claustrophobia, sweating.

tokyo

With its schizoid hybrid of Advanced Capitalism and Zen Buddhism, Japan has a magnetic pull on some people. Tokyo is a vital, edgy and exciting place to be; crowded, cramped, noisy and hectic, it is the *"archetypal concrete jungle, but with a real charm to it."* While you can get yourself the latest all-singing all-dancing mobile phone for mere pocket change, you may surprise yourself by succumbing to a six quid can of baked beans. Go in September to miss the rainy season and enjoy the skiing. March is a month of blue skies and cherry blossoms, and a time when the Japanese go to extraordinary lengths to celebrate the changing of the seasons.

work: Forget genteel tea ceremonies and Geisha entertainment, a posting to a Tokyo office slams trainees straight into finance work and lots of responsibility. There may also be energy and litigation matters. You need to have *"a lot of stamina,"* because the hours can be long, and you're quite likely to handle a number of your own files, so *"you won't feel like a trainee."* Client contact will be rare unless you are a master of oriental languages and etiquette.

rest and play: A western-style apartment is rare; most trainees reside in traditional Japanese-style accommodation complete with tatami matting. Ashurst, for example, has a central place in Hiroo, which is *"the Hampstead of Tokyo."* Socially, an e-mail list *"gives you a good base to expand from,"* but the trainee pack is far smaller in Tokyo than in other Asian destinations. While you will be invited out by colleagues from the office, the Japanese are notoriously reserved: *"They have very distinct professional and personal personas and they are difficult to get to know."* It's far too easy to work and play in the same district, so make the effort to get out of Roppongi and its expat bars and English pubs. At weekends, bullet trains can take you to Hiroshima, Miya Jima and Nikko for day trips, and in winter you can be on the slopes in an hour and a half. Gentlemen, unless you're tiny, take plenty of clothes with you, as you're unlikely to find much that fits. Ladies, retail therapy won't be in the least bit therapeutic as you'll probably need to buy size extra large unless you have the hips of a nine-year-old. Karaoke is a must, and the Japanese do it in a booth with their friends, so it's not at all embarrassing. If you want to practice before you go, there's a little Japanese-run place in Soho's Frith Street.

best things: Visual stimulation, food, cheap electronics.
worst things: Language problems, hard to get to know the Japanese.

warsaw

Often viewed as a bleak, post-communist purgatory, Warsaw suffers from a serious image problem, yet it is fast becoming one of Europe's most underrated capitals. By the end of World War II, the entire city was rubble, its spectacular old town lay in ruins and its population was decimated. The old town was painstakingly reconstructed and made it onto the UNESCO World Heritage List in 1980, though one trainee thought it was *"a bit like a film set - a little bit too perfect."* You can't escape history in Warsaw, and perhaps its most poignant testament to the past is the Jewish Ghetto, which retains a palpable sense of tragedy. The left bank of the Vistula river monopolises the main attractions - the city centre, the Royal Way and the old town - while the right bank contains the increasingly hip Praga district. Socialist realist art and architecture stand alongside renaissance and gothic styles. Poland's post-communist transformation throws up many surprises, such as former Solidarnosc leader and national president Lech Walesa presenting a weekly angling show on TV3. Visit Warsaw in summer as it becomes cold, grey and snowy in winter.

work: The trainees we spoke to found themselves doing a whole range of different work from real estate to corporate and, increasingly EU law. *"Joining the EU is really impacting on Polish business in terms of product safety, environment, etc."* The odd bit of proof reading and translation is inevitable, though *"it allows you to know what everyone else is working on and get contacts and understand how an overseas office works. In London it's like, just proof read this. But if I was reading a detailed piece of Polish tax advice I would ask them to explain it and work with them to make advice accurate and helpful."* At times you'll be treated as the resident UK law expert: *"If everyone else is out and you're from Eng-land, you will get asked questions."* The hours are slightly better than back home, although there are *"fewer people to absorb the work when things get hectic."* The atmosphere in Warsaw offices is friendly, although elements of communist bureaucratic culture remain. *"When you ask for something to be done, it's always on Poland time."*

rest and play: English is prevalent among young Warsawites, so making friends among the locals is easy, but most trainees find having a stab at learning Polish pays dividends. The city buzzes after dark, with cool and knowledgeable crowds descending on the many bars and clubs. There's everything from spit and sawdust drinking dens through to ultra hip lounge-style bars with cocktails and live DJs. Cinemas show all the latest films in English with Polish subtitles and the opera costs just £10. In summer, you can relax in leafy parks and outdoor cafes. Lazienki Park has live Chopin concerts and music is often heard in the city's main squares in the evening. For eating out, there's everything from milk bars (workmen's cafes) to more expensive restaurants, but the general view on Polish food is that it's *"pretty bland."* Those who venture further discover beautiful scenery from the Hanseatic city of Gdansk to the beach in Sopot. *"It's really sweet, like England in the 1950s, but with no beach huts. You have to visit the old Grand Hotel - everyone from Charlemagne to Hitler has stayed there."* The Mazurian Lakes and mountains are perfect for lovers of the outdoors, and the medieval city of Krakow is just two hours away. If you love history, you'll be in your element for your entire six months.

best things: Sunday morning at the Russian Market, vodka.

worst things: Pickled herrings for breakfast, communist architecture.

OVERSEAS SEATS – WHO GOES THERE?

LOCATION	FIRM
Abu Dhabi	Richards Butler, Shearman & Sterling, Simmons & Simmons, Trowers & Hamlins
Amsterdam	Allen & Overy, Baker & McKenzie, Clifford Chance, CMS Cameron McKenna, Freshfields Bruckhaus Deringer, Herbert Smith, Linklaters, Norton Rose, Slaughter and May
Athens	Norton Rose
Australia	Baker & McKenzie
Bahrain	Norton Rose, Trowers & Hamlins
Bangkok	Allen & Overy, Watson, Farley & Williams
Beijing	Freshfields Bruckhaus Deringer, Herbert Smith
Berlin	Hammonds, Linklaters
Boston	Dechert
Bratislava (Slovakia)	Allen & Overy, Linklaters
Brussels	Allen & Overy, Ashurst, Baker & McKenzie, Cleary, Gottlieb, Steen & Hamilton, CMS Cameron McKenna, Clifford Chance, Cobbetts, Coudert Bros, Dechert, Dickinson Dees, Eversheds, Freshfields Bruckhaus Deringer, Hammonds, Herbert Smith, Linklaters, Lovells, Mayer, Brown, Rowe & Maw, McGrigors, Nabarro Nathanson, Norton Rose, Olswang, Pinsents, Simmons & Simmons, SJ Berwin, Slaughter and May, Taylor Vinters, Taylor Wessing, White & Case, Wragge & Co.
Bucharest	Linklaters
Budapest	Allen & Overy, CMS Cameron McKenna, Linklaters
California	Osborne Clarke, Weil Gotshal & Manges
Chicago	Baker & McKenzie

LOCATION	FIRM
Cologne	Freshfields Bruckhaus Deringer, Osborne Clarke
Copenhagen	Slaughter and May
Dubai	Allen & Overy, Clifford Chance, Clyde & Co, Denton Wilde Sapte, Norton Rose, Trowers & Hamlins
Düsseldorf	Simmons & Simmons, Slaughter and May
Frankfurt	Allen & Overy, Ashurst, Clifford Chance, Freshfields Bruckhaus Deringer, Herbert Smith, Linklaters, Lovells, Norton Rose, SJ Berwin, Slaughter and May, White & Case
Geneva	Slaughter and May
Hamburg	Allen & Overy, CMS Cameron McKenna
Helsinki	Slaughter and May
Hong Kong	Allen & Overy, Baker & McKenzie, Barlow Lyde & Gilbert, Bird & Bird, Clifford Chance, Clyde & Co, CMS Cameron McKenna, Freshfields Bruckhaus Deringer, Hammonds, Herbert Smith, Holman Fenwick & Willan, Linklaters, Lovells, Norton Rose, Richards Butler, Shearman & Sterling, Simmons & Simmons, Slaughter and May, Stephenson Harwood, White & Case
Lisbon	Simmons & Simmons
Luxembourg	Allen & Overy, Slaughter and May
Madrid	Allen & Overy, Ashurst, Baker & McKenzie, Clifford Chance, Linklaters, SJ Berwin, Slaughter and May

OVERSEAS SEATS – WHO GOES THERE?

LOCATION	FIRM
Milan	Allen & Overy, Ashurst Morris Crisp, Clifford Chance, Freshfields Bruckhaus Deringer, Linklaters, Lovells, Norton Rose, Simmons & Simmons, Slaughter and May, White & Case
Monaco	Lawrence Graham
Moscow	Allen & Overy, Baker & McKenzie, Clifford Chance, CMS Cameron McKenna, Freshfields Bruckhaus Deringer, Herbert Smith, Linklaters, Norton Rose, White & Case
Munich	Ashurst, Bird & Bird, Clifford Chance, Dechert, Norton Rose, SJ Berwin
New York	Allen & Overy, Baker & McKenzie, Clifford Chance, Cleary Gottlieb Steen & Hamilton, Dechert, Freshfields, Lovells, Simmons & Simmons, Slaughter and May, Weil Gotshal & Manges
Oman	Trowers & Hamlins
Oslo	Slaughter and May
Paris	Allen & Overy, Ashurst Morris Crisp, Bird & Bird, Clifford Chance, CMS Cameron McKenna, Denton Wilde Sapte, Eversheds, Freshfields Bruckhaus Deringer, Hammonds, Herbert Smith, Holman Fenwick & Willan, Linklaters, Lovells, Norton Rose, Richards Butler, Shadbolt & Co, Simmons & Simmons, Slaughter and May, SJ Berwin, Travers Smith, Watson, Farley & Williams, White & Case, Weil, Gotshal & Manges
Philadelphia	Dechert
Piraeus	Clyde & Co, Holman Fenwick & Willan, Ince & Co, Norton Rose, Richards Butler, Stephenson Harwood, Watson, Farley & Williams

LOCATION	FIRM
Prague	Allen & Overy, Baker & McKenzie, Clifford Chance, CMS Cameron McKenna, Linklaters, Norton Rose, Slaughter and May, White & Case
Rome	Allen & Overy, Clifford Chance, CMS Cameron McKenna
Rotterdam	Simmons & Simmons
Sao Paulo	Clifford Chance, Linklaters, Richards Butler
Shanghai	Clifford Chance, Freshfields Bruckhaus Deringer, Herbert Smith, Stephenson Harwood
Singapore	Allen & Overy, Baker & McKenzie, Clifford Chance, Clyde & Co, Freshfields Bruckhaus Deringer, Herbert Smith, Linklaters, Norton Rose, Shearman & Sterling, Stephenson Harwood, Watson, Farley & Williams, White & Case
Stockholm	Bird & Bird, Linklaters, Slaughter and May
Stuttgart	CMS Cameron McKenna
Tokyo	Allen & Overy, Clifford Chance, Lovells, Freshfields Bruckhaus Deringer, Herbert Smith, Linklaters, Simmons & Simmons, Slaughter and May, White & Case
Turin	Hammonds
Utrecht	CMS Cameron McKenna
Vienna	CMS Cameron McKenna
Warsaw	Allen & Overy, Clifford Chance, Linklaters
Washington	Baker & McKenzie, CMS Cameron McKenna, Dechert, Freshfields Bruckhaus Deringer

notes

the true picture

the true picture

The *True Picture* is the only independent analysis of training contracts available to students. This year we report on 140 English and Welsh firms, ranging from the international giants to small regional practices that take just two new recruits per year. Most handle commercial law, although many of these also offer private client experience. A handful avoid commercial work altogether. We believe there is something for everyone in this year's *True Picture*!

how we do our research

The firms in the table on page 167 all agreed to provide complete lists of their trainees, and sometimes their NQs too. Having checked that the lists are complete, we randomly select a sample of individuals to interview over the phone. Our sources are guaranteed anonymity, as we feel this is the best way to give them carte blanche to say exactly what they want. The *True Picture* is not forwarded to the law firms prior to publication; they see it for the first time when this book is published. This makes our work unique.

We try to find out why trainees chose their firm and why others might want to. We ask about seat allocation and the character and work of different departments. We ask about working hours and after-hours fun, and we ascertain what happens to people on qualification. Aiming to capture the general mood in a firm, we look for the things trainees agree upon, or present both sides of the argument if they do not agree. Where we feel there are topics that students would wish to learn more about – say if a firm had made a significant number of redundancies – we ask trainees what we should say to readers who might be concerned about the issue. Our sources can respond however they want or elect to say nothing at all.

We're bored by the tired lines used in many recruitment brochures. You know the ones that tell you Smashing, Great & Partners is a standout firm because of its 'friendly culture' where everybody is 'down to earth' and 'approachable partners' operate an 'open-door policy'. Take it from us: these traits are not the preserve of a few firms. It constantly amazes us when our trainee sources are surprised that we hear these stock phrases every day. We try to focus on the detail of what builds a firm's character. If this is best demonstrated by telling you what happens at the Christmas party or how the senior partner turns into the Easter Bunny once a year then that's what we'll do. If we need to tell you partners are not that approachable or chatty, then we'll tell you that too.

our findings

Two years ago we found trainees were more critical of their firms than during the preceding three or four years. Last year, with the NQ job market in pretty dire health, we sensed many were either world-weary or eternally grateful to have a job on qualification. This year most of our sources were people who'd started their training since September 2002 and had only ever known the legal profession in a tough market. They are resilient, especially in the firms that have struggled with profitability or been through a lot of change. The class of 2004 take little for granted and are objective. They are also loyal to each other, which is admirable, since they could so easily have sunk to Lord of the Flies-style depths.

We try not to concentrate too much on current market conditions when writing the *True Picture*, as we recognise that things will probably have changed (particularly hours and budgets) by the time our readers start their training. However, we also recognise that the climate of 2004 affects the fortunes and market positions of law firms, and this in turn may have a bearing on what firms will be like in 2007 and beyond. If someone has a spare crystal ball lying around, we'd be very grateful for it!

The other thing we just can't predict is law firm mergers or closures. Thankfully the latter are rare, but the mergers crop up regularly. Hands up who remembers Sinclair Roche & Temperley, Gouldens and, of course, darling of the legal profession DJ Freeman. When firms merge, trainees' contracts are honoured, but of course it does mean they end up working at a different firm to the one they signed up for. Most of the high-profile mergers of the last year or two have been transatlantic tie-ups or the fusion of two regional firms or a national firm with a London firm. It's also worth noting that the international firms have reassessed the value of certain overseas offices, particularly in Asia, because the state of the local economy has not allowed these offices to be as profitable as hoped. For more on overseas seats and life as a trainee in far-flung places see our **Trainee Postcards** feature on page 147.

across the board:

• Some seats are more popular (and rarer) than others. The perfect example is employment law.

• Levels of responsibility vary between departments. In property you might have your own small files. In corporate you will generally work in a very junior capacity as part of a team.

• The experience in litigation depends entirely on the type of cases your firm handles; usually a trainee's responsibility is inversely proportional to the value and complexity of a case. If your firm handles personal injury claims, you may have conduct of matters yourself. If your firm goes in for long-running financial services litigation or multi-jurisdictional matters, you could be stuck for months on document management jobs.

• In times of plenty, corporate and finance seats mean long hours, commonly climaxing in all-nighters. Recently, there has been a shortage of corporate work, so hours have been more manageable. Again, the size and complexity of a deal will determine your role, but corporate and finance usually provide the most teamwork.

• Most firms offer four six-month seats; some six four-month seats and others their own unique systems. Trainees switch departments and supervisors for each seat. Most share a room and work with a partner or senior assistant; others sit open-plan either with the rest of the team or with other trainees. Occasionally a trainee will even have their own room (and maybe their name on the door!)

• All firms conduct appraisals, a minimum of one at the conclusion of each seat, and often halfway through as well.

• Client secondments, where offered, are a great way to find out how to be a better lawyer by learning to understand a client's needs. Often they turn out to be the highlight of a training contract.

• The Law Society requires all trainees to gain experience of both contentious and non-contentious work. Additionally, most firms have certain seats they require or prefer trainees to try. Some firms are very prescriptive, others flexible. The important thing to remember is that a training contract is a time to explore legal practice to see what you're best at and most enjoy. You will probably surprise yourself!

• The Law Society has raised its minimum salary(see page 11), but salaries in commercial firms have stayed static(ish). So have NQ salaries.

• NQ retention rates have not been brilliant in 2004. A full table of who managed what is on the Chambers Student website and also shows statistics dating back to 2000.

These terms will be useful when reading the *True Picture*

• **agency work** – making a court appearance for another firm that can't get to court
• **all-nighter** – working through the night
• **cmc** – case management conference
• **coco** – company-commercial department or work
• **dispute resolution** – litigation, mediation, arbitration etc
• **grunt work** – also known as donkey work, monkey work or even document jockeying. Administrative (and boring), yet essential, tasks including

photocopying, paginating, compiling court bundles and scheduling documents, bibling (putting together sets of all the relevant documents for a transaction), data room duty (supervising visitors to rooms full of important documents, helping them find things and making sure they don't steal them!) and proof-reading or checking that documents are intact.

- **high net worth individuals** – rich people
- **NQ** – a newly-qualified solicitor
- **PQE** – post-qualification experience
- **trainee partner** – a trainee who acts like a partner
- **mentor partner** – much better, the kind of partner who will guide you and buy you lunch
- **supervising partner** – you'll get one of these each seat, or you may be allocated a senior assistant
- **training partner** – the lucky partner who over sees the whole training scheme
- **real estate** – the newer name for property

what kind of firm do I choose?

Most students have a set of criteria that determine their choice of firm, though we did come across two novel approaches in our interviews this year. One trainee told us she worked her way through all the firms in the *True Picture*, starting at the beginning. She got a training contract when she reached the letter F. Another chose one firm from each letter of the alphabet and ended up in an S firm. We do not recommend either approach.

Your choice of firm will be based on location, size and the practice areas available...then it's a matter of chemistry. Some firms are stuffier; some are more industrious and some are very brand-aware and involve trainees heavily in marketing. Some have a strong sense of identity and others allow more freedom of expression. Some work open-plan; others occupy premises long past their sell-by date! Some focus on international business; others are at the heart of their local business communities. Some concentrate on contentious work, others transactional. The combinations of these variables are endless.

the city giants' trainees say: They are happy being among hundreds of trainees and an even greater number of staff ...They want overseas seats...They're prepared to sacrifice their social life...They want a top name on their CV...No expense should be spared on office support and facilities...Patience is a virtue – a glittering career is worth the wait...Money is important

mid-sized firm trainees say: They're names not numbers...They know most people at their firm...They don't want endless corporate/finance work...Overseas seats are not the be-all and end-all...They want to be well paid

american firm trainees say: They want top-end City/international work in a small office...The overseas seat was great...The salary is just dandy... The hours can be tough, but no more so than at the magic circle...They love the responsibility they get

national firm trainees say: They want a well-known name on their CV...They are the best paid in their region...Strength lies in numbers, even if they are spread across the UK...They are happy/unhappy about moving/not moving between cities...The mega deals aren't all they're cracked up to be...

regional firm trainees say: Rat-race London? No thanks!...They are proud of where they come from...Everyone knows them...Being managed from another city doesn't appeal...There's more to life than work – friends, family, the countryside

niche firm trainees say: They often had relevant industry experience...They had what it took to see off the competition

high street trainees say: Self-funding through law school was tough, but money isn't everything... They've grown up quickly...Corporate life is loathsome, give us real people any day

and finally...

We hope the *True Picture* will help you decide what sort of firms you want to target. No matter how hard or how easy securing a training contract turns out to be, you'll want to end up with the right one.

THE TRUE PICTURE 140 FIRMS

BY SIZE	FIRM NAME	CITY	TOTAL TRAINEES	PAGE NUMBER
1	GLS	London*	60	305
2	Eversheds LLP	London*	186	275
3	DLA LLP	London*	151	263
4	Clifford Chance LLP	London	238	236
5	Allen & Overy LLP	London	247	173
6	Linklaters	London	258	354
7	Freshfields Bruckhaus Deringer	London	212	297
8	Herbert Smith	London	165	314
9	Lovells	London	132	358
10	Hammonds	London*	82	309
11	Addleshaw Goddard	Manchester*	89	171
12	Slaughter and May	London	182	447
13	CMS Cameron McKenna	London*	123	242
14	Pinsents	Birmingham*	77	412
15	Norton Rose	London	152	395
16	Beachcroft Wansbroughs	London*	56	194
17	Denton Wilde Sapte	London*	85	256
18	Wragge & Co LLP	Birmingham*	48	498
19	Ashurst	London	97	183
20	Nabarro Nathanson	London*	60	390
21	Simmons & Simmons	London	120	443
22	Berwin Leighton Paisner	London	66	197
23	Cobbetts	Manchester*	54	244
24	Osborne Clarke	Bristol*	40	402
25	SJ Berwin	London	67	445
26	Baker & McKenzie	London	67	186
27	Mayer, Brown, Rowe & Maw LLP	London	50	374
28	Barlow Lyde & Gilbert	London	34	188
29	Masons	London*	37	371
30=	Irwin Mitchell	Sheffield*	35	334
30=	Morgan Cole	Cardiff*	26	387
32	Taylor Wessing	London*	46	462
33	Halliwells LLP	Manchester*	32	307
34	Hill Dickinson	Liverpool*	24	318
35	Clyde & Co	London*	34	239

*Firms are listed in order of size as measured by partner and assistant figures provided to Chambers UK. *Head or primary UK office*

THE TRUE PICTURE 140 FIRMS

BY SIZE	FIRM NAME	CITY	TOTAL TRAINEES	PAGE NUMBER
36	Bird & Bird	London*	25	204
37=	Mills & Reeve	Cambridge*	36	383
37=	Olswang	London*	43	398
39	Burges Salmon LLP	Bristol	36	221
40	McGrigors	Edinburgh*	37	380
41	Field Fisher Waterhouse	London	27	281
42=	Shoosmiths	Northampton*	22	436
42=	Charles Russell	London*	25	229
44	Reynolds Porter Chamberlain	London*	21	421
45	Richards Butler	London	40	423
46	Lawrence Graham LLP	London	34	342
47	White & Case LLP	London	45	491
48	Dickinson Dees	Newcastle*	28	261
49	DWF	Liverpool*	16	270
50	Stephenson Harwood	London	41	455
51	Pannone & Partners	Manchester	22	405
52	Jones Day	London	40	336
53=	Bevan Brittan LLP	Bristol*	38	200
53=	Macfarlanes	London	50	363
54=	Trowers & Hamlins	London*	29	473
56	Travers Smith	London	44	471
57	Penningtons	London*	24	409
58	Forbes	Blackburn*	15	290
59	Browne Jacobson	Nottingham*	20	219
60=	Freeth Cartwright LLP	Nottingham*	15	295
60=	Sidley Austin Brown & Wood LLP	London	16	439
62	Walker Morris	Leeds	30	478
63=	Shearman & Sterling LLP	London	15	434
63=	Withers LLP	London	25	494
65	Edwards Geldard	Cardiff/E. Midlands	20	272
66	Weil, Gotshal & Manges LLP	London	20	487
67	asb	Crawley*	10	180
68=	Farrer & Co	London	15	279
68=	Holman Fenwick & Willan	London	20	322
68=	Howard Kennedy	London	8	325

*Firms are listed in order of size as measured by partner and assistant figures provided to Chambers UK. *Head or primary UK office*

THE TRUE PICTURE 140 FIRMS

BY SIZE	FIRM NAME	CITY	TOTAL TRAINEES	PAGE NUMBER
68=	Speechly Bircham	London	10	451
72	Thomas Eggar	Chichester*	16	466
73=	Dechert LLP	London	29	253
73=	Lewis Silkin	London*	13	352
75=	Manches LLP	London*	20	366
75=	Nicholson Graham & Jones	London	20	392
77	Ince & Co	London	20	332
78	Watson, Farley & Williams	London	20	483
79	Hugh James	Cardiff*	17	327
80=	Mishcon de Reya	London	14	385
80=	TLT Solicitors	Bristol	11	468
82=	Veale Wasbrough	Bristol	10	476
82=	Ward Hadaway	Newcastle	16	483
84	Martineau Johnson	Birmingham*	19	369
85	Cripps Harries Hall	Tunbridge Wells*	14	251
86	Mace & Jones	Liverpool*	10	361
87	RadcliffesLeBrasseur	London*	10	417
88	Bristows	London	15	217
89	Brabners Chaffe Street	Liverpool*	17	213
90	Russell-Cooke	London	10	426
91	Foot Anstey Sargent	Plymouth*	15	288
92	Laytons	London*	16	345
93	Kendall Freeman	London	17	338
94	Lester Aldridge	Bournemouth*	12	349
95	Capsticks	London	11	227
96=	Bircham Dyson Bell	London*	13	202
96=	Gateley Wareing LLP	Birmingham*	14	303
98=	Bates, Wells & Braithwaite	London*	8	192
98=	Boodle Hatfield	London*	9	209
100=	McDermott Will & Emery	London	4	378
100=	Taylor Vinters	Cambridge	13	459
102=	Reed Smith LLP	London*	13	419
102=	Iliffes Booth Bennett (IBB)	Uxbridge*	10	329
104=	Anthony Collins	Birmingham	11	178
104=	Cadwalader Wickersham & Taft LLP	London	12	223

*Firms are listed in order of size as measured by partner and assistant figures provided to Chambers UK. *Head or primary UK office*

THE TRUE PICTURE 140 FIRMS

BY SIZE	FIRM NAME	CITY	TOTAL TRAINEES	PAGE NUMBER
104=	Wedlake Bell	London	11	485
107	Cleary Gotlieb Steen & Hamilton	London	8	233
108	Salans	London	7	428
109	DMH	Brighton*	13	266
110	Stevens & Bolton LLP	Guildford*	6	458
111=	Harbottle & Lewis LLP	London	8	312
111=	Finers Stephens Innocent	London	9	284
111=	Devonshires	London	10	259
114	Andrew M Jackson	Hull	11	177
115=	Fox Williams	London	8	292
115=	Coffin Mew & Clover	Fareham*	9	247
117	Clarks	Reading*	4	232
118	Shadbolt & Co	Reigate*	8	432
119	Payne Hicks Beech	London	4	408
120	Fisher Meredith	London	14	286
121	Hodge Jones & Allen	London	9	320
122	LeBoeuf, Lamb, Greene & MacRae LLP	London	9	347
123	Brachers	Maidstone*	10	215
124	Capital Law	Cardiff*	4	225
125	Prettys	Ipswich	10	415
126=	Barlows	Guildford*	7	190
126=	BPE	Cheltenham*	11	211
126=	Teacher Stern Selby	London	9	464
129	The Simkins Partnership	London	4	441
130=	Steeles (Law) LLP	Norwich*	12	453
130=	White & Bowker	Winchester	8	489
132=	Birkett Long	Colchester*	4	207
132=	McCormicks	Leeds*	8	376
134	Orchard	London	5	400
135=	Dorsey & Whitney LLP	London	8	268
135=	Wollastons	Chelmsford	4	496
137=	Coudert Brothers LLP	London	7	249
137=	Kent Jones & Done	Stoke on Trent	5	340
139	Galbraith Branley & Co	London	8	300
140	Samuel Phillips & Co	Newcastle	4	430

*Firms are listed in order of size as measured by partner and assistant figures provided to Chambers UK. *Head or primary UK office*

Addleshaw Goddard

the facts

Location: Leeds, London, Manchester
Number of UK partners/assistants: 162/358
Total number of trainees: 89
Seats: 4x6 months
Alternative seats: Secondments
Extras: Pro-bono – Manchester Uni Legal Advice Centre, Springfield Legal Advice Centre

In May 2003 Addleshaw Booth of Manchester, Leeds and London merged with City firm Theodore Goddard. Although not a merger of equals, the firm's new name recognised each legacy part. The one-year anniversary has passed without too much drama. So far, it's all looking good...

helping hands

To fill you in on the background, northern giant Addleshaw Booth resolved to develop a London office. It sent lawyers down to the capital and prized others away from City firms, but growth was too slow, so it followed the example set by rivals such as Hammonds and Pinsents. Addleshaws has now transformed itself through its merger with Theodore Goddard. Poor old TG: it was loved by many, but beset by bitterness after a series of failed mergers. What with a string of partners throwing in the towel, falling profits, and reports of private dicks being hired to stop leaks to the press, the firm needed a helping hand. Addleshaws offered two and the deal was done.

None of our friends in the northern offices had much to say about the merger. One told us bluntly: *"There was a lot of free champagne on the day, but the corporate image hasn't changed that much – seeing a different header on firm's notepaper doesn't make you feel differ-* ently."* Another agreed, saying: *"Basically it has just shown [Addleshaws'] ambition to grow and that it is progressing to hit its target."* In London, where the two firms have physically come together, change is more noticeable.

pompoms and petty cash

We're told to expect managed departures at partner level – those who can't pull in the dosh will be pushed out so that profitability can double by 2009. Some staff, whose roles were duplicated, have already left the firm, and its only overseas office (in Brussels) has closed. AG apparently has no intention of venturing beyond the UK, and will instead concentrate on developing good relationships with foreign firms, while pumping resources into its banking, corporate and employment practices.

The aim is to *"expand to survive...not wholesale, but gradually."* This might mean pinching a partner from here or a team from there. *"Everyone is concentrating on establishing a national presence and increasing the number of FTSE 350 clients."* One source announced: *"We want to attack that area below the magic circle. We've spotted the firms that are falling away, and we need to be attacking and climbing up the size ladder."* With all this ambitious talk we'd expected everyone in London to be cheering from the sidelines, but while the ex-ABC trainees were shaking the pompoms, some of the ex-TG lot were shaking their heads. *"The focus has changed to Manchester: all key decisions come down from Manchester...even petty cash has to come from Manchester!"* For a certain type of person who'd never have joined anything other than a well-established, traditional City law firm, the prospect of working at a national firm is just too much to bear. Those trainees more willing to embrace the vision of the future seemed far happier, and we doubt it's any different at partner level.

it's show time

Trainees take seats in each of the corporate, property and litigation divisions, although these need not all be mainstream seats. For example, IP and employment each count as litigation, and property lit, planning and construction all tick the property box. Mainstream corporate finance, however, is a common first seat as trainees can be eased into the work gently by assisting with the administrative elements of a deal. *"The way you start off allows you to build trust with people,"* which then leads to more demanding roles. The corporate recovery department is another potential stop-off point, described by one visitor as *"like corporate finance but with all the dull bits taken out."* Acting mainly for banks and insolvency practitioners (ie accountants), you have bags of client contact and will tackle both non-contentious and contentious work, perhaps taking on a portfolio of small debt actions or assisting with an asset disposal.

Described by one source as *"the best six months I've had at the firm,"* property seats usually go down a storm. If working on a large corporate-support job, expect *"primarily admin tasks, but you can get a feel for the subject while being very valuable."* You should quickly build up *"a solid property foundation"* by managing 30 to 40 files, including small leasehold transactions and telecoms matters. In this seat, *"it really is your show. You get the post, decide what to do next on the file, check with the supervisor and then get on with it."*

Reports on commercial litigation seats were also favourable. One trainee was amazed at how tactically lawyers had to work – *"sending out open letters and without prejudice letters at the same time; trying to think around the case."* Whenever he'd been asked to assist on a matter the supervisor sat him down and explained his role and what they needed to achieve. *"They ask your opinion – it's been a very interactive process,"* he told us. This approach is repeated elsewhere. Our source continued: *"I came out of my first seat thinking I was lucky to have a supervisor take time out of their day to talk me through things that would have taken them a quarter of the time to do themselves. In fact*

they all adopted the same approach. You get the odd person who thought their last six months was rubbish, but I have heard that in only a few cases here."

relish the eperience

Up north there are one or two private client seats covering either family or trusts and probate matters. In these, *"the style of drafting and letter writing is different to what you're used to in commercial seats. You get given files for yourself and you learn a lot about client care, letter writing and drafting..."* The oversubscribed, *"plum"* seats can be devilishly hard to get. A trainee who'd secured one of Addleshaws' three employment seats assured us that *"contrary to popular belief, no one else died in the process."* There are always going to be disappointments but, overall, trainees say the seat system is fair. A reminder to anyone hoping to tread water at some point in their training: *"If there's competition for a seat then your performance in past seats is going to play a part in their decision."* For time out of the office, you can apply for one of the client secondments, including spells at AstraZeneca and the FA.

"I wanted decent quality work and a decent-size firm with the attendant support," one trainee told us. Another echoed the sentiment, saying: *"I wanted big-name clients and work I could grow into."* The firm seeks trainees with a solid academic record and an ambitious and hard-working attitude to their careers – practical people keen to deliver results. On the vac scheme it's easy enough to spot those who'll go further with the firm: they'll be *"enthusiastic and excited – not blasé about being here."*

This keen-as-mustard attitude is prevalent in both northern offices, but there's a shade of difference between the two locations. *"Leeds is a self-contained office and people know each other better between the departments."* This is partly down to the layout of the building, which boasts a large, airy and well-used café. *"In Leeds more people eat lunch together downstairs. In Manchester it takes a bit longer to get to know people."* That said, the similarities between the two offices are greater than the differences. Three years ago Addleshaw Booth & Co codified its character and values in a document called The ABC Way. *"It was a source of much humour, though we don't hear much about it now. Corporate rebranding buggered that up!"* Putting such cynicism aside, if the satisfaction of our interviewees is anything to go by, promoting The ABC Way was a brilliant idea.

the c-words

In December 2003, the managing partner gave a speech to trainees at their annual conference. In it he likened the firm's qualities and aims to the facets of a diamond. *"There are four Cs,"* a trainee explained, *"but I can't remember them exactly."* That would be cut, clarity, colour and carat weight. A prize for anyone who can shine a light on the analogy.

The typical northern AG trainee is *"outgoing and will chat the hind legs off a donkey,"* and when we accused them of being keenos, most accepted the charge. Said one: *"We all want to do this job, so there's not a lot of moaning. We're expected to be like that though – to show a professional outlook and be willing to work hard."* And from another: *"You are probably right, but we also have a reputation for being complete idiots when we're out. We're to be avoided at TSG balls!"* Categorising the typical London trainee is more difficult. As *"classy"* as TG's reputation was, many trainees had chosen it as an alternative to the standard City offerings. With its media seats and pop star clients, it was old-school pinstripe with a twist. We suspect it'll become harder and harder to spot which legacy firm recruited a particular trainee in the next couple of years, especially as trainees start to move around offices for seats. Up and down the country, 32 of the 45 September 2004 qualifiers took jobs with the firm.

pincer movement

The Leeds local, Homarus, which has always received rave reviews in the past, has apparently *"lost its shine a bit."* When someone told us it was attached to a Travelodge, we began to understand why rebels are trying to persuade colleagues to try

trendier bars in the Calls. Over in Manchester the Pitcher & Piano beneath the office is also the subject of competition from Rain Bar. In London fortnightly drinks in the office's atrium area are well attended: *"Often it will progress to the Red Cow and then on to Extra Time."* Sporting endeavours are also well supported – five-a-side footie, bowling, rugby...you name it, people do it.

and finally...

Addleshaws has played a smart game. In merging with TG it jumped up the legal league tables and potential new clients have taken notice. In Leeds and Manchester it was always a dream ticket for students who shunned City snobbery, and we sense many London-bound students will now want the same deal.

Allen & Overy LLP

the facts

Location: London
Number of UK partners/assistants: 197 / 692
Total number of trainees: 247
Seats: 3 or 6 months long
Alternative seats: Overseas seats, secondments
Extras: Pro bono – various schmes incl. Liberty, RCJ CAB, Battersea Legal Advice Centre and death row appeals; language training

Since its foundation in 1930, Allen & Overy has grown from Mr A, Mr O, a dozen staff and a cab full of sequestered files into one of the world's largest and most respected global law firms. Today it boasts membership of the City's magic circle, top-notch teams in almost any area of commercial law you'd care to name and what many regard as the world's premier finance practice. Trainees love it for each of these reasons, and in that order. Buying into this superbrand also brings them huge salaries and the career equivalent to a 'get out of jail free card', should they later decide to work elsewhere.

champagne breakfast

Even the most cursory of glances at the handy pie chart tucked away at the back of A&O's recruitment literature reveals that nearly half the firm is dedicated to banking and international capital markets (ICM). If huge syndicated loans, or eurobonds grab your attention on your morning thumb through the *FT*, A&O should be a mouth-watering prospect, as you'll get the chance to work in *"one of the best banking practices in the world."* We don't perceive the level of obsession with being 'first and biggest' that we do with Clifford Chance, a firm which shares the limelight with A&O in the finance arena; nevertheless, this hasn't stopped A&O from guzzling up to 50% of the top jumbo financings this year. A&O's involvement on these full English breakfasts of the international loan market includes advising JPMorgan on the provision of a €15.5 billion facility for Olivetti in connection with its merger with Telecom Italia (the largest syndicated package anywhere in the world in 2003). In the past year, the firm has also advised this client on a $3 billion credit arrangement for publishing group Reed Elsivier and on a £1 billion syndicated loan for Reuters. It regularly acts for most of the world's leading investment banks including ABN AMRO, Bank of America, Barclays Capital, BNP Paribas, Citibank, Deutsche Bank, HSBC, Merrill Lynch, Société Générale and Royal Bank of Scotland.

It's a mark of the scope of A&O's finance practice that capital markets work is a distinct department from banking, which to one trainee at least meant there was *"double the amount of finance work as elsewhere."* The firm acted on the first ever eurobond issue in 1963...and it hasn't looked back. Champagne moments for the ICM team over the past year include the first ever issue of sovereign bonds for the governments of Dubai, UAE and Bahrain, a eurobond issue simultaneously listed on both the Zagreb and Luxembourg exchanges, and a £300 million bond issue for retailer Next. Anyone with recent experience of the City LPC may think they know all there is to know about distressed debt, but in the world of A&O this means projects such as the high-profile restructuring of Marconi's financial commitments and a scheme of arrangement for Drax Power Station. US securities continue to occupy many of the firm's capital markets lawyers; indeed the firm has one of the largest groups of US qualified lawyers in London. In short, A&O's pedigree in the financial world means quite simply that it can *"set the way that the market works."*

Don't worry overly if all that has left you reeling. As one trainee pointed out: *"It's a misconception of A&O that we're all about banking and ICM – we do lots of corporate finance as well."* If the banking and ICM departments allow companies to raise money, the corporate groups advise on how they spend it. As proof that A&O doesn't only act for banks, its lawyers have recently held the hands of advertising and marketing group WPP on its acquisition of Cordiant Communications Group, and Wella on its takeover by Procter & Gamble.

bolly moments

Sign up to train at A&O and you'll spend at least a year (and usually your first seat) in banking, ICM or corporate finance seats. These departments handle roughly 75% of the firm's work and some trainees actually spend 75% of their training contract in them. In a banking seat (chosen from global loans, financial services regulatory, leveraged finance, restructuring or projects) you'll be helping out on *"massive deals"*...once more for effect, *"massive deals."* What you actually do will depend on what stage of the transaction you come in on. If it's the negotiation stage, you'll amend loan documents, research markets or even draft smaller agreements yourself. When the deal is struck, you'll help with the closing arrangements and, once the champagne's been drunk, there'll be bible preparation to keep you busy. Especially as a first-seater, the huge facilities you'll be working on can be baffling: they can have *"strange, tax-driven structures,"* which *"you can't understand enough to be able to contribute."* Banking is where the firm's *"killer departments"* tend to be found – we heard whispers about demanding and hardcore leveraged finance and global loans seats. For long hours, you can't beat the securitisation seat in ICM.

Talking of ICM, most of the other seats here are very popular. Why so? *"ICM transactions are shorter, so you can get more involved and get more hands-on experience with clients."* Expect to have a go at the first drafts of agency agreements or pricing supplements for small bond issues, or you might assist by updating bonds to accommodate changes in law or the intentions of the parties. As most transactions here are done by just one lawyer, *"there's less of a team atmosphere,"* but you will get to work more closely with your supervisor.

pirhanas

The compulsory seat in litigation is just three months long, but you can ask for it to be extended to six. And sometimes that's possible. Comments on contentious work are accompanied by everything from beaming smiles (*"I really enjoyed it and got lots of legal research and good cases"*) to the gritted teethed (*"I'm trying to make the most of it"*). The fact that *"everyone has to do it and so there's a lot of trainees there"* leads to *"a feeding frenzy for work...e-mails come round saying 'can a trainee help?' and the work will be gone within a few minutes."* Interestingly, *"the people who finally end up in litigation really want to be there; you get people staying there for a long time after qualification."* The three-month stint in litigation seems to be breaking down the traditional four by six months seat structure. Several of our sources had completed two, or even four three-month seats, something they liked because *"it gives you more options."*

Your two-year seating plan is decided during the course of your first (non-optional) seat. After a series of presentations by the different departments, you'll sit down for a chat with the grad recruitment people and discuss your shopping list. Once the core basics are in the trolley, you can then cruise the aisles to pick out what else you fancy. *"HR structure every-*

thing really well; once you say 'this is my plan', they'll do what they can to accommodate it," subject to the inevitable restraint of over subscription of popular seats. An overseas posting or a secondment to a major corporate or financial institution can be easily incorporated into your shopping.

As a valued customer, you'll also be allowed to cash in the points on your loyalty card. The 'priority seat request' guarantees you your seat of choice and is usually used for the very popular niche areas such as IP litigation, employment or real estate. The firm boasts an excellent reputation in many of these areas and certainly *"plays up"* these departments to potential recruits. But bear in mind that these departments are *"support departments."* In competition, employment and tax, for example, you'll usually be assisting the progress of corporate or banking deals. Even in the real estate department, standalone property transactions account for just 30% of the work, the rest being property finance or due diligence for the corporate teams.

Be aware that a single group within banking can be *"larger than our whole property department"* and size matters as far as qualification is concerned. Trainees pointed out that *"a lot of people are quite surprised when they find out how hard it is to qualify into niche areas."* One said plainly: *"If I had been interested in a niche area – employment, tax or property – I would have applied to a more specialist firm."* Perhaps because trainees are realistic about where NQ jobs crop up, *"most people seem to get their first or second choice department."* In September 104 out of 117 qualifiers (unfortunately much lower than usual for A&O) stayed with the firm, the majority – approximately 80% – qualifying into corporate, banking and ICM.

at the feet of the masters

When working on a massive deal as a trainee, you won't take a starring role. *"You are occasionally going to have to do proof-reading and other menial tasks that need doing."* On this issue, our sources understood that *"it's unrealistic to not expect trainees to do some of this type of work;"* they appreciated that supervisors generally do their best *"to try and get you involved."* All agreed that the plentiful formal training sessions were excellent and, for most, five minutes of fame in the *FT* was seen to compensate for being lower down the work food chain. Big deals mean *"working with the really big names."* *"Some people here know they're the best, and you can learn so much from these people."*

One particularly erudite source summed up the trainee's lot by saying: *"I've done more bad work than you might do at a smaller firm, but I've done more good work as well. I've just done more work!"* That leads us to an important question: just what exactly will A&O expect of you in exchange for a fat salary? Of the hours lottery, one trainee revealed: *"I normally get to leave at 6.30pm-7pm, but I have done a fair few late nights until 11pm or 12pm. There might be people who have done less; there might be people who have done more. The hours are very unpredictable and you have to learn to work efficiently."* But if trainees did find themselves working *"from 8am to 2am again and again and again,"* the feeling was that such challenges build character. Which made us wonder if training at A&O is just a bit like being at boarding school.

Of course, you won't have to play lacrosse or sleep in a dormitory, but school spirit and discipline is definitely required. Said one source: *"I wish someone had told me how disciplined you have to be. You're not just judged on how good your work is, but also on how you get on with the team."*

A&O's current One New Change office certainly has all the facilities you'd expect at an elite educational establishment: everything from a canteen to a nurse and (in common with Eton) its very own bar...although *"it wouldn't get the best of reviews in Time Out."* And just as all decent schools have a chapel or church attached, in A&O's case it's St Paul's Cathedral. Around a third of the firm can also enjoy *"Zen Buddhist chill-out areas,"* basketball hoops and Japanese-style sleeping pods in the newer Canary Wharf outpost. However, by the time you join the firm in 2007, it will be installed in newly built premises in Spitalfields.

a good deed every day

So why choose A&O? Although trainees told us they *"hadn't met anyone not interested in the work,"* for most it was the safety of a good name: *"If you train at A&O, you can do whatever you like afterwards."* Trainees also mentioned *"the people"* and, as the megafirms go, A&O does have a reputation for being more scout camp than boot camp (though in the *Student Guide's* childhood experience, the two were pretty much indistinguishable). In many respects, the experiences of trainees at all the magic circle firms are equally indistinguishable, but we've more than a hunch that positive effects flow from the firm's Values Into Action philosophy. Some trainees feel that mottoes such as 'excellence in everyone and everything' are *"something you take the piss out of while you have to fill in the box on your appraisal form,"* whereas for the less cynical *"it generates a certain feeling and integrates the firm."* If it works for you...

As A&O has more trainees than some smaller outfits have staff, joining the firm feels *"almost like being part of a university intake."* For some this translates into a non-competitive collegiate atmosphere, and we heard about intake-wide curry nights and gangs of trainees descending on the A&O flats in Prague or Luxembourg. For others though, it's all a little too much like *"being back at school – it can get bitchy and all the Sloaney girls stick together."* But even the non-group-huggers agree that bigger is better: *"In a group of 60, you can usually find 10 people that you really like and then ignore the others."* Any trainee who doesn't click with the cohort thing can opt for departmental socialising.

and finally...

To conclude, we'll refer to founder George Allen's original criteria for recognising a future A&O star: "He is a fine chap, he is competent and he has financial ability." Apart from the chap bit, and the fact that you'll also have to flash good A-level grades and at least a 2:1, these principles hold true today. The firm can offer you dazzling opportunities, but make sure you're aware of what will be expected of you.

Andrew M Jackson

the facts

Location: Hull
Number of UK partners/assistants: 27/29
Total number of trainees: 11
Seats: 4x6 months
Alternative seats: None

Hull. Fish and a funny accent. Come on, this city has produced more than that. Off the top of our heads we came up with Fatboy Slim, Everything But The Girl and undisputed heavyweight political champ John Prescott. We also know that Hull is the only city in the UK to have its own telecommunications network, and that it's home to a certain law firm by the name of Andrew M Jackson that's been representing clients for the last hundred years or so.

northern exposure

AMJ is, according to our sources, *"a great firm to train in, if you're not massively sure what to qualify into. Generally, the quality of work is good, and you have quality of life as well."* In other words, it's *"a nice all-rounder."* The first thing to consider is the large range of seats on offer. The firm represents everyone *"from big plcs to one-man bands"* and has an active legal aid practice. There is also a smattering of international work concerning fishing vessel transactions, and the firm has been known to litigate major fishing cases across the country. Boasting national commercial clients such as MFI, Northern Foods and Express Dairies, for someone intent on a legal career in Yorkshire, AMJ can be considered a realistic East Riding alternative to working in Sheffield or Leeds.

AMJ enjoys longstanding links with the local shipping industry and is still the clear market leader in the sector. Trainees in the marine department discovered *"a mammoth area"* of interesting law and found themselves dealing with accidents on board ships, collisions and cargo disputes, drafting charter parties and selling yachts. Aside from the fact that work came in peaks and troughs, with some trainees reporting a *"famine or feast"* workload, and others declaring that *"six months wasn't really enough to get a full picture,"* shipping seats clearly go down well.

Nowadays, commercial property is the firm's largest department. Here trainees reported a *"fantastic variety of work,"* including advising on the sale and purchase of freehold properties, and drafting leases and licences to assign. You'll probably run some of your own smaller files, but equally you'll assist on some *"pretty impressive,"* large commercial deals. Taking it down a notch, domestic conveyancing is seen as *"an excellent first seat"* defined by *"lots of client contact and supportive training."*

driving tests

One thing our trainees agreed on was that, whichever department you end up in, you take something useful away from the experience. As one opined: *"No matter what seat you do, you get the chance to practice certain skills. For example, even if you don't necessarily want to do family work, it can be a really good seat to practice your client management skills. They let you do everything from initial interviews to going to court with counsel."* We got the feeling trainees were genuinely happy with the kind of work they were given. Even of the corporate department, often prone to becoming a responsibility by-pass, we were told trainees were encouraged to put themselves through a rigorous road test: *"There isn't anything too big for you to have an attempt at, even if you do get it completely wrong."* Corporate work focuses on acquisitions and disposals, with lawyers having acted on several MBOs in 2004. It seems that corporate supervisors are keen to involve their charges in as much of their work as possible, and are always willing to discuss any areas where this is not possible.

team talks

Each trainee has a 'mentor' partner with whom they meet on a monthly basis to review any problems and chat about their aspirations for the next seat. The mentors then meet up to decide which trainee should move to which department. While most of our sources were positive about its potential, we noted a degree of concern that the system is *"a bit subjective in terms of how good the mentor is that you're sending in to bat."* *"What needs to be refined is which partners are selected as mentors. Once you've got a core of 12 on a level playing field, the system will be fantastic."*

The same could be said about the appraisal system. While some interviewees had regular feedback, others noted that they hadn't had an appraisal for over a year. We understand that HR now have their beady eye on the situation. Alongside a programme of in-house seminars and lectures, the firm runs one-day skills sessions. Last year's seminars included assertiveness, presentation skills and communicating in meetings. On top of this, trainees are encouraged to get involved with marketing, which might mean sitting on the client entertainment committee or organising a run of ads in the local paper.

beverley hillbillies

The firm is going through a bit of a makeover. Apart from changing the logo to a suspiciously trendy 'amj', we heard reports of a digital dictation revolution as part of the drive to make the firm *"more efficient and more modern,"* though we were assured that this wasn't going to extend to punishing hours. Admittedly, this ultra-professional firm sometimes projects a slightly austere image; however, we were told that the reality was quite the opposite: *"We may be a bit hard on the outside, but we're smooth on the inside."*

The state of the firm's offices was the one regular gripe we heard from trainees. As one noted: *"A flash building isn't our style – we're more about keeping costs down for the clients."* AMJ is perched on the top floors of an office block that apparently suffers from *"sad building syndrome."* And any trainee anxious about looming qualification can't have been helped by having to pass the job centre on the ground floor every day. In no need of the job centre, four of the six qualifying trainees took positions with the firm in September 2004.

Hull has come out on top in polls ranging from chubbiest city to highest number of snorers. *"One league table we're top of is teenage pregnancies. That can't be good."* We couldn't help but wonder if the city is judged unfairly, yet the last time we visited we found ourselves asking a taxi driver to explain why so many small shops and pubs on the route from the station to the university were boarded up. Our learned driver hinted that the arrival of bigger businesses meant Hull was in a state of flux, and one of the trainees confirmed this, saying: *"A lot of investment is going into the city."* Chances are, if you're reading this, you'll already be familiar with Hull and all of these trends. Many staff live outside the city in smart places like Beverley, and as so many are Hull born and bred they have their own social networks, meaning that not everyone feels obliged to head straight for the pub at the end of every working day. Nonetheless, *"a few individuals are trying to kick-start a social life,"* and the trainees do make it out en masse once a month. The partners, too, do their bit to keep staff happy, laying on departmental Christmas parties and an annual fancy dress summer barbeque. Roll on summer!

and finally...

Andrew M Jackson proves you don't have to move away from the banks of the Humber to get quality commercial training.

Anthony Collins Solicitors

the facts

Location: Birmingham
Number of UK partners/assistants: 18/47
Total number of trainees: 11
Seats: 4x6 months
Alternative seats: None

Committed to a legal career but not to selling your soul? Birmingham Law Society's Firm of the Year 2003/4, Anthony Collins opens its doors to you.

care and the community

Licensing specialist Anthony Collins gave his name to the firm in 1973. Thirty years on, a new senior partner and an impending move to new premises could be seen to be ringing the changes. However, you only have to look at the firm's work to see that Collins' committed community ethos and compassionate spirit remain the lifeblood of the partnership. The firm has three main areas of practice: commercial services, private client and the intriguingly named 'Transformation'. The commercial services limb covers commercial property, dispute resolution, employment, business and licensing work, and its client list brings together local Midlands businesses with big names such as Goodyear Dunlop, Tearfund and The Restaurant Group. The private client lawyers supply not only family and probate services, but also a wealth of legal aid advice and a powerful clinical negligence practice. They have been involved in prolific matters such as Hepatitis C litigation and organ retention cases, as well as high-value claims concerning, for example, birth injuries.

The firm's most compelling cause is its utterly respected and nationally regarded Transformation group. Here, Anthony Collins' spirit is clearly visible in its work on community regeneration, local government, housing management and litigation, public-private partnerships and Best Value projects for Christian and national children's charities, housing groups and local authorities.

loop the loop

While a training contract at Anthony Collins may look like a crash course in social conscience and loving thy neighbour, it's not all about polishing your halo and the firm can offer a thoroughly commercial training. A standard four by six-month seat system works within a *"loop system,"* following the three main branches of the firm. Generally trainees undertake all four seats within one of the three limbs of the firm, the idea being that *"if you want to be a specific type of lawyer you will do seats within that stream."* Certainly, *"there is the option to switch around,"* and the varying degrees to which our sources were au fait with the whole loop thing suggest that recent years have seen a *"more flexible outlook on seats."*

Undoubtedly, Transformation is a draw, especially for recruits coming to the law from other careers. Working on Best Value projects, trainees end up drafting documentation for local authorities in the process of contracting out, say, their leisure services or entering into design-and-build projects. If working on housing litigation, a trainee would certainly attend court, as well as meetings with clients and counsel. And in a 'regeneration' seat, they would assist with housing and community projects nationwide, by researching, drafting and liasing with tenants and residents. The seat also promises site visits, which is great if you want to see the fruits of your labours first hand. Many of the projects are worth serious amounts of money – such as the redevelopment of Attwood Green for Optima CA. This is a 1,400 unit, mixed use and tenure regeneration project in inner-city Birmingham. In contrast, *"in a commercial seat, matters are smaller, and you get quite a bit of responsibility: you get your own files to run and can see through whole transactions."*

It's a similar story on responsibility in the private client stream as *"the firm does quite a lot of legal aid work and trainees tend to get the legal aid clients."* That means *"trainees in a family seat are busy going to court all the time"* and, get used to it quick – *"people phone you for your advice."*

too good to be true?

We were left in no doubt as to this being a training laden with responsibility and variety, but equally it is one in which supervisors take different approaches, ranging from the whiteboard-flowchart-painting-by-numbers school of thought, to those who are committed believers in the quick-chat-see-how-you-fare philosophy. We heard of *"brilliant day-to-day feedback"* in addition to mid and end-of-seat appraisals. And as for grunt work, apparently at Anthony Collins *"you don't do photocopying."* Those with views to express can do so at a monthly forum, and trainees *"get the impression people are listening."* Perhaps this explains the general aura of calm and satisfaction we perceived during interviews.

Happy trainees doing excellent work in a principled firm. Too good to be true? Apparently not. Our sources commented that early on in the recruitment process, the proverbial 'work-life balance' was paraded before them, with one candid source admitting: *"I was sceptical."* Nonetheless, *"at 5.15pm on the first day, the office really did empty out,"* and with the working day starting at 9am and rarely finishing later than 6pm, we eventually submitted to persistent assurances of the firm's good character. *"It is a welcoming place with a good ethos, a caring approach and a feeling you are being looked after."* There's no doubt that some folk were attracted by the idea of sharing their working life with other committed Christians, but for those of other or no faith this aspect of the firm's make-up does not appear to dominate.

form an orderly cue

Rapid expansion in staff numbers has meant the office overlooking Birmingham's Anglican cathedral has become overcrowded, and it seems that IKEA-style furniture and a few dried flower arrangements in the toilets are insufficient creature comforts for trainees. One open-minded critic described *"perfectly acceptable offices with a good view and bad coff*ee;" from a colleague came a more damning appraisal of the building as *"not unpleasantly drab, but nothing remarkable, in the closest Birmingham gets to a nice part of town."* The prospect of a move in the future is encouraging to say the least. All that said (through the *"perpetual drizzle"* of a grey March morning), Birmingham now boasts a Harvey Nicks, and with Selfridges gracing the new Bullring shopping centre, *"the temptation to shop at lunchtime is great."*

Our sources were obviously not instrumental to the city's acquisition of the title of National City of Sport. When it comes to the local TSG inter-firm pool competitions they are first in the queue, but we don't see them as serious challengers to the likes of Wragges or Eversheds on the hockey or football pitch. Preferring to sit down and socialise, ad hoc lunches at a local café supplement a comprehensive social calendar. This includes pay-day drinks and monthly firm-wide buffet lunches, an annual Christmas dinner (which takes place in January and this year collided with Burns Night, resulting in Scottish dancing) and a family day in the summer. Last year, a commemorative service at the city's cathedral marked the firm's 30th anniversary, and for the last three years, trainee induction has also involved a day-long, sponsored charity canal boat race incorporating 50 consecutive locks. If you need assurances that the boats are appropriately categorised as pleasure craft, check out the pictures on the AC website.

They had their differences, but all our sources were definitely singing from the same song sheet: Anthony Collins is not a place for someone seeking a full-bore corporate experience. One trainee noted *"a perception that Transformation is woolly work, and attracts woolly people, but we aren't a woolly bunch."* We concur. In 2004, both qualifiers stayed with the firm.

and finally...

Anthony Collins welcomes those who have made a decision to follow and endorse its beliefs and public-spirited approach, rather than just follow the corporate crowd.

asb law

the facts

Location: Brighton, Crawley, Croydon, Horsham, Maidstone
Number of UK partners/assistants: 42/72
Total number of trainees: 10
Seats: 4x6 months
Alternative Seats: None

Asb *law* prides itself on being one of the top law firms in the South East. Five offices across Surrey, Kent and Sussex offering a broad range of commercial and private client services from aviation finance and IT to personal tax and trusts and slip and trip PI, means we're inclined to agree.

in mint condition

Back in 1999, Argles Stoneham Burstows was the freshly minted coinage for three South East firms who joined forces to extend their geographical and practice boundaries. Burstows had offices in Brighton, Horsham and Crawley, Argles & Court had a Maidstone presence and Stonehams brought a Croydon office to the melting pot. Barely had the lustre of merger begun to fade, when the firm forged itself a funky new corporate identity, and the name asb *law* became common currency across the region.

Thus suited in new armour, the firm set out like a new-made knight of old to do battle with the likes of Cripps Harries Hall, DMH and Thomas Eggar for the fairest of South East commercial work. The last five years have certainly seen asb win its spurs, building an impressive reputation in corporate finance, commercial litigation, employment, IP/IT and more niche expertise in respect to aviation and travel industry clients. The recent snaffling of DMH's former head of corporate is indicative of the firm's growing strength and the corporate team regularly acts on multimillion-pound deals for clients like First Choice Holidays, ABN AMRO, Royal Bank of Scotland and Mercury Petroleum Systems. Meanwhile litigators have represented various aviation clients in the last year. Amongst its other private and public sector clients, the firm can name Wandsworth Borough Council, Titan Travel, Zenith Insurance Management and Cellular Design Services, which is one of the many software and telecoms companies that give a strong IP/IT flavour to the commercial contracts practice.

round our way

Asb has broad corporate ambitions and sees itself structurally as one firm with different teams working cross-regionally. Yet it is also happy to perpetuate the local reputation of individual offices, and each of them retains its particular client base. One trainee told us: "*You still pick up the phone to people who'll say, 'I'm using you because I remember this firm when it was Burstows.'*" Whilst commercial work does flow between Brighton, Croydon and Crawley (and to a lesser extent the other offices), it stands to reason that some work in each office is more local - "*If you're working on tax, trusts and probate in Brighton, then your clients are only going to be from Brighton.*"

With corporate, employment and commercial litigation teams in residence, the Crawley office is "*the main commercial hub*" from which expertise is dispensed to the other locations. Emphasising the benefits of mobility, one source explained how "*partners in one of the commercial groups will whizz around the other offices - our strength is in offering a service across the region.*" However, there is a bit more to the asb strategy than simply buttressing a corporate hub with high-street practices.

Pay attention, if you want to understand this next bit... The Croydon office is "*fairly similar to Crawley*" but has a good reputation for property litigation and the Brighton office has a strong commercial property department and also offers corporate insolvency expertise. Together with Maidstone, Brighton fields an important claimant PI team. A good example of the benefits of regional reach, the Maidstone planning team has not only acted for its own local council, but also represented a leading conservation society at a public inquiry into the proposed location of Brighton & Hove Albion FC's new stadium.

around the houses

"*The firm expects trainees to go around the offices for different seats,*" stated one nomadic trainee, adding: "*A car is pretty much essential.*" We did hear of one lucky so-and-so who had managed to take three of their four seats in Brighton, with the fourth a short commute away in Crawley; however, most trainees shuttle around more. Because it is the most geographically distant office in the group, the firm is careful about placing trainees in Maidstone, although the seats all need to be filled. *"One guy based in Maidstone was commuting each day to Crawley for a finance seat. It must have made his day fairly long!"*

The basic rule on seats is this: *"If it's available at the office and there is the capacity to support a trainee, you can do a seat there."* Private client seats are available across the firm but those with a strong commercial bent are likely to find themselves in Crawley, Croydon and Brighton. With only five trainees taken on per year, rotation is not a contentious issue.

The busy corporate team added a second seat recently, and it was this *"dynamic and forthright"* department that prompted trainees to talk about working hours more familiar to their City contemporaries. *"Monday 9am to Tuesday 6pm was the worst, but I was staying until 10pm almost every day,"* reported one veteran. Elsewhere a manageable *"9am-6pm is the firm standard,"* leaving plenty of time to get home, even for those with a longer commute ahead of them.

no frills on us

"Ambitious, hardworking and sociable too," was the no-frills self-assessment of a group of self-effacing trainees, the majority of whom had some prior connection to the South East. Those we interviewed felt that their ambition had been satisfied over two years at the firm and were optimistic about the future. *"It's really up and coming...you can definitely see a route through to partnership,"* said one. And with good reason: asb has an excellent track record for NQ retention. In 2004, all three qualifiers were offered jobs, with two accepting. The third chose to relocate within the UK. Yet the attraction of the firm is about more than simply climbing the ranks; indeed, *"there's a real sense that everyone is equal, partners, secretaries or trainees."* Amongst the most satisfying things for trainees is the fact that they are *"really involved in marketing and building up the client base."*

Because of the geographically diffuse nature of the firm, *"it is important to get yourself known and make sure lots of people are seeing your work."* The variables of department and office do seem to affect the quality and diversity of work that trainees experience; however, across the board our sources found that *"the times of admin rubbish"* were balanced out by more sophisticated and demanding delights. In corporate finance they were *"involved in deals all the time, attending completion meetings as well as doing company secretarial stuff."* Variety was the key in commercial contracts, where it is *"never the same day twice, with work ranging from review of terms and conditions to drafting agreements to advice on patents and copyrights."* Elsewhere, PI meant *"your own caseload, taking witness statements and attending trials, a lot of day-to-day client contact."* End-of-seat appraisals are useful for gaining *"a sense of progression,"* and our sources confirmed that *"supervisors are always accessible and generous with their time."*

Socially, each office has its own flavour, though we weren't surprised to learn that *"Brighton is the best because there's so much to do there anyway."* Volleyball and softball competitions against clients and *"bars on the beach"* explain the appeal, and thankfully the rest of the firm is allowed to play in the sand pit too. The yearly Christmas party actually takes place in January *"to lighten up those New Year blues,"* and although the annual firm wide AGM involves *"an hour-long talk about business stuff,"* it is followed by *"a meal and a disco, when everyone really lets their hair down."*

and finally...

If you've a mind to train in the South East, you'd do well to consider asb law, especially as its diversity of practice will enable you to keep your options open until you're ready to specialise. Put it at the top of your list if you want to grow up with a young partnership.

Ashurst

the facts

Location: London
Number of UK partners/assistants: 111/302
Total number of trainees: 97
Seats: 4x6 months
Alternative seats: Overseas seats, secondments
Extras: Pro bono – Islington and Toynbee Hall Legal Advice Centres, Disability Law service, Business in the Community, death row appeals, language training

In 2003 this firm backed away from a merger with a leading New York firm. Commitment phobic? You bet! This was the third time in recent years that it had considered and then rejected a proposal at the door of the church. As night follows day, this inglorious phase in the firm's long history inevitably led to a period of self-analysis followed by a rebranding exercise. We were keen to find out more...

symbolic changes

The firm formerly known as Ashurst Morris Crisp now goes by the name 'Ashurst'. But beware the dangers that lurk within this simple seven-letter word. First, you must deliver the name in the singular because way back in 1822 there was only one Mr Ashurst. And second (especially if you are even slightly dyslexic), when writing the name, never ever place the two s's side by side.

Rebranding is a good way of squandering vast sums of money on designers who'll tweak an existing logo and come up with a new corporate colour. Ashurst must have provided a fuller brief to its chosen consultants as it has used the rebranding exercise to push several important messages. Of a new-found pride in the firm's independence, one source said: "*It wants to stand on its own two feet after all the rumours of merger with Fried Frank.*" Hence the emphasis on its international offices – six in continental Europe, a small offering in NY (to be backed by a new US practice in London) and three in Asia. On becoming more

comfortable with its position in the UK market, another source said: "*I didn't like the way Ashurst was always apologising for being outside the top five because, by heck, we do enough deals with magic circle firms.*" And finally, the rebranding offered the ideal platform from which the firm can jazz up its reputation.

Ashurst had clearly grown bored with being labelled stuffy/conservative/traditional/blue-blooded, etc, etc. We'll confess we always thought the reference to Messrs Morris & Crisp rather outdated, and wrestled with images of Victorian gents gallivanting off to foreign parts to build railways and dams, or to mine their fortunes at the dusty frontiers of Great Britishness. One trainee summed it up nicely when he said: "*It's no longer appropriate that we're named after three long-dead men in capes and top hats.*" Single-word Ashurst, wants to be seen as modern, unencumbered by history, more polyglot. As for the trainee who told us: "*The bottom line is Ashurst offers top-level service,*" well, he deserves either a pay rise or a stint in the firm's marketing department.

Some trainees also sensed a drive to be "*more open-minded.*" In case they forget, all staff have been issued with circular mouse mats that read: "*Square minds can't think around corners.*"

own brand

A new seat regime now means that there are only two things a trainee must do – litigation and a transactional seat, the latter requirement being fulfilled by corporate, international finance, real estate or energy, transport and infrastructure options. Corporate is a common first seat, and is an "*absolute must-do,*" according to one trainee. For the first two to three months when you're just finding your feet the corporate department can "*support you more than others could. You're not thrown work all the time, if you can't cope; whereas in finance you are going to be put under constant pressure as it is so busy.*" First-seaters in corporate muck in on data rooms and verification exercises – things that are more time consuming than complicated. "*I was drafting things by the end of the seat,*" one trainee told us. *"Lots of people go back in a later seat if they don't want to do a specialist seat, which they see as pointless."* Anyone who's primarily interested in corporate deals might want to understand the basic differences between public company work and private equity work. Ashurst is felt to have met with greater success in the latter. That said, in 2003/4 the corporate department came through for the successful bidder in the Safeway supermarket chain sell-off, which was one of the highest profile public company deals for some time.

Specialist seats (eg employment, IP, tax), client secondments and the overseas seats go to those who make their exact requirements known early on. *"There was slight disappointment from our intake concerning overseas seats,"* one second-year admitted. *"Previously Tokyo and Singapore had been available, but we realised we'd not got the opportunities outside Europe that we thought there would be."* Seats are presently available in Brussels, Milan, Madrid, Paris, Frankfurt and Munich. Our colleagues on *Chambers Global* point to France and Germany as Ashurst's greatest continental successes.

out of the frying pan

Back in the London office, in a seat in structured finance *"it's not easy to get hold of the concepts; even after six months I'd not worked everything out."* For those trainees who take to it, there's a huge sense of satisfaction when they finally master the intricacies of collateralised debt obligations or whatever else has been occupying their time. In the real estate department, trainees look after their own files; *"they may be piddling licences, but they are yours. It was liberating knowing my supervisor trusted me."* A trainee who'd chosen the international finance option instead of property admitted to being *"jealous of people in real estate as they got their own work early on."* Looking for some heat? You should try a projects seat because *"it's a fryer,"* and consistently busy – you could end up working on a toll road in the Czech Republic or a submerged tunnel in Greece. One source was reminded of his time in the department whenever he rode the DLR.

In litigation, trainees found working on smaller cases particularly rewarding: *"There's a lot of research – reading cases, writing a memo and then talking to people about it."* On bigger cases, however, there's a certain inevitability concerning the preparation of enormous court bundles. Even so, one trainee reported how the partner he worked for had *"the grace and charm to pull me in and explain the case to me to make sure I understood the big stuff and was motivated."* Up to 20 trainees sit in litigation at any one time, each of them taking turns at 'court duty', which involves filing or serving proceedings or, if they're lucky (*"or unlucky depending on your viewpoint"*), going before a master on a small application. Those who make it known that they're eager for interesting work seem to get it.

supporting and uplifting practices

Every department has its own feel based on the key partners and how they work. We hear litigation tends to be more formal, while finance is the friendliest. What is emerging is a firm where the main departments have sufficiently equal weight that trainees can be assured of getting a balanced training. Whereas some of the biggest City firms have effectively sidelined litigation training, at Ashurst you can guarantee at least six months of it. If you want a genuinely rounded training, we suggest Ashurst is now one of the most sensible choices. Admittedly, *"the more specialist groups have a slight feel of being supporting practices,"* but that's going to be the case at any big firm.

When you first start a seat, you'll receive a couple of weeks of trainee-specific seminars led by others in the department, and practically every day there are sessions going on around the firm, be they talks from barristers or soft-skills topics like presentation techniques and stress management.

Not one interviewee spoke of a harsh environment, yet we were also warned: "*It is not a cuddly, strokey firm.*" One realist admitted: "*Ashurst has its demons – it's not a saintly firm. I've worked for assistants that I wanted to kill.*" Yet he was as big a fan of the place as the person who told us: "*I've really enjoyed the company of all my principals. I've found it easy to get to know them, chat and make jokes with them. My current one tells stories about partners she trained with herself.*" Even if you remain "*mindful of what you say in front of certain partners,*" the overall impression is of a firm in which seniors will "*thank you for what you do or hold the lift for yo*u." This is a big firm; even so, trainees point to a Tardis effect in reverse – big on the outside, intimate on the inside. Some 44 of the 54 trainees who qualified in 2004 stayed to swell staff numbers.

code of conduct

A City training is never going to be a cakewalk, and the following comment on hours was typical. "*I have had weeks where I had to stay till 12 every night and come in on Saturday, and weeks where I've gone home at 5.45pm every day.*" Of course, the worst thing about long hours is not knowing when they'll crop up and having to cancel evening plans at the last minute. "*Knowing what's coming up is dependant on who you are sitting with. Good managers will warn you, and that makes all the difference.*"

When we asked if there were any similarities between trainees, we learned of a shared "*ambition, but anti-aggressive attitude.*" We've heard people stereotype Ashurst lawyers so often that we decided to confront the clichés head on. One gem emerged – "*The image of us being posh, bumbling idiots is undeserved...personally I think it is filled with middle-class people who want to be posh! I mean a lot of really important partners here went to grammar schools.*" Alas, this view was not as widely held as we'd have liked it to be; instead the majority of sources thought the old blue-blooded reputation completely anachronistic, preferring instead to stress the importance of good manners and good conduct. Our interviewees happily consented to us presenting a picture of a firm where civility and courtesy held sway.

The ironic and the iconic

We've no idea whether courtesy is the guiding principle on the sports field, but we do know how important sporting success is to Ashurst. If you have a flare for rugby, football or any other team sport, you'll feel right at home. If food is more your thing, you might make the staff restaurant, Writs, your second home. Partners have their own dining room so, presumably, if you did get the urge to moan about your supervisor over lunch, you needn't be constantly looking over your shoulder. A full-time dress-down regime is most commonly expressed through the classic chinos-blue-shirt-timberlands look for the guys; although the tide is turning with many trainees reverting to suits and ties.

"*I don't trust places where you can't get a pint,*" was the considered opinion of one chap. You may wish to bear this in mind on a Friday afternoon as you negotiate with colleagues over which bar to visit. Ashurst's offices are just a short walk from Hoxton and Shoreditch where there are ample places to suit the anti-All Bar One crowd. Assistants go out for drinks with trainees, and every so often "*a partner may come along and play old man and then go home.*" We assume that the individual who claimed: "*People get lazy and start having families,*" will one day understand the irony of this statement.

and finally...

We were left in no doubt as to the sense of "*vibrancy*" that's been sweeping through Ashurst since the December 2003 'rebranding day'. If you can secure a vac scheme here, you'll meet plenty of people who'll happily explain exactly what has reinvigorated the firm.

Baker & McKenzie

the facts

Location: London
Number of UK partners/assistants: 71/200
Total number of trainees: 67
Seats: 4x6 months
Alternative seats: Overseas seats, secondments
Extras: Pro bono – Waterloo Legal Advice centre, UN High Commission for refugees, death row appeals, language training

"Before there was Baker & McKenzie, there was a man with a dream. Russell Baker grew up in the rugged American Southwest, travelled by cattle car to go to college, and started his legal practice years before getting his law degree..."

Thus begins the life story of Baker & McKenzie, as recounted in true Homeric style on the firm's website. Now the firm is looking for people to share that dream and contribute to the latest chapter in its colourful history. Although sadly the firm does now require its new trainees to have legal qualifications, it does also pay them enough to afford a cab.

and all that jazz

As you may have gathered, Bakers was born in the USA, but it has come a long way since those early days in Chicago. It has grown to over 8,000 staff spread across almost 40 countries and shows no sign of stopping. Acting for the likes of Estée Lauder, Cisco Systems, DaimlerChrysler and Sony, the firm has a client list that would have even Billy Flynn rubbing his hands in glee. The trainees who spoke to us were keen that we understand the classifications of the firm and their office. *"They don't like calling it an American firm – it's seen as the London office of an international firm, and it's not American in its culture."*

Known to have allowed branches across the globe to 'go native', Bakers is now adopting a new 'visual identity programme' to bring more consistency to the vast network. Perhaps aware of the unkind nickname 'McLaw', our sources insisted this wasn't going to turn the firm into yet another homogenised and soulless corporation: *"The changes are pretty much stylistic. It's mainly so that when clients get a piece of advice it has the same layout, which makes us look more professional and saves time and redrafts."*

a night out with friends

Putting global concerns to one side, we asked our interviewees to discuss Bakers' main attractions, and one of the first things they picked up on was the sheer variety of seats on offer. As well as the traditional opportunities in corporate, commercial, banking and property, trainees also discover less-frequently trodden paths to qualification. Seats in employment, IP and IT always prove popular, as do pensions. This comes as no surprise considering the firm's stellar reputation in those fields, which consequently mean trainees are exposed to excellent standalone work, rather than just corporate transaction support roles.

Invariably, trainees had understood Bakers' profile quite well before accepting a training contract offer and several we spoke to confirmed they were attracted by the firm's hotspot IP/IT and employment departments. That said, some find seats they weren't initially keen on unexpectedly enjoyable: *"Everyone dreads going to corporate as it has a reputation for long hours, though I never minded the occasional late night as there was always someone else there. Everyone in the team tends to go down for dinner together, and it can be a bit of a laugh."*

The firm asks trainees to do a stint in corporate and something contentious, usually commercial litigation. From first seat to the last, our sources were more than happy with the amount of say they had in the seat allocation procedure. If your heart's set on a particular department and you stick to your guns, you can be confident of working there at some point. Amongst the most popular options is a three-month spell working as a judicial assistant to a Court of Appeal judge.

things that go bump in the night

Our interviewees were impressed by the quality of supervision they received. Each department has a dedicated trainee supervisor who's responsible for keeping an eye on the trainees' workloads, and other people are good at remembering to contact him or her to check you're not too busy before giving you work. Nonetheless, if you're an enterprising type there's no problem with you showing interest in a case that someone else is working on. This can be particularly useful in the IP/IT department, where trainees usually start off working on one side of the line, but have the option to move to the other halfway through the seat.

Any trainee has to be fairly stoical about some of the tasks they're given: "*When you're asked to work for a client, you have to take the rough with the smooth. You do get interesting work, but on some days you may get asked to look through a bunch of files to find an advice that we wrote in 1998.*" Yet the highs more than make up for the lows of grunt work. One trainee assured us: "*You certainly get a lot of direct client contact. I was working on one agreement where I was put on the phone to the client straight away, and then followed this up and saw it through to the end as the main contact person. Although I was a bit scared, luckily the client was fee-conscious and forgiving!*" The firm is also keen for trainees to get involved in the business development, and they've been known to write articles for newspapers and journals...well, ghost write at least.

single person supplement

One of the great allures of working for a firm of this type is the option to work overseas. The temptation to regard Bakers' international directory of offices as one of the finest holiday brochures available is great, but everyone knows an overseas seat won't be six months of hammock swinging and sundowners. In the last couple of years, trainees have been sent to Chicago, Sydney, New York, Hong Kong, Tokyo, Madrid, Moscow, Brussels, Prague and Toronto. The overseas offices tend to only offer certain seats: in Chicago it's tax or corporate; Moscow offers finance or corporate; and Washington and Brussels both have competition seats. Some locations are inevitably more popular than others – for example, the opportunity to brush up on your employment or litigation skills in Sydney is always hotly contested. Wherever you go, you're guaranteed a "*fantastic social set up.*" And if you don't make it away during your training contract, the firm also runs an associate training programme which gives two-year PQE lawyers an opportunity to work in one of the other offices for up to two years.

If you're reading this before you've checked out the firm's website or training brochure, you might not know about the amazing vac scheme opportunities it has available. Forget the two weeks affairs offered by most firms, Bakers' international summer programme offers placements of 6-12 weeks split between London and an overseas office. Frankly, you'd be mad not to apply...even if you would miss that week with mum and dad in the caravan in Lyme Regis.

more ghostly goings on

We love ghost stories, so when Bakers' trainees said they had a few to tell us, we hunkered down under our desks, turned the lights off and held hands in the dark. Apparently, when the firm opened its office in Hong Kong in 1974 and learned that the locals believed a ghost inhabited the building, it imported an eight-foot tall statue from New Guinea to scare the spirit away. And there are rumours of spooky goings on in London too: "*One of the paintings in the building is of a person working at a desk with a man stood over him. Apparently that man looks like one trainee from every intake.*"

Luckily not all the London artwork borders on the paranormal. Other favourites include 'Man Looking Into Horse' and 'Sculpture of Wooden Shoes'. Well, what do you expect when you get the likes of Damien Hurst involved? The rest of the building is fittingly modern, though it gives the impression of being surprisingly small for a firm of

Bakers' stature. It is conveniently situated close to the Thames and only ten minutes away from the West End, so if you don't want to spend your evenings looking for ectoplasm with a vacuum cleaner strapped to your back, you can easily disappear off to a restaurant or the theatre.

Our sources were keen to stress that from early on they were told *"you don't earn any brownie points for staying late."* In certain departments, such as pensions or employment, they are normally out of the door by 6.30pm. In other seats, namely corporate, the work comes *"in peaks and troughs,"* so there will be occasions where you have to wave goodnight to your chums and get your nose back to the grindstone. At least the office infrastructure aids efficiency – the trainees almost idolised the library and support staff for their willingness to help out. And IT was also praised, which comes as no surprise considering the firm gives all new recruits their own laptop in the LPC year.

a bizarre nativity

The eponymous Mr Russell Baker is rumoured to have entered prize fights at county fairs in order to pay for his tuition at the University of Chicago. When we asked our trainees if they had similarly combative personalities, we were told quite the contrary. *"Generally, the firm recruits people who are very sociable, and they place a lot of importance on social skills."* This doesn't mean everyone has to conform: *"They encourage strong and individual personalities. You're not expected to put your head down and fit in. We've got some more eccentric lawyers who probably would be better off as barristers."* Obviously most NQs were suited to being solicitors at the firm, because in September 2004 19 out of 22 stayed.

And a local pub called The Blackfriar is a good place to meet them. If not there then at monthly drinks in the firm's own restaurant, with a licensed bar, or at departmental drinks at the start of every seat. Come Christmas time, it's the job of the trainees to write and perform a festive review, in which they

are encouraged to *"take the piss."* It seems that no one is safe – last year's surreal performance included a rather disconcerting sketch in which trainees dressed as Posh and Becks gave birth to Gary Senior, the firm's new managing partner.

and finally...

Year on year Baker & McKenzie's approval rating is high, and if the trainees are happy then we're happy. Do we recommend the firm? Wholeheartedly.

Barlow, Lyde & Gilbert

the facts

Location: London
Number of UK partners/assistants: 76/187
Total number of trainees: 34
Seats: 4 x 6 months
Alternative seats: Occasionally Hong Kong, secondments
Extras: Pro bono – St Botolph's Project

Barlow, Lyde & Gilbert is ranked by *Chambers UK* as king of the hill for contentious insurance, professional negligence and defendant personal injury work. Trainees were quick to remind us of this success, yet lost no time in telling us about a congenial working environment and the advantages of training the mid-size way.

stud or dud?

"Obviously anyone not interested in litigation just wouldn't fit in here," one trainee piped up. And we have to agree with them. It is a Law Society requirement that all trainees gain some contentious experience but, unusually for a firm in the Square Mile, at BLG quite a lot of your time will be spent this way. Not that things get samey – the firm's courtroom battles and dispute resolution techniques cover a slew of areas of law. In recent months, BLG has dealt with massive SARS-related claims from the Far East, secured a high-profile House of Lords victory for insurers

dragged into the mis-selling of pensions issue, and acted in a $10 million Japanese claim, brought when a prize stallion turned out to be infertile. Whether you fancy a career locking horns with other lawyers or talking your clients through complex settlement negotiations, *"as a trainee...you can't really go wrong here."*

Some things in life are inevitable – puberty, gas bills, *Songs of Praise* on a Sunday. At BLG inevitability arrives in the guise of a seat in the professional liability and commercial litigation department, or PLCL to use its snappy abbreviation. This department is the firm's largest and is split into five teams: commercial litigation, financial institutions, professional indemnity, accountants' negligence and solicitors' negligence. Yes, you did read that right – lawyers do get it wrong sometimes, and when they do, BLG is the best place to come. Its clients even include several of the firms featured in the *Student Guide*. The cases handled in PLCL are big and beefy, and much of the time the lawyers are representing the insurance company that is ultimately liable to pay damages.

talking turkey

A trainee's role on these big matters tends to be restricted to bite-sized tasks such as research questions and those old litigation favourites of document review and management. Happily, there are plenty of paralegals to do much of the grunt work, many of whom have developed thriving careers in document jockeying. They probably know more about certain long-running cases than is truly healthy. Partners are keen to take trainees along to mediations or conferences with counsel, and though you might not have the skill or gravitas of a Sumption or a Pollock, there's no need to be shy. As one trainee put it: *"I knew the case well and so felt able to chip in and give my opinion."*

Given BLG's focus on the area, a general insurance seat is also likely (though you might opt for reinsurance). In contrast to PLCL, cases here are usually smaller and less complicated with plenty of defendant slip-and-trip and road traffic matters to make trainees

feel *"like a proper solicitor."* Reinforcing the point, one source confirmed: *"It's totally different to PLCL. There's much greater independence"* and *"you get given more responsibility."* You might be let loose in court before a master to make a cost application or request for extension of time, experiences we guarantee you'll be telling your mum about on Boxing Day over the turkey sandwiches. Besides PI claims, there's interesting stuff going on in defamation, complex medical negligence and the relatively new area of failure to educate, where an individual sues a local authority for not providing proper schooling. The common thread through all these matters is the nature of the client – insurance companies. BLG has put together an impressive roster of names, including Direct Line, Churchill, Norwich Union and Lloyd's.

star quality

Trainees spoke in hushed tones of the market-leading, *"hardworking and intellectual"* reinsurance department where there are *"plenty of John Waynes and a few donkeys."* We assumed this comment to be a confused reference to big-gun partners rather than evidence that BLG the law firm is merely a front for an animal sanctuary. In this arcane and complicated area of law, lawyers deal with *"absolutely huge claims going into billions"* and engage in much *"intellectual legal debate."* Inevitably, trainee tasks are restricted to research and general assistance, but for those with true grit this area of work has a lot to offer.

The popular aerospace department also enjoys sky-high rankings in *Chambers UK*. Widely acknowledged to be among the best in the business, after the September 11 attacks, the diligent BLG team was asked to come up with and implement a major disaster strategy for UK airlines. Trainees in this department are involved in everything from *"'I banged my head on the cabin roof' claims"* to multi-million-pound satellite matters. The small and close-knit team is reputed to have the most sparkling social life of any at the firm. Not to put too fine a point on it: *"They're always going out together and get-*

ting pissed." Not at all like airline pilots then...

Despite the focus on contentious work, you mustn't assume that the *"up-and-coming"* corporate department is merely in orbit around more prominent areas of expertise. Corporate finance, banking, non-contentious insurance advice and employment law not only feature at BLG, but are being actively promoted. All trainees undertake a non-contentious seat, and some wangle two. While many clients are referred to the corporate lawyers by their litigating peers, BLG is also making the effort to foster new client relationships.Secondments for trainees are always a good way of cementing bonds with clients and these can be requested.

chocaholics

In terms of hours, generally you can expect a standard nine to sixish day in the office. Naturally things crop up that break the pattern, but litigation-led firms normally benefit from more predictable work schedules than corporate or banking-led firms. In place of impossible deadlines and long nights proofing documents, we heard of trainees worn out (poor things) by excessive partying. *"It's too much,"* sighed one, *"there are so many things organised."* Summer barbecues, karaoke, fancy-dress evenings, wine tasting, nights at the dogs, Art In The City events, birthday lunches...and as for Christmas, one particular scrooge told us: *"It doesn't seem to stop; it's never-ending and absolutely knackering."* Staff with children were able to treat them to a party complete with a chocolate fondue fountain, those without presumably gave no thought to babysitters on the night of the annual black tie ball.

Who to believe? The trainee who assured us: *"We're not all stark raving mad and drinking every day of the week,"* or the scallywag who let slip: *"We were all out last week until the early hours"*? Perhaps their behaviour has something to do with the vagaries of the recruitment formula. *"They seem to have recruited loads of people from the outer regions...we all think it's hilarious and we've really bonded."* Or perhaps it's that

the firm recruits heavily from the vac scheme so, on starting at the firm, *"we all knew each other already."* The majority, 11 of the 15, stayed with the firm on qualification in September 2004.

and finally...

If you're drawn to litigation and a good office social life is a priority, then Barlow Lyde & Gilbert is well worth investigating. Someone may have described it as *"the Hollywood of insurance litigation,"* but we don't recommend you turn up to interview in a red-carpet frock.

Barlows

the facts

Location: Guildford, Godalming, Chertsey
Number of UK partners/assistants: 12/28
Total number of trainees: 7
Seats: 4x6 months
Alternative seats: None

Surrey, home of the wealthy London commuter and a land of rich pickings for this established South East law firm. Barlows is new to the *True Picture* this year and we're delighted to be able to showcase what it has to offer to prospective trainees.

fine and dandy

Barlows is typical of many good provincial firms in that it can draw upon a loyal client base. In this case it's been nurtured since 1816, a year in which society pages would have been filled with tales of the undoing of that arbiter of Regency fashion Beau Brummell, who apparently took five hours to dress and only polished his boots with champagne. In more recent times, Barlows has followed the tried and tested route of sweeping together several smaller practices to consolidate them into a strong local brand. We love a good story, and Barlows certainly gives us just that. Back in the 1970s the son of the senior partner of Godalming firm Mellersh &

Lovelace qualified at Barlow Norris & Jenkins in Guildford. Dad wanted him back; Barlows wanted to keep him. The solution was a merger of the two firms. Michael Goodridge is still at Barlows, so on your first day as a trainee why not ask for a few tips on how to become indispensable. It's not the only father and son story in the firm's history, but we'll stop now before you wonder if you've accidentally picked up an Anthony Trollope novel.

Having swapped tailcoats for pinstripes years ago, Barlows is developing as a commercial/private client hybrid. One trainee said: *"I'd say it's now more commercial than private client, yet the private client department is incredibly profitable."* The reason for this is simple: *"Surrey is a wealthy area and there are plenty of little old ladies with a million under the bed. Barlows has the cream of that work."* Since the 1980s when a young female solicitor was charged with the task of developing a commercial practice, the transformation of the firm has been remarkable. Guildford, as the biggest of the three locations, has emerged as the commercial hub of the firm and is structured in a way that works very well for lawyers and clients alike. The commercial team is still run by the lawyer who started it, Christine Goodyear (*"the driving force of the firm"*), and is now staffed by both contentious and transactional lawyers. Working as a one-stop shop, the left hand knows what the right is doing, and the right hand knows exactly whom the left is acting for. One trainee said of the team: *"It's very strong and understands teamwork and camaraderie...there's a real feeling of togetherness."* Breaking the mould, it is *"all girls bar two partners,"* which means that when the calendar on the wall in the open-plan office is changed, *"it goes from Brad Pitt to Orlando Bloom."*

cats' homes and broken bones

With this training scheme you sign up to four seats, one in each of the main departments – commercial, property, private client and litigation. A transactional seat in the commercial team brings company forma-tions, business sales and purchases, and the drafting of commercial terms and conditions *"mainly for Surrey businesses."* Where you take your property seat determines the exact balance of commercial property and residential conveyancing. Amongst the firm's clients is a mortgage lender for whom it handles the sale of repossessed properties. Speaking of the Acacia Avenue breed of work, one trainee admitted that by the middle of the seat *"the bones of a transaction were well set and to a certain extent I began to tire of it."*

Private client seats generally mean a trip to the Godalming office, *"a more old-school part of the firm"* where you'll get *"plenty of client contact"* and a few of your own wills, probate and trusts files. And bequests to cats' homes? *"Yes, if they're on their own, a lot of people do leave money in their will to charities, including animal charities."* In this part of Surrey there's a surfeit of *"old colonels and rear admirals; Godalming has older, moneyed clients and the partners are based locally so they know a lot of them. There are charities too, such as WWF"* – the pandas not the wrestlers. Take a family seat and you'll have your own caseload there too. *"It was predominantly divorces, though I helped out on more complicated things."* The family team has different fee earners specialising in financial arrangements, non-married couples and cases involving children.

In litigation you'll encounter claimant PI and clinical negligence. Again, you'll have your own caseload of simple RTAs, with the rest of your time spent assisting other fee earners. If you were hoping to gain advocacy experience, you won't be disappointed. In PI you can attend infant settlement hearings (where the court authorises a payment to a child under 18); in a commercial lit seat there is agency work and bankruptcy hearings, and in family the odd domestic violence injunction.

giant haystacks

With so many different styles of work available, it seems almost fitting that Barlows offices are equally diverse in style, from the open-plan, female-dominated commercial environment in the Guildford office at Milkhouse Gate to the quaint, almost chocolate box-cottage affair in male-dominated, private-client led Godalming. The Chertsey office is probably the least visited by trainees as it is the smallest; it exists to serve the north Surrey client base. While most trainees have no desire to work in London, many live there and commute to the Guildford area by train or car – residence in the Home Counties can wait until they're old enough to slow down. Besides, Guildford rents are not dissimilar to those in outer London. Ditto house prices. As is typical in firms in the South East, salaries are an issue: basically, trainees wish they were higher. We also heard calls for the firm to reconsider its policy not to provide funding for law school.

We liked the people at Barlows; they had plenty to say and the confidence to speak their minds. This either means the firm recruits confident trainees or it makes them. It certainly likes to keep them: in 2003, all three qualifiers took jobs with the firm and in 2004 it was two of the three. One source outlined the kind of person who should apply: *"It has to be someone who is happy to get stuck in. You do sometimes get some rubbish work – not paginating etc, but stuff that that no one knows the answer to, so you have to use your initiative to find it…needle-in-a-haystack type things."* Another added: *"I gained a lot from the sink-or-swim philosophy…there's a feeling of satisfaction that you survived and I genuinely did feel ready to be an NQ."* Unsurprisingly, there are differences between seats in how partners train their charges. Some have it spot on; others perhaps *"look back 20 years to how they themselves were trained."* One or two of our sources said they'd welcome more standardisation.

When it rains in Godalming, one of the office's flat roofs has a tendency to flood. If you're there at such a calamitous time, we hear that you might be asked to squeeze through a window on to the roof to clear the leaves from the guttering. That said, we've no evidence that Barlows recruits on the basis of candidates' fitness for this purpose. Nor for their barnyard skills. It may just be a rumour (or a porky pie), but we heard tell of a trainee who, in his first week, was dispatched to a local farm to stick a pig on a spit for the firm's annual barn dance. We trust the event was a roaring success.

and finally...

Barlows sounds like a firm with character. Trainees clearly have a good deal of affection for the place and its quirks but they also have a good deal of respect for what it offers them by way of training.

Bates, Wells & Braithwaite

the facts

Location: London
Number of UK partners/assistants: 35/34
Total number of trainees: 8
Seats: 2x6 months + 3x4 months
Alternative seats: Occasional secondments
Extras: Numerous pro bono activities

Bates, Wells & Braithwaite is a mid-sized London firm with a heart. A reputation for serving the varied needs of the charities and voluntary sector is matched by excellent quality media, immigration, theatre, sports and commercial practices. With turnover up 17% to £7 million this year, BWB should never just be seen as a refuge for knit-your-own-yoghurt liberals.

with a small l

Over 800 charities refer more than 50% of BWB's work and the firm was recently ranked top in a Charities Aid Foundation survey of legal advisers. Age Concern, Amnesty International, the British Council, British Red Cross, Eden Project, English National Opera, The Arts Council and Shelter are just a few of the diverse charities and public bodies represented by the firm. Whether it be charity-specific constitutional, registration or lottery funding issues, or more general employment, property, litigation and commercial concerns, BWB is the best friend a charity could hope for.

This has been a resolutely do-gooding sort of firm from the first day that the Cheapside office opened its doors back in 1970, and that's as much to do with the people as the work. *"There are wonderful people here, people who you wouldn't have expected to be working in law because they're so nice."* Certainly, the majority of trainees we interviewed applied to BWB for the chance to do worthy and high-profile work in the one place. *"It's not a legal aid firm, but it is a firm with a social conscience,"* they told us. There is a definite BWB type at all levels in the firm; our sources had no problem identifying it and neither do we. In fact, the only problem is fitting all the evidence in just a line or two. So here's a brief summary: *"There have traditionally been real characters here and there still are," "people are strong in their opinions," "we're ethically committed" and "we're liberal with a small l."* Our favourite comment was: *"We're ethically aware vegetarians,"* which at first sounds like protein-deficient delirium but actually has a solid basis. For the record, roughly 65% of trainees decline to feast on our animal friends.

Given that the firm only takes on four trainees a year it can afford to be picky. This year's interviewees had previous lives in journalism, charity work, womens' and human rights organisations and teaching. Some had arrived fresh from university, but if you decide to make an application at that stage of your life, it's advisable to show *"an understanding of the work the firm does and a committed explanation of why you want to do it."* And decline that tasty sausage roll offered at interview – it's bound to be a trap.

it's for charidee mate

If we've made the firm and its employees sound a little right-on then you've come to the correct conclusion. But don't imagine for a second that BWB is populated by wishy-washy, cardigan-wearing types. Commercial law is as business-like here as anywhere. The first year for trainees comprises two six-month seats (chosen from litigation, commercial, charities/media and immigration), whilst the sec-

ond year allows some room to manoeuvre through three four-month seats (chosen from straight charity, litigation, employment and property).

As well as being the firm's mainstay and extremely popular with trainees, the charity department *"is incredibly forward-looking and has exacting standards."* Offering the chance to work on anything from company law to internal charity disputes to fundraising and tax matters, one day you might be working for the RSC, the next for the Tate Gallery and the next for Whizz-Kidz. It's here that the *"relaxed and charismatic"* partners are *"most eager to get you involved in marketing events."* The department's full title is in fact Charity and Social Enterprise, a response to the relatively new trend for socially conscious but profit-making businesses. So expert is the firm in this emergent sector that it recently seconded an associate to the Department of Trade & Industry to assist in creating a new regulatory body to support such companies.

lost in space

Elsewhere change has arisen out of exigency. Last year we reported that changes in the funding of legal advice for asylum seekers were on the horizon. Having now come into the foreground, these have left many firms unable to work in the legal aid immigration field. BWB is just one that has withdrawn because *"it was very difficult to do the work to the quality and standard we'd want under the new regime."* The firm remains committed to its business immigrant practice, which enables trainees to work with applicants for entry under the Highly Skilled Migrant Programme. One trainee had helped secure visas for *"a NASA scientist moving to the UK to continue his research into lost satellite retrieval systems,"* and the firm also acted for the rapper 50 Cent, successfully appealing against a refusal to grant him permission to enter the UK for the MOBO awards.

Recent growth in the corporate practice has resulted in a new sports and media department this year. Are trainees excited by this? You bet! *"We do* contract work and handle image rights issues for top athletes and footballers!" There's also plenty of high-profile media, film and theatre company work, and some trainees have enjoyed secondments (either part-time or short-term) with TV production companies like TalkBack and Hat Trick. Said one: "It was all media rah-rahs; a great experience and good to see how that kind of world operates." The corporate department handles a lot of work for charities, but also has a conventional client base. Trainees reported doing due diligence on a pet food company, drafting software agreements for a computer company and IP/IT work for big pharmaceutical clients. Charities are also responsible for much of the litigation department's work (eg eviction or dilapidation issues for housing associations) and the respondent portion of the employment practice. Trainees in the employment department also get to work for "high-income City workers," for whom they draft statements on unfair dismissal claims and attend tribunal or EAT hearings.

bring on the cowardly lion

Training days are run in conjunction with a group of other firms and there are "relevant" mid and end-of-seat appraisals. Trainees admitted that different supervisors have different abilities, but were very happy with the majority. The most important things a new recruit should bring to the firm are independence, self-confidence and self-motivation: "It's up to you to get involved, find out about things, get up to speed and apply yourself." One wise soul summed things up well in saying: "You're not equal as a trainee, of course, but you're seen as a valid person, doing valid work that matters."

The social life of the firm is pretty good but won't eat away too many valuable pages in your diary. The different departments each organise drinks evenings and there are "fun" firm-wide summer and Christmas parties. After the frankly weird pantomime sketches of 2002, we were curiously excited by the prospect of discovering more strange carryings on. Our disappointment that the Christmas party was a quiet boat-borne affair was tempered only when

someone mentioned that a satirical Wizard of Oz pantomime had been planned for 2004. Like the department, sports at the firm are nascent: "We're trying to convince people that they should play sport as well as work in a sports law firm...maybe softball." Drinks are to be had in any one of several locals, with The Hole in the Wall ("it's a tiny little place") popular amongst trainees, and The City Pipe a firm lunchtime favourite for partners and trainees alike.

The firm was a victim of its recruitment criteria in 2004; even though NQ jobs were available for all, only one of the four qualifiers stayed on. Those who left are now pursuing very specific (even idealogical) work, or they simply tired of London (though we hope not life). Headstrong is as headstrong does...

and finally...

If you've got a social conscience but a taste for good work then Bates, Wells & Braithwaite offers the perfect solution. It's no easy compromise, however, so make your application a good one.

Beachcroft Wansbroughs

the facts

Location: Birmingham, Bristol, Leeds, London, Manchesrer, Winchester
Number of UK partners/assistants: 131/307
Total number of trainees: 56
Seats: 4x6 months
Alternative seats: Secondments
Extras: Language training

Beachcroft Wansbroughs has a national name for insurance litigation and health sector work, and offers training in its Bristol, London, Leeds and Manchester offices.

a peaceful existence

"People think of Beachcrofts and think of insurance." So said one of the trainees we interviewed at this large national firm. Beachcrofts does perform well in many other areas of work, particularly where these interface with the public sector, but our sources seemed resigned to the fact that "we are never going to be renowned for corporate or commercial." Chambers UK ranks the firm right at the top for defendant personal injury and clinical negligence work, insurance and professional negligence. It is one of the select few firms on the NHS Litigation Authority legal panel and cites the Department of Health, NHS estates, many hospital trusts and primary care trusts among its clients. Furthermore, healthcare connections extend into its employment, PFI/PPP projects, property, and technology and commerce departments. Outside insurance and healthcare, household-name clients include Marks & Spencer, Pickfords, Unilever and Akzo Nobel.

Last year, we banged on Beachcrofts' door and loudly interrupted the firm's quiet existence. This year, trainees told us "the slumbering giant image is right; for our size people probably haven't heard of us." The firm may not be tap-dancing across the pages of the legal press, but it has not pulled up the duvet, hit snooze and gone back to sleep. Trainees alluded to the firm having "all sorts of plans" and "a lot of effort being made to make the name known." Basically, it is "trying to get out more." For starters, each year the "big bods" pack up their tour bus and head off on a nationwide road show. Sadly, all parallels with Mike Read and Bruno Brookes larging it on the beach in Weston-Super-Mare stop here; instead "the senior partners come round and do a powerpoint slide show about how we have progressed." There are no free mugs or t-shirts, but "they are making a real effort to make sure everyone knows what is going on," which let's face it is probably more useful than a bumper sticker.

crowd-pleasing moves

Beachcrofts is "a nice, non-slave-driving, non-factory-type law firm." Trainees told us: "It is not aggressive at all;" in fact, "on the whole it is quite calm." Nonetheless, "each location has its own individual style." Bristol is the administrative centre, though most of our interviewees named London as the biggest presence, and Manchester is "the most sociable," though we heard that "Leeds is trying to catch up." Trainees choose an office at the application stage and thereafter, there is little movement between them (unless, of course, you are the senior partner and towing a large trailer). One source pondered that "if you really wanted to go somewhere else you could," and indeed we did hear of trainees who had moved from London to Winchester for odd seats, but "you have to be particularly vocal." For most, the PSC is the time to meet and compare notes with peers.

Training follows a four-seat system. The first seat is "not exactly pulled out of a hat...but it's not far off;" thereafter trainees indicate their preferences. We didn't encounter any disgruntled customers, but suspect an open mind will serve you well. "Property used to be compulsory, but not any more," we heard.

Firm wide, trainees described a solid training where "you aren't left on your own." They all sit with or near their supervisors, who provide them with the bulk of their work and feedback. Mid and end-of-seat appraisals are a casual affair: after completing the necessary forms, you "go to the pub to discuss them." Formal training is a little more regimented, however; one trainee observed "an awful lot of training going on" and departmental seminars for all fee earners are regular. On qualification, an NQ training programme includes the option of studying for a master's degree. Advocacy opportunities are "fairly limited" for trainees as Beachcrofts "retains quite a few barrister types." The trainee's lot is very seat-dependent and "client exposure is very partner-driven." One source explained: "In some seats I have been treated like another fee earner, but in others I am just tidying up other people's scraps." A second said: "You are the administrator for whatever cases your supervisor does," and that can mean "grunt work." Nevertheless, we were reassured that "there is no seat where you spend the whole time in the photocopy room."

just one cornetto

In Bristol, seats in employment, property and corporate are on offer alongside clin neg, professional indemnity, projects and contentious construction. When trainees requested property litigation and non-contentious construction, a couple of seats were rustled up, and to accommodate the clamour for employment experience, a second seat was created there too. In London trainees get to choose from construction, projects, technology and commerce, corporate finance, financial services, employment, property and *"a huge amount of litigation – strategic litigation, insurance, reinsurance and general commercial litigation."* A projects seat exposes trainees to major public-sector work including LIFT projects and telecoms matters. It's always hard for a trainee to slot into a massive and long-running project, and one interviewee, at least, understood why they *"can't be trusted with complete autonomy."*

We heard much about a secondment to Unilever, which is on offer to London trainees. The six-month general commercial role sees them doing *"anything from managing PI claims in factories to huge-scale employment tribunals or disposals of businesses which aren't doing particularly well."* Trainees valued the significance of their role at Unilever, saying: *"For general experience of meeting people and learning how to interact with all levels of management in a great company, it's a huge benefit."* The other huge benefit is that *"Bird's Eye Wall's is downstairs, and on every floor there are freezers full of free ice-creams."*

Beachcrofts has a smaller London base in East Cheap and a more prominent Fetter Lane office. After hours, sources were *"ashamed to admit it, but we go to the Printer's Devil."* When someone muttered the word 'karaoke' all became clear. For a classier evening out, the bars of Smithfield are at hand and departments organise outings. There is also an office-wide summer family day and BBQ, plus a Christmas bash.

The Bristol office is *"not exactly central, but on the edge and close to the station."* If these directions leave you lost, the office has recently put up its first sign on the outside of the building. One source described the refurbished office building as *"fairly dull inside,*

very bland with white walls and grey carpet...not particularly inspiring, but not particularly ugly – just functional." The social scene is fairly low key, except that an initial trainee bonding session sees all the second-years taking the newbies off laserquesting or rock climbing, and each month 'First Friday drinks' are held at The Stonehouse. The combined effects of team building, rough terrain and heavy drinking can be seen in the annual sponsored walk in the Lake District, in which teams from each office compete against each other and then mingle in a pub. When one snitch told us: *"The Bristol office cheats,"* we felt duty bound to investigate. It seems that last year a map, a compass, a 90-minute head start and some astute navigation meant the Bristol team had made an enormous hole in the drinks kitty long before any of the other teams made it home. In the spirit of fair reporting, we put this accusation to our Bristol sources, who simply said: *"We couldn't possibly comment."*

diet coke break

The northern office pairing is considered the livelier half of the firm. In Leeds, seats in property, projects, construction, health advice, employment and professional indemnity are all on offer. In Manchester the spread includes commercial, corporate, commercial litigation, professional indemnity, commercial property, property litigation, employment and personal injury, plus a new technology and commerce seat. A bit of a *"wish-list seat,"* here the trainee works with one partner and one assistant on IP and IT, data protection and competition matters, drafting licences and franchise and outsourcing agreements. In Manchester, insurance litigation was considered to be compulsory, but seeing as it provides opportunities to go to court every week for CMCs and small applications, this is no hardship.

The Manchester office is right next door to Flannels, where the Manchester United players get kitted out. *"Every now and again you hear screams from the secretaries and everyone rushes to the windows."* Ronaldo has some work to do, as *"it was worse when Beckham was at Manchester!"* On St Anne's Square, the offices are *"hi-tech, spacious and open plan"* and trainees usually share a 'pod' with their supervisor. Some floors are decorated to particular partners' tastes; we were advised to check out the third floor for an insight into the artistic appreciation/psychology of a certain commercial litigator. Each month, the office hosts 'The Hundred Club' – a draw with a £100. Anyone who doesn't profit can console themselves with a full social calendar of monthly parties and events including wine tasting, trips to the races, karaoke and treasure hunts. With a series of sports fixtures to boot, we fully understand how Manchester acquired its lively reputation. For the truly hardy there is also a summer party, a Christmas black-tie do (complete with trainee revue) and an annual trip to Blackpool.

The Leeds office competes with its own social club and a similarly eclectic list of monthly events. When there isn't snowboarding or trips to the theatre, Alton Towers or the races to keep you out of trouble, try the *"leisure room"* with its sofas, magazines and TV. The Park Square offices in Leeds are open plan, if *"a little dated,"* but an excess of people has pushed the PI department out to the *"more modern"* Minerva House across the road.

At Beachcrofts *"the work-life balance is just fine – there is no danger of missing out on a social life." "Weekend working is a real rarity"* and a 9am-6pm day is the norm. There is *"no macho ethos"* and *"there are not a lot of egos;"* in fact, one trainee said: *"I was a very non-exceptional child at school."* Like the firm, Beachcrofts trainees' style is largely self-deprecating and a little on the quiet side. Yet with no obvious reason: once they got talking, they were witty, willing and incredibly personable. 18 of the 27 qualifiers accepted jobs at the firm in September 2004.

and finally...

Offering first-rate insurance, immersion in the health sector and a choice of several offices, Beachcrofts isn't for big voices or heavy feet, but for anyone else it's *"a sensible choice."*

Berwin Leighton Paisner

the facts

Location: London
Number of UK partners/assistants: 134/195
Total number of trainees: 66
Seats: 4x6 months
Alternative seats: Secondments
Extras: Pro bono – various projects and law centres

Profits up by 40%. Top-notch teams in property and planning. Corporate and finance departments with a growing presence and a widening web of international connections. BLP has certainly been winning headlines recently.

starring hip lion between

"The foundation of the firm is the strength in real estate." This basic tenet, as expounded by one of our trainee sources at BLP, can never be omitted from any analysis of the firm. Its relationships with trophy clients Tesco and the Royal Bank of Scotland are based heavily on the real estate work that the firm conducts for them. Every little helps, but the amount of real estate work the firm gets from Tesco is enough to keep a quarter of the firm's property lawyers busy at any one time. As for RBS, the bank puts many of its major deals BLP's way, recently hiring it to co-ordinate the acquisition and reletting of 11 major hotels, including London landmarks Grosvenor House and the Waldorf.

But BLP is no longer happy to be stereotyped: *"They're playing up corporate at the moment as the firm suffered pre and post-merger because of the focus on real estate."* Is this window dressing? Definitely not. *"There's been a genuine shift in terms of what we're about. The management wants us to be regarded as a larger firm and so want an increased corporate capacity."* The corporate finance team has grabbed a firm hold of the AIM market and recently tickled a sizeable deal from entertainment rights specialist Chorion on its £28 million acquisition of rights over the Mister Men from the Hargreaves Organisation. Corporate profits are up and the department now accounts for nearly a third of BLP's overall capacity, edging closer to the current dominance of real estate at 38%.

Perhaps influenced by Roger Hargreaves' cartoon chums, other cheery elements seem to be creeping into BLP's game plan. Over the past year, the firm has been conducting an internal review of its working culture. The process has been christened Project Leo *"because we want to be the most respected firm in London and the lion is the most respected animal in the jungle,"* muttered one trainee with barely concealed embarrassment. The aim is *"to look at how we can make the service we offer more valuable to the client"* and *"to make us more all-singing, all-dancing."* Picturing partners humming 'I just can't wait to be king' is irresistible...

phew! beginner is no trial

The law of the jungle is extended to the firm's training methods. Starting at any firm can be daunting for a young cub, especially when they don't really know what will be expected of them. *"I'm quite a cynical person,"* one trainee confessed. *"I read through the marketing literature which kept on banging on about early responsibility and thought, 'What a load of rubbish'. But now I'm here, I would say that they will give you very good quality work, if they think that you can cope."* The way you'll work in real estate is a prime example: *"I was running 46 files on my own at one point. It was a very self-contained seat, I was almost my own boss and was doing everything from drafting to negotiation to sending the project out."* Trainees reported working on simple lease renewals, licences for alterations, getting permission for Tesco to erect a new sign (*"I got overly excited as it was really near my house"*), and dealing with individual premises within shopping and leisure complexes.

Property seats can be taken with any one of four real estate teams, which can be broadly categorised as shopping centre matters, projects and Crown estate work, Tesco, and work for banking clients RBS and

Merrill Lynch. Where you end up in the real estate department determines how much of your time is devoted to assisting on larger matters. One trainee said of this aspect: *"I was doing more mundane tasks – checking in property searches, setting up the data rooms – but it was interesting to be part of much bigger sales and leases."*

A seat in real estate is a dead cert and you should bear this fact in mind on applying to the firm, not least because a large slice of qualification jobs are reserved for potential real estate stars. In September 2004, 22 out of 29 trainees stayed at the firm on qualification, eight of whom are now doing property work. However, some of the trainees we spoke to were quick to remind us that the firm has plenty of room for those interested in other areas of practice. One wit told us: *"Even though 140 property lawyers here can't be wrong, I prefer corporate work and I've been able to focus on corporate during my training contract."* We were also told that: *"It's more that if you are interested you should definitely apply rather than you shouldn't apply if you're not interested in property."* If that makes sense!

he be in no til ringer swap

The firm encourages recruits into corporate seats, often straight corporate finance, sometimes insurance, corporate recovery, banking or a seat in the business and technology services department (BTS), which has been newly created from the former commercial, technology and media groups. There's less chance for autonomy in the corporate seats, but even so some trainees were in no doubt as to the compensations. *"There wasn't the same degree of own-file work as in real estate, and maybe less client contact, but the work was of a higher level and I got really involved in partners' meetings."*

A helping of contentious experience is compulsory, but we've never sensed that trainees actively choose BLP for its litigation work. Contentious construction, real estate litigation or corporate recovery fulfil the requirement as easily as straight commercial litigation. For a fourth seat choice there are some very popular niche seats: employment, projects and planning to name three. Some seats come with the popular add-on of secondments; you could go to a worldwide engineering giant as part of your projects seat, and the firm has just begun sending trainees to investment bank Schroder. One of the most long-standing arrangements is with Tesco, which means working on general commercial matters – confidentiality agreements, data protection arrangements and controlling the rights to those familiar blue stripes. Invariably, on secondments *"you're treated just like an NQ and you can get on with your work with as much or as little support as you want."* The opportunity to *"see things from the client's perspective and really think commercially as well as legally"* is also invaluable. Proof that some trainees take to the in-house role completely is to be found in the comment that *"after three months you have the mentality 'I am Tesco'."* Scary.

no rear within belge spin

We have to say we didn't hear anyone saying 'I am Berwin Leighton Paisner'. Or even 'I am beginner piano whistler'. In fact, we didn't hear much praise for the firm's anagram-led ace pirate groom, sorry, corporate image, at all. Said one trainee in answer to our favourite role-play question: *"If I were senior partner, I would sort out the website and the branding. I don't know what marketing guru designed that – the anagrams are gibberish and the name is a problem when you're on the phone to the other side. When you say you're from Berwin Leighton Paisner you have to spend half an hour spelling it out to the secretary."* But apart from such cosmetic issues, trainees were almost uniformly full of praise for the firm's culture. We heard that the firm is *"not quite as laid back as it used to be as we're trying to be the best in London for our size and what we do'* but also that *'if I'm stressed out, these are the people I want to work with because I want to be able to laugh."* Another aspect of the firm's personality stems from its connections to the Jewish community, and this means a great deal to those trainees for whom religious observation is important. As one told us: *"If you are Jewish, it's nice because faith requirements are never a problem."*

The firm is keen to build up overseas connections in a bid to become known as an international firm. Currently there are outposts in Brussels and alliances with firms in New York, Paris, Milan and Rome. German partners have also been considered. These arrangements are beginning to add up and make sense in trainees' minds, but they're not quite there. As this trainee comment shows: *"I've had lots of contact with the New York office and some with the Italian firm. There are definitely strong links there, and there are fee-earner exchanges. At the moment we have one guy from Germany and one guy from the Brussels office, which is part of the firm but it's as if we don't know it exists. We don't know what they do and there are no opportunities to go out there."* We did hear, however, of trips to Milan, including an ill-fated football tour: *"We didn't win a single game!"* Apparently because *"we had to play two games back to back on astroturf in 30°C heat with hangovers as we'd been out until 4am the night before. One Italian team was semi-professional; they didn't bother scoring that many goals, but just made us run around like idiots. The firm paid, and in the end it was a great weekend."*

real shop win beg trinnie

Back on home turf there's also fun to be had. *"The trainees take the lion's share of the gossip, although the secretaries give them a run for their money. The partners behave, on the whole."* Sounds like there were a few stories to tell from the James Bond-themed Christmas party. Could they feel the love that night? *"Let's just say that there was plenty of love and emotion."* The minority view was that *"the real scandal was the managing partner's speech; his jokes really died a death. He's usually quite a good speaker, but his scriptwriter must have been off sick."*

As for the rest of the year, the 2003/4 crop of second-year trainees are perceived to be letting the side down as far as socialising goes: *"Our intake never really gelled. Once I ended up speaking informally to a partner who said that we should go out more – the firm feels that it's quite important to be friends as well as colleagues."* By contrast, the first-years need no encouragement: *"A lot of our socialising involves alcohol and we're all big eaters. Today we all went to Borough market and had cheese and bread and olives, which is quite a regular thing. There's also lots of lunchtime shopping trips."*

fly and nail...

Berwin Leighton Paisner has plenty to sing about at the moment, having just walked off with the Law Firm of the Year accolade from a major legal magazine. This slap on the back doesn't represent a full stop: the firm has big ambitions for the future. If you've a mind to play a part in them, start practising that Hakuna Matata for your audition.

Bevan Brittan LLP

the facts

Location: Bristol, London, Birmingham
Number of UK partners/assistants: 65/98
Total number of trainees: 38
Seats: 4x6 months
Alternative seats: Secondments
Extras: Pro bono

If you're flicking through the *Student Guide* looking for Bevan Ashford, then stop here you've found the right firm. Or one half of the right firm at least. Needless to say, big things have been happening at Bevan Brittan LLP this year.

towering indifference

Deep Impact, Armageddon, The Day After Tomorrow, Gigli – all the best disaster movies pit the indomitable spirit of plucky humankind against the almighty apocalyptic indifference of nature and fate. And always, but always, humankind emerges wiser, better, scarred but hopeful. With that in mind (and having noted the hail of meteorites that have blasted across the firm's website in recent years) we approached our interviews with the newly christened Bevan Brittan trainees ready for uplifting tales

of heroism, derring-do and triumph born of adversity. Wrong. When prompted to discuss Bevan Ashford's dramatic paring, trainees were distinctly underwhelmed. *"The demerger hasn't made and won't make any difference to us,"* they said. *"Everyone's been expecting it. The only surprise is that it didn't happen two years ago when we had an image overhaul."*

Eighteen years ago, two regional firms merged to form Bevan Ashford, but never progressed to full profit sharing between the Exeter, Plymouth and London (EPL) offices and the Bristol, Birmingham and London (BBL) offices. The two equally profitable axes had separate recruitment teams, separate IT systems, separate partner remuneration schemes, separate offices in London and few shared clients. Trainees didn't have any contact across the great divide and identified wholly with their respective halves of the firm. Since effecting the formal split in autumn 2004, EPL is now known as Ashfords, and our current subject firm, Bevan Brittan, is the new-look BBL.

a clean break

We're only giving one side of the story because Ashfords took the decision not to appear in *The True Picture* this year. Read nothing into that – we haven't – but if you do want to find out more about Ashfords, consult our 2004 edition feature on Bevan Ashford, which contains plenty of good stuff on the old EPL offices.

Bevan Brittan trainees explained the timing of the split as best they could: *"The two profit centres were beginning to compete for the same clients;" "it just made business and financial sense to demerge."* Asked why the firm dallied over the split for so long, our sources were quick to admit: *"It will mean we'll drop out of the Top 50 law firms."* However, most felt *"it might be smaller on paper, but it will feel just the same." "Probably only the stationery will change."* And continuity was the theme for the firm's new name: the 'Brittan' part belonged originally to *"one of Bevan's founding fathers from the early 20th century."*

brittan's national health service

Bevan Brittan's traditional strength has been its Bristol-based healthcare regulatory and clinical negligence litigation departments. The history buffs amongst us recall that the London and Birmingham offices initially opened to extend reach in these areas of practice. Regular PI caseloads partner the defence of complex medical claims in obstetrics, neurosurgery and infection, with a massive body of work received from the NHS Litigation Authority. The firm's expertise has earned it instructions from other healthcare organisations, but the recent NHSLA decision to handle more claims in-house "*at least halved the work of the department*" and redundancies resulted. This was undoubtedly a blow, though our sources assured us: "*All is settled down now.*" Some we interviewed suggested that the demerger will see the firm move further away from its healthcare roots, and that it is "*free to follow a more commercial focus.*"

Hard as it is to pick apart the voluntary and the expedient in this directional change, it is clear that the firm is expanding apace in its commercial departments. Across the offices, Dyson, Zurich Financial, Chesterton and the South West Regional Development Agency are among the satisfied customers, with the Welsh Development Agency having just signed up. Commercial practice has been beefed up by lateral hires at partner level in tax and banking and BB now states its intent to promote IT/IP, technology, retailing and leisure. Intel, Orange Personal Communications, Lucent Technologies and Skandia are some of the more non-traditional BB clients, and the firm acted for LMVH on copyright issues surrounding the Louis Vuitton and Celine brands this year. Licensing of technology to corporate organisations in Japan and China using complex royalty payment arrangements was another notable job. In London the employment team works for "*a massive freight forwarding company and major high street retailers,*" and the corporate and commercial teams across the company have acted on a range of transactions for major banks, manufacturers, a leading supermarket and AIM-listed companies.

Nonetheless, traditional clients aren't going to evaporate overnight. A national spread of NHS trusts from Cornwall to Kent and from the Isle of Wight to Newcastle upon Tyne includes acute trusts, mental health trusts, strategic health authorities, community and ambulance trusts, primary care trusts, the Department of Health and special health authorities. Although south focused, the Birmingham office is reaching further north, with the Black Country Strategic Health Authority now a major client. Such clients still refer around half of the firm's commercial work. Giving it full coverage in the UK healthcare market, the firm also acts for numerous other health-related organisations, including partnerships for health, the National Care Standards Commission, Commission for Patient and Public Involvement in Health, local authorities (many of which are taking on health functions as part of joint working) and private healthcare providers (such as life sciences clinics).

The firm's strongest developments have come in the much lauded projects/PFI department, which has synthesised traditional public sector expertise and newer commercial skills to break into new practice areas. BB is the sole legal adviser to the NHS Lift project, which will see the development of 500 new one-stop health centres and the refurbishment of over 3,000 GP practices. Furthermore, the Department for Education and Skills has been sufficiently impressed to appoint the firm on an equivalent project for UK schools.

cornish posties

Trainees were quick to tell us that although the location of the Bristol and London offices couldn't be bettered, "*they're both a little shabby, especially from a client's point of view.*" Fortunately, a relocation is on the cards in London and an overhaul is in progress at the warren-like Bristol city centre site. Like the ten-trainee London office, the Birmingham office currently occupies one floor of a larger building "*so it's not the same as walking into the Bristol office and*

TRUE PICTURE OUR 140 FIRMS

thinking 'This is Bevan Brittan.'" At least from their 26th-storey vantage point in Alpha Tower, the five trainees have a heck of a view of Brum. And, should they wish they can test their nerves by throwing themselves against the windows.

"They really do give you as much as you can handle," said one trainee referring to the way the firm had balanced the responsibility/experience see-saw. It was an opinion echoed by another who enthused about "good overall supervision and training that gave me so much self-belief." Alas, the menial chore of post-opening is still a trainee's lot in the Bristol office, but at least "there really is very little photocopying, and generally people are very good about making it up to you with good work if you've had a raw deal." While some interviewees recounted experiences of "being with a supervisor who you couldn't establish a rapport with...it makes you disengage," these were exceptions to the rule. Elsewhere, the firm does a good job of keeping its staff motivated and on-song: bonuses for meeting target include "away weekends for the whole department." We could almost hear the smile on the face of the trainee who remembered: "We went to Cornwall for the weekend and got trashed!"

musical chairs

Trainees are recruited specifically for each location, and hopping between sites is unusual but not impossible. Trainees were unanimous in their praise for the "unity" of the firm, especially appreciating the new CEO's monthly drinks parties at each site. In addition, videoconferenced monthly training sessions give all trainees a chance to discuss issues with HR and amongst themselves, not least the thorny matter of seat allocation. In general, those we interviewed were happy with allocations, though there were a few dark murmurs about "behind the scenes lobbying." The firm has recruited "outgoing," "motivated," "ambitious but not ruthless" people from a fair variety of backgrounds. Nine out of 14 accepted NQ job offers from the firm in 2004.

After work, Bristol trainees are rewarded by a mighty array of bars, sports, events and the general "aura of loveliness" of the city. And whether it's hectic Trainee Solicitors Society jamborees in Birmingham or kick-back, feet-up drinks at The Cartoonist in London, there's plenty for those with a social sweet tooth.

and finally...

There's only one Bevan Brittan, and without the distraction of a two-firms-in-one identity (with attendant client conflicts) the firm is now at liberty to develop in any way it chooses.

Bircham Dyson Bell

the facts

Location: London, Cardiff, Edinburgh
Number of UK partners/assistants: 43/30
Total number of trainees: 13
Seats: 4x6 months
Alternative seats: None
Extras: Pro bono – Central London Advice Centre

If you thought Westminster was all HP sauce and scandal, there's one corner of this political patch that bucks the trend. A long-established SW1 practice, Bircham Dyson Bell is described by trainees as a very decent place to work. Recently representing the interests of the family of Dr David Kelly in the Hutton Inquiry, it's well known for parliamentary and private client work, but there are other things on the agenda.

sitting in private

While none of their four seats are strictly compulsory, trainees are quite likely to visit private client as it is the biggest department. They are even more likely to spend time in the parliamentary, planning and public department, which hosts three trainees at each seat rotation. Beyond this, there are options in company/commercial, litigation, employment, property and charities. Whichever seats they'd done, the trainees we interviewed were all directly engaged with clients and pleasantly surprised by the roles they'd taken on. "*It's been an excellent foundation for a career in the law,*" one pronounced.

With 13 partners and a full bench of solicitors, Birchams' private client department is among the UK's largest. Clients include the green-welly brigade, entrepreneurs and the odd famous name, and although high net worth individuals dominate, trainees get a fair crack of the whip when acting for less wealthy clients. Hence the comment: "*It's an ideal first seat, giving you all the skills you use day to day as a solicitor.*"

Private client work can be complex, tax-based and dry, and the department is somewhere you might typecast the partners as "*Oxbridge educated and quite intimidating.*" Someone who initially held this view happily conceded: "*You soon get over that...the supervising partners are excellent and they take time out to go through your work.*" Yet trainees still whisper of a department in a world of its own – "*It is happy with its intellectual superiority. The private client floor is hushed and highbro*w," and as if to reinforce a traditional image, "*it has a ticking clock in the corridor.*"

crossing the floor

"*Commercialisation is a clear aim,*" we learned. It started in 2000 with the arrival of corporate lawyers from Bower Cotton, continued in 2001 with a move to swanky new premises, and has been pursued through lateral hires ever since. But don't get too excited...while trainees say Birchams has the mindset to change, they all appear to cherish its role as a haven from the hardcore, corporate excesses of City life. The firm's flagship deal of 2003, while worth over £50 million, was less multinational blue-chip and more cuddly Pudsey bear – it restructured BBC Children in Need as a corporate charity.

Perhaps inspired by craazy telethon behaviour, the litigation department is "*an upbeat, perky place,*" offering "*a lot of amusement*" alongside the writs and witness statements. Any trainee who wishes to sample family law can do so in this department. Partners are "*conscious of making sure you get a broad spread of cases,*" and best of all, "*you won't get cases so large that you'll be paginating for six months.*" Admittedly, trainees can't escape dull tasks entirely, but here, "*as in the whole firm, there's a good emphasis on giving experience and responsibility.*" One source had hosted a meeting alone with the client and counsel, and confirmed that it was common to have conduct of small cases from beginning to end. "*They are very keen on getting you into court – I did a couple of applications before masters and they frequently send us to take notes.*"

The property department was voted the most easygoing of all, something apparently evidenced by the fact that "*there's more laughter*" and "*you're more likely to get people wearing the same colour shirt-and-tie combo.*" You'll be kept busy on residential and commercial sales and purchases, agricultural work and commercial leases. Clients include large landed estates, retailers, charities, property companies and private individuals. "*You deal directly with clients on the phone most days,*" so if you've got both Calvin Klein and Marks & Spencer on the go at the same time, you could get your knickers in a twist.

it takes two to quango

And so to the top-ranked parliamentary department. Representing all sorts from the GLA to Scottish fishermen, these lawyers dwell in what is for most of us unfamiliar territory. "*It's quite daunting when you first arrive,*" admitted one trainee. Research tasks feature large, but trainees also attend public inquiries and liaise with counsel. Much time is spent on the promotion of, and opposition to, private and local legislation, which one sage rightly pointed out "*adds something completely different to your CV.*" The clients seemingly have a hand in every rail project in the UK; before you know it, you'll be au fait with Transport and Works Act Orders as well as Harbours Act Orders. Birchams has outposts in Cardiff and Edinburgh, located close to the National Assembly for Wales and the Scottish Parliament. But if, like us, devolved powers don't get you that excited you needn't worry about being forced to work outside London.

maiden speeches

When we asked what Birchams looked for in trainees, one source replied: *"Intelligence, independence and a sense of humour."* If you think that sounds like a lonely hearts advertisement, you might not be far off the mark. In an effort to get staff networking, the firm organised speed dating-type evenings where folk from different departments were given just three minutes to 'connect' with each other. 'Does this lead to actual dating?' we asked. *"I doubt it very much. They are not encouraging us to have affairs!"*

Of course, people who do well on blind dates are generally open, relaxed and good at talking with others. It's much the same with this firm's recruitment process: *"You can have all the 'A's in the book, but if you can't get on with people you are not going to get in."* Birchams consistently recruits an interesting blend of trainees – some youngsters (many of whom have travelled) and some with previous careers (currently exiles from the foreign office and a merchant bank, as well as a professional trumpet player). *"The firm has expectations of trainees and the fundamental reason why they recruit who they do is that they can utilise them more. As a lawyer, it is important to keep a sense of perspective, and if you are a bit more mature, you are less likely to start panicking if something goes wrong."* Hear! Hear!

A mature outlook is also required with regard to manners, conduct and appearance; there is no dress-down policy (*"and that doesn't bother anybody"*) and the watchwords are decency and respectfulness. In relations with clients, too, trainees must act like grown-ups: *"The firm likes us to take part at all levels. We are encouraged to write articles and give presentations. They place a lot of trust in us."* It may not be a fashionable thing to say, but *"Birchams has retained traditional values,"* albeit that these are *"updated with a modern slant."* Cue the firm's intranet, accessible by anyone who wants to peruse the business plan or see what other departments are up to. As one regular user explained: *"If we all know the goal we can aim for it."* Good news on the retention front in 2004: all four qualifiers stayed.

honourable friends

Bircham's offices are just a stone's throw from St James's Park, which is ideal for summer picnics and winter snowball fights. Yet, this is so obviously a firm for lunchers not fighters. At regular mid-day mingles, *"you have to be careful because it's too easy to get three or four glasses of wine down you!"* And after work? *"We don't have the same drinking-together culture as the trainees in big City firms."* On Friday nights a contingent can usually be found in The Two Chairman in Queen Anne's Gate, and if not, they'll be celebrating pay day in Zander, the overpriced bar at the fashionable Bank restaurant. *"I am fantastic friends with the trainees in my year,"* one source told us. *"We have fun meals out together after work...sometimes we trek across the park to Piccadilly."*

Behind a Georgian frontage, Birchams has created a modern office in which to develop its growing sense of commercial self. Sensitive to clients tastes, it also has meeting rooms that appeal to the tweedier, more traditional element of its constituency. One trainee recalled a partner in a panic over the prospect of taking a client into the wrong style of room, at which point we instantly pictured Basil Fawltyesque room shuffling and distractions, and were forced to conclude our interview.

and finally...

Bircham Dyson Bell easily picks up votes from applicants who want legal training the good old way – in an intimate environment where clients and legal principles are valued above all else.

Bird & Bird

the facts

Location: London
Number of UK partners/assistants: 54/160
Total number of trainees: 25
Seats: 4x6 months
Alternative seats: Overseas seats, secondments
Extras: Language training

IP, technology and communications, e-commerce and sports – Bird & Bird, with its techy clients and snappy twobirds.com web address, sounds more like one of those übercool, new kids on the block than a law firm that's been kicking around since 1846.

1846 and all that

"Gentlemen, this is no humbug!" So said one of those present at the first public demonstration of an operation under anaesthetic. If you're wondering what Mr Gilbert Abbott's jaw op in 1846 has to do with our subject firm, the answer is simple. These days, whenever there are scientific or technological advances, lawyers are on hand to assist the creators in the protection, management and exploitation of their new asset. Quite simply, Bird & Bird is renowned, worldwide, as a key legal adviser to those who are inventing, improving or buying and selling knowledge and technology. Whether you're developing a new drug, buying an ISP, employing a research scientist or selling an IT system to aid with the delivery of anything from healthcare to vehicle testing, you'd be well advised to call in the Birds.

Your first task as a prospective applicant is to visit the twobirds website to ascertain whether the firm's target sectors interest you. E-commerce, communications, IT, IP, life sciences, sport, media and aviation – it's a far cry from banks, banks and more banks, which is what you'll encounter at many a City firm.

ground-breaking cases

Trainees all take four seats chosen from a very respectable list of options. Anyone with a science degree, PhD or relevant post-graduate experience will doubtless want to sample the firm's high-flying patent litigation department, whose work other trainees will find harder to handle. Covering pharmaceutical, mechanical and biotech cases, trainees work alongside partners with planet-sized brains.

This is probably a good time to point out that trainees are the cheapest and least experienced members of the team, and as on any type of high-value litigation, end up doing their fair share of document management. In spite of this, one source reported feeling *"privileged to spend time in a top-ranked department."* Bird & Bird is frequently involved in the biggest and most complex of patent cases: recently it pulled off a favourable biotech-related judgment for Transkaryotic Therapies and Avensis in the erythropoietin litigation which had been running since 1999. Yet sometimes IP cases can be understood by even those whose scientific education stopped when *Tomorrow's World* went off the air. To illustrate, the Birdbrains recently met with success when acting for Belgian and Dutch coffee producers in a European patent action brought by Sara Lee. As a result, coffee drinkers no longer have to use Douwe Egberts products in their Senseo coffee makers.

The mainstream commercial litigation department handles some interesting cases. For example, it successfully defended Guy's & St Thomas' Hospital NHS Trust against a £1 million claim made on behalf of the child of a serviceman stationed in Germany. The MOD had outsourced secondary healthcare for British servicemen and their families to the trust, which had in turn subcontracted care to a German hospital. In another example, coincidentally also a healthcare matter, the firm advised a government body called to give evidence in the third stage of the Shipman Enquiry. It helped with written evidence, gave strategic advice and supported a senior member of staff through his oral examination.

public awareness

Aside from purely contentious work, trainees can sample real estate, coco, employment, banking, tax, communications and IT and e-commerce. In most cases, the fourth seat is a return visit to the department into which they hope to qualify. This year, as over the past two years, qualifying trainees were placed on a six-month probation. All flew through it last year, which bodes well for the 14 out of 18 that stayed on in September 2004.

The commercial department has won trainees' hearts. Within the department are two groups: commercial 1, which deals with IT projects; and commercial 2, which handles telecoms, general commercial and sports work. The lawyers in commercial 1 handle *"very large public sector contracts which run to hundreds of pages."* This equates to *"a lot of responsibility for trainees in relation to document management."* On the flipside, *"on smaller contracts, such as software sublicences, they will let you draft by yourself."* Of commercial 2, one trainee told us: *"It was brilliant. I was fortunate enough to sit with one of the best partners in the firm. He and the trainee work together reviewing documents on a transaction,"* and from the sound of things this partner is a master at developing commerciality in his charges. If you want to get out of the office for a while, why not accept the offer of a client secondment. Sometimes these are done on a part-time basis, with trainees or NQs spending two or three days a week with the client.

flight patterns

Particularly in the first year of the contract, there's a volume (verging on a surfeit) of trainee-specific seminars covering black letter law and skills subjects. On top of this, larger departments offer *"excellent seminar programmes"* including visits from barristers and lawyers in the firm's overseas offices.

Did someone mention overseas offices? An ambitious growth programme has transformed Bird & Bird from a mid-sized UK partnership into a European player that has feathered nests in Brussels, The Hague, Stockholm, Milan, Paris, Düsseldorf and Munich. And at a time when some firms are retreating from Asia, the Birds have even migrated as far as Hong Kong. The occasional trainee who chirps noisily enough is permitted to fly the London coop; in recent years people have gone to Hong Kong and Germany, and after qualification a twinning system ensures a fair degree of nest hopping around the Continent. All this said, none of our sources thought their work in the UK had been particularly influenced by the presence of the overseas network. *"It's not every day that we get cross-border transactions, but we do work with lawyers from the other offices."*

identifying the breed

The Bird & Bird trainee is *"not the classic Oxbridge type going off to Linklaters and thinking, 'Isn't it great to be a City lawyer doing big deals.'"* Rather, *"it's about coming into work and being interested in what you are doing."* Some sources described partners who tended towards the intellectual, though not to the extent of *"emphasising the legal minutiae and not looking at the bigger picture."* For the avoidance of doubt: *"The overly academic won't fit in,"* yet *"you can't be a legal lightweight at this firm."* A few of our interviewees reported having lively legal debate with their seniors. *"I won an argument over a point of interpretation,"* one trainee boasted proudly. *"He had one view and I had another and the next day he said, 'On reflection you're right.'"* Another source appreciated being treated as someone *"with four years of legal education."*

Had a past life and worry that it will spoil your chances? Far from it. Bird & Bird has an enlightened approach to recruitment. Among the current hatchlings are someone who'd worked in legal marketing and IT recruitment, a former sports agent and an ex-music producer. Don't expect trendy or cool though – that's not Bird & Bird's style. Even if some of the clients are into cutting-edge technology, others are *"huge big multinationals with formal commercial and legal departments. And at the end of the day, clients want lawyers to be lawyers and not music business impresarios."* The style of firm's premises reflect this – the main office is located in Fetter Lane and a second, housing the IP department, is located in Furnival Street. We hear a third building has also been brought into service to ease congestion. Surely it is only a matter of time before the Birds start twittering about nesting together.

Cricket, rugby, football, hockey, softball and

rounders – the Birds play it all. There's even a yoga group. If putting your legs behind your ears holds no appeal for you, below the Fetter Lane office there's a bar called Walkers, which really couldn't be more misnamed – its dark interior is frequented only by those who refuse to walk to more appealing surroundings. "*At least the beer's cheap,*" someone muttered. Every few months, the partners host a drinks party in their basement dining room. 'What's it like down there?' we asked. "*Hot and crowded,*" came the reply. Sounds like hell.

and finally...

Bird & Bird is a distinctive firm that deserves to be chosen for its defining traits. Make sure the sector focus ruffles your feathers in the right way, and if it does rest easy knowing that you'll not be perched miserably on a telegraph wire wishing you'd found a different roost.

Birkett Long

the facts

Location: Colchester, Chelmsford, Halstead
Number of UK partners/assistants: 19/16
Total number of trainees: 4
Seats: 4x6 months
Alternative seats: None

Birkett Long is one of Essex's longest standing and most well known law firms. Operating from bases in Colchester, Halstead and now Chelmsford, it offers a hybrid commercial/private client training contract.

can anyone hear a buzzing sound?

Our thanks must go to the trainee who gave us a thumbnail sketch of Birkett Long's 180-year history. Apparently, it all started in the village of Halstead way back in 1821, which a quick bit of research confirmed was also the year that saw the birth of the modern states of Greece and Peru. Without even a second thought for jokes of partners' high urnings or trainees' Andes-on experiences, we set about discovering civilisation in deepest darkest Essex.

Some of the older practice areas, particularly in Halstead, may be clinging to tradition, but the firm as a whole is "*brimming with*" new bits of technology and ideas for the future. Having set up the Colchester office in the 1980s, in 2002 the firm opened a Chelmsford office to focus purely on commercial practice. Trainees tell us Birkett Long aims to be "*The firm in Essex*" and that "*there's a definite buzz in the air regarding pushing the firm forward and doing better work.*"

life of pie

For the most part contained within the Colchester and Halstead offices, there's a very decent package of seats on offer to trainees – commercial litigation, employment, company/commercial, commercial property, residential conveyancing, rural business, family law, probate, tax and trusts, very occasionally PI and, if you're particularly keen, financial services.

Residential conveyancing in Halstead may not sound that glamorous but get it as a first seat and you might well conclude that "*it's a very good place to start because it isn't exactly rocket science and the theory is simple...if it all falls into place.*" Of course, transactions don't always fall into place and, as such, trainees become adept at fixing problems, soothing clients and juggling files. "*The phones don't stop ringing*" and you have to keep saying to yourself "*this now, this next and this can wait a bit,*" but what better introduction to the complex art of prioritisation? Best of all, "*the team is fantastic fun*" and the "*high pace*" keeps the adrenalin pumping.

Meatier and equally as busy is a seat in commercial litigation. The team is split between the main Colchester office and the all-commercial Chelmsford office. "*I've had my fingers in all sort of pies from insolvency to property litigation and professional negligence, general contract disputes and sale of goods cases,*" said one past occupant of the seat. Trainees split their time between helping other members of the department and handling smaller matters that would be uneconomical for anyone more senior. Visits to court are commonplace and our sources reported handling possession proceedings, winding-up petitions and preliminary applications to district judges. As the county court is just over the road, there's also a little 'outdoor clerking' to be done (ie filing and collecting documents).

old macdonald

Family law in Colchester brings you into contact with the kind of clients who, *"without wanting to sound snobbish, have money. The firm has dropped its legal aid divorce work and it is now referred to other firms."* The team mainly handles ancillary relief cases, but also has a couple of childcare lawyers who have a legal aid franchise. Trainees can sample both aspects of the department's activities and get stuck into drafting divorce petitions and client interviews, settlement negotiations and preparing for trials. *"I never got to do advocacy, which was a bit of a disappointment, but there are few opportunities where it comes up."* Mediations and client care are to the fore and *"it's one of those seats where the law is not very complicated so there's not much to hide behind and your client skills have to be up to scratch."*

Try a seat with the rural business team in Halstead and you'd better be ready for a few farm visits. *"Luckily there was a spare pair of wellies in back of the partner's Land Rover!"* chuckled one trainee. Essentially, the seat involves property work for farmers, though there are many issues specific to this (forgive the pun) field of law. Milk quotas, regulations on cattle movement and EU subsidies, grants for husbandry and wild heathland, etc – *"It's a complete service to farmers and rural businesses in the area, who are looking at diversification for use of their land."* What do they do with it? *"Caravan parks and student accommodation for agricultural colleges, subsidiary business, the construction of radio masts;"* it's easy to see why farmers need specialist legal advice. And the good news for those firms that do specialise is that there are not that many others with dedicated teams.

Whether it's a private client seat like tax, trusts and probate or a commercial one like coco, *"your principal expects you to work as a solicitor; they're not interested in spoonfeeding you, though they will always give you enough pointers. You speak to the clients, write the letters and make the court applications in all cases where this is possible."* What's more, you must also be prepared to lend a hand to anyone who needs one, whichever of the three offices they are in. Said one trainee: *"Everybody in the firm hears of your arrival and you end up with e-mails coming out of your ears."* There's nothing better than feeling like you're wanted, we say!

a man in uniform

As one of just four trainees, each of our sources spoke of their sense of involvement with the firm. This involvement extends to a business development role whenever the firm throws a bash for clients. And when it does, it certainly makes an effort. Our attention was drawn to a photograph in The Law Society's *Gazette* earlier in 2004; a photo, no less, of staff from Birkett Long dressed in 1940s clothes – civvies and uniformed. *"That was a 'business partners' event that we throw every year,"* explained one trainee. *"This year it was held at the East Anglia Railway Museum, trainees attended to generally help out, serve drinks and make sure people were okay."* The best part apparently was a fly-past by two WWII fighter planes, a little treat organised by a friend of one of the partners.

If you like a man (or woman) in uniform, Colchester is just the place for you as it has an abundance of them garrisoned nearby. Though some might beg to differ, we have it on good authority that the last time Colchester was truly under siege from troops it was by the New Model army in the Civil War. At Birkett Long the only thing you're likely to be enlisted for is a trip to nearby Roberto's with colleagues, though it has to be said that because many people come to work by car, Friday night partying is strictly for those with dedicated drivers to deliver them safely home. Colchester's other notable features (forgetting all that Roman history malarkey) are the Essex University campus and proximity to the coast – Clacton, Burnham on Crouch and other pretty villages are just 15 minutes away. London, too, is just an hour away on the train, which makes meeting up with mates in the City after work totally possible. In 2004. one of the two qualifiers enlisted for further service at Birkett Long.

and finally...

Birkett Long is the ideal firm for any Essex-based trainee looking to sample both commercial and private client practice. And if the increased focus on commercial business in the last decade is anything to go by, the opportunities should keep growing.

Boodle Hatfield

the facts

Location: London, Oxford
Number of UK partners/assistants: 9/69
Total number of trainees: 9
Seats: 4x6 months
Alternative seats: None

Next door to Claridge's in the heart of Mayfair, just down the road from Grosvenor Square, Boodle Hatfield's address speaks volumes – property is a distinguished asset and high net worth individuals are par for the course.

they paved paradise...

For 280 years, Boodle Hatfield has been undertaking property work for such highly prized clients as the Duke of Westminster's Grosvenor Estate. If dukes and estates all sound a little too 18th century, you should understand that this estate is an international property development and investment group that has instructed Boodles on the 42 acre, £750 million urban regeneration of Liverpool's Paradise Street among other things. A clutch of other big names such as Bedford Estates and PMB Holdings keeps the team busy with major development, construction, investment and enfranchisement projects. Property

is *"the heartbeat of the firm"* – *"you've only got to look at the floor plan of the office to see how far it sprawls compared to other departments."* One trainee told us: *"To a certain extent the rest of the firm feeds off property."* However, another saw it slightly differently: *"There is more emphasis on property, but the others aren't left behind. There is enough scope for each department to excel in their own thing."* Superb trusts and tax and family teams span the firm's two offices in London and Oxford. The trusts and tax team mixes contentious with non-contentious work and acts for old and new-money clients on both their personal and business affairs. The Oxford limb of the family team is highly regarded for its work on both finance and children's cases from the UK and overseas.

cradle to grave

The traditional four-seat training scheme successfully accommodates trainees' wishes. All sources had done a stint in both property and litigation, and most had done trusts and tax and corporate, though construction is available on request. Unfortunately, earlier this year the Boodles' employment team lost key members to Lewis Silkin and *"down-sized considerably. It needs to be rebuilt before a trainee can go back in there."* The Boodles training contract is normally a London-based affair, though a trusts and tax or family seat in Oxford can be arranged.

The near-compulsory property seat is *"one of the best seats for training"* as *"you get your own files – from opening them to archiving them."* Trainees described a jam-packed six months of leases, licences and leasehold enfranchisement, and some found the amount of responsibility they'd been given and the pace of the department *"quite a shock"* at first. *"You're not totally out of your depth as such, but you don't have much time to settle in."*

"Everyone likes to go to litigation," we're reliably informed. *"You get really involved and everyone gets into something interesting, from pesticides disputes to a dispute concerning cockles...and of course the infamous house of ill repute"* – a case concerning a client whose tenant is

running a brothel. Trainees attend court, meet clients and *"write some quite gritty letters."* Significantly smaller than property, the litigation team ensures *"you are more likely to get involved with everything that goes on there and you get a general feel of what each main fee earner is doing."* In trusts and tax, there's a steady diet of wills and probate, with some contentious work thrown in. The client base makes for some interesting encounters – *"You do get a few crazy faces, but also some bread-and-butter, less-batty stuff as well."* Variety is also the name of the game in corporate, where clients range from Britain's oldest wine and spirit merchant, Berry Bros & Rudd to Allied Irish Bank. Trainees described *"quite a lot of drafting and adminny stuff, but quite a lot of contact with clients too."*

When asked why they had chosen Boodle Hatfield one source replied: *"You hear the horror stories of paginating all day, and I wanted to actually do some work."* It sounds like he'd picked the right place. A standard day is an *"intensive"* 9ish till 6.30ish; as one astute trainee pointed out, *"in property you are busy with phones ringing and e-mails all day, but no one wants to complete at 5am."* Trainees share offices with their supervisors, who appear to be the partners *"best suited to having a trainee in their room."* Quarterly appraisals keep trainees apprised of their progress, though as the weeks go by, *"if you aren't performing well...you will be told. In your appraisal you shouldn't find out anything dramatic."*

rubber duckie

The original Mr Boodle who joined the firm in 1767 was the nephew of the founder of a famous gentleman's club in St James's – also called Boodles. This 280-year-old law firm is *"aware of its heritage,"* but apparently *"it wants to become younger."* Conveniently, *"brand new offices fitted out for Boodle Hatfield"* are in the pipeline...and the vicinity. *"We will always be based in Mayfair,"* one trainee explained, referring to the significance of the firm's relationship with the Grosvenor Estate. Trainees say the new offices will be more modern, more spacious and more practical.

"People are excited; it is a good sign and a step forward." For now, the firm's traditional Brook Street building has all the trappings of a classic, old-style law firm – moustached gents in oil-on-canvas, French polished tables and mumsie china. We hear that confused new trainees *"suffer from that first-day-at-school thing when everything looks the same."* The general mood is heads-down, except at lunchtime when Oxford Street can be a bit of a distraction, though one female trainee confessed: *"It does get a bit much at Christmas."*

Despite their firm's historic connections to the cigar-smoking and port-drinking brigade, our sources did not conform to the habits of their forebears, preferring the nearby Barley Mow, Running Horse, Pitcher & Piano or Balls Brothers for a quick drink after work. Organised events have included a Thames boat trip, a day at Kempton Park races and a golf day. Our sources described themselves as *"karaoke-phobics,"* but many at the firm take this form of 'entertainment' quite seriously – especially one associate who *"always sings something crazy like Teenage Dirtbag."* Events are also organised by the Grosvenor Estate, including dragon boat racing (*"the other teams were like rugby players – all rippling muscle types – we didn't have a chance in hell, so we came last and got a rubber duck"*) and a games night for Pictionary, Scrabble, Guess Who? and Jenga. *"Generally Grosvenor wins."*

BH attracts the type of person for whom good manners are a natural instinct. They come from very decent universities, though not all of them come straight from acadaemia. Though it's probably fair to say that none are likely to set the world alight, they do *"look out for each other."* The majority will continue to do so: five out of the six September 2004 qualifiers stayed with the firm, four of them going into property.

and finally...

Even those trainees who told us they'd hated the idea of property law before starting their training at Boodle Hatfield appear to have been persuaded of its merits. Who knows, maybe you'll think the same way if you end up in this particular corner of Mayfair.

BPE Solicitors

the facts

Location: Cheltenham, Birmingham
Number of UK partners/assistants: 18/22
Total number of trainees: 11
Seats: 4x6 months
Alternative seats: Occasional visits to Estonia

Performing well in property, commercial litigation and corporate work, Cheltenham's BPE is an energetic firm that's grown to become the largest in Gloucestershire.

chain reaction

In 1989, two established Cheltenham firms, Bretherton Price and Elgoods combined forces. Three years ago the resultant firm moved into new premises in a developing part of the town centre and then abandoned its unwieldy name to adopt the abbreviation it uses today. Since then it has left no stone unturned in its quest to take full advantage of a buoyant housing market and to build up its business services capability.

If you examine the firm's revenue and staff numbers – 250, 40 of whom are qualified solicitors and 18 of these partners – it immediately becomes apparent that the little things in life have not been forgotten. Around half of BPE's business lies in the realm of residential property: both lender services (for the most part, remortgages and sales of repossessed properties) and residential sales and purchases (most of these for clients referred by building societies and large estate agents, or plot sales for house builders). If you want an idea of the scale of the operation, the lender services division handles some 20,000 files per year and the 'resi' division around 5,000. BPE's main clients are the C&G and Chelsea building societies (both of which are headquartered locally), Bradford & Bingley, Zurich, Countrywide and Bovis Homes.

oompa loompa, doopity doo

These clients are going to be the ones you'll first encounter because almost all trainees start as paralegals in one or other of the above divisions. Whether it's for a few months or a couple of years, BPE likes to know that those who get hold of the golden ticket to a training contract are deserving and bright like Charlie Bucket not petulant social misfits like Augustus Gloop or Verucca Salt. Said one of those who'd made it through the gates after a stint as a paralegal: *"There are very few trainees here in short shorts and wet behind the ears; they expect people to have built up a high level of competence before starting."* We checked with the firm and it does also want to encourage applications from those who are still studying, be this full time or part time.

Trainees come from a variety of universities, including those among the nearest to the firm, ie Bristol, Cardiff and UWE; some but not all grew up in Gloucestershire. A few had missed the law firm applications boat when it left two years in advance of their LPC graduation, and there were others who, by virtue of unfortunate academic grades, had *"always known* [their] *way in would be by getting a foot in the door."* Interestingly, several had worked in public sector legal jobs. To a trainee, these are people who are thoroughly committed to being lawyers and fully prepared to get stuck into the task in hand, even if it is being one of the *"bums on seats"* processing bulk work for a while.

So, just imagine the scene: after a bowl of thin cabbage soup with the grandpas and grandmas in the big double bed (we always thought that was a rum set-up), you arrive at work, open the file for the sale of 66 Acacia Avenue and there lies...a golden ticket.

going, going, gone

Once in the trainee fold, your existence is changed forever. What lies ahead are four six-month seats to be taken from commercial property, corporate, commercial litigation, employment, PI, private client, residential conveyancing or even insolvency in the fledgling Birmingham office. By chance, the people we spoke to were definitely keyed into the commercial areas of practice, and so these are the ones we'll report on.

It's the biggest commercial earner for the firm, so we'll start with property. Trainees sit with a partner and assist them on their caseload, which depending on who they sit with includes retail premises, office and industrial space, residential investments and developments, and even agricultural property. One trainee spoke of *"entrepreneurial, proactive, get-up-and-go"* clients and the need to be ready to fly into action if they ring up with news of a property that's up for auction the next day. If they say, *"fancy going for it?"* – of course the answer is yes. Of the two seats in the litigation department, one focuses on general commercial disputes and the other on property lit. Trainees have to be prepared to get their hands dirty, be it on boundary disputes or claims against negligent surveyors, construction cases or injunctions for housing associations against nuisance tenants. In this seat, *"the most extraordinary things crop up:"* we heard of one trainee who was assisting on an intriguing case concerning two neighbours, some back-garden flood defences, mooring rights and weirs on the River Severn.

Corporate seats, by comparison with most others, generally allow less scope for trainees to take the lead. *"I was just shadowing my supervisor to a certain degree,"* said one; *"but I attended all the meetings and was drafting less important documents. I'd do the minutes and have a go at the agreements."* The firm targets the entrepreneurial SME market and has a foothold in the AIM market *"Usually clients were happy to communicate with me as the trainee,"* revealed one source. Another who had really flourished in corporate spoke of running a business sale by himself under the watchful eye of a partner.

suck it and see

Ah yes, the partners. Machiavellian Wonkers running a large and profitable factory or kindly Grandpa Joes that would give their last shilling to make Charlie happy? When we put this choice to one trainee, he replied: *"The partners don't look as if they are minted, not if you look at the cars in the car park...and no one feels they're getting exploited!"* Which brings us to something called Project Vampire, a scheme set up to encourage and teach young solicitors how to win new business of their own rather than simply servicing the partners' existing clients. Basically it involves a good deal of socialising and networking with non-lawyers. Such networking is one of BPE's key strengths, and if you want to get an idea of the kind of events the firm organises, there's a useful section devoted to the topic on its website.

Beyond your bog-standard golf days, there's been a paintball challenge (*"This isn't work, this is war!"*), an audience with *"Scud Stud"* Rageh Omar at the Cheltenham Literature Festival, a Nosh and Becks table football tournament, and as a *"half-term treat,"* a family day at the Slimbridge Wildfowl Centre. If the idea of putting children and birds together fills you with as much dread as the Hitchcock movie that combined the two, you might have preferred to take your chances in a light aircraft on the property department's flying day. Networking has even led to a strong relationship with an Estonian law firm and the government of that country.

We should confirm that concerning appraisals, feedback, working hours and the relatively relaxed dress code, our sources were very satisfied. They also gave their office the thumbs-up and said the single-floor, open-plan layout worked well for them. Partners, solicitors, trainees and secretaries sit together in teams (*"partners make secretaries coffee"*), and departments are demarcated by rows of filing cabinets, which lends an air of *"friendly rivalry."* This rivalry no doubt found voice at the annual summer jolly – school sports day-type races and a barbecue at a local country hotel.

And speaking of cheering loudly at the races, Cheltenham, of course, has its famous Gold Cup week, when the entire population of Ireland pitches up to gamble, win, lose and either way tip the town's waitresses ludicrous amounts of money. That's in March, but in December the firm always celebrates Christmas with a black-tie bash at the racecourse. On a more regular basis, local hostelry Jim Thompson's sees quite a lot of the staff. And it shall continue to see the 2004 qualifiers as all four of them stayed with the firm.

and finally...

BPE is undoubtedly a lively and rewarding firm to work for. However, you're going to have to earn your stripes on bulk work and accept a trainee starting salary that is no better than the Law Society's minimum (though it bounces up to a decent level for the region on qualification). We'll end with the words of one of our interviewees who, in spite of these caveats, told us: *"It would be hard to find a better place."*

Brabners Chaffe Street

the facts

Location: Liverpool, Preston, Manchester
Number of UK partners/assistants: 45/41
Total number of trainees: 17
Seats: 4x6 months
Alternative seats: None

Forming a triangle (we trust more golden than Bermudan), the Liverpool, Preston and Manchester offices of commercial firm Brabners Chaffe Street offer excellent training opportunities.

clean and jerk

Liverpool and Preston firm Brabners first set sail around 200 years ago. Since then it has managed to pick up a fair few lawyers along the way, not least a sizeable portion of Manchester partnership Chaffe Street after it disintegrated. The ship is captained from Liverpool, which has by far the largest office,

but it looks like the Manchester operation was well worth the investment in 2001. Having scooped up some of the city's best mid-market lawyers, Brabners has continued to pick up good people, most recently a property partner from Eversheds. As for the little Preston office, we were charmed by what it has to offer. But more of that later.

The firm subdivides itself into five main practice groups: corporate and commercial; employment; litigation; private client; and property. If you want a really comprehensive list of what each group actually does, we can do no better than direct you to Brabners' training brochure. Don't get sidetracked by all the pictures of sportsmen and women because you won't have to practice ballet in litigation, run relays in private client or lift really heavy weights in property. We're not entirely sure of the symbolism of the photos in the brochure – perhaps it's just a reminder of what you could have achieved if you'd kept going after that second BAGA award.

give me moor

Of the 17 trainees on board in 2004, ten were in Liverpool, two in Preston and five in Manchester. Wherever they worked (with the possible exception of Preston), all had followed the same four-seat training scheme. We didn't spot anyone who had moved offices after starting, though we're assured this is *"in the pipeline"* for the future. When we say that no seat is compulsory, what we mean is that you'll have no say in the first two and quite a lot of control over the second two. To refine this statement further, *"property is our biggest department in Liverpool and it tends to have two or three trainees, so it's odds-on you'll end up there in your first year."* For Manchester you can repeat this statement so long as you replace the word property with the word corporate.

In Liverpool property seats there is plenty of good work up for grabs as the firm has a list of cracking clients as long as your arm – JD Wetherspoon, several local authorities, Associated British Foods, NM Rothschild & Sons, Royal Bank of Scotland and

Edinburgh Woollen Mill to name but a few. One trainee who'd taken the high road straight into property told us the seat had given him *"a good grounding"* in commercial leasehold work and interesting encounters with agricultural and unregistered land for clients in Wales and the Lake District. If all that sounds a bit too John Craven for your liking, how about getting stuck into property work while on a secondment to the Mersey Docks and Harbour Authority.

A seat in the litigation department always goes down well because it's such a hands-on experience. You'll help out on the bigger cases being run by your supervisor or other members of the department (recently a human rights-angled House of Lords case involving the club Cream), but better still you'll take charge of a caseload of lower value matters for your supervisor. *"I ran them on a day-to-day basis with my partner there to bounce ideas off,"* said one trainee. *"Yes, I've done my fair share of disclosure and some bundling, but I've also done quite a few hearings – directions hearings and case management conferences – on both cases I've run by myself and agency matters. I've done everything from evicting squatters, drafting witness statements, statements of claim and serving writs."*

early retirement

Employment is a core part of the firm's business in both Liverpool and Manchester, and thankfully there are usually enough trainee seats to go around. If, by the time you get to this department, you already know whether or not you're a born litigator, you can ask for a balance of work that best matches your interests.

We were particularly impressed by reports of the Manchester corporate seat, which sees trainees sharing an office with a partner and becoming their right-hand (wo)man. *"You're not just given bits and bobs,"* we heard; *"you're working on deals from start to finish...On a typical deal there will be one partner, one fee earner and the trainee, and you'll be closest to the partner. I went to all the meetings (even if I had nothing to con-*

tribute) and I saw it all happen. I had an initial stab at all the documents, although when the partner got hold of them they would be changed radically!" As the department specialises in acting for owner-managed businesses, client contact is constant and you'll become familiar with the mindset of *"businessmen who have done well and perhaps are selling out before they retire."*

landed types and city types

In stark contrast to the national firms that dominate Manchester and encroach into Liverpool, Brabners still views private client work as a valuable element to its practice. Admittedly, in Manchester and Liverpool the clients have to be pretty wealthy to be able to afford the fees, but in Preston there is a steady flow of Joe Bloggs clients with whom a trainee can meet by themselves. When it comes to landed gentry types from Cumbria, busy professionals, celebs and the managing directors of the North West though, they're perfectly happy to just shadow a partner to a meeting and help them draft something nice and tax efficient.

It struck us that a trainee's workload depends not only on what matters become available, but also on the progress they've made in previous seats. One trainee confirmed: *"It definitely increased from the second seat onwards, when they had an idea of the work I was capable of."* Formal reviews take place at the end of each seat, but seeing as no one complained about being left in the dark over their performance, it just shows that the daily interaction between supervisor and trainee is close in almost all cases. It also struck us that despite talk of integration, trainee nights out and an annual conference to get all staff together, Brabners training is definitely an office-by-office affair. Manchester trainees and Liverpool trainees become wrapped up in their own cities and Preston trainees get used to a quieter life...even though Preston has been granted city status, something which is *"unbelievable for most people who live there!"* In September 2004, five of the eight qualifying trainees stayed with the firm.

eat, drink and be merry

It's quite easy to spot Brabners at a university law fair. Most firms have brochures and chocolates and pens on their stands, some even have umbrellas. Brabners always has a few boxes of wine. Some students just scuttle around picking up the brochures and confectionary before bolting for the nearest exit, but Brabners much prefers the people who'll accept a drink (you could ask for water) and stay for a chat – by and large, Brabners people are social animals. The firm *"wholeheartedly"* supports the TSGs in Manchester and Liverpool, and the trainees usually put themselves up for and get committee positions with the Mersey TSG. There's plenty to support claims that the firm is *"supportive of trainees generally"* and no one we spoke to sensed they were at the bottom of the heap or that there was a rigid hierarchy to contend with. *"One trainee golfs with one of the senior partners...even on the weekend."*

Close to the main Liverpool office (*"the client areas are pristine, but the rest could do with a lick of paint"*) Newz Bar pulls them in on a Friday night. Back in Manchester, the favourite haunt of the litigation and employment team is Piccolinos, which comes jampacked with *"famous football players, Corrie stars, luminaries from the Manchester music scene"* and, er, lawyers. Even on the annual firm-wide conference, only half the day is given over to the serious business of business; the rest is spent having a laugh. At the last conference there was a barbecue and an It's A Knockout contest where the games included human table football (with people hanging on bungee rope over the pitch), giant Twister and a competition to make a plasticine model of a partner. After that there was a live band, another big meal, a free bar and a bed for the night if people needed one. Which they probably did.

and finally...

In the past we've said Brabners Chaffe Street was growing into itself following its merger. We still think this is the case and don't expect any dramatic news from the firm any time soon – ideal if you like what you see right now.

Brachers

the facts

Location: Maidstone, London
Number of UK partners/assistants: 22/23
Total number of trainees: 10
Seats: 4x6 months
Alternative seats: occasionally Lille

Serving both commercial clients and private individuals, Maidstone-based Brachers also boasts a superb defendant healthcare practice, having maintained its prized position on the NHS Litigation Authority legal panel.

tunnel vision

Many trainees cite the healthcare team as the thing that drew them to Brachers so we'll start there. As well as the NHSLA, it advises 30 regional NHS trusts, primary care trusts and health authorities on issues spanning data protection, LIFT projects, pensions and employment law, and its superb clin neg team is ranked top in *Chambers UK* for its defence work. But there's more to Brachers than healthcare; the firm also has a first-class debt recovery team that acts for the biggest credit and charge card companies, and in coco it has *"a fairly good spread of clients from people starting their own tiny companies"* to companies with transactions up to the £3.5 million mark. The employment team, which bridges the Maidstone and smaller London office, acts for clients including the National Gallery, First Assist, Kimberly-Clark, and Eurotunnel...and all those NHS bodies.

The family, private client, property and agriculture departments are a strong reminder that Brachers is *"fairly traditional."* With its well-established Kentish client base, Brachers most likely *"will always have a traditional flavour,"* though this year our sources spoke of *"a palpable sense of it going through changes."* The arrival of a new corporate team in 2003 and the appointment of a new managing partner earlier this year has created *"a bubble of excitement."* Trainees said: *"We are modernising and becoming more up to date."* It seems there are plans afoot to consolidate, refocus and improve communication within the firm.

a place of your own

Training follows the common four-seat format, and *"when you first join the firm you say which two seats you would like to do."* The first seat is picked from those two and over the two-year period *"most trainees get their two preferences."* There are no compulsory seats though *"one assumption might be that property is essential, but then there are one or two people who haven't done it – it just tends to be one of the busier departments."* The new corporate team has already won trainees over, replacing employment as the favourite department. Here, trainees help out with business and share sales and purchases, and *"run all the company secretarial files."*

In the commercial property seat *"you have the most responsibility"* and your own caseload including *"the odd bit of residential conveyancing."* An employment seat may be undertaken in London or Maidstone and trainees get involved in such diverse matters as maternity rights and trade union disputes. Each year a second-year trainee also gets the opportunity to spend three months on secondment to a law firm in Lille. A coveted healthcare seat means research and client advice on staff harassment, mental health legislation, confidentiality and data protection issues. Responding to client needs here makes for *"instantaneous and quite high-pressured"* work – as one trainee explained, *"it's about trying to stop things becoming clinical negligence cases."* Despite its reputation, debt recovery is not a popular destination – *"one trainee was put there and asked to be moved after a few days!"*

Firm-wide, trainees described admirable levels of responsibility and, wherever possible, running their own files, undertaking small pieces of advocacy and *"being very much encouraged to liaise with clients directly."* The firm has taken on a number of legal execs, which has significantly reduced the amount of grunt work done by trainees. One admitted: *"I get told off if I try and do stuff myself,"* explaining that *"we are too valuable to do it, and are told to use the resources available."*

As most trainees have their own office or share with another trainee or legal exec, mid and end-of-seat appraisals with supervisors are key moments. *"Everyone is very affirmative and criticism is always constructive."* One source said: *"You never feel swamped and there is always someone to check on you,"* while another described feeling *"immersed yet supported."* The PSC is organised through Law South, a network of good firms, and in-house training is also on offer throughout the two years.

bunk up

As well as those who had been attracted to Brachers by its healthcare reputation (even if later they found something else they preferred), there are trainees who wanted *"a bigger part in smaller deals."* One chose the firm simply because of *"the atmosphere...and it was a lovely sunny day. Kent has great weather!"*

In Maidstone, Brachers occupies four buildings on London Road. Medway House is *"an old Victorian building with an extension at the back and a courtyard with benches and flowers."* It is home to the healthcare, family, civil lit and PI teams. It is also, from time to time home to a couple of trainees...literally. In the grounds, Brachers' cottage is up for grabs for stray trainees. As well as being *"a great starter place,"* the cottage is ideal for anyone who has trouble getting up in the morning as you can be at your desk in the time it takes Terry to do the 8 o'clock pips. Further up the road, Somerfield House is the main office. A *"lovely, yellowy, Kent stone building with a newer extension on the back,"* it houses private client, property and coco. Here, rather than a cosy cottage in the car park, we hear there is a nuclear bunker, inherited from previous owners The Royal Observer Corps. The bunker is allegedly haunted and is used by Brachers to store deeds and by the local fire brigade for training (though one source was pondering turning it into a nightclub). The Royal Observer Corps may have something to say about that – apparently if nuclear war breaks out *"we will be kicked out and they will move back in."* In London, nothing quite so exciting lurks behind the office on New Fetter Lane.

entertaining the troops

A quick surf on Brachers website will tell you all you could possibly want to know about life in Maidstone (including its one-way system) and a brief chat with a Brachers trainee will tell you even more. The West Kent TSG gets Brachers recruits out bowling and drinking in both Maidstone and Tunbridge Wells, while within the firm the Leeds Castle open air concert has become an annual fixture. This year, the event had a D-Day theme and was *"a bit like last night of the Proms"* with John Suchet, the Opera Babes and even a Hurricane fly-past, plus the requisite rendition of *Land of Hope and Glory*. The rest of the year, Hanrahan's up the road from the offices is a favourite haunt, and *"we usually end up in Strawberry Moon."* Pre-empting our wail of horror at this admission to poor taste, we were assured that *"the Maidstone one is a bit different to the London one."*

Also a bit different this year was the firm Christmas party, which saw Brachers bods join 1,000 like-minded souls for a haunted house party in a marquee that was *"decked out with spiders' webs, performers and professional spooky things."* Complete with ghost train and dodgems, the fancy dress bash saw the litigation team get into the spirit of things:*"There was one very impressive little devil and a ghost."* The firm's annual trip to France was replaced by a BBQ and disco this year, though the traditional weekly buffet lunch is still going strong. Perhaps reflecting the firm's desire to modernise and move on, *"the food is better than it used to be."*

and finally...

Brachers trainees are precise, thorough and thoughtful, and with no strong common theme in terms of their backgrounds or aspirations, we can only conclude that with regard to recruitment, *"it's a case of does the face fit?"* In september 2004 both qualifiers fitted the bill and stayed with the firm.

Bristows

the facts

Location: London
Number of UK partners/assistants: 29/58
Total number of trainees: 15
Seats: 3 or 6 months long
Alternative seats: Secondments
Extras: German classes

Pharmaceuticals, biotechnology, electronics, IT and telecommunications, consumer products, television: Bristows knows exactly the kind of client it wants to do business with. It is just as clear about the kind of trainee it wants to recruit.

the formula for success

See if you recognise yourself in this recollection from one of Bristows current trainee solicitors. *"I really enjoyed my science degree, but after a while I realised that I didn't want to spend my life in a lab."* At the core of Bristows' practice is top-grade patent litigation, and to feed its voracious appetite for professionals who possess dual qualifications in both law and scientific disciplines, the firm plunders the labs of leading universities. From Scotland to Oxford, students are tearing off their acid-burned white coats to take the Bristows shilling. We detected a strong preference for biochemists and microbiologists (surely only natural for a firm with an interest in biotechnology work), although Bristows also recruits physical scientists.

Law students do get a look-in (we think the firm would like to see more of them) and the odd arts or languages grad makes the grade, but as often as not they will have taken science subjects at A-level. Some four years after being recruited, the qualification decisions made by trainees are almost as predictable as their reasons for joining the firm. IP litigation is Bristows biggest department by far, and as well as offering the greatest number of trainee seats, it also absorbs the greatest number of qualifiers. Eight of the nine 2004 qualifers stayed with the firm, six of them going into IP.

patently clear

Every trainee will complete a full six months in IP litigation; by contrast, other seats can last for three or six months. Invariably, on entering the department they are assigned to assist on a couple of heavyweight pieces of patent litigation. Technical, valuable, long-running pieces of litigation, such as that relating to the Quickstep laminate flooring system and the drug Citalopram. In the latter, Bristows helped a subsidiary of Novartis to get its generic version of this antidepressant drug onto the market by defending two interim injunctions and eventually reaching a favourable settlement with the drug's original manufacturer. Said one trainee: "*It's kind of frustrating*" because the cases will invariably have started long before you arrive and "*you're not necessarily going to see the end.*" A "*read-in period*" is essential "*because there's a lot of technical information that passes between the parties and a lot of the cases involve experiments.*" After this you'll be expected to know what's going on – "*You have to be able to hit the ground running.*"

While partners try to gear tasks towards a trainee's background, so making the best use of their up-to-date technical know-how, there are always going to be spells of plodding through document administration and list maintenance. "*Of course, sometimes I felt like a grunt,*" one source admitted, "*but if there's a bundle to be done it's not going to be a three-year qualified doing it.*" These times are more than compensated for. Trainees are invited to sit in on all the meetings and phone conferences on cases and "*everyone is willing to listen to your point of view. Particularly when you are working in a smaller team, you are a real asset.*"

The other compulsory aspects to the training are three-month stints in the non-contentious commercial IP department, corporate and property. Servicing the ongoing contractual and licensing requirements of clients that "*tend to know us for IP litigation and use us for other things,*" trainees bob around the commercial IP department in the knowl-

edge that they have "*freedom to roam*" from their supervisor. Since the arrival of a new partner who's very IT-focused, there are more data protection and website-related instructions up for grabs.

time out

The existence of three-month property, commercial litigation, competition, corporate and employment seats (some of which elongate into six months) reflects the wider commercial environment. The firm even has a selection of clients that instruct these supporting departments quite independently of the IP practice, notably on property and employment matters.

The final twist to the training contract is a three-month secondment to the in-house legal department of a key client. These were defining months in the working lives of the trainees we interviewed: each had gained an unforgettable and valuable insight into the commercial imperatives of companies that keep the lights on in Bristows' Lincoln's Inn Fields offices. Time away also meant a taste of a different office environment. According to one trainee: "*It was quite a culture shock...completely dressed down and very relaxed.*" Which, naturally led us to ask about life in Lincoln's Inn.

hats off

The firm's name dates back to the mid-19th century when Ebenezer Bristow was a leading light in patents even before patent legislation was enacted. More than 150 years on and we can still smell a whiff of tradition about the place. Not that it adversely affects the general mood of the firm; it's more that old-school civility and formal dress codes ("*no ties skew-whiff*") have never been challenged. Said one trainee: "*It's old-school in terms of comfortable old pair of shoes not oppressive or restrictive; there are no barriers to liberal thinking. Everyone is incredibly polite and friendly; impeccably mannered. I like that and I like to think that's what clients want to see in their lawyers – professionalism and attention to detail.*" Indeed, the Bristows way of working is all about thoroughness and the pursuit of perfection. In patent work, it has to be that way. *"Extravagance doesn't wash here; it is intellect that is admired and respected."*

In IP lit in particular it's very much heads-down, get on with things, no winging it. The partners clearly impress trainees: *"They have to wear two hats,"* fully understanding the technical detail of cases – the actual cutting-edge science – while taking command of the litigation timetable and strategy. Essentially they need to draw on two separate skills sets...as well as managing client relationships and more junior members of staff.

new balls please

For partners, the demands of practice (and no doubt the wife and kids) don't leave an awful lot of time for nights out in the pub. That kind of activity is left to the younger staff, who spread their custom among several local hostelries on Friday nights. There's probably nothing to prevent a thirsty trainee from flitting between Bristows' five Georgian office buildings for different departmental drinks...apart from being labelled a gatecrasher that is. An annual black-tie ball unites all for an evening (and night) of glamour and glitz.

One thing that's worth pointing out (and worth noting by rivals) is the efficiency with which students' applications are processed. The firm stole the march on certain others who could have attracted its IP lit-oriented trainees simply because it was prompt in seeing applicants, offering vac schemes and issuing offers. It's also worth noting that a number of our sources had received attention from and done vac schemes at the magic circle and other big firms. The idea that *"quality of life would be a quantum leap better at Bristows"* swung it in all cases. No billing targets (the work alone dictates how long you stay in the office); a room with a fireplace and a view of Lincoln's Inn Fields (one interviewee treated us to the thwonk of tennis balls as he chatted away next to the grass courts); the knowledge that you are working with legal and scientific experts – Bristows serves aces.

and finally...

Frankly, it amazes us just how many training contract applications Bristows gets. Not because it doesn't warrant the attention, but because its scheme is so clearly suited to a particular breed of trainee. If you think you have the credentials to be a top-flight patent litigator, you absolutely must apply here...even if you subsequently choose to become a property lawyer.

Browne Jacobson LLP

the facts

Location: Nottingham, Birmingham, London
Number of UK partners/assistants: 49/95
Total number of trainees: 20
Seats: 4x6 months
Alternative seats: None

The recent expansion of Browne Jacobson's Birmingham office leaves us concluding that our subject firm is no longer content to be simply one of the 'big three' commercial practices in Nottingham. We wondered what was on the mind of this notable litigation player...

risky business

The simplest answer is litigation and lots of it. Acting for substantial insurance companies and a decent collection of general commercial clients, the firm divides its lawyers and trainee seats into four groups: property, business services, business and professional risk (BPR), and insurance and public risk (IPR). There are no compulsory seats for trainees, but we're told *"you'd have a job trying to do your training contract without doing insurance."*

IPR is a kaleidoscope of colour. Its orange team deals with employers' and public liability, including matters relating to public highways and road safety. The green team handles matters of an environmental nature. The red team deals with medical and educational negligence, as well as defending local authorities from personal injury claims. The yellow team specialises in motor claims, and the purple team defends clinical negligence actions brought against the NHS. And just as a kaleidoscope image transforms with a simple twist, in Birmingham the purple team has turned to blue and somewhere in the picture we spied indigo and violet teams. Don't be too alarmed if the arrangement leaves you cross-eyed with confusion, apparently many at the firm aren't overly sure about it all either.

What is beyond doubt is that the department's profile is first rate. BJ's place on the NHS Litigation Authority legal panel is a ringing endorsement of its abilities, and it is making inroads into the growing area of defending local authorities from 'failure to educate' cases, particularly those concerning responsibilities towards children with autism or dyslexia.

branching out

The profile of the commercial litigation team is boosted by the patronage of clients such as Express Dairies, Christian Dior, and Derby County and Nottingham Forest football clubs. Divided into general litigation, debt recovery and professional indemnity, trainees in the department are welcome to try their hand at each. *"There's a wide scope of work on offer, and you can go out and choose who you want to work with."* Some lawyers will handle contractual disputes; others will focus on defending claims against accountants, solicitors, financial advisors, brokers, surveyors, architects and engineers.

The business services department is ideal for anyone growing weary of a steady diet of litigation. The firm mainly acts for Midlands-based clients, although it also has high-street banks Barclays and Lloyds TSB on its books. A focus on management buyouts has been strengthened by the arrival from Hammonds of two private equity partners in Birmingham. The rise of the Birmingham office is a good indicator of the firm's future intentions. It suggests a broad-church business model and a refusal to sit back and rely on established insurance industry rela-

tionships. If you're wondering why the firm needed to go to Birmingham (and London) to do this, the answer is simple. The commercial opportunities in Nottingham are far fewer.

The property department boasts success in the retail sector (Louis Vuitton, Joseph, Fendi and Wilkinson), social housing (acting for over 25 housing associations) and the health, education and public sectors. The public services team, for example, recently advised De Montfort University on the disposal of its Scraptoft Campus site to a residential developer.

cool runnings

For the last couple of years, trainees have been *"heavily encouraged"* to do a seat in the London or Birmingham offices. Acknowledging that Birmingham seemed like *"a bit of an outpost"* at the moment, trainees sense the three offices are being brought closer together by an increasingly shared portfolio of work and clients. Birmingham offers seats in corporate, clinical negligence and PI, and there's potential for a hotly contested seat in employment. The single London seat is all things to all trainees, combining as it does both contentious and non-contentious work. As well as defending clinical negligence claims, you could find yourself working with the firm's French inward investment group, advising our nearest neighbours how to do business in the UK.

When working out who's getting which seat next, the trainee group likes to take control of the situation. *"We usually talk amongst ourselves, so we all know what seats people are going for. We tend to work it out beforehand and then tell the trainee principal."* When it comes to formal training, the firm takes a much firmer hand. *"I've got training coming out of my ears to be honest,"* one source revealed. *"The firm organises induction courses, as well as lunchtime sessions run by each department. We even got 'Working The Room' training, which involves tips on how to interrupt conversations to work your way into a group as well as videoing you to look at your body language."*

Outside these formal sessions you may need to be assertive in your dealings with your supervisor, particularly if you want extra feedback on your work. *"Supervisors vary to be honest, but usually there's as much help on hand as you want, so it's really up to you. The firm does expect you to get on with things."* The ability to getting on with things is a prerequisite for BJ trainees. As one advised: *"You have to make an effort to make yourself feel included. If you're outgoing you're okay; if you're otherwise you could feel a bit left out."* Proactivity is the best policy: prove your ability, put some effort in and it will pay dividends. *"In my very first seat, within three months I was running my own fast track case on my own, and I got to follow it through and sit behind counsel at the hearing."* Those who don't show vim and vigour could well find themselves left with the *"donkey work."* You have been told.

Whichever seats they'd done, trainees assured us *"your work does get noticed; it's not like you put in the hours and then it all just disappears."* But it's not all hard slog: *"They encourage you to talk to clients at social events. The best approach is to throw yourself into things. I've been out to play golf with clients, even though I was awful, and I've even been tobogganing."* How bizarre.

minor royalty

Our interviewees spoke highly of the firm's facilities (we don't mean the toilets, by the way) and seem, finally, to have worked out the floor plan. In years gone by we've heard from trainees who even after 18 months at the firm still got lost looking for the photocopier in the labyrinthine Nottingham office. Trainees usually sit with one of the equity partners, but occasionally have the privilege of their own office. Whether safety-pinned to a senior figure or left to their own devices, they buzzed with praise for the firm. *"We've got some truly excellent solicitors who are very good in their field,"* said one. *"It's quite inspirational to see how they take on new areas of law."* After hearing such adulation, it came as no surprise to learn that, having made it to Browne Jacobson, trainees are reluctant to leave on qualification. Lucky for them, in

September 2004 six of the ten did not need to.

On Friday nights it's almost compulsory to go to the Royal Children, a *"small, smoky, but welcoming"* pub opposite the Nottingham office. On a particularly jolly night, even the older partners have been known to head down to *"a scout hut full of sweaty darts players"* known as The Irish to continue the evening's festivities. Once a year the sports and social committee organises an 'It's a Knock Out' day out, at which lucky spectators can watch the head of the property department being rolled through a maze while dressed in a sumo suit. If that doesn't get a big enough laugh, how about half the employment department racing around in six pairs of Wellingtons strapped to planks of wood.

and finally...

If you've fallen in love with Nottingham, or you're seriously interested in litigation, Browne Jacobson is a hot bet. If you're willing to put the effort into your training you'll be rewarded with a healthy degree of control over the direction you want your traineeship to take.

Burges Salmon LLP

the facts

Location: Bristol
Number of UK partners/assistants: 56/151
Total number of trainees: 36
Seats: 6x4 months
Alternative seats: Secondments
Extras: Pro bono – Bristol University Law Clinic, Bristol Neurological Unit, Drug Addiction & Recovery Agency, Bristol & Avon Enterprise Agency

Beyond the smoggy shark pool of City law, Burges Salmon stands fin and scale above South West competitors. With over 75% of work coming from outside the region, the firm is no mere smear smolt. Top clients, top work, and a Cityesque atmosphere: come on in, the water's lovely...

taste the difference

Burges Salmon finds itself in the enviable position of being labelled a regional Macfarlanes. A quick glance at a client roster to make most competitors weep explains the comparison with one of London's 'golden circle' of high-profit firms. BS, like Macfarlanes, takes on a scale and quality of work seemingly beyond its size or capabilities. In 2003, it completed one of its largest ever deals, a £2.5 billion PFI project for the MoD relating to military satellite communications. In terms of well-known clients, EMI Group, English Heritage, CompuServe, Reuters, Orange, Honda and Coca-Cola all recognise that BS possesses the intellectual capital to tackle transactions they might normally reserve for bigger City outfits. Yet, for all this undoubted quality, we must point out that BS isn't securing the most prestigious and most valuable international transactions. Perhaps you could look at it this way: if the magic circle firms represent highly profitable factory farming, then BS hand rears top-quality free-range produce.

Historically, the agriculture work has been one of the firm's strongest suits, and whilst perhaps now strategically superseded by the corporate practice, agricultural concerns continue to form part of the bedrock of the firm's success. With a well-established list of clients ranging from farmers' co-operatives to the landed gentry, trainees wondered if it might represent the more cloistered "conservative" side of the firm, but reflected that "although reasonably self-contained, it does seem to filter well into other areas." We figured they were right when we noticed that the corporate department recently worked on the restructuring of several dairy co-operatives and the acquisition of a UK grain procurement business. You can take the firm out of the farm...

But fear not, the choice isn't just between wellies or brogues. If neither of these options are your cup of tea, the firm has nationally (in some cases internationally) recognised family, private client and environment departments, to name just a moo...so sorry, few.

bristol fashion

Whilst traditional Bristol rival Osborne Clarke has scattered its seed far and wide, opening offices in Reading, London and Europe with mixed results, BS has been content to till the homestead. Bristol is and will remain the firm's only site, and whilst pressures of expansion dictate a move to new premises by 2010, the postcode will remain BS1. Okay, there is a London outpost, but it's just a place to host meetings with those big city clients. Essentially, a day trip there is *"just like being in the Bristol office; everything is networked and the decor is themed."*

The significance of unity in a single location is dual. First, BS partners are confident enough to bank on national work and clients from outside Bristol coming to them, and given that lawyers recently advised on acquisitions in Glasgow, rail franchises across Yorkshire and assisted overseas private clients investing in the UK, that confidence seems well placed. Second, the firm's cohesive, clear and defined sense of self is due in no small part to its location in and deep affiliation with Bristol. Said one trainee: *"The firm is proud of being in Bristol; it doesn't apologise for not being in London,"* adding that *"it wouldn't be the same firm without everyone under one roof."* When we asked more about the firm's sense of self, the replies all followed a theme: *"quality," "right and proper," "serious and competent," "nothing skimped on," "switched on and diligent."* Propriety even finds its way onto the firm's famous pink stationery: it defers to tradition and has a vague air of the old school about it, but at the same time it is quirky, distinctive and beloved by clients and staff alike. Said one trainee: *"It's just one of the things that makes Burges Salmon, Burges Salmon."*

pic 'n' mix

BS trainees should be compared to children in a sweet shop. Do they go for the sherbet dibdabs or strawberry liquorice laces? The flying saucers or the white mice? Oh the agony of choice! Why the comparison? Simple – the firm offers them six seats of four months each, making for a potentially diffuse training. But like any good parent the firm tempers freedom with discipline. Three seats are compulsory: company/commercial, property, APLE (agriculture/property lit/environment). Trainees may then choose between either employment and pensions or tax and trusts. Once these four seats have been completed, the fifth seat is a free choice, and the sixth and final seat is taken in the area in which the trainee hopes to qualify.

Trainees generally applaud the system, believing its advantages outweigh its disadvantages – "*Four months is enough time,*" concluded one. "*You gain enough experience of an area to know whether it's for you.*" Within all this seat hopping, there is room to manoeuvre – "*You can add seats together, focus on one area, or go for a more balanced approach, then throw in a wild-card seat.*" Not for nothing did one trainee describe it as "*a mosaic of a training.*" Another source reflected: "*I think we gain a lot more than the firm does from the six-seat system.*" Yet this tried-and-tested formula pays off in spades; NQ retention is always very high and 2004 was no different, with all 19 staying at the firm.

we know what you did last summer

Sailing is just one of the many, many, many activities that a Bristol location makes possible. And trainees take full advantage of their surrounds: there are more clubs and teams than you can reasonably shake a stick at (though no one mentioned kabadi) and if you don't play a sport before you go, you soon will. With sailing for example, whether you're a novice or an old sea dog, you'll find lessons and competition to suit. The emphasis is definitely on everyone mucking in together, which is exactly what trainees did last summer. With the age-old excuse of charity as motivation, 20 of them attended a survival camp in Wales for an "*epic, mud-pit-assault-course-24-hour survival thing.*" What's more, they spent the entire time dressed as pigs. Truly bizarre.

From the meticulous and worthy to the witty and cynical, the trainees we encountered this year were all different. Alongside fresh law graduates there's an ex-theatre designer, an ex-armed serviceman and an ex-police officer...and a random ex-entrepreneur! They are united by the appeal of Bristol and demonstrate a commitment to the South West.

At the beginning of the two years, trainees spend a week together on a residential version of the PSC, which kicks off a fast-paced social scene. As one breathless trainee enthused: "*The first six months were so hectic, we'd be out all the time; we've had to slow down a bit now, but it's still busy.*" It's bars a-go-go close to BS's prime harbour-front location, and Bristol city centre is but a step away. Trainees chant the mantra of "*quality of life*" in unison, but when you end your 8.30am-6pm working day with a "*pleasant 15-minute walk home along the river with ducks and everything*" why the heck not?

and finally...

Burges Salmon is less Oo-arrrr and more Go Far. If you want a fantastic quality of work, some tasty clients and a broad training without the hours, hangups and filth of London, then it's perfect. Just remember: the firm isn't reliant on magic circle rejects so make it your first choice and prepare your application well. Any old BS just won't do.

Cadwalader Wickersham & Taft LLP

the facts

Location: London
Number of UK partners/assistants: 11/54
Total number of trainees: 12
Seats: 4x6 month seats
Alternative seats: Occasional secondments

As one of the oldest continuing US law practices, Cadwalader Wickersham & Taft is a venerable firm eager to trumpet its close involvement in the socio-economic and political changes that have shaped America. But a thriving London office is just one of the signs that old and proud doesn't mean behind the times...

american history

Wall Street was just a thoroughfare linking the East River with the Hudson and George Washington was busy not telling lies in order to getting re-elected when John Wells set up his lower Manhattan practice in 1792. Plenty has changed in the intervening 200 years, but Cadwalader has travelled the long road, adapting to and even shaping the evolving needs of US business, and enjoying a plum view of history along the way. Rockefeller, Vanderbilt and Carnegie came and went, newfangled tomfoolery like telephones and typewriters became the norm, there was the small matter of the Great Depression, and in 1930 partners acted on a copyright infringement suit involving *Gone with the Wind*. In brief, this firm is a veritable aristocrat amongst US law firms and has its political and commercial bases covered with offices in Washington DC and Charlotte. It may not top the profits tables, but when corporate, financial restructuring or capital markets plaudits are being bandied around, Cadwaladers is never far from mind.

Like many other yankee outfits, Cadwalader made a move into the UK in the late 90s. However, unlike many of those upstart rivals, the 1997 opening of a London office didn't signal the development of an international network or a dramatic break with tradition. Trainees took up the story, telling us: *"The move was about accessing capital markets in the UK and Europe." "The office has been built up by mirroring traditional US strengths, not wanting to be a one-stop-shop for clients."* If the firm was *"cautious about quick change – it apparently took a while for London to be on the letterhead"* – then perhaps it is understandable. It's often said that if the history of the world were a day, mankind would have existed for only the last 30 seconds. By a similar reckoning, London is a Cadwalader toddler.

Mirroring US expertise, London has a strong financial restructuring group, which is headed up by managing partner Andrew Wilkinson. Recently it advised the Ad Hoc Committee of British Energy bondholders in the cancellation of £408 million of guaranteed bonds in favour of new shares, and the bondholders of TXU Europe, who accounted for £1.9 billion of creditor claims. Capital Markets is another strength and here the firm represented Deutsche Bank London in its first UK commercial mortgage-backed securities transaction and Ambac Assurance UK in connection with a €600 million CDO.

The London practice has additionally met with success in projects, often energy-flavoured transactions such as the $23 million financing of the Galata Gas Project in Bulgaria and the $1.2 billion Mozambique–South Africa natural gas pipeline project, on which it acted for the lending consortium.

chest patting

Despite the cross-Atlantic similarities, trainees told us that they *"feel part of a UK firm that is connected to a US network."* Our sources did admit one thing – *"Our public image is that of an aggressive firm, but that's a mis-applied, general US tag coupled with the fact that the bondholder clients we often represent are seen as aggressive vultures."* They assured us that day-to-day office life is *"sophisticated and exacting, but people don't walk around beating their chests...there's no machismo in the hallways."* A restrained atmosphere coupled with *"the smaller, more intimate office size"* and the *"really very high salaries"* were what attracted our high-rolling sources to Cadwalader over the magic circle alternatives. *"I thought I'd get a higher level of responsibility and more detailed involvement in the work than elsewhere,"* said one, *"and so it has proved."*

Trainees say that, generally, *"you feel part of a team and work is allocated within the team, not just drip fed to you."* Close acquaintance with a transaction or case can sometimes come at the cost of autonomy and lead to research and document management tasks; at other times *"your assignments are hived off from larger* matters." One trainee told us about one of his high points: "*I prepared a detailed section of an advice to a client that took a month, but it affected the client's actions.*" In essence, "*you play a key part rather than waiting patiently for people to drop a few crumbs.*"

"*Really feeling involved in what you're doing*" is common across the office, and "*there are no dramatic differences between departments.*" Except sartorial ones. "*The exact definition of shirt and tie does seem to vary between departments – it's most relaxed in projects.*" Starched stiff or non-iron casual, trainees can choose their four six-month seats freely from financial restructuring, litigation, project finance, banking, corporate/M&A, capital markets and tax, though given the firm's strengths "*most trainees do end up in financial restructuring.*" No international network means no exotic overseas seats, and there isn't even a humdrum Stateside swoop on offer. If you get the urge to leave the office, the occasional client secondment must suffice. Interestingly, we heard that "*day to day the average trainee doesn't have a massive amount of interaction with the other offices; you tend to focus on your department.*"

independence day

Although sitting with supervisors and enjoying both mid and end-of-seat reviews and "*not infrequent drinks out to discuss progress,*" we got the impression that Cadwalader would best suit those with a certain independence of spirit. Our sources agreed, adding that "*ambition is a key factor. Everyone is very driven, capable and resourceful.*" But City slickers beware: "*There are no young pinstripes here!*"

We were told about keen efforts to establish a trainee forum this year "*to help improve the training contract.*" Trainees sounded pleasantly surprised at the swift response to some of their queries: "*We suggested that more should be done to make the buddy system more active and it happened almost immediately.*" On qualification four of the six qualifiers stayed with the firm in 2004. Said one, just a few weeks before the big day: "*Obviously the short-term goal is qualification, but five*

years down the line I see myself at the firm progressing through the PQE and getting more and more involved."

The firm occupies the top three-and-a-half floors of a "*pretty much brand-new, state-of-the-art building*" on the Strand. There's no canteen, but the kitchens on each floor offer a nice touch – "*freezers with food in and microwaves for cooking.*" Perfect for late night munchies, although not needed too often apparently as "*the average is 9am-7.30pm and staying until 11pm is not uncommon, but all-nighters are rare.*" The small size of the office is also a plus when it comes to socialising and an active social committee ensures "*there are lots of instances when the firm as a whole goes out.*" Events include a summer djs-and-posh-frocks bash, paintballing, drinks in any one of a number of local pubs, and the self-explanatory 'Curryaoke.'

and finally...

If sophisticated billion-dollar deals and the world of bondholders and capital markets are your bag, Cadwalader's relative fledgling of a London office is a canny choice. Especially if you value your independence and flinch at the idea of being a foot soldier in a trainee army.

Capital Law

the facts

Location: Cardiff, Birmingham, Southampton
Number of UK partners/assistants: 21/22
Total number of trainees: 4
Seats: 4x6 months
Alternative Seats: None

Formerly known as Palser Grossman, this expanding Cardiff Bay firm is doing much to shake off its image as a predominantly defendant insurance litigation practice. Commercial litigation, property, employment and corporate are all growth areas, thanks in no small part to the ongoing regeneration of Cardiff, and particularly the Bay.

horses for courses

The clients that have helped Capital Law develop include International Greetings, Zurich, Bridgend Council, Cardiff Magistrates Court, Clerical Medical and Persimmon. Its corporate team acts for small to medium-sized companies and entrepreneurial investors in manufacturing and technology, and the commercial litigation team acted recently for a rugby club in its dispute with the Welsh Rugby Union following its reorganisation. A cracking property team has handled some pretty big business, such as Associated British Ports' £33 million sale of assets and shares in the £100 million Cardiff Bay Partnership, and the Penarth Heights redevelopment, one of the top residential schemes in Wales.

Although defendant PI (employer's and public liability, motor and MIB claims) still accounts for a significant amount of the Capital Law's work, it is no longer the firm's policy to march trainees into the department – a decision our sources saw as reflective of its expansion. Traineeship has a more commercial focus, with seats available in property, litigation, corporate and employment. The firm is generally good at accommodating individual tastes and will "*channel you in the direction that suits your talents best.*" As one trainee told us: "*I thought that all I wanted to do was litigate, but it turned out that I had a flair for the corporate work, and so that is where I have spent a lot of my time.*" The one criticism we found was that, when it came to allocating seats, some trainees did not hear where they were headed until the last minute.

With the exception of commercial litigation, in which trainees tend to sit with a senior associate, partners supervise all seats. Everyone accepts their share of run-of-the-mill or mundane trainee tasks because of the opportunities to get involved in interesting work. Though you won't be left to your own devices entirely, some trainees reported running their own cases from start to finish. Those who'd done commercial property seats were consistently enthusiastic: "*I found that I got quite a lot of client contact. I was working alongside fee earners for a couple of major clients in big development projects, and you can see that the client is getting a feeling for your work as well.*" In larger corporate transactions much of a trainee's work is "*behind the scenes,*" but from time to time they also get an official name check as an assistant on a deal, which is always good to bring up in that weekly phone call to mum.

who let the dogs out?

Capital Law is certainly not as big as Cardiff rivals Eversheds or Morgan Cole, but then nor does it want to be. Trainees prefer being in an environment where "*you don't just become another pair of hands.*" That's not to say that Capital Law isn't prepared to fight its corner with the top firms – on the whole, it is seen as quite tenacious. As one trainee put it: "*We're like little terrier dogs who are as aggressive as the big dogs, but even better in the ring.*" But you've also got to think Andrex puppy rather than clapped out old mongrel, as the firm is "*young, fresh-faced and energetic.*" To use the words of one trainee, "*you cannot swim against the tide; you've got to be fully engaged and fully committed. If you are like that and up to scratch, you will inevitably further your career.*" If you fear this may be a cliquey place, stop now because "*it doesn't matter who you are mates with, it's the quality of your work that they care about.*"

Trainees all agreed their firm offered an environment in which "*you are valued for being able to speak your mind,*" and that they would feel quite happy "*arguing their case with one of the equity partners.*" The applicants who do well here are, surprise surprise, the "*ambitious and hardworking*" ones ("*the marks of a good trainee are creative thinking and picking up the file and just doing the next thing*"), but you'll also need to show some kind of commitment to the locality. That's not to say you have to be especially Welsh – one of the current trainees comes from Belarus. Both of those who qualified in 2004 remain with the firm.

carry on camping

Make no mistake, a training contract here will be a hard slog. The hours vary from department to department, but it's not unusual to start your day at

8am and finish at around 7pm when things are busy. By the same token, *"they're pretty flexible if they know that you've worked hard on a deal."*

Socially, Capital Law is alive and kicking. When we spoke to them, trainees had just got back from a camping weekend at the Brecon Jazz Festival, and had not long ago completed the Ty Hafan Hospice Three Peaks Challenge. If the great outdoors is your idea of hell, fear not: there is a bistro under the office, and as if things could get any better, it's owned by four of the firm's partners. Expect mates' rates at dinner and regular happy hours. The banoffee pie comes recommended! Around Cardiff Bay, there are plenty of walks to compensate for all that pie: *"We're surrounded by water, so you can go duck watching...it's a fantastic location!"* If you were wondering about the Birmingham and Southampton branches, for now no trainee seats are available in these smaller offices, which handle PI work.

and finally...

Like a breath of fresh sea air off the bay, Capital Law should reinvigorate anyone after a year at law school.

Capsticks

the facts

Location: London
Number of UK partners/assistants: 29/45
Total number of trainees: 11
Seats: 6x4 months
Alternative seats: Secondments
Extras: Pro bono – Putney Law Centre

We've said it before and we'll say it again: the Capsticks name is synonymous with first-class healthcare law and clinical negligence.

cutting edge

Capsticks has been crowned the leader for healthcare and defendant clinical negligence work, and it's easy to see why. The firm acts for around 200 NHS trusts, primary healthcare trusts (PCTs), BUPA and many other healthcare organisations. Clinical law at Capsticks is split between classic clin neg defence and clinical advisory work. On the advisory side, the firm gets to grips with everything from primary care regulation and data protection issues through to *"people wanting to take bits of their relatives home."* Recent matters have been as diverse as claims against NHS trusts for failing to recognise and handle complications during childbirth, and injuries sustained by a patient while absconding hospital. One trainee assured us: *"There is very little to worry about, if you're squeamish,"* though we found it easier to believe that *"some notes are fairly gory."* Teams advise on mental health, patient safety and child protection matters, but clinical work is *"what the firm is really famous for."*

The beauty of a firm that is committed to its cause is that *"you get to be at the forefront – you aren't divorced from the cutting edge of the business."* This firm's business is very definitely the NHS, and the trainees we spoke to could see how the relationship colours the firm's approach. *"The letters you write and the language you use are all very to the point."* More than that, one interviewee explained how *"friends in the City are always wining and dining clients; you can't do that in the NHS, the managerial side is very aware it shouldn't be seen to be too close to the people they are paying."* While the NHS may not provide trainees with unlimited opportunities to flex the corporate credit card, it does provide superb work in abundance.

Our sources were keen to point out the existence of *"other sides to Capsticks,"* and interestingly, they indicated that *"the firm is looking to broaden out and diversify a bit...into charities and stuff."* For now, at least, you can spot a public sector *"thread"* running through practically all of its work. Employment here is *"very much tied to the NHS,"* which turns out to be the biggest employer in Europe. Similarly, as a huge landowner, the NHS provides the property and commercial teams with LIFT projects in abundance – one trainee enthused about site visits, saying: *"You can actually see the hospital that is going to be built."*

doing the rounds

On your first day at Capsticks *"you arrive and are plonked in a seat."* The final seat tends to see trainees where they are going to qualify, but between the first and last *"they try and line up what you will get with what you want to get."* Six four-month seats mean plenty of opportunities. Though not strictly compulsory, trainees say *"you'll do clinical law."* Certainly all those we spoke to had been more than happy to don scrubs. One told us: *"A lot of people come here thinking they want to do clin neg, and then see the other seats and think maybe not. That's not a black mark against clin neg, but more a positive one for the others."* While clinical advisory work is popular for the *"juicy"* work, *"it does put you off ever going to hospital...or having a baby."*

It's not all white coats and antibacterial hand-wash – some trainees find their niche in the general dispute resolution seat, and employment is viewed as *"a hot and sexy subject."* One bold source even went as far as to say: *"Property rules!"* In each of these seats, the prospect of greater responsibility appealed because, as another pointed out: *"It is harder to get your own files in clin neg: million-pound baby brain-damage cases will not be given to a trainee."* In property, trainee tasks include researching titles and attending project meetings. In employment, trainees work largely on contentious matters and enjoy *"dealing with a lot of people and getting out of the office."* A steady diet of witness statements, tribunals and unfair dismissals were livened up by HC 99 Enquiries – the process through which a PCT must go in order to strike off a practitioner. Dispute resolution is *"a real mixed bag"* and quite literally *"can entail anything involving litigation."* Squatters rights and possession cases fall alongside planning appeals, with trainees describing *"getting people out of NHS property when they shouldn't be there."* A seat here also brings everything from *"defamation to zero tolerance policies in the NHS and difficult patients."*

hospital visits

A number of our interviewees had been on secondment one or two days a week to a local PCT within a clinical seat. Described by one as *"an honour,"* a secondment means *"you get a good idea of what it's like on the ground, and you get to do things rather than just advise."*

Across the board, *"you're doing substantive tasks."* Trainees accompany supervisors to client meetings, take witness statements, attend conferences with counsel and *"there are often opportunities to do advocacy in the county court."* An advocacy course and further regular training sessions ensure they are *"trained in the Capsticks way."* Inevitably, there is *"occasionally dull work,"* but *"it always goes away after a while."* We came across the odd instance of after-dark bundling, but on the whole *"you feel very valued."* More than that, sources enthused that *"they hand hold you all the way."* End-of-seat appraisals are taken more seriously than those administered mid-seat, because on a day-by-day basis *"it's more likely you would just turn around and ask your supervisor for feedback."* Trainees generally share an office with their supervisor, but receive work from all quarters; we even heard that between trainees *"it's not a case of 'This is mine, this is yours' – trainees all talk a lot and work together, which takes a lot of the pressure off."*

cherchez le cube

"The firm advertises itself as a place where you can leave at 5.30pm and have a laugh. That's not so accurate in commercial departments, but in clinical departments it is 100% accurate." A little bird whispered: *"By 5.30pm they are all playing practical jokes."* Property and commercial were frantic with LIFT projects when we called, but even so, we struggled to find anyone who was working nights and a 9.30am-6pm day was standard.

For our sources, such civilised hours were a real draw, as was the Putney location. Capsticks sits near the Thames not far from the end of the District Line, probably in part due to the fact that *"Mr Capstick is a west Londoner."* The office building wins no hearts: *"It is a 1970s office block and there is no disguising it."*

Last year we reported on the appearance of an enormous red plastic cube in the reception area. This year we were dismayed to hear that *"the red cube has mysteriously disappeared...the foyer is bare."* Panic over: the cube has moved upstairs because *"it was right in the way of people coming in and out."* Our quest to uncover its meaning remains just that as the most helpful comment we got was: *"It's symbolic...of something...ask the marketing people."* The office's only other notable feature is its lack of air con, which each summer provides the perfect excuse to ditch the suit and tie and slip into *"shorts and t-shirts."* At the end of the week, nearby bar Le Piaf remains the most-frequented watering hole despite being *"a bit of a dive."* It had better watch out as the new Putney Station is winning favour even though it is pricier.

Delve into the past lives of trainees and you will most likely uncover a previous career in healthcare or the public sector or, failing this, a degree in medicine or sciences. Even if the only link is a distant second cousin who once wanted to be a brain surgeon, all our sources had some prior interest in healthcare. They told us that *"working in healthcare and the public sector is more human and interesting, and you don't get so much lawyer guilt as you would if you were working for a big corporation."* All our interviewees were *"reasonably confident people"* and *"outgoing, lively, friendly...and short!"* We cannot vouch for the latter, but we did sense a real commitment to the firm and colleagues. A self-confessed *"really close-knit firm"* with a *"family-friendly"* feel, we were left wondering if Capsticks also offers courses in pillow plumping and bedside manners. Our congratulations to the trainee who will be swapping her white coat for a white dress next year when she marries a colleague. Three of the five 2004 qualifiers will be around to throw rice at the happy couple.

and finally...

Our diagnosis is simple: if you want high-quality clinical work or to build hospitals, you should hotfoot it over to SW15.

Charles Russell

the facts

Location: London, Guildford, Cheltenham
Number of UK partners/assistants: 86/113
Total number of trainees: 25
Seats: 4x6 months (Lon), 6x4 (G&C)
Alternative seats: Secondments
Extras: Pro bono – Bethnal Green Law Centre

A mid-sized general practice firm, Charles Russell has a middle-of-the-road appearance, which belies a well-chosen route that mixes fast-moving highways with scenic byways.

stand off

In the client reception area of CR's London HQ an oil-on-canvas Mr Russell eyeballs a plasma image of Sky News' Martin Stanford. In a firm where private client is as highly prized as telecommunications, this virtual staring match is par for the course. At least it's a friendly game not a straight fight to the death, and with both faces of the firm looking healthy and growing larger the match looks set to end in a draw.

Across its three offices in London, Guildford and Cheltenham, 70% of Charles Russell's practice is commercial, covering key areas of property, employment, corporate finance and insolvency, plus more niche areas such as media, telecommunications, sports and IP. The remaining 30% is geared towards private individuals and covers trusts and probate, rural affairs and family. Thoroughly respected private client and family teams act for high net worth individuals on multimillion-pound trust structures, settlements and some children's matters, but also *"quite a lot of people who don't necessarily have that much money."* Earlier in 2003 Stephenson Harwood's entire private client contingent joined CR, boosting the team by 20%.

boy racers and sunday drivers

It's swings and roundabouts though, as unfortunately the firm lost two of its top media lawyers in late 2003 when they left to set up their own firm. They also took some snazzy clients including magazines *Red* and *Hello!* with them. Our sources assured us: *"The firm is trying to build media up again,"* and indeed it is still handling matters for film producers, financiers and ITN. Moreover, if big names win medals in your mind, the sports team acts for Audley Harrison, Lennox Lewis and Martin Johnson, as well as the Jockey Club, Holmes Place, Channel 5 and Vodafone. Over in the telecommunications team the top clients are Cable & Wireless and ntl.

So, whether you prefer your surroundings to be oak panelled or screened in interactive technicolour, Charles Russell can cater for your tastes...which is precisely why most of our sources had opted for the firm in the first place. For everyone who said: *"I'm not a private client person,"* someone else would pipe up: *"The firm fulfils my slightly less commercial desires."* This 'please everyone all of the time' winning combination seems to have stood the test of time. As have many other aspects of the firm: as one source summed up – *"We are a modern firm, although we have been around for some time...you do have a sense of its tradition."*

central reservation

Whichever side you prefer, across the board great work is guaranteed. No seats are compulsory, and between them our sources described varied, wide-ranging and tailored contracts. The success of the standard four-seat training system in London is underpinned by astounding flexibility that saw all our sources cutting seats short, extending others, returning to favourite departments and shooting off on secondments. In Guildford and Cheltenham the same flexibility attaches to a six-seat system. Giving trainees a lot of leeway enables them to look both ways before crossing the road to qualification, something welcomed by the interviewee who admitted: *"I was convinced I wanted to do family law, but a corporate seat changed everything!"* The system is simple –

"everyone gives their first and second preference and they jiggle everyone about."

Due the size of deals in corporate, *"work comes into partners and gets delegated down."* The trainee's lot is to draft ancillary documentation and prepare due diligence reports. One source conceded: *"I was effectively running the due diligence – normally it is relatively tedious, but in spite of the paper shuffling it has been enjoyable."* The litigation department breaks down into a number of smaller groups and *"you are assigned to a group for your seat."* The options include communications, IT, commercial, insurance & reinsurance, medical negligence and contentious trusts and probate. Here, *"if there's a small matter you get to run your own file"* on which *"you do all the basic things"* such as drafting defences or claim forms and attending court. Naturally there is less independence when assisting seniors on larger cases.

It's much the same story on the private client side of the street. Here, trainees proudly announced: *"You are in charge!"* In family, for example, *"if it is a relatively small case or the client doesn't have much money you could end up virtually running the file."* Trainees described abundant client contact and plenty of court work.

The opportunity to go on a three-month secondment to Cable & Wireless or a government agency client had been taken up by several of our sources, all of whom appreciated the experience.

a wing and a prayer

CR only takes a handful of trainees each year and our sources appreciated the sense of identity this gave them, telling us: *"You feel like your opinion counts."* More than that, *"a conscious effort is made"* to keep them in the loop – one even remarked: *"I am quite surprised at how much we are kept informed."* When it comes to their own progress, trainees are given an informal mid-seat appraisal and a more thorough end-of-seat review. While trainees pondered that *"the firm's standards are quite high"* and *"quite a lot is expected of you,"* they were quick to note that *"the peo-*

ple you sit with are chosen quite carefully" and "they show you the right direction and encourage you to take on your own files."

The downside of being part of a small intake is that "we don't have the support of hundreds of paralegals" and "the buck stops with the trainees pretty much. There's nobody below you to delegate to." Yet it sounds as if trainees are seen as key team members – one confided: "I actually can't believe the responsibility I am given sometimes." Undaunted, one said: "It is challenging and the days fly by."

The London office on New Fetter Lane is a 1970s hexagonal creation that is "getting a bit on the crusty side." Aside from the eighth-floor client area being "quite traditional, almost bookish" with "a few portraits of old people, wood panelling and leather-bound volumes," the rest of the building retains an air of modernity and normality. No weird art or water features here. Exciting corporate facilities run no further than showers and "a room with a bed in it, if you are ever feeling ill." We have previously reported that the building used to belong to Robert Maxwell and, sensing our nose for intrigue, trainees were quick to conjure up some gossip. "People say there are bugs in the rooms" and that Maxwell's rooftop helipad was never granted planning permission, so the helicopters were only permitted to hover low enough for Mr Maxwell to jump off. An urban myth that benefits from the circumstances of his death, we suspect...yet, the bit about the bugs was certainly widely rumoured back then, so who knows!

the casting couch

A diverse range of work and clients calls for a diverse range of employees and at CR "there is no list of tick boxes." The firm's training contract application form has included the question 'Which film role would you most like to play and why?' We established that current recruits include Blanche Dubois, Watership Down's Fiver, and Indiana Jones. The point? "They want to wheedle out the Erin Brokoviches early on!" Despite this unlikely casting, the group melds and

"there is quite a community within the firm." As well as a recent weekend away together at Longleat Center Parcs, we heard of "quite a lot of inter-office relationships." Cricket, football, rugby, netball and softball are all on offer for the loveless, and the local pub is The White Swan for anyone needing to cry into the beer and swear off men/women. Occasionally the trainees stray further and "go up to Old Street if we're feeling adventurous." The dress code, by the way, is suits Monday to Thursday, with dress-down on Fridays and throughout August.

c. russellureus

The small Cheltenham office can accommodate one trainee with a taste for civilised town life and a penchant for horseracing (you know who you are). We didn't chat to anyone in Cheltenham this year but it sounds like a sweet deal from what we can tell. Guildford trainees find the first year of their training is "pre-planned – commercial litigation, property litigation and employment/PI. The second year is then a choice from whatever is left in the office." That would be coco, private client, family, residential conveyancing and real estate. The Guildford office is "five minutes from the town centre, so quite leafy and near the river." A smaller group of trainees enjoys its own social life, playing badminton, football and cricket and attending quarterly events organised by Surrey Law Society. Trainees in both Guildford and Cheltenham are kept in touch with their London counterparts through video-linked training sessions, and also the annual firm-wide summer ball, which this year took place at the Chelsea Physic Garden. In September 2004, nine of the 13 qualifiers came up smelling of roses and agreed to further graft for the firm.

and finally...

If keeping your options open is a priority, Charles Russell offers superb private client work and a broad and strong commercial practice to boot. Start perusing your DVD collection for inspiration.

Clarks

the facts

Location: Reading, London
Number of UK partners/assistants: 16/38
Total number of trainees: 4
Seats: 4x6 months
Alternative seats: None

Reading firm Clarks has packed up, moved home and repainted since we last visited two years ago. And the pile on the welcome mat is as thick as ever...

start rite

Clarks offers trainees a solid introduction to legal life through a four-seat training that spans its core business areas of litigation, employment, corporate and commercial property. Typically trainees work in each area, though "*if you specifically ask for a seat at a specific time they will do their best to get you there.*" Within these four areas, there is further choice – one trainee, reluctant to do straight corporate work, was given an environmental caseload instead; another secured a heavy construction bias to their litigation seat.

The litigation department allows trainees to "*stand on their own two feet*" as they take control of a portfolio of debt recovery files. In property they blend commercial transactions with a little residential conveyancing and tell us: "*You are supervised, but given the responsibility of an assistant. You basically organise yourself and decide what to do next.*" Unwilling to be left behind in the approval ratings, the corporate department also give trainees "*hands-on*" experience, mainly on deals worth up to £10m for regional clients.

Employment, however, is "*the big one.*" Or as one trainees described it, "*the driving force of the firm – the leading asset.*" The department has become so prominent that a seat here should "*now be considered compulsory.*" News International, Aegis, Carillion and BOC are just a few of the big employer clients, and on the employee side the team looks after a steady flow of top executives, many of whom have been recommended by leading City law firms. Trainees say that on more prominent matters "*you are kept a bit more distant with a more minor role.*" Nonetheless, "*you are kept informed of everything.*"

winning smile

Employment work is "*the spearhead*" of the recent changes at Clarks. It has taken the firm up the M4 to London, where a small Covent Garden office now means lawyers are closer to those hotshot City execs. Trainees say: "*We're not just a little Reading backwater anymore,*" and to prove it the firm has a new logo and letterhead. The employment team's dedicated website has long featured 'Buddies', cheery cartoon characters dedicated to helping clients solve all their employment woes. Now, the new Clarks logo, too, has a smiley face. "*When the logo first came out it was a bit controversial,*" we heard from one trainee. "*It showed a touchy-feely and fun firm, not a serious commercial one.*" Not everyone was so sceptical; another simply said: "*It just shows the friendly face behind the firm.*" Importantly, it hasn't dissuaded new clients or lateral hires: Clarks recently won the attentions of the Retail Motor Industry Federation and Scottish & Southern Energy Group, quite apart from new recruits from Clifford Chance, Richards Butler, CMS Cameron McKenna and Denton Wilde Sapte.

comic timing

A cunning 8.45am start means staff are ready, coffee in hand, to log on by 9am. And at the other end of the day "*no one will scowl at you*" for leaving on the dot of 5pm and "*most of the office goes by 5.30pm.*" If you're waiting for the 'but', yes, there is one. Corporate completions do, on occasion, keep trainees in the office till the wee hours. So long as these occasions are limited, no one minds. As one trainee put it: "*We are all people who work hard, but don't want to kill ourselves in the process.*" With London on the doorstep and the Thames Valley in the back garden, we can see that for many trainees the decision to go to Clarks was *"a lifestyle thing."* One told us that trainees were *"trying to have their cake and eat it."*

The London office has no seat for trainees, but with classy new offices in Reading, that recently enhanced slick commercial feel is abundantly clear there, too. The *"plush"* new HQ at Forbury Square replaces the *"grubby"* old one in the former Great Western Hotel. One source said the open-plan layout, with its long rows of booths and partners strategically placed at corners, was *"meant to foster great communication, but when people come and visit they are stunned by how quiet it is. It's all a bit Dilbert."* Others thought the new arrangement had brought more of a team atmosphere and enjoyed being able to listen in on others' conversations. And they obviously like chatting at Clarks because trainees have no fewer than 26 appraisals over the course of their two-year contract. You'll be sitting down for an *"open and frank"* discussion with your supervisor every month and again at the end of each year.

Socially, something is organised each month, recently a quiz, BBQ and karaoke night. The annual treasure hunt is not to be missed and gets trainees *'enthusiastically rushing around Reading"* looking for clues to earn them champagne and chocolates. The Christmas party puts them through the *"horrifying"* experience of entertaining the rest of the firm. Nothing a stiff drink won't sort out, we suspect.

In 2004, three of the four qualifiers stayed with the firm; nonetheless, from 2005, it is reducing its intake from four to two trainees. The good news is that it will offer funding for the LPC for the first time. Less is more, as they say.

and finally...

We were idly chatting about Clarks with a trainee from a firm in London. *"Where is this place?"* he exclaimed. *"I want to work there."*

Cleary Gottlieb Steen & Hamilton

the facts

Location: London
Number of UK partners/assistants: 14/48
Total number of trainees: 8
Seats: 4x6 months
Alternative seats: Overseas seats, secondments
Extras: Pro bono – LawWorks, Solicitors Pro Bono Group

Cleary Gottlieb Steen & Hamilton has come a long way in the 58 years since its inception in New York and Washington. Steady, strategic growth means it now has offices in Paris, Brussels, Cologne, Frankfurt, Milan, Moscow, Rome, Hong Kong, Tokyo and London. Though we mention it last, the London office is definitely not least, either in the firm's estimation or for prospective trainees.

kicking up dust

Clearys is no Yankee-come-lately to Europe, having ridden into town as long ago as 1947, when it was involved in the implementation of the Marshall Plan. By opening up in London in 1971, it beat the stampede of US firms determined to challenge the City establishment in the 1990s. The 60-lawyer office now has an important place in the Cleary game plan, acting as a gateway to continental Europe. Expert in international finance and corporate transactions, and with excellent lawyers in tax, financial regulation and IP, the office is able to offer a unique training contract, which includes the opportunity for those with the right qualifications to practice in the USA.

A scorching Brussels-based antitrust group is one of the firm's hottest properties, so the arrival of four partners from the group to bolster an already impressive department in London is a fair indication of good things to come. On the finance front, the firm recently acted for Bank Austria Creditanstalt in a €1 billion share offering and Vienna Stock Exchange listing, and a combined US/UK-counsel team worked on the establishment of a $4 billion short-term notes programme for Bradford & Bingley. On corporate transactions, Clearys advised an American Express subsidiary in its acquisition of Rosenbluth International, a leading global travel management company, and Deutsche Bank in its acquisition of a 40% stake in United Financial Group, a leading Russian bank. Other clients include Merrill Lynch, Citigroup, Siemens and Credit Agricole, not forgetting several sovereign governments.

all around the world

Like many a seasoned traveller, the firm has picked up a little of its style here and a little there. Trainees told us: *"It is the firm culture, not one specific national culture that informs our style most."* London clients are billed in dollars and work is measured using US time recording methods, but that's the extent of Uncle Sam's influence. Even that most stereotypical of US law firm trappings – otherworldly billing targets – are nowhere to be seen. *"We don't have targets; associates probably know roughly what they bill, but no one boasts about it."* From day one trainees are thrust into a global business environment, scooting around for work here, for a client visit there. Said one: *"I've been to Rome by myself to perform due diligence on a fruit juice provider, and was sent to Stockholm to do an acquisition in the IT sector."*

The majority of our contacts had visited the New York office, either physically or virtually through the marvels of *"constant videoconferencing,"* and all had attended one of the firm-wide capital markets or M&A conferences, which take place in a different office each year. *"They fly you and your partner* [huggy-kissy type, not boss type] *out...really it's a chance to network and help integrate all the various offices."*

flexible friends

Clearys operates in a 'departmentless' way. No office is divided by practice area and most lawyers handle a variety of work. So when we say that London's core practices are international finance and corporate, *"those terms are shorthand for what elsewhere would be a much wider range of specific departments."* For trainees, *"although you have four different supervisors during your two years, the idea of a formal seat is fairly redundant."* Daily work is dictated in part by the expertise of the supervisor of the moment (*"When I sat with an IP partner, I probably did about 40% IP"*) and in part by current business needs. This system brings trainees *"close up to the excitement of major transactions,"* providing *"amazing experiences as you're treated very like a junior associate."* It also prevents early specialisation, a flexibility that trainees appreciate and one that extends beyond qualification.

At Clearys *"you don't become an NQ in a specific department"* and, if you wish, you can remain a free agent for another four or five years. *"You find even quite senior associates with expertise in things as diverse as Russian finance and European M&A."* Reflecting on the learning process, our sources had few regrets in their choice of firm: *"I've got such a broad understanding of different areas of law...someone will say, 'We need a deal staffing, are you free?' so you learn on the job."*

very satc

Trainees are actively encouraged to take seats overseas. Spend time with the Brussels antitrust group and you may become spoiled: in the canteen *"they'll do you a steak cooked to order"* and *"you're basically parachuted in to a full social scene."* If you've set your heart on the Big Apple, you're definitely going to be spoilt because you could end up spending a good deal of time out there working and studying for the New York Bar. Although a law degree is not a strict requirement for Clearys' UK trainees generally, only those who have one have a choice as to which of two options will take them stateside.

Option one is to follow up an LLB with a masters' degree at a major American law school, then study for the Bar at the firm's expense and train on its Foreign Lawyer Programme for nine months before returning to London to complete your training. In those nine months you'll work alongside contemporaries from other European offices. One trainee who'd followed this route had also fulfilled a TV-fuelled fantasy by taking on pro bono work and doing advocacy in a New York family court. *"It was great, but a bit more Ironside than John Grisham!"* The $125,000 salary (pro-rata for the period) also enables you to get the most out of the city. *"We basically tried to nail every single bar in the Zagat's guide."* In case you're wondering, that's a guide to all the NY bars and restaurants a lawyer should *"see and be seen at."* Option two involves qualifying in the UK first, then heading across the pond to take the Bar exam.

Either option includes the small matter of actually passing the NY Bar exam, described as *"one of the worst ways you could choose to spend a summer. Most states test you on six core subjects, but in New York they make it 24!"* The *"pure elation"* of passing is some consolation, and then the only real chore is coming back to the UK. Even so, there are consolations. *"It was a bit of a culture shock, but whilst New York is the powerhouse, anonymity comes with that. London is a smaller, more friendly environment."*

all touchy cleary

Trainees described the London office as *"truly collegiate,"* though *"not in a stuffy Oxbridge sense." "It is genuinely inclusive; when we go out everyone from partners to secretaries are there."* They put this vibe down to two things: its small size and *"a strong Cleary culture of treating trainees very well."* On top of one of the highest salaries in London, trainees benefit from some pretty decent perks – *"an Amex and a Black-Berry."* And let's not forget that all-important, standard-issue leather chair. *"You sit in it on a bad morning and think 'This is what it means to be a lawyer'!"*

Although a 9.30am start isn't so bad, the hours can be long, especially when *"the US time lag comes into play."* Leaving for home at 7pm or 8pm isn't uncommon, nor is it unusual to stay far later when the pressure is on. Keen to test one trainee's assertion

that *"the firm is incredibly sensitive to work intruding on your personal life,"* we quickly found proof – they paid for his girlfriend to visit him overseas.

The free-range approach to training means feedback must sometimes be gathered from *"over 30 people who you've worked for."* But gathered it is and *"you sit down with your supervisor, discuss it exhaustively and get the chance to raise more general questions."* Training contract applicants go through a similarly exhaustive three-interview process, one of which is conducted by current trainees. After hearing this we paid special attention to our sources' comments on the firm's recruitment policy. And so should you. *"The firm dislikes arrogance; it won't stand for it."* In the same vein, *"you have to be confident to take responsibility, but confident enough to judge when you need help."* The involvement of trainees also extends to *"seeking feedback on the running of the office"* and *"having meetings to explain future plans for growth."*

we just want to be together

With over 1,200 applications a year, Clearys can afford to be picky and, indeed, is nothing if not scrupulous in its selection of trainees. Consequently, *"they always retain everyone. The major decision seems to be whether to take you on in the first place."* In the past it has even been known to fill only one of its four trainee vacancies *"because the right people weren't out there."* Such careful matchmaking makes for long-lasting relationships, with all those we interviewed comfortable with the idea of a commitment stretching way beyond qualification. True to form, all four of the qualifiers stayed with the firm in 2004.

Reflecting expansion in the London office, Clearys' premises close to London Wall have been enhanced by *"a lavish new conference centre and a cafeteria with Lavazza espresso machines and everything."* Historically, the firm has been reluctant to grow except through internal promotion, but recently lateral hires such as the recruitment of Linklaters' capital markets partner Simon Ovenden have *"developed existing practice areas and less traditional ones."*

Our sources were excited by the prospects of growth ("*In antitrust, for example, we now deal with names like BT or BA, not just financial institutions like Merrill Lynch*") and clearsighted about their attraction to the firm. As one put it: "*You get big-name experience at a smaller firm that is expanding, and you're not joining an anonymous factory firm.*" Perhaps most endearing of all (because we hear it so infrequently), they spoke of partnership as "*a realistic long-term aim.*"

and finally...

Whether you fancy dual qualification, want to live the American Dream or hope to stretch yourself in London, we reckon Cleary Gottlieb Steen & Hamilton is a fine choice. Just remember to buy one of those watches with different dials for international time zones.

Clifford Chance LLP

the facts

Location: London
Number of UK partners/assistants: 231/713
Total number of trainees: 238
Seats: 4x6 months
Alternative seats: Overseas seats, secondments
Extras: Pro bono – Hackney and Tooting Advice Centres, language training

Hands up who remembers the 80s? That's right, big hair, big mobile phones, big shoulder pads and neon everything. Okay, that's not exactly what you'll find at Clifford Chance, but at the largest law firm in the world with its undisguised ambition to be top dog across the globe, the spirit of big lives on. If you're up for the challenge, perhaps this straight-talking giant will do you a deal.

money talks

The new money of the magic circle, Clifford Chance burst onto the scene in 1987 as the result of a merger between London firms Coward Chance and Clifford Turner – we're guessing keeping the Coward bit just wasn't an option. The firm's sheer muscle is shown by its top rankings in a host of commercial areas, from capital markets to banking litigation to IT to private equity. The firm is split into six main divisions: banking and finance, capital markets, corporate finance, litigation, real estate and TPE (tax, pensions and employment), but despite the firm's apparent breadth, its original core business, finance, is still core today. The leveraged finance group barged its way into the biggest deal of 2004 and won a role advising the banks supporting Philip Green's bid for M&S. On the capital markets side, top deals included the €600 million recapitalisation of china and crystal manufacturer Waterford Wedgwood PLC and representing lenders Barclays Capital and Mediobanca on a €1,700 million refinancing of Aeroporti di Roma.

Clifford Chance's position as one of the financial heavyweights means that, as a trainee, you won't avoid a bout in this particular ring. At least one financial seat is compulsory, and many trainees will do two. In a general banking seat (where "*responsibility varies*" depending on what work is available and on how you perform), one trainee we spoke to had been lucky enough to run their own completion meeting on a small deal. More usual trainee chores might include drafting parts of documents to be reviewed by partners, proof reading and bibling (creating a comprehensive record of all the documents pertinent to a deal). The breadth of CC's banking work means that more specialised seats are available, for example project finance or regulatory work. The latter is best suited to those who are more inclined towards research than transactional work. Asset finance is the A-Team of the banking department, and in this rough and tumble, hard-working '*male-dominated*' group, which concentrates on aircraft financing, you'll do long hours and your fair share of the grunt tasks, although there are opportunities for "*some responsibility.*" When things get busy, the likelihood of any non-work-related chat with supervisors is minimal.

Many trainees also spend time in capital markets where, because the transactions are smaller, you'll tend to get more involved. The securitisation seat is where you might find people *"whingeing about the shocking hours."* Secondments to banks, including Barclays Capital and Citigroup are also on offer, providing an insight into the other-worldly life of the in-house lawyer.

what's the big deal?

As the world of finance is not enough for CC, it has muscled into the realm of top corporate deals and now boasts some highly regarded teams. The firm acted for Safeway, the subject of a fierce takover battle, which was of course finally sold to Morrisons for £3 billion. It also represented Canary Wharf Group in relation to its £1.7 billion sale. British Energy is another long-standing client and the firm recently helped out on a complex £16 billion corporate and financial restructuring. For private equity work, CC fields one of the strongest teams in London; its lawyers have acted on matters such as a £1.54 billion bid for Debenhams and an offer from Barclays Capital for a £147 million slice of Royal & SunAlliance Insurance. What can a trainee expect to do on such massive transactions? Said one: *"I did anything from proof reading to drafting board minutes, checking share certificates, updating company books, turning round documents and bits of drafting."* If corporate is your first seat, your role will be more practical and organisational than legal, but as in most other parts of the firm, your experience will depend on the attitude of your supervisor and the type of group you end up in. Supervisors are generally senior associates. As well as the big-hitting teams (corporate finance and private equity), groups in financial institutions, CMT (communications, media and technology), competition, commercial and funds also accept trainees.

be careful what you wish for

The specialised nature of the groups in both banking and corporate led us to wonder if trainees weren't missing out on the breadth of experience gained by their peers in smaller firms. When we posed the question, they suggested there were no disadvantages to early specialisation, saying: *"Lots of finance work is similar – many of the documents contain the same types of clauses."* And *"I don't feel that I've had too specialised a training – there's always the option to say that you haven't had experience in a particular area."* However, with seats so focused on particular types of transaction, you have to be careful what you ask for. Helping you to pick your way through the CC minefield is a booklet written by former trainees containing a profile of each seat. The information is *"as candid as anyone could be in a business environment. You try and allude to long hours or other problems, but obviously you don't say everyone's a dick."* Once you've picked out the seats you want, the great game of allocation seems to work relatively well. Most people we spoke to came out winners – one of them said: *"Every single time I got what I chose, but some other people got stuffed."* It probably all depends on how well your tastes match with what the firm has to offer you.

continental drift

Apart from corporate and finance, planet CC has seats in real estate, competition, tax and other specialist areas. Few of the trainees we spoke to had ventured into these unfamiliar territories and, controversially, many trainees will also complete their training contracts without setting foot in the litigation department. The Law Society requires all training contracts to include some element of contentious work, but CC now offers a week-long litigation course followed by either six months in general commercial litigation, arbitration or shipping seats or an 18-month commitment to the firm's Free Law pro bono scheme. It's hoped this new system will stop the litigation department getting clogged up with po-faced, finance-loving trainees whilst allowing those who are actually keen to get stuck in. The cases CC handles are usually pretty monolithic and it acts here for the same huge corporate entities as seen in the transactional departments.

Trainees hinted that litigation teams felt more *"old-school"* in contrast to the *"flashy Ferraris, banks and golf"* atmosphere elsewhere. They also told us involvement with the Hutton Inquiry and secondments to organisations such as Law4All and Liberty were a real contrast to the work they'd done in other seats. Is CC really the place for future litigators to target? With just two qualification jobs on offer in the department in September 2004, we'd suggest not. However, most trainees did find their spot on the CC land mass in the last round of qualifications – a very healthy 57 out of 63 of them stayed on.

CC has one of the largest global networks of offices. At the last count 28 in 18 countries. We won't list all the overseas seat options for trainees, but here are a few: Paris, Frankfurt, Prague, Warsaw, New York, Singapore, Hong Kong and Brussels. All these offices are smaller than the HQ in London, often leading seconded trainees to play a bigger role than they would at home. However, some sources suggested that in certain locations there was a tendency to use trainees as glorified proof readers or translators. In such circumstances, at least *"you get to know what everyone else is working on and how the office works."* And reading a detailed piece of foreign tax advice has got to be good for you. As has the lifestyle abroad, according to one trainee who enthusiastically recommended people try for *"easy postings where you don't have to do too much work. I'm just grateful to the firm for sending me out as they'd have made more money out of me if I'd stayed in London."* The firm's not stupid. It knows how much of an effect the overseas seat programme has on recruitment.

starting at the top

Trainees may stay with the firm on qualification, but the reality is that most fall by the wayside in the years post-qualification. This is no problem for the firm as *"for everyone who leaves, five people want to come...no one is indispensable"* and neither is it a problem for trainees. Said one: *"If I'm honest, I'd say to a student come here because it looks great on your CV and* then if you want you can leave. It gives you such flexibility in your career as although there's no way up, it's easy to move sideways or down."* As well as the kudos of having the brand name on their CV, trainees were convinced they'd got their money's worth in other ways. As one put it: *"I wanted to work abroad and I wanted to do the best deals for the biggest clients, so Clifford Chance was right for my training contract."*

Big works for these trainees. *"It would have felt restricting to be in a smaller firm. It's good to be in a situation where there are so many people with different working styles – you get to know how to work with different people who you don't know and get used to dealing with new people."* If you're a social butterfly, the huge intakes of trainees mean that (should you really want to) you can relive freshers week. One interviewee wanted *"to be cushioned a bit coming to London. The trainee camaraderie makes it a bit like uni and law school and so it's an easy transition. It's a bit like being a student again and when you're ready, you can cut free."*

We didn't sense much emotional investment in the firm; most of the trainees we spoke to felt they'd entered into a transaction with their employer. As one put it: *"You make sacrifices and you get rewards. Everyone gets their pound of flesh."* Just as at any of the big firms, the hours at CC make training here a lifestyle decision. It will depend on your supervisor and the group's workload, but in most seats you can expect to be in the office until around 7pm. In the mainstream seats you will also encounter periods where you'll work achingly late nights and weekends for stretches of varying lengths. In some seats, supervisors have a healthy attitude to work; in others *"there are stupid bosses who want to look good and so stay all hours and think trainees should as well."* In terms of formal lectures and seminars, you'll get *"the best training possible,"* but in terms of the tasks you'll be given, these will range from the exhilarating to the crappy. Few we spoke to had any sympathy for trainees who'd come to the firm expecting anything different – *"People who whinge have no commercial nous; this is a job in the real world."*

a field of poppies

While competitors in the magic circle cringe at their supposed trainee stereotypes, CC is in the fortunate position of being known as a diverse place where *"not everyone's obsessed with rugby and the girls aren't all six foot tall."* Apparently, *"if you're an outrageous snob you'll be no good here."* London managing partner Peter Charlton hails from the city that brought us that classy lass Michelle from BB5 and *"for his Christmas message he dressed up as Santa and did a piece about Alan Shearer's best goals."*

What we heard from trainees suggested there are some odd pockets in the firm where *"people's ways are tolerated only because they are senior."* From outside the firm come praise and flak in almost equal measure. One source explained: *"We're a target because we aggressively publicise ourselves."* Tall poppy syndrome is another way of putting it. CC's notorious and unabashed empire building is responsible, at least in part. Its incessant drive to be biggest and first as well as best at everything is its defining characteristic and we asked trainees for their views on this. We did wonder – after leaks to the press from associates in NY and the West Coast dream turning into an ugly nightmare of abandoned plans, departures and law suits – is being biggest, first and best at all costs sustainable? One trainee opined: *"We were a bit gung-ho. I feel we were trailblazers who inevitably encountered problems – other firms are now benefiting from those lessons."*

dock workers

In 2003, CC shifted the bulk of its London operation to a brand-new, 30-storey skyscraper in Canary Wharf. Trainees spoke of light-filled offices, juice bars, a swimming pool, shops, gourmet restaurants, spinning studio, make-your-own-pizza stall and MTV screens. To us it sounded like a cross between the Harbour Club and Beckingham Palace. As for the Docklands location, the move hasn't been as catastrophic for staff morale as some feared, although one wit told us: *"The E in the postcode could stand for Essex as we're so far away from anywhere."* On the plus side, Canary Wharf has *"everything you've ever wanted in terms of shops and on your lunch break you can walk for miles underground."* Also, *"you can go from the office into the tube without leaving the building."* On the down side, *"going out for drinks is just God awful. It's all chains – Fine Lines and All Bar Ones. It has no character and will just get worse."* However, trainees were prepared to forgive the firm for taking them out of the City because *"the lovely building compensates."*

and finally...

"If you don't want to be involved in big deals and put in long hours and work in a big shiny tower, don't come here." Such was the uncluttered thinking of one Clifford Chance trainee, and we rather like it. Long live big.

Clyde & Co

the facts

Location: London, Guildford
Number of UK partners/assistants: 91/137
Total number of trainees: 34
Seats: 4x6 months
Alternative seats: Overseas seats, secondments
Extras: Pro bono – Lambeth Law Centre

With overseas offices in Dubai, Singapore, Hong Kong, Piraeus, Paris, Nantes, Belgrade, Caracas and St Petersburg, Clyde & Co has built its reputation on the back of international trade. Although mostly recognised for its stellar shipping, insurance and reinsurance practices, this ambitious firm has more to offer the trainee who chooses to step aboard.

military manoeuvres

The trainees we interviewed were drawn to Clydes' core practice areas. As one proudly pointed out: *"In the areas where we're well known, we're either market leaders or very close to it."* Trainees should be prepared to do a seat in either shipping or insurance; however, for most this was not an unwelcome burden – they think it would be *"strange"* for anyone going to the firm to not want to work in such respected departments.

For the raw recruit, shipping law is *"incredibly complicated,"* yet shipping seats get the aye vote due to the sheer variety of work on offer. Trainees can expect to involve themselves in tussles over the ownership of goods at the time they were stolen, and are frequently found in the library poring over international conventions to discover how much loss should be apportioned to their client. Sometimes the methods used to protect the client's interests are unorthodox – last year Clydes hired former special forces personnel to prevent a cargo of rice worth £2.4 million being sold on the black market in Somalia.

Insurance litigation has a reputation for being *"incredibly document heavy"* and would appeal to anyone who's spent many a long night engrossed in the board game Diplomacy. *"There are lots of different parties all over the place, so things progress very slowly, and very tactically."* We asked our trainees to explain the difference between insurance and reinsurance, but to be honest the answer left us more confused than ever. Fear not: if ever you're at a loss, there will be plenty of people at hand to give guidance. Furthermore, *"everyone in the London market knows each other and is relatively friendly."* Though as any Diplomacy addict knows, even the firmest friendships can be broken when some cad unexpectedly invades Sevastopol.

a case in every port

As well as the usual seats in corporate, insolvency, commercial dispute resolution, tax, property and employment, the firm boasts other, more niche, departments, such as healthcare and medical negligence. The latter is *"quite an emotional department to be in, as you're dealing with clients who either have their health or their career at risk. It can be emotionally draining as it's about much more than the money."* A seat in international trade proved especially popular: *"As a trainee you will regularly be dealing with clients in Greece, cargo shipping problems in Africa or underwriters from across the world."*

A few people were disheartened that certain of the smaller departments could be a bit quiet at times, but we were assured that if a trainee ever had an unproductive seat, the graduate recruitment team did their best to make up for it at the next rotation. Clydes operates a four-seat system, and the view from some sources was that seat selections needed to be well timed – *"A lot of people look at the fourth seat as a bit of a write-off, so coming in and trying to qualify there might be dangerous."*

It is worth emphasising one more time just how litigation led this firm is. A number of trainees estimated that as much as 75% of their work was contentious in nature, with one concluding that *"although the non-contentious side is picking up and going forward, we're still very litigation heavy. That's our main focus."* Clydes was successful on the Sphere Drake case and the Metro case, which were two of the largest matters to be tried in the Commercial Court in recent years. The Metro case related to the largest cargo insurance claim (in this case oil) ever to have reached court, and started off as a group of 35 linked actions involving more than 50 parties. In 2003, 37 of Clydes' cases were reported: it is, beyond question, a litigation powerhouse. While we're on the subject of statistics, let's mention that 18 of the 21 qualifiers stayed with the firm in 2004.

Another word of warning for budding transactional lawyers: *"We're market leaders in what we do, but I don't believe we offer a full service in the way that some magic circle firms do."* Which means in essence that although the firm may do some corporate or property work, it won't necessarily be the first port of call for some of its bigger clients when they require services outside Clyde's traditional areas of expertise.

past times

Remember that New Labour battle cry? Well, here too at Clydes, there's *"a heavy emphasis on education,"* leading to plenty of lunchtime and evening training sessions at which you'll be *"expected to show your face at a good proportion."* Luckily, the majority were described as *"brilliant."* On the other hand, the degree to which supervisors stick to the system for giving their charges feedback is *"a bit hit and miss,"* with reports that a few didn't ever get round to filling in appraisal forms.

Trainees were happy with the *"superb"* levels of responsibility they enjoyed, to the extent that some even longed for the occasional hour at the photocopier to give them time to reorganise their thoughts. They were keen to impress on us that from the start they were treated as 'case handlers' rather than disposable foot soldiers, pointing to a decent number of paralegals to take much of the grunt work. Even when they do have to knuckle down to the administrative chores on a major matter, supervisors generally try to make life as interesting as possible. Said one trainee: *"When you work on the big cases, obviously you can't be the fulcrum, though that doesn't mean that you get the crap tasks. You end up doing more research, so you do learn – even if it's more theoretical."*

The atmosphere in the office was described as *"serious,"* though certainly not in any way unpleasant. *"I would describe the firm as quite old-school, but not using that as a loaded term. We are quite old-fashioned, but also down-to-earth and not at all formal."* Every day a trolley is still trundled round the corridors, loaded with confectionery and bacon butties: it's the sort of genial scene not witnessed since the days of *Are You Being Served*. We sensed disdain for the idea of *"ostentatiously"* staying in the office all hours...it's almost as though the Thatcher years never happened.

the legend of clyde's gold

On its website, Clydes describes its Guildford office as *"a viable alternative for City slickers who would rather not commute."* There are training contracts specifically for Guildford and London, but you will do six months in the other office, so if the idea of working more than a mile away from the C-zone leaves you in a cold sweat, get over it! On the whole the Guildford office received rave reviews on matters ranging from the *"stunning"* offices to the accommodating, family atmosphere.

Those who have their hearts set on a voyage overseas will be satisfied by a range of secondments to offices including Hong Kong and Dubai, where the firm has the largest presence of any international firm. An eye forever on new opportunities to expand its network, Clydes recently opened up in Abu Dhabi and is looking to build relationships with firms in India and Pakistan. Somehow we doubt that its associate office in Baghdad will take trainees any time soon, but it's worth a mention as it's a good example of the firm's willingness to exploit new market opportunities. The foray into Iraq follows on from the experience of opening in Belgrade after the cessation of conflict in the former Yugoslavia. Trainees who'd worked abroad spoke of *"extremes of experience."* On the one hand the hours can be longer and the offices less organised than in the UK, but on the other you become the recipient of *"benefits you wouldn't dream of"* back home. We're talking about the house-and-car kind of benefit rather than the £20-off-Holmes Place-membership kind.

The firm's international approach attracts an international crowd at trainee level: *"There's quite a mix of nationalities represented at the firm – Iraqi, Australian, Greek, Polish... and that's just in our year."* Avoiding the well-trodden trainee path from law degree straight to law school, a fair number have previous careers or travel experience behind them. If you're intrigued enough to want to visit them in their natural habitat, head to the The Ship or Balls Brothers in EC3. The London office also has a free bar in the canteen every Thursday night, after which people usually spill out into the pub.

and finally...

If shipping or insurance float your boat, Clyde & Co should be one of your first ports of call. Anyone inclined towards the Guildford location should be clear that this calibre of litigation is not available anywhere else in town...or indeed outside London.

CMS Cameron McKenna

the facts

Location: London, Bristol, Aberdeen, Edinburgh
Number of UK partners/assistants: 123/331
Total number of trainees: 123
Seats: 4x6 months
Alternative seats: Overseas seats, secondments
Extras: Pro bono – Islington Law Centre, language training

Is CMS Cameron McKenna magic circle lite? The big corporate deals, banking work and overseas network are all there, but trainees tell us they also get to spend more time in niche areas and work shorter hours. Too good to be true? Read on...

star in the east

Camerons is certainly keen to push its corporate practice and has won some big deals this year, including a £1.1 billion publishing merger and drug company Astex's cross-border link-up with a German pharmaceutical giant. However, as one trainee saw it: *"There are big transactions done by the firm, but not with the regularity that they are done by the magic circle. There's some frustration that corporate are not making headway...they're not actively winning work off the magic circle."* Historically, much of Camerons' strength lay in energy, utilities, property and construction, and to a certain extent the corporate teams depend on clients won by lawyers serving those industry sectors. Energy and natural resources work, and utilities companies in particular, remain a real bright spot; clients include National Grid Transco, Thames Water and several major oil companies. What's more, the firm's London office is plugged into one of the most extensive networks of Eastern European offices going, which includes outposts in the Czech Republic, Hungary, Poland, Romania, Russia, Serbia and Montenegro and Bulgaria. This allows it to take full advantage of the growing amount of oil and gas work to be found in these countries. Alongside plenty of North Sea jobs, the firm has recently advised a Polish client on the sale of Russian crude oil and Shell on its Eastern European business.

In the future, it looks like the firm will concentrate on its European links for the next few years. The firm having abandoned its Washington and Beijing offices and scaled down Hong Kong over the past year or so, it looks likely that *"the* [remaining] *Asian and American offices will stay open, but just won't get any bigger."* There has been a *"huge push"* to integrate all the offices (with partner meetings, internal publicity and football tours), but although a sizeable portion of the work trainees encounter is international, it seems that it takes a seat abroad for them to fully appreciate the firm's international reach. Overseas postings are available in Brussels, Amsterdam, Utrecht, Stuttgart, Vienna and Budapest among others, and although for some trainees an overseas seat is just *"too much hassle,"* those who did venture abroad told us the experience was a real highlight. Even of the notoriously unpopular seats in Aberdeen and Bristol, trainees said: *"Most people who go really enjoy it."* Stay-at-homes can take one of the many secondments on offer to clients including Lloyds, Nestlé, Exxon, AIG Insurance and National Australia Bank.

Explaining the ins and outs of the four-seat training scheme, trainees told us: *"The firm wants you to do at least three seats in three of the main practice areas."* Those core areas are corporate, banking, property, litigation and commercial. Energy and projects work, incidentally, come within these categories. Beyond seats in the major departments, seats can be taken *"somewhere in the 20 or so niche areas"* such as employment, insurance and health and safety. Generally the trainees that we spoke to had done seats that corresponded with their description of the basic requirements, although it looked to us as if there might be room for manoeuvre. Seat allocation has been an issue in the past; while one fourth-seater told us: *"The frustrating thing is that we feel that we haven't always been consulted,"* a more pragmatic trainee realised that *"you have to go where the business needs you"* and felt that *"people lose sight of that – it's not all about your training contract."* We're told that the grad recruitment folk *"have listened and taken on our concerns"* and, judging from the experiences of those we spoke to, most people are likely to get the seats they want.

blowing hot and cold

The real estate department takes on a fair number of first-seaters, and the word on Trainee Street is that it's *"a useful first seat as it is a baptism of fire."* Don't worry about singeing that new suit; what our sources meant was that you'll get *"lots of responsibility,"* some of your own files and a role helping out on big investment and development deals.

The prominence of the corporate department came as a surprise to several of our sources. *"You almost have to come into contact with corporate work – 75% of trainees do a seat there."* Those that dont take a seat can always take advantage of the department's standard induction training on the side, although it isn't compulsory. Yet *"the firm attracts a higher proportion of people who don't want to do corporate, but want to do good work in non-mainstream areas."* Taking the middle ground one source said: *"People view it as a useful seat rather than a career and there is a perception among trainees that if you really are a corporate person – really determined and ambitious* [for that work] *– then you would probably be at Slaughters or at Ashursts."* The trainees who spoke most enthusiastically of corporate seats liked the fact that *"the department is not divided up,"* which is *"cool for a trainee or an assistant, as you get to do lots of different kinds of work, theoretically from all across the department. I did a venture capital deal, a plc acquisition and the conversion of a company into a charity."* They reported receiving *"work of a good level"* and told us: *"It's never just 'You're a trainee, this is your job.'"* Of course, you'll be taking the role of a very junior assistant, but one source proudly told us: *"I had to do some dogsbody work, but there was a lot of drafting and plenty of interesting stuff."*

If you don't do corporate, you will do banking, which often means PFI funding issues; it's popular as you get *"real responsibility."* The department commonly acts for the big lenders that are financing projects such as street lighting schemes and the building of new schools or hospitals. As a trainee, you might be responsible for the conditions precedent on which the deal rests or the co-ordination of all the ancillary documentation. The department works closely with the projects team on matters such as the Crossrail project (the firm acts for the review group set up by the Department for Transport to consider this long-awaited scheme), and has advised the government on the financial restructuring of the Channel Tunnel Rail Link. Looking overseas, projects lawyers advised Estonian National Railway and Baltic Rail Services on the refinancing of their loans. On these *"big, big projects,"* *"trainee responsibility isn't great,"* but *"the team is very friendly and supportive."*

swimming with the fishes

We wondered how long it would be before we heard the dreaded f-word that blights the lives of the *Student Guide's* research team. Sadly there's no escaping it here (or, it seems, at 98% of the firms we review). Camerons has developed a reputation among students for being the flipper in a sea of giant killer whales and small but vicious sharks. This year, as before, trainees said the firm is *"friendly and open,"* *"friendly and relaxed,"* *"friendly and reasonable"* and (full marks for originality) *"communal and pragmatic."* Trainees also liked the firm's size: *"It's big enough to find people to get along with without being swallowed up."* If only Jonah had made an application instead of opting for fishing.

When trainees also pointed to a *"superb work–life balance,"* we felt duty bound to give the claim some context and concluded that our sources were generally making comparisons with the magic circle firms rather than small to mid-sized outfits. Said one: *"I can categorically guarantee that I do less hours than my friends at magic circle firms."* Our view, having analysed comments from these firms, is that when the waters are smooth or you're in departments with predictable schedules, you'll do the same 9am-6.30pm day that you'll find under the same conditions at the magic circle. Of course, when things get choppy you do have to stay later, and there is a difference between Camerons and magic circle firms in quite how late you have to stay and in the regularity of these very busy periods. In true lawyerly style, we'll qualify all of this by saying that the hours in all big firms are heavily dependent on seat, supervisor and workload.

chivalry is not dead

So what kind of person picks this firm? We heard that Camerons subscribes to *"gentlemanly principles"* and that *"people here aren't as outwardly ambitious as you'd get elsewhere."* Certainly trainees see themselves as having a *"balanced"* attitude to their careers and *"want to go out and enjoy themselves."* As we spoke to trainees, the vac scheme season was well and truly underway and so we heard about evening flights on the London Eye, meals at Pizza Express and, perhaps a chance to put those chivalric values into action, a medieval banquet. During the rest of the year, the centre of the CMS universe is local boozer The Hand & Shears – *"It's just nice to know that everybody will be there."* In fact, the only sour note we heard about extra-curricular life was from the chap who said: *"We're really bad at rugby sevens. We've never won a game at the Law Society championship."*

Until a year ago, the firm's next-door neighbour was Clifford Chance. Its ugly 80s building looms large over Camerons' Aldersgate Street office near to the Museum of London. Now the giant has moved away and no longer casts a shadow over Camerons, we did wonder if comparisons with the magic circle should be left in the past. Yet, they do seem to help students position the firm and assess its qualities. In 2004, 44 of the 50 qualifying trainees opted for a future with the firm.

and finally...

CMS Cameron McKenna has some top-class work and very satisfied employees. If you're fascinated by Eastern Europe, or you think that projects or energy might be the thing for you, or you simply want a good grounding in the City, put this one on your shortlist.

Cobbetts

the facts
Location: Manchester, Leeds, Birmingham
Number of UK partners/assistants: 117/162
Total number of trainees: 54
Seats: 4x6 months
Alternative seats: Brussels, secondments

Once confined to the North West and traditional property expertise, heavyweight Manchester firm Cobbetts has been merging like there's no tomorrow. First it thrust a size 12 across the Pennines into Leeds and this year it took a giant step into the Midlands by merging with Birmingham outfit Lee Crowder. The aim? *"To be the biggest regional law firm."* We'd say the game is afoot!

cobbettitis
Ebola, cholera, the black death – vicious diseases that spread like wildfire infecting all in their path with a grisly assortment of boils, pustules, general misery and then sudden death. Just as virulent, but at least ten times more benevolent, is a dose of the Cobbetts. Beware! On entering the system it instantly turns cynicism to pure elation, with its victims hugging trees or random passers-by and bursting into full-blown 1950s-style song and dance routines. Other symptoms include blurting out over enthusiastic comments and a general sense of well-being. *"From day one they want you to be happy." "They look after you incredibly carefully." "As a trainee, and at all levels, you get as much support as you need." "It feels like a family."*

"Everyone is equally enthusiastic about work and socialising." The poor blighters we interviewed had it bad...

Put simply, Cobbetts aims to treat its people well and promotes a relaxed approach that *"actively discourages the idea of a traditional lawyer stereotype."* Our sources explained that the firm's ethos is based around a set of core values: *"Integrity, honesty, teamwork, recognising the achievements of others and uniting all the offices as 'One Virtual Office'."* One trainee even went so far as to say: *"The values are sort of common sense really...how you'd want to live your life if you thought about it."* Don't worry if your natural inclination is to cringe at comments like this and to think they sound just a little too Stepford for comfort. We would think like that too, except that years of experience have taught us that this is simply the Cobbetts way.

cobbettic

And a fairly successful way it is. Whilst the vibe may be touchy-feely and the firm walked off with 12th place in the *Sunday Times'* 100 Best Companies to Work For 2004 survey, its track record of expansion speaks for itself. Traditionally possessing an excellent reputation for property law in Manchester, a groaning mantelpiece of trophy clients includes Orange, Peel Holdings and Burger King, not forgetting housing associations, charities and property developers aplenty. Even after recent expansion and diversification, property remains *"the bedrock of what we do"* and *"a fair bit of the commercial work is referred from property or construction clients."* Trainees stressed that *"the work is roughly split 50-50 between the property and other work."* However, there's little doubt that the firm has long harboured broader commercial aspirations.

With the Leeds opening having boosted these corporate ambitions, in late 2003 another merger with niche Manchester corporate finance firm Fox Brooks Marshall *"expanded our AIM-client ability."* Since then the firm has embarked on a marketing tour of Russia following a series of successful deals

for Russian client Highland Gold (one of the world's largest mining companies, which made a £200 million admission to AIM last year). The move into Birmingham – the UK's second largest legal market – was the next logical step in the cross-regional plan. In the same vein, in September 2004 Cobbetts merged with Leeds-based planning and environmental boutique Wilbraham & Co, whose clients included Land Securities and Severn Trent Property. The plan is straightforward: where you don't have a presence, merge; where you do have presence, broaden your expertise by merging some more. Either way make sure the Cobbetts cap fits to avoid a clash in cultures.

When Cobbetts goes a courtin', it goes not to rape and pillage at random, but instead to embrace and cosset a well-matched partner. The legacy of Lee Crowder trainees we interviewed in Birmingham told a very similar story to the Read Hind Stewart recruits in Leeds who had been Cobbetted a year earlier. *"We've had lots of visits from senior Cobbetts personnel,"* *"they've worked incredibly hard at keeping us in the loop"* and *"we've had presentations coming out of our ears!"* they told us. Most significantly, our sources said: *"It was really stressed pre-merger that one of the reasons for merging was the matching values of the firms."* Which perhaps explains why those washed over by the Cobbetts wave feel *"assimilated, not annihilated."* Although they scratched their heads to explain why – *"It's really hard to pin down the similarities but we are very similar."* Cobbetts types old and new told us: *"It feels like one firm across the offices."*

cobbettology

Undeniably, Cobbetts is *"very keen on a strong connection to the North West"* (or Yorkshire or the Midlands), yet we did also hear of a trainee from the south whose only reason for moving north was a job at the firm. As well as students straight from university and law school, we heard about an ex-concert musician, an ex-DJ, an ex-surveyor and ex-criminal lawyer in amongst the trainee ranks. Pre-merger the whole lot were *"put up in Malmaison in Manchester for* the night and sent on a paid-for clubbing trip." And from now on they will also all meet on the PSC course. Currently, trainees reside at one office for the duration of their contract, but "the possibility of swapping offices for seats" cannot be discounted in the future. There has already been trainee migration between the North and the Midlands when the Brum office was working flat out.

Thanks to the "One Virtual Office" ethos, Birmingham is "getting up to speed" with the Cobbetts systems, procedures and IT. Four six-month seats is standard for all trainees, whichever office they're in. In Manchester and Leeds it's "very unusual to avoid property," although not impossible, and not always desirable as the department has fab work – "I drafted leases, ran residential conveyancing from start to finish, had lots of client contact and also worked on bigger retail site deals." Seats can also be chosen from employment, licensing, banking, property finance, commercial litigation (including financial regulation and property litigation), commercial, corporate, construction and matrimonial. The Manchester matrimonial department might seem a little out of place, but is important to the firm and "always popular" with trainees. "The commercial teams are just growing and growing" with "fluidity between Leeds and Manchester." The comlit department in Leeds is, for example, "really important with an increasing leaning towards mediation; I was drafting pleadings on big contractual claims and attending a lot of client meetings for clients like Magnet Kitchens."

As of this year trainees in Brum will be able to choose seats from banking, social housing, property, litigation, corporate, commercial, construction, employment and private client. The private client department seems "at odds with the Cobbetts commercial vision...dealing with old biddies in nursing homes is a bit different." Nevertheless, "it's one of the few city-centre private client departments and it's well known," so seems likely to persist. Birmingham's strengths are in property and construction and there's a strong local authority and social housing client base. With a variety of Midlands and national charities instructing the office, this practice area is also important. The commercial department has a media slant – "I worked for a satellite TV company, service providers and a news group," confirmed one source.

cobbettechture

Across the firm, the average hours work out at 8.45am–5.30pm or thereabouts and there's a decidedly "anti-stay-late culture – my supervisor once said to me, 'Just because I'm obsessed with this contract doesn't mean you have to be: go home!'" The only major difference between cities is the office architecture: all are located in their respective city centres and close to shopping and drinking venues, but that's where the similarities end. The Manchester office is a "very ornate, grand, 19th-century canal-boom building," looming imperiously over the fashionable King Street and "sandwiched between two branches of Armani." The overspill office across the road is "open plan and modern, unlike the main building," but just as much of a des res as it's between Whistlers and Max Mara.

In Leeds there are new open-plan premises on Park Place; "they look great and are right in the centre, five minutes from Harvey Nicks, ten to Hammonds, five to Boots and five to Virgin records and any number of bars." Meanwhile, Cobbetts Birmingham is "uncomfortably bursting at the seams," so trainees are looking forward to the upcoming move to "the brand-spanking-new landmark office building in the centre of town. It's going to have a restaurant and breakout rooms and everything!"

cobbettertainment

Cobbetts trainees have long felt that they're getting a good deal both during their contracts and at the end – retention rates are traditionally very high and those for September 2004 were no different with 15 out of 16 accepting jobs at the firm. Of the many factors contributing to their satisfaction, one of the most significant is the social life: "It's stunning, much to my husband's disgust!" For an itsy-bitsy £2 per month subscription, a hyperactive social committee arranges events from worthy theatre trips to *"ridiculous things like a school disco evening"* or *"the annual trip to Doncaster races."* This year's 'merger ball' was held at Birmingham's swish ICC and had a Carnevale di Venezia theme, *"so everyone was flamboyantly masqued up!"* We heard tales of *"jugglers, acrobats, stilt walkers and a Venetian circus,"* *"mixed tables of staff from all offices"* and *"a quiz with questions specific to all offices to get everyone involved."* Even better, staff were *"challenged to build a boat from whatever was on the tables to float on the mock canal. The one that stayed afloat the longest won."*

and finally....

Consolidation may not be a word in the Cobbetts trainee vocabulary just yet, but it is going to have to be at some point when the pace of change slows. Right now, no matter which office they call home, trainees are working at a firm that *"feels like it can turbo-charge your career without any side effects."*

Coffin Mew & Clover

the facts

Location: Portsmouth, Southampton, Fareham, Gosport
Number of UK partners/assistants: 20/35
Total number of trainees: 9
Seats: 6x4 months
Alternative seats: None
Extras: Pro bono – CAB

Coffin Mew & Clover. Given this firm's rather odd and creepy name, we're surprised it's not better known by the student masses. Never mind: here's to notoriety – for all the right reasons...

mind control

In quite a short time, CMC has transformed itself from a sprawling network of neighbourhood offices into a more cohesive, increasingly commercial, four-office firm. Yesteryear's partners have been given their carriage clocks and are now digging allotments with anyone else who declined to move with the times. But in following an *"out-with-the-old"* management style, partners have taken care not to discard the baby with the bath water; the client roster is still fairly evenly split between commercial organisations and private individuals. CMC's departments range from commercial litigation to personal injury, commercial property to family and employment, and corporate to crime. As trainees do six seats, this effectively means the possibilities are endless.

Training partner Malcolm Padgett is a man who's taken his role to a new dimension. *"He absolutely loves it...it's not that he's drawn the short straw."* When it comes to seat selections, there's no possibility of being fed through a sausage machine. Mr P seems to know what seats will suit people's personalities as well as their plans for qualification. Has he supernatural powers? It was a hot topic with trainees this year: *"It sounds crazy, but I think he is psychic,"* one of them whispered.

private thoughts

Private client in Fareham is a typical first seat and offers will drafting, enduring powers of attorney and referrals from the Court of Protection concerning those with mental incapacity. *"It's nice to start with, as you get to learn how to deal with clients and office procedures."* Trainees are the first port of call for new clients and will handle all initial phone calls and many first meetings. As well as *"old people,"* they encounter everyone from the ordinary man or woman on the street to successful local businessmen and members of the armed forces past and present.

Another common stopping-off point is the claimant personal injury department. *"I didn't have my own files; instead I helped a lot on other people's by drafting witness statements and particulars of claim."* Trainees also spend time out of the office visiting clients at home or police stations for information on road traffic accidents. *"I went to see the scene of acci-*

dents too," one trainee recalled without a hint of morbid fascination. More senior members of the department handle serious, high-value claims, particularly head injuries, and the Royal Naval Dockyard in Portsmouth has also been the source of asbestos-related claims.

when push comes to shove

"Almost everyone" does a seat in commercial property. Having practised the basics on plot sales for housebuilder clients, a trainee will progress to investment landlords and commercial tenants. The supervising partner likes to present them with a series of challenges: *"As soon as I thought I was getting somewhere with the work, he pushed me further."* The social housing team is going great guns. We counted no fewer than 15 housing associations on the firm's books, and learned from our colleagues on *Chambers UK* that CMC is top of the social housing tree in the southern counties and one of the best regional practices UK-wide. Its lawyers cover everything from anti-social behaviour cases to key worker development projects. Some clients have enormous property portfolios worth hundreds of millions of pounds, and this in turn can mean hefty finance transactions. If you thought social housing work was small beer or obscure, think again.

The corporate department's instructions come from private limited and family-owned companies. *"They tend to be Southampton based, although we act for national banks,"* stressed one source. A trainee can expect to assist partners with company and share sales or purchases, corporate reconstructions and partnership matters. They may be fortunate enough to handle smaller deals by themselves, if sufficiently experienced. Forget silly, City hours though: *"I never worked really, really late – 8.30pm was the latest."* The firm is basically offering *"good-quality work, but not the corporate machine."*

Take a crime seat in the North Harbour office and you might feel like you're in an episode of *The Bill* after you've attended a couple of ID parades at the police station. The cases will be mainly general crime – trainees seem to get their fair share of motoring offences – including more serious Crown Court matters such as GBH, firearms, drugs and benefits fraud.

supermarket sweep

With so many contrasting departments, you never really know what to expect of a seat: *"The experience depends on the supervisor, but I've never felt spoon-fed or that I've no one to go and talk to."* Most trainees have their own room or sit with a junior fee earner; very few actually sit under the nose of their supervising partner. From one paranoid source: *"When you're on your own, you can sit and think and not worry about everyone watching you."*

As the commercial hub and the largest office, Southampton has a faster pace and is more sociable; the only downside is its location under the flight path for Southampton International Airport. The *"ultra-modern"* Fareham Point office hosts many of the admin departments and private client lawyers. It's near to the M27 motorway, although unlike some other rival firms, it isn't in a soulless business park. The purpose-built North Harbour office in Portsmouth has crime, family, conveyancing and childcare, and the Gosforth office doesn't take trainees, being limited to residential conveyancing work. The common theme is that each office, bar Southampton, is located close to a supermarket: Sainsbury's in Fareham, Tesco in North Harbour, and Waitrose in Gosforth. For the record, we don't recommend picking seats based on your food-shopping habits.

pyjama party

As a trainee, you'll need to set your alarm early enough to get in for 8.30am to open the post. While you may curse this chore as you stare bleary-eyed into the bathroom mirror with toothpaste dribbling down your shirt front, an hour later you'll be fully up to speed with all the soaps, the latest football scores and any gossip that's been brewing in the office. It's also a good way to meet partners.

Thinking more of the tail end of the day, one source confessed: "*I don't want it to be the be-all and end-all of my life.*" However, far from just switching off when they leave the office, "*people do a lot for the local area by way of fundraising*" – all manner of things from abseils to joining local charities' committees. "*The attitude of a lot of people here is that they want to be of help.*" On In The Pink Day for Cancer Research, staff wore pink to the office; on Comic Relief day they wore red. Apparently one time they had a pyjama day – all well and good until you've a conference with counsel. But then we were reminded that charity begins at home, and with no sponsorship from the firm, self-funding law school had clearly been a heavy burden for our sources. Which is why we are pleased to report that the firm will now consider financial assistance for the LPC.

"*Most people want to get a good balance between work and home life. It's easy to do that here because of the general attitude.*" An attitude that extends to having fun, be this at The Orange Rooms or a firm party. When we rang trainees, a school disco night was eagerly awaited and the Oscars-themed Christmas party, at which awards were given to celebrity look-alikes, was fresh in their minds. "*One partner looks like Harry Potter will in 20 years' time*" and another reminds even clients of Bryan from Westlife. We are delighted to be able to report that the trainees' tradition of dining at home lives on. Buy yourself a Jamie or Nigella book to shove next to Megarry & Wade, because you'll end up cooking dinner for your peers one school night, although presumably they visit only once if your best efforts are inedible. Thankfully, NQ job offers are made without reference to culinary skills and in September 2004 two of the three qualifiers took jobs at the firm.

and finally...

Coffin Mew & Clover offers what we can only conclude is a very palatable training. If the south coast beckons, wherever you're from, this firm is more than worth a look-see.

Coudert Brothers LLP

the facts

Location: London
Number of UK partners/assistants: 10/18
Total number of trainees: 7
Seats: 4x6 months
Alternative seats: Brussels
Extras: Solicitors Pro Bono Group, language training

You might not have heard of Coudert Bros; the snug London branch of this US/international firm keeps a relatively low profile in the City. But if you're tempted by the idea of practising your Swedish or Cantonese whilst not being part of a cast of thousands, you too could be part of the Coudert family.

upstairs downstairs

Most of Coudert's work takes place in the international business arena. Much of what goes on in the two-floor Cannon Street office is referred there from the firm's network of offices across the US, Europe and Asia. Upstairs, the focus of the corporate department is on banking, telecoms and oil and gas, but you'll also find smaller groups working on employment and data protection matters. Downstairs, lawyers work primarily on litigation and property. Pretty quickly you'll learn that working in such a compact environment has one major advantage – maintaining good communication between departments is easy and "*within a couple of weeks you'll know everyone's name.*" A word of warning though: it's best to take the stairs between floors rather than attempting to master the "*comedy lift system,*" which we're delighted to hear still "*keeps you on your toes.*"

Trainees generally do two seats taken from general coco, M&A/banking, employment and EU/competition. Typically, trainees busy themselves by setting up subsidiary companies, tackling research tasks and taking responsibility for small aspects of large banking deals. In line with Law Society requirements, a litigation seat awaits, where, as one of only a couple of trainees in the department, you'll have your fair share of note-taking and bundling duties, but you'll also find yourself in conferences with counsel and trotting along to court. We heard of trainees getting involved in everything from international arbitration to employment disputes.

As for fourth-seat possibilities, although the firm doesn't offer the jet-setting opportunities you'd expect at a magic circle firm, or indeed some other firms with worldwide networks, six months in Coudert's Brussels office is a definite possibility. Perfect if you love moules et frites but have grown bored with the Belgo chain. Of the four trainees recruited every year two will usually go, and there's an added bonus in the form of *"a lovely big corporate flat less than ten minutes' walk from work."* As you'd expect, the seat is competition-focused, which means getting stuck into the intricacies of some very specific industries. *"I had to learn all about corrugated paper and fresh tubular pasta,"* said one past occupant of the seat. Stay-at-homes might choose a property seat for their fourth stint. The department has a good reputation for training, with partners allowing you to get your feet wet by running your own residential conveyancing files. If that sounds less than exciting you might be surprised at what there is to learn from the experience. You will also assist with social housing projects and shopping centre management by drafting elements of leases or doing research into landlord and tenant law. And, as the only trainee in the department, you're guaranteed to be in the spotlight – whether that's a good or bad thing is up to you!

With so few trainees, the process of seat allocation is reasonably informal and flexible, and most trainees get what they want over the two years. However, our sources tell us that for whatever reason *"the firm is moving in the direction of laying out a reviewable, provisional seat plan from the beginning of the training contract."* Still, it doesn't sound particularly rigid to us! Regarding the small matter of qualification in 2004, all three NQs took jobs at Coudert.

'allo, 'allo

As with any international firm, the property department differs from the others in that most of its clients are domestic. Elsewhere in the office it's like the Eurovision Song Contest every day – one trainee, for example, ended up co-ordinating a banking deal with lawyers in Stockholm, Munich, Paris and Amsterdam. We presume it was nothing our source had said that led the Munich lawyers to defect to Dechert at the beginning of 2004. In litigation, too, *"it's rare for us to deal with two British parties;"* instead, matters from Africa, the US, Spain or Sweden will be on your desk. Established offices in Moscow and St Petersburg provide London with *"strong Russian links,"* particularly in oil and gas. The firm's prospects in this field have strengthened as markets have opened up in the former USSR and Central Asia. For anyone keen to extend their knowledge of the Russian language beyond the words 'vodka' and 'nazdaroviye', classes are available. Having positioned itself in Beijing in the 1970s, Coudert also has a presence in the Asia-Pacific region with *"some really big Chinese clients"* – both financial institutions and leading corporates. It recently advised on a $600 million dual-currency loan facility, evidence – were it needed – of China's growing position as a leading manufacturing economy.

It's not just Coudert's work that is international: staff are also more cosmopolitan than average. *"At least once a week you'll see an American or Russian guy walking down the corridor."* Judging from the people we've spoken to over the last few years, the firm is inclined to recruit trainees with international backgrounds, language skills or experience of living abroad. As one of them put it: *"You can't join the firm and be narrow minded. You have to understand that advice to a foreign client may have to be phrased in certain ways...you have to have an international outlook."* Links between the offices seem to run smoothly – *"There's an emphasis on making the network work,"* *"partners travel a lot and there's a lot of interchange between them."* This approach filters down to more junior staff too;

for example, *"there's a meeting of all the European offices every year."* Last year it took place in Dublin, where *"we had a football tournament and a lot of Guinness was sampled!"*

the good life

Expect a solid 9am–7pm work schedule, though there's plenty of Tom and Barbara-style *"popping next door"* for a quick catch-up with colleagues. *"It's not scowled on by partners – they often join in,"* said one source. We were touched (or should that be alarmed?) to hear one trainee describe the firm as *"my home for ten hours a day."* As a trainee, it's easy to get your views heard by the partners over lunch or coffee, and a new pastoral initiative has been put in place to formalise what is clearly an already supportive atmosphere. The policy of not sitting trainees with their supervisors, but with a junior associate, gets a thumbs-up; they appreciate having *"a safety blanket"* before having to bother a partner with what could turn out to be simple questions.

hatchett job

In the summer of 2003 Coudert celebrated its 150th anniversary and raised a few glasses to the original Coudert frères who launched the firm in their adopted home, New York, back in 1853. We were disappointed to learn that Coudert's very own vintage wine was not drunk, but there were gala dinners and cocktail parties, and the firm took the opportunity to launch a new pro bono initiative in London. Just a year after the celebrations, however, and the firm was in well-publicised merger talks with US giant Squire, Sanders & Dempsey, although these did not reach a succesful conclusion.

Coudert staff *"tend to be friends outside work."* Trainees find that with only eight of them in the office, social events are organised on a departmental rather than peer group basis. There's a tradition of meeting every few weeks for a quiz at local boozer The Hatchett, and those who need physical as well as mental exercise find an outlet in football.

and finally...

Coudert's achievements derive from its international approach to business. If you see yourself as a citizen of the world (as corny as that may sound) and you want to feel at home in an intimate London office, you should fit right in.

Cripps Harries Hall

the facts

Location: Tunbridge Wells, London
Number of UK partners/assistants: 38/54
Total number of trainees: 14
Seats: usually 6 of varying length
Alternative seats: None

Royal Tunbridge Wells. Tweed suits, tea shoppes and the odd residual gift to the local cats home? No thanks. For a City break at Cripps Harries Hall, pack your pinstripes.

making waves

Established in 1832, Cripps Harries Hall has been in expansionist mode in recent times, extending beyond its traditional private client base to make a name for itself in commercial practice. Admittedly, *"many of the clients are still in the green-welly brigade"* (the owners of large estates and farmers), but this is no longer the mainstay of the firm. The commercial client roster is made up of regional businesses, including some small plcs, and there's a healthy charitable clientele that includes Paignton Zoo, Vision Aid Overseas and the Royal Geographic Society.

Commercial property and dispute resolution (litigation) are *"the biggies"* for the firm, and it has found an excellent friend in City giant Lovells. Developed for the Prudential's property investment arm, PruPIM, a Mexican Wave scheme sees Lovells farming out less complex real estate work from the £12 billion portfolio to smaller firms that operate at lower cost. Cripps is a major recipient. The department is performing excellently all round: it retains a place on the legal panel of Land Securities, and other clients include government departments and agencies, as well as large house builders.

On the litigation front, lawyers have acted for an Indian steel manufacturer in dispute with an international banking syndicate in both London and Singapore; and for Benjamin Pell (aka Benji the Binman) in his successful defamation claim against the *Sunday Express*, which alleged that he'd sold the names of the Bloody Sunday paratroopers to the IRA.

hot property

The existence of a small London office does nothing to detract from the firm's Kent focus: "*It is committed to its Tunbridge Wells base*" and as a trainee that's exactly where you'll stay. A six-seat plan will be mapped out on your arrival – "*You don't just turn up and get stuffed into six seats.*" The seats vary in length according to the firm's requirements and your preferences: "*It is a 50:50 decision.*" As to which you'll do, Cripps likes people to experience a mix of private client and commercial work and a spell in the big and busy commercial property department is almost a dead cert. "*One person negotiated their way out of it, but it is a key place to go.*" At the other end of the spectrum, the employment and family departments are incredibly popular and have space for just one trainee, so don't expect more than a short stint in either. The system is ideal for waverers, but we were warned: "*If you don't put forward a stringent view of what you want, the firm will decide where to put you.*"

purple patch

Formal training is a serious business, with weekly sessions preceded by slightly officious e-mail reminders. On arrival at the firm, comprehensive IT training gets new recruits up to speed on Purple Pages, the firm's intranet. There's everything from client conflict checks to time recording, lost mail, staff photos, births, marriages and even reminders about overdue library books. And why Purple? "*To match our imaginative square and triangle logo.*" The firm certainly needs a well-designed intranet; between its two offices Cripps now has 38 partners and more than 300 staff, who bill around £20 million annually.

Pushing aside their enthusiasm for technology, we asked trainees about the supervision and feedback they received from their seniors. Weekly chats, monthly appraisals and end-of-seat reviews keep everyone on their toes, and between billable hours and a photocopying department, there is little chance of getting lumbered with too much grunt work. Where it is appropriate (eg private client and residential conveyancing), there's greater scope for running your own files, and we heard of trainees trotting off to court and to meetings with counsel and clients. "*Every last letter is checked,*" and trainees perceived that as the two years progress observation becomes participation.

Previously we've shown an unhealthy fascination for the firm's civilised working hours – a 9am–5.15pm day with a 75-minute lunch break. Only one source ventured to suggest they had ever worked "*the occasional longer day.*" And what is a long day in Royal Tunbridge Wells? "*I left at 6.30pm.*" Superb!

worlds apart

There is a price for such a leisurely existence, however; in Tunbridge Wells, nothing comes cheap. The firm likes its trainees to have "*a commitment to the area,*" something which commonly translates into parents who live near by. Living with mum and dad can relieve the financial burden, but this year we noted fewer stay-at-homes. Independent living in Tunbridge Wells on a trainee salary may be a case of "*getting by rather than doing brilliantly,*" but our sources took a philosophical view. One said: "*You can either go to London and get loads of money, or knock off at half five and have your weekends.*" Another reiterated the importance of choosing the firm carefully: *"You have got to want to be here – it is no good it being a second choice to the City."* In 2004, jobs were offered to six of the seven qualifiers and four accepted them.

Indeed, someone after the pure City experience will be disappointed. Sure, trainees told us: *"There's lots of testosterone flying around"* in the corporate department, and our interviews were liberally scattered with references to *"cutting edge," "dynamism and innovation"* and *"City slick."* Yet despite the presence of two partners and various assistants from the likes of CMS Cameron McKenna and Linklaters, the simple fact is that Cripps undertakes smaller ticket transactions. Typically these will be valued between £1-10 million, and occasionally up to £30 million, so we're really not talking about blood-on-boardroom-table experiences.

Cripps has *"swish"* Georgian offices and a *"very conservative"* dress code – it's what many of the clients expect. Moving around the firm every few months, trainees perceive differing atmospheres in the two limbs of the firm, although they feel that *"these aren't mutually exclusive."* Possibly in an attempt to span the traditional private client/modern commercial divide, we heard of *"a few braces-wearers, and a worrying presence of pinstripes."*

and the oscar goes to...

A healthy social calendar maximises the town centre location. For end-of-month drinks, people remain faithful to Sankey's; the Pitcher & Piano runs a close second in popularity and trainees have a love-hate relationship with Tunbridge's disco offering, Dav's. At Christmas, there is a choice of lunch in a local restaurant or dinner, or – if you have the appetite – both. The dinner is held in the basement of the office (not as gloomy as it sounds) and last year included bingo. An annual summer ball gives the second-years a chance to flex their creative muscles: in 2004 they organised an Oscar-style ceremony, complete with red carpet and awards.

Presumably after fumbling behind the sofa cush-

ions for loose change, the trainees take regular lunches together. And those worried about expanding waistbands can participate in cricket, football, and netball or join the racquet and running clubs.

and finally...

You want the Tunbridge Wells location and a thoroughly decent start to your career. Can you have both? At Cripps Harries Hall we think you can.

Dechert LLP

the facts

Location: London
Number of UK partners/assistants: 39/68
Total number of trainees: 29
Seats: 6x4 months
Alternative seats: Overseas seats, secondments
Extras: Pro bono – comprehensive in-house programme and North Kensington Law Centre

When representatives from 13 American colonies met in Philadelphia's Independence Hall in 1776 to declare independence from the English crown, we bet they never imagined that, 225 years later, sons of the city would be making a bid for control of a corner of legal London. The Dechert story makes for interesting reading...

ringing the liberty bell in london

The London arm of Dechert has been a feature on London's legal scene for many years, and it is only in the past decade that it has become Dechertised. The formal marriage with its US other half came after a long, seven-year engagement with the Philly firm, so it was hardly a rush job or a shotgun wedding.

The London office had long been known for its property prowess, more specifically retail property (though certainly at this firm we really ought to use the term real estate now). Although there have been exits at partner level, the firm still boasts the likes of

Land Securities and the Crown Estate as clients, and still has a great name in the sector. Yet since the merger, Dechert London has been reshaping its profile by building up its financial practice and fusing the real estate department with the finance department to mirror practice groups in the US. In many respects, Dechert London is beginning to look more like Dechert in the US than ever before. Indeed, trainees say: "*Quite apart from visitors from stateside, there's no getting away from the fact that the HQ is in Philly and the policy is written in the States.*"

an american revolution

"*I was pleased they had gone international,*" one source told us; "*although I wasn't quite aware of how dominant the US side was until I got here...You get the impression that London has become a piece of the Dechert jigsaw and some of the older lawyers are not pleased about that.*" Certain small practice groups that were not central to the firm's plans – construction litigation, criminal and civil investigations – have closed down; certain partners who didn't want to accept the new world order have left. That said, on the news front, nothing more alarming has "*ground out of the rumour mill.*" Everyone is now learning how to adjust to the new-style Dechert London. The IT help desk is in the US and "*you get e-mails from America addressed to 'All Attorneys', some of which are quite annoying. I remember getting one asking me to welcome Sarah, a new librarian in New York.*"

To get them in the mood, new London trainees are treated to a transatlantic jaunt. Their initial induction week is spent in Philadelphia, the city of brotherly love and birthplace of both America's revolution and its constitution. Founded by William Penn and his band of Quakers, the people of this city have a tradition of getting their own way, and in Dechert HQ they've a mind to carry on laying down the law. "*The cynics amongst us would say the Americans are hell-bent on transforming us into a magic circle firm, though we'll never be one because of the culture of the office.*" But there has been change: "*The merger enables both parties to work on bigger and better things*" and massive strides have been made in the financial services sector.

Dechert's UK financial services team has grown from a standing start in 1997 into one of the country's top departments, billing over £7.6 million in 2003. The practice helps to set up funds, management companies and distribution operations in jurisdictions around the world, and advises on the creation of domestic and offshore funds, collateralised debt obligations and membership applications to the FSA and other regulators as well as activities in the main cash and derivatives markets. One's entry into the world of equities, bonds, currency swaps, derivatives, and hedge funds can be confusing to say the least. "*You just have to sit down and read up on it all*" was the best advice we got.

spoilt for choice

Quintessentially British clients have not forsaken the firm, so you'll still be acting for the likes of *The Telegraph* and Tesco. However, as we've said, in terms of clients and transactions the benefits of the merger are being felt, not least in the corporate department. One trainee outlined his role on a US client's purchase of a UK subsidiary company in the defence sector. "*There was a massive amount of due diligence and I was able to draft a large part of the report.*" Naturally, corporate deals bring trainees into contact with data rooms and other tedious tasks; however, in a display of junior empowerment, one of our interviewees declared: "*As trainee you have to do your fair share of grunt work, but you should never be prepared to do more than your fair share.*" We got a sense that a trainee has a choice whether to rise to challenges, and if they do then good work follows. It's a natural reaction of supervisors to be "*wary for the first couple of weeks and then, if you show you want it and can do it, you get more and more responsibility.*"

Any flaws to the six-seat system are "*vastly outweighed by the positives.*" Four months may feel too short in a seat that takes a while to settle into, so a lot of trainees repeat a favoured seat, either by rolling four months over into eight or by returning to the department closer to qualification day. The only non-negotiables in the system are a corporate-type seat, a property-type seat and a litigation-type seat, each of which is deliciously vague in definition. Rather than allowing choice to spoil them, we noted a strong sense of direction in our sources, even first-years. "*I am dead set on being a litigator,*" said one. Why was he so sure? "*Many people are headstrong in that regard. They come here knowing what they want and then their gut feelings are either reinforced... or sometimes blown out of the water.*" To get the seats you want, it's not a case of playing politics or sweet-talking the relevant partners, but more a case of simply saying: "*This is the path I want to take.*"

At each rotation there's a seat in Brussels offering competition law and close working with the US attorneys. The firm is pushing extra resources on to the Continent – it recently swiped Coudert's Munich lawyers and opened up in Luxembourg. As a result, there may be an opportunity for a German-speaking trainee to do a seat in Munich. As for trips stateside, anyone qualifying into a transactional seat gets to spend the last two months of their training contract in one of the Philadelphia, Boston, New York or Washington offices.

saint bernard

Ex-College of Law head and director of training at the firm Bernard George has the firm's supervisors rigorously schooled in the art of looking after trainees. "*Bernard is The Man,*" declared one source; "*and he has such respect among the partners.*" "*Every firm needs a Bernard,*" another agreed. Membership of the Inn Group of solicitors and barristers means masses of lectures and seminars held by outside speakers as well as internal sessions. A 'panel partner' is assigned to each trainee and then committed to sitting in on every end-of-seat appraisal. Some trainees maintain regular contact with their mentors, periodically meeting with them to discuss their progress over a cup of coffee. "*They are not just figureheads; they are there to provide input into your training.*"

english manners, american vitality

"*There's no culture here of trainees should be seen and not heard. They are able to express themselves.*" If our interviews were anything to go by this is certainly the case. Without wishing to swell their egos, we were enormously impressed by their analysis and presentation of their thoughts on the firm. The qualities they deemed necessary in their breed were adaptability, excellent communication skills, a well-defined work ethic and healthy ambition. Classic head boy and girl material, if you like. Of the qualifying trainees in September 2004, eight out of 12 stayed with the firm.

Serjeants, the pub below the office, is the meeting place after work. "*We don't have a trainee-exclusive social life,*" explained one of our sources. "*Outside the office, partners and associates just talk to you as if you are on a level with them. I've never understood why trainees at some firms are nervous of partners.*" The associates run a programme of summer soirées in the courtyard, boat trips down the Thames, trips to comedy clubs, and in 2003 they staged a charity variety performance. Playing their part, the trainees performed a version of *Blankety Blank* and, much to the amusement of the audience, took the micky out of some pretty senior figures at the firm. As for the partners, to their credit one of our sources said of them: "*There's not much haughtiness.*" A fact evinced by their willingness to transform the old partners' dining room into the open-to-all Dechert Deli.

The social calendar reaches its zenith during the week-long visit to London by 60 or so American summer interns. Lord knows what they make of the quaint London premises in the Inner Temple, what with its rustic filing cabinets and phantom air conditioning. Let's hope they're won over by the tinkling fountain and show of blooms in the courtyard. There's no denying that the dated London office is "*inappropriate*" for new-look Dechert, and the task in hand is to find somewhere in keeping with the firm's aggrandised ambitions.

We should not conclude without a word or two on Dechert's commitment to good causes – the pro bono programme is one of the best-received changes emanating from Philly. Most of the trainees we chatted to had taken control of a pro bono file or two, be this a planning case or a small litigation matter. A number had worked on US death row appeals and all had high praise for Suzy Turner, the London-based partner who co-ordinates Dechert's pro bono activity worldwide.

and finally...

Until now the firm's greatest recruiting tool has been its personable nature and the positive influence of the recruitment personnel on the students they meet. While it'll be no different this year, we believe the Dechert name will be associated much more with the perceived benefits (and pitfalls) of directions from across the pond.

Denton Wilde Sapte

the facts

Location: London, Milton Keynes
Number of UK partners/assistants: 146/290
Total number of trainees: 85
Seats: 4x6 months
Alternative seats: Overseas seats, secondments
Extras: Pro bono – The Prince's Youth Trust

London outfit Denton Wilde Sapte has been forced to make some hard decisions about its global ambitions this year and last. But with a new funky image and a timely focus on traditional strengths, it could be turning the corner.

oranges and dentons

Have you ever had a friend who had a few bad months, or perhaps a break-up and felt the need to reinvent themselves? You know the kind of thing: outlandish new clothes, a bizarre haircut or a sudden determination to give it all up and run an orphanage in Chile. It's all part of the healing process. There's nothing you can do except nod approval as they stare at you with manic eyes and a fixed grin, everything about them screaming "I am SOOO not over him/it/that." Well, this year Denton Wilde Sapte is that friend.

To explain: the years following a 2000 merger culminated in a year from hell in 2003 when the firm cut 70 jobs, let 50% of trainees go upon qualification and scrapped its European network, Denton International. But this drastic action wasn't enough to boost sagging profits. So, in spring 2004 the firm announced its withdrawal from Asia, jettisoning loss-making offices in Beijing, Hong Kong, Singapore and Tokyo, a move widely perceived as the end of the firm's global model approach. At this point the firm could have licked its wounds and lain low for a while. Instead, it reached for the hair dye to effect a major image overhaul.

Orange is the colour it hit upon. Not a muted orange or an ochre, but a *"really fluorescent," "the kind that hurts your eyes in the morning," "to be honest I had boxer shorts that colour when I was thirteen and it's not a happy memory"* orange. And the firm hasn't been backward in coming forward with the new look: business cards, promotional literature and office stationery are all now themed. Orange DWS-branded taxis roam the streets of London. The firm's managing partner even wore an orange boiler suit at the summer ball, apparently oblivious to any Guantanamo Bay overtones.

The trainees we interviewed were very aware that this loud, even manic, makeover is a self-conscious attempt to draw a line under a difficult and muddled period. *"We're trying to get rid of a past era,"* one opined, whilst another told us: *"It's about raising the firm's profile after some pretty bad press."* Some felt *"it makes us too dot.commy"* and recognised *"it could take us too far from the conventional law firm feel."* But overall the feeling was that this move has been an important step towards recuperation – "*It's not just rebranding at surface level.*"

there's gold in them thar hills

One of the reasons for this confidence is that the rebranding stresses the sector-based approach pushed by the firm for the last year. DWS has four 'key-strength' sectors: financial institutions; real estate and retail; energy, transport and infrastructure; and technology, media and telecommunications (TMT). It's not an innovative approach, and it's not unusual in times of hardship to fall back on old strengths, but trainees told us: "*There's been a lot of real work towards getting the sector groups working and communicating.*" Whilst some questioned: "*I wonder quite where we're going long term with this approach,*" evidence that it is bearing fruit comes from the trainee who told us: "*I feel like I'm qualifying into my sector.*"

There are plenty of other reasons for an optimistic outlook. DWS retains an international reach with offices in Moscow, Paris, Istanbul, the CIS and the Middle East, as well as a 'close friends' network in Europe. For trainees this means there are still overseas seats, but for the firm it's all about focusing on those sector strengths. The highly rated UK energy and infrastructure practice has received new instructions from British Energy, Centrica, EDF Energy and Powergen this year, but also advised the Government of Turkey on regulatory frameworks for renewable energy sources and the AIM listing of Marakand Minerals, owners of a polymetallic deposit in Uzbekistan. Furthermore, Africa is an area where the firm has established itself as one of the main players, with associate offices in Tanzania, Zambia, Uganda, Ghana and Botswana. With clients like the Western Mining Corporation, mining may make up the bulk of work, but the financial institutions sector is boosted by instructions from major financial players on the Continent, such as Standard Bank and West LB.

On the home front, departments within each sector retain an excellent reputation and some top-notch clients. In the financial institutions sector the banking department receives instructions from Royal Bank of Scotland, Crédit Lyonnais, Barclays, Deutsche Bank and ABN AMRO. It's a measure of the success of the traditionally strong property litigation department that it recently secured a key role on the £2 billion King's Cross Central regeneration project. Furthermore, the sports and media teams work for the English Football Association as well as having advised UEFA on the official Euro 2004 song. We could go on...

extreme party games

Body blows like the ones the firm has absorbed recently are not easily shaken off. NQ retention, for example, was a relatively unimpressive 34 out of 48 in September 2004, but we got the sense the firm is heading in the right direction. Internally, our sources told a similar story. Trainees were honest in their assessment that "*it's not been an easy time,*" with some suggesting that morale had been sapped, leading to "*a little apathy about the long-term picture.*" However, "*it is turning around.*" Despite trials and tribulations, our sources (both those with and without qualification jobs) were unanimous in enthusing: "*This is a great place to work day to day.*"

A hundred strong in previous years, the trainee population is being gradually trimmed in line with the leaner DWS identity. Nevertheless, with nearly 85 trainees and four six-month seats, rotation time is like a giant game of musical chairs with everything to play for. "*There are always six or seven people who don't get what they want and end up in real estate or banking.*" It is unusual for any trainee to miss a stint in one of these big departments, but generally speaking those who don't get their preferred seat on one rotation are quite likely to get their first choice next time around. Departments like sports, media, employment, energy and tax are "*incredibly popular*" and "*for trainees the third seat is seen as the important one for where you qualify, so there can be a logjam around popular seats then."* A few casualties are inevitable, though *"most people do get to do what they want over the two years."* The new sector approach is already bringing benefits: *"I wanted IP and didn't get it, but in telecoms there was a lot of fringe IP stuff which overlapped."*

in the can

Real estate was variously described as a dosshouse (*"it's relaxed: you go in, work your hours and go home"*) and a workhouse (*"you come in, work like a dog and go home"*), but either way the 9am–5.30pm hours were less stressful than the 9am–7pm elsewhere. The sector includes property litigation, commercial property and property finance, and extends to cover some of the PFI department's work. On the whole *"it's a lot of landlord and tenant stuff, manageable work and clients, and plenty of your own files."* At the higher end of the scale, trainees assist on *"massive PFI projects,"* working with organisations like English Partnerships.

By contrast TMT is rock 'n' roll. The sports team acts for the Premier League, Rio Ferdinand and Greg Rusedski, whilst the film team offers exposure to financing and production matters for major Hollywood film studios and British and international projects. Recent films include *Girl with a Pearl Earring*, *My House in Umbria*, *Harry Potter and the Prisoner of Azkaban*, *Love Actually*, *Bridget Jones: The Edge of Reason* and *Troy*. It seems there is equal excitement for trainees in the telecommunications or IP departments. One trainee who'd sat in the latter told us: *"I ran my own small files pretty much unsupervised, and there's good experience of big clients with recognisable trade marks."* Trainees also felt *"part of the team and treated like an NQ"* in TMT, in contrast to the *"well-established hierarchy"* of real estate.

Our sources were generally satisfied with the levels of feedback and responsibility they got across the firm. In insolvency litigation there is *"lots of client contact and lots of court work on dodgy deals and scams,"* and in asset finance you might get to deliver an aeroplane or help structure an agricultural equipment deal. The banking department sometimes has a secret weapon in the form of secondments.

Last but not least, the energy, transport and infrastructure sector includes a range of highly regarded departments including aviation, rail, water and waste. This is also where the electricity, and oil and gas departments reside, with national clients including London Electricity and international clients from almost everywhere. One trainee told us: *"I did a lot of work on issues surrounding a proposed new pipeline."* For the more ecologically minded the firm has also acted on wind farm developments, and the environment department advises a varied clientele on *"things like regulatory compliance on the conservation of natural habitats."*

you've been tangoed

Split across two sites for the last four years (one in the legal artery of Chancery Lane, the other not far from Fetter Lane), the powers in orange have decided not to try and find a single office big enough for all. Instead, Chancery Lane, which is close to the High Court for the litigators, is being tarted up. Culturally, DWS hasn't got the hardcore rep of a magic circle firm, but we suggest you take suggestions that it is *"laid back"* with the pinch of salt they deserve. We rather like the summary of the trainee who said: *"It wouldn't describe itself as a lifestyle firm, and it's not just work, work, work... but you do work."* Then again, the vast range of sports clubs and the variety of social activities to be enjoyed do suggest that DWS lawyers know how to relax. From dragon boat racing to softball, from drinks at the pub to *"weekends out clubbing,"* it's all there if you make the effort.

It's also no surprise that although originating from a variety of backgrounds (not all come from the tight pool of conventionally favoured universities), recent difficulties have bred a *"tight-knit group across both years."* E-mail banter and supportive advice fly around, as do the drinks on *"raucous nights at the pub."* However, this kind of relaxation isn't a reflex action for the entire firm, and deportment often depends both on department and location. *"You might go out with TMT partners, but never real estate ones,"* and *"we avoid the Corney & Barrow; it's very partnery and we couldn't act like we normally do in front of them."* The *"mind-blowingly good"* firm-wide summer party in 2004 was a more unified, egalitarian affair – *"I danced with my supervisor and with a guy from the post room."*

and finally...

The future's bright, the future's orange? Time will tell for Denton Wilde Sapte, but we'd put money on the fact that the glow we've noticed over EC4 is not a sign of nuclear meltdown. We advise donning protective shades if you're considering an application.

Devonshires

the facts

Location: London
Number of UK partners/assistants: 18/39
Total number of trainees: 10
Seats: 4x6 months
Alternative seats: None

Devonshires is a smaller London firm with a nationally recognised business serving the variegated legal needs of social housing organisations. This is a firm that knows what it does, and does what it knows.

firm foundations

The extent of Devonshires' social housing practice can't be exaggerated: it receives instructions from over 220 registered social landlords. In case you're wondering, an RSL is any organisation taking on the job of providing affordable housing – local authority housing departments, co-operatives, charitable and non-charitable housing associations and trusts and educational and health sector housing providers all fall within the legal definition. Social housing has deep roots in the UK, and many of those involved with the sector see themselves as part of a long-

standing movement rather than an industry.

At the simplest level, Devonshires' clients all require legal advice on the purchase, sale, development and funding of affordable homes for their tenants. However, in the last 15 years the breadth and sophistication of the sector's legal needs have increased dramatically. Many local authorities have transferred their housing stock and responsibilities to housing associations in deals frequently valued in hundreds of millions of pounds. In the private sector, planning legislation increasingly requires developers to include areas of affordable housing in new developments, pushing them into working relationships with RSLs. Lately, there has even been political controversy over agreements whereby local authorities outsource repair and management responsibilities to arms length management organisations (ALMOs). It all equates to legal work that can only be carried out by specialist firms, and as such Devonshires finds itself responding to the needs of RSLs across the country. Another measure of its success is its recent appointment to the Housing Corporation's newly created national panel, which is set to invest more than £3 billion in social housing in the next three years.

playing footsie

If you think it's all straight property work, you'd be wrong. Devonshires is at the forefront of new initiatives, such as Fusion 21, a project handled by the firm's corporate lawyers whereby seven Merseyside RSLs and a local authority entered into a pioneering partnership committed to finding new ways of working with the construction industry. Having tripled in size in the past five years, Devonshires is a more complex firm than ever before. Commercial property and PFI have become important departments in their own right, although their activities generally relate to the core client base. From one trainee we heard: *"Everything I've done revolves around RSLs in some way,"* but you don't have to have experience of the sector to apply to the firm – *"People come here for the small size and for the responsibility you get."* One source admitted: *"I really wanted to do property work and I didn't cotton on to the firm's RSL expertise until I joined."* Furthermore, the RSL clientele doesn't mean a meagre diet of good work or a narrow spectrum of experience: *"With social housing clients, you've got to think of them as multimillion pound companies with equivalent turnover to FTSE 250 companies. At client events, the people I meet are focused high-flyers."*

In property, the nature of the work allows you to *"have your own files and get on with them,"* be this *"drafting shared ownership agreements"* (where tenants buy a portion of the equity in their home and pay rent on the remainder) or *"negotiating the leases for a shopping centre owner."* On larger deals like the recent £350 million financing for Orbit HA or the £210 million financing for Somer Housing Group, trainees assist more experienced lawyers, *"implementing bank charges on housing association property portfolios"* or *"working on stamp duty post completion."*

bad behaviour

Beyond property work for RSLs, trainee seats are also available in commercial property, banking/corporate, employment, PFI, property litigation, housing management, construction and general litigation. As one sage head put it: *"Much of the work we do isn't particular to housing associations; in banking for example you'd be doing exactly the same work at any other firm for any other client."* The firm acts for many of the major financial institutions such as Lloyds TSB, Bradford & Bingley and Royal Bank of Scotland. *"If you're a finance house lending to a housing association, it makes sense to come to us because we know RSLs inside out."* In PFI, the firm has recently acted for the preferred bidder on a number of NHS LIFT projects and educational schemes. In this department, a trainee's lot tends to *"revolve around document management,"* but life is better at *"all-day client meetings or when you're doing research."* The pace here can be exciting: *"There are some colourful characters with drive and personality who run the department."*

The litigation department is subdivided into housing management, general litigation and PI/family. The housing management team obtained some of the first anti-social behaviour orders (ASBOs) against tenants, acted on cases involving the closure of crack houses and dealt with complex human rights issues relating to tenants. However, it is in the other two departments that the greatest divergence from the firm's core practice can be found. Trainees in general litigation told us: *"The department gets a lot of referrals from partners' previous lives at other firms."* Such as? *"Copyright work for one of the largest bike manufacturers in the world."* The growing capacity in the employment team means that a seat is now also available here, and a seat in PI and family involves *"straightforward slip-and-trip cases."* These are not to everyone's taste (*"once you've done one from beginning to end they're all essentially the same"*), but the work *"provides excellent training in the principles of law"* and a wealth of private client contact.

home is where the heart is

Devonshires occupies several floors of a *"slightly ageing"* office in London Wall. According to one source: *"It can be quite hard to negotiate...labyrinthine even!"* That said, trainees were generally very happy with their place within what they described as a *"humane, kind and fair"* firm, and stressed the *"passion and effort"* put into their training by supervisors. Special praise was reserved for the *"inspiring, intelligent"* managing partner Julie Bradley. Many of our interviewees had spent several years paralegalling at other firms before starting at Devonshires and were thus able to compare the firm with previous employers. Their praise for its *"open and not at all political"* atmosphere was all the more credible as a result. They explained that the firm is always willing to be accommodating over seat rotation (four seats is not a strict requirement) and frequently keeps trainees not offered an NQ position until they can locate alternative employment. In 2004, two out of four stayed on a permanent basis. The most fitting praise came from the trainee who told us: *"You're given the opportu-*

nity to express your own personality."

Professional, dedicated and expert, but not yet of a size to need the most formal of procedures and systems: *"Devonshires has still got the feel of a small firm."* The social scene is equally ad hoc, but there are still people to be found in the local pub, The Scottish Pound, of an evening.

and finally...

Thank goodness for firms like Devonshires. If you want to carve a career as a business lawyer, but you also believe that some things in life go deeper than the bottom line of corporate profits, this firm might well satisfy you.

Dickinson Dees

the facts

Location: Newcastle-upon-Tyne, Stockton-on-Tees
Number of UK partners/assistants: 64/116
Total number of trainees: 28
Seats: 4x6 months
Alternative seats: Brussels, secondments

Dickinson Dees is the gentle giant of the North East, its mighty arms wrapped firmly around the region in an embrace that's part bear hug, part stranglehold. The firm offers a full-picture legal service to a range of clients from the tweed-clad private client to the bullet-proofed multinational.

a swell firm

Rather like Richard Branson at his most intrepid, Dickinson Dees has ballooned in the last few years, but unlike the bearded wonder, there's no sign of it crashing down to earth. With 25 practice groups listed in our parent publication *Chambers UK*, over half of which are ranked numero uno in the North East, the firm employs a whopping 600 or so staff. With the North East market comfortably in the bag, it now competes for national work. We thought it pru-

dent to examine the firm for signs of bloating, growing pains or stretch marks, but are pleased to report a glowing bill of health and no foreseeable easing off of the pace.

By way of illustration, partner Craig Monty, recently recruited from Lovells to the dispute resolution group, is bringing in new work in his specific field of pensions litigation. Consider, too, the up-and-coming IP, environmental and urban regeneration teams that are attracting new clients of the likes of multinational chemicals outfit Huntsman. Further proof of Dickie Dees' success beyond its region can be found in its appointment to Croydon Borough Council's legal panel and its role acting for Govia on the negotiation of new South Central rail franchise agreements valued at £670 million.

We wondered whether the firm might be tempted to plant a permanent foot in London. A couple of obliging trainees thought *"it will have to make that decision in the next few years,"* but the majority felt that, for the time being at least, Stockton-on-Tees was as far south as it would go. This doesn't mean you'll be chained to Newcastle itself; the people we interviewed had bobbed about everywhere from London to Belfast and Carlisle on various deals. Nor does a Newcastle connection seem to be as important as it was once in the recruitment process. Even if *"a core number come from the North East,"* the net is widening and current recruits hail from all over the UK. Yes, a demonstrable commitment to a career in the region is advisable, but whether you say 'haway th'lads' or 'play up Newcastle,' you'll get a look in.

dig daddy

Based on St Ann's Wharf on the tidal banks of the Tyne, trainees told us Dickie Dees prides itself on providing *"a full, tailored service. We've got specialists in all areas."* While it is *"fully aware it is the best in the area,"* the salty sharp tang of the air keeps heads clear. *"We're not complacent; it's just that there's no rivalry really; no one else is quite on our level."* Dickie Dees, as the daddy in the city, charges higher fees than others, but by comparison with London prices its overheads and fee rates are low enough to be extremely attractive to southern clients.

Dickie Dees has a 30-year connection with Newcastle, something very apparent in the make-up of its high net worth private and agricultural client base, and these departments represent the more *"conservative"* aspects of the firm. One sensible type summed it up by saying: *"We may have strong connections with the great and good of Northumberland and beyond, but it doesn't mean anyone's stalking around the office in tweeds."* Our sources were keen to emphasise that the firm is *"aware of its heritage, but not constrained by it,"* and an impressive commercial client roster backs them up. Amongst its satisfied customers the firm counts Arriva, Reg Vardy, Teesside International Airport, Go-Ahead Group, the Environment Agency, Newcastle United and Northern Electric.

tinker, tailor, soldier, spy

Training is delivered through the medium of four six-month seats, with each trainee obliged to complete compulsory stints in coco, property and litigation. In the fourth seat, trainees can return to a previously sampled area or head over to private client (where they can also sample agricultural work). *"There's loads of choice within each seat because of the breadth of practice,"* and there's always the added prospect of a secondment to an affiliated firm in Brussels or to a client. Meanwhile, the Stockton-on-Tees office, where trainees will occasionally take a seat, is an eerie identikit of the Newcastle hub *"the same beige leather chairs, the same green carpet..."*

bean count outrage

From first week lunches to the head of corporate, who'll bellow kindly at a befuddled youngster *"Oi, you're looking lost. Where do you want to go?"* trainees are in good hands. Three-monthly appraisals do the job they're supposed to and seats allow room for growth, though *"you're never flailing around going 'Help, I'm stuck now!'"* All told, experiences like

"going through a box of deeds three times to find a missing document" were exceptions to the rule. Trainees also praise the firm for being *"very responsive to legal changes...I've had at least seven seminars on new money-laundering laws."*

Contracted hours are 9am–5pm, and we can only admire the trainee who warned of the dangers inherent in *"Parkinson's law"* (which states that work expands to fill the time you allocate to it). Basically, there's no point in staying later than you really need to because you'll not get any additional work done. One ambitious type suggested you might wish to work until 6pm, saying: *"Work your arse off and you'll go far."*

On hearing about the fresh cakes and biscuits baked in house for both internal and external meetings, we wondered if there was nothing Dickie Dees wouldn't do to keep staff happy. And then we inadvertently touched a nerve: *"Blasted coffee machines,"* beefed one trainee. Another griped: *"They're tacky Gold Blend machines. You only get two free cups a day, and after that you have to pay."* By the same token, although there are a few vending machines, they are lightly scattered across the offices and *"walking half a mile to get a snack is a mite too far."* Good for the waistline though. Despite the coffee outrage, 13 of the 14 qualifiers accepted positions in September 2004.

one bum note

Gazza infamously sang: "Sitting in a sleazy snack bar sucking sickly sausage rolls. In a dirty old town on the back of the Tyne." That was back in 1990, and Newcastle is now a testament to the effects of investment and regeneration. Dickie Dees occupies Quayside offices with panoramic views over the river and a hip-and-happening European city. Discerning trainees are likely to be found picking carefully over the selection of cafes, shops and art galleries on offer – *"The Baltic for cake and coffee, Ma Maison for tea and biscuits."* Or at least the girls are; the boys *"were shocked and had to leave"* on one such genteel outing. Thankfully, the array of bars close to their workplace means there's something for even the most reluctant of new men. Trainees enthused about the quality of life in the bustling metropolis, and in stark contrast to Gazza's singing we've only detected one bum note: on a recent trip to Toon Town the *Student Guide* observed that the Metro smelled of wee. You heard it here first.

The firm organises a wealth of entertainments year round, but we always ask for an update on the annual Stars-In-Their-Eyes talent contest. Normally organised in October, and an excellent opportunity for new trainees to meet the entire firm, it is a truly star-studded night. Last year's winner was a trainee acting up as Will Young, and the training manager herself took the role of compère dressed as a Cheeky Girl. Probably inadvisable to touch her bum though.

and finally...

If you live in the North East, putting Dickinson Dees on your shortlist has always been the obvious thing to do, but these days it's an increasingly attractive option for those resident below the 54th parallel. A great firm...if you can get a foot in the door.

DLA LLP

the facts

Location: Birmingham, Leeds, Liverpool, London, Manchester, Sheffield and three other UK offices
Number of UK partners/assistants: 395/837
Total number of trainees: 151 plus more in Scotland & Hong Kong
Seats: 4x6 months
Alternative seats: Secondments
Extras: Pro bono – The Prince's Trust plus regional projects.

From humble Sheffield beginnings came a world-famous brand. No, we're not talking about the Lycra-clad Def Leppard lads. Try DLA, a fiercely proud, gravity-defying, poll-winning law firm that's made its fortune...very publicly and very rapidly.

steely determination

For a law firm that didn't even exist ten years ago, DLA has achieved considerably more than anyone expected. Anyone except its management team that is. Yet when you've a visionary in charge – in this case DLA's managing partner, Nigel Knowles – perhaps miracles are inevitable. He and the other top brass took a Sheffield-based firm and merged it with others, first in Leeds, then in other parts of the UK. After this they set their sights on continental European jurisdictions, with a view to either planting their own flag or building up exclusive relationships with established firms. Thus the DLA Group was created. Having bagged four offices in Asia, DLA is now hoping to go transatlantic through a tie-up with Chicago firm Piper Rudnick.Though when we went to press there was no concrete news. On the pace of growth, trainees say: "*It will reach a plateau or slow down, but at the moment the world is not enough.*" Exactly how the firm achieved so much in such a short space of time is a mystery to many in the profession, so we decided to delve deep into its corporate psyche by quizzing trainees and young assistants. What emerged from our interviews was rather telling...

To understand DLA is to understand the men behind DLA, particularly the charismatic managing partner. And to understand them you need to learn a thing or two about the firm's spiritual home. "*The big chiefs at DLA come from Sheffield and some of them still work here... It's where they grew up and cut their teeth.*" Much like the city, these men "*made a big push*" at a time when Sheffield was picking itself up after the malaise of the 1980s. And just like the stripping ex-steel workers in *The Full Monty*, DLA once adopted the theme tune from the movie *Flashdance*, which is itself an up-by-your-bootstraps, working-class-made-good parable. If you've consigned Sheffield to the cutlery drawer of the 1970s, you're ignoring its universities, teaching hospitals, the (arguably pointless) National Centre for Popular Music, the Meadowhall shopping complex, the stunning Derbyshire Dales, and the obvious wealth of the S10 postcode. Civic pride? Sheffield folk pity those of us who don't live there. *"And,"* quipped one Midlands-based trainee, *"it brought us Nigel Knowles!"*

pour some sugar on me

This is a firm where you are judged on what you do and not who you are or what school you went to. Encouraging the most determined and dedicated to achieve the unachievable is the firm's modus operandi. Take its charitable endeavours for the Wellchild Foundation. In an almost symbolic manner, it set itself a target figure of £500,000. And raised it. Nigel Knowles was the figurehead for that project, as he is for the DLA's business goals or 'visions'. Once upon a time, the current vision – to make it as a top-five firm in Europe by 2006 with a presence in Asia and the USA – sounded totally unattainable. These days you have to admit the firm's done rather well. *"We were never Herbert Smith,"* one trainee mused. *"Big clients never walked through our door; we always had to go out and get them...to market hard. That's the ethos that has infiltrated the firm; it's a crusading attitude that has made us expansionist."*

In case you miss out on any of Nigel's motivational speeches or the latest corporate video, a monthly magazine called *DLA: Way Ahead* will bring you up to date with the sweetest news. *"In the latest edition there was information on the opening of the Moscow office. We've had articles about the Sunday Times' good workplace survey, which we did really well in. It's propaganda I suppose, but it's always good to be able to say to clients what DLA is doing elsewhere."*

are you winding me up?

Under the four-seat system, first-years indicate their three preferred options, second-years need only give two. Mostly things work out, although you need to be a bit tactical and inevitably *"some aren't happy to get their third choice."* There are few rules on what you must do: in larger offices the only stipulation is that trainees undertake a contentious and non-con-

tentious seat. In smaller offices, seat allocation sounds a shade more prescriptive. In Liverpool, for example, you're unlikely to escape either real estate or corporate.

BS&R is the name for the business support and restructuring department, which takes its instructions from insolvency practitioners (ie accountants) and banks. In a contentious BS&R seat you'll assist on large claims against directors of insolvent companies, whilst also grabbing some of the action on smaller cases, such as chambers advocacy to withdraw winding-up petitions, or debt collection. In a non-contentious seat, you'll be selling off an insolvent company's assets, perhaps working in tandem with lawyers from the real estate department. And on the subject of real estate, it's presently one of DLA's success stories. *"The way we work here is different to a lot of firms. Departments like property are not just corporate support departments."* Indeed, no area of practice is more important than any other – *"For someone choosing where to train that's a very good thing."*

But if corporate is your thing, take note: one of our sources said he'd run his own deal. It was worth just a couple of million pounds, but the experience was an excellent contrast to the role he'd taken within a team of six lawyers working on a much bigger transaction worth a couple of hundred million pounds. In C&P (commercial and projects) the commercial bit amounts to *"smaller corporate-style deals such as asset sales, agency agreements, consumer credit, a little IP and IT contract work"* and the projects bit relates to PFI and PPP on hospitals, schools and transport projects such as the Merseyrail tram system. All the seats we've mentioned were popular with our sources. Thinking about it, we didn't actually hear of a duff seat.

connect four

Three-monthly appraisals provide *"a good vantage point to see where you have got to and where you need to go. They are not merely procedural; you do get frank and constructive comments."* Training co-ordinator Sally

Carthy spends a lot of time on the road so she can have quarterly one-on-ones with every trainee: *"It's amazing how she remembers all our names. I haven't needed her in a work-related conciliatory way, but you can talk to her frankly."*

Training sessions are run nationally, both the initial induction – at which you'll meet all the other newbies plus those starting in Hong Kong, Brussels and Scotland – and many departmental sessions. After qualification, you can go on Connect Breaks, which are subsidised weekend trips designed to promote contact with European associates. These have included *"sports in Madrid, food in Amsterdam and an art exhibition in Gothenburg."* Proving that fortune favours the brave at DLA, a few trainees who pushed hard enough have also gone.

In terms of overseas seats, for now there are none but client secondments can provide time out of the office for those who want it.

brother, where art thou?

One trainee in the capital claimed to know where the DLA power base lay: *"London is the HQ. We're trying to get away from that northern rottweiler image, and any firm that wants to portray itself as offering an international service has to have a decent London presence."* That said, even though you'll find the top brass commuting from Sheffield to their offices in London, it's not easy to pinpoint the firm's epicentre. *"Different departments are run from different places, and you don't feel like everything is centralised in one place."* Graduate recruitment and training, for example, is run from Birmingham.

While the big departments feature everywhere, certain offices have developed a stronger reputation than others for specific practice areas. *"In Leeds, the engine room is the real estate department. It billed a phenomenal amount last year...more than the whole of one of the regional offices."* And certain offices have strands that are not present in all others, such as aviation in London, healthcare in Birmingham and business crime in Leeds. Liverpool, on the other hand, has no

tax department and relies on lawyers in Manchester or elsewhere. But this, they tell us, is one of the advantages of working in a national firm; know-how and clients can be shipped in from another office as and when it suits. *"Within ten minutes I can get e-mails back from people who've done the same stuff before,"* said one source.

We sensed certain office-specific character traits. Liverpool is very active socially and Sheffield trainees aren't too proud to do low-value work in seats like insurance litigation, where they trade glamour for hands-on experience. Leeds and Birmingham trainees believe they've ended up in the hardest working law firm in their respective cities and London trainees are just as likely to come from Surrey or somewhere equally soft and southern as any of their City counterparts. There's a friendly rivalry between offices which, we must confess, we tried to stir up in our search for the best office gossip. However, either tantalising tales are thin on the ground or trainees were keeping schtum. The best we got was a tale about a Scottish office security guard who, while marshalling a crowd auditioning for George Clooney's next movie, was picked for a role himself.

it's the real thing

It's easier to see what connects DLA recruits than what distinguishes them from each other. According to our sources, you must be ambitious, bright and hard working. You have to be *"up for getting involved, keen on being part of a team,"* and *"a confident person who has enough bottle to not be intimidated. Partners react to that well."* For some people business, not law, is the prime motivation: *"Our focus is on assisting clients in commercial, business terms not in a stuffy legal way,"* one said earnestly. And from another: *"The thing I love about DLA is that I don't just give legal solutions. I have to understand what perspective my client is coming from. That follows through in the way DLA handles itself. We are a law firm and a business."*

And businesses need branding. *"The branding is*

everything. *Brands sell. They represent something."* Two trainees likened the firm to Coca-Cola. Were they repeating something they'd seen on the most recent motivational video, or did they simply want to buy the world a Coke and lead it by the hand into a new age of legal services? What did the DLA brand mean to them? *"The idea that there is a proper partnership between the clients and us; that we can improve their business; that DLA is approachable."* The implication is that other law firms are not actually meeting clients' needs and that the most successful are sitting on their laurels. Funnily enough, that was the main thrust of DLA's 2003 press campaign, in which they distanced themselves from the likes of the magic circle.

The branding, which includes a set of values that you can read on the firm's website and a prominent 'blue square' logo, is a key weapon in the battle for hearts and minds. And by that we mean the minds of clients, staff and people like you, dear reader. You can either buy into it with religious fervour or shrug it off as an evil necessary to transubstantiate visions into reality. Within DLA there are believers (*"The visions and values are backed up. They are not just empty words"*), agnostics (*"To a certain extent you see what they are trying to do"*) and even the odd atheist (*"During the induction period the visions and the values were stressed over and over again, but I am not getting carried along by the tide"*). Ultimately, there is acceptance: *"It makes business sense for us all to be behind the firm and its drive forward."* A word to the wise for the cynical: *"If you go around showing that you think it's all bullshit, you really won't get very far. You have got to be seen to share the crusading thing. I am nothing like some of the people you see here: if you cut them you'd see little blue squares coming out."* Blue squares or not, 60 of the 71 qualifiers stayed with the firm in September 2004.

and finally...

At DLA you've got to play the game, but the rules are fair and very well defined, and the prize is both attractive and exciting. Definitely not a firm for the nihilistic though.

DMH

the facts

Location: Brighton, Crawley, London
Number of UK partners/assistants: 34/25
Total number of trainees: 13
Seats: 4x6 months
Alternative seats: None

Not so long ago this was a small Brighton minnow called Donne Mileham & Haddock, but look at it now! DMH started fishing in newer waters in Crawley in the 90s and has now landed an office in the capital.

london to brighton backwards

It's all go at DMH, trainees told us. *"Two years ago we never thought we'd have a London office, and to that extent the firm might be unrecognisable in another couple of years."* The London office was created out of a merger with a small niche insurance practice and since then new partners have been recruited from Jones Day and Morgan Cole. Tellingly, we heard that management *"are always looking for good niche firms"* and *"they have changed the firm's vision from wanting to be leading in the South East to be leading in London and the South East. They want to start rivalling the mid-sizers in London."*

Bit by bit, the commercial side of DMH's Brighton operation has decamped to Crawley near Gatwick Airport; the logic is simple – there's more scope for winning new clients and business here. On the firm's books now are several retail banks and local authorities, SEEBOARD, retail giant Arcadia, Greater London Magistrates' Courts Association, Amlin Plc, a busy venture capital company called the South East Growth Fund and Reigate & Banstead Housing Trust, which owns 7,000 properties.

under the flight path

Trainees complete four six-month seats in different departments. *"There's no real competition for seats,"* one told us; "*in my year there are just five trainees so we managed to work it so we got what we wanted.*" New recruits are asked at the outset what they want from their training, and "*they've definitely taken on more people who want to be commercial lawyers recently.*" Anyone of a commercial disposition should note that "*all the good departments are in Crawley*" and Crawley itself is "*horrible.*" Ah well...

Property is the firm's biggest asset so trainees almost always end up with a seat in this field, albeit some do property litigation or planning. A commercial property seat in Crawley brings independence and your own caseload. "*I met with my supervising partner once a week and did a lot of research for others in the group...the newly qualified solicitors were also really helpful.*" Much of your time is spent working for London boroughs or landlords with retail portfolios.

Employment is another biggie, with trainees in this department covering mainly respondent work, though "*they want to keep some applicant work going so we see things from both sides.*" The operation is led by outgoing training partner Rustom Tata, who one of our sources insisted we big up, because he'd done such a good job over the last seven years. "*He takes his job very very seriously and remembers every little thing about your personal life and what you were talking about last time you saw him.*" The new training partner clearly has big shoes to fill. Wearing his hat as seat supervisor, Mr T watches trainees closely, but allows them to gets them stuck into drafting witness statements and correspondence. They also get to accompany him to client meetings and tribunals, no doubt coming to appreciate why he's rated as one of the top practitioners in the south of England.

In a coco seat most of your work will come from the commercial side – carrying out research, drafting terms and conditions and IP licences, etc. Additionally you'll assist on a couple of corporate transactions; however, trainees report that the seat can be quiet ("*they almost can't justify having a trainee at times*"). "*Things are getting better; the new American partner* [UK, NY and Florida-qualified] *is doing a lot of*

networking and bringing in deals.*" Indeed, we noted a north American angle to a number of the recent transactions. The innovation and media team concentrates on IP and IT work mostly for smaller regional businesses, but also for the likes of online insurance companies and guitar manufacturer Fender, which sought advice in relation to the promotion and sponsorship of the 50th anniversary of the Stratocaster model. A new insolvency seat London ("*it was a bit of a shock when it became available*") and a litigation seat in Crawley complete the commercial package.

pebble dash

In lovely Brighton, home to the newly re-named 'private office', seats are available in tax, trusts and probate, property, planning and PI. Not everyone wants to do PI, but that doesn't mean they won't be posted there in their first year. Said one trainee: "*I thought it would be ambulance chasing and that I'd have to be sympathetic when really I am a cynical person. Thankfully it wasn't like that at all. The seat is busy and the day goes really quickly...it's a buzz having to prioritise about 70 files.*" Almost all of your cases (on which you'll meet with clients and counsel) will be fast track worth under £15,000; for anything more complex, you'll have to elbow in on your supervisor's matters. The department sounds like a lot of fun and "*senior fee earners interact easily with juniors.*" Things are a shade more formal in tax, trusts and probate, although the experience is similar to PI in that it entails a good deal of client contact on your own files. A family seat won't disappoint on that score either.

In a sense, Brighton is a victim of its own success. "*Property prices are ridiculous and rents are almost the same as London.*" Having "*London prices and a southern wage*" can leave you with less than a third of your salary left after essential costs, which is tough if you've still got law school debts to pay. Life at DMH is "*a trade off*" between money and lifestyle. For most, finishing before half five, having an hour and a quarter for lunch and being able to walk to work – in an office just two minutes from the beach – is well worth it. This is a firm people end up at by design rather than accident: trainees almost all attended one of the nearby universities (DMH runs competitions at Sussex Uni) or have family in the area. And they tend to stay – in 2004, all four qualifiers took jobs with the firm.

saving face

Last year *"there seemed to be a bit of a cull...virtually every Friday someone high level was leaving. I think management were getting tough to become more profitable."* If so, the firm's not alone in clearing out the cobwebs. The AGM is a time for talking tactics and getting staff on board with plans for the future. Last time round, DMH brought in a local theatre company to enliven the proceedings. *"We all had to wear masks and do mimes. It was embarrassing!"* The DMH band was also unveiled to an expectant crowd – *"It's a proper band made up of ten people...partners, solicitors and secretaries. There are four female singers and a guy from the post room on drums."* Apparently they sound like The Commitments doing Britney Spears.

This year's summer party was another big knees up and staff brought their families together for a BBQ on the lawns of a stately home. An excellent social committee in Brighton is run by *"someone who loves going out,"* and when nothing's been organised or it's close to pay day and you haven't a pot to piss in, there's always the local pub-cum-chamber pot museum, The Pond, next door to the office. Forty-five minutes away in Crawley, the conveyancing team makes the most it can of the town's modest entertainment opportunities by going bowling. In all offices, DMH has a business suits dress code...unless it's scorching hot and the air con in Brighton is on the blink, when it's shorts and T-shirts. Perfect for lunchtime sunbathing? *"Yes, there are a lot of sickeningly tanned people here!"*

and finally...

With the commercial teams moving to Crawley and increasingly dominating the firm, you have to wonder if the pleasure of working in what must be one of the UK's best locations is being traded for better work and bigger profits. Ultimately, however, DMH still has the edge over the vast majority of firms in its ability to offer a lifestyle that most lawyers would kill for.

Dorsey & Whitney LLP

the facts

Location: London
Number of UK partners/assistants: 9/21
Total number of trainees: 8
Seats: 4x6 months
Alternative seats: Secondments

Dorsey & Whitney is a Minneapolis-based giant with 20 offices spanning North America, Asia and Europe. But a word of warning to those hoping to collect new stamps in their passports: the London office is a relatively self-contained outfit and the training is equally so.

the english job

The mothership may be painted with the stars and stripes, but this little extra terrestrial has bought two St George's flags for the roof of its Mini Cooper. Britcentricity is the order of the day for trainees taking up places at the firm: *"This isn't a White & Case style law firm and there's no imposing US culture."* We learned that *"almost everyone's English and English-trained."* The greatest crossover occurs in corporate, where *"probably a fifth of what you work on is for US clients,"* and the transactional nature of such work does mean that *"lawyers shuttle backwards and forwards from the States."* Second-year trainees get the chance to smudge national boundaries with a trip to the US for a *"lawyer-retreat thing, which is good for getting a sense of the massive scale of the firm."* But that is pretty much it. There are no seats overseas and *"even as an NQ, I'm not sure there is much prospect of moving to the States or Asia."*

Reconciling yourself to the fact that training isn't going to involve jetsetting is the one of the few compromises you'll have to make. The London office handles domestic and cross-border capital markets, M&A and real estate transactions as well as IP and litigation. Trainees' four six-month seats can be taken in the litigation, corporate, commercial property, tax, IP and competition teams, and there's also the possibility of client secondments. Whether it's for UK, European or multinational clients, there is ample high-quality work with which to engage. The trainees we interviewed had worked on IP issues for the UK branch of DaimlerChrysler ("I had to go out with a camera and get photographs of a rival firm's infringing logos") and M&A transactions like the recent £20 million cross-border acquisition of UK concerns by Smiths Group plc. In property, they had "run smaller transactions from inception to completion" and assisted with site purchases for a major multinational car manufacturer.

the muppet show: no strings on us

The Dorsey show also features star turns by specialist departments that very much play the music and dress up bright. This year the firm acted for EM:TV on the $78 million sale of the Jim Henson Company back to the Henson family, and has retained a working relationship with the Muppet outfit. Other notable clients include a major British film star, music artists and producers, film producers/financers and the Raindance Film Festival. A quick shifty around the firm's excellently placed offices near Liverpool Street confirms a strong link to the media and creative industries. Meeting rooms and office walls are decorated with film posters reflecting Dorsey locations – "We've got offices in Fargo and Seattle, so there's a Fargo poster and a Sleepless in Seattle poster." And clients, too, have their place: "We worked for someone involved with Lord of the Rings, so there's a premiere poster on the first floor."

the cherry harvest

Given the small size of the office, with seven partners and roughly 40 lawyers in total, work from transac-

tions like the Henson deal spills across all departments. This cross-fertilisation is reflected in seating arrangements – "although a lot of the litigation people tend to sit together, departments aren't divided between floors or geographically delineated." The firm owns its five-storey home and has filled just three floors, leaving plenty of room for future growth. That said, the current recruitment strategy is all about cherry-picking mature lawyers or teams into specialist areas. It's a principle that has served the firm well: the highly regarded IP team was recruited a couple of years ago from East of England firm Hewitsons and has done so well that a Cambridge office has been opened to challenge the likes of Eversheds, Mills & Reeve and Taylor Wessing for Silicon Fen IP/IT and venture capital work. The hire of "an experienced biotech lawyer" has bolstered the office, which it is hoped will be introduced to Dorsey's global technology expertise.

In the last few years the firm has also sneaked over the orchard wall to snaffle a six-lawyer team from PwC's allied law firm Landwell and a partner and associate from Ernst & Young's tied firm. These people have turbocharged the firm's UK tax and antitrust capability. Trainees who had sampled life in the tax department had worked first hand on a "groundbreaking class-action style case" in which the firm is representing over 60 UK plcs in a suit against the Inland Revenue for tax losses on the grounds that UK tax law does not comply with EU regulations. Don't you just love it when a plan comes together?

a mini adventure

Trainees told us that "the firm's size means you're able to gain experience very quickly," and their involvement in high-calibre work lends weight to the claim. "It pays pretty much magic circle rates, but you get a very different experience," one trainee advised, gleefully reflecting on "swathes of responsibility," whilst another admitted: "My learning curve has been very steep." Generally very happy with the support and feedback they had received, our sources did note that "the office is only just beginning to reach the size where it needs really formal processes for everything." With trainee numbers increasing to eight this year, and new arrivals now offered only a September start date, the office is clearly refining and formalising its procedures. Mid and end-of-seat appraisals are in operation, but interviewees told us: "You can normally work out from the expression on a partner's face whether you've done well or not!" More redolent of a global law firm is the programme of formal training and seminars: "It's a lot more organised than you might expect for an office this size. We've covered marketing, selling, pitching, management and people skills." "That's the US connection in play," observed one wise head.

Office life Dorsey style means "an open-minded, informal culture" with "little evident hierarchy." It is a dynamic that is also seen outside work: "When we go out, everyone goes; partners socialise with secretaries, it's really relaxed and you never feel like you're being tested." On occasion the hours can be long, though 9am-6.30pm seems average, leaving plenty of time for an evening tipple at the Red Lion or the local Corney & Barrow. Partner-organised nights out, such as a trip to Romford dog track, are not uncommon either.

Those we interviewed tended to be high-flyers from non-traditional universities and mostly came with a healthy chunk of life experience. They concluded that "technical ability and a dash of charisma" will take you far at the firm. Presumably brimming with these qualities, of the three trainees who qualified in 2004, two stayed on. The person who left went stateside to work with death row prisoners.

and finally...

It may be a dark horse for trainees thinking about a City training, but we reckon hitching yourself to Dorsey & Whitney sounds like a smart idea. As one of our sources summarised: "You're part of the team, your contribution is important and you are very well looked after."

DWF

the facts

Location: Liverpool, Manchester, Warrington
Number of UK partners/assistants: 55/123
Total number of trainees: 16
Seats: 2x6 + 3x4 months
Alternative seats: None

Having started out in 1977 as an insurance litigation practice, this growing North West firm is maturing into a broader-based commercial player. Any student set on training in either Manchester or Liverpool, but a little wary of the national behemoths, is advised to read on...

some complicated maths

Trainees usually sit out their entire two years in either Manchester or Liverpool as both offices offer the same range of seats. "Both offices are seen to be equal; it is not the case that one is the HQ," though depending on who you speak to you'll hear that "Liverpool is the place to be" or that "Manchester is easily the best." There is plenty of communication between the two cities and regular trips up and down the M62 for both work and pleasure.

The DWF seat system is not the normal four by six-months affair – it's far more complicated than that. Basically, the first seat of six months is followed by three four-month seats, and then "the idea is that your final six months are spent in the department you will qualify into." The longer first seat "helps you settle down;" as for the others, "after four months you know if you like it or not and if you do you can go back." On this last point, trainees said they appreciate being able to take a running jump into qualification, though some felt the experimental first seat of six months had been too long. They're optimistic that while "the kinks [in the system] haven't been ironed out yet, it will all get worked out neat and tidy."

Perhaps more important than their length is the type of seats available. Typically, three are taken in insurance litigation, corporate, commercial property or commercial dispute resolution. Though officially the firm doesn't stipulate that trainees must do any one seat in particular, one thought *"insurance might be compulsory...well, just about everyone does it. They like you to do corporate too."* The first seat is chosen for you and thereafter *"it is 50-50 whether or not you get what you want."*

dog bites man, man sues dog owner

The insurance litigation department is still *"dominant in terms of size"* and acts for the giants of the industry including Zurich and Royal & SunAlliance. The scope of the practice covers everything from professional indemnity to personal injury, in other words everything from *"buildings that have gone wrong"* to *"a dangerous dog."* Yet, however much insurance has traditionally been *"the big thing"* for the firm, it does not dominate the ambitions of trainees. *"Some really love it, others really hate it,"* and usually for the same reasons – *"it is really busy, you get a lot of cases and it is a case of sink or swim."* On the plus side, client contact is freely available to trainees, and *"it is certainly not the case that you just do the legwork on files for the partner to come in and claim all the glory."* On the down side *"you get a certain amount of the really rough jobs"* like photocopying or bundling, but as one trainee reasoned, *"you're only asked to do this if absolutely necessary."* While in the insurance lit seat, all our sources had made the most of the firm's in-house barrister by shadowing him at court to learn the ropes of advocacy.

in the can

DWF is pursuing a programme of general commercial growth and fermentation. Commercial property, construction, health and safety and insolvency have been the most recent departments to swell in the warmth of the DWF pot. Chunky national brands of the likes of Persimmon Homes, Carpetright, PwC, KPMG and Ernst & Young are increasingly being added to the client roster alongside regional names such as Liverpool John Moores University, Manchester Airport, and a number of food producers including Princes, Inter Link Foods and Burton's Foods.

In a corporate seat, depending on the number of deals hitting the partners' desks, *"it is either absolutely mental or dead,'* so you could either be *"rushing off to London and whatnot"* or *"twiddling your thumbs."* And while in corporate *"it takes a while to get autonomy because you have to prove yourself first,"* in commercial property when a trainee is given a file it becomes *"pretty much your own baby."* One of the smaller departments, the health and safety team is known as *"an exciting place to be, with loads of interesting court work."* A recent case involved a local school that was prosecuted after pupils went on a trip that ended in tragedy. In employment, trainees get a healthy dose of TUPE work, along with the more standard diet of drafting and checking contracts and accompanying solicitors to tribunals.

Our sources ummed and aahhed about which seats were the most popular, eventually concluding that *"it is horses for courses and everyone qualifies where they want to."* As in the past, DWF maintained an excellent NQ retention record in 2004, keeping on all eight of its qualifiers. Avoiding last minute *"jumping through hoops,"* all were told the good news early in the year.

miss congeniality

As well as rapid growth and diversification, DWF has also been through cultural and stylistic changes. *"They are getting rid of all the old logos – we have new offices and a new image,"* explained one source. Actually, all our interviewees chatted away with refreshing vigour about the firm's *"modern, progressive and trendy"* atmosphere. While *"there has been a move away from the more traditional set-up,"* the firm has not deteriorated into excitable, youthful disarray and *"there are still chains of respect."* As someone put it: *"There is definitely a hierarchy, but you don't feel like the lowest of the low. I don't get depressed about it."* Moreover, we sensed that trainees are kept well informed and are consulted on developments within the firm.

For all the change, DWF remains a distinctly northern place, and according to our sources, the North West is *"miles better than London and not like Coronation Street at all."* Manchester city centre has received a major facelift in the last decade and Liverpool is now strutting in tinsel tiara and a winners' sash reading 'European Capital of Culture 2008'. Hardly surprising then that with the games, gossip and glossy paint-job on their front step, our sources felt little need to venture beyond the end of the street.

chilling tales

Across the Liverpool–Manchester divide, trainees are a cohesive, matey group that likes to hang out at weekends; some trainees even live together. Our interviewees chattered away with a rare intimacy about their friends' interests, experiences, ability on the football pitch and choice of nail colour. One said sweetly: *"There is always some moral support on the other side of the filing cabinet if you need it."* Playing nicely and sharing their toys, *"there is an expectation that people will muck in when required."* We readily believed the trainee who claimed: *"There are no airs and graces"* and *"anyone trampling on others to get to the top wouldn't get very far."*

The hours are great – *"You can work your standard nine-to-five day"* – and this perhaps explains why DWF's social life is as full as it is. In Liverpool, Friday nights always mean Newz Bar, The Living Room or Metro, while in Manchester trainees spice things up with a trip to Persia. Highlights of the trainee social calendar are 'Young Professionals' evenings, at which DWF trainees and younger fee earners host networking events with a twist. One recent bash had a Bollywood theme, and an On the Piste party required trainees to remodel the firm's client area into a ski resort with snowballs, with eggnog on the drinks list and a strict dress code of bobble hats and goggles. Said one source: *"We were in a board room with no air con, so I got quite toasty in my bobble hat. It's very hard to get the top off a bottle of Stella with gloves on..."*

The Liverpool office is affectionately described as *"a rabbit warren"* with *"this one lift that tends to trap the unwary now and again."* In Manchester, the trainees can afford to be rather smug about their *"very plush"* new residence at Centurion House. This office is open plan with break-out rooms (ominously referred to as *"break-down rooms"*) and *"chrome, glass and shiny wood...it's beech veneer as far as the eye can see."* Huge windows give panoramic views out over the city and the Manchester Evening News building, so *"you get to see all the latest offers on the advertising board."* When we called, a holiday for two in Turkey was being plugged at £429, but for those on a tighter budget, the office also has views over Pret – *"It's great, you can see when the queue has gone down and time it perfectly."* On a strict diet? Simply take a trip to the office vending machine for 25-calorie soup washed down with a cup of watery hot chocolate.

and finally...

For solid insurance work, or an all-round general commercial experience in the North West, look out for DWF – *"they're the ones wearing bobble hats."*

Edwards Geldard

the facts

Location: Cardiff, Derby, Nottingham
Number of UK partners/assistants: 47/69
Total number of trainees: 20
Seats: 6x4 month seats
Alternative seats: None

There's a cold war going on at Edwards Geldard. Even though the partners may have emergency hotlines to each other, as far as trainees are concerned, there's not much contact between east and west. You'll have to pick your side of the dividing line but you'll find a remarkably similar ideology either way: local focus, big personalities and go-karting.

positioning the troops

While the firm deals with some *"wealthy private clients"* and a bit of residential conveyancing, business as usual means commercial work for *"medium to large-ish enterprises,"* which includes anything from *"one-off businesses"* to *"people who have branches all over the country."* The national and international *"big players"* on Edwards Geldards' side include security company Chubb and car dealer Pendragon, and these clients instruct both offices. More usually, the client base for each office is drawn from the firm's two regions.

The Cardiff office, for example, advises a host of Welsh institutions such as the National Library and the Wales Millennium Centre, and its corporate lawyers recently got themselves tangled up in nearby Chepstow Racecourse's complex reverse takeover of Northern Racing Limited. That might sound a bit like a tricky military manoeuvre, but turns out to be something to do with shareholders' interests. Over in the East Midlands, Derby County FC is a major client and the real estate team recently helped out on the Rams' sale of their former home, the incongruously named Baseball Ground. In the East Midlands, the firm splits evenly between Nottingham and Derby; corporate and property teams are found in both, but for contentious work, Derby's the place. However, if you need insolvency advice or want to say guten tag to the firm's small team of German-qualified lawyers, you'd better hotfoot it over to Nottingham.

Because both sides of the firm work for mainly regional clients, trainee *"paths haven't really crossed,"* although diplomatic relations are made during a day of joint training at the start of the contract and there are firm-wide e-mails and the odd videoconference. *"There are not firm-wide events"* but *"if one department was really busy, then maybe people would go over to help...if there was a need, we would overlap."*

corporate nerves

In both offices, there's a six-seat training scheme with the first three seats chosen for you. Only the Welsh trainees told us they could expect to have some influence in choosing their second-year seats, although in the East Midlands the firm does try to ensure that trainees spend their final seat in the department where they want to qualify. However, with six seats to be worked through, trainees are effectively guaranteed a spell in most of the main areas of work

EG likes everyone to do corporate, property and litigation. Property is a common first-year posting and trainees soon find the work here is really varied. It sounds like they get a good stab at all the basics – *"dealing with lease summaries, research, writing letters of advice, searches, insurance and registrations at the land registry."* Trainees told us breadth was also a strength of the litigation seat: *"You could be asked to look into defamation one day and then procedures in the White Book the next, and then IP or insolvency. We have a vast range of matters and you can gain experience in it all."* As well as getting you involved in the big cases, where you might be taking notes in court or working on a schedule of loss or a witness statement, the firm also makes sure you have experience of file management on smaller claims.

Trainees seemed especially wary of the corporate department in Cardiff, saying: *"People always dread going there"* as *"the heavy workload is challenging."* But once there, we sense they quickly realise it's not so bad. *"You tend to work in small sub teams of two or three on a corporate transaction rather than 12, so you feel more of a part of things. There's an effort to make sure you see a wide spread of work, and you are invited to things like completion meetings, even if you don't do very much."* The longest hours in the firm are found here: *"Things can occasionally go mad and you stay later,"* but mostly you'll be able to get out of the office between 5.30pm and 6pm wherever you're sat. Other than these core seats, there are options in IP, clinical negligence, employment, insolvency and construction. In September 2004, a healthy eight out of ten qualifying trainees found their niche and stayed with the firm.

the graveyard shift

EG's office in Cardiff used to be occupied by the Territorial Army, and some claim it still is... *"The office is supposedly haunted by a TA soldier. When the secretaries are up in corporate at midnight, they say they can feel him."* Spooky! We reckon you could film a great spine-chiller in the building – the spectacular spiral staircase running up through the atrium would definitely add atmosphere, though the open-door policy has the potential to spoil some of the fun.

In Derby, the *"very new, modern, purpose-built"* business park office seems less intriguing, but mod cons (*"showers, breakout rooms, free pens"*) are certainly appreciated by trainees. By the time readers join the firm, the Nottingham branch, currently languishing in a former hospital, will also have moved to equally flashy quarters. It's nothing much at the moment, *"just a hole in the ground, as they've only just started digging."* East Midlands trainees are expected to split their training, and sometimes even a seat, between the two offices. *"Where you end up depends on what seat you want to do and where they need a trainee, but at the beginning they will try and put you nearer to where you live."* Trainees say it is possible to spend most of your training contract in one office.

All the excitement of new buildings and the general atmosphere of positivity we detected at the firm this year left trainees in an expansive mood when it came to considering the future. *"The history of this place is that the firm looks to expand by merger..."* reflected one source in leading fashion. Our interest duly provoked, we unrolled a map to consider the options for invasion, expansion or plain old annexation. Hmm, Bristol? Or maybe an M4 corridor office would give Cardiff clout: Slough? Reading? Swindon? Chipping Sodbury? Or what about little Brum-based-boost for the Midlands axis? Pure speculation of course, but enough to make us question the firm's training partner on the matter. He reported that despite continually keeping an eye on potential areas for expansion there are no definite current plans for world domination. Our sources seemed more reliable when they spoke generally about *"just quite a big growth...certainly in Nottingham where corporate finance in particular is definitely expanding."*.

knowing the right people

On hearing that the firm has some big personalities (*"one or two of the partners are reputed for their individuality"*), we pressed our spies for further revelations. *"The insolvency partner is quite funny about all the interesting circumstances he's been in – he always talks about his heavies."* We assume they were referring to bailiffs here, although *"there is one partner who is known for being hard on the trainees, but she does it almost for the fun of it."* (Scary.) And what about the trainees? They're *"quite chatty"* (we concur), and *"there's lots of banter playing on people's personalities."* As long as you have good academics and a commitment to the region you apply to, there seems to be room for all: *"In one intake, there's one guy who's so intelligent he's on another level but quite strange, one very scatty, one chilled and relaxed, one a surfer-type and one a very hard worker."* Sounds like the perfect cast for a sitcom.

Cardiff's lawyerbar Ha!Ha! has *"gone off. It's got a bit cheap and..."* (we're not going to repeat the rest as it's a bit sleazy). The new hotspot is Incognito. Staff at the Cardiff branch enjoyed disguising their identities at the firm's *"memorable"* fancy dress Christmas quiz, and over the past year, other events have included a charity hike in Snowdonia, a summer party at Llandaff Rowing Club, a visit to Alton Towers, a Caribbean night at Chepstow Races and go-karting. Not to be outdone, over in the East Midlands, there was also the obligatory go-karting event, picnics, a quiz at Halloween and a knees-up with a big client. The last Christmas party was held at Derby County FC's new home, Pride Park, and the highlight of the evening was a spoof Oscar ceremony. Forget best art direction or best actor in a supporting role, *"there was a Mid-Life Crisis award and one trainee won Rear of the Year."*

and finally...

Trainees assured us that the firm offers "*the best*" training in the region – and we'd agree that the small trainee intake and range of work on offer certainly keeps it up to scratch in the medium firm stakes. Any training contract is going to resemble a war zone at times, so if you want yours to be more Blackadder than Apocalypse Now, start polishing those boots.

Eversheds LLP

the facts

Location: Birmingham, Cambridge, Cardiff, Ipswich, Leeds, Manchester, Norwich, Nottingham.
Number of UK partners/assistants: 328/942
Total number of trainees: 186
Seats: 4x6 months
Alternative seats: Overseas, secondments
Extras: Pro bono – various law centre and projects

In the 90s Eversheds grew into the biggest firm in the country by absorbing regional players and rebranding them as Eversheds. With the team-picking phase over, the challenge now is to ensure that all who wear the Eversheds shirt are fit to offer the same high-quality experience to clients – and their trainees.

going for gold

Whatever part of the country you come from, your local Eversheds will be a market leader in many areas. But Eversheds is reluctant to be regarded as just a chain of regional players and is making a sustained effort to get everyone feeling like they're on the same team. The final-seat trainees we spoke to thought the firm had made real progress on this front since they joined. "*When I started there was this sports day between offices, which was unbelievably competitive, and I didn't get the impression that other people liked my office very much. Now there's been a massive improvement and people work together and we're looking more like*

a unified firm." This unity has been codified in a 'Vision and Values' mission statement, setting out Eversheds' long-term aim to become a leading international law firm. Speaking of the six core behavioural values, trainees admitted that aims such as 'being client centred' and 'teamworking' are "*all common sense*" and slightly "*corny,*" but felt they were "*a good basis and very positive.*" It's not all group hugs though; competitive spirit lives on in the cash prizes awarded to those nominated by their colleagues for various reasons – "*You get £200 for a gold, £100 for a silver and £50 for a bronze.*" We're not sure if you get to stand on a podium, weeping as the strains of your favourite national anthem are piped through the tannoy.

The firm has structured its offices into four regional groupings, with each of the four operating as a unit and contributing to multi-site practice groups. It's an especially effective approach for smaller groups, such as projects or pensions, which are actually moving towards operating nationally. Yet, it does sound like there is a little point scoring between offices still. One trainee told us that weekly departmental video conferencing meetings were "*like the Eurovision Song Contest – 'Hello Manchester. Can you answer question one?'*" As a trainee, life is pretty straightforward and you'll mainly have contact with other offices in your immediate region

The bigger departments, such as property and corporate, "*have less need to contact other offices,*" but here the firm is also trying to lose the regional tag. It is trying to beef up its corporate departments outside London by doing more work for national and international clients. Trainees said they got a buzz out of being involved in "*high-value and high-quality work*" for "*big-ticket clients and major corporations*" including Next and Rolls Royce...particularly if they were doing so from somewhere that retained a small office feel. However, if you are "*a real corporate bunny*" with an eye on the biggest deals around, it may be best to hop elsewhere. What Eversheds does best is variety: "*Here you have the opportunity to get a lot of experience in* a lot of different areas." Across the network, you'll find outstanding work, but you have to analyse what is on offer. Though mouse mats and corporate rallying cries are the same across the country, individual offices have different areas of expertise and the Eversheds name does not mean the same thing everywhere. Not yet.

london: horseplay

Eversheds' "flagship" City office is smaller in the capital than many of its direct rivals: "It's a big law firm in England, but feels like a medium-sized firm [in London]. But we get bigger clients as we have more resources than other medium London firms." For a trainee, this can work to your advantage; for instance, in the general corporate seat the work may cover "public companies, equity finance, takeovers, private equity" and "you get massive deals, but you're not just looking at a teeny bit of them. You feel like you're playing a part even as a trainee." Among the massive deals done by the London office this year is Caudwell's £405m sale of Singlepoint 4U to Vodafone.

Property is also very likely to feature in your training and we heard no complaints here either. "There's always such a volume of work in this seat that you get quite a bit of responsibility. People are happy to pass stuff to you and let you sort it out. And then there's always an element of helping out the person you're sitting with, usually chasing information or getting things together." We did hear a few grumbles about the office however; the premises have a "great location" near Mansion House, but are "getting a bit past it," especially the "dingy cafe" in the basement. A refurb was underway as we wrote, partly to accommodate newcomers ...hopefully new staff and not "the mice we recently had running around on level 4."

The mice may have been exterminated, but Eversheds London hasn't forsaken the animal kingdom altogether as every week there's "the Friday night pony trek." This is no canter down Queen Victoria Street in hard hats, rather a trot "just across the zebra crossing" to favourite local, The Seahorse. In this "comfortable old shoe" of a pub you'll find "any mixture of people from the firm" and "partners aren't shy about coming forward with a pint or two."

The London AGM doubles as a Christmas party and last year trainees played a starring role. "The firm spent a silly amount of money on producing a spoof Faking It programme" where "some guy from McDonald's came in and faked it as an Eversheds trainee in front of a panel of partners." This televisual gem featured a highly accurate portrayal of life in the London office, including "the guys from construction playing with Lego blocks," "golf" and "a disco scene." And did the partners guess right? "They didn't – but good on them;" "we had a great time doing it." Apparently the feature was so successful that there are plans to produce a new video next year. The theme is top secret ("I'd be shot if I told you")...we're on the edge of our seats!

northern exposure

Newcastle has now been 'merged' with Leeds and Manchester to bring all three northern offices under the same management. The cross-Pennine ties are the strongest, with trainees from Manchester sometimes doing a seat in Leeds and vice versa. This is possible as both Leeds and Manchester currently run a six-seat system. By the time you get there, the seat pattern will have come into line with the four-seat model used in all other offices. The six-seat system has served a purpose, allowing a greater number of trainees to sample the many "niche seats" offered in these two offices. For instance, Leeds in strong on competition and local government work, while Manchester's planning and employment teams stand out. Niche seats may be shared around by way of split seats in the future. In Manchester, we were told "the partners are pushing core seats a lot as they want well-rounded trainees," which means that seats somewhere in corporate, property and litigation are almost compulsory. Most Leeds trainees also did these seats, and an extra in Leeds comes in the form of a secondment to Asda. In Newcastle, there are no obvious compulsories.

Across the northern offices, property work (which recently included the redevelopment of the King's Waterfront site in Liverpool) was particularly popular this year. *"It was really different to the conveyancing you do at law school as we were acting for big developers. When you go out there on site you can contextualise the issues, and then when you're looking at the documents, they come alive."* Exactly! Sadly, the firm's own buildings in the north are not uniformly super. In Manchester lawyers luxuriate in *"very new, very modern, very plush offices;"* over in Leeds, trainees grumbled about their geriatric building and couldn't wait for the move planned for 2006 to *"the tallest building in the north – we have to get airport approval!"* If you're beginning to sense a pattern after reports on just three office buildings, you might not be surprised to learn that *"Eversheds is on a programme of renovating or moving offices."* Newcastle's office seems to be the most spectacular, and it even boasts showbiz glamour, having been on TV a few times (most recently in ITV drama *Lawless*). As if that's not enough, there's a great comedy touch – *"There's a water feature in the atrium that people tend to walk into. They come in and look up and then go into the pool by mistake. We often get clients with soggy trousers."*

Leeds is a *"very social office"* and the newly opened bar Prohibition is *"the new Tiger Tiger."* We heard about *"a booze cruise on the River Ouse"* – trying saying that when you're three sheets to the wind – and the ball organised by the Leeds TSG is very popular as *"the firm coughs up."* Ball shenanigans always lead to *"e-mail banter that goes on for a week afterwards – the usual who's snogged who and who's embarrased themselves the most, which often involves a vomiting incident."* The firm is also happy to fund extra-curricular fun in Manchester, and this office has to get a prize for the sheer variety of fun on offer. *"We've done concerts, theatre trips, a shopping trip to New York, a ski trip, trip to Blackpool, quiz nights, weekends in Spain. People pay a monthly subscription and the firm matches that and then all events are half-price."* In Manchester, photos of the latest event go up on a notice board in the deli. Up in Newcastle, things are a bit more laid back, with trainees telling us: *"There are formal events that the firm organises, but we like to just get together ourselves as much as we can."* Local bar Destination was deemed *"a bit pink and neon – our favourite is The Apartment, but it is more expensive, so trainees tend to go to The Telegraph where it's nice and cheap."*

the ones in the midlands

The firm's Birmingham and Nottingham offices have operated hand in hand since 2002. The *"bigger and bolder"* Brum office is clearly top dog after a reorganisation of the Midlands corporate and banking departments to focus on Birmingham. We are also aware that some of the Nottingham corporate partners have left the firm altogether so we asked trainees what this meant in terms of seats and training places for Nottingham. They told us: *"There has been movement of people both ways"* and *"Nottingham fee earners often go over to Birmingham one day a week and vice versa, and there is a push for teams to be one Midlands team."* All we'll say is that if you want to work exclusively in Nottingham, keep a close eye on developments. At the moment, most trainees do all their seats in their home office, the exceptions being real estate litigation and tax in Nottingham, where trainees are encouraged to spend two days a week in Birmingham.

The real strength of the Midlands offices is real estate: *"There isn't much property development that goes on in the Midlands that we're not involved in somewhere."* Among the large-scale projects Eversheds has worked on is the redevelopment of the Birmingham Bullring. A property seat is highly likely, but trainees really enjoyed this work. Litigation is also popular: *"I got lots of responsibility on small files and also got involved in big stuff. We did everything from breach of contract to defamation to IT disputes, and there are also teams that do construction litigation, property and environment regulatory."*

Again, the big event of the year is the AGM party, last year taking on a Chicago theme. *"It was fantastic* to see all the heads of department in costume, hanging off the side of a vintage car...they all did their own piece. It was a fantastic routine." When they're not prancing around in fishnets, Utopia is the place to find trainees in Birmingham. Over in Nottingham, The Castle has well and truly triumphed over former favourite the Rotunda: "You inflate the prices and put in leather sofas and they all love it!" mused one cynic in Nottingham. Nottingham trainees love go-karting, paintballing and scaring themselves stupid at Alton Towers, whereas the Brummies seem to be more the sitting around drinking coffee types. "There's a huge group of trainees who all live together in a set of flats. It's just like being on Friends." They do come out once a year for the "renowned" BTSS ball; when we asked for details, one trainee simply said: "The best events you don't remember."

east angular

The Cambridge, Norwich and Ipswich offices are officially combined with London as an administrative group but in terms of seat structure, East Anglia operate as a separate unit. With this trio of offices, "you apply for a role on the understanding that you may be asked to work at another office." On the plus side, you are consulted about your preferences, get relocation and travel expenses, and "commuting is very possible." Even those not initially keen on venturing further afield end up enjoying the experience. Said one: "With hindsight, I'm glad I had to move...we are part of a regional network."

Some kind of property work is very likely to feature in an East of England training contract. The Ipswich office concentrates on projects, construction and litigation, and a projects seat here is known as "the big one where you have to sell your soul and give up your life." To give you just one example, Eversheds has recently been involved in the extensive redevelopment of Peterborough City centre. Norwich and Cambridge have broader practices, and in Norwich we heard that planning was popular. Working with this six-strong team, you'll get a "very hands-on expe-

rience. Once you've gone through the initial period, they'll give you very high-quality work, and if you prove you can handle it, they'll let you have charge of projects. We deal with a large number of major housebuilders and the planning requirement of developments and give assistance and planning advice for government bodies." Over in Cambridge, employment and IP/IT are prominent. Along with London, the 'Easy Anglian' offices have "particular links with the Paris office" and so are good locations to pick if you're interested in spending six months in one of the three hotly contested Paris seats (currently public international law, coco and employment).

The office in Cambridge seems to owe more to this city's hi-tech prominence than to its historical roots: the "flagship office" for East Anglia, it has "all the latest state-of-the-art equipment...everything's very slick and flat-screen." There's also a "nice café with brilliant chefs and a patisserie." Sounds like the folk moaning about the café in London should be galloping up there, or, given this office's proximity to the station, hopping on the next train from King's Cross. History buffs can get their fix in Norwich; one of the offices here is located in the shadow of the cathedral and enjoys lovely views of the city's old centre. As far as social life goes, it sounds like the tastes of the trainees could be called many things, but never traditional. The respective hangouts of the Cambridge, Ipswich and Norwich crowd are called Sauce, Curve and Orgasmic.

talking shop

A multitalented Cardiff office excels in the Welsh market in everything from banking and planning to health and safety and insolvency, although employment emerged from our interviews as winner of the popularity contest. Seats in pensions, property and IP/IT were also singled out for praise. The only seat trainees weren't so keen on was 'legal services', which processes a large volume of slip-and-trip claims, but we suspect this can be put down to the type of trainee that the firm attracts in Wales –

"trainees want to do big deals rather than a £1,000 claim." A brand-new, purpose-built office has "brightly coloured walls," "artwork by local artists" and is open plan, so "you might overhear someone talking about a matter you've worked on." We bet it's perfect for gossip too... Local bar, The Yard, is another good place for catching up on everyone's news; here "you can just turn up and guarantee that there'll be 20 Eversheds people there."

The Eversheds experience will taste slightly different wherever you go, but it will always arrive in a branded wrapper. There are many standard elements across the offices; for example, you should get a mentor in each seat (although this system is more closely adhered to in some places than others), and 'Have Your Say' meetings will take place thrice yearly. Another standard feature is the type of trainee Eversheds tends to recruit. They are "sensible," "positive" and committed to the region, if outside London. They are also "pulled from all over the shop" in terms of universities and first careers. Residential courses, held throughout the two years, allow trainees to "catch up and share experiences and mistakes. And then once you qualify you have a peer group across the firm." In September 2004, a rather good 90 out of 100 qualifiers stayed with the firm, which is pretty impressive if you factor in the pull of wrongly placed boyfriends and girlfriends. Actually, on this point, trainees predict that in the future it should be easier to apply for NQ jobs (and even seats) in other offices.

and finally...

This monster firm, which grew fat in the late 90s, is becoming sleeker and eyeing up the options abroad. Having said that, there's been no loss of regional strength. The firm will expect you to be "Evershedian to the core," so if you think you might be, get on a vac scheme and find out.

Farrer & Co

the facts

Location: London
Number of UK partners/assistants: 59/54
Total number of trainees: 15
Seats: 6x4 months
Alternative seats: Secondments

When we speak to the trainees at Farrer & Co, two words come to mind – 'character' and 'history'. The firm is famous for its private client work (it is, after all, the Queen's solicitors), but behind the venerable veneer of its grand premises in Lincoln's Inn Fields there's a whole other realm of commercial law.

slings and arrows

The firm traces its origins back to 1701 when a young attorney by the name of Tempest Slinger came to join his uncle (who shared the same rather bizarre name) to practise law in London. At that time the name Slinger & Co might have been more appropriate as the area around Lincoln's Inn was a popular spot for duellists. Indeed, Farrers' website tells of how a divorce – on which it was advising – involved an attempted duel between Lord Ligonier and his wife's lover, Count Alferi.

Although Farrers is proud of its heritage, nowadays it opts for the pen rather than the sword, and it is the firm's top-quality defamation practice that is more likely to draw blood. As one trainee noted: "The traditional aspect is certainly here, and you can't pretend otherwise. We've been around for hundreds of years, but we wouldn't have been there that long if we hadn't been able to adapt with the times. It's probably better to look at it as though we've come forward hundreds of years." But despite successfully adapting to the modern age, Farrers can't, or won't, part with its past. It is imbued with historical interest: for instance, the Charter of the Bank of England was sealed in the main boardroom in 1694, and in the client reception area hang the family trees of former resident the Duke of Newcastle and his in-laws the Marlboroughs. And trainees wouldn't have it any other way: *"The building is part of the firm's identity, and we couldn't imagine moving anywhere else."*

the old curiosity shop?

The reputed site of Dickens' Old Curiosity Shop is just around the corner, and for trainees seat selection must sometimes feel like a visit to the shop to spend their pocket money. One enthused: *"The breadth of work on offer here is extraordinary. Coming from a non-law background that struck me as an amazing advantage, as I didn't want to close off too many avenues."* This is certainly good news for those who weren't magnetically drawn to the law by a certain area of practice or for anyone wanting to avoid the corporate rat race.

Nevertheless, one mustn't be fooled into thinking that Farrers doesn't conform to the general rules of commercial law firms or have established commercial clients. It is true that *"a lot of the interesting private client work feeds into the rest of the firm,"* meaning that much of the corporate and commercial work is for wealthy entrepreneurs and investors rather than public companies. But it is also true that a number of commercial clients have nothing to do with the private client practice. Examples are News International, Haymarket, Citigroup and Emap.

The firm runs a six-seat system, in which trainees spend their first four seats in: property (commercial, private and estates options); charities or private client; commercial (including banking and employment) or litigation (family, media or general commercial). This is followed by a 'wild-card' seat of the trainee's choice, before the final four months being spent in the seat in which they hope to qualify. One observed that *"the system lets you see as much of the firm as possible and be more certain of your choice of qualification department."* We were also told the graduate recruitment team *"bend over backwards"* to ensure that trainees get the type of work that most appeals to them. It cleary pays dividends: five of the six September 2004 qualifiers stayed on for more.

elephant and cathedral

Never a dull day? One trainee said of her experience in the charities group: *"I did everything from registering cute little elephant charities to work on Canterbury Cathedral."* Other experiences included figuring out how to modernise a school charter that dated back to the early 19th century. And on the subject of tinkering around with the nation's heritage, there's even a group of lawyers called the heritage department that specialise in works of art and historical value, often the subject of probate. *"If you're interested in people, the work is fantastic. I remember trying to deal with one beneficiary who locked herself in her house for three days and wouldn't come out. You certainly come to realise how idiosyncratic people are."*

In the media department, you could be assisting with pre-publication advice given to the editor of a tabloid newspaper, filing a defamation suit or running down to court to cover a trial. *"It's a reactive environment, so it's hard to predict what's coming in next,"* one trainee explained. On the other hand the commercial litigation team has a reputation for being *"pretty chilled out,"* though one trainee's day was made after a client sent her a bottle of champagne for winning her very first case. In employment you'll attend tribunals and meet with clients to discuss discrimination claims, whereas a seat in the *"entrepreneurial"* financial services group, which handles deals for investment companies and hedge funds, will teach you a thing or two about winning new business – it is known for its *"brilliant"* marketing parties. If none of this appeals, there's always the possibility of secondments which in recent times have included the Science Museum, the British Olympic Association and Christie's the auctioneers.

horse and hounds

It's a common perception that Farrers only recruits those who've had a private education and are schooled in the ways of the privileged classes. Scotching this rumour, one trainee said: *"Some clients may be blue-blooded, but the people at the firm certainly aren't all like that."* Instead, what is required of recruits is that they are *"gregarious," "self-assured"* and *"intelligent in a lively, inquisitive sense."* They remind us of the sort of child who, rather than making the school hamster run through a maze, would be sitting it down and reading it Tennyson.

They certainly seem enamoured with their experiences at a firm where *"you're never treated as a dogsbody."* Apparently, *"you never need to go out to find work – people are usually delighted to have a trainee."* As work usually comes via your supervisor, *"they can say no if they think you're taking on too much."* And *"partners make time to go through what you've done. They understand you're there to learn and not just do the legwork."*

sport with kings

Normal working hours allow plenty of time for extra-curricular activities. One source reported they could *"make plans for the evening with 95% certainty of being able to meet them."* When detention is necessary, there is usually some sort of recompense – *"Once I was in until three in the morning, but the partner was so apologetic afterwards."* If you do have a run of late nights, we've heard that supervisors are willing to give you some time off in lieu to compensate.

After a day in the office, trainees don't have far to go for a drink in the local branch of Jamie's – it's right under the newer part of the office that fronts on to Kingsway. Otherwise they can join those heading off to the White Horse, or further afield to the Fine Line or Bierodrome. The true highlight of the social calendar is the Christmas party, for which second-year trainees write a series of satirical sketches to be performed by the whole trainee population in front of the entire firm. There are just two rules: the trainees can only pick on the partners, and the partners are not permitted to take offence. Senior partner Robert Clinton acts as editor in chief, although apparently his main role is to spice up the jokes and heckle loudly on the night. Other dates for the diary include rugby sevens, yachting with the bankers Coutts, and cricket against the Royal Household and *The Sun*.

and finally...

Farrer & Co is a firm about which much is said yet the full story is rarely told. It has its charming quirks and more history than almost any other firm; however, such aspects are merely the seasoning, the flavourings, of a successful business. If you sense a pull towards Lincoln's Inn Fields after inspecting this firm's practice areas and client base, don't let anyone stop you setting your cap at this unique institution.

Field Fisher Waterhouse

the facts
Location: London
Number of UK partners/assistants: 78/123
Total number of trainees: 27
Seats: 2x6 and 3x4 months
Alternative seats: Secondments

Field Fisher Waterhouse continues to field one of the strongest teams in London for IT and IP law, but its mix and match approach to practice has allowed the firm to survive comfortably after the burst of the dot.com bubble. Traditional corporate, property and litigation departments co-exist alongside the technology trendies and an eclectic group of niche teams.

the delicatessen

The highly regarded and fast-growing BTMT (brands, technology, media and telecoms) team is the firm's trophy practice. The start-ups, e-commerce businesses and software companies that helped propel FFW into the limelight in the 90s are still to be found on its Christmas card list, but with this work thinner on the ground these days, the firm has had to act wisely. Accordingly, it has built a public sector IT practice and now advises the Foreign and Commonwealth Office, the Cabinet Office and the new 'NHS University' on the creation of a virtual campus for NHS employees. IT outsourcing, particularly on behalf of long-time client Accenture, is also a speciality. And the 14-year-old girl in us couldn't help but notice Claire's Accessories and Schooldisco.com among the firm's clients...

Other all-star teams include the investment funds, clinical negligence, personal injury and travel and tourism groups, and backing it all up is a bedrock of respectable real estate, commercial litigation, banking and corporate work. Of the latter, one trainee said: *"You can't buy out M&S; it's mostly mid-ticket stuff."* To give you a flavour, the corporate team recently advised on a variety of AIM flotations, and along with the real estate group has a large number of clients in the hotel and leisure sector, including Whitbread.

thorough examination

The importance of this bread-and-butter work to the firm is reflected in the fact that a seat in corporate (which includes banking and finance) is compulsory. Yet we sensed trainees had greater affection for all the other seats. One summed up their experiences in the *"hardworking,"* *"serious"* and *"partner heavy"* corporate department as *"general M&A-type stuff. I found the work a bit dry and everything is checked a hundred times."* In finance, you might start on Companies House forms and bank mandates before progressing to drafting loan documentation and involvement with the funds work for which the firm is developing a pretty good name. Trainees felt they would have enjoyed these seats more had they had more client contact and if more efforts had been made to integrate them into the team. *"You'll come in and do one tiny part of a huge matter, and you're not given the whole picture,"* which *"wasn't nice when I stayed all night."*

Perhaps trainees had been spoilt by their experiences in other parts of the firm; they were positively purring when we asked them about their time in niche seats. It's no holiday, but time in travel and tourism is *"particularly good; I've dealt with my own matters from the word go and been involved in everything from investigating liability to going to the coroner's court*

and the Court of Appeal." Most of the work is contentious (*"slips and trips around swimming pools, coach crashes and some very long-term food poisoning litigation"*) as the corporate and employment aspects are passed over, but the department does deal with some business issues such as financial protection for travel companies and aviation work.

A high level of responsibility also keeps trainees happy in the PI/clin neg seats, where *"you can get involved in absolutely everything."* The department has two groups: one specialises in asbestos claims (*"very good training and you get to go to lots of conferences with counsel;"* *"going out to meet clients and take witness statements is extremely rewarding"*) and the other in defendant clin neg. In this second group, the main client is the General Medical Council, which the firm represents at disciplinary hearings and recently at the Shipman Inquiry in Manchester.

tell us about your childhood...

A five-seat system allows more freedom than usual to explore the diversity of the firm's work; other options include professional regulation, IP, IT and employment. But remember, as well as the compulsory corporate or banking and finance seat, you must do some contentious work, and real estate is also highly likely to feature. As one trainee put it: *"You have to do the firm's core commercial areas and the fact that the firm has departments in slightly random subjects is a bonus."* Also upping the firm's appeal is its growing international alliance. In 2004, FFW firmed up relationships with Spanish and Italian lawyers to supplement its existing friendships in Germany, France, Ireland and Scotland.

In the past, the differences in culture between the traditional core departments and the IP/IT whizz kids have led us to diagnose a Jekyll and Hyde complex. This year, we felt it was more a case of multiple personalities: lying on the *Student Guide* couch, trainees told us: *"The departments are quite autonomous so there isn't really a single firm personality"* and *"there are so many departments that they're almost like mini-*

firms." The effects of this are felt in *"disparity from department to department"* in the methods of training, but perhaps the best illustration of FFW's many incarnations is the complexity of its dress code. Before joining the firm, you'll need to do some clothes shopping. *"Corporate all wear suits, even though they don't go to court, which is a bit peculiar. IT and IP are dress down, which is smart trousers or skirt and a shirt, but also depends on whether they're seeing clients. Property is very casual – one partner even wears a T-shirt – and the other departments are chinos and shirts."* And if you end up working all night, feel free to slip into something more comfortable: *"During the all-nighter that I did, one of the partners was wearing pyjamas."* Normally you'll be spared this sight, as working hours are generally a wholesome 9am–7pm.

superstars and bond villains

To us, the firm's diversity can be put down to the dedication and achievement of star partners and their teams. Trainees admit that that they *"like the fact that there's a lot of individuals here. I wouldn't want to go somewhere where there's a big rah rah corporate culture where we're all best friends – it's not natural."* However, some also sense a need for *"a bit more of a corporate image that puts everyone together."* There are departmental strategy and marketing meetings and initiatives, but trainees weren't aware of an overall game plan. One said: *"I don't really have a clue – I don't know if the firm wants to approach magic circle work or whether they're happy just to stay medium or whether they want to play on specialisms or keep all departments good."* If someone is up there stroking a white cat, one trainee felt that *"it would be nice to be let in on what's going on."* Whatever the plan, nine of the 12 qualifying trainees stayed with the firm in 2004 to play their part.

It was a shame to hear it, but *"adverts on the Underground thanking the staff for the last six months"* were seen as *"a bit pointless."* More informal and conventional methods of praise hit the spot – *"I remember there was one department I was in where we'd done well*

and they got everyone together and had drinks and quickly said thanks for your contribution. It was just two hours one evening, and that's all it took."*

it's behind you!

When we conducted our interviews, the firm's main Vine Street office was undergoing an 18-month refurbishment programme. Certain to remain intact is a portion of the Roman-built London Wall that runs through the basement. *"It has to be open to public view, so we have skylights above it. We also get people walking through on the Jack the Ripper tour!"* The office should appeal to sportsfolk as well as historians because the basement houses the firm's very own squash courts. *"You get to know people through the squash league."* A lot of the firm's organised social events revolve around sport – an annual football tournament and regular softball and netball matches against clients. Trainees aren't averse to a bit of hobnobbing, and there's usually a good showing at the local Hogshead on a Friday night: *"We all know each other very well and we're all very chummy."* Sadly, the traditional Christmas panto didn't take place in 2003, but things are looking up for 2004. According to one source: *"E-mails are going round...I think the pantomime horse will rear its head."*

and finally...

Top-quality work is going on in a number of areas at Field Fisher Waterhouse, and with the five-seat system, you should have the opportunity to explore some of the firm's unusual corners as well as its mainstream areas. You won't hear the recitation of a corporate mantra here, but if substance over style appeals, that may be a blessed relief.

Finers Stephens Innocent

the facts
Location: London
Number of UK partners/assistants: 29/28
Total number of trainees: 9
Seats: 4x6 months
Alternative seats: None

West End outfit Finers Stephens Innocent is a natty little ensemble that serves both commercial and private interests. And it's not averse to the odd TV appearance.

fashionable threads
The six principal areas of FSI's practice are commercial property, litigation, corporate/ commercial, IP & Media, private client and employment. The firm prides itself on being a member of MERITAS – an international association of law firms – but at home, its operations are defined by *"entrepreneurial clients"* and *"commercial business people."* This clientele bleeds into the private client side of the firm, where high-value divorces and childrens' work emanate from *"commercial clients rather than aristos."*

FSI's media team was involved in the Hutton Inquiry, Kate Adie's case against *The Sun* and JK Rowling's action against *The New York Daily News* in relation to her fourth Harry Potter book, yet one of our sources admitted: *"It's not all glamorous and sexy; I have never ever met any popstars."* In the commercial departments, household names are the order for the day, including Boxfresh, Scope, Conran, LK Bennett and Monsoon/Accessorize, and the property department recently landed its first work for Littlewoods.

Does such an eclectic mix of work make for a firm that's more Blue Peter jumble sale than Selfridges January sale? Apparently not. *"There is definitely a thread running through it all,"* by way of departmental cross-referral and common goals.

dedicated followers
Our sources described a seat system that *"doesn't push you where you don't have leanings."* The standard four-by-six-months pattern leaves trainees reasonably free ranging. On the face of it, there are no compulsories, though property is the largest department, and for every source that said: *"Compulsory is probably too strong a word,"* another told us: *"I don't know anybody who has ever got out of it."* Despite losing six partners in the past year, property remains the largest department, accounting for more than 30% of the firm's turnover. When the department is involved in projects such as the London Olympic bid, and the development of Eastern Tower at West India Quay, and has clients of the likes of Pizza Hut and LA Fitness, a stint here should be no hardship.

Media/IP remains flavour of the month (this month, last month, next month, any old month...) and we were unsurprised when one trainee confirmed: *"I had to fight my way in."* The message for applicants is clear: *"People applying to the firm because they just want to do media will have a chance, but shouldn't pin their hopes on it."* You have been warned. FSI trainees also subscribe to the national trend for employment law worship, and here we had trainees speaking in tongues about disciplinary proceedings, redundancy, race discrimination, unfair dismissal claims and plenty of client contact. FSI's private client and family departments also end up winning the hearts of trainees. One source described how in private client *"you are seen as quite important to the department."*

not so innocent
Across the board, the firm manages to provide trainees with decent responsibility while also leaving them with a sense that they are *"quite guided."* Though happily none reported that they'd been *"shafted by bundling,"* excitement can't be guaranteed 365 days of the yea, and some trainees mentioned quieter periods in certain seats. On the plus side *"there are other times when its like 'Yeah, that's wicked. Result!'"* Steady on.

A three-monthly appraisal system involves more form filling than you can shake a stick at, all culminating in a detailed half-hour debrief with your supervisor. Equally predictable is a 9.30am–6pm day which is only adjusted according to the content of the desktop. Property is occasionally guilty of keeping people until 9pm or 10pm, and we heard of the odd night shift.

lost in translation

Close to Oxford Street on Great Portland Street, FSI's offices are ideally positioned for a little lunchtime 'research' of one's retail clients' latest lines. Behind an unassuming façade, the main office houses all bar the private client and family lawyers. Some felt its small reception *"doesn't do justice to the firm,"* despite an enormous plasma screen and life-sized man made entirely of copies of the *FT*. When we asked about his significance, the reply came: *"Nothing. He's lost."*

Over the road in the annexe in Clipstone Street, trainees sense a *"small firm atmosphere"* and a degree of isolation. To remedy this, an abundance of social events from Monday morning breakfasts (*"if you get in early enough"*) to monthly wind-down drinks keep everyone in the loop. Trainees are also encouraged to help out with marketing, and recent initiatives to foster links with young professionals saw trainees inviting their mates and contacts along to watch Euro 2004 with the rest of the firm.

For post-work drinks (and post-match commiseration) Villandry, is a favourite. On Friday nights, our sources had discovered that associates *"won't let you buy drinks as a trainee."* The annual Christmas Party is a not-entirely-standard dinner dance, last year following a 'Fancy Footwear' theme. One partner turned up in customised wellies, but he just couldn't match the creativity of the secretary who took the prize for a fantastic pair of home-made, sequinned Jimmy Choos. After the 'Sunglasses and Sunhats' summer party, we're expecting the FSI Winter 2004 collection to be hitting a high street any day now.

candid on camera

In the office, you'll be wearing a business suit, except on Fridays and during a month in the summer. However, if you're still wondering about FSI's style, this collection of thoughts from our interviewees may help. *"Quite modern with a commercial edge,"* yet *"not cut-throat"* nor *"fuddy-duddy and traditional."* And one source observed that while *"it is quite cool, inside it doesn't feel that cool."* We think we understand. At FSI musicians mix with mothers, academics with athletes. One recruit discussed the firm's application process, which invites hopefuls to present their credentials in whatever form they feel most appropriate. This is ideal because standard questions about school and university would be lost on a group that, in the main, have done considerably more interesting things since putting their books away.

At FSI, *"profile raising is very important,"* and at times our interviews resonated with wearying corporate-speak as trainees wove the firm's own slogans into conversation with the ease of a well-trained marketeer. In the past, this role has largely fallen on the shoulders of media law partner Mark Stephens, a regular on television and radio, but now partners in family and private client are also claiming their 15 minutes of fame on GMTV and Radio 5. Apparently there is often a television crew in reception *"or a camera in the taxi on the way to court."*

The people we spoke to were willing, independent, relaxed and candid. Three of our conversations started with a spontaneous fit of the giggles; others were simply interspersed with dry, ironic wit. With such a strong pool of resourceful opportunists waving the FSI banner, it seems a shame that the firm's retention figures have been decidedly under par of late: one out of five in 2002, one out of three in 2003, just two out of five in 2004. Yet, as before, our sources accepted the news with pragmatism and good grace, pointing out that a bigger role at a smaller firm, doing work that really interests them, was ultimately worth more than a guaranteed, but less inspiring, meal ticket from day one.

and finally...

Finers Stephens Innocent operates one of the best West End training schemes around. If you're looking for close engagement with interesting work, interesting partners and interesting clients, you could do far worse.

Fisher Meredith

the facts

Location: London
Number of UK partners/assistants: 9/40
Total number of trainees: 14
Seats: 4 x6 months
Alternative seats: None

Fisher Meredith is a south London legal aid firm, practising crime, family, education, employment, and civil liberties/human rights law. After living on the streets of Stockwell for nearly 30 years, the firm recently relocated to an architectural dream home in Kennington and is now embracing more lucrative, privately paying clients. Nonetheless, the prevailing ethos remains a determination to assist the disadvantaged, the disenfranchised and the wronged.

rights on

Founded in 1975, from the word go Fisher Meredith seems to have been a left-field, possibly anti-establishment, definitely idealistic, firmly 'right-on' outfit. Defending battered housewives, the wrongly imprisoned and the socially excluded, its commitment to its local community goes unquestioned, but FM has earned professional respect for more than mere dedication. Its reputation has also been built through involvement in prominent cases of public interest such as the Deptford Fire. It also advised Sonia Sutcliffe, wife of the Yorkshire Ripper, who was subjected to considerable press intrusion, and on one occasion the premises were actually raided by

police when an IRA suspect represented by the firm escaped from prison to meet with his lawyer. Never content to blend into the background, just last year regulators banned a criminal department poster campaign from the underground because it's message "Dear Bystander, we'll arrest you anyway" was deemed anti-police.

But there are signs FM is becoming less radical with age: it is repositioning itself in the legal market and attempting to attract more private and commercial clients from across and beyond London. It has recently attracted work from voluntary sector agencies, local authorities and charities, including Age Concern, Mencap and the Refugee Council. Instructions from the Royal Embassy of Saudi Arabia are perhaps the strongest proof that there is more to the firm than first meets the eye. But before you imagine betrayed ideals and vanquished idealism, consider a few facts. Over 70% of the firm's work is publicly funded despite legal aid rates having not increased, even with inflation, for 12 years. So, whereas a private client would be charged a respectable £180 pounds an hour, working for government-funded clients will net the firm only £60. It is economic exigency that has forced FM to look for other income in order to sustain its fundamental community law function. Our sources assured us that *"the ethos of commitment to individuals and rights-based work remains a strong thread across all departments."*

blue-sky thinking

The most visible sign of FM's tactical rethink is its swanky new premises, which *"represent a statement of intent and an investment against the future."* It struck us that the building's name – Blue Sky House – was more redolent of 90s' corporate-speak than 21st-century ambition. However, it made more sense when trainees suggested that the move *"was a natural progression"* in a process of evolution that had been evident for over a decade. *"We're bigger and better than the three old, high-street offices,"* one told us. In practical terms the move makes perfect sense: *"We're all together on the same site for the first time and that is really unifying."* From the client's point of view, trainees suggested: *"If the environment is professional, then clients will feel that they are getting a professional service."* One canny individual admitted that appearances might be *"more important to clients paying our full private rate."* And as we all know, burglars too target the homes of people who look like they're doing well for themselves. Sadly, thieves wasted no time in breaking in to steal FM's entire mainframe shortly after its move. Plain mean.

relatively ideal

The trainees we interviewed had all come to the firm because of its *"rights-based ethos,"* but were quick to admit that moral crusaders are in for a culture shock. *"Your ideals are quite quickly tempered by realism and an awareness of the limits of what you can actually do for the clients."* They stressed that the pointy end of legal aid work means hard graft and dirty hands – *"It's not about the intellectual niceties of human rights law."* Nevertheless, despite prison visits, endless court clerking, interviewing walk-in clients and representing repeat offenders, our sources still had the capacity to get misty eyed about *"the cases that remind you of your principles."*

FM operates in a sector of the profession that is renowned for lower salaries, and most of its trainees absorbed law school fees personally, even painfully one might say. For them, satisfaction is sought and found in very different ways to those of their peers in the City. We asked our interviewees to share their happiest memories of training in order to explain the attraction of the job. For one it was *"getting a client a community sentence instead of the usual jail sentence because of a mitigation I prepared."* And for another, *"working on asylum cases where we were challenging the very nature of the immigration system."* And it seems the desire to help people doesn't fade: *"You quite often hear partners giving free advice over the phone to people who have just called up at random."*

troubled teens

The firm operates a structured four-seat training in which crime and family/children seats are compulsory. Then, at twice-yearly meetings with the training manager and senior management, trainees can express their preferences for the other two seats. Everyone seemed happy enough with the system, but you might decide, like one Machiavellian trainee, *"to have a quiet word in the training manager's ear about your choices as well."* As well as the basic duties of a trainee in all departments – meeting and advising clients, clerking, selecting and instructing counsel, sourcing additional evidence, 9.15am–6pm hours, and preparing bundles are just a few of the universals – there are also unique experiences to be had.

Crime involves *"a very high turnover of work,"* and because *"the law is relatively easy to grasp, you can quickly feel quite confident, competent and involved in the department."* Trainees *"run cases under supervision"* and assist on weightier matters including actions against the police and murder or gun-related crimes. The public services law department is equally engaging. It has a remit to assist individuals, sometimes groups, in bringing actions against public service providers such as LEAs or social services. School exclusions, failure to provide care and special education needs are the stock in trade – *"you are trying to help people improve their lives a little."* Trainees here are the first point of contact for walk-in clients, performing initial assessments before referring the case on, a role which one trainee described as *"triage work."* One of the main attractions of public services law is that cases home in on the root causes of societal problems. For example: *"If a 13-year-old old kid is threatened with exclusion from school and doesn't get to do his GSCE's, it can be the beginning of a downward spiral. We'd rather he didn't need the services of our criminal department in the future."*

While crime and public services law allow for quick engagement, in matrimonial *"time breeds expertise."* Under the watchful eye of firm founder and almost legendary family expert Eileen Pembridge, the department focuses on divorce and marital finances. It services the largest number of private clients of any department, and trainees tell us *"you have to develop different skills to deal with them."* The firm also has dedicated child law, fraud and business crime, police and prison law, immigration, and employment teams, which add up to plenty of choice in seat selection.

birds of a feather

FM gets enough training contract applications to be very selective about who is welcomed into the fold. Online trainee biographies confirm that every single one of the current fledglings had prior experience of legal aid work. One trainee advised: *"The value of work placements and the like cannot be overestimated, and I know that without my own legal experience I wouldn't be here now."* You have been told! We spoke to trainees from as far afield as Manchester, Hull and South Africa; all understood the value of working with *"people who have similar commitment to you, and are focused on the same kind of work as you."* It's a mutual bond that fosters friendships, which are easily deepened while chewing the fat over a bacon buttie in the Parma Café or enjoying a meal at someone's house. Two of the five qualifiers stayed with the firm in 2004.

and finally...

Whilst the firm can't compete on salaries with West End or City firms, no one at Fisher Meredith is in it for the money. A career at this highly respected community law firm will allow you to make a real difference to the lives of ordinary people. This should be more than ample motivation.

Foot Anstey Sargent

the facts

Location: Exeter, Plymouth
Number of UK partners/assistants: 26/52
Total number of trainees: 15
Seats: 4x6 months
Alternative seats: None

Down the A303 trunk road past Stonehenge, onto the A30 and keep going until you hit the south Devon coast. If that route sounds familiar you're either having a flashback to when you were nine and sat in the back of a stationary, sweaty Ford Cortina with an ice lolly wrapper stuck to your foot, or you've been to visit Foot Anstey Sargent recently.

best in the west

Formed through a merger in February 2000, Foot Anstey Sargent practices in most things from corporate and commercial to childcare. Its stated aim is to be the premier firm in the West Country, and in some fields it has already achieved this accolade. Foot Anstey's profile is much the same in both its Plymouth and Exeter offices, that is to say primarily commercial but with a notable private client element. Trainees can attach themselves to either office, in the knowledge that each is capable of offering them a wide-ranging training. There are just a few provisos: marine litigation and 'advocates' (crime) are only available in Plymouth and insolvency is only offered in Exeter.

When you arrive at the firm, your first seat will have been allocated, but thereafter you'll be consulted about where you want to go. Although not able to give everyone their first choice of seat all the time, the firm does allow trainees to remain in a department for more than six months and aims to have everyone spend their final seat where they want to qualify. We spoke to trainees who had stuck to commercial departments and others who'd opted for seats that allowed them to work for real people rather than companies.

every sperm is sacred

The seat menu at Foot Anstey is pretty comprehensive and includes coco, commercial property, employment, banking, property lit, insolvency, family and childcare, crime and private client. The firm has added popular new clinical negligence option, in which trainees have been working on cases ranging from *"broken hips to sperm destruction."* As part of a wider claimant clin neg practice, the lead partner was one of the four key lawyers on the Alder Hey Royal Liverpool Children's Hospital group litigation concerning retained organs. Having settled for £5,000,000, it was the largest ever mediated settlement against the NHS.

The 'living together' law group within the family department specialises in cohabitation issues, the family finance team deals with the financial aspects of marriage breakdown, and there is also a large childcare team that acts occasionally for children but most often their guardians or parents. The private client team offers tax-planning advice to businessmen, farmers and landowners.

Elsewhere, insolvency has also proved to be a hit. According to one fan of the seat, *"it is unusual to have a good department outside London or Bristol."* Setting up companies, drafting debentures or software licence agreements, researching into partnership law or IP, liaising with clients by letter or on the phone – there's more than enough to keep a trainee busy in coco, where the department handles the business affairs of the likes of Plymouth Marine Laboratory, Devon Air Ambulance Trust, University of Plymouth and Wrigley. Meanwhile, the popular commercial property side of the firm has been getting stuck into interesting regional work such as the sale of one of Devon's greatest old properties, Endsleigh House, and the brown site redevelopment of the old Taunton railway station.

nanny state

One of the most intriguing things about Foot Anstey is its nationally renowned media practice, led by acclaimed lawyer Tony Jaffa. Counting the Northcliffe Newspaper Group, which owns the majority of UK regional titles, and *The Toronto Sun* as clients, Mr J and colleagues give pre-publication advice and help smooth away defamation actions. This footprint in the world of newspaper publishing has produced some unexpected and very welcome benefits. Recently the firm took a Privy Council case for a major Jamaican newspaper publisher and it is likely that similar matters will follow now that the firm is a member of the Commonwealth Press Union's panel of lawyers who provide pro bono legal assistance to members.

Don't expect to be inundated with work from the start: *"You're not thrown in at the deep end, but given responsibility gradually. At the same time you're not nannied along."* Somewhere in the middle then. Climbing off the fence, trainees were very happy with quality of support available to them. Regular appraisals with supervisors supplement plenty of ongoing feedback, and monthly group meetings with the training principal are a chance to discuss issues of wider importance. *"It's a very trainee-oriented firm,"* one remarked; *"All the departments are very helpful, especially the secretaries."* We did hear a couple of grumbles about not getting enough client contact in the corporate seat, but the firm more than makes up for this in the private client sphere. Trainees there spoke of running their own files and meeting clients on their own right from the start. Worried about being chained to the photocopier? *"Sometimes you have to do your fair share, but you never feel put upon. Even the partners will make the coffee or do their own photocopying if necessary."*

a tale of two cities

Although the two offices are quite far apart (an hour by train, a little longer by car), our sources assured us *"there is still a sense of firm identity and all the trainees get together at social functions."* They are free to take seats in either office, but tend to stick to the one closest to where they live. In Plymouth the firm occupies a modern, glass-fronted building, which previously served as a television studio. In Exeter, home is *"a*

Dickensian rabbit warren with rickety stairs." Still, it's not entirely without its charms: "The building's certainly got character. You can put your pen on the desk and look away, then a minute later it's rolled off onto the floor." Regrettably for anyone looking forward to hour after hour of such fun and games, the firm is soon relocating to new open-plan digs just behind Southernhay and near to the new court complex.

"Exeter is incredibly rah-rah studenty, and not exactly flush with nightclubs," so those in search of a hedonistic lifestyle should probably look elsewhere. And Plymouth? "Plymouth is Plymouth, isn't it – full of scrubbies!" (So harsh!) Yet, despite these reservations, "every now and then the trainees all go out together in Plymouth." For the young professionals at Foot Anstey, lunch is the main point of contact, and they "take any excuse to go out for a meal." Need a break from the TV studio? "You can always walk down to Plymouth Ho at lunchtime and watch the ships go by." Needless to say, anyone with an interest in sailing or surfing will be in heaven, and for the moor adventurous, there's also a certain national park on the doorstep offering "fantastic walks with fantastic pubs at the end." From the point of view of one Devon man we spoke to, "Cornwall's almost like going on holiday."

buoys and girls

Back in 1919, Nancy Astor of Plymouth became the first woman to take a seat in the House of Commons, and Foot Anstey appears to have also taken the feminist cause to heart. This year an impressive ten out of the twelve trainees were female, as are a comparatively high proportion of the partnership and half of the management board. Gender is not the determining factor in recruitment, however; instead we sensed the firm values the experience that more mature applicants can bring. One of the current trainees had spent 15 years in the police force and served as a registrar, and another had managed a chiropractor's office. Whatever their background, those wishing to train at the firm must first brave the famously rigorous recruitment day. "The interview process is a bit like Pop Idol," we were told. "All the potential trainees turn up at 9.30 in the morning, get put through their paces, then half of them get sent home at lunchtime." No wonder a couple of the current crop had chosen to get a foot in the door by first working at the firm as paralegals.

Wary of losing its brightest and best to London or Bristol firms, Foot Anstey is careful to recruit trainees who have regional ties. One trainee advised: "You have to convince the firm that you are committed to staying in the West Country. If you live in another part of the country and want to apply, make sure you can give a good reason other than wanting to learn how to surf." The approach must be working as four of the five 2004 qualifiers remain at the firm.

and finally...

If you're committed to a life in the West Country, you'll already be aware that top-quality professional opportunities don't grow on trees down here – not of this calibre at any rate.

Forbes

the facts

Location: Blackburn, Accrington, Clitheroe, Preston, Chorley, Leeds
Number of UK partners/assistants: 43/102
Total number of trainees: 15
Seats: 4x6 month seats
Alternative seats: None

One hundred and a few years young, with eight red rose offices in Lancashire and a daring new foothold across the Pennines in Leeds, Forbes is a venerable North West firm with two feet on the high street and a developing taste for slicker city ways.

local colour

Talk to a southerner about the north and monochrome images spring to mind. Industrial dereliction, grey mottled hillsides dotted with windswept sheep. Weathered faces, flat caps and gap-toothed kids with rickets kicking a pig's bladder down a steep hill. Indigestible pies made from prime gristle and pastry that could turn even a ferret's bite. The reality, of course, is quite different: just ask a Forbes trainee – they're proud to be Lancastrian through and through. *"Everyone from partners to trainees to support staff comes from a similar background;" "they're from the locality, know the area, are easy going and always ready for a good laugh."* Whilst we spoke to a few trainees who had come to study in the region from further afield, they had all embraced northern life, fitting right in with the firm's *"preference for an obvious commitment to the North West."*

Having grown through various amalgamations of smaller firms over the last century, Forbes now has offices peppered across Blackburn, Accrington, Chorley, Clitheroe and Preston, not forgetting the Leeds branch. It's fair to say that the bulk of work comes from local people and businesses, and consequently we weren't surprised to learn that no-nonsense northern values have their place. *"We don't mince our words; we take on the file, act in the client's best interests and do the best we can."* Nevertheless, inveterately local doesn't mean parochially yokel: the firm is well aware of its status as one of the biggest firms in the region and recently rebranded to *"unify our identity across the region."* *"B&Q orange"* may be the mainstay of the fancy new theme, but the makeover came with a no-frills promise to avoid legal gobbledegook. Our sources were quick to stress: *"It's about more than just image, there's been a real reorientation to focus on client needs"* and spoke of the *"professionalism, ambition and drive"* they'd found at the firm.

going public

The *"flexibility and diversity"* of the seat system is a big draw for trainees. Four six-month seats taken from crime, civil litigation (PI or employment), defendant insurance, family (including probate and tax) and non-contentious/corporate make for a training contract that *"doesn't force you into specialising before you qualify."* *"Easy-going"* trainees were happy to experience a range of work, but those with a specific ambition found that making their point at an end-of-seat appraisal (where *"they listen closely to everything you've got to say"*) could pay dividends. *"I wanted employment, made that clear and they accommodated me,"* said one. Although the recent rebranding *"put a sheen on our increasing corporate ambitions,"* the range of publicly funded work on offer is huge. Our sources saw the firm's breadth of practice as a testament to *"forward-thinking partners of the last 20 years who have led the firm into new areas without compromising our mainstay practice."*

Publicly funded work, particularly crime remains the bedrock of practice. A well-organised approach ensures good returns in an area of law where profit margins are narrow, and the firm looks well placed to weather the forthcoming criminal legal aid shake up. Not only did it recently win an appointment to the Legal Services Commission's serious fraud panel, but it is also one of only 25 firms nationally to be selected for the LSC's 'preferred supplier' pilot scheme. Trainees in crime seats revel in *"a hell of a lot of work; the whole range of magistrates court cases,"* and some had taken the opportunity to gain their police station accreditation. General crime is offered in all offices, but the firm recently consolidated Crown Court casework into the Preston office. A trainee who'd been there confirmed: *"I was working on more specialised casework like rape or serious fraud."* It was interesting to hear how the firm's *"new corporate attitudes and abilities are feeding back...we're looking to generate fee income in traditionally public funded areas."* The move into the field of white-collar crime is a perfect example.

making a meal of it

If crime is the *"bread and butter,"* then family is also a staple. Again publicly funded work is to the fore, with *"lots of clients literally coming in off the street."* Trainees find themselves *"taking initial instructions, opening the file, helping to prepare injunctions, maybe sit-*

ting behind counsel in court, even doing small-scale advocacy." Here, as elsewhere, "the support staff are amazing, so you never find yourself doing much photocopying." It is classic high-street fare, and so too is the probate and tax seat where trainees are "running the administration of estates and preparing final accounts for walk-ins and some high net worth clients." The real bonus for trainees is "the opportunity to run files yourself and have a lot of face-to-face client contact."

Defendant insurance work for clients such as the Co-op is a growth area, and one that led directly to the opening of the Leeds office. Retaining panel membership for Zurich Municipal in "a massively competitive market" this year was an important boost for the fledgling branch. Trainees who take a seat in here tend to "act for the insurer or a local authority on fast track slip-and-trip matters worth up to 15 grand. On the larger matters you'll only do isolated research." By contrast a litigation seat back on the right side of the Pennines involves applicant PI work by the bucket load. Employment seats always go down well. Generally "the firm represents large local companies," so in addition to "dealing with telephone queries from new clients," trainees also find themselves "preparing pleadings and sitting in on meetings." The non-contentious/corporate side of the firm services the needs of clients including Blackburn Rovers FC, Burnley FC and a swathe of small to medium-sized local enterprises. Trainees experience "a broad spread of work from property matters to company secretarial duties."

snug as bugs

Forbes regularly takes on trainees who have paralegalled at the firm and they are the ones most likely to experience life in the more distant offices. Well, distant is stretching a point as "all of them except Leeds are within half an hour of each other," which means a car is "a luxury not an absolute necessity." Unless they want to experience a particular seat, say with the Crown Court crime team in Preston, most trainees are likely to find themselves "contained by the three Blackburn offices." In true Coronation Street fashion, each of these are "knocked-though, three-storey terraced houses," which "get quite hot in the summer and it's easy to get lost inside them." Each building has a specific role. "Northgate House is the legal aid office right in the middle of town, it's very hectic." Marsden House is "quiet because it's where the defendant insurance work is done and no clients ever come in." And finally, there's Rutherford House: "It's the head office, but further from the town centre and the work is a mix of PI, employment, civil litigation and property."

Despite a few grumbles about the "45-minute lunch hour," trainees work a civilised 9am-5pm day though some stay until 6pm when they're particularly busy. Overall, they have plenty of time to enjoy the social distractions of Blackburn and its environs. Usually they just "get together on a Friday night for drinks at O'Neills, or maybe go out clubbing on a Saturday," but the firm has a few sports teams and an improving social committee. We heard about one trainee who was marrying a firm friend, and a little birdie told us: "There are sometimes dalliances!" We didn't push for details, but we understand it gets cold up north in the winter, so presumably people have to huddle together for warmth. Those we interviewed evidently felt as snug as bugs in rugs, because of the three qualifiers four stayed with the firm in September 2004.

and finally...

Forbes offers a training wi' now't tek'n owt. If you want top-quality publicly funded work and a chance to find your inner commercial lawyer, we recommend get on the blower to Blackburn.

Fox Williams

the facts

Location: London
Number of UK partners/assistants: 18/37
Total number of trainees: 8
Seats: 5x21 weeks
Alternative seats: None

Top-dog employment work, a broad commercial base and a full social agenda, all wrapped up in a jazzy little City location. Is this for real? You bet!

wolf in sheep's clothing

Fifteen years ago, Fox Williams – the brainchild of six City lawyers – opened for business. Now over 50 lawyers strong, the firm has a stellar reputation for partnership law, employment law and business immigration, and fares very well in mid-market corporate finance work. The firm's expertise in partnership matters was put to good effect in the Addleshaw Goddard merger and is being sought by Kirkpatrick & Lockhart in its merger with Nicholson Graham & Jones. The employment team recently advised FA chairman Mark Palios in the Svengate debacle.

While *"employment is probably the most established area of work, the others are growing and establishing themselves."* The sober-sounding commerce and technology group belies a funky fashion industry practice that acts for Mambo, Daks and Firetrap, and acted in the sale of Karen Millen Group. If you think this all sounds a bit too cool for school, be warned: Fox Williams has some serious-sounding clients too – Earls Court & Olympia Group, Reed, Amlin, Hasbro International and Caledonia Investments plc. If you need further confirmation that FW is no fickle fashionista, listen to the trainee who said: *"We like to think we are hip and cool and wear trendy clothes, but to be honest lawyers just look silly in chinos."* They said it, not us.

all i want for christmas...

At Fox Williams the maths is simple: there are *"five departments and five seats."* However, *"if there is one you have done well in or are looking to qualify into, you can do that twice."* Up and down the country, week in, week out, year after year, trainees tell us that an employment seat is top of their wish list. At FW, trainees can uncross their fingers as *"employment is practically half the firm – you can't train here without*

doing it." In fact, when we rang, half of the trainees had spent two seats in the department. The only downside of having all your Christmases come at once is that there could be a very long, dark winter to follow: there are usually few NQ positions in employment, which in 2004 made for empty stockings on qualification day. Despite there being other positions available, only two of the four qualifiers chose to stay with the firm.

So, enjoy it while you can: an employment seat means *"working with experts"* on both defendant and claimant work and also non-contentious matters. Trainees get a smattering of their own small files and are heavily involved in contentious share schemes, age and sex discrimination matters, compromise agreements, employment contracts and policy drafting for the firm's clients. And employment work is not limited to the employment department: a litigation seat also involves employment matters plus agency law and general breach of contract claims. A spell in litigation has seen trainees undertaking research into things like gardening leave (where departing staff and partners are prevented from joining their next place of work for a set period of time) and bonus payments. They also get to draft letters of advice, attend mediations and client meetings *"reasonably regularly"* and attend court, though the number of solicitor-advocates at the firm means *"there's not much chance to do advocacy"* at this early stage.

The smaller corporate and commercial property teams afford greater autonomy for trainees. In property *"they put a lot of faith in you"* and *"it is very much about juggling lots of small files."* Corporate can be a frenetic experience for the department's sole trainee. One source noted morosely: *"Someone has to do the due diligence and disclosure documents."* The flipside however is that they are third in line on £5-£100 million deals, rather than stuck at the back of the queue, near the photocopier. All up, *"the actual responsibility you get is huge, and you liaise with clients quite closely."* This is essentially true across the firm: we're told "you actually feel that trainees have a decent role" and "generally you won't get your own files, but work closely with another lawyer and end up doing the bulk of the work."

All new recruits are paired with a second-year buddy and have a partner or senior associate as mentor throughout the two years. This is in addition to a seat supervisor who sits down each month for a chat about their progress. A mid-seat review is "a slightly more serious version of the monthly meetings, and then the end-of-seat review is the big one" with two-way feedback and comments from across the department. There were no complaints about the rigorous and comprehensive training on offer, even though this means attending a training session every Monday evening.

fantastic mr fox

The firm's two-year-old den is tucked behind M&S on Moorgate. Trainees oozed with pride for their snazzy, glass-walled home, which is branded with the firm logo in every conceivable place. Each level is decorated in a different colour "so you know what floor you're on when you get out of the lift." Apart from one "dodgy salmon-pink" floor, all are quite tasteful. Dotted along the walls is artwork from Brighton University and pictures of "models in quirky clothes." "Bright and breezy" surroundings seem indicative of a convivial and easy atmosphere that filters down from senior partner and employment law guru Ronnie Fox. One trainee explained: "I know everyone from the cleaner up to Ronnie. Ronnie comes into my office for a chat...as does the cleaner."

This year FW earned itself a place in the Sunday Times' list of the 50 Best Small Companies to Work For: one trainee must have read our minds when they said "friendly is such a quaint word, and so many firms bill themselves as friendly...here there is a down-to-earth approach without compromising on quality." A standard day is 9am–7pm-ish, with one trainee boasting: "I can honestly leave at 5.30pm, and some people come in at 10am, and no one says anything." Others admitted to a few late nights and early mornings, but only for limited periods.

Check out the firm website and you'll find bold promises about the social life. When quizzed, our sources confirmed that the social committee organises regular events like softball, table football competitions, bowling, karaoke, salsa nights and sweepstakes (World Cup goal strikers, guess the weight of the baby, etc). The close-knit trainee group regularly lunches at Wagamama, and after work The Prophet, All Bar One and Digress are nearby. In addition to an annual summer party, the Christmas bash is a black-tie, sit-down do and includes a revue performed by the trainees. The FW website will tell you that this "consists of gently poking fun at different colleagues." "Less of the 'gently,'" we heard: second-year trainees write the sketches and "they are vetted by Ronnie" though "you can't make it funny without taking the piss." The revue was the "bright idea" of an outgoing trainee who was not retained on qualification one year; given that most trainees regard the experience as "nerve-racking and tense" and some even find it "excruciating," it's no surprise that "he gets a lot of abuse every year."

One trainee explained how Ronnie Fox's recruitment philosophy is based on something called the lift theory. Basically all employees have to be the kind of person you could easily spend a couple of hours with while stuck in a lift. Having jammed the doors and settled down for a chat with a few of them we'd say it's a pretty good philosophy. Our sources fitted their own description of "interesting and socially adept," and we sensed a genuine loyalty to and respect for the firm and each other. At FW you "treat people the way you'd like them to treat you."

and finally...

If your love for employment law is more than a fleeting flirtation with fashion, we definitely recommend you try Fox Williams on for size.

Freeth Cartwright LLP

the facts

Location: Nottingham, Leicester, Derby
Number of UK partners/assistants: 57/78
Total number of trainees: 15
Seats: 4x6 months
Alternative seats: none

No longer the provincial boy next door, East Midlands firm Freeth Cartwright is delivering what it promised it would just a few years ago – commercial services to really good clients alongside award-winning class action litigation.

putting away childish things

Growth spurts and boyhood aspirations all in the past, this year the *Student Guide* found Nottingham home to a young buck of enterprise and commercial success. To mark its coming of age, Freeth Cartwright has acquired a brand-spanking new office, a serious logo, LLP status and room for further growth. Upper Parliament Street is home to private litigation (clinical negligence and personal injury), and a lavish new build at Cumberland Court houses the remainder of the Nottingham departments. Most trainees are based here, although a Derby office also takes trainees into commercial property and corporate seats, and a third office in Leicester offers commercial litigation, clinical negligence and private client options.

No seat is strictly compulsory, but trainees must all spend at least one seat in either Derby or Leicester and time in the firm's burgeoning commercial property department (which *"defines the firm"*) is pretty much a dead cert. This is no hardship for anyone with an eye for big deals: the property lawyers act for Center Parcs, Coral, Multiyork and Paul Smith on transactions valued well into the several millions.

deciding what you like

In the past, the firm's prolific clinical negligence and PI practices have won the hearts of trainees. This year, however, Freeth Cartwright's role in the case of Naazish Farooq, who died following a massive overdose of drugs during cancer treatment, and the wrong diagnosis of over two hundred children at Leicester Royal Infirmary left our sources unmoved. Neither did the product liability team, which has been heavily involved in the MMR group action and Trilucent soya breast implant settlement, have their pulses racing. Immunity to the appeal of this work represents a departure from past years, and we put this down to a new breed of trainee. Put bluntly, *"a lot of us are more commercially minded now."*

Private client seats are still an option in Nottingham or Leicester, but if you have set your heart on the firm's private litigation practice, we were told *"you will struggle to find someone who will take on a trainee."* The message is clear: *"The firm is now really for people who want to do corporate and commercial work."*

the engagement

A number of our sources had initially hooked up with Freeth Cartwright as paralegals. While the firm is obviously not averse to such liaisons, we're told an offer of paralegal work by no means guarantees that a training contract will follow. For every trainee who took this route, there are others who proffered more standard chat-up lines (A levels, degree, other interests...) as fresh applicants for the training scheme. Once engaged, this is a relationship that allows trainees to retain their independence. Our sources had been to court alone, had meetings with clients alone and run their own files. Even on the bigger stuff they deny being taken for granted. One source assured us: *"I have never been to the copy room, or used a hi-lighter or stapler."* We're sceptical, but we know what they're trying to say – *"You never just do the Noddy stuff."*

In smaller departments, such as private client, expect to get work solely from your supervisor; in bigger commercial and property departments *"work comes from all directions."* Generally, all the offices are now open plan, and trainees sit at least near, if not next to, their supervisor. Appraisals come at the end of each six-month seat, though some trainees additionally ask for mid-seat reviews. Formal training is viewed with appropriate seriousness, and once the PSC is out of the way the training manager readily accommodates requests for places on relevant courses. In this area, a proactive approach will get you far.

the stag night

Admittedly, some sources regarded a stint in Leicester or Derby *"a duff choice because of the commute,"* but those who'd played the field positively endorsed their experience of these smaller pockets of the Freeth Cartwright brand. Like the best mate of the school stud, there is nothing technically inferior about either Derby or Leicester, yet Nottingham has greater pull. Cumberland Court seduces trainees with its all-singing, all-dancing, honky-tonk, hi-tech, sleek-and-sexy interior, bacon butties for breakfast, Starbucks in the canteen, air con, enormous TV and requisite great views. One more added bonus of bringing people together under one roof is that it's promoted a *"more organised, professional and motivated"* approach. That, and the fact that *"you no longer pass your colleagues in the street without knowing who they are."*

If this all sounds too good to be true, bear in mind that Nottingham is also home to 365 clubs, pubs and bars within a single square mile. Little wonder it has a reputation for being *"a stag-night haven full of marauding gangs of blokes,"* nor that Freeth Cartwright trainees have a cracking social life. At the Christmas bash trainees *"dress up, embarrass themselves and sing."* The rest of the year, the nearby Castle pub is a regular haunt for *"the same faces every Friday night."*

Trainee socialising starts early at Freeth Cartwright, with new recruits being measured up for drinking hats pretty much on leaving the interview room. Our sources firmly endorsed the tradition of starting people early, noting that it *"helps them get a foothold on how everything works."* Certainly it makes for a well-bonded group (one source even went so far as to describe it as *"cliquey"*) that extends its activities into the weekends.

the nuptuals

Following on from reports last year that the firm can be *"a little incestuous,"* passions were still running high when we rang trainees. We're reliably informed that *"if you come to Freeths and are lonely you can find someone to be your 'friend'."* One tactful soul assured us *"nothing too icky"* goes on, yet another more unabashed source admitted: *"It is quite randy here."* And you may have to remodel that drinking hat because true love has already prompted the chime of wedding bells and a recent trip up the aisle for two trainees. Together, that is.

When asked for the winning formula for an eternal love affair with Freeth Cartwright, our trainees struggled to pinpoint what they all had in common. The usual adjectives tripped off the tongue – friendly, personable, hardworking – but didn't help us come closer to profiling the ideal recruit. Perhaps more telling is that all our sources had a strong prior connection with the East Midlands, be it through family, uni or law school. *"There is a feeling that if you have come here randomly, there is less chance of you staying more than two years,"* or as one source put it: *"This is a Midlands firm with a Midland outlook – it helps if you have that too."* In September 2004, seven of the eight qualifiers renewed their vows with the firm.

Freeth Cartwright may be practising a top-dog swagger on Nottingham's Corporate Block, but certainly when it comes to comparisons with the hours and aggro of London life, it's still a poodle. The standard 9am–5pm day may be stretched in the commercial departments, but all-nighters remain unheard of even in the *"notoriously hardworking"* property and construction groups. That said, Freeth Cartwright is no pussy, and as a reminder a motivational slogan 'Only your best is good enough' rolls around on screensavers throughout the offices.

and finally...

For better or worse Freeth Cartwright has come good on its promise to change. We wish it health, happiness and prosperity.

Freshfields Bruckhaus Deringer

the facts
Location: London
Number of UK partners/assistants: 179/529
Total number of trainees: 212
Seats: 3 or 6 months long
Alternative seats: Overseas seats, secondments
Extras: Pro bono – RCJ CAB, Tower Hamlets Law Centre, FRU, Privy Council/US death row appeals, language training

Sitting with magic circle competitors at the thin-aired summit of City law, Freshfields Bruckhaus Deringer is not alone in wanting to *"be the best"* in any practice area or international jurisdiction in which it works. But all this said, it was the *"well-mannered, gentler touch"* of the recruitment process that proved the clincher for trainees casting about for a high-flying legal career.

land of the giants
Of course that gentler touch is after the manner of a velvet glove on an iron fist. Equally exceptional nationally and internationally, the firm slugs it out with other magic circle titans for the most outstanding deals in an environment that is sometimes more brutal than merely competitive. Good manners alone don't make for success in business, and body blows are traded that would leave a 20-stone heavyweight gasping for breath. This year Freshfields hit the mat hard when the High Court granted a conflict of interest injunction that booted it off Philip Green's £9 billion takeover bid for Marks & Spencer. The punishment pill was made even more bitter by an order for hefty costs to be paid to rival Slaughter and May. And to top it all, Ashursts scooped the Green instruction on the rebound. But some you win, some you lose: on the plus side, Freshfields gained a notable victory when it scooped one of Norton

Rose's trophy clients, HSBC Holdings, and instructions to advise it on the £1 billion acquisition of a 19.9% stake in Bank of Communications, China's fifth largest lender.

During the last year, Freshfields advised Group Falck on its £1.7 billion merger with Securicor, Scottish Newcastle on the £2.5 billion sale of its pub portfolio, the MoD on a £4 billion British army garrison contract and Canadian company Brascan on its hostile takeover bid for Canary Wharf. At the same time, in a legal market in which mid-rank firms have performed most strongly, Freshfields recorded a smaller drop in profits per partner than any of its magic circle rivals. In the colossal war of give and take, Freshfields is more than holding its own. In recognition of this, and the success of the firm's German merger, Freshfields scooped *Chambers Global Law Firm of the Year* award earlier in 2004 at a glittering, legal star-studded ceremony at London's Hilton Hotel. True to form, the German co-senior partner Konstantin Mettenheimer made a gracious and elegant acceptance speech.

corporate dwarfs
But what of the little people? Well, undoubtedly trainees pitch up at the firm knowing that corporate work is the heart of practice. *"It's the driver behind the whole place, make no bones about that,"* said one source, whilst another added with a slight curl of the lip: *"If you wanted to be a specialist IP/IT lawyer, then why the hell would you be here in the first place?"* Yet, in addition to mammoth corporate and finance departments, the firm also has an array of excellent supporting departments, including litigation, environment, real estate, employment, pensions and benefits (EPB), competition, and tax. Common perception has it that these areas exist only to serve the wider needs of the corporate department, and our interviewees readily admitted that *"if corporate says the word, everybody jumps to it."* However, some had been pleasantly surprised to find *"the work in more specialised departments wasn't just corporate support."* Said one: *"In employ-*

ment, I did 20% transactional work and 80% advisory work for standalone clients."

Within a "fairly flexible" seat system, trainees are expected to complete stints in corporate, finance and litigation, though corporate has many teams and "finance covers a multitude of sins from insolvency to structured finance." The training scheme is primarily a transactional one, so expect at least six months of corporate and finance work in your two years. In overseas seats the story is the same: New York offers largely finance work; Hong Kong and Singapore offer corporate seats; Moscow offers a mule-like mix.

In part due to pressure of numbers around popular seats like litigation or EPB and in part to facilitate broad experience, seats vary in length between three and six months. In practical terms that means "up to 200 people are moving seat every three months; it's a scary prospect for HR." It can also be a scary prospect for trainees as they try to plot a course to qualification. "We're all assertive people with our own ideas and losing independent control of your career path can be dissatisfying." The first seat tends to be six months in duration "to allow you time to bed down," but the more alert trainees told us: "It's a mistake to be complacent and it can be a shock to discover how competitive rotation can be." While there were some niggles that "once you've handed your choices in, the process is fairly shrouded in secrecy" and that "lobbying of partners blatantly goes on and seems to work in some cases," the majority of those we interviewed said they'd done well out of the process.

Opinion was divided over the wisdom of three-month seats. For every person who chirruped: "It's great to experience as many departments as possible" or who rationalised: "If you realise a seat isn't for you, three months is ample time to get a snapshot," there were those who suggested: "It isn't long enough for people to get to know you or feel comfortable with you." Dissatisfaction usually condensed around issues of qualification, with one trainee pointing out that "when it comes down to NQ jobs, partners make the decisions, and if they don't know you or your work, you're in trouble."

"People tend to go on secondment or to foreign offices in their last seat." With offices in Paris, New York, Moscow, Singapore and Hong Kong amongst others, and placements on offer at Reuters, IBM and Morgan Stanley, this can be a competitive process itself. But it also means an added incentive to impress early in a hoped-for qualification department. Trainees encouraged future recruits to "think strategically from day one."

talk to the hand

The trainee group is cosmopolitan and drawn from a wider range of universities than most people assume, and our interviewees confirmed the firm is "looking beyond the redbricks a lot more." The Oxbridge element accounted for around 25% of the trainee population in 2004 by our head count "not least because of the emphasis put on academic ability." We spoke to or heard of trainees from over 40 different universities including some former polys. Irrespective of their background, what unites trainees is an "outgoing," "ambitious," "driven" and "assertive" disposition. One wit said: "You see a lot of decisive hand-chopping movements from people," but another reflected on the group's diversity, saying: "There is a character type who is bookish and not outgoing or gregarious...that kind of person might make a great lawyer, but not at Freshfields."

As we mentioned at the start of this report, very many of Freshfields' trainees were attracted by the subtlety of the firm's recruitment and marketing style. Despite its slightly Victorian feel, the Freshfield family's crest remains the firm's logo and the recruitment brochure has "no whacky photos of models, no over-zealous spin." By the same token the training contract application form doesn't require endless revisionist analysis of your time at scout camp or your captaincy of the hockey team. Instead it offers a large empty box in which to write a personal statement in your own style. Combined with "a very relaxed interview style," these touches mark the firm out in a market place in which "it's very difficult to differentiate between firms." For most, "this place lets its reputation speak for itself." Our sources acknowledged that Freshfields is *"conservative in some ways...there'll never be dress down."* Stories about first week clothing advice from an imported fashion designer (*"never wear cuff links with a button collar shirt"*) or timely tips from partners (*"less of the purple shirts, you're not a mobile phone salesman"*) do play into the hands of a 'gentlemanly and proper' reputation.

working up a storm

When trying to gauge a firm's atmosphere, you have to factor in the effects of localised weather systems, and thankfully for us, trainees are excellent barometers of the variable pressures across departments. In the corporate and finance departments our interviewees found themselves *"sometimes doing crazy hours, billing 100 hours plus in a week."* They also possess a particular breed of lawyer that some went as far as describing as *"macho, red-braces, very full-on."* By contrast, others reflected that the *"intense, pressured environment"* resulted from *"the important high-profile nature of the work."* One more forthright trainee opined: *"Corporate clients tend to be investment banking males, and you're likely to go further, if you're that sort of a character."* Yet, these days, being that sort of character is a matter of personality rather than gender – *"There are women doing well there, but they tend to be the more laddish types."*

Trainees did emphasise that even across different corporate teams the exact conditions vary, but by contrast the niche departments, *"tend to all be more relaxed"* and *"partners will often refuse to work ridiculous hours."* Even litigation *"has a reputation for being less hardcore than corporate or finance,"* although the friend of one of our sources was *"working like a dog"* in their lit seat. Tax is the department with *"the real intellectuals...no-one really understands what they're talking about, but even corporate bends over backwards for them."* Employment is typical of the lighter side of the firm, and although there are more female partners here, again, the prevailing climate is as much to do with the work as with gender.

luck and timing

An important constant across the firm is the *"huge effort"* put into training. *"There are two styles of supervision. One: they keep an eye on you, but you work for other managers. Two: you work very closely with the supervisor."* Of the former, trainees said: *"You get autonomy and see a range of people...your supervisor isn't listening in to your phone calls."* Of the latter, they believe *"you get a much closer feel for each transaction,"* though much depends on the seniority of supervisors, who tend to be associates. The younger the associate, the more likely trainees are to work up close and personal with them: *"It's not laziness on the part of more senior associates, it's just that at £600 an hour billing rates, they don't have the time to waste explaining everything to you."* Mid and end-of-seat appraisals ensure that whether it's focused feedback from one person, or *"a distillation of lots of people's opinions,"* trainees have a good sense of their ongoing performance. Day to day *"if you do something wrong, someone will be pissed off at you, but you just deal with it."*

Trainees stressed, *"there is no conscious process of giving you better work over the two years,"* *"what you get is pretty arbitrary and based on luck and timing."* So the trainee in litigation we interviewed who had spent three months doing *"discrete tasks without any sense of its overall importance"* on the Bank of England-BCCI case, could only reflect with envy that *"my predecessor spent three months interviewing Lord Kingsdown."* Several said they'd occasionally enjoyed good client contact, and all were realistic that the scale of work and clients demands a lengthy apprenticeship – *"You'd be out of your league trying to entertain the head of legal at Shell."* It should also be pointed out that with large numbers of *"excellent secretaries, excellent paralegals, excellent PSLs and an excellent repro department,"* trainees are spared some of the menial drudgery that often characterises a magic circle training. Consolation for the lows of *"being at work at 2am for the third day running,"* is found in team spirit; *"you might be up in the middle of the night, but you're not working with a bunch of idiots."*

you are what you eat

Freshfields hours sound no more excessive than any magic circle rival. Our interviewees reported that *"9am–7pm is an average day;" "overall it's pretty civilised hours and the odd incredibly hard month."* However, it must be said that the source who gleefully *"felt like a part timer in EPB when leaving at 6pm"* was a rare breed, with the majority of trainees neither under illusions about the commitment demanded nor asking that any quarter be given. Our thanks to the source who introduced us to the concept of the trainee fridge: *"A few ready meals, a bit of pasta, lots of beer and no milk because you often won't be home long enough to use it before it goes off!"* If you're of the can't cook, won't cook school of eating, the canteen serves from breakfast time until late and there's even an on-site Costa Coffee. The kitchens on each floor of the office are filled with fruit, teas, and coffees (cappuccino, latte and espresso for those late nights). Add in *"free food after seven, free taxis home after nine,"* on-site doctors, dentists, opticians and masseurs and the reasons for the empty fridge become clearer.

In truth, *"many people choose to keep their lives separate from work,"* though if you're not one of them there are almost enough sports teams to sweep the medals board at the Olympics, not forgetting theatre and museum trips and departmental Christmas and summer parties. There are *"never full-firm events, probably because it would be impossible to arrange one,"* but Freshfields foots the bill for *"fantastic"* summer and winter balls for trainees. En-masse socialising fades as the two years progress, and anyway, *"out of 50-odd people there's bound to be a few you don't like. Inevitably, you see a smaller group of close trainee friends more regularly."* Just down the road on Fleet Street, The Witness Box and The Cheshire Cheese are the most frequented watering holes.

inside the hothouse

Out of duty to our readers, we really pushed to find out why a magic circle training is more attractive than the greater responsibility on offer at mid-sized London firms. The answer came loud and clear: *"When you go home and the front page of the FT is talking about the deal you're working on, it's what you want."* These trainees are the kind of people who flourish rather than wilt in the heat of transaction. Yet all those we spoke to were clear that *"making partner here is bloody hard, no one is looking that far ahead."* Without being cynical, they were detached enough to recognise that *"you buy into the brand by training here, it's a mark of quality that opens doors in the future."* Many said they'd be knocking on those doors one to two years after qualification. Out of 77 who qualified in 2004, 68 took jobs within the firm.

and finally...

Whether you're looking to scale the gargantuan peaks of the corporate world or want experience in the foothills, a training contract with Freshfields will give you a full range of nearly peerless experience. Two years of uphill endeavour will see you emerge as a lean, mean NQ with stamina to die for. And if you fully engage with the Freshfields way you'll have all the refined gloss and lightness of touch that distinguish this big boy from the crowd.

Galbraith Branley & Co

the facts

Location: London
Number of UK partners/assistants: 4/12
Total number of trainees: 8
Seats: Number varies
Alternative seats: None
Extras: Pro bono – Hendon CAB

Galbraith Branley is a pocket rocket of a North London firm: raw, punchy, no-nonsense, no let-up and just enough breathing space to nurture a few ideals. With crime the predominant practice area, the firm also has a police and prisons team as well as a burgeoning personal injury and mental health practice.

If you can hack the pace, light the blue touch paper...just don't expect to be able to retire to a safe distance.

earning your wings

Many of those we speak to describe their training contract as the perfect preparation for a legal career. They tell us how they have developed into fully-fledged solicitors through the tender two-year ministrations of their firm. At Galbraiths, day-one trainees are thrown from the back of a light aircraft with 7 square metres of silk, 15ft of twine and a dog-eared copy of *Teach Yourself How to Construct a Parachute*. In French. Or at least they might as well be, judging by the testimony of those to whom we spoke: "*It's real sink or swim...most people just manage to tread water for four months.*"

This is a train-on-the-job experience that will have you engaging at close quarters with a varied clientele dictated by the firm's Finchley Road location and chosen practice areas. The baptism of fire serves a dual purpose: on the one hand "*the partners are finding out if you're strong enough for the job*," and on the other raw recruits are knocked into shape to be "*as useful as possible, as quickly as possible*." To illustrate, all trainees are required to attain Police Station Representative Accreditation soon after joining and thereafter will be on night or weekend call two or three times a month. If you're starting to feel faint, rest assured that whilst the ethos may be sink or swim, "*most start swimming*."

dr jekyll...

Once bobbing nicely in the briny Branley Sea, you may notice something of a dichotomy between the firm's two offices, something which our sources suggest reflects both the different departments and the different personalities housed therein. Perched atop a marketing consultant's office, the newer, funkier, open-plan Archgate premises is the base of the mental health, and personal injury (including actions against the police) operations. Trainees described the

atmosphere as "*relaxed,*" mentioning that "*the partners are happy to lend an ear.*" They also emphasised that most autonomy is to be had here.

In PI the bulk of the work is referred through legal insurers and mainly comprises the sort of slip-and-trip claims that, even if not exhilarating, translate into full caseloads for trainees. "*I had around 50 cases, so lots of phone conversations, dictation and negotiating with insurance companies,*" one trainee told us. More stimulating are mistreatment in custody claims brought against the police.

Mental health law is a growth area, and trainees benefit from partners' significant experience both in representing people at mental health review tribunals and bringing actions before the High Court, Court of Appeal and House of Lords in judicial review proceedings. One trainee's experience was typical: "*I ran files from start to finish, and attended and won managers hearings by myself. It was great advocacy experience.*" Almost all of our contacts stressed that working with clients who have been hospitalised or sectioned as a result of anything from self-harm to mental impairment gave them great personal satisfaction. One yipped: "*It's really exciting – you can actually affect their quality of life.*" Another gave the following near-perfect summary: "*It's a little bit of a moral crusade. Most people are passionate about clients' rights, especially when it comes to civil liberties in mental health work.*"

....and mr hyde

By contrast, in the crime department at the Finchley Road office, "*you start off having an idealistic attitude, but get over it.*" The crime team is Galbraiths' central core, and it has a proven track record in defending fraud and serious crime. Among the firm's high-profile Old Bailey murder cases is R v Manning (Victoria Climbié), and it has also had several matters heard by the Court of Appeal, including R v Toussaint (murder outside So Solid Crew gig) and R v Plakici (the leading authority on human trafficking). Whilst trainees might assist on such cases, at the other end of the spectrum a staple diet of clients facing burglary, assault or rape charges is the daily fare. Not a menu to suit everyone's stomach, and perhaps it's understandable then that in this *"high-pressure, real-world"* department there is less room for idealism or trainee autonomy. But as one source reflected: *"It makes for very good practical training; everything has to be precise and is checked."* The usual hours of 8am to 6.30pm are exceeded regularly, bringing experiences and clients that contemporaries at commercial firms are unlikely to share. Such as? *"You have to not mind the smell of urine at three o' clock in the morning at Tottenham police station."* The law doesn't get more practical than this, and so whilst it is no surprise that the atmosphere here is more intense than down the road in Archgate, trainees did suggest that it was equally a result of the crime partner's exacting standards. A family seat is equally full-on and brings a wealth of client contact and as much autonomy as you can handle, working on divorces, custody disputes, domestic violence et al. Trainees make applications for emergency orders at court and even choose and brief counsel themselves.

miss demeanour

Female trainees now outnumber their male contemporaries, making it interesting that comments about the firm's social life were identical to those of previous years. One feisty lass told us: *"We go down the pub two to three times a week; there's definitely a drinking culture."* Another reflected that nights at local pub The Autumn House were *"how we let off steam after long hours at work."* In previous years we've used comments like this to describe a masculine culture at the firm, but upon reflection there's a more straightforward explanation. It's simply that, whether male or female, the trainees admitted to the firm are robust, committed types who, after ten hours of stressful work and with the prospect of an 8am start the next day, don't have the time or energy for more fanciful pastimes. We think this comment says it all – *"I asked the partner at my interview what they wanted in a trainee, and he said, 'Someone we could take down the pub'. I liked that."*

vocation vocation vocation

If you've got the impression that Galbraith training is an all-consuming experience then you're spot on. As one trainee admitted wryly: *"This is our entire life."* You must be unshakeable in your commitment to the work, and you must be prepared for an on-the-job apprenticeship. *"I learnt by experiencing,"* said one interviewee. *"You learn law, you learn how to speak for yourself and you learn to look things up."* Admittedly, trainees felt they could be given more structured support – for example, there is no rigid seat system (although as a rule of thumb most do two). Nevertheless, the firm keeps staff bang up to date with new legislation and case law, and *"it's widely recognised at other firms that you get an excellent practical training here."* Faint hearts need not apply because, in our view, how well you fare here depends on how much you put in and whether you show the essential qualities of *"initiative and confidence."*

There will be times when the warm glow of moral vindication in vocation isn't quite enough to salve bone-tired eyes and minds. As last year, trainees told us they'd feel happier on their ubiquitous small-hours police station visits if overtime was paid, and although the salary is above minimum requirements, no one described it as a fortune. However, it does increase every six months and there are bonuses for gaining police station accreditation and at Christmas. Trainees must own a car but a mileage allowance is paid, and interest-free loans are available to help out with the initial purchase costs. All this helps keep body and soul together, but let's face it, if you're doing this job it's about more than the money. For some people, this kind of work satisfies a soulful itch; for others it proves too uncomfortable, and we heard about two trainees who left early on in recent years. Of those who ran the full course in 2004, two of the three remain after after qualification.

and finally...

Come and have a go if you think you're hard enough...and care enough.

Gateley Wareing LLP

the facts

Location: Birmingham, Leicester, Nottingham
Number of UK partners/assistants: 25/48
Total number of trainees: 14
Seats: 4x6 months
Alternative seats: None

Gateley Wareing is turning heads...and for all the right reasons. With new partners, new premises and new clients, this is a time of great optimism for the Midlands player.

little brother

Gateley Wareing is known for the enthusiastic support it gives to entrepreneurs and small to medium-sized companies in both the east and west Midlands. This distinctive Midlands focus sees it headquartered in Birmingham with smaller *"footprint"* offices in Leicester and Nottingham that allow it to operate using its trademark *"face-to-face"* style. Unless you've lived and worked in the Midlands all your life, you'll be more familiar with the names of clients who've only recently discovered Gateleys. The property department alone boasts new relationships with Carlsberg Tetley plc, Countryside Properties plc, Wolverhampton City Council and Fairclough Homes.

The most likely explanation for the surge in big names on Gateleys' client list is a steady inflow of new partners and assistants over the last three years – a handful from Hammonds, others from Eversheds and Wragges. The latest scalp is an ex-Edwards Geldard partner who brought three of his loyal assistants to the private equity-driven Nottingham corporate team. Trainees are impressed by *"the quality of the people coming through the doors,"* and believe it is *"a reflection of the quality already here."* When compared to the major Birmingham firms, Gateleys is still a small player. One source, after some thought, described it as *"Wragges' little brother,"* because he was reminded of the top Birmingham firm before its rapid growth.

water cooler moments

You'll be hard pushed to find a trainee who's unhappy with the seat system or appraisals. The nearest thing to a compulsory seat is corporate, and even here *"you're not dragooned into it"* as a commercial seat will suffice. Corporate trainees work within a *"partner-heavy"* environment, which is great if you hate the idea of sitting somewhere at the bottom of a huge pyramid structure. After some seats, the corporate experience can be a *"drop back down to earth,"* with company secretarial duties and due diligence a regular part of the diet, but at least the size of transaction usually handled is relatively trainee-friendly and at least allows for the possibility of core involvement. To illustrate, last year Gateleys acted for the management team and then the company on the £15 million buy-in management buyout (BIMBO) of Angel Springs Holdings, which purchased four water cooler companies using funding from 3i and Royal Bank of Scotland.

card games

The property and litigation departments are roughly the same size as coco, and each brings in just under a third of the firm's annual revenue. Seats in these departments are popular with the trainee group as they offer hands-on, client-facing roles and a chance to mini-me supervising partners. One of our sources left us in no doubt as to trainees' eagerness to put into practice the raft of skills they'd been taught during their initial induction to the firm. *"The first two weeks are solid training. Even though I won't need quite a lot of the things that were covered for years, at least I know about them."* We asked for an example. *"How to walk into a room full of strangers with a pocket full of 100 business cards and to walk out with 100 new ones."* Now that's what we call working the room!

The construction team usually takes a trainee, as does the employment team, and the occasional request for a private client seat is always considered. New recruits have no input into which seat they get first, unless they already work at the firm as paralegals (something which three of the September 2004 starters had done). Second and subsequent seats are allocated only after discussions between trainees and the HR manager, whose long experience and sage words frequently influence seat choices to good effect. In case, like one of our interviewees, you were wondering whether Birmingham-dwelling trainees are required to undertake seats in Nottingham or Leicester, these postings are voluntary. There are usually one or two trainees based in the east Midlands because that's where they live.

spread the news to timbuktu

"I'd be deceiving you if I said it wouldn't count at all," one trainee admitted when we asked if applicants had to demonstrate a Midlands connection to bag a training contract. "Although, if a really good candidate came along they could come from Timbuktu." We checked with HR. They don't get many applications from the Sahara. The archetypal trainee is hardworking, capable, "outgoing and willing to get to know people." For what it's worth, some of those we spoke to were among the most erudite that we encountered in 2004, and we're certain any firm would be proud to have them. It's a good job Gateleys has recruited such people because we think it's going to need them as it moves forward. In September 2004, the firm retained four of its five qualifiers.

When firms make staff aware of future plans and business strategy it tends to help everyone "buy into it." Referring to Gateleys' annual State of The Firm address, one trainee told us: "Next week we're off to the Hyatt for a couple of hours of serious talking followed by four or five hours of serious drinking." Fair enough, we say – the firm already has much to celebrate.

that's ENTtertainment

On the subject of celebrations, after the Christmas party one year, a certain partner (who shall remain nameless) skated on thin ice when, perhaps believing he was John Curry, he dashed onto a frozen canal. "Naturally, the ice cracked and he fell into the water with a huge, panicked roar." Partners like to be in the thick of things, socially and work-wise. "They really are game for a laugh," we heard, "at social events you can spend hours talking to them." At last year's Wild West-themed Christmas party, which was – as always – organised by trainees, senior figures were put in the stocks and made to answer various charges. One paid £40 to drench another with cold water, only to find the bucket had (mysteriously) been filled with wallpaper paste. Full-throttle fun and games help to define life at Gateleys, so if you don't like fun, don't apply.

From the moment they walk through the office door on their first day, recruits are put in the spotlight. Literally. The exact detail of 'Welcome Night' varies from year to year, but typically each new trainee and their supervisor get up to entertain the assembled staff. One year the trainees were each asked to relay to their new colleagues three pieces of information their supervisor wouldn't wish anyone to know. Whilst we heard some cracking stories, we're going to stop short of embarrassing anyone further.

In September 2003 Gateleys made a symbolic move to beautifully refurbished premises in the legal heart of Birmingham. Formerly the old Ear, Nose and Throat Hospital, it is one of half a dozen old Victorian hospitals on Edmund Street. Close by, the old Eye Hospital has been converted into a bar, though we're not aware that they issue beer goggles.

and finally...

Gateley Wareing is on a roll, what else can we say? Form an orderly queue.

Government Legal Service

the facts

Location: London, Manchester
Number of lawyers: Approx 1,850
Total number of trainees: 60
Seats: 4x6 months

The choice of waking up to a leisurely breakfast with the lovely Natasha Kaplinsky or finishing work in time to catch that performance of *Tosca*, and completing a hands-on training contract with real responsibility and high-quality work – surely you must be living in a fantasy world? Or maybe you work for the Government Legal Service (GLS). With some 1,900 lawyers in 40 departments, the GLS is the agency charged with managing legal staff throughout central government.

lobsters and urchins

There's no one type of government lawyer and no one type of work. A day in the life of a GLS lawyer could include anything from drafting employment contracts for the MOD to sitting in on a House of Commons select committee and providing answers to government ministers on legal questions. Trainees are usually assigned to a single department for the duration of their traineeship, though within that department, as in an orthodox traineeship, they will move around four six-month seats. This means that for most trainees there will be exposure to different aspects of practice areas and a call for a range of skills. This is likely to continue throughout one's career as the GLS tries to avoid situations whereby lawyers become boxed into one department. As one trainee put it: *"The attraction is the huge variety...you just keep building up more and more experience...you'll never be bored."*

If you're turned on by the idea of working at the heart of politics and government, but don't think electioneering is your cup of tea, the GLS is a good way to get close to the action. A solid amount of work falls into the parliamentary and advisory category, involving a fair amount of drafting and background legal research. Take the experiences of one trainee at the Office of the Deputy Prime Minister, who was given responsibility for scrutinising local council by-laws to check on their legality. *"It covered everything from where people were allowed to leave their lobster pots in Cornwall to measures dealing with rough sleeping on the streets of London."* Lawyers don't just scrutinise the law; they're involved in drafting it too. One of our sources had just been involved in drafting regulations made under new adoption legislation, and already had three statutory instruments to his name on the statute book. There is also the chance to see the law you've drafted get churned through the parliamentary process. Going along to a parliamentary debate, sitting in the officials' box, and frantically scribbling notes to pass down to the minister in charge of a bill is all in a day's work.

Most of the trainees we spoke to had friends of the same age who had become solicitors in private practice in the City. Compared with the experiences of their peers, there was a distinct absence of horror stories of endless days chained to the photocopier. As one joked: *"I write the law: beat that, magic circle!"*

when a plan comes together

As you might imagine, the government of the day is always an active litigant. In addition to the prosecution work carried out by the CPS, many government departments regularly prosecute criminal offences, and the government is itself prosecuted. Just like any other large organisation, it is susceptible to claims for breach of contract or tort or, additionally, legislation and administrative decisions may have been made unlawfully and thus challenged by judicial review. There are a plethora of tribunals, commissions, enquiries and quasi-judicial bodies at which the government requires legal representation. Remember *Re A*, the case of the conjoined twins? Remember *ex parte Pinochet*? Remember the Hutton Inquiry? All of these cases involved lawyers acting for the government in some capacity or another.

Some departments will be more heavily involved in litigation than others, but wherever you end up, you can definitely expect some kind of contentious work, and usually at least six months of it. Some departments, including the Office of the Deputy Prime Minister, don't have their own litigators, so their trainees are sent on secondment to the Treasury Solicitor's Department (TSOL), which handles the vast majority of the government's litigation. TSOL is one of the most popular choices for training contract applicants and in many ways *"it's not dissimilar to being in the litigation department of a firm in private practice."* We got the impression that the *"young and dynamic"* TSOL trainees are the A Team of the GLS. So this presumably makes the Treasury Solicitor Mr T. Except it's a Mrs at the moment.

Litigation experiences tend to be hands-on. Whilst for larger and more complex cases, trainees work alongside senior colleagues, once settled in to the seat, *"it's not uncommon to have about ten files of your own to run."* That means *"doing everything from taking instructions from clients, arranging conferences with barristers to attending hearings, and sometimes doing some of the advocacy."* One trainee had done a six-month seat with the welfare benefits team of the Department for Work & Pensions. Part of his work included representing the Secretary of State in appeals to the Social Security Commissioners (who are usually drawn from the ranks of senior QCs and High Court judges). *"It was fantastic experience. Where else would a trainee be able to do all the advocacy in front of such an important tribunal?"*

that'll teach you

From what we've said so far, you might think trainees are left to their own devices. Not so. There is a standard trainee booklet that each trainee takes from one seat to another. At the beginning of each new posting, trainees sit down with their supervisors and set out a 'Four Job Plan' listing the learning objectives for the seat. There is a mid-seat review

after three months and a more substantial progress report at the end of each seat. As well as receiving formal feedback, the trainees we spoke to had all felt comfortable about asking questions of their supervisors (or line managers in civilservantspeak). And in true civil service style, you'll get *"oodles and oodles of training,"* all delivered by practitioners who are commonly *"the top expert in their field."*

The GLS is supportive of trainees and NQs who want to add extra strings to their bows. One trainee had just been accepted to spend six months as a judicial assistant to a Lord Justice of Appeal, while another who had developed a flair for advocacy had expressed an interest in qualifying as a solicitor-advocate and was going to be allowed to do this. As for seat allocation, you can't always get what you want, but *"if you make your interests known at an early stage, they will try hard to accommodate them."*

who's your daddy?

Not a question you'll get asked at the interview. It doesn't matter what your background is, or who you know. Trainees describe the recruitment process as *"tough, but rigorously fair."* In common with many law firms, the application form itself gives plenty of room for detail, and if you get past that first hurdle, you'll be invited to attend for a day at a GLS assessment centre. Expect an individual interview, in which applicants are required to prepare a discussion on a recent topic from current affairs, and a group problem-solving exercise. The GLS website states that applicants must have at least a 2:2, and while we did speak to someone who'd attained this, the reality is that without a 2:1 or better, you'll need to impress in other ways to stand out from the competition.

There are some distinct advantages to a career in the GLS, and job security is certainly one of them. Even though there is no guarantee of a job at the end of your training contract, the retention rate is extremely high, and no one we interviewed could think of anyone who had not been taken on at the end of the two years. Another advantage comes in the form of great hours. Though it's not unheard of to work the odd late evening, for example when a bill is being debated in parliament, this is rare. As one trainee told us: "*I can count on one hand the number of times that I've had to stay beyond seven in the evening.*" You won't earn the same amount as your magic circle mates, and there will be a cap to what you can earn in the long term, but then again, you won't be using your keyboard as a pillow at night. Some departments pay more than others, though all pay a competitive salary.

Don't expect the type of glittering social scene you might get in a big City firm – taxpayers would be enraged at the thought of young GLS lawyers grazing caviar off the backs of ice-carved swans! On the positive side, you won't be required to spend time schmoozing with clients at marketing events as you'll already have a captive clientele of civil servants. Some trainees did point out that the effect of moving departments, often involving a change of both office and e-mail address, was not conducive to social cohesion. To compensate for this trainees have set up their own inter-departmental network that meets for regular social activities. We're afraid it's buy your own pint though.

and finally...

Most students looking for a training contract concentrate on the opportunities in private practice, perhaps oblivious to what's on offer at the GLS. After a couple of days spent interviewing its trainees, we must say our heads have been turned.

Halliwells LLP

the facts

Location: Manchester, London, Sheffield
Number of UK partners/assistants: 87/144
Total number of trainees: 32
Seats: 5x21 weeks
Alternative seats: Secondments
Extras: Pro bono – Manchester Uni Advice Centre

Now recruiting for both its newer London outpost and its original Manchester office, this profitable commercial firm is undergoing a growth spurt. In 2004 it posted record profits and made up nine partners.

onward and upward

Just to set the scene, we'll tell you that several of our sources had considered both London and Manchester firms for their training, perhaps indicating the nature of their career ambitions. From one we heard: "*I chose Halliwells because it seemed so commercially driven, dynamic and it was going places.*" And from another: "*We are in the top 50, but we want to go higher up – at least top 25.*" Halliwells is fortunate enough to receive armfuls of good quality applications and consequently, "*they are picking people who have it all. The Oxbridge quota is high and the rest come from the best redbricks.*" But it also recruits from within if someone can earn the respect of partners after a period of paralegal work. Whichever route they take, trainees are the type who "*want to be best at what they do and are not afraid of anything.*" Least of all hard work.

seats you sir

A new five-seat system allows trainees to sample four different areas of practice before deciding on a final seat in their intended qualification department. Litigation is a common first seat; either insurance lit ("*smaller cases and the potential to run a couple of your own files*") or commercial lit, which comes in three varieties – mainstream commercial, construction, and the brewery team. "*Unfortunately I never actually went to a brewery,*" bemoaned one past occupant who, commenting on the frequency with which he'd gone to the pub after work, added that it was "*brewery by day and brewery by night.*" In all litigation seats, court attendance is commonplace, whether to take notes at trial or to stand up before a master or judge in chambers. These penalty-kick moments were seen as highlights by our sources; although when the opposition clearly has far more experience than you do, *"you can feel like a soldier at Rorke's Drift."*

The *"fast-paced"* corporate department will also test your mettle. *"You are given a very definite role, and quite a lot of involvement and interaction with clients. Okay, some jobs are procedural – for example, verification on a public deal – but you have to remember that if it's not done right directors could go to prison."* In corporate, as in other departments, *"you come out of a seat having done a wide range if things, and you can look after yourself."* The property department leaves some trainees in raptures. Running her own files, drafting leases and agreements as well as carrying out basic search and registration functions, one young lady was left in no doubt that she had *"developed important organisational skills."*

Also on offer are IP, employment, trusts and estates, tax and banking options plus the odd client secondment. Manchester trainees can spend a seat in London, and once London trainees have been recruited the reverse is equally likely to be the case. There is a single seat in Sheffield doing insurance litigation, though we hear it's an acquired taste. No seat is compulsory and two stints in the same department can be easily wangled. Aside from the fact that trainees want more notice of their next seat move, the system gets the thumbs-up. And to smooth the arrival into a new department, the trainees have prepared a seat-by-seat survival guide covering *"how it works, who the clients are and what to do if this or that happens."* If you are indeed wondering who the clients are, Halliwells' website will assist. For now we'll mention St Paul (lead insurer on the Paddington rail crash litigation), Thresher Group, Kwik-Fit, Focus Wickes, Karrimor, Time Computers and the owners of Blackpool Tower.

a breath of fresh air

Can you imagine yourself, midway through your training contract, telling us: *"I have thrown myself into this firm."* Or how about: *"I don't have a problem with being in a harder working firm. I really do want to learn and to be at the top of my profession... It may be politically*

incorrect to say that – what with work-life balance and all that – but it's true." We could have given you a dozen or more comments concerning trainees' eagerness to succeed, all of which left us in no doubt that you don't want to end up here by accident. Be sure your ambitions aren't surpassed by those of your classmates because, if they are, you belong somewhere less thrusting. *"When the pressure is on, you either fold or focus – we at Halliwells focus."* *"Are we aggressive? Yes, but rather than meaning we trample over the other side, I'd say we aggressively fight the client's cause."*

As a part of a compact squad of recruits, you'll learn quickly about your strengths and weakness, and *"the firm will exploit your strengths."* You must then understand that *"the more proactive you are, the more you are taken seriously."* It all adds up to one thing: *"You are definitely going to make an impression – either a good one, or by default a bad one."* Everyone believed the firm's sink or swim culture would be the making of them – as one trainee put it: *"You are allowed to wander off on your own over a precipice. There will be someone to catch you, but the precipice is there."* For a trainee with a growing workload and competing calls on their time, it is *"very easy to sit and suffer in silence until the problem becomes a monster and it takes over."* The fix? *"Having the courage to say 'I have a problem',"* which in turn requires a *"social adroitness."*

Does the need to be supertrainee equate to an unbearable burden of late nights and abandoned weekend plans? One source laughed off the idea of assistants having *"a prison pallor,"* confirming that the hours were really no worse than in any other leading Manchester firm. And how many hours is this? *"The blunt answer is how efficient are you?"* The obvious sense of dedication that we found *"can't be taught or instilled by the firm. It's not as if they are trying to browbeat you into working hard."* Apparently you're either a Halliwells type, or you're not. *"You need a sufficient level of initiative and gumption about you."* In September 2004, eight of the ten qualifiers found out they were indeed Halliwells types.

bangalaw

We asked about the calmer, more cerebral aspects of the contract – formal seminars and talks. One source joked that there was so much training *"it's almost hard to find the time to work!"* More seriously, *"there is no difficulty in going to sessions in other departments; in fact it is recommended that you go to everything, but you're not castigated for not going."* In addition to mid and end-of-seat appraisals, there are also pre-seat meetings to set objectives for the coming months.

We asked if there was any aspect to the firm that warranted criticism. A few thought the IT system *"slow and crashing;"* others wanted more advance warning on seat changes and NQ job offers. Yet it's not appropriate to paint the firm as IT resistant: it has opted for digital dictation and even ran a pilot scheme for the outsourcing of certain functions to India. Of the firm's own caste system, we heard: *"There's obviously a rigid backbone to the firm, but there are no power-hungry freaks that just want to put you down."* Which just goes to show that you can be a partner and still be one of the gang. *"As long as you don't push the boundaries too far, you don't have to hold your tongue,"* one trainee confirmed.

time gentlemen please

"The office decor could do with improving," was the honest opinion of most in Manchester. Every single floor is laid out the same. No funky artwork. Functional. Somewhat tired. But a major spruce-up seems unlikely as the firm still talks of an office move that will put everyone under a single roof. We've heard all this before, but at least the partners have instructed agents now and set a date for 2007.

For now, energy is focused on the capital. *"There's more of a drive in London: the firm is a very, very small fish in a big pond, and the Halliwells name doesn't mean anything as of right."* The London office is located near Bank tube station, and there are scores of bars to choose from after work. *"About 10 to 15 people, including a couple of partners, go out on a Thursday or a Friday each week."* Back up north, *"Halliwells' common room"*

is a bar called Time. Formerly the local branch of Chez Gerard, the firm has favoured the venue for years, but one trainee at least was ready to revolt: *"I hate the place, they do Bud on tap."* Beer snob.

Some trainees had a few things to say about the inequalities posed by Friday's dress-down policy. Girls, apparently, have it a lot easier, and the secretaries come to work ready for a Friday night out. And as for role models, the boys despair: *"One partner came in wearing brown cords and a polo shirt – which should be a crime."* It probably is.

and finally...

Sometimes we're asked which firms we'd recommend students to apply to. There is no right answer; it depends who's asking. All we'll say is there's a certain brand of applicant that will be truly suited to and fully stretched by Halliwells. If it's you, don't pass the opportunity by.

Hammonds

the facts

Location: London, Leeds, Manchester, Birmingham
Number of UK partners/assistants: 167/364
Total number of trainees: 82
Seats: 6x4 months
Alternative seats: Overseas seats, secondments
Extras: Pro bono – Paddington Law Centre, Business in the Community, language training

Top 15 nationally with increasing reach in Europe and beyond, Hammonds is a big firm with more than half an eye on the bigger picture.

keep your eyes on the horizon

First some background on the firm. In a move similar to rivals like DLA, Pinsents and Addleshaws, Hammonds has made an assault on traditional City territory through a series of mergers. However, the London market is a tough one to break into, and in the process of trying, we suspect the firm has learned the real value of its regional heartlands. More latterly, we've seen an emphasis on European expansion and the planting of a flag in Asia rather than a focus on building up London. Hong Kong and Madrid are the latest exotic additions to an impressive list of foreign offices.

Having expanded at a phenomenal rate for over 13 years, 2003-4 was somewhat bumpier for the firm. A double-digit drop in profits is bad news in anyone's book, but the firm also took flak from certain quarters of the legal press, who all but accused it of having it rougher than a ride along a potholed highway in a jeep with shot suspension. The thing to remind yourself, should you come across such reports, is that most firms have been dragged down to some extent or another by the economic malaise of the last three years. Unlike many of them, Hammonds has also been expending a great deal of money and other resources on its new territories during this time.

This year we ended up having a forthright set of *Student Guide* interviews, with good and bad feelings running high amongst trainees. One thing on which they did all agree is that across its offices *"the firm is genuinely beginning to achieve its one-firm ambition;"* however, some also felt that Hammonds *"has expanded too quickly, and lots of things like management style need to catch up."* The more analytical minds suggested some bedding down was now in order: *"It needs to consolidate the mergers, consolidate its place in the UK market, and consolidate the depth and quality of work generated by the European offices."* Trainees' eyes and minds were on the future (*"In two or three years this will be a great place to work"*) as well as the here and now (*"there's no denying the brilliant quality of training"*).

hobo carousel

Trainees spend their first three weeks together on a hotel-bound version of the PSC, a prelapsarian time of *"bonding and nights out,"* which almost immediately gives way to a nomadic two-year dash around the UK. Like the Littlest Hobo, Hammonds' trainees just keep moving on. And on. And on. This is because of the unique 'location-rotation' training scheme, which has them taking six four-month seats in a minimum of three English offices. You could even head abroad as a few seats are available in Berlin, Paris, Turin, Brussels and Hong Kong, and only Berlin and Paris require native fluency. The firm's logic is clear: shuttling trainees between offices buttresses cross-site relationships and breeds a new generation of fee earners who see Hammonds as one entity. On that score the scheme fulfils its purpose: *"You really feel part of a national firm,"* opined one source, and another reflected: *"I now find it really easy to pick up the phone and ask a colleague in Birmingham for advice."*

Whilst the firm *"wants to attract the kind of people who might not normally apply to the regions,"* the danger seems to be that a whistle-stop tour of the provinces is regarded by many of them as a gap year-type adventure before qualification in London. Whilst many did take up NQ jobs in the capital in 2004, this goal simply isn't attainable for everyone. Said one source: *"I was told there was no property qualification seat for me in London, but was offered one in Birmingham."* In the last two years pressures of London-centricity briefly led the firm to restrict the number of seats trainees could spend in the big smoke, but standard order has now been restored and up to half a training contract can be enjoyed there. Clearly recognising that location-rotation is sometimes not the best way for firm or trainee, Hammonds has introduced a quota of fixed-location contracts across every UK office except London. 15 per year to be precise. But don't read too much into that; although some trainees had a hunch that location-rotation might be on its way out, one interviewee suggested: *"You'd need to have a pretty sturdy reason, like a wife, for wanting to stick in one city."*

Once on the hobo carousel, trainees can state their seat and location preferences. Beyond the enforced moves, some office-hop with alacrity, and others spend as much as three seats in the same office. In terms of practice area, a corporate seat (banking, tax or corporate), a litigation seat and property seat are compulsory, but beyond that there is relative freedom. With over 80 trainees to be placed every four months, *"feelings run high about seat allocation"* and consequently our sources recommended taking a flexible approach. *"People who come here with a master plan in mind for every seat seem to be disappointed,"* one interviewee admitted, while a tactical player revealed his strategy: *"I was easy going about a couple of seats and then got what I wanted later."* The implications for qualification are unquantifiable: *"If you think you want to qualify into commercial dispute resolution in Manchester, and you get CDR in Birmingham for a seat it can be quite frustrating."* However, *"lots of people changed their perceptions about where and into what they want to qualify."*

who drank all the milk?

The bottom-line assessment of the tour-of-duty training contract is that *"if you go in with you eyes open, and are willing to stay footloose for a while, it's brilliant."* Six seats enable breadth of training, with the disadvantages of short assignments (*"You often don't see things through to completion"*) outweighed by the benefits of variety. *"If you don't like a seat, you're in and out quickly, whereas if you do you can always go back, and then you'll have eight months experience in that area."* Just don't bank on going back to the department in the same office.

The system best suits those who adapt quickly, the kind of trainees who set themselves the *"six-months-in-four challenge."* Meaning? *"You can't just settle in for a month, you've got to really get stuck in from day one to get the most out of it."* Frequently moving city, department and social group tests trainees' inner resources and breeds self-confidence. One trainee confessed: *"It forced me to take the initiative and to be more outgoing."*

Time spent together on the PSC pays dividends – *"As a group, we're really good at supporting one another."*

And Hammonds offers stout support as well, not least by providing accommodation for all trainees on location rotation schemes. In the past this has amounted to heavily subsidised, plush, city-centre flatshares for two, minutes from the offices. A major bugbear with trainees this year is the firm's decision to cut costs by providing trainee accommodation further from city centres. Trainees now live in slightly larger groups too, although the firm assures us that there are never more than two people to a bathroom. In Leeds, accommodation is now a 30 to 35-minute commute away in Horsforth; Manchester trainees no longer live in Salford Quays; in London the Barbican has been abandoned in favour of Docklands; and in Birmingham trainees now reside in Sutton Coldfield. Trainees had this to say: *"We were told that our accommodation, together with the savings we'd make on travel through being in the centre of town, would represent £6,000-£7,000 on top of our wages. But we worked out the rents on the new shared houses, and the firm is barely adding any subsidy on top of the rent we pay...plus we've got travel costs and longer journey times."*

They'd obviously done their maths, but in fairness, the new accommodation is of an *"excellent standard"* and the firm had been quick to resolve teething problems. Additionally it still provides *"a lorry that comes round and moves your stuff to the next location at rotation time."* Nonetheless, whilst those commuting times couldn't be described as unreasonable in anyone's book, they did make *"a big difference"* to some. If you're settling in to your third new town in 12 months, as well as getting to grips with a new seat, you might well find that your margins of tolerance become equally thin.

become as one

Trainees tell us Hammonds' UK offices are very much alike, with only small regional variations. Birmingham is *"a great office, very comfortable, if a bit 60s-ish,"* Manchester is extremely popular, *"not least for the city itself,"* and Leeds is *"friendlier even than

Birmingham." Perhaps unsurprisingly given the challenges of the City market, the *"more corporate, plush and aggressive"* London office departed most from the Hammonds mould. It is here that trainees talked of working *"ridiculous hours. I once worked until 2am every night for four weeks in commercial and IP,"* but across the office, a rigorous 9am–6.30 or 7pm was not thought uncommon.

Trainees were unequivocal in saying: *"The firm is really focused on giving you the best quality training possible,"* stressing that it *"invests so much money and time in us."* Depending on which department and/or office you are in, you may share a room with a partner, assistant solicitor or even another trainee, although a few departments work open plan. A day-to-day supervisor ensures you get the right amount and type of work, and a separate training supervisor takes a longer term view, sitting in on the beginning, mid and end-of-seat appraisals.

Of course, the exact nature of the work trainees get depends on location and department, but the following contrasting examples are fairly typical. *"In property in London I had 30 of my own files,"* one source said; another told us: *"In Birmingham in the commercial seat, I did a lot of legwork, but also got some sectioned-off bits of work on larger deals that were my responsibility."* Because Hammonds sells itself on a 'one-firm' basis, it's hard for us to pick apart the work each office is doing and so the following deals are not itemised by location. Recently, property lawyers handled Trinity Mirror's sale of Post and Mail House in Birmingham and the subsequent relocation of its West Midlands printing facility to Fort Dunlop. Meanwhile, litigators represented sports agency SFX in their dispute with David Beckham, and corporate lawyers were doing everything but snoozing on the £72.2 million recommended cash offer by Soundersleep Ltd for Silentnight Holdings.

The picture trainees paint is of a *"straightforward,"* *"no-nonsense"* firm, that still adheres to traditional northern values. Generally, this sits well with the *"outgoing and straightforward"* trainees we interviewed. One told us: *"It's a direct place – everyone knows where they stand, partners, trainees and clients."* Things are equally clear when it comes to qualification; in 2004, 25 of the 32 qualifiers accepted positions with the firm. As we observed earlier, many variables of location and department come into play on qualification. The figure should be viewed in the context that the firm went to the market to fill prime positions such as employment after trainees had made their decisions. Leavers pursued further academic, travel or specific work interests or held tight for work in the place they'd decided to call home.

and finally...

Hammonds is a robust and distinctive firm with a distinctive training scheme. If you're willing to hit the road for two years or you can secure a fixed contract in Birmingham, Manchester or Leeds, you'll be rewarded with good work, excellent formal training and a solid start to your career.

Harbottle & Lewis LLP

the facts

Location: London
Number of partners/assistannts: 22/35
Total number of trainees: 8
Seats: 4x6 months
Alternative seats: Secondments

As much a fixture in the West End as The Palace or The Haymarket, Harbottle & Lewis is a traditional London firm that's bang up-to-date with all the latest celebrity gossip and new media work.

west end story

Founded in the 50s by two theatre and film-mad partners, Harbottles has enjoyed a long run in the West End, receiving excellent notices for its sterling entertainment and media practice. Today the firm prides itself on being large enough to handle virtually any matter in the specialist fields of film, TV, sport, music, publishing, advertising and theatre, but is also highly regarded for its corporate expertise on smaller-ticket deals. Times may have changed since founding partner Laurence Harbottle spent his weekends running a professional theatre company, but there is plenty to suggest that the firm has stayed true to his desire to encourage originality and creativity. This year, one notable first-time instruction came from the highly successful Sam Mendes-founded theatre, The Donmar Warehouse.

Like any ageing thespian, Harbottles has to keep one step ahead of young whippersnappers, eager to snatch the limelight. It is at the forefront of legal developments at the sharp end of new media, interactive entertainment and mobile telephony, and with clients like Sony, Diageo and Yahoo! it is clear to us the firm will be enjoying top billing for a few years yet.

Tired theatre clichés apart, every trainee we interviewed had applied to the firm because they craved involvement in *"high-profile work."* And whether their preference was for celebrities or celebrated businesses, high-profile work is what they've had. Harbottles acts for a glittering pantheon of stars – think Kate Moss, Diana Rigg, Gary Rhodes and the England cricket team...and those are just the ones we can mention. As one trainee whispered: *"The really brilliant clients are the ones people don't know about."* We're sworn to secrecy on much of what we know, but in a *Hello!*-style EXCLUSIVE we can reveal that Harbottles also advises the likes of Chrysalis, the Prince's Trust, Manchester United, News International and Universal Studios.

Lest you imagine an application to Harbottles will propel you into an A-list fantasy playground, as if *Heat* magazine had been crossed with *The Lawyer* and brought to life, here's a timely note of caution. *"Just because you're working on the sale of a celebrity's house, it doesn't mean the law itself is any more glamorous."* One honest soul confessed: *"I've seen a Z-list celebrity in the lift, but that's all."* Yet having administered the regulation dose of realism, we fully accept that there's a reason why media work is so popular. Goodness! Who wouldn't enjoy telling their mates: *"My most recent file was running all the copyright clearances for a movie soundtrack."*

some like it hot...

Just a stone's throw from the media scrum of Soho and the bright lights of Theatreland, Harbottles' overly warm and *"slightly ramshackle"* Hanover Square office is due for (and getting) an *"air-conditioning, glass-walls refit."* For now, work boils over between its four floors, with different departments frequently serving the varied needs of the same clients. As in any relatively small firm, the brief is simple: reel in a client and cater to all their needs. Harbottles' litigation department advised David Beckham over the Rebecca Loos allegations this year, and we'd lay money they'd do anything to ease Goldenballs in the direction of their IP lawyers next time his contract with Pepsi expires.

Alas, the property department on the fourth floor left our contacts decidedly cool, perhaps because it was *"the least client facing and relatively dry."* By contrast, the third floor coco and IP/IT departments raised their temperatures. Coco is subdivided into M&A and start-ups, with trainees spending three months carrying out similar duties in each. According to one old hand, these amount to *"assisting on due diligence, lots of research and a fair bit of company secretarial."* However, start-up work exposes trainees to computer games, dotcom and media companies. Concerning second-floor litigation, trainees chose to remain philosophical about the more mundane chores, preferring to focus on the opportunities for advocacy and running their own small files.

The entertainment, sports, TV and music departments are sizzling, We particularly liked the sound of the *"hectically busy"* music team, which acts for both talent and record companies. Having lost a couple of key music partners in recent years, the team has had to reshape itself – not unlike the music industry really. These days, the traditional drafting of standard recording contracts sits alongside innovative new media work. One trainee told us how they'd been *"finding out rates for ring tones of songs; how the licences will be granted and repeat-fees collected...even though the collection agencies don't know how it will be done."* Working on the Prince's Trust 'Fashion Rocks' event, trainees were *"running about on the day making sure all the artists' release forms were signed so they could perform."*

Should they be tempted to hop out of the frying pan, a popular client secondment to Virgin Atlantic offers trainees six months in the fire. *"It's not like you're a trainee; there are all types of work from Advertising Standards Authority complaints to employment matters to aviation law to coco – you're just expected to get on with it."* The only downside is *"no free flights."*

wannabees

Trainees tend to take seats in property, litigation and commercial but the firm is flexible about its four-seat system; *"they have an idea where people will go, but if you make a preference clear they'll try to accommodate you."* A *"well-structured"* appraisal system involves monthly chats with the training partner and an end-of-seat review for more formal feedback. Whilst some felt *"it could be a bit more full on and targeted to your needs,"* others argued that *"if you're not getting the mix of work you like, it'll get sorted if you mention it at your monthly meeting."* Each trainee is also given a mentor who has *"more of a pastoral role, takes you out to lunch and makes sure everything is alright."* Contracted working hours are a theatre-friendly 10am–6pm, though 9.30am–7pm seems more the norm. The firm provides a free lunch every day, at which *"we all sit together, support staff and everyone."*

Trainees would have you believe there's no Harbottles type, but our overactive imaginations were tickled into action when one source anatomised their year group as *"one very posh one, another trendy, one loud, one quiet, another very intellectual."* Knowing that the firm acts for Simon Fuller's 19 Management, only

one conclusion could be drawn – the pop impresario is in charge of recruitment.

When not *"all yabbering away in the kitchens,"* staff can be found at the Duke of York sharing a cocktail at the monthly drinks party. *"Socialising tends to be more organised than off the cuff"* and, as one source explained, *"not all encompassing, but there if you want it."* The West End location isn't ideal for sport but Harbottles does have tennis, cricket, and football teams. After concluding our interviews we were left with the impression that staff here place a good deal of importance on their lives outside work, and part of the firm's appeal is that it allows one to strike a balance between career and real life. Historically, on qualification most trainees remain with the firm, but in September 2004 only one of the three stayed, with one of the others heading back to Virgin.

and finally...

A successful audition for Harbottle & Lewis will result in you joining a small and intimate cast. With them you'll enjoy a breadth and profile of work that should transform you into an excellent lawyer.

Herbert Smith

the facts

Location: London
Number of UK partners/assistants: 151/455
Total number of trainees: 165
Seats: 4 x6 month seats
Alternative seats: Overseas seats, secondments
Extras: Pro bono – death row appeals, Whitechapel Legal Advice Centre, language training

Herbert Smith is a phenomenally successful City practice that has become the third most profitable UK firm. Ambition and drive have seen it gain credibility at the top end of a fierce transactional market, while retaining its dominance of the litigation arena. This gladiator of a firm knows how to whup ass!

cider with herbies

Real estate is a common first seat and trainees reported great work in a welcoming environment. One recalled the seat fondly, saying: *"I was working on a large matter with three other trainees and we got 40 properties each to look after. Out of all of them this is the seat where I did manage to run my own work and had an extent of control over how I spent my time. I got on with most people and the assistants were very helpful."* Another added to the wave of euphoria by telling us: *"It would take me much longer to get to this level of responsibility in other departments. I've had daily contact with clients...large investment funds, dealing with their agents on leases and licences and some big sales or portfolios and refinancings."* That sounds about right as the property lawyers have acted on some great transactions and won some interesting new clients including UBS and Anshutz Entertainment Group, the owners of Madison Square Garden and the people who have just got their hands on the Millennium Dome.

Corporate is another likely first seat, although some trainees found it *"daunting,"* particularly if sitting with a senior-level partner. Said one: *"I would always see it as an advantage to sit with a senior assistant. My supervisor was a big character who has been here since he was a trainee."* It sounds as if the demands placed upon trainees are unpredictable. *"It was spectacularly quiet when I was there, but I caught the tail end of a deal,"* reported one. *"I attended a couple of meetings and was the contact point for some junior lawyers on the other side. To be honest I had to be pretty proactive in finding work, but I did get the obligatory drafting of board minutes, company searches and registrations and filings at Companies House."* Make a second visit to the department at a busier time and things might be very different: *"I've had to turn down work or get other trainees to help. The deals are the same, but I am trusted to do more things – to draft things and send them out without 13 people checking it. I've drafted first versions of ancillary documents and I feel like I've been allowed to behave like a real lawyer."* Among the department's most prized deals of recent times was the sale of Lukoil's $1.37 billion interest in the Caspian Sea Azeri-Chirag–Gunashli project, and the sale of HP Bulmer to Scottish & Newcastle for £278 million.

A corporate seat is compulsory, but can be substituted with a finance seat. We spoke to fewer people who had taken this alternative, but the firm is growing its finance practice and so we envisage more seats becoming available over time. In the crossover areas of capital markets and projects, there is also growth. And, notably, the energy sector has fuelled activity at the firm, accounting for many of its highest valued deals lately. It recently advised the DTI on a £48 billion nuclear clean-up programme.

Much is said of tough City hours. Our sources didn't moan; they accepted busy periods (usually in corporate) in the knowledge that they would come out of them alive. *"There have been weeks when I have done 75 hours,"* said one trainee, *"but only when everyone has been working that, including partners, on the big-ticket deals. It's just how we do things."* He put the departmental differences in hours down to this – *"Corporate has a certain mindset: clients work in a certain way and the corporate lawyers react. In litigation, the clients are much more in the hands of the lawyers and the lawyers have control."*

a-plié-ing yourself

And so we come to the litigation department, the reason why most of our sources chose Herbert Smith in the first place. It is split into four groups: A and B are general litigation; C is insurance and D is energy and arbitration. *"Litigation D was a phenomenally good seat and I got the impression that the people who inhabit the group are very, very good. The partner I sat with was very busy and had a couple of assistants working with him. Mine was an admin-based role – finding the correct documents and keeping track of them...I was a guardian of documents."* Anything more exciting? *"I attended the odd meeting and conference call and was drafting letters, which can be fun! When I was in court I was purely an observer...I didn't do any advocacy."* A particularly proactive trainee said of his general litigation seat: "*I did no more than 25% monkey work. I have seen a paginator, but I'm not sure I know how to operate one! I certainly did bundling and binding though.*"

The litigation department is seen as more traditional and hierarchical than the other parts of the firm: "*It's doors closed and heads down. It's not unfriendly; it's just that they work hard.*" It seems also that some of the bigger egos are difficult to contend with, so many don't try. When we heard that one litigation group had been nicknamed 'the fridge' because of it's chilly ambient temperature, we became somewhat confused as others had talked of a fridge in corporate. "*There's quite a few fridges,*" explained one trainee. "*They are working on it,*" another reported of the corporate fridge; "*they had a bowling night and a Christmas sketch in which trainees had to take on the role of partners in The Weakest Link.*" We also heard tell of the finance department's Christmas party at which the trainees were required to perform a dance. The firm had been sponsoring the English National Ballet and a partner called in a favour – "*two tiny ballerinas*" who taught the trainees a few steps. "*The boys were pretty inelegant though!*"

Guaranteed to be considerably more temperate are the niche departments, client secondments and overseas seats. Of employment, for example, one source said: "*I loved my seat there and I really felt part of the team, even though I did quite a lot of research and a lot of monkey work. They are all really friendly, lovely people and the hours and the supervisors are great.*" He told us he'd felt privileged to work alongside highly rated partners. Another privilege is a three-month posting to the Court of Appeal to act as a judicial assistant. Here, you'll be "*seeing things from behind the scenes and sitting down and discussing cases with the judge.*" Secondments are also available to human rights organisation Liberty, and a number of commercial clients..

parlez vous?

The international nature of Herbert Smith's practice was sometimes the thing that clinched it for trainees when accepting an offer of a training contract. Six-month overseas postings are available at each seat rotation, and the menu, which includes Paris, Amsterdam (with allied firm Stibbe), Hong Kong and Singapore, is pretty darned tasty.

The word on appraisals is good: "*They are definitely thorough enough and people are good at spotting what you do well and don't do well.*" Ongoing feedback is usually forthcoming too: "*Apart from the one I have now, I've been able to speak to my supervisors at regular intervals... they've been chatty and I've been able to have a running dialogue.*" Alas, "*there are people who don't get on with their supervisors. It just depends on the people involved.*" Away from the individual supervisor/trainee relationship, trainees all agree that the firm takes their training seriously, and we heard how "*they spend a lot of money educating us.*"

Seat allocation can feel like a lottery at times, though admittedly the odds for getting a desired seat are far higher than those offered by Camelot. One trainee told us: "*I have always got the seats I wanted, but I know that others haven't. There are frequently e-mails from the trainee discussion group saying we want more transparency and we want to know the basis of how seats are allocated – the criteria are not obvious.*" It doesn't take a rocket scientist to see the problem: the numbers wanting a second stab at litigation outnumber the opportunities to return there. In the estimation of one source: "*Most trainees want a second litigation seat. Nine out of ten don't get one.*" Sadly, one trainee reported that he'd not got to try the one seat he'd most wanted; yet, he told us: "*In retrospect there is no other firm I would rather have trained at.*" In September 2004, as in past years, there were too few litigation jobs on offer(eight to be precise) for the number of qualifiers who sought them. As such, only 41 of the 52 stayed, and even some of these compromised on the kind of job they accepted.

building bridges

"If you have time, there's plenty to do in terms of sports and culture." It's hardly high culture, but nearby is a bar called Davies. *"Everyone hates it but everyone goes...it's just there waiting for you,"* said one source with resignation in his voice. A black-tie trainee ball is held every two summers, last time at the Kensington Roof Gardens. Indeed, summer is definitely the most sociable time, with the vac scheme bringing a shower of theatre tickets as well as students. First-years go out the most, often taking lunch together, *"but then it starts to fizzle out as key people go on second-ments."* As for departmental socialising, it depends which group you are in, though all have a changeover event to mark the arrival of a new batch of trainees. And on a monthly basis, a drinks trolley will magically appear from nowhere leading most people to down tools for a glass or two and a handful of Twiglets.

The firm occupies a glass and steel building (complete with escalators as well as lifts) overlooking Exchange Square and Liverpool Street station. *"The square is fantastic in the summer as everyone sits out there at lunchtimes and in the evenings there are bands and croquet."* Hurrah! A much-needed refit is underway in the main office. When we asked one trainee to describe the decor, he said: *"I can't see it for all the wood everywhere!"* Let's just say it is very 80s, very woody and has two ugly atria with a couple of oversized and dusty looking kites in them. *"They are slowly refurbishing this building floor by floor and transporting people over to a new adjacent building via this Indiana Jones-style rope bridge."* For the record, the bridge is not made of rope.

There are worlds within worlds at Herbert Smith. Much has been written elsewhere about the battle for predominance between the litigation and corporate/banking practices, and perhaps this is inevitable in a firm that has only latterly sought to take on the rest of the City in the transactional arena. Though we hear the top brass are thinking in a more cross-firm manner these days, trainees (who are in the luxurious position of sampling life in all the main departments) remarked that there's some way to go on this front. Said one: *"They could do more to make it feel like one workplace. Often I speak to my supervisor about other departments and she won't know what I am talking about."*

slings and arrows

It sounds as if you'll always find people you like in your intake and, so far as we can see, Herbies has a tendency to recruit very likeable people. For what it is worth, we spotted a preponderance of ordinary kids who'd done very well at school and university. One source summed up the ideal trainee as someone who is *"very clever and can do the job very well. If that is the case, you will be praised and accepted and lots of other good things...if you are dedicated."* Another mused: *"In life it helps to be robust. We work in a reasonably stressful and demanding environment and it has its slings and arrows."* As in past years, we sense Herbert Smith is the wrong firm for softies or those who are prone to paranoia...or even ups and downs emotionally. These comments from a fourth-seater are a case in point: *"I am sat with a partner who will say good morning and goodbye and beyond that leaves me to my own devices. Now, I am fine with it. I have developed a tough shell!"*

and finally...

Herbert Smith is proud that it offers one of the most rounded training contracts in the Square Mile. We think it has every right to be, and for the robust applicant it is a super choice. Even so, we just wish someone would have the balls to remove from the scheme the minority of supervisors who are unsuitable for the role.

Hill Dickinson

the facts

Location: Liverpool, Manchester, Chester, London
Number of UK partners/assistants: 115/114
Total number of trainees: 24
Seats: 4x6 months
Alternative seats: None

The old money of Liverpool firms, Hill Dickinson has been a fixture in the commercial world of the North West since 1820. From a sea-salty start acting for the shipowners and traders in the port city to its post-millennial growth and diversification, here's the firm's story...

iceberg!

The ship in a glass box in the reception of Pearl Assurance House in Liverpool is a testament to Hill Dickinson's marine law origins. The firm acted in relation to the ill-fated ocean-going liners the Titanic and the Lusitania and a marine law department still thrives today. But just as 90% of an iceberg lies unseen below the water, to look only at Hill Dicks shipping work is to ignore the bulk of its activities.

The topic at the forefront of our interviews was the transformation of a litigation-dominated firm into something more rounded. Those trainees who were approaching qualification (seven out of nine of whom stayed at the firm in September 2004) remarked on how different Hill Dicks was from the time they had applied to it. Said one: "*In four years there has been an awful lot of change;*" others fully expected the change to continue: "*It's doubled in size and we want to be higher still in the top 50.*" Four years ago, litigation accounted for some 50% of business with shipping, health and clin neg bringing the tally to around three-quarters. By 2004 non-contentious work accounted for around half of business, not least because the firm has secured a string of lateral hires (from North West firms and the likes of Eversheds, Stephenson Harwood, Clyde & Co and Hammonds)

and a merger with a leading Liverpool property firm Bullivant Jones.

Many trainees had originally set their compasses for a litigation-led training, healthcare work being of particular appeal. Hill Dicks acts for scores of insurance companies including Norwich Union, Royal Liver, Sabre, Churchill and Royal & SunAlliance as well as leading insurers to the professions including St Paul and the Veterinary Defence Society. Most notably, it is one of just 14 firms on the NHS Litigation Authority's panel, so allowing it a slice of the huge clinical negligence defence pie. Changes in the firm's practice orientation won't lead to lost opportunities for trainees intent on contentious training, but it will allow them more room to manoeuvre around transactional and advisory areas of practice.

busting crime and the compensation culture

Trainees have little or no choice as to the first two of their four seats; they usually find themselves in healthcare and insurance litigation departments in Liverpool. A healthcare seat brings exposure to supervisors' work on a whole range of cases from brain-damaged babies to General Medical Council disciplinary hearings. "*Some of it was quite gruesome especially when you are reading medical reports,*" admitted one source; "*but you get immune to it. I also went to inquests into some quite horrific deaths.*" You'll meet with hospital staff, both managers and medical professionals, as they are the people who provide the evidence upon which the NHSLA's defence relies. One recent case of note relates to the claim made by over 1,100 families of babies whose organs were secretly retained by Alder Hey Children's Hospital. In non-healthcare professional indemnity litigation, Hill Dicks acts for the insurers of solicitors, barristers, surveyors, accountants, financial advisers, vets and more.

Over in public sector insurance litigation, the trainee's experience will be determined by the particular practice of their supervisor. Aside from regular employer's liability cases (asbestos claims, check-out operators with back sprain, etc), there's some pretty unique work. A small team has acted for local authorities defending allegations of abuse in children's homes in north Wales dating back to the 1960s and 70s. Several trainees also reported acting for supermarkets on public liability claims of the in-store banana-skin-slip variety. One claim was made by a severely obese woman who injured herself when a plastic chair collapsed. Said one trainee: "*I think it's definitely true that the UK is becoming a litigious society like the US.*"

Proof that the shipping work didn't go down with the Titanic, there's a seat in the department in Liverpool. Also on offer here are seats including coco, employment (private sector employers and NHS bodies, "*mainly hospital trusts and primary healthcare trusts*") and commercial property. The insurance fraud seat sounds like the coolest one to us, and if you've ever fantasised about becoming a private detective (if only to wear the gabardine raincoat and trilby hat), it's got to be the one to go for. Acting for insurance companies and employing two ex-cops, the team investigates arsons, staged accidents and potential crime rings.

manchester: a cheek on each chair

Hill Dicks' Manchester operation is smaller than the four-office Liverpool set-up and here we noted a tendency for trainees to work for two departments at a time. There seems no apparent logic to the combinations – IP with property litigation; family with employment; regulatory (health and safety) with sport and media. Doing a split seat only works if the supervisors are prepared to talk to each other and be aware of how busy the trainee is. If the departments you work for are on different floors, it can mean a good deal of running about. And the reason for split seats? Until now, several of the Manchester departments simply weren't busy enough to keep a whole trainee occupied. However, if the growth of the office continues as it has, split seats will become a thing of the past.

Looking more closely at Manchester, the obvious difference to Liverpool is the independence from insurance companies and NHS bodies. It does some of this work, but plenty more besides. Sports lawyers handle contractual and sponsorship issues for football and other sports players and clubs, including several in the Premiership. Media lawyers rub shoulders with celebrities, and family lawyers take on divorce and ancillary relief cases for *Sunday Times* rich-listers and other wealthy folk. They don't touch children's or legal aid cases, leaving these to colleagues in the tiny Chester office. Of family in Manchester, one trainee explained how the work frequently involved company law, taxation and trusts issues. "*It is the seat that stretched me most,*" they said. Amusingly, "*one old gentleman said to me 'You'll never get married now!'*" Alongside these non-core departments, the usual property and coco offerings are available.

Northern trainees work in both Liverpool and Manchester, and they suggested we emphasise that this is a North West training. Being told your next seat is in another city can mean rushing to find new accommodation and, on occasion, paying two sets of rent if you can't get out of a tenancy quick enough. The only other option is a miserable commute, particularly if you live on the wrong side of Manchester. If we were to generalise, we'd say the majority of trainees have Liverpool roots and a preference for that city. And in case you were wondering, there are trainees who have come to Hill Dicks with no prior connection to the north at all.

The two main northern offices couldn't be more different. Aside from the fact that the Liverpool operation has been drawn and quartered, and that the main office has been described as "*scabby,*" there are cultural differences between the two. Liverpool is buzzy, more informal and big on socialising. "*We have a blast,*" said one source; "*there are so many nice pubs around – The Living Room, Mosquito and the Blue Bar by the docks.*" Everyone berated the dingy bar across the road, Trials, although they all admitted to drinking there. *"Manchester is much more formal; you really know you are in an office environment."* The premises near King Street are lovely, but the social scene is practically non-existent. *"Things get put in the pipeline but they never seem to come off...I suppose people are just busy and have their own lives."*

london: ships in the night

So far we've not mentioned Hill Dicks London. There are only two trainees here and the office sings from its own song sheet, being more oriented towards traditional marine work. A seat working on goods-in-transit cases will mean claims for cargo that's been lost or damaged at sea (perhaps steel that has rusted en route from Japan to Europe) and road carriage work. Enjoy yachting? You can spend a whole six months in a seat devoted entirely to multi-million-pound gin palaces. *"The work is so broad even though the subject matter is always yachts."* On the contentious side you might have *"people crushed by boats or falling overboard, collisions and surveyors giving negligent surveys."* On the non-contentious side, *"you'll be arranging the finance of boats, drafting new-build or refit agreements and dealing with registration issues, perhaps the implications of a UK-registered yacht sailing into BVI, US and Cayman waters."* The clients are people who can afford to buy £50 million yachts and the banks who help out with extra finance.

In insurance litigation and professional indemnity seats, the experiences of northern trainees are echoed. You might be acting for *"the insurer of an electrician who has made a horrendous mistake or a housing authority with subsidence problems in buildings or train companies."* There's nothing to stop a London trainee from taking a seat up north and last year that's exactly what happened to one guy who was advised to make his way up the motorway to Liverpool to get the best possible experience of corporate transactions. His motives are obvious; the Liverpool coco team recently beat Linklaters to a £100 million deal for a Danish client that was selling off its international aerospace business.

Our source in London spoke of a welcoming environment in the office in the capital and nights out in The Jamaica Wine House being spontaneously *"rustled up."* As a small office, few things are set in stone and *"there aren't rules or policies or systems like you get in the big firms."* Having said that, there is one policy that doesn't sit well with trainees: the *"blanket ban"* on non-work-related e-mails and internet use. Nevertheless, *"parochial"* tendencies aside, the benefits of being one of two trainees are enormous because people treat you as an individual and not just 'the trainee'.

and finally...

Hill Dickinson wants to be the dominant player in the North West. We should point out that a few of its rivals also want much the same thing, so it looks like things might get interesting in the future. That said, the firm is already the biggest in the region and, if we were betting types, we'd have a flutter on this firm.

Hodge Jones & Allen

the facts

Location: London
Number of UK partners/assistants: 14/34
Total number of trainees: 9
Seats: 4x6 months
Alternative seats: None

One of the most respected and successful firms in north London, HJA has been involved in cases such as the New Cross fire inquest and compensation claims for Gulf War Syndrome. In recent years, it has branched out from its key legal aid practice to offer advice to commercial clients.

anarchy in the uk

Back in 1977, when HJA began operating as a community law firm in Camden Town, Britain was undergoing a cultural revolution. As disco divas queued round the block to see *Saturday Night Fever* at the local Odeon, The Sex Pistols were swearing and spitting at Bill Grundy on *Thames Today*. More than 25 years on and nothing's really changed. John Lydon is still hurling four-letter abuse at the camera, flares are alive and well on the High Street, and the good people at HJA are still doing the business.

There are two routes to a training contract at HJA: either apply for a traditional contract a year in advance, or prove your worth as a paralegal in one of the specialist teams such as housing or mental health. Those taking the traditional route will sit in four six-month seats chosen from crime, family, commercial or residential property, and housing.

the minute you walked in the joint...

For many, the *"busy and sociable"* criminal department is the main attraction, and the firm sometimes allows trainees to remain in the seat for a second term. Part of the appeal is the level of responsibility heaped upon them. The role typically includes advising clients on charge, taking witness statements, getting expert reports and briefing counsel. One enthused: *"For my first case I did everything from meeting the client at the police station right through to preparing the case for the Crown Court, where I clerked at the trial."* No wonder they *"learn a lot about the law really quickly."*

The way things work at HJA, *"clients always see a trainee first when they walk off the street."* If you're particularly interested in their case, you can speak to your supervisor and ask to handle the matter yourself. Of course, you'll work with a partner on more serious matters, but *"the firm is prepared to put you out there. You're not just doing small shoplifting cases, but rape and murder from the start."*

cigarettes and alcohol

Dealing with clients can be exacting but rewarding: *"You're often working with people with mental health, or drug or alcohol addiction problems. You need to have patience and understand where they're coming from, keep calm if they start shouting and screaming, and explain things carefully."* Trainees are encouraged to enrol on the police station accreditation programme, which allows them to attend stations to advise clients on charge and drop off a couple of packets of Marlboro Lights. *"You have to be tough when faced with heavy-handed police tactics, and be able to walk in there with confidence. You can't be phased by dealing with inspectors who are a lot older than you."* On the other hand, if you're struggling, help may come from the unlikeliest of sources: *"Some clients have much better knowledge than you, as they've often been in the system for years."*

Once you've completed the accreditation course, you can expect your share of nights on call – either an overnight shift or a 24-hour period over the weekend. Our sources didn't seem to mind this too much, as overtime pay is a more-than-handy £25 an hour.

love is a battlefield

In the family department you'll be involved with care proceedings and domestic violence cases, and advise on divorce. Once again, client contact is high on the agenda, and you must develop a good bedside manner as *"you're dealing with people's emotions, usually when they're at a very difficult time in their life."* Trainees are encouraged to go to court to try their hand at a spot of advocacy.

In personal injury, trainees reported working on matters ranging from traffic accidents to professional negligence. As well as a steady diet of *"trips, slips and falls,"* there are also more serious injuries, and some of our sources had been lucky enough to contribute to Gulf War Syndrome cases. A note of warning though – if your heart is set on clinical negligence work, the PI and clin neg departments are separate and the latter does not offer a trainee seat.

HJA has branched out into commercial practice, and no longer relies on publicly funded work. It's an eminently sensible move, given the uncertain climate for legal aid and its low rates of pay. Trainees must now do a seat in commercial property and the family department is taking on more privately funded clients. One source considered the general feeling within the firm: *"We're having to take on a certain type of client to get more money in. Not everyone in the firm agrees. They understand it, but don't really like it."* Rather like buying organic food, you can stick to your principles only if you can afford to.

HJA was built on the premise that law is for all, whether or not they can pay for it. Accordingly it expects recruits to have gained some experience of legal aid, or charity/voluntary work before starting at the firm. As one commented: *"People here are definitely passionate about their work, and they are committed to the principles of justice."* When asked to elaborate on notions of commitment, another dryly observed: *"The pay isn't great, so they need it!"* If you watched the BBC2 series *Make Me Honest* in the spring of 2004, you'll have seen a prime example of beyond-the-call-of-duty attitudes that prevail at HJA. One episode featured the mentoring efforts of motor-biking crime lawyer Greg Foxmith, who helped an ex-heroin addict effect a 180° turnaround in her life and put a 21-year-old serial offender back on the straight and narrow.

This firm sees itself as an essential part of the local community. According to one trainee: *"We have whole families with different files scattered between several departments. Clients use us for so many services, we're almost like part of the family."* Especially if the family is a cross between the Slaters and the Sopranos.

never mind the botox

The *Student Guide* team couldn't be more qualified to comment on life in Camden Town. Half of us live within a couple of hundred metres of HJA's offices, and we're more than familiar with the pros and cons of the area – in every sense of the words. So we asked trainees if they thought the area needed a bit of a botox injection. Although they did speak of a certain *"air of depravation"* (it's odds-on round here that you'll be accosted by someone attempting to sell you the basic constituent of a Camberwell Carrot, or asking for money to buy crack or heroin), the overall

impression was of an area with *"character."*

That 'character' is also to be found in some excellent neighbourhood hostelries. Both the Mac Bar over the road and the nearby Camden Brewing Company are popular with the firm. The crime team regularly props up the counter in the Parma café, and when money gets tight at the end of month, the nearby Camden Tandoori provides a good lunch for just £2.50. On a sunny day you might choose to spend your lunch hour strolling along the adjacent canal towpath to Camden Lock, which is just five minutes away. If you're lucky you might even have an office with a view of canal boats and waterfowl. Frequently, someone will organise, say, bowling or a quiz night, and in the summer everyone is given an afternoon off for a big picnic in nearby Regent's Park. In September 2004, one of the three qualifiers took a job with the firm.

and finally...

If you're committed to legal aid work, and are looking to make your mark in a challenging environment, this superior practice should be high up on your list.

Holman Fenwick & Willan

the facts

Location: London
Number of UK partners/assistants: 56/57
Total number of trainees: 20
Seats: 4x6 months
Alternative seats: Overseas seats, secondments
Extras: Language training

Holman Fenwick & Willan made a classic start for a shipping firm, when in 1883 it was founded by a family of merchant adventurers. Quick to see the potential in London's role in world trade, shipping and insurance, it soon developed a reputation that has carried it ever since.

watery depths: dry african plains

Far from complacent and aware that its fortunes ebbed and flowed with the tides of the shipping industry and the number of cases passing through the QBD, two years ago the firm took a good hard look at its business model and management structure. It appointed its first managing partner and divided lawyers into four divisions: shipping and transport, energy and trade, corporate, and banking and insolvency. The shipping and transport division dwarfs each of the others and, importantly for trainees' purposes, still offers the greatest number of seats.

For a major 'wet' adrenaline rush and a spell in the limelight, head for the Admiralty group, which comprises lawyers *"with sea legs"* and non-lawyer master mariners, who are qualified to captain ships. Holmans has worked on almost all the major maritime disasters that you'll have read about in the press or seen on TV and is very highly regarded for its salvage work. It acted for the Dutch salvors of *The Prestige* oil tanker, which sank 130 miles off the Spanish coast, and the Belgian owners of a ship attacked by terrorists off the Yemeni coast. *"It's very exciting to feel that you're a part of all that...seeing the pictures and hearing the reports coming in,"* explained one trainee, who'd loved the diet of collisions, salvage claims and pollution spills. *"They happen all around the world: anywhere there is water, but predominantly in the main shipping lanes, where there is most traffic – the English Channel or around the Pacific and Asian coasts."* With time and experience, lawyers and ex-mariners with the right technical know-how get to fly off to the incident scene to assess the situation and take witness statements from crew members. It can be a tough job getting the full picture, especially if there are language barriers to contend with.

The 'dry' shipping litigation group also goes by the nickname the Kruger National Park because so many South African lawyers roam there. It's busy but less dramatic than the wet group, and straight away throws trainees into research tasks on various aspects of charter and bills of lading disputes. A typical case might turn on the difficulty of terminating a long-term charter party agreement when the vessel is *"a bit of an old tub that needs to go in for repairs"* or a claim regarding a mite-infested cargo of grain from Australia. Teams usually consist of a partner, an assistant and a trainee, which means it's easier for the trainee to get up to speed on the facts and strategy of a case. As one told us: *"This area of law and the type of disputes that arise either make sense to you or they don't."* He also pointed out that Holmans' prominence in the industry ensured a constant flow of interesting cases: *"If I was in a different firm I might end up with laytime and demurrage cases* [unloading cargo late] *all the time."*

the marmite test

We were rather amused when a trainee likened all non-contentious work to Marmite: you love it or hate it, he told us. The firm has a fleet of non-contentious shipping lawyers who handle the sale, purchase and financing of vessels. Acting for both banks and borrowers (*"although not on the same deal"*), they find that ship financing is not usually a team game and involves a considerable amount of drafting. Enjoy yachting? This could be the seat for you, as Holmans has earned a name for transactions relating to pleasure craft of varying degrees of luxury.

It's all very well a firm announcing that its practice is diversifying, but at least Holmans has put its money where its mouth is. In the past two years it has hired established practitioners into its non-core areas. Partners from Osborne Clarke have joined the corporate and insolvency teams; a project finance partner has defected from White & Case and an ex-Denton Wilde Sapte partner is building up the construction team. These lateral hires have enhanced the range of trainee seat options, such that it is now possible to do two non-contentious seats should you wish. All this said, it is always worth remembering that these niche areas are small, about three-quarters of the firm's lawyers litigate, and shipping, insurance and international trade clients still dominate.

oils well that ends well

Some of the most complex litigation is to be found in the insurance/reinsurance department. You'll recall the horrendous *Exxon Valdez* oil spill that polluted large tracts of the Alaskan coastline back in 1989. Fifteen years on, through the so-called Brandywine case, Holmans helped its reinsurer client resist liability for payments to the several insurance syndicates that originally paid out damages for the clean-up, debris and property loss. It can be a daunting experience for a trainee entering into this area of law. *"You go in cold...but people are aware that you know nothing on day one. There are a lot of talks laid on for us,"* explained one source, adding that this was true of the shipping seats too. Enormous, long-running litigation has a nasty habit of embroiling trainees in endless document management, so they are thankful for the presence of paralegals. *"There were times when I had to roll my sleeve up and just get on with it,"* we heard, *"but it wasn't my lot and I also got to draft letters and attend meetings. You take the rough with the smooth."*

worldly wise

It's an obvious question: do you need a maritime background or insurance industry experience to train here? The answer is no, but should you possess either in conjunction with appropriate academic credentials and a decent manner, then the firm might just bite your hand off when you offer your application. Some of the current trainees fit this bill, having degrees in maritime studies or previous careers at sea; others showed a strong sense of adventure by travelling or teaching abroad in their gap years. Like the firm's founding fathers, they've all come to appreciate that international trade makes the world go round, and they're the type to want to get involved with the physical aspects of the global economy.

Holmans has offices in Paris, Rouens, Piraeus, Hong Kong, Singapore and Shanghai, and it has long been the case that partners and assistants can work abroad both long and short term. Trainee seats crop up in Piraeus, Paris and Hong Kong. Most trainees speak foreign languages, and we don't mean just the usual European tongues; some are non-UK nationals. In September 2004, eight of the ten qualifiers took jobs with the firm.

World outlook, language skills, sea legs – the denominators of the trainee group are more common than your average cold. Another thing that ties them together is a passion for litigating, and we were positively inspired by one trainee's analysis of the contrast with transactional law. *"Litigation is very much law heavy, more so than corporate or commercial, and it's quite an academic way of working. Litigation is inspiring; you can tell people I go to court and have cases rather than just bringing up precedents for a deal. That's what gives you a buzz, I suppose...the excitement of a dispute is important to me."*

we are sailing

Speaking of the firm's strong sense of heritage (*"ships in glass cases"* dotted around the place), one source said: *"It makes the firm stand out from others. Holmans is established; it has provenance."* The dress code is formal and the image smart. In the Georgian-fronted main office on Lloyd's Avenue, there's no chill-out area or canteen for the staff, but at least the mood is cordial and the hours aren't hideous. *"There is definitely a hierarchy,"* one source told us. *"That's quite evident when you arrive, but it doesn't limit your ability to go and deal with partners. By the end of the first year they all know who you are, and you have an identity, which is nice. Being one of nine in an intake means you are in demand and people will come and find you."* One trainee spoke of a supportive atmosphere within the trainee group, telling us how just a couple of days before another trainee had taken an urgent call from a partner to attend a conference for which he had to supply a bundle of copied documents. *"We were all happy to help, and this is just the tip of the iceberg."* We collected mixed bag of comments on how comfortable trainees felt with partners, so we'll give you one taken from the middle ground. *"Some are more easy going, some are more formidable – it depends on the individuals. All litigators have a short temper...and they have their moments, but generally people are very friendly and my current supervisor has a wonderful sense of humour."*

If the clink clink of a marina in a light breeze is music to your ears, you'll be pleased to hear, *"there's a huge sailing community here, both yachts and dinghy sailing. Loads of people are doing their yacht master course at the moment, and there are lots of client sailing events off the south coast."* Landlubbers may be in the minority at Holmans, but even they aren't averse to the odd tot of rum in a nearby pub.

and finally...

When we asked one trainee what shape he thought the firm would be in when our readers were ready to start their training contracts, he touched on an interesting point. *"I think Holmans will still be a niche firm with clients in the shipping area, but there will be new factors within shipping. Because of 9/11 and the war on terrorism charterers, owners and all the parties involved in shipping and general trade are having to change and adapt."* Something a 121-year-old firm is no doubt well used to.

Howard Kennedy

the facts

Location: London
Number of UK partners/assistants: 73/40
Total number of trainees: 8
Seats: 4x6 months
Alternative seats: None

A small West End practice with a big name for property, Howard Kennedy is gearing up in London.

that west end feel

Howard Kennedy: a Canadian Quarter-Master General, a photographer of women's body parts and an elementary school in Omaha, Nebraska. Whimsical googling on a hot Friday afternoon is a dangerous business, but rest assured, once we found what we were looking for, it was well worth the search. Established in 1936, HK has carved its own West End identity: neither *"traditional like Farrers"* nor *"the type of funky meeja-cool firm that replaced all the capitals on its letterhead with lowercase when the dot.com boom happened."* Certainly not: as the largest department and one that has grown by 24% in the past year, *"property sets the tone for the firm,"* with big-name clients including a fistful of banks and building societies, Roseberry Homes, Diageo, Etam, Frogmore Estates and City & Docklands. It is perhaps worth noting that of the four trainees who qualified in 2004, the two who stayed with the firm went into the property department.

The firm's practice also spans charities and construction, energy and employment, licensing, travel and banking; an impressive corporate finance team handles AIM flotations in the several millions' bracket and media lawyers are well known for their film finance work for major banks.

HK's merger with Amhurst Brown Colombotti in 2003 not only bolstered partner numbers in property, it brought a few extra pairs of hands to the litigation, corporate and private client departments. Further new arrivals from Bird & Bird, SJ Berwin and Lawrence Graham among others all indicate a shift in gear. The trainees we spoke to seemed unbothered about it all, so we assume the last year must have been more of a smooth slide into fourth than a kangaroo jolt forwards. One told us: *"There has been a move in terms of numbers, and perhaps a move towards a City approach."* That said, we were assured *"that West End feel"* – so appealing to our sources – had been retained. Trainees did however comment on the acquisition of *"quite a range of clients from Joe Bloggs around the corner to princes and kings and things,"* adding excitedly: *"We are constantly calling other countries."*

mind your step

Despite the ABC merger bringing a ready-made list of foreign chums as far flung as Pakistan and Russia, a four-seat training contract at HK is very much a London affair, based in offices just north of Oxford Street. Property, coco and litigation seats are all compulsory, and *"once you've covered the three core areas, it's a case of whatever works out for the fourth seat,"* though *"you can put in your bid."* A stint in coco involves trainees in private company takeover and advisory work, plus AIM flotations. This seat can be taken in the international corporate team, in which case it boils down to *"lots of company admin work with an international flavour"* and business immigration. Work permits under the Highly Skilled Migrant Programme are par for the course and *"the procedures are easy to grasp so you get plenty of client contact and manage your own files."* Working on applications for large institutional clients means less client contact and fewer of their own files, but this doesn't mean trainees can soft pedal: *"With a client who knows what they are talking about, you have to be on the ball."*

It is litigation that really wins hearts. Trainees described a *"mixed bag"* of employment, PI, family cases, building disputes and bankruptcy hearings, and talked of *"hands-on experience straight away."* One source opened the bidding by telling us: *"I was let loose on a lady who had fallen over,"* only to be trumped by a colleague with a better hand – *"One day I was dealing with someone suffering from mesothelioma, then the next day someone who fell off a ladder and then the next day an international IP case."* And when they say they were let loose, boy did they mean it. All our sources described running their own files, appearing before High Court masters and meeting the other side, counsel and clients as standard. A few of our sources had also undertaken a short, experimental seat in the private client team, and its rapid expansion means there are going to be greater opportunities here for those who want them.

peeling spuds, painting coal

The simple fact is that the firm *"needs you to do quality work"* and bill for it, though one voice of reason noted that *"any trainee who says there isn't grunt work would*

be lying," As in any other smaller firm, a little co-operation goes a long way and *"you have to be prepared for the little tasks and be prepared to chip in."*

There are appraisals at the end of each seat and a programme of regular legal updates and seminars; however, *"you are left to your own devices and you take responsibility for your career yourself, so you're not wasting time doing stuff that HR thinks is good for you."* Supervisors *"constantly check your work;"* better still, *"they thank you."* *"When you are left to do something on your own and the client is really appreciative, the partner makes it clear that it was all your work – they give you recognition."* Though sources conceded: *"There is a hierarchy,"* we were also told: *"There is no culture where you have to suck up"* and *"partners like to put themselves on the same level as you."* If it's an officious, boot camp experience you're after, we suggest you get back on the Central Line and continue east.

in the frame

In a former life, HK's main office in Cavendish Square was residential, but there are no bedrooms here now. An average day is a neat 9am-6pm and *"if you work hard and get things done, no one raises an eyebrow to you leaving at 5.30pm."* The building is *"really cool in the sense that it is not a nasty square building,"* though it has to be said that leather armchairs and *"old pictures of the founders"* in the waiting room give *"a first impression that the firm is traditional."* Trainees raved about their *"trendy West End"* location; one told us: *"I bump into famous people all the time walking to work."* Trainees usually share an office with their supervisors and *"pictures of their kids."* A second office at Chapel Place is a modern, open-plan affair, complete with air con and a third building in Harley Street contains additional meeting rooms.

With many shops, restaurants, clubs and bars to hand, we were horrified to hear that HK's social life described as *"not that spectacular."* Perhaps this is a little unfair as someone's been organising quizzes, karaoke nights and drinks parties and an annual Christmas bash at the Langham Hotel. What's more, head off to the Old Explorer on a Friday night and *"everybody will be there."* And after that there's always The Loop, Opium and Strawberry Moon... When asked why they had opted for HK, sources' responses ranged from *"I didn't want to become just another statistic"* to *"I went to lots of interviews in the City and everyone just seemed so glum."* We found no common thread amongst those we interviewed other than their decision against the trappings of the Square Mile.

and finally...

Superb property work and rapid expansion across the board provide all the evidence you need of Howard Kennedy's position as one of the best known and most successful smaller West End law firms. The only downside is the effect on the bank balance of being so close to Oxford Street.

Hugh James

the facts

Location: Cardiff, Merthyr Tydfil, Blackwood
Number of UK partners/assistants: 45/52
Total number of trainees: 17
Seats: 4x6 months
Alternative seats: None

Ensconced in its new glass palace in Cardiff, Welsh firm Hugh James has pursued a programme of growth and modernisation, acquiring some new big-name clients into the bargain. Yet, never forgetful of its long-standing mining valley clientele, it is still committed to those suffering as a result of industrial disease or serious injury.

spoilt for choice

Hugh James' work is broadly divided into four parts: claimant PI, publicly funded law, business litigation and business services. The result is a firm in which trainees find a wealth of choice – commercial property, coco, e-commerce, employment, lender services, insurance services, commercial litigation, sport, residential conveyancing, crime, family, PI, clin neg and private client. No one could possibly be left wanting and no two training contracts need be identical.

Hugh James has recently added Royal Mail to a client list that already includes KPMG, PwC, Royal Bank of Scotland, Zurich Insurance and the Welsh Rugby Union. As is to be expected of a regional firm, much of the day-to-day corporate work comes from local clients. Last year, for example, one of the firm's most notable transactions was the acquisition of Slough-based steel manufacturer Howells and Carnet by the Merthyr company RJ Sheet Metal. Another was the management buyout of the European subsidiary of the US corporation Gold Systems Inc. At the same time as the buyout, the subsidiary relocated its business from the Thames Valley to south Wales.

In start contrast to the corporate experience is Hugh James PI and clin neg practice, which handles everything from claims below £15,000 in its fast track personal injury unit to headlining group actions such as that arising out of the Gerona air crash. It is also well known for its work in the cause of mine workers suffering from Vibration White Finger and respiratory conditions. The fast-track work in particular provides trainees with *"a useful introduction to smaller dental negligence, clinical negligence and product liability claims."*

divorce, drudgery and drainage

In the past, employment has been *"the hot seat;"* this year favourites were less obvious. Some trainees enthused about the family department, where heaps of client contact and their own caseload had them handling divorces, financial matters and childcare issues, instructing experts and dealing with court appointments. Others reflected on *"proactive"* roles in commercial litigation, where *"you get to work on larger cases, drafting instructions for counsel, doing advocacy and everything."* Trainees do not escape essential drudgery, but while stints on the photocopier and bundling duties are par for the course, there were no moans. One source even ventured to say: *"You are often the person deciding what goes in the bundle."*

In previous years, news of a posting to the lender services division, with its *"process-driven remortgaging work,"* was greeted with much the same warmth as an invitation to work the graveyard shift. However, with an automated computer system taking over much of the job, it looks like the seat may sail out of the doldrums as its scope has widened to cover more interesting work. In commercial property in Cardiff you could play a part in a multi-million-pound acquisition for Barratt Homes or Wimpey, or *"do glamorous things like liaise with Welsh Water over drainage easements."* In the Merthyr office, you're more likely to find yourself *"explaining the basics of residential conveyancing to a client."*

naked ambition

"In the branch offices you tend to find other aspects of work creep in; its amazing how things overlap...what's that expression about being a jack of all trades?" In this firm *"you have to be flexible as a trainee,"* and this is brought home in the seat allocation. For the most part, the four-seat system remains intact, but *"you could be in a department for a year"* or just two brief months to cover a busy spell. Business needs take priority. That said, the firm does give you every opportunity to say where you want to go: *"It is down to you to just speak out and be enthusiastic about an area."* From afar, a Hugh James training contract may look a little like a Jamie Oliver recipe: a 'bosh' of this, a 'drizzle' of that and very little in the way of carefully measured ingredients; however, like Jamie's creations it usually turns out pretty pukka.

And when things get heated, trainees are not left to simmer in silence. They told us they feel *"supported by the firm"* and showered with *"day-to-day encouragement."* What's more, a new mid-seat review has also been introduced. In addition to an abundance of in-house training, there's a dedicated trainee website, listing useful contacts and reference points for all manner of legal and other info. A trainee's work can *"come from all directions,"* but individual supervisors are always *"easy to pester"* and in Cardiff, open-plan offices mean *"you may have to get up and walk"* to find them, though with plate-glass walls throughout the new offices, they are never far.

people in glass houses...

The Cardiff contingent of Hugh James moved to its new home in the summer of 2003. Here, the majority of the firm's corporate lawyers plus niche practices like the sports law team and the IP/IT group are all boxed up in glass, with fabulous views of the Millennium Stadium and Cardiff Castle. The move has *"created a fantastic atmosphere – you really do feel like a prominent law firm in Cardiff."* The glass theme extends throughout the building, leaving the impression that architectural brilliance and wow-factor had taken priority over acoustics. All our interviews sounded like they were conducted from the confines of a small biscuit tin.

The firm's discreet hierarchy is expressed in the most peculiar of ways. While secretaries and support staff sit in open-plan areas, trainees get a glass pod to call their own which, if their detailed descriptions are anything to go by, are a little like a transparent fence. Higher up, associates get a booth with head-height glass screens, while partners get the whole shebang – full-on glass walls, door, the works. *"They also get coat hooks."* You know you've made it in life...

In Merthyr and Blackwood, smaller offices retain a high-street feel and provide trainees with greater client contact and greater scope for running their own caseload. They even get their own offices. The sleek, hard edges of corporate Cardiff do not infiltrate here, producing a sense of *"the city slickers and the country bumpkins."* Such as it is, any rivalry appears good-natured. Within our random sample of interviewees there were staunch advocates of glossy commercial Cardiff and dedicated followers of the more local experiences to be had in Merthyr and Blackwood.

chatterboxes

Trainees informed us that *"like Heinz, there are 57 varieties of Hugh James trainee."* We beg to differ. There are in fact two: those who crossed the Severn Bridge never to return and those who just never left Wales in the first place. Our sources proudly described themselves as *"local boys and girls,"* many born and bred, and almost all educated in Cardiff. Beyond that, all sweeping generalisations fall by the lush, grassy, sheep-nibbled wayside. Trainees span the twenty-nothing to forty-something divide; interests and ambitions are as varied as the firm's practice. As ever, the people we interviewed were cheerful and enthusiastic, and could talk the hind legs off a donkey. These are not the yes/no kind of trainee that cause our hearts to sink; there is always a story to be told, and they relish the telling. Giving them plenty to talk about, nine of the ten 2004 qualifiers got jobs with the firm.

In Blackwood on Friday lunchtimes everyone nips across Market Square to Y Coed Deuon for a cheeky pint, while after work the Merthyr office ventures down to the Mumbles for *"a game of rounders on the beach while the cans chill in the sea."* Idyllic. In Cardiff, the move to a new office location has led to the discovery of a new watering hole, The Yard. Football, cricket (do they actually play that in Wales?), rugby and the Three Peaks Challenge are also attempted by those who like to work up a thirst before supping.

Singing is another favourite pastime. Especially at Christmas. The whole firm comes together at Cardiff's Corn Exchange for dinner, dancing and *"running around like idiots."* The corporate entertainment usually includes karaoke, and last year the Hugh James band did a few numbers (*"actually not so much a band as a couple of solicitors and a guitar"*). At the three separate office parties *"there's always a bit of drama,"* the Merthyr office usually providing the most. In the past, tales of the Merthyr partners' antics/cabaret performance have had us crying with laughter, so we were mightily disappointed to hear that nothing of note took place in 2003. We're assured that *"everyone formed the consensus that the show needs to be got back on the road next year."* We expect a full report.

and finally...

Quite apart from giving us an opportunity to try out our Welsh accent, the *Student Guide* really likes interviewing Hugh James trainees. They're just so chatty. But while our Welsh accents derail into a peculiar Scots-Punjabi hybrid, Hugh James is steaming ahead. For choice aplenty, this is your firm.

Iliffes Booth Bennett (IBB)

the facts

Location: Uxbridge, Chesham, Ingatestone
Number of UK partners/assistants: 22/47
Total number of trainees: 10
Seats: 4x6 months
Alternative seats: none

You're at Harrow on the Hill at the far north-west end of the Metropolitan Line and the onward journey offers two choices. At the end of one branch is Chesham, at the end of the other is Uxbridge. All routes lead to IBB.

all aboard

Just because it is at the end of the tracks doesn't mean that IBB will shunt you up a disused siding and leave your career to moulder. Instead, our sources tell us you'll be on the fast track to success at a *"dynamic and progressive"* multi-site operation that is *"committed to expanding commercially, but not at the expense of public-funded or private work."* For trainees that broad ambition means a diverse contract, which won't see them railroaded into pre-qualification specialisation: practice coverage spans corporate/commercial, commercial litigation, property, criminal (both blue and white collar), private client, PI and specialist child law expertise.

A thumbnail sketch of the firm's history explains this diversity of geography and practice. Iliffes had been providing an all-round private client and residential conveyancing service in Chesham since way back when. Even as long ago as the first days of steam, if you believe some of our sources: "*Oh yeah, it's about 200 years old.*" We venture to suggest it might not be quite this ancient, but it's a lot easier to pinpoint the birth of Booth Bennett. Whilst Margaret Thatcher was cheerfully annihilating British Rail back in 1985, Steven Booth set up his crime and family practice in Uxbridge and Slough. In the mid-90s the two firms decided to hitch their fortunes to the same engine, swopping the puffing Flying Scotsman and the ageing Intercity 125 for a sleeker, more aerodynamic corporate identity. IBB was born and since then has consolidated its combined expertise and grip on the locality, whilst adding new commercial services. Alongside clients like Norwich Union, the firm acts for property developer Bellway and for the Uxbridge-based UK arm of Coca-Cola. Most locally sourced work (often employment flavoured) is for national and international insurers and manufacturers.

all stops to qualification

Trainees boarding the IBB express had universally done so to take advantage of the flexibility of the training on offer. Said one: "*I wanted a balance of commercial and non-commercial work without compromising on the quality of either.*" We did speak to those who arrived with very focused priorities, but the willingness of both trainees and the firm to be flexible never seemed a hindrance, and was sometimes a positive delight. "*I had no ambition to do crime and the experience of a general [crime] seat really opened my eyes to a new area of law,*" reflected one. Another chirruped: "*I thought I was interested in corporate work, but after six months in family I can't imagine doing anything else.*" The only price of this flexibility is the expectation that trainees will move between the two Uxbridge offices and the Chesham branch during their four

six-month seats. The proximity of the offices means that such moves cause minimal problems and with only five trainees taken on per year, rotation is "*never a competitive business.*" Shared IT systems, well-established moving procedures ("*someone takes all your stuff to the next office*") and "*a really welcoming firm-wide atmosphere*" further minimise disruption. Nevertheless, interviewees told us that the specific practice, character and even history of each office make for distinct experiences.

lords of the manor

Residing in a stately "*country manor in beautiful grounds with a lake and ducks and geese,*" the idyllic location of the Chesham office "*perfectly reflects the work we do there: private client and residential property.*" Furthermore, "*the nature of the work means a much more sedate pace.*" We weren't surprised to hear that the local, The Queen's Head, is "*a lovely, old-fashioned place that does great food.*"

However, whilst the pace may be calm, the quality of experience is up to speed. Private client seats involve family, matrimonial and probate work, meaning "*a lot of client contact, a lot of responsibility and a high turnover of cases.*" As a department it particularly appealed to those enjoying "*close work with clients and the feeling that you've made a difference to their lives.*" The probate aspect of the residential property seat sometimes allows the same satisfaction, "*but in general it's a more analytical process.*" Assisting in "*the buying and selling of three-bed semis*" is balanced out by "*work on the portfolios of large trusts.*" This department also overlaps with a commercial property team at Lovell House that acts for Bellway and recently received an instruction from the joint venture company that is developing premises in Birmingham city centre to rent to the First Secretary of State for £1.8 million.

uxbridge #1

Over at Lovell House, in the middle of "*busy, commercial-centre Uxbridge,*" the vibe is quite different.

"It's a bustling, open-plan office over two floors" that feels "modern, dynamic and progressive." The PI team is based here, offering trainees experience on standard slip-and-trip work (referred by insurers and union clients, including TGWU) in addition to specialist brain and spinal injuries cases handled by supervisors. Lovell House is also the main commercial centre of IBB, with the coco team and the commercial team accounting for that "faster-paced atmosphere." Coco gives trainees experience of a broad mix of transactional and financing work for commercial clients ranging "from IP companies and a few international businesses to more local clients." Recent deals include the £1.7 million sale of Skynet, and acting for Advantage Insurance Company on the provision of a £20 million funding facility from Lloyds TSB.

Our interviewees told us the firm "looks around West London and as far away as Reading and High Wycombe" to expand its client base, and were keen to stress that "it's very aspiring and adapts readily." Recent internal reshufflings to create subgroups within the commercial litigation team certainly back up this view, but it has to be said that in this seat you could just as easily find yourself "acting on a boundary dispute over an overhanging tree" as for larger corporate clients.

uxbridge #2

Crime is the name of the game in the Market House offices, which are also open plan and also in Uxbridge. Unlike Lovell House, "people are often out at court or on prison visits, so it can be quite deserted." Rejigs have taken place here too, with the specialist children's law team relocated from Chesham to join the general crime team as well as the newly created (and excellently named) business investigations and governance team. That's the BIG team to you. A crime seat involves a balance of "bread and butter criminal work, a lot of drunk driving and criminal damages," and some "meatier matters." Apparently, one trainee spent two weeks taking evidence from a

suspect in the £6 million Heathrow warehouse robbery case. Commitment to general crime practice has its foil in the growing white-collar crime practice that resulted in the BIG group. This is "partly to support our corporate clients in the post-Enron environment," but also reflects the firm's place on the Very High Costs Cases (VHCC) and Serious Fraud panels of the Legal Services Commission. BIG means big, even for trainees. Said one: "I've been working on a massive case going to trial in September on allegations of VAT fraud." By contrast, dealing with little people in the children's law team can be "bittersweet. In access cases it can be difficult to feel you're the unequivocal winner because the other side has often lost out personally."

sweet thames run softly

Despite local variations, continuity was a word never far from trainees' lips when they described their experience during training. Supervisors were praised for making the appraisal process "very interactive," and there are quarterly trainee meetings with HR and senior management for raising issues of wider interest. The social scene is "consistently good," with a committee arranging events. There are cricket and football teams for the sporty and informal get-togethers amongst trainees and associates are common. "We'll go out locally, but also make an effort to head into central London or to see ex-colleagues' bands play." Last year's Christmas boat trip down the Thames was also a memorable affair: "Tower Bridge opened just for us to go through!" All in all, it seems the pleasant sounds of lapping water and happy sociability were just one more good reason to hang around upon qualification. In 2004 three of the five qualifiers stayed.

and finally...

IBB offers a broad-based training within easy striking distance of London. Whether you're a local or an arriviste from further afield, "if you put in the work the only limits at the firm are the ones you set yourself."

Ince & Co

the facts

Location: London
Number of UK partners/assistants: 49/53
Total number of trainees: 20
Seats: 4x6 months
Alternative seats: Piraeus, secondments

Established in 1870, Ince & Co has long been regarded as a leader in shipping and insurance litigation. This year, the firm has steamed ahead of competitors to claim the *Chambers UK* blue riband for wet shipping, with insurance, aviation, e-commerce, competition, international trade and professional negligence all bobbing in the wake.

incing ahead

Ince's website describes a broad practice encompassing property and private client work, but trainees stress: *"It's just piecemeal – they don't sell themselves on it."* For sure, *"some trainees show an interest in other things, but it's harder to do that; insurance and shipping is the natural work of the firm."* One trainee warned: *"You need to have made a certain number of decisions before you get here. It is not the best place to find out that you don't want to be a litigator, or think you might prefer family law."* More than that, *"you've got to have a litigious frame of mind. Non-contentious opportunities are relatively limited."* If this appeals, step forward for involvement in *"the whole swathe of litigation...applications to court, letters before action and attending actions."* On large cases trainees hang off the ropes and pulleys, while on smaller cases, they don their sou'wester and wade on in to *"conduct the correspondence and decide the next step."* At Ince there is no room behind the photocopier to hide from the elements.

An Ince training contract is anything but standard, and definitely *"not for the fainthearted."* While trainees move into the office of a new partner every six months, they do not simply take on their work. Instead, *"you go round recovering any number of cases from any number of partners."* Trainees quickly learn to get out and market themselves to the partners whose work most interests them, and *"it's really up to you to tout for business."* The system enables trainees to tailor their contract to their own interests, act as their own agent and *"have more ownership of files."* The downside is that there is no spoon feeding and *"you don't hand cases back at the end of the seat, you take them with you."* Consequently, *"you can't just offload cases that have become tricky or difficult."* Each six-month period culminates in a thorough appraisal with the training principal and another independent partner, who assess the reports written by those you've worked for. Although feedback varies from partner to partner, we were told: *"They would say if something were radically wrong."* The firm's Resource Committee also *"keeps tabs on your workload,"* checking that no one is being overloaded and, of course, that no one is hiding behind the photocopier.

thunderbirds are go!

All trainees get a two-week introductory course on all the firm's core practice areas, including shipping law and lore, helping them to learn the ropes and knots of practice. The majority view from trainees is that *"a background in shipping is not important; those with other degrees are more than able to catch up and deliver."* Acting for all the biggest cargo owners, charterers, insurers and shipowners, and with three new casualties a week, plus a wealth of international issues to be litigated, trainees get a crow's nest view of all the biggest seafaring battles and marine disasters. Ince & Co acts for the owners and P&I club of the ill-fated oil tanker *Prestige* and has played a key role in the case of *The Alambra* and GlobalSantaFe v Harland & Wolff.

For trainees, dry shipping work means charter party disputes, bill of lading conflicts and hire disputes, while wet work involves them in the preparation of fact summaries and draft advices to clients. *"You can go from taking crew statements one day to preparing a bill the next."* Wet work is *"traditionally* seen as quite glamorous," and grounding disputes and salvage cases provide more opportunities for travel, particularly if you have useful language skills or technical knowledge. Though wet work spells all the romance and cut-throat-jakery of a Patrick O'Brien best seller, one source warned that "*it's harder to get the work – it has more technical aspects.*"

We have always loved the idea of Ince's 'Emergency Response' team. "*It's not like there are 10 people jumping into a Thunderbird boat and rushing across the Atlantic,*" but hit the red emergency response button on the firm's website (actually don't) and, no matter what time it is, somewhere out in the commuter belt a shipping partner will leap from bed and spring into action. Back on dry land, some of our sources had "*shied away from shipping and really focused on non-shipping work.*" Professional Indemnity is one such option. The insurance practice sees trainees identifying issues and involved in disclosure documents on multimillion-pound matters for clients such as Amlin, AAA Insurance and Reinsurance Brokers and Europ Assistance. For those who can't bear the thought of a seat without a sea view, trainees also get their turn on marine insurance matters.

Our sources all described admirable responsibility and while "*you get your fair share of administrative document handling, there will also be cases where you are the principle assistant.*" Furthermore, "*if the opportunity arises to do advocacy and it is suitable they would encourage you to do it.*" At this firm "*you really do jump in, and the water's pretty deep.*"

a catalogue of disaster

Fancy a dive in warmer waters? No problem – Greece is your oyster. It's currently the only overseas opportunity in a network of offices that also includes Hamburg, Hong Kong, Le Havre, Paris, Shanghai and Singapore. Six months in Piraeus was described by one trainee as "*very exciting and dynamic.*"

In Ol' Blighty, the firm occupies offices near the Tower of London. One trainee admitted that our previous description of Knolly's House as shabby was "*a fair comment.*" Another hedged around the issue, saying: "*Internally it's fine, the external image requires me to be quite diplomatic.*" OK, we'll say it: it sits over a newsagent's. Trainees confirmed that "*there are lots of pictures of ships – sinking, on fire, in snowstorms...you frequently get reminded why you're here.*" Several sources had escaped for quick jaunts abroad ("*if you're required to go, you go*") and while one source tried to convince us that "*if you are stuck abroad it is probably stressful and exhausting, not glamorous and exciting,*" we sensed excitement in the voices of those who had been told to pack their bags. Unfortunately this year, five of the dozen qualifying trainees packed their bags permanently to take up NQ jobs elsewhere.

get off the fence

Ince is not a firm that will "*walk you through anything particularly delicately.*" Time and again, our sources traded in the usual flurry of nondescript adjectives ("friendly," "approachable," "relaxed"...) for "*gritty and tough*" and "*robust.*" This comes partly from a client sector that "*expects work to be done in a matter-of-fact way.*" Inevitably then, the training contract is "*very much about personal responsibility; you can't be quiet and sit back and wait for things, you must take the reins in all aspects of the work.*" Trainees say: "*If you suffer from self-doubt, this isn't the best place for you.*" All-out aggression is not the firm's style, but "*you do have to be able to – quietly or loudly – take a point of view and back it up. People respect that.*" The age range of the trainees is broad, they come from a variety of universities and they have arrived with degrees as diverse as shipping and drama. A number have first careers under their belts already, including the police and naval architecture, and while at partnership level women are poorly represented, in the lower ranks they are plentiful. The common thread? "*We're all quite confident and quite bolshy.*"

An average day hovers around the 9am-6.30pm mark with the odd weekend duty also required. One source admitted: "*I've pulled some very late ones, but they are rare."* There are office drinks once a month at Auberge, though these have *"waned a little"* in popularity, and trainees aim for a night out together a few times a year. The Christmas party is a relaxed buffet affair, with people saving themselves for the May Ball. Each year, the identity of the 'surprise speaker' from within the firm is *"always the subject of quite a few bets."* Cricket, sailing and polo are all pursued, as is rugby, which *"normally results in a few injuries."*

and finally...

For stellar shipping work and insurance, Ince & Co will give any aspiring litigator the opportunity to prove themselves. As the firm will tell you itself, "no wet fishes need apply."

Irwin Mitchell

the facts

Location: Sheffield, Leeds, Birmingham, London, Newcastle-upon-Tyne
Number of UK partners/assistants: 82/159
Total number of trainees: 35
Seats: 4x6 months
Alternative seats: None
Extras: Pro bono – Docklands Outreach, CABx

From its humble beginnings in personal injury and clinical negligence work in Sheffield, Irwin Mitchell has gained a national presence. This firm now offers one of the most diverse training programmes in the country.

taking goals to Newcastle

For the trainees we spoke to, the main attraction of the firm was its diversity and breadth of practice. For those who aren't sure which type of legal career they wish to pursue, IM caters for all tastes ranging from private client to full-on commercial work to niche areas such as business crime. There is also a strong emphasis on public sector law and clients, which treads a nice line between private client and hardcore commercial practice. Some of the current trainees were inclined to take a company and commercial route, and said they'd chosen the firm because they *"didn't want to be in a law factory."* But don't let that fool you into thinking the firm is small or suffers from a lack of ambition. It continues to expand rapidly (it now employs 1,750 people), and it is *"constantly looking for areas to exploit."*

To illustrate, IM opened a dedicated PI office in Newcastle in 2003 to take advantage of what it saw as a gap in the market. Since it opened, the number of fee earners has risen dramatically and there are signs that a trainee seat will soon be available there. Good news if you want to get out and explore the country, but not so for those hoping to stick close to home. The firm stresses that trainees should be willing to travel to another of its five offices during their two years. If you are loath to relinquish your Villa season ticket for six months, be aware – a note from your mother won't suffice. As one source put it: *"You have to have a good reason for not wanting to travel. Wanting to stay close to your boyfriend won't count."*

chain gang

So move you must, if only because some offices do not offer the full range of seats. For example, the public law and family seats are only available in Sheffield, whereas the Birmingham office has given up most of its business departments, leaving only the core PI/clin neg, insurance and employment teams plus family. We also detected a bit of a north–south divide in the corporate department. Although part of what is known as *"a Yorkshire team,"* some of the trainees in the Sheffield office weren't as chuffed as their Leeds counterparts. *"Some of the work was quite routine, as you're left at the bottom of quite a large chain. Although you're included as much as possible, a lot of the time all you can do is observe."* In contrast, upbeat London-based corporate seat trainees reported more responsibility and contact with AIM-listed clients. Of the five offices, London and Leeds have more of a commercial emphasis, but there is no doubting that Sheffield is the firm's principal office with most staff.

One of IM's real success stories, and a major contributor to its impressive turnover, is the large volume of low-value cases handled by its army of fee earners in the uninsured loss recovery and commercial legal expense insurance teams. Such work is mostly done by legal executives and paralegals, but the firm has recently allowed trainees to spend a short amount of time in these groups, with successful results. *"It's a good early seat...you get to learn about litigation and how to run cases economically."*

helping hands

Away from the volume operation, IM is known for its involvement in high-profile injury and negligence cases, notable examples being CJD and The Marchioness disaster. Trainees proudly reported involvement in *"very serious"* cases for coal miners, and those who claimed the MMR vaccine had damaged their children's health or that they had received dangerous breast implants. We heard how the realities of dealing with clients with serious head injuries can be distressing. For example: *"It's hard when they're so young and you have to calculate what potential they had."* Yet we also heard about how rewarding PI and clin neg cases can be. *"It felt like I was helping people for the first time, and not just acting as someone you had to pay to get something official done."*

Of family law, one trainee said: *"It was brilliant as a training experience, although the clients could be very demanding."* Over in employment, trainees were running their own files on race, age and sex discrimination cases. The firm acts for both employers and employees and frequently gets referrals from trade unions and professional organisations. The seat allowed trainees to *"build up a relationship with the clients. As tribunal work turns over quite quickly, you also get to see matters through to the end. It's always good to see the client's relief when you get a settlement."*

smooth criminals

Business crime is proving to be a hit with trainees. Why? Well, firstly they get client contact, either proofing witnesses or meeting them (*"very nice people – not your average criminals"*). Then they become immersed in a juicy case, which hopefully leads to the *"fantastic experience"* of clerking a trial. One convert enthused: *"You get to meet more and more people who are so passionate about what they do. It's a very small world in the profession, so you feel like you're joining a club. There's something cool about it, a bit like being a detective."* The only downside is *"having to deal with the Legal Services Commission,"* which *"should be a profession in itself."*

The public sector seat is also proving popular. *"The best thing about the seat is the range of different things you can do. Each fee earner has their own specialism, and you can go and ask them for the work that interests you."* Although the trainee task of preparing tenders can be *"a bit tedious and boring,"* rewards were apparent: *"You can draft contracts yourself, rather than being involved on a peripheral basis."*

desperately seeking susan

With so many seats on offer, we wondered how on earth trainees figured out what to ask for. We're told that each year head of training Sue "Angel of the North" Lenkowski has a devil of a time trying to place them all. During their induction course, each trainee gets a chance to be Sue for a morning, so they can appreciate the complexity of satisfying everyone's requirements. Usually seat allocation works out well, but we did hear some complaints: *"There isn't any guarantee, even for second-years, that you'll get what you want."* And moving cities can sometimes be a hassle as *"you don't get that much notice."*

One good thing about relocating to another office is that you get to meet other members of the firm. This year our sources spoke of a firm that was becoming *"increasingly nationalised,"* with a distinct IM brand in each city. Anyone worrying about making and then pining for trainee friends may take comfort in the fact that they will meet for regular training sessions at the *"flagship"* Sheffield training centre, where they can all learn how to negotiate, manage and be assertive together.

monkeying around

When in the Sheffield office, we recommend you pop next door to Bar Sola, the *"ultra-modern"* traditional office haunt. In Birmingham *"compulsory"* (if you understand our meaning) Friday night drinks are at Utopia, whereas the Leeds socialites prefer the delights of Babylon. In London, the FNPC (Friday Night Pub Club to the uninitiated) is likely to press-gang you into fun at Livebait or the Holborn Colony. Party poopers risk being *"named and shamed"* at the Christmas awards ceremony.

And talking of the festive season, the firm has traditionally shipped staff to *"a glorified sports hall"* in Sheffield for what sounded like a pretty impressive Christmas party. What the party lacked in aesthetic appeal (*"they have to hide the monkey ropes behind balloons"*) it made up for with enthusiasm. However, rumour has it that IM has now outgrown every venue in the city, and next year each office will host its own event.

Trainees would scold us for failing to mention that you'll usually have time to attend all the social events you want because working hours are very manageable. Although *"some departments require you to knuckle down more than others,"* most of our sources were out of the door by 5.30pm. As one remarked: *"You're not expected to show your face late. There'll be no one else there to look at it."* Continuing to show their faces around the firm, 11 of the 13 September 2004 qualifiers accepted NQ jobs.

and finally...

Although our interviewees were adamant there is *"no IM identikit trainee,"* the firm is likely to suit those with a hint of wanderlust. It will allow you to experience some excellent PI or clin neg work, whilst keeping your options open for a commercial career.

Jones Day

the facts

Location: London
Number of UK partners/assistants: 48/117
Total number of trainees: 40
Seats: Non-rotational
Alternative seats: None
Extras: Pro bono – Waterloo Legal Advice Centre

Jones Day (London) is the sum of a 2003 merger between international law firm Jones Day and characterful, commercial, mid-scale London independent Gouldens. Known until recently as Jones Day Gouldens, the last name was quietly dropped after a brief transition, so offering ammunition to those who predicted the annihilation of The Gouldens Way. However, our sources begged to differ...

the odd couple

If we were to describe the pre-merger firms as episodes of the now defunct TV smash *Friends*, Jones Day would be 'The One With the Global Reach' and Gouldens would be 'The One With the Weird Training Contract'. Like Chandler and Monica getting together, it initially smacked of odd scripting when the firms announced their merger. Based in Cleveland, Jones Day is a huge international firm with 2,200 lawyers spread over 29 worldwide locations. By contrast, Gouldens was a 40-partner London firm with a reputation for high-class, mid-ticket property and corporate work and for paying staff shed loads. Each had been characterised as control freakish, and many questioned what would happen when such strange bedfellows lay down together on a shared mattress. Yet the logic of the sleeping arrangement was relatively sound: Jones Day's London office would boost its profits with immediate strength in depth, whilst Gouldens would access international markets without heavy foreign investment.

It is difficult to assess exactly how successful the

pairing has been, especially in a relatively depressed London market, but there are some early indicators in terms of work. Jones Day London lawyers recently worked with counterparts elsewhere to advise Russian oil producer TNK and its shareholders on the creation of an $18 billion joint venture with BP, which represents the largest single foreign investment and the largest transaction in Russian corporate history. In a similar vein, London lawyers worked with stateside colleagues on a deal for Aquila Inc and First Energy Corporation, whereby these companies disposed of their interests in Midlands Electricity Plc to a subsidiary of Powergen.

hello ohio, goodbye gouldens?

Any merger involves a period of introspection and irritation whilst internal systems and conflicts of style are ironed out. Last year, trainees told us it was too early to assess the situation fairly; however, this time around we learned that everything is beginning to bed down, and trainees were remarkably honest in their assessments. "*It hasn't been a smooth or easy time,*" we learned. "*Over Christmas* [2003] *several fee earners left and you wondered, 'Who next?'*" They reflected on how "*the firm was different even six months ago, with lots of post-merger suspicion. But it's beginning to settle down now; people realise that Jones Day hasn't just swallowed us up.*"

Almost immediately after merger, office systems changed. Trainees had to get used to Jones Day's standard software (Lotus Notes instead of Outlook), its so-called 'Jones days nights and weekends' billing culture, and a general reorientation of Gouldens' light-touch management towards the firm grip of Cleveland. Despite "*inevitable gripes about admin and fiddly new expense reports,*" the more realistic and adaptable trainees concluded: "*We're simply part of a bigger system now. It's a bit more bureaucratic, but there are benefits too.*" Trainees told us gleefully: "*Most people have been to the States once or twice now.*" At the top of the tree, the majority of the old Gouldens personalities have settled into the new-style working

environment, but some have walked away, including, intriguingly, former joint managing partner Charters MacDonald Brown, who would have been a key architect of the merger. He operates his new firm from within the Jones Day build up.

spirit of endurance

Any institution which defines itself by its independence from the mainstream is bound to inspire loyalty, and those we interviewed who had signed up to old-style Gouldens did speak about "*a quiet determination to keep the Gouldens identity alive.*" Notably, Gouldens' unique training scheme has remained intact.

'But isn't one training contract much like another?' we hear you cry. Well, yes, a training contract is a training contract is a training contract...except this one. Whilst the Karate Kid had endless hours of fence painting, floor sweeping and patient tutelage under the watchful eye of kindly Mr Miyagi, for many years Gouldens trainees had been dodging ninja stars and fighting to the death from the moment they stepped through the door. There is no formal seat structure at the firm, so the only rotating you'll be doing is on your very own chair, all by yourself, in your very own office, given to you on your very first day. You want some work? Ask for it. You want some feedback? Ask for it. You want some help? Ask for it. We're not being dramatic; this is how it is. As one sage trainee advised: "*No amount of blurb can prepare you for it.*" At the same time, almost everyone who comes to the firm has chosen it for precisely this reason, and they are impatient to take their falls in the real world, not on the practice mat.

"*The work you get initially depends largely on geography; people just pop their heads around your door and say, 'Do you want some work?'*" So if you're sat on a corporate corridor, you'll get a lot of corporate work, and if you're near the property department, you'll...well, go figure. This isn't a system to suit the static, instead rewarding the forthright and those who arrive with a game plan. "*The idea is you go and seek work where you want.*" In other words, "*you can join the firm and target a specific area."* By the same token you can also cast about to see what suits you before homing in on your chosen area. One trainee told us: *"I knew I hated property, so I did the minimum...I've done corporate exclusively for the last eight months."* To get the best out of the system you must network furiously to earn yourself a reputation with lawyers in your chosen field.

the real deal

So that's the theory, but what's it like in practice? Well, trainees talked about *"a very, very steep learning curve,"* admitting that *"the level of responsibility we have is often frightening."* But they also enthused about the rewards inherent in the system: *"I have my own clients and I'm allowed to do what I think best."* Talk about autonom: between them our sources had run £5 million debt claims, all property management issues on a large business park and €50 million corporate transactions, all with minimal supervision. Even when working on larger transactions, they told us: *"You're expected to be fully involved and you're always treated like an associate, internally and externally."* As a result, there is client contact aplenty, sometimes even too much, as this trainee reflected: *"I do occasionally wish the phone would stop ringing!"*

The majority of trainees flourish in this system, but admit that the *"very defined culture and way of training"* is an acquired taste. *"It's not the firm for everybody"* and there are those who crave more structured support. It's not that there is no framework however; the firm's training co-ordinator works with trainees to complete a monthly checklist of areas covered and there are regular lunchtime seminars to guard against anyone slipping through the cracks.

pooped and groggy

Trainees will tell you: *"There just isn't a typical person here: some are outgoing, others shy, some really driven, others more laid back."* Our analysis differs. You clearly need to be ambitious, proactive and fearless. We were told about one trainee known to her contemporaries as 'the machine' because of her predilection for working incredibly long hours, but the majority managed 8.30am–7pm (except when nearing a completion). With a strong constitution and a following wind, your prospects at Jones Day are good. A very healthy 18 of the 20 qualifiers stayed with the firm in 2004.

This training breeds strong social ties; you'll never lack company in a nearby pub, be it partner or fellow trainee. We're pleased to report that partners regularly pick up the tab, and if they've made a fool of themselves on the dance floor one night, they're just as likely to be *"bragging about their skills"* the next day as trainees are to be *"taking the piss out of them."*

and finally...

Speaking of the merger, one trainee reflected: *"I made application to a self-contained City firm and ended up working for a global player."* If you are robust enough for the training scheme, then you could enjoy the best of both those worlds.

Kendall Freeman

the facts

Location: London
Number of UK partners/assistants: 21/35
Total number of trainees: 17
Seats: 4x6 months
Alternative seats: Secondments

A mid-sized City practice targeting the insurance industry, Kendall Freeman emerged on to the legal landscape in May 2003, following the dissolution of national treasure DJ Freeman.

policy renewal

When KF was created, there were ramifications for trainees. The firm's focus narrowed and so did the range of seats on offer – currently available are insurance litigation, construction, company/commercial, commercial litigation, public international law, insolvency and employment. *"Media and property have gone. It was a disappointment,"* one source confirmed, before cheering up – *"Actually, I don't think I wanted to do property really."*

The firm acts for an extensive list of insurance and reinsurance clients – AXA, Munich Re, Direct Line, HSBC Insurance Brokers, Equitable Life of the United States, Chubb and St Paul to name a few. *"Insurance litigation is the biggest department, so everyone does a seat there."* You'll most likely sit with a partner and do work for several assistants. In this department, *"cases are big and complex and take a bit of reading in to get your head around them."* To illustrate, KF is acting for two of the reinsurers of a $500 million asbestos liability policy in a case where the insurance company's parent is in Chapter 11 bankruptcy in the US. The case requires them to work with top US attorneys and there are other insurance and reinsurance companies involved in the suit. Far from straightforward. And then there's film finance litigation, which is worth several hundred million dollars and represents the largest raft of cases before the Commercial Court since the Lloyd's Names litigation of the early 1990s.

With matters so big, it's vital to have a band of paralegals who know the cases inside out. *"The paralegals here are good. I did the odd bit of bundling, but the big jobs are normally taken on by them."* The size of the cases prohibits trainees from getting on their feet and making small applications before masters. *"Perhaps I'll do it in commercial litigation,"* one source hoped. Others confirmed that this would indeed be the case.

you'll wish you hadn't said that

In the insurance lit seat, *"you come across a lot of discussion about the actual law. And dealing with insurance clients, there's always someone at your level to build up a relationship with."* Nevertheless, it was clear to us that most of our sources preferred their time in the smaller commercial litigation department. Here they tend to get more variety in terms of clients, and the size of cases – some of them even trainee-sized. Basically it's an easier seat to get your head around in six months. Clients include Corus, Iraqi Airways and Shell. The loss of some of the old DJF media lawyers was a disappointment to some trainees, but as one put it: *"We've still got Al Fayed and Harrods as clients, so defamation work continues!"* Last year the upmarket retailer was involved in proceedings against *The Wall Street Journal* regarding an article it published after not getting the joke in an April Fools' Day press release about the company's 'flotation'. The newspaper accused Harrods of being 'the Enron of Britain', so Harrods brought in KF. In the same vein, the firm acted for Saudi businessman Sheikh Khalid Bin Mahfouz, who successfully sued the *Mail on Sunday* for alleging that he was Osama Bin Laden's brother-in-law and a financial supporter. The newspaper was forced to pay damages and issue an apology. As one source put it: *"As well as the work being of good quality here, it is interesting."*

That's for sure. The public international law team advises governments like that of Nigeria, for which it is presently working on the recovery of assets looted by the late head of state, General Abacha. It is giving advice on a US government-led initiative to review and advise on controls over money laundering activity in a developing state that is vulnerable to terrorism. It is also assisting Somaliland in its bid for international recognition as an independent state.

While this is undoubtedly a litigation-led firm, it does handle non-contentious work. These days, no insurance law firm could realistically do otherwise as their clients increasingly want one-stop-shop legal advice. Tax, insolvency and employment law, corporate start-ups, M&A, financing, FSA issues – you can expect KF to handle it all. It does some work for non-sector clients, but nowhere near as much as for insurance companies. The employment lawyers, for example, acted for a team of brokers that moved from one broking company to another. Several issues needed to be addressed, including garden leave, payment of discretionary bonuses, restrictive covenants and other contractual issues. But away from the insurance sector, they have been advising Fulham Football Club (another Al Fayed venture) in relation to two disputes with ex-manage, Jean Tigana, one for unlawful deduction of wages and the other in relation to player transfers. Secondments to clients allow the odd trainee experiences away from the office.

talking shop

"Partners are keen to know what we think about everything, and they think we should be aware how a law firm functions." At meetings with trainees not long before we conducted our interviews, two members of the management team canvassed the youngsters' views: *"They said to us, 'Don't hold back it's off the record; tell us what you think'. And once people started speaking, a lot was said. It went on for two or three hours."* That sort of thing is simply never going to happen in a big firm. Another agreed: *"I could go to Laurence Harris* [managing partner] *and say, 'I'm really annoyed about this.' And he'd listen."* If you'd hate to be one of a hundred people shuffling through their training contract, fear not: *"People are going to know you within a week...and whether you are good or not."* As such, *"You have to be someone who feels confident enough to handle that."*

Continuing the DJF tradition, each trainee has at least four points of contact if anything is bothering them. Someone in the year above will be appointed as their 'aunt' or 'uncle' to hold their hand when they first arrive. Every six months the trainee sits with a different supervisor – generally considered to be the most useful person to turn to in almost all situations. But they are also allocated a mentor partner, who will offer as much or as little involvement as is wanted of them over the two years. Most of our sources had enjoyed the odd lunch, but never felt the need to take the mentor-partner relationship further. The trainee partner takes overall responsibility for the smooth running of the scheme. It looks as if she's doing a decent job: two of the three qualifiers stayed with the firm in September 2004.

Occupying premises on Fetter Lane (*"we kept the nicest out of three buildings that DJ Freeman was in"*), it looks as if KF has already managed to fill the place. Part of the canteen was lost to fee earning within the firm's first year, but it's not at the stage of stacking desks two-high just yet. As before the creation of KF, no one has any moans about hours: *"In litigation they are a steady 9am to 6 or 6.30pm."* By contrast, *"it's not a steady pace in corporate: when you are quiet you leave on time or earlier, but you hear a few horror stories."*

After hours, *"every week or two on a Thursday or Friday, trainees go out for a drink and assistants tag along."* Usually they frequent The Cartoonist and The White Swan. A firm-wide social committee organises events for everyone every two or three months – comedy clubs, dog racing, ice skating at Somerset House – even partners turn up. There are both men's and women's five-a-side football teams as well as softball games against insurance clients and participation in the Manches Cup sailing regatta.

and finally...

In last year's edition, we claimed we'd know by now what kind of car to compare the new Kendall Freeman to...and we'd like to keep our word. KF is the new Mini Cooper: a small, enjoyable drive. And while it is still a recognisable version of the original model, this *"sharpened-up,"* *"new-lease-of-life"* outfit looks like it's carrying a pokier engine and far less baggage.

Kent Jones & Done

the facts

Location: Stoke-on-Trent
Number of UK partners/assistants: 16/12
Total number of trainees: 5
Seats: 4x6 months
Alternative seats: None
Extras: Pro bono – Proline

Legally speaking, Kent Jones & Done is the best thing since sliced bread in Staffordshire. Any trainee hankering after a commercial experience in this part of the world should read on...

coal and china teapots

"We go back to the 1890s," one of our interviewees told us when we asked about the firm's history. "We were started by wealthy property owners – the Sutherland estate, which owns a lot of Stoke-on-Trent and most of the north of Scotland I think. There's a statue of a Duke of Sutherland just outside Stoke on the top of a hill and the estate owns practically everything you can see from the top of that hill." Rather like the Dukes of Sutherland, KJD has a dream to dominate the region. It wants to be the leading single-site commercial firm between Birmingham and Manchester. And why not? Aside from a crack property firm in Newcastle-under-Lyme, it has no major competition.

The local pottery industry and the legacy left behind by the coal industry provide a ready-made market for legal services in the area, and KJD has certainly taken advantage of this. It is renowned for its expertise in coal mining subsidence litigation, having acted on two of the major cases on the subject. "We gradually moved into ceramics," our KJD historian continued, "then Alec Done started to move into corporate and commercial work in the 1950s and from the 1960s Tony Reeves, the current senior partner, made us a full-service firm." Aside from various potteries, the client list of 2004 boasts some giant names: British Energy, The Crown Estate, Britannia Building Society, Britannic Assurance, Ticketmaster, Severn Trent Water and several borough councils. Plenty to impress your mates with when they ask you what north Staffs can offer to a hungry young lawyer.

the magic attic

Trainees take four seats, usually commercial property, litigation, coco/employment and perhaps planning (a really hot area for the firm) or a further spell in something they want to qualify into. In the property seat, "you have a few residential files for experience, but it's mostly commercial property and really varied." Assisting partners as well as handling a number of your own files, you can get involved with construction matters, leasehold transactions and lots of research. "It's refreshingly academic sometimes," one trainee reported, "and it can get a bit mad!"

Which brings us to some of the goings-on in the litigation seat. General commercial claims and debt recovery ("plenty of work in the county court and mortgage possession hearings in front of a district judge") supplemented by the speciality of the house – mines and minerals-related claims. "I spent much of my time on manorial rights," confirmed one source. "We had a client who used to run a very successful ceramics business and had property interests in Derbyshire with manorial rights running under other people's land. A supermarket wanted to build on some of the land, so he effectively had a ransom strip. It was fascinating. We had a proper historian on board to do a lot of the research into copyhold, and I had to spend one evening in the Magic Attic – a local history society above a snooker club." Full of bearded historians? "Absolutely. I arrived in my pinstriped suit, Samsonite in hand, and there was a sudden hush...a tumbleweed rolled across the floor...I was most disgruntled that the evening didn't end with a banjo player like in Deliverance."

putting yourself about

Most of the time, getting out to meet the locals is rather different. KJD likes its trainees to become fully absorbed into the Stoke chamber of commerce, so they regularly attend the chamber's events and 'spotlight' lunches to meet with other professionals and business folk. "There's a weekly diary of what's going on and you can go every week if you want. You just go along and mingle." Our sources were completely convinced of the benefits of these events, saying: "There's a lot of skill in this area and you really don't have to toddle off to Birmingham or Manchester; you just need to put yourself about a bit." One of the firm's youngest solicitors is busy setting up a north Staffs young professionals group.

We wouldn't wish to give the impression that

Stoke is the centre of the universe. Actually, our sources readily admitted that it's not the nicest of towns. "*It looks like hell.*" Was it bombed in the war? "*No, but it should have been!*" And as for the KJD offices, "*Well, you know the TV programme 'Restoration' with Griff Rhys Jones?*" one asked us. "*They ought to do one for our office called Destruction!*" Apparently, it's a typical 1960s/1970s concrete monstrosity. "*Lots of glass and no air con, so it's like being in a greenhouse...though we do have a lot of space.*" Trainees all share a large room with a partner ("*They are pretty sizeable – you could probably get three-and-a-half Clifford Chance lawyers in them*") and the views of the grassed-over slag heaps at the back of the office are actually quite pleasant. In 2004, one of the two qualifying trainees stayed to continue enjoying the view.

grey days

Perhaps because so many people choose to live on the outskirts of Stoke or away from it entirely, the after-work social scene is not exactly rug-cutting, though there is a decent local bar called Churrassco, which is "*relaxed with good food.*" The firm also has quiz nights and plays rugby and rounders. The social scene is the one thing that our sources would pep up a bit...actually, some have an issue with the greyness of the firm's branding – its offices, business cards, logo, website etc. A technicolour KJD? "*We are pushing for it! The senior partner likes grey though.*"

It was interesting to hear how many times the senior partner cropped up in our interviews; he's clearly a very influential man. After mulling things over, we reached the conclusion that KJD has made its mark through the efforts of key practitioners. Another important name for us to mention is that of Michael Servian, who has built a media practice and has acted for Ravi Shankar, Genesis Publications, the David Lean Estate and various other names in music and entertainment. "*He started out by acting for Nine Inch Nails,*" one source revealed. "*He's not actually an old rocker himself, but he has taken up the guitar.*" In case you were wondering, yes, trainees do get to see some of this media and IP work in the commercial seat.

It looks to us as if KJD does everything it can to teach trainees the importance of client relationships and immersion in the marketplace, be this through pearls of wisdom from the senior partner ("*In the first week he tells you a story about client confidentiality, but I can't tell you it*"), trips to local history societies or chamber of commerce lunches. A training contract here will be more than the sum of the files on your desk

and finally...

It was curiously fitting that as we were finalising this report, Stoke boy Robbie Williams' song *Rock D*J came on the radio. If only it had been his *Kids* duet with Kylie – we could have borrowed a really cheesy line to end with...oh all right then – Jump on board. Take a ride (yeah).

Lawrence Graham LLP

the facts

Location: London
Number of UK partners/assistants: 86/101
Total number of trainees: 34
Seats: 4x6 months, some split seats
Alternative seats: Monaco
Extras: Language training

In legal London, much-loved Lawrence Graham is known as a thoroughly nice, medium-sized firm, traditionally strongest in property. As for its training scheme, the emphasis has always been on giving recruits a good solid grounding and allowing them plenty of fresh air. In every respect, Larry G is a wholesome firm.

drinking and gambling

From its office on the Strand, LG offers a full service to a collection of good clients that range from Coffee Republic to Bank of Scotland and Encyclopaedia Britannica. The property department brings in about

35% of the firm's revenue, and it is here that the biggest deals are done. One of the highlights of the past year was a mammoth instruction from brewing giant Scottish & Newcastle concerning the £2.5 billion sale of its pub estate. Other household-name clients include Sainsbury's and Allied Dunbar. There's currently a move to beef up property finance and other financial and corporate areas. Although it still feeds off property to a certain extent, the corporate department does a lot off its own back, recently including the acquisition of the Perry Barr Greyhound Racing Stadium in Birmingham, several AIM floatations and deals for AIM-listed clients. The remaining third of the firm's muscle is split between litigation and tax and private capital. Small shipping and reinsurance departments operate from a small second office in St Mary's Axe, although this side of the business was depleted when the firm's insurance team decamped to Reynolds Porter Chamberlain recently.

In the past we've always said of LG that nothing much changes from year to year. However, changes are afoot: with the Strand lease running out in 2007, the firm is contemplating a move to More London, a prestigious office development near Tower Bridge. The firm has also been contemplating its position in the legal market and its desire for greater recognition of its capabilities and achievements. But no one rushes things at LG, and true to form, we heard: *"There's not much point in changing anything before we move."*

diplomatic relations

In the four-seat training, second-years get priority over their junior colleagues. Commonly, a trainee's first seat will be property, which swallows up about half of the trainees at any one time, and multiple stints are available if you wish. When you express your preferences for the later seats, it seems that pester power can have its place: *"I was always aware that if you wanted a seat you had to make sure you kept on asking. Quite a few people didn't really make their minds*

up and said that they would do anything in a certain area and then weren't happy." The same approach seems to apply to qualification jobs: *"If people are vague about where they want to go, they are seen as wishy washy. The firm wants you to know what you want."* While the 'quiet chat' approach to awarding qualification jobs has always worked well in the past, with retention down to a poor eight out of 16 in September 2004, we detected some bad feeling about a perceived lack of transparency.

There's a huge variety of work on offer in the core property department, from telecoms-related transactions to a geography A-level style seat where you'll be doing research into unregistered land and canals and *"lots of map work and colouring in."* Across the board, trainees gave the training in the department an A*. As part of this *"really good, really supportive team,"* you can expect several days of induction, monthly lunchtime seminars and detailed precedents to cover every possible circumstance. Trainees also like the fact that they got to handle their own files, which means *"you get to speak to clients on a daily basis;"* however, we heard whispers that this may be restricted to a degree in the future, as some clients *"want more continuity."* The only sore point is really that due to space restrictions, trainees in property are exiled to booths in an open-plan part of the office rather than sitting in an office with their supervisor. One trainee told us: *"I wouldn't make anyone sit in a pig pen!"*

Time in the corporate department is strongly encouraged. This could be a straight seat working on company matters, refinancings and flotations (which sadly doesn't involve lying in a tank listening to dolphins), corporate recovery or a commerce and technology seat (which covers competition and IP work). In corporate you might find you have slightly less independence than elsewhere and you'll have to be prepared to work hard. In this *"pressurised"* department, *"you tend to be given work to do on very short notice."* You'll work until 7pm on average and much later when things hot up. You may even have to say goodbye to the odd weekend. Elsewhere, the hours are easier, but late nights may crop up on a few occasions.

home sweet home

A reinsurance seat in St Mary Axe equals a spell in a *"quieter and calmer office,"* where the atmosphere is *"just like working for a very small firm."* In the opinion of one trainee, the work is *"more complicated than anything I've ever done."* Be prepared to go into meetings and not understand a single word...or, like one of our interviewees, hope that the outgoing incumbent is public spirited enough to leave you a glossary. A couple of trainees we spoke to had relished the experience, but others spoke of their reservations about being dispatched to EC3. *"The disadvantage of the second office is that you don't feel part of Lawrence Graham. And you want to have your face about the place as it's important to be seen, especially in your last seat. It's almost like drawing the short straw to go to St Mary Axe."* Even those who enjoyed it felt the need to touch base on a regular basis: *"I made sure I always came back for drinks on a Friday night."*

Given the consternation caused by going a few stops on the tube, we weren't surprised to hear that there was a general reluctance to spend three months in the firm's office in sunny Monaco, despite the prospect of *"watching yachts going past the office."* Those prepared to take the plunge can look forward to tax and trusts matters for racing car drivers, aristocrats, entrepreneurs and, as one trainee put it, *"let's just say entertainment people."* You'll be based in a flat two minutes from the office with beaches and casinos on your doorstep and trips to Corsica, Provence and Italy definite weekend possibilities. It sounds mad, but apparently *"it's hard to get trainees to go out to Monaco as they've all got boyfriends or are buying flats. The firm isn't desperate, but it would be fair to say that the seat is not as easy to fill as they'd hoped."*

a dizzying social whirl

Perhaps it's the social life that's keeping them in London: nearly every trainee we spoke to cited the friends they'd made at LG as one of the high points of their training contract. Centre of the legal universe, Daly's wine bar is still the venue of choice for Friday night drinks but, in sharp contrast to some previous years, trainees were very well behaved at their most recent Christmas party. *"In terms of people getting paralytic it was quite tame and the partners were the first on the dance floor."* As for departmental jollies, property organises a lot of client events, but for sheer glamour, tax and private capital win hands down with their celeb-studded champagne receptions. Some social events take place in the firm's reception area, which doubles up as an art gallery. During the week of our interviews with trainees, pictures with *"actual spikes sticking out"* were on display. The general rule is *"anyone can put something in if it's crazy enough."*

Speaking of crazy, we'd like to tell you a story about the time an LG partner and Alastair Campbell crossed swords. Picture the scene: the Grosvenor Hotel's ballroom, more than a thousand of the UK's lawyeratti gathered to celebrate the achievements of the best of their number, Mr Campbell as compère of the awards ceremony. The high point (or low point depending on your view) could have been the moment Campbell handed an award to James Dingemans QC in recognition of his role in the Hutton Inquiry. It could have been the childish retort he tossed at the evening's lifetime achievement award winner as he left the stage. But for our money, it had to be the bold heckle from the brave LG partner who could no longer stomach Campbell's endless tirade on the media. Believe it or not, the LG partner was 'invited outside', though presumably not for a game of hopscotch.

and finally...

You can rely on Lawrence Graham to give you a good all-round training, albeit one where you can't escape property. We've a hunch that it'll still be in much the same form when you get there...not something we'd say so readily about every other firm.

Laytons

the facts

Location: Bristol, Guildford, London, Manchester
Number of UK partners/assistants: 35/42
Total number of trainees: 16
Seats: 4x6 months
Alternative seats: None

What do the lunar cycle, army barracks, the financial year and cucumber sandwiches have in common? Not a whole lot, we hear you mutter. The answer, of course, is that they all come in quarters – and so does Laytons. The firm has four offices, all doing commercial work, but each with its own twist.

one for all and all for one

We sensed excitement when we spoke to trainees this year. *"Laytons is going to expand and will become much more recognised. Previously it hasn't promoted itself as much as some other firms, but now Laytons is the one to watch. Come here if you want to be somewhere with a fast-forward future. The firm has a good, solid foundation and will go great guns over the next few years."* Wow! It seems this optimism can in part be attributed to greater efforts to bond the offices together (*"Laytons used to be four firms"*). In the past year, the firm has shifted to national practice groups, which means more joined-up working for shared clients and more referrals across the network. One interviewee illustrated the point by telling us: *"I sent work to a trainee in Bristol as she's better at drafting that type of contract than me. So she did it for the client, even though they're just down the road from us."*

Having had a firm-wide ball for a few years, Laytons is now doing a lot more to promote inter-office links. Trainees are encouraged to attend the annual Laytons Trophy sailing competition on the Solent, although one poor soul didn't enjoy last year's event – *"I spent all day being seasick, so I won't be going again."* There's also increased movement between offices: *"one partner came from Guildford to London to help out on a matter, and there've been more national meetings."* Of most relevance to trainees is the opportunity to take a seat in another office. Here's what's on offer in each...

london: capital ideas

In London Laytons occupies the upper storeys of the Carmelite building on the Victoria Embankment, *"on top of Taylor Wessing;"* there's *"lots of glass everywhere"* to show off the amazing views. Founded over 125 years ago, the office boasts particularly good relations with established clients in the Square Mile – *"There's one we've acted for over a hundred years."*

After seats in coco, dispute resolution and commercial property, trainees can choose a spell in private client or a repeat of a seat they've particularly enjoyed. London has a more corporate focus than elsewhere and specialises in transactions for *"medium private companies right up to quoted clients."* As a result of this City orientation, trainees have to be prepared to work longer hours than their peers in the regions. One told us: *"I did a big company sale, which went on for about two months and involved lots of late nights and weekends."* You'll usually get away by 6pm, and once off duty people are *"always popping out for a bite to eat"* or a drink at nearby favourite The Bell.

manchester: parlour games

Alone of all Laytons' offices, Manchester handles family work. *"The majority of the work is high net worth finance. Cheshire wives, footballers' wives – we get a lot of immaculate ladies and famous people!"* A seat here is *"loads of fun. I was seeing clients with the partner from day one, and I've been drafting divorces and meeting barristers. She got me so involved; it was great."* In fact, family partner Christine Barker *"only closes her door when she's giving radio interviews,"* which happen rather often as *"she's a bit of a legal pundit and talks to the media about various things. The last one she gave was about that footballer Ray Parlour for BBC Online."* Given the expertise of Laytons' lawyers in this field, the recent appearance of the office in *Wife Swap* seems wholly appropriate.

The office seems made for fame; when we asked one trainee for more details about the building, we were treated to a virtual tour worthy of a four-page spread in *Hello!* Here's the (heavily) edited highlights: "*...Gorgeous...just off Deansgate...like walking back 100 years...lovely big entrance hall...marble-floored reception...conservatory...glass offices.*"

Expect family and coco seats in the first year, rounded off with commercial property and insolvency or employment in the second. The work may change, but in this snug office, trainees didn't notice a culture shift as they played training contract musical chairs. This is because they all sit together in the office's central open-plan area, which has the advantage that "*there's always someone right next to you who's done the seat you're doing, so we help each other.*" When we asked if there was much fun and gossip at the trainee table, we were told that that because "*everyone can hear what everyone else is saying,*" there's not much scope for Chinese whispers.

The entire Manchester branch is close-knit, and "*trainees are selected on personality as it is a small office and would only take one person to divide it.*" The last Christmas party was a cosy affair: "*We had three big tables at Stock in the old stock exchange building and it was a really friendly night. It didn't matter where you sat; everyone just mucked in together.*" During the rest of the year, there are drinks and meals at El Rincon, Persia, Dimitri's, Bar 38, Life..."*we're not alcoholics! We always come across in your pieces as big boozers, but we're just sociable.*"

bristol: wonderwalls

In Bristol, there are seats in coco, commercial property, dispute resolution and then it's a case of either another six months in coco or a shift in employment. The office is particularly hot on property matters, and speaking of a seat in this department, one trainee told us: "*We get a mixture of clients selling huge portfolios. I also worked for a client investing in 12 prop-*erties nationwide, and I personally completed a refinancing worth about a million and a half.*" A London trainee added: "*Construction work is a strength in Bristol and we refer lots of planning stuff down there.*" Employment was also praised: "*I had a number of files to do myself and got to appear at a tribunal in an unfair dismissal plus discrimination claim. It was good to be heavily involved, and towards the end there was lots of client contact.*"

Just down the road from Laytons is the Hotel Du Vin "*where all the rich and famous people stay when they're in Bristol.*" "*When Glastonbury had just finished, we saw Oasis – all the staff were looking out of the window to get a look at the Gallagher brothers, Nicole and some girl from Eastenders.*" (Who needs *Heat*?) It's not all champagne supernovas though; the high life generally means a drink at The Sugar Loaves and a meal at Pizza Express.

guildford: bricks, mortar and staples

Located in the heart of Surrey, just 45 minutes from London, the city of Guildford is dominated by the imposing red brick cathedral used in Richard Donner's classic *The Omen*. Its other claim to fame is being the home of Laytons' leading team of real estate lawyers. Residential development is the speciality here. Laytons has been appointed as the project solicitors for the Cambourne village development in Cambridgeshire, and the firm can list house building market leaders Barratt Homes and Wimpey Homes among its premier league client base. Trainees working from Guildford will ordinarily spend some of their time working in the property department, as well as doing seats in coco, dispute resolution and employment. There is also the possibility of skipping a seat in exchange for a further six months in coco.

Unfortunately, we must report that Guildford trainees have a serious complaint: "*It's frustrating not to have a stapler that works.*" Alarmed at the gravity of the situation we pressed our source for more details and suggested that an open-door policy on the stationery cupboard might be the answer. They knew themselves too well to agree, however: "*I know that if we had an open cupboard I would have 18 staplers in each drawer!*" As we pondered on why staples are so often the source of office turbulence, our interviewee continued: "*They are responsive – the managing partner took everyone in the firm for a one-to-one and they dealt with something I mentioned. That's the advantage of not having tons of people in the office.*" The disadvantage is that "*social life doesn't happen here...you get to leave work at 6pm and go off and do your own thing.*" There are some organised events (we heard of garden parties and weekends away), but "*don't come to Laytons Guildford if you want the firm to provide your social life.*"

more than pot luck

In each office trainees had their own stories to tell, but we picked out plenty of common threads. At Laytons, as one of a very small trainee population, "*you'll never have to compete to be noticed*" or "*get crap work piled on you.*" Our sources described themselves as "*chatty*" and good at tackling "*conundrums,*" nevertheless we suspect the firm is more likely to be interested in how you would banter with Richard and Carol than in your mental arithmetic. Obviously good academics are important, but this firm is wants people who they could "*leave alone with a client without wondering what they're going to say,*" and who would be happy at a marketing event "*playing snooker with some chaps from Natwest.*" In September 2004, the firm pocketed three of its five qualifiers.

and finally...

If you think you've spotted a Laytons segment that suits you, the message from trainees is "*take a chance and apply; you might be pleasantly surprised.*" You'll get plenty of attention and we guarantee that by the time you're finished you'll have a few stories to tell.

LeBoeuf, Lamb, Greene & MacRae LLP

the facts

Location: London
Number of UK partners/assistants: 16/30
Total number of trainees: 9
Seats: 4x6 months
Alternative seats: Occasional secondments, Moscow
Extras: Language training

In the 85 years since its birth in New York, LeBoeuf, Lamb, Greene & MacRae has developed a clear focus on the insurance and energy sectors. Its London office has been in business since 1995 and is now staffed by nearly 60 lawyers, most of them English or American.

that's oil folks!

Let's repeat: the firm focuses on the insurance and energy sectors. Expect this orientation to influence both the type of work and clients you encounter, and almost everything you handle to have a distinctly international flavour. With a bakers' dozen offices across the USA, LeBoeuf also operates from nine strategically located offices worldwide. Most have been set up to exploit major energy markets: why else would you go for Bishkek in the Kyrgyz Republic, Almaty in Kazakhstan or Riyadh in Saudi Arabia? And London, of course, has an important insurance market, a fact that has not escaped the firm's litigators.

It's certainly not the case that only the litigators act for insurers, or that the transactional lawyers do deals only for oil and gas companies. Last year, for example, a big dispute arose concerning the Government of Ghana on a Volta River Authority matter relating to power supply and aluminium smelting contracts. Last year, too, LeBoeuf's corporate lawyers were handling IPOs and M&A transactions for insurance companies. Of course, if you want oil and gas work, you'll be spoilt for choice. Recently, LeBoeuf acted for the Getty family's Victory Oil company in its attempt to exit the Russian oil market by selling its majority interest in a joint venture company called Stimul. The deal got into trouble with the Russian anti-monopoly authority and then became bogged down in disruptive litigation between the joint venture parties in both the UK and the US. To keep all the Getty family's bases covered, LeBoeuf fielded corporate lawyers and litigators in Moscow, New York and London.

wrong footed

All trainees do a litigation seat, often as their first. After lit, most do two corporate seats, and although these are not overly specialised, *"there are three different seats in corporate – project finance, mainstream M&A, and one with a competition bias."* Completing the picture are property and tax seats, and one or two trainees have gone on secondment to an insurance client for a few months or taken a seat in the firm's Moscow office.

In addition to its traditional areas of expertise, LeBoeuf is building up its telecoms, aviation, shipping and trade finance work. Having been boosted by a team from Weil Gotshal two years ago, the project finance group advises clients in Africa, the Middle East and Eastern Europe. Indeed, LeBoeuf is making a fair old noise in Africa, acting for example for Zambia's largest power utility company. It is also being deployed by the Government of Equatorial Guinea on a $1.4 billion liquefied natural gas project and in its efforts to establish a national oil company. That's a job for a planeload of hardcore mercenaries, some might say; we suspect they'd make a mess of the paperwork. Closer to home, and proving that some of LeBoeuf's work is UK-based, lawyers are involved in football injury litigation for insurers, agricultural issues such as foot-and-mouth disease and BSE, and PFI projects for the development of leisure centres in Brent and Lewisham.

exciting episodes

LeBoeuf London appeals to those who wish to avoid both the giants of the City and itty-bitty firms with a purely domestic agenda. One trainee explained: *"It's the size of a magic circle firm internationally, but small here in London."* The implications of this for a new recruit are immediately obvious: *"I knew everyone on my floor in three months and, within six, I knew everyone in the firm."* But there are downsides to working in a small office: while the support staff are *"excellent,"* paralegals are rarer than a thumbs-up from Simon Cowell and, sadly, this leads to times when trainees get stuck on menial tasks. One recalled a night when *"a load of us were sat around a table at 1am filing things for the next day in court, and wondering what we were getting out of the experience."* Also, *"there are no special departments to send photocopying off to,"* which means you can't be too proud to roll your sleeves up and press that green button.

Drearier tasks are shared by trainees, in the knowledge that there is always compensatory excitement in the form of visits to court. Apparently last year's top-banana Noboa trial in the High Court was a real spectacle – *"very Sunset Beach-ish,"* with witnesses calling out to God and a dramatic clash between two of the UK's top commercial QCs. Aaron Spelling would be proud. And if you're looking for excitement on the non-contentious side then you probably won't have to wait long for an impromptu business trip. You might even be offered a short exchange with a European associate, which will hopefully be nothing like that nightmare exchange you did at school, when you accidentally killed the Marceaux family's pet rabbit. The general consensus is that levels of interest, complexity of work and responsibility leap upwards in the second year, such that by the time you qualify you should feel rather proud of your achievements. In September 2004, all four of the qualifying trainees accepted jobs with LeBoeuf

the price is right

At the beginning of their second year, trainees join young European associates on a meet-the-in-laws trip to New York. Last year, this week-long induction programme included a presentation by one of the firm's co-chairmen expounding on LeBoeuf's seven-year business strategy. "*He told us they are pitching the firm at giving the best legal advice, charging high fees and having the best lawyers, being a premium brand...and in London the strategy is growth, most recently in corporate.*"

We wondered how strong the American influence was, generally, at LeBoeuf London. According to one source: "*It feels like an English firm that is owned by Americans, and then all of a sudden you hear an American walking around, which is quite cool. Actually, the Americanisms are the best aspects to the training – going to New York, being part of a big company* (sic)..." And the salary? "*Everyone assumes you are on big bucks, and it is true – you get paid more than magic circle.*" So does this also mean longer hours? "*I have worked long hours, but no longer than magic circle trainees.*"

LeBoeuf trainees commonly speak at least two languages and several have studied or lived abroad. Even within such a small group, there are always a couple of non-UK nationals, which is a clear reminder of the firm's international perspective. Working as one of ten or fewer trainees, you'll not experience the rigidity of big-City-firm training. "*If you are a person who really likes being in a big class and doing the two-week initiation thing, this is not the firm for you.*" That said, no one's saying the system is haphazard; in fact, the appraisal system has a built-in degree of sophistication that would be unachievable in a bigger firm.

whacko!

Regarding the full-time dress-down policy, one trainee told us anything goes so long as the 'no jeans, no trainers, no tank tops, no flip-flops' rule was adhered to. However, another said: "*People are coming round to the view that dress down was a dot.com era gimmick. It doesn't fit in with our push towards becoming a premium brand.*" Evidently, no one was taking fashion tips from David Blaine last year. "*We could see him in his box from the 12th floor. It was close enough that you could have hit it with a golf ball...but someone had already tried that.*"

Fridays nights mean drinks with associates, usually in Balls Bros or one of the bars in Mark Lane. Partners wait until the Christmas party to let their hair down; last year the top brass in litigation managed enthusiastic if "*cheesy*" karaoke performances that were only surpassed by the trainee who moon walked expertly across the stage.

and finally...

This highly paid, internationally oriented training will suit those who have the courage to follow their own instincts and not those of the herd. Especially if global energy issues interest you more than over-specialised finance work, or if large-scale international litigation and the London insurance market are your thing.

Lester Aldridge

the facts

Location: Bournemouth, Southampton, Milton Keynes
Number of UK partners/assistants: 37/38
Total number of trainees: 12
Seats: 4x6 months
Alternative seats: Occasional secondments

South Coast firm Lester Aldridge set itself ambitious goals in terms of growth and increased profile. Not only has it managed to achieve these things, but it's also developed a reputation for being one of the most fulfilling places to work in the UK.

family planning

Lester Aldridge advises a broad church of clients from private individuals to large commercial concerns, though its trainees view it as "*very much commercial with private client on the side.*" Most of them work in the Bournemouth HQ and three operate out of a Southampton office that has grown fast since opening in 2001. Fast Track (low-value debt recovery) and residential conveyancing are handled at a third office near Bournemouth International Airport, but trainees visit neither this nor the brand new Milton Keynes office. Nothing about the firm's four-seat training scheme is compulsory, and one old hand assured us: "I've never known anyone to be completely mortified by what they get."

Private client is a good introductory seat; it's "not so pressured with regard to time frames. As half of the clients are dead, they're not chasing you for anything." Of course, Bournemouth has no shortage of old people, but your clients won't all be Mrs Goggins-from-the-post-office types. The firm's international probate team draws them in from as far afield as Zimbabwe and South Africa, and plenty of the firm's UK clients have pots of money, which makes for interesting trusts and tax work. A word of warning about the private client team though: no fewer than three people who have sat at one particular desk have become pregnant. We're assured it has nothing to do with the seat supervisor ("he's an absolute gentleman"), but if you want to complete your training contract without having to taking maternity leave, you should perhaps steer clear.

On the subject of families, the LA family lawyers have really made a name for themselves and frequently receive big-money referrals from top London firms. They received considerable publicity recently when they were successful in the Court of Appeal for two fathers who fought for their young children to be immunised with the MMR vaccine against the mothers' wishes.

the one with the chocolate money

LA's main business is commercial law and most trainee seats are in commercial areas of practice. The banking and finance department is on to a nice little earner acting for the finance arms of major motor manufacturers, and a specialist contentious team handles debt recovery and title disputes for these clients. The trainees who work with the team get to draft pleadings and instructions to counsel, as well as attend court for charging orders, monetary judgments and bankruptcy hearings. One breathless source told us: "It is very commercially operated. Kevin Heath involves the entire team in much of the decision making and you are made aware of how important it is to understand your client and to work in a commercial way, not just a legal way, and to understand your figures and billing." Apparently, time in the department is "like being in an episode of Friends...everyone is always having a laugh and being really sociable."

Talking of hit TV shows, we rather liked the sound of one of the employment law seminars the firm organised for clients. Based on The Office, a partner took the role of David Brent, while fee earners played Gareth and Tim et al. "The whole thing was very professionally done...even down to the invitations," and was a perfect example of the lengths to which the LA marketing team will go. For other events it sent out SOS messages in bottles to Fast Track clients and missives from the tax team in the form of a mock tax return with chocolate money attached.

my people will speak to your people

A seat in the corporate department led one source to claim: "My learning curve has been virtually vertical." On one small deal they had taken charge of the disclosure exercise, amended the share purchase agreement, attended all the client meetings and drafted the warranties and other related documents. You won't be acting for an ICI or a GlaxoSmithKline on a deal worth hundreds of millions of pounds, but if you really want all that you'll have to do your time carrying boxes and curating data rooms in the Square Mile. As one trainee put it: "You have to take a zero off the end of the figures here, but you're exposed to the whole transaction." It's not all small beer though; last year the firm acted for a US/UK company called Mitsui NutriSciences in its acquisition of a £9.5 million pet food flavourings business represented by US legal giant Jones Day.

Having listened to trainees' tales of decent work and responsibility, we wondered who did all the grunt work. The answer is legal assistants – *"even the PAs here have legal assistants!"* With secretaries a thing of the past, PAs each work for three fee earners, leaving word processor operators to handle digital dictation. *"It's an excellent system,"* which has additionally had an interesting impact on trainee recruitment – a number of the current trainees used to be PAs or legal assistants before starting their contracts. Clearly LA believes in the old adage 'better the devil you know'! Perhaps the firm had this in mind when it kept three of its four qualifiers in 2004.

bog standards

An enthusiastic training director bombards everyone with e-mails about forthcoming legal training events and soft-skills sessions on topics like negotiation techniques and *"influencing people."* (Scary!) In part, these sessions make up for the fact that trainees don't sit with their supervisors and instead have their own rooms or share with their peers. *"On the first day you get a stack of business cards and your name on the door of your office: it's grown-up stuff and you realise you're going to have to act like a grown-up."* Monthly meetings with your mentor partner are a chance to chat through issues *"such as how to manage clients' expectations."* And perhaps the birds and the bees too?

Quarterly meetings between the trainees and managing partner Roger Woolley are always followed by a group dinner. These evenings have an open agenda and are designed to bring the youngsters up to speed on the developments at the firm. Woolley by name but not by nature – his monthly e-mail missives are crucial to LA's sense of cohesion. And there's more: staff attend forums to discuss everything from the bonus system and holiday entitlement to IT, *"plus we have questionnaires on how the reception should look, how well the cleaning is being done and whether we like the toilet facilities...on everything really."*

Countless nice touches make LA a really pleasant place to work. Whether it's Sparkle the office dog (*"She wandered into a completion meeting on the 7th floor one day...I didn't know whether I should mention her in the minutes"*), the Belgian chocolate eggs given to all staff at Easter, the jeans-OK Friday dress-down policy or the whole Southampton office having lunch together in The Cricketers at the end of each week – it all adds up. Needless to say, LA's appearance in the *Sunday Times'* survey of 100 Best companies to work for in 2004 was a cause for celebration.

summit to do

The Bournemouth office is only a five-minute walk from the beach, making it perfect for lunchtime sunbathing or a pre-sunset swim. People here believe evenings and weekends are for fun, sports and family, so working hours are incredibly civilised. Only the die-hards on major transactions stay much beyond 5.30pm or 6pm. On the last Friday of each month, staff ascend to the seventh floor of the Bournemouth office for happy hour drinks. Its new decor (*"corporate navy and pale blue"*) and communal toilets (*"I'm not at all sure about them"*) are supplemented by a *"fantastic"* view. The Christmas party is always themed; last time it was London Underground stations, so some of the chaps in finance dressed up as nuns (Seven Sisters), others came as 007 (Bond street), and a leather-clad property team represented Angel.

Other events include skittles nights, departmental walks across the New Forest or Dartmoor, theatre trips, a family sports day...the list goes on and on. Just before we rang them, some trainees had participated in a pinstriped sponsored hike up Scafell in the Lake District. *"One of the trainees met another hiker on his way down and asked him, 'Have you seen anyone in a business suit on the summit?' When the hiker said he had, the trainee said, 'Great – I've a meeting up there at three!'"*

and finally...

If the South Coast is somewhere you want to be, Lester Aldridge sounds like a fabulous choice. It's got a reputation for quality, a sense of fun and camaraderie and pretty good salaries. And it has just cottoned onto the clever wheeze of sponsoring students through the LPC!

Lewis Silkin

the facts

Location: London, Oxford
Number of UK partners/assistants: 43/64
Total number of trainees: 13
Seats: 4x6 months
Alternative seats: None
Extras: Language training

Well-performing. Medium-sized. Good training. Convivial working environment. Many firms tick these boxes, but Lewis Silkin also claims to offer something different. The corporate equivalent of social conscience has fostered an environment in which superb employment and housing teams flourish, and its position as the darling of the advertising industry renders it one of the most brand-aware firms around.

beer and sandwiches

Thumb through the early chapters of *An Illustrated History of Lewis Silkin* – one of our greatest fictions – and you'll find roots in legal aid work, an office in Peckham Rye and several Labour MPs. The Peckham office turned into a punchy little community law firm called Glazer Delmar and the last of the MPs probably signed off the last legal aid form five years ago. The Lewis Silkin that emerged from post-war socialism is now to be defined in commercial terms and by reference to a distinctive client base. Acting for *"people you've heard of,"* the firm has a good sprinkling of media (ad agencies *The FT*, Haymarket Group) and foodie clients (Pizza Express, Pret A Manger), as well as retailers (Harrods, House of Fraser) and law firms (our lips are sealed).

Trainees tell us they are still aware of, and were attracted by, Lewis Silkin's past – though we detected no overt political sentiments, it struck a chord with them. When asked if there was any tension between the firm's commercial profile and its traditions, one assured us that while *"any business has*

to adapt...it wouldn't be true to Lewis Silkin to not be socially aware. I can't see any evidence of the firm cutting off those limbs; it's pretty much ingrained in what the firm is."

glove's labours lost

Leading the charge of late is the seemingly unstoppable *"flagship"* employment department. They say that from tiny acorns great oak trees grow. It's a perfect metaphor for the group, which now accounts for nearly a third of the firm's fee earners. No partner has ever left the group; indeed it just keeps on growing, recently taking in the entire Boodle Hatfield Oxford employment team. Taking on applicant work on a regular basis, this year lawyers represented a former Tarlo Lyons partner in her well-publicised sex discrimination claim against the law firm. And as we went to press, client Stephanie Villalba's multi-million-pound discrimination claim against Merrill Lynch was in full swing. Despite these hold-the-front-page cases, it's worth remembering that the employment group's real strength lies in its ability to act for employers and employees with equal aplomb.

When not in or preparing for tribunal, the employment lawyers are ironing their kit in readiness for football matches against other member firms in the international employment law network Ius Laboris. Thus far they've kicked balls in Argentina and Italy, and in conjunction with lawyers in the cross-departmental sports law group they've dealt with the employment problems of leading UK players and teams. Whether or not you can explain the offside rule, and in stark contrast with the hand-of-God luck needed at many other leading firms, you've more than a sporting chance of securing one of the four employment seats. Once in the group you'll be allowed to run small cases under supervision, usually applicant matters such as pension entitlements or contractual problems. This means interviewing your own clients, doing your own admin and, just maybe, going to tribunals by yourself. You'll also be involved in meatier work, perhaps helping to draft a maternity policy for a corporate client or a settlement agreement for a high-flying exec.

decent, honest and true

Two trainees at a time are posted in corporate seats to assist partners on decent-quality medium-ticket deals such as Clara.net's recent takeover of the ISP Netscalibur, or Chez Gerard's acquisition by Paramount. On such matters, your role as a trainee is likely to involve *"the donkey work on hundreds of documents, board minutes of shareholder resolutions etc"* rather than getting your own files. If M&A doesn't tempt you, try the hybrid corporate/media, brands and technology seat for a taste of Lewis Silkin's 'mwah mwah' work. Top-ranked for advertising and marketing law, the firm counts a good number of the UK's top agencies among its clientele, from well-established Saatchi & Saatchi to edgy 90s upstart St Luke's. Doing your bit for these *"glamorous clients"* might include drafting performance rights contracts on behalf of actors' union Equity.

Trainees must undertake compulsory service in the litigation department, where they'll assist partners on large commercial claims and run much smaller cases under supervision. A quick scan of the department's work shows everything ranging from a falling out between Harrods and Essanelle, the operator of the in-store hair and beauty salon, to a House of Lords case on behalf of Glasgow City Council, which had resisted the attempts of two London boroughs to refer homeless applicants back to Scotland. The remaining six months will be taken up by a spell in property, be this in the commercial property group or the highly rated social housing group that works for large housing associations on everything from constitutional problems to inner-city redevelopment schemes. The former offers a more conventional setting in which to draft leases and licences, or assist with planning matters. Trainees loved their role here. One told us: *"You get plenty of client contact and lots of liaising with agents. You're com-*

pleting transactions yourself and dealing with the accounts side of things."

fair game

Lewis Silkin is undoubtedly one of the most self-aware firms around and a sense of style is part of its identity. Its marketing budget doesn't match that of a Linklaters or a DLA; nevertheless the firm has always placed itself carefully, be this through a well-designed website, client news updates or an annual pat on the back from *The Times* for its sassy Christmas cards.

Year after year we've tried to pin our interviewees down to a definition of the firm's so-called 'silkiness'. Is it the people? Maybe. Maybe not. One trainee said adamantly: *"I don't think the firm has any pre-set perceptions about who should work here."* Another confessed of silkiness: *"I couldn't define what it means."* For them what stood out at Lewis Silkin was *"the human element – there really is a sense of camaraderie."* And therein lies the rub. Plenty of law firms like to give the impression that the mood in their office is more like hanging out at Central Perk than being holed up with David Brent. Yet these trainees genuinely feel special efforts are made to keep them happy. Going beyond the call of duty, one supervisor administers chai latté to their charge and another is known to be *"generally a bit of a mother...which is great when you're trying to find your feet."*

A warm glow also comes from feeling that one's views are being listened to. Every month there's a pub lunch with the training partner and HR, where views are aired and suggestions made for changes to the training system. The only issue left unresolved seems to be the serious problem of lunchtime sandwiches, which always provoke *"a bit of moaning;"* *"you never really know what's in them; it's always crazy combinations with cranberry."* On a serious note, trainees found the intense NQ recruitment process (up to three separate panel interviews) no picnic; yet they understood it was designed to ensure all were treated equally and fairly. In September 2004, four of the seven qualifiers stayed with the firm.

making whoopie

Although it moved into its Gough Square office less than four years ago, the growth of the employment group means Lewis Silkin has already burst the building at the seams, forcing the property department to move into nearby premises. The offices could be made famous for *"magic taps"* that dispense fizzy water, toilets with *"sparkly walls"* and *"big round windows, which make you feel like you're on a cruise liner."* However, we've chosen to highlight the danger to public safety that is inherent in the address. Each summer a pair of seagulls nest and rear a family in the square. How sweet, you may think, but just you wait until you've had to run the gauntlet across the cobbles and scrape gull poop off your best suit.

After hours, trainees seek refreshment at the King & Keys, now known throughout the firm as the King & Trainees. The Old Cheshire Cheese is also popular, though litigators have broken away to Vanquish on Farringdon Road. As we conducted our interviews, trainees were eagerly anticipating the forthcoming firm-wide table football tournament; for those who feel overly constrained by no-spinning rules, there are always those real-life international footie games, plus netball and cricket matches, and tennis in nearby Lincoln's Inn. As ever at Lewis Silkin, fairness and diplomacy rules: *"It's not the sort of place where people get overly competitive. Here it's all about getting involved."*

and finally...

For many, Lewis Silkin's hot-spot departments are more than reason enough to jump the firm to the top of a shortlist. Essentially, the firm offers niche training opportunities within the parameters of a broader commercial environment. And while the ultimate definition of 'silkiness' must remain our Holy Grail, we suspect a training contract at this firm will be smoother than average.

Linklaters

the facts

Location: London
Number of UK partners/assistants: 202/573
Total number of trainees: 258
Seats: 4x6 months
Alternative seats: Overseas seats, secondments
Extras: Pro bono – Disability Law Service, death row appeals, RCJ CAB, Mary Ward, Toynbee Hall, Hackney and Southwark law centres, Liberty, language training

Hard against the stark concrete functionalism of the Barbican, the Linklaters' building is a sober-looking place. Enter the lobby, with its acres of African hardwood, minimalist decor and four clocks ticking ever onwards as a blunt reminder of global law forces at work, and you'll be hit by an unmistakable *"waft of professionalism and drive."* A waiter may offer you coffee, but forget niceties – Linklaters means business. If you want to train here, so should you.

on the fast train

First things first: the quality of formal training at Linklaters is second to none, and that's a process which begins even before the LPC, with new recruits gathering together at Manchester Business School for a business foundation course. Good for *"establishing the principles"* before the LPC, but just as useful for getting to know future colleagues; *"all us Links people met in Manchester, and we were much more cohesive as a group than anyone else on the LPC."* But the Linklaters' LPC (and, yes, you will have your own classes and your own course at the College of Law in London – see page 27) isn't all about making social bonds; the firm also keeps a close eye on trainees' progress and lawyers and HR personnel will work hand in hand with you throughout the year. It won't be a relaxing year! We heard opposing views from sources who'd been involved in the consultative process for the new course. Said the nays: *"It's ridiculous. If I was a student again it wouldn't attract me to Links,"* while the ayes reflected: *"It'll allow you to focus on your career and on the working world earlier."* Time will judge the success of a scheme that does seem a logical extension of the firm's desire to break down the divide between practice and the classroom.

Ever-innovating, Linklaters has always prided itself on pushing at the boundaries of legal education and training. With the PSC dealt with in a swift initial two weeks, there's also an induction week that encourages trainees to think in real-world lawyer terms. Take the 'all-night scenario', a (daytime) exercise that simulates the pressures of a busy office at deal-close time, with the phones ringing red hot and demanding clients wanting answers quickly. When our sources giggled: *"It was hard to take seriously, we laughed a lot,"* we reflected that there is an undeniably over-the-top flavour to such performances. Yet, it illustrates perfectly the way in which Linklaters seeks to encourage trainees on to the commercial and practical front foot through classroom experiences. In the two years of the training contract, you can also expect *"brilliant training when you enter each new department; they really fully immerse you in the relevant issues and law."* With litigation seats increasingly seen as less important, the firm also allows, even encourages, trainees to fulfil the contentious requirement of training on a three-week external litigation course (supplemented with some pro bono exposure). *"It's excellent and highly structured, so that you do exactly what you're supposed to practically and theoretically,"* said one corporate-minded trainee, who was only too thankful for *"not having to take a six-month seat in an area that didn't interest me."*

With all this full-on, geed-up, specialised classroom training, we weren't surprised when interviewees told us: *"People arrive with an extra something, more ambition, drive and career focus."*

a rock or a soft place?

In recent years Links has trodden a hardcore "good enough isn't good enough" path in its recruitment materials, placing an emphasis on commercial awareness and staying power. Entirely appropriate, you might think, for a firm that wants a certain brand of ambitious, hardworking trainee. It seems that message has been cast aside in favour of a new, decidedly touchy-feely approach to recruitment that will emphasise diversity in all things and present the firm as less prescriptive. In the context of the firm's training methodology and proposed new LPC, this abrupt volte-face puzzles us somewhat. Is old iron-links really going soft? Could the legendary Castle Greyskull of the legal world really become Castle Chipmunk? Will an 'open all hours', 'the deal's the thing' mentality transform into comfortable introspection over cups of hot chocolate? Probably not. When we asked our sources for their opinion, they tended to agree that the downside to constant innovation is the lack of stability. Said one: *"To be honest, we lose track of the new approaches; there have been that many of them – even grad recruitment seems to have changed five times in the last year."* Another trainee shortly to enter an NQ job raised eyes heavenwards: *"When we joined we were told we'd be doing five seats, but then that changed. There is a general scattiness that causes frustration and scepticism, but as trainees we just grit our teeth and get on with it. What else can you do?"*

financially secure

Whatever the brochure you're reading says, remember that there is at least one constant about Linklaters. It is a pure-breed, magic-circle giant that prides itself on *"being just about as good in finance as it is in corporate work."* We checked this point with our colleagues on *Chambers Global* and the view is that the firm's corporate profile still outpaces its finance profile...for now at least. Wherever the emphasis is placed, the use of the word 'good' is, we feel, an understatement of the firm's talents!

Linklaters operates around the globe from offices in over 20 countries, and the scale of its work is just about as limitless, receiving instructions from top companies like Vodafone, Shell, GKN, BAE Systems,

BA, Citigroup, Merrill Lynch and many others. On the corporate front Linklaters beat its magic circle rivals to top European M&A league tables with 78 deals totalling £66.24 billion in the first half of 2004. Representing French software supplier Cegid in a £38.2 million acquisition of CMX Holding was just one of those 78. In the same period it also knocked Clifford Chance off top spot in the Asian M&A table with deals totalling $5.4 billion. Back on the home front, the competition fights tooth and nail, but Links this year emerged as an adviser to M&S in its bid battle with Philip Green, and also elbowed CMS Cameron McKenna aside to gain the first major corporate job for National Grid Transco since its merger with energy group Lattice. Basically, if you want to work *"on the biggest headline deals and with the lawyers at the top of their field,"* then Linklaters is ideal.

you're not alone

Linklaters has an enormous trainee population. Even though it decreased last year and is to do so again, it still tops the 250 mark. Steer clear if the idea of not knowing everyone in the office by name gives you the heebie-jeebies. In fact, *"you're lucky if you even know half the trainees to talk to."* Our sources were unequivocal that *"they definitely over-recruited in the past and it impacted on the quality of work we got."* However, with a leaner trainee population, an increased number of client secondments and the shoots of an increasingly healthy market, that aspect of the training will improve.

Speaking of what it feels like to work in a huge firm, one trainee said: *"It's a diffuse experience, and it's hard to feel a great sense of firm culture – I can't distinguish one."* Another went further, saying: *"Even after 18 months there's nothing I would identify as Linklaters beyond what the marketing people put in front of us."* Not sensing emotional attachment, we asked what our sources intended for the future, and while some did stress: *"I'm here and I want to stay,"* more told us: *"I see it as somewhere that is the best place to be at the moment."* If the sense of firm identity is flimsy, Linklaters

trainees certainly speak enthusiastically about their bonds with each other. Each new intake of 75 trainees is introduced into the firm over three staggered weeks, so *"although you do get to know others you tend to be really close to your 25 people."* E-mail banter, lunches out together, drinks in the pub and even shared holidays provide intimacy and a chance to let off steam in an *"occasionally alienating environment; it can become a bit us and them."*

variety is the spice of life

Beyond uniformly high-quality formal training, what made or broke the experiences of our sources was a combination of factors: *"luck," "being in the right department at the right time," "your supervisor – some were inspiring, others less brilliant,"* and *"your attitude – if you go at it with a lot of drive then you get more out."* Some things are the same for everyone: by and large, seat rotation follows the standard pattern of four six-month postings, with corporate the only compulsory. That said, under the umbrella term 'corporate' there are a range of seats from investment management to straight corporate finance. Said one trainee: *"I was in a department that did everything from private acquisitions to public takeovers to private equity."* There are also very many secondments to a variety of clients and up to 35 trainees work in overseas offices at any one time. With offices from New York to Warsaw to Hong Kong you may feel like you're choosing from a holiday brochure, but beware. *"You have to justify your desire to go and explain how it fits into your career plan."*

Competition for overseas seats is hot, and at home too, the issue of rotation is a numbers game. Placing 250 trainees every six months is no mean feat, so it's only natural that there will be winners and losers. We spoke to several trainees who were delighted (*"I got roughly the choices I outlined to HR at the beginning, it's been a smooth ride"*), and others who were more shaken up as the giant wheels of rotation creaked round (*"A lot of us feel like we've been messed around. In my first year I did three months in one seat I* didn't want before being moved to another that I had no desire to go to for nine months"). The frustration of trainees is understandable, and isn't alleviated by the "less than transparent process of NQ job allocation." One source confided: "After a top-drawer appraisal for my third seat, I spoke to the partner in charge about potentially qualifying into the department. Even though the NQ process hadn't begun, he told me the three places in the department had already been promised to people."

response and responsibility

The experiences in different departments were summed up by one trainee as follows: "Advisory tends to equal better hours and more relaxed environments than the transactional departments, but there also tends to be less socialising." It's a broad statement, but the small print backs it up: "Employment is relaxed but quiet," "competition is quirky people, good fun in an intellectual way, but never any drinks," "projects was very male dominated," "corporate is mainstream and outgoing, lots of drinks trolleys and outings, but not laddish." The differences in atmosphere are matched by differences in the quality of trainee tasks and autonomy.

Linklaters has only a small number of paralegals, and trainees admitted: "There can be times in any department, but especially the corporate ones, where you're bibling and photocopying at godforsaken hours." That given (and it is given at many big firms), it was also common for trainees in smaller departments like real estate to be "running my own matters, fielding client calls myself, even meeting a client alone." By contrast, the corporate departments, by nature of "the massive scale of transactions," tend to see trainees doing more "piecemeal work." The consolation comes in the status of the deal, though one less impressionable soul told us: "You may be working big matters that hit the headlines, but your role is tiny." Happily it's not all scratching for crumbs, and the experience of this trainee was not that unusual: "I ran a matter relating to a US client's listing on the stock exchange single-handedly from start to finish. It was as fantastic as it was scary!"

Supervisors are the final variable in the equation, with the best examples those who were "driven, inspiring role models." Formal feedback comes in the form of an end-of-seat appraisal, and trainees really valued the "mid-seat appraisal that is more a hints-and-tips chat;" "you quite often have to fight to get it though." This struggle reflects the fact that trainees are expected to be largely self-sufficient – one told us: "My current supervisor will shut the door and go through things with me, listing good and bad points. No one else has been like that." Nevertheless, pay attention and show interest and you'll get a good response, as "most supervisors appreciate a genuine involvement in the transaction."

the long haul

The able, impressively articulate, clear-sighted trainees we interviewed remained stoic about their experiences, always able to pick the good from the bad objectively. On hours, they admit that "eating three meals a day, six days a week" at the in-house canteen, Silks, implies an unhealthy work schedule, but they also point to opportunities "to leave at 6pm if you've got no work." Typically they looked at the bigger picture, saying: "You know sometimes the lows are the highs, because when you leave at midnight thinking, 'God, what am I doing here? I'm really stressed,' those are the same times you're doing the most challenging, exciting work."

In actual fact, with a dentist, doctor, gym, manicurist, Starbucks ("somehow really reassuring at 2am") and cash machines, there isn't much reason to leave the building. Sadly, although dressed-down, the dress code is "not relaxed enough for you to wander around in your pyjamas like you would at home!" There are numerous off-site distractions: sports teams aplenty and "money to set up a team if there isn't one," occasional marketing events and even an annual trainee ball, this year at Kensington Roof Gardens on an Arabian Nights theme. Did anyone dress up? "Er, I think one person did." Memo to senior management: on-site fancy dress outfitters required. Supply immediately.

Partly of nature and partly of necessity, our sources were also objective about the small matter of NQ jobs. In 2004, 112 of the 137 qualifiers stayed with Linklaters, with qualification into niche departments highly competitive and even some corporate groups relatively stingy in dishing out jobs. It's another feature of the large trainee population, but those we interviewed who are moving on told us: "*A lot of people are offered jobs, but in an area they're not interested in. Personally I don't want to stay on for the sake of a job in a* [field of] *practice I don't like.*" Nor should they; with Linklaters on their CVs they turn heads elsewhere.

and finally...

Given the sluggish NQ market of the past two years, Linklaters clearly got its maths homework wrong at the tail end of the 90s and in the year or so after. If it can get the sums right from now on, we reckon it should earn more of the training gold stars for which it works so tirelessly. Perhaps it can stick them on the wall next to the clocks in reception.

Lovells

the facts

Location: London
Number of UK partners/assistants: 166/386
Total number of trainees: 132
Seats: 4x6 months
Alternative seats: Overseas seats, secondments
Extras: Pro bono – The Prince's Trust, Community Links, language training

Lovells is highly accomplished in a genuinely broad range of corporate and commercial areas of practice and also boasts a beautiful London home and some very polite and articulate trainees. Take into account the cachet it enjoys in the legal world and a well-connected international family of offices, and you have to conclude that this firm has it all.

red, white and green

Lovells is the tenth largest firm in the City, and with that comes the high-profile corporate and finance work that you'd expect. To illustrate, this year it acted for major client Granada on its £5.7 billion merger with Carlton Communications and on the listing of new holding company ITV plc on the Official List. The firm also gracefully accepted compliments when it acted for the Barclay brothers on their successful £665 million bid for the Telegraph Group. With offices across Europe, Asia and North America, international deals can also be handled in style; Lovells advised South African brewing giant SABMiller on its £563 million acquisition of a majority interest in Birra Peroni, the Nastro Azzuro people. On the banking side, Lovells' acquisition finance team acted for Bank of Scotland in the provision of debt facilities to allow health club chain Fitness First to go from private to public ownership, and advised Tube Lines on a £2 billion refinancing of the London Underground JNP PPP (that's the Jubilee, Northern and Piccadilly lines bit).

None of this can be disregarded, though in our conversations with the Lovells' trainees, we heard repeatedly that people at the firm are "*not all macho, red meat-eating, corporate type*s – *we're a bit everyman.*" In litigation, for instance, the firm is often caught up in the case of the moment, including the Barings litigation and the BCCI liquidators' ten-year-old claim against the Bank of England. Lovells also has one of the best defendant product liability teams in the City, which is currently advising the manufacturers of the MMR vaccine, British American Tobacco and mobile phone companies on how to fight off claims from consumers. Like Herbert Smith, Lovells has been able to build a very strong standalone litigation practice as historically it was not bound by the strong relationships with investment banks enjoyed by the magic circle. But some elements of the firm are eyeing the carnivore work longingly: "*There's a debate over whether we're going to become more corporate focused or stay fuller service,*" revealed one trainee.

The current situation – as explained by a handy pie chart in the firm's graduate brochure – is that just under half of the firm's work is made up of corporate and finance transactions, litigation brings in 21% of its business and projects, and energy and property together account for 13%. The remainder is classed as 'commerce', and encompasses a coleslaw of departments such as competition, employment, pensions, IP/IT and media. Unlike at some other big firms, these teams are not regarded as side orders, though the fact that *"a key proportion of the people there are supporting bigger practice streams"* means they're not quite a main meal in themselves.

any colour you like

Last year we revealed all the details of Lovells' then-brand-new Atlantic House offices, including the Smartie-themed meeting rooms. Sadly the bowls of sweets have gone – actually they were M&Ms *"as Mars is a client and Nestlé isn't"* – but the glass tables and brightly coloured chairs remain. Which is appropriate, as Lovells proffers fully functional seats of various hues. A corporate or finance seat is compulsory, as is six months somewhere contentious, usually litigation, but beyond that there is a wide range of options, so that *"by the time you get to the end of four seats, you feel confident that you have had a good go at most things."*

As everywhere across the City, in the corporate department you'll find *"testosterone-fuelled macho types who get really into a deal and slap each other on the back when they're done."* Your role will be *"assisting your supervisor,"* not in the backslapping, but by proof-reading and drafting. For those who like a challenge, private equity is notorious as the seat where *"you either sink or swim."* Even though *"the deal structures were complex,"* said one trainee, *"by the end I knew what was going on."* The equivalent in banking is the capital markets seat, which *"requires more brains than mainstream banking"* and where it may take you *"three or four months to understand the documents."* Trainees found that this type of work attracted *"hard-*working, driven and oddball people,"* whereas elsewhere in banking it seems that people are more easy going: *"The mainstream banking department like karaoke...they love to party!"*

On the subject of the other compulsory seat, litigation, we heard different views about Lovells involvement in mammoth cases. Some trainees loved doing research and other discrete tasks: *"It was great hearing QCs argue about something I'd done notes on – I like being involved in high-profile work where you can see its effects and its implications."* However, for others, it all boiled down to *"a lot of photocopying and menial work."* Whether they simply weren't interested in contentious work or whether they would have been more inspired by the chance to run a small claim of their own we can only guess. Suffice to say this is big-firm, big-litigation territory.

redcoats in grey suits

Real estate seems a pleasant department. *"It's full of old-duffer partners who have been there for centuries and know all there is to know about conveyancing,"* said one cheeky trainee. However, we're not recommending this quote to our parent publication *Chambers UK*, which thinks, as does the rest of the profession, a great deal of the department. The working day here is a civilised 9am–7pm and the 'social' side of the department includes an annual cricket match against mega-client Prudential. We're unconvinced that real estate is *"like Butlins,"* even though it does sound fun. No one ever forgets the quarter days when drafting a lease as there are always departmental parties to mark them. Apart from the men from the Pru, big-name clients include Waitrose and Nomura International. The department does *"everything from conveyancing to corporate support to the clever, complicated stuff I didn't really understand."* As a trainee here, and in contrast to the other big departments, trainees get *"a free rein on your own files."*

We could go on – seats in financial services, media, insolvency, construction, employment and tax are among those also available, though you may not always get what you want ("*It's probably a good idea to say 'Hi' to partners. I did and it pays off*"). There are bags of secondments available, including Merck and John Lewis. There are also popular overseas seats in Brussels, Paris, Hong Kong, New York and Tokyo among others. In total, 22 trainees are based away from Atlantic House at any one time.

pod life

The "*cartoon image*" of Lovells is that "*we're all terribly nice and friendly,*" but "*the firm doesn't like this as we're perceived as a soft touch.*" Accordingly, trainees stressed that if you pick the firm because you think you'll have an easy life, "*you won't get through graduate recruitment.*" Our sources were certainly very candid about the realities of life at a top City firm. We heard that "*the work is excellent in patches and the system is meritocratic;*" that is to say "*you have to prove yourself on little things to get the interesting stuff.*" They admitted that sometimes "*you have to grit your teeth and get through the donkey work...and think 'I'll pass it on to the trainee once I qualify!'*"

You'll need stamina and determination to get you through periods of long hours, and these periods do hit hard. One trainee told us: "*I was ill for three months after leaving corporate as I worked so hard I nearly killed myself.*" They crop up in banking too: "*During the quiet phases I'd work until 9pm, and when we were busy until 3am. One guy had to be sent out to buy new shirts because he hadn't been home for a week.*" If, like one trainee we spoke to, this type of work suits you, you'll "*get a real adrenaline rush – there were only a few times when I didn't want to be there.*" And once your stint is done, "*it's good to have something in your record that shows you've worked really hard.*" If it doesn't suit you, you'll need to choose your seats carefully to avoid the "*crazy hours.*" With a bit of luck you'll find "*you'll only do a few weeks* [of them] *across your training contract.*"

We wondered why it was that this year Lovells trainees were prepared to speak so frankly about the sometimes harsh realities of their work. After a period of reflection we've concluded that they sensed the firm had always been right behind them in good times and bad. Spending the night isn't so awful when you've a Lovells sleeping pod to slip into ("*they're like little hotel rooms with en suite bathrooms, TV and freshly laundered towels – one even has a double bed!*), and the freshly baked cookies that appear in meetings are also a nice little touch. There's also attention of a professional nature; for one interviewee, the "*very thorough, very serious training*" was "*one of the main reasons I came here.*"

A perfectly run household, Lovells operates with minimal flap. Even when we asked about Hermione the hawk, who keeps the oriental roof garden pigeon (and therefore pigeon poop) free, we were told: "*I never notice her or the pigeons, which suggests that she's doing her job.*" The feng shui influence of the top floor must be filtering down, as trainees have a Zen-like faith in their firm ("*we're pretty good at everything*") and in the future ("*I'm confident that there will still be a good, well-paying job for me here in a few years' time*"). Having said that, we did sense wounded feelings from a few of our interviewees when we asked how NQ recruitment for September 2004 had gone. "*It's a pretty murky process,*" some concluded; "*the firm gives the pretence that it's all a land of opportunity, but actually* [the departments] *are all scrapping to get the best* [qualifiers] *for themselves.*" Of the 34 trainees who came of age in September 2004, 31 stayed in the nest.

psychological profiling

The firm recruits students with outstanding academic records and, consequently, "*many people come from a certain two universities.*" It clearly likes those who've also done plenty of after-school activities – "*at university we all got involved in everything – music, sport, travelling.*" Once these requirements have been fulfilled, Lovells looks for different types of individual, so "*there's a group that is entirely academic – some of the Oxbridge lot – and they're all about to qualify into tax, which is seen as quite scary. There's a very sporty, laddish group going into banking and out of the four girls going into property, two just got married and one is just about to.*"

For those who are feeling rebellious, the traditional escape from the immaculate environs of Atlantic House has been a *"real dive"* called The Bottlescrue. *"You'll meet everyone in the Bottlescrue, from partners to trainees...in fact I've never seen anyone in there who's not from Lovells."* If trainees want to avoid bumping into their supervisors, nearby One of 2 and The Living Room are also popular. But that's not to say that the firm can't throw a party of its own: Lovells puts as much attention to detail and hard work into its social events as it does into its deals. *"The whole firm shuts down"* for the *"extravagant"* annual fancy dress ball, for which *"they pull out all the stops."* This year's Olympic-themed event saw the appearance of togas and loincloths, the 118 runners in ancient Greek costume and Manuel from Fawlty Towers. Before you ask, *"the senior partner John Young is the spitting image of Basil Fawlty and seems to have a pretty good sense of humour about it. While he was giving a speech, Manuel ran on, kissed him and ran off, which had us all reasonably amused."*

and finally...

If you're adopted by the Lovells family, you'll have access to a wealth of professional experience and CV-enhancing opportunities. Discipline can be strict at times and high standards are expected, but you can be confident that, if you work hard, you'll be nurtured to reach your full potential.

Mace & Jones

the facts

Location: Liverpool, Manchester, Huyton, Knutsford
Number of UK partners/assistants: 38/53
Total number of trainees: 10
Seats: 4x6 months
Alternative seats: Occasional secondments

Born in Liverpool over 75 years ago, the professional offspring of Messrs Mace and Jones has expanded with age. What has resulted is a well-respected, four-office commercial practice with additional specialisms in private client law, notably PI/clinical negligence and matrimonial.

building up

The commercial side of the firm stands up well to the intense scrutiny of our parent publication *Chambers UK*, winning rankings in employment, property, corporate, construction, insolvency litigation and partnership matters. Growth continues steadily, particularly in property, which recently saw the arrival of two partners from Wacks Caller, hot on the heels of two others from DLA and Addleshaw Goddard. Trainees were delighted to be with the firm at such an optimistic time. *"We could do with even more expansion,"* one trainee concluded; *"the client base is there and the firm has the capability of being on a par with the big hitters."*

Recruits take four seats from corporate, commercial litigation, property, employment, PI and family. The shortness of the list is a fair indication that seats offer general rather than specialist exposure to the different disciplines. What's more, trainees aren't averse to having a second go at something they've enjoyed, especially if they've a mind to qualify into that area. In the largest department, property, urban regeneration is big business, with the firm representing the joint venture projects responsible for the revitalisation of Runcorn Old Town Centre and the massive redevelopment of the former Advent VW site in Ancoats, Manchester. The department works closely with a burgeoning construction group in Manchester.

For a firm of its size, M&J has one heck of an employment team that acts for some pretty large employers – Shell, Littlewoods, the National Probation Service, the Health & Safety Executive and Merseyside Police. It recently advised on the nationwide transfer of motorway functions (road accidents, road closures and openings, signage etc.) from the police to the Highways Agency. With big respondent clients you're not going to get your own files; nevertheless, you do get good exposure to partners' work and *"sit in on the meetings with clients."*

oops! i did it again

Commercial litigation is a popular posting, perhaps because cases range in size from the *"30 files of photocopying"* type to the *"small stuff for trainees in front of a county court district judge"* type. There's a good chance you'll be involved with professional negligence claims, acting either for solicitors, accountants and other advisers or for the *"little old lady at risk of losing her house."* This latter category of client often finds her way to the firm's door via the Law Society. And as we always say, there's nothing like picking up the pieces after other solicitors' foul-ups (commonly residential conveyancing errors) for teaching you how to avoid making mistakes of your own. In this seat, *"there's not so much liaising with clients on your own, but plenty of drafting court and legal aid documents, and research tasks."*

To compensate for the absence of trainee-specific seminars, recruits are fully absorbed into departmental events and the programme of seminars and legal updates for clients. The revamped appraisal system now also contains mid-seat reviews and a new system of six-monthly formal meetings between the trainee group, training partner and HR allows for debate over further nips and tucks to the training scheme. Top of the trainees' list is a formal checklist of targets and achievements to be devised by the supervisors for each seat. No complaints about retention in September 2004: both qualifiers stayed with the firm

all aboard the transpennine express

One topic surfaced in each of our interviews – the greater popularity of the Manchester office. It has nothing to do with the work, clients or people and everything to do with where trainees choose to live. The main stumbling block is the commute from Manchester to Liverpool: a good hour if you live in central Manchester or any of the western suburbs, and a whopping *"two hours plus"* if you live east of the city. By road or train, it can be *"a nightmare, an absolute nightmare."* M&J is billed as a North West firm with a North West training and recruits must be prepared to work in any of the four offices. To clarify, five seats are presently available in Liverpool, three in Manchester, and one each in Huyton and Knutsford.

It's not only trainees who shuffle between offices; partners are thinking in a more pan-office way and department heads manage staff across the offices. The one-firm concept has definitely strengthened since we last spoke to trainees in 2002, yet we wonder if the popularity of the Manchester office will rise even further since moving from three cramped buildings to a new *"prestigious address."*

accidental heroes

In Huyton, nine miles from Liverpool and just off the M62, there's a small specialist claimant PI office. *"The partners have the more serious stuff, asbestos diseases and fatal accidents. Trainees handle RTAs, trips and slips and employer's liability."* Having your own busy caseload (400+ files) means no let up in the pace, but this is no production line. The world of claimant PI was put under the microscope with the collapse of claims company The Accident Group. Some uncomfortable facts emerged and many of the firms to which TAG fed work were left high and dry and out of pocket. M&J brought a test case on behalf of a claimant to establish the validity of the conditional fee arrangements signed by TAG customers, and eventually negotiated a settlement with insurance companies through mediation. The settlement benefits some 700 firms and thousands of claimants, who will now be paid by the insurance companies. Ever aware of the need to meet exacting standards, M&J trainees learn to assess, commence and manage claims wisely. Said one: *"You need to be able to determine if someone's pulling a fast one...you have to dig into a case to find out what's going on."* Having established the veracity of a client's story, it's the trainee's job to ensure the case reaches a satisfactory conclusion, including conducting any case management conferences, directions hearings and infant settlement approvals.

The Knutsford office in Manchester's wealthy Cheshire hinterland caters to a different type of private client. Here, family law (middle-class divorces, no more legal aid children's work) joins wills, probate and property (both residential and a little commercial) on the menu. Clients have pensions and tax issues to resolve, and sometimes also shareholdings in family businesses. Speaking to trainees who have done time in Huyton or Knutsford, you sense how useful the experience can be, because it not only teaches case management, court and client skills, but also assertiveness. The only trouble seems to be one of perception – that these offices are out of the way and on the sidelines.

playground antics

Our sources say M&J is a top-heavy firm: "*There's more partners and associates than assistants and trainees.*" Great from a client's perspective, and not so bad from a trainee's either – they get to share a room with a partner in most seats. Culturally, "*there's definitely still an element of conservatism or old-school feel; I notice it when meeting friends whose firms have dress-down Fridays.*" On this point, one trainee said: "*It won't sacrifice the corporate image it is working hard to build.*" Yet on the administrative side, things are gearing up: "*Just a couple of years ago we had no HR manager; now even the HR assistants have assistants!*"

On the first Friday of every month the Manchester partners pay for staff drinks in Rain Bar. In Liverpool, staff and partners mingle in Newz Bar or The Slaughterhouse, close to the dockside office where there's always something going on, be it a client event, someone's birthday or an important football match. There are two firm-wide parties each year. The summer one is held at Chester Racecourse, and this year took on a school days theme. The invitations came attached to skipping ropes for the girls and bags of marbles for the boys. "*We were cursed by the British weather, but the whole thing was well-thought out and well-prepared...so typical of this firm to put a lot of thought into whatever they do.*" If you think playground games are cute, the invites for the last Christmas party were attached as labels on cans of baked beans...though we're not exactly sure why.

and finally...

We've decided that 'Never Knowingly Unprepared' should be the motto of Mace & Jones. This highly professional North West firm is set for even bigger and better things, which makes it a very good time to consider its training contract. Just think hard about the Liverpool-Manchester commute.

Macfarlanes

the facts

Location: London
Number of UK partners/assistants: 5/112
Total number of trainees: 50
Seats: 4x6 months
Alternative seats: Secondments
Extras: Pro bono – Cambridge House & Talbot Advice Centre, Caribbean death row appeals, language training

It doesn't take much to work out why Macfarlanes is one of the most successful law firms in the UK. Small but perfectly formed, some say of this corporate powerhouse. A guaranteed winner, we say.

military precision

Trainees will typically rotate through the litigation, property and mainstream corporate departments, taking a fourth seat in private client or another, more specialised, area of corporate law, such as tax or competition. In all seats, supervisors (usually partners) will conduct appraisals, which are also reviewed by a partner from the training committee and the trainee's own mentor partner. If you think that sounds terribly organised, it is. And you'll probably pick up on the firm's efficiency from the interview day, which is *"run with military precision"* to reflect the pace of the typical lawyer's day.

The mainsteam corporate department is *"the absolute boiler room."* *"At first it was a scary place and I found myself hoping I might spend a day photocopying."* No such luck: *"It really is challenging on a daily basis and there's no patience for sloppiness."* The work ethic is described as *"very, very, very focused"* and, as elsewhere in the firm, *"the partners' biggest annoyance is people who are not prepared to stretch themselves."* Macfarlanes' smaller size has not prevented its corporate practice from earning a reputation as one of the very best in the City. No matter how many bodies the magic circle firms throw at a matter, you'll learn to face them as a part of a tight team made up of a partner and a couple of assistants, or sometimes just you and the partner. Sitting with a good novel whilst managing a data room will be something you crave, not something you've endured for the previous three weeks. In all probability you'll achieve more during your six-month stint than you imagined possible, but if that thought makes you anxious, don't be. We've never yet spoken to a Macfarlanes trainee who couldn't handle themselves.

To ensure the corporate department runs as smoothly as possible, everyone attends a weekly monitoring meeting for which they fill in a form detailing their movements and level of busyness. There are three categories, and our thanks go to the trainee who kindly interpreted them for us. 'R' is for Ready For More (*"How many times have I said that? Not very many!"*); 'B' is for Busy (*"But if you are going to push me I could take more work"*); and 'V' is for Very Busy (*"OK, look, really I am **not** going to be taking anything else on"*). Apparently some partners additionally acknowledge that there's a category of 'More Than V' or 'High V'. Trainees are in a state of B most weeks.

In addition to M&A, private equity is an important aspect of corporate practice in which Macfastlanes has earned loyalty from top venture capital companies, including 3i, Alchemy Partners, Kleinwort Capital, Gresham, Soros and Advent International. Lawyers from across the firm also act for well-known brands and companies like Kangol, Trainline, Campbell Soups, Jaguar Racing, Fitness First, Hat Trick Productions, Krispy Kreme, Reebok, the Ministry of Sound, Virgin Group and Anglian Windows. In 2003, it completed 62 corporate deals with an aggregate value of £8.8 billion.

privates on parade

Orbiting the mainstream corporate department are support departments such as tax, competition, commercial and employment. Their smaller size breeds a degree of intimacy within that impressed several of our sources. *"In competition you can tell that they really like each other. Partners have the group round to dinner every so often and they have a group ski trip to Switzerland."* In property, *"I was surprised how quickly I was expected to do things."* And frankly, so were we. Not only were they getting typical trainee fodder – licences to assign leases or make alterations to property – one source had negotiated a whole lease and conducted the sale of £90 million commercial premises. As a first seat, property can be a baptism of fire; however, the people there are described as *"obscenely nice,"* or depending on who you talk to *"complete gods...so good at what they do and such nice people."* Stop! We get the picture.

One of the things that sets Macfarlanes apart from other top corporate law firms is its impressive private client department. Ranked as the best in London by our colleagues on *Chambers UK*, it offers commercially minded trainees scope to sample trusts, personal tax and probate work. And should some take to it like ducks to water, the department is sufficiently large to keep them when they qualify. Clients are invariably well heeled, and their affairs sufficiently complicated or far flung to satisfy the hungriest of intellects.

legal gentlemen

Macfastlanes' working hours are standard for the City, which means that you can expect full days for two years and some very late nights, especially in corporate. Quite simply: *"It has a work-focused, no-nonsense attitude and that's what impresses clients."*

"Love it or loathe it, you are always surrounded by people who have trained at Macfarlanes." One trainee told us of a departmental party where they sat next to their supervising partner, who was sat next to their old supervising partner, who was sat next to theirs. Can you ever leave this firm? MacFarlanes is legendary for two reasons: it is the second most profitable UK firm (after Slaughter and May, with Herbert Smith third) and, supposedly, it doesn't have a written partnership agreement, preferring to rely on a gentlemen's agreement. Macfarlanes used to also been known for its impenetrability, but in 2003 it hired partners from other firms for the first time in forever. More specifically, it lured the head of acquisition finance from Norton Rose and the UK head of finance from US firm Kirkland & Ellis. Made to reinforce the firm's debt finance capability, the appointments were widely accepted as evidence that Macfarlanes is not as isolationist in its thinking as some would have you believe. Sure, it has no international offices, preferring to be the 'best friend' of quality overseas firms; nonetheless, even though *"it's not gone on a flag-chasing exercise,"* like any leading corporate player, much of its work has an international dimension and the firm will value your linguistic talents. If you desperately want a few months away from the office during your training contract, you could try for a secondment to 3i, which is an important client. Or if keen to sample *"life at the sharp end"* during your litigation seat, you could try for a three-month posting to the Court of Appeal to act as a judge's assistant.

Trainees were happy to discuss the firm's image with us, particularly the impressions they had at the time they applied. One praised the firm for its directness: *"They didn't bamboozle me with fun nights out and gifts...it was more, 'We like you and you like us.'"* Another mused on its conservative reputation, saying: *"It is less eager to change than many firms,"* which is perhaps why *"people think of it as a dusty place, but I have not had that opinion of it."* And a third thought that three or four intakes above her, the firm felt *"very Oxbridge and learned...I just hoped I would manage to keep up."* On this latter point, we dug around to unearth the spread of universities from which trainees come. It's broader than you probably imagine (just check out the current trainee profiles on the website), yet the firm still insists on and achieves undiluted academic excellence in its recruits. The September 2003 intake attended a Results Dinner, where prizes are traditionally awarded to those achieving a distinction or a commendation for their LPC. Everyone was awarded a prize, almost all for attaining a distinction.

Equally clever in work, beyond it trainees' lifestyles are quite different. *"I assumed everyone would do posh things at the weekends, like going skiing. Actually people do all sorts. One does a lot with the church and charity work, another is in the pub a lot, another is rugby mad."* We sorely regretted not interviewing the guy who stated in his biog that his hobbies were dinosaurs and space. As one source put it: *"A lot of people here are dark horses!"*

kings of the castle

"Socially, there isn't that much to know to be honest," was the frank admission of one of our interviewees. The Castle is a tiny pub on the corner of Norwich Street. It is generally full of lawyers on a Friday night, but other than a biennial ball, bimonthly firm-wide drinks and some departmental parties, that's about it for hoopla and highjinks. In the office, things are similarly straightforward. *"People are open and hard-working. Not serious in a straight way, but there are no hysterics...well, if there are then you know who those people are damn quickly. There's just no gossip or maliciousness, and no lack of professionalism – that's heartening."* One trainee told us she was *"so pleased*

with my firm...that sounds awful...you spend your time being concerned at being too satisfied." Like embarrassment at being middle class? *"Yes, very much like that! I am so glad I wasn't swung by the big firms; the comfort factor here is really important to me."*

We generally have a dig at Macfarlanes' office set-up. To be truthful, it's the only chink in its armour, and you may conclude that we're too harsh in our description. But when it comes to Macfarlanes, the *Student Guide* is an old dog unwilling to learn new tricks. *"We could do with a makeover,"* said one trainee; *"the premises didn't win me over at interview."* One thing that might is an art installation in the form of a wall of curiosities collected by staff. You should pass it en route for your interview, but if you end up in another of the firm's three buildings, we recommend you ask to see it anyway.

and finally...

Macfarlanes has a tendency to recruit life's winners: *"A firm of this reputation is not going to take many chances. There's not much room for error."* Turning this idea on its head, opting for Macfarlanes means there shouldn't be any surprises or disappointments. Perfect if you want to continue a winning streak.

Manches LLP

the facts

Location: London, Oxford
Number of UK partners/assistants: 47/59
Total number of trainees: 20
Seats: 4x6 months
Alternative seats: Occasional secondments

Split between Oxford and London, Manches can offer trainees a middle way between the intense corporate focus of the City and the sometimes bitterly exposed experience of general practice.

top-glass reputation

Manches was founded in the late 1930s by a double glazing magnate called Sydney Manches, and is still managed by his family. Daughter Jane Simpson is chairman and son Louis is the head of the property department, and who's to say there won't be another generation of Manches lawyers carrying on the family tradition. We're not going to get carried away though – the firm now has 50 partners and about 300 staff. More than enough to diversify the gene pool.

Diversity is actually a particularly fitting word for Manches: its practice spans both commercial and private client fields, and this is reflected in the training scheme. First-years have no choice over seats, generally getting what is left free by second-years. There's no guarantee of getting a particularly popular seat, say employment or IP/IT/media, although you can wangle two seats in a department such as family, property, construction or corporate.

family affairs

The family department has a towering reputation, which leads many to regard Manches as a niche firm. *"We are not a family firm with commercial departments; we are a commercial firm with a family department,"* countered one of our sources. That said, *"everyone is very proud of family,"* with many trainees citing it as their reason for joining the firm. As befits any top-notch team, it has *"exacting"* standards and for trainees it's not possible to take a leading role on cases where the stakes are high and the clients often guarded very closely by senior staff. The best that can be hoped for in six months – and this is not to be underestimated – is to witness and appreciate excellence. One source revealed: *"It may sound like a sad admission, but I was proud to be standing next to Jane Simpson – other lawyers and judges know who she is."*

It's not that you won't contribute to the success of the department, rather that your contribution will be made discreetly. Apart from making a few small applications in court on your own, other face-to-face interaction (with clients and barristers) will take place at your supervisor's side. The family seat is likely to bring the longest hours (*"perhaps 8.30am to 7pm or 8pm"*), but more generally around the firm, *"you are not thrashed to death in terms of hours."* Because family law is court-based with the attendant deadlines this brings, *"everything has to be done quite quickly; they seek perfection...quickly and accurately."* Clients include the rich, the famous and the super rich and super famous, some of whom will be embroiled in high-profile divorces that make the newspapers. A few of the lawyers also act for ordinary mortals (although not the legally aided), perhaps handling difficult child custody and abduction cases.

what's the game plan?

Despite having been through a wave of partner departures and reorganisation, the property department is still really big and takes four trainees. It is *"quite a relaxed department,"* with *"partners popping in and out of each other's rooms to have a cup of coffee."* They're no slouches though – it's one of the most successful parts of the firm, with a client roster bursting with big names in investment and retail property. Trainees manage many of their own files and, consequently, property has a reputation as *"a great training ground,"* where you develop client-handling, drafting and time-management skills from day one.

Manches is intent on developing a profile in construction law, and a seat here means working predominantly on *"disputes or potential disputes that are boiling up."* These days, a lot of construction spats are resolved through arbitration, so the seat is great for learning about methods of alternative dispute resolution.

The corporate team has joined forces with the media and technology group. Together they host three trainees at a time, each of whom can take snippets of work from across the department, while working mainly for one partner. *"The Oxford office has a long-standing reputation for tech work, and now we are getting more in London,"* one source explained. Anyone interested in clients such as EA Games, Eidos and Atari, or the development of mobile phone games, will fit right in. *"People are regularly asked what they think about the industry sector and where they would like Manches to be going...what areas we should be working in."*

a land of milk and honey

Manches has had its ups and downs recently, including falling profitability and a string of partner departures. Things are looking up now, and 2003 also brought a change in management when Jane Simpson took over the chairmanship from her ex-husband, who has since moved to Addleshaw Goddard. Mrs Simpson has her fans: *"Jane is milk and honey,"* said one trainee. *"She is a hard-nosed lawyer but very sweet..."* Seen as *"generally more communicative and approachable,"* some credited her with the recent increase in their holiday entitlement. There is certainly an impression of this being a new era for Manches; for example: *"We are Manches LLP now. We've changed all of our notepaper and the logo has been simplified so that it looks smarter and less 80s. It is bolder and less fussy – something the firm is trying to become too."* *"Smarter. Bolder. Better."* Sounds almost Olympian.

Trainees see themselves as *"good folk, but you just wouldn't have put us together. It's as if graduate recruitment has thrown all the potential people in the air and plucked them at random."* Surely there's more of a plan...a Manches type? Unfortunately, all our sources could agree on was that each fulfilled the criteria of meeting *"exacting academic standards"* and *"being a decent sort."* We'll add that you need to be the sort of person who, if they had a problem, would *"confront it straight on and speak to the person you work with."*

As well as being amenable to giving feedback, *"supervisors like you to ask questions."* Admittedly, *"you do the odd bit of photocopying,"* but it's a rare mid-size firm that has paralegals and admin staff in abundance. Apart from one or two calls for more paralegals to help shoulder the brunt of tasks like bundling, we heard precious few moans during our interviews. Which is perhaps why seven of the eight qualifying trainees stayed with Manches in September 2004.

oranges and lemons

The office ("*professional without being stuffy*") on the Aldwych is apparently "*phenomenally expensive.*" On the outside at least, it can hold its own in the company of some prestigious neighbours including the LSE, BBC, Australian High Commission, Waldorf Hotel, Royal Courts of Justice, St Clement Danes Church and oodles of theatres. Yet the neighbourhood hasn't always had a good reputation – 150 years ago it was the best place to buy dirty books and prints.

Back in the office, meeting rooms are interspersed throughout the building, which in turn means that clients walk past lawyers' rooms. It's an obvious reason why the dress code requires smart suits at all times: "*That may seem quite formal compared to other firms, but you don't get the impression you need to behave formally towards other people.*" Our sources happily dismissed the dress-down phenomenon as a fad. As one put it: "*All it really means is that you have to buy a third wardrobe!*"

Manches has a score of good bars and restaurants on its doorstep as Covent Garden is moments away. Whenever it takes their fancy, trainees, various assistants and the occasional partner pop out for drinks in nearby Bank or The Columbia. Don't expect regular Friday binges or karaoke nights as these are not Manches' style. Do expect a good deal of excellent fun at the annual Manches Cup sailing regatta in Cowes. A well-established event on the legal social calendar, even if you don't know your ropes from your rollocks, you'll be welcome. Another sporting highlight was Manches' triumph in the 2003 and 2004 legal softball leagues. It even beat the infamous Denton Wilde Sapte team.

ox tales

Manches is the firm you never thought you'd find in an OX postcode: great corporate, litigation and property clients, success in employment and a super media and technology practice with shoots of biotech work and loads of sexy publishing-type clients. Add in really decent hours ("*usually 9am' til

5.45pm*") and it's a sweet deal. The Oxford set-up strikes us as a mini-Manches London, just without a tax department and with a private client team. Our Oxford sources saw London trainees in first-week induction and on the occasional PSC session, but otherwise their worlds do not collide. Oxford enjoys its independence, and one trainee even claimed it was the more profitable part of the firm.

Seats in corporate and litigation are likely for first-years. After that it's usually a stint in property and a seat in media and technology, family, employment or trusts and estate planning. With just one other trainee in your intake, getting exactly what you want is usually easy, but switching seats means moving between the five different departmental buildings, each of which has its own style and a degree of insularity. "*It feels like you are starting a new job in a new office each time,*" said one trainee. A move to large, modern premises in 2005 will change all this; however, the downside is the location on the Oxford Business Park. "*It will impact on the social side. At the moment we have restaurants and shops on our doorstep. These are all going to be missed, even though they've said they will put on a minibus or a chauffeur service at lunchtimes.*" The people who've been organising the dog racing and bowling trips up till now will need to keep up the good work. Unfortunately, neither of the two Oxford qualifiers of 2004 will be around to enjoy life in the new offices.

and finally...

You can either choose Manches for something specific, such as its Oxford office or its family law; or for its general profile. One source who did the latter said: "*It's important to be one of a handful of individuals in order to get the attention and training you need. Here we have decent clients and decent work, and enough of a reputation to have on your CV.*"

Martineau Johnson

the facts

Location: Birmingham, London
Number of UK partners/assistants: 40/53
Total number of trainees: 19
Seats: 6x4 months
Alternative seats: Occasional secondments

This Birmingham-based commercial firm, which has been in the city since the early 19th century, has also always been known for its niche departments. It boasts one of the Midlands' leading private client practices and is additionally expert in education and charities matters.

cooking with gas

Martineau Johnson operates a six-seat training scheme, in which four seats are very likely to feature: private client or education, corporate or banking, litigation or employment, and finally property. This requirement should give you an idea of the firm's emphasis on different areas of work.

As you'd expect, Martineaus is very discreet about exactly what keeps its private client lawyers busy, but we can reveal that the team specialises in estate planning for both aristocratic and entrepreneurial folk. Because of the complex nature of this tax-based work, as a trainee you'll be limited to drafting simple wills and probate documents or conducting research. The firm's other star team, education, was recently rocked by the departure of its head Nicola Hart, but is still getting good marks and reported a 32% rise in billing for the financial year ending in April 2004. Martineaus acts for a host of further and higher education cients, including the University of Birmingham and the College of Law, for whom the firm sorts out anything from institutional mergers to property investment to student discrimination claims. A proportion of the work for education clients spills over into the property department, which has acted on the outsourcing of a student village to a third party and on campus redevelopment schemes. The department also takes on investment work for pension funds and private clients, and acts on development projects, often shopping centres. As a trainee, who you sit with will determine which of these strands you'll focus on, but in all cases, you'll take possession of some of your own files.

Looking at Martineaus' corporate business, on the M&A side it mainly handles deals around the £50-million mark. Lawyers here specialise in waste disposal, retail, healthcare and, very importantly, energy. In the energy sector, clients include National Grid Transco, for whom the firm is becoming increasingly important. When we rang trainees, the firm was celebrating the win of major Transco gas-related instructions away from Denton Wilde Sapte. On the private equity side, trainees will encounter share issues and transactions, but the team's party piece is the creation of venture capital trusts and publicly funded private equity funds, each worth a fair few million. All those we spoke to who'd done corporate seats talked of "*tax-focused work*" and lots of research as well as drafting board minutes and "*straightforward company secretarial stuff.*" The hours in corporate seats are slightly longer than elsewhere; you might find yourself heading home at 6.30pm rather than the standard 5.30pm.

six of the best

If you want to try finance work, you'll have the opportunity to visit the firm's small London office. Since the departure of the London banking partner, the only seat in the capital is with the partner specialising in banking litigation, who we heard is "*really busy*" and doing "*good interesting work, usually acting for major banks doing corporate recovery.*" As the office is tiny – just six to eight fee earners – you'll have to pitch in on commercial and property work and do some mundane tasks, but you'll also get responsibility: "*I got to do applications in front of masters, ran my own files (which were usually standard possession orders) and had lots of client contact."* If you're very *'Birmingham focused,'* be aware that the firm applies steady pressure for someone in each intake to head down south.

Back in Birmingham, a litigation seat could involve general commercial, property or insolvency disputes. Some of the firm's recent bigger cases have included acting for a utilities company on a £17 million dispute arising out of the supply of allegedly defective software, and a civil recovery claim after a substantial fraud was committed by an employee of a doctors' surgery. As a trainee, you'll get involved in these large matters, but you'll also get your own files such as *"debt recovery, as it's ideal for a trainee, or small partnership disputes."*

After completing your compulsory seats, the remaining eight months are usually spent in or around the department into which you want to qualify. Mostly trainees liked the flexibility of the six-seat system, with one saying: *"I think it's a really good idea – if you're in a seat you're not particularly interested in it goes really quickly. And then you've got more scope to return to the areas you are interested in."* However, some trainees did point out that *"you have less time to get into the area. As soon as you reach a peak, you have to move on."* Also, *"six seats is only great if you get variety."* The allocation of seats was generally felt to be fair, but as always in life, *"people who kick up more of a fuss get what they want."*

comings and goings

We were pleased to hear that issues raised last year about a small minority of supervisors seem to have been *"dealt with"* and *"things have improved."* This year's crop of trainees felt they had largely been given good quality work and trusted with responsibility. As well as receiving formal feedback (sometimes monthly), potential recruits can also look forward to turning the tables and giving confidential feedback on their supervisors and other aspects of the department such as secretarial support.

So this year things looked brighter for trainees...aside from the fact that from September 2004 the trainee intake will be smaller. When asked how they felt about this, trainees told us: *"The firm is definitely still committed to trainees, but maybe too many were taken on previously. In fact, reducing the number could be seen as a good thing for new trainees, as more are likely to be retained on qualification and they may get a broader training contract as there'll be more seats to choose from."* All noted, but we can't help wondering if some of the more canny *Student Guide* readers might question what this shift in recruitment says about the financial health of the firm, especially in the context of some high-profile partner departures. As well as the education team's head, Martineaus also lost the head of its pensions team and its private client team, plus a few other lawyers and secretaries in the last 18 months. When we asked trainees what we should conclude, most spoke in vague terms about the general economic downturn of the past three years. Nevertheless, each had confidence in the firm: *"I'd say to a student just what we're all thinking ourselves: the firm has been around in Birmingham for a long time, it's a stable firm and a lot of key people are still here who are loyal."* We should add that the NQ retention rate for September 2004 was a reasonable, though not stunning, eight out of 13, and the firm bucked the national trend by posting a significant hike in turnover at the end of the 2003/4 financial year.

At the time of writing, the firm was on the verge of moving into new offices in a *"flagship development"* on Colmore Square. Trainees thought that the move from an old building in the shadow of the cathedral to an *"up-to-the-minute,"* open-plan new one, complete with *"cordless phones and flat screen monitors"* would *"give the firm a push."* Said one: *"The new office is a really positive thing; it should improve morale."* When we asked what else the move would bring, one source joked: *"We'll lose the chandeliers!"* Quips aside, we sensed that trainees hope that having the entire staff working closer together in a modern environment will make internal communication easier and give the firm a marketing boost. Currently, *"we're very British about things...the firm could be a bit more dynamic.*" Yet despite all this, trainees seemed to respect much about the firm's modest style, claiming: "*Someone with an arrogant streak might not fit in here.*"

beach brums

The Birmingham Trainee Solicitors' Society is renowned for being one of the most active young professionals' groups in the country and Martineaus trainees certainly play their part. The inter-firm sports trophies are taken very seriously; over the year there are football and netball leagues and in the summer, Birmingham firms compete in a mixed sports league in which events vary from mainstream hockey and rounders to more unusual events such as water polo and an egg and spoon race. It was all looking good when we rang trainees, who told us: "*We're leading at the moment. It's generally between us and Wragges, who just pipped us at the post last year.*"

For those who are not sports-minded, the BTSS organises pub nights and an annual ball. Martineaus trainees also get involved in inter-professional social events and make the most of the firm's own social scene, the highlight of which seems to have been a Caribbean party held at the city's Botanical Gardens in March. The tropical dress code proved slightly problematic as "*lots of people ended up wearing the same outfits...it's quite hard to find Hawaiian shirts in Birmingham in the middle of winter.*" The Old Joint Stock is still the favourite watering hole after work, although trainees are often lured away by the prospect of "*cheaper drinks*" in nearby Digress.

and finally...

Martineau Johnson will never be the biggest recruiter or the biggest hitter on the Birmingham legal scene, but we reckon that with some good work coming in and a swanky new building, it's a decent alternative to the city's giants.

Masons

the facts

Location: London, Bristol, Leeds, Manchester, Glasgow, Edinburgh
Number of UK partners/assistants: 82/162
Total number of trainees: 37
Seats: 4x6 months
Alternative seats: Secondments

Masons towers over other firms in construction and engineering law and sits in the fast lane on the IT superhighway. It recently added Dubai to a list of overseas offices that already included branches in Asia and Scotland, but here we report on its English offices.

concrete decisions

Masons is "*first and foremost*" a construction firm, and is structured into four divisions: UK construction and engineering, international and energy, capital projects, and technology and business services. This latter department is comprised of dispute resolution, property, coco, information and technology, employment, tax, health and safety, insolvency and pensions. While these areas do have a degree of standalone work, much of the activity in business services supports the other three departments. Whilst not all would agree with the statement, some sources indicated that "*Masons can't claim to be a full-service firm at the moment.*" Let's take the middle ground and stress that Masons is a truly sector-focused firm that can offer its chosen client sectors an awful lot.

Any applicant with a construction background or serious IT aspirations, should place Masons at the top of their list of firms to consider for training. On the IT side, the firm acts for Invensys, London Stock Exchange and AOL Europe; it has represented Defra in connection with a major IT outsourcing project, and is advising on the National Smartcard Project. In construction, Masons works with all the biggest names: AMEC, Amey Group, Skanska, Wembley National Stadium, Ballast, Bovis Lend Lease, John Mowlem & Co...we could go on... During your time with them, the London construction team could have you working on anything from building schools in Clacton to the Indian/Malaysian Hyderabad airport joint venture.

Anyone whose priorities are less concrete is recommended to do some serious swotting-up on Masons before applying. As one trainee put it: *"There is a feeling that at Masons why on earth wouldn't you want to do construction?"* Another said: *"It is important for people to realise how construction-based Masons is. It is a long time to do construction if you don't like it."*

digging in

The seat system follows the standard four-seat pattern with everyone due a seat in UK construction and engineering or international and energy. The first seat is allocated to trainees on their arrival at the firm and, thereafter, *"they try and get your requests right."* In London, the construction department, as the hub of the firm, *"has a certain vibe."* Information and technology also wins trainee hearts for its capacity to offer *"a hell of a lot of exposure"* on major outsourcing projects and data-protection issues. Trainees found they were getting greater responsibility on smaller matters in property and enjoyed employment for its independent clients and *"a good mix of contentious and non-contentious work."* London is also home to some smaller departments such as health and safety, insolvency and tax.

The Leeds and Manchester offices have been bundled into one on the Masons map. The Leeds offering is small in terms of staff and seats: contentious construction and engineering, non-contentious construction and engineering, capital projects or energy are on offer. Leeds trainees can also opt to go to Manchester for something like pensions or property. An influx of Loiners has created a few problems regarding seat allocation in Manchester: *"Logistically it is difficult to accommodate everyone – it is a case of who*

can shout the loudest." This year the problem has been solved by squeezing in a fifth seat for all (though the training contract lasts no longer). Bristol trainees get the pick of construction, international energy and engineering, commercial property and property litigation, and capital projects. *"You have to be prepared to do three of them"* and *"if you have no preferences you will do all four."* If you do have a particular leaning, its perfectly easy to swing six months in London, though as one interviewee curtly pointed out: *"If you go to Bristol expecting to do banking or IT etc, it is your own fault. You can't go to London to do three out of four seats."*

Despite a plethora of foreign offices, and alliances with firms in the US, Spain and Iraq, Masons trainees rarely get to laugh at each other's passport photos. They may make the odd fleeting business trip, but generally a Masons traineeship is a UK-based experience. As to why in 2004 the firm closed its Dublin office and set up shop in Dubai instead, we were told: *"Offices close and open as and when they are needed."* This sense of fluidity has also been felt by trainees who have witnessed the departure of people from the London property litigation and planning teams,*"which has left a bit of a hole."* However, sources were quick to point out that while smaller departments are *"falling away, moving on or being support functions,"* the firm's core strengths of construction and IT remain very strong. The way trainees see it, *"more and more, we are going back to being a brilliant construction firm and great for IT."*

on the grapevine

Sharing an office with their supervisor, trainees mix easily with associates and senior staff – *"there is no pomp, ceremony or hierarchy."* Thankfully, partners *"don't rip your head off, even when the pressure's up"* and *"there is no aura of fear."* Mid and end-of-seat appraisals are scheduled with each supervisor, in addition to six-monthly appraisals with the training manager or training principal. If you do feel the need to consult a partner on your work, you'll not be left wanting. And for more general info and gossip, "*the grapevine is brilliant...but officially there is not very much.*" Of course not!

Put away that pen with the fluffy pink bit on the top; our sources described a gritty training contract that had them working on some phenomenal transactions. They described some periods of "*immense responsibility,*" saying "*you never feel underused.*" Admittedly, you are unlikely to lead a small army of your own files at this firm, yet even so, all our sources had done their turn close to the frontline on notable transactions. But were they just digging trenches and passing telegrams forward? It seems not. "*Of course there is grunt work too, but it all balances out...in favour of quality work.*"

Trainees spoke of "*peaks and troughs*" in the working pattern. Getting palmed off with a six-month seat next to the photocopier would be out of the question, but at times you may find you are heavily involved in marketing activities rather than a top deal. When we called, capital projects was going through a lull, leading one source to comment: "*Some days I read far too many sports reviews.*" The flipside is that in other departments, such as the current hot seat, IT, "*it seems to be bloody manic.*" There, the usual 8.30-6ish day was frequently running well into late evening.

Just like many other firms, Masons has cut the size of its trainee intake. One of the current crop raised an eyebrow at this point in conversation, saying: "*They will continue to get high-quality work, but they will be really busy – good luck to them!*" One candid source ventured to comment on another of the firm's economically exigent moves, the reduction of trainee salaries in recent times. "*There are kernels of resentment hanging around*" he revealed, however, "*they are aware of the problem and they do talk about changing it.*" In September 2004, some 20 of the 30 trainees stayed with the firm throughout the English offices.

got your number

At the start of their contracts, trainees all bunk down together for two weeks in a London hotel to complete their PSC and get on with the important business of bonding. Thereafter, socialising is an office by office thing. In Bristol that means monthly drinks in the nearest wine bar, or when the weather's nice, a BBQ on the Downs.

Manchester's quiz nights, wine tastings and trips to the dogs are only surpassed by a joint summer ball with the Leeds office. In Leeds a monthly trainee night out frequently turns into a free-for-all at Indy Joe's around the corner, and the annual trainee revue at the Christmas party "*gives you absolute free rein to take the piss out of everyone.*" The partners are "*not terribly strict when they check the script; it's just about humiliating yourself in order to give everyone else a giggle.*" In London, however, the revue is a deadly serious business. Though not all our sources were fans of this "*self-induced humiliation,*" everyone acknowledged that "*it is a bit of an institution*" and "*everyone is completely on your side – they will laugh at anything.*" This year, the London revue included a sketch called 'I'm a Solicitor: Get me out of Here' and impersonations of Ali G, Cilla Black, David Brent, and Austin Powers. The 118 Guys also made an appearance...then made a comeback at a recent karaoke night for a rendition of 'Keep on Running'. "*Absolutely crazy!*"

green and pleasant lands

A recent Summer Ball shared by the London, Bristol and Scottish offices took a Wild West theme and included a Bucking Bronco and some tequila girls. For less-hard liquor, the Crown on Clerkenwell Green is a safe bet after work, (as is the Grape, The Priory, The Bear, The Jerusalem Tavern...) and for an office location the Green is itself positively idyllic – there are "*trees and everything.*" Set back from the City, the firm has gorgeous offices with a "*sexy 'woo' client area*" and a massive atrium. The piéce de résistance is a roof terrace for "*the cheapest meal with the best view of London.*" Those whose stomachs are still left rumbling are medicated by "*the trolley lady*" who brings round chocolate and homemade cookies each noon. The dress code is *"officially formal, but it is very rare to see a man in a tie."*

A Masons trainee is *"confident and able to take the initiative"* and *"can hold their own,"* if only in the in-house trainee mooting competition. For everyone with prior experience in architecture, engineering or IT, there is another who had simply sought the embrace of a mid-sized firm. We were assured *"we don't all wear hard hats,"* and yet as in recent years our interviews with Masons have left us concluding that it is a place suited to those prepared to launch themselves into one of its core areas of work. Bottom line: Masons is no soft cushion for a crash landing into any-old-law.

and finally...

For construction and IT converts, Masons is your Jerusalem. For everyone else, we're told: *"You could cope, but it is a lot more fun if you enjoy it."* The advice? *"Do your research before you apply."* Better still, do a vac scheme.

Mayer Brown Rowe & Maw LLP

the facts

Location: London, global
Number of UK partners/assistants: 99/160
Total number of trainees: 49
Seats: 4x6 months
Alternative seats: Brussels, secondments
Extras: Pro Bono – RCJ CAB, Bar Pro Bono Unit/Liberty referrals, Islington, Fulham and Toynbee Hall law centres, language training

Mayer Brown Rowe & Maw is a Chicago-based global law firm with eight stateside offices complemented by flourishing branches across Asia and Europe. The London arm is no after-thought however, being the result of a 2002 merger between the USA's Mayer Brown & Platt and 100-year-old Limeys Rowe & Maw.

a winning combination

Many such US/UK mergers have taken place in the last five years, but none has so roundly surprised the legal market, nor appeared so harmonious. This year we interviewed the last of the trainees who applied pre-merger, and the first of the unadulterated class of MBRM. All were aware that *"the merger took everyone's breath away; the reaction was 'How the hell did old Slow & Bore manage that?' and there seemed to be a lot of jealousy and hopes that it might fail."* But MBRM ignored cruel nicknames and disappointed all those gleeful gloom merchants.

R&M absorbed the small MBP London office but there was *"no importing of a stereotypical cut-throat American attitude."* The UK end retained its own billing culture, won three seats on the global board and, at present, largely runs its own ship. Trainees told us: *"The major changes have been in making our systems and procedures globally compatible...that's only seen as a positive thing."* Significantly, the small differences in style we heard about last year seem to have been smoothed out. *"The odd one or two* [partners] *who felt displaced have either accepted and adapted to the prevailing culture, or have moved elsewhere."* One first-year trainee admitted: *"I think I had one legacy MBP partner as a supervisor, but I'm just guessing; he never mentioned it."* Charmingly, when one trainee used the word merger, he quickly corrected his slip: *"Actually we call it the combination."* And according to our sources, *"the combination has created a new beast that seems to be able to achieve things that neither of the old firms could have done individually."*

We understand that a 'three years in' review will determine the degree of autonomy that London will continue to enjoy. Those trainees who knew or had opinions on this matter were not fearful that the honeymoon period was about to end sharply. *"There's such a positive feeling that we're doing well; no one remotely thinks of the US as a harbinger of doom."*

Undoubtedly there is ample evidence to support the view that *"the London office is...feeding on a greater supply and quality of work."* The firm now boasts a client roster that is the envy of many: Nestlé, Rothschild, Société Générale, easyNet, Cable & Wireless, Bank of America, Standard Chartered Bank, Volkswagen, Dow Chemical, HMV, EMI, Virgin, Green Property, AT&T, Nationwide Building Society and Royal Bank of Scotland. At the same time, the firm's global expertise is adding weight to the London corner in areas like IP. Dealing with M&A-related IP matters for long-time clients like Reuters and ICI is nothing new, but racing to third position in the trademark filing league tables and receiving IP instructions from major US food producers and automotive manufacturers wouldn't have happened precombination.

opportunity knocks

Trainees who applied pre and post combination all told us they chose the firm *"because of the mid-scale size and because it took on 20 to 25 trainees."* On that score everyone was satisfied: *"You get a lot of attention, and by the end of your time every partner knows you."* Some were even *"freaked out!"* Why? *"Well, I bumped into the managing partner in the corridor and we chatted for 30 minutes: he not only remembered my name but also which university I'd been to!"* Mid-sized appeal now comes with the added bonus of global reach, and our sources were genuinely excited by this prospect. Said one: *"The international capacity is opening up more and more. I've dealt with people in Hong Kong, Singapore, Trinidad and the Cayman Islands."* It was clear to us that bouncing around the corridors of MBRM *"there is a sense of genuine excitement and ambition."* Last year we couldn't help feeling that trainees' ambitions were directionless, but this year a more insightful bunch of trainees had a finer eye for detail. *"When you think of change you think of dramatic events but this firm is changing as it gels, evolves and realises its strengths...You could call it opportunistic ambition."* The organic growth of the IP department is a good example, and sits in stark contrast to what

has been going on at, say, Dechert (which has deliberately shifted its focus from property to finance since its US merger).

Seat rotation is a fairly straightforward matter of four six-month seats: trainees do stints in corporate and something contentious plus two optional seats. They reflected on a *"relatively transparent process of rotation,"* but advised future recruits to *"make a play, if there's something you really want."* The firm may have a predominantly corporate practice, but there are rich pickings elsewhere. Pensions, employment, tax, construction, real estate (transactional and litigation varieties), IP, public law, com lit, finance, environmental law and insurance are all there for the choosing. Despite the firm's global stature, the only overseas posting currently on offer is at a *"highly recommended"* competition seat in Brussels. If *"monitoring EU law"* isn't to your taste then one of the regular client secondments to Unilever, AstraZeneca, Marsh & McLennan, ICI or Cabled Wireless and or Reuters could help *"to build commercial awareness and teach you what clients actually want."*

in one ear

One trainee who was thrilled about the *"mass of responsibility"* on offer on secondment admitted that the prospect of returning to a more mundane trainee role for a final seat had caused a few worries. *"At my appraisal before returning, I expressed those concerns, and the firm took them on board and have given me a lot of responsibility in the final seat."* Given that in the past trainees have griped about the lack of autonomy and quality of work they have sometimes received – corporate and litigation being particularly guilty parties – this was good to hear. Concerning *"times of pedantry and bundling,"* our sources were either pragmatic (*"you've got to expect to jump through hoops at some point"*) or inventive (*"I'd bring in my Walkman on rudimentary filing days and listen to it in the ear not facing the corridor"*). Several people had taken the bull by the horns after a period of grunt work. *"In litigation, my first three months was document management on one big* transaction, but I was very honest in my mid-seat appraisals and subsequently I got a lot of smaller matters, went to meetings and met counsel." Smaller departments like IP or pensions are appreciated for the "closer proximity to the work," with real estate especially popular because "you run landlord and tenant stuff yourself and can see a transaction through." Nevertheless, the larger departments did have their fans amongst those who are more collaboratively minded. As one of them told us: "The teamwork on those larger deals can be really exciting."

the gravy games

While the appraisal system came out of our interviews smelling of roses, on the subject of day-to-day relations with their supervisors, trainees hinted at a broader palette of aromas. "Sometimes it's blood, sweat and tears, sometimes it's all gravy." A wonderfully sticky mental image, but the general feeling was that "if you've messed up you'll be told, 'Have another go at that, try x, y and z,' and if you've done well, you'll know." Outside work, "partners aren't a breed apart," and trainees are used to mingling with them at regular drinks parties and in the "inescapable" local pub The Evangelist. "I've never done a construction seat, but I often find myself drinking in the pub with construction partners," said one source. When they do tear themselves away, there are a variety of sports teams to help work off the alcohol-added calories, but the main event is the yearly corporate v the rest of the firm football match. Apparently "everyone turns out to watch, and even the managing partner plays." We bet he puts himself up front.

The manageable size of the trainee group makes for "a sociable bunch" that is equally satisfying to those "who drop in and out, and those looking for a bit more." Our sources couldn't see themselves in generic terms, though they did recognise a variety of university backgrounds and noted that "quite a few of us have had a few years out." A more polemical subject was that of retention: with 15 out of 22 qualifiers staying on in 2004, many of those hoping for jobs in the more niche departments like IP had been disappointed – "Several smaller departments simply aren't recruiting." In fairness, we're told that two of those leaving were offered jobs but are leaving law altogether. Hopefully in future years retention will pick up, but those trainees focused on a corporate NQ life were buzzing. "There's the potential for growth here so you can see your way to partner." We particularly liked the pearl of wisdom from the trainee who told us the firm gave people "enough rope so you can either hang yourself or make yourself a hammock."

and finally...

Currently enjoying connubial bliss, Mayer Brown Rowe & Maw offers aspiring City lawyers excellent prospects. Our interviews with trainees can never be said to be a window on the future, but from where we're standing the view looks pretty good.

McCormicks

the facts

Location: Leeds
Number of UK partners/assistants: 15/20
Total number of trainees: 8
Seats: 4x6 months
Alternative seats: None

"If you're going into the law, why work for Dooley Diddle & Glum? It'll be dull as f***. You might as well work for McCormicks and put a bit of glamour in your life." So said the most characterful of our trainee sources at this lively Leeds firm.

rapier wit

When trainees describe their firm as "a glitzy, Las Vegas-like beacon in the middle of the legal desert" you can be forgiven for not taking them seriously. When they go on to describe the firm as "hip and sexy" you're tempted to snigger. However, at McCormicks the biggest laugh is that it's all true. A young whip-per-snapper of a firm, McCormicks channels its energy into commercial and charities law, and frequently outpaces the competition in the specialist fields of media and sports. As for any surplus energy, that goes into having the last laugh...

...or the first as the case may be. Monday morning meetings take on the feel of the confession box, with everyone crowding in to own up to their weekend misadventures. Friday mornings on the other hand are set aside for competitions ('Who can ping the elastic band the furthest'. 'Who can eat a Creme Egg the fastest'). Indeed, a quick look at McCormicks' website confirms that here competition is the name of the game. Liberally smattered with images of boxers and fencers, the site portrays the firm's gutsy, fighting spirit. One brave soul tried to convince us the images reflect *"intellect, culture and respectability,"* but the truth of the matter is *"if people mess with us, they'll feel the sharp edge of our sword."*

So between an early-morning belly laugh and ending the day in a cheeky headlock on the boardroom floor, is there any time to get some work done? You bet.

return to the woolpack

Lest we give the impression of a firm that can't be taken seriously, we must stress that McCormicks is stuffed with highly proficient lawyers that have earned genuine respect in the marketplace. In September 2003 Yorkshire Law Society recognised the firm as its Law Firm of the Year (under 21 partners). In order to bring trainees up to speed and up to standard, all of them complete four six-month seats drawn from property, coco, commercial litigation, IP, corporate crime, private client, employment and family law. On the whole they are able to concentrate on the areas that most interest them, although it's fair to say that the media/broadcasting and sports law practices are the common denominators in this regard. After all, what trainee would turn down the chance to act for showbiz names like Nell McAndrew, Richard Whiteley, Leslie Ash, cast members of Corrie and Emmerdale, plus footie stars and sports organisations such as Leeds United FC and the Premier League?

For the aspiring Premiership-player-cum-Pop-Idol-wannabee, McCormicks may seem like a natural choice; however, *"the firm is keen to be known for other stuff too."* A highly respected charity department acts for The Outward Bound Trust, Age Concern, The Prince's Trust and The Duke of Edinburgh's Award as well as Friends of War Memorials and a convent in Whitby. On the commercial side *"local businesses are definitely the bread-and-butter client base."* The main message is clear: don't let the celebrity side of things blind you to the firm's other business. The secondary message is this though: *"Regardless of which department you are in, you will get the run-off from the Leeds United connection."* Aware of the need to check in with reality periodically, trainees explained: *"The law is still the law;""it's not as glittery as everyone expects."* But one couldn't help admitting: *"When you find yourself sat across the table from the cast of Emmerdale, you know you've made it in life."*

popular frontman

Your working hours will normally be a brisk 8.30am-6pm with *"sporadic periods of manic nights in corporate."* Here, lawyers have been busy acting for a number of motor dealers on the acquisitions of businesses and franchises, as well as selling off the famous Drum and Monkey restaurant in Harrogate. While trainees working on bigger deals and cases inevitably end up doing more in the way of research, proof reading and *"generally helping out,"* they do get the chance to cut their teeth on smaller files, and this includes meeting clients and undertaking advocacy. Our sources were philosophical when it came to the quality of work they received. In short, *"you get the full range – when it's good it's very, very good; when it's bad, it goes with the territory."* Once a month, there are training sessions for all, and our sources reported heavy involvement in marketing events from early on. As for feedback, monthly meetings with the managing partner will mean you always know how you're getting on. On a daily basis *"people are quite blunt: you certainly know if you've done badly, and if you've done well you'll definitely get praised."*

Any grievances can be aired through MyLaw, which is a two-sided initiative by and for trainees. Externally, it helps them meet and build links with other young professionals in Yorkshire; internally, it *"acts as a little union."* Such collective power shouldn't be a threat to senior partner Peter McCormick (OBE for services to charity) – described affectionately as *"bonkers,"* our sources would all happily *"go the extra mile for him."* It seems that two of the four September 2004 qualifiers will be doing just that.

strong will, good grace

Forget strict hierarchy or airs and graces. As one trainee explained of the relationship with colleagues: *"You've seen them all drunk, and they've seen you throw up, so there's nothing to hide."* Recently reclaimed from a bunch of pretentious city types, The Vic has been reinstated as the Friday night pub of choice for McCormicks' staff. Putting visits to comedy clubs, the theatre and the dog track into the shade, the annual Christmas bash always has a fancy dress theme. In 2003, *"Bucks Fizz were there, the Ghostbusters made an appearance, and Michael Jackson turned up..."* Rest assured, sartorial extravagances are kept away from the office, which remains strictly suited and booted.

McCormicks has a small office in Harrogate, but trainees do not visit, instead spending the whole of their two years in Leeds, where the firm occupies two city centre buildings – *"a posh one, and one where all the work is done."* Britannia Chambers is an old Victorian building with lots of stairs *"providing a good thigh and buttock workout."* Next door in posh Oxford House, the commercial team have a more luxurious existence. Moves are underway to knock through the two buildings, which should even out the fitness levels between departments.

If popular opinion is anything to go by, *"you have*

to be quite robust" to fit in at this firm as *"there's a lot of banter."* Perhaps we shouldn't have been surprised to hear then that *"they used to recruit mainly on personality, now they have started to look at people's grades more seriously."* We noted that several trainees had been recruited from Leeds University, with others having come from Cambridge, Manchester, Durham and Norwich. Quick wit and caustic humour aside, all of our sources were bright, sparky and easygoing...*"incredibly intelligent, great fun, very attractive..."* You get the picture.

and finally...

If you're tempted to make an application to McCormicks simply because it sounds like masses of fun, you should pause and consider the reasons why it has become successful. In the tough Leeds legal market firms require grit, determination and good lawyers to rise to the top. This is perhaps the only sense in which McCormicks conforms.

McDermott Will & Emery

the facts

Location: London
Number of UK partners/assistants: 25/43
Total number of trainees: 4
Seats: 4x6 months
Alternative seats: None
Extras: Pro bono – Sir John Cass Foundation

Chicago-born McDermott Will & Emery is a top 12 firm on the far side of the pond, and with 15 offices spanning the Atlantic, it is every inch an international concern. Although swimming in shallower waters in the UK, the London branch is no backwater minnow. Since it was opened in 1999, the UK office has grown from scratch to 70 (mainly English) lawyers and made good inroads in certain areas of practice.

never bottom of the list

If you're thinking of McDermotts as a good back-up application in case magic circle hopes take a tumble, then don't bother printing out that generic CV and covering letter. *"We all made a clear, active choice to come here,"* our sources advised, adding forcibly: *"We all have personality, several of us have diverse past experiences, and the firm has avoided recruiting arseholes."* It's a forthright statement and, on the basis of our interviews, we have to agree with it. The fact that only two trainees are recruited each year suggests the firm can afford to be *"very strict and fussy,"* so those with the inclination and inspiration to make a tailored application here might reflect on this advice – *"Come to a definite conclusion or even conviction about what the firm could specifically offer you."*

those few, those happy few

If you are one of the select few walking through the doors of McDermotts' Bishopsgate office and into a new job one September, you'll find plenty on offer across its five *"plush"* floors. It might be the UK arm of a US firm, but trainees assured us that *"although there is a certain US bias firm-wide"* and the London office does *"draw on the international network,"* it is *"self-sufficient in generating work."* Scratch about a bit and you do unearth a very American 2,000 hours per year billing target for qualified lawyers and other US trappings. Upon arrival, new starters join their peers from across the international network for an orientation week in Chicago. *"At the orientation week, presentations explain how the process of qualification works in each jurisdiction, but because the Americans don't really understand what a trainee is, you often end up being treated as an associate when you deal with partners internationally!"* Throughout their training contract, our sources had also been invited to join qualified lawyers at *"group retreats...we had one recently in Toronto."* One interviewee said: *"It was amazing to see quite how many people had been working worldwide on a big IP transaction I'd been on for months."* With overseas seats and secondments not available until post-qualification,

these experiences add texture to the London training and promote *"a perspective that is global not insular."*

flying first class

Underlining its significance in the international set-up, the London office has a representative on the five-strong executive committee that rules the entire firm. A surprising fact when put in the context of other US firms' incursions into the UK, but not when the *"high-quality work for top clients"* and *"the flow of work both ways across the Atlantic"* is added into the equation. McDermotts likes to see itself as competing with the top City firms despite its relatively small size, a fact given credence by its high ranking for mid-scale and larger corporate deals in our parent publication *Chambers UK*. To whit, the firm this year advised the vendor in the £271 million sale of car dealer and distributor CD Bramall to prestigious retail and hire company Pendragon.

The firm also boasts superb employment and IP teams, with banking, pensions, litigation, tax, energy and competition practices also more than holding their own too. This breadth plus strength reflects the way in which the firm planted itself in the UK and recruited *"top partners from magic circle firms;" "almost every group has someone who is recognised as a leader in their field."* The firm's almost dizzying client list includes multinational and national companies and financial institutions, and suggests the firm is achieving its lofty goals. On the roster: Balfour Beatty, Levi Strauss, Marks & Spencer, the National Theatre, Sainsbury's, Oracle, United Airlines, EMI, The Diamond Trading Company (formerly DeBeers), Formula One Management, BioProgress Technology, Bradford & Bingley, O2, Alcatel, European Investment Bank and Motorola. The role of the employment and IP teams in building this list cannot be underestimated, however.

streetwise: selling yourself

Our sources spoke of *"a relatively small office with no sense of hierarchy, and an exciting atmosphere."* If you're already dribbling with excitement at this, trainees suggested we also point out that being in short supply, and therefore highly in demand, they had a lot of sway in terms of seat selection. *"We're not in a position of total power – you might sometimes have to go where you're needed – but in general it's a case of 'Make your list of choices and we'll do everything we can to facilitate that.'"* Not bad! Those we spoke to had been able to pick from any department they wanted, often varying the standard six-month seat with a few three-monthers *"to broaden experience."*

As a relatively new scheme (trainees have only existed at the firm for four years), this training best suits those *"who are prepared to be proactive;" "you need to sell yourself to the whole department in a seat and to the wider firm when you qualify."* This viewpoint rang true when trainees told us that the firm likes *"an element of streetwise-ness in us. We've probably got to be a bit more commercial than trainees elsewhere." "Inevitable trainee drudgery"* was described as *"present but not awful,"* and was more than balanced out by not infrequent words of praise. *"The ex-managing partner rang me up just to say 'This is absolutely perfect, thank you'."* On a more hum-drum note, mid and end-of-seat appraisals *"function well and your supervisor is continually assessing your progress to make sure you don't get pigeon-holed."*

Of course as well as having advantages, being at a relatively small firm has its disadvantages. Trainees admitted: *"We're not big enough to have on-site catering"* and *"the socialising tends to have less of a 'Let's all go out on a Friday night' feeling."* As one mathematical genius pointed out: *"If we arrange a trainee event and two drop out, that only leaves two!"* The compensation comes in the office culture and informal dress code – *"You dress down unless you've got a client meeting."* On visits to nearby pub, the Counting House, or at monthly drinks, what stood out for our sources was *"the absolute lack of hierarchy; everyone knows everyone."* In 2004, the two qualifying trainees both stayed on, a fact for which one nearly qualified trainee gave a simple explanation – *"They only recruit outstanding candidates who they can see as involved in the future of the firm."* Which brings us back to where we started...

and finally...

"Quality work in an exhilarating environment, and you're treated like a worthwhile member of the team – that's why I get out of bed every morning." It seems that McDermott Will & Emery has the ability to turn even lazy students into valuable tax-paying members of society!

McGrigors

the facts
Location: London
Number of UK partners/assistants: 76/129
Total number of trainees: 37
Seats: 4x6 months
Alternative seats: Brussels, Scotland, secondments

North of the border, the McGrigors clan has a 200-year history, but here we report on its London operation.

braveheart
McGrigors' office in London is the offspring of an Anglo-Scot liaison that has all the trappings of a Reformation marital saga. A quick skip through modern British legal history explains why. In 1999, international accounting giant KPMG set up a legal arm – KLegal. KLegal subscribed to the multi-disciplinary practice (MDP) school of thought, which brings accountants, lawyers, tax advisers and financial experts together to work in unison for clients. The firm's brief existence was marked by brave ideas, rapid expansion, exciting potential...and then Enron, which wasn't even anything to do with KLegal or KPMG. The bankruptcy of the seventh largest company in the US, and the implication of its auditor, Arthur Andersen, prompted the US Government to pass the Sarbanes-Oxley Act. The Act restricts the

ability of accountancy firms to perform other expert (eg legal) services for their clients. The knock-on implications rather scuppered KLegal's game plan.

In 2002 the marriage of KLegal with Scottish firm McGrigor Donald brought KLegal a new client base independent of KPMG and allowed McGrigor Donald to tap into the KPMG legal international network. It was not an entirely happy relationship and became scarred by differences, departures and rumoured power struggles that would put the Tudors and Stuarts to shame. The decision in February 2004 for the London practice to rename itself McGrigors tells much about the outcome and reflects the loosening of ties with KPMG. No one was left in any doubt that McGrigors was wearing the kilt.

more than a highland fling

Many of the trainees we spoke to had applied to the firm in 2000, when KLegal was a brave and dynamic, international (if unknown) quantity. Trainees confessed that *"the MDP thing seemed to be the way things were going. I thought it would be less regimented and more exciting than a City law firm"* and *"we didn't want to be just straightlaced lawyers, we wanted to rub shoulders with KPMG."* Inevitably then, our interviews were marred by a sense that current trainees *"signed up for a different product."* Concerning *"more influence from Scotland,"* opinion was mixed; for every one who felt that *"London isn't seen as crucial – the Scottish side is where the miracles are made,"* another felt that *"McGrigors probably raised the standards. They're well respected in Scotland and they brought that into the London office."* A move from current lodgings with 'best friend' KPMG to a home at Old Bailey looks set to cement the new identity. Said one source: *"It's high time we moved because it's a bit of a rabbit warren here. Everybody will be glad to get out of here. We won't get our free lunch in the KPMG canteen anymore, but we won't miss it!"*

They would, however, miss a steady diet of good work if the relationship with the accountants disappeared altogether. The retained link is treasured by trainees – KPMG-sourced work accounted for over 10% of the firm's turnover in 2003, but loosening the tie will enable the firm to pursue other client leads. Of late partners have brought Dunlop, Grupo Ferrovial and Bank of Tokyo-Mitsu into the fold to graze alongside established monster clients like Bank of Scotland and Imperial Tobacco.

SSSSSSS

Within the four-seat system trainees have a good deal of choice. They must all complete a spell in corporate and a contentious seat chosen from dispute resolution, construction, tax litigation and IP; beyond this, options include real estate, banking, technology, and people services (employment). We repeatedly heard that *"corporate is genuinely dreaded,"* mainly because of the hours. One particularly dramatic source said: *"It's a viper's nest. You get beasted,"* though another conceded: *"The hours are hell, but there's a buzz in there and you kind of get used to it."*

This year the most popular seats were pensions and tax litigation. These departments continue to display elements of the KLegal work ethic, and *"really operate under the MDP principle."* Of pensions, one trainee chipped in: *"It was great; I was working for a big client and got involved in employee benefits and setting up employee accommodation."* Another agreed: *"I had a fantastic time; it was very corporatey, but without the hours culture."* More than that, *"due to KPMG there was lots of interesting bonus planning and tax-incentivising."* The team works for international investment banks and FTSE 100 companies, professional services firms and overseas companies with a UK presence.

Tax lit trainees got to *"spend all day working with tax people in KPMG."* The experience was described by one enthusiast as *"totally crazy; eight single guys who work hard, play hard and make loads of money – it's just good fun."* Trainees were *"surprised by the amount of courtroom experience"* in the seat. They were drafting claim forms and researching for High Court, Court of Appeal and House of Lords cases, though understandably they don't actually undertake any advocacy themselves – *"it's too specialized."* Similarly of construction litigation, *"long and protracted disputes"* limit the extent of trainee involvement, but one source assured us *"I was playing as big a hand as I could, the next step up is strategising."*

Real estate offers trainees *"more autonomy and responsibility."* The team acts for big names in retail, such as McDonald's and French Connection, plus other large clients, such as Royal Mail and Royal Bank of Scotland. Trainees described a workload of licences to assign/make alterations plus other portfolio management tasks. People services sees trainees taking witness statements for tribunals, drafting notes of advice and getting their heads round employee benefits, pensions issues and corporate support. *"You do feel really involved, you're not just sitting in a little office waiting for people to bring you things."*

knitting together

One benefit of working for a firm that scales Hadrian's Wall is that trainees get a chance to pack a bag and a woolly jumper and swap places with Scots trainees for six months. McGrigors *"definitely actively encourages you all to swap around."* Those who had braved the GNER booking line considered the experience a real highlight and described *"upbeat, confident and well-established offices."* They got a real sense that McGrigors in Scotland *"know who they are and what they're doing; they don't need to worry about very much."* Those more inclined to travel south can try out for a competition seat involving three months in Brussels, and from September 2004 the firm will offer a whole raft of secondments to KPMG. One cynic pointed to the unwieldy size of the 2004 intake, saying: *"It is being trussed up with a nice fancy ribbon, but it is actually about locating an overspill."* Others welcomed the news: *"It means I have still got the same opportunities I signed up to."*

For better for worse, the McGrigors marriage offers a *"a ruddy good training contract."* Photocopy-

ing is a rarity, and duller chores such as bundling are balanced with admirable responsibility. Recruits attend ample formal training sessions starting with a three-day residential induction, which also provides an opportunity for a little cross-border bonding. This year, the induction took place in Bishops Stortford – not exactly halfway, but *"close to Stansted"* – and thereafter departmental training takes over. It's clearly good stuff if the level of commercial awareness amongst trainees is anything to go by.

The downside of working at a firm emerging from a management head spin is that *"transparency is atrocious."* In most firms, it would be fair to say that trainees rely heavily on the proverbial grapevine, but at McGrigors in 2004 we sensed a good deal of bewilderment: *"The issue is always communication,"* said one. A few others also hinted that paucity of communication infiltrates the training contract too, with one stating: *"There is an issue in terms of getting appraisals done"* and another saying of the level of feedback: *"I don't know if it would be there, if I didn't ask."*

Moving on to things that improve communication, departmental away days are always popular. A firm-wide corporate department bonding session followed the favoured format (hotel near airport), and we also heard that a tax department punt down the Cam was in the pipeline. Other firm-wide events have included dragon boat racing, plenty of sport and, of course, a Burn's Night supper. On a more regular basis, trainees are not averse to slinking off to the nearby Evangelist or The Blackfriar. And *"on bigger nights we all go to Bed in Smithfields."*

chalk and cheese

Our sources included *"complete shrinking violets and real alpha males:"* Our standard 30-minute interview was protracted to a feisty 65-minute deconstruction by one, and reduced to a frosty nine minutes of yes/no answers by another. *"There are very few Oxbridge, a few good redbricks and some polyversities represented,"* but *"we were all looking for the human side of law."* More than that, all our sources had been looking for something a little different and were prepared to plump for the unknown quantity, even though, ultimately, on qualification in September 2004 only one of the five stayed.

and finally...

Amongst students looking for a London training, McGrigors will be a relatively unknown name, but with strong Scottish roots, superb clients and *"no laurels to rest on"* we would agree that the firm should serve well *"someone who is not hung up on names."*

Mills & Reeve

the facts

Location: Birmingham, Cambridge, London, Norwich
Number of UK partners/assistants: 66/142
Total number of trainees: 36
Seats: 6x4 months
Alternative seats: Secondments

Here's a piece of advice from a trainee: *"People don't appreciate that ideas about what they want to do in their career can change massively. Don't limit your choices early on."* With only loose rules on seat choices, everything from private clients to biotech start-ups, and four very different offices to choose from, there's no danger of limiting your options at Mills & Reeve.

keen as mustard

Since it started in Norwich in 1880, growth has been steady for M&R. While not exactly tiring of Norfolk, the management appreciated that the firm's prospects would be limited unless it entered a more vibrant market. Norfolk has its wealthy landed agricultural classes and some non-agricultural, Norwich-based businesses, but legal empires need to be built on more fertile soil. The firm opened in Cambridge in 1987, which then put it in an ideal position to exploit new technology industry in Sili-

con Fen. Having acquired a taste for expansion, Birmingham and London offices followed.

Around 500 staff and partners are split between the four offices and the five practice groups: private client, corporate, property, insurance and healthcare. All eyes are on Birmingham at the moment. Having started as a specialist healthcare office, it has developed a broader commercial function, and some sources spoke openly of a plan to make Birmingham the lead office in the future. Moving it in early 2005 from Edgbaston to larger premises in the heart of the legal community in Colmore Row is certainly a start.

public interest

Birmingham is arguably already the lead office for public sector work. Between them the M&R offices act for over 100 NHS bodies and 70 local authorities and other regulatory agencies; last year the firm won important new clients in the shape of the NHS Purchasing and Supply Agency and the NHS Logistics Authority. For some trainees, the opportunity to act for public sector bodies was central to their choice of firm. Said one: *"I thought it would be slightly more interesting as they are more complex organisations. And I saw an ethical angle to working for public bodies that, in turn, help people."*

The London office mainly acts for insurance companies on professional negligence cases relating to solicitors, accountants, brokers, financial advisors and architects. After a period when *"things got quite stretched for a while,"* M&R went on a hiring spree, recruiting lawyers from the likes of CMS Cameron McKenna, Beachcroft Wansbroughs and Kennedys. A seat in London is an attractive proposition for any trainee who wants to know if earlier ideas about avoiding the capital still hold water. Work-wise, you will be *"given as much as you can possibly handle,"* and can expect plenty of client schmoozing on top of your own caseload. One Norwich source implied that this full-on experience was exhausting: *"When trainees come back from London they are a shadow of their former selves!"*

east is east

"Norwich has a backwatery reputation, whereas we are the bee's knees," a Cambridge trainee joked. Yet if ever there were doubt as to M&R's deep attachment to the city, its recent move to open-plan, glass and steel premises on Whitefriars next to the River Wensum should put paid to any rumours. The move was tied in with a general sprucing up of the M&R brand; nothing radical, just some tinkering with the logo and a change of corporate colour.

In Cambridge, the firm has had to adjust to market conditions. Once hi-tech and biotech industries used to be geese that laid golden eggs, these days *"technology work is chugging along...it's not the boom area that it was."* Nonetheless, trainees in the technology seat engage with university spinouts and incubator sites at the Cambridge Science Park, and work on agreements for licensing of software and web hosting. In 2004, it is a burgeoning PFI team that makes most noise and is helping the firm rack up healthy profits. The group mostly handles projects for NHS trusts and educational institutions, and recently completed a £120 million deal for the University of Hertfordshire.

In both Norwich and Cambridge, a family seat means acting for people with more cash to flash than your average man on the street. In Cambridge the typical client is connected to the university or is an entrepreneurial CEO at one of its spinout companies or another regional start-up. *"It's less green wellies, more people who ask a lot of questions!"* Their divorce settlements often have company law aspects – *"Perhaps he set up a hi-tech miracle company and she wants a part of it because she holds shares in it. Emotionally wrenching, but intellectually challenging."*

open fields

Trainees have a good-old-fashioned mentor partner and a second-year buddy for those first few weeks when they need help finding the toilet or the stationery cupboard. They undertake six four-month seats, the last of which is for most people a return to their qualification department. Trainees have no choice about their first two seats but after that the field is open: *"Here I could do corporate or family. I found the extremes of options really appealing as I knew I didn't want to do one type of corporate finance after another."* Seats are available in family, agriculture, private client, employment, insurance and healthcare litigation, technology, corporate, real estate, property litigation, planning and environment, commercial litigation, construction, education, public law, PFI, tax, charities, and regulatory and defence work. The latter seat has nothing to do with the military and everything to do with professional negligence litigation.

We heard slight criticisms from some quarters on seat allocation. *"We were told it was a transparent system – that you just make choices clear and they do their best to accommodate you. However, it turns out that you need to go and speak to the team leader...certainly in Norwich."* Gentle politicking? *"Brazen politicking I'd say. Trainees are quite cagey about which seats they want...but that's the only thing their cagey about."* According to one source: *"There is a massive disparity in terms of the level of responsibility you get in different seats. Some people spoon-feed you a bit."* Yet in London, *"to start it was really hard going and I was working really long hours – sometimes supervision was scarce."* Sounds like you need to pick seats that suit your levels of confidence and energy as well as practice preferences. Of those who qualified in 2004, 35% had worked in more than one office, but if you find yourself paying twice for somewhere to live, don't worry: the firm covers the cost of the more expensive accommodation and contributes towards travel expenses.

smoky bacon

The highlight of the M&R year is a summer party for the whole firm. Held in *"deepest Hertfordshire"* last time, it had a Wild West theme and is perhaps best remembered for the managing partner line dancing with the summer students. Have you kids no pride these days? Christmas parties are single-office affairs, and teams of lawyers will also arrange the occasional night out together. Recently Birmingham staff were treated to a self-indulgent quiz night in which the questions were based entirely on themselves. In Norwich, *"a lot of people live outside the city. The firm tries to encourage a social scene but it's not well taken up."*

Many Cambridge staff live in the city and walk or cycle to work. Others live in surrounding villages, and some even commute by train from London. *"It's a very pleasant city with a good social scene. It's got all the bars and pubs and clubs but not the rough and threatening feel that some city centres have. It's nice, middle-class and safe."* The traditionally favoured Flying Pig now has a rival in the shape of a bar called Sauce – it's newer, slightly trendier and less smoky. Trainees enjoy regular meals with colleagues, quiz nights and have a book group, which discusses literature like *The Handmaid's Tale*, *The Curious Incident Of The Dog At Night Time* and *1984*. But far be it from us to portray them as fully paid-up members of the dystopian, pan-fried, chattering classes.

signs of the times

When asked to sum up the firm's style, several sources spoke of an ultra-professional, smart-suits environment in which *"virtually no one"* is arrogant. People are *"grounded and good at what they do. They know they are good but don't behave like they know it."* Partners don't pull rank; they gain respect by being decent and knowledgeable. And in keeping with this, *"they do everything properly...nothing is slapdash,"* and *"there's a lot of focus on the training."*

Anyone considering the East of England for their training will end up looking at both M&R and Eversheds. In Cambridge the two firms sit *"on opposite sides of road and gesticulate at each other."* Surely not! Eversheds is *"more national with a more international focus and they are solely commercial. We have more of a mix of work and seats here."* Qualified lawyers hoping to quit large London firms for a better quality of life also face this same choice. The steady influx of disillusioned City hotshots eager to join M&R and climb the ladder to partnership can leave *"home-growns dis-*

incentivised," nonetheless they are one of the reasons why the firm is so successful. This is especially noticeable in Cambridge, where the core of the office are M&R natives but the majority are laterals. On the positive side, 18 of the 24 2004 NQs stayed with the firm and got their first-choice departments.

and finally...

Apparently the plan is to take M&R into the Top 50, *"not number 63 or whatever it is we are now."* As one trainee predicted: *"We won't be a huge national firm but we might be on the verge of it."* Sounds like a smart time to get on board.

Mishcon de Reya

the facts

Location: London
Number of UK partners/assistants: 44/51
Total number of trainees: 14
Seats: 4x6 months
Alternative seats: None

Mishcon de Reya makes headlines, usually for its litigation practice, which has a tendency to attract intriguing clients and cases. Beyond this it boasts some unique, quirky practice areas, so if you're searching for a *"commercial firm with a twist,"* turn your attention this way.

stars in their eyes

Much of the work here has an edge of celebrity, infamy even. Lawyers have represented everyone from saints to sinners, including Jeffrey Archer, Princess Diana, Diane Modahl and Craig David. The firm defended Penguin Group and author Deborah Lipstadt in a defamation claim brought by right wing historian David Irving, and Watford FC in its dispute with Gianluca Vialli. Of famous clients, one trainee remarked that *"at the end of the day they're clients like any other."* Which means *"everyone gets the same treatment, whether or not they're Mr. Superstar."*

There are four main departments: corporate and commercial, litigation, property and family. Trainees confessed that when it came to seat allocation *"you don't get a huge amount of choice."* Coco and litigation are both compulsory, and although property is meant to be an optional seat, everyone we spoke to had done it. The real option appears to be whether to work in the family department or return to the coco or litigation groups for a more specialised seat.

This isn't as restrictive as it sounds. In litigation there are teams dedicated to media, employment, fraud and art law. In the latter, lawyers have advised foreign governments on the return of Jewish-owned works of art stolen during the Holocaust. The corporate group is equally diverse, with teams concentrating on music and entertainment, IP and business immigration. The firm has also ventured into some new intriguing areas, including a business ethics advisory service and a cross-disciplinary group focusing on fighting IP theft at major UK companies.

opportunity knocks

If a number of these areas sound appealing, don't worry about missing out on the chance to stick your fingers into several pies: *"You just have to show initiative, and approach a particular partner to say you have capacity. The firm encourages you to go around and ask for work."* Whether you're doing a general commercial seat, or even a specialised one, it is always possible to get work from another area of the firm. As such you should be receiving *"a mixture of work all the way through."* If you keep your nose clean, you could be advising the West Indies Cricket Board one week and helping Microsoft combat online spam the next. Best keep shtum when in the pub with your mates enduring six months of over-specialised finance work at a big firm.

Trainees were enthusiastic about the tasks allotted to them; echoing peers, one said: *"If they can see you can handle it, they'll let you run with things."* In litigation this equates to *"immediate exposure to drafting and client contact,"* and court attendance. Rumour has

it one lucky so-and-so ended up in the House of Lords in their first week in the department. We've no doubt they were watching from a position of safety behind a QC's wig, but trainees do undertake advocacy themselves, sometimes at quite short notice. *"One time a fee earner had to leave urgently, so I was packed off with the file to do the application myself. It was quite nerve-wracking as I wasn't really sure what I was doing. Luckily it worked out fine and we got what we were asking for."* As any old hand will tell you, that's how it's meant to feel the first time. Much like losing your virginity really. For the record, the firm is *"quite keen"* for its litigators to gain higher rights of audience.

passionate performances

Maybe because of the need to take the initiative when hunting for work, it seems that *"the trainees that do well are the ones that can think for themselves."* Mishcons certainly won't suit someone who wants to lie back and think of qualification. As one trainee noted: *"The attitude is that if you want to work, you want to work. The firm doesn't try to sell themselves to trainees massively."* Hard sell or not, five out of the seven qualifying trainees stayed with the firm in September 2004.

The current crop described themselves as *"self-aware and savvy,"* but we also detected a group with a well-rounded set of interests. In the last few years alone the firm has welcomed people from other careers including book publishing and museum curating, and has *"a tendency to take on trainees who have seen a bit of something."* Rather than being an exclusive preserve for art lovers and culture vultures though, *"you'll be just as likely to hear people talking about the football."* Trainees considered their most important characteristic to be: *"A real interest in the law. It's actually something we're quite passionate about."*

the wrong trousers

We hope no one takes this the wrong way – the firm is home to some big personalities. For example, partner Anthony Julius recently caused a bit of a storm when he published a book about TS Eliot's anti-

Semitism, and Lord Mishcon himself still clocks in every day to charm trainees and clients alike. Interestingly, in April 2004 around a third of the equity partners were de-equitised. It's not an uncommon move these days, but it makes us even more certain of a hunch that, here, there is a group of seriously influential individuals at the top of the tree. Despite this, trainees reported that "*the firm has an egalitarian atmosphere...everyone is there to be spoken to.*" Our sources certainly had no trouble pinning down supervisors for weekly informal chats about their workload and recent cases of note.

Some interviewees admitted that every so often their jobs entailed "*drudging through documents and scheduling,*" but paralegals and secretaries should take many of the less stimulating tasks off your hands. And you'll not be chained to your desk: "*You only stay late when it's perfectly obvious that it's necessary.*"

The firm has "*modern, light and airy*" accommodation in Red Lion Square in the guise of an unusual art deco building, full of bright colours and modern art. The "*trendy*" side of Mishcons also stretches to dress-down Fridays, where the chino-haters amongst you will be pleased to hear that some departments even allow jeans. And it's all in the name of charity – there's a collection every week for the privilege of leaving your suit on the hanger for a day.

family fortunes

While the atmosphere in the office is sociable, after hours the firm is "*not hugely social.*" This may be because "*a lot of people work a long day and then want to go home to their children. We have our own lives and we want to get on with them, rather than piling into the pub every night.*" Despite this, The Overdraft next door is a welcoming place, though recalcitrant students beware – teachers from BPP have been known to frequent the same establishment. Christmas celebrations are supplemented by sporadic 'Mingles' for the whole firm downstairs in the boardroom. And at the time of writing, the football team was going great guns, having topped the Division Three of the London Legal League and gained a place in the cup final against the mighty Clifford Chance.

and finally...

In the past we've portrayed Mishcons as an out-of-the-ordinary firm and, dare we say it, unconventional. What to do this year? Let's just say that if you're likely to fit right in, both you and the firm will recognise it as soon as you step through the door.

Morgan Cole

the facts

Location: Cardiff, Swansea, Oxford, Reading, London
Number of UK partners/assistants: 56/185
Total number of trainees: 26
Seats: 4x6 months
Alternative seats: Secondments

Morgan Cole has offices along a 150-mile route that roughly follows the M4. Despite a difficult few years for the firm, trainees report on excellent work experiences.

does fortune favour the brave?

In 1999, Welsh firm Morgan Bruce merged with Oxford and Reading firm Cole & Cole. Shortly after, professional indemnity boutique Fishburn Boxer bolted on and a low-value claims outfit was added in Croydon. Morgan Cole was an ambitious project that promised great things. It had talented lawyers, excellent blue-chip clients and a clear vision for the future. But something went wrong. Fishburns' 11 partners unhooked themselves in 2002 and now operate as a separate partnership. And that's just a small part of the story; in total, over 50 partners have left Morgan Cole since it was created, most from the English offices, though key departures have occurred in Wales lately. A partnership that stood at around 100 at the time of merger is now just 60 strong and, worryingly, profitability is a shadow of its former self. We keep waiting for it all to stop, but the partners keep leaving.

In the light of all of this *"blackness"* (to use one trainee's parlance), you'd think the firm would rebuff our advances, preferring to keep trainees away from 'the press'. But perhaps the grad recruitment folk had a hunch they would do the firm proud and recount positive training experiences. As indeed they did. What's more, they were jolly chipper, and better still some nine of the 14 qualifiers were staying with the firm after qualifying in September 2004 and another had accepted a position at Fishburns. What follows is a region-by-region account of training the Morgan Cole way.

jelly and scream

If you know Wales, you'll probably already know of Morgan Cole. The firm has built a fantastic name and slugs it out with the other two South Wales giants, Eversheds and Edwards Geldard, for predominance in many commercial areas of practice. True, a handful of partners have switched allegiances of late, but the firm has maintained most of its muscle. One of its more recent corporate transactions, for example, saw it acting for the management of fan manufacturer Nu-aire in its £34m buy-out of the company

Trainees choose their seats from a wealth of different commercial options, among them commercial property, banking, corporate, dispute management, construction, employment, and health and professional indemnity. These latter two seats appear to be particular favourites, employment for obvious reasons and health and professional indemnity because it's a latex gloves-on six months that allows trainees to handle key stages in the litigation process, including case management conferences. The firm has jumped into the professional insurance market feet first and now handles solicitors', surveyors' and healthcare defence work for insurance companies and their insureds. On the health side, trainees report visiting hospitals to take witness statements on everything from *"nurses slipping on jelly to nutty patients in psychi-atric hospitals hitting each other and staff."* *"The buzz thing is mediations. I went to a few of those; in fact, I was taken on every opportunity. The team also does a lot of training for the General Midwifery Council and NHS trusts, so I got to see that side of a lawyer's job – the education side."* We have to say the seat sounds a bit gruesome at times. *"You have to read tons and tons of medical records and you get a real insight into people's lives."*

A seat in the DMG (litigation) is less icky and can be taken in either Cardiff or Swansea. The subject matter is varied and may include bankruptcy, insolvency and property litigation as well as general contract claims. Trainees get to do bags of court work – repossessions for housing associations, judgement debts and applications in chambers, much of it on an agency basis. The Cardiff mob, especially, is seen as *"a busy, young and vibrant team to work with."* They *"utilise each other's knowledge more than any other department"* and are *"very integrated."* Best of all, *"they are perfectly willing to let you be engaged with their work"* and follow them everywhere. All of this goes some way to explaining the *"bottleneck around litigation seats."* The litigation department, like others, has lunchtime seminars for anyone in the firm who wants to attend, and similarly, coco lawyers run a 'Corporate Academy' on Thursdays, which is perfect for brushing up on all the stuff you've forgotten from law school.

general naughtiness

Cardiff is home to all but two trainees and is probably the more popular of the two offices because most live nearer to the capital than Swansea. That said, the Swansea contingent is just an hour away by train and has a swanky office overlooking the marina. *"The beach is just five minutes away and the Gower Peninsular is beautiful."* Socially, there are theatre trips, meals out and a summer barbecue. Back in Cardiff, the firm's city-centre location means endless possibilities for fun and games in local bars including Ha!Ha!, Incognito and new favourite, The Steam Bar in the Hilton. Cardiff's fun reputation had obviously reached the English trainees, as just a fortnight before we interviewed, the entire trainee population blew its annual budget on a massive day out in the Welsh capital. If you want to know how to blow an entire budget in 24 hours, this is what you do: lunch and drinks, bowling and drinks, the pub, dinner, a club and then a hotel for the night. Simple when you know how. The reason for the event is also simple: the trainees so enjoyed each other's company on the residential PSC courses in Oxford (staying at Oriel and St Anthony's and *"doing what naughty children do"*) that someone suggested they all get together again.

card games

Thames Valley trainees take seats in both Reading and Oxford, though we should point out that the firm pays for the commute. It has restructured the TV offices so that Oxford has DMG, family, IP, general commercial and property, and Reading has corporate, 'IT Lawyers' and employment. As well as these choices, there are secondments to BP and a professional indemnity litigation seat with Fishburns in London.

Of an *"awesome"* employment seat, one trainee said: *"I did masses. God, I loved that seat."* Such enthusiasm was hardly surprising given the work on offer – seeing clients, drafting witness statements on discrimination claims, running and settling cases, drafting defences and *"not a single photocopying job."* On the non-contentious side of the seat, trainees are also involved in corporate support work and discover the ins and outs of TUPE and everything else that happens when two companies merge.

An IT seat brings contract work and plenty of drafting, perhaps on website terms and conditions. One trainee told us they had also been involved in the marketing side of the job, which involved plenty of trips to London and *"learning how to hand out a business card slickly."* Again, as in Wales, DMG brings a wealth of good stuff such as district judges' hearings (charging orders, CMCs etc.), witness statements and pleadings to draft, and meetings with clients and counsel.

Reading and Oxford each have their own persona, with the smaller Reading office being the more relaxed of the two. It's generally felt to be a younger more sociable environment that's helped by its single-floor open-plan layout. Socially, it's not exactly buzzing but the mood is good. Oxford is more *"old-school"* and does not have the same flow in the office, so *"you can work there for months and not meet the person who sits just a few metres above you on the next floor."* The location on the Botley side of the ring road also hampers the social scene and *"there's nowhere to go at lunchtime apart from McDonald's or the Co-Op and no outside space...unless you want to sit in the car park."*

trashed

London is the real problem. The office has withered to just three partners and four solicitors, and can offer just one seat option – property litigation. Trainees occupy the other 18 months of their contracts with secondments to clients and Fishburns and additionally have access to the Thames Valley. Sensibly, from 2004 the firm will no longer recruit for the London office.

We did ask trainees what they made of the partner exodus at Morgan Cole and they were consistent in their views. This comment is typical: *"It's had no bearing on me personally whatsoever. When there's a story in The Lawyer, I just think, 'Load of bollocks!' and into the bin it goes."* The point is this: in all the seats they'd done, trainees had been exposed to very good work and had been able to develop as lawyers. They also felt supported by the mentor-partner system and had ample contact with the training partner, wherever they were located.

Several of our sources said they thought the worst was over for Morgan Cole, and that *"it was a good thing that some people have gone...things feel firmer and more settled now."* One said: *"It was upsetting...but what has happened has happened and I never thought there would be a job for me but there is. There was a lot of turmoil, and even to this day I don't think anyone can explain it."* What this trainee did know was *"we are still offering fantastic training and that's not changed since the day*

I walked through the door. Even when things were bad my training was good. I developed a lot of confidence because I had to or I would have drowned."

and finally...

Our last word goes to the trainee who, when asked to define Morgan Cole for our readers, said: *"It's now a Welsh firm with branches in the Thames Valley and a facility in London."* As much as we'd like to, we simply can't say what the firm will be like in September 2007 when readers are ready to start their training contracts.

Nabarro Nathanson

the facts:

Location: London, Reading, Sheffield
Number of UK partners/assistants: 99/297
Total number of trainees: 60
Seats: 4x6 months
Alternative seats: Brussels, secondments
Extras: Language training

At the moment, mid-sized firms are going from strength to strength in terms of work, clients and profits. With the advantages they offer to trainees, they can seem very comfortable places to be. But as one trainee admitted, *"You get the sense that all the mid-market firms are relatively similar in terms of work and clients."* Nabarro Nathanson has solid work, a trio of offices and some star departments, but what makes it stand out from the pack?

middle of the road

Like several other firms of a similar size, Nabarros has built an all-round practice on the back of a successful real estate department. Although the firm no longer markets itself on the strength of its real estate team, word is that *"property does think, 'yeah, we are the best.'"* The firm's goal, repeated by many a trainee, is to be *"the top firm in the mid market."* One optimist among our sources told us: *"Property is already there*

and the other sectors will be in the next two or three years."* The firm acted on the largest straight real estate deal of 2003, representing a syndicate of Israeli investors in their acquisition of a portfolio of car parks from the Royal Bank of Scotland for the whopping sum of £600 million. The firm also had a hand on the wheel of some of the most prestigious projects of the last few years, including the new Wembley Stadium, Birmingham Bull Ring and the new 'Shard of Glass' London Bridge Tower.

The firm's corporate teams do their share of decent transactions too, racking up a total deal value of over £7 billion in the past year alone. However, we feel one trainee was right on the money when they said: *"The firm knows its position on the scales and exploits its reputation in property."* Recent property-flavoured deals included acting for long-standing client Pubmaster on its acquisition by Punch Taverns for nearly £1.2 billion. Much of the rest of the corporate work tends be mid-cap deals, AIM and venture capital. Most trainees were quick to praise the firm for not having ideas above its station. Whilst one trainee joked: *"I'd like an office in Singapore,"* he knew there would be no snapping at magic circle heels any time soon.

because i'm worth it

Because there are only 60 of them, our interviewees claimed this meant the graduate recruitment team and partners *"are genuinely interested in us."* They told us they felt *"valued and respected."* Bitter or cynical readers should give up now because we've bags more of that kind of comment. Trainees usually get exactly the seats they want and the firm found NQ jobs for 26 of the 30 qualifiers in 2004. Within the trainee group there are *"people who really want to get into property law, people who don't want the magic circle but who want a good firm and people who just want a good training with good supervision."*

The firm operates a six-seat system, and as we often find with this twist on the standard four-seat pattern, trainees appreciate the flexibility it gives them. *"If you're not having a great time* [in a seat] *it's only four months, but if you're really loving it, you can go back for your last seat."* It's not a system to pick for an easy life though: *"After four months, you're just starting to find your feet and then you move on and you have to start all over again. It keeps everything fresh, but it can be hard to move on when you've just got hold of something, especially if you have to move from contentious to non-contentious or vice versa."*

bring on the chippendales

All trainees spend time in litigation, corporate and property. Property seats are seen as a very solid introduction to legal life: one trainee summed up her four months as *"very busy, awful lot of client contact, excellent weekly training, good team, very social, high-profile partners."* Rest assured that she and her peers were all more than capable of mastering complete sentences. The commercial litigation team seems equally adept at giving trainees a good introduction to their work. *"That seat was really good,"* said one source. *"There was a really good mix of different sized matters – you go from assisting on large cases right down to conducting your own files."*

If you're keen on real estate work, you might want to consider going for the prestige seat in property litigation. *"Nabarros has the best property litigation team by reputation. It's quite small – only four partners – but very switched on...people are so proud of what they do."* This seat can certainly provide some unique challenges. *"You tend to get involved with very obscure things – there is no pattern. You end up going to court because something has never come up before."* Intrigued we pressed for an example and heard of a case involving a landlord's refusal to consent to a licence allowing the tenant to underlet a property. Nothing too unusual in that you might say, but *"the reason was because it was a lapdancing club. However, our client did want to grant consent to something* [else] *that held Chippendales events and so we had to do some very complex drafting to distinguish the two."*

The corporate department is split into four teams:

private capital; M&A; private equity; and public sector. *"Roughly equal in size,"* each can provide trainees with much the same type of work – *"lots of ancillary documents, letters to clients, a bit of drafting"* and *"the company secretary element is huge."*

wake up and smell the horse hair

Having completed your compulsories, for your remaining three seats the options include energy and infrastructure, banking, insolvency, construction, employment, IT/IP and telecoms. The range of seats on offer is broadly the same across the firm's three offices but there are some local differences. In Sheffield, personal injury seats are available – *"a throwback to the days when we acted for British Coal. The firm acts for the defendant, the DTI, which has set up compensation schemes."* Three PI groups each deal with different claims from miners: vibration white finger damage from drill use, lung diseases and miscellaneous injuries, including noise claims. Reading, by contrast, specialises in IT/IP and London trainees may be offered a seat there if the smaller department in the capital is oversubscribed. They may also take an employment seat there if the London department is clogged up, and a secondment is offered to Oxford University.

The London office was described as *"very modern with nice wooden tables, cream carpets and black leather chairs."* Having been there we'd say this description underplays its qualities by some way. Some of our sources were diplomatic about, yet clearly not enamoured with, some of the modern art scattered around the building. Said one: *"I wouldn't have in it my living room!"* Much preferred was the IMA (that's informal meeting area), a *"very comfy, big coffee lounge"* with *"Starbucks-trained baristas"* (that's coffee grinders, not the wig-wearers. As far as we're aware, Starbucks has yet to become a BVC provider).

Nabarros trainees may however be running into future stars at the bar on their regular sojourns to The Square Pig, a favourite pub for BPP students. And the fun doesn't stop at the swine bar: *"We go to all the* local pubs nearby;" "Friday is when it always happens – you can bump into people from all across the firm and there's always someone you know in The Perserverance." Staff in the smaller Reading office tend to join in with the London gang for organised events such as the Christmas party. Or should that be the Yule party? Last year's December shindig had a winter solstice theme – "there were Druids everywhere." We're not aware that the regular weekday dress code at Nabarros is anything out of the ordinary, but flowing white robes would sure beat chinos for dress down Friday. A prize for the first law firm to introduce them.

When we asked the trainees up north about fun and games in Sheffield, we were told rather firmly that "it's not all Full Monty and dog racing!" Actually, we were thinking more cutlery and Peter Stringfellow, possibly combined in a display of knife throwing, but maybe that's just us. As "the office isn't really in the middle of town," the Friday tradition here is to go for lunch at the nearby Bluewater Café. The highlight of the year is a Cocktails on the Quay summer party. Last year, karaoke featured heavily: "The social committee got two groups of partners to perform acts. Five women partners dressed up as Spice Girls...actually, one of them was a bloke." Apparently, these five brave souls haven't been able to live it down since – "every time I see them I think of the humilation they endured," grinned one trainee.

ripping yarns

The firm's three offices seem remarkably chummy given the miles between them. For one trainee in London, "Reading is so connected that I don't think of it as different." All new recruits are inducted together in London, and at the start of the second year there's a trainee-bonding weekend in Sheffield. Last time round some of the London trainees even went up a night earlier to spend more time with their northern counterparts. Was the weekend a success? Well, lets just say the trainees are close enough now to be prepared to reveal some embarrassing stories about each other to complete strangers. Our particular favourite was this gem: "On the Sheffield weekend, we all went into this club and were dancing in a circle. One of the trainees decided to do air guitar on his knees and ripped his trousers – sadly they were the only pair he'd taken with him." Back in London, "there's always a bit of banter" as well as regular breakfasts (!) and lunches together. In fact, "we're always doing things together that aren't anything to do with work – dinner parties, drinks at the weekend, and of course, the fantasy football league."

and finally...

To return to our original question, 'what makes Nabarro Nathanson stand out?' it really depends on what you're looking for. Some might point to the strength in property, others to the well-connected family of offices, the size of the trainee intake or the general pleasantness of the place. Whatever you plump for, the single best thing you can do to up your chances of being invited on board at this happy (though not happy-clappy) firm is to apply for a vac scheme at one of its offices. When you hear that "they try to recruit 80% of the intake from the vac scheme, maybe even more," it kind of makes sense.

Nicholson, Graham & Jones

the facts

Location: London
Number of UK partners/assistants: 51/55
Total number of trainees: 20
Seats: 4x6 months
Alternative seats: Occasional secondments
Extras: Pro bono – Battersea Law Centre, language training

In the past, we've sometimes felt this balanced City mid-sizer was a bit of an everyfirm: solid work in core areas, good training, nothing too flashy. But changes are afoot at Nicholson Graham & Jones. With a new managing partner, and the distinct possibility that by the time you read this an amazing transformation into a branch of a US superfirm will have occurred, this Clark Kent is whipping off its glasses and wearing its underpants on the outside. In more ways than one...

tongue-twister

At the time of writing, NGJ was in advanced merger talks with US giant Kirkpatrick & Lockhart. Of course, we'd already been teased by news of negotiations with rapidly growing regional player Pinsents, but these broke down in January 2004. Our interviewees claimed that the firm wasn't on the rebound and that an American link up would be a better bet. *"Let's face it, the K&L prospects are a lot sexier than some Birmingham firm – I'd much rather have New York on my letterhead,"* said one. And not just New York; the stateside network of this corporate powerhouse spans San Francisco, Washington DC, Miami, Boston and Dallas. Whilst claiming the firm doesn't need a merger and attributing financial concerns to *"the recent downturn that hit all law firms,"* trainees certainly have stars and stripes in their eyes. Said one: *"I'm looking forward to the firm going international, getting larger and moving into more areas of work; they're also talking about an event over there and any excuse to go to a party in the US has to be a good thing."* How true!

NGJ is prepared to change its name, and the official line is that the firm will be christened Kirkpatrick & Lockhart Nicholson Graham. Quite a mouthful. Trainees told us: *"We're very clear that we'll be like Mayer Brown Rowe & Maw"* (also *"a bit of a tongue-twister"*) and felt confident that their merger would be equally painless. *"We're told there won't be cuts or legions of Americans in the office."* Apart from the prospect of the name, trainees had few reservations, although one cautious soul did admit: *"I am worried that I'll have Chad from Pittsburgh phoning me up at 3am.* Seven of the nine September 2004 qualifiers will have the chance to find out.

So what's in it for the Americans? Currently without a London office, K&L must like the look of the stable, evenly balanced 51-partner London firm. Especially as, despite a huge difference in size, the two firms have certain things in common, not least similar profitability and good real estate capability.

a spin around the block

NGJ's property group has a bias towards finance, and this year has worked alongside the firm's banking department for long-standing client HSBC on a £225 million acquisition of and term loan facility for the Mayfair Intercontinental Hotel. It also numbers Nationwide Building Society and Eagle Star Mortgages among its clients. Its straight property work tends to focus around redevelopment purchases and hotel and leisure work. A seat here is a virtual certainty, and NGJ also requires all trainees to gain corporate and litigation experience. Generally done in your first year, property is seen as *"a brilliant first seat as you get all your own files straight away."* It's the usual lease and licences negotiating, commercial sales, residential sales for *"eccentric rich people"* and planning or environmental work. One trainee freely admitted: *"My first two weeks in property were horrendous,"* but felt that diving straight in was *"the only way to learn."* Said another: *"I enjoyed the fact that after years of studying you're suddenly on the phone to the client. You learn quickly, but there's not too much pressure, so you have time to get to know the files."* You will also assist your supervisor on larger matters, giving you a taste of what life might be like ten years down the track.

In addition to small but respected partnership and private equity groups, the firm's corporate department includes a healthy M&A practice. The biggest deal of 2003 saw the firm acting for the purchaser on a £107 million acquisition of mining finance and development company, Shambhala Gold, but generally NGJ cruises along the corporate A-road doing deals from £20-100 million rather than the big-ticket motorway. AIM-listed clients bring in a lot of business, and some of the most valuable deals tend to be flotations on this exchange. As a trainee you'll do the usual proof reading, Companies House forms and board minutes, but *"there's not much tedious stuff and you do get a chance to liase with clients."* As well as AIM and a few FTSE-listed plcs, the department also acts for smaller companies and individuals. *"You get a cross section of clients, which makes things exciting."*

Trainees in litigation mostly assist on large matters, but also have a few small breach of contract or debt files to look after by themselves. There are significant banking and real estate litigation groups as well as an employment team and a small, but very successful, three-strong travel group, which generally takes one trainee at every rotation. Although in litigation your focus will be on your supervisor's cases, you won't be pigeon-holed – *"The firm encourages you to seek out the work you want to do...if it is available."*

get your kit off

After you've slogged your way through all that, the firm lets up and lets you pick pretty much anything else for your fourth and final seat. Options include construction or banking (which can also replace property or corporate as a core seat) as well as tax, environment, employment or the jolly sounding IP, technology and sport. This department generally deals with branding, sponsorship and IT matters as well as supporting corporate, property or litigation lawyers. On the hi-tech side, the firm represents several mobile phone companies and is acting for internet CD sales site CDWOW! in the defence of proceedings being brought against it by the British Phonographic Society. Sports-wise, clients include the PGA Tour, the National Greyhound Racing Club and Puma UK (in respect of its long-term kit sponsorship deal with Fulham Football Club). We asked if the department was full of football fans and golfers, but were simply told that although *"if you know about sport you will appreciate the seat more,"* *"you don't have to be a sports fan – there are even a couple of girls in here!"*

Across the firm, training seems to be uniformly solid in terms of responsibility and client contact. In each seat, as well as your supervisor, you'll be allo-

cated a mentor who'll ensure you get a balance of work and is available for advice (and a free lunch), if you ever need to chat. However, uniformity in all things is not to be assumed, and we got some intriguing answers when we asked whether there was any difference in atmosphere between departments. There seem to be several distinct personalities in the NGJ family. For instance, litigation is *"quite young, chatty and buzzy"* in contrast to the *"more conservative"* property, and both are considerably less *"testosterone-fuelled"* than corporate, which although not *"arrogant and blokey"* is *"male-dominated."* One male trainee quipped: *"I may come in one day in drag and try to be the second woman on the floor."*

on a manumission

Whilst all the trainees have the excellent academic records you'd expect, there are plenty of colourful details on their CVs as well. One trainee accepted that *"most law students are kind of anal, but none of us are geeky;"* certainly the firm's civilised hours (on average 9am–6pm) leave the trainees plenty of time to pursue extra-curricular interests. We heard about a *"sports freak,"* a former *"world number three at ballroom dancing,"* a keen amateur actor who *"whips out Shakespeare quotes from time to time"* and even an individual who *"does a great Britney Spears."* As a group, the trainees are close, and we even heard there's *"romance in the water"* (shouldn't that be air?). Even those who are just good friends are very good friends indeed. As well as Friday night trips to *"dodgy dives"* like the local All Bar One and Tiger Tiger, one intake recently spent a decadent weekend in Ibiza. *"It was a random thing to do; we all just booked flights and off we went."*

The races at Windsor and a pool competition have recently featured in the NGJ social calendar, but having been sorely disappointed that it was cancelled last year, what we really wanted to hear about was the firm's infamous country house weekend. This event, still fresh in the minds of trainees when we conducted our interviews, involves the whole firm decamping to Hertfordshire stately home

Ashridge. The Saturday was spent in teams making spoof promotional videos for the firm to be shown at the heroes and villains-themed dinner. Our sources admitted that it is *"quite disturbing"* to encounter *"people who you normally see in a suit being serious all day in tights and lycra."* As far as the partners are concerned, *"there's no messing about, they spend a lot of money on their outfits."* Spectators will have spotted Robin Hood, Scooby Doo and Catwoman *"in skin-tight leather."* Steady on...

and finally...

Who knows what the US merger will bring to life at Nicholson Graham & Jones? If it does go ahead, and if you're lucky enough to get invited to interview at the firm, we recommend you use the time to ask how things are changing. For our part, we'll be on hand next year to report on what we've uncovered.

Norton Rose

the facts

Location: London
Number of UK partners/assistants: 126/319
Total number of trainees: 152
Seats: 6x4 months
Alternative seats: Overseas seats
Extras: Pro bono – Tower Hamlets Law centre, FRU, death row appeals, language training

One of the big firms loitering with intent just below the magic circle, Norton Rose should be on your shortlist if you're looking to train at one of the international City powerhouses. Recruits can look forward to overseas seats and top salaries and all the usual trappings of the City big guns.

go team

Make no mistake, Norton Rose is a *"a banking specialist firm with a strong corporate team."* Performing well in a number of corporate and banking areas, this is a firm that means business, so if the gory bits of the *FT* make you shudder, look away now. Recently, the corporate finance department acted on HSBC's $1.3 billion acquisition of the Bank of Bermuda and its $815 million acquisition of Lloyds TSB assets in Brazil. Other household name clients include BMW, Citibank and new trophy client Nestlé, for whom the firm is now primary adviser on European M&A. The firm's market-leading asset and ship finance groups advise a host of international corporations in the transport sector including P&O, Stena, KLM and HSBC Rail. The projects department continues to be involved on the PPP of London Underground; following the £1.8 billion financing last year, the firm is currently advising on the project's refinancing. Just in case you haven't yet grasped Norton Rose's focus, we'll point out that well over 50% of its work is banking and corporate finance. Litigation weighs in at just under the quarter mark, and property and other supporting departments make up the remainder.

Each of the firm's departments is organised into teams, almost always constructed around the needs of particular groups of clients: *"The firm is trying to become more industry specific,"* explained one trainee. *"For example, in asset finance, there are a lot of aviation clients and so there is a team that just does aviation. Other firms might have a more general asset finance team. There are pros and cons both ways – elsewhere you might get more experience doing a wide range of things, but here you become more specialised early on."* One of the real benefits of the team system is that it keeps things cosy – trainees told us the firm feels a lot smaller than it actually is and is *"disarmingly informal."* Another thing that helps is a mentor system that pairs each recruit with a volunteer partner who can be approached for chats about training, qualification and even personal concerns.

dizzy

Norton Rose operates a notoriously complex six-by-four-month merry-go-round. Trainees love the flexibility and added opportunities of this system, and many of our interviewees cited it as their primary reason for coming to Norton Rose. *"The advantage of having more seats is that you can try more things out. Four months is enough time to get an experience of something and then you can revisit if you want or look at other aspects of the firm's work. There are no disadvantages."* Such an assessment is corollary to the comments about how specialised seats can be.

Explaining the complexities of the seat arrangement is something we dread every year, so pay attention at the back; we're only going to say this once...You'll do at least one seat in each of the firm's main departments in London: these 'core' seats are corporate, banking and litigation and they tend to be your first three seats but need not be. The fourth seat is a free choice (subject to availability) and the only restriction in terms of the timing of seats is that you must usually first do an area of work in London if you want to focus on it during a later seat abroad. Seats abroad are much encouraged as *"the firm's viewpoint is that we are an international firm and so the more experience trainees get abroad, the better."* After the fourth seat, you can home in on an area you'd like to qualify into. This could mean more time in your department of choice or, just as the firm has recognised the benefits of industry focus, you can too by attaching yourself to an industry and tracing it through different departments. *"You could look at shipping, say, from a banking, corporate and litigation perspective. The firm is happy for you to get lots of exposure in one area when you make it clear that that's what you're interested in, but you don't have to work this way."*

Doing a specialist seat, for example IP, tax or employment, is definitely an option but if these areas appeal to you, here's a word of caution. These departments, and even perhaps litigation, are very much seen as support departments within the firm. Trainees told us that those who come to the firm with a passion for these types of work may end up disappointed: *"People who are very set on support areas would be advised to go elsewhere. They are keenly sought after [by trainees]. You might not get a seat and you might not be able to qualify there."*

Perhaps because they recognised where they'd be spending the majority of their time, the people we spoke to were pretty happy with the seats they'd been allocated. *"I was very lucky to get all my first choices"* was a refrain we heard so often we were left concluding that the tortuous nature of the seating plan inspires less confidence in those good people in HR than it ought to. Frankly, we'd rather stick pins in our eyes than have the job of sorting out who goes where at Norton Rose, so all credit to those responsible.

getting to the 19th hole

At a firm this size, it's inevitable that the food chain on big deals will be a long one. *"Generally, work passes from a partner to an associate and then you get brought in."* This may translate into grunt tasks, on which subject one trainee said quite bluntly: *"Anyone who thinks they can be a trainee and not have to do bundling and bibling is deluding themselves. It's unrealistic to think you can just start off and for it all to be schmoozing and golf days from then on."* Nevertheless, our sources were sure that the right balance was being struck in the training, saying of supervisors: *"They make an effort to include you in what's going on."* Even in corporate and banking, where the majority of the deals are huge, you'll often be given your own mini-projects within those deals. *"It depends on the relationship and rapport you have with your supervisor, but quite a lot of the corporate team are good at giving work to trainees, especially as you rise through the ranks. Later on in the two years, they'll expect more of you and carve out a role for you."* You may even get your own small offshoot files to run yourself.

The hours can be long, so expect 9.30am–7.30pm as standard, and your share of late nights and a couple of weekends during the training contract. *"When you're a trainee, someone can come in and say 'This needs to be done' and you have to drop everything."* However, several of our sources loved the adrenaline rush of working on deals that hit the headlines and most were least enthusiastic about time spent in seats when things were quieter. In the worst case, we heard how one trainee in a corporate finance seat *"didn't get much experience and had to do a lot of research and updating of know-how files, and preparing board minutes."*

ice and a slice

"As soon as you go abroad the ball game changes." So said an ex expat after time in one of the firm's overseas offices. In the larger offices, you'll probably be assigned to a particular team, but in the smaller outposts, you'll be a 'floating trainee' and so get a chance to get involved in all the types of work that the office does. Norton Rose has long had interests overseas because of its focus on international trade and shipping, particularly ship finance. Hong Kong and Singapore are the hot destinations of the moment, and after hearing about weekends in Bali or Thailand, air-conditioned taxis to the office and a maid to do your ironing, we can understand why. With seven tickets to Asia up for grabs at each seat rotation, there's plenty to go round, and Bahrain, Dubai and European cities such as Frankfurt and Paris are also available. Most offices operate in English, so language skills, although helpful, are not the be all and end all. One of the few exceptions is the corporate finance seat in Paris, where the large number of local clients make French essential.

Back in London, the firm will continue to spread itself out over several buildings in the City until its likely shift in 2007 to the trendy Foster and Partners-designed SE1 development More London. Who knows what stylistic changes it will make when it acquires the new address – for now we'd say Norton Rose is still more gin and tonic than green apple martini. Suits are still worn in the office every day with dress down strictly reserved for charity events.

curiouser and curiouser

To get a handle on the character of a firm, we're fond of asking how you'd spot the trainees in question across a crowded bar. When we put this to team NR, the response of one interviewee was that *"they'd probably be drunk."* While we took this with the pinch of salt intended, we heard from other trainees that the firm has *"a very good social element."* We were, however, concerned to find that none of the final seaters we spoke to were aware that the traditional Monday-night free trainee bar in the office has for some time been taking place on Wednesdays. To be fair, these gatherings appear to be frequented primarily by those at the beginning of their training contracts as *"when you start, it gives you the opportunity to commune. It's a good way of getting people together who can then go on elsewhere. It breaks down barriers."*

At times, and as the final seaters we spoke to fully understand, the demanding nature of the job takes its toll on after-hours fun. As one pointed out: *"If you arrange to meet up at 7pm on a Friday, something can come up at 5pm and you can't just say you can't do it."* Run-of-the-mill socialising therefore tends to be informal and low-key, although there are always a couple of very popular organised events such as the summer ball, which this year was a riverside extravaganza with an Alice in Wonderland theme. *"The soup came in a teapot and one of the puddings was a tiny chocolate milkshake that said, 'drink me'"* Cute.

The popularity of sports ensures a full complement of teams. The rugby players are particularly keen and take part in Sevens at Durham University, a competition sponsored by the firm. *"The annual grudge match"* is against Freshfields, who beat them this year. Apparently *"fitness took its toll."* There was triumph as well as defeat, however, as Norton Rose's magnificent seven emerged victorious in the Law Society's championship. Football and hockey players prefer to keep it in the family at the annual Norton Rose World Cup, which as part of the firm's efforts to integrate its overseas network, brings together lawyers from the offices across Europe and Asia. In September 2004, 48 of the 63 qualifying trainees stayed with team NR.

and finally...

Teams are central to the way Norton Rose operates. Join the firm and your mission will be to find a team that suits your work interests, preferred hours and personality. But remember, although there are many to choose from, you're unlikely to stray far from the big-ticket corporate ballpark.

Olswang

the facts

Location: London, Reading
Number of UK partners/assistants: 79/129
Total number of trainees: 43
Seats: 4x6 months
Alternative seats: Brussels, secondments
Extras: Pro bono – Toynbee Hall and Tower Hamlets law centres, language training

Olswang was always seen as an impressive, but limited, firm targeting clients in the media, technology and telecommunications industries. The arrival of a raft of partners and staff from the now defunct DJ Freeman has helped it transform into a firm with broader appeal.

bonuses and balls

When Olswang burst on to the scene back in 1981, it was viewed with the sort of envious suspicion usually confined to parents who've discovered their neighbour's three-year-old already knows how to programme the VCR. Without using the manual. In the intervening years the firm certainly suffered some growing pains. At the height of the dot.com boom it expanded by an amazing 40% in one year. Then, abruptly, the growth spurt stopped, profits took a hammering, and recruitment and retention stats took a nosedive. Although this can largely be blamed on the crash of the tech market, it did give the impression that trainee numbers had been allocated by Guinevere the National Lottery machine.

Yet this didn't stop Olswang making some bold moves. When Andersen Legal imploded after the Enron debacle, the firm negotiated and finalised a deal to take over its Reading office within just two weeks. It seemed to epitomise the firm's approach: *"We're very progressive and move forwards very quickly. Although we're not much of a 'look before you leap' firm, we seem to get away with it."* The downside is that staff sometimes come to learn of the firm's plans on a *"fait accompli"* basis. Whatever the pros and cons, the bounce back is a fact – at the time of writing, the firm was busy posting a 30% increase in turnover.

newly weds

Naturally, part of this must be down to hiring the bulk of DJ Freeman's property team, a move that caused/enabled the firm to undertake a rebranding exercise. It now wishes to be known for offering a full service to the property industry as well as its existing stock of TMT clients. The trainees we spoke to showed pride in this new persona, saying: *"Our property client list is now ridiculous. I think we now act for all the major property developers, and have got the market largely covered."* With names like Green Property, Woolworths and Land Securities Trillium on the client roster, we're almost inclined to agree.

All the same, we wondered how well the new arrivals had fitted in at a firm that was always known for its quirky, meeja image. Although admitting that some of the new partners were *"slightly older and a little bit more conventional,"* trainees seemed to think that the firm's ambience had not become unbalanced. *"Property is certainly a more mature thing than schmoozing with glam media clients,"* said one; *"but it hasn't changed the distinctive feel of the firm. We're still very young and fast moving, but now we've got a broader commercial outlook."* Contrary to some reports (and its fake fur, all-singing, all-skateboarding grad recruitment material of years gone by) Olswang was never a hideout for disaffected film directors or potential pop idols. While some of those we spoke to bemoaned the disappearance of the *"old atmosphere,"* most thought

Olswang hadn't changed radically. Putting these differences of opinion aside, what is clear is that the firm has started to market itself differently – *"The image they are trying to project now is a lot more grown-up."*

the real world

Although there are no compulsory seats, we were told that avoiding a stint in corporate is impossible due to the size and importance of the department. The in-house name for the group is 'indigo', apparently because when they were trying to think of a name for the department, half the partners were wearing blue ties and the other half lilac. Just to confuse matters, the group has been further subdivided into 'black' and 'white'. One trainee kindly tried to explain the rationale for this, but quite frankly we gave up halfway through their answer. The main thing is that the clients these lawyers work for will make your mates in the pub sit up and listen to your work stories – Miramax, MTV, Channel 4, Twentieth Century Fox... *"You get to work for companies that you've heard of, stage concerts for bands that you listen to, and negotiate opposite TV channels you actually watch."* Yeah, yeah...pass the nuts.

One of our sources had observed that *"media people can be very, very demanding,"* and working in the corporate department, you have to be prepared to *"sign your life away"* at times...which is better news than you might think. Known for having an exceptionally hardworking environment in the boom years, the firm suffered from a paucity of work after the dot.com crash. It sounds as if the right balance is being struck these days. And what better way to cope with the rigours of a growing balance sheet than by fielding a young and vital workforce and management? Note exhibit A: chief executive Jonathan Goldstein, who was appointed at an age when most lawyers are still pushing to make partner. Actually, we can think of a better way – having a raft of really top-notch partners. Funnily enough, according to our colleagues at *Chambers UK*, Olswang's got exactly that too.

moule train

Trainees acknowledged that, inevitably, they had to roll their sleeves up for some *"document shovelling,"* but on the whole they were content with their lot. *"You may have to do some of the boring stuff, but it's being boring about the next Bond Film or the staging of the World Cup. You always have an interest in the underlying commercial business you're dealing with."* And although some reported that they didn't get as much client contact as they'd like, others observed that talking to clients wasn't necessarily the *"holy grail"* of a legal career and said other types of work could be far more rewarding. It's debatable.

It's a truism that some seats are more popular than others, so you need to get your message through to the good folk in HR from the outset. As well as the standard seats in corporate, litigation, property and TMT, the firm also offers secondments to a range of clients, which at various times have included the BBC, HIT Entertainment and Film Four. And then there's always the chance to go to Brussels, where the trainee *"lives like a king"* in the partner's own apartment.

In past years, there was a policy of making trainees spend three months in a 'know-how' seat, researching and writing articles and working on precedents. While some considered it *"a menace,"* others saw it as a useful addition to their training, especially if it fell in their first seat. The main objection seemed to be that this sword of Damocles could fall at any time and, in the worst-case scenario, split a favoured seat in half. The good news is that it is no longer compulsory for all.

barking up the wrong tree

In 2003, Olswang moved to new premises on High Holborn as it had outgrown its digs in Covent Garden. The new building was designed to look like the sail of a ship, though more mischievous trainees made various other comparisons. Its *"ergonomically designed"* interior includes breakout areas on each floor where you can grab a cup of coffee in the company of one of the intriguingly named *"relaxation plinth"* sculptures. Trainee food critics raised a glass to 'Ozone', the *"immaculate"* new canteen that offers good-quality subsidised food and serves right into the evening. Even so, we doubt it's appropriate for first dates or dinner with the parents. The building also has its own branch of Starbucks, known to be frequented on occasion by the rich and famous. Well, Kevin Spacey. When on a break from dog-walking duties. The Independent Police Complaints Commission has just rented two floors in the building, so who knows what this will bring in terms of sightings at elevenses.

The firm is notoriously hard to get into since it receives as many applications as Clifford Chance, but offers only a fraction of the number of TCs. To help you out, we've tried to identify what type 'the Swang' goes for. Some interviewees did their best to help us – *"In the MCT department there's an element of 'geek chic'. People are incredibly serious about the law, and there's still an element of the little-square-glasses syndrome."* But alas, others decried our attempts to lump them together – *"There's a complete lack of an Olswang stereotype. It's pretty obvious that the reputation for designer suits and little square glasses isn't true. That's just the sort of thing that people who write guidebooks talk about."* There was no point arguing the toss, so we'll leave the final word to the person who simply said: *"The trainees here are fun loving, ambitious, intelligent, witty and humorous. There's a definite spark about them. And they're also perhaps slightly irreverent."* In September 2004, 18 of the 27 qualifiers stayed with the firm.

Outside the office, the trainees described themselves as *"clannish, rather than cliquey."* Their natural habitats include Torts, The Square Pig (*"an 80s theme bar that time forgot"*) or the Chancery Court hotel for cocktails on special occasions. Never one to shy away from a party, the firm arranges social events on its seventh-floor veranda on high days and holidays such as Halloween and St Patrick's Day. Last year its Christmas party was held at Madame Tussauds, and no expense was spared in procuring a non-waxwork Kylie-a-like to sing after supper.

and finally...

Olswang offers the chance to do *"unbelievable"* work for household-name clients. If you like the idea of working with partners who know more about music downloads than you do, this could be a name to save on your Palm Pilot. However, never ever mistake the place for anything other than an ambitious and hard-working law firm. Choosing Olswang because you think it sounds cool is so last century.

Orchard

the facts

Location: London
Number of UK partners/assistants: 14/20
Total number of trainees: 5
Seats: 4x6 months
Alternative seats: None
Extras: Language training

Abundant with the fruits of its commercial labours, EC1's Orchard provides rich pickings for trainees interested in ripening in a smaller firm.

miracle gro

Since opening in 1995, Orchard has experienced almost 30% year-on-year growth, attracting lawyers from Clifford Chance, Freshfields, Macfarlanes, KLegal, Simmons & Simmons, Coudert Bros. and Morgan Cole. Is this bumper crop due to a mild winter, some particularly potent fertilizer, or something else...

One source poetically described Orchard as *"a diamond in the rough."* We think we understand: while you won't find socking great bling bling deals here, a closer look reveals good clients and valuable matters, with plenty of experts willing to show trainees how to cut their pears and arrange their roses. Corporate and litigation are *"on a par"* in terms of the setting and *"both are large and always fairly busy. They both punch pretty hard when they want to."* The firm acts for William Hill and the Bank of England.

among others, and handles corporate transactions for a variety of domestic and overseas clients. We spotted deals relating to Vietnamese mining concerns and Scandanavian hi-tech companies.

each peach pear plum

The four-seat contract introduces trainees to the firm's core areas – coco, litigation and commercial property. *"Technically, all are compulsory"* and the firm is *"cautious about letting people stray from the path."* However, trainees meet with variety within this arrangement; for example, there is TMT work within the corporate seat. If there's something in particular you want to try, and develop, *"it is up to you to approach certain partners and remain interested."* Generally, all trainees spend time in employment, though there is more flexibility here. When we called, one trainee was spending six months in New York, though *"it is not something common or written into the training schedule. You make your case and speak to appropriate people...it is up to you to put yourself forward."*

Coco and litigation are the favourites with trainees *"simply because you get a lot of work to do and can get some quite exciting stuff too."* In coco, larger deals afford less autonomy, but trainees assured us that while *"you have a smaller part,"* it is *"a relevant part, not photocopying."* Alongside standard corporate and commercial transactions there are more glamorous media and IP matters. Litigation provides trainees with *"quite a lot of face-time in court"* and a juicy mix of construction, shipping, media and IP cases, including breach of copyright and passing off issues and some regulatory work. Orchard is also on the Law Society's panel for interventions and litigation, and a trainee in the department is automatically awarded the title of Head of Debt Collection, something that leads to a steady diet of *"good salt-of-the-earth trainee work."*

In commercial property too there is plenty of responsibility – one trainee explained: *"When you walk in there's a filing cabinet and that's basically your baby for the duration of your seat."* After a quick recap

on the subject of birds and the bees, we established that trainees *"cut their teeth on residential matters"* and are then involved in commercial leases and sales and licensing work for pubs and restaurants. Property is the firm's smallest team, and for trainees this translates into *"the highest pressure."* In employment by contrast, work *"comes in fits and spurts,"* but a large sex discrimination case had kept our sources on their toes, along with drafting compromise agreements for major investment banks, plus business immigration and general corporate support tasks.

white christmas

Describing their first day at the firm, one trainee told us: *"I came in, got a quick tour of the building, and then there was research on my desk before lunchtime for a tribunal the same week."* Recent changes to the induction process have poured cold water on this baptism of fire, and trainees now also benefit from an ongoing programme of weekly seminars. A *"large pool"* of paralegals means that grunt work is a rarity for trainees, who are encouraged to delegate bum jobs. When these just have to be done, *"everyone chips in and helps out."* For the record, we heard that *"more than once one trainee has had a deal on and four others have given up four nights to stay until 3am to help them."* Why? *"Because they all want to learn."* And Orchard offers *"a very supportive atmosphere for teaching."* Trainees usually share a room with their supervisor and mid and end-of-seat reviews keep them apprised of their progress. If feeling out of your depth, *"you just put your hand up and say so; no one expects you to know everything."* Moreover, partners *"give you whatever time you need,"* even though *"their time is worth gold dust."*

Always *"deemed to be a stop-gap"* the firm's premises on Snow Hill under Holborn Viaduct will struggle to contain everyone for much longer. One source admitted: *"It does creak a bit – you cross your fingers when you get in the lift!"* Lacking the self-conscious installations of its close neighbour Lovells, the interior lends itself to a *"slightly homey feel;" "there are no Rembrandts, but still some pretty nice things to look at."*

keep it in the family

We quite often hear firms described as 'family-friendly' but one trainee went a step further and described managing partner David Orchard as *"a bit like your dad really."* Apparently, *"people just love him,"* although like any good parent he is *"strict, and knows when to be serious and when to have fun."* Despite tempting analogies with the extended Olivio patriarchy, dining en familia in their abundant Tuscan garden, we were assured that at Orchard *"there really is no hierarchy."* Each day starts at 9am with a departmental meeting to discuss everyone's workload and for trainees it usually ends at a respectable 6pm, often *"with the senior partner asking you why you're still there."*

A recently established fee earner's forum also finds a representative from every level from 5 years PQE right down to paralegals sitting down together to put forward concerns, issues and discuss strategy proposals. They also manage to sit down together fairly frequently in one or other of the firm's *"second meeting rooms"* – The Bishop's Finger and The Butcher's Hook – and the managing partner's daughter often joins them after work for a pint. The annual Christmas party took place in a restaurant in nearby Smithfields last year and at events like this partners are *"relaxed around their junior staff, and some like to let go – there are no equity partners sitting in the corner smoking pipes!"* Less uninhibited, however, the trainees revolted when someone proposed they perform a revue; *"a secretary sang instead, which was much better."* Throughout the rest of the year there are occasional golf days, nights at the dogs and football games.

Despite their reluctance to make fools of themselves in front of the entire firm at the Christmas party, the Orchard trainees aren't wallflowers. *"We're not all mad or anything, but we are all proactive and have personality – you can't just sit in the corner here."* Indeed not – these are enterprising self-starters

who had organised their own secondments abroad, set up international corporate charity projects, arranged and executed a successful marketing initiative, co-ordinated recruitment projects and set up a new training schedule. All our sources had made an informed decision to opt for the smaller City experience, and, in Orchard, had seized the opportunity to flourish as entrepreneurs and marketeers as well as lawyers. Both of the September 2004 qualifiers stayed with the firm.

and finally...

Planted in the shadows of the City powerhouses, Orchard is a tiny shoot of a firm that will suit someone with the drive and desire to help their employer grow bigger.

Osborne Clarke

the facts

Location: Bristol, London, Reading
Number of UK partners/assistants: 85/190
Total number of trainees: 40
Seats: 4x6 months
Alternative seats: Overseas seats, secondments

The after-effects of the technology crash pushed self-confessed TMT nut and would-be global law firm Osborne Clarke into turbulent waters. But a recent 30% profits rebound suggests that new managing partner Simon Beswick's practice-broadening approach is reaping dividends.

tiger tiger burning bright

The firm's logo depicts a prowling cat of some sort, though whether it be jaguar, puma, lionness or domestic moggy is beyond us. In fact, it seems to be beyond everyone. What is beyond doubt is that Osborne Clarke roared into the limelight by hitching its fortunes to the explosive, exponentially growing star of the 90s – the technology sector. OC sprang jaws first at the market, capturing internet, computing and technology companies by offering a first-grade TMT service backed up by all-round commercial prowess. Encouraged by turbo-charged growth in Bristol, Reading and London, the firm opened in Silicon Valley and cultivated a European network. It's hunting grounds stretched from California to the Baltic Rim.

Feasting heads-down on the market, the firm's management failed to spot the approaching technology crash. As the sector was reaching critical mass, OC continued to recruit heavily and paid a stiff price when TMT went supernova and collapsed in on itself. Over 20 partners (many of them from the London office) chose or were pushed to fly, not fight. Criticisms about OC having neglected its Bristol heartland and a slump in profits followed.

A new managing partner, Simon Beswick, ushered in a phase of stock taking, consolidation and retrenchment, which is beginning to bear fruit. Although TMT remains a key part of OC's business, with work for Vodafone on its link-up with BT one of its most important instructions of the past year, the firm has been pursuing a more diversified business plan. Similarly, there has been an internal shift back to the specific strategic importance of each UK office. *"The new mantra is One Firm, Three Offices,"* revealed one of the trainees we interviewed.

The OC of 2004 is also attempting a balancing act between its regional, national and international priorities. The Frankfurt office may have defected to Taylor Wessing last year, but the Cologne arm remains; indeed, the firm's European network of allied law firms is stronger than many possessed by other top 40 UK firms. In addition to formal friendships in Barcelona, Madrid, Brussels, Paris, the Netherlands, Russia and the Baltic, OC now boasts connections in Brescia, Milan and Rome. Significantly, OC's Silicon Valley office remains integral to the firm's plans, picking up instructions locally for work on the English end of Anglo-American technology deals. Recent advice to NASDAQ-listed US data management corporation Informatica on an acquisition of rival Striva is illustrative. Not least because trainee secondments to Cologne and California are available, our sources reflected contentedly that there is still an international flavour to OC. The more commercially astute also saw its vital significance in the rehabilitative process. Said one: *"The angle of working for European and US clients is invaluable, especially for the London office. Apart from anything else US, firms can see us as a one-stop shop for the Continent."*

the IT bone's connected to the...

In order to review the fortunes of the firm, we've had to sacrifice the page anatomising the range of responsibilities and experiences on offer to trainees in the wealth of seats at their disposal. Instead we're just going to list the seats available – banking, commercial property, commercial litigation, competition, construction, corporate/private equity/M&A, employment, general commercial, health and safety, insolvency, IT/IP, licensing, media and entertainment, natural resources, pensions and share schemes, and tax. Not forgetting those popular overseas seats and secondments to a variety of clients. Whether it's working for giants like 3i in private equity, receiving instruction from wind farm developers in environmental, acting for HSBC, Bank of Ireland, Coutts & Co or Abbey National in banking, assisting on deals for massive developers such as Birse Construction or Gazeley Properties (the property arm of Asda-Walmart) in construction, or even American software companies in commercial litigation, OC offers anything and everything to satisfy the most voracious trainee appetite.

While trainees are recruited specifically to each of the UK offices, they are *"really encouraged"* to take one of their four six-month seats in another. Although trainees had shuttled in all directions for seats, this year's interviewees noticed a marked brain drain from Bristol to London. *"Quite a few people have gone there for one seat and been drawn in by City life."* Proof that the one-firm feel across offices is gathering force is evinced in one Bristol trainee's lament: *"I wish I'd gone to London for a seat, even if just to get to know people there."* Our sources were generally satisfied with arrangements for rotation, but there are *"often pile-ups around commercial litigation,"* which can result in seats split 50-50 between litigation and another area such as private equity – hardly likely to satisfy a contentious appetite. Certain seats, like film financing in London, are understandably popular, but even those who found themselves making up the numbers in property or licensing were philosophical, saying: *"It might not be your preferred area, but the skills you learn as a lawyer make it great training."*

chickens and eggs

Overall, our sources were very satisfied with the responsibility and attention they were given. *"It's an inclusive, involving atmosphere that encourages you to turn up to work,"* said one. As well as regular briefings from the managing partner, frequent meetings with HR and a firm-wide trainee forum in which to raise issues, our sources enjoyed the *"clarity and transparency,"* which they'd been promised in OC's promotional literature. Open-plan offices mean *"there is little visible hierarchy,"* and *"you don't feel like you should treat partners differently."* By the same token, *"although our no-nonsense reputation varies a bit between departments, the firm tries to be straight up and say what it thinks;" "we're quite good at admitting when things go wrong."* On a day-to-day basis that means trainees are happy to put the duller duties in context; one told us of *"a sense that when you do important work, what you do will carry weight."* That sense found a good illustration in this trainee's experience – *"At a client meeting I came up with a point that shaped the negotiations – afterwards my supervisor took me aside to say 'well done.'"*

In a classic chicken-or-egg scenario, trainees describe each other in equally no-nonsense terms. *"We're bullish and communicative." "Headstrong isn't* quite the word, but there's just an outgoing, ambitious feel to everyone."* Academic excellence is apparently *"a given,"* but the firm wants *"bright, enthusiastic, commercially switched-on types, not five-As, First-from-Cambridge, can-recite-EC-directives bores."* We hear you crystal clear. There are currently substantially more female trainees than male (*"HR says it's because the girls just do better on the assessment days"*), but aside from a tendency for Bristol trainees to have a connection to the South West, there is a fair degree of variety in the group. *"We've got public school Oxford types and state school Manchester or Cardiff types."* Perhaps most tellingly, *"they're all people you would want to be friends with; we often go away at weekends together."*

the indisputable....

Without doubt London and the Thames Valley office (TVO) in Reading play Benny and Choo Choo to Bristol's Top Cat; because of its size, dominant position in the local market and status as the historical centre of the firm, the Bristol office is *"inevitably the most important."* In marked contrast to last year, trainees told us: *"London is recovering in atmosphere and importance."* A move to new premises at One London Wall will finally unite all departments in the capital under one roof. Back home, Bristol trainees don't live in a dustbin: far from it. Their relatively new home has ample space, breakout rooms and a glass atrium that stretches from top to bottom. *"It divides all the floors into two sections with walkways across the atrium...it's really beautiful."* Less aesthetically minded trainees told us of a daily battle with their dark side: *"It's so tempting to throw a cup of coffee from the top walkway."* TVO shares a building with companies such as 3i and Ernst & Young in the centrally located Apex Plaza. Not to be outdone by Bristol, there is also an atrium here, but this one is *"filled with enormous palm trees; it's bizarre."* Whichever office they were in, trainees were emphatic that *"it does feel like the same firm across the offices."*

the oc

We had to ask – is the social life of the firm like that of its namesake California-based soap: all shiny, leggy people engaged in complex relationships with each other, each other's mothers, brothers, sisters and husbands? It seems not. The most outrageous it gets is one male trainee playing for the netball team.

There is an almost endless list of things to do in Bristol: "*sailing, cricket, rugby, netball, firm drinks, outings, weekends away...*" The Severn Shed is "*the flavour of the month*," although the connoisseur's choice is the Cornubia "*for a nice bitter.*" In TVO things are "*pretty quiet*" socially, not least because "*a lot of people commute from London.*" If it is after-work pubs you want, London is the best place to be: "*We like Chambers, Corney & Barrow, All Bar One, the Magpie & Stump...*" With the move to new offices, these locals may change but we doubt it will take long for a new portfolio to become established. In 2004, the firm-wide summer party took a Grease theme "*with fairground rides, a big wheel, dodgems, a BBQ and plenty to drink.*" It sounds like a sick-making combination to us, but by all accounts it was "*a beautiful evening, a really good atmosphere, and it really felt like the recent difficulties were completely gone.*"

We haven't mentioned much about the effect on trainees of the past few years' difficulties because our interviewees felt "*shielded from them*" and as though "*the worst passed before we arrived.*" As a sign of increasingly prosperous times, there were more NQ jobs than qualifiers in September 2004. Eleven of the 13 stayed.

and finally...

Osborne Clark has worked hard to put its house in order and balance out its regional, national and international priorities. Applicants with their hearts set on Bristol or Reading have less to weigh up as the firm sits comfortably at the top of the tree in these cities. Those with an eye on London might want to factor in the firm's style and practice strengths when surveying their options in the City.

Pannone & Partners

the facts

Location: Manchester
Number of UK partners/assistants: 77/90
Total number of trainees: 22
Seats: 4x6 months
Alternative seats: None

A self-styled "complete law firm," Pannone & Partners seems to have everything going for it: an impressive list of clients spanning commercial and private practice, and sustained growth including a 20% rise in profits in 2003/4. And heaven forbid that we forget about the firm's sixth-place gong in this year's '*Sunday Times* 100 Best Companies to Work For' survey.

winning formula

It's not that the *Student Guide* suffers from misanthropy or envy, nor does it succumb to tall poppy syndrome; in fact, we like to consider ourselves suitably even-handed in the best journalistic traditions of George Orwell and Harry Harris. However, when faced with such a unified equation of profits, happiness and all-round success we can't help being challenged to test its logic to the limit. So we set out to discover whether everything really is rosy in the garden of Pannone.

The trainees we spoke to were unanimous in their praise of a firm that offers an exciting variety of work and the opportunity to exercise ambition in a warm environment. "*It offers a good halfway house between commercial and private client work,*" one stated, whilst another added: "*It's not a high street firm, but it's big without being faceless.*" Hailing from a variety of backgrounds (a North West connection isn't a must), these are "*diverse, down-to-earth,*" sociable types, "*confident individuals*" with a communal urge. And possibly greased to the tune of a £5 tip, one trainee whispered in our shell-like that the firm stresses "*human connections with clients in terms of making and retaining business.*"

accidental heroes

On the private client side, it all adds up: PI, clinical negligence, employment, trusts and probate, family, liquor licensing and residential property departments equate to a clear focus on the individual. PI is the largest department, the traditional backbone of the firm, if you will. Showing no desire to let up on the pace, in 2004 it successfully tendered for referrals from the AA's accident insurance arm, which will mean an extra 4,500 cases each year. According to our sources, this has prompted the firm to shore up the department with extra paralegals...to the benefit of trainees who gleefully told us: "*The lower level work is run by paralegals, so we miss out on sprained ankle cases.*" The knock-on effect is that trainees now spend more of their time assisting partners on more complex claims and less on running their own small files. Autonomy has been traded for interest: "*I was assisting on cases where people were seriously injured with things like spine injuries. It was morally satisfying getting them compensation.*"

Another consequence of the changes in the PI department is that, although common, a seat there doesn't appear be compulsory anymore, although those eyeing the much-prized clinical negligence seat were keenly aware that a stint in PI can offer them a leg-up. The clin neg department has recently acted on claims brought by individual claimants against plastic surgeons, group actions by soldiers suffering from Gulf War Syndrome and victims of the 2003 outbreak of Legionnaires disease in Barrow.

hard luck stories

Much of the employment department's work is also referred from legal insurers, and a trainee's experience would typically include running smaller applicant cases on sex or race discrimination and unfair dismissal. The trainees we interviewed had also assisted seniors on large-scale respondent cases, with several noting that "*there seems to be a general move to more commercial employment law.*" The

department certainly acts for some well-known clients, including Kellogg, Texaco and the Bank of England.

Trainees amused us with their description of the privately paying family law clientele. "*The Cheshire set*" is their cover-all term for a group that includes everything from Range Rover-driving, pashmina-wrapped, countryside rahs, to Range Rover-driving, Gucci-wrapped footballers' wives. Child custody disputes, educational choice cases, divorces – it's all there. And it must be lucrative because Pannones is opening a satellite office in Hale so those sporty 4x4s don't have to grapple with central Manchester traffic.

corporate ho!

When trainees told us that Pannones' private practice is keen to be seen as "*caring, cuddly and user-friendly,*" we wanted to know if the equally important commercial stream was seen in the same way. If the firm's saintly halo were to slip anywhere, surely it would be here in cut-throat world of Manchester commercial law?

The fact that the corporate department experienced a 25% growth in profits in its 2003/4 financial year suggests Pannones isn't observing a softly-softly approach. However, trainees emphasised that whilst trying to keep pace with competitors like DLA, Addleshaw Goddard or Halliwells, the firm stays true to itself. "*We market ourselves as user-friendly, reacting appropriately to the situation, but not aggressive for aggression's sake.*" A seat in corporate equates to everything from general commercial advice for established clients, to specific IP and IT matters, M&A and equity financing. Here, you might find yourself registering trade marks all over the world for Cotton Traders, working on national asset exchange transactions for companies like Texaco, or working on the AIM admission of a big-fish Manchester client such as Community Broking Group

As a trainee in commercial litigation, you should

experience a good balance between assisting on big cases and having small cases of your own to "*cut your teeth on.*" The department works on general commercial contract and tort actions, landlord and tenant, insolvency and defamation. Cases handled by the department include everything from a judicial review brought by the Mink Farmers' Association concerning legislation which outlaws their trade, and acting for MonsterMob, the market leader in ringtones, in a copyright infringement case.

hot pannone

Reflecting on a *Sunday Times* survey that effectively labels Pannones the nicest law firm in the country, one source admitted that "*the stuff in the paper was the kind of rhetoric that a lot of firms put out. But it is all true.*" Of course, no firm is a Utopia: "*We live in the real world – tempers get frayed and sometimes a lot of work gets dumped on you.*" But even this doesn't alter the fact that Pannones' trainees seem to get a very good deal. For a start the firm sometimes bends over backward to accommodate seat preferences: last year it added an extra employment seat. Formal training, appraisals and general support were each described as excellent, and whilst most trainees didn't sit with partners, the following, slightly incredulous, comment reflected general experience: "*I've had positive feedback from partners apropos of nothing!*" Another source told us: "*The most formal it gets is knowing that your supervisor is busy, and waiting for an hour to ask for help.*"

With "*space at a premium*" the "*warren-like*" Deansgate offices were mentioned as an area for improvement, but the firm clearly works incredibly hard on the feel-good factor. If it meets a target, a team is rewarded with cakes, extra days' holiday, departmental meals and, most importantly, bonuses.

As well as having an influential and much-admired female managing partner, Joy Kingsley, women at Pannones outweigh men two to one. We left it up to one (typically) articulate trainee to suggest that there may be a link between this fact and the way the firm operates. "*With so many females, it's definitely less hierarchical than it might otherwise be...it's a meritocracy and there is a very understanding environment.*" To our mind this next comment captures the firm – "*It's cyclical: the firm presents itself as approachable and personal, that's reflected in the kind of people hired and they perpetuate the firm's approach.*"

the family that plays together stays together

Time for a quick comment from Joy Kingsley: "We do not believe that working very long hours on a permanent basis serves either our clients' interests, or makes for very interesting colleagues!" Typical corporate rhetoric you might think, but with Pannones it seems that dreams do come true. Step up Trainee X: "*I came in one Sunday at a busy time, and was e-mailed the next day by my training partner telling me not to make a habit of it!*"

The social scene is excellent, with a committee organising events from simple drinks to a night at the dogs. Trainees regularly head off to city centre bars including The Hogshead and the very chichi Living Room, although we were told Friday's dress-down code means getting in to the latter can be difficult. Throw in firm-organised shopping trips to Edinburgh and 'football' (read 'shopping') tours to play European partner firms in the Pannone Law Group, and we wonder how anyone ever gets any work done. Adding everything up, it comes as no surprise that seven of the nine trainees kept it in the family and stayed with the firm when they qualified in 2004.

and finally...

Nicely is as nicely does. If you want to keep your options open with a balance of private and commercial work, if you fancy a warm working environment and if you possess the talent and charm to get on Pannones' shortlist, then get in line.

Payne Hicks Beach

the facts

Location: London
Number of UK partners/assistants: 28/23
Total number of trainees: 4
Seats: 4x6 months
Alternative seats: None
Extras: Pro bono – Wandsworth Law Centre

LONDON. Trinity Term lately over. Implacable July weather. Hard by Temple Bar by Lincoln's Inn Hall, at the very heart of the drizzle, sit the Payne Hicks Beach trainees in 10 New Square. For venerable private clients, country estates and complex family matters, PHB gives a modern spin to a classic Dickens plot.

jarndyce v jarndyce

Commanding the attentions of illustrious clients and excelling in established areas, PHB traces its origins back to 1730. As one trainee reminded us: "*Tradition is very important. The firm is proud of its image and trades off it.*" The comment that "*the senior partner is at least 105, and other partners have been here for even longer*" was nothing more than a joke by a mischievous trainee, yet it is true that PHB is wholly, utterly established. The firm is in "*the same place it has always been, and the client base is very settled. You know it will have the same make-up and feel for a long time to come.*" Without doubt, "*PHB is comfortable in its own skin.*"

All that said, the firm has replaced the lingering smell of mothballs with the enticing aroma of contemporary issues. PHB's private client lawyers supplement a work base of historic and landed families (they are involved with the administration of the estate of Francis Bacon) with entrepreneurial types from both the UK and abroad. The family team was involved in the landmark case of White v White and a recent addition to the team, Fiona Shackleton, acted for Prince Charles in his divorce. Our interviewees felt the private client and family work set the tone for the firm, and while sensitive or prolific work affords them less autonomy, both offer a great deal of client contact.

please sir, can I have some more?

A traditional four-seat training contract gives trainees a free run of the firm's practice areas. We like the logic of a system that essentially means: "*In the first year you say what you don't want to do; then in the second year you say what you do want to do.*" Small firms are usually very good at such bespoke tailoring, and PCB is no different. The scheme is "*personalised and directed at the individual,*" and trainees get to see hand-stitched law take shape...even if that sometimes means a whole day of holding the tape measure.

As well as family and private client work, PHB offers its trainees spells in company/commercial, property and dispute resolution. The coco clientele largely comprises family businesses and private companies won off the back of the firm's private client base. Here, trainees experience "*very wide-ranging, general work*" plus non-contentious employment matters. In property, commercial clients such as Centrica Plc rub shoulders with agricultural estates and provide trainees with "*a big pile of your own files.*" In litigation, the Bloody Sunday and Guildford Four inquiries prompted the comment that "*the quality of work is superb,*" though inevitably, "*on the big stuff your role is fairly restricted – you are supporting the partners.*" But on the little stuff, one source enthused: "*They are happy for you to jump on the phone to a client and get involved – it makes you feel like a proper lawyer.*"

what's in a name?

The official working day is 9.30am–5.15pm and "*there's no feeling if you leave at 5.30pm that you've been naughty.*" More than that, "*partners are very fixed that you don't work by yourself in the office.*" All trainees share an office with a supervisor, except in the family team where trainees share their very own cubbyhole with the printer. Three-monthly appraisals and weekly training seminars keep the youngsters on their toes and the partner-led supervision ensures *"you're not out on a limb."*

Names. We've all got them, and usually they make life easier. Not so at PHB. *"One partner likes to be referred to as 'Mr', but everyone else you call by their first names."* And that's the problem. Our sources had all chosen to train at a small firm where trainees aren't just a number and *"people know your name."* However, they're *"all called Anna, and there's a million Fionas."* This has led to particular problems in the family department, where there are so many Fionas that in a cruel twist of fate they are now known by numbers.

fishy tales

The firm is *"very proud"* of its New Square base in the heart of legal London. Apparently, *"it looks wonderful, but makes terrible offices."* Our sources were philosophical about the lack of air con and central heating, and one nostalgically recalled a candle-lit client meeting during a power cut. With gas lamps on the square outside, oil paintings of former partners in the boardroom, *"old books everywhere"* and even rumours of a ghost in the post room, this is about as far removed from Feng Shui inspired minimalism as the 21st century affords. Unsurprisingly, PCB's address features in various films including *A Fish Called Wanda* and the genre classified as *"costume dramas with Colin Firth in them."* Nearby, the Knight's Templar offers good ale, and the occasional quiz evening or wine tasting brings out the fun side of the firm. Tennis, cricket, hockey and the Manches Cup sailing regatta keep the sporty types active and out of the danger zone on the scales. A good job, as every week PHB's in-house cook, FiFi, lays on a lunchtime spread for all.

The official dress code is a smart contemporary affair, that's designed to keep the clients happy. Good manners also do the trick. Generally, our sources had followed the fast track straight through school, university and law school and described themselves as *"mostly middle class, mostly privately educated and just averagely normal,"* additionally cautioning readers to *"not bother applying if you're pretty whacky – it is not a whacky kind of firm."* Indeed, PHB offers your classic Court of Chancery experience. Sadly, in 2004 the one NQ job on offer was not accepted, so none of the three qualifiers remain at the firm.

and finally...

The real beauty of a Payne Hicks Beach training is that, if you identify with the firm's practice, clients and style, you can sign on the dotted line knowing that it will all be there waiting for you on your first day...and for years to come.

Penningtons

the facts

Location: Basingstoke, Godalming, London, Newbury
Number of UK partners/assistants: 60/86
Total number of trainees: 24
Seats: 4x6 months
Alternative seats: None

Offering both commercial and private client services from London and three regional offices in the south of England, Penningtons is just the thing for the student who is unwilling to opt for one or other side of the law before trying their hand at either.

pie chart in the sky?

The following breakdown of Penningtons' activities gives us a clue why its trainees emphasise the rounded nature of their training. Property accounts for 34% of the firm's revenue, litigation 30%, corporate and commercial 18% and private client 18%. To be more specific, the firm's mission statement declares a desire to be a leading firm in commercial property, employment, clinical negligence, private client, and professional regulation and healthcare. It additionally wants to be top dog in Berkshire, Hampshire and Surrey. With goals so broad and bold, is Penningtons harking back to its glory days in the 1980s? Are we witnessing a resurgence of fortune

One trainee tried to have their cake and eat it when we asked about the firm's style. *"It's forward-looking but with traditional values,"* they told us. Perhaps what they meant was that the firm is determined to cater to clients who have been with the firm for many years, whilst also appealing to new businesses and organisations. This year, as last, we found ourselves debating a process of change at Penningtons. One NQ remarked: *"The firm has definitely changed in the time I have been here. When I arrived there were a lot of partners in their 50s and 60s and not so many younger fee earners. It is a lot bigger now and it has practically doubled at partner level."* Younger partners are entering the sphere of influence, and experienced lawyers looking to break away from larger City firms have been hired. Turnover has grown, and this in turn is bolstering a renewed sense of pride and confidence. Nevertheless, some trainees felt the firm should be portrayed as *"fairly traditional still. It is well-established and partner-led...partner-heavy even."*

Whereas 12 months before, trainee opinion was split on whether Penningtons was pushing and marketing itself hard enough, this year our sources all had a neatly laminated copy of its business plan on their desks. In trainees' minds, the firm is a name to be reckoned with. It may not be the biggest City player, but size isn't everything they told us. Penningtons acts for some substantial international clients – India's transportation giant Tata and banana kings Fyffes/Geest to name but two – but most are of the smaller, domestic variety. It additionally concentrates on the healthcare sector, acting for professional bodies such as the Royal College of Veterinary Surgeons, the Nursing and Midwifery Council and the General Chiropractic Council.

making the right connections

Penningtons' profile is broad in all offices, so trainees can opt for any of them, safe in the knowledge that a fulsome training is guaranteed. That said, certain offices have particular specialsisms. PI and clin neg, for example, are to be found only in Godalming and Basingstoke.

It's odds on that trainees will see the inside of the property and litigation departments, as these are the firm's largest; in the out-of-London offices especially, a private client seat is also likely. Reassuringly, trainees who were drawn from the outset to certain kinds of work were generally able to swing two seats in the relevant department. There was high praise for the recruitment team, who make a big effort to get to know trainees: *"Andrea Law even has us over for Sunday lunch sometimes."* There's just one major criticism relating to the firm's tendency to be *"strict and archaic"* on the IT front. *"You can't access hotmail – not even at lunch – and they have insane firewalls, so often you can't read attachments."* Sounds fixable.

The London private client team cares for large trusts and handles probate for high net worth families. *"One client is worth an excessively large amount of money,"* a source revealed. In litigation, when not managing smaller matters solo, trainees try to be as useful as possible to as many people as possible. Recalling his time there, one reported: *"I was drafting all the letters, statements of claim and other documents on my own files. I also did a couple of applications in court in front of a master."* A far cry from the experience in the big firms, trainees don't tend to take on the role of chief photocopier and bottle washer. *"I did my own bundling and the photocopying on my own files, but not other peoples."*

rash decisions

In London and elsewhere, *"partners always make time for a trainee if needs be, and it's very much appreciated because we all know their time is much sought-after."* The relationship between a Penningtons trainee and their supervisor is worthy of special mention because, with just one exception, all our sources were bowled over by the extent to which seniors involved them in work. Commonly second or third in the chain of command on a deal, corporate seat trainees found themselves at best solely responsible for due diligence exercises, and at worst shadowing a partner to meetings. *"How else do you pick things up?"* one mused.

Once a month on 'First Mondays' (actually it's now the second Monday, but no one has thought of a better name) the out-of-town trainees converge on the London office for a training seminar, swiftly followed by a drink or two in the Slug and Lettuce. This pub is the favourite, although one of the partners maintains *"an infatuation for Balls Brothers below the office,"* which trainees find baffling. *"It's painful there. I think I'm allergic to it,"* said one.

the godalming goldmine

We extend our thanks to the trainee who told us how legend has it that, on a visit to Godalming, Peter the Great's entourage of 20 Russians caused a riot at the King's Head pub. These days, the pretty, commuter-belt citadel of wealth is less turbulent, so much so that one trainee suggested we bill it as *"the Monte Carlo of Surrey."* Chris Evans and Billie, Sue Barker, Damon Hill and Anthea Turner are some of the high rollers who live there – no wonder there's a thriving private client practice *"with a large tax-planning element to the work."*

In the claimant PI and clin neg department, cases relating to serious injuries caused by medical mishaps can go on for years, which means *"you'll only see all aspects of a case by reference to different files."* Sometimes *"it can be upsetting, but like a doctor, you grow immune to it."* Had a holiday from hell? Mowed down the town mayor en route to hospital after a food-poisoning outbreak at your cockroach-infested hotel? Why not pop over to see Penningtons' travel and tourism litigators, who until recently operated as the well-known specialist firm Andreas & Co.

Socially, it's lunches with select office friends rather than big boozy nights because *"most people drive to work."* On the plus side, you're likely to develop rewarding friendships...it's that kind of place.

the hampshire hug

Keen to distinguish Penningtons from the thick soup of provincial high street firms *"where lawyers are sitting in cardigans with pipes and muddling through,"* one Basingstoke trainee assured us that *"our business clients can see we are a very commercial firm."* Doubtless the firm's relocation to new purpose-built offices reinforced this impression in the minds of loyal local enterprises and London-based companies seeking value for money. The corporate department has grown under the helm of office managing partner, Franco Bosi, who *"encourages family life and a friendly atmosphere. He's very approachable and he's indicative of the way Penningtons is going."* As comforting as chicken noodle soup, one trainee's description of supervising partners made each sound like a cross between a life coach and an old form tutor. *"If you need support – emotional support even – you get it."*

The ubiquitous private client department has that extra je ne sais quois due to the presence of two dual-qualified UK/French lawyers who work closely with the firm's small Paris office.

new-look newbury

Private client is commonly taken as a first seat in Newbury. You'll work in the background for wealthy landed individuals and large family trusts because with such clients *"it's not unreasonable for trainees to not be the face of the firm."* When it comes to more ordinary folk, you'll be able to handle probate from start to finish and draft their wills. In Newbury, too, the corporate team has been recruiting. One source revealed: *"Even in the time I've been here, I've seen a totally different team develop."* A litigation seat brings a mixed workload: employment, family, civil and commercial, and a preponderance of debt and insolvency cases is ideal trainee fodder, particularly *"if you're keen to do advocacy."*

You may be reassured to hear that *"for the size of place, Newbury has a decent business community, and you do start meeting the people you work with. There's 110% employment...and virtually everyone works for Vodafone, which has its worldwide HQ here."* It begs the question what did everyone do before Vodafone? Answers on a postcard please.

If you arrive in Newbury without a friend in the world, you're unlikely to stay lonely for long. For nights in the pub, *"everyone is invited, and although there's the crowd of usual suspects, there's no set cast or regiment at the firm."* In June 2004, Penningtons moved to new open-plan digs in the centre of town. *"We are the biggest and most prestigious firm here and will now look it,"* one trainee beamed.

Penningtons had ample jobs to offer to NQs in 2004, but due to competition for specific posts and personal relocations, only five of the ten qualifiers stayed on.

and finally...

For those with the relevant county roots, Penningtons is an obvious choice, yet the capital's trainees' motives are less clear. 'Why didn't you choose a big City firm?' we asked one of the Londoners. *"They couldn't pay me enough to go to one of them,"* he replied.

Pinsents

the facts

Location: Birmingham, London, Leeds, Manchester
Number of UK partners/assistants: 164/289
Total number of trainees: 77
Seats: 4x6 months
Alternative seats: Brussels, secondments

With offices in Birmingham, London, Leeds and Manchester, Pinsents was built through a slow and considered series of mergers. Speculation about a further merger in London suggests that there is space for extra chairs at the Pinsents table.

the proof is in the pudding

Pinsents has associations with firms in Sweden, Denmark, Poland, Estonia, France, Germany and Brussels, but it is not in any sense an international law firm and trainees mainly dine on good old British fare. Though we're assured *"there are big plans to move forward"* in Europe, save your passport for your summer holidays as the firm's gaze is fixed on the UK. More particularly, *"there is a commitment to strengthening the London presence."* Recently Pinsents conducted merger talks with Nicholson Graham & Jones, and although these negotiations eventually broke down, we repeatedly heard that *"the firm is definitely open to the prospect of more mergers."* So there we have it: Pinsents is still perusing the pudding menu. Who knows if it will plump for apple crumble or tarte aux pommes, but as a firm that *"won't take chances,"* we doubt it will order a banana flambé.

Time and again trainees dropped the words *"chosen markets"* into conversation in a bid to emphasise the firm's sectoral approach to work by building legal services around clients. We will leave you to check out Pinsents website for a more comprehensive explanation, but rest assured, trainees were fully clued up on the firm's business strategy. The mere mention of chosen markets even elicited a weak *"yeayy"* from one source.

Acting for clients such as Smith & Nephew, Barclays Private Equity, John Laing Plc, Hanson, Budgens, Argos, Thistle Hotels and Mayflower, and handling matters in the multimillion-pound bracket, Pinsents has a good reputation for corporate work. Accordingly, there are corporate seats in abundance and *"unless you have a reason why it wouldn't fit in with what you want to do, they do recommend it."* However, there are also *"lots of support departments which have learnt to stand on their own two feet."* Property, for example, is a vast entity. The Birmingham team acted for its own city council on the Masshouse Circus element of the city's redevelopment, and in Leeds the department was instructed by rival law firm Eversheds on the lease of its new digs in that city. Looking around the firm more generally you see most departments doing very well and certain departments doing extremely well – the employment departments in Leeds, competition and banking departments in Birmingham and the tax groups in each are all first class. London and Manchester each field fabulous pensions and pensions litigation teams.

ruling the roost

On applying to Pinsents, trainees specify their preferred office and can expect their training contract to be a one-site affair...unless they change their minds or find an inconveniently situated boyfriend or girlfriend, in which case they might be allowed to do one seat in another location. Despite the miles between them, an initial trainee induction followed by quarterly get-togethers for all trainees provide recruits with *"a real sense of a Pinsents identity across the UK."* Perhaps we shouldn't have been surprised then to find that trainees thought the concept of an HQ *"not that meaningful."* One source ventured: *"It is somewhere between Birmingham and London"* (surely not the Bicester Village factory outlet?), while another bluntly confessed: *"I don't really care."* Firm-wide coherence is bolstered by departmental away days and training, plus cross-office working on the part of some partners. With not a happy-clappy, group-bonding powerpointing, all-singing, all-dancing jamboree in sight, Pinsents' approach to togetherness is more *"work days than fun days."*

A training contract follows the usual four-seat pattern. At each rotation trainees get to list their top three choices and HR *"tries to fit you as much as possible with that."* As ever, employment is the must-have seat as *"you get the most responsibility and quite a lot of contact with clients."* A dearth of technology and media seats means *"people usually fight"* for the opportunity to help on government contracts and IP litigation, though one source mourned the fact that the client list was not star-studded. Conversely, tax sets few pulses racing as *"it's quite difficult as a trainee – it's so technical, and it just has a reputation for being a bit sad."* Similarly, one source contemplated pensions as an unpopular choice; *"it's not a reflection on the department, it just doesn't sound sexy."*

More attractive is a three-month competition and general EU seat in associated Brussels firm Crosby Renouf. Currently, postings further afield are only open to associates, but *"for six months, every six months"* there is the opportunity to go to a major client. We also learned of trainees doing 'virtual secondments', that is to say working for just one client but remaining office-based. Across the board, while quality tasks are interspersed with grunt work, our sources had *"never heard of any trainees just being used to do all the rubbish. You are treated as if you are part of the department, and not just there to pick up what others can't be bothered to do."* We heard of trainees running their own caseload in property, taking witness statements and attending interviews alone in employment, and taking a front row seat on a major completion in projects.

When everything is going well, leaving a favourite seat and supervisor can be a wrench. *"You really are tucked under their wing – you feel a huge part of the team and you don't feel disposable."* One trainee reminisced about a 2am stint in the office and how *"my supervisor still took the time to sit down and explain why I had to do the work."* Even during daylight hours, supervisors are generally *"good at checking your workload and making sure you aren't too overrun."* Monthly appraisals leave trainees with little doubt about how they are faring.

london: fast work

In Birmingham and Leeds *"Pinsents has had an established presence for donkey's years,"* and our sources here were clear that *"it is a regional firm. If you are looking for the absolutely huge deals you aren't going to get them."* However, the London training is more *"corporate-oriented"* than elsewhere and trainees found themselves getting to grips with some very decent deals. The main London office near Liverpool Street is home to the majority, and though trainees confessed that *"physically, the offices in the regions are nicer,"* the view is not half bad. A smaller, more *"cosy and old-fashioned"* office on Gresham Street is home to the insurance and litigation lawyers. The 15-minute walk between them is just long enough to scupper regular post-work, office-wide bevvies, but all come together each Christmas for a black-tie dinner. The London trainees described themselves as *"very cliquey."*

birmingham: the last days of disco

Home to many of Pinsents' bigwigs, the Birmingham office was about to undergo a long-awaited refurb when we called. Trainees tour around a full range of commercial seats and for them a typical day is 8.45am–6.30pm, with occasional long nights cropping up in corporate. We spotted many Birmingham Uni grads amongst our sources, and were told: *"There are not many who have no connection with Birmingham."* It came as no surprise then that they were all experts on where to go after hours. Utopia is favoured over Digress; in fact of the latter they said: *"We tend to stay away – it's dark and seedy."* One candid interviewee also admitted:*"Pinsents is not traditionally known for being hot at sport,"* so despite netball and football being played, you shouldn't expect to find a bulging trophy cabinet. They do like to have fun though: at the last Christmas Party a 70s and 80s disco theme provided the perfect excuse for Adam Ant face paint, big afros and big flares. Trainees also fully involve themselves in the Trainee Solicitors Society and other young professionals' groups, and told us of a certain speed dating event whereby lawyers got to rub up close with accountants and doctors. Spreading love inside the office, when the firm rebranded everyone received chocolates, and at Christmas there was a bottle of bubbly for all. Last Easter everyone arrived at work to find cakes on their desk from the senior partner – *"we heard he personally went and bought them."*

leeds: living in a box

In Leeds, *"basically everything"* is on offer for trainees, though *"you are told you are most likely to get property or corporate because of the size of the departments."* An 8.30am–6pm day is typical, *"with 75 minutes for lunch."* As in Birmingham, the two northern offices attract those who have a commitment to the region. The office is open plan, which means trainees sit next to their supervisor. One recruit mourned that *"there's no waterfall like there is at Addleshaws,"* but went on to tell us: *"There are glass lifts which are quite amusing – you forget people can watch you, so you have to be careful- you can't pick your nose and stuff."* With a flurry of new bars opening nearby, trainees are spoilt for choice. Friday night could see them in any one of Tiger Tiger, Firefly, Manoni's or the Living Room, and one Thursday a month each team has a night out on the tiles. The best one? Property – *"it invites all the trainees in the office."* Sounds like covert internal PR to us!

manchester: little voice

Our sources in Manchester were the first trainee intake at this newer office. Initially, *"seat choices were slightly restricted,"* but *"now it is pretty much full service."* For anything not on offer in Manchester, Leeds is close enough and trainees at the two offices *"find themselves sticking together."* At the top of King Street, the Manchester office is *"a bit dangerous on pay day – Armani is right outside."* There are also plenty of bars nearby for frittering away hard-earned pennies, Lion Bar being a current favourite. The small trainee contingent hang out with the junior lawyers, and for the annual Christmas bash the whole office parties together. Black tie and karaoke may sound a little incongruous, but apparently it's a winning combination. There are *"some real karaoke officiados"* whose a cappella rendition of *Wild Rover* is not to be missed.

and finally...

Pinsents offers all the benefits of a strong regional name combined with a City presence that will in all probability expand greatly once it has found the right match. Trainees promised us *"there are no outrageous personalities"* at the firm; indeed we sensed a mild reserve among our otherwise obliging sources. Quite typical, we feel, of a firm that considers its moves carefully. This year it kept 26 of its 34 qualifiers and took on another 14 from outside the firm.

Prettys

the facts

Location: Ipswich
Number of UK partners/assistants: 16/26
Total number of trainees: 10
Seats: 4x6 months
Alternative seats: None

Ninety-eight years old and fit as a fiddle, Prettys of Ipswich is acting more like a 20-year-old than a virtual centenarian.

classical training

Prettys is a classic example of a firm that's developed a strong commercial practice within its region and met with some success beyond. In doing so it has also stayed true to its private client roots, so acknowledging the importance of the little things in life. All this bodes well for the trainee who is keen to keep all options open until certain of their career path.

When it comes to selecting seats, trainees soon find that nothing is compulsory although, admittedly, they have no choice as to the first seat. Thereafter things usually run smoothly: *"In our trainee group we were all very set on what we wanted to do, but lucky that out interests weren't competing."* Whether or not this luck is repeated every year is open to debate; however, with seats available in property, corporate services, IT/IP, employment, commercial litigation, shipping, wills and probate, matrimonial plus claimant and defendant PI, there's plenty of room to manoeuvre.

plain sailing

Prettys' shipping department is rated highly in *Chambers UK*, and is unabashedly chasing an even better market position. *"I didn't have a clue about shipping when I started,"* one source told us; *"but I settled in really well...I had my own caseload from very early on; mostly transport work and smaller matters where the value of claim was lower. Plenty of debt actions or lien matters, arbitrations and cargo claims."* You'll get your own caseload in commercial litigation too – insolvency and property cases, construction and corporate spats, general debt and contract disputes. There's no danger of becoming overspecialised and every chance that you'll be *"settling cases and left to* [your] *own devices to run things."* Under supervision of course.

The busy property seat brings a mainly commercial caseload with a bit of residential conveyancing on the side. *"You look at some of the properties and they're lovely. The clients are rich, independently wealthy property magnates, those creating new developments, local businesses and banks."* High on client contact, trainees particularly like this seat because they get to see matters from start to finish. But we mustn't give the impression that everything you do in your training contract will be so fulfilling. As one source revealed: *"We don't have any paralegals,"* which means *"you do occasionally have to do mundane tasks like photocopying."*

A seat in claimant PI and clinical negligence will deliver *"the whole shooting match from seeing clients to going to court."* According to one past occupant, *"you need to be a little gore-proof"* when it comes to some of the photographic evidence. You also need to learn how to treat clients with sympathy – some will cry, *"and sometimes you have to speak to relatives of people who have died on a hospital trolley."*

customary behaviour

After completing the PSC in London, trainees attend regular departmental training sessions led by assistants and partners. Speaking of the bosses, we noted a paucity of female partners at Prettys and felt it only right to ask trainees what they thought of this. *"Certainly it doesn't feel like it's male-dominated on a day-to-day basis,"* one reassured us, *"but on paper it is obviously so. I think having female role models would be encouraging – it would mean you could associate with the figure, aspire to that position."* Of course, long-term aims are not always at the forefront of every trainee's mind; nevertheless, every sensible recruiter will want some kind of reassurance that those they train will be likely to commit to them for longer than it takes to qualify. In Prettys case this hasn't translated into an East Anglian-born-and-bred policy, so don't let your roots elsewhere put you off applying. The firm was disappointed to lose two of its four qualifiers this year. Jobs were offered to all, just not in the right fields for those who left.

"I was interested in being part of a team where I could make an impression," one trainee explained. And at Prettys, an impression needs to be made with clients as well as partners. If you're the sort who's keen to *"establish links early on"* and intends to make a go of it in the Suffolk business community, then you're the sort Prettys is after. You'll be involved in client seminars and entertaining, be these at large parties or cosy lunches. The 2004 annual client party was held on Ipswich's Waterfront, and included a ferry ride and guided tour around some of the town's oldest buildings, finishing up at the Custom House. The firm also throws a London client party each year, evidencing the fact that its business is not exclusively East Anglian. Proof of its overseas interests comes in the form of a niche French property department and membership of Galexy, an international association of law firms.

From the street, Prettys' office at Elm House looks like any other large Georgian townhouse, but behind the facade is a modern block. Is the building a metaphor for the firm itself? Perhaps. With a full-time, smart-suits dress code and a long-standing reputation to protect, *"it's still formal, but not old and horrible."* Never forget that the firm has client rela-

tionships that stretch back to the day Bernard Pretty founded it, and perhaps in a nod to this the general feel is *"established but not fogey."* Interestingly, in a profession that nowadays shuffles and rearranges itself as much as Lilly Savage in swimwear, we heard the words: *"We've not ever merged with anyone."*

highland flings

Trainees sense that Prettys is *"not for the real hard-core City types."* Contracted hours are 8.45am–5pm; generally people have gone by 6pm and only work later if things get particularly hectic. They work a full day by anyone's standards, so don't assume you can kick back just because you're not in EC4. One wise soul told us: *"I don't mind putting in the hours, but I want my weekends free."* Admittedly, lovely Ipswich is not the UK's wildest city, but *"it is sufficient for my needs, and London is just over an hour away." "It's great for outdoor leisure pursuits,"* and the seaside is within easy reach. Those more into the arts will discover a quaint cultural wormhole in Aldeburgh.

We've a hunch that Prettys is more sociable than your average firm. Traditionally its bar of choice has been Mannings, now The Curve is more popular with the youngsters. Organised social events appear miraculously, despite the lack of any formal social committee. In May 2004, over 30 people spent four days in Scotland, yomping up mountains in Glencoe by day and sharing a wee dram or three in lodges by night. *"It's great fun and you get to know people from different departments,"* said one Gortex convert.

Back on the flat in Suffolk (*"There are no hill starts in a driving test round here!"*), netball has really taken off, and the Prettys team now play competitively against local accountancy firms and insurance companies. We trust they make judicious decisions as to when to win and when to lose.

and finally...

Prettys is a firm that will suit someone who wants to engage fully with their career and their clients, whichever kind these turn out to be.

RadcliffesLeBrasseur

the facts

Location: London, Leeds, Cardiff
Number of UK partners/assistants: 47/42
Total number of trainees: 10
Seats: 4x6 months (2x12 in Leeds)
Alternative seats: None
Extras: Pro bono – Battersea Legal Advice Centre

For those with a hunger for responsibility or a taste for healthcare work, RadcliffesLeBrasseur offers both served up on a solid commercial plate.

le brasserie

In 2001, established Westminster firm Radcliffes merged its hybrid commercial/private client practice with Covent Garden healthcare outfit Le Brasseur J. Tickle. An offshoot in Cardiff waves the healthcare banner, and in Leeds teams serve up both property and healthcare. As for the resulting name, "*everyone is gutted they dropped the Tickle, but the Le adds a touch of class.*"

Indeed it does. The Brasseur end of the practice contributed plenty of meaty clients including NHS trusts, local health authorities, private hospital groups and health professionals' insurance companies. While most of us were still pondering the fireman/princess career dilemma, many RLB recruits had already set their heart on healthcare law. In healthcare defence litigation trainees get to instruct experts, draft witness statements and defences and help out on high-value cases for medical and dental defence organisations. We were told: "*You work on cases that have reached the Privy Council and Court of Appeal – things reported in the press.*" One trainee enthused: "*I went to the GMC when the paparazzi was outside – that was cool.*" Back in the office, there's plenty of research to be done, especially in relation to mental healthcare, where trainees assist in advising doctors how to treat patients without breaching their legal rights. This is "*where the Human Rights Act comes into play almost from the off*"

on tackling issues such as the detention or force feeding of patients. "*The work might be a bit more academic,*" but chunks of research definitely don't make for a stale experience: our sources had come face to face with "*life-or-death situations.*" After all, a diabetic on a hunger strike is about as life-or-death as it gets.

Most recently the clinical negligence team acted in a case involving a covert operation (private eye and all) to prove that a claimant was insufficiently disabled to warrant the amount claimed. They also defended an obstetrician alleged to have caused tetraplegic cerebral palsy and a neurologist involved in allegations of Methysergide-induced retro-peritoneal fibrosis. You can put that medical dictionary back on the shelf now. To complete the list of clients we should also add that it acts for nursing home providers, opticians, the National Blood Authority, the Society of Chiropodists and Podiatrists and plenty more. On the regulatory side, lawyers were involved in a House of Lords case that defined the meaning of professional misconduct in the context of NHS disciplinary cases. On the mental health side they represented an NHS trust in the House of Lords concerning the resectioning of a patient, and successfully defended a challenge under the Human Rights Act regarding the administration of ECT treatment.

If all this leaves you feeling a little off-colour, the firm has a more traditional offering of corporate mergers and acquisitions worth anything from "*a couple of million pounds*" right up to the £120 million mark on occasions. Its real estate group acts for the likes of BP, City University, Hanson Plc, Lloyds TSB, Royal Mail and Spaghetti House, and a very reputable private client team handles tax, trusts and estates matters for those who can afford central London rates, as well as family law and charities work.

ye olde property seate

In London, four six-month seats are on offer with no compulsories. There is a degree of choice, which increases markedly for second-years, and some people choose to do two stints in a favourite department.

The employment seat remains a perennial favourite, so it's generally the preserve of second-years; however, first-years must be philosophical about their seat allocations – for example, *"residential property isn't useful to healthcare, but the experience is invaluable."* In Leeds, there are just two departments (property and healthcare) and both take a trainee for 12 months. The link between the London and Leeds training is strictly video-only, though when you're having a bad-hair day, the phone will do.

A stint in property sees trainees *"surviving on their own."* In Leeds it's mostly commercial and *"a bit of domestic work, which gives greater opportunity to have your own files."* In London, standard fodder includes leases, licences and investment purchases plus *"quite a lot of unregistered land stuff for clients who own large areas of England where everything is in Ye Olde Deeds."* Property litigation means drafting proceedings, negotiating settlements and recovering unpaid rents. Here too, trainees get their own files, *"about 25 of them."* In commercial litigation too there is plenty of autonomy, especially in insolvency and personal bankruptcy cases.

In case you have any lingering doubts, at RLB *"the training and responsibility is second to none."* Our sources say: *"All those clichés about bigger fish and smaller ponds really do apply."* Aside from minimal photocopying and bundling duties (though they do still exist), one source happily observed: *"It's not like they're just throwing you bones, you're doing proper, useful work and have the role of an assistant. On qualification, the work you do won't be hugely different."* Another interviewee reflected that *"the flip side of the responsibility is that sometimes you can get a bit exposed, but it only happens every so often."* Guarding against this are mid and end-of-seat appraisals, video-linked seminars between the two training centres and in-house lunchtime sessions.

the powder puff plot

The London office is considered *"quite impressive in an old-school way."* The Westminster location requires a daily battle through the thronging school parties and protestors on Parliament Square (sometimes one and the same) and past the news crews and political commentators receiving a little last-minute powdering on College Green. One dry wit observed: *"It's a good location, if you're a tourist."* Make it through and you end up in a *"really beautiful red-brick building"* that has more wood panelling than even our boss's office...and that's a lot. One interviewee noted: *"The firm is traditional in décor and every other way, which may stem from a reputable tax and private client department, but it is modern in the same breath, reflecting the clients and law in healthcare."*

Last year, we noted that the two strands of the firm did not make an obvious pairing, and there was no getting around the news of various post-merger musical differences and departures; however, it looks as if the story has moved on from there. One trainee told us: *"We are often being asked what will make us happier and there's lots of interaction between the top people."* Trainees also described a very pleasant 9ish to 6ish working day, and though the property department may demand an extra hour, *"you don't stay late because someone is breathing down your neck; you get treated very well – it is very humane."* *"family-friendly: if someone has a baby they'll bring them in to show them off, and when kids are off school sick they come in and sit in the library watching videos."* All in all, trainees considered the Leeds side of the business less old school.

Reports on the RLB social scene are mixed. In London, it's theatre trips, wine tasting, boat cruises, and football, though according to one interviewee, *"all the pubs here are rubbish...especially the one by Westminster Tube which is terrible."* Not too far away is The Atrium, *"where Cherie Blair made her speech about Euan Blair and Peter Foster and cried."* And bless the lovely trainee who told us: *"Some trainees are genuinely trendy and go to bars I've never heard of. They're very cool."* Cool factor aside, year on year we form the same impression of RLB trainees, and as they seem to read themselves accurately, we'll use their own description – *"big characters and confident, chatty types wanting responsibility."* In september 2004, four of the six qualifiers stayed with the firm.

and finally...

It might look a bit wood panelled in SW1, but RadlciffesLeBrasseur is a great place to go for an all-you-can-eat buffet of challenges and a top-nosh healthcare practice. Bon appétit.

Reed Smith

the facts

Location: London, Coventry
Number of UK partners/assistants: 32/35
Total number of trainees: 13
Seats: 4x6 months
Alternative seats: None

A global US Giant with a gentle UK touch. Reed Smith is a Pittsburgh-based firm with 14 stateside branches from California to Virginia and UK offices in London and Coventry.

mighty blighty

There is a corner of Reed Smith that is forever Warner Cranston. We wouldn't mention the two-office *"small boutique firm"* absorbed by this US behemoth in a merger four years ago, except that its spirit is still alive and well. More importantly it is a *"harmonious and happy"* component, an example of successful integration giving the lie to the stereotyping of our cousins across the pond as purely profit driven and culturally insensitive. Whilst a US-style billing culture is in place and trainees are delighted at the expanded opportunities afforded by the relationship, they were adamant that no sacrifices have been made. *"It doesn't feel like we're working for a US giant,"* *"the US offices respect us and our way of working."* Tellingly, prospective expansion into Germany or France also seems contingent on finding a good match *"with a similar working culture."* Said one trainee, *"of course that could just be management speak, but it is what seems to have happened here."*

In the UK there has been *"careful growth, not simply pushing trendy or commercially lucrative areas erratically."* That means focusing on existing strengths in coco, real estate and finance and working for a range of clients including retailers (think Moss Bros), exclusive retailers (think Tiffany), fast food outlets (think McDonald's or Dominos), manufacturers (think Akzo Nobel or Sara Lee), pharma companies (think McNeil Nutritionals) and financial institutions (think Crédit Lyonnais). With equally impressive clients like Savoye Logistics and Soufflet Agriculture, the French expertise of the corporate team continues to be an important asset. No doubt even more so if a French connection does become permanent. Trainees told us *"growth seems to be about focusing in on the big pharmaceutical and financial services clients, then branching out more broadly with that expertise."* A burgeoning life sciences practice is a US import, and several interviewees had worked extensively in this field.

no stone throwing

Based in *"spanking"* premises at London Bridge, Reed Smith's office in the capital has a transparent working environment. Literally. *"The outside walls are made of glass, so are the inside walls, you can see right through the building."* Ideal for views of St Paul's, the Thames, Tower Bridge and Canary Wharf, but not so ideal if you've a fear of heights. Trainees here spend a year in the business and finance/corporate and commercial division (changing supervisor halfway through), six months in litigation and a final seat in either real estate or employment.

With only four trainees per year, there's never much friction over seat choices, and in any event the firm's smaller size means *"you get a wide scope of work."* Trainees sit with their supervisor, but get work from all over departments, and *"because you know everyone, you can find out what work they're doing and express an interest."* The range of work and general commercial means diversity for trainees. *"There's no possibility of getting pigeon-holed, say, finding yourself only doing securitisation,"* said one source. And another added: *"In the same day I've done a loan agreement, drafted a software licence and completed a due diligence exercise."*

Litigation does involve *"the curse of bundling,"* but the pay-off comes in the form of *"big corporate clients"* and *"very wealthy individuals who appreciate our discretion,"* (though we are allowed to mention Catherine Zeta Jones' *Hello!* spat). Over in real estate, trainees get *"a lot of files and responsibility"* and take pride in acting for big-name clients such as *The Daily Mail,* Pizza Express and many fast-food providers. The alternative option of employment, is as popular here as anywhere, offering an equally attractive range of *"top clients and responsibility."*

It's not possible for trainees to take seats in the States yet, but associates frequently hop the pond for secondments, entire departments go for retreats and there are plenty of return visits. *"The senior partners from the USA are coming over next week and we're having a firm-wide event."*

legal life in cuvontroy

No one we interviewed in the Coventry office had a strong Midlands accent, but we can rarely resist a regional stereotype. Increasingly, neither can Reed Smith. *"It's definitely looking more and more for* [trainees with] *a strong connection to the area. All the summer students are from Warwick or Birmingham Universities."* Coventry has its own atmosphere and identity, and some of its own priorities. Trainees rotate through the same departments as their contemporaries in London; that said, when we rang employment was a *"one-partner practice"* with the one partner away on maternity leave and a fill-in pending. Similarly, although B&F is beginning to gather momentum with clients like Bank of Scotland, the department is still a young one and trainees do *"a lot of paperwork and company secretarial stuff."*

The long-established real estate and commercial litigation departments are where the benefits of being *"at an international firm in the Midlands"* really come into play. The former is *"a brilliant team"* that's on the up, having recently seen the arrival of three new associates. Recently it has advised UK and US clients on matters relating to the proposed Cambridge Medipark. In real estate, trainees get *"a lot of plot sales, exchanges and completions,"* whilst in litigation they make occasional court appearances, run their own files and even use their languages – *"I've recently been translating on a French company's debt claim."*

In answering the curious question of why there's a Coventry office at all (let's face it, it's not a location usually associated with US law firms), what we can say is that it was the preferred home of the lawyers originally responsible for the old Warner Cranston/McDonald's relationship. After merger, the scope of the office broadened. The London tax partner works one day a week in the Midlands and the firm's UK real estate head is based there. It helps that *"it's easy to hop on the train from Coventry, the office is just next to the station,"* and the *"stream of exchange between the two offices"* includes regular departmental video meetings, joint Christmas and summer social events and a shared HR department.

it's a mini adventure

The theme common to trainees in both offices was their attraction to the firm's size in the UK. One source told us: *"It's really easy here to make an impression as an individual."* Others delighted in the attention their supervisors were able to give: *"[My supervisor] would give the work to me and I'd have a bash. Then we'd look at it together, and incorporate my ideas into the finished article."* Coventry and London trainees both admitted to being *"scared sometimes by the responsibility,"* but could count on the fact that *"there's always someone there to back you up."* Trainees in the Midlands seem to get more direct client contact than those in London (*"We only tend to be taken to* meetings if there is some practical work we can do"), but we did find one source in London who said jokingly of the real estate experience: "Sometimes I wish clients would stop ringing me up!"

Not least because "everyone drives to work," the social life in Coventry is less than explosive. "A social committee has been started up, but most often we're just sad and go home after work." Don't take that comment the wrong way – "the people are fantastic," it's just that compared to "full-on" London there's a slower pace. Presumably they pick up speed when competing with their colleagues in the Reed Smith Olympics, held each summer.

In London there are regular post-work trips to local pubs. What really defines the London office, however, is the rambunctious "non-hierarchical" potential in the air. "There's a monthly meeting where fee earners discuss their work in progress. It always turns into partners taking the piss out of each other and it is hilarious to watch!" Trainees were quick to stress that the style is "relaxed and fun, but suddenly very serious when the interests of the clients demand it." They clearly relish the trickle effect of such banter: "It feeds down to create a great working atmosphere." In September 2004 all five qualifiers accepted jobs with the firm.

and finally...

If you want to be at the only international law firm in Coventry, or at one of the most intimate international law firm's in the big smoke, Reed Smith is the one you're after. Especially if you want your training to be a rounded one.

Reynolds Porter Chamberlain

the facts

Location: London, Tiverton
Number of UK partners/assistants: 63/129
Total number of trainees: 21
Seats: 4x6 months
Alternative seats: Occasional secondments

A respected insurance and reinsurance firm, Reynolds Porter Chamberlain also boasts excellent defamation and family practices and a solid company/commercial offering.

clearing up after the professionals

"Do you see yourself as a litigator?" prospective trainees are asked at interview. It's a fair question given that contentious work dominates at RPC and most trainees spend three-quarters of their training contract litigating. Furthermore, "about 90% of the firm's work is insurance-related," a statistic largely due to it's long-standing relationships with the hottest names in insurance – Chubb, Heath Lambert, Hiscox and Zurich to name but a few.

Within the four-seat training contract, there are no compulsory seats but you are unlikely to avoid insurance work. Reflecting on this, one source told us: "There was one trainee who didn't do any insurance seats, but he is qualifying into it. There is no way of escaping it really." High on the agenda is professional negligence, which is divided between four specialist groups. The ADF team handles claims against accountants, directors and financial planners; PEP lawyers deal with property, construction and employers and public liability issues, and the legal group handles actions against solicitors. In these first three fields, the negligent party will almost always have an insurer, for whom RPC is acting. The fourth specialist group, health, defends the NHS against claims concerning the slip-ups of medical practitioners.

political intrigue

Away from insurance-related litigation, seats are available in coco, property, family and media. (Though the latter two are, in the main part, also contentious in nature). The family department has developed a reputation for high-profile international child abduction cases and celebrity divorces, all of which provide "lots of court experience" and good exposure to clients. It can, however, be "tough going" and left one trainee concluding: "*It's definitely put me off marriage.*" Anyone keen to sample libel and political intrigue in one six-month package should make a beeline for the media seat. In the past year the firm was drafted in for IDS on the Betsygate affair and by Prince Charles' former aide Michael Fawcett in his injunction against the *Mail on Sunday*. Here, as in all contentious seats, trainees get their names added to the outdoor clerk rota, effectively a subscription to small court appearances on both RPC matters and agency work.

In property seats, trainees told us they got plenty of contact with clients and managing agents, and the usual round of lease and licence drafting, letter writing and land registry applications. In coco, trainees assist on deals for clients including Lloyds TSB Development Capital, Apax Partners, Associated New Media and Topsy Turvey World, a children's play facilities company that received a £600,000 venture capital investment from private equity company Investory Ltd. Most of the team's work centres on private equity, AIM and smaller ticket M&A.

city slickers

The bulk of RPC's work is carried out at its Holborn base, Chichester House. A "*not particularly attractive facade*" conceals "*80s-looking*" offices that "*could do with a bit of a revamp.*" A "*marbly*" reception area leads through to "*beigey offices*" and "*stately home-ish boardrooms.*" Thankfully, trainees were far more positive about the firm's culture. Essentially they describe "*a pretty level-headed place*" where a well-earned, super-professional image is valued highly. Ask any RPC trainee how they perceive their firm and the word "*professional*" will always be the answer. It is perhaps even more strongly felt in the second office at Leadenhall. This branch is the home of the insurance/reinsurance department and offers seats to up to four trainees at a time. One past occupant described this office as "*much more heads down;*" another observed that "*over there you are right in the middle of your client base, so you have to be even more professional, as*

you're going to be seen. It's the main drive of the firm and the big guys are over there. They take it seriously."

The work of the insurance/reinsurance department sounds complicated. In the past year it has continued to receive instructions pertaining to the World Trade Center collapse and also acts for Aachen & Munich Insurance regarding the reinsurance of AIG's cover of Railtrack's liability on the Ladbroke Grove disaster. Trainees told us: "*The value of the claims and the duration of the matters makes it just impracticable to get really involved – you get interesting snapshots instead.*"

While in Holborn the civilised 9am–6.30pm day is rarely extended (except in corporate); in Leadenhall trainees said they worked longer. Certainly "*people would raise an eyebrow if you left at 5.30pm, and turning up at 9.45am would be looked on badly.*" All this said, trainees enjoy the Leadenhall experience, seeing it as a chance to get a real feel for proper-pinstriped, EC-postcode, City life. For those of you wondering about the RPC Tiverton connection, one trainee admitted: "*I don't really know what goes on in Tiverton.*" And all you need to know is that the work done there doesn't impact on the training scheme.

eats, shoots and leaves

Trainees normally share an office with a recently qualified solicitor, with their supervisor sitting next door. This doesn't mean out of sight and out of mind; indeed, supervisors are praised for making "*a big effort to take you to client things.*" As well as a seat supervisor, trainees each have a dedicated 'minder partner' to act as a sounding board, and first-years are additionally shepherded by their own 'buddy' from the second year when they first arrive. The recent introduction of mid-seat appraisals in addition to end-of-seat appraisals has been welcomed, and trainees appreciate the high level of general feedback available: "*There is no doubt your grammar improves considerably in your first six months here!*"

This attention to detail and accuracy is indicative of the RPC brand. Call it old-fashioned if you will, but doing things the proper way is important. One source confessed: *"We are perceived as being quite traditional – I think it's a consequence of having three names – but I think we are very up to date...certainly, we don't send post by pigeon!"* That said, the partners still lunch in their own dining room three times a week. And there are a few more of them around the table these days: in the last year the firm has hired five new partners, four of them coming from Simmons & Simmons, Lawrence Graham and Addleshaw Goddard.

number crunching

Any remnants of staid British reserve are quickly shrugged off after hours...even quicker when partners have their weekends away and everyone else gets to knock off at 4.30pm. RPC's local pub in Holborn is Penderell's Oak, but as *"there is an element of it being a Wetherspoon's pub and therefore not very nice,"* trainees are now leaning towards Sway. In the City, the insurance team heads off to The Counting House to tot up their weekly figures, and for when the sums get really complicated, a pub called The Abacus is also nearby.

After years of cobbling together fancy dress costumes for the summer party, in 2004 the issue was put to the vote and the answer *"came back with a resounding 'no'."* Fret not: *"The idea hasn't been scrapped forever."* As for dress-down Fridays, *"in Holborn that means smart casual, in the City it means you take your tie off."*

murder on the dance floor

Each year the firm enters the Manches Cup sailing regatta and a group of staff and partners head off to Hamble for *"a blow-out weekend and some sunbathing."* This year only one pour soul ended up in the drink...even before making it on to a boat. Everyone else ran amok at the Saturday night ball, procuring wigs and medallions from other race-goers to fit in with the Austin Powers theme. And for a grand finale, the RPC crew *"lined up to 'New York, New York' to do their high kicks."*

Irrespective of whether they have the skill or will to make a show of themselves at a party, RPC knows the kind of trainee it wants to recruit. *"The firm isn't looking for miracles nor legal genius, just an appreciation of the commercial realities and the ability to try and to learn."* Of themselves, our sources said: *"There are no hidden agendas amongst trainees; everyone is just here to learn"* and *"no one is trying to get points over each other."* Not that it's a soft environment: *"You have got to have a sense of humour and take a bit of stick...they won't pamper you."* In September 2004, seven of the ten qualifiers took positions at the firm.

and finally...

The emphasis on contentious training at Reynolds Porter Chamberlain should not be underestimated. Beyond that, all we need say is the firm will do its utmost to ensure you are properly schooled and in top condition for graduation.

Richards Butler

the facts

Location: London
Number of UK partners/assistants: 71 / 120
Total number of trainees: 40
Seats: 4x6 months
Alternative seats: Overseas seats, secondments
Extras: Pro bono – St Botolph's Project, language training

An impressive array of international offices, an established reputation for high-quality work in interesting specialisms; if you're looking for a medium-sized London firm, it might be worth getting out the compass and plotting a course in Richards Butler's direction.

changing tack

This firm started off life as a shipping practice, but has since diversified and added a host of other specialist and mainstream practice areas. Two thirds of the firm's work has an international dimension, leading one trainee to claim: "*I'm over half way through my second year now and I still haven't done any work for an English client.*"

RB's commercial litigation division has gone from strength to strength, having successfully positioned itself as a preferred referral practice, benefiting from the conflicts of interest that prevent many of the biggest firms from acting for companies in dispute with banks. One such referral led to an important instruction from the Co-operative Group when it decided to bring a claim against Merrill Lynch Investment Managers. The litigation group has had to adapt to cope with the continuing flood of "*big-ticket litigation*" by laying out open-plan offices, and at times trainees are required to work that extra bit harder in order to get through everything. One went as far as to say that the occasional late night session was enjoyable. When this comment was met with an incredulous silence from our researcher, they went on to explain: "*Even when you're bundling, it's quite fun if there are a few of you. And there's always a couple of partners bouncing around in the background.*"

jelly bellies...

Trainees appear content with their role in litigation and other departments. While they must sometimes put up with the more unenviable aspects of commercial practice, the firm does at least try to make life bearable. A corporate seat trainee said: "*I did once have to spend a while sifting through a data room, but at least they provided me with plenty of Jelly Belly beans, so it was okay.*" Recently the firm acted for Land Securities Trillium on two outsourcing deals worth £700 million. For the next 15 years LST and its partners Group 4 and Securitas will take over security services at employment benefit offices and other related government premises.

Let's not forget that other staple of commercial practice – property. RB has run some smashing deals, including the acquisition by Orient-Express Hotels of Le Manoir aux Quat' Saisons in Oxfordshire and La Residencia in Mallorca, as well as the Le Petit Blanc restaurant chain for £27.5 million. It also advised MTV on its lease of the Home nightclub in Leicester Square.

...and pork bellies

In addition to those who'd spent time in litigation, corporate and property, we managed to contact trainees who'd worked in insolvency, banking, employment, media, shipping, professional negligence and IP. "*On the whole they're very good at putting you in the seats you've asked to do,*" even if it's one of the most popular. "*Normally they only have one trainee in media, but when two trainees were set on going there, they made the extra seat available.*" As well as a seat supervisor, each trainee has a mentor partner for whom they will never work and whose primary purpose appears to be "*taking you out to lunch.*" We're told the firm picks "*the cooler, more approachable partners,*" which leaves us wondering how to describe the remainder. Training sessions are in bountiful supply, so much so that one trainee noted: "*I think I fulfilled the Law Society's criteria for two years in my first seven or eight months.*" Beware: not all sessions are suited to bed heads – "*Sometimes it can be a bit of a shocker when they're organised for 9am!*"

The firm is the unrivalled market leader for commodities work, particularly international arbitrations governing disputes over trade finance, credit risks, and the confiscation and misappropriation of goods in transit. It is particularly prominent in the futures market, acting for two European exchanges and several commodities brokers. We're reminded of the Dan Ackroyd/Eddie Murphy movie *Trading Places*, in which two old codgers in a trading firm wager on street bum Murphy, who is rehabilitated to trade pork bellies and frozen orange juice, and cosseted Ackroyd, who is turfed out into the December snow. If you're invited to visit the firm, you might want to ask a trainee if our flight of fancy has any basis in reality.

We hear that RB's managing partner had a wager of his own with the chief exec of Collyer-Bristow. The subjects of the bet were the Olympic sailors Ben Ainslie (sposored by C-B) and Mark Bulkeley and Leigh McMillan (sponsored by RB). The man whose sailor(s) fared worst in the games was required to work in his firm's post room for a day. If the sailors were equally lucky (or unlucky for that matter) the men would work in each other's post rooms. As we all know, Ainslie captured the gold medal. If the MP really enjoys his day at the franking machine, a revolutionary trainee-secondment system at the firm can only be a matter of time.

it's a hard life

RB's nautical legacy has bequeathed a network of international offices including Paris, Hong Kong, Abu Dhabi, Piraeus and São Paulo, to which trainees can be seconded. A substantial Hong Kong presence makes this one of the biggest firms in the region. Trainees who'd sampled what the island city has to offer reported being given *very commercial work with a good academic edge* in a *sociable office where there are no age barriers and you can always chat to anyone.* More importantly, the firm has its own yacht, which trainees, along with forty of their friends, can sign out for a cruise around the harbour. Similarly, trainees who'd spent time in the firm's Abu Dhabi office had the enviable task of balancing a full commercial caseload with time spent scuba diving and pursuing the *"fantastic shopping opportunities."* Vying for these popular postings is a competitive game, but we're assured that *"although there's a bit of jostling, everyone who wants to get away can go to their first or second choice place."* And if you don't get to work abroad, you can make a bid for a secondment to MTV, the BBC or Rank.

Unfortunately there is a note of caution. RB got the City's fishwives' tongues wagging by making 12 corporate lawyers redundant in the autumn of 2003. Blamed on the downbeat global M&A market, the cuts only affected transactional lawyers and other departments such as litigation were unaffected. The news had left some trainees feeling all at sea: some reported that they were less keen to take on overseas secondments when coming up to qualification as they wanted to be seen and heard around the London office. However, the general feeling is that the cuts were inevitable and the firm handled the situation as well as could be expected. *"We were kept well informed,"* said one, *"and were told that there was always someone we could talk to. The firm still aims to keep on its trainees, and our intake is small enough that there should be enough jobs to go round."* As it turns out, ten of the 13 qualifiers stayed at the firm in September 2004.

slot machine skirvy scandal

After speaking to RB trainees, we decided we liked the cut of their jib. On the whole they're honest and up front about problems at the firm (*"In the drinks machines we used to have Ribena, orange, and lemon. They took away the lemon"*), and for the most part they are exactly as they describe themselves – *"quite relaxed, chilled out and personable people."* They'll tell you they are *"not very aggressive or competitive,"* but you mustn't mistake this for lack of ambition or grit. The trainee group is cosmopolitan with a notable share of people who've had previous careers from accountancy to life aboard ship as a master mariner. There's a tendency to settle on training at RB after careful consideration of the firm's merits and, once there, to proceed with quiet determination.

After hours, many answer the call of the Slug for a common-or-garden night out. Then there's the Christmas party (for which partners have been known to dress up for 'entertainment' value), and each summer on the roof terrace there's *"a barbeque with a band and unlimited beer."* Once a month the infamous 531 club holds sway in the staff restaurant; it is so called because it opens at the exact end of the working day *"plus one minute to get down in the lift."* There are active cricket and football teams, and in the summer trainees retire to the softball field with *"two taxis full of beer, which we then carry around on wheelie trolleys stolen from the post room."* It's amazing they get anywhere in the league...

and finally...

Richards Butler's practice profile is not your standard City offering. Corporate and finance do not lead the other departments by the nose; instead, litigation and niche departments are more influential than at most firms, and your training will reflect this.

Russell-Cooke

the facts

Location: London
Number of UK partners/assistants: 36/45
Total number of trainees: 10
Seats: 4x6 months
Alternative seats: None

With a Putney High Street centre, a Kingston-Upon-Thames limb and a small outpost in the legal heartland of Bedford Row, Russell-Cooke is one of west London's finest firms. It has an excellent name in key areas such as family, charities, crime and professional discipline.

made to measure

Log on to the Russell-Cooke website, and you'll find a potted history of the firm, complete with grainy black and white illustrations of handlebar-moustached and butterfly-collared gents adopting stern poses. Waistcoats and tiepins have been replaced by casual attire (though each summer there are the usual e-mails about *"no midriffs or shoulders"*), and while *"there are a lot of partners who have been there since they were trainees and are proud of the firm"* this does not translate into anything *"stuck-in-the-mud."*

Within the standard four-seat training contract, *"no seats are compulsory per se"* and our sources had been presented with a range of work spanning PI and private client, coco, crime and employment plus a multitude of different flavours of property. But be warned: *"The firm does a fair amount of property, so that is fairly guaranteed at some point."* In fact, *"last time around five of the ten seats were in property."* Charities, crime and family were among our sources' favourites, though all those we spoke to were very clear that *"you start with the impression you have an awful lot of choice, but market forces dictate and you are put where the firm needs you."* That means *"you aren't necessarily going to get the chance to do crime, matrimonial or PI, which can be a problem if you aren't commercially minded."*

To illustrate, time and again we heard that *"there is not currently a seat in crime and not likely to be one for a while."* It's a similar story with family. Though a seat has recently been created, occupants had to *"push really hard to get it."* In short, while the offering has all the allure of a sweet shop counter with sherbet fountains, flying saucers and pink shrimps, you may find yourself stuck with half a pound of black jacks and no one to do swapsies with.

taking the plunge

All that said, in the seats that are on offer, trainees get a sharp sugar rush from a *"definitely in-at-the-deep-end"* approach to training. Thankfully, *"they don't let you drown...but they do leave you for a certain amount of time!"* Shrivel-toed trainees in residential conveyancing described *"managing the whole transaction from start to finish,"* while their counterparts in property litigation battled with portfolios of their own smaller files and assisted on supervisors' work. In commercial property, trainees are positively engulfed. One told us: *"I inherited 50-odd small files on the first day"* and got *"lots of gritty work at the bottom end of the scale."* In commercial litigation, trainees get *"a fair bit of advocacy"* mixed in with the *"more menial tasks"* that come with the territory. It is only in a private client seat that trainees paddle in the shallows. Acting for *"pretty rich clients right down to the normal everyday guy,"* the department is seen as *"a very good first seat* and good for finding your feet." This is because "generally it is quite sleepy and quiet, and there is less urgency...because the clients are dead." The charities department is really popular with trainees, perhaps because it has such impressive clients: the Charities Commission, the UN High Commission for Refugees (to advise on fundraising and governance issues), Stonewall, Barnardos, Scope and UNICEF.

On your first day "you are told you must organise yourself and get your PSC done before you qualify." Throughout the two years "you are treated as a responsible person" and "a fully fledged member of the department." But when your best doggy paddle starts to deteriorate into panic and that sinking sensation takes over, supervisors are close, lifebelt in hand. While some trainees have their own offices, the majority share with a supervisor who monitors the amount of work colleagues give the trainee and "cracks down when you are getting inundated." The two appraisals per seat are relaxed affairs and just as likely to take place in a restaurant as the office. Our sources also reported being consulted on the firm's strategy, though admittedly trainee lunches with the senior partner can be "a stilted affair." No doubt the celebrations on qualification were anything but: two of the three qualifiers stayed on.

full of potential

The "main port of call," Putney is home to three RC offices located near the High Street. No.2 Putney Hill is an old bank, and though one trainee assured us that "at Russell-Cooke we don't go in for gimmicks," we did learn that "the original vaults in the basement are where they store the deeds etc." Round the corner No.113 is "a concrete monstrosity," and a third office at the Crescent is "a rat warren [sic] with tiny staircases and crevices" situated over an estate agents, who could no doubt come up with a more appealing description. When working in the Crescent you must take care: "There are several different stairwells and [entry] codes. A trainee was actually locked in once and had to call a partner and ask to be let out."

In Putney a 9am–6.30pm day leaves plenty of time for socialising. Trainees frequently lunch together at the Blue Pumpkin or Pizza Express and recently sampled the posh new Rocket Riverside at Putney Wharf for a trainee night out. More commonly, they pile into a local pub that's become known as "the sweaty fox." Each year RC enters the Manches Cup sailing regatta and one enterprising trainee recently established a football team. On sunny summer evenings, staff play rounders "on some patch of grass down by the river" and there was once a netball team, but unfortunately it was disbanded after being declared insolvent by the firm. Apparently the team had squandered its entire budget on a trip to Bournemouth and too many chips.

upstream and downstream

Most of our sources had spent time in the Bedford Row office, which is home to a property litigation group and the professional discipline lawyers, who act for professional bodies such as The Institute of Legal Executives, the Architects Registration Board and the Office for the Supervision of Solicitors. With a younger, smaller collection of staff, there is "not such a clear demarcation between departments" and "a more sociable and relaxed atmosphere" than in Putney. One trainee even admitted: "We did have a reputation as the rebel branch...you can get away with more there." The offices are situated in a "narrow and tall" Georgian townhouse with plenty of character: one trainee amused us with tales of sloping floors – "I have to pull myself in and hold onto my desk!" And after hanging on all day, "there is a mass exodus at 5.30pm. It's religious...but people obviously have to work very hard during the day." Trail around some of the local pubs – The Dolphin, Old Nick, Rugby Tavern or Penderell's Oak – and you'll find them.

The small Kingston office houses a family law team, but doesn't usually take trainees and, consequently, was viewed by our sources with the suspicious apprehension of an airline pilot approaching the Bermuda Triangle. We sincerely hope that the trainee destined for the newly created family seat left Putney with a tracking device.

Held 'up town' at the RAC Club on Pall Mall, the annual Christmas party brings the whole firm together for a slap-up dinner and dancing. Offering valuable insight into the type of people you will find at the firm, one trainee told us: "*As soon as the disco starts, 95% of the workforce is on the dance floor. Nobody can dance very well, but they lurvve it.*" RC trainees come in all varieties and ages and from all manner of backgrounds and universities. They claimed to be "*open minded as to what we do*" and ready to "*just get on with it.*" Whatever it turns out to be. All had chosen the firm for its low-key feel and Putney base, but all valued the presence of the central London office.

and finally...

Russell-Cooke is ideal for those who haven't made a decision between commercial and private client business. Or as one trainee put it: "*If you don't know which side of the coin you want to see fall.*"

Salans

the facts

Location: London
Number of UK partners/assistants: 31/30
Total number of trainees: 7
Seats: 4 x 6 months
Alternative seats: secondments

A rather unusual international hybrid with offices from Almaty to Bucharest, Warsaw to Shanghai, Salans is clearly not entering into self-delusion when describing itself as "a truly international law firm." A New York office it may have, but don't be tempted to see Salans as another one of those US firms with a UK outpost; history and present-day reality tell a very different story.

mine's a cosmopolitan

Salans has got where it is as a firm by a process that can only be described as organic. One hazy trainee historian took up the tale: "*There was a firm in London with a renowned banking practice, Harris, Rosenblatt & Kramer. Then Salans in Paris, which was all about arbitration. So the Anglo-French merger was first.*" And then? "*And then there was Christy & Viener who had been in New York since the year dot, so incorporating them made an Anglo-French-American axis.*" But what of the Anglo-French-American-Hungarian axis? Well, suffice it to say that, in addition to its own outfits in Russia, the Far East and former Soviet bloc states, Salans last year snapped up offices from the doomed Altheimer & Gray partnership, giving it instant capacity in Bratislava, Bucharest, Istanbul, Prague and Shanghai. A smart move that the firm has been quick to build upon. In June 2004 it announced a tie-up with Hungarian firm Szabo Kovari Tercsak, whose clients include McDonald's, and it then cracked open the bubbly when it received formal approval from the Chinese government to operate out of A&G's old office in China. All in all, the firm now operates in 14 jurisdictions worldwide. Truly, truly international.

For all this cosmopolitanism, trainees talked of a distinctly British flavour to life and work in London, stressing that "*it has always retained its identity, it's not been branded.*" Day-to-day life is "*not likely to feel massively international in terms of the work you get,*" and whilst one specific client secondment is not uncommon for trainees, no one below associate level finds themselves working in an overseas office. Nevertheless, trainees were very aware that "*interplay between international offices is a feature in the upper echelons of the firm,*" and were clear sighted about the strategic importance of London. Two years ago the firm came close to merging with Theodore Goddard, and as one trainee explained: "*The proposed merger was supposed to create a large London hub for a worldwide network, but after it fell through the emphasis has really been on marketing the 'international law firm' angle.*"

Although the merger talks collapsed, six TG partners and a whole host of assistants decamped to Salans to take up residence in the employment, corporate and media departments. Such a sudden intake has had *"quite a dramatic effect on an office our size,"* and although *"it's gone very smoothly,"* trainees told us that here, as on the wider Salans stage post-A&G, *"we're going through a small period of consolidation."*

a london calling

When we asked trainees to define the atmosphere and the attraction of Salans in London, they had plenty to say. *"We're a medium-sized firm in the UK," "lean and hungry," "not run on a shoestring but with things kept tight, everyone busy, always looking for work."* Highly regarded for its employment expertise for companies like Rotary Watches, Lloyds TSB, Cadogan Tate and Parity Group, the firm also possesses significant ability in consumer asset finance, undertaking retail credit transactions, lease financings and motor finance for Nissan, Volkswagen, Barclays and Bank of Ireland amongst others. As a trainee, you'll be able to sample this kind of work and the official list of seats also includes property, banking, litigation, employment and corporate. In the last year the firm has acted for the purchaser on the sale of the entire issued share capital of retail firm Cromwells Madhouse plc and acted for DNA Films on its $50 million joint venture with Fox Searchlight Pictures. Furthermore the firm also has a niche expertise in internet betting and gaming.

As for why they chose the place, trainees spoke of *"a vibrant atmosphere"* and *"professionalism that also has a relaxed element."* Size was also important to them, as one honest type admitted. *"Simply by virtue of its smaller size and the small trainee population, you get a lot of responsibility. I knew if I went to a magic circle factory I'm so lazy I would have hidden in the corner doing due diligence."* There's little chance of hiding in any of the four six-month seats, and autonomy and responsibility come thick and fast. With its *"mix of contentious work for big institutions and non-contentious advisory work,"*

employment is a popular choice, not least because *"you're treated like an associate."* One trainee told us: *"I had four meetings yesterday; I've been to tribunal, had masses of face-to-face client contact and even taken two cases from first meeting to negotiating the final settlement."*

Our sources admitted that *"the more formalised nature of the work in litigation means your experience is more piecemeal,"* but still described it as a popular department. *"Document management is a fact of life, but you also get a good range of drafting, court visits and experience of general commercial and property litigation and pretty big-ticket arbitration."* It is additionally the department where trainees get most *"exposure to international work, liaising with New York, Warsaw and Paris particularly."* Elsewhere, insolvency might see trainees in court for bankruptcy hearings, corporate brings *"a broad mix – the standout was a £40 million fraud case"* and in commercial there is *"everything! Mining companies, water filtration companies, air conditioning companies, airlines..."*

mouthing off

Speaking to trainees, we got the impression that they are robust, sorted and unpretentious types. *"We don't seem to get people off the 'go-straight-to-university-law-school-law firm' conveyor belt."* Though formal training is *"very good"* and there are mid- and end-of-seat appraisals, the ethos of training is decidedly upfront. *"People take you to one side and say, 'This is good' or 'This isn't.' For example, my boss at the moment is quite mouthy, so we have a robust relationship to say the least!"* Whilst we wouldn't want to overstress the value placed on self-sufficiency, one of our sources summed it up perfectly: *"You get out what you put in with this firm. The harder you work, the more you ask, the more you try and do, the more they'll give you feedback, support and push you in the right direction."*

could do better

It was entirely characteristic of our sources that they were unflinching in their criticism as well as their praise. *"The offices aren't the greatest,"* said trainees of the two floors (fourth and sixth) of the EC2 building they worked in. *"It is a 1960s concrete block – the last one in an area that's been redeveloped – and it's made to look dire by the beautiful, shiny vacant premises on either side."* A move remains *"a Salans legend at present,"* but in the meantime there is always the consolation that *"the entrance or the stairway is listed or something; it got used for that BBC series The Hustle."* Hobnobbing with Adrian Lester, or a more pleasant working environment? We know which we'd choose.

Trainees were unequivocal that *"the social life is in rehabilitation. It did die for a while"* following the expansion of the office, but things are getting back on track with *"events starting to be planned for every month."* They seem to enjoy each other's company: *"with such a small group you are sort of comrades in arms."* Two pubs, the Red Herring and Fullers, are within *"a literal stone's throw"* for light post-work refreshment, but *"I don't think any of us want to be part of some incestuous trainee continuation of university or law school, it's not why we're here."* Well said, but they are here to qualify and in 2004 all three qualifiers took jobs with the firm.

and finally...

While Salans may not be the best-known name on the recruitment circuit, we'd be surprised if its popularity doesn't increase with each year of growth and change. An ideal pick for those who want to sidestep the standard City offerings.

Samuel Phillips & Co

the facts

Location: Newcastle-upon-Tyne
Number of UK partners/assistants: 5/10
Total number of trainees: 4
Seats: 4x6 months
Alternative seats: None

More quintessentially Newcastle than brown ale and black and white stripes, Samuel Phillips & Co is a firm with an excellent regional reputation. We think it's a must-consider for any North East trainee looking for a smaller firm.

a stitch in time

If you have clichéd preconceptions about Newcastle, then chances are you won't be joining the firm in two years' time. It's not that Samuel Phillips doesn't welcome people from further afield (*"several of us trainees are from the Midlands"*); it's just that *"everyone at the firm has strong connections to the North East"* either by birth or through the still-more-intense passion of the recently converted. The majority of those we interviewed had spent time on work experience placements at the firm or paralegalling.

It may be located in the heart of Grainger Town close to the centre of Newcastle, but Samuel Phillips is much more than a high-street practice. *"The range of work put it a cut above the norm,"* said one trainee. Quite rightly. With over thirty years' experience of advising hospitals on everything from consent and surgery risk-management procedures to the handling of negligence claims, the firm has a top-grade healthcare pedigree. It currently advises a variety of NHS bodies including the Newcastle-upon-Tyne Hospitals Trust, for which it handles complex and high-value clinical negligence claims, such as those arising from heart transplant operations, and the recent sad case of a baby born with half a face. Looking beyond Newcastle, *"where we can avoid conflicts of interest,"* the firm also takes on claimant work.

The Newcastle Hospitals Trust is also a significant client of the highly regarded employment department, which balances a range of applicant and respondent work as well as offering non-contentious advice. However, there's more to to this firm than health and hospitals – Wessex Taverns, Metnor Group, Ultimate Leisure and Alfas Group are all part of a glowing client roster. Furthermore, the family department enjoys not only *"an established private client base and lots of business and personal referrals,"* but also wider repute for its children in care, adoption, access rights and abduction expertise. National charities Relate and Reunite regularly draw on the firm's abilities in these areas.

a legal patchwork

Until this year, the firm's strengths have boiled down into a tri-partite trainee experience, with the two years split across three departments: civil litigation, family and clinical negligence. Each possessing *"specific strengths"* and *"all doing things slightly differently,"* our sources had been offered a textured training contract that showed them *"a real breadth of experience."* In future years a fourth 'non-contentious' seat is being added, which will offer residential conveyancing, commercial property, general commercial, and wills, tax and trusts work. The department has just been beefed up with the hiring of a partner and other staff, so time will tell exactly how this new seat pans out.

Trainees in the civil litigation seat share an office with either a paralegal or another trainee, which is *"good for support and sharing tips on work."* Although attached to a specific supervisor, duties are dispensed by all the partners in the group, so that on the one hand *"you get employment work – preparing policies and procedures for firms, helping to set up breakfast seminars and helping to conduct* [employment] *audits."* And on the other *"you'll do PI work and run your own cases under supervision."* This was the department where our sources had enjoyed most client contact, particularly on *"repossessions or debt recovery for small local businesses."*

Although also sharing an office with a paralegal, a clinical negligence seat is more 'managed', with *"tasks and memos coming to you from partners and fee earners."* That said, *"dipping in and out of a case that settled for three million"* is scarcely unexciting, and the range and sophistication of work means there is plenty to keep trainees interested. *"There's a lot of legal aid form-filling and dealing with the LSC,"* but at least *"you do get to do some advocacy at appeal hearings against case costs being reduced."* Aside from these on-your-feet experiences, trainees confirm that *"the nitty-gritty"* is the main attraction of the seat. *"Compiling medical summaries and chronologies gets you familiar with medical jargon, but they're often extensive. You have to conclude whether there's a case for negligence or not – it's a great learning experience."* Overall it's a patchwork seat, but trainees conclude that the net effect is more collage than simply rag tag: *"At the end of the seat you've done all the tasks and built a general knowledge of how a case proceeds."*

Sitting with the senior partner in family puts trainees in the thick of things. And there's action aplenty. Wheezed one trainee: *"Whereas the pace in the other departments is measured, here the nature of the work means a lot of urgent applications and more time pressure."* Once they'd got their second wind, trainees relished *"going to court to do simple directions and first appointments, and interviewing clients by yourself."* As well as learning by osmosis from the *"phenomenal"* Jennifer Goldstein, trainees reported really getting their teeth into more involved matters. *"When acting for individuals or local authorities on care or adoption issues, you're juggling social services reports and so many different people's views – it's textbook* [turned] *into practice."*

knit one, pearl one

Samuel Phillips occupies an 18th-century Grade II listed building known as Gibb Chambers, once the home of a Dr Thomas John Gibb, whose fame as a dispensing chemist was such that he's even mentioned in a Geordie ballad called *The Blaydon Races*. You'll find full lyrics on the Samuel Phillips website, but in brief it's a happy tale of the friendship, mischance and general drunken abandon of a group of locals on a day trip. And we couldn't help feel that such an association seems appropriate for a firm whose intimate *"family atmosphere"* hails almost from another era. It's not that the firm is behind the times in training, in fact the *"day-to-day feedback,"* *"monthly assessment chats with the training supervisor"* and *"thorough end-of-seat appraisals"* made our sources some of the best-assessed trainees we've encountered. Said one: *"I'm neither spoon fed nor dumped upon; when I qualify I'll feel like a fully fledged lawyer not a scared NQ."*

Socialising is *"almost always firmwide"* rather than confined to the four-person trainee population, but though small in number the trainees are big in social influence. *"We set up a club called the 501 club."* So named because? *"Because at 5.01 on a Friday we're all at Ghengis drinking together. Everyone who fancies a drink on a Friday knows there'll be Samuels people there."* And let's not forget *The Christmas Review*, a light-hearted rag written by trainees and paralegals and read by everyone at the firm as they enjoy a few drinks *"before going off for a sit-down meal."* Add in the fact that *"nearly the whole firm turned out for the evening do"* after the wedding of an employment lawyer and perhaps you see what we mean about the close-knit atmosphere. Not wishing to drop a stitch, the one trainee who qualified in 2004 was offered a position at the firm and accepted it.

and finally...

A thorough training at a firm that is thoroughly decent in every sense of the word. If you're looking for a non-corporate legal life in the North East you could do no better.

Shadbolt & Co

the facts

Location: London, Reigate
Number of UK partners/assistants: 23/30
Total number of trainees: 8
Seats: 4x6 months
Alternative seats: Paris, secondments

Yes, it's based in Reigate but this is not your average commuter-belt player. One of the top firms for construction work, Shadbolt & Co has embraced the international nature of its chosen industry.

family history

If you're sitting comfortably, we'll tell you how Shadbolts was built. *"It all dates back to when Dick Shadbolt started the firm. He used to be the head of construction at what is now CMS Cameron McKenna and left 14 years ago to retire gracefully. He kept a few clients on to finish off a couple of deals and he was enjoying the work and so kept going and was soon inundated. Another lawyer left somewhere else to join him and Shadbolt & Co was born. He rented an office in Reigate, as he lives near here – after all, he was supposed to be retiring. Then he got the offices behind that and the firm has grown and grown and grown."*

You'll still see Dick around the office *"if some heavyweight stuff comes in or if a client wants him in particular,"* although he's *"more of a figurehead to drum up business now."* Construction is still *"the main thrust of the firm"* and clients include building materials suppliers, major contractors such as Jarvis and Kier Group, and energy and transport infrastructure companies. A good chunk of the firm's work, perhaps 25%, is international; as well as French matters and Olympics-related deals in Athens, the firm has connections in Hong Kong and recently advised a Scandinavian government on a £30 million aid-funded construction project in Central America. Because *"when something's being built it can all go wrong,"* a large proportion of the construction team handles contentious work. Cases do reach the courts, but in construction world these days arbitration and adjudication are just as likely to feature.

When we asked about clients, we heard that *'quite often the company is* [an individual's] *own business, so they feel passionate about it. Even with the bigger clients, you find yourself working with the founders or their children and it's nice to be helping people to whom it means so much."* Shadbolt also fields corporate, property, commercial litigation and employment teams. Traditionally these have been reliant on the clients brought in by the construction lawyers but, some teams are managing to build independent practices: For instance, the corporate team recently acted on a £30 million share disposal for a top security company, while the commercial litigation team has worked on software disputes and problems arising out of aircraft leases.

mud and bullets

As a trainee, *"you have to be prepared to try construction."* Let's face it, why apply to Shadbolt if bricks and mortar don't appeal? When we did our interviews, around half of the current trainees had come from a background in construction, for example as site managers or surveyors. However, this type of CV is by no means obligatory and the firm won't expect you to be a ready-made expert. *"They are prepared to take you on and train you as someone who doesn't have any construction knowledge; you don't have to have read all the building journals."* For the sake of those who haven't considered this area of work, we asked the trainees to sell construction law to us. Here's what they said: *"It's big names, big deals and claims; often loads of things have gone wrong and you're sorting out a big mess, which is quite rewarding."* Another told us about the *"ooh factor"* – *"when you're driving to work, the people you see digging up the road are your clients."*

The first seat is often in contentious construction *"as it's trainee friendly."* The cases Shadbolt handles are big; trainees told us about one High Court battle where they spent *"the best part of 20 days in court"*…*"there were two QCs on each side, four parties involved and endless partners."* Aside from gawping at judges from a safe position behind a battalion of barristers, trainees draft letters and witness statements, and we even heard of one trainee being responsible for a piece of expert evidence *"about the composition of sewage."* Nasty. As ever on mammoth cases, trainees also have to do their fair share of document management chores.

Commercial litigation is also likely to feature early on in your training contract. Here *"the matters are a lot smaller"* and, with only two fee earners (compared with the 14-strong contentious construction group), so is the team. Because you'll be working very closely with those in charge, you'll have *"big*

input" on *"franchising, shareholder disagreements, commercial debt and local business issues."* The firm likes trainees to have plenty of experience in both contentious and non-contentious work, so after the former has been completed, seats await them in non-contentious construction, corporate, IP, commercial property and employment. Seat allocation works well on the whole; close attention is paid to trainees' preferences, but limitations on places mean they must be prepared to be flexible.

paris match

If you speak French *"you will get to go to Paris."* In the tiny French office you'll help out with everything that's going on, but *"the fundamental thing they do in Paris is international arbitration"* as the International Court of Arbitration is based there. Expect to research points of English law for the Parisians, perhaps giving your humble opinion where a choice of English or French jurisdiction needs to be made. Back in the UK, secondments to construction companies are also available, which our interviewees felt were *"a great way to learn."* Giving you the opportunity to be part of a small in-house legal team, *"it really teaches you to up your game; as your work won't be checked by a partner, you have to really make sure it's all right as the bottom line is you."* If things get *"hairy,"* fear not – Shadbolt's Reigate and London offices *"are there for you."* You should also expect to take one seat in the firm's expanding London branch, which is on the verge of moving to larger premises near Blackfriars. Trainees told us: *"The firm is keen to grow the London office and have more departments represented there. I think the idea is to grow the whole firm…but it may well be that some departments find this harder in Reigate."* Swelling numbers at the junior end, two of the three qualifiers took jobs in 2004.

on the clapham omnibus

Partners tend to have backgrounds in the construction industry, which is *"a draw for clients"* and means that the atmosphere in Reigate is *"more relaxed than a firm led by the needs of City bankers."* Many lawyers have, like Dick Shadbolt himself, *"all done time in the City and want to work for a good firm, but also want a higher standard of living."* Which brings us on nicely to the joys of Reigate. This small Surrey town set in *"beautiful countryside"* is *"quite refined and full of ladies who lunch."* It's *"not a kicking place,"* but it's a very manageable commute from south London via London Bridge or Victoria, and thus ideal for those not ready to leave London entirely. Amusingly, when we asked about their favourite post-work hangouts, trainees surprised us by naming the Slug and Lettuce at Clapham Junction.

The whole firm gets together at Christmas for a knees-up at that well-known party mecca Gatwick Airport. *"It's easy for people from the Paris office, Gatwick is near Reigate and people from London can get the Gatwick Express that runs all night."* Yeah, but it's still Gatwick Airport! In the summer there's usually a firm barbecue and five or six cricket fixtures against clients, where *"there is an element of letting them win...though that may just be flattering our team!'*

and finally...

Forget builders' bums – at Shadbolt & Co piles and scaffolding are glamorous With its international work, high-level arbitration and clients at the forefront of their industry, this firm is well worth putting on a hard hat for a site inspection.

Shearman & Sterling LLP

the facts

Location: London
Number of UK partners/assistants: 27/97
Total number of trainees: 15
Seats: 4x6 months
Alternative seats: None

Considered one of the US's most successful legal exports, Shearman & Sterling brandishes the scalps of an ever-growing number of UK lawyers. While traditional strengths lie in corporate/M&A and capital markets, London also offers training in international arbitration, competition, project finance, banking, financial services and tax.

yankee doodle went to town...

Shearman & Sterling prides itself on its history of excellence. Established in New York in 1873, this firm is inextricably linked with US history, and its website makes great reading. Shearmans' lawyers were heavily involved in litigation arising from the American Civil War, they advised corporate legend Jay Gould in his takeover of the Union Pacific Railroad in 1875 and they have acted for the Ford Motor Company since the days of the Tin Lizzie. Founding partner David Field won a landmark civil rights case in the wake of the American Civil War, when he acted for a civilian detained and sentenced to death by a military tribunal for aiding the confederacy. The Supreme Court found, in a decision relevant especially today, that only congress can suspend habeas corpus. His associate Thomas Shearman won a supposedly unwinnable case when he proved that the conflict was a civil war rather than a rebellion, defeating an insurance claim on a merchant ship sunk during the conflict. The firm has also acted in some of the highest profile and iconic corporate deals, restructurings and disputes in the country's history.

and called it macaroni!

Given this history, it should come as no surprise that Shearman & Sterling is renowned for its traditional 'white shoe' culture. This is a firm as American as baseball and macaroni and cheese. And yet, despite its deeply East Coast heritage, rivals look upon Shearman & Sterling as *"an example of how to crack Europe,"* and trainees told us: *"Whilst it might be a US firm by reputation, it truly is international."* Shearmans now boasts offices across Europe including Rome, Munich, Frankfurt, Mannheim, Düsseldorf, Brussels, Paris and, of course, London. This is in addition to its Beijing, Hong Kong, Tokyo, Singapore, Abu Dhabi, Toronto and US offices. The recent addition of a Sao Paolo office almost feels like wanton excess. Our sources loved the *"international vibe,"* relishing *"working closely with Germany and France on one deal, New York on another."* We heard of trainees travelling to Egypt and across Europe for work, as well as for global department get-togethers, but there are also opportunities to make a longer stay. Overseas seats are currently available in Abu Dhabi and Singapore.

The firm's back catalogue of high-profile international work is dazzling to say the least. Nor is the firm afraid to boast about it. True to all-American free-market ideals, Shearmans advised Maggie Thatcher's government on the privatisation of Britain's gas, petroleum, telecoms, steel, rail, electricity and water industries. Following the 1989 collapse of the Berlin wall, its lawyers advised the German government on the privatisation of assets of the former East Germany, and they acted for the Chinese government when, in 1979, Deng Xiaoping announced China's open-door policy. Nor is it shy about building on those initial inroads, recently acting for the Bank of China in the $2.67 billion IPO of its Hong Kong banking subsidiary.

the half-full glass

But there is a more British, more intimate side to Shearman & Sterling that is, according to our sources, typical of its international methodology – *"a true dedication to bringing up and developing a genuinely local practice."* The London office was established in 1972, and in 1996 began practising with dual capacity in UK and US law. Since then, its numbers have increased fivefold and it now boasts around 130 lawyers. The firm's aims are clear; just ask any trainee: it wants to be the market leader for US/UK legal services. But those same trainees advised: *"There is such a large UK capacity that you couldn't call it a typical US firm."* Almost half the London office's clients are non-US entities, which is of course another way of saying that more than half are. Nevertheless, it certainly doesn't get much more English than advising WestLB in the $1 billion financing of the new Wembley Stadium project. There is also *"a huge amount of multi-jurisdictional work,"* as the firm has earned a reputation as the number one in the City for complex cross-border acquisition financing. Major clients include British Gas, BT, Barclays Capital, Deutsche Bank, Citigroup, Nokia and Powergen.

The London training experience is the usual four by six-month affair, and trainees must spend at least two seats in the firm's core practice areas, choosing from banking and finance, project finance, M&A, litigation or anti-trust/competition law. Beyond that, their choices are freer, with the possibility of split seats in some areas allowing maximum breadth. In London, international arbitration is the contentious strong suit, so trainees may find themselves making the occasional trip to the Paris office. And those with a penchant for Renoir might be interested to learn that the firm has developed a niche in fine art litigation.

the back-breaking greenback?

Understandably, Shearman & Sterling is looking for excellent applicants who, as one trainee put it, *"relish hard work and intellectual challenges."* And they meant it. Whilst the word on the street is that a junior assistant is expected to do a whopping 2,200 billable hours per year (that would be around nine long, arduous hours billed each day), the truth seems a little more relaxed: *"If the transaction is there to be completed and you need 100 documents for signing, then yes you'll be in at 8am and home at 4am…if you go home at all. But on a quiet day I'll be in at 9.30am, home by 7pm."* Time in lieu is just one of the payoffs for such hardship, and our sources had been lured by *"the draw of top City work at a top international transactional firm,"* fully aware that the hours came with the territory. In exchange for your youthful energy and precious time, you'll be paid a king's ransom.

Forget production line values. Trainees are outnumbered by paralegals, thus guaranteeing little of the inane pagination and photocopying that can blight a training contract. Our sources valued *"the chance to be an individual whilst training. You're one of a small population and you get incredible attention from supervisors and HR."* In addition to mid and end-of-seat appraisals and weighty input into seat selection, trainees also enjoy the tender ministrations of *"a mentor who takes you out to lunch and makes sure you're all right."* But this is a firm that has blazed many legal trails, and it expects its trainees to continue the tradition. We weren't surprised to hear the influx of American motivational parlance, and words like *"proactive"* also came up with regularity. The firm's website proclaims that it wants "self-starters who will assume professional responsibility early in their careers," and our sources agreed, telling us: *"You do need to use your initiative."*

The atmosphere in the Liverpool Street offices is relatively informal and the dress code smart casual. You won't be swanning around in flip-flops and sarong, though one source said: *"I often wear trainers and no one cares."* The social life may be *"not force fed,"* but there is *"plenty to pick and choose from"* with Spitalfields and Farringdon close by. All too often though, *"it's All Bar One and the Corney & Barrow. Again."* Still, it's the same with the rest of the law firms in the area, so in this sense at least, Shearmans types are far from unique.

and finally...

In almost all areas of practice, and despite the downturn, which led to the lay-off of 13 associates in London and Frankfurt, Shearman & Sterling has maintained or improved its market position year on year. The good news is that the firm had jobs for all five qualifiers in 2004, though one left the law entirely. If you're committed to hard work and maintaining the firm's reputation for excellence, it's a stellar pick.

Shoosmiths

the facts

Location: Northampton, Nottingham, Reading, Solent, Milton Keynes, Basingstoke, Birmingham
Number of UK partners/assistants: 65/134
Total number of trainees: 22
Seats: 4x6 months
Alternative seats: Secondments

Increasingly a *"commercially focused"* firm, Shoosmiths has grown from small beginnings in Northampton to having offices dotted across England from Southampton to Nottingham. Having carefully considered their options, two years ago the partners agreed to invest in a new Birmingham office. After a small fall in profits last year, a whopping 66% profits rise this year tells its own story. Shoosmiths is gearing up.

shoo-per duper

Last year we got mixed messages from our interviewees. Some trainees sounded complacent and unimaginative in their attitudes towards work; by contrast we applauded the driving ambition of others. Overall, we wondered quite where the firm was pitching its recruitment drive. Everyone we interviewed this year was raring to work. *"This is a vibrant, active, young place,"* they enthused, telling us: *"We're all willing to go the extra mile for ourselves and the firm."* Largely outgoing, mainly graduates of good redbrick universities, what really marked out trainees this year was *"ambition to get on, not just the desire to finish what you're doing."*

Fortunately for them, right now Shoosmiths seems to be a good place for ambition to flourish. It has two divisions: personal injury and commercial services. The former is moving along nicely, but the latter is the place to be for excitement. Our contacts described the firm's hunger *"to grow nationally in all areas of commercial practice."* The new Birmingham office has raided rivals like Wragges and Pinsents for a succession of lateral hires at associate and partner level, boosting the property litigation team and turbo-charging the construction team. Younger partners with *"excellent experience of high-level work"* are energising the firm and enthusing Birmingham trainees, just like the *"brilliant"* ex-magic circle partner Oliver Brookshaw has done with his highly rated corporate finance work in the Nottingham office.

This energy isn't confined by region. When *"partners and associates constantly shuttle around between offices,"* both the buzz and the work quickly spread. *"Gala Casinos are a big client in Nottingham, but now if they're doing some construction work, they'll call us up in Birmingham."* Touches like generic 08700 phone numbers for all staff underline the firm's eagerness to be seen as a single entity across offices, so *"from a client's point of view you're not calling Shoosmiths Southampton, you're calling Shoosmiths."* At the same time IT systems are unified across the country, so that any staff member can log on at any computer in any office. *"It's called the hot-desk principle,"* giggled one computer-literate type. Cool-headed trainees summed up: *"It really feels like one firm."*

soft-shoo shuffle

Trainees are recruited specifically for the Reading, Nottingham, Southampton and Northampton offices, with Northampton recruits agreeing to be available for seats in Milton Keynes or Birmingham. Otherwise, there is no pressure on trainees to move between offices for their four seats, but the option is there if they fancy a change or a specific seat that's available elsewhere. Whether they stick at their home office or twist on a seat elsewhere, trainees are faced with *"a good variety of work and responsibility."* Almost a dizzying variety. On offer across the three Midlands offices, for example, are (deep breath): banking litigation and debt recovery, claimant PI and clinical negligence, construction, commercial litigation, commercial property and landlord and tenant litigation, IP and regulatory law (product liability, food law etc.), not forgetting planning and corporate.

The firm is *"generally very accommodating"* when it comes to seat selection, leaving most trainees *"more or less happy."* When an employment seat wasn't available, one Reading trainee was sent over to the Basingstoke office to fulfil their tribunal-based fantasies. There are also the occasional client secondments to companies like DaimlerChrysler.

pay attention at the back, jennings!

Although spread out over six sites, trainees describe *"a good group dynamic."* Is it the freshers' residential PSC course that fosters good relations? Well, yes and no. *"Three weeks in a country house in the middle of nowhere...it was a great bonding experience, but a bit like boarding school."* After these weeks together sharing lumpy semolina and after-class detentions, they maintain contact via *"a good bit of e-mail banter."* Subsequent training days for all trainees every two months had the distinct feel of double maths last thing on a Friday: *"They're supposed to be about learning a new legal discipline, but it's a great chance for a gossip!"* These important dates in the diary rotate between each office, so they also allow trainees to put faces to names with which they've grown familiar from *"constant phone calls to other offices."*

As well as being the longest established in the network, Shoosmiths' Northampton office at The Lakes is the HQ. It houses much of the volume personal injury practice in addition to central support staff. With over 400 people on site *"you don't know everyone."* Aside from *"the odd person in their ivory tower,"* a full-time dress-down policy and a good range of experience keep trainees here happy. Their only major gripe concerns the removal of the canteen and its replacement with *"dreadful sandwiches."* This is more serious than you might think: based in modern premises on a business park some distance from the centre of town, *"it's a long walk for a decent sandwich if you haven't brought lunch."* Trainees also missed the sense of community fostered by the canteen, saying: *"We used to have meals with each other or with partners."* Friday night drinks at the Cherry Tree are some consolation, especially when *"you time it to arrive just after a partner has put their card behind the bar."* A sports and social committee takes up the slack with frequent events, and trainees often get together at weekends to sample Northampton's copious nightlife: *"The Lube is brilliant."* We shudder to imagine.

land of milk and honey

Most of the trainees in the Brum-Milton Keynes-Northampton axis live in Northampton, so the *"easy"* commute to MK makes it a popular choice. Recently relocated to *"trendy and modern"* new premises, proximity to national and multinational companies makes for interesting clients including Barclays Bank, BP and Nike. An employment seat covers both advisory work for employers and *"tribunals for high-net-worth individuals in unfair dismissal cases."*

Our contacts felt *"there'll soon be trainees recruited to Birmingham,"* and the firm agrees. The bustling Brum practice should soon be of a size to support its own trainee population and recruitment is beginning now. The construction and property litigation practices based there are the departments of the moment, beautifully packaged in *"City-esque, glitzy and glamourous"* offices. Trainees work alongside *"dynamic young partners"* on contentious and non-contentious matters for *"large property developers and small sub-contractors, the MDs of multinationals and sole-traders."*

Situated on the canalside close to the city centre, the Nottingham arm has a novel approach to client retention – *"It was one of our clients who built the office."* Modern premises are matched by up-market work, and clients like Boots and WH Smith give a flavour of the office's national reach. The national corporate finance team is run from Nottingham, and like the large commercial property team, it is popular with trainees. In property, one of our sources had *"worked with retail sector clients from all over the country as well as on the compulsory purchase order for the largest shopping centre in Nottingham."* After hours, there's a lot going on in Nottingham. A pub connoisseur recommended a certain hostelry – *"The Trip to Jerusalem in*

the base of the old castle. It's the oldest pub in the country." And for those who like nothing better than to curl up in front of the telly: *"We all watched the England match round at the managing partner's house."* No one mention penalties...

having a crystal ball

In Southampton and Reading, as in Nottingham, trainees usually have some connection to the local area, *"but it isn't vital."* The Southampton office is tucked onto a business park just by the M27, which means *"you do really need a car."* Traditionally, seats have only been offered in litigation, property, coco and landlord and tenant, but a growing profile means more work and *"the firm has opened up seats in employment, residential conveyancing and planning."*

Reading offers seats in property, coco, litigation, construction and employment, and a Thames Valley location means *"a lot of work for small to medium-sized IT companies."* A special injuries unit in Basingstoke is also more than reachable. *"You get a good level of responsibility and a good mixture of work,"* and trainees are also encouraged to get involved in marketing – they recently helped organise a table football league for local businesses. Socially, the six trainees in Reading consult the Oracle shopping and leisure centre for everything from lunch to clothes to after-work drinks. The only thing it doesn't provide is gnomic utterances about the chance of getting a job on qualification. On this score grad recruitment were happy to report improvements on last year's figures with ten of the 13 qualifiers remaining at the firm nationally.

and finally...

If you intend to steer clear of London and are hungry for good-quality work in the specific regions in which Shoosmiths operates, this firm is more than worth a look. We've tried to avoid playing the 'nice place to work' card because in the past we sense it's made the firm sound too soft. You could always ask the recruitment team to give you a quick flash of that particular trump card though...

Sidley Austin Brown & Wood LLP

the facts

Location: London
Number of UK partners/assistants: 37/98
Total number of trainees: 16
Seats: length and number varies
Alternative seats: None

One of the corps of successful 'American firms' in London, Sidley Austin Brown & Wood offers a distinctive finance-based training contract.

it's the real thing

In 2001, the Sidley Austin bit of the firm merged with the Brown & Wood bit. The tie-up was masterminded by the two US parents, presumably looking primarily at the benefits for each partnership stateside. However, the effect in London was also significant. The combined London practice achieved critical mass, making it easier to stamp its mark in the UK market. Headquartered in the Windy City of Chicago, Sidleys is the fifth largest US firm (as measured by an annual turnover verging on $1 billion) and has some 1,500 lawyers in 14 offices in North America, Europe and Asia. The UK portion of this global player is made up of 90 lawyers, 27 of whom are partners, 80% of these UK-qualified.

Finance and capital markets, more particularly, securitisations, dominate activity in the London office. On the US securities side there are registered public offerings, Rule 144A issues, private placements, stock exchange listings and depository receipt programmes. English capital markets work includes emerging markets transactions, equity and debt financing, debt restructuring and listings on the London Stock Exchange. The firm is instructed by US and European companies, investment and commercial banks, and financing, leasing and insurance companies. To give you a flavour of the work, acting for Deutsche Bank, the team enabled Cadbury Schweppes to raise money in the US for the first time. It did so by way of a $2 billion issue of guaranteed notes through a US affiliate company and the offering was listed on the London Stock Exchange. It carried out much the same exercise in raising $900 million for a division of Coca-Cola by way of notes issued through a Dutch affiliate company and listing the offering on the Luxembourg Stock Exchange.

If you're following us so far, try this next transaction on for size. In 2003, Sidleys acted for the underwriters (led by a group of seven investment banks) of a public offering and sale of $850 million worth of exchangeable capital securities of Royal Bank of Scotland, which were listed on the New York Stock Exchange and are exchangeable for RBS's Tier 1 preference shares.

It's little wonder that when we asked a trainee to sum up securitisation in a snappy one-sentence sound bite we heard his heart sinking. "*It's phenomenally difficult and I think I'm a bright person...I should be able to master anything, depending on how much I apply myself. Sometimes I ask myself, 'Could I really become an expert and make a career out of this?'*" The obvious answer is yes – almost all trainees stay with the firm when they qualify; indeed all five of them did in 2004. "*Everyone recognises that* [the work is complicated] *and there's definitely no academic or intellectual snobbery here...my supervisor is very very supportive and encouraging, even though he is very busy. He's either putting on a good show or he is happy with the work I do.*" While it's certainly not the case that prospective trainees must be fully versed in international capital markets, "*no one should come here without realising this is quite a narrowly focused practice.*" What you need to know is that you are interested in the machinations of the international financial markets and you are prepared to work hard to develop an understanding of them.

auntie's conveyancing

Trainees spend about nine months, sometimes longer, in the firm's international finance group. For most it will be at the start of the training contract, for others their first seat will be spent with the corporate team. Sidleys is keen to grow the corporate side of its London business, so by the time you start there's every chance the scales will have tipped away from finance slightly. Last year the deals that kept the corporate lawyers busy included the disposal of the Middle Eastern, European and African Budget Rent-a-Car businesses after their parent company went into US Chapter 11 and UK administration.

Having put IFG and corporate on their CVs, trainees can choose seats from property and tax. The property team boasts two excellent partners swiped from Denton Wilde Sapte, who are *"really showing their worth now."* It works closely with IFG and corporate lawyers on deals such as the loan from Morgan Stanley and the £813 million bond issue that has provided funding for the redevelopment and sale and leaseback of the BBC's Broadcasting House. One trainee said of her experience in property: *"It's five or six lawyers working flat out to make sure a huge skyscraper in the City gets transferred from the right person to the right person."* In a move that pleases all concerned, the property trainees take on residential conveyancing instructions for Sidleys' staff and its corporate clients. It's partly why they consider the seat *"a particularly good experience for client contact."* It goes without saying that the firm's tax lawyers are indispensable. In short, nothing happens unless they give the say-so. It also goes without saying that this is a seriously intellectually demanding place to spend time as a trainee.

back to school

There is no litigation seat, so to ensure no one falls foul of Law Society stipulations, all trainees attend an intensive litigation course run by the London branch of Nottingham Law School. Admittedly, she wasn't in the best position to judge, but one trainee assured us: *"It is very useful in the sense that you understand the procedure of litigation and the skills are transferable, for example the negotiating."* The litigation classes provide a stark contrast to the style of learning in all other areas, and we spent some time discussing with trainees the pros and cons of learning on the job as opposed to filing into a seminar with scores of your peers. One source told us: *"The one thing they lack here is a trainee-specific lecture programme like you get in the magic circle. There's usually a department thing every week, but it's so high level; I wish we could have it broken into easier pieces."* A trainee in the opposing camp countered by saying: *"I do deals, not lectures!"*

whoppers v whippersnappers

And so we land upon a crucial question for anyone considering a career in the City: do you choose an established behemoth or a whippersnapper 'American firm'? Trainees were clear in their views on this matter. We heard everything from the obvious (*"In a smaller firm you have a more collegiate atmosphere and you know everybody"*) to the forceful (*"The numbers in the massive firms don't make sense to me; how can they justify intakes over a hundred or whatever it is"*) and the indignant (*"So many people go to the magic circle with their eyes shut and I find that incredible"*). For our sources, the chance to do top-level City work in a smaller office was the clincher. They also perceived that American firms were more meritocratic than their English counterparts and lacked the formality of long-held traditions and hierarchy. Speaking of the recent arrival of a top securities partner from Clifford Chance, one source said: *"I'm speculating here, but I think his move was all about making a fresh start...a lifestyle change."* One of the first things he did after arriving was take all the trainees out for a drink.

Lifestyle? People will try to convince you that if you work for an American firm you'll have no life at all, let alone any style. This is what trainees have to say on the thorny subject of hours: *"People generally work from 9.30am to 7pm, but if a deal's on you just go with it."* Also: *"When I am less busy I go at 5.30pm... when I am busy I work phenomenally long hours. A couple of weeks ago it was 80 to 90 in one week."* Avoid too much *"farting about"* and you should be fine in the normal course of business, but *"you must be prepared for the two-week stints when you will live in your office...though it won't be just you; there'll be a team of four or five all in the same boat."* Proving there is down time, we heard that *"amongst the trainees we are quite sociable and traditionally go out on a Thursday."* Sometimes associates join them, though it's rare to see a partner in the pub. Interestingly, the partners tend to give their staff breathing space even at the annual Claridges Christmas black-tie ball and summer party. *"Partners hang around for dinner"* and then leave people to it. *"One or two of them have their moments, but generally speaking they are more reserved than, say, some of the other staff...not in a bad way, mind you."*

In 2004, Sidleys swapped its two-home existence for beautiful new offices in Moorgate Exchange. Gone are *"the dark Threadneedle days"* (more wood than you could shake a stick at); it's light and airy all the way now. The best thing is a large roof terrace for evening drinks or sunny sandwich lunches when you've tired of the new canteen.

and finally...

We'll give the last word to the trainee who told us: *"I have been incredibly happy the whole time I have been here."* That's not to say everyone would be, but those who want high finance and hard work will do well to heed her words.

The Simkins Partnership

the facts

Location: London
Number of UK partners/assistants: 26/13
Total number of trainees: 4
Seats: 4x6 months
Alternative seats: None

This premier media law firm's past and present clients include Channel 4, *Wild Swans* author Jung Chang, Eddie Izzard, West Ham FC, Lee Ryan of Blue and James Brown – and these are just some of the ones we won't get shot for mentioning! We couldn't wait to have a chat with Simkins' trainees.

variety show

A large number of the lawyers at The Simkins' Partnership work exclusively on showbiz matters: film and TV, advertising, music, theatre, sports and publishing. Alongside these specialist lawyers, you'll find corporate, property and litigation departments, though even their clients are glam, being drawn mainly from the entertainment and leisure sectors.

Whatever kind of law you practise, the basics are important. Simkins likes its trainees to get a good grounding in property and litigation in their first year before moving on to more specialised areas in the second. The *"businesslike"* property seat brings commercial and residential work, and you can expect to be *"very busy"* shouldering *"lots of responsibility for your own files."* The work is *"not particularly media,"* though *"we do have some aged rock stars buying big properties...you end up having to calculate the hefty stamp duty on a £20 million house."* The litigation seat is a real *"mixed bag,"* with all trainees starting off on small debt claims and then being exposed to defamation, film-format rights disputes and even trips to the criminal courts if a celebrity client gets into a spot of bother.

The second year is for exploring Simkins' more specialised corners. How about working on management, publishing or recording agreements for major record labels and songwriters? Or perhaps production terms and crew contracts for a big film deal is of more interest. Things are *"relatively flexible"* as, with only two trainees taken on each year, there's no need for rigid seat divisions. That said, you will work in at least two distinct areas, usually chosen from coco, film and music options, but possibly also advertising, photography and theatre. Flexibility is the watch word throughout the two years, and one trainee told us: *"If you're very keen there can be a lot of movement."*

It's also possible to keep on files from a previous seat, so if you enjoyed litigation, you can stay involved on contentious files in your later seats.

learning your lines

Admit it, it was the Blue name check in the first paragraph that caught your eye. But if your heart didn't skip a beat, that's probably a good thing because *"if you're really impressed by the famous people then you're useless."* Our sources were remarkably unstarstruck, fully aware that in showbiz *"there's a lot more involved than just being on the front page of Heat."* Senior partner Julian Turton may have featured in Kevin Sampson's cult rock novel *Powder,* but you can't live your working life waiting for a mention in a client's Oscar acceptance speech. *"You're just the lawyer doing the paperwork,"* trainees reminded us. Nonetheless, one did admit that *"some of the defamation and privacy work is quite high profile, which I suppose does make it more exciting."* And another told us: *"I have met quite a few musicians."* It's all about developing a passion for the business as well as the show bit of Simkins' work; getting excited about *"how deals come together and how programmes are made and how bands get from being unsigned to radio exposure."*

Though it looks for a good academic record first and foremost, when Simkins recruits it wants people with *"a genuine interest in media,"* perhaps demonstrated by the study of IP law or work experience in TV or radio. A subscription to *Popbitch* won't suffice. *"People look at media law and think that's a sexy way of making money. But if you want to get a job here you need experience and real desire as a back-up, as the competition is so high."* Certainly the trainees we spoke to had plenty on their show reels and a depth of feeling for their work that we don't always find elsewhere. Said one: *"What I'm doing is so interesting. Working with music makes me feel alive, as it's what I'm into outside the job."* Homework is important at all levels of the firm: *"They like to know you're reading, going to gigs...even the partners have to go and see all these odd heavy metal bands."* Equally important is how well you fit in, and

muck in, because *"if there's a big case you might spend two days photocopying. You can't be too arrogant about that and you need to get people's respect to get good work."*

don't blame it on sunshine...

Trainees contrasted Simkins favourably with a certain other media-focused firm where *"it's all style over substance"* and *"people in Prada shoes doing very long hours and then going to poncy bars in the evening."* At Simkins, if you're not going to court or seeing a client, *"you can come to work in trainers and shorts,"* and *"as long as you're doing the work, you don't need to be doing long hours and can leave between 5.30pm and 6.30pm most nights."* It was all sounding too good until one trainee's sheepish confession – *"I keep it to a minimum, but I am guilty of a bit of poncy barring!"*

After initial protests that Simkins' office was simply *"full of files and computers just like anywhere else,"* trainees did admit it was awash with film posters, signed photos and platinum discs. The office is located in *"film production, ad agency territory"* just off Goodge Street, where you're liable to see *"trendy kids with trendy hair"* straying out of Soho. But *"people here are not all dead-trendy wannabe groovers; just enjoyable people to work with."* Some sing along to music at their desks, and if you pop into a certain department when a contract's just been signed you might even be treated to a dance floor number as *"there's one partner in particular who boogies when he's done a deal."* Presumably the two qualifying trainees of 2004 did at least a quick moonwalk when they heard they were both being retained.

silky smooth

As Simkins is a partner-heavy firm with a small number of associates and trainees, you won't get the freshers-week social life you'll find elsewhere. There's also *"no star-studded events,"* which put a stop to our speculation about what Robert Kilroy Silk and Alexei Sayle might chat about over the cheese and pineapple sticks. Just about the nearest the firm got recently to partying with celebs was last year's

Christmas bash at the Hard Rock Café, which was *"just an embarrassment – we're supposed to be this cutting-edge media firm!"* Winning better reviews was the annual walking weekend where 20 or so members of the firm *"get the bus from work on a Friday and go and climb a hill somewhere."* More regularly, there are casual drinks and dinners around Charlotte Street.

and finally...

If you can demonstrate a real passion for the media industry and an even greater passion for the law, this is definitely one of the best places to be seen.

Simmons & Simmons

the facts

Location: London
Number of UK partners/assistants: 111/244
Total number of trainees: 116
Seats: 4x6 months
Alternative seats: Overseas seats, secondments
Extras: Pro bono – Battersea Legal Advice Centre, RCJ CAB, language training

With a long tradition of City work, some major client names on the books and an array of international seats, Simmons & Simmons' popularity among students endures.

patience

Training seats are divided into four groups. The first is comprised of the corporate and commercial departments; the second includes the financial markets seats; and the third is litigation-based and includes commercial dispute resolution, employment and IP. The fourth group holds seats such as tax, pensions, private capital, environment and property. Trainees are meant to select one seat from each group, and the pressures of getting everyone through a contentious seat means it is a rare trainee who'll do employment and IP, as they are both in the contentious group.

Although we heard reports that some trainees managed to *"get away"* with slight alterations to the seating plan, these related to people seeking extra experience in one of the first two groups.

Summing things up well, one trainee explained Simmons' goals to our researcher: *"We're trying to market ourselves as a financial markets-based firm. It's an area where there is some really good premium work to be had, and the clients have deep pockets."* However, students looking for *"big City work in a big City firm"* beware: sometimes it pays to look beyond the names on a firm's client roster. As one trainee observed: *"We're making a big push in the corporate and financial departments... We've got good clients, but we're not doing the major work for them."* Simmons has faced this problem since the late 90s, when the firm suffered partner defections after a bout of poaching by US firms establishing themselves in the London market. It's worth remembering that Simmons' response to this was to dig in and battle on. And there are some signs of it making ground again. The *"fantastic"* private capital and hedge funds groups are particularly well regarded by the profession at large and the trainees who get the chance to work there. The firm recently got a standing ovation for creating a new way of facilitating a company acquisition (by way of an accelerated IPO, if you must know), which it used in the sale and subsequent flotation of companies such as Northumbrian Water and Center Parcs. It's also at the leading edge of advising on multimillion-pound outsourcing deals to India.

The fact that lawyers in the corporate and finance departments work in comparatively small teams can be a mixed blessing: *"You get the chance to become really involved in the deal, but when it comes to the crunch it does mean that you have no life for a week or so."* Yet at times the workload is noticeably lighter. One source revealed that *"sometimes you don't even pick up a pen. It's more of a question of playing solitaire on the computer."* Which is when the smart trainee will take matters into their own hands: *"I've had some good work, but some of that might be down to luck. I did one good deal early on, and then everyone knew that I was keen and interested. If you want to succeed, you've got to put yourself out there and get yourself known."* If you're successful, the ensuing responsibilities are rewarding: *"One of the high points for me was being told that the firm had confidence in me. They were quite happy to let me meet a client without another grown-up in the room."*

winning numbers

Elsewhere in the firm, trainees reported more regular hours and workloads. The quality of work on offer tends to increase as you progress through your training contract, but the level and quality of formal training sessions is consistently excellent. On the subject of feedback, some trainees reported having to *"badger"* supervisors for any word on their progress, whereas others were updated on a daily basis. If you do have problems, a mentor system by which each trainee is paired up with a partner from outside their department ought to assist. Again, some people reported *"not hearing a peep"* from their mentor in all their time at the firm, whereas others are doing lunch with them on a semi-regular basis. Again, the smart trainee will take matters into their own hands and introduce themselves to the mentor at the start of the contract.

Before we start to sing the praises of Simmons' niche practice areas, one thing should be made clear. Being a major City practice, the firm is led by its corporate and finance work. Which means that, although you may get a seat in its top-ranked employment or IP departments, you're going to spend twice as long working on more typical City transactions. If you do have your heart set on one of the niche areas, take heed: *"The IP department, especially, is quite small and the competition to work there, or in employment, is absolutely immense."* Make your desires known right from the start in order to avoid the *"tombola effect"* of seat allocation that can easily plague a firm this size.

If your interests lie further afield, Simmons has 18 international offices, and sends trainees to a good ten of them. Some are more popular than others; New York, Hong Kong and Paris being hardy perennials.

"If you speak the required language, you stand a much better chance of getting the seat. However, they do run language classes, so you won't go out unprepared." The firm also offers secondments to clients including Actis, UBS and Shell.

target practice

Simmons is frequently viewed and promoted as a *"cuddly"* firm. For the past few years it has made a regular appearance in the *Sunday Times'* '100 Best Companies to Work For' survey. The partnership is proud of this reputation and the majority of our sources thought justifiably so. As one said: *"They do play off their friendly image, but they also live up to it. All the people here are friendly and approachable."* Such disquiet that exists appears to stem from the fact that Simmons now wants to increase its profitability (which ultimately is the only way to keep sought-after partners faithful) and this entails making some tough decisions. *"More than a handful"* of corporate assistants were laid off in the last year, and the firm de-equitised or pushed out 11 of its equity partners. This has been coupled with a rise in assistants' target billable hours to 1,700 a year. No more or less than many of Simmons' rivals, but for some the changes have left a sour taste in the mouth. Said one: *"We realise that without the profits we won't keep the best partners, but there's just not enough work going round. Raising billable hours sends out a message, but without the work all it will do is worry people."* All this seems to have made certain people slightly more crabby than usual. A couple of our interviewees spoke of times when they felt they had been overly criticised for work that they had done, or blame was apportioned unfairly. Although they were keen to stress that these were isolated incidents.

spirit in the sky

Simmons' premises in CityPoint are modern and airy and filled with art, including pieces by some artist called Damien Hirst. Whilst some of our interviewees professed not to *"get"* the art, it always makes a worthy topic of conversation for lift journeys with strangers. Talking of lifts, pity the trainee who told us: *"If I'd change anything about the firm it'd be the lifts. One doesn't stop on the second floor; one takes you directly out of the building; and another one just goes to the canteen. One I hadn't even known existed spirited me to the third floor today, and it took me half an hour to get out again."* This aside, most of the facilities were judged to be top-drawer, with amiable canteen and print-room staff scoring highly in the popularity stakes.

By common consent, the social life at the firm is *"awesome."* There's usually a fair mix of people to be found in the local Corney & Barrow, handily located below the office. Throwing budget to the wind, Simmons organised a big summer ball in Lincoln's Inn Fields this year and told everyone to bring a loved one or spouse. Other highlights include departmental Christmas parties, plenty of sports fixtures, group ski trips and other random treats such as cake trolleys roaming around the floors. Less easy to swallow this year were the NQ retention figures: out of 54 qualifiers in 2004, 35 accepted positions with the firm.

and finally...

The firm has the ability to handle big-ticket transactions and is making waves in investment funds, but for now we sense Simmons will stay sitting just outside the top ten London firms...which might be exactly what you're looking for.

SJ Berwin

the facts

Location: London
Number of UK partners/assistants: 83/190
Total number of trainees: 67
Seats: 4x6 months
Alternative seats: Overseas seats, secondments
Extras: Pro bono – Toynbee Hall Legal Advice Centre

SJ Berwin has broken into the London top 20 and opened up a handful of international offices. Not bad for a firm that's only just passed its 21st birthday.

va va voom

One secret to SJB's success is a competitive attitude that is shared by almost everyone. Another is making sure that the client is satisfied at all times: *"We get told the client is the key factor, and we're always keen to please in whatever circumstances, irrespective of whether it has an adverse effect on us."* Trainees are expected to extend the same *"professional attitude"* to every client, irrespective of whether they are an international bank or a humble borrower. SJB has an enviable list of clients for its size. Said one source: *"Sometimes you look at clients and think 'This is such a big coup'. It's a bit like a small club signing Thierry Henry!"* On its books are the Laurel Pub Company, Royal Bank of Scotland, ABN AMRO Capital and Laura Ashley. Success has come in the field of private equity, European buyout activity in particular. Among its top deals of 2003 were Duelguide's £1.9 billion buyout of Chelsfield and Bridgepoint Capital and Permira's £250 million buyout of Holmes Place. This type of deal has been the driver for SJB's expansion into Continental Europe; as well as Madrid, Paris and Brussels, the firm has offices in Munich, Frankfurt and Berlin, all of which can be visited by trainees with the right language skills and a desire to spend six months using them.

Now the firm has established itself, our sources predicted interesting times ahead. *"We've stopped being a young firm, so now it's harder to prove ourselves. We've arrived at a crossroads, but the feeling is we want to push on."* And a better address is part of the plan. The old Gray's Inn Road offices were always considered a bit dingy and, quite frankly, in the a**e end of nowhere. At the end of 2005, the firm will move to *"pretty amazing"* premises on the north bank of the Thames opposite Tate Modern. We're told the office boasts London's biggest roof terrace.

like it or lump it

SJB runs a standard four-seat training scheme, but don't assume this will include any time spent relaxing in a sideline or niche department. The firm is driven by its corporate division and you will spend at least two of your seats there (though the options include the European offices, tax, financial services, funds and banking as well as M&A and private equity).

The corporate lawyers like to work hard and play hard. But playtime is often cancelled. Several trainees reported that they were *"constantly busy with a stream of work,"* including company and group reorganisations, share buy-backs and hive-offs. This can lead to some scary moments. One young corporate gunslinger told us: *"You just get told to do things. If you expect your hand to be held, you're going to be in trouble. It's tough, but that's better than being treated like a school kid."* Conversely, certain other trainees reported a more mundane workload of proof-reading and bible preparation.

This diversity of experience arises because success in the SJB corporate world is partly a matter of personality and partly a matter of luck. Each group has a distinct ethos that you'll either love or hate. Some trainees in private equity were thrilled by the seat: *"There is a large amount of pride and bulging chests. We know we're one of the best in the world, and people still get excited about what they do. There is still a lot hunger."* However, others described themselves as mere *"cannon fodder."* *"It's a very macho environment. They put a lot of emphasis on assertiveness."* Trainees acknowledge that while the private equity partners are on top of their game, there are a few who *"lack interpersonal skills."*

off the leash

Elsewhere in the firm, there is a softer feel. The huge real estate group was considered to be *"very warm and relaxed,"* with partners more than happy to chat about your work over a cup of coffee or game of table football. Our sources ran files by themselves from the outset and worked on matters ranging from £2 million homes to pub portfolios and shopping centres. And the client list makes for great reading: Hilton, Marks & Spencer, Land Securities, Sainsbury's. Part of the appeal for such companies is a clutch of mind-bogglingly clever partners who are renowned for

their ingenuity, particularly at the intersection of real estate, corporate transactions and finance.

In spite of all this, the smaller departments often prove to be the most popular with trainees. In the construction and commercial groups, for example, they reported building relationships with new clients and close involvement in transactions. A note of caution: if your heart is set on one particular area, you must be prepared to fight your corner. With two corporate seats and one contentious seat to complete, you'll meet with competition for optional seats. Our sources advise leaving the HR bods in no doubt as to your goal, but the more cautious view is that if you're not a fan of corporate transactions, let your dream of a training contract at SJB fade. The truth is that not everyone will necessarily get a chance to work in any particular niche area, let alone qualify into it.

mines of information

Persistence seems to be a necessary quality for any SJB trainee because the hours can be long. *"Corporate finance is like working at a coalface – people get in there and never leave! I know one group of people who were working 150 chargeable hours a week. Even when it's slow, you know you're going to get nailed at some point."* In some departments: *"You'll be a marked man if you waltz out at 5.30pm...you can feel eyes burrowing into the back of you!"* But sometimes we got the feeling that they wouldn't have it any other way. Said one trainee: *"I work the hours that I do as a personal thing. I want to get my work done, get it done well, and get it done on time."*

The good news is that dedication to the cause is noted. A number of the partners are said to be excellent at giving ongoing feedback and taking time to explain why they are amending trainees' work. There does appear to be a problem of consistency though. Training supervisors were given ratings from *"fantastic"* to *"ogreish"* by our sources, and some were quite frankly *"invisible."* A similar point can be made regarding training sessions. When they took place they were excellent, but in some groups there has been a tendency to let fee-earning work take priority.

roger ramjet

One thing all our interviewees were clear on was that "*the firm encourages individuality.*" Rather than "*an army of grey-suited lawyers straight from The Simpsons,*" SJB trainees are a diverse group, all of whom have "*a little twinkle in their eye or glint on their teeth.*" One enterprising soul went as far as to ask David Harrel, the senior partner, his opinion of what makes a good SJB trainee. Harrel's reply went something like this, according to our source: "*You all have one thing in common – the social skills that put you above others. You are rarely caught off guard, or if so you can deal with it.*"

If this sounds like you, there's a good chance the firm would be prepared to take you on, irrespective of your background. "*The firm goes more for what you're like in action rather than on paper.*" If you can show the necessary drive and desire to work in an intense corporate environment, they'll consider you whether you've come from Cambridge or a lesser-known university.

And intense it certainly is: "*People here are very into what they do; there is always a sense of urgency.*" The typical trainee at SJB decided early on in their career that they'd rather be on the phone than at the photocopier and are willing to rough it with the big boys to make sure they stay there. While one candid source revealed: "*We're not very touchy-feely. If you're easily bruised, stay away,*" the situation is more positively summed up by the idea that "*the firm would suit anyone who's enthusiastic and able to work hard. Keen people get on very well here. And it is noticed.*"

on the edge of your seat

Lawyers are commonly found over the road in the firm's favourite bar Centros and the nearby Blue Lion. The Christmas party is a typically "*raucous and drunken*" event, with the main aim of the evening being "*trying not to embarrass yourself in front of all the partners...or, more importantly, your secretary.*" Sports flourish, with active hockey, football, softball and cricket teams, as well as an annual sailing weekend.

Some of our interviewees felt the management had in recent times "*underestimated the importance*" of social events. In the past SJB has been known to treat its trainees very, very well, whilst also working them hard. If ever there was a firm with a work hard, play hard ethos then this was it. Furthermore, it was quick off the blocks to hike up trainee and NQ salaries in the late 90s. The past year or two's belt tightening on fripperies such as super-generous Christmas gifts and ad hoc treats has had the effect of making a hard-working environment feel harder, whether or not it actually is. There's also no doubt that unfortunate NQ retention statistics and a drop in profits in 2003 made 2004 an edgy time for our sources. However, profits have swung back up to previous levels and turnover has increased as a result of the activities of small to mid-market companies. Reflecting this improvement, in September 2004 retention stats were slightly up on the previous year with 26 of the 35 qualifiers taking jobs with the firm.

and finally...

Fast-paced, challenging, often exhausting, an SJ Berwin training contract is suited to those with real drive and ambition. If you sort of want to be a lawyer and sort of want to work in the City, do yourself a favour and find a different employer.

Slaughter and May

the facts

Location: London
Number of UK partners/assistants: 110/369
Total number of trainees: 182
Seats: 4x6 months
Alternative seats: Overseas seats
Extras: Pro bono – RCJ CAB, Islington and Battersea law centres, language training

Slaughter and May is usually referred to as the magic circle firm with a frostier reputation than its rivals. We donned mittens and a bobble hat, breathed on the windows and peered in...

what price success?

Austere reserve is a characteristic often attributed to Slaughters by the outside world, although many in the know and on the inside are stumped to account for it. Said one trainee: *"I just don't understand where that stuffy conservative image comes from; it is certainly not true on the basis of my experience."* Perhaps it is because, faced with a world of slick rebrandings, natty logos, all-encompassing corporate identities and brazen self publicity, Slaughters has shrugged its shoulders, raised a laconic eyebrow and carried on as before. After all, there's nothing like defying a trend to earn the suspicion of all those clinging to the overcrowded bandwagon. We're not suggesting Slaughters trainees are unfashionable, but they all admitted to feeling the frisson of pleasure upon stumbling across the *"low-key Slaughters way"* in amongst a welter of *"hectic recruitment brochures,"* *"ridiculous psychometric tests"* and *"in-your-face interviews."* Of course any applicant looking for a training contract with a leading City firm has to resign themselves to this bombardment, but no one says they have to like it. In fact, simplicity was the primary attraction for our sources; said one: *"The whole experience was really classy, very plain and straightforward,"* whilst another reflected: *"They never seemed to be trying to buy me...that really mattered."*

So that's the hook, but does two years at Slaughters throw up any surprise catches? Not really. Trainees reflected on *"a no-frills approach"* that matched up to both their ambitions and initial impressions. *"There's no marketingspeak or managementspeak or anything like that;"* *"the attitude is simply, 'We will do the law well and everything else will follow.'"* The key thing that follows, according to our sources, is a working atmosphere in which excellence is the only permissible standard.

it's a dome deal

The reason Slaughters keeps itself uncluttered is appropriately straightforward. As the most profitable firm in the UK, why waste time on trimmings and trappings when you could be focusing on working hard and maintaining exacting standards? With outstanding ability across all areas of corporate and commercial practice, *"the quality of our work and our professionalism speaks for itself."* In the last year Slaughters has scored notable new clients, scooping a huge instruction from Jarvis on its strategic review, and being appointed sole advisor to Meridian Delta, which will work with English Partnerships on the 20-year, £4 billion Millennium Dome redevelopment. A few noses were also put out of joint at Clifford Chance when Slaughters scored an instruction from CC's client Permira on the private equity firm's £900 million bid for WH Smith. In the same period Slaughters also extended existing relationships, securing a lead role on one of Europe's largest ever cross-border retail banking mergers, the £8.5 billion takeover of Abbey by Spanish Bank Santander Central Hispano. Its competition department also broke new ground in securing EC clearance for Bertelsmann Music Group's merger with Sony Music, a radical change from previous rulings.

In trainee terms, Slaughters' clarity of focus means only one thing. You come to the firm to become a corporate lawyer and a good generalist one at that. Trainees were unequivocal in their understanding that *"corporate work: it's why you're here."* A minimum of two of your four six-month seats must be taken in corporate groups (though many of our contacts had the appetite for three), and trainees get to choose from a variety of options. You can have your seat insurance-flavoured, finance and refinance-flavoured, M&A-flavoured, insolvency-flavoured or even disposals-flavoured. In fact, any flavour you like, as long as it's corporate.

With one or two seats left to play with, there is the possibility of working in a variety of supporting satellite departments such as TMT, IP/IT, financial regulation, commercial property, employment and pensions, or competition. The contentious requirement is satisfied either through six months in IP/IT or employment and pensions, or in the commercial litigation department. In the latter case it is almost standard to split a seat into two with tax. The niche departments *"do a great majority of corporate support work, but do have standalone work too."* Their smaller size also means *"they are more cohesive and a bit better at socialising than some of the bigger corporate departments,"* although the insurance corporate group was described as *"really quite feisty."*

losing your marbles

Trainees told us: *"Slaughters takes a long-term view of your training"* and confirmed they'd been asked to list their preferred seats before arriving to start their contracts. It gave them a rough idea of their likely route through to qualification and took the heat out of the twice-yearly rotation process. If pressure does build up, and an appeal to graduate recruitment fails to yield a desired change, then *"swapsies can release the steam."* Just as in the school playground, if you have your eye on your mate's aggie, and he quite likes the look of your cat's eye, then you switch. *"Grad recruitment is happy to let you swap, if you present it as a fait accompli...after all, it does their work for them."* This lack of friction at rotation goes some way to explaining the fact that *"competitiveness between trainees doesn't really exist,"* but equally important are the absence of billing targets and high levels of NQ retention. In 2004, a whopping 72 out of 76 rolled smoothly into positions at the firm.

As for the much-mythologised matter of magic circle hours, it is another example of the straightforward Slaughters approach that you work for as long as it takes and no more. In a lean corporate market, your hours will be a breeze and given the climate of the last couple of years, trainees seemed slightly ashamed as they whispered: *"I think I've got off quite lightly."* In times of plenty, by God you'll work hard – *"Everyone's had a 20-hour day followed by an 8am start the next day"* or *"a mad few weeks of working until 10 or 11pm every day."* Around work, trainees must fit in the PSC incrementally, in addition to internal training seminars and, should they want to, pro bono work and language classes. Some of those we interviewed were surprised to learn that a trainee forum exists to tackle issues of relevance to their contracts, mumbling absently: *"Well, if I had a problem I'd probably just talk to a partner myself."*

stand by for action

In contrast to several major rivals, Slaughters works on the international law firm, rather than the global law firm model. In short, three of its own overseas offices in main commercial centres are complemented by 'best-friends' relationships with international firms. These firms are the magic circle equivalents of their jurisdictions, for example Uria y Menéndez in Spain and Hengeler Mueller in Germany. Firms like Denton Wilde Sapte or Clifford Chance have recently paid heavily for the failure of costly overseas offices, while the Slaughters approach minimises the financial risk of international reach. However, proving that it's not entirely immune to trends, this year the firm announced the closure of its small New York and Singapore offices; in the latter instance the decision should be seen in the context of the primacy of the 'best friends' policy. Existing work in the area is now being channelled through an enhanced relationship with the best friend and main player in the region, Australian firm Allens Arthur Robinson.

Amongst trainees, domestic types much appreciate the fact that *"even though half our clients are multinational FTSE 100 companies, the UK base is a strong focus for the firm and a distinctive feature."* By contrast, more itinerant bods relish the chance to take a trip abroad in either their final or penultimate seat. Last year we heard mumblings of discontent from trainees about the availability of overseas seats, but our sources this year reflected: *"If you hold out for one particular office you may be disappointed, but be flexible and you're bound to go away on one occasion."* With roughly 14 overseas seats from Brussels to Hong Kong on offer at each rotation, flexibility shouldn't mean compromising on quality of experience.

On the broader subject of a trainee's lot, our sources told us of *"a general progression in the work you're given over the two years,"* especially when it comes to *"making sure that second-years get more responsibility."* Although admitting that even in your final seat you could end up as *"a small cog in the larger process,"* trainees talked enthusiastically about the occasions on which a good degree of autonomy was forthcoming. *"My supervisor would say 'This is the problem, this is where you might find a solution, go find it.'"* Nevertheless the accusation that trainees at such large firms sacrifice hands-on experience for the opportunity to watch top-class corporate lawyers at work does stick. One source told us: *"In one seat I was responsible for co-ordinating the data room side of things, collating answers to the buyer's due diligence queries. Not fascinating work, but I was speaking to clients by e-mail or phone every day."* And another explained: *"Even when you're part of a very big team, you're seeing different associates' or partners' styles and how they worked under pressure...it teaches you how to be a lawyer."*

the ice men melteth

Slaughters partners have a reputation for forbidding reserve and distance from trainees, perhaps the strongest factor informing the firm's icy reputation. Those we interviewed did understand why the firm's culture of independence and self-sufficiency could translate into a feeling of isolation for some. *"You are responsible for deciding if you're working to capacity and asking for more work if you're not,"* they told us, admitting with more or less chagrin that *"there is no real ethos of being told, day to day, how you're doing."* Some trainees do feel themselves out in the cold as a result: *"In my last seat I was told something in the end-of-seat review that, if I'd been told mid-seat, I could have put right...I felt like I'd wasted time."* The quality of end-of-seat appraisals is supervisor-dependent: *"Some partners make it a more involving process than others."* That variability of individuals is the heart of the issue really – slight

reserve may be generally pervasive, but patches of black ice are relatively and far between along Slaughters' well-salted thoroughfares. For each trainee with a tale to chill the cockles (*"being sent to buy my supervisor a toothbrush after his secretary refused to do it was a low point"*), there were two with warmer anecdotes to share (*"after a trainee was upset one day, three partners came separately to see if she was all right, and whether she wanted to go home"*). Don't it just melt your heart?

Our sources weren't overly analytical about the future. One told us: *"We don't have arrogant people saying, 'I'm going to make partner,'"* and another said: *"You're much better placed to make a decision about your career after a couple of years' NQ work."* Making partner is of course a distant, exacting prospect, but in the shorter term many trainees clearly feel a degree of loyalty towards their employer that's rare amongst the biggest firms.

the three-step plan

"There are no upturned-rugby-shirt-collar, braying idiots here," stated one trainee, with obvious pleasure and perhaps just a dash of contempt. Yet Slaughters trainees don't have to rely on negative constructions in picking out the qualities that unite them – *"We're intelligent people who aren't too brash,"* *"very confident,"* but *"understated,"* *"very bright"* with a *"good work ethic."* It's probably these qualities that lead to the bookish, aloof stereotype of a Slaughters trainee. *"These stereotypes...I was aware and even a bit fearful of them before I arrived, but I haven't encountered anything like it."* The Oxbridge element is undoubtedly strong, though there is good representation from *"the top 20 universities"* and sometimes beyond.

With regard to the firm's social life, *"the onus is on the individual."* Trainees tend to home in on *"a core group of close friends amongst your intake,"* with larger group socialising *"tailing off a bit, especially in the second-year."* Drinks in the Corney & Barrow, the nearby but *"awful!"* St Paul's Tavern and occasional expeditions to *"Farringdon, Shoreditch, even beyond"* add substance and spice to the social calendar. Regular department drinks with partners in attendance and *"making an effort to chat to everyone"* equal *"good team-building"* if slightly more restrained affairs. The highlight of the year is undoubtedly the annual black-tie Christmas ball at the Grosvenor, which gives trainees the opportunity to practise *"the three-step plan"* of socialising. *"One: everyone's sober and no one talks. Two: everyone's a bit merry and have a merry chat. Three: the partners leave and we embarrass ourselves!"*

Slaughters' superb, *"low-key premises"* at Bunhill Row have an easy-on-the-eye *"greys, muted blues and frosted glass"* theme. Minutes from Liverpool Street, many trainees rent flats within walking distance. After strolling into work for a leisurely 9.30am start, they avoid the floor-level water feature which has wetted the ankles of many an unsuspecting client. They also reserve a special curl of the lip for the *"twig-like wood sculpture,"* which has the enmity and incomprehension of all. The building is no corporate village à la Clifford Chance; an *"excellent canteen"* is the extent of the on-site provision. Meals are available there at all hours of the day, chargeable to clients if you're staying late on a deal (although we're told you might do better to pack a sandwich as *"by 9pm it's just the leftovers from lunch"*). The first time we visited Bunhill Row, we immediately felt the tidy efficiency and poise of the building captured Slaughters personality; while everything is just so, there's ample space to save you from feeling hemmed in.

and finally...

By the end of our interviews with Slaughter and May trainees, we'd shed bulky winter wear and were sitting comfortably at room temperature. Slaughters may not embrace you with overbearing bonhomie, but if you have the intellect, ability and ambition to succeed at this corporate powerhouse, you'll find more than a little verity in its handshake.

Speechly Bircham

the facts

Location: London
Number of UK partners/assistants: 47/66
Total number of trainees: 10
Seats: 4x6 months
Alternative seats: None

Speechly Bircham is a mid-sized City firm with a solid reputation in commercial areas of law that is complemented by traditional strength in private client practice. This resolutely *"straightforward"* firm offers good-quality work and fewer frills than a supermarket's-own brand of cornflake.

commonsense and sensibility

At least to our ears, the name Speechly Bircham suggests a racy cad from a Jane Austen novel, all flowing locks and devilish intentions. In fact, trainees' descriptions of the firm as being *"scrupulous," "dedicated"* and *"knowledgeable"* sound more like the sober and gentlemanly Mr Darcy than the showy Mr Wickham. *"The firm doesn't pretend to be anything it's not,"* our sources told us. *"It's been said many times, but we don't try to over-egg what we do."* It is a balance between sense of propriety and business sense that seems to pervade this firm: a place for everything and everything in its place.

Whilst it may not be ruthlessly deflowering big businesses like those magic circle rogues, trainees emphasised that *"maintaining and competing with the standards of the big City firms"* is a continual aim. The recent recruitment of partners to grow the corporate and construction teams, coupled with a 10% bounce back in profits after a big drop last year, certainly suggests that there is steel for a duel beneath that courteous exterior.

When it comes to courting new trainees, Speechlys is equally proper. It doesn't try to seduce with flashy recruitment materials or web pages, but rather solicits mature-minded applicants with a passion for the law. Our sources delighted in this *"plain, homespun not spin"* approach. Many had taken advantage of the three-week summer placements, which allow both parties to assess the other's pedigree. The proverb warns, marry in haste, repent at leisure, but such a thorough approach ensures that neither firm nor trainee is left repenting.

on the estate

Speechlys resides over six floors of a seven-floor building that is excellently situated in Holborn with views of St Andrew's Church. Each floor is colour-coded to aid navigation, although no one could actually tell us which colour pertained to which floor, let alone list the colours, *"...err, there's definitely duck egg blue, then orange, maybe mustard and purple."* We shuddered at the palette, but in truth you're unlikely to lose your bearings in the firm. Only five trainees are taken on each year and *"there's a real community feeling, you know everyone on all floors and all departments."* Many of our sources delighted in revealing that *"you never feel far from the epicentre."* In each department, trainees either share with a supervisor in an outside-edge office or slum it in a central open-plan area. As they moved around the firm for each of their four six-month seats, our sources observed how *"each department definitely has its own character."*

The firm has a well-known private client department that provides wills, tax and trusts advice to clients ranging from landed estates to loaded entrepreneurs to *"quite ordinary clients whose earnings have just tipped over the balance where tax planning is necessary."* Most trainees end up in this, the *"quietest"* of the departments, at some point, typically *"helping out on pieces of research or drafting wills."* The firm's expertise in off-the-peg tax-efficient wills and trust schemes is a key reason why the seat is so popular with trainees. *"It's quite inspiring to be at the forefront of this kind of work; you see partners devising a lot of new techniques."* Amongst others, the firm advises Howard de Walden Estates, Lord Lloyd-Webber, the

Estate of the Fifth Marquis Camden and Alexander Thyssen. It's certainly an impressive roster, but trainees invariably start off with more humble clients and their highlight will probably be *"meeting Mr and Mrs Bloggs to discuss their will."*

The corporate department offers the starkest contrast to private client, and here *"when the pressure is on you feel the buzz."* The department is divided into sub-groups – financial services, private equity, commercial and banking, with trainees taking work from *"whoever needs the help."* The financial services lawyers are particularly noted for their investment funds and insurance advisory work, recently assisting Ecclesiastical Insurance Group with a scheme of transfer for its life assurance business. This is just one of the areas in which the firm has the expertise and capacity to handle large transactions that are normally the province of bigger City firms, but there is a good quality of work across the department. Trainees *"mainly assist with company searches and due diligence, or draft confidentiality agreements,"* but felt there is room for the eager to manoeuvre.

constructive thinking

The construction department is very important to the firm, and offers trainees experience of both contentious and non-contentious work. Those we interviewed had worked on live litigation (including trials) and assessed potential claims for both blue-chip companies and private individuals. Away from contentious matters, they had helped to draft contracts and appointments for domestic and international projects. One of the more forthright trainees we interviewed told us that the seat allowed the most able to achieve a satisfying level of independence: *"Your capacity and ability determines the extent of what you get."* On the same floor, the commercial dispute resolution department has *"its fair share of menial stuff like bundling,"* but the trade-off is regular court appearances and the opportunity to run debt collection matters yourself. *"It's perhaps not earth-shattering litigation, but useful in that it teaches you the principles."*

Autonomy is more than possible in the real estate department: *"You get your own files, and you'll see them through to completion under supervision."* Trainees typically handle *"the small beer"* for large estate owners, but can be enlisted on *"larger transactions around the £30 million mark."* One of the more glamorous things we heard about was the trainee who represented the firm at a property auction at the Cafe Royal on Regent Street. Swanky!

Perched on the sixth floor, the highly popular employment department acts for major charities and banks, and recently defended Drake International Group against a redundancy claim. *"Trainees go to tribunal, if there's one on,"* and if there isn't they're kept occupied by a healthy stream of advisory work. A bottleneck does sometimes occur around this seat but, in general, seat rotation is a very well-mannered process that leaves everyone's honour intact. *"When four of us wanted to go into employment, the training supervisor told us to go away and sort it out between us. So we did."* How very Speechlys.

little bits of food

Trainees were full of praise for the mid and end-of-seat appraisal system, to which *"everyone contributes feedback, not just your supervisor."* Communal spirit is reinforced at monthly fee-earner lunches, which are whipped up by in-house chef Chris. By all accounts Chris deserves a Michelin star for his efforts – trainees variously described his food as *"excellent," "amazing," "outstanding"* and *"delicious."* No wonder he's also set the task of preparing canapés (*"mini hamburgers, samosas, satays, lots of fresh fish"*) for the firm's bimonthly drinks parties. This provoked a convoluted debate here at the *Student Guide*, as we tried to work out the difference between hors d'oeuvres and canapés. If the latter is to be eaten standing up and the former is a precursor to a sit-down meal, then does an hors-d'oeuvre become a canapé if you rise to a standing position whilst eating it? You may laugh, but questions such as this need answers. Perhaps Chris can help...by sending some of his fine fayre over to us.

An *"excellent sports and social committee organises loads of events"* from theatre trips to go-karting. Greedily, trainees mentioned that they'd like to see *"more events for the entire staff,"* like the Christmas party, which included *"a dating lottery."* Essentially, six willing types allowed themselves to be prizes in a raffle. One lucky trainee scored a hot date with a property partner, but no one we spoke to was prepared to give any details. Overall, *"it's a very sociable, communal place,"* which explains why, even though only two out of five qualifying trainees were able to remain in September 2004, none of those due to leave had a bad word to say about the firm.

and finally...

Speechly Bircham epitomises good manners, steadiness and reliability. But don't take our word for it, take a three-week placement and find out for yourself.

steeles (law) LLP

the facts

Location: Norwich, London, Diss
Number of UK partners/assistants: 18/18
Total number of trainees: 12
Seats: 4x6 months
Alternative seats: None
Extras: Pro bono – CAB, FRU

Spread over three locations in Norwich, Diss and London, Steeles offers a generous mix of commercial and private client work, with an expanding public law team and music/media practice to boot.

the way the cookie crumbles

Norwich is generally regarded as the steeles stomping ground and home to the nerve centre of the firm. Here, the offering stretches from copyright to conveyancing, acting for both regional clients and household names such as Bowater Zenith, Campbell Foods, Canon UK, Wimpey Homes and Westminster City Council. The importance of local authority clients shouldn't be underestimated, and instructions (planning, strategic advice, health and safety prosecutions, licensing, property lit, urban regeneration, debt collection, contract and corporate advice, etc.) come from a large number of these public bodies. It is estimated that they account for some 30% of the firm's business across the board.

In the south Suffolk outpost of Diss, there is civil litigation and private client work, while the London office in Holborn houses the newer sports and music/media practices in addition to substantial property and litigation teams. While *"you will have to make it clear if you want to go to London,"* and there is clearly *"flexibility to mix around,"* there's a general trend for either a London-based training contract or Norwich-with-a-bit-of-Diss-thrown-in.

Last year, we reported on an orderly queue forming at the door of the music and media department; this year company-commercial and employment are the seats *"you have to fight for."* In employment, this may be due to a steady supply of home-baked muffins and cookies that have caused trainees to *"pile on the pounds since joining the firm."* In co-com, it is down to *"a level of training that is second to none."* No seat is compulsory; *"all the way through you get asked where you want to go next,"* and *"if there is someone else after the same seats, you just agree to share things out."* Very civilised.

legal acrobatics

Steeles provides *"an environment conducive to growth;"* however, before you reach for your favourite pair of tracky bow-waps (ideal after an employment department bake-off), bear in mind that this is not a training contract for slouches. The dress code is strictly smart casual, but seeing as you'll be leaping into responsibility, juggling files and dashing between meetings and courtrooms, we'd recommend something aerodynamic and stretchy with a high Lycra content. Between them our sources had attended court alone in the first week, run up to 50 files single-handedly in property, met clients tout seul, worked on High Court matters, undertaken advocacy thrice-weekly and become the department expert on obscure areas of little-known European regulations. Who would have thought so much could be packed in between 9am and 5.30pm? Okay, in *"pacey"* co-com the day may roll on until 7pm, and legend has it that once upon a time a trainee worked on a Saturday, but we are assured they were rewarded with a day off in lieu (and a place in East Anglian folklore).

Of their dizzying assignments, our sources had nothing but praise. One said: *"It can be pretty daunting, scary stuff, but you do get plenty of training."* The upsides of such a hectic schedule are that *"only about 0.2% of your time is spent photocopying"* and *"you feel like they do trust you."* Mid-point and end-of-seat appraisals are padded out with day-to-day feedback from supervisors, and as one source noted, *"when they make changes they tell you why. Work is marked and the advice is constructive."*

give a dog a home

Flick through steeles' recruitment brochure with its pictures of high-jumping, hurdling, leggy athletes and you could be forgiven for thinking the firm is full of Olympic medallists. Sadly not. *"I'm not sporty at all,"* bragged one trainee without even a hint of embarrassment. Rest assured, *"you won't be made to run any relays,"* though if you do want the exercise, both the London and Norwich offices field footie teams and London has also been known to put up a triathlon team. In the main sporting law degrees and UEA colours (*"the firm likes to take from the local pool"*), trainees describe themselves simply as *"unpretentious team players."*

Steeles' trainees happily exercise their drinking arms and dancing feet. In Norwich drinks parties are held monthly, as are trainee meetings – usually followed by a night out, perhaps in the Cellar House.

Set in three units on an out-of-town business park, the Norwich office location boasts an eclectic range of lunchtime distractions – Homebase, Pets World...perfect if your weekend chores involve creosoting the dog kennel. To solve a sartorial crisis or sate a thirst for a cheeky pint, trainees can take the firm's free 'Fun Bus' into town on Thursday lunchtimes. In London, steeles' lawyers dwell in a legal heartland close to plenty of shops and bars. Many make a beeline for the Kings Arms at lunchtime on Fridays.

Geography and swelling numbers mean the firm is no longer able to indulge in the traditional firmwide Christmas bash. Come the festive season, in Norwich everyone piles into a local hotel for some festive cheer, leaving the London lot to do their own thing. And Diss? *"Diss has a really nice local bakery."* We're probably being a little harsh here because, in actual fact, those of our sources who'd spent time in Diss raved about the place. The small office is located in *"a pretty impressive old building with marble pillars"* and has a *"lively, jovial atmosphere"* that allows *"a greater chance to chat without feeling self-conscious."* Some trainees preferred the set-up to the open-plan layout of Norwich, where people are heads-down and careful *"not to make too much noise."*

capital ideas

Steeles has worked hard to free itself of a fusty, provincial reputation. It rebranded itself from Steele & Co. to the slinkier steeles, sought out a better address in London, converted to LLP status and signed up to internet dispute resolution with an American initiative called Cybersettle Inc. Our sources saw these developments as evidence of a *"dynamic, ever-changing"* firm that *"makes you feel as if you are at the forefront of things."* However, while such developments may be breaking figurative boundaries, geography remains something of an obstacle.

Steeles literature will tell you that its trainees are "unrestricted by bricks and mortar," yet this year, as before, some sources commented on the physical

and conceptual separation of Norwich and London trainees, saying: *"There is a slight disparity between the two bases and not a great deal of contact."* In fairness to the firm, moves are being made to bridge the gap, with joint training days and increased movement between offices, and the trainees themselves are *"making every effort to mix when we do see each other."*

The retention rate in September 2004 was not ideal; only one of the three qualifiers stayed on, though the others were offered jobs too.

and finally...

Trainees tell us that for heaps of choice and plenty of responsibility in the East of England, steeles should be *"on your horizon."*

Stephenson Harwood

the facts

Location: London
Number of UK partners/assistants: 61/113
Total number of trainees: 41
Seats: 4x6 months
Alternative seats: Overseas seats, secondments
Extras: Pro bono – Hoxton and Camden law centres, language training

Maritime and international trade, financial markets and real estate: these are Stephenson Harwood's chosen markets. Trainees with a taste for one or more of these areas are advised to read on.

no pain, no gain

In the past couple of years we must confess we've approached our interviews with Stephenson Harwood trainees with the trepidation one experiences just before a visit to the dentist. Don't get us wrong: they are lovely people (as are most dentists), but we never quite knew what we were going to hear. There was always a chance it would be uncomfortable news, and from some people that's exactly what we did hear. Hardly surprising as the firm has been through some ups and downs. A merger with shipping practice Sinclair Roche & Temperley in 2002 added a whole heap of staff and trainees whose numbers could not be supported in a poor economy, so there were redundancies and poor NQ retention rates. Profitability had fallen significantly, so there were partner exits, both voluntary and involuntary. Three large claims hung over the heads of the former SRT partners (two from former partners and one from a former client) and the firm was forever changing its business plan.

2004 has been a turnaround year in SH's fortunes; cost-cutting measures (including those redundancies and partner exits) have improved profitability and the firm has fixed on a business plan that reflects its real strengths rather than its aspirations. There has also been a symbolic change in management with the appointment of young litigation partner Sunil Ghadia as chief executive. Speaking of the clean sweep on good news and the appointment of the new chief exec, one trainee told us: "*It did go through a period of time when people were subjected to quite a lot of bad press – it sapped team morale – but it is noticeable how work has picked up in the last year and also Sunil has taken over.*" When he told us: "*A new broom can get you winning the game,*" he wasn't really referring to curling, but the likelihood of better relations with the legal press.

shipshape

Trainees were pleased that the firm was not trying to be all things to all men anymore and proud of its most successful practices. So let's look more closely at these and how they form the basis of training.

Maritime and international trade is a business sector encountered by trainees in various seats. A whole swathe of the banking and asset finance (BAF) lawyers are kept busy with the finance of ships (and increasingly aircraft too) and there are usually five trainees in the department. "*We're at the top of the tree,*" one trainee told us, "*and the quality of work is extremely high.*" Trainees loved the international element to the work and the fact that there were very few English clients. "*You're always on your toes because you have to pay attention to the different ways of working of different clients...There's a real energy in the department and the structures of deals are always changing.*" Sometimes they will have a good deal of direct client contact, particularly if registering foreign-owned ships in the English Registry. Alongside the asset finance there are general banking and PFI deals, the latter involving contact with the property department. The hours in BAF are acknowledged to be the longest, with 8.30am–8.30pm days not unheard of.

Ships also navigate their way into the sea of top-grade litigation for which SH is very highly regarded. Seats are available in either the general litigation department or the more specialised shipping lit group. One trainee spoke of the document management tasks he'd been asked to deal with in shipping lit. It was more than mere grunt work; "*you actually do achieve something. On a number of occasions I was given a vast number of documents to look at to see what we could prove and what was missing.*" Away from shipping, the firm has an impressive back catalogue of cases and has recently been chasing Dame Shirley Porter's secreted millions on behalf of Westminster City Council. Of course with important cases, trainees "*break their teeth on low-responsibility work – reading over things and bundling*" while "*learning how the litigation process works.*"

fishy tales

The firm's third target sector is real estate, though it is by no means the largest department in the firm and not all our sources had done a seat there. It is seen as a good choice for first-seaters, however, as "*your knowledge of conveyancing and property law is fresh in your mind.*" The department is full of likeable characters and responsibility for small files is a given. On the department's books at the moment are projects for the London Development Agency, one of which relates to the £1.5bn Silvertown Quays regeneration project, complete with a £60m aquarium, and the £100 million Centrale shopping centre in Croydon for St Martins Property Group. If general commercial property transactions don't float your boat, you might ask for a property finance seat instead.

The other seat options with which to fill up your dance card include corporate, employment, tax and overseas seats in Hong Kong, Piraeus and Singapore. In May 2004, SH's Hong Kong office celebrated 25 years of business in the island city with a garden party for 500. That's a lot of cucumber sandwiches. It has also been operating in mainland China for 10 years, longer than the johnny-come-latelies who've only recently latched on to the growth in the Chinese economy. Actually the firm's interests in the country go much further back. A certain Mr Harwood was doing business in Shanghai as early as the 1860s. Come to SH hoping for an overseas posting and it's odds on you will get one. By all accounts the experience is unmissable, socially as well as professionally. And if you want to develop some all-important business development skills, the firm can help you with that; it has recently set up a programme of events at which trainees can shmooze with their peers in other professions.

The trainees we spoke to had been able to do seats in the areas of practice they'd most wanted to try, although anyone looking for the private client and family option will now have to look elsewhere. At Charles Russell to be exact, as this is where the team went recently. The loss of the team accounted for one of the four trainees who departed on qualification in September 2004. The other eight stayed on.

good eggs

Boasting one of the best views in London – the front elevation of St Paul's Cathedral – SH's neighbourhood has much to offer. Nearby is the newly developed Paternoster Square and shops aplenty on Cheapside, and just over the wobbly bridge is Tate Modern. The office building has recently undergone a refit and benefits from a large roof terrace that is brought into service for parties. Best of all is that *"positivity which is starting to move freely throughout the firm."*

After hours you'll still find trainees in Shaw's the Booksellers (actually, it's a pub), though *"a splinter group"* prefers The Cock and The Rising Sun, the latter having a big screen TV for sporting events. The firm's own football team has recently been promoted, though our sources couldn't quite remember to which division in the legal league. Described as a place that prefers *"eccentrics"* to *"armies of grey men,"* the firm attracts trainees for whom the big firms hold no fascination. *"We all get on well and there are no bad eggs or trainee partners,"* said one. Few come straight through university without any time spent travelling or working, and there are always a couple of non-Brits in the group. They tell us that SH is *"a nice place to be and train because you get good experiences without being completely under the kosh."* Aside from some late nights in BAF, the hours are perfectly manageable and the dress code is a smartish but relaxed business casual.

There's something about SH that makes you think it's quite a traditional place, but not in a crusty hierarchical way and *"it's definitely not old-fashioned."* Gentlemanly is also not quite the right word as that makes it sound too male. Some of the trainees tried to help us as we scratched around for the right description of the firm's style, and one came up with a story about how he'd sat with a quite thorough and pernickety partner whose attention to detail had at first surprised him. He'd subsequently learned to see the beauty in a perfectly laid-out document, where no comma or colon was out of place or out of line. Sounds heavenly.

and finally...

While we still dread trips to the dentist, our anxiety about interviewing at Stephenson Harwood is cured. Roll on summer 2005!

Stevens & Bolton LLP

the facts

Location: Guildford
Number of UK partners/assistants: 25/33
Total number of trainees: 6
Seats: 4x6 months
Alternative seats: None

Once upon a time, there was a small Guildford high street firm called Stevens & Bolton that dreamt of fame and fortune. Over the last 15 years, it magically transformed itself into an ambitious and driven commercial success story. The firm is currently ranked in *Chambers UK* in corporate finance, trusts/tax, commercial litigation and property.

grass stains

Currently just under a third of the firm is to be found in the expanding company/commercial department which, while maintaining its core regional and medium-sized corporate client base, is also winning banking work and some publicly listed clients including national business services group Hays Plc. Together with coco, sister departments in litigation, commercial property and trusts/tax account for the bulk of the firm's revenue, although there's a Cinderella role for small employment, family and residential property groups.

S&B has recently lured a few City types into the commuter belt, including former Simmons & Simmons corporate head, Ken Woffenden and former Denton Wilde Sapte employment guru, Stephanie Dale. The firm hopes these genies from the Square Mile will conjure up big client wins and trainees told us: *"We want to be getting better quality work, more national work and to be attracting larger clients rather than just regional South East companies."* Despite this, there are no plans to move from Guildford, even if S&B outgrows its converted canalside warehouse. The powers that be clearly believe there's no place like home, and have promised *"any new offices will be in Guildford or nearby, not in London or on an industrial estate."*

Must a trainee have a regional connection? Yes and no. *"They look for people who have made conscious choices, not drifters. They want people who have thought about why they want to be doing this, and why they want to be doing it here – in Guildford and at this type of firm."* Trainees warn against equating the green and pleasant land of Surrey with being put out to pasture; *"you shouldn't have the attitude that you're at a provincial firm so you can sit back and relax,"* said one. Recent matters have included multimillion-pound takeovers, involvement in a dispute between IBM and Cable & Wireless, and representing former Crystal Palace chairman Ron Noades in an action against the club. While you won't be doing crazy hours – 9am 'til 6pm is the norm – trainees must *"be very eager to please, want to get the work done and be happy to stay late if necessary."* On the subject of those who stay, one trainee (admittedly not entirely sure of the facts) said: *"Mr Stevens is possibly still around."* After September 2004, two of the three qualifiers were too.

all rounders

Our interviewees admitted that the S&B brand might not work the same magic on your CV as the big City firms, and that the firm lacked the same opportunities to specialise and flit overseas for six months. But, generally, they had few grumbles and many positive things to report. In particular, the small number of trainees means there's flexibility in the seat system. A programme is mapped out at the beginning of the two years, but you can discuss changes at the three, four and six-monthly reviews with supervisors, training partners and HR, and three-month split seats are possible. Receiving diverse work within a single seat is typical of smaller firms. *"In coco,"* for example, *"you could do IP, corporate finance, work for energy providers and agency agreements."* One source praised their supervisor, saying: *"They made an effort to ensure I got varied work. Even if they didn't need a trainee they would still involve me, for instance, one partner kept me updated by e-mail as an agreement I'd been working on changed."*

One of the *"big three"* seats, along with litigation and property, all trainees do a seat in coco, which is described as an *"ambitious"* and *"focused"* department. In litigation too, you'll be made to feel part of the team: *"I attended all the interlocutory hearings, meetings with experts or counsel and discussions about the case,"* said one source. And you'll also run a batch of small claims by yourself, perhaps routine breach of contract cases.

retiring to the clubhouse

Trainees are also encouraged to give private client work a whirl. This represents a *"huge change"* from commercial seats; as deadlines are longer, the department is quieter and the atmosphere more relaxed – *"It's still hard work but you can take your foot off the gas."* As well as probate and domestic trusts, the team also handles offshore trusts and matters for the Court of Protection, which rules on the affairs of people who are deemed not to have legal capacity (such as the mentally ill). Seats in employment and family are also up for grabs.

Although trainees get on, there are just half a dozen of them so it's only natural that after-hours activities tend to be departmental affairs. *"We tend to go for dinners after deals or if we've met our targets; good performance is used as an excuse to go out!"* Guildford's *"trendy wine bars"* play host to drinks evenings and each year there's a summer barbecue and a Christmas ball. There's also plenty of sport to join in with, including a firm-wide, mixed-sex cricket team whose antics are always described in *"an amusing e-mail the following day."*

and finally...

Stevens & Bolton offers a pick'n'mix training contract and has a reassuringly ambitious management. If you're bewitched by Guildford, it could provide a fairytale ending to your search for a training contract.

Taylor Vinters

the facts

Location: Cambridge
Number of UK partners/assistants: 28/40
Total number of trainees: 13
Seats: 4x6 months
Alternative seats: Brussels

Come off the A14 from Newmarket and take the fourth exit from the roundabout. Doesn't sound that exciting, does it? But this hi-tech Cambridge firm might change your mind.

breadwinners

Taylor Vinters' capabilities include personal injury and clinical negligence, commercial property, corporate, employment, tax and trusts, IP, litigation, debt recovery, matrimonial, financial services and planning. Add in some intriguing niches in rural affairs, life sciences, food law and an associate specialising in bloodstock and equestrian law and what you have is a firm that can only be described as a good all rounder. It doesn't just look good on paper: a quarter of all the firm's qualified lawyers are ranked for their expertise by our parent publication *Chambers UK*, making the firm one of the very best in the region.

TV's location could be the key to its success. Just across the road from the U-shaped glass and steel nerve centre of Cambridge's Science Park (fondly known in the city as the Toast Rack), the firm's IP and IT teams are perfectly placed to meet the needs of the locally based hi-tech and biotech boffins. These include microchip experts Cambridge Silicon Radio and IT start-up Hypertag. And it doesn't stop at Silicon Fen. TV is also instructed by techy clients from further afield, such as the £780 million MoD technology spin-out QinetiQ and the Massachusetts Institute of Technology. Tech clients also have a direct impact on the rest of the firm: *"The technology teams will deal with the tech element – IP rights, patents etc – and then corporate will do the restructuring of the company or sale of elements of it, and there might be property expansion or a sale of the site. And if* [the owners of the company] *have made a lot of money, we'll give them private advice about wills and tax planning."*

that's not all folks

Now that the dot.comedy is well and truly over, no firm can survive purely on technology work, and TV is no exception. It also counts the University of Cambridge, Wisdom Toothbrushes and...er...Isleham Carrot Growers among its clients.

TV's biggest departments are actually PI and clinical negligence, and your first seat is likely to be spent in one or other of them. In PI, you can expect your own files straight away (usually slip and trips or minor road accidents) and in addition you'll help with larger cases, perhaps calculating the quantum of damages or preparing a schedule of loss for a serious head injury claim. Head injuries are the main speciality, but certain solicitors work in niche areas such as riding accidents and military claims. In clinical negligence *"there are a lot of children's cases – difficulties at birth and cerebral palsy."* Here, it's more a case of trainees being taken along to meet clients and *"taking notes and learning"* rather than running their own files. Most find these seats *"a really good opportunity to have lots of client contact and get used to working life and practices,"* although for those set on commercial work, they can seem like *"baby seats to ease you in."*

A property seat is also likely in your first year. Its popularity firmly dispels the *"visions of AP1s and transfers and nothing else"* that some have before starting. In commercial property, one trainee said: *"I was doing 100+ files; lots of easements, lease negotiations and purchases of plots of land."* Expect to be thrown a couple of residential conveyancing files and perhaps a bit of planning or construction work. The successful rural services department also falls under the ambit of property, and a seat here could mean working on rights of way, shooting rights and even attending meetings of the Game Conservancy Trust. You may well find yourself writing summaries of the latest edition of *Farmers Weekly*, but forget the Archers; the landowner clients you'll encounter here can be phenomenally wealthy. It's said that you can travel from Cambridge city centre to Oxford without leaving Trinity College land, and there's also a tradition at Trinity of reminding freshers that their college owns the island of Manhattan. We're not sure how many of them are gullible enough to swallow that fact, but it's certainly fair to say that university landowners are extremely important clients to TV. As are the many agribusinesses, aristocratic estates and smaller tenant farmers that instruct it.

steam training

The corporate department is a popular second-year choice. Trainees start off on company secretarial work for biotech and local industry clients, and then become involved in setting up new companies or restructuring work, perhaps getting a small file (such as a sale of partnership or a management buyout) to run under their own steam. Although the quality of the work here depends on how busy the department is, it was felt that *"they try and push you."* Said one trainee: *"My supervisor said, 'You've done fine so far, but let's give you a challenge.'"* In this seat, *"you get out what you put in."*

The commercial litigation team is known simply as 'disputes', and you can take a seat here or in the employment, private client and matrimonial departments. There's also a secondment from June to September each year to Brussels firm Crosby Renouf. If you can tear yourself away from regulatory and international trade work, you can enjoy the beer and excellent restaurants with a gaggle of trainees from other UK firms.

porridge, punting and pantomime

The firm is housed in *"a massive grey building"* that's *"quite imposing when you first get here."* Before you get too excited, you must understand that it has also been described as looking like a prison. It's not the kind of architecture you'd expect on the outskirts of a city that can boast King's College Chapel and the Wren Library, but trainees appreciate the benefits of being located on the outskirts. For employees and clients alike, its position means avoiding the ordeal of negotiating the city centre's tortuous traffic system.

The traffic and hordes of annoying tourists were practically the only complaints trainees had about Cambridge. It may not have *"cutting-edge nightlife,"* as anyone who's roamed the desolate city centre past 11.30pm can testify, but this small and beautiful, *"chilled-out"* city has many other attractions. Unlike some other regional centres, the atmosphere is *"cosmopolitan because the university brings lots of different people here."* And as a student city, Cambridge *"caters for young people and there are always balls and parties going on;"* during term time, your weekend isn't complete until you've seen a gaggle of champagne-soaked students in black tie. Trainees get involved in the active TSG and Young Professionals Group, which organise punting trips and pub nights and provide a social network if you're new to Cambridge.

TV places no particular emphasis on a connection to the region or the university, being more concerned that applicants have the right qualifications and, rather ominously, *"aren't afraid to make fools of themselves at social events."* This requirement is likely to include the firm's annual Christmas pantomime, *"a skit on the partners and anything that's happened over the year."* All of our interviewees had made a conscious decision to choose TV *"because we didn't want to be in London and a part of that scene, but wanted to get a good standard of work from good clients."* They are most keen for readers to know that they are *"not people who couldn't get into London firms!"* Continuing their attachment, four of the five trainees stayed on qualification in September 2004.

let's do lunch

Because most people drive to work and the local pub scene is limited to the intriguingly named Q'Ton bar in the Science Park's conference centre, you're more likely to find TV employees meeting up at one o'clock than at half past five. Trainees grumbled about having to eat their sandwiches around someone's desk, as there's no canteen or eating areas, but those who want a break from the greyness can head for the green spots in the Science Park. Or they can drive over to the pond at Histon, where marshmallow brownies from the nearby branch of local coffee shop Nadia's come highly recommended. Three Fridays a month, a buffet lunch is laid on for fee earners and is designed to be *"a chance for everyone to chat and relax."* Perhaps we shouldn't say this, but *"after having main, dessert, cheese and coffee, we all come back and fall asleep."*

Organised social events include trips to Newmarket races, quizzes and, last summer, a garden party in the grounds of Queen's College. As a memento of this civilised occasion, a photograph of the managing partner on a bucking bronco hangs in pride of place above one of the office photocopiers. There are active sports teams – the boys play football and cricket, and (apologies for calling you lazy last year) some of the *"very proactive"* girls have set up a hockey team.

Every year, we learn a little more about TV's best-hidden delight – a secret beer fridge. This *"infamous,"* *"invitation-only"* refreshment facility is *"an advantage of being in a certain department."* We won't reveal its location (though we do know it), but rest assured that if you're in the right place at the right time and you know the right people, *"on most days"* you'll be offered a beverage.

and finally...

Taylor Vinters has built a very successful practice around the special opportunities to be found in Cambridge. If the challenge of locating the firm's most famous secret asset isn't enough, you could apply for its technological wizardry, an interesting range of seats and the good life in a pretty unique city.

Taylor Wessing

the facts

Location: London, Cambridge
Number of UK partners/assistants: 95/138
Total number of trainees: 46
Seats: 4x6 months
Alternative seats: Overseas seats, secondments
Extras: Language training

Taylor Wessing has a great reputation for IP and life sciences work plus well-developed mainstream commercial capability. It's also embraced a European business strategy wholeheartedly.

legal manoeuvres

The Taylor Wessing story is one of Anglo-German co-operation. Back in 2002, the then Taylor Joynson Garrett took over Andersen Legal's Cambridge office. Then it merged with a rather similar German firm called Wessing. Having developed a taste for growth, it went on to raid Osborne Clarke's Frankfurt office and grabbed 30 lawyers from Landwell in Paris. The firm now says that it wants to build a *"significant presence"* in at least five major European jurisdictions.

With all this going on, there was bound to be a hiccup somewhere. As hiccups go, TW's wasn't so bad and seems to have arisen from confusion as to how it should be defined by the watching world. After a couple of well-publicised technology partner departures, stories surfaced to the effect that the firm was moving away from this core focus. These were then countered by arguments that the firm was having a change of emphasis rather than a full-blown change of direction.

sophie's choice

So, what does all this mean for your average TW trainee? Initially, some of our sources were concerned that they had applied to a well-defined, medium-sized firm that was now having an identity crisis. By the time we spoke to them in 2004, such

concerns had melted away and they were able to assure us that the firm's character had not changed. The overwhelming feeling was that the German merger had been a really positive move. Said one trainee: *"To be honest, it doesn't make a massive amount of difference to me on a daily basis...though there are lots of social events between the firms* [sic]*, and people flying over to play football matches. You also see work coming round that is a collaboration between the different offices, which potentially might not have happened before."* Qualified lawyers can go on secondments to the other offices, but although thus far trainees have been limited to London and Brussels, there is talk of secondments to Paris and Germany.

In stark contrast to previous years, we're delighted to inform readers that seat allocation is a model of harmonious working. Full marks to Sophie Ferguson, who came over from Linklaters to sort out what was, in all honesty, a bit of a mess. The new system works as follows: *"You have a meeting right at the start to give grad recruitment an impression of the work you want to do. Then you draw up a rough plan for how you want your contract to progress. They don't hold you to this, but they do take it into account when planning seat changes. The current policy is that you don't cherry-pick a partner, but you do get to choose the department. You also get a say in what kind of work you get to do within that department."* Every trainee we spoke to had got the seats they wanted, even if not always in the desired order. There was some disappointment on the jobs front in 2004 however; too many NQs were chasing jobs in the niche departments and so only 11 of the 17 qualifiers stayed.

jingle all the way

In the corporate seat (which is compulsory), trainees were impressed by the work on offer to them. *"I thought it would just be a photocopying and proof-reading seat,"* said one, *"but I got to work on a joint venture by myself and a couple of sale and purchase agreements... though you should expect to have to do the lower end work sometimes."* The team has developed a name for working with American technology companies – often West Coast ventures – looking to invest or open operations in the UK.

Real estate is known as *"the best seat from a training perspective"* since you get to run your own files and speak to clients regularly. Alternatively, you could help out on some of the firm's bigger deals, such as the £130 million sale of Kensington High Street's shopping arcade or renegotiating the lease for the London Eye (which, incidentally, you can see from the office). The pensions group is also regarded as *"a hidden gem,"* and buried beneath the bigger departments are small private client teams working in the fields of family law and tax and trusts for *"old families with large landed estates, as well as more modern high net worth individuals."*

Trainees who'd experienced a 'soft' IP seat reported an exciting and variable workload of copyright and trademark matters. For example, the firm acted for Pepsi against a company producing a 7-UP look-alike soft drink, and the Mechanical Copyright Protection Society in respect of a claim for copyright infringement for an arrangement of *Jingle Bells*. Someone who'd had a taste of defamation law for newspaper publishers told us: *"Even if you had no interest in the law, you'd find something to attract your interest."*

For patent litigation seats there is *"a definite preference"* for people with science backgrounds. Admittedly, one source advised us that *"if you really want to do a patent seat, there are no prerequisites, apart from an interest in science;"* however, TW is a top-ranked firm in patent litigation and it works on some exceptionally complex matters. Without the requisite skills and understanding of the subject matter, you might struggle. Recently, TW has successfully acted for Apotex Inc. against GlaxoSmithKline in patent infringement proceedings relating to the lucrative anti-depressant drug Seroxat.

As in most firms, trainees who undertake client secondments find them to be of great benefit. One trainee who'd slipped free for a seat told us: *"It's a really nice change of lifestyle: you get your own car to drive to the client's offices, and your work develops much faster as you become more autonomous."* There is also a corporate seat in the firm's Cambridge office for anyone missing the dreaming spires. Or punts.

home and improvements

The offices on the north bank of the Thames just opposite the Oxo Tower tend to go down well with trainees. *"The location makes a massive difference. When you leave work it's great to have some fresh air and the river in front of yo*u." And there is a chance you might manage to make it out of the office to enjoy it: *"If you've got work, they expect you to do it, but never be scared of going home. If you've finished everything you can leave at 5.30pm."* Facilities are also up to scratch: *"The library is comprehensive, the support staff are helpful and we've got good access to online resources."* And, as befits a technology-strong firm, all trainees are issued with laptops.

In a previous edition of the *Student Guide*, trainees complained about the attitudes of some rather *"old-school"* partners; this year they seemed far more content with the cadre of supervisors charged with developing their potential. Younger partners and senior associates, whom trainees find it *"easier to relate to,"* are now being enlisted to the task. The firm is also tackling what one source described as a *"horribly low"* proportion of female partners by setting up a working party to examine how the ratio can be improved.

The appraisal system gets improved reviews: *"You do get good feedback, but sometimes it's difficult to pin down your supervisors. They're very good at performing the appraisals, but you just have to chase them up for the written report."* The firm is also *"very hot"* on training, with compulsory lunchtime sessions for trainees at the start of each seat, as well as regular know-how meetings in all departments.

all change

After a decent innings, it's bad news for one of the firm's favoured haunts. *"Recently the hardcore Witness*

Box crew have been beaten by those wanting to go to the Evangelist or over the river to Doggetts." And for its fanfare moment, the firm is moving its big celebration from Christmas to the summer. When we rang, preparations were underway for a jamboree with a marquee and dodgems. We must confess to liking the sound of the annual quiz night – the top prize is two extra days' holiday! Teams are also rallied for football, hockey and netball amongst other sports.

and finally...

If you know the periodic table from back to front, you probably already have this firm high up on your list. But even if you can't tell your Ag's from your Fe's there's more than enough going on to make Taylor Wessing a good choice.

Teacher Stern Selby

the facts

Location: London
Number of UK partners/assistants: 20/20
Total number of trainees: 9
Seats: 4x6 months
Alternative seats: None
Extras: Pro Bono – Toynbee Hall Legal Advice Centre

To the casual eye, Teacher Stern Selby is a quiet and restrained practice, occupied largely with property work. However, on closer examination it becomes apparent that the firm possesses a capacity for the grand flourish.

weighing it up

Finding a workable balance between the old and new, between a 30-year heritage and fresher ambitions, is entirely characteristic of the firm, according to our sources. "It's traditional on some levels, but then it can surprise you on others with its modernity." On the one hand TSS occupies four storeys of a Georgian property "close to the Inns of Court and lots of barris-

ters;" indeed, the office could itself "easily be mistaken for a barristers chambers." On the other hand, our colleagues at Chambers UK tell us the firm has forged ground-breaking expertise in educational litigation, particularly in the expanding field of educational negligence. And while it maintains a "family feel" and more than a dash of "old-school values," trainees tell us that the firm is clear sighted about the punch it can pack commercially. "We definitely get work that is way better than you might expect for our size."

Happily, the various aspects "co-exist; there isn't any schizophrenia about the firm." In fact, the equilibrium that our sources detected, whether during a vacation placement or at interview, was one of the main factors that had drawn them to the firm. Said one: "I knew I didn't want to be just another anonymous face in a massive, massive firm doing boring work. At TSS you know everyone, and although the responsibility you get can be daunting, for me it's the best way to learn." Trainees were unanimous in praising the balance struck between responsibility and supervision, saying: "You don't hide behind your supervisor; we're introduced to clients, and if we've done the work we're encouraged to call them." By all accounts, this "teaches you to be versatile and makes you very confident."

oiled wheels

The process of seat rotation is never at any risk of descending into friction or discord for the simple reason that it's blissfully simple. Trainees spend one six-month seat in property, one in coco and another in litigation. This leaves six months to spare, and these are usually spent gaining a more thorough grounding in the department into which the trainee hopes to qualify. Our sources were quick to stress that there's more to each seat than you might think. "Exactly what you do in each depends on the expertise of your supervisor." And besides, "because of the size of the place there's always the potential for you to be called in, no matter what your seat, for the big transactions."

A property seat is universally recognised as "the most valuable in terms of getting responsibility," although trainees did advise that *"as a first seat it could be a shock."* The exact nature of the trainee's role is supervisor-specific, as one interviewee reflected: *"My supervisor's portfolio was mainly small commercial transactions, so I got my own caseload of 30–40 files."* The satisfaction of *"running the lease or sale of a pub or commercial property from pre-contract enquiries through to completion and post-completion"* is not to be underestimated. Trainees are also drawn into the larger transactions that are the hallmark of this well-established department, for instance the recent £167 million acquisition of Cannon Bridge House and the acquisition of a £38 million central London hotel.

mixing it up

In both of the other departments variety is the spice of life. Coco gives trainees experience of M&A, disposals and AIM listings, as well as media and IP work. As well as handling IT and e-commerce matters, TSS advises a whole host of music, film, TV and cable companies, with this year's instruction from Cable Telecom on its acquisition by Telstra Europe illustrative. We're informed that *"it would be unusual to do a seat in litigation without at least some property flavour,"* a state of affairs that reflects the firm's historical connection with real estate investors and asset managers dealing with shopping centres, industrial estates, offices, pubs and residential portfolios. A trainee is likely to take on *"residential landlord and tenant matters like debt recovery,"* whilst *"joining in to assist on the bigger, more strategic work."* The department also offers the chance to experience employment and straight commercial litigation.

Some lucky so-and-sos engage with the work of expert educational and clinical negligence lawyer Jack Rabinowicz, who has been at the forefront of TSS' burgeoning practice in this area. He is currently acting on several cases concerning cerebral palsy resulting from poor birth management, which have a combined value in excess of £10 million. With his schools hat on, he has been acting for a 23-year-old man detained under the Mental Health Act in a failure to educate claim, and for a 14-year-old girl who was denied LEA contributions to her private schooling. Other trainees get the chance to work with wise counsel to star footballers and sports personalities, Graham Shear. With *"signed football shirts on his wall from grateful clients,"* Shear's practice is undeniably glamourous. He acted for the three footballers involved in the Grosvenor House rape allegations, advised both Dwain Chambers and Rio Ferdinand on their alleged contraventions of drugs testing regulations and also has links with Stellar Management, a sports personalities management agency. Getting injunctions preventing tabloid revelations and battling against their after-effects are all in a day's work for him. We interviewed trainees who had spent time with both lawyers and learned that *"unless there is a massive case on, when you'll do hands-on work, you tend to be in more of an observational role...but it is fantastic experience!"*

well-prepared speeches

Speaking of the mid and end-of-seat appraisals that mark each seat, trainees said they particularly valued the halfway check-up because *"it gives you the opportunity to put right anything that is going wrong."* They emphasised how *"if you're doing day-to-day work wrongly, you'll be put on the right track not lambasted."* But don't start imagining anything too fluffy; we were left in no doubt that *"a strong personality,"* *"adaptability,"* and *"a willingness to take on the responsibility"* were essential in any trainee. The expectation that they will make a written or oral presentation on specific topics at departmental meetings is a good example; *"it's scary, but you get used to it and you realise the benefits in the end."*

At this *"family-oriented"* firm, which has a *"strong Jewish contingent,"* *"lots of people have full lives outside of work."* Reasonable working hours of 9am-6.30pm make that possible, as does the *"take it or leave it social scene."* Once a month, the entire firm is invited to Friday drinks in the boardroom, and there are annual summer and Christmas parties and *"the occasional sporting event."* Last year's Christmas do was an Oscars-style bash at a swanky Park Lane hotel, giving everyone the opportunity to let their hair down – or put it up, if preferred.

Trainees spoke of *"the sense of community"* among their group of nine, and they can often be found in The Old Monk enjoying an after work pint or sharing a lunchtime coffee somewhere around Holborn. The downside of such conviviality at a relatively small firm is that when it comes to qualification, it can be hard to say goodbye to friends. In 2004 only two of the five qualifiers stayed with TSS, both of them qualifying into the litigation department.

and finally...

At Teacher Stern Selby it sounds as if there's plenty of Teacher and not too much Stern. Whether they want a rare peek at educational issues, some of the glamour of media and sports work or simply a thorough grounding in all the basics, this firm has something to offer a willing pupil. And whether they stay beyond qualification or not, it sounds as if they are more than well equipped for the challenges of commercial practice.

Thomas Eggar

the facts

Location: Chichester, Horsham, Worthing, London, Reigate
Number of UK partners/assistants: 54/54
Total number of trainees: 16
Seats: 4x6 months
Alternative seats: Secondments

Surrey and West Sussex: Home Counties hell or South Downs satisfaction? With Thomas Eggar we'd venture it's the latter.

location location location

To understand Thomas Eggar's origins requires a degree in history, a sound understanding of local geography and a fine grasp of interplanetary movements. The abridged version goes something like this: in 1981 a Brighton firm going by the name of Eggars since 1881 merged with two other outfits. Around the same time, two small firms in Worthing hooked up, and a London practice dating back to 1746 eloped with an equally ancient Reigate practice. In 1998 the whole lot collided, resulting in a star-shower of offices across the South East. The current Chichester-Horsham-Worthing-London-Reigate constellation now bears a striking resemblance to the Plough.

TE balances its skill equally between private clients and general commercial work. *"It is split 50-50 really; we are a full-service firm."* The impending birth of a new star near Gatwick is unlikely to change that balance – we heard that the whole Horsham office, Reigate's commercial practice and the Worthing commercial litigation team are *"soon to move to the delightful town of Crawley."* However, the firm looks set to retain a presence in all three towns, presumably to cater for the personal needs of the locals.

Although Chichester is the largest of the firm's offices and home to its admin departments, none of our sources would actually acknowledge it as the HQ. Each office is seen as important in its own right and each has a distinct character, despite the firm's best efforts for them all to be *"uniform."* Chichester is *"businesslike and formal"* and the London office is *"busy, dynamic and always trying to get out there"..."it's not just a show office."* As for the smaller county offices, Horsham has *"a heck of a lot of different and interesting private client stuff,"* Reigate was described as *"not quite high street, but very small and family-friendly"* and, depending on which trainee you talk to, Worthing is either *"generally unpopular because it's full of old people"* or dedicated to *"really big international litigation work, high-powered cases and highly motivated people."* In Worthing? *"Yes! It's a weird thing."*

northern exposure

Within a standard four-seat training scheme, everyone undertakes private client, litigation, coco and commercial property. A new employment option is in the pipeline and we heard rumour of increased choice in the future, but *"the main, broad four will be the same."* Before starting, all trainees are sent a comprehensive plan outlining which seats they will be doing and where. Up until now, TE has allocated them either to the north circuit (London, Horsham and Reigate) or the south circuit (Chichester and Worthing, and presumably Gatwick soon). Essentially, both loops offered the same merry-go-round of seats, though there are subtle differences. Private client isn't on offer in London, and *"if you're on the south circuit you'd be scuppered for pensions and PI."* Across the board *"a family seat is quite difficult to get hold of"* as demand outstrips supply. *"Basically it is set in stone: once you start it is quite hard to change,"* but the firm does try to place people according to where they live. Unfortunately, the system did not cater for that girlfriend in London or a granny in Bognor when your conscience calls and you're riding a Waltzer that's heading the wrong way.

We heard of people who'd *"kicked up a fuss"* and been allowed to jump from one circuit to the other, and with new face Mark James now policing the system it looks as if everything's about to change. Confirming that *"they are trying to listen more,"* from now on, after accepting an offer from the firm, trainees will sit down with Mark to map out their training contract. Presumably the London office will remain popular – many of our sources confirmed they'd picked TE for a 'non-City' training that offered a little *"London exposure."* Unfortunately, there is a maximum load sign on the ride to the capital.

where there's a will there's a way

In all offices, *"supervisors keep an eye on what goes on to make sure you're not out of your depth."* But this is not to say trainees can't dive from the high board. The first-rate private client practice allows *"responsibility, client contact and running your own files."* Acting for *"an old guard of landowners and titled people"* plus a newer breed of entrepreneurs, the department's work covers inheritance tax, charity issues and offshore trusts matters, sometimes quite meaty stuff. As one trainee explained: *"I was drafting trusts, dealing with the appointment and retirement of trustees and tax planning issues for classic car collections and art collections – I didn't have to draft a single will!"* All offices bar London handle regular private client work, but London and Worthing both deal with contentious trust and probate cases turning on fraud and negligent management.

A coco seat offers *"a mish-mash of commercial, employment, IP and pensions."* According to one trainee, the pace of work *"depends on what's in at the time. I had quite a fallow period, but now it's a heck of a lot more busy."* You may be rolling your sleeves up to change a local partnership into a company, or grabbing your cufflinks to join partners at meetings, where *"the volume and quality of the work means clients would be insulted if a trainee went along on their own."* Clients would include Abacus Asset Management and iTrain; recent deals have included the refinancing of Futuremedia, which is listed on NASDAQ, and Allied Irish Bank's £14 million loan to the University of Sussex. All five offices house a commercial property team, allowing trainees to dip into the usual *"leases and licences and whatnot"* plus some residential conveyancing. On the property client list are Barclays Bank and Network Rail.

A litigation seat in London or Reigate will involve *"quite a lot of building litigation"* for clients such as Hamptons International. A lit seat in Chichester is more of a smorgasbord: *"Landlord and tenant stuff, a bit of advocacy, agency hearings and exposure to the court, a bit of ADR and mediation."* Clients here include Pfizer and the Change Group. However, it is the Worthing litigation team that gets the biggest cheer. One trainee detailed its remit as contentious private client, personal injury and commercial litigation. The commercial team handles international fraud in conjunction with other member firms in the Avrio European network, so trainees *"come to court in London a lot and constantly meet with international lawyers."*

back to basics

The way our sources chatted easily about partners and supervisors suggests that this really isn't a firm where anyone pulls rank. Monthly appraisals are simply *"a chat with the partner, usually over a beer,"* and at the more formal end-of-seat appraisals *"there are no shocks because they are honest during the six months."* Trainee lunches each quarter provide a diplomatic forum to raise niggles. It seems to be effective: from 2004, all trainees get £200 per month in travel expenses. Many ascribe a recent upsurge in employee-friendly initiatives to the influence of the *"can-do, pragmatic"* managing partner, Tony Edwards. Trainees rarely describe their managing partner with the fondness of a favourite uncle, but here at TE, you get the sense that this is exactly how he's seen. *"He's good fun and takes us out for a beer,"* and he recently joined all the trainees on a touch-typing course – *"It was just all the trainees and him."*

Every year, the entire firm attends a 'Grand Day Out'. The descriptions we were given of the last one conjured up frightening images of a Playdays-Alpha crossbreed. The day is designed to get everyone together to *"create a firm culture and identity"* and ensure everyone is singing from the same song-sheet...literally. Memories of a rehashed version of 'London's Burning' with full orchestral accompaniment caused one source to mutter something dismissive and resentful about an American lifestyle coach. Another simply observed that *"a cross-office do should involve alcohol and there was none."* So did it work? Well, *"it is now the butt of all jokes,"* so in that respect, yes. Needless to say, the next firm-wide event will be a good old-fashioned Christmas dinner. Trainees do their best to get out together every few months, but the firm's approach to socialising sounds fairly low-key. Every office has its own respective local pub, there are football and cricket teams, and *"the blokes go off and do their golf."* One guy assured us: *"We have invited the girls, but they all said no."*

For everyone who said of TE *"there are aspects where I think it is still regional,"* another piped up: *"It's a London firm in the South East. We're on our way to that if not already there."* We liked the observation of one trainee, who declared: *"We are a confident firm. We're not trying to be American or multinational or a massive, big player. We realise our core areas and how to grow in them without having a revolution."* At Thomas Eggar *"everyone is on board."* In the case of NQs, literally: in 2004, all six qualifiers stayed with the firm.

and finally...

Don't be blinded by the London address because most of Thomas Eggar's business and trainees are bound to the Home Counties. However, if you want to train in the South East, this is one of the best options around.

TLT Solicitors

the facts

Location: Bristol
Number of UK partners/assistants: 38/57
Total number of trainees: 11
Seats: 4x6 months
Alternative seats: None

Winning plaudits from the profession and new commercial clients is Bristol up-and-comer TLT's new hobby.

happy talky talky

When Trumps merged with Lawrence Tucketts four years ago, the resulting firm entered a transition phase. We wondered whether the firm was still changing or if it had achieved its goals and was ready to settle back and enjoy the fruits of its labour.

"The transition has finished," thought one commentator, *"but the growth will carry on. It's not all about getting bigger though, the firm is looking to keep on improving its services to make sure the client is happy."* It took soundings from clients, and *"one of the messages coming through is clients like what we give them. It's standard across the board that things are written in a language the client can understand. Delivering the law is what we are here for, but clients like the other side of what we are giving them too."*

All our sources were excited about the Best Regional Firm award the firm had recently received from a legal magazine; it gave them some of the glitz and glamour usually reserved for Bristol's two biggest law firms, Burges Salmon and Osborne Clark. Since its merger, TLT has been jostling for the position of Bristol's third-placed commercial firm, but it is not *"biting on the heels"* of the lead pair just yet. Some of our sources concluded that their firm is far more regionally focused than the multi-site, international OC, and though it is similar in focus to BS (which one described as *"more masculine and more formal"*), it is not as developed or well known nationally.

blowing in the wind

Allowing us a glimpse of what the future might hold for TLT, trainees told us the management has chosen to develop in the fields of retail and leisure, construction, financial services and technology and media. For now, the banking and lender services department (possibly the biggest of its kind in the South West) pulls in around a quarter of TLT's income. As well as acting for retail banks and building societies on both debt recovery and new lending work, it has less familiar lenders on its books. One such client is Triodos Bank, which TLT has helped lend on not-for-profit projects including a £3.9 million facility to Greenpeace and a series of wind farms. Trainees in the lender services seat are given quite a lot of their own smaller files – debt recoveries worth anything from £500 to £15,000 and mortgage repossessions.

Consequently they end up making solo appearances before district judges in chambers in the county court. *"There's nothing that complex, so it's a good first seat,"* said one trainee.

hung out to dry

The corporate and commercial lawyers are winning instructions from a smattering of well-known names such as Imperial Tobacco and First Choice, though more commonly they cater to the needs of smaller, regional clients such as Severn Delta, a manufacturer of wipes and tumble-dryer sheets, which underwent a management buyout in 2003. A certain one-man-and-his-dog outfit, Aardman Animations, has gone from strength to strength since it first instructed the firm. Perhaps spurred on by the rise of existing clients and having gained a taste for bigger business, TLT has plumped up its corporate capabilities by hiring the former head of Martineau Johnson's corporate tax team.

If the day-to-day workings of a company interest you more than one-off mergers or management buyouts, a general commercial seat will be right up your street. Past occupants spoke of having a broad-based experience focusing primarily on drafting skills and ranging from basic terms and conditions to IP and IT transactions and the odd piece of competition advice. The client base includes computer companies and government bodies. Corporate defence is another interesting area of work, and one lucky trainee gets to assist clients on the wrong end of health and safety claims or other types of corporate liability.

whose round is it?

Time in one of the commercial property seats brings trainees into contact with some of TLT's biggest clients, for example pub chain Punch, which has a huge portfolio of properties. This particular client gets Slaughter and May to run its big corporate deals, yet its loyalty to TLT illustrates perfectly how good regional firms have the edge over London firms for more routine work as they can keep costs low. It's a similar story with the holiday company First Choice, which sends its biggest corporate deals to Herbert Smith, but uses TLT for property deals and smaller pieces of advice. *"You get to work for smaller clients too,"* one trainee assured us, *"Bristol-based business a lot of them."* Again, offering a lot of drafting experience and your own files, property is *"quite a positive experience...Yes you do get some tasks which are a bit menial, but you get quality work too."*

If you care about Bristol's landmarks and heritage, you'll be delighted to learn that TLT lawyers gave planning and development advice on the creation of the controlled preservation environment around the SS Great Britain, which is moored in the docks. It also advised on the regeneration of Queen's Square, once blighted by a dirty great road that cut a concrete swathe through its centre. As for The Watershed arts complex, TLT advises it on everything from IP to employment.

murderous intent

Of course, securing a seat in the employment department can, in many firms, be likened to playing a hideous game of Cluedo, in which the bludgeoning of Miss Scarlett with the lead piping is replaced by some equally murderous act toward your rivals – strychnine in the water cooler perhaps. Thanks to sustained growth over the last three years, TLT's employment department can now offer two seats at each rotation, thus obviating the need for skulduggery.

The private business group is comprised of family lawyers and those specialising in probate and personal tax and trusts. Acting for wealthy landowners, entrepreneurs, local professionals and the odd notable from London and beyond, the family practice is deemed one of the best in the South West. The trainees who'd done either family or private client seats had actively chosen them rather than been dragged kicking and screaming away from commercial areas.

a plaice where everybody knows your name

The *"soft, fresh"* open-plan layout of TLT's Redcliff Street office is *"a friendly arena to work in."* Trainees tend to dress formally as they don't have complete control over their diaries, but after qualification many slip into something more comfortable. Unfortunately only two of the for qualifiers took jobs with the firm in 2004, however. *"From partner level to trainee level there's no big divide, no real hierarchy,"* though *"people do have respect for the partners."* Significantly upping trainee salaries has certainly boosted their standing!

TLT is described as a social firm that likes to go out on a Friday and to play cricket and softball on balmy summer evenings. Perhaps this is why the ideal applicant is someone who *"shows willing"* and is *"ready to pick up the bat and run."* A committee organises weekend trips to destinations that could be described as reasonably exotic (Bruges), or indeed truly exotic (Tamworth Snow Dome). Not everyone wants to return to work battered and bruised on a Monday morning, only to realise they are now known as the worst snowboarder in the office, so for them there are *"less epic events"* such as karaoke or nights at Jongleurs. The most regularly visited pub is The Old Fish Market, though it doesn't appeal to all – the person who described it as *"big and near and not that nice"* was one of a number who prefer *"little, old-man pubs."* Wherever they choose to go, the likelihood of being delayed in the office is minimal. One trainee had only worked beyond 6pm twice during her entire training contract.

Each year, the trainee group performs an entertaining sketch at the firm's Christmas party. The cast of 2003 was somewhat handicapped by the fact that there was just one male amongst them, although the comment *"It just so happened that the guys the firm took on were all girls"* shouldn't be read literally. The *"regimented rehearsals"* of the previous year were deemed unnecessary, and trainees took to the stage knowing the performance risked being *"shambolic."* In spite of all of this, one claimed they *"stole the show,"* but omitted to tell us they were the entire show – the partners' failure to perform their own annual skit was noted by disapproving staff. If they cry off again next year, there will be a mutiny.

and finally...

If you're intent on a quality commercial career in Bristol, TLT is a very creditable option, but do be certain of your decision to shun the bright lights of the capital. We suspect we're preaching to the converted...

Travers Smith

the facts

Location: London
Number of UK partners/assistants: 51/100
Total number of trainees: 44
Seats: 4x6 months
Alternative seats: Paris
Extras: Pro bono – ICSL and Paddington law centres, death row appeals, language training

Choosing Travers Smith is a simple task. Consistently popular with high calibre applicants, this mid-size City firm offers a golden hello to corporate law and a culture that leaves its trainees thankful for the day they signed on the dotted line.

vel primus vel cum primis

You may hear the term 'golden circle' applied to Travers Smith (which by the way, no longer uses the Braithwaite bit of its name). No need to look blankly; it simply means the firm is one of an elite of smaller corporate-led firms that commands real respect for its achievements. This reputation alone makes the firm an exceptional proposition for students seeking quality training, quality deals and quality clients. For those who worry that the big City giants have become too bloated to retain the abracadabra of quality of life and the alakazam of intimacy, Travers

Smith may just be capable of pulling the right rabbit out of the hat. Training here is like watching a table magician performing tricks at close quarters instead of craning your neck from the back of the Siegfried and Roy show. As one trainee explained: *"They've never taken the route of larger firms that are there to churn out transactions."* And from another: *"It offered manageable size coupled with excellent quality."*

audio, video, disco

If you were lucky enough to have one-on-one tutorials when at university you'll already appreciate the value of personalised training. In such an environment, you are the focus of the learning experience, but by the same token there's no room for shirking. It's the same here. Travers Smith will sit you in a room with a partner and a junior assistant, each of whom has a hand in transforming you from nervous novice into accomplished acolyte. *"I could hardly think of a better way of doing things,"* said one source. *"You don't have to pester a partner with day-to-day, mundane questions, but you see the way they work and how a file is managed at a high level."* This doesn't mean the partner won't interact with you, far from it: *"You are encouraged to ask questions and show you are curious and interested."*

Your four seats will always include corporate (*"the core of the firm, the engine room"*), litigation, and property or banking. For the other seat you can opt for, say, tax, financial services, commercial or employment. If the choice of seats is narrower than in larger firms, this doesn't mean a narrow training, and every six-month posting comes with regular departmental training sessions and three-monthly appraisals.

ut prosim

The corporate department hosts ten trainees. Some of its partners specialise in private equity, some in corporate finance and a few are *"crossover partners."* Typically you will assist with due diligence and verification exercises, draft small documents and board minutes, attend client meetings and completions and, yes, you will have to take your turn at managing data rooms and page turning when there are massive documents to go through. Among the firm's recent deals are the £1.5 billion management buyout of mobile satellite communications company Inmarsat Ventures, and the £47 million public-to-private buyout of kiddie paradise Hamleys. Long-standing client ntl was saved from Chapter 11 bankruptcy in the US with a little help from Travers Smith lawyers, and any of you that enjoy using those lovely Molton Brown soaps will be interested to hear that the firm acted on the company's £73 million sale last year.

Interviewees spoke enthusiastically about the banking department. One wanted to commend a partner *"who took so much time talking me through the commercial rationale of transactions."* Breadth of training is promoted in a department that covers property finance, acquisition finance and a little capital markets work. In the property department, the work lends itself to a *"your-client, your-deal"* approach on sales, purchases and lease assignments, which is always good for one's self-confidence and skills development.

Financial services (compliance work and regulatory advice) is a seat that will initially *"hurt your head as you think about it,"* and strikes trainees as *"one of the less accessible areas of law."* However, the department is *"prestigious"* and one of the most successful in the City. Employment is as popular here as it is in every other firm in Britain, and tax is yet another big-brain department for those who relish black-letter challenges. The commercial seat brings you into contact with *"joint ventures, IT and IP, competition...you do a bit of everything and you rotate rooms after three months. Tax rotate as well, and employment."* Do bear in mind that *"these specialist departments orbit around the corporate department and are largely used as support. If you are not driven by the idea of being a corporate animal, if you are driven by socially aware things, it's not the firm for you."*

nil sin labore

The litigation lawyers are embroiled in everything from property disputes to class actions involving hundreds of claimants. The Maxwell pension fund litigation is one of the UK's longest running cases, although as one source pointed out, *"not as long running as Jarndyce and Jarndyce."* The only problem with massive, long-running cases is that trainees only ever witness one particular stage of the proceedings, and if you pitch up at the disclosure stage there can be a heck of a lot of document scheduling; or if a trial date is looming, it will be trial bundles that beckon. So if you were *"thinking you would come here and never have to do grunt work,"* take heed of the trainee who said: *"That ruby was shattered."* As it turned out, we failed to find anyone who'd been absolutely buried by mundane tasks, and some had even been given their own small cases to progress under supervision.

"We're not all lying in hammocks and magically still managing to be good and profitable," laughed one trainee when we asked about hours. Another recalled: *"There are times when you are so busy that you think, 'Oh my God! I wish this could stop.'"* We saw the point made by the trainee who felt things could get *"pressured but not stressed,"* yet we wondered how to reconcile this with comments from others who said they'd happily left the office at 5.30pm. In answer, one trainee picked up on Travers' claim to offer trainees the best of both worlds. *"Buy in to that,"* he said, *"but with your head screwed on. It's a City firm and corporate here will not give you the best of both worlds – it can't do, as we are on the other side to A&O, CC and Slaughters. But the experience will not be tough going across the two years."* We learn that trainees and assistants do not have billing targets and *"the fact that your light is on at 1am is not an indication of how good you are."* If your work is good, *"in a huge firm, only your supervisor will know about it. In a smaller firm your reputation is made and spread more easily."*

manners makyth man

Our sources were perfectly amenable to us asking if their firm was too posh for some of our readers. We learned that while some partners are *"really rah!...so posh,"* you can be a Travers Smith type whether or not your school had its own Latin motto and centuries of tradition. Polite, respectful, confident, anything but brash, serious about being successful, committed, interested: these are the traits the firm looks for. In past years we've suggested that Travers Smith has a collegiate atmosphere, and our sources were quite happy for us to continue giving this impression. As one source put it: "*It's a virtuous circle: you are taken in and become a part of it.*" But don't assume the firm wants only Oxbridge recruits – we'd venture to suggest it is now beyond all that. Such graduates no longer make up the rump of each new intake as the firm increasingly finds its type at a number of the better universities. By limiting its intake each year to less than 25, it can hand pick only the kind of applicant who will fit in.

If you have a passion for sport then all the better. Here's a plea from one trainee: "*We have three or four pretty handy guys, but we need to recruit some great new rugby players to sort the team out.*" And here's a warning from us: linger too long in the property department and you'll be wearing Pringle sweaters and comfortable slacks. "*The property department is a breeding ground for golfers!*" Apparently it's "*a client thing,*" but not so all pervasive that you need to indicate your handicap on your application form.

meliora petens

Travers' office is well located close to Smithfield and Clerkenwell. "*The office is smart, functional and understated. They take a certain amount of pride in not being brash.*" One trainee said he'd have no qualms about the firm being a shade less traditional and understated and installing a huge plasma screen TV in the canteen, "*but I am not about to move firms for that!*" The trainee group is well known for its cohesiveness. Believe it or not, this has led to several weddings. So, is it a hive of inbreeding? The legal world's equivalent of the Forest of Dean? "*That certainly was true, but these days we are all doing alright in the outside world!*" Socially, there aren't as many organised trainee jollies as at larger competitor firms; instead there's a come-as-you-are, come-if-you-like attitude to fun. Convivial in the office and relaxed out of it probably sums things up. Trainees maintain the tradition of visiting The Bishops Finger, a local pub so synonymous with the firm's name that we truly believe the sky will fall in should they ever stop.

On deals, our sources proudly squared up to their peers at the biggest firms, but to them these firms are factories; in rowing terms, galleys not eights. Of course, neither craft moves at all without intense training and hard work, but at least in an eight both bow and cox may look each other in the eye. On qualification in September 2004, 12 of the 16 trainees stayed at the firm.

and finally...

Travers Smith has much to be proud of, so in a market that has witnessed more legal marriages than Elizabeth Taylor's best friend, should we worry that it will be snapped up by a suitor? "*The firm is committed to organic growth,*" a trainee reassured us; "*despite the fact that we have offers from American firms all the time.*" Another concurred: "*I'll go out on a limb and say a merger defies logic...we will stay the same as we are.*" That works for us.

Trowers & Hamlins

the facts

Location: London, Manchester, Exeter
Number of UK partners/assistants: 63/100
Total number of trainees: 29
Seats: 4x6 months
Alternative seats: Overseas seats
Extras: Pro bono – Toynbee Hall Legal Advice Centre

Did you enjoy studying land law at university? Do you think working in the Middle East for six months could be pretty cool? If you can answer 'yes' to one or other of these questions, mid-sized London firm Trowers & Hamlins should grab your attention.

knowing your market

Trowers & Hamlins has a formidable reputation for public sector and social housing work, much of it linked with real estate issues. Consequently, at least one of your four six-month seats will be property based, and your experience in other departments may be influenced by the firm's exceptional list of property-oriented clients. Fear not, social housing matters are a far cry from your average residential conveyancing transaction. Large-scale voluntary transfers from local authorities to housing associations can be worth many millions of pounds, and the resulting maintenance contracts millions more. As a trainee involved in such transfers, there's every chance you'll be able to travel to different parts of the country to visit local authorities or meet with tenants. In particular, the latter can be a valuable experience as *"you have to explain the agreement to a layman in clear and uncomplicated language."*

Sometimes you'll be acting for the housing associations (the official term is registered social landlord), and once a voluntary transfer has taken place the work really begins. Of course, RSLs don't all acquire local authority housing stock; they have property portfolios of their own and will require legal advice on the purchase, sale, development and funding of affordable homes for their clients. You're likely to be given your own files, as well as working on more substantial matters that entail *"six people running round tearing their hair out at the same time."* Messy. In the property litigation department, you could end up learning a thing or two about human frailties as you steer RSLs through the minefields of anti-social behaviour orders, rent arrears and repossessions. The thing to remember though is that as complicated and troublesome as such issues get, your client contact will be a rational and conscientious housing officer and not some Rackman-style landlord out for a quick buck.

But if you find property is not to your taste, the firm has plenty of other slots for the curious trainee, including corporate and commercial, employment, projects and construction, litigation and private client. The corporate department, especially, is said to be *"progressing steadily"* and increasing its profile in the niche but growing market of Islamic finance. For those unfamiliar with the concept, this method of finance is designed to avoid those aspects to lending that fall foul of Sharia law.

In all departments, trainees felt that *"if you go around and make yourself known to people, they are always happy to give you work, especially if they don't have their own trainee."* Our interviewees were impressed by the range of work with which they were entrusted. As one commented: *"Trainees are not just there to assist with menial tasks. You get to play a more hands-on role and people take your ideas on board."*

a place in the sun

One of Trowers' biggest selling points is its network of offices in the Middle East, where it has acquired a top-notch reputation. Trainees are currently offered six-month placements in the Abu Dhabi, Dubai, Bahrain and Oman offices, all of which are considerably smaller than the London headquarters. Trainees always come back raving about the levels of responsibility and quality of work they received. One told us: *"You work harder in an overseas seat...but you also learn more as you take on the role of a qualified solicitor."* And for those who fall in love with the experience, the firm lets its newly qualified lawyers spend a few further years in one of the overseas offices. Surprisingly, none of the trainees we spoke to cited this as a major factor in their choosing the firm. So, anyone with a fascination for the Arab world, take note: with four postings on offer at any one time, booking your seat on that outbound plane is likely to be easier than you'd imagine.

For those wanting their travels to keep them closer to home, how about a housing or property litigation seat in the Manchester office? Again, it's nowhere near as big as the London office, so the atmosphere tends to be more relaxed and everyone can genuinely say that they know each other. It has also been known to take on its own full-time trainees, but it may be necessary for them to pop down to the capital to get some corporate experience under their belts.

sitting tenants

Trowers takes its training commitments seriously. Every Monday there's a trainee lunch with an industry-based talk, as well as frequent internal and external seminars. Trainees also get mid and end-of-seat appraisals to discuss their current progress and make a pitch for their next seat. Inevitably, certain departments are over-subscribed, so although the general feeling is that you get your first choice department in the end, we did hear reports of a *"random"* element to seat placement when demand and availability are mismatched.

If things do go wrong, there is an active trainee solicitors' committee through which you can vent frustration. It even gets results: *"The trainees wanted to be able to give feedback on the supervisors as well, and now we get forms to fill in about them. And the senior partner even took some of us out to lunch to talk about how we feel about our training contracts."* (We'd have loved to have been a fly on the wall there.) Such direct access pays dividends – *"I'm glad I'm not at a massive firm,"* one source reflected. Yet, if it keeps pinching whole departments from elsewhere – like Nabarro Nathanson's public law team in summer 2004 – it's going to grow.

For whatever reason, people stick around at Trowers. In September 2004 it was ten of the 13 qualifiers (half of whom went into property-related work). *"It's a very stable institution, and people tend to stay from birth to death. A lot of the senior partners are the children of the firm."* The international offices lend a cosmopolitan air in London, and we were further assured that the office had a *"relaxed and egalitarian"* feel about it. Considering the principles by which so many of the local authority and RSL clients operate, there's a good chance they'll also expect to see these traits reflected in their lawyers' style and approach.

Of course, the public sector famously adopts family-friendly hours, and although some trainees said they'd feel uncomfortable making tracks at 5.30pm every day, the general sense was that, once your work was done, you could head off at a reasonable time with a free conscience.

going for a song

The London office has a great location, with some lucky trainees having a view of Tower Bridge and the Thames. On the other hand, its distinctive triangular shape and fetching pink hue have often led to it being referred to as *"the largest traffic island in London."* We've already questioned the wisdom of playing Heart FM in the canteen; trainees were known to bolt down their roly-poly pudding in double quick time for fear of being serenaded by the flame-haired Beelzebub of popular entertainment (Mick Hucknall or indigestion...it's a tough choice.) Matters reached a *"nadir"* when Holding Back the Years was played on a loop for three consecutive weeks and someone finally got off their seat and turned over to Magic instead. Well, it's a start...

Once a year the firm manages to gather together in the same place for the traditional summer party. And in between times there are departmental Christmas parties and regular karaoke nights, when even the occasional partner has been known to knock back a few too many and entertain the troops. As for the common-or-garden night out in the pub, Trowers' trainees are a fickle lot. Every time we think we can pin them down to one drinking establishment they up sticks and switch allegiance to another. Last year's hot haunt, The Minories, is now referred to as 'The Miseries'. We give up.

and finally...

If you're simply looking for a pleasant, mid-sized firm in the City, you could do far worse than Trowers & Hamlins. However, this firm can offer so much more than the standard package and, because of that, it warrants closer inspection.

Veale Wasbrough

the facts

Location: Bristol
Number of UK partners/assistants: 24/70
Total number of trainees: 10
Seats: 4x6 months
Alternative seats: None
Extras: Bristol Law Centre, Young Enterprise

What's black and white and red all over? One answer is a sunburnt penguin but these are also the firm colours of Veale Wasbrough. You're more likely to see seagulls than penguins if you choose to train at this medium-sized Bristol firm, but few are complaining here and we're not surprised.

school uniform

Around half of VW's work is both non-contentious and commercial, and the rest is divided between litigation and services for individuals, including estates and tax planning, family and PI, which, thanks to a steady stream of work from union TGWU, is one of the firm's largest departments. The property department is also prominent and its clients include landowners, developers and institutional investors. On the corporate front, work mostly comes from local owner-managed businesses, but some bigger companies do come knocking. Last year VW acted for Destini Financial Services Group plc on a 15-transaction acquisition programme with a total value of £11 million, and for the management team of a large educational software supplier in their buy-out of the company from its founders. This latter deal reflects one of the firm's real strengths; highly ranked in *Chambers UK* for education work in the South West, the firm acts for a host of independent schools. Furthermore, the client list also includes police authorities, the MOD and many local authorities – Bath and North East Somerset Council, Wiltshire County Council and Bristol City Council to name just three.

Trainees can take seats in a wealth of departments including corporate, commercial, commercial property, litigation, schools, IP/IT, employment and PI. *"The firm takes the view that in PI you can get certain skills that you wouldn't get elsewhere, such as client contact on a daily basis and your own files,"* and so you are likely to do a seat here. *"You'll get involved straight away"* and will be *"constantly busy"* managing road accident and trip-and-slip cases. The good news is that you'll get to go to court and interview clients by yourself from the off. Up to 95% of the work comes from the TGWU, and in one of the three seats in the PI department, you'll also be involved in employment work for union members. This applicant work is kept separate from the main employment team, which acts predominantly for employers and with whom seats are also available.

A seat in the firm's schools department may also come early on in the training contract. Only one partner works exclusively for these clients, but partners in other departments also have extensive experience in education insofar as it pertains to their primary areas of practice. In the schools seat trainees encounter *"lots of different elements of law"* from *"employment and IP issues"* to *"corporate and charity stuff"* to *"general advice on crisis management."* The latter, we understand, does not include the dog-ate-my-homework variety, but rather *"anything that happens in a school environment"* – expulsions, A-level marking scandals and the fallout when *"senior figures get into trouble over pornography or relations with students."*

toughening up

As it's a big department, the firm also likes trainees to spend time in property, *"drafting leases and sale agreements, and also doing exchange of contracts and completions."* You may get your own clients: *"I had a nice lady with a portfolio of rent charges. I acted for her in selling them and also on some more general lease renewals."* If you think that transactional property work isn't your thing, you can request property litigation instead. As far as straight commercial litigation goes, there's *"big variety,"* including *"a lot of work for the police, civil actions, allegations of harassment, data protection and debt collection…and enough responsibility without ever being in too deep."*

Coco seats have a reputation for being tougher *"because of the nature of the work and the hours."* One trainee admitted: *"My corporate seat was probably the hardest seat, but as an experience, what I got from it was definitely worth it. It really took me up a level."* Here you'll be *"supporting the partner you're working for,"* but will get significant responsibility. Said one source: *"I worked on one transaction that carried on throughout the seat. The buyer was quite twitchy about risk and I was pretty much responsible for all the document management, which sounds dry but was actually really important."* Over in commercial, you should expect lots of contract drafting and to assist on PFI transactions. As there is *"crossover"* between corporate and commercial, whichever seat you're in you'll probably also get work from the other.

bristol fashion

As they are every year, our interviews with VW trainees were interspersed with seagull noises. Basically, *"they always squawk away in the background,"* and there's nothing you can do about it. One trainee guiltily admitted: *"We try to keep up the pretence that we're on the beach somewhere,"* but the *Student Guide* isn't gullible (sorry!) enough to believe such nonsense and we're fully aware that VW's office is located just behind the Bristol Hippodrome. It may not be a beach hut, but on the plus side the *"cramped and tired"* courtyard buildings are currently undergoing a refurbishment. The growing PI team has been booted next door *"to leave space for the rest of the firm to expand."* Alas, expansion won't mean opening in Tahiti or even Taunton any time soon; this one-city firm is definitely committed to Bristol.

Just like its trainees. Everyone we spoke to absolutely loved the place: *"It's got all the advantages of any city, but it's not that big,"* they told us; *"you can be out in the countryside within 15 minutes and you can walk to work."* We learned that most trainees had either studied in Bristol or grown up locally, and it's understandable that the firm looks for people who are *"quite well settled and want to stay when they qualify."* VW puts its money where its mouth is with regard to qualification jobs, and in September 2004 all eight NQs stayed on.

If you're a die-hard Bridget Jones-type you may be in for a rough ride: we were told that the shortly-to-qualify intake of 2002 were *"all really good friends and all in long-term relationships or married; we go round to each other's houses for dinner parties."* And when a little bird told us romance was blossoming in the intake below, we went straight out and bought hats. (You know where to send the invite.) When we pressed the trainees as to why they were all such good mates, they explained: *"We're all quite hardworking with an easy-going manner"* and *"everyone has the same bubbly and willing-to-get-involved personality."* Is this beginning to sound like Stepford to anyone else?

penguin suits

VW encourages its trainees to get involved in client events, and they're happy to oblige. *"I went off to an energy company to do marketing on my own,"* said one trainee with great pride, and as for the local TSG, *"all the trainees in my year have had positions on the committee."* As going home time will nearly always be between 5pm and 6pm, there's plenty of time for extra-curricular activities. Several of the trainees we spoke to were involved in VW's various sports teams, though when we conducted our interviews, the netballers had unfortunately just been *"crushed by Bond Pearce."* At least the footballers were *"doing quite well;" "we just played Bevan Ashford and beat them."* For those who hate sport, *"drinks on a Friday are open to everyone,"* and you'll normally find a collection of *"trainees, other younger people and the older, but single, people who don't need to go home as quickly"* at one of the nearby waterfront bars. The highlight of the social calendar is the September party. Last year's party took its theme from the firm's red, black and white corporate colours, which sort of brings us back to the penguin gag. Alarmingly, when we spoke to trainees in August, the September 2004 party theme hadn't yet been revealed. Don't they realise it takes time to plan a good fancy dress costume?

and finally...

Just about the only bad thing we can say about VW is that the firm still doesn't provide free tea and coffee. So if the prospect of forking out for your own Earl Grey doesn't put you off, you can look forward to a rewarding variety of work and the benefits of a full professional life in Bristol.

Walker Morris

the facts

Location: Leeds
Number of UK partners/assistants: 40/86
Total number of trainees: 30
Seats: 6x4 months
Alternative seats: Occasional secondments

The only independent firm in the Leeds 'big six', Walker Morris is a solid choice for anyone set on forging a career in commercial law in Yorkshire.

marching on together

Leeds is a tough market for any law firm, and at the top of the game where WM fights its corner on the biggest deals and cases, the market is dominated by the so-called national firms. These organisations have placed themselves in the UK's major commercial centres – London, Manchester, Birmingham, Leeds, etc. – and sell themselves on the basis of national coverage twinned with regional knowledge and sympathies. Walker Morris is defiant in its rejection of this approach and sticks to a single-site strategy. The trainees we spoke to at WM were each convinced of the wisdom of this approach; they sim-

ply don't buy the argument that a firm benefits from having most of its lawyers in other cities. From a trainee's perspective, *"being at a single-site firm has immediate benefits. When you come in at the lowliest end, it is difficult enough to get noticed...but 75% or more of the partners know my first name and know me. You are in constant daily contact with the senior people."* So, for example, *"it's a lot easier to just ring the head of tax if you need to."* Some even argued that the national firms had spread themselves too thinly.

Independence, stability and strong management have served WM well for more than 120 years so why go changing things? It recently acted for the consortium that purchased ailing Leeds United. Perhaps it should have been asked to advise the club a lot earlier. While the law firm is riding high in Yorkshire's legal premiership, the club took a financial battering and a season's-end elevator down to Division One in 2004. By contrast, WM is the UK's eighth most profitable firm (and the most profitable outside the City of London), though admittedly this has much to do with the fact that, for a firm of its size, it has a small partnership, the equity members of which are a tight and exclusive clique. Even so, something about the firm induces loyalty; it's the kind of place people join with a view to staying long term.

best seats in the house

In addition to knowing that your career will start and end in Leeds, the other thing that sets WM apart from most of the other top Leeds players is its six-seat training scheme. First-years have no choice as to their seats and visit three areas – property, corporate/commercial and litigation – but after this they have control. For each second-year seat change, *"everyone e-mails their top two choices to Nick Bates [training partner], and we all then sit round and talk about how seats will be allocated."* In a good year conflict is non-existent, but the meetings can induce sweaty palms as *"no one likes to be reminded that they are in competition with their friends."* The trick is to identify which seats most interest you and target them for the fourth or fifth rotation, when *"you need to get the experience and visibility in the right departments to convince them that you should be taken on there when you qualify."* Appraisals are scheduled for the end of each seat, and anyone wanting a mid-seat chat just asks.

Property is a core part of WM's business (*"Lots of our larger clients are in the property arena"*), and in this department seats come in a variety of flavours: retail, finance, development and planning. Retail property is *"a volume-driven department where you have your own files."* As well as acting for well-known retailers, the property team has assisted in the redevelopment of various city centres – Bradford's Fraser Square, the Northern Ballet's theatre and surrounds in Leeds, and York's Barbican Centre. For one trainee, the experience opened his eyes to urban evolution: *"By the end of my property seat I was seeing cranes everywhere."* In property finance you'll see how banks are generally more risk averse than investors or developers. Deals for banks can be enormous – the refinancing of a portfolio of hundreds of properties, for example, entails a mammoth title-investigation and reporting exercise. Perfect for putting a trainee through their paces.

shedding light on the matter

A seat spent working on public sector projects like the £180 million Wakefield street lighting PFI is no picnic either. It can be hard finding your way in such long-running matters in the space of a four-month seat, but needs must as *"there's so much work."* When a trainee moves to their next seat, their replacement has to *"come in and pick up where they left off. You are expected to get up and running with it straight away, although it's a supportive group and everyone understands the situation."* This scenario illustrates perfectly the benefits of repeating a seat in a favoured department, and it's telling that everyone we spoke to had doubled-up where they intended to qualify.

Corporate-seat trainees often work on deals worth between £10 and £20 million. A partner or senior associate negotiates the main agreement with the trainee concentrating on disclosure or due diligence, and perhaps also drafting any ancillary documents. *"It means lots of late nights and long hours, but you find yourself speaking to your opposite number and discovering they are three years' qualified."* In their view, WM encourages trainees to achieve more than they might at some other firms.

the x factor

Partners supervise just over half of the trainees, with senior associates picking up the remainder. *"If you're sitting with a partner they'll have partnership business as well as fee earning business,"* so sometimes an associate can make for a better room-mate. With partners, *"some are more approachable than others,"* though luckily, *"those who shouldn't have trainees don't!"* Also speaking of partners, one trainee said: *"Their position and what they have done demands respect,"* but far from having to kowtow to these big fish, it seems easy enough to get to know them.

To borrow a line from heavyweight philosopher John Prescott, tectonic plates have shifted since the retirement of the last managing partner, and nowadays more decisions are made by committee. Apparently, a little while back management consultants made a house call to WM. And their diagnosis? *"There was a general feeling within the firm that it had grown particularly rapidly in recent years, and that we needed a different structure in place to manage that growth. It's not that our values have changed, but our circumstances have."* On the cards are extra vitamins and supplements but no amputations: *"They're reviewing the idea of professional development...career breaks after a certain length of time and a bonus scheme. Things will be reorganised wherever we are slightly behind the times."* We're waiting for a modest rebrand...

On the subject of brands, we must throw in a reference to the lighter side of WM's work. It seems the IP team has been hobnobbing with 19 Entertainment and registering trade marks for Pop Idol, Gareth Gates, Will Young and Kelly Clarkson. And in a sense, the firm has been running a talent contest of its own – each year a trickle of paralegals make the grade and are allowed to convert to trainee status. Thankfully the judges are less wounding than Cowell, Walsh et al. So what does it take to make it here? *"Real teamwork and dedication. If you get on with people, work hard and show commitment to the firm, the partners will love you."* Generally, people are *"direct and to the point,"* yet during a networking course the trainees all took a personality test, the results of which fly in the face of the gruff, northern stereotype we'd have expected. *"Amazingly,"* said one, *"our year split evenly into the four personality types. Somehow the firm has recruited a good balance of people!"* Nonetheless, this is a *"proud"* firm: *"We're proud of the quality of service we deliver; we're not a run-of-the-mill law firm...Oh wait, that sounds like an Alastair Campbell-type comment. Remove that!"* No chance.

paint the town red

8.30am until 6 or 7pm is a normal working day, and everyone we spoke to commented on how busy certain departments were, especially property and projects. All good news for qualification: in September 2004 the firm retained 11 of its 15 NQs.

Trainees have their own social committee with a budget that allows *"half a dozen reasonably large and expensive"* events. *"We try to make sure two of them also involve the supervisors."* One such 'bring dad' event is a hotly contested pool competition that teams trainees with their bosses. Who won this year? *"Some hustler!"* That would be a construction litigation partner. Partners stump up for end-of-month drinks in one of the many local bars, but any night of the week you can take *"ten steps from the back door of the office for the cheapest, nicest pint of Tetleys in Leeds."* That pint is to be found at Wharf Street (no one uses the new name 'Bar Work' and, frankly, we can understand why) along with a liberal sprinkling of partners, fee earners and support staff, *"especially in the summer when half the firm will be standing outside."*

WM is a paid-up patron of the arts through its involvement with student YBAs from the Royal Academy. However, if you're left with the impression that the work hung in its offices could have been executed by a seven-year-old, that's because it probably was. Every year the firm runs a competition for kids, with the winners enjoying widespread celebrity and a jelly and ice cream party. Thankfully one trainee halted the melt of our researcher's frozen heart by telling her: *"We're not one of those awful, cheesy, regional firms that go on about being really in touch with the community."* Sponsorship of the Barbarians rugby team – that's more like it.

and finally...

No-muss, no-fuss Walker Morris is a little softer on the inside than one might expect from a firm with such high profitability. But make no mistake; this is firm for someone who's serious about making a go of their career...so long as it's in Leeds.

Ward Hadaway

the facts

Location: Newcastle-upon-Tyne, South Shields
Number of UK partners/assistants: 48/46
Total number of trainees: 16
Seats: 4x6 months
Alternative seats: None

Monday, 9am. Overcast with scattered showers. Interview with Ward Hadaway trainee. Cue sunshine, youthful enthusiasm and all the bounce of a Labrador puppy.

tyne spirit

The product of a romantic encounter between Hadaway & Hadaway and Septimus G Ward & Rose in 1988 was the firm of Ward Hadaway. Since its arrival on Newcastle's legal landscape, the firm has experienced one growth spurt after another and is now a robust, *"team-spirited"* business. *"Never content with standing still,"* the firm runs rings around most of the local competition.

WH leads the regional pack in litigation and has won the loyalty of clients such as Pride Valley Foods and Newcastle City Council. It also represented ship recycling company Able in cases relating to its contract to dismantle US-imported ghost ships carrying dangerous chemicals. Beyond litigation, there's everything from agricultural and planning advice to corporate finance and healthcare law. We heard that *"property is booming with the market, planning is really busy, so is commercial, PFI and healthcare...and employment. In fact, they're all growing."* The firm is not letting the regeneration of the North East pass it by: *"Everyone here is determined to get new work,"* and *"the firm is fighting the competition and wants to prove itself."* The property practice is making the most of things by involving itself with a great deal of housing development and regeneration projects. On the commercial side, clients include international software giant Sage, Barratt Developments, Zytronic (touch screen technology), Surface Innovations and Durham Pipeline Technologies.

super, smashing, great

When we called, trainees were popping with enthusiasm for the firm. Every interview was liberally peppered with words like *"brilliant" "fantastic"* and *"great."* We put this down to two things – the fact that all eight qualifiers were being retained by the firm and a *"flexible"* training programme that had allowed them to tap into a full range of work. Seats in property, litigation and commercial are to be expected, though are *"not set in stone,"* allowing you to *"sort things out as you go along."*

A seat in commercial property means knuckling down with leases, licenses, work for banks on secured lending, and *"a little residential stuff, but not for Joe Bloggs on the street, more investors of buy-to-lets and stuff."* In the planning team, trainees are involved in compulsory purchases by local authorities, issues over rights of way and drafting planning agreements between developers and local authorities. In both these seats, *"you get a lot of responsibility, but are never left to fend for yourself,"* and a spell in property development brings a *"heavily residential"* caseload to handle by solo. *"If you want responsibility it is there; if you shy away from it, it's not great."*

In litigation, too, trainees enthused about a role that's *"not just sitting on the outskirts looking in."* They take responsibility for claims involving small businesses and lend a hand on healthcare and family cases. A commercial seat tells a different story though. While trainees get to help out by setting up companies and drafting letters of advice on directors' duties, data protection and confidentiality issues, *"there's not your own clients, caseload or the responsibility here."* The same is true of corporate, where trainees sneak a peek at acquisitions, sales and AIM flotations for a client base dominated by owner-managed businesses.

blood and guts

While employment ends up becoming the cool place to hang out, some trainees apply to WH for its healthcare practice, and particularly clinical negligence work. The firm is just one of 14 on the NHS Litigation Authority's panel and undertakes defence work for primary care and NHS trusts. Whereas *"some people have avoided medical negligence because they are a little bit squeamish,"* one hardy soul told us: *"Now I can watch Holby City and know what they're talking about."*

Across the board, trainees are *"encouraged to get stuck in;"* and though in dire straits *"you all muck in,"* a whole gang of 'juniors' exist to do the mundane admin, so that trainees don't have to. Apparently a bit of sweet talking goes a long way – *"the juniors are really good...especially if you're nice to them."* Client contact is a given, and advocacy is definitely an option: *"If something comes up, you are asked if you want to try it. It's your call whether you feel able to do it."* All trainees sit with or near their supervisor, who *"makes sure you aren't taking on too much or trying to be too clever,"* and a two-pronged, six-monthly appraisal system sees trainees receiving a long appraisal from their supervisor and short appraisals from others they have worked for.

to know a veil

While you may get the odd long night or weekend stint, the average working day is a straightforward 9am-6.30pm affair. A good job, too, because Newcastle has plenty to offer after hours. Their accents led us to believe that trainees weren't entirely impartial when they told us just how *"up and coming and vibrant"* Newcastle is. We were assured that *"it's absolutely fantastic...as evidenced by the amount of stag and hen parties happening."* And *"it's got everything you need – a beautiful quayside, great shopping, everything..."* The only down side is that *"it can get a bit chilly."* All the same, we were enthusiastically told: *"You should come up here, it's brilliant!"* If you take the trainees' advice, rather than a veil, false boobs and L-plates, you should pack a duffel coat.

Set on the Quayside, WH's offices have views of the Tyne and Millennium bridges, and directly opposite is the recently refurbished old Baltic Flour Mills and the Foster & Partners designed Sage concert hall, which was named after its sponsor, WH's client, and affectionately described by one source as *"a giant slug."* Apparently, *"here on the Quayside you really are part of the vibe."* The firm occupies two buildings, Sandgate House and Keel Row, although *"from a certain angle it looks like they're joined together."* One helpful source commented that the premises were *"all modern, reflecting that the firm is trying to be modern and useful – more like a business than a stuffy, antiquey old law firm."* Of course, just two doors away is the granddaddy of the region's law firms, Dickinson Dees. Said one trainee: *"Compared to Dickie Dees, we are very young. We have an enthusiastic approach: the outlook and general persona of the firm is more modern."*

the hole truth

It's not all business, as the landlord of the nearby Pitcher & Piano will testify. When half a shandy will not satisfy, there is always the annual treasure hunt, which one honest source admitted was actually *"a pub crawl...but you have to collect things along the way."* An annual It's a Knockout competition is also a thinly disguised opportunity for opening a few bottles. Said one trainee: *"It's a little bit like a school sports day, but there's a bar and people mill about after they've dried off."* To fill in the blanks in that comment you need to know that there's a bouncy castle and water shoots; in fact the only proper races seem to involve sacks and buckets with holes in them. For more serious sportsmen, the firm enters the UK Corporate Games, which involves *"proper hardcore sports – tennis, triathlon, dragon boating, go-karting..."*

All our sources were as high as a kite about their choice of firm, perhaps because it selects people who are *"up for a laugh, realistic, encouraging and pretty sporting"* (even if only in the hole-in-my-bucket sense of the word). We heard that *"no one is stand-offish or arrogant,"* and that trainees are *"dead friendly and willing to help each other out."* Despite protestations to the contrary, we concluded that they did all have prior connections to Newcastle, be it through family or university, which is something you might wish to bear in mind before you waste the time putting WH at number 74 on your 'shortlist'.

and finally...

When we asked one trainee if there were any low points during their time at the firm, they pondered a while before replying: *"Only Monday-morning syndrome."* And as we all know, you can get that anywhere!

Watson, Farley & Williams

the facts

Location: London
Number of UK partners/assistants: 41/57
Total number of trainees: 20
Seats: 6x4 months
Alternative seats: Overseas seats
Extras: Pro bono – Toynbee Hall Legal Advice Centre, language training

Watson, Farley & Williams (note the punctuation) is a one-time niche shipping practice that has expanded its core business to cover asset finance, aviation, telecoms, and power and energy work. And if that hasn't turned your head already, you're guaranteed a seat abroad.

taking the plunge

"The City seemed monolithic and dull. I thought shipping would add a bit of colour!" If you've a nagging doubt that this trainee knows something you don't, you might want to read WFW partner Tony Rooth's thoughts on the hues of a shipping lawyer's life on page 138. If it leaves you green with envy there's nothing to stop you dosing up on shipping industry work; if it leaves you moody blue be reassured that there's more than simply ship finance on the WFW palette.

Within the six seat system, some trainees seemed slightly confused over which seats were compulsory, but it would appear that you need to do one contentious seat, one in corporate and one in finance, although most trainees were encouraged to attempt both pure and shipping finance. The latter is still acknowledged to be *"the core of the firm,"* but while it appeals to some, others had mixed feelings about their experiences. One thought: *"It can be a bit too formulaic. There's not much more to learn than creating perfect documents and executing flawless transactions."* Another disagreed, saying: *"Each transaction has its own nuances. Something always happens at closing meet-*ings, *especially when dealing with several different time zones."* What's more, *"there can be some tense moments when a vessel is waiting to be delivered and it's got some mechanical problems over in Hong Kong."* One thing everyone agreed on, *"you don't call them boats; they're definitely ships."*

If you balk at finance, there's plenty going on elsewhere in the firm. *"Litigation is really growing,"* one source enthused. *"You can see that it's going to be a really good team."* You should be able to strike a decent balance between key responsibility for smaller cases and a *"small cog"* role on a massive dispute. WFW is currently representing Vivendi in some major arbitrations in Europe, and has been involved in substantial litigation arising from ships refusing to deliver goods in the Gulf due to the outbreak of war in Iraq. Frankly, we'd be happy to settle for small-cog duties on such matters.

Much the same can be said for time spent in the projects department. Here you could be working on a large overseas energy project for most of your seat or helping on deals relating to golf courses, hotels and health spas. One can only hope there were plenty of essential site visits on the latter. Speaking of visits, and this is particularly directed at those hoping to boost their air-miles collection, WFW's network of offices and bank of overseas clients led one trainee to observe: *"Every piece of work I've done here has had an international basis to it."*

heartbreak hotel

One of the major attractions of the firm is the guaranteed seat abroad. In marked contrast to some other firms, certain seats are even reported to be undersubscribed. This has the advantage that you can often be told *"on the spot"* whether you can make it to your destination of choice, which is surely better than agonising weeks spent wondering if a rival will poison your tea when you leave your desk to go to the toilet. On offer: Paris, Piraeus, Singapore or Bangkok. The Piraeus seat is dominated by ship finance, although this differs from the London version of the same.

According to one trainee: "*At one level they're quite relaxed and don't like to hurry anything, but when transactions have to be done, they have to be done very quickly.*" If the pressure can pile up in Piraeus, the Paris seat has been quite quiet. However, seeing as the firm has recently poached partners from Weil, Gotshal & Manges, we expect things are already beginning to look lively. Asian postings sound unforgettable, not least because if you end up in Bangkok, you'll stay in a five-star hotel just minutes away from the office.

With overseas offices come overseas clients, and what an experience that can be. One trainee had clients addressing him in three separate languages in a taxi ride to a meeting. "*Unfortunately, much of the meaning was lost on me, but you do get some real characters. It brightens up your day.*" According to another trainee, it can sound as though lawyers are "*enjoying the ceremonials of a Greek wedding*" when engaged in a particularly energetic meeting. There are times when reality bites unexpectedly: "*It sounds glamorous to start with, but dealing with very rich clients can be demanding. You become more conscious of their whims than you would do with a banking client. When you're dealing with a big tycoon, you're both very aware that it's his money.*"

the six million dollar man

Whether you're "*running a £6 million transaction, largely single-handedly*" or coming to terms with your inexperience in the tax department, the really positive news is that you're likely to have a defined role and defined responsibilities. No one felt they'd been subject to the whim of a particular supervisor, which take it from us is not to be sniffed at. In departments where the level of involvement fluctuated, we were assured that partners often sought trainees out to participate in the more interesting work. Even when asked to do the "*classic trainee tasks,*" our interviewees took a pragmatic attitude, saying: "*You don't mind as you know it won't be long until something good lands on your desk.*" Trainees also felt that they were able to "*direct their training contract,*" claiming that

they "*didn't know anybody who hasn't got a seat where they've requested.*" The firm also gives you a chance to spend your last seat in the department that you wish to qualify into.

WFW is said to look favourably on applicants who have spent time abroad, and language skills are "*certainly a bonus.*" Apart from that, trainees described themselves as "*relaxed, but ambitious*" and "*not particularly competitive with each other, even in the lead up to qualification.*" Speaking of which, although the firm kept on seven of its ten trainees in 2004, there were still some fears: "*Unless you're interested in the core shipping, finance or litigation seats, you might not be taken on.*"

food for thought

Harmony in the workplace is rarely accidental, and we doubt that it is here. "*Everybody respects the layer above, but it comes willingly and isn't forced. You can chat to the partners about anything.*" The six-seat system means that mid- and end-of-seat appraisals come round fast. If anything, the only complaint is that "*no one gives criticism.*" However, the firm certainly listens to complaints. A trainee forum meets every four months to discuss topics ranging from the serious ("*qualification concerns*") to the extremely serious ("*sandwich mixtures*"). Perhaps a better example is the time when trainees voiced their concerns at being "*quite overwhelmed*" by the "*sink or swim*" environment at the start of the shipping seat. Those in command immediately devised a more structured induction.

No gripes about the heavily subsidised restaurant...unless you count the trainee who (denying her own contributory negligence) claimed: "*The chocolate trolley is doing serious damage to my health. A lady comes round once a day waving a Flake at me. Resistance is useless.*" Elsewhere, the firm scored praise for "*funky new meeting rooms*" with "*magic buttons that make the glass go frosty when they're in use.*" It's official – the *Student Guide* team is quitting Smithfield and moving in.

hooray for hollywood

Although reluctant to use the phrase, we can only conclude that the firm is the embodiment of 'work hard, play hard'. *"If you've won a case they don't mind you going awol,"* and sometimes no excuse is necessary. We heard rumours of a trainee who went out for lunch to meet the team on the first day of their new seat, and didn't make it back into the office until 9pm. Our favourite tale, however, relates to the Bangkok Christmas party, which had a Hollywood theme. Not only were all the support staff in professional make-up and costumes, but the firm also hired photographers and actors to play journalists and autograph hunters to clamour for your attention as you strode down the red carpet.

and finally...

Some firms brag noisily and annoyingly about having a good working environment. We're wondering if Watson, Farley & Williams shouldn't crank up the volume a bit.

Wedlake Bell

the facts

Location: London
Number of UK partners/assistants: 33/32
Total number of trainees: 11
Seats: 4x6 months
Alternative seats: None

You could say that Wedlake Bell is like a good old-fashioned variety show – not quite City, not exactly West End. A solid corporate client base allows it to flirt with Square Mile work, while successful private client and employment departments and a *"smart and sexy"* media team are also key to the performance.

channel crossings

Seats in corporate, property and litigation are likely to feature on the bill during your training, allowing you a peep at all aspects of the firm's expertise. A corporate seat isn't strictly enforced, but *"there are two trainees in the department and so it would be hard to go two years at the firm and not end up there at some point."* One trainee summarised the department's repertoire: *"We do the work of a City firm, but on a smaller scale."* That means mid-market M&A, AIM-listed clients and the odd plc. The firm's finance capability includes specialisations in hedge funds (google if you need to) and a wealth of offshore work involving the creation and administration of trusts outside the UK. Wedlake Bell is the only English law firm to operate from a Guernsey base, and this small office also handles property and private client instructions. We say wangle a business trip there and spend the afternoon on the beach!

There's a financial bent to the work of the real estate department, which takes on two trainees. It is expert at raising finance for property investors and recently negotiated a revolving credit facility on behalf of long-standing client Bank of Scotland. Operating in the usual realm of leases and leasebacks, recent deals have involved the likes of Harrods and Surrey County Cricket Club. In this seat, trainees applaud great supervision and *"masses of responsibility."*

orange glow

In the commercial litigation seat you could be dealing with incidences of breach of contract and fiduciary duty, or picking up the pieces on Customs & Excise litigation. On top of the usual trainee tasks of organising documents and managing disclosure, trainees are gifted *"little bits of advocacy like extension-of-time applications."* One trainee proudly declared: *"I met counsel by myself!"* We were intrigued to hear that *"the commercial lit department is known as the charm school."* Why so? *"You're supposed to be charming by the time they're done with you!"* Litigation experience can also be gained in the fields of business recovery (insolvency), construction or, if you know the right people to ask, MIPCOM. This media, IP and commercial team is regarded as a star turn within the firm and high kicks its way through matters involving intellectual property rights and commercial issues for clients as varied as the Motion Picture Association, Cheapflights Ltd and the Law Society. Recent cases have included a High Court punch-up between Tesco and Weight Watchers over skinny food, and a catfight between Select Models and Fantasy Tan, the 'pioneers' of spray-on tanning. There is no requirement to sample any of these products, unless of course you particularly want to acquire the appearance of an orange stick.

As one of the two trainees in litigation, you can't expect to be taking the lead, but those we interviewed seemed generally happy with their supporting roles. Most had been given the chance to show off their talents elsewhere, particularly in private client and property, the departments in which trainees have the most client contact – one trainee working on trusts and tax files had *five people ringing me up every day.* In this curious mixed-metaphor world: *"They give you as much rope as you can handle, so you can learn to fly at some point."* Looks like acrobatic skills are worth putting down on your application form.

We did hear a couple of gripes about grunt work and the absence of paralegals, particularly in connection with the busy employment department, where one source grumbled: *"I had to work out lists of documents and do paginating, which was pretty boring."* The hours tend to be longer here than across the rest of the firm – you might well find yourself staying until 8pm or 9pm when the department is busy. On the plus side, normally representing the employer, trainees enjoyed perusing the juicy details of contentious claims, drafting witness statements and attending tribunals.

magic act

Most of our interviewees seemed suspicious about the goings on in larger firms: *"I was concerned I might disappear,"* one confided. By contrast, they assumed, *"they treat you decently here – people end up staying for a*

long time." In 2003, the firm found jobs for all its qualifying trainees, and repeated the act for five out of six in 2004. While everyone spoke enthusiastically about their working lives, we got the distinct impression they weren't the type to compromise on their personal lives. Despite the fact that Dairy Crest is one of Wedlake Bell's biggest clients, one trainee told us: *"I got the feeling* [at interview] *that it's not all about milking you."* It's great to hear that the firm places weight on recruiting all-rounders (*"Our minds aren't channelled totally on law"*), but the assertion that the firm is full of *"fantastically good-looking people with hidden brains who can charm clients"* is taking things a little far, we feel! More credible is the claim that *"you won't get very far if you tick all the boxes academically, but can't sell yourself."*

For some students, choosing a medium-sized firm over one of the giants can feel like a bold move. Hopefully they will take comfort from the words of one of our sources at Wedlake Bell. *"Sometimes,"* they told us, *"you have doubts – although it's not like I think I'm a failure because I'm not at Clifford Chance – but the more time you spend here the better you realise you have it. The feeling at Wedlake Bell is that in terms of hours, money and clients we have a fantastic deal. The bottom line is that your life doesn't revolve around work enough for you to hate it."* Anyone still labouring under the illusion all training contracts are the same, or that job satisfaction increases with the size of a firm, might want to go for a drink and a chat with this person.

lamb chopped for mint pub

A prevailing good mood contributes to Wedlake Bell's professional effectiveness: *"The large majority of people are very sociable and socialising is important here; it's all about the art of getting along with people. If you can't get along with your colleagues, you won't be able to get along with clients."* No one stands on ceremony and *"there's no knocking on doors."* Apparently, *"the partners will just come along and say, 'Fancy a pint, mate?' It's phenomenal how many nights you spend in the pub with work colleagues."* The notorious Lamb & Flag (*"grotty pub that it is"*) has given way as the venue of choice since the firm relocated from Covent Garden to nearby Bedford Row. A shame perhaps as *"most of the partners are on first-name terms with the bar staff. They even know all their nicknames."*

Overall, a clear sense of excitement and anticipation surrounded the move: *"There was a big stir when the new desks were released,"* and surprise at the shift to open-plan working. *"It's a good thing to have a shake-up,"* mused one source; *"it's part of the move away from being traditional towards being modern...without being too modern."* A case in point, the leather sofas and the partners' private dining room remain.

and finally...

If you're one of those people who hates being stuck behind a pillar or in the back row of an auditorium, Wedlake Bell's front row seats should appeal. Especially if you're up for a drink after the show.

Weil, Gotshal & Manges LLP

the facts

Location: London
Number of UK partners/assistants: 24/91
Total number of trainees: 20
Seats: 4x6 months
Alternative seats: Overseas seats, secondments
Extras: Pro bono – RJC CAB, FRU, Bar Council and Solicitors pro bono units

In the eight years of its London residency Weil, Gotshal & Manges has made an excellent name for itself. Part of the wave of 'overpaid and over here' US firms that assaulted the UK market in the 90s, it has overcome the prejudices of a suspicious legal profession, rippled the market and earned respect.

ambrosia: riced out of the market

With 16 offices worldwide (the most recent addition being a base in Shanghai), Weil Gotshal is a firm that should properly be described as international rather than American. However, London is a bit of an anomaly in the worldwide Weil operation. In the US it's known as **the** insolvency and reconstruction firm, not least because of it's major role in picking up the pieces after the superscale collapses of Enron, WorldCom and Global Crossing. Though lawyers in London assist on these matters as well as Europe's own corporate shockers, Parmalat and the Eurotunnel restructuring, Weil's UK operation is not known first and foremost for insolvency expertise. Here, it has developed as a corporate finance firm, excelling particularly in private equity work.

Leveraged buyout house Hicks, Muse, Tate & Furst and GE Capital are, among others, responsible for propelling the London lawyers into the limelight. In 2003, it acted for Hicks Muse companies on the acquisitions of Weetabix, Ambrosia and Brown & Polson. When a bidding war for control of Canary Wharf took hold, Weil's London corporate lawyers pulled in colleagues from the real estate and tax departments to go all out for the major investor, businessman Simon Glick. A deal was eventually struck at £1.7 billion, but not until the eleventh bid had been made did the rival party concede defeat. Ask a trainee why they thought Weil Gotshal offers them as much as any of the magic circle or other top English firms, and they'll point out that they work opposite lawyers from all of them.

the trainee world: small is beautiful

Which begs the question, what's the difference between this and a magic circle training? Here's what the trainees think: *"In corporate I was sat with a partner and we had the head of corporate and Mike Francies* [managing partner] *working on a deal with us as well. Your personal exposure within this firm is very, very good."* Similarly: *"Given the size of the firm, you can easily get to know people. I have worked in most areas of the firm now."* And: *"You'll hear people above us who have trained elsewhere say we have it easy in terms of the hierarchy. Obviously there is a hierarchy, but not an oppressive one; you are free to get on with people at all lev-*

els." Smaller office, smaller teams, freedom from long-held office traditions and mores – it does sound appealing...

Trainees all spend six months in straight corporate, litigation and finance seats; beyond this they choose from property, competition, tax, technology, environmental, employment, restructuring, securitisation and international corporate finance. Here's what one trainee had to say about a busy time in securitisation: "*You do have a lot of fun and people are really nice. The team is headed by Jacky Kelly...I think you'd speak to her as if you were speaking to your future mother-in-law.*" (Intriguing) "*We were doing a lot of mortgage-backed securisisations and my main task was liaising with the FSA, and specifically the listing department. I was also liaising with the London Stock Exchange. The good thing about working on repeat deals is that you get to know the characters. I was running closing meetings and drafting the global notes.*" How easy was it getting your head around the jargon of the transactions? "*I had a manual of basic terms, which I pinned down pretty quickly.*"

Another trainee told us about life in banking: "*I was exposed to a lot of different work and different members of the department. I shared a room with an associate who was six years qualified and worked on a lot of his deals as if I were a junior assistant. He always explained things, so I had a good idea of what the deal was about...I wasn't just in my own trainee world. I did do trainee-type things like preparing bibles and board minutes, but I also got stuck in with meeting clients and the other side.*"

sunseekers: unfreezing your assets

The litigation department (which has adopted an internal barristers chambers approach) is as good a place as any for us to demonstrate how much of your time is spent working on cross-border transactions and cases. In the last year, London litigators discharged two worldwide freezing orders made by the UK courts and worth over $400 million. The orders had been made in support of a $3 billion claim made in New York against two businessmen, and the said claim had prompted litigation and arbitration in multiple jurisdictions including Paris, Switzerland, Turkey, Germany, the Channel Islands and Bermuda. On another matter, and acting for Diners Club, the team obtained an important ruling regarding the confidentiality of credit and debit card transactions. This case was run in conjunction with South African proceedings.

Our sources had all worked in tandem with other Weil lawyers, mostly in Europe and the USA. Some trainees go one step further and take a seat in a US office, usually New York (for corporate) or California's Silicon Valley (for IP). If you can get your tongue around a foreign language and put up a convincing business case, you should be able to hop over to channel to Paris or another European office, and a few secondments are also available to GE Capital. Every two years, the entire complement of European lawyers and trainees converges somewhere sunny for a weekend of shop talk and partying.

&more: love at first bite

Moleskin jeans, fine champagne and rioja from Spain is all available downstairs in the in-house Marks & Spencer store. Pretty handy if you want to pop away from your desk and buy a new pair of chinos for the office...a shame though that those pesky members of the public are also allowed access. Listen to some people and they'll try and convince you that the reason the firm operates above a large knicker drawer is because its lawyers work around the clock and never get home for fresh clothes. The truth of the matter is that your hours will mirror those of your mates in the magic circle – steadier in some departments, prone to peaks and troughs in corporate and banking. "*I'm always in for 9.30am,*" said one trainee; "*and if it's quiet I can leave bang on 5.30pm. If we were in the earlier stages of a transaction then I'd leave at 7pm (that's about 50% of the time) and if we're at or near a closing, it could be any time. In corporate, deal announcements were going out at 7 o'clock in the morning so that did mean all-night working.*"

Weil Gotshal strikes us as a good-natured place, and one where people enjoy each other's company, whether they're piling into the Corney & Barrow or Sosho Match or playing softball in the summer. And, as if running the office isn't enough, Mike Francies is not averse to inviting the entire staff to his house for a summer party.

fair trade: your money or your life?

Want to know what's happening in the big Weil world? Get yourself along to one of Mr F's quarterly reviews. "*Last time they combined that with a slide show of the partnership retreat to Las Vegas, which made it more interesting!*" Want to mug up on a bit of hard law or some soft skills? There's a trainee-specific programme of sessions, departmental programmes and "*PSLs [professional support lawyers] will send round e-mails asking what topics people want to brush up on.*" Want to know what your supervisor and other lawyers in the department actually think of you? Three monthly appraisals should do the job – "*Jillian [grad recruitment manager] pushes for you to get them done on time*" – and many of the supervisors are happy to give feedback on a "*piece-by-piece*" basis too. Want to put something back? Weils London has imported a healthy attitude towards pro bono from the USA, and as well as the opportunities mentioned above in the fact box, it has devoted time to gratis advice and representation for Oxfam on the issue of potentially damaging agricultural subsidies in Europe and the USA.

Having achieved full retention in 2003, the firm didn't do half as well with its qualifiers in 2004, when only three of the seven stayed on. Not everyone took to City life and the people that left are now pursuing other styles of career. The advice of one trainee is that it's pointless applying to this or any other hard-core City firm on a whim: "*You've got to want to be a corporate lawyer.*" Another agreed, saying: "*If you are going to pursue a career in the City you need to go in knowing what to expect. If you are then prepared to really get involved, you will get a lot out of it.*" We say do a vac scheme, keep your eyes open and ask questions. Trainees add: "*Be realistic about the academic background you have. The firm has become a lot more cut-throat in who they take on, so if you've not got the grades there's little point in applying...unless you're older with a standout CV and you're incredibly well rounded.*"

and finally...

Training at Weil Gotshal & Manges is rather like ending up in the first-class lounge at Heathrow airport. You don't take off any quicker than the hordes whiling away the hours in the economy lounge or thumbing through the Argyles in Sock Shop, but at least your wait is comfortable and you'll get plenty of attention from staff. Of course, there's also that little matter of being able to afford a first-class ticket, but this shouldn't be a problem on a Weil's salary!

White and Bowker

the facts

Location: Winchester, Chandlers Ford
Number of UK partners/assistants: 16/20
Total number of trainees: 8
Seats: usually 4x6 months
Alternative seats: None

The solicitors firm of White and Bowker settled in Winchester in 1750. Home to Jane Austen and sufficient men of large fortune to allow the practice to flourish in Regency times, this little cathedral city can now offer the discerning 21st-century trainee considerably more than country living and social climbing.

little persuasion required

Although well known for its top-notch agriculture and environment practice and impressive private client work, White and Bower also handles family law, crime, company/commercial transactions, commercial litigation and employment law. There is enormous scope for meeting and working with a wealth of clients including the owners of large farms and estates, charities, house builders, hoteliers and housing associations. If individuals are more your client of choice, in crime you'll encounter murderers or those facing prosecutions linked to the Human Fertilisation and Embryology Act, and in family people going though divorce or adoption and those who have suffered domestic violence or whose children have been abducted. In the PI department you'll meet people with injuries or illnesses arising from road accidents or exposure to asbestos at work. The firm has taken on a number of particularly interesting and groundbreaking matters over the years, including the case of gender-reassigned Sergeant Major Joanne Wingate, who sued the army for unfair treatment.

The only areas that are compulsory are litigation and property. The latter may be residential conveyancing for a major mortgage company client, which provides *"an adrenaline rush because there are lots of deadlines,"* though by the same token it can be *"quite formulaic."* Inevitably, business needs dictate the running of the four-seat training scheme, and we heard of seats cut short or extended depending on which departments were run off their feet at the time. Generally, however, the firm is seen to be *"fairly flexible in letting you go where you have an interest."* Seats are available in all groups save for the small charities team.

praise & prejudice

Our sources sang the praises of a new, more coherent approach to training, which introduces future trainees to White and Bowker society before they start, and provides new arrivals with a 'buddy' for companionship (though one candid source confessed *"that only really lasts as long as the first lunch"*). Trainees sit with or near their supervisor in each seat and, on top of *"quick chats as and when,"* monthly meetings keep everyone on track until its time for a comprehensive review at the end of the seat. To our ears the role of trainee sounded very much like that of junior lawyer rather than spare wheel: we heard from trainees who had attended employment tribunals, gained advocacy experience, run their own files and written articles on new law. They also had billable-hours targets, though *"these are very achievable and really just act as a guide."* A flexitime system is in operation, but that said, it seems to be so flexible that our sources couldn't tell us how it worked or to whom it applied. We'll assume it is a nine-to-five day with a little discretion at either end.

playing sardines

Best known for a large public school and a cathedral, Winchester is an agreeable place to visit, and White and Bowker's Georgian townhouse office is also unlikely to disappoint those with an appreciation of Regency architecture. The inside was described by one source as *"a higgledy-piggeldy rabbit-warren,"* and new recruits have been known to end up in the office broom cupboard (generally by accident). As the venue for the firm's residential conveyancing, private client, agriculture and family law services, it is felt to have *"quite a staid and reserved atmosphere."* The car park has a two-year waiting list, but look on the bright side – this means qualification could entail more than just a pay rise. As the office is just a short promenade from some great shops, lunch risks taking more than an hour.

In contrast, the firm's office at Chandlers Ford is a ten-minute drive out of town. Here, modern premises house the crime, employment and commercial practices. Trainees portrayed Chandlers Ford as *"the more vibrant"* and sociable of the two offices, probably because it is open plan. At this office, not only is there plenty of parking, *"there's even a valet, a dry-cleaning service and a choice of two sandwich services."* The downside is that lunchtime window-shopping is limited to Asda.

Does this arrangement result in a split personality? Apparently not. Our sources spoke of a firm that is *"promoting its age, but with a more modern spin;"* one that is *"moving with the times, but isn't ignoring those clients who don't want to."* While *"there is a very sharp distinction between them,"* we were assured that the existence of two very different offices *"doesn't jar"* and that people do mix.

a suitable match

Trainees maintain that a local connection is not a prerequisite for working at White and Bowker; nonetheless, many did have a link with the area, be it through home or university. They all fall into the category of *"people who have made a definite decision not to train in London,"* but who weren't enamoured with the idea of being the sole trainee in a high-street practice. Financially, choosing this kind of firm over London is *"a big decision to make"* but, like Ms Austen, these trainees understand that a large income is not always the best recipe for happiness. Instead they reap the rewards of hands-on, broad-ranging experience and good levels of responsibility. That said, Winchester is a pricey place and consequently many staff live further afield in Southampton or the surrounding countryside.

Typically twenty-somethings, a number of them with a period of paralegalling before starting training, we noted a distinct White and Bowker type. *"Training here, you need to be quite self-motivated,"* so *"anyone who has no confidence might struggle."* Our sources were articulate, self-assured and willing, and we've no doubt Austen could have had them all married off in minutes. Two of the three trainees who qualified in 2004 stayed with the firm.

pleasures and diversions

Alas, trainees could not entertain us with tales of Austen-style heaving bosoms at the photocopier, dead faints or meaningful glances across a crowded office. Yet despite a lack of romance in the air, they clearly enjoyed the social side of the firm. Staff from both offices gather in Winchester's Slug and Lettuce, and there's the standard Friday lunchtime pub routine. The firm beat the rush by getting its annual Christmas bash out the way early this year...in January. Clearly planned by someone intending to buy a new frock in the sales, the event brought the whole firm together at the Rosebowl (Hampshire County Cricket Club to the uninitiated). The summer AGM party was held at the Winchester Guildhall. Regular football fixtures keep sports fans happy, and when we called a cricket team was in the pipeline. We must say we rather admired the brave-bottomed Bowker Bikers, who cycled over 500 miles across France for charity.

and finally...

Whether it's Regency etiquette or commercial acumen that inspires you, you'd do well to consider White and Bowker for a southern English training. Sadly, we cannot guarantee an appearance by local lad, Colin Firth, either with or without wet shirt.

White & Case LLP

the facts

Location: London
Number of UK partners/assistants: 52/129
Total number of trainees: 45
Seats: 4x6 months
Alternative seats: Overseas seats, secondments
Extras: Pro bono – RCJ CAB, The Prince's Trust, language training

Born in the USA maybe, but this 39-office, 26-nation-state law firm is most definitely not looking to be called a US firm. White & Case epitomises a class of firm that has put its all into international practice.

going native

White & Case has been operating in London since 1971, proving that globalisation wasn't actually invented in the 1990s after all. As a matter of fact, the firm had a presence in Paris as early as the 1920s, moved to Brussels in the 1960s, and was quick to clamber over the rubble of the Berlin Wall into Eastern Europe. In its quest for a place in world legal markets, it's left few stones unturned; yet it hasn't behaved in the manner of a colonising power – it's gone native. Its offices are staffed mainly by domestic-qualified lawyers and over half of the partners are of a non-US persuasion. In London this equates to an office full of Brits with the odd American or Swede or Italian, or whoever else may have stopped by for a week or a month or a year.

Long known as a banking and finance outfit, White & Case has made no secret of its desire to dominate in other spheres. Its 'sovereign practice' – through which it acts for heads of states and governments around the world – has been very successful, and wherever there have been political developments likely to lead to economic growth, the firm has been quick to take advantage. The worldwide managing partner says on the firm's website that White & Case wants to be "the pre-eminent global law firm by the end of this decade." No small task, but we don't doubt his sincerity.

or world domination?

The global theme of growth and market dominance is apparent in the London office. One trainee said of the office's ambitions: "It wants to cement itself as one of the top firms in London." In September 2004, the trainee population will hit 45; long gone are the days when choosing White & Case was the dare-to-be-different move of the maverick student who would have joined the magic circle were it not for their obtuse views ("I won't be corporate robot trainee no. 73"). The firm has earned its training stripes in London and can give the establishment firms a run for their money.

Following a four-by-six-month seat system, trainees are ushered through a finance seat and something contentious. Nothing else is compulsory, though we've never yet spoken to someone who's not spent six months working abroad in either Asia or Europe. The firm boasts that at any one time 25%

of its trainees are away in one of its many overseas offices. Most of the things you'll work on will involve people from different cultures and countries, and "it would be a strange choice for someone who didn't want to do a seat abroad." Unless you're interested in international work and clients, turn the page because this is not the firm for you.

one sausage or two?

A banking seat brings the occupant into contact with "a whole range" of transactions – acquisition finance, unsecured credit agreements, bog-standard secured lending... One source, who'd spent time assisting with the finance for a merger, explained how she'd drafted many of the guarantees herself and contributed some of the provisions of the main agreement: "It really hits you that this is the big time!" she told us. Also on offer is asset finance (aeroplanes, plant and machinery, etc.) and project finance. Indeed, it's international projects a-go-go at White & Case London.

"Projects is a very good department and traditionally one of the most high-profile here," said one old hand. Not only do you get to work on things like the $11 billion Sakhalin II (Phase 2) Russian oil and gas project and Algeria's first international syndicated loan deal, the €436.5 million financing of Orascom Telecom Algeria's GSM network, you're also likely to be supervised by the firm's training partner, Philip Stopford. Each week Mr S (assisted by the grad recruitment team) scrutinises reports submitted by each of the trainees. They must tell him exactly how their time has been spent, and "he'll get straight on the phone if he thinks you're not getting the right kind of work." When he's not keeping a watchful eye over the kids, or running his own practice, he can be found slaving away over a hot barbecue in his garden. Each summer he cooks for his colleagues in the projects department, the trainee group and whoever else has blagged an invitation. We're not sure if he's a martyr or just plain mad.

Corporate seats – not everyone does them, and

those that do may find the deals *"not as large-scale as those say in project finance."* Three lawyers per deal is not uncommon, and you're likely to be the number three. *"I had excellent-quality work from the start,"* enthused a trainee who'd taken great pleasure in attending a closure meeting at a magic circle firm where she and her two colleagues were greeted by a room full of 12 lawyers with not a trainee among them. Legal assistants do most of the grunt work, and apparently, *"there's a guru who will do your Companies House filings and searches. You only need to do basic corporate tasks once, so that you could do them if you needed to when she was off sick. But if you've got 20 filings to make, why would you want to waste time doing them all?"* Why indeed?

A capital markets seat can be *"a baptism of fire;"* one of our contributors admitted he'd not had a clue about the work of this department (which is growing like *"an evil empire taking over the building"*) until his supervisor gave him a *"crash course."* Although some trainees worried that friends at the biggest City firms were getting more classroom-style training, we couldn't help wondering if White & Case's one-on-one, in-the-field training was more effective.

Most trainees visit the commercial litigation department (the other contentious alternatives are IP and employment). Trainees are *"not pushed aside and given menial tasks"* because the legal assistants are *"a huge part of the support network."* Instead they can be found assisting with witness interviews, drafting witness statements, attending court hearings and doing research for clients and other White & Case offices. *"I worked a lot with Paris,"* one trainee recalled. *"It has a strong arbitration group and trainees who go out to Paris do a lot of arbitration."*

a home at last

After a long delay, in October 2004 White & Case finally moved to a single-site office at 5 Old Broad Street near Bank. The buildiers had stumbled across some 2,000-year-old relics, which are now in the Museum of London should you wish to see them.

When we interviewed a few months earlier, the firm was *"bursting at the seams"* of its five old buildings, so the move came not a moment too soon. It was symbolic in some ways – *"My only experience of this firm is change and growth...it's never been stable,"* said one trainee. *"This move will give us a root...a base...it will say, 'We're here now, don't mess with us.'"*

Trainees tell us the atmosphere in the office is *"relaxed."* Perhaps reading our researcher's mind, one source continued: *"People don't believe you when you say that. They say, 'You work too hard' or 'It's a US firm!'"* Lacking in formality is perhaps a better description. *"Part of it is the fact that we're dressed down five days a week,"* which up till now has allowed people to wear jeans or whatever else fell out of the wardrobe in the morning. In anticipation of the office move, *"they were talking about having a stricter dress code as we'll be working close to the Stock Exchange."*

Trainees exchange info on seats and supervisors – *"what they are like and how much you can talk to them."* Not that any horrors await: the firm has *"a flat hierarchy, certainly socially."* The major challenge is the demanding work – trainees receive a lot of *"personalised attention,"* but *"you end up becoming confident to survive here."* Some trainees are refreshingly ambitious; for example, one said quite simply: *"I want to make it here and see how far I can progress."* Their hours are fairly standard for top City firms – 9.30am to 7.30pm is common. Then again, White & Case's sociable side is likely to keep you from going home. *"On a weekly basis, a big group of people will go to the Corney & Barrow underneath the office,"* and every month there are in-house drinks, although sometimes they are themed and can be *"a bit naff. For example, on Halloween the lights were dimmed and there were some paper cut-outs..."* What did they expect? A real haunting?

White & Case now needs to focus on the *"mechanics of getting bigger,"* certainly insofar as this affects the training scheme. On seat allocation and NQ job awards, the right results used to happen naturally when there were fewer trainees; now formal systems and procedures need to be followed more closely. Yet, one of the best things about training here is that there's very little chance of slipping through the cracks, and *"everyone knows what you are doing."* The firm must do whatever it takes to hang on to this advantage, including, if necessary, cloning Philip Stopford.

and finally...

Any White & Case trainee will tell you their firm is a realistic alternative to the magic circle. Small teams, front-line action and a flat hierarchy – it's a potent and appealing mix, even before you consider the whopping great salary!

Withers LLP

the facts

Location: London
Number of UK partners/assistants: 56/68
Total number of trainees: 25
Seats: 4x6 months
Alternative seats: None

With a traditional bedrock of private clients and estates on which to rely, Withers LLP is easing itself away from the landed-gentry tag by sniffing out new-money clients worldwide and repositioning itself as a hybrid commercial/private client firm.

family tree

Those traditional practice areas really are the core of Withers' business, with the private client department alone bringing in over 40% of the firm's revenue...and that's without taking into account the trickle effect of wealthy individuals who subsequently instruct it on corporate matters. Factor in a mature portfolio loaded with heavyweight estates such as the Duke of Marlborough and Guy's & St. Thomas' Charitable Trust and it's easy to see why Withers remains true to its roots and is loath to adopt a prune-and-graft

approach in broadening its client-base. However, alongside this characteristic work, it is branching out and winning first-time instructions from 'rich-list' clients. Growth may be organic, but Withers is not content to simply sit and watch the grass grow. Speaking of the firm's transatlantic tie-up with a similarly focused US partnership in 2002, one told us: *"The stuffy landed-gentry, shooting-and-fishing-fraternity reputation has really been blown out of the water in the last few years. The merger moved us forward at a rate of knots."*

It's a fulsome analysis for a trainee, but we have to agree that Withers is dedicated to developing itself as a hybrid, equally at ease with commercial deals and *"anything the private individual can throw at us."* Long-standing Italian links have brought a steady stream of clients including *"trendy small-scale designers whom you'd see in Selfridges;"* the New York/New Haven merger opened up New World money; now Withers is turning its attentions to the billionaire Russian oligarchs wishing to invest outside the motherland. Yet, a reinvigorated sense of purpose and direction needn't mean a dramatic change of style. Trainees claim the Withers ethos (*"We aim to provide a personal touch"*) remains the same as ever. This emphasis is common throughout the firm, no matter how commercial the instructions, and creates *"a real sense of continuity between departments."* Equally, and happily for trainees, cohesion needn't rule out diversity: during their four-seat training there's plenty of variety on offer.

taxing times

Time in the private client department isn't exactly compulsory, but it's a strange trainee that applies to Withers with no desire to sample its work. *"It's where the real intellectuals of the firm hide away; there are some exceptionally bright people there in terms of grey matter,"* gushed one trainee. Drafting wills and structuring trusts makes this *"a very technical department...tax day-in, day-out."* No yawning at the back; the required research and tactical decision-making sound as engrossing as a good game of chess. Referring to tax manuals rather than telephone directories, one trainee told us: *"You go through the Yellow Books, picking out the loopholes and second guessing the Inland Revenue."* At other times you'll be tailoring wills for wealthy entrepreneurs who subsequently *"go forward to instruct the firm on corporate work."* Trainees are adamant the department *"isn't at all stuffed shirt,"* but admit that if a faint odour of conservatism hangs anywhere in the firm, it is here.

In sharp contrast to these cloistered environs, the busy, buzzy litigation department is stuffed with commercial minds *"who will think their way out of a problem creatively."* Or put another way: *"Will say, 'Screw that, we'll find a way'."* We laughed out loud when one trainee told us: *"My partner in litigation was great; he was really motivational and would shout things like 'We're going to beat them!' He really knew how to make you feel involved."* Last year the litigators acted for the wealthy Egyptian El Nasharty family in their dispute with Sainsbury's, the purchaser of their supermarket chain. In an arms-related matter, they represented an Italian organisation in a claim about the production of multi-warhead systems. The case involved questions concerning the UK Official Secrets Act and US arms-trafficking regulations.

hedging your bets

One trainee described the family department as *"fun;"* an analysis that led us to seek help from other, more polysyllabic, colleagues. They told us: *"It's easy to get a grip on the law quickly; you see more clients, have more responsibility and the turnover of your work is really high...it boosts your self-esteem."* Alongside Manches, Withers is judged by *Chambers UK* to have the best family law team in the UK. Many of its clients are either mind-bogglingly rich people that you've never heard of or super-rich celebrities. Unfortunately we can't reveal any of their names, but suffice to say their divorce settlements can run to many tens of millions and beyond. It's a reminder that family law is a serious and lucrative business and not high-brow social work. Megabucks to one side, Withers

has also made strides in the specialist areas of surrogacy, child abduction and same-sex relationships.

Property promises polar opposites of experience. On the one hand it *"offers heavyweight transactional experience,"* and on the other it is possessed of *"very technical aspects."* The real beauty of the property department is that its client base says so much about the firm. Last year it secured instructions from the Swiss Hauser & Wirth Gallery, which was opening its first UK retail premises. And designers flock to the firm: Lulu Guinness, Matthew Williamson and Eskandar Nabavi to name but three. Doubtless their work can be found at Ascot races; as can Withers' own – it is handling the legal aspects of the new £180 million grandstand. When not assisting on heftier commercial transactions such as this, trainees are allowed to run small files themselves, prompting the wonderful admission: *"I sold a lot of fields!"*

up close and personal

The trainee who told us: *"I wanted to talk to individual clients, rather than the lawyers of faceless corporations,"* neatly summed up the motivation of the whole trainee group. That word 'faceless' recurred again and again, each time underscoring a trainee's desire to apply a personal touch to their work. It also typifies the firm's approach to training: an excellent appraisal system *"goes far beyond just ticking the boxes"* and is buttressed by the support of *"very experienced people who invest a lot of time in training you."* Quite clearly, *"a real effort is made in picking supervisors who can dedicate time to you and are right for you."*

In broader terms, whenever you are farmed out to others, *"people will always let your partner know you've done well."* And progress is rewarded with greater responsibility and autonomy: *"I've always been happy with the level of work I've had, but if I went back to my first seat now it would probably be a shock how little I did!"*

ging gang gooly

As a group Withers' trainees display balanced, grown-up tendencies – someone we know even likened the females among them to girl guides. One trainee summed it up saying: *"Everyone is engaging – they're people you'd want to talk to and find out about"* though *"we don't live in each other's pockets."* Don't expect the firm to offer *"the all-encompassing social experience"* you might find at the likes of Lovells or one of the firms with trainee hordes. Withers people enjoy departmental drinks when organised, and might well be found together in the local Corney & Barrow or aboard the clipper from Blackfriars en route to share a few drinks in the sun at West India Quays, but lives and interests outside the firm remain intact.

Although a dress-down policy is supposedly in place, *"everyone wears suits."* And although an 8.30am–7pm day is commonplace, hard work is not welcomed if it is at the expense of social interaction. For example, *"it's frowned upon to eat your lunch at your desk; everyone is encouraged to go and use the canteen."*

In past years trainees have likened the layout of Withers' office to a pair of trousers, confirming that directions are sometimes given by reference to left or right legs, turn-ups and pockets. This year we're thankful for the poetic insight of the trainee who judged that the building offers a neat metaphor for the firm itself. That is to say an orderly meshing of old and new. The way the listed atrium with silk-clad walls and high-fashion magazines links seamlessly to *"slick lifts and glass offices"* neatly encapsulates the firm's style – *"halfway between old and new."* When it comes to retention, Withers is doing just as good a balancing act; in September 2004, ten of the 12 NQs accepted jobs.

and finally...

The dominance of the private client and family law practices will (and should) determine who applies to Withers. Beyond that, no one should be scared off by concerns their training won't be commercial enough for them to keep their post-qualification options open.

Wollastons

the facts

Location: Chelmsford
Number of UK partners/assistants: 16/17
Total number of trainees: 4
Seats: 4x6 months
Alternative seats: None

Nineteen years after Richard and Kate Wollaston and Nick Cook started a small corporate/commercial boutique in Chelmsford, the firm is going great guns and offers a lucky few trainees an excellent start in life.

life on wollastons mountain

Who remembers the Waltons? Pa was a successful entrepreneur; Ma held the home together and nurtured ambitious, well-adjusted kids. Then there was Grandpa, who fixed things and grew the vegetables, and Grandma, always in the kitchen rustling up wholesome grub and laundering red-checked tablecloths. The happy, ever-expanding Walton family was the envy of all from Rockfish to Charlottesville.

The similarities between Chelmsford's most prestigious law firm and the Waltons are too obvious to be ignored. Life at senior partner Richard Wollaston's firm is made all the sweeter by the influence of his wife and the firm's managing partner Kate Wollaston. *"The firm is their baby,"* said one trainee, *"and they want people to feel as though they are part of the Wollastons' family."* Just like the Waltons, the Wollastons have grown such that they now occupy a large and impressive home, though in the law firm's case it's on the edge of the centre of Chelmsford. The mock Georgian building (photo on website) *"looks like a beautiful old country house at the end of a long driveway, but inside it's as modern as Ikea, with all the latest IT."* Built ten years ago for the firm, it was recently extended by some 75%. The grounds are tended lovingly by a full-time handyman, and there's even an in-house caterer to lay on lunch every day. *"You can put your order in and Ann will have it ready for the time you say. The nicest thing is that whenever it's someone's birthday she will make a selection of cakes."* When we remarked that catering in a firm of Wollastons' size was rare, a source pointed to the benefits of family meals. *"Even in a relatively small firm, if everyone is busy and getting their heads down to work, they might not see people on the other side of the building."*

the family that plays together...

If you thought all that sounds appealing, there's more. Aside from regular trips to local pubs with colleagues, a summer barbecue on the office lawn, rounders, boules and a spot of dragon boat racing, the Wollastons like nothing better than to go off on a country walk together. *"I went on a group walk with the cocom department,"* said one trainee. *"We started off in a pub in Margaretting and walked though the fields to another pub for a meal. It was the whole department and their wives and kids...all on a Thursday evening after work."* Could there be more of a contrast to City life?

And yet, lawyers come to Wollastons because they don't want to abandon the City entirely. The firm was started as a corporate boutique and corporate is still its primary area of practice. The message from trainees is that you need not abandon your desire for M&A, MBOs and BIMBOs just because you choose to work in Chelmsford. The cocom department has six partners and even acts for the odd plc or two, though its main purpose is to cater to smaller enterprises. One trainee gave us a quick summary of the firm's development, explaining how the firm gained a foothold in Essex through transactional work and general commercial advice and *"after a while it became obvious that clients had property needs and then wanted the firm to sort out their employees. Then they came to us with disputes and so a litigation department was bolted on and then private client...and then Melanie came recently to do family work."* So there you have it: a firm that has become full-service by starting out on the big stuff and working its way to the small stuff – the opposite way round to most regional firms.

bless you!

As it is *"the hub"* of the firm, all trainees undertake a seat in cocom, working closely with the partners and usually as their right hand (wo)man on a transaction. In this department *"everyone rallies round"* when a big deal gets underway, and if the enthusiasm of one of our sources is typical then they do so with gusto and no moans about staying in the office until the job is done. Cocom is the one place where at crucial times you can be kiss goodbye to really decent hours of 9am–5.30 or 6pm. For instance, *"if you're in London doing a completion, you might not get back until one or two in the morning."* And that's not because London is particularly far away; it's actually only 35 minutes to Liverpool Street on the train.

When not doing deals, trainees learn how to give commercial advice on everything from IT/IP issues to partnership or consultancy agreements and starting up new businesses. One trainee reported that her work had also touched upon competition advice. Commercial property is another likely seat, though trainees also try their hand at a little residential conveyancing. Offices, factories and housing estates; purchases, sales and options over land; Essex property, East Anglian property and property *"all over the shop"* – this is a busy and varied six months. And you'd better bring a box of tissues with you on your first day as *"you come across unregistered land every now and then and you're sneezing all over the place when you get dusty deeds!"*

perry mason moments

The dispute resolution experience here is a whirl of general commercial claims, insolvency and property litigation. There's even a spot of claimant personal injury and clinical negligence. Our sources had all earned their advocacy wings on winding up applications, infant settlements, possession hearings and a range of small county court matters, such as setting aside default judgements. One trainee said the experience had matched up to the dreams she'd had when she used to watch lawyers on the TV. Of course they don't find themselves in court every day, and back in the office their role, as in other departments, is to assist the partners.

Wollastons is not a firm to throw a cabinet full of files at a trainee and just expect them to get on with things. *"They are always checking on you and asking how you are doing. You always know they are responsible for you."* So, while *"at the beginning of each seat you may feel like a spare wheel,"* by the end *"you really feel part of the team."* Employment and private client seats are also an option, the latter team acting for *"the landed and people who have made their own money."* The firm also acts for charities, insolvency practitioners such as KPMG, and a number of clients in the education sector, including Anglia Polytechnic University.

Mid and end-of-seat appraisals come as standard and lawyers at all levels are encouraged to sign up to externally run training courses, which for trainees includes the PSC. Back at base, weekly team meetings are used to discuss all matters of relevance to each group and, of course, there's all that lunchtime chat in the canteen. In 2004, one of the two qualifying trainees took a job with the firm.

and finally...

Our sources made a point of telling us how quickly they'd felt at home at Wollastons, concluding that the managing partner had a knack for recruiting the right type for the firm. Quite simply: *"She likes to recruit happy people."* It seems fitting that we end on a gentle note – after all, every episode of *The Waltons* did.

Wragge & Co

the facts

Location: Birmingham, London
Number of UK partners/assistants: 110/310
Total number of trainees: 48
Seats: 4x6 months
Alternative seats: Brussels, secondments
Extras: Pro bono – College of Law, BERAL, LaW-WorksWeb, language training

The story at Birmingham-based Wragge & Co has always been a compelling one of wholesome values, vibrant ascendancy and positive vamp. With outposts in London and Brussels, the tale is being retold far beyond the traditional Midlands audience.

having your cake and eating it

It would be easy to bang on at length about how Wragges is an unmitigated success: the firm is ranked by our parent publication *Chambers UK* in over 30 practice areas. However, for our sources, the real draw was the firm's impressive tutelage and supportive environment.

At Wragges, employee care is a serious business. Again this year, the firm featured in the *Sunday Times'* list of the 100 Best Places to Work, and we heard of an abundance of initiatives that explain why. From a loan to help you kit out your new legal wardrobe to *"transparency"* over pay and NQ retention, at every stage our interviewees felt the firm's caring hand guiding them along. With a principal, supervisor and minder for each trainee, there are also plenty outstretched to catch you should you fall.

The trainee committee is just one of many focus groups that keep employees *"in the loop,"* and while *"trainees are shielded"* from the pressures of profit margins, on everything else consultation is a part of their world. Everything down to the brands served in the new coffee bar is open to the floor. What prevents the caring, sharing subtext of this commercial success story from deteriorating into tree-hugging delirium is an ingrained and mutual *"high professional respect."* Trainees say: *"You are never introduced as a trainee, always a colleague"* and *"your secretary is simply another member of staff."* Equally *"the management reward people, so you respect them more. And people don't mind giving 110% when they know it is being appreciated."*

weight watchers

In a tough market Wragges has done well to retain its staff-oriented ethos as it scrabbles with London firms for the finest work, but we wonder if it will now be sharpening its elbows and starving its sweet tooth in a bid to protect its portion of the meaty plc pie. Trainees think not, saying: *"It is quite a tough job to maintain that* [ethos] *as well as drive the firm forward, and toughen it up, but it is working."*

In the past ten years, Wragges expanded like the British waistline. Admittedly, it was less down to a steady diet of balti and chips than its healthy relationship with clients including Lloyds TSB, British Airways, Powergen, Geest, 3i, Easygroup, Cadbury Schweppes and Alliance & Leicester. But this year the firm has hopped on the dieting bandwagon and the effects have been noted. Maintaining its previous good record, in September 2004 all 17 of the qualifying trainees accepted jobs and the firm took six NQs from elsewhere. However, it did shed a few pounds of fat at other levels. When asked about the trimmer look, trainees told us: *"The firm grew really really quickly. You can't do that forever, it's not a game of Risk.'* Indeed not.

no, no...after you

All trainees spend time in the company/commercial, property and litigation departments, after which they are free to take their fourth seat where they choose. Despite a few murmurings about tax being regarded with some trepidation and property being *"not everyone's idea of a crazy life,"* there are *"no horror seats,"* no general views as to best and worst, and no need to plot and scheme to get what you want. Selflessly, remarkably even, *"if someone else wanted to go to a seat and knew someone else wanted to qualify there, they would stand back."* Client secondments are offered to second-years, and for those drawn to the bright lights of London, there are seats in property, corporate and IP at the firm's Holborn location. For now, trainees seem reluctant to up sticks and head south, so anyone who wants to can undertake two or even three seats there. While there has been no seat in Brussels lately, a competition seat in Birmingham is likely to see you paying short visits to the Belgian capital.

All our sources enthused about *"exciting"* work across the range of seats. Wherever possible, trainees are given their own caseload of smaller files, but are also engaged on more complex matters. As one explained: *"You might not get right to the heart of a big deal, but the opportunities to be involved are there. People are keen for you to get involved...they want you to get excited too and join in."* Small-time advocacy, client meetings and dinners, completion meetings and even tramping about building sites in wellies are all on the trainee agenda.

Training is a thorough process, *"the firm is really focused on developing your personal skills as well as your legal skills,"* and training sessions once a fortnight help recruits brush up on their letter-writing, networking and client-winning skills, as well as the odd bit of law. The appraisal system is a 360-degree experience in which *"feedback goes both ways."* Added to that there are plenty of people – from your minder-trainee right up to a senior supervisor – to ask for help. *"When work gets plonked on your desk, your first thought includes a number of expletives, but then they do go through it with you."*

hi-ho silver lining

At Wragges, every grey cloud is neatly flipped inside out to reveal its silver lining. A couple of years ago, it alleviated a space crisis by knocking out walls and lumping everyone together open-plan style. Somewhere along the line this strategy was re-spun as a team-building exercise and is now enthusiastically championed as a way of *"encouraging an informal environment."* The open-plan office does reflect non-hierarchical attitudes as trainees, assistants and partners share the same floor space and *"everyone gets the same-sized desk."* We also heard of one trainee who, on joining a new department, warmed to the very kind gentleman who made the tea. It was several weeks before he realised the man who played mother was in fact a partner.

Of themselves, trainees say they are *"confident,"*

"*lively*" and "*good all-rounders*" who "*want to do well.*" All come from top-notch universities, some straight-away, others following a brief dabble in something different. They come from across the country and boast a range of backgrounds and interests – crick-eters, violinists, horse riders, rowers. Our interviewees frequently referred to themselves as "*people-people.*" Normally unwilling to bow to hol-low clichés, in this case we submit. Wragges trainees were the cool babysitters who let you stay up late; they were the popular head girl whom the teachers adored but who still got wasted at the Christmas Ball; they are the flatmate who can carry off sobriety when the neighbours come round to complain about the noise. Wragges' trainees are unashamedly enthu-siastic, mature and mischievous in equal measures and very, very funny.

tanks, trousers and that tache

Wragges trainees are apparently "*the first to the bar and the first on the dance floor.*" They certainly get plenty of practice as quarterly trainee nights out are subsidised by the firm. On a recent away day they ended up driving tanks and shooting bows and arrows before tucking into a barbecue and plenty of booze. On Friday nights the hordes descend on Utopia or Digress, and trainees happily admitted to making the most of Birmingham's "*really cheesy and ridiculously cheap*" student nightlife. Everyone expressed a fondness for Birmingham, with one trainee saying: "*I thought it was going to be rubbish and concrete, but actually I've had a really good time. The Brummy accent is a downside, but otherwise it's really moving forward.*"

In the past, the annual firm-wide Christmas bash at the ICC has involved a bouncy castle. The curious incident of a partner breaking his leg put an end to that. Another year, "*a trainee sat on the decks and killed the music.*" This year, to resurrect that festive feeling, and to humour "*a few of the guys who wanted to dress up as James Bond,*" a 007 theme (and a few casino tables) were introduced. While most saw this as an excuse to wear a posh frock or black tie, one woman arrived in a wetsuit ("*she got too hot and took it off pretty quickly*") and the senior partner turned up in combat gear. For the rest of the year the dress code in the office is smart casual. Which is what, exactly? "*Well, that's open to debate. Probably a suit without a jacket and tie...so, a shirt...oh, and trousers.*" And staying on the subject of the perfect look for the office, we have to share the thoughts of one trainee who, when asked what he'd do if made senior partner for the day, told us: "*Hmm...I'd lose the moustache.*"

and finally...

Picking Wragge & Co may be one of the smartest decisions you ever make. Quality? "*It is almost branded on to you!*"

solicitors a-z

Addleshaw Goddard

150 Aldersgate Street, London, EC1A 4EJ
Sovereign House, PO Box 8, Sovereign Street, Leeds LS1 1HQ
100 Barbirolli Square, Manchester, M2 3AB
Tel: (0161) 934 6000 / (020) 7606 8855
Fax: (0161) 934 6060 / (020) 7606 4390

firm profile
As a major force on the legal landscape, Addleshaw Goddard offers extensive and exciting opportunities to all its trainees. Across the entire spectrum of commercial law from employment and banking to property, corporate finance, entertainment, PFI and litigation, as a trainee with this firm, you'll be a key member of the team from day one. Whether based in the Leeds, London or Manchester offices (or out on secondment), you'll work closely with blue-chip clients within a supportive yet challenging environment, part of a structured training programme designed to ensure your success - now and in the future.

main areas of work
The firm has five main business divisions, finance, commercial, corporate, litigation and employment and property. Within these divisions as well as the main practice areas it also has specialist areas such as sport, media and entertainment and private client services such as family and trust and tax.

trainee profile
Graduates who are capable of achieving a 2:1 and can demonstrate commercial awareness, motivation and enthusiasm. Applications from law and non-law graduates are welcomed, as are applications from mature students who may be considering a change of direction.

training environment
During each six-month seat, there will be regular two-way performance reviews with the supervising partner or solicitor. Trainees have the opportunity to spend a seat in one of the firm's other offices and there are a number of secondments to clients available. Seated with a qualified solicitor or partner and working as part of a team, enables trainees to develop the professional skills necessary to deal with the demanding and challenging work the firm carries out for its clients. Practical training is complemented by high-quality training courses provided by both the in-house team and external training providers.

sponsorship & benefits
CPE and LPC fees are paid, plus a maintenance grant of £4,500. Benefits include corporate gym membership, season ticket loan, subsidised restaurant, pension and private healthcare.

vacation placements
Places for 2005 - 75; Duration - 2 weeks; location - all offices; Apply by 11 February 2005.

Partners	170
Associates	500+
Trainees	89

contact
Mrs Niki Lawson
 Graduate Manager

selection procedure
Interview, assessment centre

closing date for 2007
31 July 2005

application
Training contracts p.a. 50
Applications p.a. 2,000
% interviewed 10%
Required degree grade 2:1

training
Salary
1st year (2004)
Manchester/Leeds £20,000
London £28,000
2nd year (2004)
Manchester/Leeds £22,000
London £30,000
Holiday entitlement 25 days
% of trainees with
a non-law degree p.a. 45%

post-qualification
Salary (2004)
Manchester/Leeds £33,000
London £48,000
% of trainees offered job
on qualification (2004) 81%

other offices
Leeds, London,
Manchester

Allen & Overy LLP

One New Change, London EC4M 9QQ
Tel: (020) 7330 3000 Fax: (020) 7330 9999
Email: graduate.recruitment@allenovery.com
Website: www.allenovery.com/careeruk

firm profile
Allen & Overy LLP is an international legal practice with 4,800 people in 25 major centres worldwide comprising of Allen & Overy LLP and its affiliated undertakings. The practice's client list includes many of the world's leading businesses, financial institutions, governments and private individuals.

main areas of work
Corporate; banking; international capital markets; litigation; real estate; private client; tax; employment and related areas.

trainee profile
Intellectual ability is a prerequisite but as Allen & Overy LLP is a commercial practice, it also looks for people with a good level of business understanding. The practice looks for creative, problem solving people who can quickly identify salient points without losing sight of detail. You will need to be highly motivated, demonstrate initiative and the ability to alternate between leading and being part of a team.

training environment
Within a highly pressurised environment, trainees obtain a balance of practical and formal tuition. You will experience at least four different areas of work, but will spend a significant amount of time in at least two of the following departments: banking, corporate and international capital markets. Your preferences will be balanced with the practice's needs. Seminars provide practical advice and an introduction to each area of law. International placements are available. A positive, open and co-operative culture is encouraged both professionally and socially. A range of sporting activities is available.

benefits
Private healthcare scheme, private medical insurance, season ticket loans, subsidised restaurant, gym membership, six weeks unpaid leave on qualification.

vacation placements
Places for 2005: 75; Duration: 3 weeks; Remuneration: £250 p.w.; Closing Date: 31 January 2005. Places available in London.

sponsorship & awards
GDL and LPC fees and £5,000 maintenance p.a. (£4,500 outside London, Oxford and Guildford).

Partners	431*
Associates	1448*
London Trainees	247

*Denotes world-wide number

contact
Graduate Recruitment

method of application
Online application form

selection procedure
Interview

closing date for 2007
GDL candidates
End Jan 2005
Law students End Aug 2005

application
Training contracts p.a. 120
Applications p.a. 3,000
% interviewed p.a. 10%
Required degree grade 2:1

training
Salary
1st year (2003) £29,000
2nd year (2003) £33,000
Holiday entitlement 25 days
% of trainees with a
non-law degree p.a. 45%
% of trainees with a
law degree p.a. 55%
No. of seats available
in international offices
32 seats twice a year and
6 client secondments

post-qualification
Salary (2003) £50,000
% of trainees offered job
on qualification (as at
31/3/04) 90%
% of partners (as at
31/1/04) who joined as
trainees 32%

international offices
Amsterdam, Antwerp, Bangkok, Beijing, Brussels, Bratislava, Budapest, Dubai, Frankfurt, Hamburg, Hong Kong, Luxembourg, Madrid, Milan, Moscow, New York, Paris, Prague, Rome, Shanghai, Singapore, Tokyo, Turin, Warsaw

A - Z

SOLICITORS

Arnold & Porter (UK) LLP

Tower 42, 25 Old Broad Street, London EC2N 1HQ
Tel: (020) 7786 6100 Fax: (020) 7786 6299
Email: graduates@aporter.com
Website: www.arnoldporter.com

firm profile

With eight offices and almost 700 lawyers worldwide practising in over 25 practice and industry areas Arnold & Porter (UK) LLP is able to bring clients a sophisticated understanding of changing environments at the intersection of business, law and public policy. The firm was established in Washington DC in 1946 and the London office was initially opened in 1997, and has grown rapidly over the past few years. As of mid-2004 there are almost 40 lawyers in the London office.

main areas of work

Arnold & Porter (UK) LLP is a full-service law firm providing legal services worldwide. In the London office the practice areas include litigation, telecommunications, information technology, intellectual property, competition, corporate, life sciences, product liability and healthcare. The firm's clients include multinationals, UK and European concerns ranging from start-ups to Fortune 500 companies. Chambers and Partners presented the firm with their 'USA Antitrust Firm of the Year' Award in 2003, for the second time in three years.

trainee profile

The firm's commitment to excellence means that it expects its trainees to be well-rounded individuals with an outstanding academic background.

training environment

The London office reflects the environment of the firm generally. It has a collegial and informal atmosphere which is enhanced by twice-weekly informal social gatherings and other events, a casual dress policy and team-based assignment policies. Trainees will be expected to work on several matters at once and to assume responsibility quickly. The office emphasises teamwork and trainees will be quickly exposed to working for a variety of partners and fee-earners throughout the office and the firm. The London office's first trainees started in September 2004.

sponsorship & benefits

Sponsorship is provided for CPE/LPC. Private health insurance, a season ticket loan and life assurance are amongst the benefits offered by the firm.

vacation placements

Summer vacation schemes are on offer. Please apply on the firm's application form by 4 February 2005.

Partners	12
Assistant Solicitors	17
Total Trainees	2

contact
Graduate Recruitment

method of application
Firm's application form

selection procedure
Interview

closing date for 2007
29 July 2005

application
Training contracts p.a. 2
Required degree grade 2:1

training
Salary minimum £30,000
Holiday entitlement 25 days

post-qualification
Salary £55,000 (tbc)

overseas/regional offices
Washington DC, New York, Denver, Los Angeles, Century City, Northern Virginia, Brussels

ARNOLD & PORTER

asb *law*

Innovis House, 108 High Street, Crawley, West Sussex RH10 1AS
Tel: (01293) 603603 Fax: (01293) 603666
Email: human.resources@asb-law.com
Website: www.asb-law.com

firm profile

asb law, a top-100 law firm and the largest in the South East, provides legal services to a diverse range of clients including high net worth individuals, businesses, financial institutions, government and public sector bodies. It has offices in Brighton, Crawley, Croydon, Horsham and Maidstone. Following a three-way merger in late 1999, asb law's turnover has increased by over 60% in four years. The firm's prestigious clients and the range of the services provided demonstrate that it is possible to enjoy a challenging and rewarding career without the grind of a daily commute to the City.

main areas of work

Principal types of work are banking, corporate finance, commercial contracts, commercial litigation, commercial property/planning, employment, environment, technology/e-commerce, insolvency/corporate recovery, intellectual property, licensing, personal injury - claimant and defendant, family, residential property, tax, trust and probate.

trainee profile

The firm is looking for strong intellectual ability, drive and initiative in people who are client-focused, commercially minded and have strong interpersonal skills. You should relish the prospect of early responsibility and contact with clients in a supportive environment.

training environment

The programme is divided into four six-month seats, tailored to your strengths/ interests. Training is structured to empower you to learn, take responsibility and interact with clients from an early stage and includes workshops/seminars as part of the firm's professional development programme. Some flexibility is required as seats can be in any of the five offices. A structured career path from trainee to partner is in place for the right candidates. asb law is proud of its history of retaining its trainees on qualifying.

sponsorship & benefits

An interest-free loan is available for the LPC, repayable over the period of the training contract.

Partners	47
Vacancies	5
Total Trainees	10
Total Staff	347

contact
Ms Gill Whensley
Tel: (01293) 601441

method of application
CV/covering letter; may be required to complete an application form

selection procedure
2 interviews, psychometric test and written exercise

closing date for 2006
28 February 2005

application
Training contracts p.a. **10**
Applications p.a **500**
% interviewed **12%**
Required degree grade **2:1**
training
£17,500 (Year 1 2004)

offices
Brighton, Crawley, Horsham, Croydon, Maidstone

A-Z

SOLICITORS

Ashurst

Broadwalk House, 5 Appold St, London EC2A 2HA
Tel: (020) 7638 1111 Fax: (020) 7859 1800
Email: gradrec@ashurst.com
Website: www.ashurst.com

firm profile

An international City practice, smaller than its principal competitors, yet consistently ranked amongst the top few firms in terms of the work in which it is involved and clients for whom it acts.

main areas of work

Corporate; commercial; competition; energy, transport and infrastructure; international finance; litigation; real estate; and tax. Specialist groups include construction and engineering; employment, employee benefits and incentives, and pensions; environment and health and safety; insurance and reinsurance; intellectual property and IT; planning; product liability; reconstruction and insolvency; sport; and telecommunications.

trainee profile

Candidates should want to be involved in the highest quality work that a City firm can offer. The firm is looking for high achievers academically as the work is intellectually challenging. Candidates should show common sense, good judgement, a willingness to take on responsibility, a sense of humour and an outgoing nature.

training environment

During the training contract each trainee solicitor will sit with a partner or senior solicitor. The training contract consists of four six-month seats, one of which will be in a contentious area of practice and one in a transaction-based department. Trainees will then be able to choose the remaining areas of practice or departments in which they would like to gain experience. Trainees also have the opportunity to spend one of their seats abroad or in-house with one of the firm's major clients.

benefits

Benefits include private health insurance, pension, life assurance, interest-free season ticket loan, gym membership and 25 days holiday per year during training.

vacation placements

Places for 2005: 2-week Easter placement scheme primarily aimed at final-year non-law undergraduates and all graduates. Two 3-week summer placement schemes primarily aimed at penultimate year law undergraduates. Remuneration £250 p.w. Closing date 31 January 2005.

sponsorship & awards

CPE and LPC funding, plus £5,000 maintenance allowance p.a. (£4,500 outside London and Guildford). LPC Distinction award of £500. Language tuition bursaries.

Partners	162
Assistant Solicitors	470
Total Trainees	100

contact
Stephen Trowbridge
Graduate Recruitment Manager

method of application
Online

selection procedure
Interview with 1 assistant followed by interview with 2 partners

closing date for 2007
31 July 2005

application
Training contracts p.a. 45-50
Applications p.a. 2,500
% interviewed p.a. 20%
Required degree grade 2:1

training
Salary
(2004)
First six months
£28,000
Second six months
£29,000
Third six months
£31,000
Fourth six months
£32,000
Holiday entitlement 25 days
% of trainees with a non-law degree p.a. 45-50%
Number of seats abroad available p.a. 10

post-qualification
Salary (2004) £48,000
% of trainees offered job on qualification (2004) 90%

overseas offices
Brussels, Frankfurt, Madrid, Milan, Munich, New Delhi, New York, Paris, Singapore, Tokyo

Baker & McKenzie

100 New Bridge Street, London EC4V 6JA
Tel: (020) 7919 1000 Fax: (020) 7919 1999
Email: london.graduate.recruit@bakernet.com
Website: www.ukgraduates.bakernet.com

firm profile

Baker & McKenzie is a leading global law firm with more than 65 locations in 38 countries. In London, Baker & McKenzie is an established City firm of solicitors with a strong domestic and foreign client base providing legal services to multinational and domestic corporations, financial institutions, governments and entrepreneurs.

main areas of work

Corporate; commercial; dispute resolution; banking and finance; EC, competition and trade; employment; intellectual property and information technology; pensions; tax; projects; property. In addition the firm has cross-departmental practice groups, such as media and communications, insurance and reinsurance, business recovery and environmental law.

trainee profile

The firm is looking for trainee solicitors who are stimulated by intellectual challenge and want to be 'the best' at what they do. Effective communication together with the ability to be creative and practical problem solvers, team players and a sense of humour are qualities which will help them stand out from the crowd.

training environment

Four six-month seats which include corporate and a contentious seat, usually within the firm's highly regarded dispute resolution department. There is also the possibility of a secondment abroad or to a client. At the start of your training contract you will have a meeting to discuss individual seat preferences and during each seat you will have formal and informal reviews to discuss your progress. Your training contract commences with a highly interactive and practical induction programme which focuses on key skills including practical problem solving, interviewing, presenting and the application of information technology. The firm's training programmes include important components on management and other business skills, as well as seminars and workshops on key legal topics for each practice area. There is a Trainee Solicitor Liaison Committee which acts as a forum for any new ideas or raises issues which may occur during your training contract. Trainees are actively encouraged to participate in a variety of pro bono issues and outside office hours there is a varied sporting and social life.

benefits

Permanent health insurance, life insurance, private medical insurance, group personal pension, subsidised gym membership, season ticket loan, subsidised staff restaurant.

Partners	73
Assistant Solicitors	189
Total Trainees	60

contact
Kate Calcutt

method of application
Online application form

selection procedure
Candidates to give a short oral presentation based on the facts of a typical client problem, interview with two partners, meeting with a trainee

closing date for 2007
Non-law 18 Feb 2005
Law 31 July 2005

application
Training contracts p.a. 30
Applications p.a. 2,000
% interviewed p.a. 10%
Required degree grade 2:1

training
Salary
1st year (2004) £29,000 +
£3,000 'golden hello'
2nd year (2004) £32,000
Holiday entitlement 25 days
% of trainees with a
non-law degree p.a.
Approx 50%
No. of seats available
abroad p.a. Variable

post-qualification
Salary (2004) £50,000
% of trainees offered job
on qualification (2004) 82%

vacation placements

London Summer Placement - Places for 2005: 30; Duration: 3 weeks; Remuneration: £250 p.w.; Closing date: 31 January 2005.
International Summer Placement - Places for 2005: 3-5; Duration: 6-12 weeks divided between London and an overseas office; Remuneration: £250 p.w.; Closing date: 31 January 2005.

sponsorship & awards

CPE funding: fees paid plus £5,000 maintenance.
LPC funding: fees paid plus £5,000 maintenance and choice to receive either an additional £2,000 or a laptop computer.

additional information

As mentioned, trainees have the opportunity to spend three months working in one of the firm's overseas offices. Trainees have already been seconded to its offices in Sydney, Hong Kong, Frankfurt, Chicago, Washington DC, Brussels and Moscow. In addition, the firm also operates an Associate Training Programme which enables lawyers with 18-24 months pqe to spend between 6-24 months working in an overseas office.

trainee comments

"I chose Baker & McKenzie because of the unique package it offers to potential trainees. On the one hand, it is a global firm that offers the opportunity to be involved in high calibre commercial work for large corporate clients. On the other, it has a relatively small trainee intake. This means that trainees can expect to take on a good deal of responsibility from the outset, whilst gaining experience of working with lawyers worldwide." Katherine Pawson [2nd Seat Trainee]

"My training so far has involved working on a broad range of complex issues and I have had plenty of opportunity to take on challenging responsibilities. There has been friendly support available from all areas of the firm and this has been a great encouragement to me during my first months. The range of international work I undertake on a day to day basis remains exciting and makes the occasional request to down tools and catch a flight all the more enjoyable." Ben Crook [3rd Seat Trainee]

"Throughout my training contract, I have been struck by the quality of training. As well as the formal training we receive at a firm-wide and departmental level, we are given continual guidance and feedback from associates and partners - the firm's "open-door" policy means that there is always someone to ask for advice. We are also encouraged to be pro-active in seeking out the kinds of work we are particularly interested in, and we have regular (formal and informal) meetings with our supervisors and departmental training partners to ensure that we are gaining the experience that we want. It is an extremely supportive and friendly atmosphere in which to work." Jo McGarvey [4th Seat Trainee qualifying into the Corporate department]

overseas offices

Almaty, Amsterdam, Antwerp, Bahrain, Baku, Bangkok, Barcelona, Beijing, Berlin, Bogotá, Bologna, Brasilia, Brussels, Budapest, Buenos Aires, Cairo, Calgary, Caracas, Chicago, Dallas, Düsseldorf, Frankfurt, Geneva, Guadalarjara, Hanoi, Ho Chi Minh City, Hong Kong, Houston, Jakarta, Juarez, Kuala Lumpur, Kyiv, Madrid, Manila, Melbourne, Mexico City, Miami, Milan, Monterrey, Moscow, Munich, New York, Palo Alto, Paris, Porto Alegre, Prague, Rio de Janeiro, Riyadh, Rome, St Petersburg, San Diego, San Francisco, Santiago, São Paulo, Shanghai Singapore, Stockholm, Sydney, Taipei, Tijuana, Tokyo, Toronto, Valencia, Vienna, Warsaw, Washington DC, Zürich

Barlow Lyde & Gilbert

Beaufort House, 15 St Botolph Street, London EC3A 7NJ
Tel: (020) 7247 2277 Fax: (020) 7643 8500
Email: grad.recruit@blg.co.uk
Website: www.blg.co.uk

firm profile

Barlow Lyde & Gilbert is a leading international business law firm with more than 300 lawyers and 80 partners. The firm's principal office in the UK is in Aldgate in the City of London. BLG is particularly well known for its expertise in insurance law having first started to practise in this area in the 19th century. The firm has long been recognised as pre-eminent in all aspects of this field and it has formed the bedrock from which the firm has expanded into virtually all areas of business law. Today BLG is widely based with strong practices in corporate, financial and commercial law, as well as in all kinds of commercial litigation. The firm also has highly rated aerospace, shipping and international trade, information technology and employment teams.

trainee profile

BLG recruits 16-18 trainees each year and looks for intelligent and motivated graduates with good academic qualifications and with the social skills that will enable them to communicate effectively and get along with their colleagues and clients.

training environment

During your training contract you will have six-month seats in four different areas of the firm. The firm will always try to accommodate a trainee's preference for a particular type of work and there may be opportunities to spend time in its other offices, on secondment with clients or on exchange programmes with overseas law firms. A capable trainee will be given responsibility from an early stage in his or her training, subject of course to supervision, and will have to deal regularly with clients. Social activities play an important role for BLG and successful candidates can look forward to a variety of sporting and social events which ensure that people in different parts of the firm have a chance to meet and stay in contact with each other. Trainees are also encouraged to participate in the firm's various pro bono activities.

vacation placements

An increasing number of BLG's trainees come to the firm through its vacation schemes. Whether you are a law or non-law student the firm will introduce you to a City practice. You will be given the opportunity to become really involved and you can even choose which department you want to spend time in. The closing date for applications is 31 January 2005. The firm also runs open days and drop in days throughout the year. Application is by way of a covering letter and application form.

sponsorship & awards

Full payment of fees and a maintenance grant are provided.

Partners	86
Assistant Solicitors	195
Total Trainees	35

contact
Caroline Walsh
Head of Graduate
Recruitment & Trainee
Development

method of application
Application form &
covering letter

selection procedure
Interview day

closing date for 2006
29 July 2005

application
Training contracts p.a.
16-18
Applications p.a. **2,000**
% interviewed p.a. **10%**

training
Salary
1st year **£28,000**
2nd year **£30,000**
Holiday entitlement
5 weeks

post-qualification
Salary **£47,000**
Trainees offered job
on qualification (2004)
11 out of 15

other offices
Hong Kong, Shanghai

Barlow Lyde & Gilbert

Beachcroft Wansbroughs

100 Fetter Lane, London EC4A 1BN
Tel: (020) 7242 1011 Fax: (020) 2831 6630
Email: bwtrainee@bwlaw.co.uk
Website: www.bwlaw.co.uk

firm profile

Beachcroft Wansbroughs provides an integrated and consistent national service capability across its strong regional office network and its major offices in the City of London. The firm offers contentious and non-contentious comprehensive legal services to clients in the corporate, commercial, financial, health, insurance and public sectors.

main areas of work

The firm is managed in two divisions: Litigation and Commercial. These divisions cover a wide range of law including Injury Risk, Professional Risk, Property, Financial Services, Insolvency, Projects, Health, Public Law, Employment and many more.

The firm has created a partnership with a strong sense of purpose and shared value; client service is its guiding principle. It has cultivated a reputation for leading rather than following and this is evident in its IT applications and its approach to training.

trainee profile

The firm looks for outgoing, commercially minded people preferably with 2:1 honours degree in any subject. You will need to be an excellent team player, possess a mind capable of analysing, interpreting and applying complex points of law.

training environment

Training takes place over a two-year period in London, Bristol, Manchester or Leeds, during which time you'll pursue a demanding study programme, whilst occupying 4 x 6 months seats in some of the key areas of commercial law. Responsibility will come early and the firm provides the supervision and support to enable you to develop and grow.

benefits

The firm operates a flexible benefits scheme including holiday, pension and private health care.

vacation placements

BW run a paid placement scheme for 16 students per year. Selection is from CV and covering letter, closing date - 1 May each year.

sponsorship & awards

Beachcroft Wansbroughs provides payment for GDL, LPC, and £3,500 bursary.

Partners	136
Assistant Solicitors	375
Total Trainees	55

contact
Naomi Birch
Graduate Recruitment and
Development Officer
Admin Centre
PO Box 2048
One Redcliff Street
Bristol BS99 7UR
Email: bwtrainee@bwlaw.co.uk

method of application
Apply online at
www.bwlaw.co.uk for an
application form

selection procedure
Assessment centre and
panel interview

closing date
1 August each year

application
Training contracts per annum
28
Required degree
2:1 preferred

training
Salary
1st year, regions-£20,000 pa
2nd year, regions-£22,500 pa
1st year, London-£28,000 pa
2nd year, London-£30,000 pa

offices
Birmingham, Bristol,
Brussels, Leeds, London,
Manchester, Winchester

SJ Berwin

222 Gray's Inn Road, London WC1X 8XF
Tel: (020) 7533 2268 Fax: (020) 7533 2000
Email: graduate.recruitment@sjberwin.com
Website: www.sjberwin.com/gradrecruit

firm profile

Since its formation in 1982, SJ Berwin has established a strong reputation in corporate finance. It also has a number of niche specialisms in areas such as private equity and film finance. Much work is international and clients range from major multinational business corporations and financial institutions to high net worth individuals.

main areas of work

Corporate 45%; real estate 20%; litigation 17%; EU and competition 8%; commercial media and IP 7%; tax 3%.

trainee profile

The firm wants ambitious, commercially-minded individuals who seek a high level of involvement from day one. Candidates must be bright and determined to succeed. They should be likely to achieve a 2:1 or first.

training environment

Four seats of six months each will be completed, and the seats are set, ideally, to the needs of the trainee. Two seats will be in the corporate finance arena, which includes Frankfurt, Paris and Madrid. The firm has a dedicated training department and weekly training schedules coupled with training designed specifically for trainees allow a good grounding in legal and non-legal skills and knowledge. Overseas seats are available in Paris, Madrid, Brussels, Munich and Frankfurt.

benefits

Corporate sports membership, free lunch, health insurance.

vacation placements

Places for 2005: 60; Duration: 2 weeks; Remuneration: £225 p.w.; Closing Date: 31 January 2005.

sponsorship & awards

PgDL and LPC fees paid and £4,500 maintenance p.a.(£5,000 in London).

Partners	119
Assistant Solicitors	270
Total Trainees	72

contact
Graduate Recruitment Team

method of application
online application form

selection procedure
2 interviews (early September)

closing date for 2007
31 July 2005

application
Training contracts p.a. **30**
Applications p.a. **2,000**
% interviewed p.a. **10%**
Required degree grade **2:1**

training
Salary
1st year **£28,000**
2nd year **£32,000**
Holiday entitlement
50 days over 2 years
% of trainees with
a non-law degree p.a. **40%**
No. of seats available
abroad p.a. **8**

post-qualification
Salary **£50,000**
% of trainees offered job
on qualification (2004) **76%**
% of assistants who joined
as trainees **26%**
% of partners who joined
as trainees **12%**

overseas offices
Brussels, Frankfurt, Madrid, Berlin, Paris, Munich

Berwin Leighton Paisner

Adelaide House, London Bridge, London EC4R 9HA
Tel: (020) 7760 1000 Fax: (020) 7760 1111
Email: traineerecruit@blplaw.com
Website: www.blplaw.com

firm profile

Berwin Leighton Paisner is a top 15 City practice. It is a commercial law firm with expertise in many major industry and service sectors. The firm is a modern growing practice that puts a premium on commercial, as well as technical advice, client relations and transactional care. The firm is entrepreneurial and innovative. The firm recently won The Lawyer Magazine award for 'Law Firm of the Year' 2004.

main areas of work

Corporate finance; business & technology services; employment, incentives & pensions; commercial real estate; planning & environment; regulatory; construction and engineering; banking and capital markets; property finance; asset finance; PFI/projects; and litigation and dispute resolution.

trainee profile

The firm is looking for intelligent, energetic, positive and hard-working team players who have an interest in business and gain a sense of achievement from finding solutions.

training environment

Training starts with an induction covering all the practical aspects of working in a law firm from billing to client care. Comprehensive technical education programmes have been developed for each department and trainees attend weekly seminars supplemented by trainee lunches and skills sessions. You will undertake a tailor-made Professional Skills Course which is run in-house. Trainees spend six months in four seats and your progress will be reviewed every three months. The office environment is relaxed and friendly and trainees can enjoy early responsibility secure in the knowledge that they are fully supervised.

benefits

Flexible benefits package including permanent health insurance, private medical insurance, subsidised gym membership, 25 days holiday a year.

vacation placements

Places for 2005: Interviews held during March and April at either university campus or the firm's London office, application by online application form before 28 February 2005. The interviews could lead to a two-week placement in the summer vacation. There are 50 places available on the summer placement scheme.

sponsorship & awards

CPE/GDL and LPC fees paid and £4,500 maintenance p.a.

Partners	140
Assistant Solicitors	182
Total Trainees	67

contact
Debbie Campion

method of application
Firm application form online

selection procedure
Assessment day & partner interview

closing date for 2007
31 July 2005

application
Training contracts p.a. **35**
Applications p.a. **2,000**
% interviewed p.a. **5%**
Required degree grade **2:1**

training
Salary
1st year (2004) £28,000
2nd year (2004) £32,000
Holiday entitlement **25 days**
% of trainees with a
non-law degree p.a. **18%**
No. of seats available
abroad p.a. **0**

post-qualification
Salary (2004) **£50,000**
% of trainees offered job
on qualification (2004) **80%**
% of assistants who joined
as trainees (2004) **47%**
% of partners who joined
as trainees (2004) **30%**

european offices
Brussels, associated office
in New York, Paris, Rome,
Milan

Bevan Ashford

(from 1 November Bristol, Birmingham and London will become Bevan Brittan)

35 Colston Avenue, Bristol BS1 4TT
Tel: (0117) 918 3050 Fax: (0117) 918 8954
Email: hr.training@bevanashford.co.uk
Website: www.bevanashford.co.uk

firm profile

Bevan Ashford has firmly established itself as a truly national law firm and continues to attract high profile national and international clients and challenging, groundbreaking work. The firm is nationally recognised for its expertise in providing legal advice to clients in both the public and private sectors and is notable for being one of the very few practices whose work is equally strong in both sectors. From 1 November 2004 the two practice centres of Bevan Ashford will separate and become two individual partnerships. The Bristol, Birmingham and London (BBL) division will become Bevan Brittan and at the same time become a limited liability partnership (LLP).

main areas of work

The firm is structured around four primary areas of the UK economy: built environment, public sector, insurance and finance and technology and manufacturing. The firm operates in cross- departmental teams across these markets, harnessing the full range of skills and experience needed to provide top quality legal advice in the context of a specialist knowledge of both the sector concerned and the client's business. Claims 18%; Commercial (Projects and Regulatory) 42%; Commercial Litigation 10%; Construction 6%; Employment 7%; Real Estate 17%.

trainee profile

Bevan Ashford recognises that the firm's success depends upon a team of lawyers dedicated to service excellence. Its success is maintained by attracting and keeping enthusiastic, bright people with sound common sense, plenty of energy and the ability to work and communicate well with others. Language and IT skills are also desirable.

training environment

During each six-month seat, the core of your training will be practical work experience in conjunction with an extensive educational programme. Together the training is aimed at developing attitudes, skills and legal and commercial knowledge which is essential for your career success. You are encouraged to take on as much work and responsibility as you are able to handle, which will be reviewed on a regular basis with your supervising partner. The firm is friendly and supportive with an open-door policy along with a range of social, sporting and cultural activities.

vacation placements

Places available for 2005: 60 across the three offices. Closing date: 31st March 2005.

sponsorship & awards

Bursary and funding for PgDL and LPC.

| Partners | 63 |
| Total Trainees | 29 |

contact
HR and Training
(0117) 918 3050

method of application
Application form (available from the firm's website)

closing date for 2007
31 July 2005

post-qualification
% of trainees offered job on qualification (2004) 85%

other offices
Birmingham, Bristol, London

Bird & Bird

90 Fetter Lane, London EC4A 1JP
Tel: (020) 7415 6000 Fax: (020) 7415 6111
Website: www.twobirds.com

firm profile

Bird & Bird is a 114-partner international law firm, employing approximately 600 staff including 25 trainees with offices in Beijing, Brussels, Dusseldorf, Hong Kong, London, Milan, Munich, Paris, Stockholm and The Hague. The firm's size ensures a friendly but stimulating environment where legal, business and inter-personal skills can be developed and recognised. The firm has a clear business focus to provide a full range of legal services to specific industry sectors: aviation and aerospace, banking and financial services, communications, e-commerce, IT, life sciences, media and sports. This focus, combined with the firm's international ability, will enable you to work across borders and within fast-moving industry sectors.

main areas of work

Company 56%; intellectual property 23%; litigation 12%; property 8%; private client 1%.

trainee profile

The firm looks for high-calibre recruits – confident individuals capable of developing expert legal skills and commercial sense.

training environment

Following an introduction course, you will undertake four seats of six months. The choice of final seat is yours. You will share an office with a partner or senior assistant who will guide and advise you. You will hone drafting and legal research skills and gain familiarity with legal procedures. The firm encourages you to make an early contribution to case work and to meet clients immediately. Internal seminars and external lectures are arranged to cover the PSC. Trainees are welcome to join the number of sports teams at the firm and to attend various social events and outings.

benefits

BUPA, season ticket loan, subsidised sports club membership, life cover, PHI, pension.

vacation placements

Places for 2005: 14; Duration: 3 weeks; Remuneration: £220 p.w.; Closing Date: 29 January 2005.

sponsorship & awards

LPC and CPE fees paid and a yearly maintenance grant of £3,500.

Partners 114*
Assistant Solicitors 257*
Total Trainees 25*
denotes worldwide figures

contact
Lynne Walters
lynne.walters@twobirds.com

method of application
Online application form

selection procedure
Assessment mornings

closing date for 2007
29 July 2005

application
Training contracts p.a. 14
Applications p.a. 1,500
% interviewed p.a. 10%
Required degree grade 2:1

training
Salary
1st year (2004) £26,000
2nd year (2004) £28,000
Holiday entitlement
25 days
% of trainees with
a non-law degree p.a.
Varies

post-qualification
Salary (2004) £46,000
% of trainees offered job
on qualification (2004) 75%
% of assistants (as at
1/9/04) who joined as
trainees 20%
% of partners (as at 1/9/03)
who joined as trainees 17%

overseas offices
Beijing, Brussels,
Dusseldorf, Hong Kong,
Milan, Munich, Paris,
Sweden, Stockholm, The
Hague

Boodle Hatfield

61 Brook Street, London, W1K 4BL
Tel: (020) 7629 7411 Fax: (020) 7629 2621
Email: hr@boodlehatfield.com
Website: www.boodlehatfield.com

firm profile

Boodle Hatfield is a highly successful medium-sized firm who have been providing bespoke legal services for more than 275 years. They still act for some of their very first clients and are proud to do so. The firm has grown into a substantial practice, serving the full spectrum of commercial and private clients, both domestically and internationally.

main areas of work

The ethos of facilitating private capital activity underpins the work of the who firm and the interplay of the skills between five major areas – tax and financial planning, property, corporate, litigation and family – makes Boodle Hatfield particularly well placed to serve these individuals and businesses.

trainee profile

The qualities the firm look for in their trainees are commitment, flexibility and the ability to work as part of a team. Students with 2.1 or above and high A levels should apply

training environment

Trainees spend six months in four of the firm's main areas: Property, Corporate, Tax & Financial Planning and Litigation. Boodle Hatfield is well known for the high quality of its training. All trainees are involved in client work from the start and are encouraged to handle their own files personally as soon as they are able to do so, with the appropriate supervision. The firm's trainees therefore have a greater degree of client contact than in many firms with the result that they should be able to take on more responsibility at an early stage. Trainees are given formal appraisals every three months which are designed as a two-way process and give trainees the chance to discuss their progress and to indicate where more can be done to help in their ongoing training and development.

benefits

Private healthcare, life assurance, season ticket loan, pension scheme, private health insurance, conveyancing grant.

vacation placements

Two week placement between June and September, for which 10 students are accepted each year. Applicants should apply via the application form on the website at www.boodlehatfield.com from 1 January 2005.

sponsorship & awards

LPC and GDL/CPE plus maintenance grant.

Partners	24
Assistant Solicitors	39
Total Trainees	10

contact
Emma Turner
020 7318 8133

method of application
Online application

selection procedure
Interviews with the Training Principal, a Partner and the HR Director plus an ability test in verbal reasoning

closing date for 2007
31 July 2005

application
Training contracts p.a. 4
Required degree grade 2:1

training
Salary
1st year £27,500
(Sept 2004)
2nd year £29,500
Holiday entitlement
25 days

post-qualification
Salary £44,000
% of trainees offered job on qualification (2004) 80%

regional offices
Oxford

BOODLE
HATFIELD

BESPOKE LEGAL SERVICES

Boyes Turner

Abbots House, Abbey Street, Reading RG1 3BD
Tel: (0118) 959 7711 Fax: (0118) 957 3257
Email: graduates@boyesturner.com
Website: www.boyesturner.com

firm profile

Boyes Turner is a leading Thames Valley practice, renowned for its insolvency and medical negligence work and well respected for corporate and commercial, commercial property, intellectual property, employment, personal injury, family law, planning, wills, private. While the focus for growth has been commercial work, the firm retains a commitment to its private clients.

main areas of work

Company/commercial (including employment) 20%; commercial property 20%; medical negligence/personal injury 20%; litigation 15%; insolvency 10%; family 5%; private client 10%.

trainee profile

Boyes Turner regards its trainees of today as its assistant solicitors and beyond of tomorrow and expects a high level of commitment, hard work and resourcefulness. Trainees must be responsive to the firm's mission to provide an excellent quality of service to both commercial and individual clients and also contribute to the team-working philosophy.

training environment

Training seats are currently organised into four six month seats; trainees gain experience in both commercial and private client practice areas. Work covers both individual and commercial clients, with as much client contact as possible, supervised by a partner or a senior solicitor. Andrew Chalkley, the Training Principal and Helen Barnett, the HR Manager oversee all aspects of the programme, while each trainee is assigned a tutor (one of the partners) who reviews their progress monthly. This is on two levels – first in assessing how the trainee is developing as a lawyer and secondly how the trainee is developing as an individual, including communication and negotiating skills.

benefits

Firm pension scheme, life assurance, 25 days holiday.

sponsorship & awards

LPC loan of £4,000 and only one loan per applicant. Interest free and repaid over training contract.

Partners	25
Assistant Solicitors	32
Total Trainees	8

contact
Graduate Recruitment Team

method of application
Letter & CV, online facility via website

selection procedure
2 interviews & 1 week work placement

closing date for 2007
31 May 2005

application
Training contracts p.a. 4
% interviewed p.a. 1%+
Required degree grade 2:1

training
Salary
1st year (2004) £18,000
2nd year (2004) £19,200
Holiday entitlement 25 days
% of trainees with
a non-law degree p.a. Varies

post-qualification
% of trainees offered job
on qualification (2003) 100%
% of assistants (as at 1/9/04) who joined as trainees 22%
% of partners (as at 1/9/04) who joined as trainees 16%

B P Collins

Collins House, 32-38 Station Road, Gerrards Cross SL9 8EL
Tel: (01753) 889995 Fax: (01753) 889851
Email: jacqui.symons@bpcollins.co.uk
Website: www.bpcollins.co.uk

firm profile

B P Collins was established in 1965, and has expanded significantly to become one of the largest and best known legal practices at the London end of the M4/M40 corridors. At its main office in Gerrards Cross, the emphasis is on commercial work, with particular strengths being company/commercial work of all types, commercial conveyancing and general commercial litigation. Alongside this there is a highly respected private client department specialising in tax planning, trusts, charities, wills and probates, and an equally successful family law team.

main areas of work

Company/commercial, employment, IT/IP, civil and commercial litigation, commercial conveyancing, property development, private client and family law.

trainee profile

Most of the partners and other fee-earners have worked in London at one time or another but, tired of commuting, have opted to work in more congenial surroundings and enjoy a higher quality lifestyle. Gerrards Cross is not only a very pleasant town with a large number of high net worth private clients but it is also a convenient location for serving the extremely active business community at the eastern end of the Thames Valley including West London, Heathrow, Uxbridge, Slough and Windsor. The firm therefore looks for trainees who are likely to respond to this challenging environment.

training environment

The firm aims to have six trainee solicitors at different stages of their training contracts at all times. Trainees serve five months in four separate departments of their choice. The final four months is spent in the department handling the sort of work in which the trainee intends specialising. The firm has a training partner with overall responsibility for all trainees and each department has its own training principal who is responsible for day to day supervision. There are regular meetings between the training principal and the trainee to monitor progress and a review meeting with the training partner midway and at the end of each departmental seat. The firm also involves its trainees in social and marketing events including golf and cricket matches, go-karting and racing and other sporting and non-sporting activities and has its own six-a-side football team.

sponsorship & awards

50% LPC costs refunded once trainee starts contract.

Partners	18
Assistant Solicitors	22
Total Trainees	6

contact
Jacqui Symons

method of application
Handwritten covering letter
& CV

selection procedure
Screening interview &
selection day

training
Salary
1st year £18,000
2nd year £19,000

A-Z

SOLICITORS

Brabners Chaffe Street

1 Dale St, Liverpool L2 2ET
Tel: (0151) 600 3000 Fax: (0151) 227 3185
Brook House, 77 Fountain Street, Manchester M2 2EE
Tel: (0161) 236 5800 Fax: (0161) 228 6862
7-8 Chapel Street, Preston PR1 8AN
Tel: (01772) 823921 Fax: (01772) 201918
Email: trainees@brabnerscs.com
Website: www.brabnerschaffestreet.com

firm profile
One of the top North West commercial firms, Brabners Chaffe Street, in Liverpool, Manchester and Preston, has the experience, talent and prestige of a firm that has a 200-plus-year history. Brabners Chaffe Street is a dynamic, client-led specialist in the provision of excellent legal services to clients ranging from large plcs to private individuals.

main areas of work
The firm carries out a wide range of specialist legal services and Brabners Chaffe Street's client base includes plcs, public sector bodies, banks and other commercial, corporate and professional businesses. Brabners Chaffe Street is organised into five client-focused departments: corporate (including commercial law); employment; litigation (including media); property (including housing association and construction); private client.

trainee profile
Graduates and those undertaking CPE or LPC, who can demonstrate intelligence, intuition, humour, approachability and commitment.

training environment
The firm is one of the few law firms that holds Investor in People status and has a comprehensive training and development programme. Trainees are given a high degree of responsibility and are an integral part of the culture of the firm. Seats are available in the firm's five departments and each trainee will have partner-level supervision. Personal development appraisals are conducted at six-monthly intervals to ensure that trainee progress is valuable and informed. The training programme is overseen by the firm's Director of Training and Development, Dr Tony Harvey, and each centre has a designated Trainee Partner. It is not all hard work and the firm has an excellent social programme.

sponsorship & awards
From 2006 assistance with LPC funding will be available.

Partners	45
Assistant Solicitors	46
Total Trainees	16

contact
Liverpool office:
Dr Tony Harvey
Director of Training and
Development

method of application
Application form (please
request by email, fax or
post only)

selection procedure
Interview & assessment day

closing date for 2007
Apply by 31 July 2005 for
training contracts
commencing in September
2007

application
Training contracts p.a. 7
Required degree grade
2:1 or post-graduate degree

training
Salary
1st year (2006) £19,000
Holiday entitlement 25 days

offices
Liverpool, Manchester,
Preston

Brachers

Somerfield House, 59 London Road, Maidstone ME16 8JH
Tel: (01622) 690691 Fax: (01622) 681430
Email: info@brachers.co.uk
Website: www.brachers.co.uk

firm profile
Brachers is a leading firm in the South East with an established City office. The firm is principally involved in corporate and commercial work although it has a niche private client practice. The firm has a leading healthcare team, one of 14 on the NHSLA panel.

main areas of work
Company/commercial, general litigation, medical negligence, commercial property, employment, private client and family.

trainee profile
Candidates need to have a strong academic background, common sense and be team players. Both graduates in law and non-law subjects are considered as well as more mature candidates.

training environment
Trainees have four six-month seats out of company/commercial, property, general civil litigation, defendant insurance, medical negligence, family, employment, and private client. Trainees have two appraisals in each seat. The firm has an open door policy and is committed to developing a long-term career structure. Social events are organised.

sponsorship & awards
LPC/CPE £6,000 discretionary award.

Partners	22
Assistant Solicitors	28
Total Trainees	9

contact
Mary Raymont

method of application
Online application from
www.brachers.co.uk

selection procedure
Interview day with partners

closing date for 2007
31 July 2005

application
Training contracts p.a. **6**
Applications p.a. **400**
% interviewed p.a. **7.5%**
Required degree grade **2:1**

training
Salary
1st year (2003) **£16,975**
2nd year (2003) **£18,565**
Holiday entitlement **23 days**

post-qualification
Salary (2004)
£30,000
% of trainees offered job
on qualification **90%**

other offices
London

Bristows

3 Lincoln's Inn Fields, London WC2A 3AA
Tel: (020) 7400 8000 Fax: (020) 7400 8050
Email: info@bristows.com
Website: www.bristows.com

firm profile

Bristows specialises in providing legal services to businesses with interests in technology or intellectual property. The firm acts for some of the largest companies in the world and helps protect some of the most famous brands. Its work reaches beyond intellectual property law to corporate and commercial law, property, tax, employment law and litigation.

main areas of work

Intellectual property 54%; company/corporate finance/commercial 15%; IT 16%; commercial litigation (including employment) 10%; commercial property (including environmental) 5%.

trainee profile

Bristows is looking for applicants with outstanding intellects, with strong analytical skills and engaging personalities. It is also looking for people who will contribute to the ethos of the firm. Bristows is a very friendly firm and believes that you get the best from people if they are in a happy and supportive working environment.

training environment

The firm's training programme gives you the knowledge and skills to build on the extensive hands-on experience you will gain in each of its main departments. You will be working closely with partners, which will accelerate your training. Part of this training may also involve a secondment to one of a number of leading clients. With the international spread of its clients, the probability of overseas travel is high, especially upon qualification.

benefits

Excellent career prospects, a competitive package, firm pension scheme, life assurance and health insurance.

vacation placements

Schemes are run for one week during Christmas and Easter breaks, two weeks during the Summer break. Remuneration: £200 p.w.; Closing Date: Christmas –26 November; Easter/Summer – 28 February.

sponsorship & awards

CPE/LPC fees plus £5,000 maintenance grant for each.

Partners 29
Assistant Solicitors 61
Total Trainees 15

contact
Graduate Recruitment Officer

method of application
Application form

selection procedure
2 individual interviews

closing date for 2007
31 January 2005 for February interviews,
31 August 2005 for September interviews

application
Training contracts p.a.
Up to 10
Applications p.a. **3,500**
% interviewed p.a. **6%**
Required degree grade
2:1 (preferred)

training
Salary
1st year (2003) **£26,000**
2nd year (2003) **£28,000**
Holiday entitlement
4 weeks
% of trainees with
a non-law degree p.a. **86%**

post-qualification
Salary (2004) **£43,000**
% of trainees offered job on qualification (2004) **89%**
% of assistants (as at 1/9/01) who joined as trainees **41%**
% of partners (as at 1/9/01) who joined as trainees **53%**

Browne Jacobson

Nottingham, Birmingham, London
Tel: (0115) 976 6000 Fax: (0115) 947 5246
Email: info@brownejacobson.com
Website: www.brownejacobson.com

firm profile

One of the largest law firms in the midlands, offering an extensive range of legal and business services; working with a wide variety of midlands and national clients in the public, commercial and insurance sectors. The genuine open and supportive environment translates into delivery of a client service experience that is professional, flexible and tailored to client needs and culture. Recent accolades include finalist in the Insurance Times Insurance Law Firms of the Year Awards and Best Use of IT in the Managing Partners Forum European Practice Management Awards. Recognised as an Investor In People and voted one of the ten best places to train in the UK (LEX magazine) for two years running.

main areas of work

A complete legal service for commercial, insurance and public sector clients. Key areas include corporate finance, banking, trade and innovation, tax, financial planning, property, employment, pensions, construction, commercial and property litigation, planning, personal injury, fraud, local authorities, environmental, French inward investment, medical negligence, social housing and education. The firm has a national profile across many sector groups including countryside and environment, freight and logistics, professional indemnity, health and retail.

trainee profile

Trainees must have high academic ability, enthusiasm, energy and commitment, coupled with the ambition to achieve 100% client satisfaction. They will have a practical approach, ability to work as part of a team and work under pressure.

training environment

Training is practical and structured, taking place in a friendly and supportive environment. Trainees spend four periods of six months working in some of the principle areas of the firm, experiencing the realities and pressure of working in a leading law firm.

sponsorship & awards

PgDL fees, LPC fees plus maintenance grant.

| Partners | 49 |
| Assistant Solicitors | 97 |

contact
Carol King
Training Manager

method of application
Apply online at
www.brownejacobson.com

selection procedure
Assessment Centre

closing date
31 July two years before
the training contract is due
to commence

application
Training contracts p.a. 8
Applications p.a. 1,500
% interviewed p.a. 5%
Required degree grade 2:1

training
Salary £19,000
Holiday entitlement 23 days
% of trainees with a
non-law degree p.a. 5%

post-qualification
Salary Regional variations
Holiday entitlement
5 weeks

A-Z SOLICITORS

Browne Jacobson

Burges Salmon

Narrow Quay House, Narrow Quay, Bristol BS1 4AH
Tel: (0117) 902 2766 Fax: (0117) 902 4400
Email: heather.stallabrass@burges-salmon.com
Website: www.burges-salmon.com

firm profile

"…the Firm has managed to win work that other national rivals would kill for, and all without sacrificing quality on the altar of ambition. With client wins such as EMI Group, Reuters, and Coca Cola HBC, Burges Salmon has quietly built the elite firm outside London." - A Leading Awards Body.

Based in Bristol, with a facility in London, Burges Salmon is one of the UK's leading law firms offering an exceptional quality of life combined with a concentration of legal talent unsurpassed by any other firm in the country. More than 75% of its top 100 clients are based outside the South West, and the firm is consistently ranked amongst the UK's most profitable. Burges Salmon's success is based on a simple strategy: a focus on quality people, a breadth of practice areas and a single site approach. This ensures a cohesive culture combining skill, enthusiasm and a supportive environment which attracts and retains lawyers and clients alike.

main areas of work

The practice comprises six broadly based, interacting departments: corporate and financial institutions (CFI), commercial, property, tax and trusts, commercial disputes and construction (CDC), and agriculture, property litigation and environment (APLE). Specialist areas include: banking, competition, corporate finance, employment, IP and IT, and transport. The firm is ranked top tier by Chambers and Partners for 16 of its practice areas.

trainee profile

Successful candidates are motivated and hardworking, with a high degree of commercial acumen alongside a genuine enthusiasm for the law. They must show evidence of a strong academic background as well as significant achievements in non-academic pursuits which demonstrate an ability to build relationships with clients as well as colleagues.

training environment

The Law Society recently accredited the firm's training programme with six points of good practice where the previous maximum in assessments of other firms had been two. This underlines Burges Salmon's reputation for having one of the best training programmes in the country. Training is personalised to suit each individual, and the firm's six seat structure means that you are given the opportunity to experience a wider range of practice areas before making a decision on qualification. This dedication to trainees is highlighted by a 100% retention rate.

Partners	57
Assistant Solicitors	150
Total Trainees	36

contact
Heather Stallabrass,
Graduate Development
Officer

method of application
Employer's application
form available on website

selection procedure
Penultimate year law
students, final year
non-law students, recent
graduates or mature
candidates are considered
for open days, vacation
placements and/or training
contracts

closing date for 2007
31 July 2005

application
Training contracts p.a.
20-25
Applications p.a. **1,500**
% interviewed p.a. **10%**
Required degree grade **2:1**

training
Salary
1st year (2004) **£21,000**
2nd year (2004) **£22,000**
Holiday entitlement **24 days**
% of trainees with
a non-law degree p.a. **40%**

post-qualification
Salary (2004) **£34,500**
% of trainees offered job
on qualification (2004) **100%**
% of assistants who joined
as trainees (2004) **60%**
% of partners who joined
as trainees (2004) **30%**

Burges Salmon continued

Trainees are given early responsibility balanced with an open door policy for advice and guidance. Supervisors are partners or senior lawyers who are highly trained to ensure trainees get as much as possible out of every seat and will tailor the workload to fit with each individual's interests and abilities. There are many opportunities for trainees to take an active role in cases involving high profile clients including Orange, Ministry of Defence, and Honda, as well as running their own files on smaller cases. Secondments to many of these clients are also encouraged to offer new perspectives on the profession as well as enabling trainees to build relationships with clients.

benefits
Annually reviewed competitive salary, 24 days paid annual leave, bonus scheme, Christmas gift, pension scheme, private heath care membership, mobile phone, laptop, corporate gym membership, sports and social club.

vacation placements
Places for 2005: 40, Duration: 2 weeks, Remuneration £200/wk, Closing Date: 31 January 2005. Selection for Vacation Placements is via Open Days which take place in February 2005.

sponsorship and awards
The firm pays GDL and LPC fees at the institution of your choice. Maintenance grants of £4,500 are paid to LPC students, and £9,000 to students studying for both the GDL and LPC (£4,500 p.a.).

comments
"Burges Salmon has one of the most proactive practices I have come across. Their style, culture and professionalism are very hard to beat, and these qualities are very important to Honda." Christopher Morgan, Head of Legal, Honda UK.

"The firm employs a relatively small number of trainees which means that you feel very highly valued. The emphasis on training and development ensures you will not be left doing menial tasks which are a waste of your time, and a waste of the firm's investment in you. Trainees are able to enjoy a high level of responsibility due to the time supervisors and other lawyers are willing to invest in providing you with the support you need for each case." Thomas Boyce, 2nd Year Trainee.

Cadwalader, Wickersham & Taft LLP

265 Strand, London WC2R 1BH
Tel: (020) 7170 8700 Fax: (020) 7170 8600
Email: hrdept@cwt-uk.com
Website: www.cadwalader.com

firm profile

Cadwalader, Wickersham & Taft LLP, a leading international law firm, has sought to anticipate and meet clients' changing legal needs for 200 years. The firm has earned a reputation for crafting innovative business and financial solutions and developing precedent-setting legal strategies. Cadwalader's London office, staffed with UK and US lawyers, was established in 1997 to serve clients interested in capitalising on European and worldwide markets, as well as those seeking US-style services and access to American capital markets.

main areas of work

The firm represents leading international commercial and investment banks, multi-national corporate groups and high net worth clients, in multi-jurisdictional transactions. Practice areas include financial restructuring, litigation, banking and finance, project finance, corporate/M&A, capital markets and tax.

trainee profile

Candidates need to demonstrate that they are intellectually bright and ambitious, and must have excellent communication skills and a commitment to the law. The firm looks for well-rounded individuals with a desire to succeed and a robust and resilient personality.

training environment

The two-year training programme consists of four six-month seats, taking into account the trainee's preferences. In each seat, trainees share an office with, and work alongside senior lawyers whose skills, experience and feedback is invaluable in trainee development and progression towards professional qualification. Formal reviews are carried out each six months. Elements of the Professional Skills Course (PSC) begin right from day one, and continue over the course of the training contract. The firm is friendly and supportive, with an open door policy, business casual dress code, and a varied sporting and social calendar.

benefits

Private dental & health insurance, life assurance, season ticket loan.

sponsorship & awards

GDL Funding: Fees paid plus £4,500 maintenance.
LPC Funding: Fees paid plus £4,500 maintenance.

Partners	11
Assistant Solicitors	55
Total Trainees	8

contact
Human Resources Department

method of application
CV & covering letter

selection procedure
Two interviews

closing date for 2007
Please refer to website

application
Training contracts p.a. 4-6

training
Salary
1st year £30,000
2nd year £33,600
Holiday entitlement 24 days

post-qualification
Salary £65,000

overseas offices
New York, Washington DC, Charlotte NC

Capsticks

77-83 Upper Richmond Road, London SW15 2TT
Tel: (020) 8780 2211 Fax: (020) 8780 4811
Email: career@capsticks.co.uk
Website: www.capsticks.com

firm profile
Rated as the country's leading healthcare law firm by the Chambers Guide and other leading directories, Capsticks handles litigation, administrative law, employment, commercial and property work for a wide range of healthcare bodies, including almost 250 NHS Trusts, PCTs, Strategic Health Authorities, private sector health providers, health-related charities and regulatory bodies.

main areas of work
Clinical law 54%; commercial 6%; commercial property 15%; dispute resolution 7%; employment law 18%.

trainee profile
Successful candidates possess intellectual agility, good interpersonal skills and are capable of taking initiative.

training environment
Six four-month seats, which may include clinical negligence/advisory; commercial property; commercial; employment and dispute resolution. Trainees take responsibility for their own caseload as well as assisting on larger cases and work with clients from an early stage. There are also opportunities to contribute to the firm's marketing and management processes. There are numerous in-house lectures for all fee earners. There is an open door policy, and trainees receive informal feedback and supervision as well as regular appraisals. Despite the firm's rapid expansion, it has retained a friendly atmosphere and a relaxed working environment. There are frequent informal social and sporting activities.

benefits
Bonus scheme, pension, PHI, death in service cover, interest-free Season Ticket Loan.

vacation placements
Places for 2005: Yes; Duration: 2 weeks; Closing Date: 28 February 2005.

sponsorship & awards
Scholarship contributions to GDL and LPC courses.

Partners	30
Assistant Solicitors	55
Total Trainees	11
Other Fee-earners	4

contact
Sue Laundy

method of application
Application form

selection procedure
Candidates are encouraged to participate in the firm's summer placement scheme. Final selection is by interview with the Training Principal & other partners

closing date for 2007
31 July 2005

application
Training contracts p.a. 4-5
Applications p.a. c.300
% interviewed p.a. c.12%
Required degree grade
2:1 or above

training
Salary
1st year TBA
2nd year TBA
Holiday entitlement
22 days p.a. (increased by 1 day p.a. to max 25 days)
% of trainees with a non-law degree p.a. 45%

post-qualification
Salary (2004)
£41,000 + benefits
% of trainees offered job on qualification (2004) 60%
% of assistants (as at 1/9/04) who joined as trainees 35%
% of partners (as at 1/9/04) who joined as trainees 10%

Charles Russell

8–10 New Fetter Lane, London EC4A 1RS
Tel: (020) 7203 5000 Fax: (020) 7203 5307
Website: www.charlesrussell.co.uk

firm profile

Charles Russell is one of the UK's top 50 firms, providing a full range of services to UK and international companies and organisations, while its renowned private client and family practices continue to thrive. It has regional offices in Guildford and Cheltenham. The firm is known for its client care, high quality, expertise and family approach. The strategy is simple – to help clients achieve their goals through excellent service. Many lawyers are ranked as leaders in their field. Experienced in carrying out cross-border corporate and commercial work, the firm also provides clients with access to 150 recommended law firms across the world as part of the two major legal networks, ALFA International and the Association of European Lawyers. The firm's lawyers and staff are highly motivated and talented people. The firm's commitment to training and development and strong team spirit is a key ingredient to being known as a friendly firm with work with and work at.

main areas of work

75% of the firm's work is commercial. Principle areas of work include media and communications, employment and pensions, charities, private client/family, corporate/commercial, intellectual property, dispute resolution, real estate and insurance/reinsurance.

trainee profile

Trainees should be balanced, rounded achievers with an excellent academic background.

training environment

For a firm of its size, a small number of trainees are recruited each year. This allows trainees to undergo the best possible training. Trainees usually spend six months in four of the following training seats – dispute resolution, corporate/commercial, real estate, private client, family, employment/pensions and intellectual property. Secondments to clients are also often available. Wherever possible the firm will accommodate individual preferences. You will be seated with a partner/senior solicitor. Regular appraisals are held to discuss progress and direction. Trainees are encouraged to attend extensive in-house training courses. The PSC is taught both internally and externally. Trainees are encouraged to take on as much responsibility as possible. A social committee organises a range of activities from quiz nights through to sporting events.

benefits

BUPA; PHI and Life Assurance: pension plan; season ticket loans; 25 days holiday plus additional day for house moves; dress-down Fridays; dry cleaning collection service; croissants and muffins are available between 8:00am and 9:00am each Friday in London.

sponsorship & awards

In London and Guildford, the firm pays for course fees whilst you are at law school and a grant of no less than £4,500 per annum. In Cheltenham, the firm pays a contribution of up to £5,000 towards your course fees.

Partners	86
Associates	27
Assistant Solicitors	95
Total Trainees	26

contact
Graduate Recruitment Line
020 7203 5353

method of application
Online application

selection procedure
Assessment days to include an interview & other exercises designed to assess identified performance criteria

closing date for 2007
30 July 2005

application
Training contracts p.a. **12-14**
Applications p.a.
Approx 2,000
% interviewed p.a. **3%**
Preferred degree grade **2:1**

training
Salary
1st year (2003) £27,000
2nd year (2003) £29,500
Holiday entitlement
25 days + additional day for house moves

post-qualification
Salary (2004) **£44,000**

regional offices
Also offers training contracts in its Cheltenham & Guildford offices. Applications are dealt with by the London office

Cleary Gottlieb Steen & Hamilton

City Place House, 55 Basinghall Street, London, EC2V 5EH
Tel: (020) 7614 2200   Fax: (020) 7600 1698
Email: lonlegalrecruit@cgsh.com
Website: www.clearygottlieb.com

firm profile

Cleary Gottlieb is a leading international law firm with more than 800 lawyers practising in the world's major financial centres. Founded in 1946, the firm operates as a single, integrated partnership, serving a clientele comprising many of the world's largest multi-national corporations, financial institutions and sovereign governments, as well as small start-ups, private clients and charitable organisations.

main areas of work

Mergers and acquisitions, capital markets and finance, tax, competition/antitrust and intellectual property.

trainee profile

Successful candidates must have an excellent academic background including at least a 2:1 from a top UK or Irish university. Language skills are an advantage. Occasionally entrance is possible via a US LLM and the New York Bar exam. Such candidates start by spending nine months in the New York office.

training environment

There are no departments at Cleary Gottlieb. Trainees sit with partners and senior solicitors and work on a mix of M&A, capital markets, finance, tax, regulatory, competition and intellectual property work. Seats change every six months. There are opportunities to travel, work in other offices and go on secondment to clients in the UK and abroad. Qualified solicitors are from time to time seconded to the New York and Hong Kong offices. Trainees may have the opportunity to take the New York Bar exam and financial assistance is provided for this. Trainees are encouraged to take responsibility early and in most respects fulfill the same role as first year lawyers in other offices.

benefits

Pension, health insurance, long-term disability insurance and health club.

sponsorship & awards

LPC fees and £5,000 maintenance award.

Partners	15
Solicitors	48
Total Trainees	8

contact
Legal Recruitment

method of application
Cover letter and CV

selection procedure
Usually 2 interviews

closing date for 2007
July 31 2005

application
Training contracts p.a. 4
Applications p.a. **1,000**
% interviewed p.a. **2%**
Required degree grade
**2:1 from a top UK or Irish
university required and
excellent A levels**

training
Salary
1st year (2003) £33,000
2nd year (2003) £39,000

post-qualification
Salary £74,000

overseas offices
New York, Washington DC,
Paris, Brussels, Moscow,
Frankfurt, Cologne, Rome,
Milan, Hong Kong and
Tokyo

CLEARY
GOTTLIEB

Clifford Chance

10 Upper Bank Street, Canary Wharf, London, E14 5JJ
Tel: (020) 7006 1000 Fax: (020) 7006 5555
Email: graduate.recruitment@cliffordchance.com
Website: www.cliffordchance.com/gradsuk

firm profile

Clifford Chance is a truly global law firm, which operates as one organisation throughout the world. Its aim is to provide the highest quality professional advice by combining technical expertise with an appreciation of the commercial environment in which its clients operate.

main areas of work

Banking and finance; capital markets; corporate; litigation and dispute resolution; real estate; tax, pensions and employment.

trainee profile

Consistently strong academic profile (minimum 2:1 degree), a broad range of interpersonal skills and extra curricular activities and interests, commitment to the career.

training environment

The Clifford Chance training contract has been devised to provide students with the technical skills and experience needed to contribute to the firm's success on a daily basis, to achieve professional qualification and to progress to a rewarding career. The two year training contract consists of four six month seats. Most trainees will spend a seat on a secondment at an international office or with a client. In each seat trainees will be working alongside senior lawyers. Trainees are encouraged to use initiative to make the most of expertise and resources available to the firm. Three-monthly appraisals and monitoring in each seat ensure trainees gain a range of work and experience.

benefits

Prize for first class degrees and distinction in LPC, interest-free loan, private health insurance, subsidised restaurant, fitness centre, life assurance, occupational health service, and permanent health assurance.

vacation placements

Places for 2004-2005: Residential Christmas Workshops, vacation placements during Easter and summer break. There is a strong social element to the programme; Duration: 2 days for Christmas Workshops, 2-4 weeks for other schemes; Remuneration: £270 pw; Closing Date: 19 November 2004 for Christmas Workshops; 31 January 2005 for other schemes. A number of international placements will also be available during the summer. Selected candidates will have the opportunity to spend two weeks in London, followed by two weeks in one of the firm's European offices.

sponsorship & awards

GDL and LPC fees paid and currently £5,000 maintenance p.a. for London, Guildford and Oxford, £4,500 p.a. elsewhere.

London office	
Partners	231
Lawyers	713
Trainees	238

contact
Sarah McKinlay
Graduate Recruitment Officer

method of application
Online application

selection procedure
Assessment day comprising an interview with a partner & senior solicitor, a group exercise & a verbal reasoning test

application
Training contracts p.a. 120
Applications p.a. 2,000
% interviewed p.a. 25%
Required degree grade 2:1

training
Salary
1st year £29,000 (Aug 2004)
2nd year £33,000
Holiday entitlement 25 days
% of trainees with a non-law degree p.a. 45%
No. of seats available abroad p.a. 86

post-qualification
Salary (Aug 2004) £50,000
% of trainees offered job on qualification (2003) 90%

overseas offices
Amsterdam, Bangkok, Barcelona, Beijing, Berlin, Brussels, Budapest, Dubai, Düsseldorf, Frankfurt, Hong Kong, Luxembourg, Madrid, Milan, Moscow, Munich, New York, Padua, Palo Alto, Paris, Prague, Rome, São Paulo, Shanghai, Singapore, Tokyo, Warsaw, Washington DC

Clyde & Co

51 Eastcheap, London EC3M 1JP
Tel: (020) 7623 1244 Fax: (020) 7623 5427
Email: theanswers@clydeco.com
Website: www.clydeco.com/graduate

firm profile

Clyde & Co is a leading international law firm with particular strengths in insurance, reinsurance, marine, transport, trade and energy. The firm's dispute resolution practice is one of the largest in the UK. The firm provides a full corporate and commercial service in its core areas and to businesses involved in international trade. Trainees are recruited to work in London and Guildford during their two-year training contract.

main areas of work

Insurance and reinsurance, marine, transport, trade and energy, property, corporate commercial and tax, commercial litigation and employment.

trainee profile

The firm is looking for graduates with excellent academic records, outgoing personalities and keen interests. Trainees need to have the social skills that will enable them to communicate effectively and build relationships with clients and colleagues. The firm is looking for at least a 2:1 degree in any discipline. The ability to analyse problems, apply common sense and provide solutions to situations are all qualities the firm seeks. Ultimately Clyde & Co recruits to retain and it is seeking candidates who will remain with the firm beyond qualification.

training environment

Clyde & Co is a friendly and supportive environment and the firm encourages its trainees to take on responsibility as early as possible. It offers four six-month seats in the London and Guildford offices, as well as opportunities for secondments to national and international clients. The firm is also able to offer seats in its overseas offices. Regular appraisals are held with your supervising partner to assess your progress, skills and development needs. With such a small number of trainees, the firm is usually able to accommodate individual preferences when it comes to choosing seats.

benefits

Subsidised sports club, interest free ticket loan and subsidised restaurant.

legal work experience

The firm runs a two-week summer vacation scheme for 15 students. Please visit the website for the exact date. Applications are made online and the closing date for the scheme is 31 January 2005.

sponsorship & awards

CPE and LPC fees and a maintenance grant are paid where no LEA funding is available

Partners	120
Fee-earners	430
Total Trainees	38

contact
Claire Kohler
Graduate Recruitment Manager

method of application
Online via website
www.clydco.com/graduate

selection procedure
Assessment session with Graduate Recruitment followed by interview with 2 partners

closing date for 2007
31 July 2005

application
Training contracts p.a. **20**
Applications p.a. **1,400 +**
% interviewed p.a. **5%**
Required degree grade **2:1**

training
Salary
1st year (2004) **£27,000**
2nd year (2004) **£30,000**
Holiday entitlement **25 days**
% of trainees with
a non-law degree p.a. **60%**

post-qualification
Salary (2004) **£46,000**

overseas offices
Abu Dhabi, Belgrade, Caracas, Dubai, Hong Kong, Nantes, Paris, Piraeus, Singapore, St Petersburg*
* Associated office

CMS Cameron McKenna

Mitre House, 160 Aldersgate Street, London EC1A 4DD
Tel: (0845) 300 0491 Fax: (020) 7367 2000
Email: gradrec@cmck.com
Website: www.law-now.com

firm profile

CMS Cameron McKenna focuses upon helping its clients find the right legal solutions for their business issues. The firm believes that to give the best advice, lawyers must clearly understand the industry, marketplace and concerns of their clients. All lawyers have a special interest in at least one major industry sector and are committed to building long-term relationships with their clients.

Clients want advice to be delivered clearly, concisely, and in a manner that fully reflects their needs. The firm agrees the best way to communicate with its clients at the outset and its comprehensive feedback programme checks that clients are happy this is being applied consistently.

It's not the structure of the firm that matters, it's what it delivers. That's why the firm places so much emphasis on creating the right service team, with the right levels of experience, for the client, no matter where they sit within the business. This approach has helped CMS Cameron McKenna build a strong reputation across a range of legal disciplines and industries, and foster strong client relationships, recognised in a number of prestigious awards: Best Education Project (above £20m), Best Accommodation/Property Project (below £20m), Best PPP Project, Domestic Deal of the Year, Eastern European Banking and Finance Law Firm of the Year, Pension Team of the Year, Construction Team of the Year and Best Trainee Working at a City (London) Firm.

main areas of work

The firm's clients benefit from an extensive range of tailored services, delivered through offices in the UK, Central Europe, North America and Asia. CMS Cameron McKenna's membership of CMS, an alliance of independent law firms in Europe, provides clients with access to like-minded lawyers in over 24 jurisdictions. The firm's services include: banking and international finance, corporate, real estate, commercial, commercial litigation, tax and employee benefits, energy projects and construction and insurance and reinsurance.

trainee profile

The firm looks for high-achieving team players with good communication, analytical and organisational skills. You will need to show initiative and be able to accept personal responsibility, not only for your own work, but also for your career development. You will need to be resilient and focused on achieving results.

Partners	180
Assistant Solicitors	460
Total Trainees	112

contact
Graduate Recruitment
Team (0845) 300 0491

method of application
Online application form
www.law-now.com/gradrec

selection procedure
2 stage selection
procedure. Initial interview
and verbal reasoning test
followed by assessment
centre

closing date
31 July 2005

application
Training contracts p.a. **80**
Applications p.a. **1,500**
% interviewed p.a. **27%**
Required degree grade **2:1**

training
Salary
1st year (2003) £28,000
2nd year (2003) £32,000
Holiday entitlement
25 days + option of
flexible holiday
% of trainees with
a non-law degree p.a. **40%**
No. of seats available
abroad p.a. **Currently 15**

post-qualification
Salary (2003) £49,000
% of trainees offered job
on qualification (2003) **90%**

CMS Cameron McKenna continued

training environment

The firm is friendly and supportive and puts no limits on a trainee's progress. It offers four six-month seats, three of which will be in the firm's main area of practice. In addition you may gain experience of a specialist area or opt for a secondment to a national or international client. In each seat you will be allocated high quality work on substantial transactions for a range of government and blue-chip clients. Regular appraisals will be held with your seat supervisor to assess your progress, skills and development needs. The three compulsory modules of the PSC will be completed before joining, allowing trainees to become effective and participate on a practical level as soon as possible. The Professional Skills Course is complemented by a comprehensive in-house training programme that continues up to qualification and beyond.

vacation placements

Places for 2004/2005: 55; Duration: 2 weeks; Remuneration: £225 p.w.

sponsorship & awards

PgDL and LPC Funding: Fees paid and a maintenance grant of £5,000 (London, Guildford and Oxford), £4,500 (elsewhere).

trainee comments

"The firm has an incredibly wide base of areas to choose from, varying from healthcare and biotechnology to energy, projects and construction to the more traditional areas of banking, corporate and litigation. You'll find yourself in a pleasant and down-to-earth working environment where you'll be offered a variety of different opportunities, both in and out of work." (Trainee solicitor, Real Estate).

"The most rewarding thing about the international opportunities here, whether it's before or after qualification, is the sheer scope the firm can offer you. There is no doubt that an international perspective is a massive selling point for law firms. Clients don't want to be dealing with one firm in London and any number of others overseas. And that's great news when you're a trainee because you have more chance to travel during your training contract, and then after qualification. My overseas experience was an invaluable part of my contract. I completed a seat in Hong Kong in our Corporate Recovery Group and worked in Orissa, India on the restructuring of the electricity industry. I doubt I'd get those kind of opportunities elsewhere." (Solicitor, Corporate).

branch offices
Visit www.law-now for further information

A-Z SOLICITORS

C'M'S' Cameron McKenna

Coffin Mew & Clover

Fareham Point, Wickham Road, Fareham PO16 7AU
Tel: (01329) 825617 Fax: (01329) 825619
Email: sarajlloyd@coffinmew.co.uk
Website: www.coffinmew.co.uk

firm profile

Founded more than a century ago, the firm has grown to become one of the larger legal practices in the South East with major offices located in the cities of Portsmouth and Southampton and just off the M27 Motorway at Fareham. The firm is in the enviable position of operating a balanced practice offering private client and business services in approximately equal volume and is particularly noted for a number of niche practices with national reputations.

main areas of work

The firm is structured through eight core departments: corporate/commercial; employment; commercial litigation; personal injury; commercial property; family/crime; residential property; trust/probate. Niche practices include intellectual property; finance and business regulation; social housing and medical negligence.

trainee profile

The firm encourages applications from candidates with very good academic ability who seek a broad-based training contract in a highly progressive and demanding but friendly and pleasant environment.

training environment

The training contract is divided into six seats of four months each which will include a property department, a litigation department and a commercial department. The remainder of the training contract will be allocated after discussion with the trainee concerned. The firm aims to ensure that the trainee spends the final four months of his or her training contract in the department in which he or she hopes to work after qualification.

sponsorship & awards

CPE and LPC funding available by discussion with candidates.

vacation placements

Open week in July each year; application as per training contract.

Partners	21
Assistant Solicitors	35
Total Trainees	9

contact
Sara Lloyd
Director of HR & Administration

method of application
CV & covering letter

selection procedure
Interview

closing date for 2007
31 July 2005

application
Training contracts p.a. 4-5
Applications p.a. 400+
% interviewed p.a. 5%
Required degree grade
2:1 (save in exceptional circumstances)

training
Salary
1st year
Competitive market rate
2nd year
Competitive market rate
Holiday entitlement 20 days
% of trainees with a
non-law degree p.a. 25%

post-qualification
Salary (2004) £27,750+
% of trainees offered job
on qualification (2004) 50%
% of assistants who joined
as trainees 20%
% of partners who joined
as trainees 60%

Coudert Brothers

60 Cannon Street, London EC4N 6JP
Tel: (020) 7248 3000 Fax: (020) 7248 3001
Email: recruitlondon@coudert.com
Website: www.coudert.com

firm profile
150 Years of Excellence, Innovation and Global Service. Founded in 1853, Coudert Brothers is a global partnership with 30 offices in 18 countries worldwide. In London the firm was one of the first English multinational partnerships of English solicitors and registered foreign lawyers. The firm advises on all aspects of national and international business law.

trainee profile
The quality and complexity of legal work undertaken by the firm demands that it recruits only individuals of the highest calibre. It is essential that trainees are enthusiastic, confident and outward going individuals, able to perform in a fast-moving and challenging environment. Early responsibility is routine and broad-based experience guaranteed. Coudert Brothers accepts law and non-law graduates. Applicants should have at least three A-level passes at grades A and B and a 2:1 degree. In view of the international nature of the firm's work and clients, language skills are an advantage, but not essential.

training environment
The training at Coudert Brothers comprises four six month placements. Three of these will be with the firm's core practices: corporate and commercial, banking and finance, litigation and property. The fourth will be drawn from one of the firm's other disciplines: energy and utilities, telecommunications, tax and funds and competition law. There is an opportunity for a secondment to one of the firm's overseas offices, usually Brussels. Partners and senior assistants ensure that trainees gain practical experience in research, drafting, procedural and client-related skills by working closely with them during each placement. There are regular appraisals during the two year training contract. Legal and professional training is provided through an in-house training programme and external conferences.

benefits
Pension, health insurance, subsidised gym membership, season ticket loan, private medical and dental care.

sponsorship & awards
CPE Funding: Fees paid plus £4,000 p.a. maintenance (discretionary).
LPC Funding: Fees paid plus £4,000 p.a. maintenance (discretionary).

Partners	10
Assistant Solicitors	20
Total Trainees	7

contact
Simon Cockshutt

method of application
Letter & CV

selection procedure
2 interviews with partners

closing date for 2007
31 July 2005

application
Training contracts p.a. 4
Required degree grade 2:1

training
Salary (Subject to review)
1st year (2004) £28,000
2nd year (2004) £32,000
Holiday entitlement 20 days

post-qualification
Prospects are good as the firm only takes a small number of trainees each year

overseas offices
Almaty, Antwerp, Bangkok, Beijing, Berlin, Brussels, Frankfurt, Ghent, Hong Kong, Los Angeles, Milan, Moscow, New York, Palo Alto, Paris, Rome, San Francisco, Shanghai, Singapore, Stockholm, St Petersburg, Sydney, Tokyo, Washington DC

associated offices
Budapest, Prague, Mexico City, Jakarta

A-Z

SOLICITORS

Covington & Burling

265 Strand, London WC2R 1BH
Tel: (020) 7067 2000 Fax: (020) 7067 2222
Email: graduate@cov.com
Website: www.cov.com

firm profile
Covington & Burling is a leading US law firm, founded in Washington, with offices in London, New York, San Francisco and Brussels. The London office was established in 1988 and has continued to grow progressively since then.

main areas of work
In London, the main areas of work are corporate & commercial, employment, insurance, tax, life sciences, litigation & arbitration, IP/IT, and competition. The firm is known worldwide for its remarkable understanding of regulatory issues as well as its depth and expertise in areas including IT, e-commerce and life sciences. In such work, the firm represents many blue-chip clients including Microsoft, Bacardi, Krispy Kreme, Business Software Alliance and Info NXX (118 118).

trainee profile
The firm is looking for outstanding students who demonstrate genuine commitment to the legal profession and who have not only excellent academic ability, but also imagination, and the necessary practical and social skills required to respond to the evolving needs of its clients. In return, the firm can offer innovative and fascinating work in a stimulating and supportive environment.

training environment
The firm offers a unique and personal training programme to suit the individual needs of each trainee. Following a comprehensive introduction, trainees will spend six months in each of corporate, litigation and arbitration, and IP/IT departments. The fourth seat will be spent in one of the life sciences, employment or tax practice areas. The firm encourages trainees to take early responsibility in order to get the most out of their training period and trainees will receive regular feedback to enhance their development.

benefits
Penions, permanent health insurance, private health cover, life assurance and season ticket loan.

vacation placements
16 places during summer vacation. Closing date for applications 28 February 2005.

sponsorship & awards
CPE, PgDL and LPC fees paid. Maintenance grant of £5,000 per annum.

Partners: 163*
**Associate Lawyers &
Other Fee-earners:** 345*
Total Trainees: 4 (2004)
* denotes worldwide figures

contact
Graduate Recruitment Manager
(020) 7067 2089
graduate@cov.com

method of application
Application form & covering letter

selection procedure
1st & 2nd interview

closing date for 2007
31 July 2005

application
Training contracts p.a. 4
Required degree grade 2:1

training
Salary:
1st year £30,000
2nd year £33,000
(subject to review)

overseas offices
Brussels, New York, San Francisco, Washington

Cripps Harries Hall

Wallside House, 12 Mount Ephraim Road, Tunbridge Wells TN1 1EG
Tel: (01892) 506006 Fax: (01892) 506360
Email: aol@crippslaw.com
Website: www.crippslaw.com

firm profile

A leading regional law firm and one of the largest in the South East, the firm is recognised as being amongst the most progressive and innovative regional practices. Although long established, this is a young firm where the atmosphere is professional and forward thinking while friendly and informal. The firm is regarded by many businesses, institutions and wealthy individuals as the natural first choice among regional law firms.
The firm achieved the Lexcel quality mark in January 1999, the first 'Top 100' firm to do so.

main areas of work

Commercial 42%, dispute resolution 31%, private client 27%. Its associated company, Cripps Portfolio, provides financial services.

trainee profile

Individuals who are confident and capable, with lively but well organised minds and a genuine interest in delivering client solutions through effective and pragmatic use of the law; keen to make a meaningful contribution both during their contract and long term career with the firm; and ambitious to build a career combining 'quality work' with 'quality life'.

training environment

The firm offers a comprehensive induction course, a well structured training programme, frequent one-to-one reviews, regular in-house courses and seminars, good levels of support and real responsibility. The training programme is broader than most other firms and typically includes six seats in both commercial and private client areas. Trainees will usually share a room with a partner and gain varied and challenging first hand experience.

sponsorship awards

Discretionary LPC funding: Fees – 50% interest free loan, 50% bursary.

Partners	38
Assistant Solicitors	51
Total Trainees	14

contact
Annabelle Lawrence
Head of Human Resources

method of application
application form available on website

selection procedure
1 interview with Managing Partner and Head of Human Resources

closing date for 2007
31 July 2005

application
Training contracts p.a. 8
Applications p.a. Up to 750
% interviewed p.a. 6%
Required degree grade 2:1

training
Salary
1st year (2004) £17,000
2nd year (2004) £19,500
Holiday entitlement 25 days
% of trainees with a non-law degree p.a. 7%

post-qualification
Salary (2004) £30,000
% of trainees offered job on qualification (2004) 85%
% of assistants/associates (as at 1/5/04) who joined as trainees 30%
% of partners (as at 1/5/04) who joined as trainees 21%

associated firms
A network of independent law firms in 18 European countries. Cripps Portfolio

A-Z

SOLICITORS

CRIPPS HARRIES HALL

Davenport Lyons

30 Old Burlington Street, London W1S 3NL
Tel: (020) 7468 2600 Fax: (020) 7437 8216
Email: dl@davenportlyons.com
Website: www.davenportlyons.com

firm profile
Davenport Lyons is a leading entertainment and media law practice and combines this work with strong company/commercial (including IP/IT), litigation, property and private client departments. The firm adopts a keen commercial and practical partner-led approach and builds on long-term partnership with its clients.

main areas of work
Media/entertainment; music; litigation (defamation/IP/IT/contentious/property/general commercial/dispute resolution/insolvency/entertainment licensing); company and commercial (IP/IT); commercial/residential property; tax and trust; matrimonial; employment.

trainee profile
2:1 or above; interesting background; business acumen; practical with breadth of interests; sociable; knowledge of foreign languages an advantage.

training environment
Four seats of six months each. Three-monthly assessments. Supervision from within departments. Ongoing programme of in-house lectures and professional skills training. Davenport Lyons offers interesting hands-on training. Trainees are treated as junior fee-earners and are encouraged to develop their own client relationships and to handle their own matters under appropriate supervision.

benefits
Season ticket loan; client introduction bonus; contribution to gym membership; discretionary bonus; 23 days holiday.

vacation placements
Places for 2005: 12; Duration: 2 weeks; Remuneration: £175 p.w.; Closing Date: January 2005.

sponsorship & awards
The firm does not normally offer financial assistance.

Partners	35
Assistant Solicitors	44
Total Trainees	13

contact
Marcia Mardner
HR/Training Manager
Michael Hatchwell
Training Partner

method of application
CV & covering letter

selection procedure
Interviews

closing dates
Closing date for 2006
December 2004
Closing date for 2007
October 2005

application
Training contracts p.a. **5**
Applications p.a. **2,000**
% interviewed p.a. **2%**
Required degree grade **2:1**

training
Salary
Currently under review
Holiday entitlement **23 days**
% of trainees with a
non-law degree p.a. **40%**

post-qualification
% of trainees offered job
on qualification (2004) **75%**
% of assistants (as at
2004) who joined as
trainees **15%**
% of partners (as at 2004)
who joined as trainees **3%**

Davenport Lyons

Davies Arnold Cooper

6–8 Bouverie Street, London EC4Y 8DD
Tel: (020) 7936 2222 Fax: (020) 7936 2020
Email: daclon@dac.co.uk
Website: www.dac.co.uk

Partners	63
Total Fee-earners	111
Total Trainees	7
Total Staff	331

firm profile
Davies Arnold Cooper is a commercial law firm. It has offices in the City of London, Manchester, Madrid and Mexico City. Its aim is to be recognised as a strong provider of legal services in two areas: commercial disputes, whatever their nature; and property, every aspect of it.

main areas of work
Commercial disputes: 70%; property: 30%.

trainee profile
If you secure a training contract with Davies Arnold Cooper you will most probably have a 2:1 degree, either in law or in another academic subject, as well as good A level grades. You will definitely be a self-starter with plenty of energy and common sense. What you've done with your life so far counts for much more than where you went to school/university. The firm likes maturity and in the past has awarded several contracts to those for whom the law is a second career: doctors, accountants, ex-public service and armed forces.

training programme & environment
The firm encourages you to take on responsibility as soon as you join and will give you as much as you can handle, although you will always be supervised and never left alone to struggle. You will experience both contentious and non-contentious work and because the firm only takes on a handful of trainees every year, the chances are you will be able to select your preferred seats.

benefits
Current first year salary is £26,000. 22 days holiday, private medical insurance and season ticket loan.

sponsorship & awards
CPE and LPC fees paid plus maintenance grants.

Dechert LLP

2 Serjeants' Inn, London EC4Y 1LT
Tel: (020) 7775 7625 Fax: (020) 7775 7322
Email: lynn.muncey@dechert.com
Website: www.dechert.com

firm profile

Dechert LLP is an international law firm with 17 offices throughout the US and Europe. It has over 300 staff in London, and over 1500 worldwide. The largest offices are in Philadelphia, London, New York and Washington. Other offices are in Boston, Brussels, Charlotte, Frankfurt, Harrisburg, Hartford, Luxembourg, Munich, Newport Beach, Palo Alto, Paris, Princeton and San Francisco. Dechert has a long established London practice, built up over more than sixty years. It also increasingly represents clients from the United States and Continental Europe, alongside its UK client base. It has particular strengths in banking, corporate, employment, financial services, intellectual property, litigation (including defamation, insurance and property litigation), property finance, real estate and tax.

main areas of work – London

Business law (including corporate, IP, employment and tax) 36%, financial services 15%, litigation 20% and finance and real estate 29%.

trainee profile

Candidates should be able to empathise with a wide range of people, as their clients come from all walks of life. Dechert looks for enthusiasm, intelligence, an ability to find a practical solution to a problem and for powers of expression and persuasion. Also wanted are those with a desire and ability to promote the firm's business at every opportunity. Dechert wants people who will remain on qualifying and make their careers with the firm.

training environment

Dechert invests heavily in training with trainees having the opportunity to work on high-profile national and cross-jurisdictional projects. Unusually training is divided into six four-month periods. The six seats are discussed with each trainee individually so that training reflects his/her own interests and needs. Some trainees are regularly seconded to the Brussels office, and also from time to time to Munich and US offices. The greater number of seats makes it easier to fit in with any special requests to work in specific areas of the firm. The firm has a dedicated training programme managed by its Director of Training (a former Director of the College of Law, London). The PSC is provided in a tailored format by the firm, with some modules taking place in-house. That apart there is an extensive training programme in which trainees are encouraged to participate (numerous aspects being particularly aimed at trainees).

benefits

Free permanent health and life assurance, subsidised membership of local gym and interest-free season ticket loans.

Partners (London)	36
Assistant Solicitors	
(London)	82
Total Trainees (London)	29

contact
Lynn Muncey

method of application
Online application form available on website

selection procedure
Communication exercises & interviews with partners & assistant solicitors

closing date for 2007
30 July 2005

application
Training contracts p.a. **up to 12**
Applications p.a. **Approx 1,500**
% interviewed p.a. **Approx 9%**
Required degree grade
2:1 (or capability of attaining a 2:1)

training
Salary
1st year (2004) **£28,000**
2nd year (2004) **£32,000**
(to be reviewed September 2005)
Holiday entitlement **20 days**
% of trainees with a non-law degree p.a. **Varies**
No. of seats available abroad
p.a. **6 (plus shorter secondments to US offices)**

post-qualification
Salary (2004) **c.£48,000**
(to be reviewed July 2005)
% of trainees offered job on qualification (2004) **75%**
% of partners (as at 1/7/04) who joined as trainees **25%**

Dechert LLP continued

vacation placements - 2 programmes

Date: 4-15 July and 18 -29 July; Places for 2005: up to 16 (up to 8 on each programme); Remuneration: no less than £225 p.w.; Closing Date: 28 February 2005.
Assessment days: Dates: 6 April 2005 and October (date TBC); Number of places: 20-30 on each.

number of vacancies

The firm recruits up to 12 trainees per year (one intake in September). Applications for the 2007 intake will be considered between 1 June and 31 July 2005.

sponsorship & awards

LPC fees paid and £4,500 maintenance (where local authority grants unavailable).

trainee comments

"Life as a Trainee at Dechert starts in a rather unique manner with all new trainees spending five days in Philadelphia taking part in the firm wide orientation; which is a great way for trainees to get to know each other before they start their training contract. The firm also has a thorough programme of training on both seat-specific and general legal issues which are presented by both internal and external experts. I have had a highly rewarding two years." (James Spencer, Newly Qualified, read Law at University of Leeds)

"The six seat system, coupled with the guidance of Bernard George, the dedicated Director of Training, allows trainees to mould a diverse training contract taking in areas of work that will most enhance the trainee's progress at any particular stage. Throughout my training contract, supervisors encouraged me to take the initiative, under responsible tutelage, and I undertook a wide variety of challenging work." (James Kaufmann, Newly Qualified, read Chemical Engineering at Birmingham)

"Dechert's rotation system allows you to gain experience in a wide variety of practice areas, and locations (including Munich and Brussels). Because Dechert takes on a relatively small number of trainees, this can involve a significant level of responsibility and client contact. Trainees are not left to fend for themselves, however, as supervisors and others are always available to provide support." (Sarah Pritchard, Newly Qualified, read History at Cambridge university)

overseas offices
Boston, Brussels, Charlotte, Frankfurt, Harrisburg, Hartford, Luxembourg, Munich, Newport Beach, New York, Palo Alto, Paris, Philadelphia, Princeton, San Francisco, Washington

A-Z SOLICITORS

Denton Wilde Sapte

Five Chancery Lane, Clifford's Inn, London EC4A 1BU
Tel: (020) 7242 1212 Fax: (020) 7320 6555
Email: jo.wilson@dentonwildesapte.com
Website: www.dentonwildesapte.com

firm profile

Denton Wilde Sapte is a large commercial law firm based in London with offices in Europe, the Middle East and the CIS. The firm's strengths lie in its sector focus, and its practice areas are as strong and diverse as its client list.

main areas of work

Banking & finance; corporate; dispute resolution; EU & competition; employment & pensions; energy & infrastructure, real estate, tax; technology, media & telecommunications.

trainee profile

The firm looks for candidates who are team players with a strong academic and extra curricular record of achievement.

training environment

Four six month seats, including at least one transactional and one contentious seat. Most trainees also spend one seat in the Banking & Finance and/or Real Estate Department. The firm aims to offer trainees as much choice as possible with their seats, one of which may be spent in one of the international offices or with one of the firm's clients. You will be given as much responsibility as you can handle, working with the law, with the team and with clients in real business situations. The firm works hard to maintain a friendly and open working environment where ideas are shared and people work together to achieve goals.

benefits

Flexible benefit scheme. Meal away from home allowance. Season ticket loan.

vacation placements

Open days during December 2004 and summer schemes during June and July 2005. Closing date for applications for open days is 26 November 2004 and for summer schemes 11 February 2005.

sponsorship & awards

GDL and LPC tuition fees covered plus £4,500 maintenance grant for each year of study, £5,000 if studying in London.

Partners	196
Fee-earners	666
Total Trainees	100

contact
Jo Wilson

method of application
Application form

selection procedure
First interview; selection test; second interview & case study

closing date for 2007
31 July 2005

application
Training contracts p.a. **35**
Applications p.a. **2,000**
% interviewed p.a. **10-15%**
Required degree grade **2:1**

training
Salary
1st year **£28,000**
2nd year **£31,000**
Holiday entitlement **24 days**
% of trainees with a
non-law degree p.a. **40%**
No. of seats available
abroad p.a. **Currently 4**

post-qualification
Salary (2004) **£48,000**
% of trainees offered job
on qualification (2004) **70%**

overseas offices
Abu Dhabi, Almaty, Cairo, Dubai, Gibraltar, Istanbul, Moscow, Muscat, Paris, Tashkent

Devonshires

Salisbury House London Wall London EC2M 5QY
Tel: (020) 7628 7576 Fax: (020) 7256 7318
Email: training@devonshires.co.uk
Website: www.devonshires.com

firm profile

Devonshires has been in the City of London for more than 150 years. The firm prides itself on its reputation for providing all its clients - who are based throughout England, Wales, the Channel Islands and the Isles of Scilly - with expert, cost-effective advice. The firm is a recognised leader in the social housing market and currently advises over 220 registered social landlords. The firm also advises financial institutions and stock exchange listed debt issuers; charities; corporations; government - domestic and international; insolvency practitioners; NHS trusts; private clients; professional service providers; property developers and investors, including financial institutions.

main areas of work

Property 30%; litigation 25%; banking and corporate 20%; PPP/PFI 10%; construction 5%; employment 5%; religious charities 5%.

trainee profile

The firm recruits high calibre trainees who are all-rounders. You don't have to be a law graduate - the firm welcomes applications from all disciplines and all universities. What you must have are keen commercial and technical qualities and proven academic abilities. You will also be able to show a demonstrable interest in a legal career and have a wide range of interests outside the office.

training environment

Training usually involves four seats of six months each, working with partners and senior staff in departments such as banking (company and commercial), church/charity, construction, employment, family/matrimonial, housing management litigation, personal injury, litigation/dispute resolution, PFI and property. You will be required to cover a minimum of three practice areas and have a minimum of three months' contentious experience.

benefits

Interest-free season ticket loans, healthcare scheme membership, trainee social group, subsidised health-club membership, dress down Fridays, life assurance, dental care.

sponsorship & awards

Under review.

Partners	18
Total Number of Fee-earners	83
Total Trainees	6

contact
Angela Hall
Human Resources Manager
(020) 7628 7576

method of application
Online application form at
www.devonshires.com

application
Training contracts p.a. **5**
Applications p.a. **500**
% interviewed p.a. **5%**
Required degree grade
2:1 and higher

training
salary for each year of
training
Year 1: **£24,500**
Year 2: **£25,500**
holiday entitlement **22 days**

post-qualification
Salary   **competitive**
% of trainees offered job
on qualification (2003) **80%**

A-Z SOLICITORS

541

Dickinson Dees

St. Ann's Wharf, 112 Quayside, Newcastle upon Tyne NE99 1SB
Tel: (0191) 279 9000 Fax: (0191) 279 9100
Email: law@dickinson-dees.com
Website: www.dickinson-dees.com

firm profile
Dickinson Dees enjoys an excellent reputation as one of the country's leading commercial law firms based in the North East with offices in Newcastle upon Tyne and the Tees Valley with an associated office in Brussels. The firm prides itself on the breadth of experience and expertise within the firm which enables it to offer services of the highest standards to its clients. Whilst many of the clients are based in the North, the firm works on a national basis for national and internationally based businesses and organisations.

main areas of work
Corporate 30%; property 30%; private client 20%; litigation 20%.

trainee profile
The firm is looking for intellectually able trainees with good communication skills. Successful applicants will understand the need to provide practical, commercial advice to clients. They will share the firm's commitment to self-development and teamwork and its desire to provide clients with services which match their highest expectations.

training environment
Trainees are relatively few for the size of the practice. You are fully integrated into the firm and involved in all aspects of firm business. The training contract consists of four seats - one in each of the commercial property, company/commercial and litigation departments. You may be able to specialise for the fourth seat. Trainees sit with their supervisors and appraisals are carried out every three months. The firm has its own Training Manager as well as a Graduate Recruitment Adviser and a Graduate Programme Adviser. There are induction courses on each move of department with opportunities for trainees to get involved in the firm's training programme. The firm offers a tailored in-house Professional Skills Course which is run in conjunction with the College of Law. The working environment is supportive and friendly with the benefits of working in the vibrant, bustling city of Newcastle yet within 15 minutes from unspoilt countryside.

vacation placements
Places for 2005: 36; Duration: 1 week; Remuneration: £125 p.w.; Closing Date: 28 February 2005. Apply online at www.trainingcontract.com. Applicants are selected for work placements by interview.

sponsorship & awards
GDL/LPC fees paid and £4,000 interest free loan.

Partners 64
Total Staff 675
Total Trainees 28

contact
Sally Brewis, Graduate Recruitment Adviser

method of application
Apply online at www.trainingcontract.com

selection procedure
Aptitude and ability tests, negotiation exercise, personality questionnaire, interview

closing date for 2007
31 July 2005

application
Training contracts p.a.
up to 15
Applications p.a. **750**
% interviewed p.a. **10%**
Required degree grade **2:1**
in either law or non-law

training
Salary
1st year (2004) **£18,000**
2nd year (2004) **£19,500**
Holiday entitlement **23 days**
% of trainees with
a non-law degree p.a. **40%**
No. of seats available
abroad p.a. **2**
(3-month secondments)

post-qualification
Salary (2004) **£30,000**
% of trainees offered job
on qualification (2004) **93%**
% of partners (as at
1/9/04) who joined as
trainees **27%**

other offices
Tees Valley, Brussels

Dickinson Dees continued

trainee comments

"The most striking aspect of the firm for me has been the atmosphere in the office. The rooms are airy and spacious, and people wander in and out of each others rooms for a chat or a discussion. It took me a while to realise who was the partner and who was the secretary, because everyone is so relaxed and friendly." (Huw Russell, Second Year trainee, read Law at Newcastle University)

"As a trainee at Dickinson Dees, we are encouraged to strike an important balance between working hard during the day and taking advantage of the excellent social opportunities of the Newcastle nightlife. We are given access to high quality work for first class clients and the friendly and social office environment ensures that there is never a dull moment! I was really pleased to be offered a job as a Newly Qualified Solicitor at the firm as I can't imagine wanting to work elsewhere." (Jennifer Stephens, NQ Solicitor, Litigation – Environmental, read Law at Lancaster University)

"The 'hands-on' work, exciting marketing events, opportunities for court work, strong commercial reputation and the huge variety of specialties made Dickinson Dees my first choice for a law firm in the North. Each seat has brought new challenges and exciting opportunities and in every seat I have been treated as a team member with something valuable to add to the equation. All in all, the firm offers an exciting, dynamic, friendly and challenging working environment offering substantial personal development." (Jaimie Blueman, Second Year trainee, read Law at Manchester University)

"Every firm promises its trainees high quality work in a friendly and supportive atmosphere, but what made Dickinson Dees stand out for me when I came here on a vacation placement was that it keeps those promises. Two years later and I feel proud to work in a firm where I am given the right balance of responsibility and support; where I am encouraged to think for myself and take the initiative whilst knowing that I will always be able to ask for help. The quality of work has far exceeded my expectations and given the emphasis the firm places on having a life outside of work, I feel that there simply isn't anywhere else I would rather be." (Catherine Lamb, NQ Solicitor, Company & Commercial – Commercial, read Law and Spanish at Cardiff University)

"I have been here for just over a year now and am thoroughly enjoying myself. The variety of work has been stimulating and interesting. It has ranged from research into septic tanks to attending a high profile sentencing at the Old Bailey, with masses in between. Outstanding!" (Harry Chrisp, Second Year Trainee, read Archaeology at Edinburgh University)

"I suppose I was in an unfamiliar position to other graduates in that I had already decided to specialise in the area of Private Client tax and trust law long before my legal studies were completed. As a result of Dickinson Dees' enviable reputation in the Private Client world, the decision to qualify as a solicitor with them made itself." (Malcolm Emery, NQ Solicitor, Private Capital Group, Private Client, read Law at Northumbria)

DLA LLP

Victoria Square House, Victoria Square, Birmingham B2 4DL
Tel: (020) 7796 6677   Fax: (0121) 262 5793
Email: recruitment.graduate@dla.com
Website: www.dla.com/recruitment

firm profile
DLA is one of the UK's largest commercial law firms with offices in eight UK cities as well as 17 international locations. The firm's impressive client base combined with an emphasis on high quality service and teamwork, provide a challenging, fast-paced working environment. With modern values and a clear structure for the future, DLA is a firm that is going places. DLA was ranked 10th in the Financial Times list of the 50 Best Workplaces in the UK. For the fourth year running, the firm has appeared in the Sunday Times survey of the '100 Best Companies to Work for', demonstrating the firm's commitment to its employees and their ongoing development.

main areas of work
DLA has nine main areas of work: banking; business support and restructuring; commercial and projects; corporate; human resources; litigation; real estate; regulatory; technology, media and communications.

trainee profile
The firm is looking for individuals from either a law or non law background who have a minimum of three Bs at A-level or equivalent and expect to, or have already achieved a 2:1 degree classification. DLA wants highly motivated and energetic team players with sound commercial awareness, outstanding communication and organisational skills, and above all, an appetite for life with a desire to succeed in business.

training environment
DLA provides a first class training environment. From induction to qualification and beyond, DLA ensures that its employees develop the necessary skills and knowledge to survive in a busy, client-driven environment. If it's responsibility you want, DLA will give you as much as you can handle. Trainees complete four six-month seats and progress is monitored through regular reviews and feedback. The compulsory Professional Skills Course is run in-house and is tailored to meet the needs of the firm's trainees. This combined with on-the-job experience, provides trainees with an excellent grounding on which to build their professional careers.

vacation placements
Places for 2005: 200; Duration: 2 weeks; Remuneration (2004 figures) £210 per week (London), £170 per week (regions and Scotland); Closing Date: 28 February 2005.

sponsorship & awards
Payment of LPC and GDL fees plus maintenance grant in both years, is offered to future trainees who have yet to complete these courses.

Partners	373
Associates	362
Assistant Solicitors	440
Total Trainees	171

contact
Sally Carthy National Graduate Recruitment Manager

method of application
Application form

selection procedure
First interview, second interview assessment afternoon

closing date for 2007
31 July 2005

application
Training contracts p.a. **85+**
Applications p.a. **2,500**
% interviewed p.a. **10%**
Required degree grade **2:1**

training
Salary (2003)
1st year £28,000 (London)
£20,000 (Regions)
£16,000 (Scotland)
2nd year £31,000 (London)
£22,000 (Regions)
£18,000 (Scotland)
% of trainees with a
non-law degree p.a. **40%**

post-qualification
Salary (2004)
£48,000 (London)
£32,500 (regional offices)
£30,000 (Scotland)
% of trainees offered job
on qualification 2004 **82%**

uk offices
Birmingham, Edinburgh, Glasgow, Leeds, Liverpool, London, Manchester, Sheffield

overseas offices
Offices in 17 locations across mainland Europe and Asia

DMH

100 Queens Road, Brighton BN1 3YB
Tel: (01273) 744270 Fax: (01273) 744404
Email: personnel@dmh.co.uk
Website: www.dmh.co.uk

firm profile

DMH is an approachable and innovative firm with an open culture which encourages personal development and provides its personnel with a high level of support in order to achieve this. The firm offers expertise and service comparable to City firms to a range of commercial organisations, non-profit institutions and individual clients. By focusing on the client's needs DMH provides practical and creative solutions. DMH operates from offices in Brighton, Crawley and London.

main areas of work

Corporate/commercial; commercial property, planning and environmental; employ-ment, intellectual property/IT; litigation; residential conveyancing; personal injury; private client.

trainee profile

The firm welcomes applications from motivated graduates from all backgrounds and age groups. Enthusiasm, a mature outlook and commercial awareness are as prized as academic ability, and good communication skills are a must. Ideal applicants are those with the potential to become effective managers or strong marketeers.

training environment

Usually four six month seats taken from the following areas: employment, intellectual prop-erty/IT, corporate/commercial, planning and environmental, commercial property, commercial litigation, property litigation, personal injury, civil litigation, residential con-veyancing and private client. Trainees are closely supervised by the partner to whom they are attached but have every opportunity to work as part of a team and deal directly with clients.

vacation placements

Places for Summer 2006: Priority given to trainee interviewees with a limited number of unpaid places; Duration: 1 week; Closing Date: 31 January 2006.

Partners	32
Assistant Solicitors	28
Total Trainees	13

contact
Jessica Leigh-Davis

method of application
Application form
Selection Procedure: First interview and assessment day (March/April), work experience, then second interview (August).

closing date for 2007
31 December 2005

application
Training contracts p.a. 6-7
Applications p.a. 400
% interviewed p.a. 4%
Required degree grade 2:1

training
Salary
1st year (2004) £17,500
2nd year (2004) £20,250
Holiday entitlement 23.5 days
% of trainees with a non-law degree p.a. 66%

post-qualification
Salary (2004) £30,000
% of trainees offered job on qualification (2004) 100%
% of assistants (as at 1/7/03) who joined as trainees 46%
% of partners (as at 1/7/03) who joined as trainees 47%

A-Z

SOLICITORS

545

Dorsey & Whitney

21 Wilson Street, London EC2M 2TD
Tel: (020) 7588 0800 Fax: (020) 7588 0555
Website: www.dorsey.com

firm profile

Dorsey & Whitney is amongst the largest law firms in the world with more than 20 offices situated across three continents. The firm has over 650 lawyers worldwide. The London office of Dorsey & Whitney has over 40 lawyers and trainees. It continues to build on its traditional strengths in corporate law, litigation and intellectual property work through its wide range of practice groups.

main areas of work

The London office offers the full range of legal services including corporate finance, cross border M&A, commercial litigation, tax, employment, real estate, intellectual property and competition law.

trainee profile

Dorsey & Whitney is looking for 'self-starters', capable of meeting the intellectual and business challenges of a successful multi-national practice. Candidates should be committed team players who enjoy rewarding client work. An honours degree at 2:1 level or above and some relevant work experience is also required.

training environment

The training contract is split into four individual 'seats' of six months each. Each trainee will be required to complete litigation and corporate seats. Secondments to major clients are available. All trainees are supplied with the encouragement and support necessary to maximise their potential. Through the mentoring, professional development and evaluation programmes, the firm strives to develop and retain the highest calibre lawyers.

benefits

Non-contributory pension schemes; health insurance and life insurance.

Partners	11
Assistant Solicitors	23
Total Trainees	8

contact
Andew Rimmington,
Partner 020 7588 0800

method of application
Application by letter with a current curriculum vitae addressed to Andrew Rimmington.

closing date for 2006
30 September 2005

application
Training contracts p.a. 4
(currently under review)

training
Salary
1st year (2005) £28,500
2nd year (2005) £31,500
Holiday entitlement 22 days plus public holidays

post-qualification
Salary (2004) £52,000
(under review)
Dorsey & Whitney aims to offer a qualified position to all candidates who have shown the appropriate level of performance during training, subject to the needs of the firm

DWF

5 Castle Street, Liverpool L2 4XE
Tel: (0151) 907 3000 Fax: (0151) 236 3088
Email: trainees@dwf-law.com
Website: www.dwf.co.uk

firm profile

DWF delivers a complete menu of legal services for businesses, providing innovative solutions and strategies - whatever and wherever the problem or opportunity. The firm possesses specialist technical know-how and industry sector expertise. It has a reputation for efficient and business-friendly service and for delivering outstanding value for money. DWF is a top tier law firm of choice for businesses based or operating in England and Wales, with a credible and effective national and international capability. Through its work with successful and growing businesses, DWF has become one of the fastest growing law firms in the UK.

main areas of work

Services cover asset finance, banking, business recovery, commercial agreements, competition, construction, corporate, debt management, dispute resolution, employee incentive planning, employment law, food law, health safety and environment, insurance, intellectual property, internet and technology, legal training, licensing, pensions, planning, property and wealthcare. These services are delivered by specialist teams - including leading experts in their field - supported by state-of-the-art technology. DWF has a client base covering a wide range of industries and is known for its service innovation as its DWF HR Horizons, DWF Maxima and Advantage service demonstrate. Information about the industry sector groups and innovative services can be found at www.dwf.co.uk.

trainee profile

DWF wants trainee solicitors to play a part in building on its success. The firm is looking for trainees who enjoy working as part of a busy team, respond positively to a challenge and have what it takes to deliver results for clients. The firm is looking for its partners of the future and in recent years virtually all of its qualifying trainees have been offered jobs.

training environment

All trainees commence life at DWF with a welcome programme, designed to provide a clear picture of the firm and its services, before moving to their first seat. The firm provides a flexible seat rotation including employment, corporate, property, commercial litigation and insurance, with agreed options which focus on post-qualification aspirations. This is supplemented by general training as well as specific training relevant to the particular seat using in-house and external courses. Appraisals are carried out during each seat to review progress and development. Trainees will have the opportunity to join in the busy social life within the offices and with local trainee solicitors' groups.

Partners	56
Assistant Solicitors	129
Total Trainees	16

contact
Sarah Fielding
HR Officer
(Manchester address)

method of application
DWF application form

selection procedure
2 stage interview/selection process

closing date for 2006/2007
2 August 2005

application
Training contracts p.a. 8
Applications p.a. c.1000
% interviewed p.a. 5%
Required degree grade 2:1
in any discipline

training
Salary
1st year £18,000
Holiday entitlement
25 days p.a. minimum

post-qualification
% of trainees offered job
on qualification (2003) **100%**

benefits
Life Assurance, pension scheme

vacation placements
Open day events at each office

sponsorship & awards
LPC funding for tuition fees

Eversheds

Senator House, 85 Queen Victoria Street, London EC4V 4JL
Tel: (020) 7919 4761 Fax: (020) 7919 4919
Application Form Online at www.eversheds.com
Email: gradrec@eversheds.com
Website: www.eversheds.com

firm profile
Eversheds LLP has over 2,000 legal and business advisers providing services to the private and public sector business and finance community. Access to all these services is provided through the firm's international network of offices. Eversheds combines local market knowledge and access with the specialisms, resources and international capability of one of the world's largest law firms.

main areas of work
Corporate, commercial, litigation and dispute management, real estate, human resources (employment and pensions) and legal systems group. In addition to these core areas each office provides expertise in a further 30 business and industry sectors.

trainee profile
Eversheds' people are valued for being straightforward, enterprising and effective. The firm listens to its clients. It likes to simplify rather than complicate. It expects trainees to be business-like, unstuffy and down-to-earth. You will need to display commercial acumen, imagination and drive and, above all, you will need to be results-driven. As a trainee you will get as much responsibility as you can handle and will benefit from the 'hands on, learning by doing' philosophy. The firm takes your training very seriously but expects it to be fun too.

training environment
You will be encouraged to play a major part in the direction your training and development takes, with advice and supervision always available. In each department you will sit with a partner or a senior assistant and participate from an early stage in varied, complex and high-value work. Eversheds aims to retain as many trainees as possible on qualifying and many of the partners were trainees with the firm. A steep learning curve begins with a week of basic training followed by departmental seats – three of which will cover the firm's main practice areas. During your training you will also complete an Eversheds designed Professional Skills Course and, on qualification, follow a progressive career structure.

benefits
Regional variations.

vacation placements
Places for 2005: 180; Duration: 2 weeks in Summer, 1 week at Easter; Remuneration: regional variations; Closing Date: 31 January 2005.

sponsorship & awards
GDL/LPC fees and maintenance grants in accordance with the terms of the firm's offer.

Partners 400+
Assistant Solicitors 2,000+
Total Trainees 200+

contact
gradrec@eversheds.com

method of application
Apply online at
www.eversheds.com

selection procedure
Selection days include group
and individual exercises,
presentations and interview

closing date for 2007
31 July 2005

application
Training contracts p.a. **86**
Applications p.a. **4,000**
% interviewed p.a. **15%**
Required degree grade **2:1**

training
Salary
1st year London (2004)
£28,000
2nd year London (2004)
£31,000
Holiday entitlement **25 days**
% of trainees with
a non-law degree p.a. **45%**
No. of seats available
abroad p.a. **Up to 12**

post-qualification
Salary London (2004)
£48,000
% of trainees offered job
on qualification (2004) **82%**

offices
Barcelona*, Birmingham,
Brussels, Budapest*,
Cambridge, Cardiff,
Copenhagen, Doha** Ipswich,
Leeds, London, Madrid*,
Manchester, Milan*, Newcastle,
Norwich, Nottingham, Paris,
Rome*, Shanghai*,
Singapore*, Sofia* Valladolid*,
Vienna*
* Associated office
** In co-operation

Farrer & Co

66 Lincoln's Inn Fields, London WC2A 3LH
Tel: (020) 7242 2022 Fax: (020) 7242 9899
Email: graduates@farrer.co.uk
Website: www.farrer.co.uk

firm profile
Farrer & Co is a mid-sized London law firm. The firm provides specialist advice to a large number of prominent private, institutional and commercial clients. Farrer & Co has built a successful law firm based on the goodwill of close client relationships, outstanding expertise in niche sectors and a careful attention to personal service and quality.

main areas of work
The firm's breadth of expertise is reflected by the fact that it has an outstanding reputation in fields as diverse as matrimonial law, offshore tax planning, employment, heritage work, charity law, defamation and sports law.

trainee profile
Trainees are expected to be highly motivated individuals with keen intellects and interesting and engaging personalities. Those applicants who appear to break the mould – as shown by their initiative for organisation, leadership, exploration, or enterprise – are far more likely to get an interview than the erudite, but otherwise unimpressive, student.

training environment
The training programme involves each trainee in the widest range of cases, clients and issues possible in a single law firm taking full advantage of the wide range of practice areas at Farrer & Co by offering six seats, rather than the more usual four. This provides a broad foundation of knowledge and experience and the opportunity to make an informed choice about the area of law in which to specialise. A high degree of involvement is encouraged under the direct supervision of solicitors and partners. Trainees attend an induction programme and regular internal lectures. The training partner reviews trainees' progress at the end of each seat and extensive feedback is given. The firm has a very friendly atmosphere and regular sporting and social events.

benefits
Health and life insurance, subsidised gym membership, season ticket loan.

vacation placements
Places for 2005: 30; Duration: 2 weeks at Easter, two schemes for 2 weeks in summer; Remuneration: £230 p.w.; Closing Date: 31 January 2005.

sponsorship & awards
CPE Funding: Fees paid plus £4,500 maintenance. LPC Funding: Fees paid plus £4,500 maintenance.

Partners	59
Assistant Solicitors	54
Total Trainees	15

contact
Graduate Recruitment Manager

method of application
Firm's application form and covering letter

selection procedure
Interviews with Graduate Recruitment Partner and partners

closing date for 2007
31 July 2005

application
Training contracts p.a. **8-10**
Applications p.a. **1,000**
% interviewed p.a. **5%**
Required degree grade **2:1**

training
Salary
1st year (2004) **£26,000**
2nd year (2004) **£28,500**
The firm operates a performance related bonus scheme based on both personal and firm performance
Holiday entitlement **25 days**
% of trainees with non-law degrees p.a. **50%**

post-qualification
Salary (2004) **£43,000**
trainees offered job on qualification (2004) **83%**
% of assistants (as at 1/9/01) who joined as trainees **72%**
% of partners (as at 1/9/01) who joined as trainees **70%**

A-Z SOLICITORS

Field Fisher Waterhouse

35 Vine Street, London EC3N 2AA
Tel: (020) 7861 4000 Fax: (020) 7488 0084
Email: graduaterecruitment@ffw.com
Website: www.ffw.com

firm profile
Field Fisher Waterhouse is a leading mid-sized City law firm. The practice is primarily commercial and the firm's clients are wide-ranging across many sectors. The firm acts for a substantial number of overseas clients and as part of The European Legal Alliance it has a strong presence across 20 European cities.

main areas of work
The firm is particularly well known for its three core practice areas of Corporate, Real Estate, and Brands Technology Media & Telecommunications (BTMT). It is also highly regarded for its specialist expertise in commercial litigation, medical litigation, investment funds, aviation, travel and tourism, employment, pensions, tax, and professional regulation.

trainee profile
The firm is looking to recruit trainees from both law and non-law backgrounds who have excellent communication skills, enthusiasm and the ability to work as part of a team. Trainees must be able to respond creatively to problems and demonstrate initiative and commercial awareness.

training environment
The training contract is split into five seats and the range of practice areas enables the firm to offer outstanding opportunities for training. Trainees share an office with a supervising partner or solicitor and are treated as a valued part of the team. Trainees benefit from high quality work as they are encouraged to take responsibility at an early stage of their training contracts. Practical training is complemented by a comprehensive programme of in-house seminars, workshops and external courses, accompanied by regular feedback and a formal assessment at the end of each seat. The firm is proud of its friendly, relaxed and supportive working environment and there are always numerous sporting and social events to take part in throughout the year.

sponsorship & benefits
Tuition fees plus £4,500 maintenance grant paid for both GDL and LPC. Benefits include 25 days holiday, BUPA, life assurance, season ticket loan, subsidised gym membership, GP service, pension.

vacation placements
Candidates are encouraged to apply for a place on the July 2005 summer vacation scheme. Apply online via the firm's website at www.ffw.com, by 31 January 2005.

Partners	78
Assistant Solicitors	121
Vacancies	12
Total Trainees	27

contact
Graduate Recruitment

method of application
Apply online via the firm website, www.ffw.com

selection procedure
Interview

closing date for 2007
31 August 2005

application
Training contracts p.a. **12**
Applications p.a. **1,200**
Required degree grade **2:1**

training
Salary
1st year (2004) **£27,000**
2nd year (2004) **£30,000**
Holiday entitlement
25 days

post-qualification
Salary (2004) **£46,000**
% of trainees offered job on qualification (2004) **80%**
% of assistants (2004) who joined as trainees **40%**
% of partners (2004) who joined as trainees **40%**

Finers Stephens Innocent

179 Great Portland St, London W1N 6LS
Tel: (020) 7323 4000 Fax: (020) 7580 7069
Email: gradrecruitment@fsilaw.co.uk
Website: www.fsilaw.co.uk

firm profile
Finers Stephens Innocent is an expanding practice based in Central London providing a range of high quality legal services to corporate and commercial clients. The firm offers a range of services focused to meet the requirements of its primarily commercial client base. The firm's philosophy includes close partner involvement and a commercial approach in all client matters. Dedicated teams create services that are supplied in a cost effective manner with a working style which is personable, client supportive and informal. The firm is a member of the Network of Leading Law Firms and of Meritas.

main areas of work
Commercial property; litigation; media; employment; family; defamation; company/commercial; private client. See the firm's website for further details.

trainee profile
The firm looks for academic excellence in applicants. It also looks for maturity, an interesting personality, strong communication skills, ability to think like a lawyer and an indefinable 'it' which shows that you have the potential to become a long-term member of the firm's team. Mature applicants are especially encouraged.

training environment
After your induction programme, you will complete four six month seats, sharing a room with either a Partner or Senior Assistant. The firm has two Training Partners who keep a close eye on the welfare and progress of trainees. There are regular group meetings of trainees and an appraisal process which enables you to know how you are progressing as well as giving you a chance to provide feedback on your view of your training.

benefits
20 days holiday, pension, private medical insurance, life insurance, long-term disability insurance, season ticket loan.

sponsorship & awards
LPC and CPE course fees.

Partners	30
Assistant Solicitors	37
Total Trainees	9

contact
Personnel Department

method of application
CV & covering letter

selection procedure
2 interviews with the Training Partners

closing date for 2007
30 July 2005

application
Training contracts p.a. **5**
Applications p.a. **800**
% interviewed p.a. **3%**
Required degree grade **2:1**

training
Salary
1st year
Highly competitive
2nd year
Highly competitive
Holiday entitlement **20 days**
% of trainees with a non-law degree p.a. **0-50%**

post-qualification
Salary
Highly competitive
% of trainees offered job on qualification (2003) **40%**

Fisher Meredith

Blue Sky House, 405 Kennington Road, London SE11 4PT
Tel: (020) 7091 2700 Fax: (020) 7091 2800
Email: michellem@fishermeredith.co.uk
Website: www.fishermeredith.co.uk

firm profile

The firm was founded almost 30 years ago and has grown steadily, particulary in the last few years. With over 105 staff including 67 lawyers, the firm's strength lies in its national reputation for high quality litigation and dispute resolution. Although a good proportion of work is publicly funded, the firm is increasingly acting for organistions, institutions, government bodies and agencies, charities, foreign embassies, local authorities and small to medium size businesses as well as fee paying private individuals.

The firm has had the 'Investors in People' kitemark since 2000 and the Law Society Practice Management kitemark since 2003. The firm was runner up in the Law Society Gazette's centenary awards for 'Excellence in Practice Standards' and has contracts with the Legal Services Commission in 11 areas of law.

main areas of work

Family, children, fraud, crime, police & prison law, public services law, immigration, residential & commercial conveyancing, housing law, employment law, public law, professional negligence and civil litigation. See the firm's website for details.

trainee profile

The firm seeks candidates prepared to undertake and with an interest in family and crime. The firm looks for academic excellence in all its trainees. It seeks a mature outlook, well rounded and interesting individuals, excellent communication skills and the ability to 'think outside the box'. Fisher Meredith wants team players who will be committed to the firm.

training environment

Each two year training contract is split into four seats. These seats are not set in stone and may change according to the business needs of the firm although there will always be seats in family and crime.

During your training contract, you will be sharing the caseload of your principal. This is not a 'sink or swim' environment, as the firm wishes to turn out credible, knowledgeable and skilled individuals after their training. There are a number of internal training events, and quarterly trainees' meetings attended by the Managing Partner and Business Manager where trainee specific issues can be raised. The firm has a track record of keeping on a high proportion of its trainees, offering the chance to work with leading lawyers in a well-managed, congenial atmosphere.

Partners	9
Assistant Solicitors	40
Total Trainees	7

contact
Michelle Matthias, Human Resources Administrator
michellem@fishermeredith.co.uk

method of application
Trainee Solicitor application form on firm website

selection procedure
Psychometric assessments, written assessment and competitive interviews

closing date for 2006
End of April 2005

application
Training contracts p.a.
Variable

post-qualification
Salary
Competitive

Foot Anstey Sargent

21 Derry's Cross, Plymouth PL1 2SW
Tel: (01752) 675000 Fax: (01752) 675500
4-6 Barnfield Crescent, Exeter EX1 1RF
Tel: (01392) 411221 Fax: (01392) 685220
Email: training@foot-ansteys.co.uk
Website: foot-ansteys.co.uk

firm profile

Foot Anstey Sargent is one of the leading full-service law firms in the South West and has a strong reputation and prominence in the region. With a growing national and international client base the firm is recognised for its expertise in many sectors.

main areas of work

Commercial property, property litigation, commercial litigation, company and commercial, banking, employment, insolvency, clinical negligence, criminal advocates, family and childcare and private client. Niche areas include media, marine, charities, e-commerce and immigration.

trainee profile

The firm welcomes applicants from all law and non-law graduates who have a strong academic background, established communication skills and who are committed to achieving excellent standards of customer service. A strong team ethos is paramount to the firm. Trainees can expect to be welcomed into a friendly and supportive environment where they will find the quality and variety of work both challenging and rewarding.

training environment

The wide range of legal services provided offers trainees opportunities in many areas of law, sitting in either the Exeter or Plymouth offices. Trainees undertake four seats of six months and, excepting the first, trainees are normally able to select their seat. All trainees attend an induction course. Individual monthly meetings are held with supervisors and a quarterly group meeting with the training principal. Appraisals are conducted halfway through each seat. New trainees are given a second year buddy to help them find their feet. Regular communication between the trainees and supervisors ensures an open and friendly atmosphere. The PSC is taught externally. The firm holds an Investors in People accreditation and has an excellent training and development programme.

benefits

Contributory pension, 25 days holiday.

vacation placements

The deadline for the summer placement scheme is 31 March 2005.

sponsorship & awards

£8,000 grant towards LPC and living expenses.

Partners	26
Assistant Solicitors	47
Total Trainees	15

contact
Richard Sutton
(01752) 675151

method of application
CV and covering letter to Richard Sutton at the Plymouth office address. Alternatively email it to: training@foot-ansteys.co.uk or apply online at www.foot-ansteys.co.uk

selection procedure
Assessment day

application
Training contracts p.a. **8**
Required degree grade
2:1 (preferred)

closing date for 2007
24 August 2005

training
Salary
1st year (2004) **£16,750**
2nd year (2004) **£19,000**
Holiday entitlement **25 days**

post-qualification
Salary (2004) **£28,500**
% of trainees offered job on qualification (2002) **100%**
% of assistant solicitors who joined as trainees
(as at 30/04/04) **25%**
% of partners who joined as trainees (as at 30/04/04) **26%**

A-Z SOLICITORS

Forbes

73 Northgate, Blackburn BB2 1AA
Tel: (01254) 580000 Fax: (01254) 222216
Email: graduate.recruitment@forbessolicitors.co.uk

firm profile

Forbes is one of the largest and most respected practices in the north with 27 partners and over 350 members of staff based in eight offices across the north of England. The firm has a broad based practice dealing with both commercial and private client work and can therefore provide a varied and exciting training contract. The firm is however especially noted for excellence in its company/commercial; civil litigation; defendant insurer; crime; family and employment departments. It has a number of Higher Court Advocates and the firm holds many Legal Service Commission Franchises. Underlying the practice is a strong commitment to quality, training and career development – a commitment underlined by the fact that Forbes was one of the first firms to be recognised as an Investor in People and its ISO 9001 accreditation. For applicants looking for a 'city' practice without the associated hassles of working in a city then Forbes could be it. The firm can offer the best of both worlds - a large firm with extensive resources and support combined with a commitment to quality, people and the personal touch.

main areas of work

Company/commercial, civil litigation, defendant insurer, crime, family and employment services.

trainee profile

Forbes looks for high-calibre recruits with strong Northwest connections, good academic records, who are also keen team players. Candidates should have a total commitment to client service and enjoy working in a progressive environment.

training environment

A tailored training programme involves six months in four of the following: crime, civil litigation, defendant insurer in Leeds or Blackburn, matrimonial, and non-contentious/company commercial.

Partners	27
Assistant Solicitors	50
Total Trainees	15+

contact
Graduate Recruitment Manager

method of application
Handwritten letter and CV

selection procedure
Interview with partners

closing date for 2007
31 July 2005

application
Training contracts p.a. 4
Applications p.a. 350 plus
% interviewed p.a. Varies
Required degree grade 2:1

training
Salary
1st year At least Law Society minimum
2nd year (2003) £17,200
Holiday entitlement
20 days pa

post-qualification
Salary
Highly competitive
% of trainees offered job on qualification (2004) 100%

Ford & Warren

Westgate Point, Westgate, Leeds, LS1 2AX
Tel: (0113) 243 6601 Fax: (0113) 242 0905
Email: clientmail@forwarn.com
Website: www.forwarn.com

firm profile

Ford & Warren is an independent, single office commercial law firm based in Leeds. Over the last 10 years the firm has sustained a rapid and generic growth without mergers or acquisitions so that it now occupies the whole of the prestigious Westgate Point office block in the heart of the commercial centre of Leeds. The firm has 22 partners, 88 solicitors and paralegals and a total staff of over 200. Ford & Warren has the following departments: Employment; Road and Rail; Transportation; Corporate; Commercial Litigation; Commercial Property; Insurance and PI; Tax and Inheritance; Matrimonial. The firm has a significant presence in the public sector particularly in health and education. The firm has areas of high specialisation where its lawyers have a national reputation and its client base includes the largest limited companies and PLCs. These areas include transportation and the licensed and leisure industries.

main areas of work

Employment and industrial relations; road and rail transportation; corporate; insurance and personal injury; commercial property/real estate; public sector; tax and inheritance; matrimonial. The Dispute Resolution/Commercial Litigation Department has five sections: commercial dispute resolution, property litigation, finance litigation, insolvency and debt recovery.

trainee profile

The firm is looking for hard working, self-reliant and enthusiastic individuals who will make a contribution to the firm from the outset. Applicants must have a strong academic background, a genuine enthusiasm for the law and the social abilities required to work effectively with colleagues and clients. The majority of lawyers practising at the firm joined as trainees.

training environment

The firm offers seats in employment, commercial litigtion, corporate, insurance and personal injury, commercial property and private client. Usually, trainees will undertake four seats of six months, although split seats may sometimes be available. The final six months takes place in the department into which the trainee wishes to qualify. The firm has a comprehensive in-house training programme for all lawyers and the PSC is also provided internally.

selection procedure

First interviews and exercise held with Practice Manager and a Partner in September and early October. Successful candidates are invited to a second interview with the Managing Partner, including a further exercise and presentation.

Partners	22
Assistant Solicitors	88
Total Trainees	12

contact
Caroline Verriez

method of application
Handwritten letter and CV or email

selection procedure
Interviews and exercise

closing date for 2007
31 August 2005

application
Training contracts p.a. **6**
Applications p.a. **700**
Required degree grade **2:1**

A-Z SOLICITORS

Forsters

67 Grosvenor Street, London W1K 3JN
Tel: (020) 7863 8333 Fax: (020) 7863 8444
Email: ajfairchild@forsters.co.uk
Website: www.forsters.co.uk

Partners	23
Assistant Solicitors	45
Total Trainees	8

contact
Alison Fairchild

method of application
Application form

selection procedure
First interview with HR
Manager & Graduate
Recruitment Partner; second
interview with 2 partners

training
Salary
1st year (2004) £25,000
2nd year (2004) £27,000
Holiday entitlement 22 days

post-qualification
Salary (2004) £42,500
% of trainees offered job
on qualification (2004) 100%

firm profile

Forsters opened for business in 1998 with 11 of the 23 founding partners previously being partners of Frere Chomley Bischoff. It is a progressive law firm with a strong reputation for its property and private client work as well as thriving commercial and litigation practices. The working atmosphere of the firm is friendly and informal, yet highly professional. A social committee organises a range of activities from quiz nights to sporting events as Forsters actively encourages all its staff to have a life outside of work!

main areas of work

The firm has a strong reputation for all aspects of commercial and residential property work. The groups handle investment funding; development; planning; construction; landlord and tenant; property taxation and residential investment and development. Forsters is also recognised as one of the leading proponents of private client work in London with a client base comprising a broad range of individuals and trusts in the UK and elsewhere. The firm's commercial practice specialises in acquisitions and financing for technology, communication and media companies whilst its litigation group conducts commercial litigation and arbitration and advises on a broad spectrum of matters.

trainee profile

Successful candidates will have a strong academic background and either have attained or be expected to achieve a good second class degree. The firm considers that factors alongside academic achievements are also important. The firm is looking for individuals who give a real indication of being interested in a career in law and who the firm feels would readily accept and work well in its team environment.

training environment

The first year of training is split into three seats of four months in three of the following departments: commercial property, private client, company commercial or litigation. In the second year the four month pattern still applies, but the firm discusses with you whether you have developed an area of particular interest and tries to accommodate this. The training is very 'hands on' as you share an office with a partner or assistant who will give you real responsibility alongside supervision. At the end of each seat your progress and performance will be reviewed by way of an appraisal with a partner from the relevant department.

sponsorship & benefits

22 days holiday p.a., season ticket loan, permanent health insurance, life insurance, subsidised gym membership. No sponsorship for CPE or LPC courses is currently provided.

Freeth Cartwright LLP

Cumberland Court, 80 Mount Street, Nottingham NG1 6HH
Tel: (0115) 901 5504 Fax: (0115) 859 9603
Email: carole.wigley@freethcartwright.co.uk
Website: www.freethcartwright.co.uk

firm profile
Tracing its origins back to 1805, Freeth Cartwright LLP became Nottingham's largest firm in 1994 with successful offices now established in Derby and Leicester. Whilst Freeth Cartwright LLP is a heavyweight commercial firm, serving a wide variety of corporate and institutional clients, there is also a commitment to a range of legal services, which includes a substantial private client element. This enables it to give a breadth of experience in training which is not always available in firms of a similar size.

main areas of work
Property and construction, commercial services, private client and personal litigation.

trainee profile
Freeth Cartwright LLP looks for people to bring their own perspective and individuality to the firm. The firm needs people who can cope with the intellectual demands of life as a lawyer and who possess the wider personal skills which are needed in its diverse practice.

training environment
Freeth Cartwright LLP is committed to providing comprehensive training for all its staff. The firm's training programme is based on in-house training covering technical matters and personal skills, supplemented with external courses where appropriate. The firm endeavours to give the best possible experience during the training period, as it believes that informal training on-the-job is the most effective means of encouraging the skills required in a qualified solicitor. One of the firm's senior partners takes responsibility for all its trainees and their personal development, overseeing their progress through the firm and discussing performance based on feedback. Normally, the training contract will consist of four six month seats in different departments, most of which are available in the firm's Nottingham offices, although it is possible for trainees to spend at least one seat in another location.

Members	59
Assistant Solicitors	67
Total Trainees	14

contact
Carole Wigley

method of application
Online application form

selection procedure
Interview & selection day

closing date for 2007
31 July 2005

training
Starting salary (2004)
£17,000

offices
Nottingham, Leicester, Derby

Freeth
Cartwright
LLP

Freshfields Bruckhaus Deringer

65 Fleet Street, London EC4Y 1HS
Tel: (020) 7936 4000 Fax: (020) 7832 7001
Email: graduates@freshfields.com
Website: www.freshfields.com/graduates

firm profile
Freshfields Bruckhaus Deringer is a leading international firm with a network of 28 offices in 18 countries. The firm provides first-rate legal services to corporations, financial institutions and governments around the world.

main areas of work
Corporate; mergers and acquisitions; banking; dispute resolution; joint ventures; employment, pensions and benefits; asset finance; real estate; tax; capital markets; intellectual property and information technology; project finance; private finance initiative; US securities; antitrust, competition and trade; communications and media; construction and engineering; energy; environment; financial services; restructuring and insolvency; insurance; international tax; investment funds.

trainee profile
Excellent academic qualifications, a broad range of skills and a good record of achievement in other areas. Language skills are also an advantage.

training environment
The firm's trainees receive a thorough professional training in a very broad range of practice areas, an excellent personal development programme and the chance to work in one of the firm's international offices or on secondment with a client in the UK or abroad. It provides the professional, technical and pastoral support necessary to ensure that you enjoy and make the most of the opportunities on offer.

benefits
Life assurance; permanent health insurance; group personal pension; interest-free loan; interest-free loan for a season travel ticket; free membership of the firm's private medical insurance scheme; subsidised staff restaurant; gym.

vacation placements
Places for 2005: 100; Duration: 2 weeks; Remuneration: £550 (net); Closing Date: 31 January 2005 but apply as early as possible after 1 December 2004 as there may not be places left by the deadline.

sponsorship & awards
GDL and LPC fees paid and £5,000 maintenance p.a. for those studying in London and Oxford and £4,500 p.a. for those studying elsewhere.

Partners 522
Assistant Solicitors 1,620
Total Trainees 212
(London based)

contact
Maia Riley

method of application
Application form

selection procedure
2 interviews and written test

closing date for 2007
31 July 2005

application
Training contracts p.a. **100**
Applications p.a. **c.2,500**
% interviewed p.a. **c.12%**
Required degree grade **2:1**

training
Salary
1st year £29,000
2nd year £33,000
Holiday entitlement **25 days**
% of trainees with a
non-law degree p.a. **c.45%**
No. of seats available
abroad p.a. **c.70**

post-qualification
Salary **£50,000**
% of trainees offered job
on qualification **c.95%**

overseas offices
Amsterdam, Bangkok, Barcelona, Beijing, Berlin, Bratislava, Brussels, Budapest, Cologne, Düsseldorf, Frankfurt, Hamburg, Hanoi, Ho Chi Minh City, Hong Kong, Madrid, Milan, Moscow, Munich, New York, Paris, Rome, Shanghai, Singapore, Tokyo, Vienna, Washington DC

Gateley Wareing

One Eleven, Edmund Street, Birmingham B3 2HJ
Tel: (0121) 234 0121 Fax: (0121) 234 0079
Email: wwarburton@gateleywareing.com
Website: www.gateleywareing.comwwarburton@gateleywareing.com

firm profile

A 28-partner, Midlands-based practice, with an excellent reputation for general commercial work and particular expertise in corporate, plc, commercial, employment, property, construction, insolvency, commercial dispute resolution, banking and tax. The firm is expanding (206 staff) and offers a highly practical, commercial and fast-paced environment. The firm prides itself on its entrepreneurial style and its work hard, live life to the full reputation. The firm focuses on owner-led businesses, but also counts some household names and internationals amongst its clients.

trainee profile

Applications are invited from second year law students and final year non-law students and graduates. Applicants should have (or be heading for) a minimum 2.1 degree, and should have at least three Bs (or equivalent) at A-level. Individuals should be hardworking team players capable of using initiative and demonstrating commercial awareness.

training environment

Four six month seats with ongoing supervision and appraisals every three months. PSC taken internally. In-house courses on skills such as time management, negotiation, IT, drafting, business skills, marketing, presenting and writing in plain English.

benefits

Current trainee offered as a 'buddy' - a point of contact within the firm, library available, invitation to summer party prior to joining.

vacation placements

12 two-week placements over the summer. Deadline for vacation placement scheme is 11 February 2005 and for training contracts is 31 July 2005. Apply online at www.gateleywareing.com.

sponsorship & awards

CPE/LPC and a LPC maintenance grant of £4,000.

Partners	28
Vacancies	6
Total Trainees	12
Total Staff	206

contact
Mrs Wendy Warburton
HR Manager

closing date for 2007
Vacation placements:
11 February 2005
Training contracts:
31 July 2005

training
Salary
1st year £20,000 (as of September 04)
2nd year £22,000 (as of September 04)

post-qualification
Salary £32,000 (as of September 04)

offices
Birmingham, Leicester, Nottingham

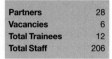

A-Z SOLICITORS

Government Legal Service

Queen Ann's Chambers, 28 Broadway, London SW1H 9JS
Tel: (020) 7649 6023
Email: glstrainees.tmp.com
Website: www.gls.gov.uk

firm profile

The Government Legal Service (GLS) joins together some 1900 lawyers and trainees working in around 40 government departments and bodies. A GLS lawyer's work is quite unique, and reflects the huge range of Government activities. GLS lawyers work in the public interest and have the rare opportunity to make a positive contribution to the well-being of the country. They also have the opportunity to move around government departments as they progress, developing skills and acquiring knowledge of new areas of the law.

trainee profile

As well as a good academic background, the GLS seeks analytical minds that can get to the root of a problem, along with good communications skills. Because GLS lawyers work as part of a team, people skills are important, as is the potential to become a good manager when you progress and take on further responsibility.

training environment

The GLS provides a training environment for trainees and pupils. Generally, trainee solicitors work in four different areas of practice over a two-year period in the Government department to which they are assigned. Pupil barristers divide their time between their department and chambers. The GLS prides itself on involving trainees and pupils in the full range of casework conducted by their department. This frequently includes high profile matters and will be under the supervision of senior colleagues.

benefits

These include professional development opportunities, excellent pension scheme, civilised working hours, generous holiday entitlement and subsidised canteen facilities.

vacation placements

Summer 2005 vacation placement scheme; approx 70 places. Duration: 2-3 weeks. Closing date 31 March 2005. Remuneration: £200-£250 pw.

sponsorship & awards

LPC and BVC fees as well as other compulsory professional skills course fees. Funding may be available for the CPE. The GLS provides a grant of around £5-7,000 for the vocational year.

Total Trainees around 50

contact
glstrainees@tmp.com or visit www.gls.gov.uk

method of application
Online application form

selection procedure
Day at assessment centre to undertake a group discussion exercise, a written question and an interview

closing date for 2007
1 August 2005

application
Training contracts p.a. **30**
Applications p.a. **1,200+**
% interviewed p.a. **10%**
Required degree grade
Min 2.2 (some Government departments require a 2.1)

training
Salary
1st year (2004) £18,500 - 22,000
2nd year (2004) £20,200- 25,000
Holiday entitlement 25 days on entry

post-qualification
Salary (2004) £27,000- £38,000
% of trainees accepting job on qualification (2004) **98%**

Halliwells

St. James's Court, Brown St, Manchester M2 2JF
Tel: (0870) 365 9492 Fax: (0870) 365 9493
Email: carrie.taylor@halliwells.com

firm profile
Halliwells is one of the largest independent commercial law firms in the North West. Over the last few years the firm has increased substantially in both size and turnover and now has in excess of 180 fee-earners and 80 partners. This development leads to a continuing requirement for solicitors and has given rise to more internal promotions to partnerships.

main areas of work
Corporate/banking 24%; commercial property 18%; commercial litigation 22%; insurance litigation 16%; intellectual property 4.8%; trust and estates 4.5%; employment 3.7%; financial institutions 6.9%.

trainee profile
Candidates need to show a good academic ability but do not necessarily need to have studied law at university. They should demonstrate an ability to fit into a hardworking team. In particular, Halliwells is looking for candidates who will continue to develop with the firm after their initial training.

training environment
Each trainee will have five seats in at least three separate departments. These will usually include commercial litigation, corporate and commercial property. Individual requests from trainees for experience in a particular department will be accomodated where possible. The trainee will work within one of the department's teams and be encouraged to assist other team members to help broaden their experience. Specific training appropriate to each department will be given and trainees are strongly encouraged to attend the firm's regular in-house seminars on legal and related topics. A supervisor will be assigned to each trainee to support their development throughout the seat. Each trainee will be assessed both mid-seat and end of seat.

benefits
A generous pension scheme plus a subsidised gym membership is available.

vacation placements
45 places are available for Summer 2005. There are four schemes each lasting for two weeks. Schemes commence first week in July. Renumeration £133 per week. Closing date for applications is 31 March 2005.

sponsorship & awards
The firm pays PgDL fees and LPC fees plus a £4,500 maintenance grant for each course.

Partners	80
Assistant Solicitors	189
Total Trainees	27

contact
Carrie Taylor
(Graduate Recruitment Assistant)
carrie.taylor@halliwells.com

method of application
Application form only

selection procedure
Group exercise, presentation and interview

closing date for 2007
31 July 2005

application
Training contracts p.a. **10 (Manchester); 3 (London)**
Applications p.a. **1,000**
% interviewed p.a. **5%**
Required degree grade **2:1**

training
Salary
1st year (2004) **£21,500**
2nd year (2004) **£22,500**

post-qualification
Salary (2003) **£32,000**
% of trainees offered job on qualification (2003) **80%**

A-Z SOLICITORS

Hammonds

Rutland House, 148 Edmund Street, Birmingham B3 2JR
7 Devonshire Square, Cutlers Gardens, London EC2M 4YH
2 Park Lane, Leeds LS3 1ES
Trinity Court, 16 Dalton Street, Manchester M6O 8HS
Tel: (0870) 839 0000 Fax: (0870) 839 3666
Website: www.hammonds.com

firm profile

Hammonds is one of Europe's largest corporate law firms and a member of the Global 100. In the UK alone, the firm advises over 200 London Stock Exchange quoted companies and 40 FTSE 100 companies. The firm has offices in London, Birmingham, Leeds, Manchester, Brussels, Paris, Berlin, Munich, Rome, Milan, Madrid, Turin and Hong Kong. The firm has 1,500 staff, including 212 partners, 518 solicitors and 82 trainees. It is regarded as innovative, opportunistic and highly successful in the markets in which it operates.

main areas of work

Corporate; commercial dispute resolution; construction, engineering and projects; employment; EU and competition; finance law (including banking); intellectual property and commercial; media/IT; pensions; property; sports law; tax.

trainee profile

Hammonds seeks applications from all disciplines for both vacation work and training contracts. It looks for three characteristics: strong academic performance, work experience in the legal sector and significant achievement in non-academic pursuits.

training environment

Around 40 trainee solicitors are recruited each year who each carry out six four-month seats during their training contract. There are both fixed location and rotational training contracts available. Trainees on a rotational contract are eligible for subsidised accommodation and experience three UK locations during the contract. Trainees can choose their seats as they progress through the training contract.

benefits

Subsidised accommodation for rotational trainees. Flexible benefits scheme which allows trainees to choose their own benefits from a range of options.

vacation placements

Places for 2005: 64; Duration: 2 weeks; Remuneration: £230 p.w. (London), £180 p.w. (Leeds, Manchester, Birmingham); Closing Date: 31 January 2005.

sponsorship & awards

PgDL and LPC fees paid and maintenance grant of £4,500 p.a.

Partners	212
Assistant Solicitors	518
Total Trainees	86

contact
The Graduate Recruitment Team

method of application
Online application form

selection procedure
Assessment and interview

closing date for 2007
31 July 2005

application
Training contracts p.a. **40**
Applications p.a. **1,500**
% interviewed p.a. **10%**
Required degree grade **2:1**

training
Salary
1st year (2004) **£20,500+**
subsidised accommodation
for rotational contract
2nd year (2004) **£23,000+**
subsidised accommodation
for rotational contract
Holiday entitlement **23 days**
% of trainees with a non-law
degree p.a. **25%**
No. of seats available
abroad p.a. **15**

post-qualification
Salary (2004)
London **£46,000**
Other **£33,000-£34,000**
% of trainees accepting job
on qualification (2004) **85%**

overseas offices
Brussels, Paris, Berlin,
Munich, Rome, Milan,
Turin, Hong Kong, Madrid

Harbottle & Lewis LLP

Hanover House, 14 Hanover Square, London W1S 1HP
Tel: (020) 7667 5000 Fax: (020) 7667 5100
Email: kathy.beilby@harbottle.com
Website: www.harbottle.com

firm profile
Harbottle & Lewis LLP is recognised for the unique breadth of its practice in the entertainment, media, travel (including aviation) and leisure industries. It undertakes significant corporate commercial and contentious work for clients within these industries including newer industries such as digital mixed media.

main areas of work
Music, film and television production, theatre, broadcasting, computer games and publishing, sport, sponsorship and advertising, aviation, property investment and leisure.

trainee profile
Trainees will have demonstrated the high academic abilities, commercial awareness, and initiative necessary to become part of a team advising clients in dynamic and demanding industries.

training environment
The two year training contract is divided into four six-month seats where trainees will be given experience in a variety of legal skills including company commercial, litigation, intellectual property and real property, working within teams focused on the firm's core industries. The firm has a policy of accepting a small number of trainees to ensure they are given relevant and challenging work and are exposed to and have responsibility for a full range of legal tasks. The firm has its own lecture and seminars programme in both legal topics and industry know-how. An open door policy and a pragmatic entrepreneurial approach to legal practice provides a stimulating working environment.

benefits
Lunch provided; season ticket loans.

sponsorship & awards
LPC fees paid and interest-free loans towards maintenance.

Partners	22
Assistant Solicitors	40
Total Trainees	8

contact
Kathy Beilby

method of application
CV & letter

selection procedure
Interview

closing date for 2007
31 July 2005

application
Training contracts p.a. 4
Applications p.a. 800
% interviewed p.a. 5%
Required degree grade 2:1

training
Salary
1st year £25,000 (2004)
2nd year £26,000 (2004)
Holiday entitlement
in the first year 23 days
in the second year 26 days
% of trainees with
a non-law degree p.a. 40%

post-qualification
Salary (2004) £43,000

A-Z SOLICITORS

Henmans

116 St. Aldates, Oxford OX1 1HA
Tel: (01865) 722181 Fax: (01865) 792376
Email: welcome@henmans.co.uk
Website: www.henmans.co.uk

firm profile

Henmans is a well-established Oxfordshire-based practice with a strong national reputation, serving both corporate and private clients. Henmans' philosophy is to be extremely client focused to deliver exceptional levels of service. The firm achieves this through an emphasis on teamwork to ensure clients always have access to a specific partner with specialist support, and through an ongoing programme of recruitment and training to guarantee clients optimum advice and guidance. Henmans has invested heavily in IT and has implemented a case management system to enhance services and client care. Henmans' policy of bespoke services and controlled costs ensure that both corporate and private clients benefit from City level litigation standards at competitive regional prices. The firm is now accredited as an Investor in People.

main areas of work

The firm's core service of litigation is nationally recognised. The personal injury and clinical negligence litigation is strong, as is professional negligence work. Professional negligence and commercial litigation: 29%; personal injury: 26%; property: 17%; private client (including family)/charities/trusts: 18%; corporate/employment: 10%.

trainee profile

Commercial awareness, sound academic accomplishment, intellectual capability, IT literate, able to work as part of a team, good communication skills.

training environment

Trainees are introduced to the firm with a detailed induction and overview of the client base. Experience is likely to be within the PI. Property, family, professional negligence/commercial litigation and private client departments. The firm values commitment and enthusiasm both professionally and socially as an integral part of its culture. The firm provides an ongoing programme of in-house education and regular appraisals within its supportive friendly environment.

Partners	23
Other Solicitors &	
Fee-earners	38
Total Trainees	6

contact
Viv J Matthews (Mrs)
MA CH FCIPD
Human Resources Manager

method of application
Application form on website

selection procedure
Interview with HR Manager
& partners

closing date for 2007
31 July 2005

application
Training contracts p.a. 3
Applications p.a. 450

training
Salary
1st year (2004) £17,000
2nd year (2004) £18,650
Holiday entitlement 20 days
in 1st year, 21 in 2nd year.
BUPA and pension also
provided.
% of trainees with a
non-law degree p.a. 30%

post-qualification
Salary (2004) £29,000
% of assistants who joined
as trainees 28%
% of partners who joined
as trainees 15%

Herbert Smith

Exchange House, Primrose Street, London EC2A 2HS
Tel: (020) 7374 8000 Fax: (020) 7374 0888
Email: graduate.recruitment@herbertsmith.com
Website: www.herbertsmith.com

firm profile

Herbert Smith is an international law firm with over 1,000 lawyers and a network of offices in Europe and Asia. In addition, it works closely with two premier European firms with whom it has an alliance - the German firm Gleiss Lutz and the Dutch and Belgian firm Stibbe.

The firm has a diverse, blue-chip client base including FTSE 100 and Fortune 500 companies, major investment banks and governments. What makes Herbert Smith stand out is its culture: a collegiate working environment, a pre-eminent market reputation in key practices and industry sectors and an ambition to be consistently recognised as one of the world's leading law firms.

main areas of work

Corporate (including international mergers and acquisitions); finance and banking (including capital markets); international litigation and arbitration; energy; projects and project finance; EU and competition; real estate; tax; employment and trusts; construction and engineering; insurance; investment funds; IP and IT; US securities.

trainee profile

Trainees need a strong academic record, common sense, self-confidence and intelligence to make their own way in a large firm. They are typically high-achieving and creative thinking – language skills are an advantage.

training environment

Structured training and supervision are designed to allow experience of a unique range of contentious and non-contentious work. You will be encouraged to take on responsibilities as soon as you join the firm. You will work within partner-led teams and have your own role. Individual strengths will be monitored, developed and utilised. On-the-job training will be divided into four six-month seats; one seat will be in the corporate division, one in the litigation division and you will have a choice of specialists seats such as IP/IT or EU and competition, as well as an opportunity to go on secondment to a client or an overseas office. Great emphasis is placed on professional and personal development and the firm runs its own legal development and mentoring programme.

sponsorship & benefits

CPE/GDL and LPC fees are paid plus a £5,000 maintenance grant p.a. Benefits include profit share, permanent health insurance, private medical insurance, season ticket loan, life assurance, subsidised gym membership, group personal accident insurance and matched contributory pension scheme.

vacation placements

Places for 2004/05: 115. Christmas 2004 (non-law students only), Easter and Summer 2005 (law and non-law students). Closing Dates: 12 November 2004 for Christmas scheme; 31 January 2005 for Easter and Summer schemes. Opportunities in some of the firm's European offices.

Partners	204*
Fee-earners	577*
Total Trainees	195*
*denotes worldwide figures	

contact
Kerry Jarred, Graduate Recruitment Manager

method of application
Online application form

selection procedure
Case study and interview

closing date for Sept 2007/Mar 2008
31 July 2005

application
Training contracts p.a. up to 100
Applications p.a. 2,027
% interviewed p.a. 21%
Required degree grade 2:1

training
Salary
1st year £28,500
2nd year £32,000
Holiday entitlement
25 days, rising to 27 on qualification
ratio of law to non-law graduates is broadly equal

post-qualification
Salary (2004) £50,000
% of trainees offered job on qualification (Mar & Sept 2004) 84% (based on no. of jobs offered)

overseas offices
Bangkok, Beijing, Brussels, Hong Kong, Moscow, Paris, Shanghai, Singapore, Tokyo

associated offices
Amsterdam, Berlin, Frankfurt, Jakarta, Munich, New York, Prague, Stuttgart, Warsaw

Hewitsons

42 Newmarket Road, Cambridge CB5 8EP
Tel: (01604) 233233 Fax: (01223) 316511
Email: mail@hewitsons.com (for all offices)
Website: www.hewitsons.com (for all offices)

firm profile

Established in 1865, the firm handles mostly company and commercial work, but has a growing body of public sector clients. The firm has three offices: Cambridge, Northampton and Saffron Walden.

main areas of work

Three sections: corporate technology, property and private client.

trainee profile

The firm is interested in applications from candidates who have achieved a high degree of success in academic studies and who are bright, personable and able to take the initiative.

training environment

The firm offers four six-month seats.

benefits

The PSC is provided during the first year of the training contract. This is coupled with an extensive programme of Trainee Solicitor Seminars provided by specialist in-house lawyers.

vacation placements

Places for 2005: A few placements are available, application is by way of letter and CV to Caroline Lewis; Duration: 1 week.

sponsorship & awards

Funding for the CPE and/or LPC is not provided.

Partners	51
Assistant Solicitors	47
Total Trainees	13

contact
Caroline Lewis
7 Spencer Parade
Northampton NN1 5AB

method of application
Firm's application form

selection procedure
Interview

closing date for 2007
End of August 2005

application
Training contracts p.a. **8**
Applications p.a. **1,400**
% interviewed p.a. **10%**
Required degree grade
2:1 min

training
Salary
1st year (2003) **£17,500**
2nd year (2003) **£18,500**
Holiday entitlement **22 days**
% of trainees with a
non-law degree p.a. **50%**

post-qualification
Salary (2003) **£31,500**
% of trainees offered job
on qualification (2003) **70%**
% of assistants (as at
1/9/03) who joined as
trainees **54%**
% of partners (as at 1/9/03)
who joined as trainees **32%**

Hill Dickinson

Pearl Assurance House, 2 Derby Square, Liverpool L2 9XL
Tel: (0151) 236 5400 Fax: (0151) 236 2175
Email: recruitment@hilldickinson.com
Website: www.hilldickinson.com

firm profile
Hill Dickinson is a leading UK law firm offering a comprehensive range of services from offices in Liverpool, Manchester, London and Chester. It is a market leader for commercial property and related disciplines, and a major force in NHS clinical negligence/health-related litigation. It has one of the leading specialist shipping and transport practices in the UK, a thriving corporate and commercial practice and a national profile for litigation, especially in the insurance sector where its reputation is for forward thinking and innovation.

main areas of work
With a wealth of specialists, the firm advises a range of clients including corporates, the private sector, individuals and the public sector and is structured into four specialist groups: commercial, insurance and litigation, health, and marine and transit. Specialisms include sport and media, corporate law, employment, pensions, PFI, intellectual property and technology, private client, professional indemnity, fraud and policy and regulation, clinical negligence, mental health, shipping, goods in transit and yachting.

trainee profile
Commercial awareness and academic ability are the key factors, together with a desire to succeed. Trainees are viewed as the partners of the future and the firm is looking for personable individuals with whom it wants to work.

training environment
Trainees spend six months in each of the four main areas of the practice and will be given the chance to specialise in specific areas. You will be given the opportunity to learn and develop communication and presentation skills, legal research, drafting, interviewing and advising, negotiations and advocacy. Trainees are encouraged to accept responsibility and are expected to act with initiative. The practice has an active social committee and a larger than usual selection of competitive sporting teams.

vacation placements
One week structured scheme with places available for 2005. Apply by CV and covering letter to Philip Bradbury (Partner) by 30 April 2005.

sponsorship & awards
LPC funding provided. Further funding and maintenance awards are under review.

Partners	115
Assistant Solicitors	114
Total Trainees	23

contact
Peter Barlow (North West)
Jamie Monck-Mason
(London)

method of application
CV with supporting letter
by email

selection procedure
Assessment day

closing date for 2007
31 July 2005

training
Salary
1st year (2004) £18,000
2nd year (2004) £19,500
London weighting £3K
(where applicable)
Salaries are currently
under review
Holiday entitlement
4 weeks

post-qualification
% of trainees offered job
on qualification (2002) **80%**

offices
Liverpool, Manchester,
London, Chester

A-Z SOLICITORS

567

Hodge Jones & Allen

31-39 Camden Road, London, NW1 9LR
Tel: (020) 7482 1974 Fax: (020) 7267 3476
Email: hja@hodgejonesallen.co.uk
Website: www.hodgejonesallen.co.uk

firm profile

Hodge Jones & Allen was founded in Camden Town in 1977. It is now one of the largest legal firms in north London, having grown from four to over 160 staff. Although the firm has private and commercial clients, it also has contracts with the Legal Services Commission in many areas of practice and is known as one of the leading, predominantly publicly funded law practices in the Country. The firm is led by one of its founding partners, Patrick Allen. It has been involved in a number of high profile cases including, the King's Cross fire, the Marchioness disaster, Broadwater Farm riots, Real IRA BBC-bombing trial, the second inquest into the New Cross fire, MMR vaccine litigation and Gulf War Syndrome. The firm is located in a single modern office next to the canal, in a lively and trendy part of Camden Town.

main areas of work

Crime, personal injury, multi party actions, public law, police actions, miscarriage of justice claims, human rights, medical negligence, family, housing, mental health, property, wills and probate, prison law.

trainee profile

Trainees will have an excellent academic record, enthusiasm and a positive approach, good communication skills and a commitment to access to justice for all, regardless of ability to pay.

training environment

Trainees have a full induction on joining HJA covering the work of the firm's main departments, procedural matters and professional conduct. Training consists of four six-month seats and trainees normally share an office with a partner who assists them and formally reviews their progress at least once during each seat. The training is well structured and trainees have the benefit of a mentoring scheme. The firm provides good secretarial and clerking support so trainees can concentrate on legal work rather than administration. The firm has an excellent IT infrastructure and continues to invest heavily in IT to keep pace with innovation.

benefits

Pension scheme, Life Assurance, disability insurance, quarterly drinks, summer outing and Christmas party.

Partners	15
Assistant Solicitors	41
Total Trainees	9

contact
HR Department

method of application
Application form (available online)

selection procedure
Interview with 2 Partners

closing date for 2007
26 August 2006 (apply one year in advance)

application
Training contracts p.a. **3-4**
Applications p.a. **400**
% interviewed p.a. **5%**
Preferred degree grade **2:1 min**

training
Salary: **£20,000**
Holiday entitlement 20 days p.a.

post-qualification
Salary: **£25,750**
% of trainees offered job on qualification: **75%**

Holman Fenwick & Willan

Marlow House, Lloyds Avenue, London EC3N 3AL
Tel: (020) 7488 2300 Fax: (020) 7481 0316
Email: grad.recruitment@hfw.co.uk

firm profile

Holman Fenwick & Willan is an international law firm and one of the world's leading special-ists in maritime transportation, insurance, reinsurance, energy and trade. The firm is a leader in the field of commercial litigation and arbitration and also offers comprehensive commercial advice. Founded in 1883, the firm is one of the largest operating in its chosen fields with a team of over 200 lawyers worldwide, and a reputation for excellence and innovation.

main areas of work

The firm's range of services include marine, admiralty and crisis management, insurance and reinsurance, commercial litigation and arbitration, international trade and commodi-ties, energy, corporate and financial.

trainee profile

Applications are invited from commercially minded undergraduates and graduates of all disciplines with good A levels and who have, or expect to receive, a 2:1 degree. Good for-eign languages or a scientific or maritime background are an advantage.

training environment

During your training period the firm will ensure that you gain valuable experience in a wide range of areas. It also organises formal training supplemented by a programme of in-house seminars and ship visits in addition to the PSC. Your training development as an effective lawyer will be managed by the HR and Training Partner, Ottilie Sefton, who will ensure that your training is both successful and enjoyable.

benefits

Private medical insurance, permanent health and accident insurance, subsidised gym membership, season ticket loan.

vacation placements

Places for 2005: 16; Duration: 2 weeks. Dates: 27 June - 8 July / 18 July - 29 July; Remuneration (2004): £250 p.w.; Closing Date: Applications accepted 1 Jan - 14 Feb 2005.

sponsorship & awards

GDL Funding: Fees paid plus £5,000 maintenance; LPC Funding: Fees paid plus £5,000 maintenance.

Partners	**80+**
Other Solicitors &	
Fee-earners	**120+**
Total Trainees	**16**

contact
Graduate Recruitment Officer

method of application
Online application form

selection procedure
2 interviews with partners & written exercise

closing date for 2007
31 July 2005

application
Training contracts p.a. **8**
Applications p.a. **1,000**
% interviewed p.a. **5%**
Required degree grade **2:1**

training
Salary (Sept 2004)
1st year **£28,000**
2nd year **£30,000**
Holiday entitlement **22 days**
% of trainees with
a non-law degree p.a. **50%**

post-qualification
Salary **£46,000** (Sept 2004)
% of trainees offered job
on qualification
(Sept 2004) **88%**

overseas offices
Hong Kong, Nantes, Paris, Piraeus, Rouen, Shanghai, Singapore

Howes Percival

Oxford House, Cliftonville, Northampton NN1 5PN
Tel: (01604) 230400 Fax: (01604) 620956
Email: katy.pattle@howespercival.com
Website: www.howespercival.com

firm profile

Howes Percival is a 36-partner commercial law firm with offices in Leicester, Milton Keynes, Northampton and Norwich. The firm's working environment is young, progressive and highly professional and its corporate structure means that fee-earners are rewarded on merit and can progress to associate or partner status quickly. The type and high value of the work that the firm does places it in a position whereby it is recognised as being a regional firm by location only. The firm has the expertise, resources, and partner reputation that match a city firm.

main areas of work

The practice is departmentalised and the breakdown of its work is as follows: corporate 30%; commercial property 25%; commercial litigation 20%; insolvency 10%; employment 10%; private client 5%.

trainee profile

The firm is looking for six well-educated, focused, enthusiastic, commercially aware graduates with a minimum 2:1 degree in any discipline. Howes Percival welcomes confident communicators with strong interpersonal skills who share the firm's desire to be the best.

training environment

Trainees complete four six month seats, each one in a different department. Trainees joining the Norwich office will remain at Norwich for the duration of their training contract. Within the East Midlands region, there is the opportunity to gain experience in each of the three East Midlands offices. Trainees report direct to a partner, and after three months and again towards the end of each seat they will be formally assessed by the partner training them. Trainees will be given every assistance by the fee-earners in their department to develop quickly and will be given responsibility as soon as they are ready.

benefits

Contributory pension scheme. Private health insurance. LPC/CPE funding, maintenance grant.

vacation placements

Vacation placements are available in June, July and August. Please contact Katy Pattle for further details.

Partners	36
Solicitors	70
Total Trainees	12

contact
Miss Katy Pattle
HR Assistant

method of application
Online application form

selection procedure
Assessment centres including second interview with training principal and partner

closing date for 2007
31 July 2005

application
Training contracts p.a. 6
Applications p.a. 300
% interviewed p.a. 10%
Required degree grade 2:1

training
Salary
1st year (as at June 2004)
£19,300
2nd year (as at June 2004)
£20,800
Holiday entitlement
23 days p.a.

post-qualification
% of trainees offered job on qualification (2004) 100%
% of assistants (as at 1/9/02) who joined as trainees 42%
% of partners (as at 1/9/01) who joined as trainees 7.5%

Hugh James

Hodge House, 114-116 St. Mary Street, Cardiff CF10 1DY
Tel: (029) 2022 4871 Fax: (029) 2038 8222
Email: training@hughjames.com
Website: www.hughjames.com

firm profile

Hugh James is one of the UK's leading law firms and was recently named 'Large Law Firm of the Year' at the inaugural Welsh Law Awards. Formed in 1960, Hugh James is ranked in the top 100 law firms in the UK. The firm provides a comprehensive range of commercial and private client services throughout Wales and the UK.

main areas of work

The practice is divided up into four divisions: business litigation (26%); business services (32%); claimant litigation (28%); public funded (14%). Specialist teams have been established to service niche areas of the law and the firm has a multidisciplinary and dynamic approach to the provision of legal services.

trainee profile

Hugh James welcomes applications from law and non-law undergraduates with a good class degree. Candidates must possess first class legal knowledge and an ability to apply that with practical skills. In addition, good interpersonal and IT skills are required. The majority of trainees are retained upon qualification and are seen as an integral part of the future of the firm. Hugh James is proud of the fact that the vast majority of its present partners were trained at the firm.

training environment

Trainees generally undertake four seats of not less than six months which may be in any of the firm's offices. Broadly, experience will be gained in all four main work categories. The breadth of work dealt with by the firm enables it to ensure that over-specialisation is avoided.

benefits

Company contribution to stakeholder pension scheme.

vacation placements

Available Summer 2005.

Partners	47
Assistant Solicitors	53
Total Trainees	16

contact
John McManus
HR Director

method of application
Application form available from HR Manager or website

selection procedure
Interview and presentation

closing date for 2007
31 March 2005

application
Training contracts p.a. 10
Applications p.a. 350
% interviewed p.a. 30%
Required degree grade 2:2

training
Salary
Competitive & reviewed annually

other offices
Merthyr Tydfil, Blackwood

Ince & Co

Knollys House, 11 Byward Street, London EC3R 5EN
Tel: (020) 7623 2011 Fax: (020) 7623 3225
Email: claire.kendall@incelaw.com

firm profile

Since its foundation in 1870, Ince & Co has specialised in international commercial law and is best known for its shipping and insurance work.

main areas of work

Shipping and trade, aviation, energy and engineering 52%; insurance & reinsurance 32%; business and finance and commercial disputes 16%.

trainee profile

Hardworking competitive individuals with initiative who relish challenge and responsibility within a team environment. Academic achievements, positions of responsibility, sport and travel are all taken into account.

training environment

Trainees sit with four different partners for six months at a time throughout their training. Under close supervision, they are encouraged from an early stage to meet and visit clients, interview witnesses, liaise with counsel, deal with technical experts and handle opposing lawyers. They will quickly build up a portfolio of cases from a number of partners involved in a cross-section of the firm's practice and will see their cases through from start to finish. They will also attend in-house and external lectures, conferences and seminars on practical and legal topics.

benefits

STL, corporate health cover, PHI, contributory pension scheme.

vacation placements

Places for 2005: 18; Duration: 2 weeks; Remuneration: £250 p.w.; Closing Date: 14 February 2005.

sponsorship & awards

LPC fees, £4,750 grant for study in London, £4,000 grant for study elsewhere. Discretionary sponsorship for CPE.

Partners	68*
Assistant Solicitors	86*
Total Trainees	28*

denotes worldwide figures

contact
Claire Kendall

method of application
Typed/handwritten letter & CV, containing full breakdown of degree results & A-level grades, with contact details of 2 academic referees

selection procedure
Interview with HR professional & interview with 2 partners from Recruitment Committee & a written test

closing date for 2007
31 July 2005

application
Training contracts p.a. 8-10
Applications p.a. **1,500**
% interviewed p.a. **5%**
Required degree grade **2:1**

training
Salary
1st year (2004) £27,000
2nd year (2004) £30,000
Holiday entitlement **22 days**
% of trainees with a non-law degree p.a. **55%**

post-qualification
Salary (2003) £47,000
% of trainees offered job on qualification (2004)
58.3%. All accepted!
% of partners (as at 2002) who joined as trainees
Approx 73%

overseas offices
Hamburg, Hong Kong, Le Havre, Paris, Piraeus, Shanghai, Singapore

Irwin Mitchell

St. Peter's House, Hartshead, Sheffield S1 2EL
Email: enquiries@irwinmitchell.co.uk
Website: imonline.co.uk

firm profile

Irwin Mitchell is a rapidly expanding national practice with 83 partners and over 1,750 employees with offices in Birmingham, Leeds, London, Newcastle and Sheffield. It is particularly well known for commercial law, commercial litigation, insurance law, business crime and claimant personal injury litigation. The firm's strong reputation for dealing with novel and complex areas of law and handling developmental cases such as vibration white finger, CJD and the Matrix-Churchill 'arms to Iraq' affair means that it can offer a broad range of experience within each of its specialist departments, giving trainees a high standard of training.

main areas of work

Corporate services 24%; claimant personal injury 26%; insurance litigation 37%; private client 11%.

trainee profile

The firm is looking for ambitious, well motivated individuals with a real commitment to the law and who can demonstrate a positive approach to a work/life balance. It recruits law and non-law graduates. Foreign languages and IT skills are an asset. Irwin Mitchell believes trainees to be an investment for the future and endeavours to retain trainees upon qualification.

training environment

The two year training contract consists of four seats. The firm's trainees also benefit from a structured induction programme, monthly training events and the Professional Skills Course which is run in-house and financed by the firm. Each trainee has a quarterly review with their supervising partner to focus on performance and development ensuring progress is on track.

vacation placements

Places for 2005: 50; Duration: 1 week; Remuneration: £75 p.w.; Closing Date: 31 January.

sponsorship & awards

Payment of PgDL and LPC fees plus a £3,000 maintenance grant.

Partners	83
Assistant Solicitors	180
Total Trainees	27

contact
Sue Lenkowski

method of application
Firm's application form & covering letter, visit imonline.co.uk between 1 April & 31 July

selection procedure
Assessment centre & interview during July & August. Successful candidates invited to attend second interview

closing date for 2007
31 July 2005

application
Training contracts p.a. 15
Applications p.a. 1,000
% interviewed p.a. 7%

training
Salary
1st year £18,000
2nd year £20,000
(outside London)
reviewed annually
Holiday entitlement
24.5 days
% of trainees with a non-law degree p.a. 25%

post-qualification
% of trainees offered job on qualification 80%
% of assistants who joined as trainees 41%
% of partners (2003) who joined as trainees 22%

Jones Day

21 Tudor Street, London, EC4Y 0DJ
Tel: (020) 7039 5959 Fax: (020) 7039 5999
Email: recruit.london@jonesday.com
Website: www.jonesdaylondon.com/recruit

firm profile

Jones Day operates as one firm worldwide with 2,200 lawyers in 30 offices. Jones Day in London is a key part of this international partnership and has around 200 lawyers, including around 50 partners and 40 trainees. This means that the firm can offer its lawyers a perfect combination - the intimacy and atmosphere of a medium sized City firm with access to both UK and multinational clients.

main areas of work

Jones Day has five core departments: corporate; banking and finance; real estate; litigation and tax. There are specialist groups for competition, construction, environment, planning and insolvency, insurance, employment and pensions.

trainee profile

The firm looks for candidates with either a law or non-law degree who have strong intellectual and analytical ability and good communication skills and who can demonstrate resourcefulness, drive, dedication and the ability to engage with clients and colleagues.

training environment

The firm operates a unique, non-rotational system of training and trainees receive work simultaneously from all departments in the firm. The training is designed to provide freedom, flexibility and responsibility from the start. Trainees are encouraged to assume their own workload, which allows early responsibility, a faster development of potential and the opportunity to compare and contrast the different disciplines alongside one another. Work will vary from small cases which the trainee may handle alone (under the supervision of a senior lawyer) to larger matters where they will assist a partner or an associate solicitor. The firm runs a structured training programme with a regular scedule of seminars to support the thorough practical training and regular feedback that trainees receive from the associates and partners they work with.

vacation placements

Places for 2004/05: Christmas (non-law): 20 places; 2 weeks; £275; closing date 31 October.
Easter 2005 (non-law): 16 places; 2 weeks; £275; closing date 14 February.
Summer 2005 (law): 40; 2 weeks; £275; closing date 14 February.
Placements last for two weeks with an allowance of £275 per week. Students get to see how the firm's non-rotational training system works in practice by taking on real work from a variety of practice areas. They also get to meet a range of lawyers at various social events.

benefits

Private healthcare, season ticket loan, subsidised sports club membership, group life cover.

sponsorship & awards

CPE/PgDL and LPC fees paid and £5,000 maintenance p.a.

Partners	50
Assistant Solicitors	80
Total Trainees	40

contact
Natalie Zschokke
Recruitment Manager

method of application
CV and letter online at
www.jonesdaylondon.com/recruit

selection procedure
2 interviews with partners

closing date for 2007
31 August 2005 - please apply by end of July to ensure an early interview slot

application
Training contracts p.a. **20**
Applications p.a. **1,500**
% interviewed p.a. **12%**
Required degree grade **2.1**

training
Salary
1st year (2004) **£33,000**
2nd year (2004) **£37,000**
Holiday entitlement
5 weeks

post-qualification
Salary (2004) **£55,000**
% of trainees offered job on qualification (2004) **82%**

overseas offices
Continental Europe, Asia, North America **Partners**

	50
Assistant Solicitors	80
Total Trainees	40

Kendall Freeman

43 Fetter Lane, London, EC4A 1JU
Tel: (020) 7583 4055 Fax: (020) 7353 7377
Email: graduaterecruitment@kendallfreeman.com
Website: www.kendallfreeman.com

firm profile
Kendall Freeman handles high value and complex matters for corporates, banks and clients in the insurance and reinsurance industry and public sectors. The firm was awarded the LCN/TSG 2004 award for Best Trainer at a Medium-Sized City Law Firm.

main areas of work
Arbitration, ADR, banking, charities, commercial litigation, company and commercial, construction, corporate finance, corporate tax, employment, energy and offshore engineering, insolvency, restructuring, insurance/reinsurance, mergers and acquisitions and international law.

trainee profile
The firm is small by City standards with 21 partners, but successfully competes and acts alongside the largest international and UK firms of solicitors in its work. It can therefore offer excellent training with high quality work in a more personal environment than the larger firms. The firm seeks energetic individuals with initiative and commercial sense who do not want to be one of a crowd. Trainees need to have a very strong academic backround and excellent people skills as they will have early client interaction.

training environment
Trainees spend six months of their training contract in four of the firm's major practice areas and once a month are able to discuss their progress with a partner. Believing supervised, practical experience to be the best training, the firm soon gives trainees the chance to meet clients, be responsible for their own work and join in marketing and client development activities. Regular workshops in each seat help develop basic skills in the different practice areas. There is a trainee solicitors' committee which meets regularly and which is attended by two trainee representatives where any suggestions or concerns can be voiced. Each trainee is allocated a partner as a mentor.

vacation placements
The firm will not be offering summer placements this year. Instead, the firm will offer several open days to university students both in law and other disciplines to enable them to find out more about the firm and experience its culture. Applications are particularly encouraged from law students who are about to start their last year at university and students in other disciplines who are about to commence the law conversion course.

sponsorship & awards
Full CPE/GDL and LPC funding and a maintenance grant of £5,000 (London) / £4,500 (outide London).

Partners	21
Assistant Solicitors	31
Total Trainees	17

contact
Graduate Recruitment
(020) 7583 4055

method of application
Firm's online application form

selection procedure
One interview with two partners

closing date for 2007
31 July 2005

application
Training contracts p.a. 8
Minimum required degree grade 2:1

training
Salary
1st year £28,500
2nd year £32,000

post-qualification
Salary (2004) £49,000

KENDALL FREEMAN

Keoghs

2 The Parklands, Bolton BL6 4SE
Tel: (01204) 677000 Fax: (01204) 677111
Email: info@keoghs.co.uk

firm profile

Keoghs is one of the UK's leading insurance litigation firms offering national coverage to clients and acts for most of the UK's major insurance companies. The company and commercial team specialise in commercial business advice serving a client base ranging from the private individual to small growing businesses and national blue chip organisations. The high standard of service given to new and existing clients has enabled the firm to achieve ISO 9001 accreditation. Keoghs ranked 25th in the 2004 Sunday Times 100 best companies to work for.

main areas of work

The main practice areas are personal injury litigation, commercial litigation and company commercial (which includes corporate, employment, intellectual property commercial property and private client).

trainee profile

The firm is looking to recruit the partners of the future and indeed many current partners and assistant solicitors joined the firm as trainees. Applicants should be able to demonstrate a high academic standard (at least a 2:1 degree but not necessarily in law), an ability to work in a team, and good communication and decision-making skills. The firm welcomes commercially aware, enthusiastic and self motivated candidates with good IT skills and a sense of humour.

training environment

Trainees undertake a flexible programme of six-month periods in each of the firm's three main practice areas of defendant personal injury litigation, commercial litigation and company commercial work. The trainee will work as part of a specialist team, receiving specific training from their departmental supervisor. The supervisor will also assess the trainee during and at the end of their placement to review progress and development of their drafting, research, communication, advocacy and negotiation skills. The firm's Training and Development department runs a comprehensive programme of in-house training designed to complement the compulsory Professional Skills Course.

Partners	29
Trainees	8
Total Staff	364

contact
Mrs Frances Cross
Director of HR

method of application
Apply by sending a CV & covering letter

selection procedure
By 2 stage interview

closing date for 2007
August 2005

application
Training contracts p.a.
3 in Bolton, 1 in Coventry
Applications p.a. 800
% interviewed p.a. 3.5%
Required degree grade 2:1

training
Salary for each year of training
Currently under review (in excess of Law Society minimum)
Holiday entitlement
25 days + 8 statutory days

post-qualification
Salary (2004) £27,500
% of trainees offered job on qualification The firm aims for 100%

offices
Bolton, Coventry

Lawrence Graham

190 Strand, London WC2R 1JN
Tel: (020) 7379 0000 Fax: (020) 7379 6854
Email: graduate@lawgram.com
Website: www.lawgram.com

firm profile

Lawrence Graham is a leading London based firm with an outstanding reputation in commercial property transactions and mid-market corporate transactions. The firm's main departments are real estate and business and finance. The firm also has a top rated tax and private capital department and a highly regarded dispute resolution team. Through Lawrence Graham International, the firm works with a number of independent law firms in Europe. Lawrence Graham also works with a number of US firms.

main areas of work

Real estate 35%; business and finance 29%; dispute resolution 21%; tax and private capital 14%.

trainee profile

The firm is looking for individuals who can demonstrate a commitment to a career in the commercial application of law and an understanding of the rigours of professional practice. A strong academic track record with a minimum 2.1 degree is a basic requirement. In addition, the firm expects a good record of achievement in other areas, indicative of the ability to succeed in a demanding career. Evidence of team working skills and the ability to handle responsibility are also essential.

training environment

Under partner supervision students will be given early responsibility. Training is structured to facilitate the ability to manage one's own files and interact with clients. In addition to the Professional Skills Course, there are departmental training and induction sessions. Training consists of four six-month seats. A real estate, business & finance and contentious seat are compulsory. The final seat can be either in tax and private capital or back to either real estate or business and finance as they are the largest departments.

benefits

Season ticket loan, on-site gym.

vacation placements

Places for 2005: 32; Duration: 2 weeks during Easter break and 3 x 2 weeks between June and August; Remuneration: £220 p.w.; Closing Date: 31 January 2005.

sponsorship & awards

GDL Funding: Course fees and £4,000 maintenance grant.
LPC Funding: Course fees and £4,000 maintenance grant.

Partners	86
Assistant Solicitors	105
Total Trainees	34

contact
Graduate Recruitment Officer

method of application
Firm's application form.
For law **After 2nd year results**
For non-law **After final results**

selection procedure
Interview

closing date for 2007
31 July 2005

application
Training contracts **18**
Applications p.a. **1,000**
Required degree grade **2:1**

training
Salary
1st year (2003) **£28,000**
2nd year (2003) **£32,000**
% of trainees with a
non-law degree p.a. **88%**

post-qualification
Salary (2003) **£46,000**
% of trainees offered job
on qualification (2003) **98%**
% of assistants (as at
1/9/01) who joined as
trainees **42%**
% of partners (as at 1/9/01)
who joined as trainees **32%**

A-Z SOLICITORS

Laytons

Carmelite, 50 Victoria Embankment, Blackfriars, London EC4Y 0LS
Tel: (020) 7842 8000 Fax: (020) 7842 8080
Email: london@laytons.com
Website: www.laytons.com

firm profile

Laytons is a commercial law firm whose primary focus is on developing dynamic business. The firm's offices in Bristol, Guildford, London and Manchester provide excellent service to its commercial and private clients who are located throughout the UK. The firm's approach to legal issues is practical, creative and energetic. The firm believes in long-term relationships, they are 'client lawyers' rather than 'transaction lawyers'. The key to its client relations is having a thorough understanding of businesses, their needs and objectives. Working together as one team, the firm is mutually supportive and plays to each others' strengths.

main areas of work

Corporate and commercial, commercial property (including land development and construction), dispute resolution, debt recovery, insolvency, employment, intellectual property, technology and media, private client and trusts.

trainee profile

Successful candidates will be well-rounded individuals, commercially aware with sound academic background and enthusiastic and committed team members.

training environment

Trainees are placed in four six-month seats, providing them with an overview of the firm's business, and identifying their particular strengths. All trainees have contact with clients from an early stage, are given challenging work, working on a variety of matters with partners and qualified staff. Trainees will soon be responsible for their own files and are encouraged to participate in business development and marketing activities. The firm works in an informal but professional atmosphere and its philosophy is to invest in people who will develop and become part of its long-term success.

vacation placements

Places for summer 2005: 6. Duration: 1 week. Closing Date: 31 March 2005.

sponsorship & awards

LPC and CPE funding: consideration given.

Partners	35
Assistant Solicitors	51
Total Trainees	12

contact
Anita Coaster (Bristol)
Neale Andrews (Guidford)
Stephen Cates &
Lisa McLean (London)
Christine Barker (Manchester)

method of application
Application form

selection procedure
Usually 2 interviews

closing date for 2007
31 August 2005 (although posts are filled as soon as suitable candidates are identified)

application
Training contracts p.a. 8
Applications p.a. **2,000**
% interviewed p.a. **5%**
Required degree grade
1 or 2:1

training
Salary
1st year (2004) Market rate
2nd year (2004) Market rate
Holiday entitlement
23 days on entry

post-qualification
Salary (2004) **Market rate**
% of trainees offered job
on qualification (2004) **80%**
% of assistants (as at 1/9/04)
who joined as trainees **46%**
% of partners (as at 1/9/04)
who joined as trainees **37%**

regional offices
Training contracts are offered in each of Laytons' offices. Apply directly to desired office. See website for further details: www.laytons.com

LeBoeuf, Lamb, Greene & MacRae

1 Minster Court, Mincing Lane, London EC3R 7YL
Tel: (020) 7459 5000 Fax: (020) 7459 5099
Email: traineelondon@llgm.com
Website: www.llgm.com

firm profile
LeBoeuf, Lamb, Greene & MacRae is an international law firm with over 600 lawyers worldwide in offices across Europe, the US, Africa, Middle East and Asia. The London office, established as a multinational partnership in 1995 employs almost 60 lawyers and is the hub office for the firm's European and international practice. The London office handles varied, interesting work and will suit people who want early responsibility in a relaxed but hard working environment.

main areas of work
General corporate, litigation and dispute resolution, energy, corporate finance, project finance, capital markets, private equity, insurance, insolvency, real estate, tax, intellectual property, employment, trusts and estates.

trainee profile
LeBoeuf, Lamb, Greene & MacRae is looking for outstanding people in the broadest possible sense. The firm welcomes applications from varied, non-traditional backgrounds. Interpersonal skills are very important: the firm likes bright, engaging people. Linguistic skills are useful (but not crucial). The firm wants proactive people who will contribute from day one.

training environment
Trainees spend six months in four seats. The firm's training programme is comprehensive and covers an induction programme, participation in internal seminars and training sessions and attendance at external courses, including the Professional Skills Course. You will be encouraged to act on your own initiative from an early stage. Trainees sit with a senior lawyer, often a partner, who can give ongoing feed back and guidance and progress is reviewed every six months.

benefits
Firm contributes to health, life and disability insurance, season ticket loan, business casual year round.

sponsorship & awards
Full payment of CPE/LPC fees and maintenance grant of £4,500 provided.

Partners	17
Counsel	3
Assistant Solicitors	28
Total Trainees	9

contact
Andrew Terry

method of application
CV & covering letter

selection procedure
2 interviews

closing date for 2007
31 July 2005

application
Training contracts p.a. 5
Applications p.a. 1,300
% interviewed p.a. 3%
Required degree grade
2:1, A,B,B 'A'Level
Equivalent

training
Salary
1st year £33,000
2nd year £37,000
Holiday entitlement 20 days
% of trainees with a
non-law degree p.a. 50%

post-qualification
Salary (2004) £65,000

overseas offices
Albany, Almaty, Beijing, Bishkek, Boston, Brussels, Harrisburg, Hartford, Houston, Jacksonville, Johannesburg, Los Angeles, Moscow, New York, Newark, Paris, Pittsburgh, Riyadh, Salt Lake City, San Francisco, Washington

A-Z SOLICITORS

Lester Aldridge

Russell House, Oxford Road, Bournemouth BH8 8EX
Tel: (01202) 786161 Fax: (01202) 786110
Email: juliet.milne@LA-law.com
Website: www.lesteraldridge.com

firm profile
Lester Aldridge is a dynamic business providing both commercial and private client services across central southern England. The firm also operates in a number of niche markets nationally including asset finance, corporate finance, licensing, marine and retail. The effective corporate management structure ensures LA is focused on delivering pragmatic solutions to their clients. LA places great emphasis on a positive working environment, and the work/life balance, understanding that this will ultimately be of benefit to clients.

main areas of work
Corporate, banking and finance 32%; litigation 30%; private client 21%; commercial prorerty 12%; investments 5%.

trainee profile
Candidates should have strong intellectual capabilities, be commercially aware, resourceful and able to relate easily to other people. IT skills and a team approach are also required.

training environment
Training consists of four six-month seats across the firm. About half way through each seat trainees discuss their preferences for the next seat and every attempt is made to match aspirations to the needs of the firm. Trainees have a training principal for the duration of the contract who will discuss progress every month. They receive a formal comprehensive appraisal from their team leader towards the end of each seat, and the managing partner meets all trainees as a group every three months.

benefits
Life assurance and pension schemes.

vacation placements
Places for 2005: 8; Duration: 2 weeks; Remuneration: £75 p.w.; Closing Date: 31 March 2005.

sponsorship & awards
LPC.

Partners	36
Total Trainees	11
Total Staff	330

contact
Juliet Milne

method of application
Letter, CV & completed application form

selection procedure
Interview by a panel of partners

closing date for 2007
31 July 2005

application
Training contracts p.a. **10**
Applications p.a. **300**
% interviewed p.a. **5%**
Required degree grade **2:1**

training
Salary
Starting: **£16,500** at present, increasing by £500 after each seat
Holiday entitlement **22 days**
% of trainees with a non-law degree p.a. **20%**

post-qualification
Salary (2004) **£29,000**
% of trainees offered job on qualification (2003) **100%**
% of assistants (as at 1/9/01) who joined as trainees **30%**
% of partners (as at 1/9/03) who joined as trainees **25%**

offices
Bournemouth (2), Southampton, Milton Keynes

Lewis Silkin

12 Gough Square, London EC4A 3DW
Tel: (020) 7074 8000 Fax: (020) 7832 1200
Email: train@lewissilkin.com

firm profile

Lewis Silkin places the highest priority on its relationship with clients, excellent technical ability and the commercial thinking of its lawyers. As a result, it is a profitable and distinctive firm, with a friendly and lively style.

main areas of work

The firm has a wide range of corporate clients and provides services through four main departments: corporate, employment and incentives, litigation and property. The major work areas are: construction; corporate services, which includes company, commercial and corporate finance; commercial litigation and dispute resolution; employment; housing and project finance; marketing services, embracing advertising and marketing law; property; technology and communications, which includes IT, media and telecommunications.

trainee profile

The firm looks for trainees with keen minds and personality, who will fit into a professional but informal team. Law and non-law degrees considered.

training environment

Lewis Silkin provides a comprehensive induction and training programme, with practical 'hands-on' experience in four six-month seats. At least three of these seats will be in one of the main departments. The fourth seat can be in one of the specialist areas. Trainees usually sit with a partner who can give ongoing feedback and guidance and progress is formally reviewed every three months. Trainees have the opportunity to get involved in the firm's social and marketing events and also to represent the firm at local trainee solicitors' groups and Law Centres.

benefits

Life assurance, critical illness cover, health insurance, season ticket loan, group pension plan, subsidised gym membership.

vacation placements

Places for summer 2005: 12.

sponsorship & awards

Full fees paid for LPC.

Partners	43
Assistant Solicitors	60
Total Trainees	13

contact
Lucie Rees
HR Officer

method of application
Application form

selection procedure
Assessment day, including an interview with 2 partners & an analytical exercise

closing date for 2007
30 July 2005

application
Training contracts p.a. 7
Applications p.a. 1,000
Required degree grade 2:1

training
Salary
1st year £28,000
2nd year £30,000
Holiday entitlement 25 days

post-qualification
Salary (2004) £43,000

A-Z SOLICITORS

Linklaters

One Silk Street, London EC2Y 8HQ
Tel: (020) 7456 2000 Fax: (020) 7456 2222
Email: graduate.recruitment@linklaters.com
Website: www.linklaters.com/careers/ukgrads

firm profile

Linklaters is a law firm that advises the world's leading companies, financial institutions and governments on their most challenging transactions and assignments.

main areas of work

The firm's work is divided into three main areas – corporate, finance & projects and commercial. While many law firms will have strengths in particular areas, Linklaters is strong across the full range of business law. This is one of the factors that makes Linklaters such a challenging and rewarding place to train as a lawyer.

trainee profile

This is a firm that achieves exceptional things for clients, but it is also a community in which individuals are encouraged to be themselves. Experienced people are generous with their time when supporting and coaching their less experienced colleagues. If you ask anyone from Linklaters what they most enjoy about the firm, the answer is usually the same: "it's the people".

training environment

Linklaters recruits graduates in both law and non-law disciplines. Those graduates who don't have a law degree take the CPE/Diploma in Law conversion course, which involves a year at law college. The next step is the year-long Legal Practice Course (LPC) which all trainees have to complete before they begin their training contracts. The training contract itself is built around four six-month seats or placements. The seat system gives trainees front-line exposure to a range of practice areas. This develops versatile, well-rounded lawyers, but it also gives trainees a good idea of the kind of law they want to do when they qualify. There are also opportunities for client secondments or overseas placements – usually during the third or fourth seat.

sponsorship & benefits

PgDL and LPC fees are paid in full, plus a maintenance grant of £5,000. Profit- and performance-related bonus schemes; 25 days' holiday; health and worldwide travel insurance; life assurance; pension scheme; interest-free season ticket loan; subsidised gym membership.

vacation placements

Christmas scheme for 30 final year non-law students and two summer schemes for 60 penultimate year law students. £275 pw. Summer schemes offer opportunity to spend two weeks in another European office.

Partners	500
Associates	1,547
Trainees	257*
*(London)	

contact
Claire Cherrington

method of application
Application form
(available online)

selection procedure
2 interviews plus
commercial case study
(same day)

application
Training contracts p.a. **130**
Applications p.a. **4,000**
% interviewed p.a. **15%**
Required degree grade **2:1**

training
Salary
1st year (2004) **£29,100**
Holiday entitlement **25 days**
% of trainees with a
non-law degree p.a. **33%**
No. of seats available
abroad p.a. **75**

post-qualification
Salary **£51,000 +**
performance related bonus

offices
Alicante, Amsterdam, Antwerp, Bangkok, Beijing, Berlin, Bratislava, Brussels, Bucharest, Budapest, Cologne, Frankfurt, Hong Kong, Lisbon, London, Luxembourg, Madrid, Milan, Moscow, Munich, New York, Paris, Prague, Rome, São Paulo, Shanghai, Singapore, Stockholm, Tokyo, Warsaw

Lovells

Atlantic House, Holborn Viaduct, London EC1A 2FG
Tel: (020) 7296 2000 Fax: (020) 7296 2001
Email: recruit@lovells.com
Website: www.lovells.com

firm profile
Lovells is one of the world's leading international law firms based in the City of London, with offices in Asia, Europe and North America. The firm's strength across a wide range of practice areas sets it apart from most of its competitors.

main areas of work
The firm's core areas of practice are corporate, litigation, commercial property and specialist groups (including EU/competition, intellectual property, media and telecommunications, employment, tax).

trainee profile
High calibre candidates who can demonstrate strong academic/intellectual ability, ambition, drive, strong communication and interpersonal skills. Professional/commercial attitude.

training environment
Trainees spend six months in four different areas of the practice to gain as much experience as possible. They have the option of spending time in their second year of training in an international office or on secondment to the in-house legal department of a major client. A comprehensive part of the programme of skills training is run for trainees both in-house and externally, placing a particular emphasis on advocacy and communication. Trainees are offered as much responsibility as they can handle as well as regular reviews, six-monthly appraisals and support when they need it.

benefits
PPP medical insurance, life assurance, PHI, season ticket loan, in-house gym, staff restaurant, access to dentist, doctor and physiotherapist, discounts at local retailers.

vacation placements
Places for 2005: 90. Placements available at Christmas 2004 (closing date 12 November), Easter and Summer 2005 (closing date 11 February).

sponsorship & awards
GDL and LPC course fees are paid, and a maintenance grant is also provided of £5,000 for London and Oxford and £4,500 elsewhere. In addition, £500 bonus on joining the firm; £1,000 advance in salary on joining; £500 prize for a First Class degree result.

Partners	364
Assistant Solicitors	1600
Total Trainees	135

contact
Clare Harris
Recruitment Manager

method of application
Online application form

selection procedure
Assessment day: critical thinking test, group exercise, interview

closing date for 2007
31 August 2005

application
Training contracts p.a. **90**
Applications p.a. **2,000**
% interviewed p.a. **17%**
Required degree grade **2:1**

training
Salary
1st year (2004) **£28,000**
2nd year (2004) **£32,000**
Holiday entitlement **25 days**
% of trainees with a non-law degree p.a. **40%**
No. of seats available abroad p.a. **22**

post-qualification
Salary (2004) **£50,000**

international offices
Alicante, Amsterdam, Beijing, Berlin, Brussels, Budapest, Chicago, Düsseldorf, Frankfurt, Hamburg, Ho Chi Minh City, Hong Kong, London, Milan, Moscow, Munich, New York, Paris, Prague, Rome, Singapore, Shanghai, Tokyo, Vienna, Warsaw, Zagreb

Lupton Fawcett

Yorkshire House, Greek Street, Leeds LS1 5SX
Tel: (0113) 280 2000 Fax: (0113) 245 6782
Email: elizabeth.brown@luptonfawcett.com
Website: www.luptonfawcett.co.uk

firm profile

Lupton Fawcett is a well-established yet dynamic and integrated practice. The firm offers a full range of legal services to both commercial and private clients alike on a quality-driven and client-led basis with the emphasis on providing first-class cost-effective and practical solutions which exceed the clients expectations. The firm was one of the first in Leeds to hold both Investors in People and the Law Society's Lexcel quality standard.

main areas of work

The commercial division offers the chance to gain experience in corporate, commercial property, employment, intellectual property, insolvency and commercial and chancery litigation. On the private client side, opportunities are available in financial services, trusts and probate, family and residential conveyancing. Further specialist areas of the firm include employment, licensing and advocacy, IT and e-commerce, sports law, debt recovery, insurance litigation and specialist personal injury.

trainee profile

Although strong academic achievements are required, the firm places a high value on previous experience and interests which have developed commercial awareness, maturity and character. Trainees will also be able to demonstrate enthusiasm, confidence, good interpersonal and team skills, humour, initiative, commitment and common sense.

training environment

Training at Lupton Fawcett is normally split into four six-month seats. Trainees office share with the partner or associate with whom they are working and are an integral part of the team, assuming a high degree of responsibility. Appraisals following each seat take place to ensure that progress is monitored effectively. A full in-house training programme enables continual development as well as from training gained from excellent hands-on experience. Trainees will have the chance to meet clients and be responsible for their own work, as well as being involved in and actively encouraged to join in marketing and practice development initiatives. There is a full social programme in which the trainees are encouraged to participate as well as sporting events organised by the office and an excellent informal social culture.

benefits

Health insurance, season ticket loans, interest free loans towards LPC funding available by discussion with candidates.

Partners	25
Assistant Solicitors	28
Total Trainees	5

contact
Doug Robertson
(0113) 280 2107 or
Elizabeth Brown
(0113) 280 2251

method of application
Employer's application
form & handwritten letter

selection procedure
Interviews & assessment
days

closing date for 2007
31 July 2005

application
Training contracts p.a. 2-3
Applications p.a. 300
% interviewed p.a. 10
Required degree grade 2:1
preferred

training
Salary
Competitive with similar
size/type firms
Holiday entitlement 20 days

post-qualification
Salary
Competitive with similar
size/type firms
% of trainees offered job on
qualification (2003-04) 90%

Mace & Jones

19 Water Street, Liverpool L2 0RP
Tel: (0151) 236 8989 Fax: (0151) 227 5010
Email: donal.bannon@maceandjones.co.uk
14 Oxford Court, Bishopsgate, Manchester M2 3WQ
Tel: (0161) 236 2244 Fax: (0161) 228 7285
Website: www.maceandjones.co.uk

firm profile

Mace & Jones is a leading regional practice in the North West and remains a full service firm while enjoying a national reputation for its commercial expertise, especially in employment, litigation/insolvency, corporate and property. The firm's clients range from national and multinational companies and public sector bodies to owner managed businesses and private individuals, reflecting the broad nature of the work undertaken. Sound practical advice is given always on a value-for-money basis.

main areas of work

Commercial litigation/insolvency 15%; commercial property 15%; company/commercial 15%; employment 35%; personal injury/private client/family 20%.

trainee profile

The firm seeks to recruit highly motivated trainees with above average ability and the determination to succeed. The right calibre of trainee will assume responsibility early in their career. The firm provides a comprehensive internal and external training programme.

training environment

Trainees complete an induction course to familiarise themselves with the work carried out by the firm's main departments, administration and professional conduct. Training consists of four six-month seats in the following departments: company/commercial, employment, commercial litigation/personal injury litigation, property law, family law. Strenuous efforts are made to ensure that trainees are able to select the training seat of their choice. A trainee will normally be required to share an office with a partner who will supervise their work and review the trainee's progress at the end of the seat. The PSC is taught externally. The firm operates an open door policy and has various social events.

Partners	38
Assistant Solicitors	51
Total Trainees	10

contact
Donal Bannon
Liverpool Office

method of application
Online

selection procedure
Interview with partners

closing date for 2007
31 March 2006

application
Training contracts p.a. varies
Applications p.a. **1,500**
% interviewed p.a. **2%**
Required degree grade **2:1**

training
Salary
1st year (2004) **£16,000**
2nd year (2004) **£16,500**
Holiday entitlement **20 days**
% of trainees with a
non-law degree p.a. **40%**

post-qualification
Salary (2003) **Negotiable**
% of trainees offered job
on qualification (2003) **75%**
% of assistants (as at
1/7/03) who joined as
trainees **30%**
% of partners (as at 1/9/03)
who joined as trainees **25%**

Macfarlanes

10 Norwich Street, London EC4A 1BD
Tel: (020) 7831 9222 Fax: (020) 7831 9607
Email: gradrec@macfarlanes.com
Website: www.macfarlanes.com

firm profile

Macfarlanes is a leading City law firm practising at the forefront of many areas of commercial endeavour. The firm is instructed by major businesses, industrial enterprises and high net worth individuals who appreciate the distinctive benefits of working with a firm which offers a cohesive and focused approach. Much of their work has a significant international element.

main areas of work

The firm's areas of practice are broadly defined under the four main headings of corporate; property; litigation and dispute resolution; and private client.

trainee profile

It is Macfarlanes' belief that the strongest firm will be achieved by choosing a mix of people, reflecting different styles so as to meet the needs that they – and their varied range of clients – will have in the future. Macfarlanes does not just need its trainees to show intelligence and imagination, but also a high level of self-reliance, energy and enthusiasm.

training environment

Anyone joining Macfarlanes cannot expect to lose themselves in the crowd. Because they recruit fewer trainees, each individual is expected to play their part and everyone's contribution counts. There are other benefits attached to working in a firm of this size: It helps retain an informal working atmosphere – people quickly get to know one another and are on first name terms across the board. There is the sense of community that comes from working closely together in smaller teams. Everyone at Macfarlanes has a vested interest in getting the best out of each other, including their trainees.

benefits

A comprehensive benefits package is provided.

vacation placements

Places for 2005: 36; Duration: 2 weeks; Remuneration: £250 p.w.; Closing Date: 28 February 2005.

sponsorship & awards

CPE and LPC fees paid in full and a £5,000 maintenance allowance for courses studied in London, Guildford and Oxford and £4,500 for courses studied elsewhere. Prizes for those gaining distinction or commendation on the LPC.

Partners	62
Assistant Solicitors	125
Total Trainees	50

contact
Graham Stoddart

method of application
Online via website

selection procedure
Assessment day

closing date for 2007
31 July 2005

application
Training contracts p.a. **25**
Applications p.a. **1,500**
% interviewed p.a. **15%**
Required degree grade **2:1**

training
Salary
1st year (2004) **£28,000**
2nd year (2004) **£32,000**
Holiday entitlement **21 days**
% of trainees with a
non-law degree p.a. **45%**

post-qualification
Salary (2004) **£50,000**
% of trainees offered job
on qualification (2004) **90%**
% of partners (as at 1/9/04)
who joined as trainees **65%**

Manches

Aldwych House, 81 Aldwych, London WC2B 4RP
Tel: (020) 7404 4433 Fax: (020) 7430 1133
Email: sheona.boldero@manches.com
Website: www.manches.com

firm profile
Manches is a London and Oxford-based commercial firm with strengths across a range of services and industry sectors. The firm's strategy has seen a greater concentration and focus on the firm's core commercial industry sectors of technology and media, property, construction and retail, while continuing to be market leaders in family law. The firm offers 10 trainee places each September.

main areas of work
Industry Sectors: Technology and media, property and construction.
Legal Groups: Corporate finance (emphasis in technology); commercial property; commercial litigation; construction; family; employment; intellectual property; information technology; biotechnology (Oxford office only); trusts and estates (Oxford office only).

trainee profile
Manches looks for candidates with a consistently good academic record who are enthusiastic, committed and with an outgoing engaging personality. They should display a strong sense of commercial awareness, the ability to think for themselves and excellent interpersonal/social skills.

training environment
The firm provides high quality, individual training. Trainees generally sit in four different seats for six months at a time (one of which is usually in a niche practice area). The firm's comprehensive in-house training programme enables them to take responsibility from an early stage, ensuring that they become confident and competent solicitors. Trainees have the opportunity to actively participate in departmental meetings and briefings and receive regular appraisals on their progress.

benefits
Season ticket loan, BUPA after six months, permanent health insurance, life insurance, pension after three months.

vacation placements
Places for 2005: 24 approx.; Duration: 1 week; Remuneration: Under review; Closing Date: 31 January 2005.

sponsorship & awards
CPE/PgDL and LPC fees are paid in full together with an annual maintenance allowance (currently £4,000 p.a. - under review).

Partners	48
Assistant Solicitors	62
Total Trainees	20

contact
Sheona Boldero
Tel: (020) 7872 8690
(Graduate Recruitment line)

method of application
Application form

selection procedure
1st interview with HR,
second Interview with 2
partners.

closing date for 2007
31 July 2005

application
Training contracts p.a. **10**
Applications p.a. **860**
% interviewed p.a. **10%**
Required degree grade **2:1**

training
Salary (Under review)
1st year (2004)
London **£26,500**
2nd year (2004)
London **£30,000**
Holiday entitlement **24 days**

post-qualification
Salary (Under review)
London **£43,000 (2004)**
% of trainees offered job
on qualification (2004) **77%**

Martineau Johnson

No 1 Colmore Square, Birmingham B4 6AA
6 Cannon Street, London, EC4N 4NQ
Tel: (0870) 763 2000 Fax: (0870) 763 2001
Email: emily.dean@martjohn.co.uk
Website: www.graduates4law.co.uk and www.martineau-johnson.co.uk

firm profile

Martineau Johnson combines a dynamic and commercial approach with a traditional and caring attitude. It is now based in the most prestigious new offices in Birmingham city centre, where there is room for the expansion planned by the firm and where staff will benefit from the latest working methods. And it also has growth plans for the London office too. Its vision is built on matching legal know-how to clients' needs through building partnerships with them and based on a detailed understanding and knowledge of their businesses.

main areas of work

Commercial 25%; corporate services 23%; commercial disputes management 18%; property 15%; private client 19%.

trainee profile

Trainees are vital to Martineau Johnson's future and no effort is spared to give the best possible experience and support to them, whilst treating them as individuals. There is a very high retention rate at the end of training contracts, when trainees are generally offered roles in their preferred departments and specialisms.

training environment

Martineau Johnson's aim is to work in partnership with trainees, providing them with mentoring, supervision, support and an exposure to the key areas of the firm's practice. Trainees are actively encouraged to be an integral part of the team delivering legal solutions to its clients whilst benefiting from quality work, flexible seat rotation in a small and friendly team environment. Generally, the firm's trainees are given experience in its chosen sectors: commercial, corporate services, commercial disputes management, property and private client – they are then given the opportunity to carry out further work in areas of their choice and specialism. There are opportunities for Birmingham-based trainees to be exposed to the London scene. Trainees benefit from a structured career training programme tailored to their personal development needs - and it covers not only legal technical matters, but also a business and commercial approach which have never been more central to successful professional careers. In giving training and offering experience that matches the best city firms, Martineau Johnson offers a rare opportunity for trainees to lay great foundations for their legal career in a fast-moving, ever-changing but caring environment.

Partners	42
Assistant Solicitors	85
Total Trainees	22

contact
Emily Dean

method of application
Online application form
www.graduates4law.co.uk

selection procedure
Assessment centre - half day

closing date for 2007
31 July 2005

application
Training contracts p.a. **10-12**
Applications p.a. **500**
% interviewed p.a. **10%**
Required degree grade **2:1**

training
Salary
1st year (2004) c. **£20,000**
2nd year (2004) c. **£21,500**
Holiday entitlement **23** days
% of trainees with a
non-law degree (2004) **50%**

post-qualification
Salary (2004) **£34,000**
% of trainees offered job
on qualification (2004) **62%**
% of assistants (as at
1/9/04) who joined as
trainees **44%**
% of partners (as at 1/9/04)
who joined as trainees **40%**

MARTINEAU JOHNSON

Masons

30 Aylesbury Street, London EC1R 0ER
Tel: (020) 7490 4000 Fax: (020) 7490 2545
Email: graduate.recruitment@masons.com
Website: www.masons.com and www.out-law.com

firm profile

Masons is one of the most highly regarded specialist law firms in Europe and the Asia Pacific region. The firm has nine offices across four countries, as well as alliances in Spain, the US and Dubai.

main areas of work

Masons provides a complete legal service to clients operating in the construction and engineering, projects, energy and infrastructure industries and to users and suppliers of information and technology. Masons' lawyers provide a comprehensive service in these sectors, as well as to clients in the following areas: commercial property and development; corporate and commercial, e-commerce/new media; employment, data protection, dispute resolution (property and commercial), facilities management, freedom of information; health and safety, insolvency, pensions and taxation.

trainee profile

The firm is seeking bright, motivated self-starters, looking to work for a firm which combines excellent training and support with early responsibility.

training environment

After induction, your two-year training contract will be divided into a number of 'seats'. Each seat will involve sharing an office with a partner or solicitor selected from one of the outlined practice areas. Your rotation throughout the firm will ensure that you are exposed to a range of areas of law and to a variety of approaches. Wherever possible the firm tries to tailor the arrangement to meet individual needs. Work/life balance is also an important part of your career and regular social events are part of our culture, whichever office you join. These range from Summer Balls, Christmas and Halloween Parties to Pop Idol and Beer & Curry Nights. For the more sporty, the firm participates in an annual charitable London to Paris Triathlon.

benefits

Life assurance, private healthcare (all offices), subsidised restaurant and season ticket loan (London).

vacation placements

Approx 12 places in London for 2005 for a two week duration. Closing Date: 18 February 2005.

sponsorship & awards

Fees are paid for CPE and LPC courses and maintenance grants.*

*benefits may vary in Scotland.

Partners	90
Total Staff	606
Total Trainees	49

contact
Graduate Recruitment Team, London Office

method of application
Apply online at www.masons.com/graduaterecruitment

selection procedure
An interview and an assessment day

closing date for 2007
31 July 2005 in England, 21 October 2005 in Scotland

application
Training contracts p.a.
15-18 across UK
Applications p.a. **1,600**
% interviewed p.a. **5%**
Required degree grade **2:1**

training
Salary
£25k-£27k in London.
Please note that salaries & benefits vary throughout UK offices
Holiday entitlement
23 days (1st year)
24 days (2nd year)

post-qualification
Salary £44,500 in London

overseas offices
Brussels, Hong Kong, Shanghai

uk offices
Bristol, Edinburgh (LSS), Glasgow (LSS), Leeds, London, Manchester

Mayer, Brown, Rowe & Maw LLP

11 Pilgrim Street, London EC4V 6RW
Tel: (020) 7248 4282 Fax: (020) 7782 8790
Email: graduaterecruitment@mayerbrownrowe.com
Website: www.mayerbrownrowe.com/london/careers/gradrecruit

firm profile

Mayer, Brown, Rowe & Maw LLP is one of the ten largest legal practices in the world. The practice serves its international client base from its 13 offices worldwide, including representation in the world's major financial centres: London, Paris, Frankfurt and New York. The practice has a reputation for delivering pragmatic commercial advice, and is praised for its professionalism.

main areas of work

The practice's client base is diverse and includes blue-chip corporates, multinationals, private companies, partnerships, financial institutions and intermediaries. The practice has an excellent reputation in a diverse range of practice areas, receiving recognition in numerous prestigious legal awards. Major practice areas include: construction; competition and trade; corporate and securities; employment; environment; finance and banking; insurance and reinsurance; intellectual property; litigation and arbitration; oil and gas; pensions; real estate; regulated industries, securitisation and tax.

trainee profile

The practice is interested in motivated students with a good academic record and a strong commitment to law. Commercial awareness gained through legal or business work experience is an advantage.

training environment

Students looking for a leading international law practice that offers exposure to a multitude of blue chip companies and a wide range of international work, combined with the confidence of knowing they have a place in its future, should contact Mayer, Brown, Rowe and Maw LLP. Trainees will participate in a lively, energetic and positive business culture, spending time in four six-month seats including the corporate and litigation departments. The practice's culture of getting immersed in a client's business means that there are excellent secondment opportunities. In addition to the Professional Skills Course, the practice offers an individual professional development and training programme. Three-monthly appraisals assist trainees in reaching their true potential.

benefits

Benefits include 25 days holiday per annum, interest free season ticket loan, subsidised sports club membership and private health scheme.

vacation placements

Places for 2005: 25; Duration: 2 weeks during Easter and summer vacations. Experience in two of the principal work groups plus a programme of seminars, visits and social events.

sponsorship & awards

GDL and LPC fees, plus a maintenance grant of £4,500 (£5,000 for London and Guildford).

Partners	99
Assistant Solicitors	152
Total Trainees	49

contact
Maxine Lawrence

method of application
Online application form

selection procedure
Selection workshops including an interview, a business analysis exercise & a group exercise

closing date for 2007
31 July 2005

application
Training contracts p.a.
Approx 25-30
Applications p.a. **720**
% interviewed p.a. **9%**
Required degree grade **2:1**

training
Starting salary (2004) **£28,000**
Holiday entitlement **25 days**
% of trainees with a
non-law degree p.a. **45%**
No. of seats available
abroad p.a. **1**

post-qualification
Salary (2004) **£50,000**
% of trainees offered job
on qualification (2004) **65%**
% of partners who joined
as trainees **35%**

overseas offices
Brussels, Charlotte, Chicago, Cologne, Frankfurt, Houston, London, Los Angeles, Manchester, New York, Palo Alto, Paris, Washington DC

McCormicks

Britannia Chambers, 4 Oxford Place, Leeds LS1 3AX
Tel: (0113) 246 0622 Fax: (0113) 246 7488
Wharfedale House, 37 East Parade, Harrogate HG1 5LQ
Tel: (01423) 530630 Fax: (01423) 530709
Email: l.jackson@mccormicks-solicitors.com
Website: www.mccormicks-solicitors.com

firm profile

McCormicks is a unique legal practice at the heart of a vibrant commercial region. With core traditional values of integrity, technical excellence and hard work, the firm is committed to deliver an unrivalled quality of service and innovation to its clients and quality of life to its people. McCormicks combines the full range and depth of skills across its entire practice with the firm's renowned fearlessness and ability to punch above its weight in order to deliver the best possible result.

main areas of work

With a diverse range of clients from private individuals to high profile international organisations its work is never dull. Trainees are exposed to all its practice areas including sports law, media and entertainment law, corporate and commercial, commercial property, commercial litigation, charity work, family, corporate crime, insolvency and intellectual property.

trainee profile

Intellectual achievement, ambition, a sense of humour and commitment to hard work are crucial qualities of a McCormicks trainee. The firm will challenge you but support you at every step of the way.

training environment

Trainees are assigned to one of six departments and supervised throughout by a mentor. The firm's training work will develop skills, knowledge and ambition within a friendly, progressive and supportive environment. Your development will be reviewed regularly by the mentor, team supervisor and the training partner. There is an open door policy and a great team spirit.

vacation placements

Places for 2005: Available in summer vacation. Closing Date: Application forms by 25 February 2005.

Partners	12
Assistant Solicitors	24
Total Trainees	8

contact
Linda Jackson

method of application
Application form

selection procedure
Assessment Day &
Interview with two partners

closing date for 2007
29 July 2005

application
Training contracts p.a. **4**
Applications p.a. **350**
% interviewed p.a. **22%**
Required degree grade **2:1**

training
Salary
highly competitive

post-qualification
Salary (2004)
Highly competitive
trainees offered job
on qualification (2004) **2 of 4**
% of partners (as at 1/1/2004)
who joined as trainees **40%**

McDermott Will & Emery

7 Bishopsgate, London EC2N 3AR
Tel: (020) 7577 6900 Fax: (020) 7577 6950
Website: www.mwe.com/london
Email: graduate.recruitment@europe.mwe.com

firm profile
McDermott Will & Emery is a leading international law firm with offices in Boston, Brussels, Chicago, Düsseldorf, London, Los Angeles, Miami, Milan, Munich, New York, Orange County, Rome, San Diego, Silicon Valley and Washington DC. The firm's client base includes some of the world's leading financial institutions, largest corporations, mid-cap businesses, and individuals. The firm represents more than 75 of the companies in the Fortune 100 in addition to clients in the FTSE 100 and FTSE 250. Rated as one of the leading firms in The American Lawyer's Top 100, by a number of indicators, including gross revenues and profits per Partner.

London Office: The London office was founded in 1998. It is already recognised as being in the top 10 of the 100 US law firms operating in London by the legal media. The firm has over 65 lawyers at present in London, almost all of whom are English-qualified. The firm provides business oriented legal advice to multinational and national corporates, financial institutions, investment banks and private clients. Most of the firm's partners were head of practice at their former firms and are recognised as leaders in their respective fields by the most respected professional directories and market commentators.

main areas of work
Banking and finance; corporate, including international corporate finance and M&A; private equity, EU competition; employment, IP, IT and e-business; litigation and arbitration; pensions and incentives; taxation; telecoms and US securities. London is the hub for the firm's European expansions.

trainee profile
The firm is looking for the brightest, best and most entrepreneurial trainees. You will need to convince the firm that you have made a deliberate choice.

training environment
The primary focus is to provide a practical foundation for your career with the firm. You will experience between four and six seats over the two-year period and the deliberately small number of trainees means that the firm is able to provide a degree of flexibility in tailoring seats to the individual. Trainees get regular support and feedback.

benefits
Private medical and dental insurance, life assurance, permanent health insurance, season ticket loan, subsidised gym membership, employee assistance programme, 25 days holiday.

sponsorship & awards
CPE and LPC funding and mainenance grant.

Partners	585*
	22 (London)
Associate Lawyers &	
Other Fee-earners	427*
	45 (London)
Total Trainees	2 in 2003
	2 in 2004

denotes worldwide figures

method of application
CV and covering letter. See website for selection criteria

closing date for 2007
31 July 2005

training
Salary
1st year (2004) £30,000

McDermott
Will & Emery

McGrigors

1-1 Dorset Rise, London, EC4Y 8EN
Tel: (020) 7694 2675
Email: graduate.recruitment@mcgrigors.com
Website: www.mcgrigors.com

firm profile

In March 2004 McGrigors became the new name for the previously known practices of KLegal and McGrigor Donald, providing a common brand name across all the offices. McGrigors operates in all UK jurisdictions. The firm continues to have strong links with KPMG and works with them on a "best friends" basis which means it has a strong and effective business relationship in some key areas such as tax litigation, people services and private equity.

main areas of work

McGrigors provides the legal services that you would expect from a City law firm. Practice areas include banking and finance, construction, corporate, dispute resolution, intellectual property, people services, pensions, private equity, projects, real estate, tax litigation, technology and telecommunications.

trainee profile

In an environment of constant change and development, it is important that people joining the firm deal with change confidently, and all staff are required to display ambition and enthusiasm in equal measure. Trainees need to prove that they are interested in business not simply black letter law and, in addition, the firm's trainees are highly visible in the firm and expected to get actively involved, whether in business or social events.

training environment

McGrigors' training is based upon a standard rotation of seats of six months in four main practice areas. Trainees are encouraged to spend a seat in Edinburgh or Glasgow rather than spend a full two years in London and there may also be the opportunity for a seat on secondment to a client. The firm is part of a consortium of City firms who deliver the PSC in-house. McGrigors' commitment is to provide an enjoyable experience, where learning is very hands-on and trainees are viewed as key contributors to all practice areas.

benefits

McGrigors offers life assurance, pension, a daily lunch allowance and 25 days' holiday. The firm also has a very active Social Committee with subsidised monthly events.

sponsorship & awards

CPE and LPC fees paid plus maintenance of £4,500 for each year.

Partners	52
Assistant Solicitors	90
Total Trainees	60

contact
Georgina Bond
(020) 7694 2675

method of application
Form available on website
www.mcgrigors.com

selection procedure
Assessment Day

application
Training contracts p.a.12-15
BBA at A level or equivalent
with realistic estimate of 2.1

training
Salary
1st year (2004) £28,000
2nd year (2004) £32,000
Holiday entitlement
25 days p.a.

post-qualification
Salary (20030 £48,000

offices
London, Edinburgh,
Glasgow, Belfast

Mills & Reeve

112 Hills Road, Cambridge CB2 1PH
Tel: (01223) 222336 Fax: (01223) 335848
Email: graduate.recruitment@mills-reeve.com
Website: www.mills-reeve.com

firm profile
Mills & Reeve is one of the UK's leading commercial law firms, providing a comprehensive range of services to a mix of regional and national businesses, institutions and individuals in the UK and internationally. It operates from offices in Birmingham, Cambridge, London and Norwich.

main areas of work
The firm offers a full range of corporate, commercial, property, litigation and private client services. Areas of work where trainees currently sit include: corporate, banking, corporate tax, education and public law, technology, real estate, planning & environment, PFI, construction, insurance, commercial disputes, probate & trust administration, agriculture and estates, private tax, employment, family & matrimonial, litigation, real estate disputes and regulatory defence.

trainee profile
The firm welcomes applications from both law and non-law disciplines. Candidates should already have or expect a 2.1 degree or equivalent. Trainee solicitors should display energy, maturity, initiative, enthusiasm for their career, a professional approach to work and be ready to accept early responsibility.

training environment
At Mills & Reeve trainees complete six four-month seats and are recruited to the Birmingham, Cambridge and Norwich offices. Subject to business needs, the firm is happy for those trainees with a desire to undertake a seat not practised in their base office to temporarily move to another office, including London, and supports the move with an accommodation allowance. During each seat trainees sit with a partner or senior solicitor and performance is assessed by a mix of informal reviews during the seat and a more formal review at the end of each seat. A full induction integrates trainees quickly into the firm and ongoing in-house lectures and training by Professional Support Lawyers support the PSC.

benefits
Life assurance at two times pensionable salary, a contributory pension scheme, 25 days holiday, bonus scheme, discounted rate for BUPA, corporate gym membership, social club.

vacation placements
Applications for two-week placements during the summer must be received by 1 March 2005.

sponsorship & awards
The firm pays the full costs of the CPE/GDL and LPC fees and offers a maintenance grant for the LPC year.

Partners	68
Assistant Solicitors	146
Total Trainees	36

contact
Graduate Recruitment

method of application
Firm's application form

selection procedure
Normally one day
assessment centre

closing date for 2007
31 July 2005 for training
contracts
1st March 2005 for work
placements

application
Training contracts p.a.15-20
Applications p.a. **Approx 600**
% interviewed p.a. 10%
Required degree grade 2:1

training
Salary
1st year (2004) £20,000
2nd year (2004) £21,000
Holiday entitlement
25 days p.a.
% of trainees with a non-
law degree 36%

post-qualification
% of trainees offered job
on qualification (2004)
90%
% of assistants (as at
1/9/04) who joined as
trainees 30%
% of partners (as at
1/9/04) who joined as
trainees 20%

Mishcon de Reya

Summit House, 12 Red Lion Square, London WC1R 4QD
Tel: (020) 7440 7198 Fax: (020) 7430 0691
Email: graduate.recruitment@mishcon.co.uk
Website: www.mishcon.co.uk

firm profile

Mishcon de Reya is a mid-sized London law firm offering a diverse range of legal services. While widely known for its high profile private client work, the firm's foundation is based upon a dynamic range of corporate and entrepreneurial businesses. By combining its expertise and entrepreneurial spirit with its clients' own drive and ambitions, the firm delivers innovative legal and commercial solutions that help businesses fulfill their strategies.

main areas of work

Mishcon de Reya's expertise falls into four main areas: Corporate, Litigation, Property and Family. The firm also has a large number of specialist groups including Arbitration, Brands & Rights, Corporate Recovery & Insolvency, Culture Media & Sport, Employment, Financial Services, Immigration, Investigations & Asset Recovery, Information Technology and Private Client.

trainee profile

Applications are welcome from penultimate-year law students, final year non-law students and other graduates wishing to commence a training contract in two years time. The firm wants people who can meet the highest intellectual and business standards, while maintaining outside interests. Candidates should be cheerful, enterprising and ambitious – they should see themselves as future partners.

training environment

Trainees have the opportunity to experience four different 'seats' of six months each. All trainees get exposure to at least three of the four core departments and are also able to gain experience in specialist groups during their time with the firm. Trainees share a room with a partner or assistant solicitor and the firm's style is friendly and informal. Because of the relatively few training contracts offered, trainees can expect to be exposed to high quality work with early responsibility. In order to support this, the firm has a wide-ranging training programme and provides extensive internal training in addition to the Professional Skills Course. Three-monthly appraisals and monitoring in each seat ensures trainees gain a range of work and experience.

benefits

Medical cover, subsidised gym membership, season ticket loan, permanent health insurance, life assurance and pension.

vacation placements

Places for 2005: 12; Duration: 2 weeks; Expenses: £200 p.w.; Closing Date: 15 March 2005.

sponsorship & awards

CPE and LPC funding with bursary.

Partners	42
Assistant Solicitors	53
Total Trainees	14

contact
Human Resources Department

method of application
Application form

closing date for 2007
31 July 2005

application
Training contracts p.a. 6-8
Applications p.a. 800+
% interviewed p.a. 6%
Required degree grade 2:1

training
Salary
1st year £27,000
2nd year £29,000
Holiday entitlement
25 days p.a.
Occasional secondments available

post-qualification
% of trainees retained
(2003) 75%
% of assistants who joined as trainees 42%
% of partners who joined as trainees 15%

Morgan Cole

Apex Plaza, Forbury Road, Reading RG1 1AX
Tel: (0870) 3664610 Fax: (0870) 3662653
Email: recruitment@morgan-cole.com
Website: www.morgan-cole.com

firm profile

Morgan Cole is one of the leading commercial law practices in the country, providing a comprehensive service to both individual and corporate clients in both the public and private sectors. The firm has a reputation for excellence and therefore attracts the highest quality of staff from all fields. The firm enjoys strong connections throughout the UK and the USA and is a founder member of the Association of European Lawyers, one of five leading UK law firms responsible for establishing a network of English speaking lawyers throughout Europe. The firm's areas of work are covered by eight practice areas: commercial; corporate and banking; employment; insurance; private client; health; commercial property; and dispute management. As a modern practice, the firm strives to meet the legal needs of clients in all sectors of industry, but places a specific emphasis on four main sectors: insurance; energy; health; and technology. Within these practice areas the firm's work includes: acquisitions and disposals; technology and intellectual property work; corporate finance; employment; energy; information technology; joint ventures; landlord and tenant litigation; management buy-outs and buy-ins; partnerships; PFI; public law; commercial property; construction; environmental/ planning/health and safety; heath and social care (including medical negligence); commercial litigation; licensing; family litigation and alternative dispute resolution.

trainee profile

Successful candidates should be commercially aware, self motivated individuals with drive and initiative who are able to apply a logical and common-sense approach to solving client problems. The firm is seeking applications from graduates/undergraduates in both law and non-law subjects, preferably with at least a 2:1 degree.

training environment

Trainees spend six months in four different practice areas, and since each practice area handles a wide variety of work within its constituent teams, there is no danger of over-specialisation. Trainees also have the opportunity to be seconded to some of the firm's major clients for one of their seats.

open days

Six in total: two in London, two in Oxford and two in Cardiff. Applications to be made online before 31 March 2005.

sponsorship & awards

The firm offers full funding of fees for attendance on the CPE/PgDL and LPC as well as making a contribution towards maintenance.

Partners	67
Lawyers	346
Total Trainees	28

Trainee Places for 2007:

Cardiff/Swansea	5
Oxford/Reading	5
Total	10

contact
Janice Okuns

method of application
Apply online at www.morgan-cole.com/careers

selection procedure
Assessment Centre & interview

closing date for 2007
31 July 2005

application
Required degree grade Preferably 2:1

training
Salary
1st & 2nd year (2004)
Competitive for the London, Thames Valley and South Wales regions which are reviewed annually in line with market trends

other offices
Cardiff, Croydon, London, Oxford, Swansea

Nabarro Nathanson

Lacon House, Theobald's Road, London WC1X 8RW
Tel: (020) 7524 6000 Fax: (020) 7524 6524
Email: graduateinfo@nabarro.com
Website: www.nabarro.com

firm profile

One of the UK's leading commercial law firms with offices in London, Reading and Sheffield. The firm is known for having an open but highly professional culture and expects its lawyers to have a life outside work.

main areas of work

Company and commercial law; commercial property; planning; pensions and employment; corporate finance; IP/IT; commercial litigation; construction; PFI; environmental law.

trainee profile

Nabarro Nathanson welcomes applications from law and non-law undergraduates. Candidates will usually be expecting a minimum 2:1 degree. As well as strong intellectual ability graduates need exceptional qualities. These include: enthusiasm, drive and initiative, common sense, strong interpersonal skills and teamworking skills.

training environment

Trainees undertake six four-month seats which ensures maximum exposure to the firm's core practice areas (company commercial, commercial property and litigation). The firm aims to retain all trainees on qualification. In addition to the core seats, trainees have the opportunity to gain further experience by spending time in specialist areas (eg pensions, IP/IT, tax, employment), possibly in Germany or Brussels, or completing a further seat in a core area. In most cases trainees will return to the seat they wish to qualify into for the remaining four months of their contract. This ensures a smooth transition from trainee to qualified solicitor.

benefits

Trainees are given private medical insurance, pension, 25 days holiday entitlement per annum, a season ticket loan, access to a subsidised restaurant and subsidised corporate gym membership. Trainee salaries are reviewed annually.

vacation placements

Places for 2005: 60; Duration: 3 weeks between mid-June and end of August; Closing Date: 28 February 2005.

sponsorship & awards

Full fees paid for GDL and LPC and a maintenance grant (London and Guildford: £5,000; elsewhere: £4,500).

Partners	107
Assistant Solicitors	219
Total Trainees	61

contact
Anna Roberts

method of application
Online application form

selection procedure
Interview & assessment day

closing date for 2007
31 July 2005

application
Training contracts p.a. **25**
Applications p.a. **1,500**
Required degree grade **2:1**

training
Salary
1st year (2004)
London & Reading £28,000
Sheffield £20,000
2nd year (2004)
London & Reading £32,000
Sheffield £22,000
Holiday entitlement **25 days**

post-qualification
Salary (2004)
London £48,000
Sheffield £32,000
(reviewed annually)

overseas offices
Brussels

A-Z SOLICITORS

Nicholson Graham & Jones

110 Cannon Street, London EC4N 6AR
Tel: (020) 7648 9000 Fax: (020) 7648 9001
Email: traineerecruitment@ngj.co.uk
Website: www.ngj.co.uk

firm profile
A successful mid-sized City law firm which has a strong commercial practice but also acts for private individuals.

main areas of work
The firm is divided into industry sector groups: finance; real estate and construction; projects; technology, media and sport; travel and leisure; manufacturing, distribution and retail.

trainee profile
Highly motivated intelligent graduates of any discipline.

training environment
Trainees spend six months in four of the following training seats: company; litigation; intellectual property; construction; private client and property. The firm aims to allow choice of seats where possible. Each trainee sits with a supervisor and is allocated an additional mentor to ensure all round supervision and training. The firm has a wide induction scheme and recently won an award for its career development programme. Trainees are encouraged to participate fully in all the activities of the firm. High importance is placed on the acquisition of practical skills with considerable emphasis on client contact and early responsibility. The training programme consists of weekly legal education seminars, workshops and a full programme of skills electives. Language training is also available. The annual training weekend is a popular event when the firm gets together for broader skills-based training and socialising.

benefits
Life assurance, season ticket loan, subsidised gym membership and BUPA.

vacation placements
The firm runs Open Days in the Easter and Summer Vacations. Online application.

sponsorship & awards
CPE and LPC fees paid plus annual maintenance grant £4,500 (2004).

Partners	52
Assistant Solicitors	54
Total Trainees	18

contact
Tina Two

method of application
Online only

selection procedure
Interview & assessment

closing date for 2007
31 July 2005

application
Training contracts p.a. **10**
Applications p.a. **1,500**
% interviewed p.a. **5%**
Required degree grade **2:1**

training
Salary
1st year (2004) **£28,000**
2nd year (2004) **£31,000**
Holiday entitlement **25 days**
% of trainees with a
non-law degree p.a. **Varies**

post-qualification
Salary (2004) **£46,000**
% of trainees offered job
on qualification (2003)
100%

overseas offices
Brussels

Norton Rose

Kempson House, Camomile Street, London EC3A 7AN
Tel: (020) 7283 6000 Fax: (020) 7283 6500
Email: grad.recruitment@nortonrose.com
Website: www.nortonrose.com

firm profile

Norton Rose is a leading city and international law firm. They provide an integrated business law service from a network of offices located across Europe, Asia and the Middle East. The firm works primarily for international corporates and financial institutions on large, complex, cross-border transactions, offering them the full range of business legal services.

main areas of work

Corporate finance; banking; dispute resolution; property, planning and environmental; taxation; competition; employment, pensions and incentives; intellectual property and technology.

trainee profile

Successful candidates will be commercially aware, focused, ambitious and team-orientated. High intellect and international awareness are a priority, and language skills are appreciated.

training environment

Norton Rose operates an innovative six-seat system. The first four seats (16 months) include one seat in each of the firm's core departments - corporate finance, banking and dispute resolution - plus an optional seat in one of the firm's other, non-core, departments - employment, pensions and incentives, tax, competition and EC, intellectual property and technology, or property, planning and environmental. The remaining eight months can be spent in the department in which you wish to qualify, or you can visit a different practice area for four months to help you to decide, and spend the last four months in your qualification seat. Alternatively, from your third seat onwards, you can elect to spend four months in one of the firm's international offices or apply for a client secondment. The firm's flexible seat system makes the transition from trainee to qualified solicitor as smooth as possible. The system has won the firm's trainees' approval, and from their point of view, develops associates with the adaptability and expertise the firm need for its future.

benefits

Life assurance (21+), private health insurance (optional), season ticket loan, subsidised gym membership.

vacation placements

Places for 2005: 45 Summer, 15 Christmas; Duration: Summer: Three weeks, Christmas: Two weeks; Remuneration: £250 p.w.; Closing Date: 31 January 2005 for Summer, 31 October 2004 for Christmas. Five or six open days per year are also held.

sponsorship & awards

£1,000 travel scholarship, £800 loan on arrival, four weeks unpaid leave on qualification. LPC/CPE fees paid plus a £5,000 maintenance grant.

Partners	217*
Assistant Solicitors	600*
Total Trainees	147

denotes worldwide figures

contact
Shaun Savory

method of application
Employer's application form (available on-line)

selection procedure
Interview and group exercise

closing date for 2007
31 July 2005

application
Training contracts p.a. 60-70
Applications p.a. 3,500+
% interviewed p.a. 7%
Required degree grade 2:1

training
Salary
1st year £28,500
2nd year £32,000
Holiday entitlement 25 days
% of trainees with a non-law degree p.a. 40%
No. of seats available abroad p.a. 22 (per seat move)

overseas offices
Amsterdam, Athens, Bahrain, Bangkok, Beijing,* Brussels, Cologne, Dubai, Frankfurt, Greece, Hong Kong, Jakarta,* London, Milan, Moscow, Munich, Paris, Piraeus, Prague,* Singapore, Warsaw
* Associated office

A - Z SOLICITORS

Olswang

90 High Holborn, London WC1V 6XX
Tel: (020) 7067 3000 Fax: (020) 7067 3999
Email: graduate@olswang.com
Website: www.olswang.com

firm profile

Forward thinking and progressive, Olswang's ethos has always focused on realising the potential of its clients, of all of its people and the potential within every situation. The firm's aim is simple: to be the preferred law firm of leading companies in the technology, media, telecommunications and property sectors. Olswang knows the players, knows the business and above all, understands the issues. Established in 1981, the firm has a total staff of more than 500 and has offices in London, the Thames Valley and Brussels.

main areas of work

Advertising; banking; bio-sciences; commercial litigation; corporate and commercial; media litigation; e-commerce; employment; EU and competition; film finance and production; information technology; intellectual property; music; private equity; property; sponsorship; sport; tax; telecommunications; TV/broadcasting.

trainee profile

Being a trainee at Olswang is both demanding and rewarding. The firm is interested in hearing from individuals with a 2:1 degree and above, exceptional drive and relevant commercial experience. In addition, it is absolutely critical that trainees fit well into the Olswang environment which is challenging, busy, energetic, individualistic, meritocratic and fun.

training environment

Olswang wants to help trainees match their expectations and needs with those of the firm. Training consists of four six-month seats in the corporate, media, communications and technology, litigation or property groups. You will be assigned a mentor, usually a partner, to assist and advise you throughout your training contract. In-house lectures supplement general training and three-monthly appraisals assess development. Regular social events not only encourage strong relationship building but add to the fun of work.

benefits

Immediately: life cover, medical cover, dental scheme, subsidised gym membership, season ticket loan. After six months: pension contributions. After 12 months: PHI.

vacation placements

Places for 2005: June & July; Duration: 2 weeks; Remuneration: £250 p.w.; 17 students per scheme; Closing Date: 31 January 2005.

sponsorship & awards

LPC and CPE fees paid in full. Maintenance grant of £4,500 (inside London), £4,000 (outside).

Partners 75
Assistant Solicitors 139
Total Trainees 43

contact
Victoria Edwards
Graduate Recruitment
Manager

method of application
Online

selection procedure
Business case scenario, interview, psychometric test and written exercises

closing date for 2007
31 July 2005

application
Training contracts p.a.
Up to 20
Applications p.a. 2,500
% interviewed p.a. 4%
Required degree grade 2:1

training
Salary
1st year (2004) £28,000
2nd year (2004) £32,000
Holiday entitlement 24 days
% of trainees with a non-law degree p.a. 50%

post-qualification
Salary (2004) £48,000

overseas offices
Brussels

Orchard

6 Snow Hill, London EC1A 2AY
Tel: (020) 7246 6100 Fax: (020) 7246 6101
Website: www.orchardlaw.com

firm profile

Established in 1995, Orchard has quickly made its name as one of the most vibrant firms in London. Built on the expertise of a highly experienced team, Orchard has already won the business of many household-name clients. The firm is committed to growth through focused recruitment.

main areas of work

Commercial litigation, white collar crime, regulatory and investigations, corporate finance, mergers and acquisitions, banking, financial services, corporate insolvency, commercial, commercial property, employment, IT/telecommunications and media.

trainee profile

Successful candidates will immediately form part of the professional team and gain early client contact alongside partners and qualified solicitors. Orchard's trainees are valued, fee-earning, members of the team, responsible for managing their own caseloads as well as assisting others. In a firm of Orchard's size, trainees have the opportunity to make a significant contribution to the running of the firm and its development. High standards of academic achievement are important but so too are commercial awareness and enthusiasm. Essential qualities are flexibility of approach and a sense of humour.

training environment

Trainees will spend six months in four of the firm's main practice areas sitting with a partner. Trainees benefit from a system which allows them to work both independently and as part of a team. Each trainee is assigned a personal mentor to assist them throughout their contract period and regular appraisals are conducted on both an informal and formal basis. Continuing education is encouraged and is supplemented by in-house seminars. Trainees are invited to join in the busy social life within the office and take part in client entertaining.

benefits

Under review.

vacation placements

Individual arrangements may be made in writing to Lisa Mills at:
lisa.mills@orchardlaw.com.

Partners	14
Assistants	24
Total Trainees	6

contact
Lisa Mills

method of application
Application form

selection procedure
Two interviews

closing date for 2007
September 2005

application
Training contracts p.a.4-6
Applications p.a. 350
% interviewed p.a. 8%
Required degree grade 2:1

training
Salary
1st year: market rate
2nd year: market rate
Holiday entitlement 20 days
% of trainees with a non-law degree p.a. 20%

post-qualification
% of trainees offered permanent employment 100%

A-Z SOLICITORS

Osborne Clarke

2 Temple Back East, Temple Quay, Bristol BS1 6EG
Tel: (0117) 917 4322
Email: graduate.recruitment@osborneclarke.com
Website: www.osborneclarke.com

firm profile
Osborne Clarke will challenge your preconceptions about law firms. Energetic, forward thinking and client-focused, it uses a unique mix of technical excellence, sector knowledge and outstanding service to support clients on a broad range of issus. As well as looking after its clients, Osborne Clarke is committed to looking after its people by giving them the opportunity to develop their potential as far as they want it to go. Providing interesting and rewarding careers is high on the agenda. The firm has been commended for its 'human touch', winning several awards over the years to reflect this, including '100 Best Companies to Work For' (Sunday Times), and, more recently, the 'Best Corporate Workplace 2003 Award' (British Council for Offices).

main areas of work
Principal areas of work include corporate, banking, commercial, property, employment, pensions and incentives, dispute resolution and tax. Osborne Clarke acts on sector 'insider' knowledge, bringing educated market solutions to the legal advice given. Sectors include construction, financial services, leisure, media, natural resources, retail, technology and telecoms and transport.

trainee profile
Take it as read that you should have intelligence, commercial focus and the ability to communicate with clients and colleagues alike. To succeed at Osborne Clarke you should also be down to earth, enthusiastic, committed and able to think independently. Trainees come from a wide background, with some joining after a first, or even second career.

training environment
Trainees can expect early responsibility. The firm takes an individual approach to ensure training is relevant to each trainee and offers a well-structured programme. Trainees are encouraged to spend time in at least two of the UK offices, in addition to which international opportunities to Europe and the US are available.

benefits
25 days holiday entitlement, employer's pension contributions, private healthcare cover, season ticket loan, permanent health insurance, group life assurance cover.

vacation placements
20–25 one week placements in April or July 2005, during which you will meet trainees, solicitors and partners, get involved with some real work and experience first-hand life at Osborne Clarke. Remuneration: £175 - £200 per week, depending on location. Closing date: 31 January 2005.

sponsorship & awards
CPE/PgDL and LPC course fees paid and £3,000 maintenance grant for each, some conditions apply.

Partners	95
Solicitors	109
Trainee Solicitors	39
Total Staff	660

contact
Graduate Recruitment Team

method of application
Online application form

selection procedure
Assessment day: group exercises, one-to-one interview and selection testing. Final stage: one-to-one partner interview and presentation

closing date for 2007
31 July 2005

application
Training contracts p.a. 20-25
Applications p.a. 1,000-1,500
% interviewed p.a. 8%
Required degree grade
2:1 preferred

training
Salary (2003)
1st year £26,500
London & Thames Valley,
£20,500 Bristol
Holiday entitlement 25 days
% of trainees with a non-law degree p.a. Approx 40%

post-qualification
Salary (2003)
£34,000 Bristol
£47,000 London
£43,000 Thames Valley

overseas offices
Germany: Cologne;
USA: Silicon Valley;
International (Alliance Member) Locations:
France (Paris), Belgium (Brussels), Spain (Barcelona, Madrid), The Netherlands (Rotterdam), Nordic Region (Copenhagen, Helsinki, Tallinn), Russia (St Petersburg) and Italy (Milan, Rome and Brescia)

Pannone & Partners

123 Deansgate, Manchester M3 2BU
Tel: (0161) 909 3000 Fax: (0161) 909 4444
Email: julia.jessop@pannone.co.uk
Website: www.pannone.com

firm profile

A high profile Manchester firm continuing to undergo rapid growth. The firm prides itself on offering a full range of legal services to a diverse client base which is split almost equally between personal and commercial clients. The firm was the first to be awarded the quality standard ISO 9001 and is a founder member of Pannone Law Group – Europe's first integrated international law group. Pannone & Partners was voted 6th in the 'Sunday Times' 100 Best Companies to Work For in 2004 and is the highest placed law firm in the survey.

main areas of work

Commercial litigation 18%; personal injury 30%; corporate 13%; commercial property 6%; family 8%; clinical negligence 7%; private client 13%; employment 5%.

trainee profile

Selection criteria include a high level of academic achievement, teamwork, organisation and communication skills, a wide range of interests and a connection with the North West.

training environment

An induction course helps trainees adjust to working life, and covers the firm's quality procedures and good practice. Regular trainee seminars cover the work of other departments within the firm, legal developments and practice. Additional departmental training sessions focus in more detail on legal and procedural matters in that department. Four seats of six months are spent in various departments and trainees' progress is monitored regularly. Trainees have easy access to support and guidance on any matters of concern. Work is tackled with gusto here, but so are the many social gatherings that take place.

vacation placements

Places for 2004: 50; Duration: 1 week; Remuneration: None; Closing Date: Easter 28 January 2005, Summer 29 April 2005.

sponsorship & awards

Full grant for LPC fees.

Partners	73
Assistant Solicitors	74
Total Trainees	19

contact
Julia Jessop

method of application
Application form & CV

selection procedure
Individual interview, second interview comprises a tour of the firm & informal lunch

closing date for 2007
1 August 2005

application
Training contracts p.a. **10**
Applications p.a. **900**
% interviewed p.a. **9%**
Required degree grade **2:1**

training
Salary
1st year (2004) £20,000
2nd year (2004) £22,000
Holiday entitlement **23 days**
% of trainees with a non-law degree p.a. **20%**

post-qualification
Salary (2004) **£32,000**
% of trainees offered job on qualification (2004) **85%**
% of assistants who joined as trainees **35%**
% of partners who joined as trainees **33%**

A-Z

SOLICITORS

Payne Hicks Beach

10 New Square, Lincoln's Inn, London WC2A 3QG
Tel: (020) 7465 4300 Fax: (020) 7465 4400
Email: apalmer@paynehicksbeach.co.uk
Website: www.paynehicksbeach.co.uk

firm profile

Payne Hicks Beach is a medium-sized firm based in Lincoln's Inn. The firm acts for both private clients and businesses. It is highly rated for private client and matrimonial advice and also specialises in commercial litigation, property and corporate and commercial work.

main areas of work

Private client 41%; matrimonial 22%; property 17%; commercial litigation 13%; corporate and commercial 7%.

trainee profile

The firm looks for law and non-law graduates with a good academic record, an ability to solve practical problems, enthusiasm and an ability to work hard and deal appropriately with their colleagues and the firm's clients.

training environment

Following an initial induction course, trainees usually spend six months in four of the firm's departments. Working with a partner, they are involved in the day to day activities of the department, including attending conferences with clients, counsel and other professional advisers. Assessment is continuous and trainees will be given responsibility as they demonstrate ability and aptitude. To complement the PSC, the firm runs a formal training system for trainees and requires them to attend lectures and seminars on various topics.

benefits

Season travel ticket loan, life assurance 4 x salary, permanent health insurance, contribution to personal pension plan.

sponsorship & awards

Fees for the CPE and LPC are paid.

Partners	28
Assistant Solicitors	21
Total Trainees	5

contact
Mrs Alice Palmer

method of application
Letter & CV

selection procedure
Interview

closing date for 2007
1 August 2005

application
Training contracts p.a. **3**
Applications p.a. **1,000**
% interviewed p.a. **3%**
Required degree grade **2:1**

training
Salary
1st year (2004) **£26,500**
2nd year (2004) **£28,500**
Holiday entitlement
4 weeks
% of trainees with a
non-law degree p.a. **50%**

Penningtons

Bucklersbury House, 83 Cannon Street, London EC4N 8PE
Tel: (020) 7457 3000 Fax: (020) 7457 3240
Website: www.penningtons.co.uk

firm profile

Penningtons is a thriving, modern law firm with a 200-year history and a deep commitment to top quality, partner-led services. Today, the firm is based in London and the South East with offices in London, Basingstoke, Godalming and Newbury.

main areas of work

In the business sphere, Penningtons advise on matters relating to all aspects of commercial property, intellectual property, management buy-outs and buy-ins, mergers, acquisitions and joint ventures, as well as litigation and dispute resolution. Advice is also given on information technology, business recovery, commercial contracts, agricultural and environmental law, and company secretarial services are offered. The firm also helps families and individuals with advice on property, tax and estate planning, family law, general financial management, the administration of wills and trusts, charities, personal injury, clinical negligence and immigration. Clients often ask Penningtons to advise on both their private and commercial affairs.

trainee profile

Penningtons seeks high calibre candidates with enthusiasm and resilience. A high standard of academic achievement is expected: three or more good A level passes and preferably a 2:1 or better at degree level, whether you are reading law or another discipline.

training environment

You will be given a thorough grounding in the law, spending time in three or four of the firm's departments - corporate and commercial, litigation, property and private client. The firm ensures a varied training is given, avoiding too specialised an approach before qualification. Nonetheless, the experience gained in each department gives you a solid foundation, equipping you to embark on your chosen specialisation at the end of your training contract with the firm. Penningtons knows its trainee solicitors are happiest and most successful when busy with good quality work. The firm believes in introducing trainees to challenging cases. The value of giving its trainees responsibility, and allowing direct contact with clients is recognised. However, experienced solicitors are always ready to give support when needed.

benefits

Life assurance, critical illness cover, pension, private medical insurance, 23 days holiday, interest free season ticket loan, sports and social events.

vacation placements

The firm offers both summer vacation placements and information days. Applications are accepted from 1 December 2004 to 31 March 2005.

sponsorship & awards

Full fees and maintenance for the LPC plus a maintenance grant of £4,000.

Partners	61*
Assistant Solicitors	100*
Total Trainees	25

denotes worldwide figures

contact
Andrea Law

method of application
Online via firm's website

closing date for 2007
31 July 2005

application
Training contracts p.a. **12**
Applications p.a. **1,000**
% interviewed p.a. **5%**
Required degree grade **2:1**

training
Salary
1st year (2004)
£26,500 (London)
2nd year (2004)
£28,500 (London)
Holiday entitlement 23 days

overseas offices
Paris

Pinsents

Dashwood House, 69 Old Broad Street, London EC2M 1NR
3 Colmore Circus, Birmingham B4 6BH
1 Park Row, Leeds LS1 5AB
The Chancery, 58 Spring Gardens, Manchester M216 1EW
Email: gradrecruiting@pinsents.com
Website: www.pinsents.com/graduate

firm profile

Pinsents is a leading corporate law firm that is committed to sector growth through its industry-recognised business model: the Chosen Market Strategy. This strategy aligns the firm to specific business sectors to achieve market-leading positions. As a result the firm has developed a successful and innovative approach to building strong, broad and deep corporate relationships. Client service is the cornerstone of the Pinsents business.

main areas of work

Corporate; dispute resolution and litigation; employment; insurance and reinsurance; pensions; projects and commercial; property; tax; technology and media.

trainee profile

The firm welcomes applications from both law and non-law graduates with a good honours degree. In addition to a strong academic background the firm is looking for problem solvers with a sharp commercial acumen, who as committed team players can use their initiative and common sense to get to the heart of the clients' business and legal needs.

training environment

Trainees sit in four seats of six months across the practice groups and are supervised by partners or associates. There are also opportunities for trainees to be seconded to clients. There is a supportive team structure where hands-on experience is an essential part of the learning process, with early responsibility and contact with clients encouraged. In addition to the PSC the firm has a structured development programme designed to broaden trainee business and legal knowledge. This is the first stage of the firm's focused legal management development programme that supports individuals through to partnership. The firm has an open-door policy and informal atmosphere with a positive focus on work/life balance.

summer vacation placements

Places for 2005: 90; Duration: 2 weeks; Closing Date: 31 January 2005.

sponsorship & awards

CPE/ LPC fees are paid. In addition to this, maintenance grants of £3,000 for CPE and £5,000 for LPC are offered.

Prettys

Elm House, 25 Elm Street, Ipswich IP1 2AD
Tel: (01473) 232121 Fax: (01473) 230002
Email: agage@prettys.co.uk
Website: www.prettys.co.uk

firm profile

Prettys is one of the largest and most successful legal practices in East Anglia. The firm is at the heart of the East Anglian business community, with the expanding hi-tech corridor between Ipswich and Cambridge to the west, Felixstowe to the east and the City of London 60 minutes away to the south. The firm's lawyers are approachable and pragmatic. It provides expert advice to national and regional businesses.

main areas of work

Prettys' broad-based practice allows it to offer a full-service to all its clients. Business law services: company, commercial, shipping, transport, construction, intellectual property, information technology, property, property litigation, employment, commercial litigation, insurance, professional indemnity, health and safety and executive immigration. Personal law services: French property, personal injury, clinical negligence, financial services, estates, agriculture, conveyancing and family.

trainee profile

Prettys' trainees are the future of the firm. Applicants should be able to demonstrate a desire to pursue a career in East Anglia. Trainees are given considerable responsibility early on and the firm is therefore looking for candidates who are well motivated, enthusiastic and have a good common sense approach. Good IT skills are essential.

training environment

A two-week induction programme will introduce you to the firm. You will receive continuous supervision and three-monthly reviews. Training is in four six-month seats with some choice in your second year and the possibility of remaining in the same department for two seats. Trainees work closely with a partner, meeting clients and becoming involved in all aspects of the department's work. Frequent training seminars are provided in-house. The PSC is taken externally. The Law Society's Monitoring of Training Officer recently visited the firm and concluded "Pretty's offers a very strong commitment to training within a supportive environment."

additional information

One day placements are available (apply to Angela Gage).

sponsorship & awards

Discretionary.

Partners	16
Total Trainees	10

contact
Angela Gage

method of application
Application letter & CV

closing date for 2007
July 31 2005

application
Training contracts p.a. 5
Required degree grade
2:1 preferred in law or
other relevant subject.
Good A Levels

training
Salary
**Above Law Society
guidelines**

A-Z

SOLICITORS

Pritchard Englefield

14 New St, London EC2M 4HE
Tel: (020) 7972 9720 Fax: (020) 7972 9722
Email: po@pe-legal.com
Website: www.pe-legal.com

firm profile

A medium-sized City firm practising a mix of general commercial and non-commercial law with many German and French clients. Despite its strong commercial departments, the firm still undertakes family and private client work and is known for its strong international flavour.

main areas of work

All main areas of commercial practice including litigation, company/commercial (UK, German and French), property and employment, also estate and trusts, personal injury and family.

trainee profile

High academic achievers with fluent German and/or French.

training environment

An induction course acquaints trainees with the computer network, library and administrative procedures and there is a formal in-house training programme. Four six-month seats make up most of your training. You can usually choose some departments, and you could spend two six-month periods in the same seat. Over two years, you learn advocacy, negotiating, drafting and interviewing, attend court, use your language skills and meet clients. Occasional talks and seminars explain the work of the firm, and you can air concerns over bi-monthly lunches with the partners comprising the Trainee Panel. PSC is taken externally over two years. Quarterly drinks parties number amongst popular social events.

benefits

Some subsidised training, luncheon vouchers.

sponsorship & awards

Full funding for LPC fees.

Partners	21
Assistant Solicitors	11
Total Trainees	6

contact
Graduate Recruitment

method of application
Standard application form available from Graduate Recruitment or online

selection procedure
1 interview only in September

closing date for 2007
31 July 2005

application
Training contracts p.a. **3**
Applications p.a. **300–400**
% interviewed p.a. **10%**
Required degree grade **Generally 2:1**

training
Salary
1st year (2004) £21,750
2nd year (2004) £22,250
Holiday entitlement **25 days**
% of trainees with a non-law degree p.a. **Approx 50%**

post-qualification
Salary (2004)
Approx £40,000
% of trainees offered job on qualification (2002) **75%**
% of assistants (as at 1/9/03) who joined as trainees **50%**
% of partners (as at 1/9/03) who joined as trainees **40%**

Reed Smith

Minerva House, 5 Montague Close SE1 9BB
Tel: (020) 7403 2900 Fax: (020) 7403 4221
Email: tclaxton@reedsmith.com
Website: www.reedsmith.com

firm profile

Reed Smith is a leading international law firm and one of the 20 largest firms worldwide. The firm has grown rapidly over the past few years through a series of strategic mergers and lateral additions, with the result that it now has over 1,000 lawyers located in 14 US offices and two UK offices located in London and the Midlands. The firm has a strong presence on both the east and west coasts and its transatlantic capabilities mean it is strategically positioned to provide teams of US and UK lawyers who work together on major transactions crossing both continents. In the UK the firm has over 80 dedicated staff and continues to focus on building upon its capabilities and strengthening its European expertise.

main areas of work

Its core services in the UK are European corporate, which encompasses a full corporate/commercial service including financial services, corporate finance, competition, M&A, reinsurance and corporate tax, litigation, employment and real estate.

trainee profile

Enthusiastic, proactive, bright, commercially-minded graduates who want to work in a friendly atmosphere where personality, a sense of humour and a hands-on approach are encouraged.

training environment

To help trainees build a strong career, the firm invests heavily in training (approximately one training session per week) covering a range of skills including advocacy, drafting and marketing. The firm provides an informal but fast-paced working environment where trainees are immediately given access to clients and fulfilling work, often with an international bias. Trainees who are fluent French speakers will be given opportunities to develop these skills. The firm has four seats available in business and finance, international litigation, real estate and employment. Progress is reviewed regularly by the Training Principal.

benefits

BUPA, IFSTL, life assurance, permanent health insurance & pension contribution available after qualifying period.

vacation placements

Places for Summer 2005: 12; Duration: 3 weeks (London), 2 weeks (Midlands); Remuneration: £600 (London), £300 (Midlands); Closing Date: 31 January 2005.

sponsorship & awards

CPE/LPC fees and maintenance grant of £2,500 for CPE/PgDL students and £5,000 for LPC students.

Partners	32
Assistant Solicitors	34
Total Trainees	12
960 lawyers internationally	

contact
Tassy Claxton
Recruitment Co-ordinator

method of application
Online

selection procedure
Assessment day:
2 interviews, aptitude test
& presentation

closing date for 2007
31 July 2005

application
Training contracts p.a.
6 (London 4, Coventry 2)
Applications p.a. 700
% interviewed p.a. 3%
Required degree grade 2:1

training
Salary
London
1st year (2004) £27,000
2nd year (2004) £31,000
Coventry
1st year (2004) £19,500
2nd year (2004) £22,000
Holiday entitlement 25 days
% of trainees with a non-law
degree 25%

post-qualification
Salary (2003) £48,000

Reynolds Porter Chamberlain

Chichester House, 278-282 High Holborn, London WC1V 7HA
Tel: (020) 7242 2877 Fax: (020) 7242 1431
Email: training@rpc.co.uk
Website: www.rpc.co.uk/training

firm profile

Reynolds Porter Chamberlain is a leading commercial law firm with approximately 250 lawyers. In addition to its main offices in Holborn, the firm has an expanding office at Leadenhall Street in the City which serves its insurance clients. Best known as a major litigation practice, particularly in the field of insurance, RPC also has thriving corporate, commercial property, construction and private client departments. Another rapidly expanding part of the firm is its media and technology practice. This handles major defamation actions and has dealt with some of the biggest internet deals to date.

main areas of work

Litigation 60%; corporate 10%; commercial property 10%; construction 10%; media and technology 5%; family/private client 5%.

trainee profile

The firm appoints 15 trainees each year from law and non-law backgrounds. Although proven academic ability is important (the firm requires a 2:1 or above), RPC also values flair, energy, business sense, commitment and the ability to communicate and relate well to others.

training environment

As a trainee you will receive first rate training in a supportive working environment. You will work closely with a partner and be given real responsibility as soon as you are ready to handle it. At least six months will be spent in each of the three main areas of the practice and the firm encourages trainees to express a preference for their seats. This provides a thorough grounding and the chance to develop confidence as you see matters through to their conclusion. In addition to the internally provided Professional Skills Course the firm provides a complimentary programme of in-house training.

benefits

Four weeks holiday, bonus schemes, private medical insurance, income protection benefits, season ticket loan, subsidised gym membership, active social calendar.

vacation placements

Places for July 2005: 18; Duration: 2 weeks; Remuneration: £250 p.w.; Closing Date: 28 February 2005.

sponsorship & awards

CPE/PgDL Funding: Fees paid plus £4,500 maintenance; LPC Funding: Fees paid plus £4,500 maintenance.

Partners	62
Assistant Solicitors	200
Total Trainees	21

contact
Kate Gregg
Graduate Recruitment Officer

method of application
Online application system

selection procedure
Assessment days held in September

closing date for 2007
12 August 2005

application
Training contracts p.a. 15
Applications p.a. 900
% interviewed p.a. 6%
Required degree grade 2:1

training
Salary
1st year (2003) £28,000
2nd year (2003) £30,000
Holiday entitlement 20 days
% of trainees with a non-law degree p.a. Approx 25%

post-qualification
Salary (2003) £47,000
% of trainees offered job on qualification (2003) 80%
% of assistants (as at 1/9/03) who joined as trainees 30%
% of partners (as at 1/9/03) who joined as trainees 35%

Richards Butler

Beaufort House, 15 St. Botolph Street, London EC3A 7EE
Tel: (020) 7247 6555 Fax: (020) 7247 5091
Email: gradrecruit@richardsbutler.com

firm profile
Established in 1920, Richards Butler is noted for the exceptional variety of its work. It has acknowledged strengths in commercial disputes, commodities, competition, corporate finance, energy law, insurance, media/entertainment, property and shipping, in each of which it has international prominence. Over two thirds of the firm's work has an international dimension.

main areas of work
Banking/commercial/corporate finance 27%; insurance/international trade and commodities/shipping 29%; commercial disputes 30%; commercial property 14%.

trainee profile
Candidates should be players rather than onlookers, work well under pressure and be happy to operate as a team member or team leader as circumstances dictate. Candidates from diverse backgrounds are welcome, including mature students with commercial experience and management skills.

training environment
Four or five seat rotations enable Richards Butler to provide practical experience across as wide a spectrum of the law as possible. Trainees can also apply for secondment to one of the firm's overseas offices, Hong Kong, Paris, Abu Dhabi, São Paulo, Piraeus or to one of their client's in-house legal teams.

benefits
Performance related bonus, life insurance, BUPA, interest-free season ticket loan, subsidised staff restaurant, staff conveyancing allowance.

vacation placements
Places for 2005: 30; Duration: 2 weeks; Remuneration: £200 p.w.; Closing Date: 6 February 2005. In addition, the firm offers overseas scholarships to Paris, Hong Kong, Abu Dhabi and Athens. The scholarship consists of a return airfare, accomodation, living expenses and two weeks of work experience. Please see website for further information.

sponsorship & awards
CPE Funding: Fees paid plus £5,000 maintenance.
LPC Funding: Fees paid plus £5,000 maintenance.

Partners	108*
Fee-earners	395*
Total Trainees	64*

denotes worldwide figures

contact
Mark Matthews

method of application
Online application form

selection procedure
Selection exercise & interview

closing date for 2007/08
31 July 2005

application
Training contracts p.a. 20
Applications p.a. 2,000
% interviewed p.a. 5%
Required degree grade 2:1

training
Salary
1st year (2004) £28,000
2nd year (2004) £31,000
Holiday entitlement 25 days
% of trainees with a
non-law degree p.a. 25%
No. of seats available
abroad p.a. 10

post-qualification
Salary (2004)
£48,000 plus bonus
% of assistants who
joined as trainees 59%
% of partners who
joined as trainees 54%

overseas offices
Abu Dhabi, Athens,
Beijing, Brussels, Hong
Kong, Muscat*, Paris,
Piraeus, São Paulo
Associated office

Salans

Clements House, 14-18 Gresham Street, London EC2V 7NN
Tel: (020) 7509 6000 Fax: (020) 7726 6191
Email: london@salans.com

firm profile
Salans has an open and friendly culture, and an informal, but hardworking environment.
It is a multinational law firm with full-service offices in the City of London, Paris and New
York, together with further offices in Almaty, Baku, Bratislava, Bucharest, Istanbul, Kyiv,
Moscow, Prague, Shanghai, St Petersburg and Warsaw, and an affiliated office in
Budapest. The firm currently has over 560 fee-earners, including 128 partners worldwide,
with 30 partners residing in the London office. Salans was named East European Law
Firm of the Year at the Chambers Awards 2004, and were runners-up in the Litigation
Team of the Year award at The Lawyer Awards.

main areas of work
London Office: Banking and finance; corporate; litigation; employment; real estate; insolvency and corporate recovery; information technology and communications; betting and
gaming; and media and film finance.

trainee profile
You will have high academic qualifications, including good A-Level (or equivalent)
results, and the ability to approach complex problems in a practical and commercial way.
The firm is looking for highly motivated, creative and enthusiastic team players. It looks
to recruit trainees who make a difference, want early responsibility and live life in the fast
lane of the ever-changing legal world. Relevant work experience demonstrating a desire
to pursue a career in law will be viewed positively, and language and computer skills are
also valued.

benefits
Private healthcare, pension, life assurance, critical illness cover, season ticket loan.

sponsorship & awards
LPC tuition fees paid.

Partners 128
(Worldwide)
Assistant Solicitors
(Worldwide) 560+
Total Trainees
(London) 7

contact
Vicky Williams
HR Manager

method of application
Handwritten letter & CV

selection procedure
interview programme and
selection workshop

closing date for 2007
31 July 2005

application
Training contracts p.a. **3-4**
Applications p.a. **500+**
% interviewed p.a. **3%**
Required degree grade **2:1**

training
Salary
1st year (2004) **£26,500**
2nd year (2004) **£28,500**
Holiday entitlement **25 days**
% of trainees with a
non-law degree p.a. **Variable**
No. of seats available
abroad p.a. **None at present**

post-qualification
Salary (2004) **Variable**
% of trainees offered job
on qualification (2004) **100%**

overseas offices
Almaty, Baku, Bratislava,
Bucharest, Budapest*,
Istanbul, Kyiv, Moscow,
New York, Paris, Prague,
Shanghai, St Petersburg
and Warsaw

*affiliated office

Shadbolt & Co

Chatham Court, Lesbourne Road, Reigate RH2 7LD
Tel: (01737) 226277 Fax: (01737) 226165
Email: mail@shadboltlaw.com
Website: www.shadboltlaw.com

firm profile

Shadbolt & Co is an award-winning, dynamic, progressive firm committed to high quality work and excellence both in the UK and internationally. The atmosphere at the firm is friendly, relaxed and informal and there are various social and sporting activities for staff. The firm comprises a lively and enterprising team with a fresh and open approach to work. The firm's qualified staff have a high level of experience and industry knowledge and some are widely regarded as leading practitioners in their field.

main areas of work

The firm is well known for its strengths in major projects, construction and engineering and dispute resolution and litigation with established expansion into corporate and commercial, employment, commercial property and IT and e-commerce. The firm provides prompt personal service and its client list includes some of the world's best known names in the construction and engineering industries.

trainee profile

Applicants must demonstrate that they are mature self-starters with a strong academic background and outside interests. Leadership, ambition, initiative, enthusiasm and good interpersonal skills are essential, as is the ability to play an active role in the future of the firm. Linguists are particularly welcome, as are those with supporting professional qualifications. The firm welcomes non-law graduates.

training

Four six month seats from construction and commercial litigation, arbitration and dispute resolution, major projects and construction, employment, corporate and commercial and commercial property. Where possible individual preference is noted. Work has an international bias. There are opportunities for secondment to major clients and work in the overseas offices. Trainees are treated as valued members of the firm, expected to take early responsibility and encouraged to participate in all the firm's activities, including practice development. The firm is accredited by the law society as a provider of training and runs frequent in-house lectures. The PSC is taught externally.

sponsorship & benefits

Optional private healthcare, permanent health insurance, group life assurance, paid study leave, season ticket loan, discretionary annual bonus of up to 5% of salary, paid professional memberships and subscriptions, 50% refund of LPC upon commencement of training contract.

vacation placements

Places for 2005: 6; Duration: 2 weeks; Remuneration (2004): £170 p.w.; Closing Date: 28 February 2005; Interviews: April 2005.

Partners	23
Assistant Solicitors	21
Total Trainees	8
Total Staff	110

contact
Andrea Pickett

method of application
Application form

selection procedure
Interview & written assessment & group exercise

closing date for 2007
31 July 2005 (interviews September 2005)

application
Training contracts p.a. 4
Applications p.a. 100
% interviewed p.a. 20%
Required degree grade 2:1 (occasional exceptions)

training
Salary
1st year (2004) £24,000
2nd year (2004) £28,000
Holiday entitlement
20 days rising to 25 on qualification, with opportunity to 'buy' an additional 5 days holiday p.a.
% of trainees with a non-law degree p.a. 50%
No. of seats available abroad p.a. 1

post-qualification
Salary (2004) £42,000
% of trainees offered job on qualification (2004) 66%
% of assistants (2004) who joined as trainees 33%
% of partners (2004) who joined as trainees 0%

other offices
Reigate, City of London, Paris, Dar es Salaam, Athens

Shearman & Sterling LLP

Broadgate West, 9 Appold Street, London EC2A 2AP
Tel: (020) 7655 5000 Fax: (020) 7655 5500

firm profile
Shearman & Sterling LLP is one of New York's oldest legal partnerships, which has transformed from a New York-based firm focused on banking into a diversified global institution. Recognised throughout the world, the firm's reputation, skills and expertise are second to none in its field. The London office, established in 1972, has become a leading practice covering all aspects of English and European corporate and finance law. The firm employs over 130 English and US trained legal staff in London and has more than 1,000 lawyers in 18 offices worldwide.

main areas of work
Banking, leveraged finance and securitisation. Project finance. M&A. Global capital markets. International arbitration and litigation. Tax. EU and competition.Financial Institutions Advisory & Asset Management (legal and regulatory advice to financial institutions and infrastructure providers, both in a retail and wholesale context, and both on-line and off-line). Executive Compensation & Employee Benefits (sophisticated advice on the design and implementation of compensation and benefits arrangements).

trainee profile
The firm's successful future development calls for people who will relish the hard work and intellectual challenge of today's commercial world. You will be a self-starter, keen to assume professional responsibility early in your career and determined to become a first-class lawyer in a first-class firm. The firm's two year training programme will equip you with all the skills needed to become a successful commercial lawyer. You will spend six months in each of four practice areas, with an opportunity to spend six months in Abu Dhabi, Hong Kong or Singapore. You will be an integral part of the London team from the outset, with your own laptop and mobile phone. The firm will expect you to contribute creatively to all the transactions you are involved in. The firm has an informal yet professional atmosphere. Your enthusiasm, intellect and energy will be more important than what you wear to work. The firm will provide you with a mentor, arrange personal and professional development courses and give you early responsibility. The firm wants to recruit people who will stay with it; people who want to become partners in its continuing success story.

sponsorship & awards
Sponsorship for the CPE/PgDL and LPC courses, together with a maintenance grant of £5,000.

Partners	26
Assistant Solicitors	96
Total Trainees	15

contact
Kirsten Davies
Tel: (020) 7655 5082

method of application
Application form

selection procedure
Interviews

closing date for 2007
31 July 2005

application
Training contracts p.a. 10
Required degree grade 2:1

training
Salary
1st year (2004) £35,000
2nd year (2004) £37,500
Holiday entitlement
24 days p.a.
% of trainees with non-law
degree p.a. 50%
No of seats available
abroad 3

post-qualification
Salary (2004) £55,000
% of trainees offered job
on qualification (2004) 100%

overseas offices
Abu Dhabi, Bejing,
Brussels, Düsseldorf,
Frankfurt, Hong Kong,
Mannheim, Menlo Park,
Munich, New York, Paris,
Rome, San Francisco,
Singapore, Tokyo, Toronto,
Washington DC

Shoosmiths

The Lakes, Bedford Road, Northampton NN4 7SH
Tel: (0870) 086 3223 Fax: (0870) 086 3001
Email: join.us@shoosmiths.co.uk
Website: www.shoosmiths.co.uk

firm profile

Growing steadily, with seven offices across the country, 72 partners and 1,200 staff, Shoosmiths is one of the big players outside London. By joining the firm you can expect to experience a full range of interesting and challenging commercial work. In a demanding legal market, Shoosmiths has developed exciting, even radical, services helping it to exceed the highest expectations of its clients. The firm supports and encourages its people to develop exhilarating, balanced careers. Shoosmiths' workplace culture offers a stimulating environment, time for family and the opportunity to put something back into the community.

main areas of work

Corporate/commercial; commercial property; dispute resolution; employment; planning; banking; financial institutions; private client; personal injury.

trainee profile

You will be confident, motivated and articulate with natural intelligence and the drive to succeed, thereby making a real contribution to the firm's commercial success. You will want to be a part of a winning team and will care about the kind of service you give to your clients, both internal and external.

training environment

You will be involved in 'real' work from day one of your training contract. Sitting with a Partner who will oversee your training and career development, you will have direct contact with clients and will draft your own letters and documents. Your experience will build through your daily, practical, workload complemented by the training you would expect from a leading national law firm. In addition to the compulsory Professional Skills Course, the firm offers a comprehensive internal training programme that includes managerial, legal and IT training as standard. Over the course of two years, you will complete four seats of six month duration to help you decide which area you would like to qualify into.

benefits

Flexible holidays, pension (after 3 months service), life assurance, various staff discounts, Christmas bonus.

vacation placements

Places for 2005: 30; Duration: 2 weeks; Remuneration: £200 p.w.; Closing Date: 28 Feb 2005.

sponsorship & awards

LPC funding: £12,500 – split between fees and maintenance.

Partners	72
Assistant Solicitors	106
Total Trainees	23

contact
Sarah Woods

method of application
Application form via website

selection procedure
Selection centre - full day

closing date for 2007
31 July 2005

application
Training contracts p.a. **11**
Applications p.a. **1,000**
% interviewed p.a. **10%**
Required degree grade **2:1**

training
Salary
Competitive
Holiday entitlement
23 days + option to flex

post-qualification
Salary **Market rate**

offices
Northampton, Nottingham, Reading, Fareham, Milton Keynes, Basingstoke, Birmingham

Sidley Austin Brown & Wood

Woolgate Exchange, 25 Basinghall Street, London EC2V 5HA
Tel: (020) 7360 3600 Fax: (020) 7626 7937
Email: itabraham@sidley.com
Website: www.sidley.com

firm profile

Sidley Austin Brown & Wood is one of the world's largest full-service law firms combining the strengths of two exceptional law firms. With more than 1,550 lawyers practising in 13 offices on three continents (North America, Europe and Asia), the firm provides a broad range of integrated services to meet the needs of its clients across a multitude of industries. The firm has over 90 lawyers in London and is expanding fast.

main areas of work

Corporate securities; corporate finance; investment funds; tax; banking regulation; securitisation and structured finance; corporate reconstruction; property and property finance.

trainee profile

Sidley Austin Brown & Wood is looking for focused, intelligent and enthusiastic individuals with personality and humour who have a real interest in practising law in the commercial world. Trainees should have a 2:1 degree (not necessarily in law) and three A levels at A and B grades. Trainees would normally be expected to pass the CPE (if required) and the LPC at the first attempt.

training environment

Sidley Austin Brown & Wood is looking to recruit six to eight trainee solicitors to start in September 2007/March 2008. The firm is not a typical City firm and it is not a 'legal factory' so there is no risk of being just a number. The team in London is young, dynamic and collegiate. Everyone is encouraged to be proactive and to create their own niche when they are ready to do so. Trainees spend a period of time in the firm's specialist groups: international finance, tax and property. Sidley Austin Brown & Wood in London does not have a separate litigation department, although some litigation work is undertaken. The firm does, however, organise external litigation training for all trainees. In each group trainees will sit with a partner or senior associate to ensure that students receive individual training that is both effective and based on a real caseload. In addition, there is a structured timetable of training on a cross-section of subjects and an annual training weekend.

benefits

Healthcare, disability cover, life assurance, contribution to gym membership, interest-free season ticket loan.

sponsorship & awards

CPE and LPC fees paid and maintenance p.a.

Partners	31
Assistant Solicitors	65
Total Trainees	16

contact
Isabel Tabraham, Legal and Graduate Recruitment Manager

method of application
Covering letter & employee application form

selection procedure
Interview(s)

closing date for 2007
29 July 2005

application
Training contracts p.a. 6-8
Applications p.a. 500
% interviewed p.a. 15
Required degree grade 2:1

training
Salary
1st year (2004) £28,500
2nd year (2004) £32,000
Holiday entitlement 25 days
% of trainees with a non-law degree p.a. 50%

overseas offices
Beijing, Chicago, Dallas, Geneva, Hong Kong, London, Los Angeles, New York, San Francisco, Shanghai, Singapore, Tokyo, Washington DC

Simmons & Simmons

CityPoint, One Ropemaker Street, London EC2Y 9SS
Tel: (020) 7628 2020 Fax: (020) 7628 2070
Email: recruitment@simmons-simmons.com
Website: www.simmons-simmons.com

firm profile

Simmons & Simmons is a worldclass law firm providing advice to financial institutions, corporates, public and international bodies and private individuals through its international network of offices. It provides a comprehensive range of legal services with strength and depth. The ability to provide technically excellent, commercial and high quality advice is expected of leading law firms. Simmons & Simmons aims to provide an additional dimension by focusing on the way it works with its clients and by shaping its services to fit the clients' needs.

main areas of work

The firm provides 10 legal services including: commercial, corporate, dispute resolution, EU & competition, employment & benefits, finance, intellectual property, projects, real estate & environment and tax. The firm works with particular focus in eight key industries: Aerospace & Defence, Consumer Goods, Energy & Utilities, Financial Markets, Pharmaceutical & Biotechnology, Real Estate & Construction, TMT and Transport.

trainee profile

A good academic record and sound commercial judgement is essential, but strength of character and outside interests are also taken into consideration.

training environment

The firm will make sure you have the right skills to join its team of worldclass legal professionals. Simmons & Simmons really wants you to succeed so you'll find a warm welcome as well as genuine levels of support from your new colleagues. The firm has put together a friendly, supportive and approachable team of people who will accompany you throughout your training. There will be a supervisor to help with your everyday work and also a dedicated personnel officer who looks after you from the minute you join.

benefits

Season ticket loan, fitness loan, group travel insurance, group accident insurance, death in service, medical cover, staff restaurant.

vacation placements

Vacation scheme opportunities available. Remuneration £250 per week; deadline 31 January 2005.

sponsorship & awards

In the absence of local authority funding LPC fees and GDL fees are paid, plus a maintenance grant of £5,000 for London, Oxford or Guildford and £4,500 elsewhere.

Partners	213
Assistant Solicitors	503
Total Trainees	209

contact
Vickie Chamberlain
Graduate Recruitment
Manager

method of application
Online application

selection procedure
Assessment days:
document exercise,
interview & written exercise

closing date for 2007
29 July 2005

application
Training contracts p.a.50
Applications p.a. 2,500
% interviewed p.a. 10%
Required degree grade 2:1

training
Salary
1st year (2004) £28,000
2nd year (2004) £32,000
Holiday entitlement 25 days
% of trainees with a
non-law degree p.a. 50%
No. of seats available
abroad p.a. 30

post-qualification
Salary (2004) £48,000
% of trainees offered job
on qualification (2004) 70%

overseas offices
London, Rotterdam, Paris,
Lisbon, Milan, Rome,
Dusseldorf, Frankfurt,
Brussels, Madrid, Padua,
Oportu, Madeira, Abu
Dhabi, Qatar, Hong Kong,
Shanghai, Tokyo, New
York.

Slaughter and May

One Bunhill Row, London EC1Y 8YY
Tel: (020) 7600 1200 Fax: (020) 7090 5000
Website: www.slaughterandmay.com

firm profile
One of the leading law firms in the world, Slaughter and May enjoys a reputation for quality and expertise. The corporate and financial practice is particularly strong and lawyers are known for their business acumen and technical excellence. As well as its London office, in order that the firm provides the best advice and service across the world, it nurtures long-standing relationships with the leading independent law firms in other jurisdictions. This means there are opportunities for secondments to these law firms as well as the firm's offices in Paris, Brussels and Hong Kong.

main areas of work
Corporate, commercial and financing; tax; competition; financial regulation; dispute resolution; technology, media and telecommunications; intellectual property; commercial real estate; environment; pensions and employment.

trainee profile
The work is demanding and the firm looks for intellectual agility and the ability to work with people from different countries and walks of life. Common sense, a mature outlook and the willingness to accept responsibility are all essential. The firm expects to provide training in everything except the fundamental principles of law, so does not expect applicants to know much of commercial life. Trainees are expected to remain with the firm on qualification.

training environment
Four or five seats of six months duration. Two seats will be in the field of commercial, corporate and financial law with an option to choose a posting overseas (either to one of the firm's offices or to a "best friend" firm), or competition or financial regulation. One seat in either dispute resolution, intellectual property, tax or pensions and employment is part of the programme and a commercial real estate seat is also possible. In each seat a partner is responsible for monitoring your progress and reviewing your work. There is an extensive training programme which includes the PSC. There are also discussion groups covering general and specialised legal topics.

benefits
BUPA, STL, pension scheme, subsidised membership of health club, 24 hour accident cover.

vacation placements - summer 2005
Places: 60; Duration: 2 weeks; Remuneration: £250 p.w.; Closing Date: 28 January 2005 for penultimate year (of first degree) students only.

sponsorship & awards
CPE and LPC fees and maintenance grants are paid.

Partners	128
Associates	414
Total Trainees	179

contact
Charlotte Houghton

method of application
Online (via website) preferred or by posting to the firm a CV and covering letter

selection procedure
Interview

application
Training contracts p.a.
Approx 85
Applications p.a. **2,500+**
% interviewed p.a. **20%**
Required standard
Good 2:1 ability

training
Salary (May 2004)
1st year £29,000
2nd year £32,500
Holiday entitlement
25 days p.a.
% of trainees with a
non-law degree **Approx 50%**
No. of seats available
abroad p.a. **Approx 35-40**

post-qualification
Salary (May 2004) **£50,000**
% of trainees offered job
on qualification (2003) **94%+**

overseas offices
Paris, Brussels and Hong Kong.

Speechly Bircham

6 St Andrew Street, London EC4A 3LX
Tel: (020) 7427 6400 Fax: (020) 7353 4368
Email: trainingcontracts@speechlys.com
Website: www.speechlys.com

firm profile
Speechly Bircham is a mid-sized City law firm with an excellent client base. Its strong commercial focus is complemented by a highly regarded private client practice. The firm handles major transactions as well as commercial disputes and has a good reputation for several specialist advisory areas, notably private client and corporate tax. Speechly Bircham's strengths lie in the synergy of the relationships between its four main departments, private client, corporate and tax, litigation and property.

main areas of work
Corporate and tax 25%; property 25%; litigation 25%; private client 25%.

trainee profile
Both law and non-law graduates who are capable of achieving a 2:1. The firm seeks intellectually dynamic individuals who enjoy a collaborative working environment where they can make an impact.

training environment
Speechly Bircham divides the training contract into four six-month seats. Emphasis is given to early responsibility and supervised client contact providing trainees with a practical learning environment.

benefits
Season ticket loan, private medical insurance, life assurance.

vacation placements
Places for 2005: 12. The firm's summer placement scheme for students gives them the chance to experience a City legal practice. In a three-practice placement, students will be asked to research and present on a legal issue at the end of their placement; Duration: 3 weeks; Remuneration: £250 p.w.; Closing Date: 14 February 2005.

sponsorship & awards
CPE and LPC fees and a maintenance grant.

Partners	47
Assistant Solicitors	66
Total Trainees	10

contact
Nicola Swann
Human Resources Director

method of application
Application form (available by request or online)

selection procedure
Interview

closing date for 2007
31 July 2005

application
Training contracts p.a. **5**
Applications p.a. **1,000**
% interviewed p.a. **5%**
Required degree grade **2:1**

training
Salary
1st year (2004)
£26,000-£27,000
2nd year (2004)
£28,000-£29,000
Holiday entitlement **20 days**
% of trainees with a
non-law degree p.a. **50%**

post-qualification
Salary (2004) **£45,000**

steeles (law)

3 Norwich Business Park, Whiting Rd, Norwich NR4 6DJ
Tel: (01603) 598000 Fax: (01603) 598111
Email: personnel@steeleslaw.co.uk
Website: www.steeleslaw.co.uk

firm profile

steeles is an innovative and progressive commercial practice with a growing national client base. It is recognised in particular for the strength of its employment and commercial practitioners and for the range and quality of its services to local authorities and business.

main areas of work

steeles offers a full range of corporate, property, litigation and public sector services. The practice is dedicated to delivering high quality value for money services to its clients regardless of location.

trainee profile

Candidates will be highly motivated, commercially astute, with a strong academic record and previous relevant experience.

training environment

The aim is to ensure that every trainee will wish to continue their career with steeles. The training programme consists of four six-month seats in the following departments: company commercial, commercial property, civil litigation, commercial disputes, employment, music and media and public sector. You will have some choice in the order of your seats. Trainees are encouraged to take on as much responsibility as possible with considerable client contact early on in their training contract. Bi-monthly meetings provide a forum for discussion of topical issues. The offices are open-plan, providing a supportive and learning environment which reflects the practice's accreditation to both ISO 9001 and Investor in People. Trainee solicitors are appraised at the end of each seat and are included in the firm's mentor scheme. There is an active sports and social life.

benefits

Private medical cover, accident insurance, legal services, interest-free season ticket loan, gym membership loan.

vacation placements

Places for 2005: Places offered throughout the Summer vacation.

Partners	13
Assistant Solicitors	31
Total Trainees	12

contact
Ann Chancellor
Human Resources Manager

method of application
Online or CV & covering letter

selection procedure
Interview/assessment day

application
Training contracts p.a. 6
Applications p.a. 300-400
Required degree grade 2:1

post-qualification
% of trainees offered job on qualification (2004) 100%

Stephenson Harwood

One St Paul's Churchyard, London EC4M 8SH
Tel: (020) 7329 4422 Fax: (020) 7606 0822
Email: graduate.recruitment@shlegal.com
Website: www.shlegal.com

firm profile
Established in the City of London in 1828, Stephenson Harwood has developed into a large international practice, with a commercial focus and a wide client base.

main areas of work
Corporate (including corporate finance, funds, corporate tax, business technology); employment, pensions and benefits; banking and asset finance; dry and wet shipping litigation; commercial litigation; and real estate.

trainee profile
The firm looks for high calibre graduates with excellent academic records and an outgoing personality.

training environment
As the graduate intake is relatively small, the firm gives trainees individual attention, coaching and monitoring. Your structured and challenging programme involves four six month seats in areas of the firm covering contentious and non-contentious areas, across any department within the firm's practice groups. It may also involve a secondment to one of the overseas offices or to a client in London. These seats include 'on the job' training, sharing an office and working with a partner or senior solicitor. In-house lectures complement your training and there is continuous review of your career development. You will have the opportunity to spend six months abroad and have free language tuition where appropriate. You will be given your own caseload and as much responsibility as you can shoulder. The firm plays a range of team sports, offers subsidised membership of a City health club (or a health club of your choice) and has privileged seats for concerts at the Royal Albert Hall and the London Coliseum and access to private views at the Tate Gallery.

benefits
Subsidised membership of health clubs, private health insurance, BUPA membership, season ticket loan and 25 days paid holiday per year.

vacation placements
Places for 2005: 16; Duration: 2 weeks; Remuneration: £250 p.w.; Closing Date: 18 February 2005.

sponsorship & awards
Fees paid for CPE and LPC and maintenance awards.

Partners	80*
Assistant Solicitors	219*
Total Trainees	43

* denotes world-wide figures

contact
Caroline Thompson
(Graduate Recruitment)

method of application
Online application form only

selection procedure
assessment centre

closing date for
Sept 2007/ March 2008
31 July 2005

application
Training contracts p.a. **12**
% interviewed p.a. **10%**
Required degree grade **2:1**

training
Salary
1st year (2004) **£26,000**
2nd year (2004) **£29,000**
Holiday entitlement **25 days**
% of trainees with a
non-law degree p.a. **46%**
No. of seats available
abroad p.a. **10-12**

post-qualification
Salary (2004) **£46,000**
% of trainees offered job
on qualification (2002) **75%**
% of assistants (as at
1/9/01) who joined as
trainees **37%**
% of partners (as at 1/9/01)
who joined as trainees **46%**

overseas offices
Bucharest, Paris, Piraeus,
Singapore and in the
People's Republic of China
- Guangzhou and Hong
Kong, with an associated
office in Shanghai.

Stevens & Bolton LLP

The Billings, Guildford, Surrey GU4 1YD
Tel: (01483) 302264 Fax: (01483) 302254
Email: gradrec@stevens-bolton.co.uk
Website: www.stevens-bolton.co.uk

firm profile

Stevens & Bolton LLP is a leading South East law firm based in Guildford. The firm provides clients with a City-calibre service and offers its trainees a supportive culture and excellent training. This was recently recognised when the firm won Best Trainer (medium regional firm) awarded by LawCareers.net and the TSG. The firm has 25 partners and over 130 staff in total. The firm has grown rapidly in the past five years and is one of the major firms in the region, described recently by The Legal 500 as a 'regional heavyweight'. The firm's work is 80% commercial, the remainder being private client work advising medium and high net worth individuals. The firm acts for a diverse range of clients. These include FTSE 100 businesses, subsidiaries of major international groups and growing, owner managed companies. The firm receives instructions from household names such as Gallaher Group plc, Hays plc, The BOC Group and Morse plc to name a few!

main areas of work

Corporate and commercial, property, litigation and dispute resolution, employment, private client and family.

trainee profile

The firm requires a good academic record and individuals with interests such as music, sport, travel and who have a genuine enthusiasm to work in the law.

training environment

Usually you will sit with a partner who will act as your supervisor and you will get real responsibility early on. There is a comprehensive cross-departmental training programme and regular reviews of performance.

benefits

Private medical insurance, life assurance, pension, rail or car park season ticket loan, permanent health insurance.

sponsorship & awards

Providing no local authority grant is available, full fees for the GDL and LPC plus £4,000 maintenance grant each year.

Partners	25
Assistant Solicitors	37
Total Trainees	6

contact
Julie Bounden
(01483) 302264

method of application
Graduate application form and covering letter, available from the website or by request

selection procedure
Two interviews

closing date for 2007
31 August 2005

application
Training contracts p.a. 3
Applications p.a. 450
% interviewed 5%
Required degree grade 2:1
& one grade A at 'A' Level

training
Salary
1st year (2004) £21,500
2nd year (2004) £23,500
Holiday entitlement 25 days

post-qualification
Salary (2004) £38,000
% of trainees offered job on qualification (2004) 70%

overseas/regional offices
Guildford only

STEVENS & BOLTON LLP

Tarlo Lyons

Watchmaker Court, 33 St John's Lane, London EC1M 4DB
Tel: (020) 7405 2000 Fax: (020) 7814 9421
Email: trainee.recruitment@tarlolyons.com
Website: www.tarlolyons.com

firm profile

Tarlo Lyons is a modern London firm focused on delivering creative commercial solutions for technology-driven businesses. The firm has a leading reputation for its technology work and its expertise provides real benefits for its clients across a range of sectors.

main areas of work

Tarlo Lyons continues to focus confidently on technology and other developments for our commercial clients. It has particular strengths in areas such as IT and outsourcing, hotels, leisure and gaming and financial services. Clients include global corporates, UK listed and unlisted corporates, entrepreneurial businesses and individuals. The main practice areas are commercial property, commercial technology, corporate, dispute resolution and employment and resourcing.

trainee profile

Tarlo Lyons lawyers can be identified as smart, commercially savvy, fun and professional – they aren't defined by the school they went to or their examination results. The firm welcomes applicants who have taken a gap year or who have had work experience in business. It values the differences in skills, strengths and ideas each person brings.

training environment

Opportunities for learning are provided throughout the training contract. You will gain work experience in most departments, including at least three months in the firm's Dispute Resolution Department, with the PSC taught externally. Your work experience will be interactive and varied and you will participate in a wide range of business development and marketing activities.

benefits

Tarlo Lyons offers competitive compensation and your salary may be enhanced by a discretionary bonus payment. The firm's benefits package includes a 50% subsidy to a nearby gym, private health cover, death in service cover and participation in a pension plan.

sponsorship & awards

LPC fees paid.

Partners	23
Assistant Solicitors	14
Total Trainees	6

contact
Trainee Recruitment
Co-ordinator

method of application
Application form available from website

selection procedure
2 interviews

closing date for 2007
6 August 2005

application
Training contracts p.a. 3
Applications p.a. 200
% interviewed p.a. 10%
Required degree grade 2:1

training
Salary
1st year (2003) £27,000 on average
2nd year (2003) £29,000 on average
Holiday entitlement 25 days
% of trainees with a non-law degree p.a. 50%

post-qualification
Salary (2003) £42,000
(Salary levels may increase subject to market conditions)

A-Z SOLICITORS

Taylor Walton

28-44 Alma Street, Luton LU1 2PL
Tel: (01582) 731161 Fax: (01582) 457900
Email: luton@taylorwalton.co.uk
Website: www.taylorwalton.co.uk

Partners	25
Assistant Solicitors	32
Total Trainees	10

contact
Jim Wrigglesworth

method of application
CV with covering letter

selection procedure
First & second interview
with opportunity to meet
other partners

closing date for 2007
30 July 2005

application
Required degree grade
2:1 or above

firm profile

Strategically located in Luton, Harpenden, St Albans and Hemel Hempstead, Taylor Walton is a major regional law practice advising both businesses and private clients. Its strengths are in commercial property, corporate work and commercial litigation, whilst maintaining a strong private client side to the practice. It has a progressive outlook both in its partners and staff and in its systems, training and IT.

main areas of work

Company/commercial 15%; commercial property 20%; commercial litigation 15%; employment 5%; personal injury 5%; family 5%; private client 10%; residential property 20%; direct conveyancing 5%.

trainee profile

Candidates need to show excellent intellectual capabilities, coupled with an engaging personality so as to show that they can engage and interact with the firm's clients as the practice of law involves the practice of the art of communication. Taylor Walton sees its partners and staff as business advisers involved in clients' businesses, not merely stand-alone legal advisers.

training environment

The training consists of four six-month seats. The trainee partner oversees the structural training alongside a supervisor who will be a partner or senior solicitor in each department. The firm does try to take trainees' own wishes in relation to seats into account. In a regional law practice like Taylor Walton you will find client contact and responsibility coupled with supervision, management and training. There is an in-house training programme for all fee-earning members of staff. Trainees are given the opportunity to discuss their progress with their supervisor at a montly appraisal meeting. In addition, at the end of each seat there is a post seat appraisal conducted by the trainee partner. The PSC is taught externally. The firm is friendly with an open door policy and there are various sporting and social events.

vacation placements

Places for 2005: 8; Duration: Up to 3 weeks; Remuneration: £150 per week; Closing Date: 30 March 2005.

sponsorship & awards

September 2006: full LPC sponsorship.

Taylor Wessing

Carmelite, 50 Victoria Embankment, Blackfriars
London EC4Y 0DX
Tel: (020) 7300 7000 Fax: (020) 7300 7100
Website: www.taylorwessing.com

firm profile

Taylor Wessing is a powerful source of legal support for organisations doing business in and with Europe. Regarded as 'one of the first names outside the Magic Circle', it is a market leader in advising IP and technology-rich industries, with a strong reputation in the corporate, finance and real estate sectors. The firm provides clients with in-depth experience across the full range of commercial legal services including tax, employment and dispute resolution. Theirs is a straightforward vision: to be an outstanding European law firm trusted by its clients to deliver success.

main areas of work

Corporate, intellectual property, finance & projects, real estate, dispute resolution, employment & pensions and private client.

trainee profile

High intellectual ability is paramount and the firm seeks a minimum of ABB grades at A Level and a 2.1 degree in any discipline. The firm looks for team players who have excellent communication skills, energy, ambition, an open mind and a willingness to learn. Applicants will also need to demonstrate a commitment to a career in law and a genuine interest in business.

training environment

Trainees will spend six months in four different departments, including a seat in either the corporate or finance & projects department. There is also the possibility of a secondment to another office or a client. Trainees work closely with a number of partners and associates in the departments and are provided with plenty of opportunity for early responsibility. At the beginning of the training and throughout trainees have ongoing discussions about their interests and how they fit in with the growth and needs of the departments. They also receive regular feedback and are appraised in the middle and at the end of each seat. All trainees attend the Professional Skills Course, which is run in-house, and other training courses as necessary during the two years.

benefits

Private medical care, permanent health insurance, season ticket loan, subsidised staff restaurant, non-contributory pension scheme.

vacation placements

Places for 2005: 20 Duration: 2 weeks; Remuneration: £225 per week; Closing date: Middle of February 2005.

sponsorship & awards

PgDL and LPC fees paid in full. Maintenance grant £4,500 per annum.

Partners	191
Fee-earners	574
Trainees	40 (UK)

contact
Graduate Recruitment Department

method of application
online application form

selection procedure
two interviews, one with a partner

closing date for 2007
31 July 2005

application
Training contracts p.a. **20**
Applications p.a. **1,150**
% interviewed p.a. **8%**
Required degree grade **2:1**

training
Salary
1st year **£28,000**
2nd year **£31,000**
Holiday entitlement **25 days**
% of trainees with a non-law degree p.a. **30%**

post-qualification
Salary (2003) **£48,000**
% of trainees offered job on qualification (2003-04) **60-65%**

overseas offices
Berlin, Brussels, Cologne Dusseldorf, Frankfurt, Hamburg, Munich, Paris and representative offices in Alicante and Shanghai. Associated office in Dubai.

Teacher Stern Selby

37-41 Bedford Row, London WC1R 4JH
Tel: (020) 7242 3191 Fax: (020) 7242 1156
Email: r.raphael@tsslaw.com
Website: www.tsslaw.com

firm profile

A central London-based general commercial firm, with clientele and caseload normally attributable to larger firms. It has a wide range of contacts overseas.

main areas of work

Commercial litigation 25%; commercial property 38%; company and commercial 16%; secured lending 12%; private client 4%; clinical negligence/education/judicial review 5%.

trainee profile

Emphasis falls equally on academic excellence and personality. The firm looks for flexible and motivated individuals, who have outside interests and who have demonstrated responsibility in the past.

training environment

Trainees spend six months in three departments (company commercial, litigation and property) with, where possible, an option to return to a preferred department in the final six months. Most trainees are assigned to actively assist a partner who monitors and supports them. Trainees are fully involved in departmental work and encouraged to take early responsibility. Trainees are expected to attend in-house seminars and lectures for continuing education. The atmosphere is relaxed and informal.

vacation placements

Places for 2005: Approximately 10 places to those that have accepted or applied for training contracts.

sponsorship & awards

Possible but unlikely.

Partners	20
Assistant Solicitors	17
Total Trainees	9

contact
Russell Raphael

method of application
Letter & application form

selection procedure
2 interviews

closing date for 2007
30 September 2005

application
Training contracts p.a. **3-6**
Applications p.a. **1,000**
% interviewed p.a. **5%**
Required degree grade
2:1 (not absolute)

training
Salary
1st year (2007) **£25,000**
Holiday entitlement
4 weeks
% of trainees with a
non-law degree p.a. **50%**

post-qualification
Salary (2006) **£36,000**
% of trainees offered job
on qualification (2004) **40%**
% of assistants (as at
1/5/03) who joined as
trainees **35%**
% of partners (as at 1/5/03)
who joined as trainees **38%**

Thomas Eggar

The Corn Exchange, Baffins Lane, Chichester PO19 1GE
Tel: (01243) 813253
Email: mark.james@thomaseggar.com
Website: www.thomaseggar.com

firm profile
Thomas Eggar is rated as one of the top 100 law firms in the UK. Based in the South East, it is one of the country's leading regional law firms with a staff of over 400. The firm offers both private client and commercial services to a diverse range of clients, locally, nationally and internationally. It also offers financial services through Thesis, the firm's investment management arm, which is the largest solicitor-based investment unit in the UK.

main areas of work
Apart from its strength in the private client sector, the firm handles property, commercial and litigation matters; among its major clients are banks, building societies and other financial institutions, railway and track operators and construction companies.

trainee profile
The firm seeks able trainees with common sense, application and good business acumen, with a 2.1 degree in any discipline. Applications can be made up to 1 August 2005 for training contracts to commence in September 2007 and March 2008. Applications should be in the form of a CV and covering letter. You should give details of your attachment to the South East region in your covering letter.

training environment
Trainees would normally have four seats covering commercial property, commercial, litigation and private client. In order to give good exposure to various specialisations, some of the seats are likely to be in different offices.

vacation placements
There is a very limited vacation scheme in July and August each year: this runs for 5 days, three days in the Horsham office and two days in the London office. Applications should be made with CV and covering letter to Mark James by 31 March 2005. Please give details of your accommodation plans in your covering letter. Travel expenses are paid.

sponsorship & awards
LPC 50% grant, 50% loan.

Vacancies	8
Partners	55
Trainees	16
Total Staff	400

contact
Mark James BEM

method of application
Letter & CV

selection procedure
Assessment centre & interview

closing date for 2007/2008
1 August 2005

training
The firm aims to pay the going rate for a South Eastern provincial firm. A London weighting is paid to those who undertake seats in the London office. The firm also pays a taxable travel allowance to all its trainees. Required degree grade
2:1 (any discipline)

other offices
Chichester, Horsham, Lodon, Reigate, Worthing

A-Z

SOLICITORS

Thomson Snell & Passmore

3 Lonsdale Gardens, Tunbridge Wells, Kent TN1 1NX
Tel: (01892) 510000 Fax: (01892) 549884
Email: solicitors@ts-p.co.uk
Website: www.ts-p.co.uk

firm profile

Thomson Snell & Passmore continues to be regarded as one of the premier law firms in the South East. The firm has a reputation for quality and a commitment to deliver precise and clear advice which is recognised and respected both by its clients and professional contacts. It has held the Lexcel quality mark since January 1999. The firm is vibrant and progressive and enjoys an extremely friendly atmosphere. Its offices are located in the centre of Tunbridge Wells and attract clients locally, nationally and internationally.

main areas of work

Commercial litigation 13%; corporate and employment 12%; commercial property 12%; private client 21%; personal injury/clinical negligence 19%; residential property 15%; family 8%.

trainee profile

Thomson Snell & Passmore regards its trainees from the outset as future assistants, associates and partners. The firm is looking for people not only with strong intellectual ability, but enthusiasm, drive, initiative, strong interpersonal and team-working skills, together with good IT skills.

training environment

The firm's induction course will help you to adjust to working life. As a founder member of Law South your training is provided in-house with trainees from other Law South member firms. Your two-year training contract is divided into four periods of six months each. You will receive a thorough grounding and responsibility with early client exposure. You will be monitored regularly, receive advice and assistance throughout and appraisals every three months. The Training Partner will co-ordinate your continuing education in the law, procedure, commerce, marketing, IT and presentation skills. Trainees enjoy an active social life which is encouraged and supported.

sponsorship & awards

Grant and interest free loan available for LPC.

Partners	32
Assistant Solicitors	60
Total Trainees	8

contact
Human Resources
Manager
Tel: (01892) 510000

method of application
Letter & application form available from website

selection procedure
Assessment interview

closing date for 2007
31 July 2005

application
Training contracts p.a. 4
Applications p.a.
Approximately 500
% interviewed p.a. 5%
Required degree grade
2:1 (any discipline)

training
Salary for each year of training
1st year (Sept 2004)
£17,250
2nd year (Sept 2004)
£18,750
Holiday entitlement 25 days

post-qualification
% of trainees offered job on qualification 75%

overseas/regional offices
Network of independent law firms throughout Europe and founding member of Law South

TLT Solicitors

One Redcliff St, Bristol BS99 7JZ
Tel: (0117) 917 7777 Fax: (0117) 917 7778
Email: graduate@TLTsolicitors.com
Website: www.TLTsolicitors.com

firm profile

During 2004 TLT won the Legal Business UK Regional Law Firm of the Year. This award was in recognition for a strong performance both regionally and nationally in the past 12 months. In addition, The Lawyer also selected Managing Partner, David Pester, as one of the UK's Hot 100 leading individuals. These accolades reflect TLT's reputation which is built on an eagerness to understand client businesses and a 'whatever it takes' approach to client service.

main areas of work

An impressive national and international client base ensures high quality work in a broad range of specialist areas: Banking, capital markets, commercial dispute resolution, construction, corporate, employment, family, insolvency and business breakdown, intellectual property, lender services, mergers and acquisitions, partnerships, pensions, planning and environmental, property, tax, technology and media.

trainee profile

Strong academic background together with commitment and drive to succeed.

training environment

TLT's commitment to excellence will ensure that trainees benefit from a well developed and challenging training programme. Training is delivered through four seats of six months duration, chosen in consultation with the trainee. In each seat the trainee will sit with a lawyer although their work will be drawn from all members of the team in order to gain the widest possible experience. Regular monitoring and development planning ensures that trainees get the most out of their training and helps them to identify their long term career path from the varied specialisms on offer.

benefits

Pension, life assurance. and subsidised sports/health club membership.

vacation placements

12 paid summer placements available, each lasting one week. Apply online by 31st March 2005.

sponsorship & awards

LPC fees plus maintenance payment.

Partners	39
Assistant Solicitors	60
Total Trainees	12

contact
Catherine Wiltshire
Human Resources

method of application
Firm's application form
online or paper

selection procedure
Assessment Centre

closing date for 2007
15 August 2005

application
Training contracts p.a. 8
Applications p.a. 500+
% interviewed p.a. 5%
Required degree grade
2:1 prefered
non-law degree p.a. 50%

post-qualification
Market rate

A-Z SOLICITORS

Travers Smith

10 Snow Hill, London EC1A 2AL
Tel: (020) 7295 3000 Fax: (020) 7295 3500
Email: graduate.recruitment@traverssmith.com
Website: www.traverssmith.com

firm profile

A leading City firm with a major corporate and commercial practice. Although less than a quarter of the size of the dozen largest firms, Travers Smith is renowned for handling the highest quality work, much of which has an international dimension.

main areas of work

Corporate law (including takeovers and mergers, financial services and regulatory laws), commercial law (which includes competition and intellectual property), dispute resolution, corporate recovery/insolvency, tax, employment, pensions, banking and property.
The firm also offers a range of pro bono opportunities within individual departments and on a firm-wide basis. In 2004, solicitors from the firm were awarded two separate national awards in recognition of their outstanding contributions to pro bono work.

trainee profile

The firm looks for people who combine academic excellence with plain common sense; who are articulate, who think on their feet, who are determined and self-motivated and who take their work but not themselves seriously. Applications are welcome from law and non-law graduates.

training environment

The firm has a comprehensive training programme which ensures that trainees experience a broad range of work. All trainee solicitors sit in rooms with partners and assistants, receive an individual and extensive training from experienced lawyers and enjoy client contact and the responsibility that goes with it from the beginning of their training contract.

benefits

Private health insurance, permanent sickness cover, life assurance cover, season ticket loan, subsidised firm bistro, subsidised gym membership .

vacation placements

45 places for summer 2005: Duration: two weeks; Remuneration: £250; Closing Date: 31 January 2005. The firm also offers Christmas and Easter placements.

sponsorship & awards

GDL and LPC paid in full plus maintenance of £5,000 per annum to those in London and £4,500 per annum to those outside London.

Partners	51
Assistant Solicitors	129
Total Trainees	44

contact
Germaine VanGeyzel

method of application
CV and covering letter online or by post

selection procedure
Interviews (2 stage process)

closing date for 2007
31 July 2005

application
Training contracts p.a. Up to 25
Applications p.a. 2,000
% interviewed p.a. 12%
Required degree grade 2:1

training
Salary
1st year (2004) £28,000
2nd year (2004) £32,000
Holiday entitlement 20 days

post-qualification
Salary (2004) £50,000
% of trainees offered job on qualification (2004) 71%
% of assistants (as at 1/9/04) who joined as trainees 68%
% of partners (as at 1/9/03) who joined as trainees 61%

Trowers & Hamlins

Sceptre Court, 40 Tower Hill, London EC3N 4DX
Tel: (020) 7423 8000 Fax: (020) 7423 8001
Email: gradrecruitment@trowers.com
Website: www.trowers.com

firm profile

Trowers & Hamlins is a substantial city and international firm. Particular strengths include housing and housing finance, local government, UK and international projects, company commercial, construction, commercial property and public/private sector initiatives including private finance. Other specialisations include the health sector, environmental law, employment and charities.

main areas of work

Property (housing, public sector, commercial) ; company and commercial/construction; litigation; private client.

trainee profile

Personable, enthusiastic candidates with a good academic record and wide-ranging outside interests. The ability to work under pressure and with others, combined with versatility, are essential characteristics.

training environment

Trainees will gain experience in four seats from: company/commercial, construction, property, international, litigation, employment and private client. Trainees are encouraged to learn from direct contact with clients and to assume responsibility. The training programme is flexible and, with reviews held every three months, individual preferences will be considered. A training officer assists partners with the training programme and in-house lectures and seminars are held regularly. There are opportunities to work in Manchester and the Middle East. The firm encourages a relaxed atmosphere and blends traditional qualities with contemporary attitudes. Activities are organised outside working hours.

benefits

Season ticket loan, private healthcare after six months service, Employee Assistance Programme and discretionary bonus, Death in Service.

vacation placements

Places for 2005: 25-30; Duration: 2 weeks; Remuneration: £225 p.w.; Closing Date: 1 March (Summer). Open Day: June/July.

sponsorship & awards

CPE and LPC fees paid and £4,250-£4,500 maintenance p.a.

Partners	72
Assistant Solicitors	121
Total Trainees	30

contact
Graduate Recruitment Office

method of application
Letter, application form & CV

selection procedure
Interview(s), essay & practical test

closing date for 2007
1 August 2005

application
Training contracts p.a. **12–15**
Applications p.a. **1,600**
% interviewed p.a. **4%**
Required degree grade **2:1+**

training
Salary (subject to review)
1st year **£26,000**
2nd year **£27,500**
Holiday entitlement **25 days**
% of trainees with a non-law degree p.a. **40%**
No. of seats available abroad p.a. **Between 4-6**

post-qualification
Salary (2004) (subject to review) **£43,500**
% of trainees offered job on qualification (2003) **80%**
% of assistants (as at 1/7/04) who joined as trainees **44%**
% of partners (as at 1/7/04) who joined as trainees **34%**

overseas offices
Abu Dhabi, Dubai, Oman, Bahrain, Cairo

A-Z SOLICITORS

631

Walker Morris

Kings Court, 12 King Street, Leeds LS1 2HL
Tel: (0113) 283 2500 Fax: (0113) 245 9412
Email: traineerecruit@walkermorris.co.uk
Website: www.walkermorris.co.uk

firm profile

Based in Leeds, Walker Morris is one of the largest commercial law firms in the North, with over 750 people, providing a full range of legal services to commercial and private clients both nationally and internationally.

main areas of work

Commercial litigation 30%; commercial property 25%; company and commercial 25%; building societies 16%; private clients 2%; tax 2%.

trainee profile

Bright, articulate, highly motivated individuals who will thrive on early responsibility in a demanding yet friendly environment.

training environment

Trainees commence with an induction programme, before spending four months in each main department (commercial property, corporate and commercial litigation). Trainees can choose in which departments they wish to spend their second year. Formal training will include lectures, interactive workshops, seminars, interactive video and e-learning. The PSC covers the compulsory elements and the electives consist of a variety of specially tailored skills programmes. Individual IT training is provided. Opportunities can also arise for secondments to some of the firm's major clients. Emphasis is placed on teamwork, inside and outside the office. The firm's social and sporting activities are an important part of its culture and are organised by a committee drawn from all levels of the firm. A trainee solicitors' committee represents the trainees in the firm but also organises events and liaises with the Leeds Trainee Solicitors Group.

vacation placements

Places for 2005: 45 over 3 weeks; Duration: 1 week; Remuneration: £165 p.w.; Closing Date: 28 February 2005.

sponsorship & awards

LPC & PGDL fees plus maintenance of £4,500.

Partners	42
Assistant Solicitors	98
Total Trainees	30

contact
Nick Bates

method of application
Application form

selection procedure
Telephone & face-to-face interviews

closing date for 2007
31 July 2005

application
Training contracts p.a. **15**
Applications p.a.
Approx. 800
% interviewed p.a.
Telephone **16%**
Face to face **8%**
Required degree grade **2:1**

training
Salary
1st year (2004) **£20,000**
2nd year (2004) **£22,000**
Holiday entitlement **24 days**
% of trainees with a non-law degree p.a.
30% on average

post-qualification
Salary (2004) **£33,000**
% of trainees offered job on qualification (2004) **73%**
% of assistants (as at 1/7/04) who joined as trainees **60%**
% of partners (as at 1/7/04) who joined as trainees **55%**

Ward Hadaway

Sandgate House, 102 Quayside, Newcastle upon Tyne NE1 3DX
Tel: (0191) 204 4000 Fax: (0191) 204 4098
Email: recruitment@wardhadaway.com
Website: www.wardhadaway.com

firm profile
Ward Hadaway is one of the most progressive commercial law firms in the North of England. The firm is firmly established as one of the North East region's legal heavyweights.

main areas of work
Litigation; property; company/commercial; private client.

trainee profile
The usual academic and professional qualifications are sought. Sound commercial and business awareness are essential as is the need to demonstrate strong communication skills, enthusiasm and flexibility. Candidates will be able to demonstrate excellent inter-personal and analytical skills.

training environment
The training contract is structured around four seats (property, company/commercial, lit-igation and private client) each of six months duration. At regular intervals, and each time you are due to change seat, you will have the opportunity to discuss the experience you would like to gain during your training contract. The firm will always try to give high pri-ority to your preferences. You will share a room with a partner or associate which will enable you to learn how to deal with different situations. Your practical experience will also be complemented by an extensive programme of seminars and lectures. All trainees are allocated a 'buddy', usually a second year trainee or newly qualified solicitor, who can provide as much practical advice and guidance as possible during your training. The firm has an active Social Committee and offers a full range of sporting and social events.

benefits
23 days holiday (26 after five years service), death in service insurance, contributory pension.

vacation placements
Applications for summer vacation placements should be received by 30 April 2005. Duration one week.

sponsorship & awards
CPE & LPC fees paid and £2,000 interest-free loan.

wardhadaway

| Partners | 48 |
| Total Trainees | 16 |

contact
Carol Butts
Human Resources Manager

method of application
Application form &
covering letter

selection procedure
Interview

closing date for 2007
31 July 2005

application
Training contracts p.a. 8
Applications p.a. 400+
% interviewed p.a. 10%
Required degree grade 2:1

training
Salary
1st year (2004) £17,500
2nd year (2004) £18,500
Holiday entitlement 23 days
% of trainees with a
non-law degree p.a. Varies

post-qualification
Salary (2004)
£31,000 minimum

Watson, Farley & Williams

15 Appold Street, London EC2A 2HB
Tel: (020) 7814 8000 Fax: (020) 7814 8017
Email: graduates@wfw.com
Website: www.wfw.com

firm profile

Established in 1982, Watson, Farley & Williams has its strengths in corporate, banking and asset finance, particularly ship and aircraft finance. The firm aims to provide a superior service in specialist areas and to build long-lasting relationships with its clients.

main areas of work

Shipping; ship finance; aviation; banking; asset finance; corporate; litigation; e-commerce; intellectual property; EC and competition; taxation; property; insolvency; telecoms; project finance.

trainee profile

Outgoing graduates who exhibit energy, ambition, self-assurance, initiative and intellectual flair.

training environment

Trainees are introduced to the firm with a comprehensive induction course covering legal topics and practical instruction. Seats are available in at least four of the firm's main areas, aiming to provide trainees with a solid commercial grounding. There is also the opportunity to spend time abroad, working on cross-border transactions. Operating in an informal, friendly and energetic atmosphere, trainees will receive support whenever necessary. You will be encouraged to take on early responsibility and play an active role alongside a partner at each stage of your training. The practice encourages continuous learning for all employees and works closely with a number of law lecturers, producing a widely-read 'digest' of legal developments, to which trainees are encouraged to contribute. All modules of the PSC are held in-house. The firm has its own sports teams and organises a variety of social functions.

benefits

Life assurance, PHI, BUPA, STL, pension, subsidised gym membership.

vacation placements

Places for 2005: 30; Duration: 2 weeks; Remuneration: £200 p.w.; Closing Date: 25th February 2005.

sponsorship & awards

CPE and LPC fees paid and £4,500 maintenance p.a. (£4,000 outside London).

Partners	56
Assistant Solicitors	150
Total Trainees	20

contact
Graduate Recruitment Manager

method of application
Online application

selection procedure
Assessment centre & Interview

closing date for 2007
29 July 2005

application
Training contracts p.a. **10**
Applications p.a. **1,000**
% interviewed p.a. **10%**
Required degree grade
Minimum 2:1 & 24 UCAS points or above

training
Salary
1st year (2004) £28,500
2nd year (2004) £32,500
Holiday entitlement **22 days**
% of trainees with a non-law degree p.a. **50%**
No. of seats available abroad p.a. **12**

post-qualification
Salary (2004)
Not less than £50,000 at the time of writing
% of trainees offered job on qualification (2004) **80%**
% of assistants (as at 1/9/04) who joined as trainees **60%**
% of partners (as at 1/9/04) who joined as trainees **4%**

overseas offices
New York, Paris, Piraeus, Singapore, Bangkok, Rome

Wedlake Bell

52 Bedford Row, London, WC1R 4LR
Tel: (020) 7395 3000 Fax: (020) 7395 3100
Email: recruitment@wedlakebell.com
Website: www.wedlakebell.com

firm profile

Wedlake Bell is a medium-sized law firm providing legal advice to businesses and high net worth individuals from around the world. The firm's services are based on a high degree of partner involvement, extensive business and commercial experience and strong technical expertise. The firm has over 80 lawyers in central London and Guernsey, and affiliations with law firms throughout Europe and in the United States.

main areas of work

For the firm's business clients: Banking and asset finance; corporate; commercial property; media, IP and commercial; internet and e-business; employment services; pensions and share schemes; construction; litigation and dispute resolution.
For private individuals: Tax, trusts and wealth protection; offshore services.

trainee profile

In addition to academic excellence, Wedlake Bell looks for commercial aptitude, flexibility, enthusiasm, a personable nature, confidence, mental agility and computer literacy in its candidates. Languages are not crucial.

training environment

Trainees have four seats of six months across the following areas: corporate, banking, construction, media and IP/IT, employment, litigation, property and private client. As a trainee the firm encourages you to have direct contact and involvement with clients from an early stage. Trainees will work within highly specialised teams and have a high degree of responsibility. Tainees will be closely supervised by a partner or senior solicitor and become involved in high quality and varied work. The firm is committed to the training and career development of its lawyers and many of its trainees continue their careers with the firm often through to partnership. Wedlake Bell has an informal, creative and co-operative culture with a balanced approach to life.

sponsorship & benefits

LPC and CPE fees paid and £2,500 maintenance grant where local authority grant not available. During training contract: pension, travel loans, subsidised gym membership. On qualification: 25 days holiday, life assurance, medical insurance and PHI.

vacation placements

Places for 2005: 6; Duration: 3 weeks in July; Remuneration: £150 p.w.; Closing Date: End of February.

Partners	33
Assistant Solicitors	37
Total Trainees	12

contact
Natalie King

method of application
CV & covering letter

selection procedure
Interviews in September

closing date for 2007
End August 2005

application
Training contracts p.a. **6**
Required degree grade **2:1**

training
Holiday entitlement
1st year **20 days**,
2nd year **21 days**
% of trainees with a
non-law degree p.a. **50%**

post-qualification
% of trainees offered job
on qualification (2004) **83%**
% of assistants (as at
1/9/04) who joined as
trainees **40%**

overseas offices
Guernsey

Weightmans

India Buildings, Water Street, Liverpool L2 0GA
Tel: (0870) 241 3512 Fax: (0151) 227 3223
Email: HR@weightmans.com
Website: www.weightmans.com

Partners	74
Assistant Solicitors	112
Trainees p.a.	12

method of application
online with
www.weightmans.com

closing date for 2007
31 July 2005

other offices
Birmingham, Leicester,
London, Manchester

firm profile

Weightmans is a top 100 UK law firm with 74 partners and nearly 550 staff. With offices in Birmingham, Leicester, Liverpool, London and Manchester, the firm offers a comprehensive range of legal services to both public sector organisations and private sector companies. In addition to being one of the largest litigation practices in the UK, the firm has a thriving commercial practice. The firm develops successful relationships with its clients, based on a spirit of partnership and trust. The firm encourages innovation and strives to achieve excellence in all its activities. Above all, it listens, keeps its promises, and dedicates itself to providing a complete value for money service for every client, large or small.

main areas of work

The firm's areas of commercial expertise include company commercial, commercial litigation, property, employment, licensing, construction, intellectual property and IT. Litigation expertise includes workplace, transport and large loss claims. Specialist teams within the firm service the healthcare, professional indemnity, public sector and police markets.

trainee profile

Weightmans is a friendly firm, with a strong commitment to a team environment and a culture that encourages early, decisive and effective action from all its staff. The firm is looking for enterprising commercially-minded people, who share its commitment to client service and will contribute to the spirit of the firm by demonstrating their support for its values. Applications from a wide variety of academic backgrounds are considered. Those with a track record that demonstrates an ability to study with discipline and common sense to achieve results will have a distinct advantage. The firm believes in rewarding all of its people well. It pays a highly competitive salary that is reviewed annually. The firm offers a benefits package, which includes a pension, health cover and life assurance.

training environment

Weightmans expects its trainees to make a positive contribution from the outset. Four six-month seats, with focused training and regular review meetings, provides a progressive learning environment for its young lawyers.

Weil, Gotshal & Manges

One South Place, London EC2M 2WG
Tel: (020) 7903 1074 Fax: (020) 7903 0990
Email: graduate.recruitment@weil.com
Website: www.weil.com

firm profile

Weil Gotshal & Manges is a leader in the marketplace for sophisticated, international legal services. With more than 1,100 lawyers across the US, Europe and Asia, the firm serves many of the most successful companies in the world in their high-stakes matters and transactions.

main areas of work

Established in 1996, the London office now has over 130 lawyers. It has grown rapidly to become the second largest of the firm's 17 offices - it is the hub of the firm's European practice. Key areas are private equity, M&A, business finance and restructuring, capital markets, securitisation, banking and finance, litigation and tax. The firm's expertise covers most industries including real estate, manufacturing, financial services, energy, telecommunications, pharmaceuticals, retailing and technology. In the firm's work on private equity, leveraged finance and principal finance transactions, it advises clients on the acquisition, the raising of the requisite financing and on any subsequent high yield or equity offerings. Due to the international nature of the business, the firm's lawyers are experienced in working closely with their colleagues from other offices - this ensures a co-ordinated approach to providing effective legal solutions efficiently.

vacation placements

Places for 2005: 12 in summer vacation. Closing date for applications by online application form: 14 February 2005.

Partners	24
Assistant Solicitors	82
Total Trainees	20

contact
Jillian Singh

method of application
online application form

closing date for 2007
31 July 2005

application
Training contracts p.a. **12**
Required degree grade **2:1**

training
Salary
1st year (2004) £35,000
Holiday entitlement **23 days**

overseas offices
Austin, Boston, Brussels, Budapest, Dallas, Frankfurt, Houston, Silicon Valley, Miami, Munich, New York, Paris, Prague, Singapore, Warsaw, Washington DC

A-Z

SOLICITORS

White & Case

7-11 Moorgate, London EC2R 6HH
Tel: (020) 7600 7300 Fax: (020) 7600 7030
Email: trainee@whitecase.com
Website: www.whitecase.com

firm profile
White & Case is a global law firm with over 1,800 lawyers in 38 offices worldwide. The London office has been open for over 30 years and boasts over 180 UK and US qualified lawyers who work with financial institutions, multinational corporations and governments on major international corporate and financial transactions and complex disputes.

main areas of work
In the London office: acquisition finance, arbitration, asset and aircraft finance, banking, capital markets, corporate finance, construction, employment, intellectual property, litigation, M&A, project finance, real estate, structured finance and securitisation, tax, and telecoms media and technology.

trainee profile
Trainees should be enthusiastic, be able to show initiative and work closely with others in a team environment. You should also have an understanding of international commercial issues and have a desire to be involved in innovative and high profile legal matters.

training environment
The firm's trainees are important and valued members of the London office and frequently work on multijurisdictional matters requiring close co-operation with lawyers throughout the firm's established global network. You will spend six months in each seat and cover the majority of work dealt with in the London office during the course of your training contract. You will sit with a senior associate or partner and hands-on experience will be complemented by formal internal training sessions. You are encouraged to spend six months in one of the firm's overseas offices to gain a fuller understanding of the global network.

benefits
BUPA, gym membership contribution, life insurance, pension scheme, season ticket loan, discretionary bonus scheme, sign on bonus.

vacation placements
Places for 2005: 40-50; Duration: 2 weeks; Remuneration: £300; Closing Date: End of January 2005.

sponsorship & awards
CPE and LPC fees paid and £5,500 maintenance p.a. Prizes for commendation and distinction for LPC.

Partners	47
Assistant Solicitors	132
Total Trainees	44

contact
Ms Emma Fernandes

method of application
Online application via firm website

selection procedure
Interview

closing date for 2007
31 July 2005

application
Training contracts p.a. 20-25
Applications p.a. 1,500
Required degree grade 2:1

training
Salary
1st year (2004) £33,000,
rising by £1,500 every 6 months
Holiday entitlement 25 days

All trainees are encouraged to spend a seat abroad

post-qualification
Salary (2004) £60,000

overseas offices
Almaty, Ankara, Bangkok, Berlin, Bombay, Bratislava, Brussels, Budapest, Dresden, Düsseldorf, Frankfurt, Hamburg, Helsinki, Ho Chi Minh City, Hong Kong, Istanbul, Jakarta, Johannesburg, London, Los Angeles, Mexico City, Miami, Milan, Moscow, New York, Palo Alto, Paris, Prague, Riyadh, Rome, San Francisco, São Paulo, Singapore, Shanghai, Stockholm, Tokyo, Warsaw, Washington DC

Wiggin and Co

95 The Promenade, Cheltenham GL50 1WG
Tel: (01242) 224114 Fax: (01242) 224223

6 Cavendish Place, London, W1G 9NB
Tel: (020) 7612 9612 Fax: (020) 7612 9611
Email: law@wiggin.co.uk Website: www.wiggin.co.uk

firm profile

Founded in 1973, Wiggin & Co has for many years been known for the high quality of its practice. It has an international reputation for its expertise, with many of the partners being regarded as leaders in their field. In November 2003 the firm demerged the Private Client practice such that it could focus solely on the Media and Technology sector. Wiggin & Co is recognised as a major player in many areas of media and technology law including television and radio broadcasting, broadcast regulation, technology (both broadcast related and IT and software related), online and interactive gaming and betting, publishing, defamation, privacy and contempt, music, film, and sport, as well as corporate/commercial, property and commercial litigation. Based in Cheltenham and London, the firm continues to build upon its expertise and is developing new teams in areas such as radio, music and film.

main areas of work

Media (including media litigation) 77%; Corporate 12%; Commercial Litigation 7%; Property 4%.

trainee profile

If you can demonstrate a passion for media and the law then the firm is interested. If you can top that with strong academics and demonstrable commitment to success then Wiggin & Co definitely want to hear from you. The firm can offer you first-class training and experience and the opportunity to qualify at an exciting, friendly, cutting-edge firm, which has the ambition to be nothing less than the best.

training environment

Training is divided into four seats. Trainees will be based in the firm's Cheltenham office and will work in the company/commercial, non-contentious media (two seats), media litigation and property departments. Trainees are encouraged to take an active role in transactions, assume responsibility and deal directly with clients. In-house lectures and seminars are held regularly and training reviews are held every three months. The firm offers the attraction of Cheltenham combined with technical ability and experience akin to a large City firm. Its relatively small size encourages a personal approach towards staff and client relations.

benefits

Life assurance, private health cover, pension scheme, permanent health insurance, subsidised gym membership.

sponsorship & awards

PgDL and LPC fees and £3,500 maintenance p.a.

Partners	11
Assistant Solicitors	12
Total Trainees	6

contact
Human Resources Manager

method of application
CV & covering letter

selection procedure
Two-day selection exercise which incorporates a panel interview

closing date for 2007
31 July 2005

application
Training contracts p.a. 3
Applications p.a. 500
% interviewed p.a. 8%
Required degree grade 2:1

training
Salary
1st year (2004) £26,500
2nd year (2004) £31,500
Holiday entitlement 20 days
% of trainees with a
non-law degree p.a. 50%

post-qualification
Salary (2004) £41,600
% of trainees offered job
on qualification (2004) 100%
% of assistants (as at 2004)
who joined as trainees 17%
% of partners (as at 2004)
who joined as trainees 28%

overseas office
Los Angeles

A - Z SOLICITORS

Withers LLP

16 Old Bailey, London EC4M 7EG
Tel: (020) 7597 6000 Fax: (020) 7597 6543
Email: emma.heycock@withersworldwide.com
Website: www.withersworldwide.com

firm profile

Withers LLP is the first international law firm dedicated to the business, personal and philanthropic interests of successful people, their families and advisers. The firm has offices in London, New York, New Haven (Connecticut) and Milan, and is known as Withers LLP in the UK and internationally, and Withers Bergman in the US. The firm provides integrated answers to the US, UK and international legal and tax needs of its clients whether this means restructuring their own assets, buying or selling businesses and properties, coping with divorce, termination of their employment or setting up charitable foundations. The exciting mix of work creates a diverse and interesting place in which to train. Withers LLP has the largest team of specialist private client lawyers in Europe and more Italian speakers than any other City law firm. In 2002 the firm extended its presence in Milan, opening a new office there.

main areas of work

Private client and charities 39%; family 14%; litigation 23%; corporate, company and commercial 12%; property 12%.

training environment

Trainees spend six months in four of the firm's five departments (family, property, private client, corporate and litigation). On the job training is supplemented by the firm's departmental and trainee-specific training. Buddy and mentor systems ensure that trainees are fully supported from the outset.

benefits

Interest-free season ticket loan, private medical insurance, pension, life assurance, Christmas bonus, social events, subsidised café facilities.

vacation placements

Easter and Summer vacation placements are available in the firm's London and Milan offices in 2005. Students spend two weeks in two different departments. The closing date for applications is 31 January 2005. In the London office there are 24 places available during the summer and six at Easter. It also has a number of places available throughout the year (except August) in its Milan office.

sponsorship & awards

CPE/PgDL and LPC fees and £4,500 maintenance p.a. are paid. A cash prize is awarded for a distinction or commendation in the CPE/PgDL and/or LPC.

Partners	81
Legal Staff	233
Total Trainees	24

contact
Emma Heycock
Senior Recruitment Officer

method of application
Application form (available online)

selection procedure
2 interviews

closing date for 2007
training scheme:
29 July 2005
Closing date for 2005
vacation scheme:
31 January 2005

application
Training contracts p.a. 14
Applications p.a. 1,000
% interviewed p.a. 10%
Required degree grade 2:1

training
Salary
1st year (2004) £27,000
2nd year (2004) £30,000
Holiday entitlement 23 days
% of trainees with a
non-law degree p.a. 50%

post-qualification
Salary (2004) £45,000

overseas offices
Milan, New York, New Haven

Wollastons

Brierly Place, New London Road, Chelmsford, Essex CM2 0AP
Tel: (01245) 211211 Fax: (01245) 354764
Email: recruitment@wollastons.co.uk
Website: www.wollastons.com

firm profile

Wollastons is a dynamic, regional law firm, widely recognised as the leading, commercial practice in Essex. Wollastons has a strong reputation as a forward-thinking and energetic organisation, offering high levels of service to both businesses and private clients. The firm's first-class resources, including sophisticated IT, and the lively atmosphere attracts high calibre lawyers, keen to work in a modern, professional environment. The Investors in People accreditation demonstrates a strong commitment to staff development and training at all levels.

main areas of work

Main practice areas include corporate and commercial; commercial property; commercial disputes; employment; planning and property disputes; private client and family.

trainee profile

Applications are welcomed from able and ambitious graduates with 24 UCAS points and a 2:1 degree. Candidates should have a commercial outlook, be confident, outgoing and able to demonstrate a wide range of interests. A link with the Essex area would be useful.

training environment

Trainees have four six-month seats. These will normally include: company and commercial; commercial disputes; commercial property and employment. Trainees sit with a partner or a senior solicitor and form an integral part of the team. Trainees are fully involved in a wide range of interesting work and, although work is closely checked, trainees are encouraged to take responsibility from an early stage. The firm is very friendly and informal and trainees receive a great deal of individual attention and support. Progress is kept under constant review with mid-seat and end of seat appraisals.

sponsorship & awards

LPC fees paid.

Partners	15
Fee-earners	23
Total Trainees	4 (2 p.a.)

contact
Jo Salt - HR Manager
(01245) 211253

method of application
CV and application form, see website for details

selection procedure
3 stage interview process

closing date for 2007
Continuous recruitment

application
Training contracts p.a. **2**
Applications p.a. **Approx 500**
Interviewed p.a. **Approx 50**
Required degree grade
2:1 & 24 UCAS points

training
Salary
1st year £20,000
2nd year £21,000

Wollastons
solicitors

INVESTOR IN PEOPLE

Wragge & Co LLP

55 Colmore Row, Birmingham B3 2AS
Tel: Freephone (0800) 096 9610
Email: gradmail@wragge.com
Website: www.wragge.com/graduate

firm profile

Wragge & Co is a top 20 UK law firm providing a full-service to some of the world's largest and most successful organisations. Only by providing the highest quality of work and excellent client service can the firm list 33 of the FTSE 100 as its clients. With its main base in Birmingham and offices in London and Brussels over 70% of the firm's work is generated outside the Midlands and over 25% is international. Much has been said and written about the firm's culture. People who work at Wragge & Co will tell you it has a strong culture based on: (a) Integrity and honesty - in the firm's relationships by working to a set of values and commitments. (b) Working as a team - by ensuring everyone at Wragge & Co feels valued, can play a part in the firm going forward and act as a single team. (c) Making a commitment to its people - by communicating openly so they understand the business they are contributing to and can buy into the firm's overall aims. Wragge & Co encourage a balanced and flexible approach to work which results in lower stress levels and greater retention rates. Wragge & Co is a 'relationship' firm. The firm was 22nd in The Sunday Times "100 best companies to work for 2004" and one of the best workplaces in the UK in a recent Financial Times survey. Wragge & Co was also voted "The Law Firm With the Best Training Environment" at a leading lawyer awards ceremony in 2003 and 2004.

main areas of work

The firm has a national reputation in many areas, including dispute resolution, employment, tax, media, project finance and transport and utilities. It also has the UK's third largest real estate group and leading practices in corporate, construction, banking and intellectual property. Other "top five" areas include EU/competition, public law and regulation and pensions. The quality of its work is reflected in the firm's client list, which includes AT&T, British Airways, Cadbury Schweppes, Cap Gemini Ernst & Young, Carlton UK Television, H J Heinz, HSBC, Marks & Spencer, McDonald's, Powergen, and Royal Bank of Scotland. The firm has nearly 1,000 employees, including 111 partners. While its main base remains in Birmingham the firm also has two other offices. Its Brussels office supports the EU/competition team, and the London office deals with intellectual property, private equity, real estate and employment and pensions. You'll be given the opportunity to spend at least six months in the London office. More than a quarter of the firm's work is international and it is formally associated with German independent Graf von Westphalen Bappert & Modest. Many of its solicitors have broadened their experience and their language skills by undertaking international secondments in law firms across the world.

Partners	111
Assistant Solicitors	300
Total Trainees	47

contact
Julie Caudle, Graduate
Recruitment & Training Manager

method of application
Applications are made online at www.wragge.com/graduate (paper application form available on request)

selection procedure
Telephone discussion & assessment day

closing date
Sept 2007/March 2008: 31 July 2005. If you are a non-law student, please return your form as soon as possible, as the firm will be running assessment days over the forthcoming year

application
Training contracts p.a. 25
Applications p.a. **1,000**
% interviewed p.a. **25%**
Required degree grade 2:1

training
Salary Birmingham (Sept 2004)
1st year £21,000
2nd year £24,000
Salary London (Sept 2004)
1st year £28,000
2nd year £31,000
Holiday entitlement **25 days**
% of trainees with a non-law degree p.a. **Varies**

post-qualification
Salary (2004)
Birmingham £34,000
London £48,000
% of trainees offered job on qualification
(2003 & 2004) **100%**
% of associates (as at 1/7/03) who joined as trainees **55%**
% of partners (as at 1/7/03) who joined as trainees **52%**

Wragge & Co LLP continued

trainee profile
The firm is looking for graduates of 2:1 standard at degree level, with some legal or commercial work experience gained either via a holiday job or a previous career. You should be practical, with a common sense and problem solving approach to work, and be able to show adaptability, enthusiasm and ambition.

training environment
The firm aims to transform its trainees into high quality, commercially-minded lawyers. You will spend six months in four different practice areas, usually including real estate, corporate and litigation, with a chance to specialise in a seat of your choice. From day one, you will work on live files with direct contact with clients and other solicitors, and be responsible for the management of the transaction and its ultimate billing. The more aptitude you show, the greater the responsibility you will be given. You will be supported by the graduate recruitment team, a partner who acts as a mentor to you throughout your training contract and a supervisor who will co-ordinate your work and give you weekly feedback. Introductory courses are provided at the start of each seat in addition to the professional skills course training requirements. This formal training complements "on the job" learning and it is more than likely that the firm's commitment to your development will extend well past the number of days recommended by the Law Society. Some of the courses will be residential, allowing you to reflect on your work practices, forge relationships and compare notes without the disturbances of your daily work. The firm's excellent trainee retention rates are the greatest testament to its training programme.

benefits
Wragge & Co's benefits include prizes for 1st class degree and LPC distinction, £1,000 interest free loan, pension scheme, life insurance, permanent health insurance, 25 days holiday a year, travel schemes, private medical insurance, sports and social club, independent financial advice, corporate gym membership rates and a Christmas gift.

sponsorship
The firm will provide your tuition fees for LPC and GDL (where relevant) and a maintenance grant of £4,500 for each year of study for LPC and GDL.

vacation placements
Easter and summer vacation placements are run at Wragge & Co. As part of its scheme, you will get the opportunity to experience different areas of the firm, attend client meetings and get involved in real files. There are also organised social events with the firm's current trainees. Again, you can apply on-line at www.wragge.com/graduate (paper application form available on request). The closing date for applications is 31 January 2005.

Wragge & co LLP is a Limited Liability Partnership

notes

barristers

BARRISTERS TIMETABLE

	LAW STUDENTS • Penultimate Undergraduate Year	NON-LAW STUDENTS • Final Year
Throughout the year	Start thinking about getting some relevant work experience. Do plenty of research into chambers/mini pupillages	
By the end of January		Apply for the CPE
By the end of April	Apply for a pupillage under the year early scheme on Olpas	
May		Apply for a CPE scholarship from an Inn of Court. If successful, join that Inn
June to September		Do pre-CPE mini-pupillages
September/October 2005	Start final year of degree	Start CPE
November	By November apply through BVC Online for the BVC. Apply to an Inn of Court for a BVC scholarship	
During final year/CPE	Apply for pupillage to non-OLPAS sets. Do mini pupillages	
April	Before 30th April apply for pupillage through OLPAS	
June	Apply for Inn membership	
September 2006	Start the BVC. Apply through the September tranche of OLPAS; make further pupillage applications to non-OLPAS sets	
April	If unsuccessful last year, apply for pupillage before 30th April	
June	Finish BVC	
September	Apply for pupillage through OLPAS if you have yet to be successful	
October 2007	Start pupillage	
Summer	Be offered tenancy at your pupillage chambers or apply for tenancy or a 3rd siv elsewhere	
October 2008	Start tenancy	
2038	Be appointed to the High Court Bench	
2048	Get slapped on the wrist by DCA for falling asleep in court	

so you want to be a barrister...

barcode

Don't let the often curious terms used at the Bar confuse or intimidate you!

bar council – the professional body that regulates barristers

barrister – a member of the Bar of England and Wales; an advocate

bench – the judiciary

bencher – a senior member of an Inn of Court. Usually silks and judges, known as masters of the bench

brief – a case; the documents setting out instructions to a barrister

bvc online – the BVC online application system run by the Bar Council and GTI. CACH was the old disk based application system for the BVC (the old term is likely to linger for some time)

call – the ceremony whereby you become a barrister

chambers – a group of barristers in independent practice who have joined together to share common costs of practice such as clerks' fees and building rents; the word refers both to the physical building and to the group of barristers

clerk – administrator/manager in chambers who organises work for barristers and payment of fees, etc

counsel – a barrister

devilling – (paid) work done by a junior member of chambers for a more senior member

inns of court – four ancient institutions, which alone have the power to 'make' barristers

junior – a barrister not yet appointed silk. Note: older juniors are known as senior juniors

keeping term – eating the dinners in hall required to be eligible for call to the bar

mini-pupillage – a short period of work experience spent in chambers

olpas – the Online Pupillage Application System

pupil – essentially a 'trainee'; a barrister in pupillage

pupillage – the year of training undertaken after Bar school and before tenancy. It is divided into two consecutive six-month periods, hence 'first six' and 'second six'. These are commonly taken at the same set of chambers but may, especially in Chancery practice, be taken separately. The main distinction is that a pupil can start earning for himself during second six. Occasionally, and particularly in criminal practice (such is the difficulty of attaining tenancy), a pupil may have to take a third six.

pupilmaster – a senior barrister with whom a pupil sits and who teaches the pupil. The Bar Council is encouraging the term pupil supervisor.

QC – Queen's Counsel; a silk

set – as in a 'set of chambers'

silk – one of Her Majesty's Counsel, appointed on the recommendation of the Lord Chancellor; so named after the silk robes they wear. The Lord Chancellor is considering scrapping the appointment

tenant/tenancy – a tenant is a barrister who is a member of chambers. Tenancy is essentially permission from chambers to join their set and work with them. This means you have to pay your fair share of the rent, hence the word. A 'squatter' is someone who is permitted to use chambers' premises, but is not actually a member of the set. A 'door tenant' is someone who is affiliated with the set, but who does not conduct business from chambers' premises

treasury counsel – barristers appointed to work for the Government. They are graded on various panels and there are different lists for different areas of practice

reality check

Dolly Parton once said that working nine to five is no way to make a living. If you agree with her, it's probably a good indication that the Bar isn't for you. If on the other hand you're looking for a job that is intellectually challenging, fast-moving and rewarding, you could do a lot worse. Be warned though, the path to your seat on the High Court bench may well be a sharp and stoney one.

Pursuing a career at the Bar is only for the determined. A quick look at the statistics says it all. In the year that this book went to print, a record 2,570 students applied for the Bar Vocational Course (BVC). Unfortunately, it's a case of too many bums and not enough seats. A glance at the figures for 2003 reveals that some 711 would-be barristers gained pupillage. As for tenancy, the pupil-barrister's equivalent of the Holy Grail, the figure drops down again to around the 500 mark. Of course, not everyone who does the BVC wants to go into private practice; some people enter the profession with the sole intention of becoming an employed barrister, working in a law centre, or as in-house counsel for a company. But the truth is that this is a highly competitive profession, and a significant number of people who set out to become practising barristers end up rethinking their career plans.

And for those with aspirations of living in a house with gold taps, now is perhaps the time to think carefully. The early days for many practising barristers are financially turbulent – there is the BVC to pay for and the income stream at the start can be barely more than a trickle. Help is available from the Inns in the form of scholarships and awards, but it's worth bearing in mind that there's a good deal of competition for these and they will only ever cover part of your costs. In line with Bar Council rules, all pupillages must now be funded. True, some of the top sets are offering 'golden hellos' that easily compete with funding from the magic circle law firms, but for many chambers, particularly those undertaking a large volume of publicly funded work, there just isn't the money to go around.

Nor are the early years of practice a get-rich-quick scheme for most young barristers. The recent move by the Department of Constitutional Affairs to introduce new graduated fee schemes for publicly funded crime and family work has caused a tidal wave of disapproval at the Bar. The current proposals will mean reductions in the fees that barristers can earn in these areas, which have traditionally been the staple diet of junior practitioners. Immigration work is facing a similar fate following proposals to place a cap on the amount of time lawyers can spend doing publicly funded immigration work. All this leads to what Nigel Bastin, head of education and training at the Bar Council, described as the "double financial squeeze" of accumulated debt and low rates of pay. For would-be barristers from low-income backgrounds without generous family support, this can be enough to deter them from pursuing a career in the profession altogether; something the Bar Council is becoming painfully aware of following a recent review on funding entry to the Bar by Sir David Calvert-Smith QC.

Yet it's not the same story for everyone. Many new entrants to the profession are finding pupillage in niche, highly specialised sets where the rates of remuneration are very attractive. It tends to support the view held by many that the Bar of the future will be increasingly specialist. To sum things up, it's not all bad; there is every chance that if you are determined, persistent and academically strong there will be a bright future ahead for you at the Bar.

What follows here is an epic journey from the students' union bar to a career at the Bar of England and Wales. We give you the low down on mini-pupillages and work experience, the dreaded OLPAS application process and the strange world of the Inns of Court. Finally, we do the rounds in some of the leading barristers sets in the UK to let you know what life is really like for pupils and junior tenants. Trust us when we say that we leave no wig unturned.

getting started

Partying until 6am and setting your alarm clock for Trisha Extra, isn't that what university is all about? Of course, university should be about more than just going to lectures and burying yourself in the Weekly Law Reports, but beware: a quick look at our timetable (page 645) will be enough to remind you that the application process for the Bar moves pretty quickly. Applicants thinking of heading for the Bar straight after their degree will be filling in those all important OLPAS forms in April of their final year, and will need to have put their CVs together already. A strong academic record should be taken as a given. Most (though not all) chambers will expect candidates to achieve a minimum 2:1 in their degree. If you are lucky and bag yourself a First then all the better.

But a strong academic background is not enough – chambers want to see that applicants have a commitment to becoming professional advocates, which means that they will expect to see relevant work experience on your CV. Most also say they are looking for well-rounded applicants with some experience of life that extends beyond the legal profession. In short, they are looking for people who, for one reason or another, stand out from the crowd. So, after recovering from the perpetual hangover that is the first year of university, it's a good idea to take stock, have a good look at your CV, and think about some ways of fleshing it out. We've given you a few pointers below to start you in the right direction.

mini-pupillage

Recruiters expect you to have done these, but what are they? Essentially, a mini-pupillage is a snapshot of life in chambers. You will be assigned to one or more members of chambers for anything from two days to a week, and essentially shadow them in everything they do. Mini-pupillages fall into two breeds: assessed and unassessed. An assessed mini-pupillage is rather like a sheep dog trial – it's all about performance. As well as observing the work of your supervisor, you can expect to be given a set of papers to read and offer your opinion on, or in some cases to produce a piece of written work. Some sets now insist that applicants undertake assessed mini-pupillage as part of their recruitment process. An unassessed mini-pupillage sounds like a softer option, but it isn't. Though there is no necessary connection between doing a mini-pupillage in a set and being successful in an application for full pupillage, it's still an excellent opportunity to make your face known to chambers and make a good impression.

what will i be doing?

This really depends on whom you shadow. You could spend a day watching a QC arguing a novel point of law in the House of Lords, or, like one student we spoke to, a morning in Thameside Magistrates Court "warding off a delinquent seven-year-old who kept jabbing me with a biro, whilst waiting for a client who didn't turn up." Don't be put off when something like this happens; if anything it's a more realistic picture of what life at the junior Bar can be like. It's not unheard of for mini-pupils to go through three days without seeing any courtroom advocacy because lawyers are negotiating a settlement, or because fresh evidence has been produced. The important thing is to soak it all up, observing how the barristers interact with one another, with their instructing solicitors and with their clients, and getting to grips with the papers. Take plenty of notes, and don't be afraid to ask questions of your supervisor at an appropriate time if you see or read something that you don't understand or need clarifying.

how do i get one?

There is no central system to apply to for mini-pupillage. Applications are made directly to individual chambers, usually by way of CV and covering letter. Details of who to contact can be found by checking chambers' websites. Plan things well ahead as spaces for mini-pupils in some of the more popular or specialised sets fill up quickly, and many (Doughty Street being a good example) require you to apply at least three months in advance. Send out plenty of applications and be prepared for a few rejections. If you are still struggling, make use of any potentially useful contacts. If you have already joined an Inn of Court, ask to be assigned a sponsor; they will often be able to give you a helping hand. Alternatively, ask the teaching staff in your university law department.

stepping forward

So you are well on the way to getting a top First and you've done a handful of mini-pupillages; what else can you do to give yourself the edge? The answer:

pro bono work. There are plenty of ways to do this, but becoming a member of the Free Representation Unit (FRU) is an obvious choice for budding barristers, as it provides the invaluable opportunity for advocacy experience in front of a real tribunal. Remember, again, to plan ahead; it's no good saying that you trained as a FRU representative if you have never signed out a case. FRU allows LLB students to train as social security representatives in the summer prior to their final year, so get in there early and start building up experience. There are plenty of other ways to get involved in pro-bono work and we've set out a non-exhaustive selection of the options on page 22. It's well worth getting your finger into as many pies as your spare time will allow.

other things extra-curricular

Almost every university law department has a mooting society, and if yours doesn't, why not get together with other students and set one up. You'll probably come across plenty of opportunities from internal university moots to large inter-university competitions like Essex Court Chambers' National Mooting Competition. Debating also makes for good advocacy experience, whether it be with the university debating society, or through the hotbed that is student union politics. Making the most of the plethora of societies available at university can only be a good idea.

olpas: getting a foot in the door

The Online Pupillage Application Service has been up and running since 2001. It's not compulsory for chambers offering pupillage to be a member of the scheme, but every pupillage provider is required by the Bar Council to advertise vacancies on the website at **www.pupillage.com**. The same information is also produced in the Pupillages and Awards Handbook, published to coincide with the opening of the on-line system and the National Pupillage Fair in March.

The online application process has two seasons: summer and autumn. The summer season closing date is 30th April (didn't we say it would come around quickly?), allowing three months for interviews, with offers being made from 31st July. The autumn season opens at the end of August and closes on 30th September, with just a month for interviews and offers being made on 31st October. Chambers can only take part in one season. Most LL.B candidates will make their applications during their final year of university, though some of the top commercial sets (otherwise known as 'The Ninjas') allow applicants to apply in their second year in an attempt to snap up the best candidates. There are 12-month and six-month pupillages available. The 12-month pupillages are increasingly the most common, and from an applicant's point of view, the more convenient option, saving the hassle of searching for a 'first six' and a 'second six' in different sets. For that personal touch, all correspondence regarding interviews and offers is sent via email, which will make checking your inbox a nail-biting experience.

an exercise in form filling?

As one barrister said to us: "Think of the OLPAS form as a skeleton argument about yourself." There is an art to filling it in. The first part of the form is pretty much a box-checking exercise, but the second part gives you the opportunity to wax lyrical, talking about your reasons for wanting to become a barrister, the work experience you've accumulated and your other interests and achievements. There is no right or wrong way to answer these questions, but a few things are worth bearing in mind. Most sets will receive at least 200 applications, so think about the person who will have to read them all, often at the end of a long day. Also bear in mind that the way your application looks on the screen is not how it churns out when it gets sent to each individual chambers. Instead, it arrives along with a ream of other applications, all in the same font and the same 10pt size. Try to make sentences short, concise and persuasive, after all that is one of the skills chambers will be looking for in potential recruits. Keep paragraphs short and clearly separated. Finally, check, check and triple check for spelling and grammar errors. As a senior QC put it: "Given that this is a job in which a strong command of the English language is paramount, we are often amazed at some of the fundamental errors that crop up in the OLPAS applications."

tailoring your application

After having spoken about yourself, you can pick your bunch of 12 seats for the season, and give individual reasons for applying to each. Obviously, the sets you apply to will depend on where your interests lie, but try to avoid choosing a combination of practice areas that go together like King Herod and Mothercare. For example, applicants who indicate that they are interested in IP or commercial law on the OLPAS form will have difficulty convincing a specialist criminal set to look any further. Also, research each chambers thoroughly. Recruiters frequently tell us of applicants who state they are interested in an area of law with which chambers has absolutely no connection. If you are still not entirely sure of where a chambers' expertise lies having looked at their website or read their brochure, you have a problem.

non-olpas sets

These are clearly identified on the OLPAS website. A set's decision not to be part of the online scheme says nothing about its quality, and indeed many of the top-flight commercial sets choose to recruit outside of the system. Applicants may apply to as many non-OLPAS sets as they wish, and are not tied down by the pro forma of the online system (though many chambers have their own application forms). The application process at each set will be different, and will operate on a different timescale. Research things well in advance to make sure you don't miss any deadlines.

expect the spanish inquisition

So you've bagged that pupillage interview. What to expect? No two interviews will be the same, and the stories we're told are a mixed bag of the positive and the negative. Some candidates leave feeling they've had the best brought out of them by the panel; others describe a *Weakest Link*-style walk of shame. What we can say is that the process tends to be in one of two formats. Some chambers have two rounds of interviews, the first being a brief, informal affair designed to shortlist further, and the second being a more intense grilling. Others do much of the shortlisting on paper, opting for a longer interview with fewer candidates. Most spell out the interview format and selection criteria on their website or in their brochures, but if in doubt, ring up and ask.

a few insiders' tips

Be prepared for anything. The panel will want to see that you can hold your own under pressure, because that is part of the job. Often there will be a Devil's Advocate to ask deliberately difficult questions. At longer interviews you may be asked to prepare an answer to a legal problem to discuss at the interview. If you are given a problem well in advance of the interview, take the time to prepare a written summary of your answer, both as an aide-memoire and to give to the interview panel. Find out how many people will be on the panel, and provide them each with a copy.

Whatever the format of the interview, it's worth brushing up on the basic principles of contract, crime and tort, especially if you are an LLB student for whom these subjects form part of the dim and distant past. Keep yourself informed of what is going on in the legal press by reading publications like The Lawyer or Legal Week, and make sure you read a good newspaper; current affairs are often a hot topic.

Obviously you must avoid offers of sexual favours or cash – they don't sit well with the Bar Code of Conduct, with which, by now, you should have at least a passing familiarity (see **www.barcouncil.org.uk**). Expect at least one question about professional ethics at most interviews. Finally, dress to impress. A smart appearance (leave the Homer Simpson tie in the drawer) won't get you the pupillage, but it will lend you a certain credibility. Take care with those finishing touches, and don't forget to moisturise.

the inns of court

Like Yorkshire pudding and cricket, the four ancient Inns of Court (Inner Temple, Middle Temple, Lincoln's and Gray's) are one of those great British institutions that seem to have withstood the sands of time. Bearing a striking similarity to Oxbridge colleges, with the customary chapel, hall and library, the Inns were originally conceived as a place of residence and learning for young barristers-to-be. Now the BVC providers have assumed responsibility for the vast majority of academic training for the Bar, but the Inns still perform some important functions. To pardon the pun, you've got to be Inn it to win it, because the power to 'call' a person to the Bar is vested with the Treasurers of the four Inns. And that doesn't come for free. Before you can be called to the Bar, you must 'keep term' by attending dinners or other breeds of qualifying session. As the current regulations stand, students must complete a total of 12 sessions, and inevitably you'll end up eating some kind of meal at all of them. Prepare your liver.

brideshead regurgitated?

It may all sound a bit stuffy, but actually, the Inns can perform a very useful function for those students willing to get themselves involved. All four Inns offer an opportunity to get involved in mooting, whether it be at internal, inter-Inn or national competition level. Those in need of career advice can take advantage of mentoring schemes, whereby students are assigned practising barristers. The Inns also run a scheme known as marshalling, giving students the opportunity to spend a week sitting alongside a judge, observing the proceedings and discussing the case at the end of the day. For those who enjoy a weekend in the country, all of the Inns run advocacy workshops and seminars at Cumberland Lodge, a conference centre in the heart of Great Windsor Park

(pack your waxed jackets for that one). There are cultural and sporting activities on offer too, and the Inns' various students' associations all arrange an active social calendar for their members. Importantly, the Inns are also the providers of compulsory advocacy training throughout the pupillage year.

Students must join an Inn by the June before they start their BVC, but the earlier they join the earlier they can make the most of everything on offer.

lining your pockets

The Inns are one of the main sources of funding for the academic stages of training, and all four offer substantial scholarships for the CPE and BVC years. You don't have to be a member of the Inn to apply for these, but you must undertake to join in the event that you are successful. The highly competitive selection process includes an interview. Further funds are available for the pupillage year, and there is normally money reserved in the kitty to help students from the regional BVC institutions to meet their accommodation and travel costs when visiting the Inn, and to pay for qualifying sessions. In addition, many of the Inns offer miscellaneous awards to fund overseas internships. For specific details of the amounts on offer, students should contact the Inns directly or check their websites. For more general advice on funding for the BVC and CPE years, refer to page 43.

which inn is for me?

The Inns have similar things to offer, and it would be wrong to say that one is any better than the other. As deputy under-treasurer of Lincoln's Inn, Joanna Robinson told us: *"The best way to decide is to come and visit us all, take a look around, get a feel for the place and meet the administrative staff."* After quizzing students and staff, we did find some subtle differences between the four.

lincoln's inn

Contact: Judith Fox, 020 7405 0138

www.lincolnsinn.org.uk

Sandwiched between the hustle and bustle of Holborn and Fleet Street, Lincoln's Inn is an oasis of calm amid a sea of chaos. The biggest of the Inns, it boasts some 'A' list celebrities from the world of law and politics including Cherie and Tony, and the late Lord Denning MR. Noted more for the drinking than the dinner, students here recommend the Inn for its *"free-flowing wine and the great atmosphere."* Students also say that the environment here is an inclusive one, and that the Cumberland Lodge Weekend is like *"going on a family holiday."* As well as the usual activities, the Inn organises an annual trip to visit the European Court of Justice, the Court of Human Rights and the Hague Tribunals. Lincoln's is known for its international membership, and as one member who grew up in Pakistan told us: *"It's the only Inn people have heard of in Pakistan because the founder of our nation was a member."*

inner temple

Contact: Clare Drewett, 020 7797 8210

www.innertemple.org.uk

From Chaucer to Charlie Falconer, this Inn has more history than we've had hot dinners. Inner Temple is a place for firsts: the first female barrister was a member, as was the first female Treasurer, Dame Elizabeth Butler-Sloss P. According to student officer Clare Drewett, it's the *"wonderful personalities of the administrative staff,"* combined with the culinary credentials of *"former chef to the stars"* Martin Cheesman that makes Inner Temple special. The Inner Temple Students Association packs a busy social diary, focusing its attentions on the twin vices of liquor and gambling, and the mooting society is a regular contender in international competitions, including the recent Jessup Public International Law Moot. The Inn also offers its students LAMDA voice training as part of its education and training programme.

middle temple

Contact: Marion Howard, 020 7427 4800

www.middletemple.org.uk

As former member Charles Dickens put it, the Middle Temple has *"something of a clerkly monkish atmosphere, which public offices of law have not disturbed, and even legal firms have failed to scare away."* Students here will find themselves mixing with members of the profession from day one, the common room being open to barristers and students alike. Among the range of activities on offer, debating is a particular forte. When we visited, the Inn was fresh from its victory in the World Debating Championships, boasting a rather sinister looking bust crafted in the image of Ming the Merciless as their trophy. There is an active social scene, which includes the notorious 'Christmas Revels' sketch show. Students recommend lecture nights for *"copious amounts of food and wine and excellent guest speakers,"* who in recent years have included former DPP Sir David Calvert-Smith and *"the lovely"* Anna Ford.

gray's inn

Contact: Rachel Isaac, 020 7458 7900

www.graysinn.org.uk

Gray's Inn has achieved infamy amongst Bar students for being the most traditional of the Inns. Toasting is the order of the day here, including the annual passing of the 'loving cup' on Grand Day, in which a giant chalice of backwashed wine is passed down the table, with members paying tribute to *"the glorious and pious memory of good Queen Bess,"* (Elizabeth I was a patron of the Inn). Be warned; in true Ibiza Uncovered style, the person at the end of the table finishes whatever is left over! Despite sounding like a scene from a Jane Austen novel, the students say that the mood here is *"friendly and laid back."* Also, as the smallest of the Inns, *"you get to know other students and Benchers really quickly, and there are always familiar faces around the table at dinner."*

pupillage and the tenancy decision

You've emerged from OLPAS and the BVC with your sanity intact and that all-important pupillage in the bag. The fledgling steps of your career at the Bar begin here.

what to expect?

The general consensus seems to be a long and challenging year of hard work! Pupillage is a game of two halves: in the first six months, pupils will be assigned to a supervisor (commonly called a 'pupil-master'). They will shadow and assist them in everything they do, which in the ordinary course of events will include attending court, carrying out legal research and drafting paperwork. Many chambers will also run their own in-house advocacy training exercises throughout the pupillage year, in addition to the compulsory training organised by the Inns of Court.

You can expect to spend your first six under the supervision of more than one supervisor; the purpose of the year is to give you as wide an experience of chambers' work as possible. At the end of the first six months, pupils who have obtained 'second sixes' in a different set will be packing their bags. Those who remain in their original set will notice a few changes in how they spend their time. The second six usually provides an opportunity for pupils to handle work in their own right (though under the 'L' plate of their supervisor's insurance policy). The amount and nature of the work will vary from set to set. In a criminal set, pupils will find themselves in the magistrates' court on a regular basis, whereas in some commercial sets the opportunity for pupils to do work that is entirely their own will be less regular (and sometimes entirely absent).

As well as learning the tools of the trade, you'll also have to worry about the looming tenancy decision, which for most pupils will come towards the end of the second six months. We've reproduced the Bar Council's statistics for you because, as you're probably aware already, securing a pupillage does not guarantee you a job at the end of the year. It may well be the case that three or more pupils are competing for one tenancy. It may be the case that, for whatever reason, a set will not be in a position to offer a tenancy to anyone.

NUMBER OF:	1998-1999	1999-2000	2000-2001	2001-2002	2002-2003	2003-2004
BVC applicants	2,696	2,370	2,252	2,119	2,067	2,570
BVC enrolments	1,459	1,490	1,407	1,386	1,332	n/a
Students passing the BVC	1,238	1,201	1,110	1,182	1,121	n/a
First six pupils	706	681	695	812	683	n/a
Second six pupils	694	704	700	724	700	n/a
Pupils awarded tenancy	541	511	527	490	*	n/a

Source: The Bar Council

*At the time of writing, the Bar Council were unable to provide a figure for the year 2002-3

Exactly what chambers look for in a new tenant varies from set to set, and pupil supervisors will no doubt give their pupils a few hints along the way. Generally, however, all sets value certain basic skills and attributes, so we hope the following tips will stand you in good stead:

Try to establish a good relationship with the clerks. They are the people that will be pushing work in your direction, and senior clerks often have an influential voice when it comes to the tenancy decision. Especially in the second six, try to give instructing solicitors a good impression. Word of how you perform and your bedside manner will get back to chambers via them. Barristers' chambers are businesses, and if a firm of solicitors is suitably pleased with you and wants to instruct you again, it's all good news.

It is easy to see yourself as being in competition with the other pupils in chambers. In some sets this is definitely not the case; in others...well, yes you probably are. Either way, there is more to be gained by providing each other with mutual support and encouragement than there is from tying their shoelaces together when they aren't looking!

For those who find themselves at the end of their pupillage without an offer of tenancy, do not despair. Clerks and members of chambers will have connections at other sets, and are normally happy to help pupils secure tenancy or a further period of tenancy elsewhere. Many chambers will allow pupils to stay on for a third six months of pupillage. Squatting (that is, conducting work from chambers without officially being a member) is often another possibility. Unfortunately for some pupils, despite persistence and hard work, becoming a tenant in private practice just doesn't happen. This doesn't mark the end of your legal career as there are still plenty of career opportunities for qualified barristers in employed practice, whether it be in local or central government, or as an in-house lawyer in the private sector. Furthermore, the solicitors' side of the profession is increasingly employing those who come from the Bar, whether or not they wish to requalify as solicitors.

practice areas at the bar

chancery

The Chancery Division of the High Court has traditionally heard cases with an emphasis on legal principles, foremost among them the concept of equity. Chancery work epitomises legal reasoning; it is an area for those who love the law and love to grapple with its most complex aspects. The tools of the Chancery practitioner's trade are legal arguments and their skills lie in the application of these tools to real-life situations. Chancery practice may have ancient roots, but as Catherine Addy at Maitland Chambers was keen to point out: *"You are often looking at ancient principles but you will be applying them to modern situations and, of course, the principles themselves often evolve over time. It is not at all uncommon to be referring, in the same case, to authorities from the nineteenth century as well as to those handed down in 2004."*

type of work
Chancery can be divided into 'traditional' (trusts, probate, real property, charities and mortgages) and 'commercial' (company law, shareholder disputes, partnership, banking, pensions, financial services, insolvency, professional negligence, tax, media and IP,). Most Chancery sets will undertake both types, albeit with varying emphases. Furthermore, the division between Chancery practice and commercial practice is less apparent than before. Barristers at commercial sets can frequently be found on Chancery cases and vice versa, though some areas, such as tax and IP, often beg specialisation.

At first, small commercial and property-related cases (eg possession proceedings) will see you in and out of county courts up and down the country. You can also expect your fair share of winding up applications in the Companies Court and appearances before the bankruptcy registrars. In the more promi-

nent sets, you might be brought in as second or third junior on larger, more complex cases – possibly even an overseas case.

Your lay client could be anyone from a little old lady to the finance director of a blue-chip company. *"Variety is the spice of life,"* Catherine reminded us. *"Sometimes it's nice to have a human side to a case."* Indeed, if this is a key motivation for you, you could orient your practice more to traditional Chancery work.

The thing to remember is that although advocacy will be a core element of your work, you will spend the majority of your time in chambers, perusing papers, considering arguments, drafting pleadings, skeletons and advices, or conducting settlement negotiations. While some instructions fly into chambers, need immediate attention and then disappear just as quickly, others can rumble on for years – although not quite as long as the infamous case of Jarndyce and Jarndyce in Dickens' blockbusting Chancery saga, *Bleak House*.

skills needed
Invariably, Chancery lawyers are pretty hot in the brains department; they are high fliers with a real affinity with the law. Catherine thinks that when trying to find your *"inner Chancery persona,"* you should consider whether you are most interested in equity, trusts, company and insolvency law. She also ventures that you'll enjoy the analytical process involved in constructing an argument and evaluating the answers to legal problems. *"Of course, quite often there isn't a straightforward answer, and that's why you end up in court trying to find one."*

Solicitors will come to you with complex and puzzling cases. Once you've unravelled and analysed them you'll then need to explain legal arguments and principles in such a way that the solicitor and lay client both understand the advice you are giving. At the same time, you also need to be able to present your argument to the judge in a persuasive and sophisticated manner. Far from being a legal boffin, you need to be a master of communication and practical in the legal solutions you offer.

Unlike your peers practising crime, your weekly agenda won't be set by last-minute briefs for next-day court appearances. Instead, you'll need self-discipline and an instinctive sense of exactly how much time and energy you need to devote to each of the instructions on your desk.

prospects

This is a highly competitive area of practice to break into. An excellent academic record is a must; most pupils in leading sets will have a First-class degree, although this is certainly not a pre-requisite, and do bear in mind that this need not be in law. You should also demonstrate an aptitude for public speaking and, if a law undergrad, this should include mooting experience. You should also be able to show that you've completed at least a couple of mini-pupillages – with or including Chancery sets. The Chancery Bar seems to be fairly immune to the bad-news stories about shrinking work and tumbling brief fees. This is the Rolls Royce end of the Bar and it continues to attract not only plenty of domestic work, but also a considerable amount of offshore and cross-border instructions.

commercial bar

The Commercial Bar is a self-defined group that handles a variety of business disputes spanning a range of industry sectors. In its purest definition, commercial cases are those heard by the Commercial Court or one of the Mercantile Courts or Business Lists; however, a broader definition includes matters dealt with by both the Queen's Bench and Chancery Divisions of the High Court, and the Technology and Construction Court (TCC). Many commercial disputes are arbitrated, which is similar to litigation, but a little more flexible and conducted in private. Also, alternative methods of dispute resolution, such as mediation, are becoming more popular as they can have the advantage of preserving commercial relationships that might otherwise have been destroyed by the litigation process.

type of work

We spoke to Sean O'Sullivan, a tenant at 4 Pump Court, about the nature of the job. Likening commercial litigation to playing "*a giant game of chess,*" he spoke about guiding the client through the litigation process, and selecting the most appropriate manoeuvres to put them in a better position with their opponent. The role blends advice and paper advocacy with courtroom advocacy. Sean explained how the client positions itself through statements of case, witness statements, and interlocutory skirmishes. In this sense, life as a commercial barrister is a far cry from that of a criminal practitioner, who might be in court every day. As the majority of disputes settle, "*it's all about assessing the prospects of success...and then doing a deal which reflects or exceeds that assessment.*"

Very junior barristers will, at least in some commercial sets, get to handle their own small cases – perhaps initially including common law cases such as road traffic, PI or employment disputes – while gaining exposure to larger commercial cases by assisting more senior colleagues. As a 'second junior' they will carry out research and prepare first drafts of documents to assist the first junior and the QC leading the case. Just as importantly, they will have the opportunity to observe silks in action in court, learning how to cross-examine witnesses and how best to present arguments. Then, in time, their own cases will increase in value and complexity: claims relating to shipping, insurance and reinsurance, commodities, banking, and general contractual matters are all standard fare. At seven years' call, Sean has handled all these types of case, as well as professional negligence, shipbuilding and entertainment industry disputes.

The fundamentals of almost all matters are contract and tort, and the area remains rooted in common law, although domestic and European legislation is also important. Commercial barristers' incomes now reflect the popularity of the English courts with overseas litigants, and cross-border issues including competition law, insolvency and conflicts of laws are all increasingly relevant.

skills needed

You need to be very bright to stand a chance at the commercial Bar and you'll have to work long hours, often under pressure. Sean suggested that: *"The real skill is in spotting the argument that most people won't see or identifying the argument that is most likely to be persuasive."* Written skills are just as important as oral advocacy, possibly more so. And yet, brainpower is only half of the story: *"You can't necessarily expect to have developed any commercial acumen as a student, but you will need to pick it up quickly in practice; you'll have to understand the client's business objectives in order to see how you can help them to achieve them."* Your service standards must be impeccable and your style user-friendly: *"This means putting yourself out for solicitors and clients,"* Sean explained. *"Sometimes they'll send you something in a hurry and you have to pick it up and run with it, even if it isn't in the form you would prefer. And if they call you late in the evening or at weekends, you take the call. The commercial firms of solicitors don't want pomp and ceremony. They are not instructing barristers because they are impressed by the wigs, they just want to get the job done. If you are going to help them do that, great; if not, they will find someone who will."*

prospects

Much has been said about shrinking small-end work, and while this has indeed impacted on the livelihood of junior barristers in common law sets, the commercial Bar is faring well. Get yourself into a good set and there's nothing to stop you making an exceedingly good living. Consciously or not, most barristers tend to specialise to a degree by building up expertise on cases for a particular industry sector, for example shipping or banking. It gives them the added value that solicitors look for when deciding who to instruct.

Competition for pupillage at the commercial Bar is as tough as it gets. A First-class degree is commonplace and you'll need to offer ample evidence of mooting and debating. You'll also need impressive references and a willingness to work extremely hard.

common law

English common law derives from the precedents set by judicial decisions rather than from the contents of statutes. Most of the cases run by common law barristers turn on principles of tort and contract, and are dealt with in the Queen's Bench Division (QBD) of the High Court and the county courts. At the edges, this type of practice blurs into both Chancery and commercial law.

type of work

As any junior in a common law set will tell you, one of the major attractions is the variety of work that lands on their desk: employment, PI, inquests, crime, landlord and tenant, small commercial and contractual disputes – it's all there for the taking. According to Akash Nawbatt from Devereux Chambers: *"Employment and PI are your bread and butter, but you get to cover different areas of the law and each case has its different facts. This is both challenging and interesting."* Common law barristers tend to carry on practising on a full range of cases throughout their careers, but there is an opportunity to begin to specialise between five and ten years' call.

Prospects for advocacy are good, and on average you could expect to be in court two to three days per week. As Akash says: *"Most people come to the Bar to be on their feet and arguing cases."* Not only can pupils expect to have their own cases during their second six, but also their pupilmasters or senior barristers could select them to be a junior on a more complex case. It is undeniable that a recent drive towards mediation has reduced the number of cases going to court, and that some solicitors have made strides in advocacy, but on the whole the role of the barrister is still valued. Solicitor advocates may frequently attend directions hearings, but are still rarely seen at trial. Legal Aid cutbacks and conditional fee agreements – especially for PI claims – both affect remuneration, but if you can get tenancy at a good set, you'll still be able to earn a pretty good living.

skills needed

Akash observes: "*Personal skills cannot be underestimated. Often the client won't have been to court before and will be very nervous. It's your responsibility to put them at ease, so a good bedside manner is crucial. They may be expecting someone older than you, so you have to inspire confidence at an early stage.*"

As you will be dealing with a variety of cases, you will need a nimble mind to assimilate the factual details of each one, and a good long-term memory when it comes to the law itself. You must be flexible in your working practices: "*At the junior end the work comes in at very short notice, but you have to be able to meet your deadlines. The night before the case you may have to read a lever arch file and digest what's important.*" On the downside, this means it is difficult to plan too far ahead, and your friends may have to get used to you bailing out on them at short notice. On the upside, the chances of you ever growing bored are minimal.

prospects

The market is fiercely competitive at the junior end and you have to make your mark to secure your next set of instructions. If you want to specialise in a certain area, make sure that you have thoroughly researched the sets you apply to for pupillage. As ever, mini pupillages are advised.

crime

Such is the number of TV shows portraying criminal briefs that the general public could be forgiven for assuming that the entire Bar practises crime. It's an area that cries out for individuals of a certain disposition and specific talents though...

type of work

Pupils can expect to cut their teeth on motoring offences, committals and directions hearings in the magistrates' courts. From humble beginnings, things progress quickly such that, by the end of their second six, pupils should expect to be instructed in their own right. Over the first two or three years junior tenants will be exposed to the entire gamut of cases: initially trial work is restricted to smaller offences such as common assault, but this soon turns into ABH, robbery and possession of drugs with intent to supply. Perform well and impress your instructing solicitor and this could lead to a role as a junior on a major Crown Court trial.

It's advisable to apply to be included on the CPS list so that you can prosecute as well as defend. Oliver Blunt QC from Furnival Chambers notes that, apart from a regular source of income, "*working on both sides of the street tends to make you a better advocate.*"

Joining the criminal Bar will ensure you have ample opportunity to develop your nascent advocacy skills. According to Oliver: "*Advocacy skills are the same for the minor cases as the major ones. Indeed, convincing a hard-core bench of cynical justices can be more difficult than a credulous jury.*" Many advocates start off their careers reading from a script, only much later feeling sufficiently confident in their oratory flair to improvise their performance. But even the most skilful advocate knows that success rests on effective case preparation, and never forget that the law and sentencing policies evolve constantly.

skills needed

Arguably criminal barristers need an appreciation for theatre and an innate sense of dramatic timing. Oliver told us: *"Defence work appeals to the iconoclast – the prosecution attempts to create an impenetrable edifice, and you have to smash a hole in the side. In a sense you have a captive audience in the jury, and the impact of a closing speech can swing the result either way."* Criminal barristers must be able to relate to people, whether they are defendants, witnesses, victims, judges or members of a jury. They must also impress the instructing solicitor and gain their trust, particularly when still a junior looking to build a practice. Sometimes dealing with defendants requires a great deal of patience. Oliver explained: *"You have to be receptive to your client's arguments, even if you have no faith in them. You need to be prepared to explain the ramifications of what they are seeking, and sometimes make it clear that their application really is hopeless."*

A good team ethic is important in chambers – pupils and juniors are effectively kept afloat by the relationships that their seniors have built with instructing solicitors' firms. Oliver has a simple piece of advice – *"Although it is important to market yourself, don't denigrate others or get a reputation as a 'diary watcher'. This always gets back to the clerks."*

prospects

The criminal bar tends to provide more pupillages than other areas, but these don't necessarily translate into tenancies, because the market is so competitive. It is also worth noting that life at the junior Bar is becoming more demanding than ever before: the inception of graduated fees (paid by the Legal Services Commission) and the rise of solicitor advocates have both had a negative effect. However, if you're willing to accept the more limited financial rewards, the allure of the stage could still prove irresistible. The best advice for students is to try to get some mini-pupillage experience as early as possible.

employment

"Employment legislation is blooming." These words from Littleton Chambers junior, Eleena Misra, help to explain the good fortune of employment barristers. It's also true that people are more aware of their employment rights than ever before as *"cases are more widely reported now. People see a Metro headline: 'Chef wins £10,000 from employer' and they think it's worth having a bash."* Legal representation is not required in an employment tribunal, and only rarely will there be a costs penalty for the unsuccessful party, so there are fewer barriers to bringing a case. *"And consider the effect of the internet,"* Eleena added. *"You can even issue a claim online!"* True, accessibility is one of the aims of the employment tribunal system; however, cases are often of such complexity that specialist legal advice is absolutely essential.

type of work

Few juniors limit themselves solely to employment practice – most will also undertake civil or commercial cases. Eleena's set is known for its employment expertise, and she spends up to 75% of her time on this type of work. Few juniors nail their colours to the mast, only acting for applicants (employees) or respondents (employers). However, at senior level this changes a bit because respondents can generally afford to pay higher legal fees.

Straightforward tribunal claims, such as unfair dismissals, discrimination cases and relatively low-value contract claims are interspersed with more complex matters such as whistle blowing, injunctions to prevent the breach of restrictive covenants, and cases that cross over with company law actions that involve shareholders. Eleena is *"frequently dealing with redundancy dismissals and race and sex discrimination claims."* Other forms of discrimination claims are coming on stream as a result of new EU legislation concerning age, religion and sexual orientation.

Most advocacy takes place in an employment tribunal or the Employment Appeals Tribunal, as opposed to the courts, and the atmosphere and proceedings in each are deliberately less formal. *"Hearings are conducted with everyone sitting down,"* Eleena explained. *"They follow the basic examination-in-chief, cross-examination and closing submissions, so even though you're not on your feet, you're still advocating."* A barrister has to modify his or her style when appearing against someone who is unrepresented as *"no tribunal likes to see a barrister intimidating an applicant in person."* The boot is on the other foot when, as a junior, you meet a silk on the other side – what an opportunity to go up against a senior advocate! Solicitor advocates, by the way, have been kicking around employment tribunals for some years.

skills needed

Of course you've got to love advocacy, but beyond that there are skills and personality traits that a good employment lawyer will possess and develop. The say no one expects the Spanish Inquisition, but equally, no one can predict what they'll encounter in a tribunal. As Eleena rightly points out: *"The majority of people spend more time in the workplace with colleagues than they do with their nearest and dearest. The situations and conflicts that can arise have endless, endless variations."*

The cases she's worked on have ranged from *"the very, very sad and distressing to the hilarious."* One case involved an investigation into the throwing of a Cadbury's CrÉme Egg while another required a site visit to a public house in Mayfair. And then consider for a moment how distressing it must be to cross-examine someone with a disability about sensitive medical issues. *"You have to do your job but it's never pleasant to see someone burst into tears,"* Eleena admitted.

Keeping abreast of developments in the law is crucial because sometimes you'll have precious little time to prepare your case for trial. Furthermore, with new directives, regulations and cases appearing all the time, you'll be forever having your cases stayed while others with similar points are being heard on appeal.

prospects

The future looks pretty bright for employment lawyers, and there are many good sets that offer the work as a part of the pupillage package. Look up the people at the Free Representation Unit (see page XX) sooner rather than later – they have a lot to offer students and pupils by way of first-hand experience.

family

Packed with emotionally charged issues, family law is a demanding practice area for a barrister, who is likely to be involved only in the most complex or combative cases. A huge amount of court time is allotted to divorce, separation, adoption, child residence and contact orders, financial provision and domestic violence. However, increasingly mediation is used to resolve disputes in a more efficient and less unsettling fashion. The family Bar had been concerned that this, and an increase in solicitor advocates, would lead to a downturn in work yet, with the exception of children's cases in which solicitors have always been encouraged to do their own advocacy, instructions for the Bar appear to have continued largely unabated.

type of work

Barristers learn the ropes on simple county court matters, progressing to complex matters in the Family Division of the High Court. In the early years, there will be a lot of private law children work (disputes between parents), small financial cases and injunctions in situations of domestic violence.

Ellen Saunders, a tenant at One Garden Court, explained how ancillary relief (financial arrangements), and public and private law children's work each offer their own unique challenges and intellectual demands. In the area of Ancillary relief it helps to have an interest in understanding pensions and shares and a good grounding in the basics of trusts and property. Meanwhile, private law children's cases can sometimes involve serious allegations between parents and require the input of child psychologists; the public law counterpart (care proceedings between local authorities and parents) invariably includes detailed and often harrowing medical evidence. Ellen advises checking the orientation of a set before applying for pupillage, though she also cautions against narrowing your options too early.

The legislation affecting this area is both comprehensive, but there's also a large and flourishing body of case law. You must keep abreast of all new decisions because while no two families are identical, the basics remain the same in relation to the problems they experience. The job is, therefore, more about negotiating general principles than adhering strictly to precedents.

skills needed

Ellen believes that "*you can't be someone who needs predictability,*" as "*what your client wants at 5pm is often different to what they wanted at 9am.*" The emotional subtext calls for communication, tact and maturity in abundance. "*You have to develop empathy for clients and personal resilience in equal measures.*" Inevitably, the work involves asking clients for intimate details of unpleasant aspects of their private life, and breaking devastating news to the emotionally fragile. As Ellen explained: "*In most cases, this is a once-in-a-lifetime experience for your client and they rely on you have to hold their hand throughout, even when you have to give them advice that they don't want to hear.*"

The end result of these cases will have a truly significant impact on each of the lives touched by it, so it is crucial to find the most appropriate course of action for each client. The best advocates are those who can "*differentiate between a case and client requiring a bullish approach, and those which cry out for settlement and concessions to be made.*" Don't underestimate the importance of teamwork. As the link between the client, the opposing barrister, the judge, solicitors and social workers, it is important that you win the trust and confidence of them all.

prospects

We're told that one in three marriages breaks down in the UK, yet the family Bar is quite small and competition for pupillage is hot. "*Going straight into family law from university, it can seem daunting to advise on mortgages, marriages or children when you've never experienced these things yourself.*" As such, those embarking on a second career, or those who have delayed a year or two and acquired other life experiences, may have an advantage. Ellen stressed that pupillages don't always go to those with starred Firsts, saying: "*No one will get in on exam results alone.*" Improve your chances by doing at least one mini-pupillage in a family law set and consider how working with a voluntary organisation that deals with family and relationship issues might benefit you. Finally, bear in mind that family cases are not the most lucrative as legally aided work is generally poorly paid, but the satisfaction to be gained from assisting a client at such a crisis point in their life can be incalculable.

public law

Public bodies operate within statutory constraints and are bound by the principles of public law. Their decisions may be challenged on procedural or other public law grounds: maybe they haven't considered the relevant facts in reaching their decisions; have made an unreasonable decision; perhaps the body or officer didn't have the authority to make the decision in the first place; or they won't reveal to you how and why they have made a decision. If you are pioneer for justice and the advancement of the law, read on.

type of work

For those not yet happy to plump for a pigeonhole and sit in it, public law interlocks with an array of different areas of law, such as competition, European, employment or general common law. Maya Lester at Brick Court Chambers explained how "*most chambers doing public law have other specialisms too: some have a criminal emphasis, and others a more commercial emphasis, some focus on employment law or human rights.*" Remember, some sets that do not profess to be public law specialists undertake judicial review work. For example, criminal barristers will often handle issues relating to prisoners or breaches of procedure by police. And a set concentrating on commercial work might handle judicial reviews of DTI or other regulatory decisions. Accordingly, cases can range from "*pro bono or legal aid work for an individual, to commercial judicial review for magic circle firms, or government instructions.*"

Barristers with a local authority clientele act for a number of different departments on a range of work, sometimes relating to planning, housing or environmental matters and education, health, prisons and children. There has been a recent spate of cases concerning community care issues and the provision of social services by local authorities. Judicial reviews of immigration decisions also make up a significant chunk of the Administrative Court's case list, and at the other end of the spectrum sit some high-profile and contentious cases, such as that of Jodie and Mary the conjoined twins, whose surgeons applied for judicial review in respect of the decision to prosecute if they were to separate them.

Where an event is of great public importance, inquiries are sometimes commissioned by the Government and then operate independently. The Bloody Sunday Inquiry and the Hutton Inquiry into the death of David Kelly illustrate well the different types of issue that come under scrutiny. The Human Rights Act has undoubtedly affected public law and, as Maya explains: "*Its first few years have shown that many areas still need to be sorted out; for example, issues relating to privacy are arising all the time but the law is still not clear.*"

With such a variety of work falling under the public law umbrella, it is unsurprising that "*everyone has a different experienc*e" but the split between advisory work and advocacy is quite distinct. About half of Maya's time is spent giving opinions rather than doing oral advocacy, and she stresses that "*you won't be getting on a train to go to court every day. A lot of your life will be spent in chambers on written advocacy, drafting skeleton arguments and opinions, advising public bodies on the implications of the Human Rights Act, or whether their structures comply with public law principles.*" That said, there will be opportunities to get stuck into advocacy early on in your career. The preliminary permissions stage of judicial review proceedings provides the junior barrister with "*a short 30-minute hearing that they can do alone.*" Perfect.

Public international law appeals to many students, but openings in relevant chambers are limited. Traditionally it's been the preserve of academics – the leading names are predominantly sitting or ex-professors at top universities, but also include Foreign Office veterans and the occasional more senior barrister. Governments want tried-and-tested counsel and will expect those they instruct to be recognised, published authors. This is not an area of work you'll fall into by accident, nor is it one you're likely to get into until you're much more experienced. If the academic route is not for you, good luck in your search for pupillage specialising in public international law.

skills needed

...a desire to battle through red tape...genuine interest in the fundamental laws by which we live...knowledge of administrative and constitutional law...familiarity with EU and international law...creativity...common sense...rationality...keen intellect...

If you are interested in the academic legal arguments but want to apply them practically, public law provides the forum for debating those issues. Maya says: "*You can get a real sense that you are helping people – there is a human interest.*" But providing real remedies for real people demands a very practical mind and a broad perspective combined with common sense. *"You have to be able to stand back and look at the broader implications of what you are saying."* Both applicants and public bodies have *"an equally valid interest in proper decision-making processes, and you have to be able to see both sides of the coin."*

The Administrative Court is one of the most inundated branches of the High Court, so you'll need to develop an efficient style of advocacy. Long and dramatic performances are rarely well received; you must learn how to cut to the chase and deliver the pertinent information, draw on the relevant case law or statutory regulations and present your arguments promptly. Importantly though, while an inquiring and analytical mind is essential, public law is *"not as precise a science as commercial law or tax...it requires using the principles of reasonableness, fairness, rationality. It is a more discursive thing, and is as much* about finding interesting and creative arguments rather than a precise answer."*

prospects

Focusing your studies on constitutional law subjects is one way of demonstrating your enthusiasm for public law practice. However, Maya warns against closing your mind to everything else because *"your practice will probably be mixed with other areas of the law."* Get a few mini-pupillages under your belt, do as much mooting as possible and read quality newspapers to familiarise yourself with the public law issues raised in them. Maya *"wouldn't discourage anyone from doing something else, such as a Masters degree, before going to the Bar – people should take the opportunity, while they can, to become a broader lawyer."* Lastly, don't forget to look at the opportunities available within the Government Legal Service.

ADMINISTRATIVE & PUBLIC LAW • London

1. **Blackstone Chambers** (Presiley Baxendale QC & Charles Flint QC)

2. **Brick Court Chambers** (Christopher Clarke QC)
   Doughty Street Chambers (Geoffrey Robertson QC)
   39 Essex Street (Richard Davies QC & Richard Wilmot-Smith QC)
   11 King's Bench Walk Chambers (Tabachnik QC & Goudie QC)
   Landmark Chambers (Patrick Clarkson QC)
   Matrix

3. **1 Crown Office Row** (Robert Seabrook QC)
   Two Garden Court (Owen Davies QC & Courtenay Griffiths QC)
   4-5 Gray's Inn Square (Elizabeth Appleby QC & Timothy Straker QC)
   3 Hare Court (James Guthrie QC)
   1 Temple Gardens (Ian Burnett QC)

CHANCERY: TRADITIONAL • London

1. **Wilberforce Chambers** (Edward Nugee QC)

2. **5 Stone Buildings** (Henry Harrod)

3. **Maitland Chambers**
   (Lyndon-Stanford QC & Aldous QC & Driscoll QC)
   11 New Square (Sonia Proudman QC)
   New Square Chambers (Charles Purle QC)
   10 Old Square (Leolin Price CBE QC)
   11 Old Square (Grant Crawford/Jonathan Simpkiss)
   Serle Court (Lord Neill of Bladen QC)

4. **24 Old Buildings** (Martin Mann QC & Alan Steinfeld QC)
   9 Stone Buildings (Michael Ashe QC)

CHANCERY: COMMERCIAL • London

1. **Maitland Chambers**
   (Lyndon-Stanford QC & Aldous QC & Driscoll QC)

2. **Serle Court** (Lord Neill of Bladen QC)
   4 Stone Buildings (George Bompas QC)

3. **3/4 South Square**
   (Michael Crystal QC & Lord Alexander of Weedon QC)
   Wilberforce Chambers (Edward Nugee QC)

4. **Enterprise Chambers** (Bernard Weatherill QC)
   New Square Chambers (Charles Purle QC)
   24 Old Buildings (Martin Mann QC & Alan Steinfeld QC)
   3 Stone Buildings (Geoffrey Vos QC)
   11 Stone Buildings (Edward Cohen)

COMPETITION/EUROPEAN LAW • London

1. **Brick Court Chambers** (Christopher Clarke QC)
   Monckton Chambers (Kenneth Parker QC & Paul Lasok QC)

BANKING & FINANCE • London

1. **Fountain Court** (Michael Brindle QC & Michael Lerego QC)
   3 Verulam Buildings (Christopher Symons QC & John Jarvis QC)

2. **Brick Court Chambers** (Christopher Clarke QC)
   Essex Court Chambers (Gordon Pollock QC)
   One Essex Court (Lord Grabiner QC)

3. **Erskine Chambers** (Robin Potts QC)
   20 Essex Street (Iain Milligan QC)
   Serle Court (Lord Neill of Bladen QC)
   3/4 South Square (Michael Crystal QC & Lord Alexander of Weedon QC)

COMMERCIAL (LITIGATION) • London

1. **Brick Court Chambers** (Christopher Clarke QC)
   Essex Court Chambers (Gordon Pollock QC)
   One Essex Court (Lord Grabiner QC)
   Fountain Court (Michael Brindle QC & Michael Lerego QC)

2. **Blackstone Chambers** (Presiley Baxendale QC & Charles Flint QC)
   3 Verulam Buildings (Christopher Symons QC & John Jarvis QC)

3. **20 Essex Street** (Iain Milligan QC)
   7 King's Bench Walk (Gavin Kealey QC & Julian Flaux QC)

CONSTRUCTION • London

1. **Atkin Chambers** (Robert Akenhead QC)
   Keating Chambers (Vivian Ramsey QC)

2. **4 Pump Court** (David Friedman QC & Christopher Moger QC)

3. **Crown Office Chambers** (Spencer QC & Purchas QC)
   39 Essex Street (Richard Davies QC & Richard Wilmot-Smith QC)

4. **Four New Square** (Justin Fenwick QC)

COMPANY • London

1. **Erskine Chambers** (Robin Potts QC)

2. **Maitland Chambers**
   (Lyndon-Stanford QC & Aldous QC & Driscoll QC)
   Serle Court (Lord Neill of Bladen QC)
   3/4 South Square (Crystal QC & Lord Alexander of Weedon QC)
   4 Stone Buildings (George Bompas QC)

3. **Enterprise Chambers** (Bernard Weatherill QC)
   24 Old Buildings (Martin Mann QC & Alan Steinfeld QC)

CRIME • London

1. **2 Bedford Row** (William Clegg QC)
Doughty Street Chambers (Geoffrey Robertson QC)
Hollis Whiteman Chambers (QEB) (Vivian Robinson QC & Peter Whiteman QC)
6 King's Bench Walk (Roy Amlot QC)
3 Raymond Buildings (Clive Nicholls QC)

2. **25 Bedford Row** (Rock Tansey QC)
2 Hare Court (David Waters QC)
18 Red Lion Court (Peter Rook QC)

3. **Atkinson Bevan Chambers, 2 Harcourt Buildings** (Nicholas Atkinson QC & John Bevan QC)
7 Bedford Row (David Farrer QC)
9-12 Bell Yard (Lord Carlile of Berriew QC)
23 Essex Street (Charles Miskin QC)
Furnival Chambers (Andrew Mitchell QC)
Two Garden Court (Owen Davies QC & Courtenay Griffiths QC)
Matrix
Tooks Court Chambers (Michael Mansfield QC)
2-4 Tudor Street (Richard Ferguson QC)

4. **36 Bedford Row** (Michael Pert QC)
9 Bedford Row (formerly 4 Brick Court) (Anthony C Berry QC)
10 King's Bench Walk (David Nathan QC)
187 Fleet Street (Andrew Trollope QC)
5 Paper Buildings (Godfrey Carey QC & Jonathan Caplan QC)
3 Temple Gardens (Joanna Greenberg QC)

CLINICAL NEGLIGENCE • London

1. **1 Crown Office Row** (Robert Seabrook QC)
3 Serjeants' Inn (Robert Francis QC & John Grace QC)

2. **Doughty Street Chambers** (Geoffrey Robertson QC)
6 Pump Court (Kieran Coonan QC)

3. **Cloisters** (Robin Allen QC & Brian Langstaff QC)
Crown Office Chambers (Michael Spencer QC & Christopher Purchas QC)
Hailsham Chambers (Michael Pooles QC & Eleanor Sharpston QC)
2 Temple Gardens (Andrew Collender QC)

4. **7 Bedford Row** (David Farrer QC)
Outer Temple Chambers (Philip Mott QC)
No. 1 Serjeants' Inn (Edward Faulks QC)
199 Strand (David Phillips QC)

ENVIRONMENT • London

1. **39 Essex Street** (Richard Davies QC & Richard Wilmot-Smith QC)
Landmark Chambers (Patrick Clarkson QC)
Old Square Chambers

2. **Blackstone Chambers** (Presiley Baxendale QC & Charles Flint QC)
2 Harcourt Buildings (Robin Purchas QC)
Matrix

3. **Brick Court Chambers** (Christopher Clarke QC)
1 Crown Office Row (Robert Seabrook QC)
4-5 Gray's Inn Square (Elizabeth Appleby QC & Timothy Straker QC)
6 Pump Court (Stephen Hockman QC)

EMPLOYMENT • London

1. **Blackstone Chambers** (Presiley Baxendale QC & Charles Flint QC)
11 King's Bench Walk Chambers (Eldred Tabachnik QC & James Goudie QC)
Littleton Chambers (Michel Kallipetis QC)

2. **Cloisters** (Robin Allen QC & Brian Langstaff QC)
Devereux Chambers (Colin Edelman QC)
Matrix
Old Square Chambers

3. **Essex Court Chambers** (Gordon Pollock QC)
Fountain Court (Michael Brindle QC & Michael Lerego QC)

FAMILY/MATRIMONIAL • London

1. **1 Hare Court** (Bruce Blair QC)
One King's Bench Walk (Anthony Hacking QC)
Queen Elizabeth Building (Andrew Moylan QC)

2. **4 Paper Buildings** (Jonathan Cohen QC)
29 Bedford Row Chambers (Nicholas Francis QC)
One Garden Court Family Law Chambers (Eleanor F Platt QC & Alison Ball QC)

3. **14 Gray's Inn Square** (Sarah Forster & Gillian Brasse)
Renaissance Chambers (Brian Patrick Jubb & Henry Setright QC)

FRAUD: CRIMINAL • London

1. **Hollis Whiteman Chambers (QEB)** (Vivian Robinson QC & Peter Whiteman QC)

2. **2 Bedford Row** (William Clegg QC)
   3 Raymond Buildings (Clive Nicholls QC)

3. **9-12 Bell Yard** (Lord Carlile of Berriew QC)
   23 Essex Street (Charles Miskin QC)
   18 Red Lion Court (Peter Rook QC)

4. **7 Bedford Row** (David Farrer QC)
   Charter Chambers (Stephen Solley QC)
   Doughty Street Chambers (Geoffrey Robertson QC)
   6 King's Bench Walk (Roy Amlot QC)
   Matrix
   187 Fleet Street (Andrew Trollope QC)
   5 Paper Buildings (Godfrey Carey QC & Jonathan Caplan QC)

HUMAN RIGHTS • London

1. **Blackstone Chambers** (Presiley Baxendale QC & Charles Flint QC)
   Doughty Street Chambers (Geoffrey Robertson QC)
   Matrix

2. **Brick Court Chambers** (Christopher Clarke QC)
   39 Essex Street (Richard Davies QC & Richard Wilmot-Smith QC)

3. **1 Crown Office Row** (Robert Seabrook QC)
   Two Garden Court (Owen Davies QC & Courtenay Griffiths QC)
   11 King's Bench Walk Chambers (Eldred Tabachnik QC & James Goudie QC)
   Tooks Court Chambers (Michael Mansfield QC)

INFORMATION TECHNOLOGY • London

1. **11 South Square** (Christopher Floyd QC)

2. **Atkin Chambers** (Robert Akenhead QC)
   4 Pump Court (David Friedman QC & Christopher Moger QC)

3. **Henderson Chambers** (Roger Henderson QC)
   Three New Square (Antony Watson QC)
   8 New Square (Mark Platts-Mills QC)

MEDIA & ENTERTAINMENT • London

1. **Blackstone Chambers** (Presiley Baxendale QC & Charles Flint QC)

2. **8 New Square** (Mark Platts-Mills QC)

3. **Essex Court Chambers** (Gordon Pollock QC)
   Hogarth Chambers (Christopher Morcom QC & Kevin Garnett QC)

IMMIGRATION • London

1. **Two Garden Court** (Owen Davies QC & Courtenay Griffiths QC)

2. **Doughty Street Chambers** (Geoffrey Robertson QC)
   Matrix
   Tooks Court Chambers (Michael Mansfield QC)

3. **Blackstone Chambers** (Presiley Baxendale QC & Charles Flint QC)
   39 Essex Street (Richard Davies QC & Richard Wilmot-Smith QC)
   6 King's Bench Walk (Sibghat Kadri QC)
   Renaissance Chambers (Brian Patrick Jubb & Henry Setright QC)

INTERNATIONAL ARBITRATION: GENERAL COMMERCIAL & INSURANCE • London

1. **Essex Court Chambers** (Gordon Pollock QC)
   20 Essex Street (Iain Milligan QC)

2. **One Essex Court** (Lord Grabiner QC)
   7 King's Bench Walk (Gavin Kealey QC & Julian Flaux QC)

3. **Brick Court Chambers** (Christopher Clarke QC)
   Quadrant Chambers (Nigel Teare QC)
   Fountain Court (Michael Brindle QC & Michael Lerego QC)
   3 Verulam Buildings (Christopher Symons QC & John Jarvis QC)

INTELLECTUAL PROPERTY • London

1. **Three New Square** (Antony Watson QC)
   8 New Square (Mark Platts-Mills QC)
   11 South Square (Christopher Floyd QC)

2. **Hogarth Chambers** (Christopher Morcom QC & Kevin Garnett QC)

3. **One Essex Court** (Lord Grabiner QC)
   19 Old Buildings (Alastair Wilson QC)
   Wilberforce Chambers (Edward Nugee QC)

INSURANCE • London

1. **Brick Court Chambers** (Christopher Clarke QC)
   Essex Court Chambers (Gordon Pollock QC)
   7 King's Bench Walk (Gavin Kealey QC & Julian Flaux QC)

2. **Fountain Court** (Michael Brindle QC & Michael Lerego QC)
   3 Verulam Buildings (Christopher Symons QC & John Jarvis QC)

3. **Devereux Chambers** (Colin Edelman QC)
   20 Essex Street (Iain Milligan QC)
   4 Pump Court (David Friedman QC & Christopher Moger QC)

PUBLIC INTERNATIONAL LAW • London

1. **Blackstone Chambers** (Presiley Baxendale QC & Charles Flint QC)
   Essex Court Chambers (Gordon Pollock QC)
   20 Essex Street (Iain Milligan QC)
2. **Matrix**

REAL ESTATE LITIGATION • London

1. **Falcon Chambers** (Jonathan Gaunt QC & Paul Morgan QC)
2. **Maitland Chambers (incorporating 9 Old Square)**
   (Michael Lyndon-Stanford QC & Charles Aldous QC & Michael Driscoll QC)
3. **Landmark Chambers** (Patrick Clarkson QC)
   Wilberforce Chambers (Edward Nugee QC)
4. **Enterprise Chambers** (Bernard Weatherill QC)
   Henderson Chambers (Roger Henderson QC)
   Selborne Chambers (Romie Tager QC)
   Serle Court (Lord Neill of Bladen QC)
   Tanfield Chambers (Peter Hughes QC)

TAX • London

1. **Gray's Inn Tax Chambers** (Milton Grundy)
   Pump Court Tax Chambers (Andrew Thornhill QC)
2. **11 New Square** (John Gardiner QC)
3. **One Essex Court** (Lord Grabiner QC)
   Monckton Chambers (Kenneth Parker QC & Paul Lasok QC)
   24 Old Buildings (Rex Bretten QC)
   3 Temple Gardens Tax Chambers (Richard Bramwell QC)

PERSONAL INJURY • London

1. **39 Essex Street** (Richard Davies QC & Richard Wilmot-Smith QC)
   Farrar's Building (John Leighton Williams QC)
   12 King's Bench Walk (Richard Methuen QC)
   2 Temple Gardens (Andrew Collender QC)
2. **Crown Office Chambers** (Michael Spencer QC & Christopher Purchas QC)
   Devereux Chambers (Colin Edelman QC)
   Doughty Street Chambers (Geoffrey Robertson QC)
   9 Gough Square (John Foy QC)
   Old Square Chambers
   Outer Temple Chambers (Philip Mott QC)

SHIPPING • London

1. **Quadrant Chambers** (Nigel Teare QC)
2. **Essex Court Chambers** (Gordon Pollock QC)
   20 Essex Street (Iain Milligan QC)
   7 King's Bench Walk (Gavin Kealey QC & Julian Flaux QC)
3. **Stone Chambers** (Steven Gee QC)

INSOLVENCY/CORPORATE RECOVERY • London

1. **3/4 South Square** (Crystal QC & Lord Alexander of Weedon QC)
2. **Erskine Chambers** (Robin Potts QC)
   Serle Court (Lord Neill of Bladen QC)
   4 Stone Buildings (George Bompas QC)
3. **Enterprise Chambers** (Bernard Weatherill QC)
   Essex Court Chambers (Gordon Pollock QC)
   Maitland Chambers (Lyndon-Stanford QC/Aldous QC/Driscoll QC)
   24 Old Buildings (Martin Mann QC & Alan Steinfeld QC)
   11 Stone Buildings (Edward Cohen)

These are just a sample selection of the tables included in *Chambers UK*. The book also contains rankings for the circuits and individual barristers in many areas of practice.

chambers reports

chambers reports

The Student Guide knows it can be difficult to decide which sets to apply to for pupillage. On paper it's impossible to gauge how they will differ and whether you will be suited to the style of each, and who has the time and opportunity to do mini-pupillages at them all? We visited 44 sets in 2003/4 to speak to pupils, barristers and clerks and to inspect the places where they work. The ones we've chosen are among the most successful in their fields of practice, though we do not suggest that the following are the best 44 sets. Such a list would be impossible to compile.

Our selection includes crime, family, common law, commercial and Chancery chambers plus some that specialise in human rights and public law. Most of those we visited are in London, simply because this is where the majority of pupillages are offered. However, after a letter from someone on the Northern Circuit, we raced to King's Cross and took the Pendolino to Piccadilly Station. This year's selection includes three Manchester sets plus the two we visited in Birmingham in 2003.

On our visits, we were given a tour of chambers, sampled the coffee, interrogated pupillage committees, silks and pupilmasters, probed pupils and juniors and even patted dogs. Many of our subject sets had developed into modern businesses or were on their way – a far cry from the outdated stereotype that many assume is still standard at the Bar.

Pupillage is an important time for any young barrister and we hope that what you will read in this part of the book will be encouraging and perhaps even reassuring. The pupillage year is hard work and has an uncertain ending (though it is less uncertain outside London), but it can be made easier by commitment and consistency in performance. Some people say it's a year-long interview; generally we found chambers to be more forgiving and willing to commit a good deal to bringing pupils on, professionally and personally – none expect perfectly formed barristers to arrive at their door on day one.

The first six of a pupillage is more or less standard whichever set you look at, though differences are more apparent in the second six, particularly when it comes to chambers' policies on whether pupils should take their own paid work. There are also differences in the breadth of practice to which pupils are exposed in different sets. And importantly there are differences in the feel of each set. This was the main reason we launched the Chambers Reports section and we hope our findings (and gut instincts) are of interest.

Finding the right set and type of practice for you is the key to career satisfaction and success. To some extent, chambers' recruiters will help you with this as they have a great deal of experience in spotting who is right for them. Mostly, it's down to you to pick wisely at the application stage. Good luck!

THE 'CHAMBERS REPORTS' SETS

NO.	SET	LOCATION	HEAD OF CHAMBERS	(QCS/JUNIORS)
1	2 Bedford Row	London	William Clegg	54 (15/39)
2	Blackstone Chambers*	London	Baxendale/Flint	64 (28/36)
3	Brick Court Chambers*	London	Christopher Clarke	65 (29/36)
4	Cloisters*	London	Langstaff/Allen	44 (4/40)
5	Crown Office Chambers*	London	Spencer/Purchas	76 (16/60)
6	Devereux Chambers*	London	Colin Edelman	46 (7/39)
7	Doughty Street Chambers*	London	Geoffrey Robertson	84 (18/66)
8	Erskine Chambers*	London	Robin Potts	24 (9/15)
9	Essex Court Chambers*	London	Gordon Pollock	67 (30/37)
10	One Essex Court*	London	Anthony Grabiner	56 (22/34)
11	20 Essex Street*	London	Iain Milligan	49 (17/32)
12	39 Essex Street	London	Davies/Wilmot-Smith	62 (19/43)
13	Fountain Court*	London	Brindle/Lerego	58 (20/38)
14	Furnival Chambers	London	Andrew Mitchell	66 (8/58)
15	One Garden Court	London	Platt/Ball	47 (6/41)
16	Two Garden Court*	London	Davies/Griffiths	81 (8/73)
17	Government Legal Service	London/Manchester	n/a	n/a
18	2-3 Gray's Inn Square	London	Porten/Scrivener	52 (9/43)
19	2 Hare Court	London	David Waters	47 (11/36)
20	Hollis Whiteman Chambers*	London	Bevan/Whiteman	53 (19/34)
21	7 King's Bench Walk	London	Kealey/Flaux	40 (11/29)
22	11 King's Bench Walk*	London	Tabachnik/Goudie	43 (12/31)
23	Maitland Chambers*	London	Lyndon-Stanford/Aldous	65 (15/50)
24	Matrix*	London	n/a	50 (15/35)
25	Monckton Chambers	London	Parker/Lasok	34 (11/23)
26	Four New Square	London	Justin Fenwick	53 (11/42)
27	Old Square Chambers	London	John Hendy	53 (10/43)
28	Pump Court Tax Chambers	London	Andrew Thornhill	26 (8/18)
29	4 Pump Court	London	Friedman/Moger	45 (12/33)
30	Quadrant Chambers	London	Nigel Teare	47 (14/33)
31	Queen Elizabeth Building*	London	Andrew Moylan	28 (3/25)
32	3 Raymond Buildings	London	Clive Nicholls	46 (15/31)
33	Serle Court*	London	Lord Neill of Bladen	46 (12/34)
34	3 Serjeants' Inn	London	Francis/Grace	41 (7/34)
35	3/4 South Square*	London	Crystal/Alexander	50 (16/34)
36	4 Stone Buildings *	London	Philip Heslop	26 (8/18)
37	2 Temple Gardens	London	Andrew Collender	42 (8/34)
38	3 Verulam Buildings*	London	Symons/Jarvis	56 (10/46)
39	Wilberforce Chambers*	London	Edward Nugee	39 (16/23)
40	No.5 Chambers*	Birmingham	Gareth Evans	151 (14/137)
41	St Philips Chambers*	Birmingham	John Randall	134 (12/122)
42	Deans Court	Manchester	Stephen Grime	57 (9/48)
43	Kings Chambers	Manchester	Frances Patterson	64 (8/56)
44	St Johns Buidings	Manchester	Michael Redfern	92 (10/82)

These sets were visited during 2003. All others were visited 2004.

chambers reports

2 Bedford Row

the facts

OLPAS: summer season **Pupillages:** 4 x 12 months
Applications: 370+ **mini pupillages:** Unlimited
First Interview: 60 **Second Interview:** 15
Award: In line with the Bar Council minimum
Tenancies awarded in 2004: Not yet known, 2 in 2003
Chambers UK Rankings: Crime, criminal fraud

There's something inherently serious about 2 Bedford Row. Perhaps it's the photograph of blindfolded Justice – sword in one hand, scales in the other – on chambers' website. Perhaps it's chambers' waiting room, on the walls of which hang two large and imposing court artist's sketches depicting scenes from the bewigged hall of fame that is chambers past. However you judge it, serious crime is what this set excels at. Wipe the dust from your first-year criminal law textbook, take a look at the Table of Cases, and you will soon discover that 2 Bedford Row has featured heavily in a good number of them. R v Brown, The Herald of Free Enterprise, Kebeline v DPP, Prosecutor v Tadic – it's all there.

Since the day the set was founded in 1983 by current head of chambers and much sought after defence lawyer William Clegg QC, solicitors, defendants, the Crown and statutory bodies have relied on the courtroom skills of 2 Bedford Row's barristers. Whether prosecuting for the Health & Safety Executive or defending the perpetrators of alleged war crimes in the International Criminal Tribunal for Former Yugoslavia, they have the necessary gravitas and experience. In every field of criminal law, they are unashamedly good at what they do.

A pupillage with this set concentrates primarily on crime, though chambers is involved in public inquiry work and sports disciplinary matters.

Pupils start their careers swimming with the bigger fish in chambers, and as such the first six is, as one pupils explained, a process of *"learning by osmosis."* Spending the vast majority of their time with a single pupilmaster, they feel *"like a spare part at times,"* but the important thing is to soak it all up. *"You learn so much just by watching how counsel interact with each other in the robing room, and by seeing them deal with solicitors or the CPS."* What pupils actually encounter depends on the luck of the draw. While one junior tenant spent the entirety of his first six assisting in the preparatory stages of a complex fraud trial, another had done the rounds of London's Crown Courts, observing much shorter *"knock-about, three to four-day trials."* Everyone agrees that it is advisable to take on work for other members as a way of getting your face known, particularly as when you undertake legal research for a senior member *"it's not uncommon for you to be invited along to court to see the fruits of your labour put into action. That's very satisfying."*

The set's standing is reflected in the kind of work pupils see in their second, practising six months. *"As a pupil here, you'll get your hands on the kind of work that you just wouldn't expect to see in other sets,"* we were told. One pupil recalled her first appearance in court – a baptism of fire that consisted of prosecuting a defendant for breach of a Community Punishment Order in front of an Old Bailey judge. If you're worried about being asked to run before you can even walk, rest assured there will also be plenty of standard-fare magistrates' court work, though this in itself may feel like a hundred-metre sprint with little time to catch your breath. As we were warned by a young pupil who'd just got back from court: *"It's a gruelling schedule. I'm usually in one court in the morning and another in the afternoon, then it's back to chambers to prepare for the next day."* For those who are not fortunate enough to be taken on as a tenant at the end of the year, this *"nuts-and-bolts"* experience becomes invaluable.

For those who do achieve a qualifying time in the pupillage race and progress to tenancy the change in pace is an *"exponential"* one. The baby junior we interviewed observed that *"before you know it, you'll go from facing three lay magistrates to standing up in front of three Lord Justices arguing an appeal against sentence...it really does happen that quickly."* The tenancy decision is made in September and by a full vote of all members. There is no formal assessment programme during the pupillage year; instead, *"pupils are encouraged to apply to solicitors who have instructed them for references."* Effectively the assessment takes place in the field.

Despite 2 Bedford Row's success and standing, this is not a place in which senior members *"go around flaunting their egos."* Indeed, on our brief visit we found the atmosphere unstuffy and understated. We also sensed that while there is a reasonable social scene, people like to get their heads down and work hard during the day. *"We're definitely workaholics; we're sociable with it, but the job itself is all-consuming."* Easy and understated are words that would best describe the relationship between clerks and juniors. First name terms are the norm, and those at the junior end of the food chain told us they were perfectly happy discussing their career ambitions with the senior clerks, who in any event *"know our practices inside out."*

If you want your application form to be plucked from what is always a pretty big pile, you'll need to be hardworking too. You must also show a firm commitment to criminal practice. It wouldn't appear to matter where your degree is from, though anything below a 2:1 and you should be very impressive in other aspects. On top of all this, you'll also need to have *"something a bit different from the norm."* A brief glance at the CVs of current members bears out one junior tenant's observation that *"we don't fit the traditional mould of a barrister."* One pupil had been a tabloid journalist before changing career, and several members had experiences outside the law. No one is suggesting that a first career is prerequisite, but it clearly helps if you have experience of the real world beyond acadaemia. In the words of one pupil: *"You need to be lucid and intelligent, but you also need to have that human touch, and be on the same wavelength as your client. It's through being able to understand your client that you get decent instructions from them."*

A good application form will only get you so far; what these recruiters are really interested in is how you perform at interview. There's a two-round process, the first interview being a fairly brief chat, usually with a topical/legal theme, and the second incorporating an advocacy exercise handed out four hours in advance. If you're one of the lucky ones that gets this far, don't worry if you come out of the interview room feeling utterly harangued. The job is all about thriving under pressure, so the interview is designed to reflect this. We chatted to one pupil who was convinced he'd flunked the whole thing after a *"grilling."* Obviously not!

We'll end with the endorsement of the junior tenant who told us: *"It's true that pupillage can be stressful and hard work, but if you revel in that pressure, and in the fact that for the first time you're doing the job for real, then you'll love it here."*

Blackstone Chambers

the facts

OLPAS: summer season **Pupillages:** 5x12 months
Applications: 350 **Mini pupillages:** 40-45
Interviews: 12-14
Award: £35,000, (£9,000 can be advanced for BVC)
Tenancies offered in 2004: 2
Chambers UK rankings: Administrative law, commercial litigation, employment, environment, financial services, civil fraud, human rights, immigration, media & entertainment, professional discipline, public international, sport

Blackstone Chambers has a dominant position in public law and leading commercial and employment practices. It has big-name QCs like Barbara Dohmann, Charles Flint and David Pannick, and you might be aware of co-head Presiley Baxendale's rebirth as a mediator. The set is instructed by all manner of firms from the magic circle to smaller provincial outfits. It also receives direct instructions from local authorities and in-house lawyers.

Blackstone attracts all those who apply to the magic circle commercial sets and plenty more besides. For many students, it's the set's public law reputation but, whatever motivates you, be aware that pupillage and the first few years of tenancy will involve all aspects of the set's work. So, *"if you don't want commercial practice you'll get a nasty shock!"* The first step to admission is an assessed mini pupillage, from which 12 lucky candidates will step up for a pupillage interview. They should have plenty to talk about as there's a sincere attempt to integrate even mini-pupils into chambers life. Yet, despite lunches and drinks with members, the pupillage committee assures us that the process of selection is based solely on objective criteria. *"There's a temptation to want to work with people you like as, on the balance of probabilities, they will be here forever,"* but *"we're not trying to recreate the set's image for the next generation."* So what is it aiming for? According to one source: *"It's not a magic circle commercial set, but it desperately wants to be."* Don't assume you'll have to come from a 'standard' background. You need first-class ability but this doesn't always equate to a First in a law degree from Oxbridge. Among the juniors at Blackstone, there is an ex-banker, an ex-journalist and an ex-bouncer.

The process of selecting pupils is just the first in a long line of examples of this set's preoccupation with fairness…and systems to ensure fairness. Apparently, there's a rumour going round that the performance of pupils is displayed in a league table in the clerks' room. While a performance chart does exist (pupils are required to take two-day formal assessments every month), it is available only to the pupillage committee and is designed to ensure the tenancy decision is based on performance rather than favouritism and face time. Our sources spoke positively of this intense 'under the microscope' approach: *"It provides a framework and that's comforting in a way. It's so fair…sometimes it's too fair and you can perhaps feel that there's no room for personality to sway the decision."* Being constantly assessed may colour your pupillage year, but *"it cuts down the need for any internecine warfare between pupils…you're so much in the same boat."*

Four pupilmasters take pupils for three months each – last year, an employment guru, an insurance specialist and two barristers with mixed commercial/public law practices. Depending on which one you're with, you'll either be haring in and out of county courts and employment tribunals or you'll be more chambers-based, researching, writing advices and pleadings etc. Work for other members is banned, as is paid work. Expect to stay within the secure confines of a carefully structured scheme, free from the need to impress all and sundry. And there's no chambers tea to which you must dutifully troop in order to be seen but not heard.

Chambers is open and relaxed and, so long as you keep a *"scramble suit"* hanging behind your door, you can happily parade around in your 501s. *"The impression an outsider gets is of a very informal and lively bunch of people who have a great deal of affection and respect for each other. Wandering along the corridors you hear laughter and lively conversation."* This youth and vitality seems to have sprung into life in the 1990s when a constitution was established, along with a new mood for nurturing younger members and pupils. This latter phenomenon has been attributed to senior junior Pushpinder Saini, who started taking the kids out for lunch and drinks. It has now evolved into a full-blown social scene to which even senior members have attached themselves. Often, there are drinks in chambers on a Friday, and if it's a fine summer evening they'll retire to the roof to enjoy the view over the Thames. But spare a thought for the chambers' goldfish that only have a view of the clerks' room. We heard a fishy tale of clerks and barristers scrabbling around under desks following a piscine bid for freedom.

In 1998, when Blackstone moved to its current home, the set skipped a generation of older members and appointed the two (younger) current heads of chambers. It was *"a reflection of a desire to be modern and forward thinking. The set was very comfortable with having younger people as figureheads."* This is a set that no one (except maybe the fish) ever leaves. *"The last time someone went to the bench was in 1979…and then in the mid-80s someone became a Master of the Queen's Bench."* Why? *"Because we're argumentative and bloody-minded advocates!"* As for moving to other sets, that's not on either. *"Michael Beloff left. But then he came back."*

"We particularly pride ourselves on our advocates," one silk told us. *"That's where we outstrip the opposition."* Certainly the juniors are encouraged to experience advocacy as early as possible, and the volume of employment work assists in this aim. Of course, a toptastic academic record is absolutely essential for pupils, but unless you're the sort that enjoys questioning things and then standing up and arguing your point, you're not really Blackstone material. Some of the members run the Gray's Inn advocacy course for pupils as well as additional in-house advocacy training for Blackstone pupils.

The tenancy decision in the summer can be an emotional moment. One source told us: *"You worry that if you have to go somewhere else, you'll spend the first three months hating them for not being Blackstone."* So what do they fear they will miss? The support network of Julia Hornor, Doreen and her chocolate biscuits, fellow pupils and junior tenants, the opportunity to have *"blazing rows"* with your pupilmaster on work/non-work related topics (*"You're supposed to stand up for your views"*) and the notion that they belong to **the** set for public law matters.

Brick Court Chambers

the facts

OLPAS: summer season **Pupillages:** 4x12 months
Applications: 370 **Mini pupillages:** 110
Interview: 20-25
Award: £35,000 (funds can be advanced for BVC)
Tenancies offered in 2004: None (2 in 2003)
Chambers UK rankings: Administrative, aviation, banking & finance, commercial litigation, competition/European law, energy & natural resources, environment, civil fraud, human rights, insurance, international arbitration, professional negligence, sport

If you're aiming for top-level European, commercial or public law, then try Brick Court. It boasts some of the biggest names at the Bar, including Jonathan Sumption QC and five others in the million-a-year club. This magic circle set has a fearsome reputation for breadth of work and calibre of lawyers. Name a big commercial case from the last 15 years and there's a good chance Brick Court was involved.

EU law is in vogue with students and huge numbers of them apply for pupillage at this set. As one source told us: *"Applicants have to be outstanding in all areas; we can afford to be picky."* Wanted: *"Excellent brains and an ability to express oneself clearly in writing, while being articulate, attractive and persuasive orally."* Contrary to rumours, what is not required is a parent on the bench – this idea probably sprang from the fact that four senior members are the offspring of judges. Just like the Bar as a whole, this set is departing from the elitist, old-fashioned stereotype. That said, barristers don't dress in jeans and trainers, many still get the 'Mister' and 'Sir' treatment from clerks, and there's no attempt to convince the outside world of its being hip…or anything much else for that matter. Brick Court's work speaks for itself.

Some might say that the work is everything at Brick Court. People make friends, and two of the barristers recently made a baby, but there's a take it or leave it approach to spending time with colleagues. *"There might be a chambers party or dinner once or twice a year, and there's a tradition that junior tenants arrange an evening out for pupils a couple of times a term."* There's no chambers tea (described by one pupil as an *"ordeal"* to be *"suffered"*) and no chambers lunch – togetherness is not force-fed. Sure, barristers are collaborative when it comes to discussing legal matters, but pulling together to raise the profile of chambers? No need. A common goal to take on other sets, to speed towards infinity and beyond? Already there. Take away the need to hype or heavily promote the set and you're left with the business of getting on with business. Unfortunately, this cool, calm and collected approach is sometimes misinterpreted by outsiders as coldness or austerity. There is a film of seriousness over the set; most of the pupils we spoke to were a shade more earnest (although possibly less anxious) than their peers elsewhere.

"Our USP is diversity of work," said a pupilmaster, cringing at her use of marketing jargon. And she's right: Brick Court has real variety in its commercial work, superset status for EU matters and a thoroughly impressive record in public law. You can find sets of equal standing in each of these areas, but none that competes at the same level in all of them. Some of our sources stressed that while they felt they could get the calibre of public law experience elsewhere, they had no desire to mix it with employment work or even personal injury. They told us that for a commercial/public law pupillage Brick Court has to be the top choice. Those hell-bent on an EU/commercial caseload were even less tempted by other sets.

Each pupil sits with a pupilmaster for three months, also doing bits and pieces of work for other members. The pupillage committee has tight control of the demands on pupils and performance monitoring. *"There's enough stress on pupils already, so they shouldn't have to worry about being seen by the right people."* The system is designed to contain sufficient objective measures to nullify the 'face fits' phenomenon. As one pupil confirmed: *"The fitting-in thing is not a big requirement. People who make good barristers can be fun to be with or complete nerds who spend all their time in their rooms. It doesn't go against you to be friendly or nerdy."* Excellent news. Pupils rub along together quite well; indeed, three of them were nipping off for lunch together when we visited. *"People are human and so there is bound to be an element of comparison, but every effort is made so you don't feel like you are in direct competition."* Monthly, assessed advocacy exercises aren't divisive, even though pupil advocates against pupil. *"We're faced by a panel, who are all attempting to trip us up with awkward questions. We're all going through the same thing together."*

Advocacy exercises are all well and good, but you'll doubtless want the real thing. In your second six there's ample opportunity to represent clients on social security and possession proceedings through Law4All. Brick Court knows that much of its work is way beyond the reach of pupils and that 12 months spent researching discrete points of law on fragments of cases doesn't make for a rounded training. It might be *"inspiring"* to work with the big names and to *"see them in their thinking context,"* but you'll need some smaller matters of your own. In July, the pupillage committee recommends who should be given tenancy, but three months beforehand, pupils will have had an indication of their long-term prospects. Whether or not it's good news, *"a pupillage here is recognised as a very good training,"* so even those who don't get the right signals usually stay a full year. While *"they can be quite hard-nosed about who they keep on,"* we understand the set is looking to grow at the junior end. And on the subject of youth, the two senior clerks are relatively young. One of their predecessors, a very famous clerk called Burley (*"Ah, yes, Burley"*) was a traditional and powerful figure, *"a mega-force in chambers."* And now? *"The power is definitely with the barristers."*

Brick Court inspires strong reactions. Intense praise from clients. Respect from competitors. Looks of abject horror from those who don't understand or would not be suited to the Brick Court style. That style is somewhat formal, efficient, clever and businesslike.

It is not buffed and polished to catch the light and it is not seeking popularity for the sake of it. When a set becomes known for its profitability, its exceptional law-making cases and the variety of its activities, such distractions would seem ridiculous. If you're keen to build a serious career in one of Brick Court's core areas, apply for an assessed mini pupillage (they are mandatory and form part of the recruitment process). A week here will give you all the insight you need.

Cloisters

the facts

OLPAS: summer season **Pupillages:** 3x12 months
Applications: 450 **Mini pupillages:** 20
First interview: c.70 **Second interview:** 15
Award: £25,000 (£3,000 can be advanced for BVC)
Tenancies offered in 2004: 2
Chambers UK rankings: Clinical negligence, employment, product liability

Cloisters was founded 51 years ago with the goal of "fighting for the individual." Its well-known former head of chambers, Laura Cox, was recently appointed as one of only seven female High Court judges out of a total of 107.

Located in the classical confines of Pump Court, Cloisters enjoys a tranquil existence next to Temple Church. Inside, the set has adopted a Sunday brunch approach to chambers decor: red-checked sofas and Utterly Butterly yellow wallpaper, *The Guardian* and *The Times* (each read many times over) strewn across the waiting room coffee table. It's bright, warm and welcoming, and very lived-in. It even doubles up as an art gallery, so who knows, you might walk away with legal advice and a new painting.

Cloisters delights in its reputation for *"creative"* legal argument and has long been associated with a commitment to difficult cases. Even before the introduction of the Human Rights Act, its members were active in civil liberties cases, *"extending the ambit of the*

law." To this day, it retains a willingness to *"have a fight."* In particular, two members embody this ethos: disability and discrimination expert Robin Allen QC and the charming PI and employment guru Brian Langstaff QC.

Pupils sit with between two and four supervisors, but are encouraged to work for others in chambers, so exposing them to *"a spread of work and working styles."* There is an element of matching: if you're boisterous, you might find yourself sitting with an equally boisterous supervisor; *"if you are diffident, we'll sit you with someone who might bring you out."*

Your bread-and-utterly-butterly work will be PI and employment matters, although pupils can play an instrumental role in major reported cases. When Brian Langstaff QC argued the leading case on capacity – Masterman-Lister v Jewell – a pupil assisted. Later, when it went before the Court of Appeal, she was again involved, this time as a tenant. Her name appears in the reported judgment. Although *"slow to start off,"* pupils can expect to be on their feet up to three times a week by the middle of their second six. A formal 'No Photocopying for Pupils' decree is policed vigorously.

Breathe easy, because during the first part of pupillage, you're free to make some mistakes. After this, pupils sit through formal assessments consisting of written and advocacy tests followed by an interview with the tenancy committee. Pupils are assessed against a universal standard, not each other, and any pupil who attains a final mark over 80% is usually offered tenancy. It's a truism that this system avoids the culture of competition that can otherwise thrive like a noxious weed. Unsurprisingly, Cloisters is committed to transparent decision-making and pupils are free to examine the marking schedules.

In 2000, tired of paying for facilities they never used, Cloisters' criminal barristers left for another set. The absence of criminal work is one thing that now distinguishes Cloisters from its peers – 2 Garden Court and Tooks Court. But if criminal advocacy is important to you, you can participate in an exchange scheme with Tooks. Cloisters now regards its competitors as the big civil (and especially employment) sets and is marketing itself appropriately. In a bid to compete with them, it increased its pupillage award to £12,500 for the first six, with guaranteed earnings of £12,500 in the second. This caused some pique among existing pupils and juniors, while others felt that it might dilute the altruistic ethos of the set.

Cloisters receives bags of pupillage applications and can afford to be picky. Academic credentials are the single most important criteria for recruiters, but mooting, public speaking, legal or volunteer work are all considered favourably. In all, you must be bright, enthusiastic and curious. Cloisters says it's a diverse set, but look a little closer and an archetype emerges. Members here don't carry *"much truck for conventions or pomposity. We take things with a pinch of salt, we're nonconformist."* One pupil told us how she is not afraid to *"speak up at bail hearings or walk into the advocates' lounge and ask for advice."* This is a brave set, but one in which juniors feel comfortable asking questions and *"revealing the chink in their academic armour."*

Cloisters represents both claimants and defendants and it is perhaps because its feet are firmly planted in both camps that it is not *"on a political mission."* Whatever your politics, if you pass muster, you'll be accepted. The commitment to equal opportunities is notable and the set recently passed a resolution requiring each member to complete one week's worth of pro bono work per annum.

A dizzying social agenda has caused raised eyebrows among pupils' flatmates. One nicknamed Cloisters *"Bolly Chambers."* And not without good reason it seems. For its 50th anniversary year, chambers rent was increased by half a per cent to cover the anticipated increase in alcohol consumption. There are drinks to celebrate new artists being exhibited in chambers, welcoming parties for pupils and new tenants, and regular trips to local hostelries *"whenever someone's had a hell of a day."* Chez Gerard, Hodgsons, Gaucho Grill and The Cock are the usual suspects. On occasions, pupils even get together with the pupillage committee for breakfast.

The dress code is *"strictly informal."* Tenants *"never wear suits"* unless appearing in court or in conference. On the day we visited, juniors wore jeans and trainers. One of them told us about the time he forgot his court clothes and cobbled together a suit consisting of size nine shoes (waaaay too small), a jacket from here, trousers from there, and a tie from someone else. He won't make the same mistake again: *"It's hard to do the barrister's swagger when you're hobbling in shoes three sizes too small."* This sartorial informality is indicative of something deeper.

You'd never know that Cloisters is 52 years old. Like Isabella Rossellini, who was also born in 1952, it seems so much younger. The joking and jibing we witnessed between members was the perfect illustration of the collective spirit that binds this set. As we were leaving, we passed a little girl rolling over the red-checked sofas, and a suited man singing 'Baa Baa Black Sheep' to her. We're not sure quite why we're ending on this note, but somehow it seems appropriate.

Crown Office Chambers

the facts

OLPAS: No   **Pupillages:** up to 4x12 months
Applications: 150 **Mini pupillages:** c.100
First interview: 30 **Second interview:** 15
Award: £35,000 (up to £10,000 advanced for BVC)
Tenancies offered in 2004: 2
Chambers UK rankings: Clinical negligence, construction, personal injury, product liability, professional negligence

Crown Office Chambers came into existence in 2000, following the merger of One Paper Buildings with 2 Crown Office Row. It's a large set with an emphasis on personal injury, construction, professional and clinical negligence and product liability, topped off with general commercial and insurance/reinsurance cases. Among its silks are joint heads of chambers Michael Spencer and Christopher Purchas, Roger ter Haar and a number of other respected names. Members have been involved in most of the major product liability issues of recent years – tobacco, oral contraceptives, MMR, organophosphate sheep dip – as well as public enquiries into major rail crashes.

So why did the two sets merge? Basically, much of their work came from insurance companies and their solicitors, a sector that has seen a lot of consolidation and cost cutting. Each of the two legacy sets realised that they'd be better off working together instead of remaining as competitors. As plans go, it was a smart one.

The set has a long client list with half a dozen firms at its core: Berrymans Lace Mawer, Beachcroft Wansbroughs, CMS Cameron McKenna, Lovells, Morgan Cole and Vizards Wyeth. In addition to an army of PI lawyers, there are also specialists in construction and those handling general commercial cases. In the early years, and *"before people start fitting into one area,"* junior barristers remain generalists. Indeed, the bulk of pupillage applications come from students for whom this approach is the main attraction. Most practices at Crown Office Chambers sit neatly on the halfway point between the paper-intensive work of commercial sets and the rapid-response, court-every-day experience of crime sets.

Full marks to the pupilmasters, who are regarded by their charges as *"gateway guardians,"* only allowing other members to give pupils useful work. *"Their principal concern is that the requirements and demands on you are fair."* One pupil described the first weeks as *"like doing finals every day. You go to the Bar to be the master of your own destiny and, initially, you are absolutely not; you are totally apprenticed to your pupilmaster."* Another talked of *"excellent attention from pupilmasters. I've almost been embarrassed at how seriously I've been taken."* A PM told us: *"I make a point of talking to them about VAT and getting an accountant. They need exposure to all aspects of life as a barrister, including ethics."* In the event of there being something you

don't particularly want to ask your PM, you can turn to one of the 'uncles and aunts' (junior tenant mentors) who will take you under their wing.

In the first six you'll have two PMs and your time will be split between observing them in court and settling pleadings on a variety of their matters – *"mostly PI, insurance and construction."* Additionally, each pupil undertakes standardised written assessments and four weeks of advocacy training, which all adds to the feeling of being under close supervision. This gives way to a *"radically different"* second six. Our pupil interviewees were just a few weeks into their second sixes, but had already met with the challenge of advocacy several times. They start off with RTA small claims trials (worth under £5,000, no wigs, no gowns) and quickly progress to fast-track hearings (worth up to £15,000 – eg an assessment of damages in a PI case). Pupils tell us that *"a lot is expected of you,"* but that getting stuck in is *"the only way you learn."*

Formal feedback at Easter gives pupils a hint as to their chances of securing tenancy. Determined by a committee rather than chambers as a whole, tenancy is certainly not guaranteed; however, the set is in expansion mode. Despite the absence of *"cultural presentism,"* pupils do experience long days and they clearly feel pressure to perform both well and consistently. We asked about the principles their guardians were instilling in them. *"Thoroughness," "taking pride in your work,"* and *"professional ethics"* won most mentions. Amusingly, we heard that it used to be said of 2 Crown Office Row that they took their work so seriously that *"every trial was a state trial."* One silk stressed: *"We try very hard to fulfil our ethical responsibilities. With pupils, we do draw particular attention to the fact that the primary duty is to the court."* Commendable.

Some barristers act only on the side of the angels – the disadvantaged and oppressed, those without culpability. Not here. Much of the time barristers defend insurance companies from claims brought by those seeking compensation for pain and suffering following an accident, medical malpractice or the use of a drug that is alleged to have been harmful. Their job is to minimise the amount their client must pay or to ensure that they are not held liable at all. *"You should make sure you are comfortable with that proposition,"* one source warned. When acting for the business interest in the business of misfortune, it's our guess that barristers need solid moral ground on which to stand. Is this why we found such a strong emphasis on professional ethics and conduct at Crown Office Chambers?

The set still occupies its two pre-merger addresses so, to assist integration, various members moved between the buildings. The southern end of the Temple is a beautiful location and, even though baby barristers get pokey rooms and QCs must often share the larger rooms with views of the Thames, overall there is a spacious feel to chambers. Good news for technophiles: the IT system is pretty hot, even down to a system which tells you who's got what from the library. We asked one junior if he ever visited the other building. *"Yes, to see my mates over there,"* he replied, so raising the topic of friendships within chambers. *"We're not in the pub every day"* trading *"gallows humour"* like criminal barristers, he said, but it sounds as if most members do rather like each other's company. Characters range from *"the profoundly intelligent to knockabout PI practitioners."* There's no forced bonding; instead it's more a case of easy interaction along the corridors, with people frequently swapping advice and insights. While we interviewed a number of barristers in their rooms, phones rang and heads poked around doors…a lot.

Although not a particularly traditional set, there are traditional elements to the place. Clerks call senior members 'Sir', but this practice has slipped at the junior end, and while it's proud of past members who've gone to the Bench, including Lord Justice Otton who sat in the Court of Appeal, and High Court judges Popplewell and Tucker, there's no rogues gallery of portraits in reception. There's also no chambers tea and little to indicate that juniors are overly deferential towards their seniors. Hardcore traditionalism wouldn't wash with the set's major clients these days, we suspect. An executive committee of 11 barristers – some very junior – runs the place, with *"day-to-day matters 80% clerk-managed."* That's unsurprising given that both senior clerks have 25 years' experience and know the insurance market inside out. Rest assured that in your early years, they are more than capable of keeping you very busy in courts up and down the country. The pupillage selection process follows a standard two-interview pattern; however, don't be disarmed by a charming interview panel – you still need to show you're as sharp as a razor.

Devereux Chambers

the facts

OLPAS: summer season **Pupillages:** 2x12 months
Applications: c.300 **Mini pupillages:** through the year
First interview: 35-40 **Second interview:** 10-12
Award: £30,000 (£8,000 can be advanced for the BVC)
Tenancies offered in 2004: 2
Chambers UK rankings: Employment, insurance, personal injury

Employment, personal injury and general commercial cases are the building blocks of practice at Devereux and leading silk Colin Edelman QC and others also draw in major insurance matters. There is an even mix of claimant/applicant and defendant/respondent instructions, although much of the most profitable defendant work goes to senior tenants. Timothy Brennan QC recently acted for former Cantor Fitzgerald employee Steve Horkulak in his £1.5 million claim for constructive dismissal following abuse and bullying at work. Once, the set had key public law silk Richard Clayton among its number, but applicants looking for a public law set should be aware that there is now little work in this area. A solid institutional client base includes BT, Royal Mail, a number of trade unions and transport giant Stagecoach.

If you're visiting Devereux Chambers, take our advice and leave yourself an extra half-hour to find it. After you've wandered aimlessly around Middle Temple and Queen Elizabeth Building, you'll need at least ten minutes to find your way up through Devereux Court, and then another ten to negotiate the hordes of tourists being led by a mockney-accented woman dressed in Victorian garb. But when you do locate chambers, down a cobbled alleyway opposite the Royal Courts of Justice, you'll be delighted. Behind the unassuming exterior, the reception room – coir matting, dark wood, sleek black leather – serves a set that is split over two premises. While most members and staff are in Devereux Court, a cluster of juniors occupies rooms in Queen Elizabeth Building on the Embankment.

On arriving at the room of one senior junior, he proudly proclaimed in a cry reminiscent of Axel Rose: *"Welcome to the dungeon!"* Actually, it was far from dungeon-like, with CDs scattered on the desk (The Streets, Tears For Fears, Jazz Greats) and a fan humming away in the corner. Instantly, you appreciate that Devereux prides itself on its *"friendly, unstuffy culture."* As the head of the pupillage committee told us: *"It's not our style to drone on with the 'hereinbefores' and the 'humbly craves.'"* *"On the basis that advocacy is about communication, it works better if you're downbeat rather than highfalutin'."* This is a set that is *"not afraid of being funny in court,"* so long as it's not *"trivialising or disrespectful."* Indeed, a former member, now a judge, once said: *"One of the most effective things you can do as an advocate is make your tribunal like you."*

The set receives almost 300 pupillage applications each year. The usual academic and extra-curricular achievements are considered alongside *"a good turn of phrase."* Those who impress at first interview (CV-based discussion plus ethical conundrum) progress to a second, more rigorous, test of advocacy skills based on a problem handed out half an hour beforehand. Last year's question was set in the fictional jurisdiction of

Utopia, a place singularly unused to legal drama. Clarity of thought and expression are the main qualities recruiters seek. As one told us: *"You hear an awful lot of verbal ticks. That doesn't help. Obviously people are nervous, and this is why fluency and clarity are impressive."* More important than clarity of speech is clarity of analysis, since *"speaking can be learned more easily than thinking."*

Pupils rotate around the same three supervisors, one from each of the set's core areas of practice. The assessment regime has been *"smartened up"* in past years and there are now formal tests throughout pupillage. There are two advocacy assessments in which pupils are given 24 hours to prepare a skeleton and present before a panel. One member of the panel is a judge, and pupils perform against a junior tenant who recently argued the same facts in court. It is, as one junior told us, *"terribly nerve-wracking,"* but great practice, and a way for pupils to hone their advocacy skills before embarking on real-life hearings. Despite the assessment regime, former pupils were adamant that pupillage did not feel like a miserable exercise in perpetual grovelling and self-abasement: *"You feel they want you to be taken on. You feel they're on your side."* To this end, feedback is *"honest and forthright"* and given with a view to improving the skills of pupils.

The tenancy decision is made in July, and pupils start working in their own name from the start of the second six. During this period, you can expect to be on your feet up to twice a week, feasting on a diet of small claims, RTAs and applications concerning expert evidence. Court appearances are mixed in with paper and advisory work for members of chambers. Second-six pupils also work closely with baby juniors to prepare them for tenancy. Employment and personal injury form the bread and butter for inexperienced juniors, who will also occasionally assist more senior members on larger commercial matters. There are no guaranteed minimum earnings for juniors, because they don't need to be. Happily, for the most part, they are busy from the outset and clients pay up relatively quickly.

Life at the Bar can be an isolated existence; indeed, many barristers tell us they are attracted by the idea of *"individual challenges."* As we sat in the stark office of one baby junior over in the QEB annexe, it was hard not to feel distanced from the action up in Devereux Court. That is until the dungeon keeper we'd met earlier cheerily poked his head through the open window: *"Just checking in on you!"* When barristers tell us that their set is *"like a family"* we're always a little wary; after all, families can bring out the worst in each other as well as the best. Yet, something rang true when we heard the claim at Devereux. It was a Friday afternoon when we visited and, as we said our goodbyes, members and staff were packing up and preparing to head to the pub. Aside from The Puzzle (run by one member's wife), The Edgar Wallace is a den of choice, as is 'The Dev', from which members can practically order beers from their office windows. We left the barristers standing around, drinks in hand, chatting in the mottled sunlight – just as they've probably done for hundreds of years.

Doughty Street Chambers

the facts

OLPAS: summer season **Pupillages:** 4x12 months
Applications: 420 **Mini pupillages:** 24
First interview: c.40 **Second interview:** 16
Award: £15,500
Tenancies offered in 2004: 1
Chambers UK rankings: Administrative & public law, clinical negligence, crime, human rights, immigration, personal injury, police law, product liability

"Defending freedom and citizens' rights" is this set's raison d'être. Founded in 1990, its reputation is inextricably linked with that of the inimitable Australian legal personality Geoffrey Robertson QC. Members are renowned as human rights' crusaders, advising in major prisoners' rights, sentencing, mental health, extradition and death row cases. Members were involved in the Hughes, Reyes and Fox cases that were influential in the abolition of mandatory life sentences in the Caribbean, while Geoffrey Robertson QC has been appointed as Appeal Judge for the Special Court in Sierra Leone, set up to try cases of war crimes and crimes against humanity. Some members, including Geoffrey Robertson, feature in *Chambers UK*'s defamation rankings for their work with newspapers and journalists.

The self-proclaimed *"warm and cuddly"* end of the Bar, Doughty Street is, according to some, the ideal antidote to the stuffiness, conservatism and pomposity that characterises certain other sets. It prides itself on a commitment to equal opportunities so don't bother dry-cleaning the old school tie for your pupillage interview. It may be recognised for its egalitarian and rather self-consciously informal culture, but don't be deceived. Like the iron fist in the velvet glove, this is a seriously and ambitious set with a commitment to client service and quality, supported by an organised and efficient administration. As one pupil put it: *"The atmosphere is laid back, but work-wise, it's very intense."*

Eighty-four members are housed in a Georgian terraced property on the moral high ground of Doughty Street, not far from Russell Square. The area has as much in common with the arts and literature as the Bar: Charles Dickens published *The Pickwick Papers*, *Oliver Twist* and *Nicholas Nickleby* while living a few doors away. Could the ghosts of social crusaders past have swept through the set? The premises are basic, neutral and non-threatening; instead of grandiose oil paintings, there's just some fairly simple art adding a modicum of interest to the plain white walls. Think neat and tidy B&B or law centre.

Mini pupillages are structured as a week-long course, during which you'll follow a single case of your choosing. By day you'll conduct research, attend conferences and sit in court; each evening, there are seminars given by specialists in different areas of law. Academic credentials, while important, are by no means the be-all and end-all at this set. More importantly, applicants must demonstrate a commitment to welfare and human rights, either through voluntary or community work or overcoming personal challenges. Few pupils come fresh out of university, since the set *"tends towards people with more life experience."* The youngest pupil we spoke to was 26. Around ten per cent of applicants make it to the first interview – a casual getting to know you. Those who reach stage two must give a presentation on a topical legal or ethical question. It is designed to test your knowledge of current affairs, analytical ability and presentation skills. Questions usually have a human rights or civil liberties bent, eg 'Do paedophiles have a right to privacy?' We doubt it's wise to respond 'No! They should all be outed on the evening news before being chemically sterilised.' And a word of advice: do not walk into this interview without having revised the Human Rights Act.

Your first six will be paper-intensive, and chances are you'll cut your teeth on smaller immigration matters. You will be given feedback on each piece of work you do, and while you're allocated a supervisor for the entire pupillage, pupils are also encouraged to do work for other members. Whereas some people believe pupils should be seen and not heard, those at Doughty Street are *"never made to feel small."* If you want to work with a particular tenant, just ask, and pupils are often included on the sexier international and human rights matters. Our sources spoke of a *"supportive"* atmosphere, with one junior tenant commenting: *"The preparation is incredible. As a junior, when I appear for someone else, the case is always amazingly well prepared…I never feel like I've been dropped in it."* And the support extends to a unique commitment to the personal and career development of members and staff. Apparently, most people feel comfortable telling clerks: *"I won't be in on Thursday this week, I'm doing voluntary work at a shelter."* This flexible approach enables members to work with international tribunals, on death row cases and in public interest matters. Tenants here are positively encouraged to have exciting, high-profile careers.

Pupils must go through the whole year before finding out about tenancy. The whole set makes the decision, basing it on a formal written assessment and an interview. Pupils are tested in a range of legal areas and papers are marked blind. You don't need us to tell you the process is hugely stressful, with only one in four pupils usually attaining tenancy. However, those we interviewed insisted that there is no tension between pupils. Friendships form around professional relationships, and where some sets boast formal afternoon tea, Doughty Street has Friday night drinks in the local pub, which often turn into late nights at one or other of the barristers' homes.

All pupils boast impressive resumés and all have had first-hand experience in human rights or welfare-related fields. When we visited, one was a trained mental health nurse and NHS consultant; one was a consultant on Russian development and two others taught in Africa. The junior tenant we spoke to worked for two years as a volunteer at the centre for Advice on Individual Rights in Europe (AIRE). He applied for pupillages prior to his work at AIRE and got nothing. Disheartened, he embarked on two years of penury as a volunteer and later found himself with a slew of offers from chambers. It's a lesson for anyone wanting to get into Doughty Street or similar sets.

Just remember that this is human rights at a distance: if it is direct client contact you want, you should consider going to a solicitors firm. But whether it's the set's inspirational and high-profile crusaders, its reputation for progressive attitudes or the *"electric"* energy of the place, for its pupils at least, Doughty Street remains the *"cool"* set.

Erskine Chambers

the facts

OLPAS: No **Pupillages:** 2x12 months
Applications: over 100 **Mini pupillages:** no limit
First interview: 10 **Second interview:** 4-5
Award: £35,000 (funds can be advanced for BVC)
Tenancies offered in 2004: None
Chambers UK rankings: Banking & finance, company, financial services, insolvency

Erskine Chambers is a one-off. After a modest start in 24 Old Buildings, it moved in the 1980s to the premises in the north-east corner of Lincoln's Inn Fields, from which it took its name, before moving to prestigious premises on Chancery Lane. We were greatly disappointed to learn this as we'd hoped the set's pedigree stretched back to the early 19th century Lord Chancellor Erskine who, rumour has it, trained his dog to wear a wig and sit with his paws on an open book.

To say that this is the leading company law set doesn't emphasise sufficiently its dominance of that field. So let's put it like this: no other set comes close to commanding the respect that Erskine does for advice and advocacy on company law matters. Its barristers are so in demand that a higher than usual proportion of cases are fought against other members of the set. Nine members are QCs, including head of chambers Robin Potts. The previous head, Richard Sykes, was a real influence: *"In City circles he was an oracle and his advice would be treated with the respect it deserved."*

Erskine receives fewer applications than other leading commercial sets and it is seen by many students as too specialised, too company law-led and too advisory-based. We put this to the secretary of the pupillage committee. *"It's not true to say that all our stuff is out of the Companies Act,"* he told us. *"Traditionally we've had a leaning towards advisory work,"* but now *"most barristers here do a mix of advisory work and litigation."* In fact, at the junior end, the opportunities

for advocacy are considerable. If you have a general interest in business matters, this is a set to consider alongside the usual suspects of the commercial Bar.

Erskine barristers have adapted to the way in which their instructing solicitors do business. With the rise of IT systems and the general advance in the volume of corporate transactions over the last two decades, solicitors recycle the structures of deals wherever possible. This leaves the role of the company law barrister as that of underwriter. Where there is an issue on a point of principle or concerns about the effect or legality of changes made to a transaction, the call will go out to an Erskine barrister. *"It's not unusual to get that call at 5pm, and you've got to deal with it immediately because the client will want to complete the transaction that night."* Consequently to succeed here you've got to be *"responsive"* and *"commercially minded."*

On the contentious side, the work spills over into commercial disputes, especially where there is a company law angle. Indeed, an Erskine barrister may have the edge over their peers in that they might go looking for such an angle and find it before anyone else. Naturally twinned with company law, insolvency and corporate restructuring feature often, and in the early years you'll see more than your fair share of winding-up petitions, leading on to full-day court appointments and injunctions to prevent the advertisement of petitions. Directors' disqualifications and shareholder disputes will also come in thick and fast. *"We always have lots of little stocking fillers to keep them busy,"* a pupilmaster told us in typically understated style. Amazingly, we heard: *"We have no demand for dogsbodies to trawl through mountains of disclosure. If we do get it, we will get in a junior from another set."* Result! And there's more: *"As a junior here, very quickly you'll find yourself against someone more senior."* But, *"we are good about not sending people into battle without the right armour."*

Erskine has a rather kindly approach to its pupils. It will keep them out of the spotlight during the initial three-month period with their first pupilmaster. In the second three months, another PM will gradually ease them into the mainstream and the pupil will also start to take on work for other members. Of PMs, one source said: *"Some have a more advisory leaning and others have more commercial litigation than pure company law cases."*

The set will normally tell pupils whether or not they are *"still in the running for a tenancy"* at the end of their first six, giving them the option of seeking a second six elsewhere if they don't stand a fighting chance of getting in. And how does the set know if it has picked a winner? *"It's a cocktail. You know when you see too much of one thing and too little of another."* Our interpretation of this cryptic comment is slightly bookish but with a businesslike mind, a steady, logical thinker, confident, calm and reassuring, happy to be alone much of the time, and very likeable. As for the work, ask yourself if you really enjoy the academic study of law. Think about how you'd enjoy *"some horribly knotty problem and spending a week or so tackling it to the exclusion of all else."*

In spite of – who knows, perhaps because of – the set's phenomenal success, it immediately strikes you as a calm and almost gentle place. No rushing around, no egos bumping off the corridor walls like pinball bearings. Our theory is that the frequency with which members act against each other has led to the erection of more Chinese walls than were ever built by the Ming Dynasty. They may take chambers tea at 5pm and chat about the weather and what judge so-and-so probably thought about such-and-such a case, but this is pretty much it for socialising and our younger sources found the job a fairly solitary experience. The doors to barristers' rooms were mostly closed when we visited, and we noted that the phone calls our sources received were almost always on their personal mobiles. This is definitely a set where you get your head down and work, and you learn to be self-reliant, yet there is a network of colleagues to call upon so you shouldn't feel like you've been set adrift.

Erskine's character is not heavily influenced by a handful of instructing firms; work comes from all quarters. It's a *"pretty egalitarian"* set that is member-driven and *"pretty close to one person, one vote."* At

chambers tea, pupils tend to keep quiet in the early months, but if one did pipe up with something, *"it's not like everyone would turn around and stare as if the dog had just spoken!"* We must confess, we liked the place and we liked the people we met. In this quiet and measured chambers, carefulness and brainpower fuse into something utterly impressive.

Essex Court Chambers

the facts

OLPAS: summer season **Pupillages:** 4x12 months
Applications: not disclosed **Mini pupillages:** 30
Interviews: not disclosed
Award: £37,500 (funds can be advanced for BVC)
Tenancies offered in 2004: 2
Chambers UK rankings: Aviation, banking & finance, commercial litigation, employment, energy & natural resources, civil fraud, insurance, international arbitration, media & entertainment, public international law, shipping

Set up in 1961 by five *"bright but disparate self-made men"* who proceeded to have illustrious careers and took leading judicial positions, Essex Court Chambers is one of the magic circle of commercial sets. It boasts some of the big names at the Bar: QCs Gordon Pollock, VV Veeder and Andrew Hochhauser, and new silk Joe Smouha. Recent big cases include Lloyd's v Jaffray, Barings v Coopers & Lybrand and BCCI v Bank of England.

If you're wondering how Essex Court's practice differs from close rivals then note that, in addition to mainstream commercial work, there's a strong emphasis on insurance, reinsurance, shipping and international arbitration. Firms like Clyde & Co, Barlow Lyde & Gilbert, Ince & Co and Holman Fenwick & Willan instruct the set on behalf of clients that include foreign shipowners, P&I clubs and reinsurance companies. One of our more senior sources told us that his work was commonly *"off-beam – a bit more* _fun"_ and required an _"imaginative"_ approach.

In pupillage, the first six months is a period of observation when you'll work for your main pupilmaster for three months and then for a maximum of five others in your second three. All pupils work for the same group of barristers. Sometimes you'll be in court shadowing your PM, but it's more likely that you'll be in the library researching points of law or their room writing a skeleton argument or opinion. By the end of March you will be told whether or not you have a future at Essex Court. All our sources thought this to be an extremely practical arrangement. Unsuccessful pupils are not forced to leave, but are unlikely to stay as the advantage of moving to another set for the second six is clear. Clutching persuasive references, they commonly slip into other well-respected sets becoming _"cuckoos in the nest elsewhere."_

The pupils who stay can heave a sigh of relief and concentrate on another six months of learning…but not earning. _"We don't encourage paid work or advocacy in the second six,"_ one pupilmaster told us. _"They cut their teeth on that once they are a tenant."_ So while your peers at other sets will be on their feet in court, you'll still be at your master's side, observing and researching smaller points on their mega-sized, mega-value cases. Patience is required. Our sources assured us that the approach pays off. Occasionally, a second-sixer might be loaned out to a law firm or sent to visit Lloyd's of London for a spell. The average working day stretches from 8.30am-7pm, and, although it's fair to say that some members choose to drive themselves rather hard, pupils don't appear to be bent out of shape by long hours.

The set's caseload is broad – some barristers specialise, but there is a prevailing generalist ethos, particularly at the junior end. It's not really possible to pigeonhole members either by background or personality: apparently, _"the poshest people around work alongside people with entirely working-class backgrounds."_ Our sources used various words to describe the set: _"a meritocracy," "pink-tinged but with some Tories too,"_ and _"a broad church/synagogue."_

Whether you're _"left, right, snobbish or violently egalitarian,"_ what counts is that you're talented. And confident. Brave even. We wondered if the idea of working with the big names at the commercial Bar was at all intimidating. _"No! That's what's great about it,"_ a pupil explained. _"You've got to be in it to win it,"_ another source said of his decision to apply to a set that's at the top of the commercial tree. _"The cost of trying is not that high, but the prize is huge."_ Another benefit is an absence of competitive behaviour within chambers. _"People don't have things to prove to each other. At lesser sets, barristers are keen to let each other know how busy they are and how good they are."_

Having established that there are eccentrics, legendary advocates and highly academic boffins all co-existing within the set's five adjoining buildings on the north side of Lincoln's Inn Fields, we turned our attention to the eclectic premises. Visitors to the set (which people refer to as having broken away from the Temple) are first presented with the old: leather armchairs and marble columns in the waiting room, and then the new: stylish, modern conference rooms that feel more City than Inns of Court. As for the remainder of chambers, it's somewhat warren-like, and everyone's room is different – from ornamental trees, chandeliers and flowing curtains to shrines to minimalism and modern art.

There's no chambers tea; instead, on Fridays, 30-40 barristers will gather for lunch to chat about their cases…or maybe their weekend plans. Pupils are welcome and can end up in conversation with senior members quite easily. _"Gordon Pollock is always there telling stories,"_ one pupil revealed. The social scene could never be described as big, but some of the juniors go out for drinks on Friday night.

Clerks generally call members by their surnames, particularly seniors, but with juniors this tradition is easing. Actually, no commentary on Essex Court would be complete without a reference to its impressive clerking. Senior clerk David Grief (who's been doing the business since 1980) is an important figure and highly respected in the profession. You'll meet him on the four-to five-strong pupillage interview panel. Essex Court picks its pupils after a single interview, so you'll need to make the most of your one shot at getting into the set. It will be tough, but remember that the other applicants will be in the same boat. How you approach and tackle the problem question you'll be set is crucial. As is talent and a self-belief, so prepare as fully as you can and put your best foot forward.

One Essex Court

the facts

OLPAS: summer season **Pupillages:** 4 x12 months
Applications: 200-250 **Mini pupillages:** 20
Interview: 40
Award: £40,000 (£13,250 can be advanced for BVC)
Tenancies offered in 2004: 3
Chambers UK rankings: Banking & finance, commercial litigation, energy & natural resources, civil fraud, intellectual property, international arbitration, tax

In the four decades since One Essex Court was established, it has transformed from a general common law set into one of the magic circle of commercial players. Its head of chambers is the inimitable Lord Grabiner QC; fellow silks, including Nicholas Strauss, Mark Barnes and Laurence Rabinowitz, also enjoy much of the limelight.

In the 1970s Sam Stamler QC and two of his former pupils, Grabiner and Strauss, took the lead in developing the set's commercial work, initially through a relationship with Slaughter and May. The way in which Stamler worked and taught his pupils is responsible for the set's approach today: *"One case at a time with plenty of preparation beforehand and gaps between cases…quality conscious and really rigorous."* The fees may be at the higher end of the scale, but *"you can absolutely rely on the barrister you have instructed being available to do the job properly."* 30 years on and important work still comes from Slaughters, as well as firms like Herbert Smith, Freshfields, Clif-

ford Chance and Baker & McKenzie. Rather like Slaughters, OEC believes that the best lawyers can turn their hand to all manner of commercial matters. *"The generalist ethos is very strong."*

This set believes advocates are made not born, but as one pupilmaster stressed: *"We can turn someone into a fine advocate, but they have to get a buzz out of standing up and giving it some welly."* Don't underestimate the amount of written advocacy that will be required of you: *"Everything you do is advocacy; every opinion you write, every skeleton argument – they all require you to persuade."* The complexity of cases means that the most important thing a pupil can possess is a practical problem-solving ability. As one explained: *"The facts of cases can be so complicated; you might have up to 14 parties to a single case."*

Cerebral it may be, but ivory-towered it isn't. *"We don't want a brain in a jar,"* said one barrister. *"It's not about giving dry legal advice; a client in conference wants a solution to their problem. How can we improve things? Where do we go from here?"* *"If you like things to be fast-paced and you are happy to work really hard,"* then *"you can be yourself."* We suspect it's important to be exactly that; a 40-year masquerade would certainly fray the nerves. Of his seniors, one pupil told us: *"Mostly they are smiling, chirpy people rather than great brooding intellects."* While we don't doubt that OEC is stuffed full of interesting and personable characters who show a healthy respect for each other, the very fact that pupils are experiencing life at the pointy end of the commercial Bar can induce a fair few knee wobbles. *"The biggest nightmare is doing something wrong for someone important."* Pupils have to work hard to adapt to the high standards of this set and to learn how to produce excellent work on complicated cases. All this and making sure you get your name known around chambers.

You'll have a minimum of three pupilmasters, each of whom will have a broad practice (although you might request an IP specialist if that were your bag). Your first six will be reasonably chambers-based – legal research, drafting opinions and skeleton arguments etc. *"It's not just disembodied parts of larger cases,"* we were told. In the second six you'll also tackle your own paid work. *"There's a huge emphasis on getting people on their feet in court – wherever or whatever – because hearing your own voice is crucial."* Many of the set's cases are huge, so juniors take a second or third counsel role, but the clerks also encourage smaller instructions, allowing juniors to run cases by themselves. Over 2,000 firms send instructions, although 35% of the fees come from half-a-dozen City firms. These clients expect their barristers to have plenty of confidence and to be decisive. Maybe this is why the pupillage interview was likened by one source to *"cruel torture."*

The decor at One Essex Court (and Nos.2, 3 and now 4) gives a nod to tradition, but we got the impression that this was simply the default setting for commercial sets in the Temple. OEC doesn't appear to be trying hard to create an image for itself. We'd also guess that precious little time is devoted to committees with a remit to expanding chambers' business. *"I don't think in terms of where I want chambers to be,"* one barrister told us. The fact is, OEC is already at the top of its game. Big-name barristers generate more than enough work for themselves, and an impressive clerking system obviates the need to put on a song and dance to attract clients. *"Solicitors love our clerks,"* one barrister boasted of the administrative team. *"Generous staffing levels"* reflect the set's unhurried approach. For 'unhurried' don't read 'slow', read 'calm'. Sources outside chambers say that the power of the senior clerks should never be underestimated at OEC; indeed, our sources inside the set readily admitted that they have a *"huge influence"* on all aspects of the business.

OEC doesn't parade a long list of old members who've gone to the bench: *"Most of us are people from pretty ordinary backgrounds who have done well academically…we like to think that we're not stuffy."* But as in most sets, there's the odd eccentric and the place is no doubt the richer for them. The wise pupil will attend Friday evening drinks in chambers. One-off events aside, this is where the social scene stops. However, *"you don't come in, clock on, do your timesheets and leave."* There is a reasonable amount of interaction between colleagues and *"plenty of e-mail exchanges!"* As for the dress code, the wise pupil errs on the side of the wardrobe where smart suits hang.

Some final advice: first, show a positive disposition at all times. In such a well-run set with such great opportunities, you really oughtn't to have anything to complain about. And second, good enough isn't actually good enough – chambers values complete attention to detail and rigour of analysis. Reflect these traits in your application.

20 Essex Street

the facts

OLPAS: summer season **Pupillages:** 3-5x12 months
Applications: 133 **Mini pupillages:** 30
Interview: 25
Award: £36,000 (£11,000 can be advanced for BVC)
Tenancies offered in 2004: 1
Chambers UK rankings: Banking & finance, commercial litigation, insurance, international arbitration, public international law, shipping

Established in 1926, 20 Essex Street is the UK's premier shipping and international law set. Huddled amidst the other commercial heavyweights in Essex Street, No.20 boasts some of the biggest names in their fields. Its list of members past and present reads like a Who's Who of international and shipping law. Former judges in the International Court of Justice Lord Arnold McNair and Sir Hersch Lauterpacht were door tenants, and international law gurus continue to pad the corridors today. Sir Elihu Lauterpacht maintains the family tradition, and Sir Arthur Watts QC has appeared in major international disputes, acting as counsel for New Zealand against France in the Nuclear Tests cases, and as counsel for Nigeria in its boundary dispute with

Cameroon. But we must stop. While the set is undoubtedly outstanding in public international law, it is wary of *"over-promoting"* this area of practice to prospective pupils. *"You don't go into law and then decide to practice PIL. It's not like commercial law."* Most in this game have a diplomatic or academic career under their belts before embarking on practice.

While its reputation largely revolves around shipping and international law, this is more than just a shipping set. Yes, it is instructed by the biggest names in the shipping world – Holman Fenwick & Willan, Ince & Co, Richards Butler and Clyde & Co – but No.20 is now receiving more instructions from the likes of Linklaters, Allen & Overy and Herbert Smith. Its involvement in the £2.5 billion claim by Equitable Life against former auditors and directors is a perfect example of its general litigation.

Behind a Queen Anne façade, the interior of No.20 is refined, if not conservative. In reception, steel grey carpet meets walls of leather-bound law reports and, conforming to stereotype, the set has hung a gilt-framed oil depicting a lighthouse in a tempest. Sinking into a faded red damask sofa, visitors can leaf through *The Spectator*, *Country Life*, the *FT* or, the joker in the pack, *The Magnificent 92: Indiana Courthouses*. (And magnificent they are.) A potted palm sits motionless in the corner and the noise and flurry of Fleet Street seems a mile away from this silent room. Silent, but for the rhythmic tick-tock-tick of the clock and the shloop of pages turning slowly.

It should come as no surprise that in this law library atmosphere pupillage is a highly academic affair. If you're hankering after the cut and thrust of courtroom advocacy in your second six, go elsewhere. Read on if complex legal problems and opinion writing in an intellectual environment appeal.

No.20 takes between three and five pupils annually, each of whom sit with a different pupilmaster each term. During your first 'finding your feet' term, your work will come almost exclusively from your PM and you'll be blessedly free of advocacy exercises. After the New Year, these begin and continue every month or two until the end of pupillage. Meanwhile, your PM's job becomes less about giving you work and more about supervising your diary. You will not work in your own name during your second six, and you certainly won't be on your feet. Shortly before the end of the first six, tenancy prospects are reviewed; those not making the grade are advised to set up a second six elsewhere. The tenancy decision is made in July and based on the views of anyone who has seen the work of pupils. As to whether or not there's a quota for tenancies: *"Good people will make a name for themselves. There's no point turning them away because there's not enough work at that particular time."* In the early years, you can expect to assist senior members, although clerks have built relationships with solicitors doing small, routine work for big commercial clients. You should also be aware that around half of the set's work is comprised of arbitrations.

On most days, pupils arrive at 8.30am and leave at around 6pm. Even if they wanted to work on weekends, they'd have some trouble, since no one gets a key to chambers until they are made a tenant.

The set receives only a modest number of pupillage applications, and this may in part be due to its fearsome reputation for intellectual vigour. *"It sounds terrible,"* one insider told us, *"but you need to be more than a solid 2:1 person to cope with our work."* No, not so terrible. What marks one excellent applicant out from the others is *"a well-rounded CV"* that shows you are *"more than just a library bookworm."* The interview consists of a problem question based on a real case that a member of chambers has worked on. It aims to identify an understanding of first principles, logical/analytical ability and interpretative skills. To introduce a spanner into the works, the panel will make regular interjections, not unlike those a judge would make in court. Time to produce the three 'C's – clarity, coherence and calm. Be sure to keep abreast of current issues: in 2003, the panel were unable to resist asking applicants for their views on the abolition of the Lord Chancellor's role and Blair's constitutional reshuffle. You'll need academic ability teamed with *"a personality that will be effective in court and effective in front of clients."*

One tenant remarked: *"We are a club, a collection of equals."* The social life is suitably warm and low-key. There is chambers tea at 4.30pm in the common room – a chance to have a cup of tea (*"and cake if we're lucky"*) in front of the cricket or the golf on Sky. Every now and then there are drinks parties and groups of juniors will occasionally head out for a beer together. Chambers football matches are a competitive affair; in the bitter rivalry between clerks and barristers, clerks seem to have the edge.

20 Essex Street is refined and academic without being arrogant. We found its members to be charming, polite and unassuming, but fiercely intelligent and legally gifted. Apparently, people used to say of this set: *"There are gentlemen and players, and you people are gentlemen."* And ladies, of course.

39 Essex Street

the facts

OLPAS: summer season **Pupillages:** up to 3x12 months
Applications: 350 **Mini-pupillages:** 37 assessed
Interview: 30-40
Pupillage award: £30,000 (£8,000 can be advanced for BVC)
Tenancies awarded in 2004: 2
Chambers UK rankings: Administrative and public, construction, environment, human rights, immigration, local government, personal injury, planning, professional discipline, professional negligence

Whether by design or by coincidence, 39 Essex Street has built itself a profile not dissimilar to that of, dare we say it, Blackstone Chambers. So much so that the two could be sisters, though we express no opinion as to which one is the better looking. As the former home of civil liberties guru and director of Liberty, Shami Chakrabarti, the set has long been known as a heavyweight in the fields of administrative and public law, human rights and immigration. But

chambers is becoming equally at home in the fields of commercial law, employment, media, sports and professional negligence among other things. A pupillage here will inevitably be split between the public and private arenas, and for this reason it makes an ideal choice for anyone unwilling to put too many eggs in one basket.

The cosy, lamp-lit Victorian charm of Essex Street stops at the front door of No.39, where a trad exterior gives way to a modern and businesslike interior. It's smart, it's tidy and it is spacious. Words that could apply equally to chambers' website, which as well as being easy to navigate does a very thorough job of flagging up the recent activities of members, including their landmark cases, publications and other achievements. This is probably in no small part due to the fact that 39 Essex has complemented the traditional clerking system with a management team, bringing in not only a chambers director but also a practice development manager.

39 Essex likes to move its pupils around chambers during their 12 months. In order for them to see as much work as possible, they are assigned to four different supervisors, spending three months with each. Inevitably that means swapping from public to private law work, which pupils say is *"mentally challenging"* because *"you have to get your head around a whole new area of law."* When not observing their supervisors in court, pupils attempt first drafts of the paperwork for a case and conduct legal research. Sometimes supervisors will actually use their pupils' work, though *"this depends entirely on the pupil supervisor that you are with."* We're also told that it's not unheard of for a pupil to come up with a point that their supervisor hadn't thought of before, and for that point to be adopted in a legal argument in court.

Opportunities for advocacy do arise in a pupil's second six, though because of the nature of public law proceedings – being conducted almost entirely in the High Court – *"you're not going to be doing your own judicial review applications."* Instead, expect the odd small claim here or case management conference there. Pupils do not undertake work for other members of chambers on an ad hoc basis; the pupillage committee takes the view that it is better for them to follow the same person for *"a sustained amount of time"* so as to *"build up a rapport"* with them. To expose pupils to other members, a body that is ominously named the 'Shadow Pupillage Committee' has been established. Pupils must complete four *"quite intensive"* pieces of written work for the committee during their second six, and these form a not insubstantial part of the formal assessment for the tenancy decision, which is made in July.

Chambers has developed close working relationships with a number of local authorities and it is common for pupils and juniors to be seconded to their legal departments. The management also has other tricks up its sleeve for promoting its junior members to clients. In fact, we got the impression that becoming a junior tenant here is rather like being one of those poor stage-school kids, dragged from audition to audition by their pushy mother. In his first year in chambers, one junior tenant had (on top of his ordinary workload) drafted a series of consultation paper responses for Liberty, advised on a pro-bono basis on the presentation of evidence to the Soham Inquiry (also for Liberty), contributed to two leading texts for a legal publisher and appeared in three episodes of Casualty. Okay, that last one was a joke, but you get the point – chambers is serious about getting juniors' careers off to a flying start.

If we've made life at 39 Essex Street sound full on, we should qualify our report by saying that chambers enforces a strict 9am 'til 6pm policy for pupils (including an hour for lunch). One junior recalled how, when working late in the library one evening, he was discovered by a senior QC who, staring at him in disbelief, asked what he was doing so late. We heard no complaints of pupils being chained to the photocopier or lugging books about, and first-name terms are the norm amongst most members. There's a smart but casual dress code, so long as you keep a bat suit for meeting clients or going out to court. This

seems in keeping with the way that 39 Essex tenants – at the junior end at least – see themselves as *"modern and forward looking."* To bring everyone together, there are either lunches or drinks on alternate Fridays, which are well attended *"from the most junior clerks to the most senior silks."* The pupils tell us that at these events even such household names as Richard Clayton QC (whose accolades include acting for Cold War spy George Blake in AG v Blake) are amenable to having their ears bent on difficult human rights points.

There's no point in beating about the bush: to stand a chance of getting into 39 Essex Street your CV needs to be pretty hot...okay, very hot. Take a look on the website at the sort of experiences recent tenants gained before arriving in chambers. One had worked as an assistant for a leading public international lawyer to prepare submissions for the International Court of Justice in the case of Croatia v Yugoslavia. Another had spent a few months as an intern at the European Court of Human Rights. As everyone we spoke to agreed: *"If there's one thing that we've got in common, we've nearly all done other things before we came here."* Pro bono work is highly valued too. The head of chambers is a trustee of the Free Representation Unit, and most members commit at least 20 hours a year to pro bono activities.

A mini-pupillage is highly recommended. Chambers runs a season of week-long assessed minis from January to June to coincide with the Olpas recruitment process. As well as accompanying barristers to court, mini-pupils will undertake formally assessed written work and a group advocacy exercise, which this year took the form of a hearing before a mock Court of Appeal. The deadline for applications falls in the November of the previous year so apply early, because while a mini-pupillage is not strictly speaking a precondition for pupillage selection, it is clear that chambers places great weight on the process. The good news is that if you make it through the pupillage application paper-sifting stage, there will only be one interview, including the customary legal problem. The verdict on the interview? *"It was an argument with five barristers...not exactly heated, but everything that I said was challenged."* We reckon if you manage to get as far as a pupillage interview here, a small challenge like that will probably be water off a duck's back.

Fountain Court

the facts

OLPAS: summer season **Pupillages:** up to 4x12 months
Applications: 200 **Mini pupillages:** 30-40
First interview: 35 **Second interview:** 17
Award: £37,000 (funds can be advanced for BVC)
Tenancies offered in 2004: 1
Chambers UK rankings: Aviation, banking & finance, commercial litigation, employment, civil fraud, insurance, international arbitration, professional negligence.

One of the Bar's magic circle of heavyweight commercial sets, Fountain Court straddles Essex Street and sits in the shadows of the RCJ. Originally a common law set, it moved into commercial work during the practising heyday of Lord Bingham (senior Law Lord, formerly Lord Chief Justice and Master of the Rolls), but still retains the generalist approach of its past. It boasts some big-name QCs, such as Anthony Boswood, Michael Brindle, Bankim Thanki and the Attorney General, Lord Goldsmith.

Most members have a broad commercial practice, although a few specialise, most notably in insurance. Your pupillage experience will reflect this breadth, although you could sit with a specialist pupilmaster if their practice matched your career aspirations. In your first three months, you'll stick to your PM's side and can breathe easy as none of your gaffes will count against you in the following June's tenancy decision. In the second three, you'll see pupil-sized chunks of a new PM's work and you'll also do things for other members. After this, a third

PM will be notionally responsible for you, and then for your final months (after the tenancy decision), you'll return to your first PM to show them just how far you've developed. Your diet of work will include banking, insurance, general commercial/contractual matters, aviation (eg the DVT case), professional negligence and, if you're lucky, perhaps some copyright or employment. Expect an average day of 9am-7pm.

Apply elsewhere if you want to be on your feet in court every other day as *"mostly you'll be sitting at your desk doing paperwork."* Also, *"there's very little contact with [lay] clients; conferences are usually with the solicitor."* Very good relationships exist with magic circle firms like Freshfields, Slaughter and May and Linklaters, plus others like Barlow Lyde & Gilbert, CMS Cameron McKenna and Herbert Smith. Think big-money, high-profile instructions: BCCI and spin-offs including Three Rivers, Cape v Lubbe (first group action by foreign claimants and the largest), and the Britvic benzene contamination case. Your involvement as a pupil or very junior member of chambers will be low-level and paper-based. Patience is a virtue at Fountain Court.

A big, fierce and full-on set? Yes, no and sort of. Chambers is spread across four buildings – the main one behind the fountain in the appropriately named courtyard and just around the corner from Temple Church, the other three annexes at 11, 14 and 35 Essex Street. The premises appear neutral and businesslike. The library in the basement is well organised, if a touch claustrophobic. The tearoom is modern and large enough to hold most members, but the 4pm tea ritual apparently declined after Lord Falconer (Lord Chancellor and Secretary of State for Constitutional Affairs) left in 1997. Members are more likely to be in their rooms writing advices than gathering to discuss their day in court. The dress code? Most will be suited; others might opt for smart casual. The reaction of friends might be *"Oh God, you poor thing!"* when you tell them you've got pupillage here; they might see the set as *"a ruthless law machine where you'll be worked to death."* However, those we spoke to were categorical in their rebuttal. *"Pupillage is much better than I expected,"* said one. *"People are not stuffy and barristerial. Yes, they are keen and some are over-achievers, but they are not arrogant."* As a seasoned member told us: *"People are quite decent to each other…considerate…pupils are well treated and respected. The job can be stressful, so we make it as nice as it can be."*

Which sounds like a fair description of the first-round interview for pupillage. *"It was very informal with more junior people,"* said one pupil. *"I was quite surprised as it was more of a chat."* But be prepared for a more exacting experience if you are asked back. *"The second one is much more formal…and there will always be someone on the panel who will be devil's advocate."*

The ideal applicant will have a top-notch academic record. Those wondering if they are cut out for this set should ask themselves if they enjoy an academic challenge and can hold their own among those who are used to success. Do you relish the process of writing an essay – the research, structuring and argument and building up the end product? As with essays, the written work you'll handle in chambers requires that *"you enjoy the challenge for itself, irrespective of whether or not you are interested in the subject matter."* This is an intellectual set that prides itself on thorough preparation and impeccable conduct of the litigation process. *"People here are clever, but they wear it quite lightly."* Pushy, ruthless or over-pompous types will soon encounter deflating comments, we heard, but we sensed a touch of self-satisfaction. Maybe that's fair – make it here and you've a lot to be satisfied with. Junior members are a mixed bag of old Etonians and the state educated and, to pass muster and make it as one of them, you must display *"consistency, thoroughness and a good written style."* Your 'solicitor appeal' is also crucial as litigators from the biggest City firms will instruct you on mammoth cases and you'll deal with them over extended periods of time. They must like and trust you, and you must be able to add something to their team…both intellectually and in terms of 'presence'.

While new pupils are welcomed with a drinks party, this is not a set that parties non-stop. The pupils we met hinted that they weren't joined at the hip and realised that, ultimately, they'd be in direct competition with each other for tenancy. However, generally, a collaborative ethos pervades chambers. Indeed, we were delighted to discover a Highgate Massive – quite a number of members live in this part of north London, some within a few streets of each other…even sharing the same cleaning lady. And while we're on the subject of cleaning, we are reliably informed that Tuesday is shoeshine day. Don't worry, pupils are not expected to run around with a tin of Kiwi – someone comes in to perform the task.

"This is not a clerk-driven set," we heard; members are definitely in control. In part, this means that clerks are less pushy in terms of foisting work on barristers or foisting particular barristers on instructing solicitors. Clerks do call members by their surnames, particularly seniors, although pupils were a bit unsure as to correct forms of address (or indeed if there were any). This is certainly not a stuffy old set, but we did sense pupils needed to ease themselves into the place slowly and discreetly.

Furnival Chambers

the facts

OLPAS: summer season **Pupillages:** 3x12 months
Applications: 200 **Mini pupillages:** unlimited
First Interview: 60 **Second Interview:** 25
Award: £15,000
Tenancies offered in 2004: 3
Chambers UK rankings: Crime

Founded in 1985, this leading criminal set of over 60 barristers specialises in all kinds of serious crime, including a niche in the growing field of asset confiscation. Senior members of chambers have appeared in some of the most publicised criminal trials in recent years, not least among them the Millennium Dome diamond heist, which achieved widespread media attention when the Old Bailey judge nodded off during the closing speeches. Other well-known cases include the Sarah Payne murder and the 'Beauty in the Bath' appeal.

Chez Furnival there's not an oil on canvas or chaise longue in sight: chambers has a modern, light and airy feel to it, which seems to go hand in hand with the set's ethos. As one barrister told us: *"Furnival Chambers is far from being stuffy; we pride ourselves on being informal, but at the same time professional."* New recruits will be disappointed if they're expecting a rigid hierarchy, and can expect to be welcomed into chambers life from the very beginning of pupillage. QCs make a habit of showing pupils around on their first day, and all newcomers have a reception thrown in their honour. *"Everyone makes a real effort to get to know you."*

Once the welcome drinks and tour are over, pupils *"knuckle down to some hard work."* Everyone agrees that the pupillage year is a tough one, and that what you see is what you get. The first six is spent with a single pupilmaster, though there is also a compulsory two-month secondment to the asset forfeiture team. Expect to be exposed to serious crime and hope you have the stomach for it. There will be plenty of paperwork, including writing written advices on sentencing or appeal, drafting skeleton arguments and summarising the evidence in trial bundles. If a pupilmaster has a lengthy trial on the circuits, chambers *"won't waste pupils' time by sending them along too if there isn't much to be done,"* but will instead turn to others to find alternative work. This is a good way for pupils to get their faces known.

A 40-hour in-house advocacy course runs throughout the first six and covers the kind of situations likely to be encountered in the early years of practice. Pupils and juniors agree that this training is *"very, very thorough, and really worthwhile."* In addition to their pupilmaster, pupils will also be assigned a junior tenant to act as godparent, another point of contact, who usually proves to be an invaluable source of advice and guidance. It works so well because the godparents are entirely detached from the tenancy decision.

We were particularly impressed with the *Hi-De-Hi!*-style tannoy used by the clerking team to announce the availability of new work. Yet a second six is no holiday, and pupils must zip up their boots for a dawn 'til dusk trawl of London's magistrates' courts. In court every day, it's not uncommon for them to get through nine or ten different clients in a single morning's work. Ever heard the motto, 'Pupil barristers: love the jobs you hate'? Furnival's pupils know it well, and are expected to take part in a Saturday court duty rota. There really is no rest for the wicked! And as you'd imagine, there will be challenging and unpredictable clients to deal with from the word go. One pupil told us of a client (one of her first) who, when asked to plead guilty or not guilty to a minor offence, began masturbating in front of the magistrates. Needless to say he was taken down to the cells pretty sharpish. Her advice: *"It can be pretty devastating when things go wrong, but it's a real learning curve...and if you really don't know what to do next, there will always be someone from chambers available on the end of the phone to guide you through it."*

With all those briefs flooding into their pigeonholes, surely these pupils must be raking it in. Not so, we were told; *"in the second six, you've got to be prepared to go at least two to three months without getting paid a thing. When you get your chambers grant, save some of it for the later months."* The good news is that the fees do eventually trickle in, and during the latter months of the second six, pupils start getting Crown Court briefs in their own name for routine work like sentences and 'mentions'.

For anyone considering tenancy here, a third six is considered a must. In a job where being excellent on your feet in court is everything, *"six months of advocacy experience just isn't long enough to see what you're made of."* For those who make the grade, the dial is turned up a notch and *"you start to build up a practice of your own."* Furnival won't offer third sixes to pupils unless they consider them to have a realistic prospect of tenancy, so make it through to a third six and it's a really good sign. To quote one pupil: *"I feel like here they are really trying to mould you into a future tenant."*

So who would fit the Furnival mould? When we probed into the backgrounds of the barristers and pupils we met, we found a complete absence of academic snobbery – this is not an Oxbridge-only set. What everyone did have in common was a certain fieriness, and we sensed they were the sort who'd definitely give you a really good fight in court. Chambers looks for applicants who can perform well under pressure. As we were told by one member of the pupillage committee: *"There's a complete cross-section of personalities here...academic ability is only worth so much, and we place a lot of emphasis on how candidates perform at interview."*

First-round interviews are short and sweet. To try and make things as fair as possible, everyone is asked the same five questions, often including an ethical or legal topic. Be prepared to fight your corner and to argue things from an alternative point of view as well as the one you hold instinctively. Make it through to the second round and you'll note that the interview panel likes to *"do a bit more heckling."* There will also be an advocacy exercise to prepare, usually a plea in mitigation or a bail application. Applicants who are still at university are at no disadvantage because *"it's not the content that's being judged, it's the style and the delivery that we're interested in."* You'll also be required to give a three-minute speech on the topic of your choosing. Apparently, previous topics have included 'bog snorkelling on my gap year' and 'why playing poker is a skill not a game of chance.' In other words, you've got free rein to talk about anything under the sun as long as you can engage and persuade your audience. Despite sounding like a mediaeval trial by ordeal, everyone we interviewed spoke positively about the interview experience: *"The process was well structured, and I knew what to expect. I think that brought the best out in me."*

We think that if you're bright and outgoing, are

good at putting together a persuasive argument and have a passion for criminal law, Furnival Chambers will bring out the best in you too.

One Garden Court

the facts
OLPAS: No **Pupillages:** 2x12 months
Applications: 200 **Mini pupillages:** 35
Interview: 20-25
Award: £15,000
Tenancies offered in 2004: not yet known
Chambers UK rankings: Family

Turn your back to Middle Temple Hall, dive between the roses and sneak through the narrow doorway: One Garden Court is unassuming from the outside, and within there is little to remind you of the grandeur of the Temple. The set spares its visitor all the self-conscious trappings of a chambers determined to wow with stylish sofas and interesting artwork. Instead, it chooses to impress by relying on its successes in the family law courts. One Garden Court can trace its roots back to family and civil set Lamb Building, established in the 1950s; however, in 1989 an *"ideological schism"* led to the departure of a family law contingent. The breakaway group blossomed into what is now the largest set of chambers in which all members specialise in family law.

Chambers' 47 tenants cover *"a healthy dose of ancillary relief and care work,"* plus adoption, child abduction, international children's law, mediation, human rights issues and family-related crime. Our colleagues on *Chambers UK* inform us that the set's four silks are all expert in children's work (including tough-end care cases) and that its reputation for ancillary relief work has also grown in stature, with many of the juniors very well regarded in this field also. The client base is as diverse as the work: *"There are two different faces – the posh, moneyed clients and the care clients. They have a variety of professional needs."*

Sitting with four pupilmasters for three months each ensures that pupils are *"exposed to the full spectrum within the narrow field of family law,"* including both publicly and privately funded work, ancillary relief, contested divorces, care work and private children's work. Pupils generally stick close to their PMs, though *"if you have a spare moment you can do work for others too."* Inevitably, both their workload and their autonomy grow as the months pass. *"In the first six they kick you out by 6.30pm, but you then get busier with your own practice,"* so that *"by the end of the second six months you barely see your pupilmaster."* You won't be left to flounder around though; *"you really can phone members at home, and late at night, to cry for help."* With PMs, *"feedback comes if you specifically ask for it,"* and *"if you screw up, it's okay – everyone knows it takes a while to get into family practice."* While there are *"no gold stars for excellence,"* *"you will get invited for coffee to go over stuff."*

Over the course of the year, pupils *"definitely do money, and care, and a seat with a more junior junior with a broader practice, plus another seat to mop up and make sure you've seen everything."* A cracking case-a-day schedule sees second six pups cutting their teeth on Family Law Act (domestic violence) and children's cases, with the agenda including non-molestation orders, contact hearings and removals from the jurisdiction. Pupils enthused about *"quite juicy stuff"* that puts them *"on the frontline from the start."* This pattern continues in the early years of tenancy, when *"as a junior, care work keeps you busier."* Money cases, it seems, come later on.

Chambers has a space problem, so members shoehorn themselves behind desks and tuck themselves into cupboards under stairs, stoically remarking: *"It's fine – there's plenty of room for me and my laptop!"* The cheerfulness with which members bunk up and knuckle down is indicative of *"a real camaraderie, and sense that you are all part*

of the gang." Possibly this feeling stems from the nature of family practice, the clientele and the type of people attracted to the work.

Various people took pride in telling us how chambers is *"not traditional for the sake of it."* One interviewee described it as *"open to change;"* another as *"more liberal"* than most and *"a grown-up, co-operative affair."* However, any suggestion that family practice equates to little more than highbrow social work is dismissed with a reminder that a human touch does not mean a soft touch. Chambers' style artfully combines the requisite good bedside manner with a *"straight-down-the-line, no-messing-around"* approach.

But this is where any sense of authority or old school ends; *"there's none of that Mister-Miss-Madam stuff"* and *"no standing on ceremony."* Furthermore, between barristers and clerks there is *"a mutual respect,"* with neither taking the upper hand. *"It is a very democratic place, right down to the tenancy decision."*

The set has an annexe in Exeter, which for those of a few years, call may provide a desirable *"lifestyle option."* Back in the Temple, the lifestyle is caffeine fuelled. The formal post-court afternoon tea ritual plays no part here and is viewed as just another *"horror story from Chancery."* Instead, *"you just go for coffee with the people you like"* ...unless it's been a particularly harrowing day at court, in which case Daly's wine bar is close to hand. A self-confessed *"loose-knit community,"* members are *"not cloyingly sociable"* and assured us that *"we don't live in each other's pockets"* (possibly because they live in each other's desk drawers). Our thanks to the wit who said: *"We recognise new arrivals and we recognise retirements, and if there's been nothing to recognise for a while, we recognise that."*

The set takes on three pupils every two years. The interview is a relaxed affair and *"there is no grilling on the law; we just want to put people at ease and relax them to give them a chance to show themselves."* Those who had been through the process said: *"They were inter-*

ested and asked questions I could respond to, rather than presenting me with an ethical dilemma with no answer." One sensed "a genuine empathy" from the interviewers. Leaving academic standards to one side, the set seeks out those who will fare well in the family law context, because "you are putting yourself quickly on to a very narrow track." It wants pupils who can "click into the service orientation," and those who are "clued up about life, able to ask the right questions and able to talk to people." Aware of the value of a little life experience, the set welcomes those with previous careers just as much as those who have fast-tracked through academia. And with a varied client base demanding differing approaches, we can see why "there is no magic formula."

The tenancy committee makes its decision based on a more rigorous procedure involving a mock brief and interview, plus written reports from all pupil-masters and other interested parties. The committee's recommendation is then put to a full vote of the members and so "anyone too aloof wouldn't get on – you need to make yourself known." Pupils are not linked up to chambers intranet (by which votes are cast), and although this is "not an insurmountable problem," it does act as a reminder that one's position is temporary.

While heavily glossed fire doors and magnolia walls took us back to our school days, and some of those we met reminded us of the type of well-meaning and chatty teacher who always made themselves accessible, there's no sense of pupils being tested, examined or league-tabled. Then again, we did learn of a spelling test, which has been taken by all members at one stage or another. The ten-word test has been devised by one of the barristers (just for fun) and includes words like "miniscule, supersede, moccasin and fuchsia." A written note is made of all scores!

After a long day in court and a cross-examination from us, we left our sources to put the kettle on and reach for the dictionary to mug up on a few tricky words.

Two Garden Court

the facts

OLPAS: summer season **Pupillages:** 6x12 months
Applications: 700 **Mini pupillages:** 46
Interviews: 30-40
Award: £12,000 plus earnings
Tenancies offered in 2004: 2
Chambers UK rankings: Administrative & public law, crime, human rights, immigration, police law, social housing

Hatched in the liberal dreamscape of the mid-1970s, Two Garden Court has made good on its promise to undertake morally and socially progressive work. From its self-proclaimed "revolutionary, if not subversive" beginnings, the set has grown from six barristers pretty fresh out of pupillage to some 79 tenants. Its immigration practice is pre-eminent, boasting the man Chambers UK described as the "guru and greatest brain in the field," Laurie Fransman QC. The courage and zeal of the set is reflected in its motto "Do right, fear no one."

Members and pupils pride themselves on working for "vulnerable people," and although the set is unabashed about its values, it is not self-righteous or superior. Modesty is scarcely a barristerial trait, but we found a trace of it here. In age and ethnic background, the members are a diverse lot, and the fact that many joined the Bar later in life may explain the lack of "Bar culture."

The set's chief premises overlook the idyllic Garden Court and Middle Temple Hall. Yet we found that even the scent of roses and lavender wafting through the windows of the reception area did nothing to soften its alarming resemblance to the waiting room of an NHS dental surgery. The framed certificates on the walls (Quality Mark, Bar Mark, Certificate of Registration), and a pinboard boasting such fascinating reading as 'You and your barrister' and 'Having a job understanding employment law?' left us with a decided feeling of dental unease. Perhaps that's the way its clients like it – housing advice and root canal work all in one day.

Under its new regime, the set will offer six 12-month pupillages. There are no tenancies offered at the end of pupillage – if a place for a junior tenant arises, it is advertised to all-comers. The reasoning behind this system is to ensure equal opportunity for all and to guarantee that the set sees the best applicants. It means that this pupillage is regarded first and foremost as a training, rather than as the entry point for tenancy. Luckily, the set's pupils have a high success rate elsewhere and, if necessary, are permitted to squat for a further six months while searching for permanent membership at another chambers.

Here, your expectations will be both fulfilled and confounded. The junior tenant we met was kitted out in a Gap T-shirt, rolled up jeans and sandals, but the senior member was suited. One of the pupils we met was a mature Oxbridge graduate, while the other was a 25-year-old from Aberdeen. And the work itself is diverse – from criminal to social housing, administrative and public law, family, human rights and immigration. Chambers tries to ensure that its pupils work in at least three areas of practice.

The set receives more applications than any other we've investigated, and to make it into the class of 30 or so that are interviewed, you must have a seriously impressive CV. A rare entity at the Bar, this appears to be a set that couldn't care less where you went to university. Furthermore, as one member of the pupillage committee told us: *"We don't care if someone had a poor degree when they were 21. We are looking for experience and commitment to the principles of the set."* And boy, have they found it. Those we spoke to own CVs that would make even Kofi Annan weep with envy. One enjoyed a successful career as a humanitarian monitor for the UN, Human Rights Watch and more non-government organisations than you can shake a stick at, while somehow managing to squeeze in a masters in international relations at Columbia University. Another worked for £12,000 a year at a legal

charity, while studying part-time for an LLM, before working as a volunteer on capital punishment cases in New Orleans. There are several lessons to be learned from this. One is that, if at first you don't succeed (at getting pupillage), try, try again. Another is that age and experience are no impediment.

The pupillage interview consists of an advocacy exercise (eg a bail application) followed by a discussion of current legal issues. You should brush up on your knowledge of new and proposed criminal justice legislation and the HRA. As one member told us: *"Lack of knowledge and understanding of things in the wider world is a real turn-off for us."* And in keeping with its ethos of fairness and transparency, unsuccessful applicants can request feedback on their interview performance.

The set boasts a very organised and well-structured training scheme. Pupils are exposed to advocacy training and lectures on substantive areas of law, courtroom etiquette and legal developments. You'll change pupil supervisors after your first six, but are encouraged to maintain contact with your old mentor. In your second six, you'll have a two-week induction before appearing in court for the first time. After this, you'll be clerked for, on your feet, and *"on your own."* But not entirely. Pupils are encouraged to take the telephone numbers of members with them to court, and to use them. The set strives to ensure that second-sixers see a good dose of both criminal and civil (mostly immigration) work, to ensure remunerative equity. As you'd expect with criminal work, the hours are long as papers tend not to arrive until the end of the day.

With its elaborate bureaucracy and management structure (committees for the library, administration, personnel, professional administrators, the list goes on…), it is a quintessential child of the 70s. A largely member-driven and democratic set, even baby barristers can stroll into the lion's den of the clerks' room without fear. However, it's a large set and being spread over three sites puts it at a risk of fragmentation. As one member told us: *"If you are not careful, you risk seeing people only from your practice group."*

Perhaps this is why there is a strong social dynamic, with organised dinners and weekends away. Chambers also organises women's nights out and annual summer and Christmas parties. The summer party – held in a nightclub – has achieved notoriety at the Bar.

Two Garden Court is replete with contradictions. While its motto may be "Do right, fear no one," it lacks the same reputation for all-out crusading of some of its competitors. The system of tenancy selection serves the set and outsiders well, but whether it is as ideal for its own pupils as it could be, we couldn't say. What we can say is that a pupillage here is extremely well regarded.

Government Legal Service

the facts

OLPAS: No **Pupillages**: 30 trainees a year, of whom around 5 are pupils
Applications: 1,200 (for all posts) **Vacation placements available**
Interviews: 120
Salary: £18,500 – £22,500 (plus BVC fees and £5-7,000 grant)

There was a time when becoming a barrister meant finding a home in chambers as a self-employed practitioner and nothing else. In fact, not so long ago, the very idea of a barrister being 'employed' would have had senior judges and barristers choking on their sherry. A pupillage in the Government Legal Service (GLS) provides an alternative to the orthodox route of a 12-month pupillage in chambers. The GLS employs about 1,850 lawyers, around a third of whom are barristers, and of the 30 people lucky enough to make it through the GLS recruitment process each year, a small handful of them will train as pupil barristers. We asked a few of them to shed some light on what, for us, was undiscovered territory.

The GLS recruitment process gets going a full two years in advance of the start of pupillage. Whether you want to be a solicitor or a barrister, the procedure is the same: shortlisted candidates are called to spend a day at the GLS assessment centre. During an individual interview applicants are asked to discuss pre-prepared topics, both legal and non-legal. There is also a group problem-solving exercise. The pupils we spoke to confirmed that this process compared very favourably with their experiences of interviews in chambers. Said one: *"The pupillage panel is chaired by a non-lawyer with human resources training. While it was certainly challenging, I felt that the panel brought the best out in me, and I didn't feel under attack, as in some pupillage interviews."*

For applicants who impress on the assessment day, the next hurdle is being accepted by a government department. Just like trainee solicitor applicants, potential GLS pupils are given the opportunity to indicate their preferred department, though because some departments are more willing to take pupil barristers than others, it's probably a good idea to find out which ones are likely to have an opening before making an application. As with a conventional pupillage, GLS pupils normally spend their first six months in chambers, a placement that is usually organised by the sponsoring department (though it is also possible for applicants to arrange their own first six independently with the agreement of their department). In some cases, is might also be possible to arrange three sets of four months so that the first and last four months are served within the department, thus enabling pupils to spend part of their practising second six in chambers. If you're wondering why a set would want to take on a pupil in full knowledge that they would be leaving after six months, bear in mind that there's probably something in it for them too. After all, government work often makes up a substantial proportion of the work of some chambers. While a pupil in chambers, you should see the full range of your supervisor's work in line with the Bar Council Common Checklist, and be treated in exactly the same way as any other pupil. It's also worth noting that whilst in chambers, GLS pupils are not in competition with their peers, as they don't have to fight tooth and nail for tenancy. As one GLS pupil told us: *"It made my relationship with the other pupils and my experience in chambers much more relaxed knowing that I wasn't a part of the competition."*

In the second six, GLS pupils make the transition from the world of private practice to the world of an employed government lawyer. In line with *"the GLS mantra that you must never stay in your comfort zone for too long,"* this will often mean that you are exposed to a very different area of law to the one you saw in your first six. A predominantly civil first six might well be followed by a second six in a department whose work is heavily prosecution based.

The second-six experience will vary from one department to another. Some departments conduct a lot of their own litigation from beginning to end, giving pupils the opportunity to get on their feet in court. A typical week for a pupil in the Department of Trade and Industry might well include everything from making decisions to prosecute and drafting indictments to actually prosecuting regulatory offences under the Companies Act in a magistrates' court. The role of a barrister in other departments (the Home Office or the Department of Constitutional Affairs being good examples) is more likely to be entirely advisory. Here, you might be asked for your opinion on the compliance of a new piece of legislation with the Human Rights Act or the legality of a new immigration policy.

Wherever you go, you will be given a significant amount of responsibility. Take the experiences of a pupil in the Solicitors Office of HM Customs and Excise. *"In my first week, I was given complete control over a VAT Tribunal appeal involving points of human rights law and EU law."* Though pupils say that they *"appreciate being trusted with important work,"* they also say that *"there is a very high level of support from training supervisors throughout pupillage, and work always gets checked before it is sent out."*

There are some subtle differences in the way that GLS pupils work as lawyers within a government department. Unlike their colleagues in private practice, who will often only meet their clients at the door of the court, barristers in the GLS have much more direct contact with the 'client', who will ordinarily be a civil servant within their department. Like it or lump it, as a lawyer there will always be bureaucracy to deal with, and in the GLS, chambers bureaucracy gets replaced by civil service bureaucracy. There are no clerks to deal with, meaning that your workload will be assigned by a 'line manager' instead. No briefs being dumped on your desk at 6 o'clock on a Friday night here though – the pupils tell us that *"the system for allocating work is much more regularised."* That means that it's usual to know what you'll be doing from one day to the next, and regular office hours are the norm. We also noticed a structured approach to pupils' training. At the start of training, pupils sit down with their supervisors and agree *"measurable objectives"* against which they will be assessed throughout the year. As well as informal day-by-day feedback, there are formal written appraisals at the middle and end of the pupillage.

If donning a wig and gown on a daily basis is part of your game plan, a career as a barrister within the GLS probably isn't for you. Though, as we mentioned above, several government departments handle their own litigation from beginning to end, *"in longer, more complicated cases, it's seen as more cost effective to instruct counsel from the Treasury Panel."* In other words, the opportunities for GLS barristers to gain advocacy experience in the higher courts (the Crown Court, High Court, Court of Appeal etc) are going to be limited. No one we spoke to had gone into the job for the advocacy. As one pupil told us: *"I've really enjoyed the advocacy that I've done, but it's not part of my overall career plan."* Instead, both had been attracted to the job by the prospect of being able to get their hands on high-quality work that involved a regular exposure to public and EC law, which *"is incredibly difficult to get into in private practice."* But did they regret not having the same autonomy as their self-employed contemporaries in chambers? Apparently not, and in fact, it seems that at the early stages of their careers at least, GLS pupils are able to exercise a fair degree of choice as to the type of work they do. As a case in point, the pupil that we interviewed in Customs & Excise had chosen to specialise in civil work at an early stage, whereas, by contrast, many of her colleagues at the same stage of their careers in chambers found themselves *"at the whim of their clerks."* A caveat though: for those who see themselves specialising in the long term, think again. GLS barristers are kept on their toes, and it's certainly the norm to move from one department to another after a couple of years. It remains possible for GLS pupils to cross the boundary from public to private later on in their careers, in the event of a change in heart, as the completion of pupillage leads to a full practising certificate from the Bar Council.

If you are looking for a practice that is largely advisory, the GLS is well worth serious consideration. While there's no guarantee of being taken on at the end of the year, and your supervisors will expect high standards, it's clear that the GLS recruits pupils with a view to retaining them. The pupils we spoke to clearly felt less uncertain about the future and less insecure than the majority of those we encountered in chambers. And with a salary and a pension scheme to boot, it's little wonder.

2-3 Gray's Inn Square

the facts

OLPAS: summer season **Pupillages:** 2x12 months
Applications: c200 **Mini pupillages:** c20
First Interview: 25 **Second Interview:** 10
Award: £25,000
Tenancies offered in 2004: 1
Chambers UK rankings: Consumer law, health and safety, local government, planning

It was a typical summer's day when we strolled across the lawns of Gray's Inn Square towards numbers 2 and 3 – brilliant sunshine the one minute, torrential downpour the next the freshness in the air gave clarity to the sights and sounds of the Inn. Upon leaving chambers we couldn't help but reflect on the aptness of this backdrop to a set where an awareness of heritage and tradition is retained, even as the breeze of modernity wafts through. Whilst it is happy to be celebrating its 150th birthday this year, nostalgic myopia has no place at this set; it is *"clear sighted about where it wants go to"* and aware that *"there is no set quite like us."*

Criminal practice has been important *"since the year dot"* and remains so through the expertise of senior members like chambers head Anthony Scrivener. But his parallel stature in planning law reflects the other traditional pillars that support *"a very diverse set,"* which *"has an increasing sense of corporate identity"* and *"a definite business plan."* The set is highly regarded for public and local government law, planning, consumer law, health and safety and civil litigation, serving over 300 local authorities, government departments and private companies. Licensing and environmental work are also strong suits.

Consolidating and strengthening expertise in these areas of practice has been at the heart of chambers expansion from 34 to 52 members in the last two years, but the set has its wits about it. Changes in licensing law have prompted the recruitment of two barristers and a solicitor in the last year *"to expand and diversify the practice."* And not just any solicitor; no less than Jeremy Phillips, former head of licensing at Eversheds and Osborne Clarke. He might as well have written the book in the subject and, in fact, he has: *"He's the author of 'Phillips on Licensing.'"*

Clearly chambers recruits carefully, and it's no less careful about the pupils it takes on. An initial meeting with two or three barristers is followed by a longer second-stage interview at which applicants face an advocacy test and general grilling from a panel of up to eight people. The set says it looks for types with *"hunger and the ability to get on with people, a must given our diverse client base,"* so we were interested to know what aspirations and ambitions mark successful applicants out from the crowd. After all, as our sources were quick to admit, there's no easy handle on the work – *"We're no Doughty Street human rights set."* So should you claim a life-long obsession with planning and local authority work at interview? *"No, we'd frankly view that with suspicion. We like to see that people have taken the trouble to find out and understand what we do, inasmuch as you can."* That's easier for some than others. There are former local authority employees and town planners at the set, but chambers takes on just as many recent university graduates, and the advice to this type of applicant is that *"you should feel able to discuss the major issues in government and planning, but don't obsess about the particulars."*

As for why the uninitiated might find chambers' work attractive, one source reflected that *"the variety appealed to me from the beginning, but across the board the public-personal element of work is what engages and challenges."* True, we observed a less ideological commitment to the law than one might expect at, say, Doughty Street. Nonetheless it was universally agreed that *"if you're full-on commercial, you wouldn't be happy here."*

Particularly in the early years of practice, juniors are kept busy covering an awful lot of bases. *"There's a lot of written and court work at the junior end, whether it's county court, civil or criminal work, and plenty of briefs from seniors."* Pupils find themselves *"doing minor local residents' issues, or even small inquiries in planning," "RTAs, social security tribunals and repossessions,"* and *"a lot of applicant immigration work."* And if you're not entirely sure what local authority instructions will entail, trust us: it's anything and everything *"from employment to elections, health and safety enforcement to finance, education to community care."* Getting the picture? Or perhaps it's more of a tapestry. As one pupil enthused: *"One of the joys of the set is the challenge of suddenly being given work on an area of law you know nothing about."*

Another *"major attraction"* is chambers' insistence *"that pupils are on their feet in court four to five days a week in the second six."* It is a very different approach to some other sets, and pupils and supervisors both admit that it makes for *"a very difficult six months, balancing out your own work with your responsibilities to others as you're approaching the tenancy decision."* Pupils reported working 8.30am-7pm with *"periods of greater intensity"* and an increasing number of weekends in the second six. But whilst they work hard, pupils insist that *"supervisors and the chambers director are protective of you getting overloaded."* One supervisor concurred, saying: *"We try to provide a lot of support before and after court, to be proactive in discussing issues and to be aware that even the simplest matter can hold hidden terrors."*

Pupils move between supervisors three times in the year, *"partly for maximum exposure to members, partly for breadth of experience, partly to satisfy their preferences."* Each pupil sits with the same three supervisors so as to create a level playing field for the tenancy decision. This is typical of *"a very open chambers that gives you the chance to improve and doesn't leave you in the dark with your paranoias and insecurities for company!"* Seniors confirmed that mistakes *"are expected, not just tolerated,"* with emphasis placed on a pupil's subsequent reaction. Halfway through their time together pupil and supervisor share informal feedback, and at the end of their cohabitation the supervisor writes a review, which the pupil is allowed to read and respond to. Together with *"reports from anyone else you've worked for"* and even *"letters of praise from solicitors,"* these reviews form the bedrock of the pupillage committee's recommendations for tenancy. *"Often 20-30 pages long"* and structured around *"strict criteria that ask, 'Is this candidate outstanding?'"* all our sources were confident there were *"no hidden surprises and you'd understand the final decision."* The set is genuinely *"supportive if you don't get tenancy."* One pupil was allowed to stay on until she found other work. Another was even luckier – *"Chambers recognised the ability of the candidate, but felt that the maturity wasn't quite there. The pupil agreed to stay on for a further six, and at the end of that period was accepted into chambers and is now very successful."*

A senior told us: *"One of the great things is the culture of putting your pen down if someone needs help. A junior pupil or tenant can always have an informal discussion with a 20-to-30-year called."* Wondering how easy that might feel at the junior end, we quizzed a pupil on the point. *"Well, my supervisor told me to take a licensing point to the resident expert, and obviously I felt like a nervous idiot, but it ended up in him explaining what it would have taken me three days to work out."* Support can be found in all quarters of the chambers, and everyone is on *"first-name terms throughout."* There is always an exception that proves the rule though. The one person who is not referred to by first name is Malcolm Spence QC. But it's not because he's an ogre or a staunch traditionalist, rather he's *"a wonderful grandfather figure who lives in the flat upstairs and comes down twice a day. You just couldn't call him Malcolm!"*

Tales of treats from Konditer & Cook ("Fabulous cakes...the sort you'd make yourself if only you had the time, inclination and energy" – Nigella Lawson, *Vogue*) and *"5pm gatherings at the fax machine in reception"* give an insight into the almost cosy side of chambers life. One source even admitted: *"Coming back after court feels like coming home to a family. You can moan or boast about the day."* In terms of its social scene, chambers *"doesn't pressure you to go out at all; in fact, it could do with being ramped up."* Although relieved that *"it's not like a criminal set where you're judged on the strength of your bladder and liver,"* pupils and juniors do recognise the value of socialising together, *"so we're trying to organise more casual events more often to improve connections and communication."*

We started out by saying that 2-3 Gray's Inn Square values both tradition and modernity, and we think it balances these two aspects of its character well. Despite huge growth in the ranks of members, there has been *"an increasing sense of loyalty to the set over recent years."* Chambers has a clear idea of where it is going, and it's going there come rain or shine.

2 Hare Court

the facts

OLPAS: summer season **Pupillages:** 2x12 months
Applications: 250 **Mini pupillages:** 70
Award: £18,000
Tenancies offered in 2004: Not known
Chambers UK rankings: Crime

The site upon which 2 Hare Court is built has long been associated with crime and punishment. It was here that former Lord Chief Justice and Lord Chancellor Judge Jeffreys, otherwise known as the hanging judge of the bloody assizes, kept his chambers during the 17th century. In modern times, 2 Hare Court has also earned a reputation as a leading set for serious crime, though whilst an impressive 14 of the senior members have taken up judicial appointments, we have it on good authority that none has a penchant for hanging.

Having been invited to take a seat on the (almost too) comfortable brown leather sofa, we took the time to soak up the atmosphere in the busy reception area. It's a well-turned-out gaff, and whoever calls the shots here is careful to ensure that the generous vases of fresh cut flowers complement the tastefully decorated interior. There are some grand finishing touches, including a marvellous fireplace in the main conference room.

Chambers style is reflected again in the design of its brochure, which closely resembles the cocktail menu of a smart hotel bar. We ordered Orlando Pownall QC followed by a sweet sherry, but unfortunately he wasn't on the menu that day, and so we busied ourselves with interviewing the pupils instead. Definitely a mixed bag of people, all of them had gone down the CPE route and boasted first degrees that included sociology and computer sciences. As for their universities, well, all of them were well known, but there certainly wasn't a hint of elitism. All three of the pupils we met were slightly older than the norm, which they felt gave them a distinct advantage as criminal practitioners – *"It's probably a good thing in this job to come across as being closer to 30 rather than 20. It makes dealing with clients that bit easier."*

The road to tenancy at 2 Hare Court requires pupils to complete the standard 12 months of pupillage and, in common with many criminal sets, a further third six for those that show the potential to become future tenants. Each pupil sits with three different supervisors to expose them to as much of chambers' work as possible. As one of the supervisors told us: *"The first few months of pupillage are about giving pupils a cradle-to-grave guide to criminal practice. We teach them the skills necessary to master a brief, we teach them how to get all the important issues out of their client in conference, and we try to guide them through the court process from beginning to end."* As you might expect in a busy criminal set, there will always be plenty of people looking for a spare pair of hands to help with important or time-consuming cases, and these are allocated to pupils on a rota basis to ensure that everyone gets a bite of the cherry. There is also an opportunity to shadow a judge (usually a former member of chambers) for a week.

The second six brings plenty of court work, and to smooth pupils into their new role, chambers provides advocacy training throughout the year. When the dreaded first day in court arrives, pupils have a *"real support network in place."* One pupil recalled her second day in the magistrates' court, telling us: *"A senior member of chambers sat down with me beforehand and we went through the brief together, making a checklist of the most important issues."* The second six also means a good deal of travelling: though 95% of chambers' work is in London, it is not unheard of for pupils to be sent to places as exotic as Wantage and the Isle of Wight. On the plus side, the clerks *"don't generally accept the kind of briefs that are just there to abuse pupils,"* and chambers will pay pupils' travel expenses, so that the financial return for, say, a Norwich Crown Court mention (worth about £45) is not swamped by the train fare. The second six also

includes a compulsory two-week secondment to the CPS, during which pupils get a shed load of prosecution work and can expect up to three trials in an average day.

Once the official 12-month pupillage is up, chambers asks people to complete a further six months before applying for tenancy. Pupils are automatically considered for a third six *"unless we don't think that they have a hope of getting a tenancy at the end of it."* The tenancy decision is made after a lengthy consideration of written work, performance in court (yes, that man sat in the public gallery dressed as Groucho Marx was a spy!) and feedback from instructing solicitors and judges.

The three pupils we met were just coming to the end of their second six when we spoke to them. Each reflected positively on their time at 2 Hare Court, and certainly there were no horror stories of endless days of menial chores. They had been given full access to the chambers intranet and their own electronic diaries in their second six months; *"we feel that we're respected as professionals, and as part of the team,"* they told us. Their early days in court had been helped along by an *"approachable and practical"* team of clerks, who regularly offer feedback via instructing solicitors. All up, though it was a tough year, they agreed it had not been all hard work and no play. The social scene, particularly at the junior end, is active and on most nights of the week you'll find 2 Hare Court tenants haunting at least one of the local bars. Chambers operates an informal, but rigorously enforced, policy of never allowing a pupil to buy the drinks, and at Christmas it treats them to a slap-up meal and drinks in a swanky restaurant. Pupils also find themselves invited along to solicitors' parties in order to do some of that all-important networking. Remarkably, given all the canapés they must have eaten, they looked in pretty good shape.

This is definitely a diverse set: there's no particular face that fits here. What recruiters are looking for is *"an appropriate level of dedication and a real determination to succeed."* The pupils' verdict is that you would do well to reflect this in your application form and that *"the more you tailor your application towards sets that specialise in crime, the better."* Importantly, your application will not be thrown in the bin if you came out of university with a 2:2, so long as you can show that you didn't waste your academic years in the pub. As one pupil supervisor explained: *"Sometimes academic high-flyers don't make great advocates. We're looking for people with a personality too; after all, we will be spending a substantial amount of time with them."* In the two-round interview process, the first meeting allows the panel to check that the candidate who looks brilliant on paper is right in the flesh. The second interview is more rigorous with a legal problem or two thrown in for good measure. Tips? Without giving too much away, it would be a good idea to brush up on your first-year criminal law, and keep up to date with current affairs. Couple that with *"a bit of self-confidence and a bit of charm,"* and don't forget to take a look at that cocktail menu we mentioned!

Hollis Whiteman Chambers

the facts

OLPAS: summer season **Pupillages:** 5x15 months
Applications: 300 **Mini pupillages:** available
First interview: 95 **Second interview:** 10
Award: £12,500 plus earnings
Tenancies offered in 2004: 1
Chambers UK rankings: Crime, criminal fraud, professional discipline

A leading crime set, Hollis Whiteman undertakes all areas of criminal law, both for the prosecution and defence. It has a particular emphasis on corporate and financial fraud, which has earned it top-dog status in *Chambers UK*. Recent high-profile matters include acting for the prosecution in the Sarah Payne murder trial, and in the trials of Meziane and Benmerzouga (Al Quaeda fund-raising) and Paul

Burrell. The set has recognised expertise in professional tribunals and public inquiries, appearing in the Victoria Climbié, Bloody Sunday and Stephen Lawrence inquiries.

The Hollis Whiteman story begins in 1947, when five barristers set up shop in Middle Temple Lane. By the 1950s, the set had grown to 12 and had to split to comply with Bar Council rules. The two sets later reunited to create a criminal megaset – the first with over 30 members – and moved into brand-new premises at Queen Elizabeth Building next to the Thames and the greenery of Middle Temple Gardens. Chambers is decorated with the ubiquitous green upholstery and law reports lining the walls. Back issues of *Hello!* and *Better Homes & Gardens* are piled in the waiting room. It's traditional yet contemporary, conservative but not stifling.

Hollis Whiteman tenants are *"almost exclusively home grown,"* and while this has given it a reputation for *"self-containment and impenetrability,"* it has also lent it a *"harmonious family atmosphere."* Tenants are deeply loyal to the set and proud of its reputation for quality and commitment to *"the correct way of behaving."* Hollis Whiteman's identity is drawn from its ethos, rather than from a legacy of great names or eccentric characters. There are no prima donnas here: *"This set is bigger than the sum of its parts."* Members speak proudly of *"fairness in prosecution, honesty and diligence,"* and of a willingness to fight hard. *"Once work comes in, it will get done properly. There is a sense of pride in the name, and a collective responsibility for maintaining that."*

If it's advocacy training you're after, Hollis Whiteman is ideal. The pupillage lasts for 15 months and is organised into two parts. The first seven months of shadowing are paper-intensive, but you'll also receive weekly advocacy training and observe court hearings. Pupils share a room with their pupilmaster, but are encouraged to work for as many members as possible. After this, buy yourself some comfortable shoes, because you can expect to be on your feet every day for the next eight months. You're not alone, however, and remain under the guidance and support of your PM, who is there to allay any *"heebie-jeebies."*

We won't lie to you: the hours are long and the work can be stressful and challenging. Because Hollis Whiteman deliberately keeps pupil numbers low and refuses to accept squatters, pupils are on their feet and carry a lot of responsibility right from the outset. After a day in court or travelling, you should expect to return to chambers and perhaps end up staying until fairly late at night preparing for the next day in court. If the idea of *Law & Order*-style courtroom battles lured you to the Bar, you'll probably not find a better training ground, and by the end of pupillage, you will have appeared in at least 200 different hearings.

The tenancy decision is made in January, 15 months after the start of pupillage. This delay is to allow pupils the chance to work for the CPS, since to do this you must have completed 12 months of pupillage. There is no formal assessment procedure in determining who gets tenancy. Instead, pupils are observed on a daily basis throughout pupillage, are interviewed by the pupillage committee, and have a mock trial in the Old Bailey, during which aspiring Rumpoles *"get the chance to strut their stuff."* The opinions of tenants and clerks are canvassed, and uniquely, the committee also consults with solicitors, judges and Crown prosecutors.

The pupillage interview can take some applicants by surprise. You will be given a topical legal or ethical issue to address. Recent examples have included the separation of conjoined twins and the implications of holding suspected terrorists indefinitely without charge. One year, applicants were asked to pretend they were the public relations executive of Bristol Royal Infirmary and to explain why the hospital needed to take the organs of babies without their parents' consent.

It's probably okay for us to say that academic credentials are secondary to advocacy skills at Hollis Whiteman. The interview is designed to test applicants' clarity of thought and expression. It's also essential to know *"when to stop talking!"* Personality and a sense of humour are vital, since in criminal work barristers must be able to relate to *"drunks, jurors and judges"* alike. One member of the pupillage committee told us: *"You must make us laugh. The real test is: 'Do I want to spend the next 30 years in a room with this person?'"* Having said that, don't try and be Jim Carrey. The set wants pupils, not court jesters.

Pupils are diverse in age, education and background, but share a confident, outgoing manner. These are advocates first and foremost, and they boast buckets of charm. Rather than antagonism and suspicion between pupils competing for tenancy, we sensed warmth amongst the Hollis Whiteman bunch. One pupil was given reams of urgent photocopying by her PM. She asked a fellow pupil to help and together the two of them stayed until 8pm. He was repaid when she introduced him to his current girlfriend that very night!

Pupils sometimes socialise with their PMs – one told us how she was taken to a gentleman's club. Push grotesque images of spearmint and rhinoceroses from your mind; this is the Reform Club, an ornate, Corinthian-columned monument to the passing of the 1832 Reform Act and its exponents. Keen sportsmen can participate in an annual chambers cricket match, while those more at home with a glass in their hand enjoy regular drinks with colleagues. There is little to indicate a rigid hierarchy here, and clerks address all barristers, whether juniors or silks, on a first-name basis. When asked to sum up the character of the set, one pupil described Hollis Whiteman as *"friendly and old-school."* Seems like a pretty accurate description to us.

7 King's Bench Walk

the facts

OLPAS: summer season **Pupillages:** up to 4x12 months + unfunded pupillages for o/seas students
Applications: 125-150 **Mini pupillages:** available
Interview: Not disclosed
Award: £34,000 (up to £5,000 advanced for BVC)
Tenancies offered in 2004: 1
Chambers UK rankings: Commercial litigation, insurance, international arbitration, shipping

Seven King's Bench Walk has the kind of history people write books about. In fact we're surprised the BBC hasn't produced a Sunday evening drama about the goings on in this part of the Temple. The set's own website is a fascinating read, and we're sure it won't mind us giving you a taster...

In 1666, the buildings on the walkway to the office of the Court of King's Bench were destroyed in the Great Fire of London, so the premises occupied by our subject set date back only to 1685. Since then it's been one legal inferno after another due to the prominence of successive residents. In 1819, Serjeant Wilde defended and saved Queen Caroline's honour and life in the face of an accusation of adultery; in the mid-19th century Lord Halsbury occupied rooms here with crack prosecutor Sir Harry Bodkin Poland, and together they defended a former Governor of Jamaica on a murder charge.

The last 40 years have less to do with sex scandals and death and everything to do with breeding masterful judges. Lords Denning, Brandon, Hobhouse and Goff were all members of the modern-day 7KBW, which formed in 1967 through an amalgam of two sets. With its origins in shipping work, latterly the set has been much less reliant on this area of practice. It had a major breakthrough into the insurance world with the mammoth Lloyd's litigation in the 90s, and since then has driven up its reputation in the field, with members taking core roles in both the Barings cases and the recent swathe of film finance litigation. Other cases include the insurance liabilities for breast implants and asbestos-related illnesses. Shipping cases now amount to just a quarter of the set's work; insurance accounts for another 60% or so and the remainder is made up of general commercial cases. Some barristers do more shipping and others more insurance and reinsurance work, but whatever their orientation, their caps are set at "*top-end work not knock-about work.*" Such instructions beg "*excellence in performance,*" and 7KBW's instructing solicitors (Cyde & Co, Ince & Co, BLG, Richards Butler and other top firms) expect – and are prepared to pay for – nothing less.

"*Honesty and excellence,*" is how one source described this small set's core principles; another told us: "*We're regarded as academic and technically rigorous on the law...we're trusted to put the case straight.*" Concepts of integrity and not pushing the boundaries of the law fit with a style that is "*not particularly flamboyant; rather conservative.*"

Pupils sit with five pupilmasters over the course of the year. The first PM will supervise the pupil for three months, the second for two and the other three will take six-week turns. "*Some are more talkative, some quieter. Some give you more academic research, some more practical procedural things.*" If you're writing an opinion on the merits of a case, it may take a few days to read through several A4 files before you can start, or you may be asked to make some notes on a point of law which takes just a few hours. Either way, you will spend most of your time doing paperwork. The learning curve is described as "*almost vertical*" and the work "*complicated,*" with issues and facts "*expressed in obscure terminology.*"

Quite separately, month by month, five QCs acting as 'pupillage assessors' and the two joint heads of chambers give each pupil a set piece of work. Additionally, from Christmas onwards any member of chambers who has suitable work is encouraged to request pupils' assistance. The end result is a pupillage system that is neither confined to PMs nor reliant on pupils getting on with their supervisors. Before the end of the first six pupils are given an indication of whether they have a real shot at building a career at 7KBW. It seems hard to predict – in 2003 none of the pupils were ultimately taken on; in 2004 one made the grade.

The second six of most pupillages is a time for getting on your feet in court and earning; here, pupillage is a full 12 months of learning. One of the youngest juniors extolled the virtues of this approach, saying: *"It's important to be somewhere where you become good at what you do."* The instructions he'd received had all been directly relevant to his future practice, so there had been no winding up applications or treks to Wolverhampton for mortgage repossessions. The clerks hadn't fed him scraps just to give him court time; they'd secured low-end work (often direct instructions from P&I Clubs) that was *"pertinent to the reality of practice."* He was currently handling his own carriage of goods case in Norwich, while also assisting more senior members of chambers as a second junior.

The work requires barristers to apply black letter law to contractual situations and to be *"very practical and think about what the parties to the contract wanted. Law is very academic, but as barristers we are required to be practical and pragmatic."* And if you ever begin to lose sight of the practical side of things, sometimes the paperwork you'll receive on a shipping case will include pictures of the vessels in question.

Describing the people she worked with, the pupil told us: *"They are very, very clever,"* yet *"not arrogant or pretentious. Even if you're working for a silk, they'll take you seriously (although I imagine the temptation is not to). As pupils we can't expect to be on a level as we don't have the experience, but they lay a lot of emphasis on the fact that you'll improve."* Simply put: 7KBW looks for pupils who can meet its exacting standards of intellectual ability and technical accuracy. It's fitting, then, that the problem question students must tackle at a pupillage interview (eg preparing a skeleton argument for an appeal to the House of Lords on a reported Court of Appeal case) is sent to them a week beforehand, allowing ample time to consider,

research and draft a high-quality response. It's not about showmanship or proving you can wing it on short notice; *"you've got to get to the right answer. All the oral advocacy in the world is not going to help you if you've got the answer wrong."*

The set is conventional in its structure: there's no formal constitution, no chief exec and the management committee has a light touch. It's not overrun with subcommittees and full meetings of members are rare; if there is a meeting, it will most likely be for the annual tenancy decision, taken in July. One member told us there was surprisingly little in the way of politics: *"We're too busy getting on with our own practices."* Another added: *"There's an expectation you'll give it your all."*

While actively discouraged from attending chambers tea on the basis that it can make them feel *"awfully uncomfortable,"* pupils are welcome, indeed urged, to join members for a monthly buffet lunch. Clerks prove to be after-hours allies and drinking companions in The Witness Box, although this might not feel the case the morning after the traditional clerks-and-pupils night out *"on the lash."* We presume the senior clerk's housewarming party, to which many members of chambers were invited, was a more sober affair. You might have guessed from all this that clerks will address you by your first name, not your surname.

Conventional in so many ways from its location in the Temple, its traditional-to-a-tee decor and long history of sending QCs to the Bench, 7KBW is your classic barristers' chambers. We rather like conducting our interviews in barristers' rooms, amongst the piles of papers and the invitations to garden parties. It made our visit less clinical than they can sometimes seem in the sterile surrounds of sleek meeting rooms, where our interview notes are written with chambers' own-brand pens on their own-brand paper. We're not so sure 7KBW has commissioned items so peripheral to legal practice. This is the commercial Bar straight up, no cocktail umbrellas (or parties for that matter) and no marketing spiel. What you see is what you get and 7KBW isn't planning to change any time soon.

11 King's Bench Walk

the facts

OLPAS: summer season **Pupillages:** 2 - 3x12 months
Applications: 400 **Mini pupillages:** 40
Interview: 12
Award: £35,000 (advance for BVC considered)
Tenancies offered in 2004: 2
Chambers UK rankings: Administrative & public law, education, employment, human rights, local government

Not to be confused with the common law set of the same name, 11 KBW, led by Eldred Tabachnik QC and James Goudie QC, is a highly regarded employment and public law set.

Despite its old-school appearance, 11 KBW is a relative baby among chambers. In 1981, former Lord Chancellor Derry Irvine founded the set with nine juniors, including Tony Blair. Today it has 43 tenants, 12 of them silks. It is renowned for its strong cadre of juniors and for a helpful and professional clerking service. Situated in the Temple in a small terraced building, the premises are quaint, warm, low key, and very lived-in. Worn brown chairs line the walls of the waiting room and newspapers are scattered on a table, the French polish on which has seen better days. Members' rooms are dark and dusty, law reports clinging to every wall.

11 KBW's beginnings give the set a distinctive sense of pride and cohesion. The *"intellectually rigorous"* legacy of Derry Irvine remains to this day, and the set boasts a wealth of eminent practitioners who are respected for their academic excellence. In some senses, 11 KBW feels more like a law faculty than a barristers chambers. Legal debate is a part of the fabric of chambers; one pupil told us: *"Some tenants are quite donnish in their approach."*

An 11 KBW pupillage is intensely paper-driven. From your first day, you'll be in the library researching in order to go on to draft opinions, skeleton arguments and notes for cross-examination. The work is *"intellectually hardcore"* and, at times, of undeniable importance – one pupil prepared a skeleton argument for the House of Lords and was gutted when the matter settled. Pupils feast on a smorgasbord of work, consisting mainly of employment matters, but including a decent helping of public and commercial law. The idea is that you *"get the law right"* before embarking on advocacy; however, pupils are encouraged to get involved in FRU cases.

Pupils sit with a new pupilmaster every three months. Personality-wise, there is an element of matching PMs to pupils, although almost every pupil will sit with 'Treasury Devil' Philip Sales. He is the junior with possibly the most diverse and interesting practice in chambers, and a *"rigorous"* tutor. In the first three months, you'll belong entirely to your PM, but thereafter, during each three-month period, you must aim to complete three pieces of work for your PM and six for other members. Written pieces for others are double marked, such that most tenants will have seen your work before the tenancy decision is made. This is a heavily assessed and highly academic pupillage: expect to spend most of your working hours in the library *"living out a permanent essay crisis!"* As one pupil put it: *"There is no learning by mistake here!"*

Despite being high achievers, all those we met were quietly spoken and unaffected. It's no secret that outstanding academic credentials are *"essential, non-negotiable"*– you'll probably need a First and you'll also need to demonstrate exceptional analytical skills and the ability to apply these in practice. Because of the nature of its work, the client base is varied. The set takes instructions from most of the leading City firms, and from central government, local government, NHS bodies and trade unions. Employment clients can range from low-wage, blue-collar workers to CEOs of large companies, so the ability to relate to a range of people is essential.

You'll be given an indication as to how you're getting on at the start of your second six. On the rare occasion that pupils are not performing, it will be suggested that they look for another set. The tenancy decision is made in July, and in addition to the assessed written work that pupils have produced, the committee considers their performance in an advocacy exercise – usually a mock EAT hearing. Pupils are assessed against *"a universal standard, not each other."* If accepted as a tenant, earnings will be good from the outset, and for the first year no chambers' fees are payable. Employment law is the bread and butter of juniors up to five years' call, with the possibility of some public law matters thrown in. Since 11 KBW has barristers on the Treasury Panels, juniors can also see some Treasury work.

Pupillage selection consists of a single, fairly rigorous interview lasting for about half an hour. Applicants, who will ideally already be known to the panel through a mini pupillage, are asked about a case or a law they would like to change, or a case they felt was wrongly decided. Far from being a test of knowledge, this gauges your ability to reason with legal concepts and give your views persuasively. The ideal applicant will demonstrate *"strong academic ability, even if not expressed in legal terms,"* and the capacity to become a *"top-flight advocate."*

We found 11 KBW to be hospitable and gracious. This set is certainly not slick and modern like some, but it is modest and unaffected. If it's a kicking post-work social life you're after, look elsewhere: apart from a low-key Christmas dinner, the scene is far from riotous. Nevertheless, there is camaraderie between tenants, and silks will often join juniors and pupils for lunch in Hall. While a pupillage here will undoubtedly be challenging, for applicants of the highest academic calibre it will stimulate and reward.

Maitland Chambers

the facts

OLPAS: No   **Pupillages:** up to 3x12 months
Applications: 200 **Mini pupillages:** 45
First interview: 30 **Second interview:** 10-16
Award: £40,000 (£10,000 can be advanced for BVC)
Tenancies offered in 2004: 2
Chambers UK rankings: Commercial Chancery, traditional Chancery, charities, company, insolvency, partnership, professional negligence, real estate

Following its merger with 9 Old Square in October 2004, commercial Chancery giant Maitland Chambers stakes its claim as the largest Chancery set at the Bar. With over 60 tenants in all this is a set that is without doubt pitching itself alongside the magic circle of the commercial Bar. If you're drawn to commercial Chancery work, you're going to be choosing between a small clutch of sets, and some at Maitland would say that this one offers the best environment in which to stand up and fight rather than sit down and draft opinions. At the time of its creation in 2001 (through the merger of 13 Old Square and 7 Stone Buildings), it had former members sitting in each division of the High Court plus the Court of Appeal and the House of Lords.

The distinction between Chancery and straight commercial cases is blurring and Maitland's work spans both areas, with a large percentage of instructions coming from Herbert Smith, Lovells, A&O, and Slaughter and May. Of the £20 million fees billed in 2002, £1.4 million related to overseas cases, most notably in Hong Kong, the Isle of Man, the Cayman Islands and Singapore. Leading cases have included Lloyd's v Jaffray, BCCI v Bank of England and the Barings claim against Coopers & Lybrand & Ors.

So what can you expect as a new pupil? Your first six is predominantly chambers and paper-based. In your second six you might average a couple of days a week in court, but the rest will be spent sat at your desk. PMs are *"quite good at farming you out to others.*

One of the most important things is to impress as many people as you can." We asked one PM what it took to succeed at Maitland. His answer: *"You need to really want to litigate, and you need to be fantastically determined and work hard."* After six months, all pupils undertake an advocacy test in front of the pupillage committee. It's part and parcel of the ongoing assessment, although it is *"handled to make it feel like training."* We've come to the conclusion that it's a mistake to consider pupillage at a Chancery set a specialised training – *"The generalist tradition in this chambers is still going strong. Half the fun is that you never know what's coming through the door next!"* As a pupil, you'll cover company law, land law, trusts, insolvency (*"going to court to freeze assets"*), and *"possibly some landlord and tenant stuff depending on who you are sitting with."* The good news is that *"nearly everyone resists the temptation to take advantage of pupils."*

The set was named after the Victorian legal historian FW Maitland, in an attempt to come up with something independent of each of the two legacy sets from which it was created. 13 Old Square and 7 Stone Buildings are a stone's throw from each other and both are beautiful architecturally. Parallel to Chancery Lane and just a moment from Lincoln's Inn Fields, the sweeping white terrace of Stone Buildings leads up to High Holborn, while the impressive red-brick houses in Old Square study each other across the cobbles. Just like the set's name, its premises give a nod to tradition, although the contemporary glass name board and up-to-the-minute IT network remind you that Maitland is a new venture…of sorts. Perhaps Chancery work begs tradition the grand but not opulent country-house-drawing-room-style reception area; conference rooms with open fires; the rituals of afternoon tea and morning coffee in the library (*"as a pupil it is probably important to be seen there"* but to *"listen rather than talk"*) – these things fuel the notion that Maitland is a stuffy set. But is it really, or is the traditional image studied?

We perceived a hint of polite reserve in most of those we met in chambers but, then again, maybe it

was nothing more than good manners. One source said there was *"no undue deference"* between seniors and juniors, but *"a degree of respect."* Almost everyone we met seemed to have arrived at the law via the classics, and a high proportion of members have earned a First. To say that people here are bright is a statement of the obvious: *"If your intellect is up to it, everyone in chambers will respect you. It's more important than where you come from. No one looks down their nose at anyone."* The recruitment process focuses on how well you present your views and arguments. Does your application communicate a good enough reason to get you an interview? The first interview tests how well you can express your views on current affairs (past examples include Jo Moore, Pinochet and Guantanamo Bay). Those who make it through to the second interview must tackle an unusual problem – one year, Wind in the Willows was subjected to the Badger Act. Applicants need to spot all the issues lurking within: *"It's not a test of law, but analytical ability."*

Clerks call senior members by their surnames, but increasingly juniors are insisting on first names. Pupils weren't entirely sure of the drill on nomenclature. In their first 12 months, tenants have a guaranteed minimum income of £70,000, yet pay nothing at all to chambers. The ethos was described by one established member as *"paternalistic."* We asked how decisions were made in chambers and learned that *"big decisions are made in general meetings: it's one man, one vote and everyone says exactly what they think in words of one syllable. You have to trust the people you work with."* That's not to diminish the role of a chief exec or any number of committees – Manco (management); Pupco (pupillage); Tenco (tenancy) and a relatively recent addition Pubco (Thursday night drinks).

To sum up Maitland you must overlay the benefits of the merger (economies of scale, increased market profile, a renewed focus on management practices) on the best of what the past held for each legacy set. You must also factor in the presence of more than 60 legal minds that can only be described as sharp, organised and elegant.

Matrix

the facts

OLPAS: summer season **Traineeships:** 2
Applications: 500 **Student placements:** 10
First interview: 40 **Second interview:** 10
Award: £25,000 (£5,000 can be advanced for BVC)
Tenancies offered in 2004: None (2 in 2003)
Chambers UK rankings: Administrative and public law, crime, education, employment, environment, criminal fraud, human rights, immigration, police law, public international law

The first thing you are told upon entering Matrix is to get the phraseology right. *"We're trying to shake things up a bit. We don't want you to say clerk or pupillage. We have practice managers and traineeships."* Okey dokey! Established in May 2000, Matrix is a self-professed *"progressive"* set. It made a huge splash at its inception and has since grown to 50 members. *Chambers UK* puts it at the top of the human rights tree alongside its main rivals, Doughty Street and Blackstone Chambers. High-profile engagements include acting for detainees at Camp X-Ray in Guantanamo Bay, and advising on the exclusion order on Nation of Islam minister Louis Farrakhan. One of its leading lights, Rabinder Singh QC, led the calls for a judicial inquiry into the legality of war on Iraq. The set also has a distinctly academic bent, and boasts many of the top academic minds in its areas of expertise. Among them, public international law gurus Professor James Crawford SC and Philippe Sands QC. Of course, it is well known that Cherie Booth QC is, as well as being a leading silk, married to someone fairly high up in government.

"New century," "innovate," "value" and *"efficient business organisation"* are not words normally associated with the Bar, but these are the buzzwords at Matrix. This is a stylised, sleek organisation whose offices feel more advertising agency than barristers chambers. You'll find the set in a newly renovated former police station in Gray's Inn, now renamed the Griffin Building. Aside from some fairly impressive security measures, there is little else to remind the visitor that this was once a cop shop. The inside is a cross between a trendy Clapham bar and a fish tank – all iridescent blue, modern art and blond wood floors, followed by striking fuchsia walls in meeting rooms. Less charitable (and possibly envious) commentators have described it as *"like Apollo 13 – no atmosphere!"*

Although best known as a human rights set, Matrix lacks the righteousness of some competitors. Happy to act for both the government and for applicants, it has come under criticism from some quarters for compromising its commitment to human rights. And so we arrive at an important issue. Matrix barristers, we learned, commonly take an academic, rather than a campaigning 'human' interest in human rights issues. We don't intend this to make the set sound overly clinical; it's more a case of fighting a cause on principles rather than naked passion or moral outrage. The set harnesses the brains and resources of academic lawyers, of which it boasts an impressive list as members. One junior told us: *"I can e-mail* [human rights lawyer] *Conor Gearty and he'll send me a list of articles on theory."* This is a set that *"keeps engaged with academic thinking."*

Traineeships are divided into four three-month portions, each of which is spent with a different member of chambers, so allowing you to see different areas of specialism. Most trainees sit with specialists in employment, public law and human rights, although the traineeship committee will try and accommodate preferences. While you are able to work for other members of chambers, it's rare for trainees to do too much for anyone other than their supervisor. Much of the time you'll be involved in legal research and drafting, writing opinions and observing court proceedings. There is nothing to stop you from getting on your feet from the first day of your second six, and trainees often get their first advocacy experience in small employment tribunal matters. The work is intellectually stimulating and conducted in a collegial atmosphere. The hours are a regular 9-6pm, and trainees who are seen in the office past 6.30pm are *"positively kicked out."*

The set receives a huge number of traineeship applications for its two places. From the outset, academic excellence is critical, yet Matrix strives to be inclusive and takes socio-economic background and other factors into consideration. A commitment to, and interest in, the work Matrix handles is vital; however, as one pupil told us: *"They're not worried if you haven't been to sub-Saharan Africa to save the world."* On the contrary, a member of the committee noted: *"Not everyone can afford to take a gap year."* In the first interview, conducted with three members, applicants may be asked to discuss a recent case that they find interesting. One year, applicants were asked what they would add to the new Criminal Justice Bill; in another they were asked about the challenges facing the Bar in the years ahead. The second interview involves a written test based on a legal problem, which is then followed by an interview with up to five members. It's a pretty intensive process, and one you can't prepare for, since the problem is deliberately based on an area of which few applicants will have any knowledge. One member of the traineeship committee told us: *"We're attracted to applicants with creative minds who think strategically...those with a lively intellect who are articulate."*

Trainees are formally assessed throughout the 12 months and, by the end of their first nine, will have completed two written and two oral assessments. There is no quota for membership, and the official policy is vague, but Matrix deliberately keeps its trainee numbers low. The set imposes a *"threshold of excellence"* and those who reach this threshold will be offered membership. For those lucky enough to become junior members, the hours are intensive; however, there is no *"culture of perpetual grind."* Barristers feel able to tell their practice manager when they're simply too busy to take instructions.

It could be because of this intense work ethic that the Matrix social scene is pleasant, without being full-on. There is a Christmas dinner and last year staff went ice-skating at Marble Arch. And although there are parties to celebrate the arrival or departure of staff, there are no regular Friday night drinks. The offices have a *"chill-out room"* complete with sofas, newspapers, a coffee machine and a float tank (Okay, not really).

Matrix prides itself on its innovation, progressive values, non-hierarchical structure, commitment to quality service and efficient management. It becomes palpably clear that this set runs itself as a business, and business ethics predominate. Those we spoke to were well aware of the set's almost Orwellian reputation (also described as *"snooty, sleek, businesslike and soulless"*), but they were adamant that *"this is absolutely not the case."* Certainly Matrix does seem to have a preoccupation with image and branding, but it feels it has something different to offer clients: a highly academic take on matters that is, at the same time, wrapped up in pragmatism and cool business efficiency. It is this melding of law as a business with law as a discipline that makes Matrix so distinctive. That and the fuchsia walls, of course.

Monckton Chambers

the facts

OLPAS: summer season **Pupillages:** 2x12 months
Applications: 200 **Mini pupillages:** 24-36
First Interview: 32 **Second Interview:** 16
Award: £32,000
Tenancies offered in 2004: 2
Chambers UK rankings: Competition and European law, tax

Monckton Chambers traces its roots back to the 1930s, when it was headed by two-time cabinet minister and valued advisor to Edward VIII, Sir Walter Monkton. After a career as a barrister and all-round good guy (penning the King's abdication speech among other things), Sir W became chairman of

Midland Bank and eventually earned the title of Viscount. In Gray's Inn since the sixties, the set only adopted the Monckton moniker in 1998. But more of that later.

The most important thing to understand about Monckton is its practice profile: this is a go-to set for European law issues, competition and VAT. *Chambers UK* speaks of the intellectual firepower of members, and only one other set – at best, two – competes at this level. The next most important thing to know is that a lot of work comes from government departments, an aspect of chambers' business that dates from the mid-80s and a QC called Christopher Bellamy who forged good relations with the Treasury Solicitor. All Monckton's juniors now aim to get on one or more of the government's lists of approved counsel. A knock-on effect, according to one member, is that *"it's important for us to remain apolitical."*

Government departments have a different agenda from private sector clients, who are primarily *"concerned with winning and costs."* By contrast, *"the government is more sensitive to doing the right thing"* and *"establishing precedents."* Ultimately, *"if they lose, they can change the law,"* but wherever necessary they want the law on a particular point to be well defined and, of course, decided in their favour. No barrister would admit that winning isn't important to them, but at Monckton we also concluded that establishing legal precedent is as important...to some at least.

"We have a reputation for being thorough, detailed and conscientious," a pupilmaster told us, adding: *"What we look for in pupils is attention to detail."* They need it in spades because the work is frequently *"intricate."* He reminded us (not that we needed him to) that there were *"no end of pedants at the Bar,"* yet if you're in the business of making or establishing law, and your client wants *"certainty,"* perhaps a dose of pendantry is healthy. No one actually blushed when they said the word, but almost all our sources at Monckton referred to the set as having a *"cerebral"* quality. *"It's an intellectually challenging place,"* one of

the two pupils conceded. The other nodded in agreement. We rather liked the fact that they could sit together without eyes like daggers – competitive sensitivities were absent between them...even though the July tenancy decision was just weeks away. Each felt confident that chambers hadn't recruited two pupils with the deliberate intention of offering just one tenancy. And they were right to be confident as both now have tenancy.

Monckton's pupillage isn't advocacy-heavy, yet we mustn't give the impression you'll never go to court. One of the pupils told us about a number of one-day judicial review hearings he'd been taken along to and was soon to sit in on a 15-day trial. Nonetheless, advisory work and legal research define the year, with a typical instruction being to advise on how the competition authorities would view a merger of two companies. Over the year, you'll sit with four different PMs and work for many other members of chambers. Reflecting on her pupillage, the newest tenant said: *"I wasn't just a research assistant; I was drafting opinions and pleadings...even though they were crawled over by my pupilmaster or whoever I worked for."* In the second six, you can push for some of your own cases, maybe acting for the VAT Man on an appeal from someone who's been caught with bootleg alcohol.

The real drama is to be found in the set's big competition cases. The replica football kit case is a great example. Its complexity is demonstrated by the multitude of parties in the action brought by the OFT against Manchester Utd, the FA and several retailers, which it claimed had entered into a price-fixing arrangement. In all, some seven members of chambers acted for four different parties, so underscoring the set's standing in competition law while at the same time highlighting the need to maintain Chinese walls between members. With fines of £18.6 million at stake, it was no surprise that the OFT's decision was referred to the Competition Appeals Tribunal (CAT), so setting in motion its first ever witness trial. Both of the 2003/4 pupils sat with one of the key barristers on the case. The first met witnesses, read their statements and attended strategic meetings with the OFT. After three months, he went to sit with a different PM and the other pupil took his place. The temperature of the case rose as it progressed towards trial, and our second pupil found himself tackling parts of the first draft of the cross-examination script and then attending the trial itself. Not wanting to miss out, the first pupil also attended parts of the trial.

We uncovered no painful or archaic traditions to make their lives a misery, and established that they don't suffer the embarrassment of being called Mr or Miss by the clerks, who reserve such formality for the most senior members. We were assured that Monckton was a *"democratic set; at chambers meetings, juniors' voices are listened to. There's not a couple of autocrats at the top saying like it or lump it."* Many of the juniors choose to dress casually when not seeing clients or going to court; one chap was in cropped combats and sandals when we met him. After work on Thursdays or Fridays, people slip into the local pub and there's even a social programme of sorts, although it can probably be best described as ad hoc.

If you make it to a pupillage interview, the panel won't be so interested in digging around in your CV; instead it will engage in some *"rigorous questioning"* on a problem question. It looks for *"academically confident people who can express themselves in a coherent manner...we want to see if the points made are sensible and that someone can hold their own."* Interestingly, we heard: *"We're not keen on overly pushy pupils."* Academic excellence (commonly a First, though not necessarily an Oxbridge degree) is paramount, yet in only a minority of cases do pupils fly through academia on autopilot and straight into practice. One of the current crop had spent a year at the Law Commission; the other had worked at the Lord Chancellor's Department. The previous year's pupil qualified at Freshfields as a competition solicitor and worked as a référendaire at the ECJ. Two new tenants joined the set in the summer of 2004 – one had been the legal secretary to the president of the Competition Appeals Tribunal and the other a référendaire at the ECJ. This sort of thing impresses the clients.

Monckton has been very strategic: back in the late 90s it took on its first practice manager and has since developed roles for PR and business development managers. It also coined the distinctive Monckton name. Since embracing professional managers, members' earnings have headed skywards.

In the autumn of 2004 chambers settled into extra premises at Nos. 1 and 2 Raymond Buildings, which just like the base at No 4 have sash windows that bring the gardens of Gray's Inn right into chambers. On the day we visited Monckton, the temperature soared to 32°C. Sunbathers packed the lawns, doubtless many of them observing that day's astronomical phenomenon – a transit of Venus. Who knows, in 2012 when Venus next transits the sun, you might be climbing through the sash window of your own room and onto the lawns. If so, don't forget your special glasses.

Four New Square

the facts
OLPAS: no Pupillages: 3x12 months
Applications: 300 **Mini pupillages:** 40 assessed
Interview: 20
Award: £32,500 (up to a £11,000 advanced for BVC)
Tenancies offered in 2004: 2
Chambers UK Rankings: Construction, financial services, product liability, professional negligence

In 1999, professional negligence supremo Four New Square upped sticks from the Temple and moved to the heart of Chancery territory – Lincoln's Inn. Its intention was simply to move into better, roomier accommodation, but it ended up developing a hitherto unexplored area of practice. Though the set originally drifted into Chancery work, it has given legs to the drift by recruiting a few Chancery practitioners. *"Our location has definitely influenced our work* profile," we were told. However, professional indemnity cases of all types (though predominantly solicitor-related) still account for 60% of business.

Professional indemnity instructions come from litigation stalwarts such as Barlow Lyde & Gilbert, Kennedys and Reynolds Porter Chamberlain, leading provincial and national firms and the in-house legal teams of large insurers such as Zurich and St Paul. Beyond this, chambers holds its own in construction, general insurance and reinsurance, general commercial litigation and product liability. In the latter area, members have been involved in litigation concerning vCJD, tobacco, BSE, MMR and numerous pharmaceutical products. Additionally, a few barristers pursue more specialist practices, including financial services and clinical negligence.

Each pupil has three supervisors: the first until Christmas, the second until Easter and the third with a looser grasp on their time in the second six. "*People expect anyone who does pupillage here to have done professional indemnity,*" though because all supervisors do a range of other work, pupils' experiences are reasonably broad. We also learned that "*pupillage will be studded with unique experiences*" whenever the opportunity arises. We had to chuckle when someone said: "*Pupillage can be a bit like running for office for a year,*" but at least at Four New Square you don't have to shake the hands and kiss the babies of every member of chambers. Or try and work for them all. As one supervisor said: "*It's not helpful for silks to come along and poach pupils.*"

Pupils tend to stick close to their supervisors, sharing their rooms and shadowing their practices. Said one supervisor: "*The pupil will do a piece of written work, e-mail it to me and then we'll go through it together.*" It's a time for absorbing necessary skills and techniques, for learning the law and developing a good manner with solicitors and other members of chambers. "*Getting the law right is the base starting point; commercial nous grows over time.*" The year is spent drafting skeleton arguments and pleadings, and preparing notes on obscure points of law; basically feeling "*pretty involved*" and even "*jointly responsible for what is going on.*"

After three months you'll receive an informal appraisal and after six a full-on review with the chair of the pupillage committee, who'll have collected written reports from your supervisors. Also marked on the calendar are a week's marshalling in the High Court and three moots, the last of which takes place in the High Court in front of former member of chambers Mr Justice Jackson. With anything up to three-quarters of chambers coming along to watch you perform, it's acknowledged to be "*a pretty bizarre form of torture.*" We wondered if the moots added to a sense of competition between pupils, but one of them assured us that while these tests were "*emotional,*" "*there have been no bad tempered or difficult periods between us.*"

Pupils are allowed to earn in the second six, and usually get to court once or twice a week on something pretty simple, such as an application to set aside a judgment in default, a debt claim or a small RTA hearing. The progression into the first year of tenancy appears seamless. "*Clerks will deliberately seek out small work for pupils and juniors,*" including employment cases, which are excellent for cross-examination experience. In the early days as a junior you'll encounter contract claims, building disputes ("*dodgy double glazing, for example*"), PI and mortgage possessions amongst other things. Your own prof neg cases will be "*phased in*" – at first just arguments about quantum rather than liability, and drafting pleadings. In this field, cases rarely get as far as trial.

There's no need to worry about striking out on your own straight away, because for the first three years you'll have your own mentor. They will be someone you've chosen yourself, not the loser in a game of buggins' turn. Juniors also undertake placements with solicitors to see how mammoth litigation matters are managed and experience "*life inside a solicitors firm.*"

At the interface between solicitor and barrister is the clerk, and an examination of a set's clerking style and function informs on so much. Four New Square operates a team clerking system, with each clerk having their own PA. You only have to meet the senior clerk for a few minutes to realise that claims of *"sympathetic clerking"* don't ring hollow. *"It's all about understanding what a barrister wants from his or her life,"* she told us, *"and being honest about someone's suitability and availability."* If all this makes life in chambers sound easy, take note: after speaking to several people, we were left in no doubt that they work extraordinarily hard.

As well as being hardworking, chambers is run with determined efficiency. *"The head of chambers is quite strong and decisive,"* we heard. And unusually for a barrister, *"he's a fantastic businessman."* We're not suggesting he's managing chambers – there are staff for that – but having a clued-up head gives the right lead. The set as a whole is *"conscious of the importance of marketing and having a brand."* Accordingly, it is not averse to a spot of judicious socialising with solicitors and insurers, nor organising lectures and seminars for them. As a pupil put it: *"You get a sense of a growing chambers in terms of reputation and standards."*

Set against a backdrop of good relations all round, where *"there's no big divide"* between members and staff, twice each year there are big parties. At Christmas it's a champagne reception, and in the summer a family day with a magician, bouncy castle and face painting (presumably for the kids, though we can't be certain). A couple of members are really into horse racing and have invested in a runner called Wasted Costs, which sports Sunderland FC colours. Several other members have also been dragooned into the venture; *"some have just a 2% stake...probably just a nostril!"* On the subject of horses we prised a bit more information from a pupil, who told us one of her PM's was an amateur jockey. Unfortunately, as a tall man, he has to keep his weight to a minimum: *"I always felt very guilty eating my lunch in front of him."* She had no lunchtime dilemmas with a different PM though; he bought her a sandwich every day. Except on the days he and other PMs took all three pupils out to lunch.

If Four New Square interests you, you must apply for a week-long assessed mini pupillage. Do well and you'll be invited to a formal pupillage interview at a later date, which amounts to a short advocacy exercise (*"no more than five minutes"*) and a discussion about what you did in your mini. The chair of the pupillage committee told us: *"I want to see if they can express themselves confidently and clearly,"* though he warns: *"there's no point in acting like an old-fashioned barrister."* To understand the full significance of this statement you probably need to understand that here a great deal of weight is placed on commercial and strategic advice – *"getting the law right is just stage one, then it's a case of developing a focus on what to do next and why."* In this set, the emphasis is *"half court work and half strategic advice."* It sounds as if most pupils grasp this principle, as usually two out of three get tenancy each year, and *"there's no shilly-shallying around about the decision, it's all very fair."*

You can form a fair impression of Four New Square within moments of walking into its light and spacious reception. Imagine Heals does Georgian in a subtle, contemporary, mushroomy kind of way, then add an infectiously chirpy receptionist who's juggling three phones while charming a steady stream of clients. It looks effortless, though we doubt it is.

Old Square Chambers

the facts

OLPAS: summer season Pupillages: 2x12 months
Applications: c100 Mini pupillages: available
Interview: 15-20
Award: £28,000
Tenancies offered in 2004: 1
Chambers UK rankings: Employment, personal injury

When we pitched up at Old Square Chambers and saw our contact decked out in jeans and sweater, it became immediately clear that hidebound conservatism is inimical to this set. Its members were unanimous that *"we are very far from a traditional set of chambers,"* stressing *"we're informal, unpretentious, very focused, very driven."* Chambers never allows the dust to settle: not long in its current, utterly business-like digs, it is hoping to move again to larger premises that will allow further expansion. The set also has 11 tenants in a second base in Bristol, located in *"breezy premises, very close to solicitors."* All in all, this is a mobile set, ready and willing to adapt to changing times and proud of its recently attained Legal Services Commission Quality Mark, which demands *"high standards in everything from equal opportunities to complaints procedures."*

Back in the late 70s, chambers took a long hard look at itself and jettisoned its crime practitioners, leaving a common law practice that became defined by its claimant PI, applicant employment work and strong trade union links. More recently it has *"achieved a balance between applicant and respondent work,"* whilst also developing environmental, product liability, clinical negligence and public enquiries expertise. While holding onto relationships with unions, the set now also receives instructions from the in-house legal teams of Ford and Rover, and solicitors firms from Lovells to Farrer & Co. We were unsurprised to hear how *"some departments run the way a modern business should, and overall we are run how a modern set should be run."* Nevertheless, whilst *"there's a strong idea of who we are as a corporate entity,"* clerks and tenants alike stressed, *"people are individuals, there are blends of interests, tastes, desires and ambitions."*

In terms of work, individuals can control the composition of their practice; we even heard of a pupil who asked for, and got, only employment matters. In terms of the set's composition, there's a good gender balance and a refreshing diversity that can only have resulted from an open recruitment process. When one senior on the pupillage committee told us: "We *don't recruit people in our mould,"* it clearly wasn't hot air – members past lives include accountancy, academia and trade union work. However, would-be pupils would be well advised to show *"a demonstrable interest in our specialist work."* Pupillage interviews mean 30-35 minutes in front of a slender three-person panel because *"we like to let the person relax into the process."* A verbal reasoning section assesses *"potential as an advocate,"* but the emphasis is on a candidate's ability to justify his or her thoughts; *"it often doesn't matter if the answer itself is wrong as long as there's a clear line of thought."*

Pupils can expect a supportive 12 months at Old Square, and both they and their supervisors happily agreed that *"it's not a year-long interview."* The set encourages all eligible members to become accredited as supervisors, and with pupils changing supervisor four times over the year, every last one is required. Spending three months per supervisor, pupils gain exposure to different aspects of practice. Said one: *"Of my two employment supervisors, one did discrimination and the other commercial employment."* The system aims to *"cater to peoples' interests,"* but also allows the open-minded pupil *"a broad range of work."*

Whilst everyone else is free to dress as they choose, pupils wear suits at all times in case of unexpected client contact. In the first six, there's a steady stream of calls from court requiring research, skeleton arguments and advices to be drafted. Pupils said: *"The good thing is that your work actually gets used."* And they didn't feel as if they were in last chance saloon over getting things right: *"You're always given development points, given a chance to improve."* This is not least down to the efforts of the pupil supervisors, who offer *"guidance, feedback and mentoring, identifying people the pupil needs to work for who haven't seen the pupil's work."*

Second-six pupils are restricted to two or three court attendances per week to ensure they keep on top of things. Supervisors liaise with clerks to make sure their charges don't get overloaded; after all, *"it could affect people's impressions if work starts coming late."*

The past year's pupil traditionally hands over his

or her phone number, creating the safety net of "*someone to phone and ask the idiot questions.*" The large volume of small PI and employment work makes for "*good knockabout advocacy experience*" at tribunals and county courts, contrasting with "*coming back and working on much more cerebral issues.*" Whether it's unfairly dismissed celebrities or recently fired joe bloggs, slip-and-trip PI claimants or work for trade unions or local authorities, "*an ability to relate to people and express yourself clearly*" is important.

The clerks emphasised "*the deluge of good-quality work for pupils,*" mentioning particularly that applicant trade union PI or employment work could offer excellent experiences "*because they don't want to pay full whack for a top-end barrister.*" It sounds good on paper, but be sure you're ready for the reality. Said one pupil: "*I turned up at tribunal and was facing a silk – what a nightmare!*" The set also sends pupils along to observe specialist cases when they arise. Having recently included product liability cases for Sainsbury's and L'Oreal, and public inquiries such as the Ladbroke Grove Rail Crash and a major organ-retention scandal, the attraction for pupils is obvious.

When it does come to tenancy, the set is thorough in its decision making. No gut instincts here! The number of vacancies is decided in April, each of the pupils then makes a formal application and goes through an interview process in June that incorporates a written appraisal and an advocacy test. The panel also takes into consideration feedback from members above seven to eight years' call before recommending its findings to the entire set. At least one person each year is given tenancy, and the early decision in June gives those not selected the chance to look elsewhere.

Pupils generally work a reasonable 9am-6.30pm and "*one weekend in four,*" but things rapidly get busier upon gaining tenancy. For all its non-traditional feel, this is a "*committed and hard-working*" set. Nevertheless we found plenty of evidence to suggest a convivial atmosphere. First names are used throughout and the notion of afternoon tea was scoffed at – "*we just don't have it!*" Summer and Christmas drinks parties are "*very relaxed and normally at someone's house,*" and pupils are welcomed along to regular drinks with juniors at various Gray's Inn locals. It is definitely not an all-encompassing social scene, but mature working and personal friendships are all part of chambers' balanced environment. One member told us: "*We're very supportive of each other; I'll go along to a colleague's book launch even though there's nothing in it for me,*" whilst another reflected: "*I've got a lot of friends in chambers.*"

These last two comments sum up Old Square Chambers well – balanced, modern and businesslike with a sense of community.

Pump Court Tax Chambers

the facts

OLPAS: summer season **Pupillages:** 3x6 months
Applications: Not stated **Mini pupillages:** unlimited
Interview: Not stated
Award: £20,000
Tenancies offered in 2004: None
Chambers UK rankings: Tax

As Benjamin Franklin said: "In this world nothing is certain but death and taxes." There can be no place where the latter is more certain than at Pump Court Tax Chambers. As the set's senior clerk told us: "*We cover every area of tax going.*" When instructions stray into insurance or company law, "*we don't touch them;*" on trusts matters, however, Pump Court is in direct competition with Chancery sets. It was interesting for us to hear that "*because everyone here does the same thing there is a sense of collective identity.*"

This is a small, tight-knit, QC-heavy set. It is in the fairly unique position of receiving the lion's share of its work from accountants rather than solicitors; indeed some of its members started life as accountants themselves. At least 60% of business comes from the big four and smaller accountancy firms, or direct from industry from companies such as Diageo. According to one member, with such professionals *"you can be more interactive, have closer relationships...less formal ones even. In that sense the barrister – professional client relationship breaks down and you can just talk to them as a person and build up a rapport."* The government, too, seeks advice from Pump Court, and chambers currently provides the First Chancery Junior to the Inland Revenue as well as barristers on the B and C panels.

As for the solicitors firms that instruct the set, these range from the giants of the magic circle to one-man bands in the provinces. With the exception perhaps of the smallest law firms, all who instruct are themselves well versed in tax law. It follows then that what they expect from a barrister is a highly sophisticated service – not something that can be developed with ease or speed, and certainly not in a single year. Pupils at Pump Court take no paid work and new junior tenants are embargoed for a year from taking their own instructions. As a pupilmaster put it: *"You're in a vicious circle at the start of practice. The law is very complicated and/or there's a huge amount of money involved. The client wants a safe pair of tried-and-tested hands...so how do you get onto the bottom rung of the ladder?"* The answer is by devilling for more senior members. A baby junior admitted the system left them feeling *"shielded,"* but that compensation lay in the fact that *"you learn so much more by devilling for silks and senior juniors."* Certainly, one must be patient because there's no getting around the fact that *"tax law has a longer incubation period."* At least juniors pay no chambers rent until their income reaches £75,000 pa. At senior level, however, and particularly on the corporate tax side, the per-head income is way above the average in commercial sets.

It sounds to us as if tax lawyers play a lifelong game of chess against the Chancellor of the Exchequer. *"Every year the finance bill cuts off a piece of our work and we have to look for other sources."* Luckily, finance bills have a habit of changing tax regimes and opening and closing loopholes. The other thing that strikes you when you talk to a tax lawyer is that their work is anything but abstract. *"We're not working in a vacuum,"* explained one; *"we're advising on the tax consequences of family trusts or big tax avoidance schemes."* For example, members of chambers recently advised Debenhams and other retailers on VAT liability on credit card payments.

Alas, *"tax is not perceived as sexy"* and Pump Court receives surprisingly few pupillage applications. A PM analysed the problem for us, saying: *"There's a perception that tax is all about numbers, and for the majority of students it's an unknown quantity. Compare it with shipping, which is applied tort and contract – charter parties and ships crashing into each other – students will be applying existing knowledge. Most people haven't studied tax as an option, but that doesn't matter to us."* A young junior agreed: *"They told me not to worry about having no prior knowledge."* Nevertheless, she added: *"It's been a steep learning curve...reading everything and trying to understand it. Thankfully pupilmasters gave me enough guidance."*

Light on facts and evidence, heavy on law and its interpretation – that's how the work of a tax lawyer looks to us. *"Sometimes instructions come in and they're just a page long: here's the facts now how does this piece of legislation apply? We are asked to give statutory interpretation; our work amounts to very pure legal problem solving."* This couldn't be more different from the work on offer in commercial sets where instructions can sometimes be accompanied by rooms full of boxes of evidence. As one barrister put it: *"The nice thing about tax is that you are arguing about law not fact."*

What does it take to be a tax lawyer? Attention to detail and the ability to think around a problem. Sloppiness is disastrous, but pupillage should help you to tie down your thinking. *"It's all very well to vaguely feel what the answer is, but you have to know exactly how, step by step, you get to that answer."* As one pupil so charmingly put it: *"There is no woolly half ground in tax opinion."*

Another thing you should appreciate is that in tax practice there is far less advocacy, and if a matter litigates then it does so at a very high level. Yet, "*if there were no advocacy at all, ever, there would be no point in being a barrister.*" In the early years, advocacy comes in the shape of VAT tribunals, either before the Special Commissioners (legislative interpretation) or the General Commissioners (cases turning on facts). You might end up in tribunal because Customs alleges a restaurateur hasn't paid his VAT, or in a county court hearing where Customs is enforcing a payment due from a building company. But remember: the majority of your career will be spent in chambers, albeit that Pump Court's full programme of seminars for clients could give you a taste for public speaking!

Pupils are assigned to several PMs, the first for three months, the others for two months each. This gives them as much exposure as possible to different work and "*ensures no single person is playing God in relation to someone's career...it safeguards against a clash in personalities.*" The same group of PMs see the work of each pupil, and the pupils each undertake the same two pieces of assessed work, submitting it anonymously. These assignments are copied to every member of chambers and play a significant role in the tenancy decision, which is made in July. Reports from PMs and a general sense of how the pupil interacts with other members are also considered. Here, as in many sets, if things are not going well in your first six, you'll be advised to cut and run to another area of practice for your second.

Pupils sit together (presently in the library) rather than with their PMs, but this is in no way due to any unwillingness to include them in chambers life. The presumption, rarely rebutted, is that if something's going on pupils are invited – seminars, lunches (not always in hall as "*hall is a bit stuffy and full of barristers*"), drinks and a recent concert in Middle Temple church followed by a garden party. Pump Court's own version of chambers tea is morning coffee at 11am, and for pupils it's the perfect opportunity to find out who's who. They aren't expected to chip in with conversation, and frankly they'd be unable to as it is limited to esoteric tax points. We asked how uncomfortable this daily ritual could be for a pupil and were told: "*You can't be your normal loud self, but I don't dislike it...yesterday KP was hilarious!*" Pupils always remove the trolley at the end of the break; according to one of them it provides a reason to stay without worrying about when is the polite time to leave. Aside from the obvious comedy value of the tradition, it does sound a bit antiquated; indeed from where we sat in the trad-as-they-come premises we sensed it could be easy to stereotype Pump Court as old school. Yet all those we spoke to assured us: "*There's no stiffness about the place.*" And for the antidote to the leather-bound, wood-panelled Bedford Row building, all you need do is slip through the small courtyard to the rear and into a modern and stylish annexe.

Clearly it takes a particular kind of person to suit tax law, yet we left Pump Court wondering if too many students are writing off the idea before giving it sufficient thought. A mini pupillage is definitely the way forward.

4 Pump Court Chambers

the facts

OLPAS: No **Pupillages:** 4x12 months
Applications: 200 **Mini pupillages:** 65
Interview: 20
Award: £35,000 (part can be advanced for BVC)
Tenancies offered in 2004: 1
Chambers UK rankings: Construction, information technology, insurance, professional negligence

Can a leopard change its spots? It seems so. If we'd written about 4 Pump Court 15 years ago, you'd now be reading a feature on criminal and family practice. It's remarkable how complete the change in this set's activities has been; practice now rests on four sturdy pillars: construction, insurance, technology and professional negligence. More than this, 4 Pump Court has pushed its way to the top of the rankings for technology cases, and many of the set's dozen QCs sit as deputy judges in the High Court or in the Technology and Construction Court. Yet chambers hasn't forgotten its roots; junior members learn their trade on humble RTAs and sale of goods cases, fully aware that their seniors had also cut teeth in the county and magistrates' courts. No one here is too proud to talk of such matters; indeed they take pride in a strong legacy of advocacy.

It can be no coincidence that changes in the set's orientation have occurred under the watch of the current chambers director, who as well as having provided continuity for the last 14 years used to be a partner in a law firm. It is beyond doubt that her experiences on the other side of the professional fence have ensured that the benefits of modern commercial management came to this set earlier than most. Having established a new direction, we heard how *"aggressive, but low-key, marketing has paid dividends – we're not sitting on our laurels."*

Pupillage is equally well managed, though the system deliberately avoids the clinical objectivity to be found at certain other sets. The chairman of the pupillage committee sat on the Bar Council's pupillage review panel, and chambers has been funding its pupils since the 1980s. Stressing that the set wishes to grow from the bottom up and by recruiting tenants from amongst it own pupils, several people reminded us that in 2003 three of the four pupils gained tenancy. The harvest is not always so plentiful, but each year the set does welcome four pupils, who follow a carefully planned routine that is designed to offer breadth and practical experience.

The first six is split into two equal parts, with the pupil sitting with two pupilmasters who each specialise in one or other of the four main pillars of practice. Bearing in mind that the PMs will be instructed on reasonably complex cases, time with them is largely chambers based. That said, if a barrister is embarking on a very large case, they will not be allocated a pupil until they are once again able to supply an interesting mix of smaller matters. We spoke with one PM about how she involved her pupil in construction matters. *"If I have a case management conference,"* she said, *"I make them write the skeleton argument beforehand. Or they'll do the notes for a conference with a client, advices and pleadings if they are not too big and legal research for a break."* If you're thinking of applying here, don't underestimate the importance of written work, because these days *"there is much more emphasis on paper advocacy...skeletons are so important, and therefore it is also so important that pupils can write."* Each of chambers' four pillars represents a different world, but in construction, as in technology and insurance work, the barrister must effectively be two experts in one. Knowing the law is not enough; one has to also become embedded in the industry sector, interact easily and confidently with expert witnesses, specialist solicitors and their lay clients. As many of the cases involve mountains of technical information and evidence, pupils must have an appetite for detail.

Pupils are set a series of four exercises (two written, two advocacy) to assess how they are developing and to prime them for a much more hands-on second six. *"We aim to give them feedback within a week of each exercise...positive and negative."* *"Of course you go in nervous to the pit of your stomach,"* one baby junior recalled the experience, adding that in his experience pupils had not become overly competitive with each other, preferring instead to have *"preliminary discussions to chat about points of law."*

Given the set's commitment to continual feedback, pupils shouldn't be shocked by sudden bad news: *"I can't remember anyone leaving us at the six-month stage,"* the pupillage committee chair told us. A brief period of shadowing the most junior members of chambers marks the halfway stage and allows pupils to see first-hand what their second, practising six will hold. Pupils have their own clerks for the second-six and a single PM acts more as a guardian than a tutor. Soon enough they are dealing with a flurry of small instructions, usually county court PI matters such as one-day fast track trials or infant settlements. Because *"your work is entirely dependent on the clerks,"* it's easy to see the importance of the rule that insists the first thing pupils must do every day is pop into the clerks' room to say good morning and have a chat. It's patently clear that *"they are keen to get us into court at the junior end."* As for what it takes to cope, *"it requires personal responsibility and confidence, because you are the one who has to talk to the solicitors – people who have been doing their job for years – and you have to give them a steer as to where you think the case is going."*

The tenancy decision is made by a committee, not the entire set; indeed, as one silk told us: *"I can't remember the last time we had a full meeting of all members."* New tenants always share a room with someone slightly more experienced, but also find any number of people are willing to sit down and talk them through things. *"If I have a few bankruptcy hearings,"* one baby junior said, *"I go and see the king of bankruptcy. People here have a sense of duty...obligation to help others in chambers."*

There's ample opportunity to chat on a Friday night over drinks in the waiting room (unfussy, clean lines, TV usually on). Sometimes after work, a few people will slip into The Devereux or Daly's, and because several members have caught the sailing bug, there's always a voyage or regatta to plan. Look at the set's website and you'll see the yacht it sponsors. We'll weigh anchor on this point for a moment because it says much about chambers. Just as on a boat you don't wave cheerily as one of your fellow crew members tumbles overboard, at 4 Pump Court you don't allow your colleagues to drown...or, worse still, push their head underwater as you struggle to rise above the waves.

Seeking permission to come aboard? Here's the drill. References are sought and considered for every applicant. About 10% are called for a thorough but not unpleasant interview at which they tackle a problem and are expected to chat intelligently on a current legal topic. No prior construction, technology or insurance industry experience is necessary and non-law graduates fare equally well. In truth, there's nothing especially unique about the ideal candidate for chambers; 4 Pump Court wants exactly the same type of pupil as the other good quality commercial sets. One's background seems unimportant so long as it is replete with academic success, and one's personality need not conform to a chambers mould, though we'd suggest that chambers wants to perpetuate the good conduct and care it has always shown towards the Bar, courts and clients alike.

You can't help but leave 4 Pump Court with the idea that it is a happy ship, and seeing as we've already sunk to the use of clichés, we might as well add that the decks are nicely scrubbed, the crew financially healthy and the navigators running a wise course.

Quadrant Chambers

the facts
OLPAS: No **Pupillages:** 4x12 months
Applications: 120 **Mini pupillages:** available
First Interview: 20 **Second Interview:** 10
Award: £30,000 (£4,000 can be advanced for BVC)
Tenancies offered in 2004: 1
Chambers UK rankings: Aviation, international arbitration, shipping, travel

Known as 4 Essex Court until 2004, Quadrant Chambers has moved into what is undoubtedly the most spectacular accommodation known to the Bar. Four Grade II listed buildings on Fleet Street opposite the Royal Courts of Justice and backing onto the Temple have been drawn together and linked by a modern atrium. To secure the move, Quadrant had to compete with other sets and convince the landlord, Middle Temple, of its good prospects. The new address looks likely to boost and broaden the set's profile, if only because it contains an extensive suite of fully kitted-out meeting rooms suitable for ADR proceedings or as a base for out-of-town solicitors with business in the RCJ or the Commercial Court. An abundance of space will allow Quadrant to grow at a self-dictated pace, though for now members are happy to rattle around their new home.

As befits a set with roots in shipping and insurance, two of the four component buildings started life as 17th-century coffee houses. In time they developed grand Georgian dining rooms, frequented by judges, solicitors and barristers. As we craned our necks up towards the ornate ceiling in Quadrant's library, we imagined conversations between long-dead counsel rolling around the room in a rich fog of coffee fumes and pipe tobacco smoke. Yet what is most striking about chambers' new home is that it juxtaposes perfectly the trappings of past success and the symbols of a bright future.

Away from its adopted bricks-and-mortar history, Quadrant does have a past of its own. No.s 1-4 Essex Court had long housed shipping barristers, and at No.2, the set's founder Barry Sheen QC developed a wet shipping practice after quitting the navy at the end of WWII. In 1978 he was appointed as a judge in the Admiralty Court, so starting a tradition of sending senior QCs to the Admiralty Bench. He was followed by Sir Anthony Clarke QC (now in the Court of Appeal) and Sir David Steel QC, who between them moved chambers into the thick of the insurance world via Lloyd's of London. Traditionally, chambers' business has centred on international trade and shipping claims, pretty much all of which are insurance-related; however, in the late 90s it acquired new members from niche aviation law set 5 Bell Yard. As well as developing this field, Quadrant has also been encouraging more general commercial instructions.

The house style is not overly academic or abstract; it's more of a *"sleeves-rolled-up approach."* *"We're known for our integrity,"* one barrister remarked, *"and for playing with a straight bat."* The aim is simply to give *"concise and helpful assistance to the client,"* using a *"Commercial Court style...there's no room for grandstanding at all."* For what it's worth, after visiting the set we concluded that these comments were equally applicable to pupillage and *"the pups,"* as the chambers director so endearingly called them. Much of chambers' work turns on the construction of contract terms and statutes. But this is only part of the equation: a barrister here must also have the knack of *"untangling the factual issues in a case"* as well as *"the ability to wrestle with jurisprudential issues."*

As an acknowledgement that they may not have studied shipping or insurance law in any detail, new pups undergo a 12-part induction. Then, over the course of the year, they sit with four pupilmasters (the term 'supervisor' drifts in and out of Quadrantspeak), each of whom produces a written report on the pupil, who can in turn comment on its content. A moot in the second three months will usually involve a fairly short summary judgment application based on a real set of papers. The assessment regime is an open one and almost all pupils sail through the six-month break period to complete a full year's training. To stand a chance in the July tenancy decision, they must demonstrate that *"on picking up a set of papers, they can confidently and persuasively argue a point of view,"* even if their PM, playing devil's advocate, chooses to see things differently.

Nothing about Quadrant led us to conclude that pupillage was a particularly unpleasant process. Typically a 9am – 6.30pm routine, the demands of the working day didn't strike us as overly rigorous either. As one pupil quipped: *"They're trying to train you up not kill you!"* During the second six, pupils are allowed to do pieces of work for other members of chambers, though it is not policy to provide them with paid work. *"We don't view them as unpaid devils, but pupillage is all about educating and training the pupil, and it takes a full 12 months to get them fully up to speed."* Chambers has a large pool of potential supervisors to call upon, the more experienced of whom will be assigned to the pupils who need the most help. The basic idea is that pupils see at least two distinct areas of practice, so no one drowns in a sea of shipping cases.

Always remember that here, as in any other commercial set, most of your time will be spent on paperwork. "*It's not the sort of practice for someone who doesn't like looking at things in the library*," someone said. "*You've got to like black-letter law...it's technical, intricate and detailed.*" A young junior estimated 75% of her time was spent in chambers, much of it drafting pleadings for disputes over charter parties and bills of lading – good old-fashioned spats over cargo damaged on board ships or consignments of rotten grain. To boost her time in court, she had also been instructed on banking matters and consumer credit cases. "*It's all good court experience!*" she told us.

Towards the end of pupillage and in the early part of tenancy, "*you've got to be exceptionally organised because you'll be working for a lot of people.*" You have to be sensible about what you take on and perhaps also take guidance from the real professionals in chambers – the practice managers. Musing on this, a young junior said: "*You have to have a very personal relationship with your practice manager. For example, they've got to know what's going on at home...it's not that they pry, but it's useful for them to know if you are having a terrible time.*" In the first couple of years juniors handle a broad range of commercial work and only then see where their practice is going and what they most enjoy. If at any time they need a few words of wisdom, their 'Godfather' (usually a senior junior) is the first port of call for pastoral care. "*Even when they're really busy, they have to help you.*"

If you make it to the two-stage pupillage interview, you'll find that much the same will be demanded of you as in any other commercial set. However, it is worth bearing in mind all that we have said about chambers' style of advocacy and the value it places on common sense.

The social scene is characterised by close circles of friends, and in summer months the pavement opposite Daly's wine bar ("*which does very well out of us!*") is positively staked out. Pupils, barristers and staff all attend a monthly chambers lunch, which pupils say is great for getting to know people. "*We all rub along very well together,*" one PM revealed. He also considered the set to be "*egalitarian and meritocratic...and the seniors are not stuffed shirts, they don't stand on ceremony.*" Something perhaps typified by a refusal to countenance rituals such as chambers tea. Finally coming together in one building has increased the likelihood of bumping into people in the normal course of the day, and reinforced "*a general feeling of corporate care.*" Practice managers, who once suffered in silence in grim rooms in separate buildings, now "*feel more a part of the new corporate image*" – an image in which it is hoped that "*our history will be less obvious*" so "*people will no longer see us as just a shipping set.*"

Chambers has long suffered from "*poor-relation*" syndrome in comparison to the magic circle commercial sets. "*When we had grubby premises, we had a difficult job arguing against that,*" one barrister admitted. Nowadays all you need do is take one look inside 10 Fleet Street to be left in no doubt as to Quadrant's vision of the future.

Queen Elizabeth Building

the facts
OLPAS: summer season **Pupillages:** 3-4x12 months
Applications: 116 **Mini pupillages:** 40
Interview: 25
Award: £25,000 plus earnings
Tenancies offered in 2004: 1
Chambers UK rankings: Family

A long held reputation for excellence makes QEB a target for any crack Bar student looking for a family law pupillage. Unsurpassed on top-end financial cases, QEB barristers act for the wealthy, the famous and the influential.

QEB has just three QCs at present and this is in no small part due to the regularity with which senior members take up judicial appointments. The set has a long tradition in this regard, boasting names like Sir Harry Philimore (Nuremberg War Trials/Lord Justice of Appeal) and Sir Roger Ormerod (CA). The most recent appointment to the High Court is that of Florence Baron QC, the former head of Chambers. She is succeeded in that role by Andrew Moylan QC. White v White and Cowan v Cowan (if you don't know the cases by now, do your homework) were handled here, as were some of the highest profile divorces of the last few years: The Prince of Wales, Geldof v Yates, Jagger v Hall, Picasso and more. The work at the top end is distinctly big-money, frequently stylish and often has an international dimension. Matters pertaining to children figure less frequently. A few members handle PI and clinical or professional negligence, but don't head for QEB if this is what you are really after.

From the windows of QEB you'll survey the Thames and the full extent of Middle Temple Gardens. Once inside, it's hard to believe that chambers' home was built as recently as the 1950s. Its reception area is lined with enormous oil paintings of the venerable and ancient. Bewigged Lord Chancellors of centuries gone by glower down on well turned out and conservatively dressed members. *"There is a traditional side to QEB and they make an effort to maintain that – clients want that."*

QEB may appear traditional, but it is not oppressively so. Meeting junior members (who make up a very high proportion of the set) enables you to pull the buttoned-up public image apart from the set's internal workings. The hard edge to be found in commercial sets is softened by the type of person that is drawn to family work. Yet QEB barristers are no soft touch: our sources described characters ranging from *"the feisty to the gentle and calm; the pragmatic to the academic; and the ambitious to the not so."* One junior explained that while family work was commonly billed as *"children and care cases…and social work,"* this was far from the reality at QEB. *"We're much more commercial in orientation and handle more moneyed clients. A lot of cases involve legal issues not immediately associated with family work: trusts, conflicts of law etc."* Indeed, when your clients are company directors with extensive assets (possibly overseas), you'll need to grapple with company law issues, pension rights and jurisdiction questions. Some juniors do handle divorces for ordinary folk, even those on legal aid, but this is how teeth are cut and not the end goal.

Top-ranked solicitors firms have instructed members of chambers since time immemorial and, provided you put the effort into maintaining these existing relationships, you'll receive quality instructions from them when you're ready. You can expect the best, but the best will be expected of you…after all, QEB has a reputation to protect. While this could feel like a burden, those we spoke to seemed unfazed and, importantly, lacked the arrogance that might come with such a prestigious position. *"That kind of attitude doesn't cut the mustard in Watford County Court,"* one junior remarked, reminding us that even the set's leading silks would have paid their dues in common or garden county court matters. Clerks may cling to the tradition of using surnames when addressing even the lowliest of pupils but, between themselves, barristers at all levels in this small set are supportive of each other. Perhaps the best example of the sense of camaraderie is the daily ritual of gathering for afternoon tea. *"It keeps everybody chatting"* and enables fresh-faced pupils to strike up conversation with senior members and even the odd High Court judge who's popped back for a cuppa.

In the last three or four years, the senior end of chambers has loosened its grip and committees have sprung up for everything – marketing, the library, pupillage selection etc. – yet the decision as to who gets tenancy is taken by the whole set. Officially, talent and hard work are the key to success. Unofficially, we heard: *"Working hard is not enough. There is an element of luck in what work you get, although chambers are fair. Try to build up contacts, but do so appropriately – don't be too forthright."* Aside from a couple of book groups, QEB isn't cliquey. It strives to make pupils feel a part of things, and in addition to their pupil supervisors (three for four months each), they will also have a very junior 'minder' who will frequently take them to court. Pupils are also able to work for any other member of chambers. Our sources reported days averaging 9am-6pm and, depending on the practice of their supervisor, anything from two to four days a week in court: *"Many clients are disappointed that we don't wear wigs!"*

We didn't leave QEB with the impression that you had to have the same background, tastes and attitudes as many of its very wealthy clients. Commitment to the family Bar, intellectual ability, a bit of charm and a knack for communication are what counts. The best advice we can give is to get relevant voluntary experience on your CV and a few mini pupillages. You could also read *Family Law* (monthly) so you know what cases are hot. At interview, remember the financial emphasis of work and show that you have the ability and confidence to interact with everyone from legally aided clients to Appeal Court judges. We'll leave the final word to the barrister who said: *"In your 25 or so years here, you and chambers will be involved in the best work the family Bar has to offer."*

3 Raymond Buildings

the facts

OLPAS: summer season **Pupillages:** 4x12 months
Applications: 300 **Mini pupillages:** Unlimited
First Interview: 80 **Second Interview:** 15
Award: £7,500 + £7,500 guaranteed earnings
Tenancies offered in 2004: Not known
Chambers UK rankings: Crime, criminal fraud, licensing

Three Raymond Buildings is home to many a big name at the criminal Bar, and since its formation in 1926 it has lent its name to many of the most notorious criminal trials and extraditions. Matrix Churchill, Jonathan Aitken, the Carl Bridgewater Appeal and Pinochet's removal to face charges in Chile are just a few of its claims to fame. Think serious blue and white collar crime and then mix it with a complementary medley of extradition, licensing, judicial review and civil actions against the police.

Spread over four floors of a Victorian terrace overlooking Gray's Inn Fields, 3 Raymond Buildings is exactly as you imagine barristers chambers ought to be. We were led in through a sturdy front door, via the lobby and into a tastefully furnished drawing room complete with a regulation-issue French-polished table. Clearly no one had been shopping at Ikea lately. In such elegant surroundings, you expect barristers to be dressed in regulation-issue pin-striped suits. Instead (with the exception of the pupil, who had just got back from a morning in court) the young and up-beat juniors we met were dressed in smart but casual summer wear. Their ensembles, they advised us, were in keeping with chambers' policy of cultivating a *"relaxed, open and friendly atmosphere."*

A 12-month pupillage at 3 Raymond Buildings should give most pupils an introduction to a good range of chambers' work. The year is divided equally into four, with pupils spending time with a quartet of pupilmasters. In the first six, they spend a substantial amount of their time in court observing and assisting their PM. There will also be written work, starting with small pieces of legal research, and moving on to noting briefs and more substantial pieces of legal drafting. As one pupil explained: *"You're really encouraged to go and do written work and research for other members of chambers. It's been a good way to meet members of chambers and make my face known."* Another good way is through the in-house advocacy exercises that take place throughout the year.

In their second six, pupils are up on their feet from the get-go and in court most days, sharpening their advocacy claws on routine magistrates' court work, particularly licensing applications. As the months progress, they don wigs and gowns for pleas in mitigation and short preliminary hearings at the

Crown Court. The briefs for these normally arrive the afternoon before, so it's not unusual to have to stay up late to prepare for the hearing. On the plus side, most of chambers' work is in London, so nasty 10am appointments in Swindon tend to be the exception rather than the rule. It all sounded very pleasant, but what we really wanted was a good horror story and so we got a pupil to tell us about one of his first ever court appearances. "*It was a plea in mitigation prior to sentence,*" he said. "*I had never met my client before, and it was my job to tell the judge what a thoroughly nice guy he was. When he emerged from the cells, I noticed that he was brandishing a tattoo reading 666 on the back of his head.*"

The junior tenants we met were all very positive about their formative years at the criminal Bar. One had been led by QCs on three occasions in the House of Lords, and had also made trips to the Court of Appeal and the High Court. As she explained: "*You soon get an idea of where you want to specialise. I was interested in extradition and public law, and the clerks and other members of chambers were really pleased to help foster me in the right direction. There's a huge support network here.*" Apparently senior members provide more than just a support network; they also operate a round-the-clock ethics Batphone for young lawyers in distress. No matter where you are in the country, you can always count on the silky tones of a QC at the other end of the line, talking you through that professional conduct nightmare. Readers: don't go getting any ideas – the service is for 3 Raymond Buildings' pupils and members only.

Advocacy exercises aside, there is no formal assessment process throughout the year, but pupils do get feedback on all written work, and each member who receives work from a pupil will report back to the tenancy committee. The grand finale takes the form of an advocacy assessment in front of the committee, followed by an 'informal' interview. The entire membership then cast their votes and may, or may not, take up the recommendations of the committee. The unlucky souls who aren't taken on are often allowed to squat or do a third six.

Chambers has a social dimension, which (certainly amongst the juniors) is alive and kicking. The highlight is a monthly drinks party, affectionately known as the Last Thursday Club...for obvious reasons. Pupils are not reduced to serving canapés or doing the washing-up; as one of the pupilmasters was keen to stress: "*There's no real delineation here. If you are a pupil, we treat you as an adult and as a member of chambers.*" Old habits die hard and clerks still refer to their barristers as Mr and Miss, though more junior members are called by their first names "*as long as solicitors and clients aren't around.*"

If you're wondering whether you're cut out for 3 Raymond Buildings, apparently there is no particular 'type' in chambers. These people see themselves as an "*eclectic and diverse bunch of people.*" Certainly the contrast between the top and bottom ends of chambers would seem to suggest that this is the case. The combination of "*landed gentry*" at the more senior end with the bright young things at the junior end must make for some interesting dinner party conversations. As well as a commitment to becoming a criminal advocate, successful pupillage applicants must demonstrate "*an ability to communicate to people on all levels. We're looking for people with charm, intelligence, persuasion and above all, level headedness.*" Applicants' forms are read by two different people, both of them applying uniform criteria. If they disagree on a candidate, the application will be read and vetted by a third. First-round interviews consist of general questions followed by a discussion of a topical issue, usually on a legal theme and notified to the interviewee half an hour beforehand. Make it through to the final 15, and you'll be invited to a 'get to know you' evening to meet other members of chambers in a more informal setting. Sound like hell to you? It did to us, and apparently the first ten minutes of the soirée can often be a "*sheepish, hands in pockets affair.*" But everyone assured us that, in fact, it proves to be a good way of bringing the best out in the young hopefuls. Best get practising with the wine and Twiglets.

Serle Court

the facts

OLPAS: No **Pupillages:** 2x12 months
Applications: 120 **Mini pupillages:** 30
First interview: 20-30 **Second interview:** 5-12
Award: £40,000 (£12,500 can be advanced for BVC)
Tenancies offered in 2004: None
Chambers UK rankings: Banking & finance, commercial chancery, traditional chancery, company, civil fraud, insolvency, partnership, professional negligence, real estate

As we've mentioned before, the distinction between commercial and Chancery work is blurring. Serle Court epitomises that blur. In 2000, a Chancery set from 13 Old Square merged with a smaller commercial set, 1 Hare Court, taking Serle Court as its new home and its new name. The smaller set filled some gaps in the larger one and came dripping with quality silks, including Michael Briggs, the man who is ranked by *Chambers UK* in more practice areas than any other barrister.

Cases come from a wide range of instructing solicitors (Richards Butler, Bird & Bird and Clifford Chance are all good customers), and barristers deal with both commercial clients and individuals from all walks of life, including little old ladies with troublesome wills, and families and ex-lovers reduced to warring over the beneficial ownership of property. However, most of the bigger cases are for commercial clients and the set defines itself by its commercial work. Banking, financial services, company law, partnership law, professional negligence, insolvency and plain old contract disputes; it's all there. There's even a spot of public law and human rights work.

Standing outside in New Square, nothing suggests that Serle Court will offer anything other than the usual maze of barristers, rooms and an old-fashioned waiting area. However, prior to moving in, the set asked award-winning architect Niall McLaughlin to leave his mark on its new home. The result is beautiful. Glass and pale wood are set off by large pieces of modern art painted by the wife of one of the barristers. Serle Court has also used this clean, calm and modern look in its branding. We sensed it was reflective of the attitudes and approach of the barristers. *"High quality, modernity, and being receptive to customers' needs"* are, apparently, the guiding principles. You know that expression about tidy desk, tidy mind? That's the kind of feel Serle Court has.

One pupil explained his reason for choosing the set: *"I wanted interesting, high-powered work in a comfortable environment."* Is it really that simple? Almost. The other important consideration is that, along with a few others, the set offers its pupillages *"far in advance."* There it is again – simple, uncluttered logic. The recruitment process is the usual two-interview affair. Expect both outings to be fairly rigorous.

The set claims to offer *"one of the more progressive pupillages at the Bar,"* and we found supporting evidence. The interaction between members and pupils is particularly easy. Nowhere to be found are the awful school desk-sized folding tables at which some of their peers must sit, as if to reinforce a sense of lowliness. Pupils are invited to chambers parties and out for drinks even before they've finished Bar school, so *"the initial discomfort about starting pupillage is not there."* We were delighted to learn that groups of barristers regularly negotiate the vast open spaces of Chancery Lane to settle in the Gaucho Grill or slip into the nearby Seven Stars for a pint. *"It's a tradition that pupils are not allowed to spend a penny,"* we were told. To avoid any confusion we agreed to change the quote to *"…not allowed to spend any money."*

Another thing the Serle youngsters are not allowed to do is appear in court until they've completed a full 12 months of pupillage. It's seen as a time for learning not earning. This does lead to feelings of being *"left behind"* as *"friends are on their feet being barristers while I am still a pupil."* Instead, pupils undertake advocacy exercises within chambers in front of senior members who hold part-time judicial positions.

The two sixes do not differ greatly. In each, the pupil will have two PMs and will work for others in chambers. They tackle a mixture of real work and set pieces designed to test their progress. One told us: *"You are taught to be a quality product and to produce quality products…they are punctilious about written style."* And so we arrive at the crux of the matter: there's an awful lot of thinking and written work involved in this pupillage. A very junior tenant told us: *"You need self-motivation and you mustn't mind sitting in libraries for hours, working on your own, buckling down."* But this is no ivory tower – good judgement and being *"rigorous in examining your client's case"* are key. Getting the right answer is only part of the job; it then needs to be turned into practical advice, which, after all, is why the client instructed you in the first place.

We looked for the quirks and scraps of humour that sometimes help define a set. Sadly our sources fell silent when asked for hilarious stories; they painted a rather earnest picture of daily life. That said, we must congratulate the prankster who tossed three yellow plastic ducks into the pigeon netting above the courtyard behind chambers. *"We're a serious business,"* one barrister told us. We thought about the ducks. We nodded.

Many sets sneer at the tradition of chambers tea, regarding it as anachronistic. This set loves it enough to also indulge in a morning coffee version, which it holds in the nearby St George's cafe. Apparently tea is a stand-up affair, but one sits down for coffee. *"It fosters a non-hierarchical atmosphere,"* a baby junior told us, *"…and yes, pupils can speak at tea!"* So, expect plenty of chattering – whether it's about work or football, it's all fair comment.

We were fortunate enough to collar one of the top bods on the management committee who, after discussing the leap that was made at the time of the merger, explained: *"Any change here is evolutionary; people are broadly happy with the set as it is, but we will continue recruiting talented people."* Broadly happy? We'd guess that the folk at Serle Court are utterly delighted with the way things are. Carry on.

3 Serjeants' Inn

the facts
OLPAS: summer season **Pupillages:** 2
Applications: 170 **Mini pupillages:** 30
First Interview: 20-35 **Second Interview:** 8-13
Pupillage award: £25,000
Tenancies offered in 2004: Not known
Chambers UK rankings: Clinical negligence, police law, professional discipline

Excuse the tasteless surgical gag, but 3 Serjeants' Inn really is at the cutting edge of medical law. A brief perusal of the Lloyds Medical Law Reports and the popular press will reveal that members of this set have been recurrent players in the litigation that has shaped the modern law of medicine. *Bland, Re A (Conjoined Twins: Separation), Sidaway,* the Bristol Royal Infirmary Inquiry and the Harold Shipman murders have all involved tenants from 3 Serjeants' Inn in one capacity or another.

It's not all doctors and nurses though. In recent years, the set has also developed a leading practice in police law, in which it acts predominantly for police authorities. Typically this work involves defending police in civil actions, judicial reviews and disciplinary proceedings, or pursuing court orders on behalf of the police in applications to, say, close down a crack den or get an anti-social behaviour order. Chambers also has a small, but nonetheless significant, team of construction and commercial lawyers.

The move from more modest premises in the Temple to the set's current home on Fleet Street gives 3 Serjeants' Inn an appearance of grandeur that most other chambers lack the space to pull off. Indeed, at first glance, visitors could be forgiven for thinking that they'd arrived at the wrong building. Occupying the premises of an old bank, the open-plan reception area-cum-clerks' room is spacious and high ceilinged with solid brass lanterns descending on chains, faux stone columns and a collection of rather gaudy frescoes depicting lusty scenes from classical mythology. The overall impact? A bit like Quadrant Chambers after a surprise ambush by Lawrence Llewelyn-Bowen.

Pupillage follows a three by four-month programme and where a pupil has a particular interest, they can normally expect to spend at least part of the year working in that area. The nature of chambers' specialisation ensures exposure to a variety of tribunals. As well as standard-fare clinical negligence actions in the High Court, it's not uncommon for members to be involved in *"life or death"* telephone applications for 'without notice' injunctions in emergency treatment decisions.

Unsurprisingly for a predominantly civil set, there's a heavy emphasis on drafting. Practice makes perfect, and chambers is beginning to adopt a uniform way of giving feedback to its pupils. For a typical piece of work like, say, drafting a statement of case, the pupil's finished draft is returned to them by e-mail with additions and corrections marked clearly in red, accompanied by an additional page of commentary at the end. According to the pupils this system works very well: *"The feedback is always constructive"* and *"expectations are built up gradually."* The development of pupils' written work is an important factor in the tenancy decision, but that said, one pupil told us: *"Everyone emphasised that it's okay to make mistakes as you're learning...as long as you don't make the same mistake twice."*

Advocacy skills are also considered *"a major thing,"* and these barristers are *"known for being tough trial advocates."* Pupils are eased into things gradually, and to use a clinical analogy, the first few months will be more about practising sutures than full-on brain surgery. At the time of writing, there was no formal in-house advocacy training over and above that provided by the Inns, though there were suggestions that it might be introduced in the near future. However, it sounds as if there's no shortage of opportunities to practice. Chambers is particularly fortunate in that it enjoys a steady stream of instruc-

tions from one of its probation service clients to prosecute breaches of community sentences in the Crown and magistrates' courts. This work has become a staple for second six pupils, who describe it as *"a fantastic opportunity to develop advocacy skills."*

When it comes to work, it's a case of 'have brief, will travel'. From Norwich to Newcastle, the pupils we met had certainly done the rounds. From time to time, the value of the brief is outstripped by the cost of travel, which means pupils are effectively *"paying for the privilege of doing a piece of work,"* but our sources accepted this as a necessary evil in the very early stages of practice. And anyway, the competitive pupillage award should certainly take the sting out of the tail.

Pupil supervisors enforce a nine 'til six policy rigidly...in the first six at least, and pupils say that socially they feel very much a part of chambers and are welcomed along to the regular and informal lunches, as well as drinks on a Friday. Pupils also told us that, on their arrival, juniors made a real effort to take them under their wing. Each was allocated their own aunt or uncle to act as a mentor, and a sounding board for niggling concerns.

The dreaded tenancy decision is made a little later than in most other sets, coming at the beginning of October. 3 Serjeants' Inn believes that *"12 months, pupillage should mean 12 months, pupillage,"* and so that is what pupils are assessed on. If, for whatever reason, tenancy isn't on the cards, people are allowed to squat while they plan their next move. Once your name is on the door, the clerking team won't waste a moment in promoting it to clients. Personal letters and profiles are sent out to instructing solicitors, and juniors are encouraged to take part in regular seminars and lectures. The style of clerking here is hands-on, with the senior clerk making it his business to know about all the barristers on his books. He sits down with each new tenant in order to ascertain their expectations in terms of income and their desired specialisation. Juniors say that in the early years of practice *"the clerks are more than happy to steer you in the direction that you want your career to take."*

While we are always assured on our various visits to different chambers that there is no one type of person whose face fits, we're damned if we don't come out finding something that brings a set together. What we noticed in everyone we met at this set was a real sense of ambition coupled with a desire to deliver the goods. These barristers are driven towards getting their hands on better and better instructions, and then producing the best work possible. As one pupil supervisor put it: *"You need to have a certain passion for doing well and working smart. It's about attention to detail, determination and a desire to really do your best."*

Apply to this set and you'll need to provide a good reason for wanting to specialise in its chosen areas of practice. If you find that you are about to write 'I am applying to this set because I'm really interested in clinical negligence' but you don't have anything to back that up with, your CV probably needs a shot of botox. It's definitely a good plan to apply to this set, and others with similar areas of specialisation, for mini-pupillage. If that doesn't work out, seek out some other relevant experience. You could try, for example, a work experience placement with the police, CPS or an NHS Trust. A 2:2 needn't prevent you from applying here, and in fact, a few senior (and highly successful) members of chambers didn't quite manage to bag a 2:1 themselves. But you will need to persuade the person reading your application that there are other things about you that will make you a good pupil/tenant. As for the interview, it will come in either one or two rounds, depending on how many candidates come through the initial screening process. There will certainly be some form of legal problem to tackle, as well as a discussion of something of topical interest. No shrinking violets please: the pupils' advice was to *"be prepared to demonstrate your reasoning and hold your corner."*

If you do go under the knife at 3 Serjeants' Inn and come out the other end with a pupillage, we think that you'll have done pretty well.

3/4 South Square

the facts
OLPAS: No **Pupillages:** Up to 4x12 months
Applications: 300 **Mini pupillages:** Up to 10 funded
First interview: 34 **Second interview:** 16
Award: £35,000 (funds can be advanced for BVC)
Tenancies offered in 2004: 2
Chambers UK rankings: Banking & finance, Chancery, company law, insolvency

3/4 South Square is the UK's premier insolvency set and the first point of call for many clients. This is a good pick for anyone *"with an interest in the workings of business."* BCCI, Maxwell, Polly Peck, Olympia & York, Lloyd's of London, Barings, Enron, Railtrack, Marconi, NTL and Global Crossing – you name it, if it's a corporate disaster, 3/4 has been involved in some capacity.

The set is located in Gray's Inn, overlooking the blazing floral displays of South Square. The jarring late-80s decor has given way to a more contemporary look. The reception area has been *"smartened up,"* though rest assured that there is no glitz, marble or *"Lovells-style great metal sculptures or towering atrium."* Said one senior member of chambers: *"We don't want our clients thinking we're prohibitively expensive."*

The set's core area of practice is insolvency, and most of its members specialise in one brand or other of insolvency law. Members relish work that requires you to *"go into a company for a time, understand its business, see the human drama and the whole range of problems of a business in distress."* And, invariably, some of these businesses will be at the centre of commercial drama and intrigue. Speaking of his work on the ITV Digital collapse, one member told us: *"That touched millions of people's lives…Not being able to watch the football makes life scarcely worth living!"*

If you're curious about life at the insolvency Bar, the set now has a system of funded mini pupillages, designed to give prospective pupils *"a feeling of what it's like to be here."* And it is, according to one QC, *"informal, friendly and approachable."* These clichés trip off the tongue very easily, but we saw no reason to doubt him. While the work is *"serious"* (*"there's no arsing about"*), this is a young set, defined by its relationships with clients. Said one member: *"The big thing is how you get along with them."* The work involves grappling with complex legal issues; nonetheless, *"it's not about finding an academic, theoretical solution."* *"We pride ourselves on offering practical business solutions. Our clients want to know what to do next."* Readers need only look at the set's website to get a taste of its practical approach. The 'Links' and 'London' pages in particular are packed with all the relevant information an out-of-town instructing solicitor or client would need: hotels, restaurants, travel info, weather etc. Someone's been thinking ahead…'What will a visitor from Hong Kong/Texas/Newcastle need to know?'

When we asked chambers' recruiters what qualities they sought in prospective pupils, the answer was *"a hybrid."* The editor of *Chambers UK* confirmed this hybrid theory, when she described insolvency barristers as both *"analytical and deal-driven."* *"There is a deal-doing mentality, but we're also there to help. After all, we're there to save the company in many cases."* And to do so, in court *"you have to be able to present a case clearly and attractively, and in the best possible light."* Fans of *The Simpsons* fantasising about Lionel Hutz-style court appearances, be warned: this is *"not stuff you can pick up five minutes beforehand."* The work is *"complicated, factually and legally,"* and your success will depend *"90% on preparation."*

Pupils are assigned to a different pupilmaster every six to eight weeks, so enabling them to see a range of practices and working styles, and to ensure that as many members as possible see their work. During the second six, pupils spend more time interacting with the most junior tenants *"to give them a better picture of life at the junior end,"* but it'll be no holiday as you'll also do pieces of work for silks on major matters. If the cut and thrust of regular advocacy is what really appeals to you, this is perhaps not the best pupillage. Few pupils can expect to be on their feet at all during the second six, since *"the work*

is sufficiently demanding to require a full 12 months of training." At the six-month mark, pupils are informed as to their chances of gaining tenancy, and some are advised (although never required) to seek a second six elsewhere. There are no formal assessments: all your work will be taken into account, as will feedback from the pupilmasters and anyone else who has had dealings with you.

The set's main clients are City law firms, although for juniors there's an endless list of instructing firms from outside the capital. In their early years, juniors spend a lot of time *"traipsing around the county courts and district registries,"* and can expect a good cross-section of smaller corporate and personal insolvency matters – winding-up petitions, setting aside statutory demands, injunctions and the like. They can also expect to work as part of a team on much larger cases and, indeed, 3/4 South Square prides itself on its team ethos and team approach to staffing large matters. As one source stressed, while there are *"lots of good, competent people around,"* personality and the ability to work in a team will take you over the line.

Some chambers are highly individualistic in their style and culture; others are cohesive to the point of conformism. We sensed that 3/4 South Square is a mixture of both. The social life is full and fabulous for those who want it, but there is no element of compulsion. Except, that is, when it comes to an annual tradition whereby junior tenants take the wide-eyed, bushy-tailed pupils out and *"get them very drunk."* It's a way of demonstrating that the set is *"not just a place where you turn up and work."* There is also a chambers function once a year, at which everyone gets together.

Pupillage applicants with *"past lives"* are embraced. Among the members, we weren't surprised to hear of a former Bank of England employee and an actuary. The BBC producer and the hairdresser were an unexpected delight. As with most things at 3/4, there is generally an *"easy"* relationship with clerks. Overall, we sensed a warm, informal atmosphere in a set that is neither contrived nor unnervingly slick. Definitely one for those with a fascination for business.

4 Stone Buildings

the facts

OLPAS: No **Pupillages:** 2x6 months
(pupillages may be extended to 12 months)
Applications: c. 100 **Mini pupillages:** 24
Interview: 20
Award: £35,000 (funds can be advanced for BVC)
Tenancies offered in 2004: None
Chambers UK rankings: Commercial Chancery, company, energy & natural resources, financial services, civil fraud, insolvency/corporate recovery

4 Stone Buildings is a small but rock-solid company and commercial law set with a host of stars within its ranks. Brightest among them is head of chambers George Bompas QC, who acted in such mammoth cases as the Blue Arrow affair, the Barlow Clowes affair and the BCCI litigation.

Occupying elegant Georgian premises overlooking the green expanse of Lincoln's Inn Fields, the set's vibe is serene and traditional. Inside, Barristers 'R Us strike again on the decoration front. It's all law reports, spectacular marble fireplaces and French polish. 4 Stone Buildings started life as a Chancery set, but like other Chancery outfits, it recognised that to remain successful and profitable it needed to diversify. Over the last two decades, it has shifted its focus to company and commercial law, with a strong emphasis on corporate insolvency. The plan has paid off and today its members act in some of the highest profile and most valuable international insolvencies. The set takes instructions from several leading City firms, and maintains strong contacts with regional firms.

Company law instructions cover takeover disputes, building society mergers, share transfers, directors, duties, freezing injunctions and issues of management control (such as that of Tottenham Hotspur FC). Many of the cases are very large, requiring second or third juniors to assist a silk. The work necessitates close contact with instructing solicitors, bringing about a real team ethos. But this is not a case of barristers trying to replicate solicitors' offices. A pupil told us: *"I steered clear of solicitors' firms because of that group culture. I wanted a bit of that, but not to the extent of it being obligatory."* In a similar vein, a junior told us: *"I like the intellectual stimulation of the Bar, being out on your own and challenged individually."* A rolling stone gathers no moss, and neither, it seems do the members of this set. With strong international connections, barristers are active in such glamorous and exotic locations as Hong Kong, Bermuda, the Cayman Islands, Trinidad and Singapore. One lucky junior spent eight weeks in Bermuda on the BCCI insolvency, juxtaposing his time at work with relaxation on the beach.

Chambers' recruiters were adamant that they *"don't care what university you went to."* Additionally, *"we don't distinguish between a First and a 2:1,"* since *"often students with Firsts have no common sense."* And the job, we were informed, is as much about common sense as pure brains. Many sets make claims to fairness in recruitment, but 4 Stone Buildings is surely unique in that it phones the referees of every single applicant for pupillage, as *"references are really telling."* From here, the set interviews around 20 lucky applicants. The interview panel is large and includes the set's influential senior clerk, David Goddard. We won't lie to you, the interview process is rigorous and the questions fairly tough. This is a set that prides itself on its common sense and commerciality – *Chambers UK* doesn't describe it as *"user friendly"* for nothing – so you should argue with your client's needs in mind. We sneaked a peek at the 4 Stone Buildings recruitment guidelines: chief among the characteristics it seeks are *"quality, agility, fluency and potential."* As one junior tenant told us: *"Potential is the hardest thing to judge. We're trying to spot the next Lord Hoffman."* Following this, you'll have a general discussion with the panel, and you'll get your chance to take revenge on the recruiters with hard-hitting enquiries of your own. You might want to tone down the pomposity – *"Very occasionally we get someone who is full of themselves,"* and that doesn't appeal.

Although a mini pupillage is advisable, it's not a prerequisite (it seems that few things are!). *"It's a chance for students to decide whether they like us."* In keeping with this approach, minis are not assessed, although someone will write a brief appraisal of your work. Those pupillage interviewees who perform well, but have not undertaken a mini, will be invited to spend a couple of days in chambers to see how they rub along.

Chambers only offers six-month pupillages. At the end of the first six, the pupillage committee reviews your progress, and depending on your chances of tenancy, might offer you a second. While most comparable sets effectively offer 12-month pupillages with a break clause at six months, at 4 Stone Buildings, you're encouraged to have an alternative second six arranged beforehand. Until Christmas, you'll sit with your first pupilmaster, switching to a second in January. All work from other members of chambers passes through your PM, who will ensure it is appropriate. The assessment regime is light, since *"the emphasis is on training and work rather than marking."* You're unlikely to work in you own name during a second six; some pupils get on their feet during this time but, in this is a paperwork-heavy pupillage, it's far from the norm. As a junior you can expect to work on mammoth cases with senior members and to run your own smaller matters. Clerks maintain relationships with regional solicitors to ensure a good flow of baby junior-sized instructions. At this stage of your career, it is likely that insolvency work will feature heavily.

4 Stone Buildings prides itself on its warmth. There is chambers tea every afternoon, although we're told it bears no resemblance to the funereal affairs that have become the stuff of legend at the Bar. A pupil told us that 'Treasury Devil' Jonathan Crow *"tells the most amusing anecdotes at tea."* We're reliably informed that the *"treacle-like"* liquid prepared by the clerks is unfit for human consumption. Apparently the recipe consists of 23 teabags for each member plus four for the pot. Outside work, there are occasional parties, ice-skating expeditions to Somerset House in winter, and every August the whole set goes out to lunch…in Paris. Apparently one member has earned his pilot's licence and is threatening to take everyone hot air ballooning.

Shortage of space in No.4 dictates that some members must reside in No.6 Stone Buildings. In spite of this separation, we found a set with a degree of intimacy and congeniality that is to be applauded. Courteous and traditional certainly, but far from stuffy, 4 Stone buildings is one of Lincoln's Inn's finest offerings.

2 Temple Gardens

the facts

OLPAS: summer season **Pupillages:** 3x12 months
Applications: c200 **Mini pupillages:** Available
First Interview: 40 **Second Interview:** 15
Award: £40,000 grant (£10,000 paid in the BVC year)
Tenancies offered in 2004: 2
Chambers UK Rankings: Clinical negligence, personal injury, professional discipline, professional negligence

Don't allow the chunky pupillage award offered by 2 Temple Gardens to leave you thinking that this set will occupy a magic circle law firm-style glass and steel palace. From outside it's more a case of blink and you'll miss it. Tucked away at the end of Middle Temple Lane, the way in is certainly understated. Sure, the interior is smart, modern and airy, but there's nothing boastful about the décor. Yet, given that this leading common law set is among the top players in at least four different practice areas, there is plenty to boast about.

If you are looking for a pupillage that will give you an all-round experience of civil practice, 2tg is worth serious consideration. Chambers is organised into 10 different practice groups. On the one hand, there is a commercial edge to the practice, with groups specialising in banking, construction, insurance and reinsurance, and on the other there's a strong common law base that includes, among other things, clinical and professional negligence, personal injury and an expanding employment team. The practice groups have become quite close knit, and we got the feeling that, although self-employed, these barristers see themselves as part of a wider team and are keen to work together to steer chambers forwards. As one of the practice managers explained: *"There's a real sense of cohesion within the different groups, and senior QCs will often organise training weekends for more junior members of chambers."*

Within a 12-month pupillage, every pupil will be guaranteed time in at least three practice groups, the year being split into three four-month 'seats'. The pupil we met was in the twilight hours of her pupillage and had just been offered a tenancy at 2tg. She had begun the year shadowing a clinical negligence practitioner: *"As well as going to the High Court, I saw disciplinary proceedings in the General Medical Council and went to the Privy Council on an appeal."* Being a civil practice, there will be plenty of paperwork, whether it be drafting letters of claim (the kind of letter you don't want to get in the post), statements of case or written advices. The approach at 2tg is 'I'll show you mine, if you show me yours'. Pupils have a stab at a first draft of a piece of written work, and then sit down with the pupilmaster to compare it with the boss's version.

In the practising, second six, the paperwork continues as before, but the difference is that some of it will start getting sent out to real clients. There will also be some court work. In an average week, pupils can expect to see the inside of a courtroom around three times, usually for quite straightforward things to start off with – small claims arising out of road traffic accidents or short interim applications in cases belonging to other members of chambers. To prepare pupils for D-Day, they all get the opportunity to go out and about with a junior tenant for a week. There are also three advocacy exercises to prepare, in which a 2tg QC sits as 'judge'. As a member of the pupillage committee explained: *"The advocacy exercises are there to help pupils. Their performance wouldn't be taken into account when making the tenancy decision, unless the pupil hadn't been doing well in other things, and their advocacy was especially good."*

When it came to real advocacy, the pupil we met had her own set of top tips for the first appearance in court. First, *"get there early;"* second, *"bring plenty of photocopies of anything that you need to rely on;"* and finally, if all else fails, try *"winking at the judge."* And they say that flattery will get you nowhere….

Of course, flattery won't get you a tenancy at 2tg. The tenancy decision is arrived at after a strict and comprehensive analysis of the work pupils have done for their PMs or others in chambers, and we were left in no doubt that the committee discounts remarks made by members unless they are based upon a piece of work.

As for getting your foot in through the door as a pupil, the recruitment process is similarly rigorous in its assessment of candidates' potential. The first round of the selection process brings together the 40 people who looked best on paper for something not dissimilar to a corporate weekend away. Spread over a whole Saturday, the lucky 40 will be invited to chambers, where, under close scrutiny, they will be divided into small groups and asked to perform a *Crystal Maze*-style challenge. Don't worry, there's nothing physical or gloopy involved and not a barmy host in sight – 2tg is interested only in applicants' grey matter. Though we are under strict instructions not to say any more, what we are permitted to reveal is that there are also individual written tests and a series of talks by barristers and clerks. Oh, and a free lunch! The purpose of the day is to whittle the crowd down to 15 people, who will be subsequently be given an individual interview with an attendant legal problem to discuss. Apparently, those who are relatively new to the study of law shouldn't lose any sleep as the important thing at this stage is not simply regurgitating reams of statute and case law, but showing your potential to think like a barrister. Our source on the pupillage committee expanded on this point, telling us the panel was interested in *"an applicant's ability to see, in massive amounts of detail, what is relevant and what isn't."*

So what makes a potential 2tg barrister? Obviously, the potential to become a great advocate is important. Think precision and detail rather than wowing the jury with your best Perry Mason because *"a Commercial Court judge is far more interested in someone who can master a bundle and get to the point really quickly.* There's no doubt that *"raw intellectual grit"* is valued too, and we couldn't help but notice a heavy preponderance of Firsts from Oxbridge amongst the last ten junior tenants, but character will also take you a fair distance. 2tg is not simply looking for brainboxes, they're also looking for someone who is *"self-aware, personable and friendly."*

Like many sets, 2tg has become streetwise about marketing itself to solicitors. As a pupil, you can guarantee that you'll be packed off for a week to one of the many leading firms that regularly instruct chambers in order to provide them with an extra pair of hands (and showcase your talents and general appeal). As the practice managers told us: *"It's certainly important for solicitors to get to meet people at the junior end of chambers."* The various practice groups also run series of seminars for solicitors that all pupils are encouraged to attend. To facilitate chit-chat afterwards, there are usually drinks and a finger buffet at which the smart pupil will grab a pinwheel sandwich and network like crazy!

It's not all about impressing potential clients; these barristers know how to let their wigs down too, and regular Friday night drinks in chambers allow pupils, members and clerks to mingle. When asked to describe the atmosphere at 2tg, pupils and juniors agreed on this: *"It's not like some chambers where everyone keeps their doors shut, or some chambers where everyone is all over each other. It's a happy medium."* Happy medium it may be, middle of the road it is not.

3 Verulam Buildings

the facts

OLPAS: summer season **Pupillages:** 3x12 months
Applications: 200 **Mini pupillages:** 25
First interviews: 50 **Second interviews:** 20
Award: Min £40,500 (£15,000 can be advanced for BVC)
Tenancies offered in 2004: 2
Chambers UK rankings: Banking & finance, commercial litigation, financial services, civil fraud, insurance, international arbitration, media & entertainment, professional negligence

3 Verulam Buildings is best known for first-class banking and finance litigation; however, success stacks up in an impressive range of other commercial areas. Headed by John Jarvis QC and the immensely popular Christopher Symons QC, its notables include former FSA general counsel Michael Blair QC, William Blair QC (brother of Tony, no relation to Michael, and current chairman of the Commercial Bar Association), and a veritable brat pack of junior silks and senior juniors.

3VB's pre-WW1 roots lie in the Temple and we're sure it won't mind us saying that nothing much distinguished it until the late 1970s. At this time, the set underwent aggressive expansion under the leadership of Andrew Leggatt QC, who moved it away from common law in the Temple to commercial practice, more particularly financial cases, in Gray's Inn. Also worth mentioning is former head of chambers Mr Justice Cresswell who, with Bill Blair and Mr Justice Silber, recruited many of the current 'names' and continued the banking focus with a view to using it as a base from which to develop other commercial areas. Members have acted on Maxwell, BCCI, Prince Jefri, Polly Peck, and the undue influence cases of Barclays Bank v O'Brien and Royal Bank of Scotland v Etridge. Then there was the spat between Italian scooter manufacturer Aprilia and the Spice Girls, the Dubai Aluminium professional negligence action and the Britvic benzine product liability litigation.

The Bar is facing change on a number of fronts and 3VB strikes us as a set that understands the importance of adapting to these changes. Some sets boast a Hotel California ethos, which is to say that no one ever leaves. Not 3VB. While it has sucked in tenants from other good sets, when Matrix Chambers was formed four members joined it to pursue public law practice amongst other like-minded souls. In a similar vein, it is interesting to note that the set has more than one ex-solicitor among its ranks and, intriguingly, in the past a couple of juniors have jumped the fence. The comings and goings at 3VB are not what defines it – it's hardly a revolving door scenario – but there's evidence to show that the set has a restless gene in its DNA.

When trying to identify a particular chambers' house style, it helps to know which firms of solicitors have aligned themselves with the set. Here, the Lovells link is strong, as is that with Herbert Smith and A&O. In large commercial cases, solicitors need the barristers they instruct to assist them by *"collaborating on the management of litigation,"* as if they were a part of the team. Perhaps this is why new tenants are commonly sent on secondment to City firms (Slaughter and May for one) to see things from the instructing solicitor's perspective. If there is a 3VB Way then it should perhaps be defined by the word 'efficiency'. Our sources all emphasised the importance of being well organised and prepared, and as a pupil that's just what you'll learn to be. After all, *"nobody wants to be taken be surprise."* Expect an emphasis on *"anticipating the needs of case timetables and work schedules."* It all sounds so precise, so Swiss. Just without the cuckoo clocks.

The clerking system operates around groups of barristers organised by practice area. Team clerking came in with the arrival of practice manager Nick Hill in 1999, and both he and Chris Symons are seen to be very much on top of the management game. Each practice group holds three-monthly review meetings and implements a programme of continuing education and marketing through seminars. It all smacks of a set that's continually assessing its own performance and following a plan. But, if all this is true, who's in the driving seat? In a fair approximation of democracy, committees are the order of the day. There's the management committee, the pupillage committee, the tenancy committee and so on; however, our favourite has to be the practice development committee (aka the family planning committee), which handles lateral hires and the set's direction and goals.

Last year we reported that 3VB boasted *"possibly the tiniest waiting room at the Bar."* Not so anymore – the public areas of chambers have recently been subjected to an extensive remodelling. All in the best possible taste though: *"It's not selling itself as a corporate hothouse: all glass and blond wood and Swedish chairs."* Equally, it is *"not Gordon Gekko-macho-bravado"* and *"not hard-nosed or uptight-establishment."* Fine. Some hints on how the set does see itself? *"Relaxed in its relations with people,"* but with *"a pretty serious ambition to make chambers a leading set in as many fields as possible."* One tenant communicated *"a strong sense of identity with chambers as a whole and what you do mattering for chambers. It matters to me if senior juniors and silks are doing well."* As well as minding each other's business, these barristers are, it seems, lunching and visiting the local pub together. Some even go on the piste together.

We met two of the pupils, each of whom had studied masters' degrees at top overseas universities. Among the juniors there are those who've turned to the law after other careers, including a former philosophy lecturer and a film producer. Whether or not you possess a novel CV, only academic excellence will see you through to an interview, and then you're going to have to show that you have self-confidence and all the usual powers of analysis and reasoning that are essential at the commercial Bar. The first of the two interviews will be a relaxed stroll through your CV, and if the panel like what they see, you'll be invited back to tackle a problem-based interview. *"We're not overbearing,"* the pupillage committee secretary reassured us: *"It's not my experience as a barrister that you're bounced around the room."*

Pupils rotate around the same group of pupilmasters, sampling banking, general commercial, telecoms, insurance and reinsurance, civil fraud and insolvency work as they go. After the first three months, pupils may take on matters from around chambers, and in the second six may also get started on bits and pieces of paying work – masters' appointments, small claims, etc. While *"a premium is placed on your drafting skills,"* it's not the case that you'll be chambers-bound with your nose to paper every day. Pupillage is *"not sedentary at all;"* what with your PM's conferences and sitting in on trials, you'll be *"out of chambers once or twice a week at least."* More often, we sensed, than their peers in magic circle sets. This is perhaps due to the involvement of shadow pupilmasters, a breed of mini-me PM, whose cases are smaller and more easily understood by pupils.

You leave this set with a strong sense that it is looking only at its future. None of the *"flash"* of some commercial sets, but instead *"a quiet confidence"* from people *"quietly focused and going about it."* As the magic circle of solicitors' firms has its aspirants, so too does the so-called magic circle of commercial sets. 3VB is clearly pursuing membership.

Wilberforce Chambers

the facts

OLPAS: No   **Pupillages:** 2x12 months
Applications: 85 **Mini pupillages:** 21
First interview: 27 **Second interview:** 9
Award: £37,500 (up to £12,500 can be advanced for BVC)
Tenancies offered in 2004: 4
Chambers UK rankings: Commercial Chancery, traditional Chancery, intellectual property, pensions, professional negligence, real estate litigation

Although certain members will have additional spe-cialisms, the main business is Chancery work. Even as a new pupil you'll be familiar with the names of the senior members: *"You meet the people you've been reading about in the law reports"* – QCs like Edward Nugee, Jules Sher, Michael Bloch, Terence Mowschenson. Notable cases of recent years include Grupo Torras, Barings, BCCI and Bermuda Fire & Marine. Members of chambers regularly work abroad in the Bahamas and the Cayman Islands. In addition to taking on last year's three pupils as tenants, in a widely publicised move Wilberforce Chambers' already strong IP capability has been augmented by Anna Carboni (formerly London Head of IP at Linklaters) and Alan Bryson (former partner at Clifford Chance).

In New Square's south-west corner, and just yards from Lincoln's Inn's Old Hall, No.8 is home to most of the set. As you descend from the newest tenants' tiny garret-like rooms on the fourth floor, down the broad wooden staircase you pass ever larger and grander accommodation until you reach the wood-panelled rooms of top QCs. The set has also taken over part of Nos.7 and 9 and a modern building on the other side of the square at No.16. Built on the site of 'The Boghouse' – communal toilets that dated back to 1693 – No.16 houses many of the juniors. It also plays host to afternoon tea, which is a very informal affair with anything up to a dozen people congregating outside the kitchen to chat about what they're up to. lunch (every fortnight for members) is when most people catch up. Social get-togethers tend to coincide with marketing events rather than having a strong life force of their own.

As we walked around chambers, we observed that some members were very smartly dressed while others had climbed out of the casual side of the bed. Michael Bloch sometimes brings his dog Gladstone into chambers, and Terence Mowschenson will occasionally be joined by his two King Charles Spaniels, Ruby and Carlo (who were lazing by an open fire when we dropped into their room). Our afternoon at Wilberforce left us with the feeling that we'd been to visit some rather welcoming long lost relatives, so we were intrigued when one pupilmaster said: *"We don't pretend we're a family; we're working colleagues. Being a family can make administration very difficult."* A sizeable proportion of the members have moved here from other sets, yet while no one has ever left except to go to the bench, *"we don't see ourselves as a tight knot who have been together forever and will be till death us do part…"* As for its self-image: *"We've ditched a lot of the old traditions that make you feel uncomfortable."* Instead, a modern management structure and a *"heads-down"* ethos have been adopted. How different from the Dickens' portrayal of the Chancery Bar in *Bleak House*.

First-six pupils move between pupilmasters every two months and work on papers that have recently come to their PM. Days are spent drafting opinions, skeleton arguments and particulars of claim or defence, or *"sometimes a QC will ask you to do a bit of research for them."* If their work is good enough, it may end up being used. *"Most pieces of pupil-friendly work are small self-standing matters."* No Jarndyce v Jarndyce stuff. Should you stay for a second six, you might receive noting briefs (to attend court to take notes) or smaller county court hearings. The firms that instruct chambers range from small high street practices to the giants of the magic circle and, consequently, the subject matter of the cases is extremely varied. Pensions, gas exportation, public law, overseas trusts, probate, property, landlord and tenant, housing associations… *"The work is cerebral – you're dealing with the more difficult areas of the law like land and trusts, but then you get into things like pensions and you soon realise that you'll not find much in a trusts book on pensions."* You do encounter the occasional little old lady with a will, but a lot of the time you'll be instructed by large commercial landlords. A junior whose practice contains traditional Chancery work will handle plenty of smaller cases, *"where you are in charge and not being led."* Commonly the cases relate to somebody's home or something very personal to them, but the cut and thrust of mainstream commercial work must not be underemphasised.

Anyone thinking of applying here has to be aware that success comes in *"a more complex package than a starred First."* Yes, pupils usually have near-perfect academic credentials, but they also have a fascination for the law. One source hinted that winning scholarships or essay prizes and mooting or debating competitions would look good on your application. Another explained the heightened degree of sophistication required by Chancery advocates as opposed to, say, their criminal colleagues. *"This is not the place for bluff and bluster. A jury advocate needs to grasp the layman's attention and not let it go for several days; in Chancery you need to get across difficult concepts to a judge – this requires poise."* Remember, open and shut cases are few and far between. Excellent paper advocacy is even more important, and a tip from one successful ex-pupil is that *"you need to be consistently good rather than occasionally amazing."* No need to clock up hours and hours of face-time: *"They're not looking for bumptious Lord Flashheart types."* Like many other leading sets, Wilberforce takes its tenancy decision after just six months so that those who are unsuccessful have the chance to move elsewhere for a second six. *"It's better than drinking in the last chance saloon, if you have to go for a third six!"* A word of recommendation: go all out for one of the mini pupillages.

In February 2003, esteemed former Law Lord Wilberforce (great-great-grandson of the social reformer William Wilberforce) died aged 95. His obituary in *The Guardian* portrayed him as *"One of the most civilised and balanced judges of the 20th century."* While no one we spoke to in chambers mentioned Lord Wilberforce, we concluded that civilised and balanced were words that described the set very well. Maybe it's the dogs. Maybe it's the people. Whatever it is, there's something pretty good going on at Wilberforce. If Dickens had met modern day Chancery barristers, *Bleak House* would have been a different book altogether…

No.5 Chambers, Birmingham

the facts

OLPAS: No   **Pupillages:** 2x12 months
Applications: 200 **Mini pupillages:** c.50
First interview: 30 **Second interview:** 10-16
Award: £15,000 + earnings (advance considered for BVC)
Tenancies offered in 2004: 1 to a No.5 pupil
Chambers UK ranks members in: Chancery, clinical negligence, commercial litigation, construction, crime, employment, energy and natural resources, environment, family, intellectual property

The largest in the UK, Birmingham's No.5 Chambers is an impressive and audacious set. A big, bold set like this needs big, noticeable words to describe it, and just over a decade ago one word that was used was 'Frankenstein'. The profession was shocked that barristers should choose to incorporate. Of course, they are now no longer alone…

A corporate structure is by no means the only thing that gets No.5 noticed. An ambitious growth strategy has seen the set climb from under 30 members in the early 1980s to over 150 today. No mergers here, it's a case of drawing in 'names' to continue feeding the six practice groups: commercial & Chancery, crime & licensing, employment, family, PI & clin neg, and planning and environment. Each of these teams has its own head, deputy, recruitment plan, marketing plan, budget and clerking team. Clerks get legal training too.

A whopping £22 million turnover puts it into the top ten sets in the UK, as measured by income. This income is supplemented by earnings from conferences and training as well as case handling; indeed the planning group managed an away weekend in Barcelona on the proceeds of one conference.

There was only one pupil at the time we investigated No.5. His solitude was, at least, saving him from the Lord of the Flies-style moral disintegration that some London pupils get drawn into. (We did bump into a second pupil at a party in London some months after our visit to Birmingham. He'd only stayed a week, having discovered he'd left his soul in London.) Back in Brum, the pupil offered up his views on the set. His thoughts on the quality of management (*"the dark art of clerking"*) and the attention he'd received from pupilmasters confirmed our suspicions that this is the kind of place where no stone is left unturned in the quest to create good barristers. *"You have to be outgoing and independent in action and thought"* to survive here, but you will be welcomed by the set, particularly by junior members. Many of the barristers sit and eat lunch together in the common room; it's a good spot for picking up on the feel of the set. And that is? *"Well, even though there are people of exceptional talent who are highly focused on their jobs, chambers doesn't lose a certain lightness of being…especially on social occasions."*

At times you must expect to get lost in the labyrinthine premises. Perhaps a bag of breadcrumbs might assist in negotiating the endless corridors and stairs, most of which are parquet-floored and likely to inspire flashbacks to your old junior school assembly hall. Thankfully, in your first three months you'll stick closely to your pupilmaster. You'll do bits and pieces for other members when they are desperate for another pair of hands, but *"you are farmed out on only a very occasional basis."* Your PM is likely to take a *"do it for yourself"* attitude. Working on their briefs, you'll be invited to go away and have a stab at producing something. *"The first six is good preparation for the second. By then you'll have experience of getting a brief, reading through it and handling things quickly."* After the first three months, you'll have two month-long spells with other PMs who can offer an insight into entirely different areas of practice. And then, as you creep towards your second, practising six, you'll have a month-long float with junior tenants from around chambers. *"So far, I've done commercial and Chancery, employment, crime and PI…in fact, everything apart from planning and family."*

The second six is going to be a whirl of briefs and court appearances, and it won't let up. You'll occupy the common areas of chambers, particularly the 'Bedouin Area'. The tenancy decision is made after ten months, and then you have *"two months grace to see out your triumph or to seek alternative employment."* And once tenancy is settled? *"Relative to other sets it's probably true that we specialise quite early. Juniors settle into their way and it happens quite naturally."* Never one to let things drift, practice director Tony McDaid (who should probably be called Tony McDude given his influence) has cosy *"tea and biscuits chats"* with members…regularly. As your career develops Mr McDude will ask you about where you want to go and what kind of work/life balance you're looking for. We heard that our man McDude sits with a copy of the *Bar Guide* putting crosses next to the barristers he'd like to draw to the set. Apparently he's got a good hit rate.

"No.5's outlook is a progressive one, couched within a more traditional appearance." A fair statement, we'd say. To illustrate: it has set up a London annexe; it has designs on a national network; it is diverse in all respects; and it embraces developments in practice management earlier than most sets. Barmark, Investors in People, an equal ops officer…No.5 gives a damn about these things, but it doesn't wear them as badges of correctness. And yet this is a set where clerks refer to barristers as 'Sir' and 'Miss', except on the football pitch or the golf course. There's a whiff of formality and traditionalism, which underscores the respect that the administrative corp accords to the lawyering corp, and it's easy to misread such signals and assume austerity and backwardness. Avoid this trap.

Whichever one of the six core practice groups appeals to you, so long as you are prepared to commit to Birmingham, this set would be a canny choice. Early applications are encouraged and you should try for a mini pupillage. One pupilmaster described the set as *"courageous, principled and forward thinking."* We concur

St Philips Chambers, Birmingham

the facts

OLPAS: No **Pupillages:** Up to 4x12 months
Applications: 250 **Mini pupillages:** Unlimited
First interview: 21 **Second interview:** 8
Award: £12,500 plus earnings
Tenancies offered in 2004: 4
Chambers UK ranks members in: Chancery, commercial litigation, consumer law, crime, employment, environment, family, insolvency, personal injury, planning

One of Birmingham's two super sets, St Philips has grown through a series of mergers. In 1998, Nos. 7 and 2 Fountain Court merged and adopted chambers' current moniker. In 2002, it fused with criminal specialists No.1 Fountain Court and, in so doing, pumped its numbers up to match those of rival set No.5 Chambers. Currently it is home to over 130 barristers. In such a large set, structured practice groups become a necessity and this is exactly how St Philips has chosen to organise itself. The largest group is crime, boasting over 65 members of chambers. Following in its wake are the family, employment, commercial, immigration, public law and PI groups. The set's website gives an indication of the size of each.

The first thing that strikes you about St Philips (other than stuff of legend, Dave the doorman) is that it looks like a swanky solicitors firm with its spacious, hi-tech reception. Artwork is eschewed in favour of the blank walls and clean lines that appeared on the architect's drawing board. *"We're a business and we need to be different,"* is the explanation. *"We consciously took a modern, bold approach."* St Philips was an early participant in the trend for chambers to employ a chief executive and he, along with the five practice area heads, comprise the management committee. Taking administrative functions away from the barristers – the set has full-time staff to handle accountancy, IT, HR, marketing and library services – enables the barristers to get on with lawyering and adds a certain slickness to the operation. Nothing much, it seems, is the product of the past and the word 'tradition' is rarely spoken. As one pupil supervisor told us: *"There's a definite feeling that we're all in this big project together."* Abandoning the Birmingham Bar's traditional home in Fountain Court and moving to the present location was a wrench for some, but what has emerged is an organisation with more clout, more drive and more plans. *"Things don't evolve here, they are designed, and there's a system for everything. If a problem arises and there is no system to deal with it then a system is created."*

St Philips is incorporated: the barristers are the shareholders of the company and the company owns its own premises outright. Depending on how much they want to pay in 'rent', they choose between a room (most of which are shared by two barristers), dedicated desk space in an open-plan area, or fashionable vagrancy (ie hot-desking). It's a system that suits variable earnings within the set and there's a further graduated discount on fees for barristers of up to five years' call. We visited on a Friday afternoon when St Philips was having a mellow moment, but we understand that it can get cramped and rather busy. Over the road, extra space has been found in Windsor House, aka Bleak House as it scores much lower on the swish-o-meter.

Communal areas and a chambers-wide drinks party one Friday each month lend weight to the claim that *"people here go out of their way to be very friendly."* *"There's ample opportunity to chat, but chambers is too big to know everyone's business inside out,"* one pupil told us. Certain bars benefit from St Philips' brief fees: Hotel du Vin (when your clerk has got a decent price for you), Utopia (if you're feeling sufficiently chic) and the Old Joint Stock (which packs enough lawyers to qualify as Dante's seventh circle of hell).

They didn't differ much from the London pupils we interviewed, but one thing struck us about St Philips' pupils: they were completely at ease with each other. It's relatively rare for a pupil to not get tenancy; consequently, they don't see pupillage as a lottery or 12 months of stiff competition with peers. Friendships grow easily between them, assisted by the fact that most live in one or other of the lawyerburbs of Harborne and Moseley. If chambers is not looking for winners and losers, it can concentrate on bringing all pupils on: *"Trying to get you to do your best."*

In your first three or four months, you'll work with your main pupil supervisor, accompanying them to court and getting a feel for paperwork – perhaps preparing a chronology for a multi-day employment case or drafting a statement of claim or defence on a PI matter. You'll then move in with two other supervisors for a month each to experience different areas of work. In the final couple of weeks of your first six, you'll hook up with more junior tenants to see first hand exactly what you'll be doing in your second, practising six. The second half of pupillage is when you'll be set loose, but previous supervisors will maintain a watching brief to ensure that you stay on the right track. In crime there's a fair bit of West Midlands Probation Service work in the Magistrates' Courts and mentions in the Crown Court. Some pupils have even undertaken three-month secondments to the CPS. On the civil side, small claims will see you in the County Courts and family work will centre around local authority care proceedings, contact orders and directions hearings. *"Everyone intends to specialise,"* we learned, *"but in your first three years you'll do a bit of everything; after all, you can't know what you want to do until you've tried things."* Tell that to pupils embarking on a specialist training in London…A more senior source told us: *"We've been debating offering specialist pupillages, but the view seems to be that general ones are better."*

Of course, you'll need to consider what practice in Birmingham has to offer you long term. Crime is the biggest practice group at St Philips, but commercial work is more profitable and the set is determined to edge itself in that direction. Maybe this is why the decision to deal crime specialists at 1 Fountain Court into the game was so hotly debated at the time. The real task ahead is to win more Midlands-based commercial instructions (around 65% of them still go to London sets), and there are signs that St Philips is making headway. Recent commercial highlights have included some hefty Mercantile Court cases, such as a £35 million Dunkin Donuts franchising dispute and a case between Landrover and one of its suppliers. About 80% of instructions come from firms within a 50-mile radius of the city and there will also be work from London solicitors with business in Birmingham courts. You'll not be restricted in where you work either; it's a case of 'have brief will travel' – Manchester, Leeds, Lincolnshire...the universe!

They may have been on the bliss pills before we met them, but our junior and pupil sources seemed very satisfied and quite at home, speaking of how their seniors and administrative staff made a positive effort to help them grow into chambers. *"There's a genuine mix of personalities within each group,"* one told us, *"so you're not taken on because you'll fit into one or other group."* If there's a St Philips Way then it was best put by the pupil who said: *"It's not about traditional values, it's about surviving at the modern Bar."* Whatever changes the Bar faces in the future – handling cases from cradle to grave, block-contract crime work from the Legal Services Commission – we'd bet St Philips will be there before most.

Deans Court Chambers, Manchester

the facts

OLPAS: summer season **Pupillages:** 2x12 months
Applications: 300 **Mini pupillages:** available throughout the year
First interview: 20 **Second interview:** 6
Award: £25,000 (£7,500 + £17,500 guaranteed earnings)
Tenancies offered in 2004: 2
Chambers UK ranks members in: Crime, family, health and safety, personal injury

For 10 points, what links footballer and impromptu kung fu legend Eric Cantona with mass-murderer Harold Shipman? You guessed it: their criminal trials both involved barristers from Deans Court chambers (defending Cantona and prosecuting Shipman, in case you wondered). High-profile work is something this leading Manchester set is well accustomed to receiving, which is understandable given its pedigree. With a history that goes back a good hundred years, chambers has produced its fair share of silks over the decades and, in turn, sent its fair share of them to the senior judiciary. At the time of writing, there were three former members sitting on the High Court Bench, including Mr Justice Ryder who we understand to be a bit of a spring chicken as judges in the Family Division go.

As the name suggests, chambers used to occupy premises within the confines of Deans Court, close to the law courts. However, gradual expansion (currently there are nearly 60 tenants) lead to a move to roomier accommodation in the legal enclave of St John's Street. We get the feeling that, when it comes to painting and decorating at least, there's a certain amount of keeping up with the Joneses amongst the residents of the street. Rather than Vera Duckworth stone cladding, the look is a subtle blend of the modern with the traditional. The smart glass tablet bearing the names of the tenants blends in discreetly with the grand, columned Georgian entranceway. Inside, the theme continues, comfortable leather furniture mingling with linear vases, garnished with giant Linda Barker twiglets. A solicitor coming here for the first time would instantly recognise a set doing rather well for itself.

For anyone looking for a pupillage that will give them a taste of both civil and criminal work, this is a good place to apply; though as the senior clerk was eager to stress, members see themselves as *"multidisciplinary specialists rather than generalists."* Deans Court is divided into a series of practice groups, including civil litigation (PI being a particular forte), family, crime, and health and safety and regulatory, which is apparently a booming area at the moment. Win a pupillage here and the assumption is that you are here to stay unless something pretty unexpected happens: in the last three years, all six of the pupils have been given tenancy. With this in mind, the pupillage committee *"tends to recruit pupils with a view to filling a space within a particular practice area,"* and so it is advisable to check that the spaces available at the bottom end of the members' list match with your career aspirations before putting in an application.

Pupils will normally spend the pupillage year with just one common law pupil supervisor, but throughout the first six, they will also be seconded to the family and criminal groups for a month each. Chambers also tries to accommodate individual's interests where possible. One of the pupils we met had followed the CPE route to the Bar; *"I knew that crime interested me, but I hadn't had much exposure to civil work."* He was allowed to split his time between a civil and a criminal supervisor.

This is a year of metamorphosis. Your supervisor will of course help you to develop the bare bones of your drafting skills and expose you to plenty of advocacy, but being a barrister is about much more than this, and *"the interpersonal dynamic is important too."* You may have achieved a double First from Oxford, but can you strike up a good relationship with instructing solicitors and clerks? At Deans Court, pupillage is just as much about learning to be commercially minded and client-focused as it is about honing legal skills. To quote one of the supervisors: *"The barrister that solicitors keep coming back to will be the one who they, and ultimately their client, can get on with."*

Once the second six comes, *"they keep you on your toes;"* indeed the clerks *"would have you on their feet every-day if they had their way!"* Pupils usually have a second six practice that is predominantly civil or predominantly criminal, though it's com-

mon for them to undertake a bit of both if required. There's no such thing as a typical week here: you could be in the Crown Court in the morning doing a plea in mitigation, then off to the county court in the afternoon to deal with a PI small claim. What makes the experience of Manchester pupils different from their London counterparts is the sheer volume of available court work, even for pupils who undertaking a largely civil training. So much so that *"on occasion, we have to ask the clerks to take us out of court for a day or so, so that we can get the paperwork done."*

On gaining tenancy things change, and the baby juniors will normally become a part of one or more of the closely knit practice groups. The work gets progressively more demanding so that, instead of handling interim applications for other peoples' cases, juniors are given small trials of their own. An acknowledgement that there is still much to be learnt, baby juniors will be led by more senior members of chambers on more complex cases. And whenever a QC picks up a particularly interesting case, *"the clerks will try to find time out for juniors so that they can sit in and observe."*

There are plenty of formal and informal opportunities for young barristers to market themselves, whether this is through giving seminars at solicitors firms or through the regular dinners and quiz nights held for solicitors, which we are told *"regularly descend into debauchery."* We didn't dare ask for details.

While pupils and junior tenants alike agree that they managed to maintain a social life as well as a working life, some supervisors will inevitably crack the whip harder than others, including one who makes a point of *"shaking the student hangover out of his pupils."* Be prepared to convert that student hangover into a barrister's hangover at times though, because *"the Northern Circuit is a very sociable place to be."* The Manchester Bar is nowhere near as vast as the London Bar and the 40 or so Mancunian pupils maintain contact throughout the year, frequently getting together in the pub to swap notes. There are also formal social events organised by chambers, such as the annual Christmas meal, and the practice groups regularly organise Friday night trips to the pub. Apparently, for the criminal group *"any night of the week will do."*

If you're serious about applying to Deans Court, a mini-pupillage is highly recommended. We noticed that the academic backgrounds of many of the tenants betray a rather northern flavour, and whilst Oxbridge is certainly represented, its presence is well in proportion to other universities. In recent years, many recruits have opted for Manchester Metropolitan BVC, and it's probably fair to say that studying at MMU will provide students with a good opportunity to expose themselves (and their advocacy skills) to members of chambers, many of whom lecture there from time to time. We should also point out that there are people here who have no direct connection with Manchester at all. Understandably though, chambers expects applicants to be able to show that they are committed to the idea of living in the area and working on the Northern Circuit.

We can see the draw of the Manchester Bar. A lower cost of living and practising in a city that now gives London a run for its money in terms of entertainment and culture; the opportunity to rise up the ranks to the dizzy heights of the High Court – it's a miracle that the London Bar hasn't upped and left. Indeed that's exactly what one of Dean's Court's pupil supervisors had done. Born and bred in Manchester, he first knocked on the door of chambers (that's how it used to be done) for some work experience when he was still in short trousers. He then went to London to seek his fortune, but the draw of the North, and with it a more varied practice, became irresistible. Now, some 20 years after being called, he's back to stay. We say, why wait the 20 years?

Kings Chambers, Manchester

the facts

OLPAS: Summer **Pupillages:** up to 3x12 months
Applications: c.300 **Mini pupillages:** 25
Interview: 15
Award: £25,000 (grant and guaranteed earnings)
Tenancies awarded in 2004: 1
Chambers UK ranks members in: Chancery, clinical negligence, commercial litigation, environment, insolvency, partnership, planning

As they say at Old Trafford: if you can see the Pennines it's going to rain, and if you can't it's already raining. The day we visited Manchester's most upmarket set, Kings Chambers, it was bucketing down. Thankfully (and appropriately), the set shares King Street with Armani, Pink's, Whistles and a score of other lovely retailers with terribly convenient doorways in which to 'shelter' from the downpour.

Before settling in King Street, Kings Chambers tried several Manchester addresses on for size over the 60-odd years since it was established by Charles Norman Glidewell just after WWII. Town and country planning legislation was, of course, one of the new initiatives introduced by the post-war government, and CNG and his colleagues wasted no time in getting involved and developing a name as a specialist planning set. Practice has broadened over the years to incorporate all manner of local government work – public inquiries, education (including school expulsions), highways, residential care homes and environmental prosecutions. Today, around a third of chambers' business falls into this category.

Some 40% of business falls within the commercial/Chancery sphere and emanates from big national firms of solicitors (DLA, Eversheds, Addleshaws etc) right down to sole practitioners. The set also receives instructions from London firms with business in the Manchester District Registry. The remaining quarter of chambers' work is made up of common law matters. To clarify, no one handles family or crime work so, effectively, chambers operates exclusively in the privately funded arena. It's a deliberate policy and one that marks Kings Chambers out from the majority of Manchester sets. The plan for the future is to boost the commercial and Chancery work and to continue building a reputation for PI – all through organic growth and individual lateral hires. Said the senior clerk: "*We may not be the biggest in Manchester, but we are the strongest. Though we don't want to be a megaset.*"

Yet chambers is a sizeable set with eight silks among its 64 members. It is also worth noting that chambers additionally has premises at 5 Park Square in Leeds; "*everyone is expected to work in both places and people can voluntarily physically locate themselves in Leeds.*" Its three practice groups operate quite distinctly. Members generally only work in one field, though frequently they share rooms with colleagues from another practice group. Pupils are recruited only after the needs of each group have been assessed and all pupillages are specialist. When we visited, chambers had just one pupil, who was being trained as a commercial and Chancery practitioner. While there is no guarantee of tenancy at the end of the year, no pupil has been disappointed in the past six years. "*If we take three pupils, it's because there is room for three tenants,*" said one of chambers' recruiters; "*it means pupils can support each other and not worry about showing weakness to each other.*" As for bidding farewell to a pupil showing slower progress in their first six, we were told by one pupilmaster: "*I've seen people turn around after fairly shaky first sixes and become great on their feet.*"

Recruits are allocated to two PMs for six months each. In the first six, it sounds as if the pupil is looked after very well; "*they're not like a puppy you get for Christmas and put in a shoebox!*" Indeed, the current pupil told us: "*My first six pupilmaster made a lot of sacrifices for me: not having holidays and picking me up in the mornings before going to court...I felt like my pupilmaster was in loco parentis.*" As he or she will be in court most days, so will you. The rest of the time you'll have a stab at the PM's written work and generally be "*housetrained.*" One explained her approach: "*I set the pupil some work at the beginning of the week, having made an assessment of the time they'll have available. I'm really hot on encouraging them to learn to time-manage and work to deadlines.*" As for accompanying her to court, "*they see all the papers and then I'll set them an exercise to summarise the key points of the case or to prepare a written piece outlining the cross-examination. After the hearing we'll have a debrief and I'll explain to them that's why I did what I did.*" She continued: "*We make sure they maintain absolute, utmost propriety, because if you don't have your reputation...*" Well indeed, but what exactly is this set's reputation? "*We're seen as the big swots; a bit geeky!*" A certain degree of aloofness stems from the fact that "*we've the biggest turnover and because we don't do crime, we're not sitting around in the robing room chatting for three hours with other barristers.*"

Towards the end of the first six, pupils are encouraged to go to court and conferences with baby juniors in order to experience small claims hearings, case management conferences, fast track trials and any kind of district judge's appointment. Second six pupils gain independence (though they still sit with and are guided by a PM) and begin to earn their own living. We asked the current pupil how he'd spent the previous week and his response might surprise someone in a London second six. Monday had been spent on half a dozen winding-up applications and a directions hearing. On Tuesday he'd resisted an application for the stay of a warrant for possession of a residential property. On Wednesday a multi-track trial had been scheduled, though it settled; on Thursday he'd applied to set aside a judgement in default concerning the enforcement of a guarantee on a loan, and then he finished up the week with a bankruptcy and a small claim. "*The difference between London and Manchester at the junior end,*" he told us, "*is that we're in court on at least a daily basis.*"

The pace is certainly frenetic and "*you'll prepare things the night before.*" This means long hours. "*Chambers won't tolerate anything that is not excellent – that's the benchmark and that's what chambers is built on." He also thought that while the first six was all about teaching him "clarity of thought," his second-six PM was intent on teaching him a "combative and competitive" style and "imbuing me with resilience."

Everyone uses first names around chambers (clerks too), and when work allows there are visits to the pub and five-a-side football matches. "People have always got time for each other and there are no door-slammers." We're told chambers has "a mixed bag of members," which makes for "interesting debates at lunch." These relate to everything from "Coronation Street, football and gossip to stories about judges...there's a great oral tradition on the Northern Circuit." Pupils are more than welcome to join in, and as a matter of fact, they have central role in the lunchroom – making the tea. The idea is that it helps them to get to know people, but we dare say it's a chore no one misses after the pupillage year is out.

The first step for any student hopeful is to attend the set's annual 'mini-pupillage fair', a three-day event for around 25 students. Everyone in chambers is involved and students are put in groups for court visits, advocacy workshops, guest speakers (a district judge, the local law society, the old head of chambers telling circuit stories), tea with each practice group and a night in the pub. When we suggested it sounded like the legal version of Glastonbury, no one disagreed. "There's no drugs though!" Make it to a pupillage interview and you can expect a gentle chat about your CV, more testing questions about the area of law in which you're interested and some questions on current issues. "We want people who are personable and have a real interest in chambers and the area of law they're applying for. And they need a bit of backbone; they must be able to justify their position."

One other day you'll need a bit of backbone is the day chambers holds its Christmas lunch. At 11am, members and staff decamp to a restaurant in Chinatown, leaving the pupils "home alone" to man the phones. Every year without fail the partygoers play pranks on them. The current pupil had taken a call from a Court of Appeal judge's clerk who sounded suspiciously like the senior clerk. After their ordeal, pupils join their colleagues to eat, drink and sing karaoke. What more could you ask for?

St Johns Buildings, Manchester

the facts
OLPAS: Autumn **Pupillages:** 2x12 months
Applications: up to 500 **Mini pupillages:** 150
First interview: 20 **Second interview:** 10
Award: £26,000 (£6,000 grant + £20,000 guaranteed earnings)
Tenancies offered in 2004: 3
Chambers UK ranks members in: Clinical negligence, crime, family, personal injury

Guarded at one end by Deansgate and pouring into one of the few inner-city parks at the other is St John Street, a pocket of Manchester that's full of Georgian charm. Our subject set plays a distinct and noteworthy part in this microcosm of the Bar. Having folded three chambers into one superset in the last three years, it is now the largest in Manchester. Some 85 members (including 10 silks) handle common law, crime, family, mental health and commercial cases.

A quick romp through SJB's history informs much. The rump of the set was originally formed in the late 1940s at No.28 by a group of Jewish barristers, frustrated at not being able to find tenancy elsewhere. Their legacy can be seen today in SJB's diversity of membership and belief in the importance of fairness and respect. Now that many other parts of the Bar have discovered such concepts, there's less need for chambers to be defined by these traits. However, any reader concerned about whether they are male enough, white enough, straight enough, or had passed through a sufficiently established school or university, should stop worrying. As one source said: *"No.28 had an equal opportunities policy before the phrase was ever devised."* Yet from quirky, nonconformist beginnings 28 grew into an establishment set and delivered more than its fair share of senior members to the bench, including the first female High Court judge, Dame Joyanne Bracewell.

In 2002, No.28 merged with its next-door neighbour at 24a, a set that came into existence a quarter of a century earlier. Forget any notions of 70s' idealism, we were left concluding that *"hungrier"* crime-heavy 24a had more in common with Thatcher's ambition-driven 80s than the philosophical liberalism of the preceding decade. And now, two years on from the first coupling, the doors have been opened to Merchant Chambers' commercial barristers. What has resulted is a well-structured organisation with distinct clerking teams and formalised practice groups. In the civil group there are 30 members (some of whom only handle employment law); the family group has 22; crime weighs in at 35 members and the commercial group has ten. The mergers were not based merely on practice considerations, but also on a belief that, culturally, the three sets could mesh together.

SJB is nothing if not well managed...masterminded even. The relationship between barrister and senior clerk is always an intriguing one, and SJB's Chris Ronan is clearly one part business heavyweight and one part agony aunt. Every month pupils climb on to his metaphorical couch for a deconstruction of their progress and goals, and it doesn't stop when they gain tenancy. One barrister was quite happy to admit: *"Chris rules your life...he shows you all the feedback, what you did and what you billed."* We heard no complaints. There's also a safety net in the shape of the practice groups – *"You are never on your own as you work in teams, and you're constantly up against each other in court. In the Salford robing room, you'll see five, six or even seven other members of chambers...you could almost hold a meeting."*

Believing that attempting anything other than a specialised pupillage would be nonsensical, SJB recruits pupils only after assessing the business needs of each practice group and matching the recruit's character to the particular pupilmaster to whom they'll be assigned. This approach stems from a fundamental principle that every pupil should secure tenancy. The chair of the pupillage committee couldn't remember when someone had last been refused it, and told us: *"If someone goes off the rails in pupillage, it's our job to get them back on...if they are here, we want to look after them and develop them, inculcating them with chambers' ethos."*

Which leads us nicely to the subject of what SJB now believes in after its transformation into a superset. Using members' own words, it goes something like this: *"Absolutely proper preparation, consistency every time you turn out for a client, careful marshalling of thoughts, always checking the law, aspiring to the highest standards, being non-judgmental about the people you meet."* And for pupils, *"recognising that everyone* [at court] *has more experience than you...including the lady behind the sandwich counter."* SJB runs a two-stage pupillage interview process, and those who make the *"dispiritingly long"* shortlist for the first interview will be sent a problem to prepare. Make it to the second stage and, an hour before facing the interview panel, you'll be handed a mock brief for, say, a plea in mitigation. With experience as a recorder, the chair of the pupillage committee is perfectly placed to play the judge. *"I'm looking for good logical analysis,"* he told us; *"someone who can identify a good point from a bad one. If I challenge people, I like someone to know when to push a point and when to stop."*

When we visited SJB, two pupils were midway through tornado-like second sixes, one specialising in civil matters and the other in crime. We spoke with the latter about life on the first rung of the ladder and a second six with more court time than your average tearaway teenager. *"I have worked every day,"* he said; *"mostly mags' work and two thirds of it prosecuting for the CPS, which is a lot of work in a short space of time and* good experience for fact management and time management." You'll get into court for 10am having had the papers for just a couple of hours. "You've an early start because there's a lot to do," although the magistrates' court is notorious for defendants or witnesses not showing up. If you have seven sets of instructions and all but two are no shows, "you could be done by 11am." Much of the time you're up against a solicitor who could have had the case for a year, and you have "maybe 12 minutes to read the file and then be ready to fight against this person and conduct a cross-examination." Everything about the first six is designed to prepare you for the onslaught of the second. "I was in court every day then too, the majority of the time with my pupilmaster, although I also got time with other criminal practitioners." First-six pupils must all experience some work outside their chosen field; in the case of a crime pupil this might mean two weeks spent with a civil practitioner working on personal injury cases.

A young junior specialising in family law (with a bit of crime thrown in for good measure) talked of an equally full-on schedule. "I am in court every day...I have to ask if I want days out." You really have to drive, because your patch is extensive: "You could be in Preston for a hearing and you'll get a call asking 'Can you go to Lancaster for a bench warrant?' Or you'll be asked to do an ex parte domestic violence injunction when you've just put your bag down after a day in court." Sometimes you'll end up scribbling down directions on the back of a paper towel and tearing off to arrive at the next venue, where you'll be handed the file just as the bench

comes in. In what can only be described as an understatement, our source said: "You've got to be adaptable!"

Will a career at the Manchester Bar ringfence you into the Northern Circuit? Apparently not. Although for our pupil, Manchester was big and crime-ridden enough to keep him in the city's courts most of the time, a family law QC told us he'd also appeared in Derby, Nottingham, Birmingham and London in the past year. Yet the strength of their desire to be in Manchester was obvious in all those we met. The silk spoke of "a village atmosphere where most barristers know each other." He also felt that, in a city of Manchester's size, better relationships could be made with the wider professional community – "You get to know most of the paediatricians, solicitors and social workers." Our junior told us: "I would have gone to London if I thought for one moment that being in Manchester would have impeded me." She readily admitted: "I am ambitious," but after joining SJB: "I knew I would spend 40 years here without having to move." From up north, the London Bar isn't something to aspire to.

In the basement of SJB is a room with a large red table. It is no ordinary table. It is the epicentre of everything. Here at this table, you and your lunchtime sandwich will make friends and grow comfortable with your seniors. You will be initiated into the fine traditions of black humour and general gossip. You will become accepted as a colleague. Your mission, should you be awarded pupillage, is to find that table on your first day and to sit and eat. The rest of your career will unfold from there...

barristers a-z

Blackstone Chambers (P Baxendale QC and C Flint QC)

Blackstone House, Temple, London EC4Y 9BW   DX: 281
Tel: (020) 7583 1770   Fax: (020) 7822 7350
Email: pupils@blackstonechambers.com
Website: www.blackstonechambers.com

No of Silks   **28**
No of Juniors   **34**
No of Pupils 4 (current)

contact
Ms Julia Hornor
Practice Manager

method of application
OLPAS

pupillages (p.a.)
12 months 4-5
Required degree grade
Minimum 2:1
(law or non-law)

income
Award £35,000
Earnings not included

tenancies
Junior tenancies offered
in last 3 years **72%**
No of tenants of 5 years
call or under **10**

chambers profile
Blackstone Chambers occupies modern, fully networked premises in the Temple.

type of work undertaken
Chambers' formidable strengths lie in three principal areas of practice: commercial, employment and public law. Commercial law includes financial/business law, international trade, conflicts, sport, media and entertainment, intellectual property and professional negligence. All aspects of employment law, including discrimination, are covered by Chambers' extensive employment law practice. Public law incorporates judicial review, acting both for and against central and local government agencies and other regulatory authorities, all areas affected by the impact of human rights and other aspects of administrative law. Chambers recognises the increasingly important role which mediation has to play in dispute resolution. Two members are CEDR accredited mediators.

pupil profile
Chambers looks for articulate and intelligent applicants who are able to work well under pressure and demonstrate high intellectual ability. Successful candidates usually have at least a 2:1 honours degree, although not necessarily in law.

pupillage
Chambers offers four (or exceptionally five) 12 month pupillages to those wishing to practise full-time at the Bar, normally commencing in October each year. Pupillage is divided into three or four sections and every effort is made to ensure that pupils receive a broad training. The environment is a friendly one; pupils attend an induction week introducing them to the Chambers working environment. Chambers prefers to recruit new tenants from pupils wherever possible. Chambers subscribes to OLPAS; applications should be made for the summer season.

mini pupillages
Assessed mini pupillages are available and are an important part of the application procedure. Applications for mini pupillages must be made by 30 April; earlier applications are strongly advised and are preferred in the year before pupillage commences.

funding
Awards of £35,000 per annum are available. The pupillage committee has a discretion to consider applications for up to £9,000 of the pupillage award to be advanced during the BVC year. Since Chambers insists on an accessed mini pupillage as part of the overall application procedure, financial assistance is offered either in respect of out of pocket travelling or accommodation expenses incurred in attending the mini pupillage, up to a maximum of £200 per pupil.

No5 Chambers

Fountain Court, Birmingham, B4 6DR, DX 16075
Tel: (0870) 203 5555 Fax: (0121) 606 1501
Email: pupillage@no5.com
Website: www.no5.com

chambers profile
In response to an ever-increasing workload, No5 has grown to be one of the biggest chambers in the country, with offices in Birmingham, London and Bristol.

type of work undertaken
Chambers is divided into seven main practice groups (Crime, Personal Injury, Clinical Negligence, Planning, Family, Chancery & Commercial, and Employment) each with dedicated clerking and marketing resources.

pupillage
No5 offers two 12 month pupillages every year and seeks candidates of a high academic calibre, preferably with experience of advocacy in the form of debating and/or moots and with the determination to succeed. In return for the exceptional opportunities that are offered, the set expects its applicants to be well-qualified and highly motivated with good interpersonal skills and an appetite for work. Tenancy following pupillage at No5 Chambers is not a formality by any means, but it is not the policy to recruit pupils merely for the sake of it.

mini-pupillage
No5's scheme of mini-pupillages seeks to give students a week long insight into the working life, benefits and burdens of a practising barrister. Chambers does not accept applications for work experience by students below the age of 18.

sponsorship/funding
An award of £15,000 is made during the first six months of pupillage and pupils can earn an average of £30,000 during their second six months. In addition to these sums, loans are available if required and bursaries or advances for the BVC year will be considered.

No of Silks	15
No of Juniors	145
No of Pupils	2

contact
Tim Mayer (Pupillage)
Paul Evans (Mini Pupillage)

method of application
By letter or email, to
pupillage@no5.com

pupillages (p.a.)
2 x 12 months

tenancies
Pupillages are offered with a view to tenancy provided appropriate benchmark requirements are met.

offices
Birmingham, London and Bristol

A-Z BARRISTERS

Erskine Chambers

33 Chancery Lane, London WC2A 1EN
Tel: (020) 7242 5532   Fax: (020) 7831 0125
Email: clerks@erskine-chambers.co.uk
Website: www.erskine-chambers.co.uk

chambers profile
Erskine Chambers is widely recognised as the leading specialist company law set and undertakes litigation and advisory work in all areas in which company law arises.

type of work undertaken
Company and related commercial law, including, in particular, shareholder disputes, corporate insolvencies, directors' duties, takeovers, corporate reconstructions, loan capital and banking securities, financial services, accounting and auditing, professional negligence and corporate fraud.

pupil profile
Chambers seek ambitious, intellectually able students, ordinarily with a first or good upper second class degree and preferably some knowledge or experience of company law.

pupillage
Each pupil will spend three months with one pupil supervisor before moving to another pupil supervisor. Increasingly, they will begin to work for other members of Chambers. There are opportunities throughout for pupils to become involved in particularly interesting or high-profile work being done by members of Chambers.

mini pupillages
Available throughout the year on both an assessed and a non-assessed basis.

sponsorship & awards
Two awards of up to £35,000 are made each year in respect of the 12-month pupillage period. Applications should be made on Chambers' standard application form available from the above address. Applications for 2006/2007 should be made by 31 May 2005.

No of Silks	8
No of Juniors	16
No of Pupils	2

contact
Nigel Dougherty
(020) 7242 5532

method of application
Chambers' standard application form

pupillages (p.a.)
Up to 2, up to 12 months

tenancies
Up to 2

Furnival Chambers

32 Furnival Street, London EC4A 1JQ
Tel: (020) 7405 3232 Fax: (020) 7405 3322
Website: www.furnivallaw.co.uk

chambers profile

Furnival Chambers (previously 171 Fleet Street) is a young (established 1985), energetic and progressive leading criminal set and the leading set in the field of asset forfeiture and confiscation.

type of work undertaken

Members of Chambers regularly appear in high-profile cases (defending and prosecuting). Prosecution work includes work undertaken by Treasury Counsel at the Central Criminal Court. Many members undertake high-profile work on behalf of HM Customs and Excise, the Department of Trade and Industry, the Serious Fraud Office, the Department of Work & Pensions, Inland Revenue and the Crown Prosecution Service. The asset forfeiture team comprises approximately 10 members specialising in money laundering prosecutions, mutual assistance and confiscation proceedings in the criminal courts, and injunctive and receivership work in the civil courts. Members of the team include the authors of the leading practitioners' textbook and regularly conduct cases in Commonwealth and Caribbean jurisdictions.

pupil profile

Applicants are expected to have excellent academic qualifications and an ability to absorb complex documentary material.

pupillage

Pupillage follows a well-defined process so that the same opportunities are afforded to all at every level. Chambers have simple and robust procedures in place that ensure that decisions affecting pupils are fair, and reinforce these with a clear complaints procedure. Further information regarding Chambers' pupillage policy is available on the Chambers website. Chambers operate a compulsory in-house advocacy course which pupils must pass before being permitted to practise in their second six months. Pupils can, therefore, expect to be well prepared for an exceptionally busy second six.

mini pupillages

Assessed mini-pupillages are available. Mini-pupils must expect to travel to courts in London. Applications should be made in writing to Clara Milligan (Chambers Administrator) with accompanying CV. Student visits are not possible. Sponsored students are not accepted.

funding

Chambers offer three funded (12 month) pupillages at £15,000 (£7,500 payable at the beginning of each six).

contact
Clara Milligan
(Chambers Administrator)
cmilligan@furnivallaw.co.uk

method of application
OLPAS summer season
2005 for 2006

pupillages (p.a.)
3 Funded

income
1st 6 months
£7,500
2nd 6 months
£7,500

tenancies
6

A-Z

BARRISTERS

2 Hare Court

2 Hare Court, Temple, London EC4Y 7BH
Tel: (020) 7353 5324 Fax: (020) 7353 0667
Email: clerks@2harecourt.com
Website: www.2harecourt.com

chambers profile
2 Hare Court is well established as one of the leading sets specialising in criminal law. Members of Chambers defend and prosecute at all levels in London, throughout England and Wales and overseas, and are experienced in advising parties from the commencement of the investigation, including issues arising from international judicial assistance. Chambers has a strong tradition of representation both on the Bar Council and Criminal Bar Association.

type of work undertaken
Chambers has considerable experience in high profile cases involving murder, corporate manslaughter, terrorism, police corruption, drug trafficking, sexual offences and internet pornography as well as those involving child witnesses and has increasingly specialised in commercial fraud and international money laundering. Individual tenants also provide specialist expertise in associated fields including immigration, licensing and health and safety.

pupil profile
Chambers select as pupils articulate and well motivated individuals of high intellectual ability who can demonstrate sound judgement and a practical approach to problem solving. Candidates should have at least a 2.1 honours degree.

pupillage
Chambers normally offers two 12 month pupillages starting in September. The year is divided into two six month periods although pupils are assigned to a different pupil master for each of the four months to ensure experience in different areas of crime. Chambers pays for the "Advice to Counsel" course and runs their own in-house advocacy training.

mini pupillages
The programme runs throughout the year with one mini pupil taken each week and two each week in the summer. Applicants must be at least 18 years old and either be studying for Higher Education qualification or on or about to start CPE or BVC course.

funding
12 month pupils will be sponsored through a combination of an award scheme, guaranteed earnings and additional earnings. No clerks' fees or deductions are taken from earnings.

No of Silks	11
No of Juniors	36
No of Pupils	2

contact
Jeremy Benson QC

method of application
OLPAS (summer)

pupillages (p.a.)
Two 12 month pupillages
Minimum degree 2:1

tenancies
According to ability

annexes
None

2 HARE COURT

Community
Legal Service

Quality Mark - Legal Services
Accredited Chambers

Maitland Chambers (incorporating 9 Old Square)

7 Stone Buildings, Lincoln's Inn, London WC2A 3SZ
Tel: (020) 7406 1200 Fax: (020) 7406 1300
Email: clerks@maitlandchambers.com
Website: www.maitlandchambers.com

No of Silks	15
No of Juniors	50
No of Pupils	3

contact
Valerie Piper
(Pupillage Secretary)
pupillage@
maitlandchambers.com

method of application
See chambers website
from January 2005.
Application deadline for
pupillage in 2006-07 is 7
February 2005.

pupillages (p.a.)
Up to 3 funded

income
£40,000 p.a.

tenancies
5 in last 3 years

chambers profile
On 1 October 2004 Maitland Chambers and 9 Old Square merged to form the largest commercial Chancery set in London.

type of work undertaken
Chambers is instructed on a very wide range of cases – from major international litigation to county court disputes. Much of the work is done in London, though the set frequently advises and appears for clients in other parts of the United Kingdom and abroad. Members are recommended as leaders in their field in commercial Chancery, company, charities, insolvency, media and entertainment, traditional Chancery, property litigation, partnership, pensions, banking, energy, tax, agriculture and professional negligence.

pupil profile
Academically, Maitland Chambers looks for a first or upper second. Pupils must have a sense of commercial practicality, be stimulated by the challenge of advocacy and have an aptitude for and general enjoyment of complex legal argument.

pupillage
Pupils sit with at least three different barristers but spend their first few months with one supervisor in order that the pupil can find his or her feet and establish a point of contact which will endure throughout the pupil's time in chambers. Pupils also undertake a structured advocacy training course which consists of advocacy exercises conducted in front of other members of chambers.

mini pupillages
Applications are considered twice a year with a deadline of 30 April for the period June to November, and 31 October for December to May. Applications should be made with a covering letter and cv (listing university grades) to the Pupillage Secretary.

funding
Chambers offers up to three, 12-month pupillages, all of which are funded (£40,000 for pupils starting in October 2006). Up to £10,000 of the award may be drawn down in advance during BVC year.

maitland
CHAMBERS
INCORPORATING
9
OLD
SQUARE

Quadrant Chambers (Nigel Teare QC)

(formerly 4 Essex Court)

Quadrant House, 10 Fleet Street, London EC4Y 1AU
Tel: (020) 7583 4444 Fax: (020) 7583 4455
Email: pupillage@quadrantchambers.com
Website: www.quadrantchambers.com

No of Silks	12
No of Juniors	34

contact
Secretary to Pupillage
Committee

method of application
Chambers' application
form

pupillages (p.a.)
1st 6 months 4
2nd 6 months 4
12 months
(Reviewed at 6 months)
Required degree
Good 2:1+

income
1st 6 months
£15,000
2nd 6 months
£15,000
Earnings not included

tenancies
Current tenants who
served pupillage in
Chambers 18
Junior tenancies offered
in last 3 years 6
No of tenants of 5 years
call or under 7
Income (1st year)
c. £40,000

chambers profile

Quadrant Chambers is one of the leading commercial chambers. Chambers offers a wide range of services to its clients within the commercial sphere specialising particularly in maritime and aviation law. Quadrant Chambers is placed in the first rank in both specialisms by Chambers Guide to the Legal Profession 2001-2002. In shipping law, seven silks and nine juniors were selected by Chambers, and Chambers concluded that 'these highly commercial barristers are at the forefront of the aviation field'. In both these areas the set had more 'leaders in their field' selected than any other set of chambers. Quadrant Chambers advises on domestic and international commercial litigation and acts as advocates in court, arbitration and inquiries in England and abroad.

type of work undertaken

The challenging and rewarding work of chambers encompasses the broad range of commercial disputes embracing arbitration, aviation, banking, shipping, international trade, insurance and reinsurance, professional negligence, entertainment and media, environmental and construction law. Over 70% of chambers work involves international clients.

pupil profile

Quadrant Chambers seeks high calibre pupils with good academic qualifications (at least a 2.1 degree) who exhibit good written and oral skills.

pupillage

Chambers offer a maximum of four funded pupillages of 12 months duration (reviewable at six months). Pupils are moved amongst several members of Chambers and will experience a wide range of high quality commercial work. Outstanding pupils are likely to be offered a tenancy at the end of their pupillage. Further information can be found on the website.

mini pupillages

Mini pupillages are encouraged in order that potential pupils may experience the work of Chambers before committing themselves to an application for full pupillage.

funding

Awards of £30,000 p.a. are available for each funded pupillage – part of which may be forwarded during the BVC, at the Pupillage Committee's discretion.

Serle Court

Serle Court, 6 New Square, Lincoln's Inn, London WC2A 3QS
Tel: (020) 7242 6105   Fax: (020) 7405 4004
Email: pupillage@serlecourt.co.uk
Website: www.serlecourt.co.uk

No of Silks	12
No of Juniors	33
No of Pupils	2

contact
Hugh Norbury
Tel (020) 7242 6105

method of application
Chambers application
form, available from
website or Chambers.
Not a member of OLPAS

pupillages (p.a.)
Two 12 month pupillages

tenancies
Up to 2 per annum

chambers profile
'Excellent for all aspects of general business law…' Chambers & Partners Guide 2002-3.
Serle Court is one of the leading commercial chancery set with 45 barristers including 12
silks. Widely recognised as a leading set, Chambers is recommended in 17 different areas
of practice by legal directories. Chambers has a stimulating and inclusive work environment and a forward looking approach.

type of work undertaken
Litigation, arbitration, mediation and advisory services across the full range of chancery
and commercial practice areas including: administrative and public law, banking, civil
fraud, commercial litigation, company, financial services, human rights, insolvency,
mediation, partnership, professional negligence, property, regulatory and disciplinary,
trusts and probate.

pupil profile
Candidates are well-rounded people, from any background. Chambers looks for highly
motivated individuals with first class intellectual ability, combined with a practical
approach, sound judgment and the potential to become excellent advocates. Serle Court
has a reputation for 'consistent high quality' and for being 'responsive and able team
members' and seeks the same qualities in pupils.

pupillage
Pupils sit with different pupil supervisors in order to experience a broad a range of work.
Two pupils are recruited each year and Chambers offers: an excellent preparation for successful practice; a genuinely friendly and supportive environment; the opportunity to
learn from some of the leading barristers in their field; a real prospect of tenancy.

mini-pupillages
About 30 available each year. Apply with CV to pupillage@serlecourt.co.uk.

funding
Serle Court offers awards of £40,000 for 12 months, of which up to £12,500 can be drawn
down during the BVC year. It also provides an income guarantee worth up to £100,000
over the first two years of practice.

serle court

3/4 South Square

3/4 South Square, Gray's Inn, London WC1R 5HP
Tel: (020) 7696 9900 Fax: (020) 7696 9911
Email: pupillage@southsquare.com
Website: www.southsquare.com

chambers profile

Chambers is an established successful commercial set, involved in high-profile international and domestic commercial litigation and advice. Members of Chambers have been involved in some of the most important commercial cases of the last decade including Barings, BCCI, Lloyds, Maxwell and Polly Peck.

type of work undertaken

3/4 South Square has a pre-eminent reputation in insolvency and reconstruction law and specialist expertise in banking, financial services, company law, professional negligence, domestic and international arbitration, mediation, European Union Law, insurance/reinsurance law and general commercial litigation.

pupil profile

Chambers seek to recruit the highest calibre of candidates who must be prepared to commit themselves to establishing a successful practice and maintaining Chambers' position at the forefront of the modern Commercial Bar. The minimum academic qualification is a 2:1 degree.

pupillage

Pupils are welcomed into all areas of Chambers' life and are provided with an organised programme designed to train and equip them for practice in a dynamic and challenging environment. Pupils sit with a number of pupil masters for periods of six-eight weeks and the set looks to recruit at least one tenant every year from its pupils.

mini pupillages

Chambers also offers funded and unfunded mini-pupillages – please see the set's website for further details.

sponsorship & awards

Currently £35,000 per annum (reviewable annually).

No of Silks	16
No of Juniors	29
No of Pupils	2

contact
Pupillage Secretary
Tel (020) 7696 9900

method of application
CV with covering letter

pupillages (p.a.)
Up to four, 12 month
pupillages offered
each year

4 Stone Buildings

4 Stone Buildings, Lincoln's Inn, London WC2A 3XT
Tel: (020) 7242 5524   Fax: (020) 7831 7907
Email: d.goddard@4stonebuildings.com

No of Silks	**5**
No of Juniors	**19**
No of Pupils	**2**

contact
David Goddard
(020) 7242 5524

method of application
On Chambers own
application form

pupillages (p.a.)
2 x six months

tenancies
At least 1 per year

annexes
None

chambers profile
An established friendly company/commercial set involved in high profile company/commercial litigation and advice.

type of work undertaken
4, Stone Buildings specialise in the fields of company law, commercial law, financial services and regulation and corporate insolvency.

pupil profile
Candidates are expected to have first class, or good second class degrees. But mere intellectual ability is only part of it: a successful candidate must have the confidence and ambition to succeed, the common sense to recognise the practical advice a client really needs, and an ability to get on well with clients, solicitors and other members of Chambers - and the clerks.

pupillage
The set aim to give all pupils the knowledge, skills and practical experience they need for a successful career at the Bar. They believe that it is important for all pupils to see as much as possible of the different kinds of work in Chambers. This enables pupils to judge whether their work suits them, and enables different members of Chambers to assess the pupils. Each pupil therefore normally spends time with two or more pupil-masters within any six month period. If other members of Chambers have particularly interesting cases in Court, pupils will be encouraged to work and attend Court with them. All pupils work in their pupil masters' rooms, read their papers, attend their conferences, draft pleadings and documents, write draft opinions and accompany their pupil masters to Court. Pupils are treated as part of Chambers, and are fully involved in the activities of Chambers while they are with 4 Stone Chambers.

mini pupillages
Up to 20 mini-pupillages offered per year of up to a weeks duration. Application by letter and cv.

sponsorship & awards
£17,500 per six months.

funding
As above.

3 Verulam Buildings (Christopher Symons QC/John Jarvis QC)

3 Verulam Buildings, Gray's Inn, London WC1R 5NT DX: LDE 331
Tel: (020) 7831 8441 Fax: (020) 7831 8479
Email: chambers@3vb.com
Website: www.3vb.com

No of Silks	19
No of Juniors	36
No of Pupils	4

chambers profile

3 Verulam Buildings is a large commercial set with a history of expansion by recruitment of tenants from amongst pupils. Over the past 10 years, on average, two of its pupils have become tenants every year. Chambers occupies recently refurbished, spacious offices overlooking Gray's Inn Walks with all modern IT and library facilities. Chambers prides itself on a pleasant, friendly and relaxed atmosphere.

type of work undertaken

A wide range of commercial work, in particular banking and financial services, insurance and reinsurance, commercial fraud, professional negligence, company law, entertainment, arbitration/ADR, as well as other general commercial work. Members of Chambers regularly appear in high profile cases and a substantial amount of Chambers' work is international.

pupil profile

Chambers looks for intelligent and ambitious candidates with strong powers of analysis and reasoning, who are self confident and get on well with others. Candidates must have at least a 2:1 grade in an honours subject which need not be law.

pupillage

Chambers seeks to recruit three or four funded 12 months pupils every year through OLPAS. Each pupil spends three months with four different members of Chambers to gain experience of different types of work. Chambers also offers unfunded pupillages to pupils who do not intend to practise at the Bar of England and Wales.

mini pupillages

Mini pupillages are available for university, CPE or Bar students who are interested in finding out more about Chambers' work. Chambers considers mini pupillage to be an important part of its recruitment process. Candidates should have, or expect to obtain, the minimum requirements for a funded 12 month pupillage. Applications are accepted throughout the year and should be addressed to Matthew Parker.

funding

In the year 2005-06 the annual award will be at least £40,500, up to £15,000 of which may be drawn during the BVC year.

contact
Mr Peter Ratcliffe (Pupillage)
Mr Matthew Parker (Mini Pupillage)

method of application
OLPAS & mini pupillage
CV & covering letter stating dates of availability

pupillages (p.a.)
12 months **4**
Required degree grade **2:1**

income
In excess of £40,500 (which was the award for 2005-06)
Earnings not included

tenancies
Current tenants who served pupillage in Chambers **Approx 40**
Junior tenancies offered in last 3 years **7**
No of tenants of 5 years call or under **8**

Wilberforce Chambers

8 New Square, Lincoln's Inn, London WC2A 3QP
Tel: (020) 7306 0102   Fax: (020) 7306 0095
Email: lbillins@wilberforce.co.uk
Website: www.wilberforce.co.uk

No of Silks	**16**
No of Juniors	**27**
No of Pupils 1 (2004/05)	

contact
Louise Billins
(020) 7306 0102

method of application
Online via website or in
writing to Louise Billins,
Pupillage Secretary

pupillages (p.a.)
Two x 12 months

tenancies
4 (2004)

chambers profile

As a leading commercial chancery Chambers, the set has 43 members (16 QCs) involved in some of the most commercially important and cutting edge advice and advocacy undertaken by the Bar today. Most members are recognised as leaders in their field by the key legal directories. Instructions come from top UK and international law firms with a complex and rewarding range of work for international companies, financial institutions, sports and media organisations, private individuals and well-known names. While clients demand high intellectual performance and client care standards the rewards are a successful career at the Bar. The atmosphere in Chambers, which is guarded with great care, is one of a united and friendly 'family'.

type of work undertaken

Chambers commercial chancery practices include commercial litigation, company, financial services and banking, insolvency, pensions, trusts and tax, property litigation, planning, professional negligence, sports and media, intellectual property and charities work.

pupil profile

Trainees should possess high intellectual ability, strong motivation and excellent communication skills. They need to have maturity and confidence with the ability to work with others and analyse legal problems clearly, demonstrating commercial and practical good sense. Chambers looks for people who possess real potential to join Chambers as a tenant at the end of their pupillage. A 2.1 degree (in Law or another subject) is a minimum requirement. Chambers has a track record of taking CPE students.

pupillage

Chambers operates a structured pupillage programme with continual assessment aimed at giving a broad experience of commercial chancery practice under the several pupil masters, with whom you are able to develop your skills. It offers 12-month terminable pupillages and aims to reach a decision about tenancy after six months of pupillage. Chambers website explains this programme in greater detail.

mini-pupillages

Chambers encourage interested students to visit for a week in order to learn how it operates, to meet members of Chambers and to see the sort of work it does. Chambers run three separate mini-pupillage weeks (two in December and one in July). See the website for more details.

funding

The award for 2004/2005 is £37,500 pa (£18,750 for a six-month pupillage). The award is paid monthly. A proportion of the pupillage award (up to £12,500) can be drawn down during the BVC year.

WILBERFORCE CHAMBERS

notes

notes

notes

notes

notes